BEETON'S BOOK

OF

HOUSEHOLD MANAGEMENT

BEETON'S BOOK

OF

HOUSEHOLD MANAGEMENT

Comprising Information for the

MISTRESS,	COACHMAN,	LAUNDRY-MAID,
HOUSEKEEPER,	VALET,	NURSE AND NURSE-
COOK,	UPPER AND UNDER	MAID,
KITCHEN-MAID,	HOUSE-MAIDS,	MONTHLY, WET, AND
BUTLER,	LADY'S-MAID,	SICK NURSES,
FOOTMAN,	MAID-OF-ALL-WORK,	ETC. ETC.

ALSO, SANITARY, MEDICAL, & LEGAL MEMORANDA;

WITH A HISTORY OF THE ORIGIN, PROPERTIES, AND USES OF ALL THINGS
CONNECTED WITH HOME LIFE AND COMFORT.

BY MRS. ISABELLA BEETON.

Nothing lovelier can be found
In Woman, than to study household good.—MILTON.

CHANCELLOR
PRESS

ORIGINALLY PUBLISHED IN
1859-61
IN MONTHLY SUPPLEMENTS TO
S.O. BEETON 'S
'THE ENGLISHWOMAN 'S DOMESTIC
MAGAZINE '
FIRST PUBLISHED BY
S.O. BEETON IN 1861
AS ONE VOLUME ENTITLED
'THE BOOK OF HOUSEHOLD MANAGEMENT '

THIS ENLARGED EDITION
FIRST PUBLISHED IN GREAT BRITAIN
IN 1982 BY
CHANCELLOR PRESS
MICHELIN HOUSE
81 FULHAM ROAD
LONDON SW3 6RB

REPRINTED 1984, 1985, 1986, 1987, 1989, 1991

ISBN   0 907486 18 5
PRINTED AT THOMSON PRESS (INDIA) LTD.,
FARIDABAD

PREFACE.

—◆◆—

I MUST frankly own, that if I had known, beforehand, that this book would have cost me the labour which it has, I should never have been courageous enough to commence it. What moved me, in the first instance, to attempt a work like this, was the discomfort and suffering which I had seen brought upon men and women by household mismanagement. I have always thought that there is no more fruitful source of family discontent than a housewife's badly-cooked dinners and untidy ways. Men are now so well served out of doors,—at their clubs, well-ordered taverns, and dining-houses, that in order to compete with the attractions of these places, a mistress must be thoroughly acquainted with the theory and practice of cookery, as well as be perfectly conversant with all the other arts of making and keeping a comfortable home.

In this book I have attempted to give, under the chapters devoted to cookery, an intelligible arrangement to every recipe, a list of the *ingredients*, a plain statement of the *mode* of preparing each dish, and a careful estimate of its *cost*, the *number of people* for whom it is *sufficient*, and the time when it is *seasonable*. For the matter of the recipes, I am indebted, in some measure, to many correspondents of the " Englishwoman's Domestic Magazine," who have obligingly placed at my disposal their formulæ for many original preparations. A large private circle has also rendered me considerable service. A diligent study of the works of the best modern writers on cookery was also necessary to the faithful fulfilment of my task. Friends in England, Scotland, Ireland, France, and Germany, have also very materially aided me. I have paid great attention to those recipes which come under the head of " COLD MEAT COOKERY." But in the department belonging to the Cook I have striven, too, to make my work something more than a Cookery Book, and have, therefore, on the

best authority that I could obtain, given an account of the natural
history of the animals and vegetables which we use as food. I
have followed the animal from his birth to his appearance on the
table; have described the manner of feeding him, and of slaying
him, the position of his various joints, and, after giving the recipes,
have described the modes of carving Meat, Poultry, and Game.
Skilful artists have designed the numerous drawings which appear
in this work, and which illustrate, better than any description,
many important and interesting items. The coloured plates are a
novelty not without value.

Besides the great portion of the book which has especial
reference to the cook's department, there are chapters devoted
to those of the other servants of the household, who have all, I
trust, their duties clearly assigned to them.

Towards the end of the work will be found valuable chapters
on the " Management of Children "—" The Doctor," the latter
principally referring to accidents and emergencies, some of which
are certain to occur in the experience of every one of us; and the
last chapter contains " Legal Memoranda," which will be serviceable in cases of doubt as to the proper course to be adopted in
the relations between Landlord and Tenant, Tax-gatherer and
Tax-payer, and Tradesman and Customer.

These chapters have been contributed by gentlemen fully entitled to confidence; those on medical subjects by an experienced
surgeon, and the legal matter by a solicitor.

I wish here to acknowledge the kind letters and congratulations
I have received during the progress of this work, and have only
further to add, that I trust the result of the four years' incessant
labour which I have expended will not be altogether unacceptable
to some of my countrymen and countrywomen.

ISABELLA BEETON.

GENERAL CONTENTS.

⸻◆◆⸺

ERRATA.

Page 657, last line but one from bottom of page, *for* 8*d. read* 8*s.*

,, 121, first line, *for* " one tablespoonful " *read* "one small teaspoonful."

,, 705, eleven lines from bottom, *for* 2*s. read* 3*s.* 6*d.*

,, 707, twelfth line from bottom, *for* 1*s.* 8*d. read* 3*s.* 3*d.*

,, 715, eighth line from bottom, *for* 1*s.* 6*d. read* 2*s.*

,, 716, seven lines from top, *for* 2*s. read* 3*s.* 6*d.*

,, 718, first line from top, *for* 2*s. read* 4*s.* 6*d.*

,, 719, second line from bottom, *for* 3*s. read* 4*s.* 6*d.*

,, 720, eleventh line from bottom, *for* 2*s.* 3*d. read* 3*s.* 6*d.*

ANALYTICAL INDEX.

—◆—

NOTE.—Where a "*p*" occurs before the number for reference, the *page*, and not the paragraph, is to be sought.

c

ENGRAVINGS.

THE BOOK

OF

HOUSEHOLD MANAGEMENT.

———◆———

CHAPTER I.

THE MISTRESS.

"Strength and honour are her clothing; and she shall rejoice in time to come. She openeth her mouth with wisdom; and in her tongue is the law of kindness. She looketh well to the ways of her household; and eateth not the bread of idleness. Her children arise up, and call her blessed; her husband also, and he praiseth her."—*Proverbs*, xxxi. 25—28.

1. AS WITH THE COMMANDER OF AN ARMY, or the leader of any enterprise, so is it with the mistress of a house. Her spirit will be seen through the whole establishment; and just in proportion as she performs her duties intelligently and thoroughly, so will her domestics follow in her path. Of all those acquirements, which more particularly belong to the feminine character, there are none which take a higher rank, in our estimation, than such as enter into a knowledge of household duties; for on these are perpetually dependent the happiness, comfort, and well-being of a family. In this opinion we are borne out by the author of "The Vicar of Wakefield," who says: "The modest virgin, the prudent wife, and the careful matron, are much more serviceable in life than petticoated philosophers, blustering heroines, or virago queens. She who makes her husband and her children happy, who reclaims the one from vice and trains up the other to virtue, is a much greater character than ladies described in romances, whose whole occupation is to murder mankind with shafts from their quiver, or their eyes."

2. PURSUING THIS PICTURE, we may add, that to be a good housewife does not necessarily imply an abandonment of proper pleasures or amusing recreation; and we think it the more necessary to express this, as the performance of the duties of a mistress may, to some minds, perhaps seem to be

B

incompatible with the enjoyment of life. Let us, however, now proceed to describe some of those home qualities and virtues which are necessary to the proper management of a Household, and then point out the plan which may be the most profitably pursued for the daily regulation of its affairs.

3. EARLY RISING IS ONE OF THE MOST ESSENTIAL QUALITIES which enter into good Household Management, as it is not only the parent of health, but of innumerable other advantages. Indeed, when a mistress is an early riser, it is almost certain that her house will be orderly and well-managed. On the contrary, if she remain in bed till a late hour, then the domestics, who, as we have before observed, invariably partake somewhat of their mistress's character, will surely become sluggards. To self-indulgence all are more or less disposed, and it is not to be expected that servants are freer from this fault than the heads of houses. The great Lord Chatham thus gave his advice in reference to this subject:—"I would have inscribed on the curtains of your bed, and the walls of your chamber, ' If you do not rise early, you can make progress in nothing.' "

4. CLEANLINESS IS ALSO INDISPENSABLE TO HEALTH, and must be studied both in regard to the person and the house, and all that it contains. Cold or tepid baths should be employed every morning, unless, on account of illness or other circumstances, they should be deemed objectionable. The bathing of *children* will be treated of under the head of "MANAGEMENT OF CHILDREN."

5. FRUGALITY AND ECONOMY ARE HOME VIRTUES, without which no household can prosper. Dr. Johnson says: "Frugality may be termed the daughter of Prudence, the sister of Temperance, and the parent of Liberty. He that is extravagant will quickly become poor, and poverty will enforce dependence and invite corruption." The necessity of practising economy should be evident to every one, whether in the possession of an income no more than sufficient for a family's requirements, or of a large fortune, which puts financial adversity out of the question. We must always remember that it is a great merit in housekeeping to manage a little well. "He is a good waggoner," says Bishop Hall, "that can turn in a little room. To live well in abundance is the praise of the estate, not of the person. I will study more how to give a good account of my little, than how to make it more." In this there is true wisdom, and it may be added, that those who can manage a little well, are most likely to succeed in their management of larger matters. Economy and frugality must never, however, be allowed to degenerate into parsimony and meanness.

6. THE CHOICE OF ACQUAINTANCES is very important to the happiness of a mistress and her family. A gossiping acquaintance, who indulges in the

scandal and ridicule of her neighbours, should be avoided as a pestilence. It is likewise all-necessary to beware, as Thomson sings,

> "The whisper'd tale,
> That, like the fabling Nile, no fountain knows;—
> Fair-faced Deceit, whose wily, conscious eye
> Ne'er looks direct; the tongue that licks the dust
> But, when it safely dares, as prompt to sting."

If the duties of a family do not sufficiently occupy the time of a mistress, society should be formed of such a kind as will tend to the mutual interchange of general and interesting information.

7. FRIENDSHIPS SHOULD NOT BE HASTILY FORMED, nor the heart given, at once, to every new-comer. There are ladies who uniformly smile at, and approve everything and everybody, and who possess neither the courage to reprehend vice, nor the generous warmth to defend virtue. The friendship of such persons is without attachment, and their love without affection or even preference. They imagine that every one who has any penetration is ill-natured, and look coldly on a discriminating judgment. It should be remembered, however, that this discernment does not always proceed from an uncharitable temper, but that those who possess a long experience and thorough knowledge of the world, scrutinize the conduct and dispositions of people before they trust themselves to the first fair appearances. Addison, who was not deficient in a knowledge of mankind, observes that "a friendship, which makes the least noise, is very often the most useful; for which reason, I should prefer a prudent friend to a zealous one." And Joanna Baillie tells us that

> "Friendship is no plant of hasty growth,
> Though planted in esteem's deep-fixèd soil,
> The gradual culture of kind intercourse
> Must bring it to perfection."

8. HOSPITALITY IS A MOST EXCELLENT VIRTUE; but care must be taken that the love of company, for its own sake, does not become a prevailing passion; for then the habit is no longer hospitality, but dissipation. Reality and truthfulness in this, as in all other duties of life, are the points to be studied; for, as Washington Irving well says, "There is an emanation from the heart in genuine hospitality, which cannot be described, but is immediately felt, and puts the stranger at once at his ease." With respect to the continuance of friendships, however, it may be found necessary, in some cases, for a mistress to relinquish, on assuming the responsibility of a household, many of those commenced in the earlier part of her life. This will be the more requisite, if the number still retained be quite equal to her means and opportunities.

9. IN CONVERSATION, TRIFLING OCCURRENCES, such as small disappointments, petty annoyances, and other every-day incidents, should never be mentioned to your friends. The extreme injudiciousness of repeating these will be at once apparent, when we reflect on the unsatisfactory discussions which they too frequently occasion, and on the load of advice which they are the cause of being tendered, and which is, too often, of a kind neither to be useful nor agreeable. Greater events, whether of joy or sorrow, should be communicated to friends ; and, on such occasions, their sympathy gratifies and comforts. If the mistress be a wife, never let an account of her husband's failings pass her lips ; and in cultivating the power of conversation, she should keep the versified advice of Cowper continually in her memory, that it

> " Should flow like water after summer showers,
> Not as if raised by mere mechanic powers."

In reference to its style, Dr. Johnson, who was himself greatly distinguished for his colloquial abilities, says that "no style is more extensively acceptable than the narrative, because this does not carry an air of superiority over the rest of the company ; and, therefore, is most likely to please them. For this purpose we should store our memory with short anecdotes and entertaining pieces of history. Almost every one listens with eagerness to extemporary history. Vanity often co-operates with curiosity ; for he that is a hearer in one place wishes to qualify himself to be a principal speaker in some inferior company ; and therefore more attention is given to narrations than anything else in conversation. It is true, indeed, that sallies of wit and quick replies are very pleasing in conversation ; but they frequently tend to raise envy in some of the company : but the narrative way neither raises this, nor any other evil passion, but keeps all the company nearly upon an equality, and, if judiciously managed, will at once entertain and improve them all."

10. GOOD TEMPER SHOULD BE CULTIVATED by every mistress, as upon it the welfare of the household may be said to turn ; indeed, its influence can hardly be over-estimated, as it has the effect of moulding the characters of those around her, and of acting most beneficially on the happiness of the domestic circle. Every head of a household should strive to be cheerful, and should never fail to show a deep interest in all that appertains to the well-being of those who claim the protection of her roof. Gentleness, not partial and temporary, but universal and regular, should pervade her conduct ; for where such a spirit is habitually manifested, it not only delights her children, but makes her domestics attentive and respectful ; her visitors are also pleased by it, and their happiness is increased.

11. ON THE IMPORTANT SUBJECT OF DRESS AND FASHION we cannot do better than quote an opinion from the eighth volume of the " Englishwoman's

Domestic Magazine." The writer there says, " Let people write, talk, lecture, satirize, as they may, it cannot be denied that, whatever is the prevailing mode in attire, let it intrinsically be ever so absurd, it will never *look* as ridiculous as another, or as any other, which, however convenient, comfortable, or even becoming, is totally opposite in style to that generally worn."

12. IN PURCHASING ARTICLES OF WEARING APPAREL, whether it be a silk dress, a bonnet, shawl, or riband, it is well for the buyer to consider three things : I. That it be not too expensive for her purse. II. That its colour harmonize with her complexion, and its size and pattern with her figure. III. That its tint allow of its being worn with the other garments she possesses. The quaint Fuller observes, that the good wife is none of our dainty dames, who love to appear in a variety of suits every day new, as if a gown, like a stratagem in war, were to be used but once. But our good wife sets up a sail according to the keel of her husband's estate ; and, if of high parentage, she doth not so remember what she was by birth, that she forgets what she is by match.

To *Brunettes*, or those ladies having dark complexions, silks of a grave hue are adapted. For *Blondes*, or those having fair complexions, lighter colours are preferable, as the richer, deeper hues are too overpowering for the latter. The colours which go best together are green with violet ; gold-colour with dark crimson or lilac ; pale blue with scarlet ; pink with black or white ; and gray with scarlet or pink. A cold colour generally requires a warm tint to give life to it. Gray and pale blue, for instance, do not combine well, both being cold colours.

13. THE DRESS OF THE MISTRESS should always be adapted to her circumstances, and be varied with different occasions. Thus, at breakfast she should be attired in a very neat and simple manner, wearing no ornaments. If this dress should decidedly pertain only to the breakfast-hour, and be specially suited for such domestic occupations as usually follow that meal, then it would be well to exchange it before the time for receiving visitors, if the mistress be in the habit of doing so. It is still to be remembered, however, that, in changing the dress, jewellery and ornaments are not to be worn until the full dress for dinner is assumed. Further information and hints on the subject of the toilet will appear under the department of the " LADY'S-MAID."

The advice of Polonius to his son Laertes, in Shakspeare's tragedy of " Hamlet," is most excellent ; and although given to one of the male sex, will equally apply to a " fayre ladye :"—

" Costly thy habit as thy purse can buy,
But not express'd in fancy ; rich, not gaudy ;
For the apparel oft proclaims the man."

14. CHARITY AND BENEVOLENCE ARE DUTIES which a mistress owes to herself as well as to her fellow-creatures ; and there is scarcely any income so small, but something may be spared from it, even if it be but " the widow's mite." It is to be always remembered, however, that it is the *spirit* of charity

which imparts to the gift a value far beyond its actual amount, and is by far its better part.

> True Charity, a plant divinely nursed,
> Fed by the love from which it rose at first,
> Thrives against hope, and, in the rudest scene,
> Storms but enliven its unfading green ;
> Exub'rant is the shadow it supplies,
> Its fruit on earth, its growth above the skies.

Visiting the houses of the poor is the only practical way really to understand the actual state of each family ; and although there may be difficulties in following out this plan in the metropolis and other large cities, yet in country towns and rural districts these objections do not obtain.   Great advantages may result from visits paid to the poor ; for there being, unfortunately, much ignorance, generally, amongst them with respect to all household knowledge, there will be opportunities for advising and instructing them, in a pleasant and unobtrusive manner, in cleanliness, industry, cookery, and 'good management.

15. IN MARKETING, THAT THE BEST ARTICLES ARE THE CHEAPEST, may be laid down as a rule ; and it is desirable, unless an experienced and confidential housekeeper be kept, that the mistress should herself purchase all provisions and stores needed for the house.   If the mistress be a young wife, and not accustomed to order "things for the house," a little practice and experience will soon teach her who are the best tradespeople to deal with, and what are the best provisions to buy.   Under each particular head of FISH, MEAT, POULTRY, GAME, &c., will be described the proper means of ascertaining the quality of these comestibles.

16. A HOUSEKEEPING ACCOUNT-BOOK should invariably be kept, and kept punctually and precisely.   The plan for keeping household accounts, which we should recommend, would be to make an entry, that is, write down into a daily diary every amount paid on that particular day, be it ever so small ; then, at the end of the month, let these various payments be ranged under their specific heads of Butcher, Baker, &c. ; and thus will be seen the proportions paid to each tradesman, and any one month's expenses may be contrasted with another.   The housekeeping accounts should be balanced not less than once a month ; so that you may see that the money you have in hand tallies with your account of it in your diary.   Judge Haliburton never wrote truer words than when he said, "No man is rich whose expenditure exceeds his means, and no one is poor whose incomings exceed his outgoings."

When, in a large establishment, a housekeeper is kept, it will be advisable for the mistress to examine her accounts regularly.   Then any increase of expenditure which may be apparent, can easily be explained, and the housekeeper will have the satisfaction of knowing whether her efforts to manage her department well and economical'y, have been successful.

17. ENGAGING DOMESTICS is one of those duties in which the judgment of the mistress must be keenly exercised.   There are some respectable registry-offices, where good servants may sometimes be hired ; but the plan rather to be recommended is, for the mistress to make inquiry amongst her

circle of friends and acquaintances, and her tradespeople. The latter generally know those in their neighbourhood, who are wanting situations, and will communicate with them, when a personal interview with some of them will enable the mistress to form some idea of the characters of the applicants, and to suit herself accordingly.

We would here point out an error—and a grave one it is—into which some mistresses fall. They do not, when engaging a servant, expressly tell her all the duties which she will be expected to perform. This is an act of omission severely to be reprehended. Every portion of work which the maid will have to do, should be plainly stated by the mistress, and understood by the servant. If this plan is not carefully adhered to, domestic contention is almost certain to ensue, and this may not be easily settled; so that a change of servants, which is so much to be deprecated, is continually occurring

18. IN OBTAINING A SERVANT'S CHARACTER, it is not well to be guided by a written one from some unknown quarter; but it is better to have an interview, if at all possible, with the former mistress. By this means you will be assisted in your decision of the suitableness of the servant for your place, from the appearance of the lady and the state of her house. Negligence and want of cleanliness in her and her household generally, will naturally lead you to the conclusion, that her servant has suffered from the influence of the bad example.

The proper course to pursue in order to obtain a personal interview with the lady is this:—The servant in search of the situation must be desired to see her former mistress, and ask her to be kind enough to appoint a time, convenient to herself, when you may call on her; this proper observance of courtesy being necessary to prevent any unseasonable intrusion on the part of a stranger. Your first questions should be relative to the honesty and general morality of her former servant; and if no objection is stated in that respect, her other qualifications are then to be ascertained. Inquiries should be very minute, so that you may avoid disappointment and trouble, by knowing the weak points of your domestic.

19. THE TREATMENT OF SERVANTS is of the highest possible moment, as well to the mistress as to the domestics themselves. On the head of the house the latter will naturally fix their attention; and if they perceive that the mistress's conduct is regulated by high and correct principles, they will not fail to respect her. If, also, a benevolent desire is shown to promote their comfort, at the same time that a steady performance of their duty is exacted, then their respect will not be unmingled with affection, and they will be still more solicitous to continue to deserve her favour.

20. IN GIVING A CHARACTER, it is scarcely necessary to say that the mistress should be guided by a sense of strict justice. It is not fair for one lady to recommend to another, a servant she would not keep herself. The benefit, too, to the servant herself is of small advantage; for the failings which she possesses will increase if suffered to be indulged with impunity. It is hardly necessary to remark, on the other hand, that no angry feelings on the part of a mistress towards her late servant, should ever be allowed, in the slightest degree, to influence her, so far as to induce her to disparage her maid's character.

21. THE FOLLOWING TABLE OF THE AVERAGE YEARLY WAGES paid to domestics, with the various members of the household placed in the order

in which they are usually ranked, will serve as a guide to regulate the expenditure of an establishment:—

	When not found in Livery.		When found in Livery.	
The House Steward	From £40 to £80		—	
The Valet	,,	25 to 50	From £20	to £30
The Butler	,,	25 to 50	—	
The Cook	,,	20 to 40	—	
The Gardener	,,	20 to 40	—	
The Footman	,,	20 to 40	,,	15 to 25
The Under Butler	,,	15 to 30	,,	15 to 25
The Coachman	—		,,	20 to 35
The Groom	,,	15 to 30	,,	12 to 20
The Under Footman	—		,,	12 to 20
The Page or Footboy	,,	8 to 18	,,	6 to 14
The Stableboy	,,	6 to 12	—	

	When no extra allowance is made for Tea, Sugar, and Beer.		When an extra allowance is made for Tea, Sugar, and Beer.	
The Housekeeper	From £20 to £45		From £18	to £40
The Lady's-maid	,,	12 to 25	,,	10 to 20
The Head Nurse	,,	15 to 30	,,	13 to 26
The Cook	,,	14 to 30	,,	12 to 26
The Upper Housemaid	,,	12 to 20	,,	10 to 17
The Upper Laundry-maid	,,	12 to 18	,,	10 to 15
The Maid-of-all-work	,,	9 to 14	,,	7½ to 11
The Under Housemaid	,,	8 to 12	,,	6½ to 10
The Still-room Maid	,,	9 to 14	,,	8 to 12
The Nursemaid	,,	8 to 12	,,	5 to 10
The Under Laundry-maid	,,	9 to 14	,,	8 to 12
The Kitchen-maid	,,	9 to 14	,,	8 to 12
The Scullery-maid	,,	5 to 9	,,	4 to 8

These quotations of wages are those usually given in or near the metropolis; but, of course, there are many circumstances connected with locality, and also having reference to the long service on the one hand, or the inexperience on the other, of domestics, which may render the wages still higher or lower than those named above. All the domestics mentioned in the above table would enter into the establishment of a wealthy nobleman. The number of servants, of course, would become smaller in proportion to the lesser size of the establishment; and we may here enumerate a scale of servants suited to various incomes, commencing with—

About £1,000 a year—A cook, upper housemaid, nursemaid, under housemaid, and a man servant.

About £750 a year—A cook, housemaid, nursemaid, and footboy.

About £500 a year—A cook, housemaid, and nursemaid.

About £300 a year—A maid-of-all-work and nursemaid.

About £200 or £150 a year—A maid-of-all-work (and girl occasionally).

22. HAVING THUS INDICATED some of the more general duties of the mistress, relative to the moral government of her household, we will now give a few specific instructions on matters having a more practical relation to the position which she is supposed to occupy in the eye of the world. To do this the more clearly, we will begin with her earliest duties, and take her completely through the occupations of a day.

23. HAVING RISEN EARLY, as we have already advised (see 3), and having given due attention to the bath, and made a careful toilet, it will be well at once to see that the children have received their proper ablutions, and

are in every way clean and comfortable. The first meal of the day, breakfast, will then be served, at which all the family should be punctually present, unless illness, or other circumstances, prevent.

24. AFTER BREAKFAST IS OVER, it will be well for the mistress to make a round of the kitchen and other offices, to see that all are in order, and that the morning's work has been properly performed by the various domestics. The orders for the day should then be given, and any questions which the domestics desire to ask, respecting their several departments, should be answered, and any special articles they may require, handed to them from the store-closet.

In those establishments where there is a housekeeper, it will not be so necessary for the mistress, personally, to perform the above-named duties.

25. AFTER THIS GENERAL SUPERINTENDENCE of her servants, the mistress, if a mother of a young family, may devote herself to the instruction of some of its younger members, or to the examination of the state of their wardrobe, leaving the later portion of the morning for reading, or for some amusing recreation. "Recreation," says Bishop Hall, "is intended to the mind as whetting is to the scythe, to sharpen the edge of it, which would otherwise grow dull and blunt. He, therefore, that spends his whole time in recreation is ever whetting, never mowing; his grass may grow and his steed starve; as, contrarily, he that always toils and never recreates, is ever mowing, never whetting, labouring much to little purpose. As good no scythe as no edge. Then only doth the work go forward, when the scythe is so seasonably and moderately whetted that it may cut, and so cut, that it may have the help of sharpening."

Unless the means of the mistress be very circumscribed, and she be obliged to devote a great deal of her time to the making of her children's clothes, and other economical pursuits, it is right that she should give some time to the pleasures of literature, the innocent delights of the garden, and to the improvement of any special abilities for music, painting, and other elegant arts, which she may, happily, possess.

26. THESE DUTIES AND PLEASURES BEING PERFORMED AND ENJOYED, the hour of luncheon will have arrived. This is a very necessary meal between an early breakfast and a late dinner, as a healthy person, with good exercise, should have a fresh supply of food once in four hours. It should be a light meal; but its solidity must, of course, be, in some degree, proportionate to the time it is intended to enable you to wait for your dinner, and the amount of exercise you take in the mean time. At this time, also, the servants' dinner will be served.

In those establishments where an early dinner is served, that will, of course, take the place of the luncheon. In many houses, where a nursery dinner is provided for the children at about one o'clock, the mistress and the elder portion of the family make their luncheon at the same time from the same joint, or whatever may be provided. A mistress will arrange, according to circumstances, the serving of the meal; but the more usual plan is for the lady of the house to have the joint brought to her table, and afterwards carried to the nursery.

27. AFTER LUNCHEON, MORNING CALLS AND VISITS may be made and received. These may be divided under three heads: those of ceremony, friendship, and congratulation or condolence. Visits of ceremony, or courtesy, which occasionally merge into those of friendship, are to be paid under various circumstances. Thus, they are uniformly required after dining at a friend's house, or after a ball, picnic, or any other party. These visits should be short, a stay of from fifteen to twenty minutes being quite sufficient. A lady paying a visit may remove her boa or neckerchief; but neither her shawl nor bonnet.

When other visitors are announced, it is well to retire as soon as possible, taking care to let it appear that their arrival is not the cause. When they are quietly seated, and the bustle of their entrance is over, rise from your chair, taking a kind leave of the hostess, and bowing politely to the guests. Should you call at an inconvenient time, not having ascertained the luncheon hour, or from any other inadvertence, retire as soon as possible, without, however, showing that you feel yourself an intruder. It is not difficult for any well-bred or even good-tempered person, to know what to say on such an occasion, and, on politely withdrawing, a promise can be made to call again, if the lady you have called on, appear really disappointed.

28. IN PAYING VISITS OF FRIENDSHIP, it will not be so necessary to be guided by etiquette as in paying visits of ceremony; and if a lady be pressed by her friend to remove her shawl and bonnet, it can be done if it will not interfere with her subsequent arrangements. It is, however, requisite to call at suitable times, and to avoid staying too long, if your friend is engaged. The courtesies of society should ever be maintained, even in the domestic circle, and amongst the nearest friends. During these visits, the manners should be easy and cheerful, and the subjects of conversation such as may be readily terminated. Serious discussions or arguments are to be altogether avoided, and there is much danger and impropriety in expressing opinions of those persons and characters with whom, perhaps, there is but a slight acquaintance. (See 6, 7, and 9.)

It is not advisable, at any time, to take favourite dogs into another lady's drawing-room, for many persons have an absolute dislike to such animals; and besides this, there is always a chance of a breakage of some article occurring, through their leaping and bounding here and there, sometimes very much to the fear and annoyance of the hostess. Her children, also, unless they are particularly well-trained and orderly, and she is on exceedingly friendly terms with the hostess, should not accompany a lady in making morning calls. Where a lady, however, pays her visits in a carriage, the children can be taken in the vehicle, and remain in it until the visit is over.

29. FOR MORNING CALLS, it is well to be neatly attired; for a costume very different to that you generally wear, or anything approaching an evening dress, will be very much out of place. As a general rule, it may be said, both in reference to this and all other occasions, it is better to be under-dressed than over-dressed.

A strict account should be kept of ceremonial visits, and notice how soon your visits have been returned. An opinion may thus be formed as to whether your frequent visits are, or are not, desirable. There are, naturally, instances when the circumstances of old age or ill health will preclude any return of a call; but when this is the case, it must not interrupt the discharge of the duty.

30. IN PAYING VISITS OF CONDOLENCE, it is to be remembered that they

should be paid within a week after the event which occasions them. If the acquaintance, however, is but slight, then immediately after the family has appeared at public worship. A lady should send in her card, and if her friends be able to receive her, the visitor's manner and conversation should be subdued and in harmony with the character of her visit. Courtesy would dictate that a mourning card should be used, and that visitors, in paying condoling visits, should be dressed in black, either silk or plain-coloured apparel. Sympathy with the affliction of the family, is thus expressed, and these attentions are, in such cases, pleasing and soothing.

In all these visits, if your acquaintance or friend be not at home, a card should be left. If in a carriage, the servant will answer your inquiry and receive your card; if paying your visits on foot, give your card to the servant in the hall, but leave to go in and rest should on no account be asked. The form of words, "Not at home," may be understood in different senses; but the only courteous way is to receive them as being perfectly true. You may imagine that the lady of the house is really at home, and that she would make an exception in your favour, or you may think that your acquaintance is not desired; but, in either case, not the slightest word is to escape you, which would suggest, on your part, such an impression.

31. IN RECEIVING MORNING CALLS, the foregoing description of the etiquette to be observed in paying them, will be of considerable service. It is to be added, however, that the occupations of drawing, music, or reading should be suspended on the entrance of morning visitors. If a lady, however, be engaged with light needlework, and none other is appropriate in the drawing-room, it may not be, under some circumstances, inconsistent with good breeding to quietly continue it during conversation, particularly if the visit be protracted, or the visitors be gentlemen.

Formerly the custom was to accompany all visitors quitting the house to the door, and there take leave of them; but modern society, which has thrown off a great deal of this kind of ceremony, now merely requires that the lady of the house should rise from her seat, shake hands, or courtesy, in accordance with the intimacy she has with her guests, and ring the bell to summon the servant to attend them and open the door. In making a first call, either upon a newly-married couple, or persons newly arrived in the neighbourhood, a lady should leave her husband's card together with her own, at the same time, stating that the profession or business in which he is engaged has prevented him from having the pleasure of paying the visit, with her. It is a custom with many ladies, when on the eve of an absence from their neighbourhood, to leave or send their own and husband's cards, with the letters P. P. C. in the right-hand corner. These letters are the initials of the French words, "Pour prendre congé," meaning, "To take leave."

32. THE MORNING CALLS BEING PAID OR RECEIVED, and their etiquette properly attended to, the next great event of the day in most establishments is "The Dinner;" and we only propose here to make a few general remarks on this important topic, as, in future pages, the whole "Art of Dining" will be thoroughly considered, with reference to its economy, comfort, and enjoyment.

33. IN GIVING OR ACCEPTING AN INVITATION FOR DINNER, the following is the form of words generally made use of. They, however, can be varied in proportion to the intimacy or position of the hosts and guests :—

Mr. and Mrs. A——— present their compliments to Mr. and Mrs. B———, and request the honour, [or hope to have the pleasure] of their company to dinner on Wednesday, the 6th of December next.

A——— STREET,
November 13*th*, 1859.   *R. S. V. P.*

The letters in the corner imply "*Répondez, s'il vous plaît;*" meaning, "an answer will oblige." The reply, accepting the invitation, is couched in the following terms :—

Mr. and Mrs. B——— present their compliments to Mr. and Mrs. A———, and will do themselves the honour of, [or will have much pleasure in] accepting their kind invitation to dinner on the 6th of December next.

B——— SQUARE,
November 18*th*, 1859.

Cards, or invitations for a dinner-party, should be issued a fortnight or three weeks (sometimes even a month) beforehand, and care should be taken by the hostess, in the selection of the invited guests, that they should be suited to each other. Much also of the pleasure of a dinner-party will depend on the arrangement of the guests at table, so as to form a due admixture of talkers and listeners, the grave and the gay. If an invitation to dinner is accepted, the guests should be punctual, and the mistress ready in her drawing-room to receive them. At some periods it has been considered fashionable to come late to dinner, but lately *nous avons changé tout cela.*

34. THE HALF-HOUR BEFORE DINNER has always been considered as the great ordeal through which the mistress, in giving a dinner-party, will either pass with flying colours, or, lose many of her laurels. The anxiety to receive her guests,—her hope that all will be present in due time,—her trust in the skill of her cook, and the attention of the other domestics, all tend to make these few minutes a trying time. The mistress, however, must display no kind of agitation, but show her tact in suggesting light and cheerful subjects of conversation, which will be much aided by the introduction of any particular new book, curiosity of art, or article of vertu, which may pleasantly engage the attention of the company. "Waiting for Dinner," however, is a trying time, and there are few who have not felt—

" How sad it is to sit and pine,
The long *half-hour* before we dine !
Upon our watches oft to look,
Then wonder at the clock and cook,
         *   *   *   *   *
And strive to laugh in spite of Fate !
But laughter forced soon quits the room,
And leaves it in its former gloom.
But lo ! the dinner now appears,
The object of our hopes and fears,
         The end of all our pain !"

In giving an entertainment of this kind, the mistress should remember that it is her duty to make her guests feel happy, comfortable, and quite at their ease; and the guests should also consider that they have come to the house of their hostess to be happy. Thus an oppo tunity is given to all for innocent enjoyment and intellectual improvement, when also acquaintances may be formed that may prove invaluable through life, and information gained that will enlarge the mind. Many celebrated men and women have been great talkers; and, amongst others, the genial Sir Walter Scott, who spoke freely to every one, and a favourite remark of whom it was, that he never did so without learning something he didn't know before.

35. DINNER BEING ANNOUNCED, the host offers his arm to, and places on his right hand at the dinner-table, the lady to whom he desires to pay most respect, either on account of her age, position, or from her being the greatest stranger in the party. If this lady be married and her husband present, the latter takes the hostess to her place at table, and seats himself at her right hand. The rest of the company follow in couples, as specified by the master and mistress of the house, arranging the party according to their rank and other circumstances which may be known to the host and hostess.

It will be found of great assistance to the placing of a party at the dinner-table, to have the names of the guests neatly (and correctly) written on small cards, and placed at that part of the table where it is desired they should sit. With respect to the number of guests, it has often been said, that a private dinner-party should consist of not less than the number of the Graces, or more than that of the Muses. A party of ten or twelve is, perhaps, in a general way, sufficient to enjoy themselves and be enjoyed. White kid gloves are worn by ladies at dinner-parties, but should be taken off before the business of dining commences.

36. THE GUESTS BEING SEATED AT THE DINNER-TABLE, the lady begins to help the soup, which is handed round, commencing with the gentleman on her right and on her left, and continuing in the same order till all are served. It is generally established as a rule, not to ask for soup or fish twice, as, in so doing, part of the company may be kept waiting too long for the second course, when, perhaps, a little revenge is taken by looking at the awkward consumer of a second portion. This rule, however, may, under various circumstances, not be considered as binding.

It is not usual, where taking wine is *en règle*, for a gentleman to ask a lady to take wine until the fish or soup is finished, and then the gentleman honoured by sitting on the right of the hostess, may politely inquire if she will do him the honour of taking wine with him. This will act as a signal to the rest of the company, the gentleman of the house most probably requesting the same pleasure of the ladies at his right and left. At many tables, however, the custom or fashion of drinking wine in this manner, is abolished, and the servant fills the glasses of the guests with the various wines suited to the course which is in progress.

37. WHEN DINNER IS FINISHED, THE DESSERT is placed on the table, accompanied with finger-glasses. It is the custom of some gentlemen to wet a corner of the napkin; but the hostess, whose behaviour will set the tone to all the ladies present, will merely wet the tips of her fingers, which will serve all the purposes required. The French and other continentals have a habit of gargling the mouth; but it is a custom which no English gentlewoman should, in the slightest degree, imitate.

38. WHEN FRUIT HAS BEEN TAKEN, and a glass or two of wine passed round, the time will have arrived when the hostess will rise, and thus give

the signal for the ladies to leave the gentlemen, and retire to the drawing-room. The gentlemen of the party will rise at the same time, and he who is nearest the door, will open it for the ladies, all remaining courteously standing until the last lady has withdrawn. Dr. Johnson has a curious paragraph on the effects of a dinner on men. "Before dinner," he says, "men meet with great inequality of understanding; and those who are conscious of their inferiority have the modesty not to talk. When they have drunk wine, every man feels himself happy, and loses that modesty, and grows impudent and vociferous; but he is not improved, he is only not sensible of his defects." This is rather severe, but there may be truth in it.

In former times, when the bottle circulated freely amongst the guests, it was necessary for the ladies to retire earlier than they do at present, for the gentlemen of the company soon became unfit to conduct themselves with that decorum which is essential in the presence of ladies. Thanks, however, to the improvements in modern society, and the high example shown to the nation by its most illustrious personages, temperance is, in these happy days, a striking feature in the character of a gentleman. Delicacy of conduct towards the female sex has increased with the esteem in which they are now universally held, and thus, the very early withdrawing of the ladies from the dining-room is to be deprecated. A lull in the conversation will seasonably indicate the moment for the ladies' departure.

39. After-dinner Invitations may be given; by which we wish to be understood, invitations for the evening. The time of the arrival of these visitors will vary according to their engagements, or sometimes will be varied in obedience to the caprices of fashion. Guests invited for the evening are, however, generally considered at liberty to arrive whenever it will best suit themselves,—usually between nine and twelve, unless earlier hours are specifically named. By this arrangement, many fashionable people and others, who have numerous engagements to fulfil, often contrive to make their appearance at two or three parties in the course of one evening.

40. The Etiquette of the Dinner-party Table being disposed of, let us now enter slightly into that of an evening party or ball. The invitations issued and accepted for either of these, will be written in the same style as those already described for a dinner-party. They should be sent out at least three weeks before the day fixed for the event, and should be replied to within a week of their receipt. By attending to these courtesies, the guests will have time to consider their engagements and prepare their dresses, and the hostess will, also, know what will be the number of her party.

If the entertainment is to be simply an evening party, this must be specified on the card or note of invitation. Short or verbal invitations, except where persons are exceedingly intimate, or are very near relations, are very far from proper, although, of course, in this respect and in many other respects, very much always depends on the manner in which the invitation is given. True politeness, however, should be studied even amongst the nearest friends and relations; for the mechanical forms of good breeding are of great consequence, and too much familiarity may have, for its effect, the destruction of friendship.

41. As the Ladies and Gentlemen arrive, each should be shown to a room exclusively provided for their reception; and in that set apart for the

ladies, attendants should be in waiting to assist in uncloaking, and helping to arrange the hair and toilet of those who require it. It will be found convenient, in those cases where the number of guests is large, to provide numbered tickets, so that they can be attached to the cloaks and shawls of each lady, a duplicate of which should be handed to the guest. Coffee is sometimes provided in this, or an ante-room, for those who would like to partake of it.

42. AS THE VISITORS ARE ANNOUNCED BY THE SERVANT, it is not necessary for the lady of the house to advance each time towards the door, but merely to rise from her seat to receive their courtesies and congratulations. If, indeed, the hostess wishes to show particular favour to some peculiarly honoured guests, she may introduce them to others, whose acquaintance she may imagine will be especially suitable and agreeable. It is very often the practice of the master of the house to introduce one gentleman to another, but occasionally the lady performs this office; when it will, of course, be polite for the persons thus introduced to take their seats together for the time being.

The custom of non-introduction is very much in vogue in many houses, and guests are thus left to discover for themselves the position and qualities of the people around them. The servant, indeed, calls out the names of all the visitors as they arrive, but, in many instances, mispronounces them; so that it will not be well to follow this information, as if it were an unerring guide. In our opinion, it is a cheerless and depressing custom, although, in thus speaking, we do not allude to the large assemblies of the aristocracy, but to the smaller parties of the middle classes.

43. A SEPARATE ROOM OR CONVENIENT BUFFET should be appropriated for refreshments, and to which the dancers may retire; and cakes and biscuits, with wine negus, lemonade, and ices, handed round. A supper is also mostly provided at the private parties of the middle classes; and this requires, on the part of the hostess, a great deal of attention and supervision. It usually takes place between the first and second parts of the programme of the dances, of which there should be several prettily written or printed copies distributed about the ball-room.

In private parties, a lady is not to refuse the invitation of a gentleman to dance, unless she be previously engaged. The hostess must be supposed to have asked to her house only those persons whom she knows to be perfectly respectable and of unblemished character, as well as pretty equal in position; and thus, to decline the offer of any gentleman present, would be a tacit reflection on the master and mistress of the house. It may be mentioned here, more especially for the young who will read this book, that introductions at balls or evening parties, cease with the occasion that calls them forth, no introduction, at these times, giving a gentleman a right to address, afterwards, a lady. She is, consequently, free, next morning, to pass her partner at a ball of the previous evening without the slightest recognition.

44. THE BALL IS GENERALLY OPENED, that is, the first place in the first quadrille is occupied, by the lady of the house. When anything prevents this, the host will usually lead off the dance with the lady who is either the highest in rank, or the greatest stranger. It will be well for the hostess, even if she be very partial to the amusement, and a graceful dancer, not to participate in

it to any great extent, lest her lady guests should have occasion to complain of her monopoly of the gentlemen, and other causes of neglect. A few dances will suffice to show her interest in the entertainment, without unduly trenching on the attention due to her guests. In all its parts a ball should be perfect,—

> " The music, and the banquet, and the wine ;
> The garlands, the rose-odours, and the flowers."

The hostess or host, during the progress of a ball, will courteously accost and chat with their friends, and take care that the ladies are furnished with seats, and that those who wish to dance are provided with partners. A gentle hint from the hostess, conveyed in a quiet ladylike manner, that certain ladies have remained unengaged during several dances, is sure not to be neglected by any gentleman. Thus will be studied the comfort and enjoyment of the guests, and no lady, in leaving the house, will be able to feel the chagrin and disappointment of not having been invited to "stand up" in a dance during the whole of the evening.

45. WHEN ANY OF THE CARRIAGES OF THE GUESTS ARE ANNOUNCED, or the time for their departure arrived, they should make a slight intimation to the hostess, without, however, exciting any observation, that they are about to depart. If this cannot be done, however, without creating too much bustle, it will be better for the visitors to retire quietly without taking their leave. During the course of the week, the hostess will expect to receive from every guest a call, where it is possible, or cards expressing the gratification experienced from her entertainment. This attention is due to every lady for the pains and trouble she has been at, and tends to promote social, kindly feelings.

46. HAVING THUS DISCOURSED of parties of pleasure, it will be an interesting change to return to the more domestic business of the house, although all the details we have been giving of dinner-parties, balls, and the like, appertain to the department of the mistress. Without a knowledge of the etiquette to be observed on these occasions, a mistress would be unable to enjoy and appreciate those friendly pleasant meetings which give, as it were, a fillip to life, and make the quiet happy home of an English gentlewoman appear the more delightful and enjoyable. In their proper places, all that is necessary to be known respecting the dishes and appearance of the breakfast, dinner, tea, and supper tables, will be set forth in this work.

47. A FAMILY DINNER AT HOME, compared with either giving or going to a dinner-party, is, of course, of much more frequent occurrence, and many will say, of much greater importance. Both, however, have to be considered with a view to their nicety and enjoyment ; and the latter more particularly with reference to economy. These points will be especially noted in the following pages on "Household Cookery." Here we will only say, that for both mistress and servants, as well in large as small households, it will be found, by far, the better plan, to cook and serve the dinner, and to lay the tablecloth and the sideboard, with the same cleanliness, neatness, and scrupulous exactness, whether it be for the mistress herself alone, a small family, or for "company." If this rule be strictly

adhered to, all will find themselves increase in managing skill; whilst a knowledge of their daily duties will become familiar, and enable them to meet difficult occasions with ease, and overcome any amount of obstacles.

48. OF THE MANNER OF PASSING EVENINGS AT HOME, there is none pleasanter than in such recreative enjoyments as those which relax the mind from its severer duties, whilst they stimulate it with a gentle delight. Where there are young people forming a part of the evening circle, interesting and agreeable pastime should especially be promoted. It is of incalculable benefit to them that their homes should possess all the attractions of healthful amusement, comfort, and happiness; for if they do not find pleasure there, they will seek it elsewhere. It ought, therefore, to enter into the domestic policy of every parent, to make her children feel that home is the happiest place in the world; that to imbue them with this delicious home-feeling is one of the choicest gifts a parent can bestow.

Light or fancy needlework often forms a portion of the evening's recreation for the ladies of the household, and this may be varied by an occasional game at chess or backgammon. It has often been remarked, too, that nothing is more delightful to the feminine members of a family, than the reading aloud of some good standard work or amusing publication. A knowledge of polite literature may be thus obtained by the whole family, especially if the reader is able and willing to explain the more difficult passages of the book, and expatiate on the wisdom and beauties it may contain. This plan, in a great measure, realizes the advice of Lord Bacon, who says, "Read not to contradict and refute, nor to believe and take for granted, nor to find talk and discourse, but to weigh and consider."

49. IN RETIRING FOR THE NIGHT, it is well to remember that early rising is almost impossible, if late going to bed be the order, or rather disorder, of the house. The younger members of a family should go early and at regular hours to their beds, and the domestics as soon as possible after a reasonably appointed hour. Either the master or the mistress of a house should, after all have gone to their separate rooms, see that all is right with respect to the lights and fires below; and no servants should, on any account, be allowed to remain up after the heads of the house have retired.

50. HAVING THUS GONE FROM EARLY RISING TO EARLY RETIRING, there remain only now to be considered a few special positions respecting which the mistress of the house will be glad to receive some specific information.

51. WHEN A MISTRESS TAKES A HOUSE in a new locality, it will be etiquette for her to wait until the older inhabitants of the neighbourhood call upon her; thus evincing a desire, on their part, to become acquainted with the new comer. It may be, that the mistress will desire an intimate acquaintance with but few of her neighbours; but it is to be specially borne in mind that all visits, whether of ceremony, friendship, or condolence, should be punctiliously returned.

52. YOU MAY PERHAPS HAVE BEEN FAVOURED with letters of introduction from some of your friends, to persons living in the neighbourhood to which you have just come. In this case inclose the letter of introduction in an envelope with your card. Then, if the person, to whom it is addressed, calls in the course of a few days, the visit should be returned by you within the week, if possible. Any breach of etiquette, in this respect, will not readily be excused.

In the event of your being invited to dinner under the above circumstances, nothing but necessity should prevent you from accepting the invitation. If, however, there is some distinct reason why you cannot accept, let it be stated frankly and plainly, for politeness and truthfulness should be ever allied. An opportunity should, also, be taken to call in the course of a day or two, in order to politely express your regret and disappointment at not having been able to avail yourself of their kindness.

53. IN GIVING A LETTER OF INTRODUCTION, it should always be handed to your friend, unsealed. Courtesy dictates this, as the person whom you are introducing would, perhaps, wish to know in what manner he or she was spoken of. Should you *receive* a letter from a friend, introducing to you any person known to and esteemed by the writer, the letter should be immediately acknowledged, and your willingness expressed to do all in your power to carry out his or her wishes.

54. SUCH ARE THE ONEROUS DUTIES which enter into the position of the mistress of a house, and such are, happily, with a slight but continued attention, of by no means difficult performance. She ought always to remember that she is the first and the last, the Alpha and the Omega in the government of her establishment; and that it is by her conduct that its whole internal policy is regulated. She is, therefore, a person of far more importance in a community than she usually thinks she is. On her pattern her daughters model themselves; by her counsels they are directed; through her virtues all are honoured;—" her children rise up and call her blessed; her husband, also, and he praiseth her." Therefore, let each mistress always remember her responsible position, never approving a mean action, nor speaking an unrefined word. Let her conduct be such that her inferiors may respect her, and such as an honourable and right-minded man may look for in his wife and the mother of his children. Let her think of the many compliments and the sincere homage that have been paid to her sex by the greatest philosophers and writers, both in ancient and modern times. Let her not forget that she has to show herself worthy of Campbell's compliment when he said,—

> " The world was sad ! the garden was a wild !
> And man the hermit sigh'd, till *woman* smiled."

Let her prove herself, then, the happy companion of man, and able to take unto herself the praises of the pious prelate, Jeremy Taylor, who says,— " A good wife is Heaven's last best gift to man,—his angel and minister of graces innumerable,—his gem of many virtues,—his casket of jewels—her voice is sweet music—her smiles his brightest day;—her kiss, the guardian of his innocence;—her arms, the pale of his safety, the balm of his health, the balsam of his life;—her industry, his surest wealth;—her economy, his safest steward;—her lips, his faithful counsellors;—her bosom, the softest pillow of his cares; and her prayers, the ablest advocates of Heaven's blessings on his head."

Cherishing, then, in her breast the respected utterances of the good and the great, let the mistress of every house rise to the responsibility of its management; so that, in doing her duty to all around her, she may receive the genuine reward of respect, love, and affection!

Note.—Many mistresses have experienced the horrors of house-hunting, and it is well known that "three removes are as good (or bad, rather) as a fire." Nevertheless, it being quite evident that we must, in these days at least, live in houses, and are sometimes obliged to change our residences, it is well to consider some of the conditions which will add to, or diminish, the convenience and comfort of our homes.

Although the choice of a house must be dependent on so many different circumstances with different people, that to give any specific directions on this head would be impossible and useless; yet it will be advantageous, perhaps, to many, if we point out some of those general features as to locality, soil, aspect, &c., to which the attention of all house-takers should be carefully directed.

Regarding the locality, we may say, speaking now more particularly of a town house, that it is very important to the health and comfort of a family, that the neighbourhood of all factories of any kind, producing un-wholesome effluvia or smells, should be strictly avoided. Neither is it well to take a house in the immediate vicinity of where a noisy trade is carried on, as it is unpleasant to the feelings, and tends to increase any existing irritation of the system.

Referring to soils; it is held as a rule, that a gravel soil is superior to any other, as the rain drains through it very quickly, and it is consequently drier and less damp than clay, upon which water rests a far longer time. A clay country, too, is not so pleasant for walking exercise as one in which gravel predominates.

The aspect of the house should be well considered, and it should be borne in mind that the more sunlight that comes into the house, the healthier is the habitation. The close, fetid smell which assails one on entering a narrow court, or street, in towns, is to be assigned to the want of light, and, consequently, air. A house with a south or south-west aspect, is lighter, warmer, drier, and consequently more healthy, than one facing the north or north-east.

Great advances have been made, during the last few years, in the prin-ciples of sanitary knowledge, and one most essential point to be observed in reference to a house, is its "drainage," as it has been proved in an end-less number of cases, that bad or defective drainage is as certain to destroy health as the taking of poisons. This arises from its injuriously affecting the atmosphere; thus rendering the air we breathe unwholesome and deleterious. Let it be borne in mind, then, that unless a house is effectually drained, the health of its inhabitants is sure to suffer; and they will be susceptible of ague, rheumatism, diarrhœa, fevers, and cholera.

We now come to an all-important point,—that of the water supply. The value of this necessary article has also been lately more and more recognized in connection with the question of health and life; and most houses are well supplied with every convenience connected with water. Let it, however, be well understood, that no house, however suitable in other respects, can be desirable, if this grand means of health and comfort is, in the slightest degree, scarce or impure. No caution can be too great to see that it is pure and good, as well as plentiful ; for, knowing, as we do, that not a single part of our daily food is prepared without it, the importance of its influence on the health of the inmates of a house cannot be over-rated.

Ventilation is another feature which must not be overlooked. In a general way, enough of air is admitted by the cracks round the doors and windows ; but if this be not the case, the chimney will smoke ; and other plans, such as the placing of a plate of finely-perforated zinc in the upper part of the window, must be used. Cold air should never be admitted under the doors, or at the bottom of a room, unless it be close to the fire or stove ; for it will flow along the floor towards the fireplace, and thus leave the foul air in the upper part of the room, unpurified, cooling, at the same time, unpleasantly and injuriously, the feet and legs of the inmates.

The rent of a house, it has been said, should not exceed one-eighth of the whole income of its occupier ; and, as a general rule, we are disposed to assent to this estimate, although there may be many circumstances which would not admit of its being considered infallible.

CHAPTER II.

THE HOUSEKEEPER.

55. As second in Command in the House, except in large establishments, where there is a house steward, the housekeeper must consider herself as the immediate representative of her mistress, and bring, to the management of the household, all those qualities of honesty, industry, and vigilance, in the same degree as if she were at the head of *her own* family. Constantly on the watch to detect any wrong-doing on the part of any of the domestics, she will overlook all that goes on in the house, and will see that every department is thoroughly attended to, and that the servants are comfortable, at the same time that their various duties are properly performed.

Cleanliness, punctuality, order, and method, are essentials in the character of a good housekeeper. Without the first, no household can be said to be well managed. The second is equally all-important; for those who are under the housekeeper will take their "cue" from her; and in the same proportion as punctuality governs her movements, so will it theirs. Order, again, is indispensable; for by it we wish to be understood that "there should be a place for everything, and everything in its place." Method, too, is most necessary; for when the work is properly contrived, and each part arranged in regular succession, it will be done more quickly and more effectually.

56. A necessary Qualification for a Housekeeper is, that she should be thoroughly able to understand accounts. She will have to write in her books an accurate registry of all sums paid for any and every purpose, all the current expenses of the house, tradesmen's bills, and other extraneous matter. As we have mentioned under the head of the Mistress (*see* 16), a housekeeper's accounts should be periodically balanced, and examined by the head of the house. Nothing tends more to the satisfaction of both employer and employed, than this arrangement. "Short reckonings make long friends," stands good in this case, as in others.

It will be found an excellent plan to take an account of every article which comes into the house connected with housekeeping, and is not paid for at the time. The book containing these entries can then be compared with the bills sent in by the various tradesmen, so that any discrepancy can be inquired into and set right. An intelligent housekeeper will, by this means, too, be better able to judge of the average consumption of each article by the household; and if that quantity be, at any time, exceeded, the cause may be discovered and rectified, if it proceed from waste or carelessness.

57. Although in the department of the Cook, the housekeeper does not generally much interfere, yet it is necessary that she should possess a good knowledge of the culinary art, as, in many instances, it may be requisite for her to take the superintendence of the kitchen. As a rule, it may be stated, that the housekeeper, in those establishments where there is no house steward or man cook, undertakes the preparation of the confectionary, attends

to the preserving and pickling of fruits and vegetables; and, in a general way, to the more difficult branches of the art of cookery.

Much of these arrangements will depend, however, on the qualifications of the cook; for instance, if she be an able artiste, there will be but little necessity for the housekeeper to interfere, except in the already noticed articles of confectionary, &c. On the contrary, if the cook be not so clever an adept in her art, then it will be requisite for the housekeeper to give more of her attention to the business of the kitchen, than in the former case. It will be one of the duties of the housekeeper to attend to the marketing, in the absence of either a house steward or man cook.

58. THE DAILY DUTIES OF A HOUSEKEEPER are regulated, in a great measure, by the extent of the establishment she superintends. She should, however, rise early, and see that all the domestics are duly performing their work, and that everything is progressing satisfactorily for the preparation of the breakfast for the household and family. After breakfast, which, in large establishments, she will take in the "housekeeper's room" with the lady's-maid, butler, and valet, and where they will be waited on by the still-room maid, she will, on various days set apart for each purpose, carefully examine the household linen, with a view to its being repaired, or to a further quantity being put in hand to be made; she will also see that the furniture throughout the house is well rubbed and polished; and will, besides, attend to all the necessary details of marketing and ordering goods from the tradesmen.

The housekeeper's room is generally made use of by the lady's-maid, butler, and valet, who take there their breakfast, tea, and supper. The lady's-maid will also use this apartment as a sitting-room, when not engaged with her lady, or with some other duties, which would call her elsewhere. In different establishments, according to their size and the rank of the family, different rules of course prevail. For instance, in the mansions of those of very high rank, and where there is a house steward, there are two distinct tables kept, one in the steward's room for the principal members of the household, the other in the servants' hall, for the other domestics. At the steward's dinner-table, the steward and housekeeper preside; and here, also, are present the lady's-maid, butler, valet, and head gardener. Should any visitors be staying with the family, their servants, generally the valet and lady's-maid, will be admitted to the steward's table.

59. AFTER DINNER, the housekeeper, having seen that all the members of the establishment have regularly returned to their various duties, and that all the departments of the household are in proper working order, will have many important matters claiming her attention. She will, possibly, have to give the finishing touch to some article of confectionary, or be occupied with some of the more elaborate processes of the still-room. There may also be the dessert to arrange, ice-creams to make; and all these employments call for no ordinary degree of care, taste, and attention.

The still-room was formerly much more in vogue than at present; for in days of "auld lang syne," the still was in constant requisition for the supply of sweet-flavoured waters for the purposes of cookery, scents and aromatic substances used in the preparation of the toilet, and cordials in cases of accidents and illness. There are some establishments, however, in which distillation is still carried on, and in these, the still-room maid has her old duties to perform. In a general way, however, this domestic is immediately concerned with the housekeeper. For the latter she lights the fire, dusts her room, prepares the breakfast-table, and waits at the different meals taken in the housekeeper's room (see 58). A still-room maid may learn a very great deal of useful knowledge from her intimate connection with the housekeeper, and if she be active and intelligent, may soon fit herself for a better position in the household.

60. IN THE EVENING, the housekeeper will often busy herself with the necessary preparations for the next day's duties. Numberless small, but still important arrangements, will have to be made, so that everything may move smoothly. At times, perhaps, attention will have to be paid to the breaking of lump-sugar, the stoning of raisins, the washing, cleansing, and drying of currants, &c. The evening, too, is the best time for setting right her account of the expenditure, and duly writing a statement of moneys received and paid, and also for making memoranda of any articles she may require for her store-room or other departments.

Periodically, at some convenient time,—for instance, quarterly or half-yearly, it is a good plan for the housekeeper to make an inventory of everything she has under her care, and compare this with the lists of a former period; she will then be able to furnish a statement, if necessary, of the articles which, on account of time, breakage, loss, or other causes, it has been necessary to replace or replenish.

61. IN CONCLUDING THESE REMARKS on the duties of the housekeeper, we will briefly refer to the very great responsibility which attaches to her position. Like "Cæsar's wife," she should be "above suspicion," and her honesty and sobriety unquestionable; for there are many temptations to which she is exposed. In a physical point of view, a housekeeper should be healthy and strong, and be particularly clean in her person, and her hands, although they may show a degree of roughness, from the nature of some of her employments, yet should have a nice inviting appearance. In her dealings with the various tradesmen, and in her behaviour to the domestics under her, the demeanour and conduct of the housekeeper should be such as, in neither case, to diminish, by an undue familiarity, her authority or influence.

Note.—It will be useful for the mistress and housekeeper to know the best seasons for various occupations connected with Household Management; and we, accordingly, subjoin a few hints which we think will prove valuable.

As, in the winter months, servants have much more to do, in consequence of the necessity there is to attend to the number of fires throughout the household, not much more than the ordinary every-day work can be attempted.

In the summer, and when the absence of fires gives the domestics more leisure, then any extra work that is required, can be more easily performed.

The spring is the usual period set apart for house-cleaning, and removing all the dust and dirt, which will necessarily, with the best of housewives, accumulate during the winter months, from the smoke of the coal, oil, gas, &c. This season is also well adapted for washing and bleaching linen, &c., as, the weather, not being then too hot for the exertions necessary in washing counterpanes, blankets, and heavy things in general, the work is better and more easily done than in the intense heats of July, which month some recommend for these purposes. Winter curtains should be taken down, and replaced by the summer white ones; and furs and woollen cloths also carefully laid by. The former should be well shaken and brushed, and then pinned upon paper or linen, with camphor to preserve them from the moths. Furs, &c., will be preserved in the same way. Included, under the general description of house-cleaning, must be understood, turning out all the nooks and corners of drawers, cupboards, lumber-rooms, lofts, &c., with a view of getting rid of all unnecessary articles, which only create dirt and attract vermin; sweeping of chimneys, taking up carpets, painting and whitewashing the kitchen and offices, papering rooms, when needed, and, generally speaking, the house putting on, with the approaching summer, a bright appearance, and a new face, in unison with nature. Oranges now should be preserved, and orange wine made.

The summer will be found, as we have mentioned above, in consequence of the diminution of labour for the domestics, the best period for examining and repairing household linen, and for "putting to rights" all those articles which have received a large share of wear and tear during the dark winter days. In direct reference to this matter, we may here remark, that sheets should be turned "sides to middle" before they are allowed to get very thin. Otherwise, patching, which is uneconomical from the time it consumes, and is unsightly in point of appearance, will have to be resorted to. In June and July, gooseberries, currants, raspberries, strawberries, and other summer fruits, should be preserved, and jams and jellies made. In July, too, the making of walnut ketchup should be attended to, as the green walnuts will be approaching perfection for this purpose. Mixed pickles may also be now made, and it will be found a good plan to have ready a jar of pickle-juice (for the making of which all information will be given in future pages), into which to put occasionally some young French beans, cauliflowers, &c.

In the early autumn, plums of various kinds are to be bottled and preserved, and jams and jellies made. A little later, tomato sauce, a most useful article to have by you, may be prepared ; a supply of apples laid in, if you have a place to keep them, as also a few keeping pears and filberts. Endeavour to keep also a large vegetable marrow,—it will be found delicious in the winter.

In October and November, it will be necessary to prepare for the cold weather, and get ready the winter clothing for the various members of the family. The white summer curtains will now be carefully put away, the fire-places, grates, and chimneys looked to, and the house put in a thorough state of repair, so that no "loose tile" may, at a future day, interfere with your comfort, and extract something considerable from your pocket.

In December, the principal household duty lies in preparing for the creature comforts of those near and dear to us, so as to meet old Christmas with a happy face, a contented mind, and a full larder ; and in stoning the plums, washing the currants, cutting the citron, beating the eggs, and MIXING THE PUDDING, a housewife is not unworthily greeting the genial season of all good things.

CHAPTER III.

ARRANGEMENT AND ECONOMY OF THE KITCHEN.

62. "THE DISTRIBUTION OF A KITCHEN," says Count Rumford, the celebrated philosopher and physician, who wrote so learnedly on all subjects connected with domestic economy and architecture, " must always depend so much on local circumstances, that general rules can hardly be given respecting it ; the principles, however, on which this distribution ought, in all cases, to be made, are simple and easy to be understood," and, in his estimation, these resolve themselves into symmetry of proportion in the building and convenience to the cook. The requisites of a good kitchen, however, demand something more special than is here pointed out. It must be remembered that it is the great laboratory of every household, and that much of the "weal or woe," as far as regards bodily health, depends upon the nature of the preparations concocted within its walls. A good kitchen, therefore, should be erected with a view to the following particulars. 1. Convenience of distribution in its parts, with largeness of dimension. 2. Excellence of light, height of ceiling, and good ventilation. 3. Easiness of access, without passing through the house. 4. Sufficiently remote from the principal apartments of the house, that the members, visitors, or guests of the family, may not perceive the odour incident to cooking, or hear the noise of culinary operations. 5. Plenty of fuel and water, which, with the scullery, pantry, and storeroom, should be so near it, as to offer the smallest possible trouble in reaching them.

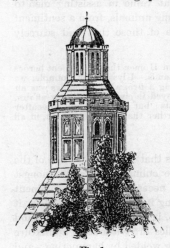

Fig. 1.

The kitchens of the Middle Ages, in England, are said to have been constructed after the fashion of those of the Romans. They were generally octagonal, with several fireplaces, but no chimneys ; neither was there any wood admitted into the building. The accompanying cut, fig. 1, represents the turret which was erected on the top of the conical roof of the kitchen at Glastonbury Abbey, and which was perforated with holes to allow the smoke of the fire, as well as the steam from cooking, to escape. Some kitchens had funnels or vents below the eaves to let out the steam, which was sometimes considerable, as the Anglo-Saxons used their meat chiefly in a boiled state. From this circumstance, some of their large kitchens had four ranges, comprising a boiling-place for small boiled meats, and a boiling-house for the great boiler. In private houses the culinary arrangements were no doubt different ; for Du Cange mentions a little kitchen with a chamber, even in a solarium, or upper floor.

63. The Simplicity of the Primitive Ages has frequently been an object of poetical admiration, and it delights the imagination to picture men living upon such fruits as spring spontaneously from the earth, and desiring no other beverages to slake their thirst, but such as fountains and rivers supply. Thus we are told, that the ancient inhabitants of Argos lived principally on pears; that the Arcadians revelled in acorns, and the Athenians in figs. This, of course, was in the golden age, before ploughing began, and when mankind enjoyed all kinds of plenty without having to earn their bread "by the sweat of their brow." This delightful period, however, could not last for ever, and the earth became barren, and continued unfruitful till Ceres came and taught the art of sowing, with several other useful inventions. The first whom she taught to till the ground was Triptolemus, who communicated his instructions to his countrymen the Athenians. Thence the art was carried into Achaia, and thence into Arcadia. Barley was the first grain that was used, and the invention of bread-making is ascribed to Pan.

The use of fire, as an instrument of cookery, must have been coeval with this invention of bread, which, being the most necessary of all kinds of food, was frequently used in a sense so comprehensive as to include both meat and drink. It was, by the Greeks, baked under the ashes.

64. In the Primary Ages it was deemed unlawful to eat flesh, and when mankind began to depart from their primitive habits, the flesh of swine was the first that was eaten. For several ages, it was pronounced unlawful to slaughter oxen, from an estimate of their great value in assisting men to cultivate the ground; nor was it usual to kill young animals, from a sentiment which considered it cruel to take away the life of those that had scarcely tasted the joys of existence.

At this period no cooks were kept, and we know from Homer that his ancient heroes prepared and dressed their victuals with their own hands. Ulysses, for example, we are told, like a modern charwoman, excelled at lighting a fire, whilst Achilles was an adept at turning a spit. Subsequently, heralds, employed in civil and military affairs, filled the office of cooks, and managed marriage feasts; but this, no doubt, was after mankind had advanced in the art of living, a step further than *roasting*, which, in all places, was the ancient manner of dressing meat.

65. The Age of Roasting we may consider as that in which the use of the metals would be introduced as adjuncts to the culinary art; and amongst these, iron, the most useful of them all, would necessarily take a prominent place. This metal is easily oxidized, but to bring it to a state of fusibility, it requires a most intense heat. Of all the metals, it is the widest diffused and most abundant; and few stones or mineral bodies are without an admixture of it. It possesses the valuable property of being welded by hammering; and hence its adaptation to the numerous purposes of civilized life.

Metallic grains of iron have been found in strawberries, and a twelfth of the weight of the wood of dried oak is said to consist of this metal. Blood owes its colour of redness to the quantity of iron it contains, and rain and snow are seldom perfectly free from it. In the arts it is employed in three states,—as *cast* iron, *wrought* iron, and *steel*. In each of these it largely enters into the domestic economy, and stoves, grates, and the general implements of cookery, are usually composed of it. In antiquity, its employment was, comparatively speaking, equally universal. The excavations made at Pompeii have proved this. The accompanying cuts present us with specimens of stoves,

Fig. 2.

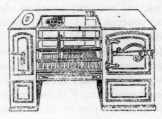

Fig. 3.

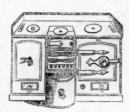

Fig. 4.

Fig. 5 .

both ancient and modern. Fig. 2 is the remains of a kitchen stove found in the house of Pansa, at Pompeii, and would seem, in its perfect state, not to have been materially different from such as are in use at the present day. Fig. 3 is a self-acting, simple open range in modern use, and may be had of two qualities, ranging, according to their dimensions, from £3. 10s. and £3. 18s. respectively, up to £4. 10s. and £7. 5s. They are completely fitted up with oven, boiler, sliding cheek, wrought-iron bars, revolving shelves, and brass tap. Fig. 4 is called the Improved Leamington Kitchener, and is said to surpass any other range in use, for easy cooking by one fire. It has a hot plate, which is well calculated for an ironing-stove, and on which as many vessels as will stand upon it, may be kept boiling, without being either soiled or injured. Besides, it has a perfectly ventilated and spacious wrought-iron roaster, with movable shelves, draw-out stand, double dripping-pan, and meat-stand. The roaster can be converted into an oven by closing the valves, when bread and pastry can be baked in it in a superior manner. It also has a large iron boiler with brass tap and steam-pipe, round and square gridirons for chops and steaks, ash-pan, open fire for roasting, and a set of ornamental covings with plate-warmer attached. It took a first-class prize and medal in the Great Exhibition of 1851, and was also exhibited, with all the recent improvements, at the Dublin Exhibition in 1853. Fig. 5 is another kitchener, adapted for large families. It has on the one side, a large ventilated oven; and on the other, the fire and roaster. The hot plate is over all, and there is a back boiler, made of wrought iron, with brass tap and steam-pipe. In other respects it resembles Fig. 4, with which it possesses similar advantages of construction. Either may be had at varying prices, according to size, from £5. 15s. up to £23. 10s. They are supplied by Messrs. Richard & John Slack, 336, Strand, London.

66. FROM KITCHEN RANGES to the implements used in cookery is but a step. With these, every kitchen should be well supplied, otherwise the cook must not be expected to "perform her office" in a satisfactory manner. Of the culinary utensils of the ancients, our knowledge is very limited; but as the art of living, in every civilized country, is pretty much the same, the instruments for cooking must, in a great degree, bear a striking resemblance to each other.

On referring to classical antiquities, we find mentioned, among household utensils, leather bags, baskets constructed of twigs, reeds, and rushes; boxes, basins, and bellows; bread-moulds, brooms, and brushes; caldrons, colanders, cisterns, and chafing-dishes; cheese-rasps, knives, and ovens of the Dutch kind; funnels and frying-pans; handmills, soup-ladles, milk-pails, and oil-jars; presses, scales, and sieves; spits of different sizes, but some of them large enough to roast an ox; spoons, fire-tongs, trays, trenchers, and drinking-vessels; with others for carrying food, preserving milk, and holding cheese. This enumeration, if it does nothing else, will, to some extent, indicate the state of the simpler kinds of mechanical arts among the ancients.

In so far as regards the shape and construction of many of the kitchen utensils enumerated above, they bore a great resemblance to our own. This will be seen by the accompanying cuts. Fig. 6 is an ancient stock-pot in bronze, which seems to have been

Fig. 6.   Fig. 7.   Fig. 8.

made to hang over the fire, and was found in the buried city of Pompeii. Fig. 7 is one of modern make, and may be obtained either of copper or wrought iron, tinned inside. Fig. 8 is another of antiquity, with a large ladle and colander, with holes attached. It is taken from the column of Trajan. The modern ones can be obtained at all prices, according to size, from 13s. 6d. up to £1. 1s.

67. IN THE MANUFACTURE OF THESE UTENSILS, bronze metal seems to have been much in favour with the ancients. It was chosen not only for their domestic vessels, but it was also much used for their public sculptures and medals. It is a compound, composed of from six to twelve parts of tin to one hundred of copper. It gives its name to figures and all pieces of sculpture made of it. Brass was another favourite metal, which is composed of copper and zinc. It is more fusible than copper, and not so apt to tarnish. In a pure state it is not malleable, unless when hot, and after it has been melted twice it will not bear the hammer. To render it capable of being wrought, it requires 7 lb. of lead to be put to 1 cwt. of its own material.

The Corinthian brass of antiquity was a mixture of silver, gold, and copper. A fine kind of brass, supposed to be made by the cementation of copper plates with calamine, is, in Germany, hammered out into leaves, and is called Dutch metal in this country. It is employed in the same way as gold leaf. Brass is much used for watchworks, as well as for wire.

68. The braziers, ladles, stewpans, saucepans, gridirons, and colanders of antiquity might generally pass for those of the English manufacture of the present day, in so far as shape is concerned. In proof of this we have placed together the following similar articles of ancient and modern pattern, in order

that the reader may, at a single view, see wherein any difference that is between them, consists.

Fig. 9. Modern.   *Fig.* 11. Modern.   *Fig.* 13. Modern.

Fig. 10. Ancient.   *Fig.* 12. Ancient.   *Fig.* 14. Ancient.

Fig. 15. Modern.   *Fig.* 16. Modern.   *Fig.* 17. Ancient.   *Fig.* 18. Ancient.

Figs. 9 and 10 are flat sauce or *sauté* pans, the ancient one being fluted in the handle, and having at the end a ram's head. Figs. 11 and 12 are colanders, the handle of the ancient one being adorned, in the original, with carved representations of a cornucopia, a satyr, a goat, pigs, and other animals. Any display of taste in the adornment of such utensils, might seem to be useless; but when we remember how much more natural it is for us all to be careful of the beautiful and costly, than of the plain and cheap, it may even become a question in the economy of a kitchen, whether it would not, in the long run, be cheaper to have articles which displayed some tasteful ingenuity in their manufacture, than such as are so perfectly plain as to have no attractions whatever beyond their mere suitableness to the purposes for which they are made. Figs. 13 and 14 are saucepans, the ancient one being of bronze, originally copied from the cabinet of M. l'Abbé Charlet, and engraved in the Antiquities of Montfaucon. Figs. 15 and 17 are gridirons, and 16 and 18 dripping-pans. In all these utensils the resemblance between such as were in use 2,000 years ago, and those in use at the present day, is strikingly manifest.

69. SOME OF THE ANCIENT UTENSILS represented in the above cuts, are copied from those found amid the ruins of Herculaneum and Pompeii. These Roman cities were, in the first century, buried beneath the lava of an eruption of Vesuvius, and continued to be lost to the world till the beginning of the last century, when a peasant, in digging for a well, gradually discovered a small temple with some statues. Little notice, however, was taken of this circumstance till 1736, when the king of Naples, desiring to erect a palace at Portici, caused extensive excavations to be made, when the city of Herculaneum was slowly unfolded to view. Pompeii was discovered about 1750, and

being easier cleared from the lava in which it had so long been entombed, disclosed itself as it existed immediately before the catastrophe which overwhelmed it, nearly two thousand years ago. It presented, to the modern world, the perfect picture of the form and structure of an ancient Roman city. The interior of its habitations, shops, baths, theatres, and temples, were all disclosed, with many of the implements used by the workmen in their various trades, and the materials on which they were employed, when the doomed city was covered with the lavian stream.

70. Amongst the most essential Requirements of the kitchen are scales or weighing-machines for family use. These are found to have existed among the ancients, and must, at a very early age, have been both publicly and privately employed for the regulation of quantities. The modern English weights were adjusted by the 27th chapter of Magna Charta, or the great charter forced, by the barons, from King John at Runnymede, in Surrey. Therein it is declared that the weights, all over England, shall be the same, although for different commodities there were two different kinds, Troy and Avoirdupois. The origin of both is taken from a grain of wheat gathered in the middle of an ear. The standard of measures was originally kept at Winchester, and by a law of King Edgar was ordained to be observed throughout the kingdom.

Fig. 19.   Fig. 20.

Fig. 19 is an ancient pair of common scales, with two basins and a movable weight, which is made in the form of a head, covered with the pileus, because Mercury had the weights and measures under his superintendence. It is engraved on a stone in the gallery of Florence. Fig. 20 represents a modern weighing-machine, of great convenience, and generally in use in those establishments where a great deal of cooking is carried on.

71. Accompanying the Scales, or weighing-machines, there should be spice-boxes, and sugar and biscuit-canisters of either white or japanned tin. The covers of these should fit tightly, in order to exclude the air, and if necessary, be lettered in front, to distinguish them. The white metal of which they are usually composed, loses its colour when exposed to the air, but undergoes no further change. It enters largely into the composition of culinary utensils, many of them being entirely composed of tinned sheet-iron; the inside of copper and iron vessels also, being usually what is called *tinned*. This art consists of covering any metal with a thin coating of tin; and it

requires the metal to be covered, to be perfectly clean and free from rust, and also that the tin, itself, be purely metallic, and entirely cleared from all ashes or refuse. Copper boilers, saucepans, and other kitchen utensils, are tinned after they are manufactured, by being first made hot and the tin rubbed on with resin. In this process, nothing ought to be used but pure grain-tin. Lead, however, is sometimes mixed with that metal, not only to make it lie more easily, but to adulterate it—a pernicious practice, which in every article connected with the cooking and preparation of food, cannot be too severely reprobated. — The following list, supplied by Messrs. Richard & John Slack, 336, Strand, will show the articles required for the kitchen of a family in the middle class of life, although it does not contain all the things that may be deemed necessary for some families, and may contain more than are required for others. As Messrs. Slack themselves, however, publish a useful illustrated catalogue, which may be had at their establishment *gratis*, and which it will be found advantageous to consult by those about to furnish, it supersedes the necessity of our enlarging that which we give :—

	s.	d.		s.	d.
1 Tea-kettle	6	6	1 Dripping-pan and Stand	6	6
1 Toasting-fork	1	0	1 Dustpan	1	0
1 Bread-grater	1	0	1 Fish and Egg-slice	1	9
1 Pair of Brass Candlesticks	3	6	2 Fish-kettles	10	0
1 Teapot and Tray	6	6	1 Flour-box	1	0
1 Bottle-jack	9	6	3 Flat-irons	3	6
6 Spoons	1	6	2 Frying-pans	4	0
2 Candlesticks	2	6	1 Gridiron	2	0
1 Candle-box	1	4	1 Mustard-pot	1	0
6 Knives and Forks	5	3	1 Salt-cellar	0	8
2 Sets of Skewers	1	0	1 Pepper-box	0	6
1 Meat-chopper	1	9	1 Pair of Bellows	2	0
1 Cinder-sifter	1	3	3 Jelly-moulds	8	0
1 Coffee-pot	2	3	1 Plate-basket	5	6
1 Colander	1	6	1 Cheese-toaster	1	10
3 Block-tin Saucepans	5	9	1 Coal-shovel	2	6
5 Iron Saucepans	12	0	1 Wood Meat-screen	30	0
1 Ditto and Steamer	6	6			
1 Large Boiling-pot	10	0	The Set	£8 11	1
4 Iron Stewpans	8	9			

72. As not only Health but Life may be said to depend on the cleanliness of culinary utensils, great attention must be paid to their condition generally, but more especially to that of the saucepans, stewpans, and boilers. Inside they should be kept perfectly clean, and where an open fire is used, the outside as clean as possible. With a Leamington range, saucepans, stewpans, &c., can be kept entirely free from smoke and soot on the outside, which is an immense saving of labour to the cook or scullery-maid. Care should be taken that the lids fit tight and close, so that soups or gravies may not be suffered to waste by evaporation. They should be made to keep the steam in and the smoke out, and should always be bright on the upper rim, where they do not immediately come in contact with the fire. Soup-pots and kettles should be washed immediately after being used, and dried before the fire, and they should be kept in a dry

place, in order that they may escape the deteriorating influence of rust, and, thereby, be destroyed. Copper utensils should never be used in the kitchen unless tinned, and the utmost care should be taken, not to let the tin be rubbed off. If by chance this should occur, have it replaced before the vessel is again brought into use. Neither soup nor gravy should, at any time, be suffered to remain in them longer than is absolutely necessary, as any fat or acid that is in them, may affect the metal, so as to impregnate with poison what is intended to be eaten. Stone and earthenware vessels should be provided for soups and gravies not intended for immediate use, and, also, plenty of common dishes for the larder, that the table-set may not be used for such purposes. It is the nature of vegetables soon to turn sour, when they are apt to corrode glazed red-ware, and even metals, and frequently, thereby, to become impregnated with poisonous particles. The vinegar also in pickles, by its acidity, does the same. Consideration, therefore, should be given to these facts, and great care also taken that all *sieves, jelly-bags,* and tapes for collared articles, be well scalded and kept dry, or they will impart an unpleasant flavour when next used. To all these directions the cook should pay great attention, nor should they, by any means, be neglected by the *mistress of the household,* who ought to remember that cleanliness in the kitchen gives health and happiness to home, whilst economy will immeasurably assist in preserving them.

73. WITHOUT FUEL, A KITCHEN might be pronounced to be of little use; therefore, to discover and invent materials for supplying us with the means of domestic heat and comfort, has exercised the ingenuity of man. Those now known have been divided into five classes; the first comprehending the fluid inflammable bodies; the second, peat or turf; the third, charcoal of wood; the fourth, pit-coal charred; and the fifth, wood or pit-coal in a crude state, with the capacity of yielding a copious and bright flame. The first may be said seldom to be employed for the purposes of cookery; but *peat*, especially amongst rural populations, has, in all ages, been regarded as an excellent fuel. It is one of the most important productions of an alluvial soil, and belongs to the vegetable rather than the mineral kingdom. It may be described as composed of wet, spongy black earth, held together by decayed vegetables. Formerly it covered extensive tracts in England, but has greatly disappeared before the genius of agricultural improvement. *Charcoal* is a kind of artificial coal, used principally where a strong and clear fire is desired. It is a black, brittle, insoluble, inodorous, tasteless substance, and, when newly-made, possesses the remarkable property of absorbing certain quantities of the different gases. Its dust, when used as a polishing powder, gives great brilliancy to metals. It consists of wood half-burned, and is manufactured by cutting pieces of timber into nearly the same size, then disposing them in heaps, and covering them with earth, so as to prevent communication with the air, except when necessary to make them burn. When they have been sufficiently charred, the fire is extinguished by stopping the vents through which the air is admitted. Of *coal* there are various species;

as, pit, culm, slate, cannel, Kilkenny, sulphurous, bovey, jet, &c. These have all their specific differences, and are employed for various purposes; but are all, more or less, used as fuel.

The use of coal for burning purposes was not known to the Romans. In Britain it was discovered about fifty years before the birth of Christ, in Lancashire, not far from where Manchester now stands; but for ages after its discovery, so long as forests abounded, wood continued to be the fuel used for firing. The first public notice of coal is in the reign of Henry III , who, in 1272, granted a charter to the town of Newcastle, permitting the inhabitants to dig for coal. It took some centuries more, however, to bring it into common use, as this did not take place till about the first quarter of the seventeenth century, in the time of Charles I. A few years after the Restoration, we find that about 200,000 chaldrons were consumed in London. Although several countries possess mines of coal, the quality of their mineral is, in general, greatly inferior to that of Great Britain, where it is found mostly in undulating districts abounding with valleys, and

Fig. 21.

interspersed with plains of considerable extent. It lies usually between the *strata* of other substances, and rarely in an horizontal position, but with a *dip* or inclination to one side. Our cut, Fig. 21, represents a section of coal as it is found in the stratum.

74. To be acquainted with the Periods when things are in season, is one of the most essential pieces of knowledge which enter into the " Art of Cookery." We have, therefore, compiled the following list, which will serve to show for every month in the year the

TIMES WHEN THINGS ARE IN SEASON.

JANUARY.

Fish.—Barbel, brill, carp, cod, crabs, crayfish, dace, eels, flounders, haddocks, herrings, lampreys, lobsters, mussels, oysters, perch, pike, plaice, prawns, shrimps, skate, smelts, soles, sprats, sturgeon, tench, thornback, turbot, whitings.

Meat.—Beef, house lamb, mutton, pork, veal, venison.

Poultry.—Capons, fowls, tame pigeons, pullets, rabbits, turkeys.

Game.—Grouse, hares, partridges, pheasants, snipe, wild-fowl, woodcock.

Vegetables.—Beetroot, broccoli, cabbages, carrots, celery, chervil, cresses, cucumbers (forced), endive, lettuces, parsnips, potatoes, savoys, spinach, turnips,—various herbs.

Fruit.—Apples, grapes, medlars, nuts, oranges, pears, walnuts, crystallized preserves (foreign), dried fruits, such as almonds and raisins; French and Spanish plums; prunes, figs, dates.

FEBRUARY.

Fish.—Barbel, brill, carp, cod may be bought, but is not so good as in January, crabs, crayfish, dace, eels, flounders, haddocks, herrings, lampreys, lobsters, mussels, oysters, perch, pike, plaice, prawns, shrimps, skate, smelts, soles, sprats, sturgeon, tench, thornback, turbot, whiting.

MEAT.—Beef, house lamb, mutton, pork, veal.

POULTRY.—Capons, chickens, ducklings, tame and wild pigeons, pullets with eggs, turkeys, wild-fowl, though now not in full season.

GAME.—Grouse, hares, partridges, pheasants, snipes, woodcock.

VEGETABLES.—Beetroot, broccoli (purple and white), Brussels sprouts, cabbages, carrots, celery, chervil, cresses, cucumbers (forced), endive, kidney-beans, lettuces, parsnips, potatoes, savoys, spinach, turnips,—various herbs.

FRUIT.—Apples (golden and Dutch pippins), grapes, medlars, nuts, oranges, pears (Bon Chrétien), walnuts, dried fruits (foreign), such as almonds and raisins; French and Spanish plums; prunes, figs, dates, crystallized preserves.

MARCH.

FISH.—Barbel, brill, carp, crabs, crayfish, dace, eels, flounders, haddocks, herrings, lampreys, lobsters, mussels, oysters, perch, pike, plaice, prawns, shrimps, skate, smelts, soles, sprats, sturgeon, tench, thornback, turbot, whiting.

MEAT.—Beef, house lamb, mutton, pork, veal.

POULTRY.—Capons, chickens, ducklings, tame and wild pigeons, pullets with eggs, turkeys, wild-fowl, though now not in full season.

GAME.—Grouse, hares, partridges, pheasants, snipes, woodcock.

VEGETABLES.—Beetroot, broccoli (purple and white), Brussels sprouts, cabbages, carrots, celery, chervil, cresses, cucumbers (forced), endive, kidney-beans, lettuces, parsnips, potatoes, savoys, sea-kale, spinach, turnips,—various herbs.

FRUIT.—Apples (golden and Dutch pippins), grapes, medlars, nuts, oranges, pears (Bon Chrétien), walnuts, dried fruits (foreign), such as almonds and raisins; French and Spanish plums; prunes, figs, dates, crystallized preserves.

APRIL.

FISH.—Brill, carp, cockles, crabs, dory, flounders, ling, lobsters, red and gray mullet, mussels, oysters, perch, prawns, salmon (but rather scarce and expensive), shad, shrimps, skate, smelts, soles, tench, turbot, whitings.

MEAT.—Beef, lamb, mutton, veal.

POULTRY.—Chickens, ducklings, fowls, leverets, pigeons, pullets, rabbits.

GAME.—Hares.

VEGETABLES.—Broccoli, celery, lettuces, young onions, parsnips, radishes, small salad, sea-kale, spinach, sprouts,—various herbs.

FRUIT.—Apples, nuts, pears, forced cherries, &c. for tarts, rhubarb, dried fruits, crystallized preserves.

MAY.

FISH.—Carp, chub, crabs, crayfish, dory, herrings, lobsters, mackerel, red and gray mullet, prawns, salmon, shad, smelts, soles, trout, turbot.

MEAT.—Beef, lamb, mutton, veal.

POULTRY.—Chickens, ducklings, fowls, green geese, leverets, pullets, rabbits.

VEGETABLES.—Asparagus, beans, early cabbages, carrots, cauliflowers, cresses, cucumbers, lettuces, pease, early potatoes, salads, sea-kale,—various herbs.

FRUIT.—Apples, green apricots, cherries, currants for tarts, gooseberries, melons, pears, rhubarb, strawberries.

JUNE.

FISH.—Carp, crayfish, herrings, lobsters, mackerel, mullet, pike, prawns, salmon, soles, tench, trout, turbot.

MEAT.—Beef, lamb, mutton, veal, buck venison.

POULTRY.—Chickens, ducklings, fowls, green geese, leverets, plovers, pullets, rabbits, turkey poults, wheatears.

VEGETABLES.—Artichokes, asparagus, beans, cabbages, carrots, cucumbers, lettuces, onions, parsnips, pease, potatoes, radishes, small salads, sea-kale, spinach,—various herbs.

FRUIT.—Apricots, cherries, currants, gooseberries, melons, nectarines, peaches, pears, pineapples, raspberries, rhubarb, strawberries.

JULY.

FISH.—Carp, crayfish, dory, flounders, haddocks, herrings, lobsters, mackerel, mullet, pike, plaice, prawns, salmon, shrimps, soles, sturgeon, tench, thornback.

MEAT.—Beef, lamb, mutton, veal, buck venison.

POULTRY.—Chickens, ducklings, fowls, green geese, leverets, plovers, pullets, rabbits, turkey poults, wheatears, wild ducks (called flappers).

VEGETABLES.—Artichokes, asparagus, beans, cabbages, carrots, cauliflowers, celery, cresses, endive, lettuces, mushrooms, onions, pease, radishes, small salading, sea-kale, sprouts, turnips, vegetable marrow, — various herbs.

FRUIT.—Apricots, cherries, currants, figs, gooseberries, melons, nectarines, pears, pineapples, plums, raspberries, strawberries, walnuts in high season, and pickled.

AUGUST.

FISH.—Brill, carp, chub, crayfish, crabs, dory, eels, flounders, grigs, herrings, lobsters, mullet, pike, prawns, salmon, shrimps, skate, soles, sturgeon, thornback, trout, turbot.

MEAT.—Beef, lamb, mutton, veal, buck venison.

POULTRY.—Chickens, ducklings, fowls, green geese, pigeons, plovers, pullets, rabbits, turkey poults, wheatears, wild ducks.

GAME.—Leverets, grouse, blackcock.

VEGETABLES.—Artichokes, asparagus, beans, carrots, cabbages, cauliflowers, celery, cresses, endive, lettuces, mushrooms, onions, pease, potatoes, radishes, sea-kale, small salading, sprouts, turnips, various kitchen herbs, vegetable marrows.

FRUIT.—Currants, figs, filberts, gooseberries, grapes, melons, mulberries, nectarines, peaches, pears, pineapples, plums, raspberries, walnuts.

SEPTEMBER.

FISH.—Brill, carp, cod, eels, flounders, lobsters, mullet, oysters, plaice, prawns, skate, soles, turbot, whiting, whitebait.

MEAT.—Beef, lamb, mutton, pork, veal.

POULTRY.—Chickens, ducks, fowls, geese, larks, pigeons, pullets, rabbits, teal, turkeys.

GAME.—Blackcock, buck venison, grouse, hares, partridges, pheasants.

VEGETABLES.—Artichokes, asparagus, beans, cabbage sprouts, carrots, celery, lettuces, mushrooms, onions, pease, potatoes, salading, sea-kale, sprouts, tomatoes, turnips, vegetable marrows,—various herbs.

FRUIT.—Bullaces, damsons, figs, filberts, grapes, melons, morella-cherries, mulberries, nectarines, peaches, pears, plums, quinces, walnuts.

OCTOBER.

FISH.—Barbel, brill, cod, crabs, eels, flounders, gudgeons, haddocks, lobsters, mullet, oysters, plaice, prawns, skate, soles, tench, turbot, whiting.

MEAT.—Beef, mutton, pork, veal, venison.

POULTRY.—Chickens, fowls, geese, larks, pigeons, pullets, rabbits, teal, turkeys, widgeons, wild ducks.

GAME.—Blackcock, grouse, hares, partridges, pheasants, snipes, woodcocks, doe venison.

VEGETABLES.—Artichokes, beets, cabbages, cauliflowers, carrots, celery, lettuces, mushrooms, onions, potatoes, sprouts, tomatoes, turnips, vegetable marrows,-- various herbs.

FRUIT.—Apples, black and white bullaces, damsons, figs, filberts, grapes, pears, quinces, walnuts.

NOVEMBER.

FISH.—Brill, carp, cod, crabs, eels, gudgeons, haddocks, oysters, pike, soles, tench, turbot, whiting.

MEAT.—Beef, mutton, veal, doe venison.

POULTRY.—Chickens, fowls, geese, larks, pigeons, pullets, rabbits, teal, turkeys, widgeons, wild duck.

GAME.—Hares, partridges, pheasants, snipes, woodcocks.

VEGETABLES.—Beetroot, cabbages, carrots, celery, lettuces, late cucumbers, onions, potatoes, salading, spinach, sprouts,—various herbs.

FRUIT.—Apples, bullaces, chestnuts, filberts, grapes, pears, walnuts.

DECEMBER.

FISH.—Barbel, brill, carp, cod, crabs, eels, dace, gudgeons, haddocks, herrings, lobsters, oysters, perch, pike, shrimps, skate, sprats, soles, tench, thornback, turbot, whiting.

MEAT.—Beef, house lamb, mutton, pork, venison.

POULTRY.—Capons, chickens, fowls, geese, pigeons, pullets, rabbits, teal, turkeys, widgeons, wild ducks.

GAME.—Hares, partridges, pheasants, snipes, woodcocks.

VEGETABLES.—Broccoli, cabbages, carrots, celery, leeks, onions, potatoes, parsnips, Scotch kale, turnips, winter spinach.

FRUIT.—Apples, chestnuts, filberts, grapes, medlars, oranges, pears, walnuts, dried fruits, such as almonds and raisins, figs, dates, &c.,—crystallized preserves.

75. WHEN FUEL AND FOOD ARE PROCURED, the next consideration is, how the latter may be best preserved, with a view to its being suitably dressed. More waste is often occasioned by the want of judgment, or of necessary care in this particular, than by any other cause. In the absence of proper places for keeping provisions, a hanging safe, suspended in an airy situation, is the best substitute. A well-ventilated larder, dry and shady, is better for meat and poultry, which require to be kept for some time; and the utmost skill in the culinary art will not compensate for the want of proper attention to this particular. Though it is advisable that animal food should be hung up in the open air till its fibres have lost some degree of their toughness, yet, if it is kept till it loses its natural sweetness, its flavour has become deteriorated, and, as a wholesome comestible, it has lost many of its qualities conducive to health. As soon, therefore, as the slightest trace of putrescence is detected, it has reached its highest degree of tenderness, and should be dressed immediately. During the sultry summer months, it is difficult to procure meat that is not either tough or tainted. It should, therefore, be well examined when it comes in, and if flies have touched it, the part must be cut off, and the remainder well washed. In very cold weather, meat and vegetables touched by the frost, should be brought into the kitchen early in the morning, and soaked in cold water. In loins of meat, the long pipe that runs by the bone should be taken out, as it is apt to taint; as also the kernels of beef. Rumps and edgebones of beef, when bruised, should not be purchased. All these things ought to enter into the consideration of every household manager, and great care should be taken that nothing is thrown away, or suffered to be wasted in the kitchen, which might, by proper management, be turned to a good account. The shank-bones of mutton, so little esteemed in general, give richness to soups or gravies, if well soaked and brushed before they are added to the boiling. They are also particularly nourishing for sick persons. Roast-beef bones, or shank-bones of ham, make excellent stock for pea-soup.—When the whites of eggs are used for jelly, confectionary, or other

purposes, a pudding or a custard should be made, that the yolks may be used. All things likely to be wanted should be in readiness : sugars of different sorts ; currants washed, picked, and perfectly dry ; spices pounded, and kept in very small bottles closely corked, or in canisters, as we have already directed (72). Not more of these should be purchased at a time than are likely to be used in the course of a month. Much waste is always prevented by keeping every article in the place best suited to it. Vegetables keep best on a stone floor, if the air be excluded ; meat, in a cold dry place ; as also salt, sugar, sweet-meats, candles, dried meats, and hams. Rice, and all sorts of seed for puddings, should be closely covered to preserve them from insects ; but even this will not prevent them from being affected by these destroyers, if they are long and carelessly kept.

CHAPTER IV.

INTRODUCTION TO COOKERY.

76. As in the Fine Arts, the progress of mankind from barbarism to civilization is marked by a gradual succession of triumphs over the rude materialities of nature, so in the art of cookery is the progress gradual from the earliest and simplest modes, to those of the most complicated and refined. Plain or rudely-carved stones, tumuli, or mounds of earth, are the monuments by which barbarous tribes denote the events of their history, to be succeeded, only in the long course of a series of ages, by beautifully-proportioned columns, gracefully-sculptured statues, triumphal arches, coins, medals, and the higher efforts of the pencil and the pen, as man advances by culture and observation to the perfection of his faculties. So is it with the art of cookery. Man, in his primitive state, lives upon roots and the fruits of the earth, until, by degrees, he is driven to seek for new means, by which his wants may be supplied and enlarged. He then becomes a hunter and a fisher. As his species increases, greater necessities come upon him, when he gradually abandons the roving life of the savage for the more stationary pursuits of the herdsman. These beget still more settled habits, when he begins the practice of agriculture, forms ideas of the rights of property, and has his own, both defined and secured. The forest, the stream, and the sea are now no longer his only resources for food. He sows and he reaps, pastures and breeds cattle, lives on the cultivated produce of his fields, and revels in the luxuries of the dairy ; raises flocks for clothing, and assumes, to all intents and purposes, the habits of permanent life and the comfortable condition of a farmer. This is the fourth stage of social progress, up to which the useful or mechanical arts have been incidentally developing themselves, when trade and commerce begin. Through these various phases, *only to live* has been the great object of mankind ; but, by-and-by, comforts are multiplied, and accumulating riches create new wants. The object, then, is not only to *live*, but to live economically, agreeably, tastefully, and well. Accordingly, the art of cookery commences ; and although the fruits of the earth, the fowls of the air, the beasts of the field, and the fish of the sea, are still the only food of mankind, yet these are so prepared, improved, and dressed by skill and ingenuity, that they are the means of immeasurably extending the boundaries of human enjoyments. Everything that is edible, and passes under the hands of the cook, is more or less changed, and assumes new forms. Hence the influence of that functionary is immense upon the happiness of a household.

77. In order that the duties of the Cook may be properly performed, and that he may be able to reproduce esteemed dishes with certainty, all

terms of indecision should be banished from his art. Accordingly, what is known only to him, will, in these pages, be made known to others. In them all those indecisive terms expressed by a bit of this, some of that, a small piece of that, and a handful of the other, shall never be made use of, but all quantities be precisely and explicitly stated. With a desire, also, that all ignorance on this most essential part of the culinary art should disappear, and that a uniform system of weights and measures should be adopted, we give an account of the weights which answer to certain measures.

A TABLE-SPOONFUL is frequently mentioned in a recipe, in the prescriptions of medical men, and also in medical, chemical, and gastronomical works. By it is generally meant and understood a measure or bulk equal to that which would be produced by *half an ounce* of water.

A DESSERT-SPOONFUL is the half of a table-spoonful; that is to say, by it is meant a measure or bulk equal to a *quarter of an ounce* of water.

A TEA-SPOONFUL is equal in quantity to a *drachm* of water.

A DROP.—This is the name of a vague kind of measure, and is so called on account of the liquid being *dropped* from the mouth of a bottle. Its quantity, however, will vary, either from the consistency of the liquid or the size and shape of the mouth of the bottle. The College of Physicians determined the quantity of a drop to be *one grain*, 60 drops making one fluid drachm. Their drop, or sixtieth part of a fluid drachm, is called a *minim*.

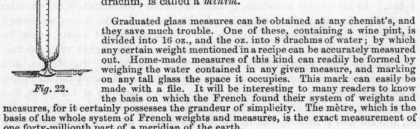

Graduated glass measures can be obtained at any chemist's, and they save much trouble. One of these, containing a wine pint, is divided into 16 oz., and the oz. into 8 drachms of water; by which any certain weight mentioned in a recipe can be accurately measured out. Home-made measures of this kind can readily be formed by weighing the water contained in any given measure, and marking on any tall glass the space it occupies. This mark can easily be made with a file. It will be interesting to many readers to know the basis on which the French found their system of weights and measures, for it certainly possesses the grandeur of simplicity. The mètre, which is the basis of the whole system of French weights and measures, is the exact measurement of one forty-millionth part of a meridian of the earth.

Fig. 22.

78. EXCELLENCE IN THE ART OF COOKERY, as in all other things, is only attainable by practice and experience. In proportion, therefore, to the opportunities which a cook has had of these, so will be his excellence in the art. It is in the large establishments of princes, noblemen, and very affluent families alone, that the man cook is found in this country. He, also, superintends the kitchens of large hotels, clubs, and public institutions, where he, usually, makes out the bills of fare, which are generally submitted to the principal for approval. To be able to do this, therefore, it is absolutely necessary that he should be a judge of the season of every dish, as well as know perfectly the state of every article he undertakes to prepare. He must also be a judge of every article he buys; for no skill, however great it may be, will enable him to make that good which is really bad. On him rests the responsibility of the cooking generally, whilst a speciality of his department, is to prepare the rich soups, stews, ragouts, and such dishes as enter into the more refined and

complicated portions of his art, and such as are not usually understood by ordinary professors. He, therefore, holds a high position in a household, being inferior in rank, as already shown (21), only to the house steward, the valet, and the butler.

In the luxurious ages of Grecian antiquity, Sicilian cooks were the most esteemed, and received high rewards for their services. Among them, one called Trimalcio was such an adept in his art, that he could impart to common fish both the form and flavour of the most esteemed of the piscatory tribes. A chief cook in the palmy days of Roman voluptuousness had about £800 a year, and Antony rewarded the one that cooked the supper which pleased Cleopatra, with the present of a city. With the fall of the empire, the culinary art sank into less consideration. In the middle ages, cooks laboured to acquire a reputation for their sauces, which they composed of strange combinations, for the sake of novelty, as well as singularity.

79. THE DUTIES OF THE COOK, THE KITCHEN AND THE SCULLERY MAIDS, are so intimately associated, that they can hardly be treated of separately. The cook, however, is at the head of the kitchen; and in proportion to her possession of the qualities of cleanliness, neatness, order, regularity, and celerity of action, so will her influence appear in the conduct of those who are under her; as it is upon her that the whole responsibility of the business of the kitchen rests, whilst the others must lend her, both a ready and a willing assistance, and be especially tidy in their appearance, and active in their movements.

In the larger establishments of the middle ages, cooks, with the authority of feudal chiefs, gave their orders from a high chair in which they ensconced themselves, and commanded a view of all that was going on throughout their several domains. Each held a long wooden spoon, with which he tasted, without leaving his seat, the various comestibles that were cooking on the stoves, and which he frequently used as a rod of punishment on the backs of those whose idleness and gluttony too largely predominated over their diligence and temperance.

80. IF, AS WE HAVE SAID (3), THE QUALITY OF EARLY RISING be of the first importance to the mistress, what must it be to the servant! Let it, therefore, be taken as a long-proved truism, that without it, in every domestic, the effect of all things else, so far as *work* is concerned, may, in a great measure, be neutralized. In a cook, this quality is most essential; for an hour lost in the morning, will keep her toiling, absolutely toiling, all day, to overtake that which might otherwise have been achieved with ease. In large establishments, six is a good hour to rise in the summer, and seven in the winter.

81. HER FIRST DUTY, in large establishments and where it is requisite, should be to set her dough for the breakfast rolls, provided this has not been done on the previous night, and then to engage herself with those numerous little preliminary occupations which may not inappropriately be termed laying out her duties for the day. This will bring in the breakfast hour of eight, after which, directions must be given, and preparations made, for the different dinners of the household and family.

82. IN THOSE NUMEROUS HOUSEHOLDS where a cook and housemaid are only kept, the general custom is, that the cook should have the charge of the

dining-room. The hall, the lamps and the doorstep are also committed to her care, and any other work there may be on the outside of the house. In establishments of this kind, the cook will, after having lighted her kitchen fire, carefully brushed the range, and cleaned the hearth, proceed to prepare for breakfast. She will thoroughly rinse the kettle, and, filling it with fresh water, will put it on the fire to boil. She will then go to the breakfast-room, or parlour, and there make all things ready for the breakfast of the family. Her attention will next be directed to the hall, which she will sweep and wipe; the kitchen stairs, if there be any, will now be swept; and the hall mats, which have been removed and shaken, will be again put in their places.

The cleaning of the kitchen, pantry, passages, and kitchen stairs must always be over before breakfast, so that it may not interfere with the other business of the day. Everything should be ready, and the whole house should wear a comfortable aspect when the heads of the house and members of the family make their appearance. Nothing, it may be depended on, will so please the mistress of an establishment, as to notice that, although she has not been present to see that the work was done, attention to smaller matters has been carefully paid, with a view to giving her satisfaction and increasing her comfort.

83. BY THE TIME THAT THE COOK has performed the duties mentioned above, and well swept, brushed, and dusted her kitchen, the breakfast-bell will most likely summon her to the parlour, to "bring in" the breakfast. It is the cook's department, generally, in the smaller establishments, to wait at breakfast, as the housemaid, by this time, has gone up-stairs into the bedrooms, and has there applied herself to her various duties. The cook usually answers the bells and single knocks at the door in the early part of the morning, as the tradesmen, with whom it is her more special business to speak, call at these hours.

84. IT IS IN HER PREPARATION OF THE DINNER that the cook begins to feel the weight and responsibility of her situation, as she must take upon herself all the dressing and the serving of the principal dishes, which her skill and ingenuity have mostly prepared. Whilst these, however, are cooking, she must be busy with her pastry, soups, gravies, ragouts, &c. Stock, or what the French call *consommé*, being the basis of most made dishes, must be always at hand, in conjunction with her sweet herbs and spices for seasoning. "A place for everything, and everything in its place," must be her rule, in order that time may not be wasted in looking for things when they are wanted, and in order that the whole apparatus of cooking may move with the regularity and precision of a well-adjusted machine;—all must go on simultaneously. The vegetables and sauces must be ready with the dishes they are to accompany, and in order that they may be suitable, the smallest oversight must not be made in their preparation. When the dinner-hour has arrived, it is the duty of the cook to dish-up such dishes as may, without injury, stand, for some time, covered on the hot plate or in the hot closet; but such as are of a more important or *recherché* kind, must be delayed until the order "to serve" is given from the drawing-room. Then comes

haste; but there must be no hurry,—all must work with order. The cook takes charge of the fish, soups, and poultry; and the kitchen-maid of the vegetables, sauces, and gravies. These she puts into their appropriate dishes, whilst the scullery-maid waits on and assists the cook. Everything must be timed so as to prevent its getting cold, whilst great care should be taken, that, between the first and second courses, no more time is allowed to elapse than is necessary, for fear that the company in the dining-room lose all relish for what has yet to come of the dinner. When the dinner has been served, the most important feature in the daily life of the cook is at an end. She must, however, now begin to look to the contents of her larder, taking care to keep everything sweet and clean, so that no disagreeable smells may arise from the gravies, milk, or meat that may be there. These are the principal duties of a cook in a first-rate establishment.

In smaller establishments, the housekeeper often conducts the higher department of cooking (*see* 58, 59, 60), and the cook, with the assistance of a scullery-maid, performs some of the subordinate duties of the kitchen-maid.

When circumstances render it necessary, the cook engages to perform the whole of the work of the kitchen, and, in some places, a portion of the house-work also.

85. WHILST THE COOK IS ENGAGED WITH HER MORNING DUTIES, the kitchen-maid is also occupied with hers. Her first duty, after the fire is lighted, is to sweep and clean the kitchen, and the various offices belonging to it. This she does every morning, besides cleaning the stone steps at the entrance of the house, the halls, the passages, and the stairs which lead to the kitchen. Her general duties, besides these, are to wash and scour all these places twice a week, with the tables, shelves, and cupboards. She has also to dress the nursery and servants'-hall dinners, to prepare all fish, poultry, and vegetables, trim meat joints and cutlets, and do all such duties as may be considered to enter into the cook's department in a subordinate degree.

86. THE DUTIES OF THE SCULLERY-MAID are to assist the cook; to keep the scullery clean, and all the metallic as well as earthenware kitchen utensils.

The position of scullery-maid is not, of course, one of high rank, nor is the payment for her services large. But if she be fortunate enough to have over her a good kitchen-maid and clever cook, she may very soon learn to perform various little duties connected with cooking operations, which may be of considerable service in fitting her for a more responsible place. Now, it will be doubtless thought by the majority of our readers, that the fascinations connected with the position of the scullery-maid, are not so great as to induce many people to leave a comfortable home in order to work in a scullery. But we are acquainted with one instance in which the desire, on the part of a young girl, was so strong to become connected with the kitchen and cookery, that she absolutely left her parents, and engaged herself as a scullery-maid in a gentleman's house. Here she showed herself so active and intelligent, that she very quickly rose to the rank of kitchen-maid; and from this, so great was her gastronomical genius, she became, in a short space of time, one of the best women-cooks in England. After this, we think, it must be allowed, that a cook, like a poet, *nascitur, non fit.*

87. MODERN COOKERY stands so greatly indebted to the gastronomic propensities of our French neighbours, that many of their terms are adopted and applied by English artists to the same as well as similar preparations of their own. A vocabulary of these is, therefore, indispensable in a work of this kind. Accordingly, the following will be found sufficiently complete for all ordinary purposes :—

EXPLANATION OF FRENCH TERMS USED IN MODERN HOUSEHOLD COOKERY.

ASPIC.—A savoury jelly, used as an exterior moulding for cold game, poultry, fish, &c. This, being of a transparent nature, allows the bird which it covers to be seen through it. This may also be used for decorating or garnishing.

ASSIETTE (plate).—*Assiettes* are the small *entrées* and *hors-d'œuvres*, the quantity of which does not exceed what a plate will hold. At dessert, fruits, cheese, chestnuts, biscuits, &c., if served upon a plate, are termed *assiettes*.— ASSIETTE VOLANTE is a dish which a servant hands round to the guests, but is not placed upon the table. Small cheese soufflés and different dishes, which ought to be served very hot, are frequently made *assiettes volantes*.

AU-BLEU.—Fish dressed in such a manner as to have a *bluish* appearance.

BAIN-MARIE.—An open saucepan or kettle of nearly boiling water, in which a smaller vessel can be set for cooking and warming. This is very useful for keeping articles hot, without altering their quantity or quality. If you keep sauce, broth, or soup by the fireside, the soup reduces and becomes too strong, and the sauce thickens as well as reduces ; but this is prevented by using the *bain-marie*, in which the water should be very hot, but not boiling.

BÉCHAMEL.—French white sauce, now frequently used in English cookery.

BLANCH.—To whiten poultry, vegetables, fruit, &c., by plunging them into boiling water for a short time, and afterwards plunging them into cold water, there to remain until they are cold.

BLANQUETTE.—A sort of fricassee.

BOUILLI.—Beef or other meat boiled ; but, generally speaking, boiled beef is understood by the term.

BOUILLIE.—A French dish resembling hasty-pudding.

BOUILLON.—A thin broth or soup.

BRAISE.—To stew meat with fat bacon until it is tender, it having previously been blanched.

BRAISIÈRE.—A saucepan having a lid with ledges, to put fire on the top.

BRIDER.—To pass a packthread through poultry, game, &c., to keep together their members.

CARAMEL (burnt sugar).—This is made with a piece of sugar, of the size of a nut, browned in the bottom of a saucepan ; upon which a cupful of stock is gradually poured, stirring all the time a glass of broth, little by little. It may be used with the feather of a quill, to colour meats, such as the upper part of fricandeaux ; and to impart colour to sauces. Caramel made with water instead of stock may be used to colour *compôtes* and other *entremets*.

CASSEROLE.—A crust of rice, which, after having been moulded into the form of a pie, is baked, and then filled with a fricassee of white meat or a purée of game.

COMPOTE.—A stew, as of fruit or pigeons.

CONSOMMÉ.—Rich stock, or gravy.

CROQUETTE.—Ball of fried rice or potatoes.

CROUTONS.—Sippets of bread.

DAUBIÈRE.—An oval stewpan, in which *daubes* are cooked ; *daubes* being meat or fowl stewed in sauce.

DÉSOSSER.—To *bone*, or take out the bones from poultry, game, or fish. This is an operation requiring considerable experience.

ENTRÉES.—Small side or corner dishes, served with the first course.

ENTREMETS.—Small side or corner dishes, served with the second course.

ESCALOPES.—Collops ; small, round, thin pieces of tender meat, or of fish, beaten with the handle of a strong knife to make them tender.

FEUILLETAGE.—Puff-paste.

FLAMBER.—To singe fowl or game, after they have been picked.

FONCER.—To put in the bottom of a saucepan slices of ham, veal, or thin broad slices of bacon.

GALETTE.—A broad thin cake.

GÂTEAU.—A cake, correctly speaking ; but used sometimes to denote a pudding and a kind of tart.

GLACER.—To glaze, or spread upon hot meats, or larded fowl, a thick and rich sauce or gravy, called *glaze*. This is laid on with a feather or brush, and in confectionary the term means to ice fruits and pastry with sugar, which glistens on hardening.

HORS-D'ŒUVRES.—Small dishes, or *assiettes volantes* of sardines, anchovies, and other relishes of this kind, served to the guests during the first course. (*See* ASSIETTES VOLANTES.)

LIT.—A bed or layer ; articles in thin slices are placed in layers, other articles, or seasoning, being laid between them.

MAIGRE.—Broth, soup, or gravy, made without meat.

MATELOTE.—A rich fish-stew, which is generally composed of carp, eels, trout, or barbel. It is made with wine.

MAYONNAISE.—Cold sauce, or salad dressing.

MENU.—The bill of fare.

MERINGUE.—A kind of icing, made of whites of eggs and sugar, well beaten.

MIROTON.—Larger slices of meat than collops ; such as slices of beef for a vinaigrette, or ragout or stew of onions.

MOUILLER.—To add water, broth, or other liquid, during the cooking.

PANER.—To cover over with very fine crumbs of bread, meats, or any other articles to be cooked on the gridiron, in the oven, or frying-pan.

PIQUER.—To lard with strips of fat bacon, poultry, game, meat, &c. This should always be done according to the vein of the meat, so that in carving you slice the bacon across as well as the meat.

POÊLÉE.—Stock used instead of water for boiling turkeys, sweetbreads, fowls, and vegetables, to render them less insipid. This is rather an expensive preparation.

PURÉE.—Vegetables, or meat reduced to a very smooth pulp, which is afterwards mixed with enough liquid to make it of the consistency of very thick soup.

RAGOUT.—Stew or hash.

REMOULADE.—Salad dressing.

RISSOLES.—Pastry, made of light puff-paste, and cut into various forms, and fried. They may be filled with fish, meat, or sweets.

ROUX.—Brown and white ; French thickening.

SALMI.—Ragout of game previously roasted.

SAUCE PIQUANTE.—A sharp sauce, in which somewhat of a vinegar flavour predominates.

SAUTER.—To dress with sauce in a saucepan, repeatedly moving it about.

TAMIS.—Tammy, a sort of open cloth or sieve through which to strain broth and sauces, so as to rid them of small bones, froth, &c.

TOURTE.—Tart. Fruit pie.

TROUSSER.—To truss a bird ; to put together the body and tie the wings and thighs, in order to round it for roasting or boiling, each being tied then with packthread, to keep it in the required form.

VOL-AU-VENT.—A rich crust of very fine puff-paste, which may be filled with various delicate ragouts or fricassees, of fish, flesh, or fowl. Fruit may also be inclosed in a *vol-au-vent*.

SOUPS.

CHAPTER V.

GENERAL DIRECTIONS FOR MAKING SOUPS.

88. LEAN, JUICY BEEF, MUTTON, AND VEAL, form the basis of all good soups; therefore it is advisable to procure those pieces which afford the richest succulence, and such as are fresh-killed. Stale meat renders them bad, and fat is not so well adapted for making them. The principal art in composing good rich soup, is so to proportion the several ingredients that the flavour of one shall not predominate over another, and that all the articles of which it is composed, shall form an agreeable whole. To accomplish this, care must be taken that the roots and herbs are perfectly well cleaned, and that the water is proportioned to the quantity of meat and other ingredients. Generally a quart of water may be allowed to a pound of meat for soups, and half the quantity for gravies. In making soups or gravies, gentle stewing or simmering is incomparably the best. It may be remarked, however, that a really good soup can never be made but in a well-closed vessel, although, perhaps, greater wholesomeness is obtained by an occasional exposure to the air. Soups will, in general, take from three to six hours doing, and are much better prepared the day before they are wanted. When the soup is cold, the fat may be much more easily and completely removed; and when it is poured off, care must be taken not to disturb the settlings at the bottom of the vessel, which are so fine that they will escape through a sieve. A tamis is

the best strainer, and if the soup is strained while it is hot, let the tamis or cloth be previously soaked in cold water. Clear soups must be perfectly transparent, and thickened soups about the consistence of cream. To thicken and give body to soups and gravies, potato-mucilage, arrow-root, bread-raspings, isinglass, flour and butter, barley, rice, or oatmeal, in a little water rubbed well together, are used. A piece of boiled beef pounded to a pulp, with a bit of butter and flour, and rubbed through a sieve, and gradually incorporated with the soup, will be found an excellent addition. When the soup appears to be *too thin* or *too weak*, the cover of the boiler should be taken off, and the contents allowed to boil till some of the watery parts have evaporated; or some of the thickening materials, above mentioned, should be added. When soups and gravies are kept from day to day in hot weather, they should be warmed up every day, and put into fresh scalded pans or tureens, and placed in a cool cellar. In temperate weather, every other day may be sufficient.

89. VARIOUS HERBS AND VEGETABLES are required for the purpose of making soups and gravies. Of these the principal are,—Scotch barley, pearl barley, wheat flour, oatmeal, bread-raspings, pease, beans, rice, vermicelli, macaroni, isinglass, potato-mucilage, mushroom or mushroom ketchup, champignons, parsnips, carrots, beetroot, turnips, garlic, shalots, and onions. Sliced onions, fried with butter and flour till they are browned, and then rubbed through a sieve, are excellent to heighten the colour and flavour of brown soups and sauces, and form the basis of many of the fine relishes furnished by the cook. The older and drier the onion, the stronger will be its flavour. Leeks, cucumber, or burnet vinegar; celery or celery-seed pounded. The latter, though equally strong, does not impart the delicate sweetness of the fresh vegetable; and when used as a substitute, its flavour should be corrected by the addition of a bit of sugar. Cress-seed, parsley, common thyme, lemon thyme, orange thyme, knotted marjoram, sage, mint, winter savoury, and basil. As fresh green basil is seldom to be procured, and its fine flavour is soon lost, the best way of preserving the extract is by pouring wine on the fresh leaves

90. FOR THE SEASONING OF SOUPS, bay-leaves, tomato, tarragon, chervil, burnet, allspice, cinnamon, ginger, nutmeg, clove, mace, black and white pepper, essence of anchovy, lemon-peel, and juice, and Seville orange-juice, are all taken. The latter imparts a finer flavour than the lemon, and the acid is much milder. These materials, with wine, mushroom ketchup, Harvey's sauce, tomato sauce, combined in various proportions, are, with other ingredients, manipulated into an almost endless variety of excellent soups and gravies. Soups, which are intended to constitute the principal part of a meal, certainly ought not to be flavoured like sauces, which are only designed to give a relish to some particular dish.

SOUP, BROTH, AND BOUILLON.

91. IT HAS BEEN ASSERTED, that English cookery is, nationally speaking, far from being the best in the world. More than this, we have been frequently told by brilliant foreign writers, half philosophers, half *chefs*, that we are the *worst* cooks on the face of the earth, and that the proverb which alludes to the divine origin of food, and the precisely opposite origin of its preparers, is peculiarly applicable to us islanders. Not, however, to the inhabitants of the whole island ; for, it is stated in a work which treats of culinary operations, north of the Tweed, that the " broth" of Scotland claims, for excellence and wholesomeness, a very close second place to the *bouillon*, or common soup of France. " *Three* hot meals of broth and meat, for about the price of ONE roasting joint," our Scottish brothers and sisters get, they say ; and we hasten to assent to what we think is now a very well-ascertained fact. We are glad to note, however, that soups of vegetables, fish, meat, and game, are now very frequently found in the homes of the English middle classes, as well as in the mansions of the wealthier and more aristocratic ; and we take this to be one evidence, that we are on the right road to an improvement in our system of cookery. One great cause of many of the spoilt dishes and badly-cooked meats which are brought to our tables, arises, we think, and most will agree with us, from a non-acquaintance with " common, every-day things." Entertaining this view, we intend to preface the chapters of this work with a simple scientific *résumé* of all those causes and circumstances which relate to the food we have to prepare, and the theory and chemistry of the various culinary operations. Accordingly, this is the proper place to treat of the quality of the flesh of animals, and describe some of the circumstances which influence it for good or bad. We will, therefore, commence with the circumstance of *age,* and examine how far this affects the quality of meat.

92. DURING THE PERIOD BETWEEN THE BIRTH AND MATURITY OF ANIMALS, their flesh undergoes very considerable changes. For instance, when the animal is young, the fluids which the tissues of the muscles contain, possess a large proportion of what is called *albumen*. This albumen, which is also the chief component of the white of eggs, possesses the peculiarity of coagulating or hardening at a certain temperature, like the white of a boiled egg, into a soft, white fluid, no longer soluble, or capable of being dissolved in water. As animals grow older, this peculiar animal matter gradually decreases, in proportion to the other constituents of the juice of the flesh. Thus, the reason why veal, lamb, and young pork are *white, and without gravy* when cooked, is, that the large quantity of albumen they contain hardens, or becomes coagulated. On the other hand, the reason why beef and mutton

E

are *brown, and have gravy*, is, that the proportion of albumen they contain, is small, in comparison with their greater quantity of fluid which is soluble, and not coagulable.

93. THE QUALITY OF THE FLESH OF AN ANIMAL is considerably influenced by the nature of the *food on which it has been fed;* for the food supplies the material which produces the flesh. If the food be not suitable and good, the meat cannot be good either ; just as the paper on which these words are printed, could not be good, if the rags from which it is made, were not of a fine quality. To the experienced in this matter, it is well known that the flesh of animals fed on farinaceous produce, such as corn, pulse, &c., is firm, well-flavoured, and also economical in the cooking ; that the flesh of those fed on succulent and pulpy substances, such as roots, possesses these qualities in a somewhat less degree ; whilst the flesh of those whose food contains fixed oil, as linseed, is greasy, high coloured, and gross in the fat, and if the food has been used in large quantities, possessed of a rank flavour.

94. IT IS INDISPENSABLE TO THE GOOD QUALITY OF MEAT, that the animal should be *perfectly healthy* at the time of its slaughter. However slight the disease in an animal may be, inferiority in the quality of its flesh, as food, is certain to be produced. In most cases, indeed, as the flesh of diseased animals has a tendency to very rapid putrefaction, it becomes not only unwholesome, but absolutely poisonous, on account of the absorption of the *virus* of the unsound meat into the systems of those who partake of it. The external indications of good and bad meat will be described under its own particular head, but we may here premise that the lyer of all wholesome meat, when freshly killed, adheres firmly to the bone.

95. ANOTHER CIRCUMSTANCE GREATLY AFFECTING THE QUALITY OF MEAT, is the animal's treatment *before it is slaughtered.* This influences its value and wholesomeness in no inconsiderable degree. It will be easy to understand this, when we reflect on those leading principles by which the life of an animal is supported and maintained. These are, the digestion of its food, and the assimilation of that food into its substance. Nature, in effecting this process, first reduces the food in the stomach to a state of pulp, under the name of chyme, which passes into the intestines, and is there divided into two principles, each distinct from the other. One, a milk-white fluid, — the nutritive portion,—is absorbed by innumerable vessels which open upon the mucous membrane, or inner coat of the intestines. These vessels, or absorbents, discharge the fluid into a common duct, or road, along which it is conveyed to the large veins in the neighbourhood of the heart. Here it is mixed with the venous blood (which is black and impure) returning from every part of the body, and then it supplies the waste which is occasioned in the circulating stream by the arterial (or pure) blood having furnished matter for the substance of the animal. The blood of the animal having completed its course through all parts, and having had its waste recruited by the digested food, is now received

into the heart, and by the action of that organ it is urged through the lungs, there to receive its purification from the air which the animal inhales. Again returning to the heart, it is forced through the arteries, and thence distributed, by innumerable ramifications, called capillaries, bestowing to every part of the animal, life and nutriment. The other principle—the innutritive portion—passes from the intestines, and is thus got rid of. It will now be readily understood how flesh is affected for bad, if an animal is slaughtered when the circulation of its blood has been increased by over-driving, ill-usage, or other causes of excitement, to such a degree of rapidity as to be too great for the capillaries to perform their functions, and causing the blood to be congealed in its minuter vessels. Where this has been the case, the meat will be dark-coloured, and become rapidly putrid ; so that self-interest and humanity alike dictate kind and gentle treatment of all animals destined to serve as food for man.

THE CHEMISTRY AND ECONOMY OF SOUP-MAKING.

96. STOCK BEING THE BASIS of all meat soups, and, also, of all the principal sauces, it is essential to the success of these culinary operations, to know the most complete and economical method of extracting, from a certain quantity of meat, the best possible stock or broth. The theory and philosophy of this process we will, therefore, explain, and then proceed to show the practical course to be adopted.

97. AS ALL MEAT IS principally composed of fibres, fat, gelatine, osmazome, and albumen, it is requisite to know that the FIBRES are inseparable, constituting almost all that remains of the meat after it has undergone a long boiling.

98. FAT is dissolved by boiling ; but as it is contained in cells covered by a very fine membrane, which never dissolves, a portion of it always adheres to the fibres. The other portion rises to the surface of the stock, and is that which has escaped from the cells which were not whole, or which have burst by boiling.

99. GELATINE is soluble : it is the basis and the nutritious portion of the stock. When there is an abundance of it, it causes the stock, when cold, to become a jelly.

100. OSMAZOME is soluble even when cold, and is that part of the meat which gives flavour and perfume to the stock. The flesh of old animals contains more *osmazome* than that of young ones. Brown meats contain more than white, and the former make the stock more fragrant. By roasting meat, the osmazome appears to acquire higher properties ; so, by putting the remains of roast meats into your stock-pot, you obtain a better flavour.

101. ALBUMEN is of the nature of the white of eggs; it can be dissolved in cold or tepid water, but coagulates when it is put into water not quite at the boiling-point. From this property in albumen, it is evident that if the meat is put into the stock-pot when the water boils, or after this is made to boil up quickly, the albumen, in both cases, hardens. In the first it rises to the surface, in the second it remains in the meat, but in both it prevents the gelatine and osmazome from dissolving; and hence a thin and tasteless stock will be obtained. It ought to be known, too, that the coagulation of the albumen in the meat, always takes place, more or less, according to the size of the piece, as the parts farthest from the surface always acquire *that degree* of heat which congeals it before entirely dissolving it.

102. BONES ought always to form a component part of the stock-pot. They are composed of an earthy substance,—to which they owe their solidity,—of gelatine, and a fatty fluid, something like marrow. *Two ounces* of them contain as much gelatine as *one pound* of meat; but in them, this is so incased in the earthy substance, that boiling water can dissolve only the surface of whole bones. By breaking them, however, you can dissolve more, because you multiply their surfaces; and by reducing them to powder or paste, you can dissolve them entirely; but you must not grind them dry. We have said (99) that gelatine forms the basis of stock; but this, though very nourishing, is entirely without taste; and to make the stock savoury, it must contain *osmazome*. Of this, bones do not contain a particle; and that is the reason why stock made entirely of them, is not liked; but when you add meat to the broken or pulverized bones, the osmazome contained in it makes the stock sufficiently savoury.

103. In concluding this part of our subject, the following condensed hints and directions should be attended to in the economy of soup-making :—

I. BEEF MAKES THE BEST STOCK; veal stock has less colour and taste; whilst mutton sometimes gives it a tallowy smell, far from agreeable, unless the meat has been previously roasted or broiled. Fowls add very little to the flavour of stock, unless they be old and fat. Pigeons, when they are old, add the most flavour to it; and a rabbit or partridge is also a great improvement. From the freshest meat the best stock is obtained.

II. IF THE MEAT BE BOILED solely to make stock, it must be cut up into the smallest possible pieces; but, generally speaking, if it is desired to have good stock and a piece of savoury meat as well, it is necessary to put a rather large piece into the stock-pot, say sufficient for two or three days, during which time the stock will keep well in all weathers. Choose the freshest meat, and have it cut as thick as possible; for if it is a thin, flat piece, it will not look well, and will be very soon spoiled by the boiling.

III. NEVER WASH MEAT, as it deprives its surface of all its juices; separate it from the bones, and tie it round with tape, so that its shape may be preserved, then put it into the stock-pot, and for each pound of meat, let there be one pint of water; press it down with the hand, to allow the air, which it contains, to escape, and which often raises it to the top of the water.

IV. PUT THE STOCK-POT ON A GENTLE FIRE, so that it may heat gradually. The albumen will first dissolve, afterwards coagulate; and as it is in this state lighter than the liquid, it will rise to the surface; bringing with it all its impurities. It is this which makes *the scum*. The rising of the hardened albumen has the same effect in clarifying stock as the white of eggs; and, as a rule, it may be said that the more scum there is, the clearer will be the stock. Always take care that the fire is very regular.

V. REMOVE THE SCUM when it rises thickly, and do not let the stock boil, because then one portion of the scum will be dissolved, and the other go to the bottom of the pot; thus rendering it very difficult to obtain a clear broth. If the fire is regular, it will not be necessary to add cold water in order to make the scum rise; but if the fire is too large at first, it will then be necessary to do so.

VI. WHEN THE STOCK IS WELL SKIMMED, and begins to boil, put in salt and vegetables, which may be two or three carrots, two turnips, one parsnip, a bunch of leeks and celery tied together. You can add, according to taste, a piece of cabbage, two or three cloves stuck in an onion, and a tomato. The latter gives a very agreeable flavour to the stock. If fried onion be added, it ought, according to the advice of a famous French *chef*, to be tied in a little bag: without this precaution, the colour of the stock is liable to be clouded.

VII. BY THIS TIME we will now suppose that you have chopped the bones which were separated from the meat, and those which were left from the roast meat of the day before. Remember, as was before pointed out, that the more these are broken, the more gelatine you will have. The best way to break them up is to pound them roughly in an iron mortar, adding, from time to time, a little water, to prevent them getting heated. It is a great saving thus to make use of the bones of meat, which, in too many English families, we fear, are entirely wasted; for it is certain, as previously stated (No. 102), that two ounces of bone contain as much gelatine (which is the nutritive portion of stock) as one pound of meat. In their broken state tie them up in a bag, and put them in the stock-pot; adding the gristly parts of cold meat, and trimmings, which can be used for no other purpose. If, to make up the weight, you have received from the butcher a piece of mutton or veal, broil it slightly over a clear fire before putting it in the stock-pot, and be very careful that it does not contract the least taste of being smoked or burnt.

VIII. ADD NOW THE VEGETABLES, which, to a certain extent, will stop the boiling of the stock. Wait, therefore, till it simmers well up again, then draw it to the side of the fire, and keep it gently simmering till it is served, preserving, as before said, your fire always the same. Cover the stock-pot well, to prevent evaporation; do not fill it up, even if you take out a little stock, unless the meat is exposed; in which case a little boiling water may be added, but only enough to cover it. After six hours' slow and gentle simmering, the stock is done; and it should not be continued on the fire, longer than is necessary, or it will tend to insipidity.

Note.—It is on a good stock, or first good broth and sauce, that excellence in cookery depends. If the preparation of this basis of the culinary art is intrusted to negligent or ignorant persons, and the stock is not well skimmed, but indifferent results will be obtained. The stock will never be clear; and when it is obliged to be clarified, it is deteriorated both in quality and flavour. In the proper management of the stock-pot an immense deal of trouble is saved, inasmuch as one stock, in a small dinner, serves for all purposes. Above all things, the greatest economy, consistent with excellence, should be practised, and the price of everything which enters the kitchen correctly ascertained. The *theory* of this part of Household Management may appear trifling; but its practice is extensive, and therefore it requires the best attention.

RECIPES.

◆

CHAPTER VI.

FRUIT AND VEGETABLE SOUPS.

[It will be seen, by reference to the following Recipes, that an entirely original and most intelligible system has been pursued in explaining the preparation of each dish. We would recommend the young housekeeper, cook, or whoever may be engaged in the important task of "getting ready" the dinner, or other meal, to follow precisely the order in which the recipes are given. Thus, let them first place on their table all the INGREDIENTS *necessary; then the* modus operandi, *or* MODE *of preparation, will be easily managed. By a careful reading, too, of the recipes, there will not be the slightest difficulty in arranging a repast for any number of persons, and an accurate notion will be gained of the* TIME *the cooking of each dish will occupy, of the periods at which it is* SEASONABLE, *as also of its* AVERAGE COST.*

The addition of the natural history, and the description of the various properties of the edible articles in common use in every family, will be serviceable both in a practical and an educational point of view.

Speaking specially of the Recipes for Soups, it may be added, that by the employment of the BEST, MEDIUM, *or* COMMON STOCK, *the quality of the Soups and their cost may be proportionately increased or lessened.]*

STOCKS FOR ALL KINDS OF SOUPS.

RICH STRONG STOCK.

104. INGREDIENTS.—4 lbs. of shin of beef, 4 lbs. of knuckle of veal, $\frac{3}{4}$ lb. of good lean ham; any poultry trimmings; 3 small onions, 3 small carrots, 3 turnips (the latter should be omitted in summer, lest they ferment), 1 head of celery, a few chopped mushrooms, when obtainable; 1 tomato, a bunch of savoury herbs, not forgetting parsley; $1\frac{1}{2}$ oz. of salt, 12 white peppercorns, 6 cloves, 3 small blades of mace, 4 quarts of water.

Mode.—Line a delicately clean stewpan with the ham cut in thin broad slices, carefully trimming off all its rusty fat; cut up the beef and veal in pieces about 3 inches square, and lay them on the ham; set it on the stove, and draw it down, and stir frequently. When the meat is equally browned, put in the beef and veal bones, the poultry trimmings, and pour in the cold water. Skim well, and occasionally add a little cold water, to stop its boiling, until it becomes quite clear; then put in all the other ingredients, and simmer very slowly for 5 hours. Do not let it come to a brisk boil, that the stock be not wasted, and that its colour may be preserved. Strain through a very fine hair sieve, or tammy, and it will be fit for use.

Time.—5 hours. *Average cost,* 1s. 3d. per quart.

MEDIUM STOCK.

105. INGREDIENTS.—4 lbs. of shin of beef, or 4 lbs. of knuckle of veal, or 2 lbs. of each; any bones, trimmings of poultry, or fresh meat, $\frac{1}{2}$ a lb. of lean bacon or ham, 2 oz. of butter, 2 large onions, each stuck with 3 cloves; 1 turnip, 3 carrots, $\frac{1}{2}$ a leek, 1 head of celery, 2 oz. of salt, $\frac{1}{2}$ a teaspoonful of whole pepper, 1 large blade of mace, 1 small bunch of savoury herbs, 4 quarts and $\frac{1}{2}$ pint of cold water.

Mode.—Cut up the meat and bacon or ham into pieces about 3 inches square; rub the butter on the bottom of the stewpan; put in $\frac{1}{2}$ a pint of water, the meat, and all the other ingredients. Cover the stewpan, and place it on a sharp fire, occasionally stirring its contents. When the bottom of the pan becomes covered with a pale, jelly-like substance, add 4 quarts of cold water, and simmer very gently for 5 hours. As we have said before, do not let it boil quickly. Skim off every particle of grease whilst it is doing, and strain it through a fine hair sieve.

This is the basis of many of the soups afterwards mentioned, and will be found quite strong enough for ordinary purposes.

Time.—5$\frac{1}{2}$ hours. *Average cost,* 9d. per quart.

ECONOMICAL STOCK.

106. INGREDIENTS.—The liquor in which a joint of meat has been boiled, say 4 quarts; trimmings of fresh meat or poultry, shank-bones, &c., roast-beef bones, any pieces the larder may furnish; vegetables, spices, and the same seasoning as in the foregoing recipe.

Mode.—Let all the ingredients simmer gently for 6 hours, taking care to skim carefully at first. Strain it off, and put by for use.

Time.—6 hours. *Average cost,* 3d. per quart.

WHITE STOCK.

(To be Used in the Preparation of White Soups.)

107. INGREDIENTS.—4 lbs. of knuckle of veal, any poultry trimmings, 4 slices of lean ham, 1 carrot, 2 onions, 1 head of celery,

12 white peppercorns, 1 oz. of salt, 1 blade of mace, 1 oz. butter, 4 quarts of water.

Mode.—Cut up the veal, and put it with the bones and trimmings of poultry, and the ham, into the stewpan, which has been rubbed with the butter. Moisten with ½ a pint of water, and simmer till the gravy begins to flow. Then add the 4 quarts of water and the remainder of the ingredients; simmer for 5 hours. After skimming and straining it carefully through a very fine hair sieve, it will be ready for use.

Time.—5½ hours. *Average cost*, 9*d.* per quart.

Note.—When stronger stock is desired, double the quantity of veal, or put in an old fowl. The liquor in which a young turkey has been boiled, is an excellent addition to all white stock or soups.

BROWNING FOR STOCK.

108. INGREDIENTS.—2 oz. of powdered sugar, and ½ a pint of water.

Mode.—Place the sugar in a stewpan over a slow fire until it begins to melt, keeping it stirred with a wooden spoon until it becomes black, when add the water, and let it dissolve. Cork closely, and use a few drops when required.

Note.—In France, burnt onions are made use of for the purpose of browning. As a general rule, the process of browning is to be discouraged, as apt to impart a slightly unpleasant flavour to the stock, and, consequently, all soups made from it.

TO CLARIFY STOCK.

109. INGREDIENTS.—The whites of 2 eggs, ½ pint of water, 2 quarts of stock.

Mode.—Supposing that by some accident the soup is not quite clear, and that its quantity is 2 quarts, take the whites of 2 eggs, carefully separated from their yolks, whisk them well together with the water, and add gradually the 2 quarts of boiling stock, still whisking. Place the soup on the fire, and when boiling and well skimmed, whisk the eggs with it till nearly boiling again; then draw it from the fire, and let it settle, until the whites of the eggs become separated. Pass through a fine cloth, and the soup should be clear.

Note.—The rule is, that all clear soups should be of a light straw-colour, and should not savour too strongly of the meat; and that all white or brown thick soups should have no more consistency than will enable them to adhere slightly to the spoon when hot. All *purées* should be somewhat thicker.

ALMOND SOUP.

110. INGREDIENTS.—4 lbs. of lean beef or veal, ½ a scrag of

mutton, 1 oz. of vermicelli, 4 blades of mace, 6 cloves, ½ lb. of sweet almonds, the yolks of 6 eggs, 1 gill of thick cream, rather more than 2 quarts of water.

Mode.—Boil the beef, or veal, and the mutton, gently in water that will cover them, till the gravy is very strong, and the meat very tender; then strain off the gravy, and set it on the fire with the specified quantities of vermicelli, mace, and cloves, to 2 quarts. Let it boil till it has the flavour of the spices. Have ready the almonds, blanched and pounded very fine; the yolks of the eggs boiled hard; mixing the almonds, whilst pounding, with a little of the soup, lest the latter should grow oily. Pound them till they are a mere pulp, and keep adding to them, by degrees, a little soup until they are thoroughly mixed together. Let the soup be cool when mixing, and do it perfectly smooth. Strain it through a sieve, set it on the fire, stir frequently, and serve hot. Just before taking it up, add the cream.

Time.—3 hours. *Average cost* per quart, 2s. 3d.

Seasonable all the year.

Sufficient for 8 persons.

ALMOND & BLOSSOM.

THE ALMOND-TREE.—This tree is indigenous to the northern parts of Asia and Africa, but it is now cultivated in Europe, especially in the south of France, Italy, and Spain. It flowers in spring, and produces its fruit in August. Although there are two kinds of almonds, the *sweet* and the *bitter*, they are considered as only varieties of the same species. The best sweet almonds brought to England, are called the Syrian or Jordan, and come from Malaga; the inferior qualities are brought from Valentia and Italy. *Bitter* almonds come principally from Magadore. Anciently, the almond was much esteemed by the nations of the East. Jacob included it among the presents which he designed for Joseph. The Greeks called it the Greek or Thasian nut, and the Romans believed that by eating half a dozen of them, they were secured against drunkenness, however deeply they might imbibe. Almonds, however, are considered as very indigestible. The *bitter* contain, too, principles which produce two violent poisons,—prussic acid and a kind of volatile oil. It is consequently dangerous to eat them in large quantities. Almonds pounded together with a little sugar and water, however, produce a milk similar to that which is yielded by animals. Their oil is used for making fine soap, and their cake as a cosmetic.

APPLE SOUP.

111. INGREDIENTS.—2 lbs. of good boiling apples, ¾ teaspoonful of white pepper, 6 cloves, cayenne or ginger to taste, 3 quarts of medium stock.

Mode.—Peel and quarter the apples, taking out their cores; put them into the stock, stew them gently till tender. Rub the whole through a strainer, add the seasoning, give it one boil up, and serve.

Time.—1 hour. *Average cost* per quart, 1s.

Seasonable from September to December.

Sufficient for 10 persons.

THE APPLE.—This useful fruit is mentioned in Holy Writ; and Homer describes it as valuable in his time. It was brought from the East by the Romans, who held it in the highest estimation. Indeed, some of the citizens of the "Eternal city" distinguished certain favourite apples by their names. Thus the Manlians were called after Manlius, the Claudians after Claudius, and the Appians after Appius. Others were designated after the country whence they were brought; as the Sidonians, the Epirotes, and the Greeks. The best varieties are natives of Asia, and have, by grafting them upon others, been introduced into Europe. The crab, found in our hedges, is the only variety indigenous to Britain; therefore, for the introduction of other kinds we are, no doubt, indebted to the Romans. In the time of the Saxon heptarchy, both Devon and Somerset were distinguished as *the apple country;* and there are still existing in Herefordshire some trees said to have been planted in the time of William the Conqueror. From that time to this, the varieties of this precious fruit have gone on increasing, and are now said to number upwards of 1,500. It is peculiar to the temperate zone, being found neither in Lapland, nor within the tropics. The best baking apples for early use are the Colvilles; the best for autumn are the rennets and pearmains; and the best for winter and spring are russets. The best table, or eating apples, are the Margarets for early use; the Kentish codlin and summer pearmain for summer; and for autumn, winter, or spring, the Dowton, golden and other pippins, as the ribstone, with small russets. As a food, the apple cannot be considered to rank high, as more than the half of it consists of water, and the rest of its properties are not the most nourishing. It is, however, a useful adjunct to other kinds of food, and, when cooked, is esteemed as slightly laxative.

APPLE AND BLOSSOM.

ARTICHOKE (JERUSALEM) SOUP.

(*A White Soup.*)

112. INGREDIENTS.—3 slices of lean bacon or ham, ½ a head of celery, 1 turnip, 1 onion, 3 oz. of butter, 4 lbs. of artichokes, 1 pint of boiling milk, or ½ pint of boiling cream, salt and cayenne to taste, 2 lumps of sugar, 2½ quarts of white stock.

Mode.—Put the bacon and vegetables, which should be cut into thin slices, into the stewpan with the butter. Braise these for ¼ of an hour, keeping them well stirred. Wash and pare the artichokes, and after cutting them into thin slices, add them, with a pint of stock, to the other ingredients. When these have gently stewed down to a smooth pulp, put in the remainder of the stock. Stir it well, adding the seasoning, and when it has simmered for five minutes, pass it through a strainer. Now pour it back into the stewpan, let it again simmer five minutes, taking care to skim it well, and stir it to the boiling milk or cream. Serve with small sippets of bread fried in butter.

Time.—1 hour. *Average cost* per quart, 1s. 2d.

Seasonable from June to October.

Sufficient for 8 persons.

ASPARAGUS SOUP.

I.

113. INGREDIENTS.—5 lbs. of lean beef, 3 slices of bacon, ½ pint of pale ale, a few leaves of white beet, spinach, 1 cabbage lettuce, a little mint, sorrel, and marjoram, a pint of asparagus-tops cut small, the crust of 1 French roll, seasoning to taste, 2 quarts of water.

Mode.—Put the beef, cut in pieces and rolled in flour, into a stew-pan, with the bacon at the bottom ; cover it close, and set it on a slow fire, stirring it now and then till the gravy is drawn. Put in the water and ale, and season to taste with pepper and salt, and let it stew gently for 2 hours ; then strain the liquor, and take off the fat, and add the white beet, spinach, cabbage lettuce, and mint, sorrel, and sweet marjoram, pounded. Let these boil up in the liquor, then put in the asparagus-tops cut small, and allow them to boil till all is tender. Serve hot, with the French roll in the dish.

Time.—Altogether 3 hours. *Average cost* per quart, 1s. 9d.

Seasonable from May to August.

Sufficient for 8 persons.

II.

114. INGREDIENTS.—1½ pint of split peas, a teacupful of gravy, 4 young onions, 1 lettuce cut small, ½ a head of celery, ½ a pint of asparagus cut small, ¼ a pint of cream, 3 quarts of water : colour the soup with spinach juice.

Mode.—Boil the peas, and rub them through a sieve ; add the gravy, and then stew by themselves the celery, onions, lettuce, and asparagus, with the water. After this, stew altogether, and add the colouring and cream, and serve.

Time.—Peas 2½ hours, vegetables 1 hour ; altogether 4 hours. *Average cost* per quart, 1s.

ASPARAGUS.—The ancients called all the sprouts of young vegetables asparagus, whence the name, which is now limited to a particular species, embracing artichoke, alisander, asparagus, cardoon, rampion, and sea-kale. They are originally mostly wild seacoast plants ; and, in this state, asparagus may still be found on the northern as well as southern shores of Britain. It is often vulgarly called, in London, *sparrowgrass;* and, in its cultivated form, hardly bears any resemblance to the original plant. Immense quantities of it are raised for the London market, at Mortlake and Deptford ; but it belongs rather to the classes of luxurious than necessary food. It is light and easily digested, but is not very nutritious.

ASPARAGUS.

BAKED SOUP.

115. INGREDIENTS.—1 lb. of any kind of meat, any trimmings or odd pieces; 2 onions, 2 carrots, 2 oz. of rice, 1 pint of split peas, pepper and salt to taste, 4 quarts of water.

Mode.—Cut the meat and vegetables in slices, add to them the rice and peas, season with pepper and salt. Put the whole in a jar, fill up with the water, cover very closely, and bake for 4 hours.

Time.—4 hours. *Average cost*, 2½d. per quart.

Seasonable at any time.

Sufficient for 10 or 12 persons.

Note.—This will be found a very cheap and wholesome soup, and will be convenient in those cases where baking is more easily performed than boiling.

BARLEY SOUP.

116. INGREDIENTS.—2 lbs. of shin of beef, ¼ lb. of pearl barley, a large bunch of parsley, 4 onions, 6 potatoes, salt and pepper, 4 quarts of water.

Mode.—Put in all the ingredients, and simmer gently for 3 hours.

Time.—3 hours. *Average cost*, 2½d. per quart.

Seasonable all the year, but more suitable for winter.

BARLEY.

BARLEY.—This, in the order of cereal grasses, is, in Britain, the next plant to wheat in point of value, and exhibits several species and varieties. From what country it comes originally, is not known, but it was cultivated in the earliest ages of antiquity, as the Egyptians were afflicted with the loss of it in the ear, in the time of Moses. It was a favourite grain with the Athenians, but it was esteemed as an ignominious food by the Romans. Notwithstanding this, however, it was much used by them, as it was in former times by the English, and still is, in the Border counties, in Cornwall, and also in Wales. In other parts of England, it is used mostly for malting purposes. It is less nutritive than wheat; and in 100 parts, has of starch 79, gluten 6, saccharine matter 7, husk 8. It is, however, a lighter and less stimulating food than wheat, which renders a decoction of it well adapted for invalids whose digestion is weak.

BREAD SOUP.

(*Economical.*)

117. INGREDIENTS.—1 lb. of bread crusts, 2 oz. butter, 1 quart of common stock.

Mode.—Boil the bread crusts in the stock with the butter; beat the whole with a spoon, and keep it boiling till the bread and stock are well mixed. Season with a little salt.

Time.—Half an hour. *Average cost* per quart, 4d.

Seasonable at any time.

Sufficient for 4 persons.

Note.—This is a cheap recipe, and will be found useful where extreme economy is an object.

BREAD.—The origin of bread is involved in the obscurity of distant ages. The Greeks attributed its invention to Pan; but before they, themselves, had an existence, it was, no doubt, in use among the primitive nations of mankind. The Chaldeans and the Egyptians were acquainted with it, and Sarah, the companion of Abraham, mixed flour and water together, kneaded it, and covered it with ashes on the hearth. The Scriptures inform us that leavened bread was known to the Israelites, but it is not known when the art of fermenting it was discovered. It is said that the Romans learnt it during their wars with Perseus, king of Macedon, and that it was introduced to the "imperial city" about

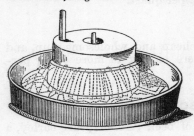

QUERN, OR GRINDING-MILL.

200 years before the birth of Christ. With them it no doubt found its way into Britain; but after their departure from the island, it probably ceased to be used. We know that King Alfred allowed the unfermented cakes to burn in the neatherd's cottage; and that, even in the sixteenth century, unfermented cakes, kneaded by the women, were the only kind of bread known to the inhabitants of Norway and Sweden. The Italians of this day consume the greater portion of their flour in the form of *polenta*, or soft pudding, vermicelli, and macaroni; and, in the remoter districts of Scotland, much unfermented bread is still used. We give a cut of the *quern* grinding-mill, which, towards the end of the last century, was in use in that country, and which is thus described by Dr. Johnson in his "Journey to the Hebrides:"—"It consists of two stones about a foot and a half in diameter; the lower is a little convex, to which the concavity of the upper must be fitted. In the middle of the upper stone is a round hole, and on one side is a long handle. The grinder sheds the corn gradually into the hole with one hand, and works the handle round with the other. The corn slides down the convexity of the lower stone, and, by the motion of the upper, is ground in its passage." Such a primitive piece of machinery, it may safely be said, has entirely disappeared from this country.—In other parts of this work, we shall have opportunities of speaking of bread and bread-making, which, from its great and general use in the nourishment of mankind, has emphatically been called the "staff of life." The necessity, therefore, of having it both pure and good is of the first importance.

CABBAGE SOUP.

118. INGREDIENTS.—1 large cabbage, 3 carrots, 2 onions, 4 or 5 slices of lean bacon, salt and pepper to taste, 2 quarts of medium stock No. 105.

Mode.—Scald the cabbage, cut it up and drain it. Line the stew-pan with the bacon, put in the cabbage, carrots, and onions; moisten with skimmings from the stock, and simmer very gently, till the cabbage is tender; add the stock, stew softly for half an hour, and carefully skim off every particle of fat. Season and serve.

Time.—1½ hour. *Average cost,* 1s. per quart.

Seasonable in winter.

Sufficient for 8 persons.

THE CABBAGE.—It is remarkable, that although there is no country in the world now more plentifully supplied with fruits and vegetables than Great Britain, yet the greater number of these had no existence in it before the time of Henry VIII. Anderson, writing under the date of 1548, says, "The English cultivated scarce.y any egetables before the last two centuries. At the commencement of the reign of Henry VIII. neither salad, nor carrots, nor cabbages, nor radishes, nor any other comestibles of a like nature, were grown in any part of the kingdom; they came from Holland and Flanders." The original of all the cabbage tribe is the wild plant *sea-colewort*, which is to be found *wasting* whatever sweetness it may have on the desert air, on many of the cliffs of the south coast of England. In this state, it scarcely weighs more than half an ounce, yet, in a cultivated state, to what dimensions can it be made to grow! However greatly the whole of the tribe is esteemed among the moderns, by the ancients they were held in yet higher estimation. The Egyptians adored and raised altars to them, and the Greeks and Romans ascribed many of the most exalted virtues to them. Cato affirmed, that the cabbage cured all diseases, and declared, that it was to its use that the Romans were enabled to live in health and without the assistance of physicians for 600 years. It was introduced by that people into Germany, Gaul, and, no doubt, Britain; although, in this last, it may have been suffered to pass into desuetude for some centuries.

CABBAGE SEEDING.

The whole tribe is in general wholesome and nutritive, and forms a valuable adjunct to animal food.

SOUP A LA CANTATRICE.

(An Excellent Soup, very Beneficial for the Voice.)

119. INGREDIENTS.—3 oz. of sago, ½ pint of cream, the yolks of 3 eggs, 1 lump of sugar, and seasoning to taste, 1 bay-leaf (if liked), 2 quarts of medium stock No. 105.

Mode.—Having washed the sago in boiling water, let it be gradually added to the nearly boiling stock. Simmer for ½ an hour, when it should be well dissolved. Beat up the yolks of the eggs, add to them the boiling cream; stir these quickly in the soup, and serve immediately. Do not let the soup boil, or the eggs will curdle.

Time.—40 minutes. *Average cost,* 1s. 6d. per quart.

Seasonable all the year.

Sufficient for 8 persons.

Note.—This is a soup, the principal ingredients of which, sago and eggs, have always been deemed very beneficial to the chest and throat. In various quantities, and in different preparations, these have been partaken of by the principal singers of the day, including the celebrated Swedish Nightingale, Jenny Lind, and, as they have always avowed, with considerable advantage to the voice, in singing.

CARROT SOUP.

I.

120. INGREDIENTS.—4 quarts of liquor in which a leg of mutton or beef has been boiled, a few beef-bones, 6 large carrots, 2 large onions, 1 turnip; seasoning of salt and pepper to taste; cayenne.

Mode.—Put the liquor, bones, onions, turnip, pepper, and salt, into a stewpan, and simmer for 3 hours. Scrape and cut the carrots thin, strain the soup on them, and stew them till soft enough to pulp through a hair sieve or coarse cloth; then boil the pulp with the soup, which should be of the consistency of pea-soup. Add cayenne, Pulp only the red part of the carrot, and make this soup the day before it is wanted.

Time.—4½ hours. *Average cost* per quart, 1½*d.*
Seasonable from October to March.
Sufficient for 10 persons.

II.

121. INGREDIENTS.—2 lbs. of carrots, 3 oz. of butter, seasoning to taste of salt and cayenne, 2 quarts of stock or gravy soup.

Mode.—Scrape and cut out all specks from the carrots, wash, and wipe them dry, and then reduce them into quarter inch slices. Put the butter into a large stewpan, and when it is melted, add 2 lbs. of the sliced carrots, and let them stew gently for an hour without browning. Add to them the soup, and allow them to simmer till tender,—say for nearly an hour. Press them through a strainer with the soup, and add salt and cayenne if required. Boil the whole gently for 5 minutes, skim well, and serve as hot as possible.

Time.—1¼ hour. *Average cost* per quart, 1*s.* 1*d.*

THE CARROT.—There is a wild carrot which grows in England; but it is white and small, and not much esteemed. The garden carrot in general use, was introduced in the reign of Queen Elizabeth, and was, at first, so highly esteemed, that the ladies wore leaves of it in their head-dresses. It is of great value in the culinary art, especially for soups and stews. It can be used also for beer instead of malt, and, in distillation, it yields a large quantity of spirit. The carrot is proportionably valuable as it has more of the red than the yellow part. There is a large red variety much used by the farmers for colouring butter. As a garden vegetable, it is what is called the orange-carrot that is usually cultivated. As a fattening food for cattle, it is excellent; but for man it is indigestible, on account of its fibrous matter. Of 1,000 parts, 95 consist of sugar, and 3 of starch.—The accompanying cut represents a pretty winter ornament, obtained by placing a cut from the top of the carrot-root in a shallow vessel of water, when the young leaves spring forth with a charming freshness and fullness.

TAZZA AND CARROT LEAVES.

CELERY SOUP.

122. INGREDIENTS.—9 heads of celery, 1 teaspoonful of salt, nutmeg to taste, 1 lump of sugar, ½ pint of strong stock, a pint of cream, and 2 quarts of boiling water.

Mode.—Cut the celery into small pieces; throw it into the water, seasoned with the nutmeg, salt, and sugar. Boil it till sufficiently tender; pass it through a sieve, add the stock, and simmer it for half an hour. Now put in the cream, bring it to the boiling point, and serve immediately.

Time.—1 hour. *Average cost*, 1*s.* per quart.

Seasonable from September to March.

Sufficient for 10 persons.

Note.—This soup can be made brown, instead of white, by omitting the cream, and colouring it a little. When celery cannot be procured, half a drachm of the seed, finely pounded, will give a flavour to the soup, if put in a quarter of an hour before it is done. A little of the essence of celery will answer the same purpose.

CELERY.—This plant is indigenous to Britain, and, in its wild state, grows by the side of ditches and along some parts of the seacoast. In this state it is called *smallage*, and, to some extent, is a dangerous narcotic. By cultivation, however, it has been brought to the fine flavour which the garden plant possesses. In the vicinity of Manchester it is raised to an enormous size. When our natural observation is assisted by the accurate results ascertained by the light of science, how infinitely does it enhance our delight in contemplating the products of nature! To know, for example, that the endless variety of colour which we see in plants is developed only by the rays of the sun, is to know a truism sublime by its very comprehensiveness. The cause of the whiteness of celery is nothing more than the want of light in its vegetation, and in order that this effect may be produced, the plant is almost wholly covered with earth; the tops of the leaves alone being suffered to appear above the ground.

CHANTILLY SOUP.

123. INGREDIENTS.—1 quart of young green peas, a small bunch of parsley, 2 young onions, 2 quarts of medium stock No. 105.

Mode.—Boil the peas till quite tender, with the parsley and onions; then rub them through a sieve, and pour the stock to them. Do not let it boil after the peas are added, or you will spoil the colour. Serve very hot.

Time.—Half an hour. *Average cost,* 1*s.* 6*d.* per quart.

Seasonable from June to the end of August.

Sufficient for 8 persons.

Note.—Cold peas pounded in a mortar, with a little stock added to them, make a very good soup in haste.

PARSLEY.—Among the Greeks, in the classic ages, a crown of parsley was awarded, both in the Nemæan and Isthmian games, and the voluptuous Anacreon pronounces this beautiful herb the emblem of joy and festivity. It has an elegant leaf, and is extensively used in the culinary art. When it was introduced to Britain is not known. There are several varieties,—the *plain*-leaved and the *curled*-leaved, *celery*-parsley, *Hamburg* parsley, and *purslane*. The curled is the best, and, from the form of its leaf, has a beautiful appearance on a dish as a garnish. Its flavour is, to many, very agreeable in soups; and although to rabbits, hares, and sheep it is a luxury, to parrots it is a poison. The celery-parsley is used as a celery, and the Hamburg is cultivated only for its roots, which are used as parsnips or carrots, to eat with meat. The purslane is a native of South America, and is not now much in use.

CHESTNUT (SPANISH) SOUP.

124. INGREDIENTS.—$\frac{3}{4}$ lb. of Spanish chestnuts, $\frac{1}{4}$ pint of cream; seasoning to taste of salt, cayenne, and mace; 1 quart of stock No. 105.

Mode.—Take the outer rind from the chestnuts, and put them into a large pan of warm water. As soon as this becomes too hot for the fingers to remain in it, take out the chestnuts, peel them quickly, and

F

immerse them in cold water, and wipe and weigh them. Now cover them with good stock, and stew them gently for rather more than ¾ of an hour, or until they break when touched with a fork; then drain, pound, and rub them through a fine sieve reversed; add sufficient stock, mace, cayenne, and salt, and stir it often until it boils, and put in the cream. The stock in which the chestnuts are boiled can be used for the soup, when its sweetness is not objected to, or it may, in part, be added to it; and the rule is, that ¾ lb. of chestnuts should be given to each quart of soup.

Time.—Rather more than 1 hour. *Average cost* per quart, 1s. 6d.

Seasonable from October to February.

Sufficient for 4 persons.

THE CHESTNUT.—This fruit is said, by some, to have originally come from Sardis, in Lydia; and by others, from Castanea, a city of Thessaly, from which it takes its name. By the ancients it was much used as a food, and is still common in France and Italy, to which countries it is, by some, considered indigenous. In the southern part of the European continent, it is eaten both raw and roasted. The tree was introduced into Britain by the Romans; but it only flourishes in the warmer parts of the island, the fruit rarely arriving at maturity in Scotland. It attains a great age, as well as an immense size. As a food, it is the least oily and most farinaceous of all the nuts, and, therefore, the easiest of digestion. The tree called the *horse* chestnut is very different, although its fruit very much resembles that of the other. Its " nuts," though eaten by horses and some other animals, are unsuitable for human food.

CHESTNUT.

COCOA-NUT SOUP.

125. INGREDIENTS.—6 oz. of grated cocoa-nut, 6 oz. of rice flour, ½ a teaspoonful of mace; seasoning to taste of cayenne and salt; ¼ of a pint of boiling cream, 3 quarts of medium stock No. 105.

Mode.—Take the dark rind from the cocoa-nut, and grate it down small on a clean grater; weigh it, and allow, for each quart of stock, 2 oz. of the cocoa-nut. Simmer it gently for 1 hour in the stock, which should then be strained closely from it, and thickened for table.

Time.—2¼ hours. *Average cost* per quart, 1s. 3d.

Seasonable in Autumn.

Sufficient for 10 persons.

THE COCOA-NUT.—This is the fruit of one of the palms, than which it is questionable if there is any other species of tree marking, in itself, so abundantly the goodness of Providence, in making provision for the wants of man. It grows wild in the Indian seas, and in the eastern parts of Asia; and thence it has been introduced into every part of the tropical regions. To the natives of those climates, its bark supplies the material for erecting their dwellings; its leaves, the means of roofing them; and the leaf-stalks, a kind of gauze for covering their windows, or protecting the baby in the cradle. It is also made into lanterns, masks to screen the face from the heat of the sun, baskets, wicker-work, and even a kind of paper for writing on. Combs, brooms, torches, ropes, matting, and sailcloth are made of its fibres. With these, too, beds are made and cushions stuffed. Oars are supplied by the leaves; drinking-cups, spoons, and other domestic utensils by the shells of the nuts; milk by its juice, of which, also, a kind of honey and sugar are prepared. When fermented, it furnishes the means of intoxication; and when the fibres are burned, their ashes supply an alkali for making soap. The buds of the tree bear a striking resemblance to cabbage when boiled; but when they are cropped, the tree dies. In a fresh state, the kernel is eaten raw, and its juice is a most agreeable and refreshing beverage. When the nut is imported to this country, its fruit is, in general, comparatively dry, and is considered indigestible. The tree is one of the least productive of the palm tribe.

COCOA-NUT PALM.

NUT & BLOSSOM.

SOUP A LA CRECY.

126. INGREDIENTS.—4 carrots, 2 sliced onions, 1 cut lettuce, and chervil; 2 oz. butter, 1 pint of lentils, the crumbs of 2 French rolls, half a teacupful of rice, 2 quarts of medium stock No. 105.

Mode.—Put the vegetables with the butter in the stewpan, and let them simmer 5 minutes; then add the lentils and 1 pint of the stock, and stew gently for half an hour. Now fill it up with the remainder of the stock, let it boil another hour, and put in the crumb of the rolls. When well soaked, rub all through a tammy. Have ready the rice boiled; pour the soup over this, and serve.

Time.—1¾ hour. *Average cost*, 1s. 2d. per quart.

Seasonable all the year.

Sufficient for 8 persons.

THE LENTIL.—This belongs to the leguminous or *pulse* kind of vegetables, which rank next to the corn plants in their nutritive properties. The lentil is a variety of the bean tribe, but in England is not used as human food, although considered the best of all kinds for pigeons. On the Continent it is cultivated for soups, as well as for other preparations for the table; and among the presents which David received from Shobi, as recounted in the Scriptures, were beans, lentils, and parched pulse. Among the Egyptians it was extensively used, and among the Greeks, the Stoics had a maxim, which declared, that "a wise man acts always with reason, and prepares his own lentils." Among the Romans it was not much esteemed, and from them the English may have inherited a prejudice against it, on account, it is said, of its rendering men indolent. It takes its name from *lentus*, 'slow,' and, according to Pliny, produces mildness and moderation of temper.

LENTIL.

CUCUMBER SOUP (French Recipe).

127. INGREDIENTS.—1 large cucumber, a piece of butter the size of a walnut, a little chervil and sorrel cut in large pieces, salt and pepper to taste, the yolks of 2 eggs, 1 gill of cream, 1 quart of medium stock No. 105.

Mode.—Pare the cucumber, quarter it, and take out the seeds; cut it in thin slices, put these on a plate with a little salt, to draw the water from them; drain, and put them in your stewpan, with the butter. When they are warmed through, without being browned, pour the stock on them. Add the sorrel, chervil, and seasoning, and boil for 40 minutes. Mix the well-beaten yolks of the eggs with the cream, which add at the moment of serving.

Time.—1 hour. *Average cost,* 1s. 2d. per quart.

Seasonable from June to September.

Sufficient for 4 persons.

THE CUCUMBER.—The antiquity of this fruit is very great. In the sacred writings we find that the people of Israel regretted it, whilst sojourning in the desert; and at the present time, the cucumber, and other fruits of its class, form a large portion of the food of the Egyptian people. By the Eastern nations generally, as well as by the Greeks and Romans, it was greatly esteemed. Like the melon, it was originally brought from Asia by the Romans, and in the 14th century it was common in England, although, in the time of the wars of "the Roses," it seems no longer to have been cultivated. It is a cold food, and of difficult digestion when eaten raw. As a preserved sweetmeat, however, it is esteemed one of the most agreeable.

EGG SOUP.

128. INGREDIENTS.—A tablespoonful of flour, 4 eggs, 2 small blades of finely-pounded mace, 2 quarts of stock No. 105.

Mode.—Beat up the flour smoothly in a teaspoonful of cold stock, and put in the eggs; throw them into boiling stock, stirring all the time. Simmer for ¼ of an hour. Season and serve with a French roll in the tureen, or fried sippets of bread.

Time.—½ an hour. *Average cost,* 11d. per quart.

Seasonable all the year.

Sufficient for 8 persons.

SOUP A LA FLAMANDE (Flemish).

I.

129. INGREDIENTS.—1 turnip, 1 small carrot, ½ head of celery, 6 green onions shred very fine, 1 lettuce cut small, chervil, ¼ pint of asparagus cut small, ¼ pint of peas, 2 oz. butter, the yolks of 4 eggs, ½ pint of cream, salt to taste, 1 lump of sugar, 2 quarts of stock No. 105.

Mode.—Put the vegetables in the butter to stew gently for an hour with a teacupful of stock; then add the remainder of the stock, and simmer for another hour. Now beat the yolks of the eggs well, mix with the cream (previously boiled), and strain through a hair sieve. Take the soup off the fire, put the eggs, &c. to it, and keep stirring it well. Bring it to a boil, but do not leave off stirring, or the eggs will curdle. Season with salt, and add the sugar.

Time.—2½ hours. *Average cost*, 1s. 9d. per quart.

Seasonable from May to August.

Sufficient for 8 persons.

CHERVIL.—Although the roots of this plant are poisonous, its leaves are tender, and are used in salads. In antiquity it made a relishing dish, when prepared with oil, wine, and gravy. It is a native of various parts of Europe; and the species cultivated in the gardens of Paris, has beautifully frizzled leaves.

II.

130. INGREDIENTS.—5 onions, 5 heads of celery, 10 moderate-sized potatoes, 3 oz. butter, ½ pint of water, ½ pint of cream, 2 quarts of stock No. 105.

Mode.—Slice the onions, celery, and potatoes, and put them with the butter and water into a stewpan, and simmer for an hour. Then fill up the stewpan with stock, and boil gently till the potatoes are done, which will be in about an hour. Rub all through a tammy, and add the cream (previously boiled). Do not let it boil after the cream is put in.

Time.—2½ hours. *Average cost*, 1s. 4d. per quart.

Seasonable from September to May.

Sufficient for 8 persons.

Note.—This soup can be made with water instead of stock.

SOUP A LA JULIENNE.

131. INGREDIENTS.—½ pint of carrots, ½ pint of turnips, ¼ pint of onions, 2 or 3 leeks, ½ head of celery, 1 lettuce, a little sorrel and chervil, if liked, 2 oz. of butter, 2 quarts of stock No. 105.

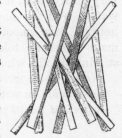

Mode.—Cut the vegetables into strips of about 1¼ inch long, and be particular they are all the same size, or some will be hard whilst the others will be done to a pulp. Cut the lettuce, sorrel, and chervil into larger pieces; fry the carrots in the butter, and pour the stock boiling to them. When this is done, add all the other vegetables, and herbs, and stew gently for at least an hour. Skim off all the fat, pour the

STRIPS OF VEGETABLE.

soup over thin slices of bread, cut round about the size of a shilling, and serve.

Time.—1½ hour. *Average cost*, 1s. 3d. per quart.

Seasonable all the year.

Sufficient for 8 persons.

Note.—In summer, green peas, asparagus-tops, French beans, &c. can be added. When the vegetables are very strong, instead of frying them in butter at first, they should be blanched, and afterwards simmered in the stock.

SORREL.—This is one of the *spinaceous* plants, which take their name from spinach, which is the chief among them. It is little used in English cookery, but a great deal in French, where it is employed for soups, sauces, and salads. In English meadows it is usually left to grow wild; but in France, where it is cultivated, its flavour is greatly improved.

KALE BROSE (a Scotch Recipe).

132. INGREDIENTS.—Half an ox-head or cow-heel, a teacupful of toasted oatmeal, salt to taste, 2 handfuls of greens, 3 quarts of water.

Mode.—Make a broth of the ox-head or cow-heel, and boil it till oil floats on the top of the liquor, then boil the greens, shred, in it. Put the oatmeal, with a little salt, into a basin, and mix with it quickly a teacupful of the fat broth: it should not run into one doughy mass, but form knots. Stir it into the whole, give one boil, and serve very hot.

Time.—4 hours. *Average cost*, 8d. per quart.

Seasonable all the year, but more suitable in winter.

Sufficient for 10 persons.

LEEK SOUP.

I.

133. INGREDIENTS.—A sheep's head, 3 quarts of water, 12 leeks cut small, pepper and salt to taste, oatmeal to thicken.

Mode.—Prepare the head, either by skinning or cleaning the skin very nicely; split it in two; take out the brains, and put it into boiling water; add the leeks and seasoning, and simmer very gently for 4 hours. Mix smoothly, with cold water, as much oatmeal as will make the soup tolerably thick; pour it into the soup; continue stirring till the whole is blended and well done, and serve.

Time.—4½ hours. *Average cost*, 4d. per quart.

Seasonable in winter.

Sufficient for 10 persons.

II.

COMMONLY CALLED COCK-A-LEEKIE.

134. INGREDIENTS.—A capon or large fowl (sometimes an old cock, from which the recipe takes its name, is used), which should be

trussed as for boiling; 2 or 3 bunches of fine leeks, 5 quarts of stock No. 105, pepper and salt to taste.

Mode.—Well wash the leeks (and, if old, scald them in boiling water for a few minutes), taking off the roots and part of the heads, and cut them into lengths of about an inch. Put the fowl into the stock, with, at first, one half of the leeks, and allow it to simmer gently. In half an hour add the remaining leeks, and then it may simmer for 3 or 4 hours longer. It should be carefully skimmed, and can be seasoned to taste. In serving, take out the fowl, and carve it neatly, placing the pieces in a tureen, and pouring over them the soup, which should be very thick of leeks (a *purée* of leeks the French would call it).

Time.—4 hours. *Average cost*, 1s. 6d. per quart; or, with stock No. 106, 1s.

Seasonable in winter.

Sufficient for 10 persons.

Note.—Without the fowl, the above, which would then be merely called leek soup, is very good, and also economical. Cock-a-leekie was largely consumed at the Burns Centenary Festival at the Crystal Palace, Sydenham, in 1859.

THE LEEK.—As in the case of the cucumber, this vegetable was bewailed by the Israelites in their journey through the desert. It is one of the alliaceous tribe, which consists of the onion, garlic, chive, shallot, and leek. These, as articles of food, are perhaps more widely diffused over the face of the earth than any other *genus* of edible plants. It is the national badge of the Welsh, and tradition ascribes its introduction to that part of Britain, to St. David. The origin of the wearing of the leek on St. David's day, among that people, is thus given in "BEETON'S DICTIONARY OF UNIVERSAL INFORMATION :"—"It probably originated from the custom of *Cymhortha*, or the friendly aid, practised among farmers. In some districts of South Wales, all the neighbours of a small farmer were wont to appoint a day when they attended to plough his land, and the like; and, at such time, it was the custom for each to bring his portion of leeks with him for making the broth or soup." (*See* ST. DAVID.) Others derive the origin of the custom from the battle of Cressy. The plant, when grown in Wales and Scotland, is sharper than it is in England, and its flavour is preferred by many to that of the onion in broth. It is very wholesome, and, to prevent its tainting the breath, should be well boiled.

LEEKS.

MACARONI SOUP.

135. INGREDIENTS.—3 oz. of macaroni, a piece of butter the size of a walnut, salt to taste, 2 quarts of clear stock No. 105.

Mode.—Throw the macaroni and butter into boiling water, with a pinch of salt, and simmer for ½ an hour. When it is tender, drain and cut it into thin rings or lengths, and drop it into the boiling stock. Stew gently for 15 minutes, and serve grated Parmesan cheese with it.

Time.—¾ hour. *Average cost*, 1s. per quart.

Seasonable all the year.

Sufficient for 8 persons.

MACARONI.—This is the favourite food of Italy, where, especially among the Nea-politans, it may be regarded as the staff of life. "The crowd of London," says Mr. Forsyth, "is a double line in quick motion; it is the crowd of business. The crowd of Naples consists in a general tide rolling up and down, and in the middle of this tide, a hundred eddies of men. You are stopped by a carpenter's bench, you are lost among shoemakers' stalls, and you dash among the *pots of a macaroni stall.*" This article of food is nothing more than a thick paste, made of the best wheaten flour, with a small quantity of water. When it has been well worked, it is put into a hollow cylindrical vessel, pierced with holes of the size of tobacco-pipes at the bottom. Through these holes the mass is forced by a powerful screw bearing on a piece of wood made exactly to fit the inside of the cylinder. Whilst issuing from the holes, it is partially baked by a fire placed below the cylinder, and is, at the same time, drawn away and hung over rods placed about the room, in order to dry. In a few days it is fit for use. As it is both wholesome and nutritious, it ought to be much more used by all classes in England than it is. It generally ac-companies Parmesan cheese to the tables of the rich, but is also used for thickening soups and making puddings.

MACARONI.

SOUP MAIGRE (i.e. without Meat).

136. INGREDIENTS.—6 oz. butter, 6 onions sliced, 4 heads of celery, 2 lettuces, a small bunch of parsley, 2 handfuls of spinach, 3 pieces of bread-crust, 2 blades of mace, salt and pepper to taste, the yolks of 2 eggs, 3 teaspoonfuls of vinegar, 2 quarts of water.

Mode.—Melt the butter in a stewpan, and put in the onions to stew gently for 3 or 4 minutes; then add the celery, spinach, lettuces, and parsley, cut small. Stir the ingredients well for 10 minutes. Now put in the water, bread, seasoning, and mace. Boil gently for 1½ hour, and, at the moment of serving, beat in the yolks of the eggs and the vinegar, but do not let it boil, or the eggs will curdle.

Time.—2 hours. *Average cost*, 6d. per quart.

Seasonable all the year.

Sufficient for 8 persons.

THE LETTUCE.—This is one of the acetarious vegetables, which comprise a large class, chiefly used as pickles, salads, and other condiments. The lettuce has in all antiquity been distinguished as a kitchen-garden plant. It was, without preparation, eaten by the Hebrews with the Paschal lamb; the Greeks delighted in it, and the Romans, in the time of Domitian, had it prepared with eggs, and served in the first course at their tables, merely to excite their appetites. Its botanical name is *Lactuca*, so called from the milky juice it exudes when its stalks are cut. It possesses a narcotic virtue, noticed by ancient physicians; and even in our day a lettuce supper is deemed conducive to repose. Its proper character, however, is that of a cooling summer vegetable, not very nutritive, but serving to correct, or as a diluent of animal food.

LETTUCE.

MILK SOUP (a Nice Dish for Children).

137. INGREDIENTS.—2 quarts of milk, 1 saltspoonful of salt, 1 tea-spoonful of powdered cinnamon, 3 teaspoonfuls of pounded sugar, or more if liked, 4 thin slices of bread, the yolks of 6 eggs.

Mode.—Boil the milk with the salt, cinnamon, and sugar; lay the bread in a deep dish, pour over it a little of the milk, and keep it hot over a stove, without burning. Beat up the yolks of the eggs, add them to the milk, and stir it over the fire till it thickens. Do not let it curdle. Pour it upon the bread, and serve.

Time.—¾ of an hour. *Average cost*, 8d. per quart.

Seasonable all the year.

Sufficient for 10 children.

ONION SOUP.

138. INGREDIENTS.—6 large onions, 2 oz. of butter, salt and pepper to taste, ¼ pint of cream, 1 quart of stock No. 105.

Mode.—Chop the onions, put them in the butter, stir them occasionally, but do not let them brown. When tender, put the stock to them, and season; strain the soup, and add the boiling cream.

Time.—1½ hour. *Average cost*, 1s. per quart.

Seasonable in winter.

Sufficient for 4 persons.

CHEAP ONION SOUP.

139. INGREDIENTS.—8 middling-sized onions, 3 oz. of butter, a table-spoonful of rice-flour, salt and pepper to taste, 1 teaspoonful of powdered sugar, thickening of butter and flour, 2 quarts of water.

Mode.—Cut the onions small, put them in the stewpan with the butter, and fry them well; mix the rice-flour smoothly with the water, add the onions, seasoning, and sugar, and simmer till tender. Thicken with butter and flour, and serve.

Time.—2 hours. *Average cost*, 4d. per quart.

Seasonable in winter.

Sufficient for 8 persons.

THE ONION.—Like the cabbage, this plant was erected into an object of worship by the idolatrous Egyptians 2,000 years before the Christian era, and it still forms a favourite food in the country of these people, as well as in other parts of Africa. When it was first introduced to England, has not been ascertained; but it has long been in use, and esteemed as a favourite seasoning plant to various dishes. In warmer climates it is much milder in its flavour; and such as are grown in Spain and Portugal, are, comparatively speaking, very large, and are often eaten both in a boiled and roasted state. The Strasburg is the most esteemed; and, although all the species have highly nutritive properties, they impart such a disagreeable odour to the breath, that they are often rejected even where they are liked. Chewing a little raw parsley is said to remove this odour.

ONION.

PAN KAIL.

140. INGREDIENTS.—2 lbs. of cabbage, or Savoy greens; ¼ lb. of

butter or dripping, salt and pepper to taste, oatmeal for thickening, 2 quarts of water.

Mode.—Chop the cabbage very fine, thicken the water with oatmeal, put in the cabbage and butter, or dripping; season and simmer for 1½ hour. It can be made sooner by blanching and mashing the greens, adding any good liquor that a joint has been boiled in, and then further thicken with bread or pounded biscuit.

Time—1½ hour. *Average cost,* 1½d. per quart.

Seasonable all the year, but more suitable in winter.

Sufficient for 8 persons.

THE SAVOY.—This is a close-hearted wrinkle-leaved cabbage, sweet and tender, especially the middle leaves, and in season from November to spring. The yellow species bears hard weather without injury, whilst the *dwarf* kind are improved and rendered more tender by frost.

PARSNIP SOUP.

141. INGREDIENTS.—1 lb. of sliced parsnips, 2 oz. of butter, salt and cayenne to taste, 1 quart of stock No. 106.

Mode.—Put the parsnips into the stewpan with the butter, which has been previously melted, and simmer them till quite tender. Then add nearly a pint of stock, and boil together for half an hour. Pass all through a fine strainer, and put to it the remainder of the stock. Season, boil, and serve immediately.

Time.—2 hours. *Average cost,* 6d. per quart.

Seasonable from October to April.

Sufficient for 4 persons.

THE PARSNIP.—This is a biennial plant, with a root like a carrot, which, in nutritive and saccharine matter, it nearly equals. It is a native of Britain, and, in its wild state, may be found, in many parts, growing by the road-sides. It is also to be found, generally distributed over Europe; and, in Catholic countries, is mostly used with salt fish, in Lent. In Scotland it forms an excellent dish, when beat up with butter and potatoes; it is, also, excellent when fried. In Ireland it is found to yield, in conjunction with the hop, a pleasant beverage; and it contains as much spirit as the carrot, and makes an excellent wine. Its proportion of nutritive matter is 99 parts in 1,000; 9 being mucilage and 90 sugar.

PEA SOUP (GREEN).

142. INGREDIENTS.—3 pints of green peas, ¼ lb. of butter, 2 or three thin slices of ham, 6 onions sliced, 4 shredded lettuces, the crumb of 2 French rolls, 2 handfuls of spinach, 1 lump of sugar, 2 quarts of common stock.

Mode.—Put the butter, ham, 1 quart of the peas, onions, and lettuces, to a pint of stock, and simmer for an hour; then add the remainder of the stock, with the crumb of the French rolls, and boil for another hour. Now boil the spinach, and squeeze it very dry. Rub the soup through a sieve, and the spinach with it, to colour it.

Have ready a pint of *young* peas boiled; add them to the soup, put in the sugar, give one boil, and serve. If necessary, add salt.

Time.—2½ hours. *Average cost*, 1s. 9d. per quart.

Seasonable from June to the end of August.

Sufficient for 10 persons.

Note.—It will be well to add, if the peas are not quite young, a little sugar. Where economy is essential, water may be used instead of stock for this soup, boiling in it likewise the pea-shells; but use a double quantity of vegetables.

WINTER PEA SOUP (YELLOW).

143. INGREDIENTS.—1 quart of split peas, 2 lbs. of shin of beef, trimmings of meat or poultry, a slice of bacon, 2 large carrots, 2 turnips, 5 large onions, 1 head of celery, seasoning to taste, 2 quarts of soft water, any bones left from roast meat, 2 quarts of common stock, or liquor in which a joint of meat has been boiled.

Mode.—Put the peas to soak over-night in soft water, and float off such as rise to the top. Boil them in the water till tender enough to pulp; then add the ingredients mentioned above, and simmer for 2 hours, stirring it occasionally. Pass the whole through a sieve, skim well, season, and serve with toasted bread cut in dice.

Time.—4 hours. *Average cost*, 6d. per quart.

Seasonable all the year round, but more suitable for cold weather.

Sufficient for 12 persons.

THE PEA.—It is supposed that the common gray pea, found wild in Greece, and other parts of the Levant, is the original of the common garden pea, and of all the domestic varieties belonging to it. The gray, or field pea, called *bisallie* by the French, is less subject to run into varieties than the garden kinds, and is considered by some, perhaps on that account, to be the wild plant, retaining still a large proportion of its original habit. From the tendency of all other varieties "to run away" and become different to what they originally were, it is very difficult to determine the races to which they belong. The pea was well known to the Romans, and, probably, was introduced to Britain at an early period; for we find peas mentioned by Lydgate, a poet of the 15th century, as being hawked in London. They seem, however, for a considerable time, to have fallen out of use; for, in the reign of Queen Elizabeth, Fuller tells us they were brought from Holland, and were accounted "fit dainties for ladies, they came so far and cost so dear." There are some varieties of peas which have no lining in their pods, which are eaten cooked in the same way as kidney-beans. They are called *sugar* pease, and the best variety is the large crooked sugar, which is also very good, used in the common way, as a culinary vegetable. There is also a white sort, which readily splits when subjected to the action of millstones set wide apart, so as not to grind them. These are used largely for soups, and especially for sea-stores. From the quantity of farinaceous and saccharine matter contained in the pea, it is highly nutritious as an article of food.

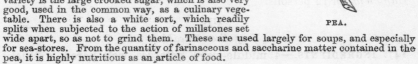

PEA.

PEA SOUP (inexpensive).

144. INGREDIENTS.—¼ lb. of onions, ¼ lb. of carrots, 2 oz. of celery, ¾ lb. of split peas, a little mint, shred fine; 1 tablespoonful of coarse brown sugar, salt and pepper to taste, 4 quarts of water, or liquor in which a joint of meat has been boiled.

Mode.—Fry the vegetables for 10 minutes in a little butter or dripping, previously cutting them up in small pieces; pour the water on them, and when boiling add the peas. Let them simmer for nearly 3 hours, or until the peas are thoroughly done. Add the sugar, seasoning, and mint; boil for ¼ of an hour, and serve.

Time.—3½ hours. *Average cost,* 1½d. per quart.

Seasonable in winter.

Sufficient for 12 persons.

POTATO SOUP.

I.

145. INGREDIENTS.—4 lbs. of mealy potatoes, boiled or steamed very dry, pepper and salt to taste, 2 quarts of stock No. 105.

Mode.—When the potatoes are boiled, mash them smoothly, that no lumps remain, and gradually put them to the boiling stock; pass it through a sieve, season, and simmer for 5 minutes. Skim well, and serve with fried bread.

Time.—½ hour. *Average cost,* 10d. per quart.

Seasonable from September to March.

Sufficient for 8 persons.

II.

146. INGREDIENTS.—1 lb. of shin of beef, 1 lb. of potatoes, 1 onion, ½ a pint of peas, 2 oz. of rice, 2 heads of celery, pepper and salt to taste, 3 quarts of water.

Mode.—Cut the beef into thin slices, chop the potatoes and onion, and put them in a stewpan with the water, peas, and rice. Stew gently till the gravy is drawn from the meat; strain it off, take out the beef, and pulp the other ingredients through a coarse sieve. Put the pulp back in the soup, cut up the celery in it, and simmer till this is tender. Season, and serve with fried bread cut into it.

Time.—3 hours. *Average cost,* 4d. per quart.

Seasonable from September to March.

Sufficient for 12 persons.

III.

(*Very Economical.*)

147. INGREDIENTS.—4 middle-sized potatoes well pared, a thick

slice of bread, 6 leeks peeled and cut into thin slices as far as the white extends upwards from the roots, a teacupful of rice, a teaspoonful of salt, and half that of pepper, and 2 quarts of water.

Mode.—The water must be completely boiling before anything is put into it; then add the whole of the ingredients at once, with the exception of the rice, the salt, and the pepper. Cover, and let these come to a brisk boil; put in the others, and let the whole boil slowly for an hour, or till all the ingredients are thoroughly done, and their several juices extracted and mixed.

Time.—2½ hours. *Average cost,* 3d. per quart.

Sufficient for 8 persons.

Seasonable in winter.

POTATOES.

THE POTATO.—Humboldt doubted whether this root was a native of South America; but it has been found growing wild both in Chili and Buenos Ayres. It was first brought to Spain from the neighbourhood of Quito, in the early part of the sixteenth century, first to England from Virginia, in 1586, and first planted by Sir Walter Raleigh, on his estate of Youghal, near Cork, in Ireland. Thence it was brought and planted in Lancashire, in England, and was at first recommended to be eaten as a delicate dish, and not as common food. This was in 1587. *Nutritious Properties.*—Of a thousand parts of the potato, Sir H. Davy found about a fourth nutritive; say, 200 mucilage or starch, 20 sugar, and 30 gluten.

PRINCE OF WALES'S SOUP.

148. INGREDIENTS.—12 turnips, 1 lump of sugar, 2 spoonfuls of strong veal stock, salt and white pepper to taste, 2 quarts of very bright stock, No. 105.

Mode.—Peel the turnips, and with a cutter cut them in balls as round as possible, but very small. Put them in the stock, which must be very bright, and simmer till tender. Add the veal stock and seasoning. Have little pieces of bread cut round, about the size of a shilling; moisten them with stock; put them into a tureen and pour the soup over without shaking, for fear of crumbling the bread, which would spoil the appearance of the soup, and make it look thick.

Time.—2 hours.

Seasonable in the winter.

Sufficient for 8 persons.

THE PRINCE OF WALES.—This soup was invented by a philanthropic friend of the Editress, to be distributed among the poor of a considerable village, when the Prince of Wales attained his majority, on the 9th November, 1859. Accompanying this fact, the following notice, which appears in "BEETON'S DICTIONARY OF UNIVERSAL INFORMATION," may appropriately be introduced, premising that British princes attain their majority in their 18th year, whilst mortals of ordinary rank do not arrive at that period till their 21st.—"ALBERT EDWARD, Prince of Wales, and heir to the British throne, merits a place in this work on account of the high responsibilities which he is, in all probability, destined to fulfil as sovereign of the British empire. On the 10th of November, 1858, he was gazetted as having been invested with the rank of a colonel in the army. Speaking of this circumstance, the *Times* said,—'The significance of this event is, that it marks the period when the heir to the British throne is about to take rank among men, and to enter formally upon a career, which every loyal subject of the queen will pray may be a long and a happy one, for his own sake and for the sake of the vast empire which, in the course of nature, he will one day be called to govern. The best wish that we can offer for the young prince is, that in his own path he may ever keep before him the bright example of his royal mother, and show himself worthy of her name.' There are few in these realms who will not give a fervent response to these sentiments. B. November 9th, 1841."

POTAGE PRINTANIER, OR SPRING SOUP.

149. INGREDIENTS.—½ a pint of green peas, if in season, a little chervil, 2 shredded lettuces, 2 onions, a very small bunch of parsley, 2 oz. of butter, the yolks of 3 eggs, 1 pint of water, seasoning to taste, 2 quarts of stock No. 105.

Mode.—Put in a very clean stewpan the chervil, lettuces, onions, parsley, and butter, to 1 pint of water, and let them simmer till tender. Season with salt and pepper; when done, strain off the vegetables, and put two-thirds of the liquor they were boiled in to the stock. Beat up the yolks of the eggs with the other third, give it a toss over the fire, and at the moment of serving, add this, with the vegetables which you strained off, to the soup.

Time.—¾ of an hour. *Average cost*, 1s. per quart.

Seasonable from May to October.

Sufficient for 8 persons.

RICE SOUP.

I.

150. INGREDIENTS.—4 oz. of Patna rice, salt, cayenne, and mace, 2 quarts of white stock.

Mode.—Throw the rice into boiling water, and let it remain 5 minutes; then pour it into a sieve, and allow it to drain well. Now add it to the stock boiling, and allow it to stew till it is quite tender; season to taste. Serve quickly.

Time.—1 hour. *Average cost*, 1s. 3d. per quart.

Seasonable all the year.

Sufficient for 8 persons.

EARS OF RICE.

RICE.—This is a plant of Indian origin, and has formed the principal food of the Indian and Chinese people from the most remote antiquity. Both Pliny and Dioscorides class it with the cereals, though Galen places it among the vegetables. Be this as it may, however, it was imported to Greece, from India, about 286 years before Christ, and by the ancients it was esteemed both nutritious and fattening. There are three kinds of rice,—the Hill rice, the Patna, and the Carolina, of the United States. Of these, only the two latter are imported to this country, and the Carolina is considered the best, as it is the dearest. The nourishing properties of rice are greatly inferior to those of wheat; but it is both a light and a wholesome food. In combination with other foods, its nutritive qualities are greatly increased; but from its having little stimulating power, it is apt, when taken in large quantities alone, to lie long on the stomach.

II.

151. INGREDIENTS.—6 oz. of rice, the yolks of 4 eggs, ½ a pint of cream, rather more than 2 quarts of stock No. 105.

Mode.—Boil the rice in the stock, and rub half of it through a tammy; put the stock in the stewpan, add all the rice, and simmer gently for 5 minutes. Beat the yolks of the eggs, mix them with the cream (previously boiled), and strain through a hair sieve; take the soup off the fire, add the eggs and cream, stirring frequently. Heat it gradually, stirring all the time; but do not let it boil, or the eggs will curdle.

Time.—2 hours. *Average cost*, 1s. 4d. per quart.

Seasonable all the year.

Sufficient for 8 persons.

SAGO SOUP.

152. INGREDIENTS.—5 oz. of sago, 2 quarts of stock No. 105.

Mode.—Wash the sago in boiling water, and add it, by degrees, to the boiling stock, and simmer till the sago is entirely dissolved, and forms a sort of jelly.

Time.—Nearly an hour. *Average cost*, 10d. per quart.

Sufficient for 8 persons.

Seasonable all the year.

Note.—The yolks of 2 eggs, beaten up with a little cream, previously boiled, and added at the moment of serving, much improves this soup.

SAGO PALM.

SAGO.—The farinaceous food of this name constitutes the pith of the SAGO tree (the *Sagus farinifera* of Linnæus), which grows spontaneously in the East Indies and in the archipelago of the Indian Ocean. There it forms the principal farinaceous diet of the inhabitants. In order to procure it, the tree is felled and sawn in pieces. The pith is then taken out, and put in receptacles of cold water, where it is stirred until the flour separates from the filaments, and sinks to the bottom, where it is suffered to remain until the water is poured off, when it is taken out and spread on wicker frames to dry. To give it the round granular form in which we find it come to this country, it is passed through a colander, then rubbed into little balls, and dried. The tree is not fit for felling until it has attained a growth of seven years, when a single trunk will yield 600 lbs. weight; and, as an acre of ground will grow 430 of these trees, a large return of flour is the result. The best quality has a slightly reddish hue, and easily dissolves to a jelly, in hot water. As a restorative diet, it is much used.

SEMOLINA SOUP.

153. INGREDIENTS.—5 oz. of semolina, 2 quarts of boiling stock, No. 105, or 106.

Mode.—Drop the semolina into the boiling stock, and keep stirring, to prevent its burning. Simmer gently for half an hour, and serve.

Time.—½ an hour. *Average cost,* 10*d.* per quart, or 4*d.*

Seasonable all the year.

Sufficient for 8 persons.

SEMOLINA.—This is the heart of the *grano duro* wheat of Italy, which is imported for the purpose of making the best vermicelli. It has a coarse appearance, and may be purchased at the Italian warehouses. It is also called *soojee*; and *semoletta* is another name for a finer sort.

SOUP A LA SOLFERINO (Sardinian Recipe).

154. INGREDIENTS.—4 eggs, ½ pint of cream, 2 oz. of fresh butter, salt and pepper to taste, a little flour to thicken, 2 quarts of bouillon, No. 105.

Mode.—Beat the eggs, put them into a stewpan, and add the cream, butter, and seasoning; stir in as much flour as will bring it to the consistency of dough; make it into balls, either round or egg-shaped, and fry them in butter; put them in the tureen, and pour the boiling bouillon over them.

Time.—1 hour. *Average cost,* 1*s.* 3*d.* per quart.

Seasonable all the year.

Sufficient for 8 persons.

Note.—This recipe was communicated to the Editress by an English gentleman, who was present at the battle of Solferino, on June 24, 1859, and who was requested by some of Victor Emmanuel's troops, on the day before the battle, to partake of a portion of their *potage.* He willingly enough consented, and found that these clever campaigners had made a most palatable dish from very easily-procured materials. In sending the recipe for insertion in this work, he has, however, Anglicized, and somewhat, he thinks, improved it.

SPINACH SOUP (French Recipe).

155. INGREDIENTS.—As much spinach as, when boiled, will half fill a vegetable-dish, 2 quarts of very clear medium stock, No. 105.

Mode.—Make the cooked spinach into balls the size of an egg, and slip them into the soup-tureen. This is a very elegant soup, the green of the spinach forming a pretty contrast to the brown gravy.

Time.—1 hour. *Average cost,* 1*s.* per quart.

Seasonable from October to June.

SPINACH.

SPINACH.—This plant was unknown by the ancients, although it was cultivated in the monastic gardens of the continent in the middle of the 14th century. Some say, that it was originally brought from Spain; but there is a wild species growing in England, and cultivated in Lincolnshire, in preference to the other. There are three varieties in use; the round-leaved, the triangular-leaved, and

Flanders spinach, known by its large leaves. They all form a useful ingredient in soup; but the leaves are sometimes boiled alone mashed, and eaten as greens.

TAPIOCA SOUP.

156. INGREDIENTS.—5 oz. of tapioca, 2 quarts of stock No. 105 or 106.

Mode.—Put the tapioca into cold stock, and bring it gradually to a boil. Simmer gently till tender, and serve.

Time.—Rather more than 1 hour. *Average cost*, 1*s.* or 6*d.* per quart.

Seasonable all the year.

Sufficient for 8 persons.

TAPIOCA.—This excellent farinaceous food is the produce of the pith of the cassava-tree, and is made in the East Indies, and also in Brazil. It is, by washing, procured as a starch from the tree, then dried, either in the sun or on plates of hot iron, and afterwards broken into grains, in which form it is imported into this country. Its nutritive properties are large, and as a food for persons of delicate digestion, or for children, it is in great estimation. "No amylaceous substance," says Dr. Christison, "is so much relished by infants about the time of weaning; and in them it is less apt to become sour during digestion than any other farinaceous food, even arrowroot not excepted."

TURNIP SOUP.

157. INGREDIENTS.—3 oz. of butter, 9 good-sized turnips, 4 onions, 2 quarts of stock No. 106, seasoning to taste.

Mode.—Melt the butter in the stewpan, but do not let it boil; wash, drain, and slice the turnips and onions very thin; put them in the butter, with a teacupful of stock, and stew very gently for an hour. Then add the remainder of the stock, and simmer another hour. Rub it through a tammy, put it back into the stewpan, but do not let it boil. Serve very hot.

Time.—2½ hours. *Average cost*, 8*d.* per quart.

Seasonable from October to March.

Sufficient for 8 persons.

Note.—By adding a little cream, this soup will be much improved.

TURNIP.

THE TURNIP.—Although turnips grow wild in England, they are not the original of the cultivated vegetable made use of in this country. In ancient times they were grown for cattle by the Romans, and in Germany and the Low Countries they have from time immemorial been raised for the same purpose. In their cultivated state, they are generally supposed to have been introduced to England from Hanover, in the time of George I.; but this has been doubted, as George II. caused a description of the Norfolk system to be sent to his Hanoverian subjects, for their enlightenment in the art of turnip culture. As a culinary vegetable, it is excellent, whether eaten alone, mashed, or mixed with soups and stews. Its nutritious matter, however, is small, being only 42 parts in 1,000.

VEGETABLE-MARROW SOUP.

158. INGREDIENTS.—4 young vegetable marrows, or more, if very small, ½ pint of cream, salt and white pepper to taste, 2 quarts of white stock, No. 107.

G

Mode.—Pare and slice the marrows, and put them in the stock boiling. When done almost to a mash, press them through a sieve, and at the moment of serving, add the boiling cream and seasoning.

Time.—1 hour.   *Average cost*, 1*s.* 2*d.* per quart.

Seasonable in summer.

Sufficient for 8 persons.

THE VEGETABLE MARROW.—This is a variety of the gourd family, brought from Persia by an East-India ship, and only recently introduced to Britain. It is already cultivated to a considerable extent, and, by many, is highly esteemed when fried with butter. It is, however, dressed in different ways, either by stewing or boiling, and, besides, made into pies.

VEGETABLE MARROW.

VEGETABLE SOUP.

I.

159. INGREDIENTS.—7 oz. of carrot, 10 oz. of parsnip, 10 oz. of potato, cut into thin slices; 1¼ oz. of butter, 5 teaspoonfuls of flour, a teaspoonful of made mustard, salt and pepper to taste, the yolks of 2 eggs, rather more than 2 quarts of water.

Mode.—Boil the vegetables in the water 2½ hours; stir them often, and if the water boils away too quickly, add more, as there should be 2 quarts of soup when done. Mix up in a basin the butter and flour, mustard, salt, and pepper, with a teacupful of cold water; stir in the soup, and boil 10 minutes. Have ready the yolks of the eggs in the tureen; pour on, stir well, and serve.

Time.—3 hours.   *Average cost*, 4*d.* per quart.

Seasonable in winter.

Sufficient for 8 persons.

II.

160. INGREDIENTS.—Equal quantities of onions, carrots, turnips; ¼ lb. of butter, a crust of toasted bread, 1 head of celery, a faggot of herbs, salt and pepper to taste, 1 teaspoonful of powdered sugar, 2 quarts of common stock or boiling water. Allow ¾ lb. of vegetables to 2 quarts of stock, No. 105.

Mode.—Cut up the onions, carrots, and turnips; wash and drain them well, and put them in the stewpan with the butter and powdered sugar. Toss the whole over a sharp fire for 10 minutes, but do not let them brown, or you will spoil the flavour of the soup. When done, pour the stock or boiling water on them; add the bread, celery, herbs, and seasoning; stew for 3 hours; skim well and strain it off.

When ready to serve, add a little sliced carrot, celery, and turnip, and flavour with a spoonful of Harvey's sauce, or a little ketchup.

Time.—3½ hours. *Average cost,* 6*d.* per quart.

Seasonable all the year. *Sufficient* for 8 persons.

III.

(*Good and Cheap, made without Meat.*)

161. INGREDIENTS.—6 potatoes, 4 turnips, or 2 if very large; 2 carrots, 2 onions; if obtainable, 2 mushrooms; 1 head of celery, 1 large slice of bread, 1 small saltspoonful of salt, ¼ saltspoonful of ground black pepper, 2 teaspoonfuls of Harvey's sauce, 6 quarts of water.

Mode.—Peel the vegetables, and cut them up into small pieces; toast the bread rather brown, and put all into a stewpan with the water and seasoning. Simmer gently for 3 hours, or until all is reduced to a pulp, and pass it through a sieve in the same way as pea-soup, which it should resemble in consistence; but it should be a dark brown colour. Warm it up again when required; put in the Harvey's sauce, and, if necessary, add to the flavouring.

Time.—3 hours, or rather more. *Average cost,* 1*d.* per quart.

Seasonable at any time. *Sufficient* for 16 persons.

Note.—This recipe was forwarded to the Editress by a lady in the county of Durham, by whom it was strongly recommended.

VERMICELLI SOUP.

I.

162. INGREDIENTS.—1½ lb. of bacon, stuck with cloves; ½ oz. of butter, worked up in flour; 1 small fowl, trussed for boiling; 2 oz. of vermicelli, 2 quarts of white stock, No. 107.

Mode.—Put the stock, bacon, butter, and fowl into the stewpan, and stew for ¾ of an hour. Take the vermicelli, add it to a little of the stock, and set it on the fire, till it is quite tender. When the soup is ready, take out the fowl and bacon, and put the bacon on a dish. Skim the soup as clean as possible; pour it, with the vermicelli, over the fowl. Cut some bread thin, put in the soup, and serve.

VERMICELLI.

Time.—2 hours. *Average cost,* exclusive of the fowl and bacon, 10*d.* per quart.

Seasonable in winter.

Sufficient for 4 persons.

VERMICELLI.—This is a preparation of Italian origin, and is made in the same way as macaroni, only the yolks of eggs, sugar, saffron, and cheese, are added to the paste.

II.

163. INGREDIENTS.—¼ lb. of vermicelli, 2 quarts of clear gravy stock, No. 169.

Mode.—Put the vermicelli in the soup, boiling; simmer very gently for ½ an hour, and stir frequently.

Time.—½ an hour. *Average cost*, 1s. 3d. per quart.

Seasonable all the year.

Sufficient for 8 persons.

WHITE SOUP.

164. INGREDIENTS.—¼ lb. of sweet almonds, ¼ lb. of cold veal or poultry, a thick slice of stale bread, a piece of fresh lemon-peel, 1 blade of mace, pounded, ¾ pint of cream, the yolks of 2 hard-boiled eggs, 2 quarts of white stock, No. 107.

Mode.—Reduce the almonds in a mortar to a paste, with a spoonful of water, and add to them the meat, which should be previously pounded with the bread. Beat all together, and add the lemon-peel, very finely chopped, and the mace. Pour the boiling stock on the whole, and simmer for an hour. Rub the eggs in the cream, put in the soup, bring it to a boil, and serve immediately.

Time.—1½ hour. *Average cost*, 1s. 6d. per quart.

Seasonable all the year.

Sufficient for 8 persons.

Note.—A more economical white soup may be made by using common veal stock, and thickening with rice, flour, and milk. Vermicelli should be served with it.

Average cost, 5d. per quart.

USEFUL SOUP FOR BENEVOLENT PURPOSES.

165. INGREDIENTS.—An ox-cheek, any pieces of trimmings of beef, which may be bought very cheaply (say 4 lbs.), a few bones, any pot-liquor the larder may furnish, ¼ peck of onions, 6 leeks, a large bunch of herbs, ½ lb. of celery (the outside pieces, or green tops, do very very well) ; ½ lb. of carrots, ½ lb. of turnips, ½ lb. of coarse brown sugar, ½ a pint of beer, 4 lbs. of common rice, or pearl barley ; ½ lb. of salt, 1 oz. of black pepper, a few raspings, 10 gallons of water.

Mode.—Cut up the meat in small pieces, break the bones, put them in a copper, with the 10 gallons of water, and stew for ½ an hour. Cut up the vegetables, put them in with the sugar and beer, and boil for 4 hours. Two hours before the soup is wanted, add the rice and raspings, and keep stirring till it is well mixed in the soup, which simmer gently. If the liquor reduces too much, fill up with water.

Time.—6½ hours.   *Average cost*, 1½*d*. per quart.

Note.—The above recipe was used in the winter of 1858 by the Editress, who made, each week, in her copper, 8 or 9 gallons of this soup, for distribution amongst about a dozen families of the village near which she lives.   The cost, as will be seen, was not great; but she has reason to believe that it was very much liked, and gave to the members of those families, a dish of warm, comforting food, in place of the cold meat and piece of bread which form, with too many cottagers, their usual meal, when, with a little more knowledge of the "cooking" art, they might have, for less expense, a warm dish every day.

MEAT, POULTRY, AND GAME SOUPS.

BRILLA SOUP.

166. INGREDIENTS.—4 lbs. of shin of beef, 3 carrots, 2 turnips, a large sprig of thyme, 2 onions, 1 head of celery, salt and pepper to taste, 4 quarts water.

Mode.—Take the beef, cut off all the meat from the bone, in nice square pieces, and boil the bone for 4 hours.   Strain the liquor, let it cool, and take off the fat; then put the pieces of meat in the cold liquor; cut small the carrots, turnips, and celery; chop the onions, add them with the thyme and seasoning, and simmer till the meat is tender.   If not brown enough, colour it with browning.

Time.—6 hours.   *Average cost*, 5*d*. per quart.

Seasonable all the year.

Sufficient for 10 persons.

THYME.—This sweet herb was known to the Romans, who made use of it in culinary preparations, as well as in aromatic liqueurs.   There are two species of it growing wild in Britain, but the garden thyme is a native of the south of Europe, and is more delicate in its perfume than the others.   Its young leaves give an agreeable flavour to soups and sauces; they are also used in stuffings.

CALF'S-HEAD SOUP.

167. INGREDIENTS.—½ a calf's head, 1 onion stuck with cloves, a very small bunch of sweet herbs, 2 blades of mace, salt and white pepper to taste, 6 oz. of rice-flour, 3 tablespoonfuls of ketchup, 3 quarts of white stock, No. 107, or pot-liquor, or water.

Mode.—Rub the head with salt, soak it for 6 hours, and clean it thoroughly; put it in the stewpan, and cover it with the stock, or pot-liquor, or water, adding the onion and sweet herbs.   When well skimmed and boiled for 1½ hour, take out the head, and skim and strain the soup. Mix the rice-flour with the ketchup, thicken the soup with it, and simmer for 5 minutes. Now cut up the head into pieces about two inches long, and simmer them in the soup till the meat and fat are quite tender. Season with white pepper and mace finely pounded, and serve very hot. When the calf's head is taken out of the soup, cover it up, or it will discolour.

Time.—2½ hours. *Average cost,* 1*s.* 9*d.* per quart, with stock. No. 107.

Seasonable from May to October.

Sufficient for 10 persons.

Note.—Force-meat balls can be added, and the soup may be flavoured with a little lemon-juice, or a glass of sherry or Madeira. The bones from the head may be stewed down again, with a few fresh vegetables, and it will make a very good common stock.

GIBLET SOUP.

168. INGREDIENTS.—3 sets of goose or duck giblets, 2 lbs. of shin of beef, a few bones, 1 ox-tail, 2 mutton-shanks, 2 large onions, 2 carrots, 1 large faggot of herbs, salt and pepper to taste, ¼ pint of cream, 1 oz. of butter mixed with a dessert-spoonful of flour, 3 quarts of water.

Mode.—Scald the giblets, cut the gizzards in 8 pieces, and put them in a stewpan with the beef, bones, ox-tail, mutton-shanks, onions, herbs, pepper, and salt; add the 3 quarts of water, and simmer till the giblets are tender, taking care to skim well. When the giblets are done, take them out, put them in your tureen, strain the soup through a sieve, add the cream and butter, mixed with a dessert-spoonful of flour, boil it up a few minutes, and pour it over the giblets. It can be flavoured with port wine and a little mushroom ketchup, instead of cream. Add salt to taste.

Time.—3 hours. *Average cost,* 9*d.* per quart.

Seasonable all the year.

Sufficient for 10 persons.

GRAVY SOUP.

169. INGREDIENTS.—6 lbs. of shin of beef, a knuckle of veal weighing 5 lbs., a few pieces or trimmings, 2 slices of nicely-flavoured lean ham; ¼ lb. of butter, 2 onions, 2 carrots, 1 turnip, nearly a head of celery, 1 blade of mace, 6 cloves, a bunch of savoury herbs, with endive, seasoning of salt and pepper to taste, 3 lumps of sugar, 5 quarts of boiling soft water. It can be flavoured with ketchup, Leamington sauce (*see* SAUCES), Harvey's sauce, and a little soy.

Mode.—Slightly brown the meat and ham in the butter, but do not

...urn. When this is done, pour to it the water, and as the scum ...ake it off; when no more appears, add all the other ingredients, ...let the soup simmer slowly by the fire for 6 hours without stir-...ng it any more from the bottom; take it off, and let it settle; skim off all the fat you can, and pass it through a tammy. When perfectly cold, you can remove all the fat, and leave the sediment untouched, which serves very nicely for thick gravies, hashes, &c.

Time.—7 hours. *Average cost*, 1s. per quart.
Seasonable all the year.
Sufficient for 14 persons.

ENDIVE.

ENDIVE.—This plant belongs to the acetarious tribe of vege-tables, and is supposed to have originally come from China and Japan. It was known to the ancients; but was not introduced to England till about the middle of the 16th century. It is consumed in large quantities by the French, and in London,—in the neighbourhood of which it is grown in abundance;—it is greatly used as a winter salad, as well as in soups and stews.

HARE SOUP.

I.

170. INGREDIENTS.—A hare fresh-killed, 1 lb. of lean gravy-beef, a slice of ham, 1 carrot, 2 onions, a faggot of savoury herbs, $\frac{1}{4}$ oz. of whole black pepper, a little browned flour, $\frac{1}{4}$ pint of port wine, the crumb of two French rolls, salt and cayenne to taste, 3 quarts of water.

Mode.—Skin and paunch the hare, saving the liver and as much blood as possible. Cut it in pieces, and put it in a stewpan with all the ingredients, and simmer gently for 8 hours. This soup should be made the day before it is wanted. Strain through a sieve, put the best parts of the hare in the soup, and serve.

OR,

II.

Proceed as above; but, instead of putting the joints of the hare in the soup, pick the meat from the bones, pound it in a mortar, and add it, with the crumb of two French rolls, to the soup. Rub all through a sieve; heat slowly, but do not let it boil. Send it to table immediately.

Time.—8 hours. *Average cost*, 1s. 9d. per quart.
Seasonable from September to February.
Sufficient for 10 persons.

THE COMMON HARE.—This little animal is found throughout Europe, and in most of the northern parts of the world; and as it is destitute of natural weapons of defence, Providence has endowed it with an extraordinary amount of the passion of fear. As if to awaken the vigilance of this passion, too, He has furnished it with long and tubular ears, in order that it may catch the remotest sounds; and with full, prominent eyes, which enable it to see, at one and the same time, both before and behind it. The hare feeds in the evenings, and sleeps, in its form, during the day; and, as it generally lies on the ground, its feet, both below and above, are protected with a thick covering of hair. Its flesh, though esteemed by the Romans, was forbidden by the Druids and by the earlier Britons. It is now, though very dark and dry, and devoid of fat, much esteemed by Europeans, on account of the peculiarity of its flavour. In purchasing this animal, it ought to be remembered that both hares and rabbits, when old, have their claws rugged and blunt, their haunches thick, and their ears dry and tough. The ears of a young hare easily tear, and it has a narrow cleft in the lip; whilst its claws are both smooth and sharp.

HARE.

HESSIAN SOUP.

171. INGREDIENTS.—Half an ox's head, 1 pint of split peas, 8 carrots, 6 turnips, 6 potatoes, 6 onions, 1 head of celery, 1 bunch of savoury herbs, pepper and salt to taste, 2 blades of mace, a little allspice, 4 cloves, the crumb of a French roll, 6 quarts of water.

Mode.—Clean the head, rub it with salt and water, and soak it for 5 hours in warm water. Simmer it in the water till tender, put it into a pan and let it cool; skim off all the fat; take out the head, and add the vegetables cut up small, and the peas which have been previously soaked; simmer them without the meat, till they are done enough to pulp through a sieve. Add the seasoning, with pieces of the meat cut up; give one boil, and serve.

Time.—4 hours. *Average cost*, 6d. per quart.

Seasonable in winter.

Sufficient for 16 persons.

Note.—An excellent hash or *ragoût* can be made by cutting up the nicest parts of the head, thickening and seasoning more highly a little of the soup, and adding a glass of port wine and 2 tablespoonfuls of ketchup.

MOCK TURTLE.

I.

172. INGREDIENTS.—½ a calf's head, ¼ lb. of butter, ¼ lb. of lean ham, 2 tablespoonfuls of minced parsley, a little minced lemon thyme, sweet marjoram, basil, 2 onions, a few chopped mushrooms (when obtainable), 2 shallots, 2 tablespoonfuls of flour, ¼ bottle of Madeira or sherry, force-meat balls, cayenne, salt and mace to taste, the juice of 1 lemon and 1 Seville orange, 1 dessert-spoonful of pounded sugar, 3 quarts of best stock, No. 104.

Mode.—Scald the head with the skin on, remove the brain, tie the head up in a cloth, and let it boil for 1 hour. Then take the meat from the bones, cut it into small square pieces, and throw them into cold water. Now take the meat, put it into a stewpan, and cover with stock; let it boil gently for an hour, or rather more, if not quite tender, and set it on one side. Melt the butter in another stewpan, and add the ham, cut small, with the herbs, parsley, onions, shallots, mushrooms, and nearly a pint of stock; let these simmer slowly for 2 hours, and then dredge in as much flour as will dry up the butter. Fill up with the remainder of the stock, add the wine, let it stew gently for 10 minutes, rub it through a tammy, and put it to the calf's head; season with cayenne, and, if required, a little salt; add the juice of the orange and lemon; and when liked, ¼ teaspoonful of pounded mace, and the sugar. Put in the force-meat balls, simmer 5 minutes, and serve very hot.

Time.—4½ hours. *Average cost*, 3s. 6d. per quart, or 2s. 6d. without wine or force-meat balls.

Seasonable in winter.

Sufficient for 10 persons.

Note.—The bones of the head should be well stewed in the liquor it was first boiled in, and will make good white stock, flavoured with vegetables, &c.

II.

(*More Economical.*)

173. INGREDIENTS.—A knuckle of veal weighing 5 or 6 lbs., 2 cow-heels, 2 large onions stuck with cloves, 1 bunch of sweet herbs, 3 blades of mace, salt to taste, 12 peppercorns, 1 glass of sherry, 24 force-meat balls, a little lemon-juice, 4 quarts of water.

Mode.—Put all the ingredients, except the force-meat balls and lemon-juice, in an earthen jar, and stew for 6 hours. Do not open it till cold. When wanted for use, skim off all the fat, and strain carefully; place it on the fire, cut up the meat into inch-and-a-half squares, put it, with the force-meat balls and lemon-juice, into the soup, and serve. It can be flavoured with a tablespoonful of anchovy, or Harvey's sauce.

Time.—6 hours. *Average cost*, 1s. 4d. per quart.

Seasonable in winter.

Sufficient for 10 persons.

THE CALF.—The flesh of this animal is called veal, and when young, that is, under two months old, yields a large quantity of soluble extract, and is, therefore, much employed for soups and broths. The Essex farmers have obtained a celebrity for fattening calves better than any others in England, where they are plentifully supplied with milk, a thing impossible to be done in the immediate neighbourhood of London.

MARJORAM.—There are several species of this plant; but that which is preferred for cookery is a native of Portugal, and is called *sweet* or knotted marjoram. When its leaves are dried, they have an agreeable aromatic flavour; and hence are used for soups, stuffings, &c.

BASIL.—This is a native of the East Indies, and is highly aromatic, having a perfume greatly resembling that of cloves. It is not much employed in English cookery, but is a favourite with French cooks, by whom its leaves are used in soups and salads.

MULLAGATAWNY SOUP.

174. INGREDIENTS.—2 tablespoonfuls of curry powder, 6 onions, 1 clove of garlic, 1 oz. of pounded almonds, a little lemon-pickle, or mango-juice, to taste; 1 fowl or rabbit, 4 slices of lean bacon; 2 quarts of medium stock, or, if wanted very good, best stock.

Mode.—Slice and fry the onions of a nice colour; line the stewpan with the bacon; cut up the rabbit or fowl into small joints, and slightly brown them; put in the fried onions, the garlic, and stock, and simmer gently till the meat is tender; skim very carefully, and when the meat is done, rub the curry powder to a smooth batter; add it to the soup with the almonds, which must be first pounded with a little of the stock. Put in seasoning and lemon-pickle or mango-juice to taste, and serve boiled rice with it.

Time.—2 hours. *Average cost*, 1*s*. 6*d*. per quart, with stock No. 105.

Seasonable in winter.

Sufficient for 8 persons.

Note.—This soup can also be made with breast of veal, or calf's head. Vegetable Mullagatawny is made with veal stock, by boiling and pulping chopped vegetable marrow, cucumbers, onions, and tomatoes, and seasoning with curry powder and cayenne. Nice pieces of meat, good curry powder, and strong stock, are necessary to make this soup good.

CORIANDER.—This plant, which largely enters into the compor-sition of curry powder with turmeric, originally comes from the East; but it has long been cultivated in England, especially in Essex, where it is reared for the use of confectioners and druggists. In private gardens, it is cultivated for the sake of its tender leaves, which are highly aromatic, and are employed in soups and salads. Its seeds are used in large quantities for the purposes of distillation.

CORIANDER.

A GOOD MUTTON SOUP.

175. INGREDIENTS.—A neck of mutton about 5 or 6 lbs., 3 carrots, 3 turnips, 2 onions, a large bunch of sweet herbs, including parsley; salt and pepper to taste; a litte sherry, if liked; 3 quarts of water.

Mode.—Lay the ingredients in a covered pan before the fire, and let them remain there the whole day, stirring occasionally. The next day put the whole into a stewpan, and place it on a brisk fire. When it commences to boil, take the pan off the fire, and put it on one side to simmer until the meat is done. When ready for use, take out the meat, dish it up with carrots and turnips, and send it to table; strain the soup, let it cool, skim off all the fat, season and thicken it with a tablespoonful, or rather more, of arrowroot; flavour with a little sherry, simmer for 5 minutes, and serve.

Time.—15 hours. *Average cost,* including the meat, 1s. 3d. per quart.

Seasonable at any time.

Sufficient for 8 persons.

THE SHEEP.—This animal formed the principal riches of the patriarchs, in the days of old, and, no doubt, multiplied, until its species were spread over the greater part of Western Asia; but at what period it was introduced to Britain is not known. It is now found in almost every part of the globe, although, as a domestic animal, it depends almost entirely upon man for its support. Its value, however, amply repays him for whatever care and kindness he may bestow upon it; for, like the ox, there is scarcely a part of it that he cannot convert to some useful purpose. The fleece, which serves it for a covering, is appropriated by man, to serve the same end to himself, whilst its skin is also applied to various purposes in civilized life. Its entrails are used as strings for musical instruments, and its bones are calcined, and employed as tests in the trade of the refiner. Its milk, being thicker than that of the cow, yields a greater quantity of butter and cheese, and its flesh is among the most wholesome and nutritive that can be eaten. Thomson has beautifully described the appearance of the sheep, when bound to undergo the operation of being shorn of its wool.

" Behold, where bound, and of its robe bereft
By needy man, that all-depending lord,
How meek, how patient, the mild creature lies !
What softness in his melancholy face,
What dumb complaining innocence appears !"

OX-CHEEK SOUP.

176. INGREDIENTS.—An ox-cheek, 2 oz. of butter, 3 or 4 slices of lean ham or bacon, 1 parsnip, 3 carrots, 2 onions, 3 heads of celery, 3 blades of mace, 4 cloves, a faggot of savoury herbs, 1 bay-leaf, a teaspoonful of salt, half that of pepper, 1 head of celery, browning, the crust of a French roll, 5 quarts of water.

Mode.—Lay the ham in the bottom of the stewpan, with the butter; break the bones of the cheek, wash it clean, and put it on the ham. Cut the vegetables small, add them to the other ingredients, and set the whole over a slow fire for ¼ of an hour. Now put in the water, and simmer gently till it is reduced to 4 quarts; take out the fleshy part of the cheek, and strain the soup into a clean stewpan; thicken with flour, put in a head of sliced celery, and simmer till the celery is tender. If not a good colour, use a little browning. Cut the meat into small square pieces, pour the soup over, and serve with the crust of a French roll in the tureen. A glass of sherry much improves this soup.

Time.—3 to 4 hours. *Average cost,* 8d. per quart.

Seasonable in winter.

Sufficient for 12 persons.

THE OX.—Of the quadrupedal animals, the flesh of those that feed upon herbs is the most wholesome and nutritious for human food. In the early ages, the ox was used as a religious sacrifice, and, in the eyes of the Egyptians was deemed so sacred as to be worthy of exaltation to represent Taurus, one of the twelve signs of the zodiac. To this day, the Hindoos venerate the cow, whose flesh is forbidden to be eaten, and whose fat, supposed to have been employed to grease the cartridges of the Indian army, was one of the proximate causes of the great Sepoy rebellion of 1857. There are no animals of greater use to man than the tribe to which the ox belongs. There is hardly a part of them that does not enter into some of the arts and purposes of civilized life. Of their horns are made combs, knife-handles, boxes, spoons, and drinking-cups. They are also made into transparent plates for lanterns; an invention ascribed, in England, to King Alfred. Glue is made from their gristles, cartilages, and portions of their hides. Their bones often form a substitute for ivory; their skins, when calves, are manufactured into vellum; their blood is the basis of Prussian blue; their sinews furnish fine and strong threads, used by saddlers; their hair enters into various manufactures; their tallow is made into candles; their flesh is eaten, and the utility of the milk and cream of the cow is well known.

OX-TAIL SOUP.

177. INGREDIENTS.—2 ox-tails, 2 slices of ham, 1 oz. of butter, 2 carrots, 2 turnips, 3 onions, 1 leek, 1 head of celery, 1 bunch of savoury herbs, 1 bay-leaf, 12 whole peppercorns, 4 cloves, a tablespoonful of salt, 2 tablespoonfuls of ketchup, ½ glass of port wine, 3 quarts of water.

Mode.—Cut up the tails, separating them at the joints; wash them, and put them in a stewpan, with the butter. Cut the vegetables in slices, and add them, with the peppercorns and herbs. Put in ½ pint of water, and stir it over a sharp fire till the juices are drawn. Fill up the stewpan with the water, and, when boiling, add the salt. Skim well, and simmer very gently for 4 hours, or until the tails are tender. Take them out, skim and strain the soup, thicken with flour, and flavour with the ketchup and port wine. Put back the tails, simmer for 5 minutes, and serve.

Time.—4½ hours. *Average cost*, 1s. 3d. per quart.

Seasonable in winter.

Sufficient for 10 persons.

PARTRIDGE SOUP.

178. INGREDIENTS.—2 partridges, 3 slices of lean ham, 2 shred onions, 1 head of celery, 1 large carrot, and 1 turnip cut into any fanciful shapes, 1 small lump of sugar, 2 oz. of butter, salt and pepper to taste, 2 quarts of stock No. 105, or common, No. 106.

Mode.—Cut the partridges into pieces, and braise them in the butter and ham until quite tender; then take out the legs, wings, and breast, and set them by. Keep the backs and other trimmings in the braise, and add the onions and celery; any remains of cold game can be put in, and 3 pints of stock. Simmer slowly for 1 hour, strain it, and skim the fat off as clean as possible; put in the pieces that were taken out, give it one boil, and skim again to have it quite clear, and add the sugar and seasoning. Now simmer the cut carrot and turnip in 1 pint of stock; when quite tender, put them to the partridges, and serve.

Time.—2 hours. *Average cost*, 2s. or 1s. 6d. per quart.

Seasonable from September to February.

Sufficient for 8 persons.

Note.—The meat of the partridges may be pounded with the crumb of a French roll, and worked with the soup through a sieve. Serve with stewed celery cut in slices, and put in the tureen.

THE PARTRIDGE.—This is a timorous bird, being easily taken. It became known to the Greeks and Romans, whose tables it helped to furnish with food. Formerly, the Red was scarce in Italy, but its place was supplied by the White, which, at considerable expense, was frequently procured from the Alps. The Athenians trained this bird for fighting, and Severus used to lighten the cares of royalty by witnessing the spirit of its combats. The Greeks esteemed its leg most highly, and rejected the other portions as unfashionable to be eaten. The Romans, however, ventured a little further, and ate the breast, whilst we consider the bird as wholly palatable. It is an inhabitant of all the temperate countries of Europe, but, on account of the geniality of the climate, it abounds most in the Ukraine.

PHEASANT SOUP.

179. INGREDIENTS.—2 pheasants, ¼ lb. of butter, 2 slices of ham, 2 large onions sliced, ½ head of celery, the crumb of two French rolls, the yolks of 2 eggs boiled hard, salt and cayenne to taste, a little pounded mace, if liked; 3 quarts of stock No. 105.

Mode.—Cut up the pheasants, flour and braise them in the butter and ham till they are of a nice brown, but not burnt. Put them in a stewpan, with the onions, celery, and seasoning, and simmer for 2 hours. Strain the soup; pound the breasts with the crumb of the roll previously soaked, and the yolks of the eggs; put it to the soup, give one boil, and serve.

Time.—2½ hours. *Average cost*, 2s. 10d. per quart, or, if made with fragments of gold game, 1s.

Seasonable from October to February.

Sufficient for 10 persons.

Note.—Fragments, pieces and bones of cold game, may be used to great advantage in this soup, and then 1 pheasant will suffice.

PORTABLE SOUP.

180. INGREDIENTS.—2 knuckles of veal, 3 shins of beef, 1 large faggot of herbs, 2 bay-leaves, 2 heads of celery, 3 onions, 3 carrots, 2 blades of mace, 6 cloves, a teaspoonful of salt, sufficient water to cover all the ingredients.

Mode.—Take the marrow from the bones; put all the ingredients in a stock-pot, and simmer slowly for 12 hours, or more, if the meat be not done to rags; strain it off, and put it in a very cool place;

take off all the fat, reduce the liquor in a shallow pan, by setting it over a sharp fire, but be particular that it does not burn; boil it fast and uncovered for 8 hours, and keep it stirred. Put it into a deep dish, and set it by for a day. Have ready a stewpan of boiling water, place the dish in it, and keep it boiling; stir occasionally, and when the soup is thick and ropy, it is done. Form it into little cakes by pouring a small quantity on to the bottom of cups or basins; when cold, turn them out on a flannel to dry. Keep them from the air in tin canisters.

Average cost of this quantity, 16s.

Note.—Soup can be made in 5 minutes with this, by dissolving a small piece, about the size of a walnut, in a pint of warm water, and simmering for 2 minutes. Vermicelli, macaroni, or other Italian pastes, may be added.

THE LAUREL, OR BAY.—The leaves of this tree frequently enter into the recipes of cookery; but they ought not to be used without the greatest caution, and not at all, unless the cook is perfectly aware of their effects. It ought to be known, that there are two kinds of bay-trees,—the Classic laurel, whose leaves are comparatively harmless, and the Cherry-laurel, which is the one whose leaves are employed in cookery. They have a kernel-like flavour, and are used in blanc-mange, puddings, custards, &c.; but, when acted upon by water, they develop prussic acid, and, therefore, but a small number of the leaves should be used at a time.

RABBIT SOUP.

181. INGREDIENTS.—2 large rabbits, or 3 small ones; a faggot of savoury herbs, ½ head of celery, 2 carrots, 1 onion, 1 blade of mace, salt and white pepper to taste, a little pounded mace, ½ pint of cream, the yolks of 2 eggs boiled hard, the crumb of a French roll, nearly 3 quarts of water.

Mode.—Make the soup with the legs and shoulders of the rabbit, and keep the nice pieces for a dish or *entrée*. Put them into warm water, and draw the blood; when quite clean, put them in a stewpan, with a faggot of herbs, and a teacupful, or rather more, of veal stock or water. Simmer slowly till done through, and add the 3 quarts of water, and boil for an hour. Take out the rabbit, pick the meat from the bones, covering it up to keep it white; put the bones back in the liquor, add the vegetables, and simmer for 2 hours; skim and strain, and let it cool. Now pound the meat in a mortar, with the yolks of the eggs, and the crumb of the roll previously soaked; rub it through a tammy, and gradually add it to the strained liquor, and simmer for 15 minutes. Mix arrowroot or rice-flour with the cream (say 2 dessert-spoonfuls), and stir in the soup; bring it to a boil, and serve. This soup must be very white, and instead of thickening it with arrowroot or rice-flour, vermicelli or pearl barley can be boiled in a little stock, and put in 5 minutes before serving.

Time.—Nearly 4 hours. *Average cost,* 1s. per quart.

Seasonable from September to March.

Sufficient for 10 persons.

REGENCY SOUP.

182. INGREDIENTS.—Any bones and remains of any cold game, such as of pheasants, partridges, &c. ; 2 carrots, 2 small onions, 1 head of celery, 1 turnip, ¼ lb. of pearl barley, the yolks of 3 eggs boiled hard, ¼ pint of cream, salt to taste, 2 quarts of stock No. 105, or common stock, No. 106.

Mode.—Place the bones or remains of game in the stewpan, with the vegetables sliced ; pour over the stock, and simmer for 2 hours ; skim off all the fat, and strain it. Wash the barley, and boil it in 2 or 3 waters before putting it to the soup ; finish simmering in the soup, and when the barley is done, take out half, and pound the other half with the yolks of the eggs. When you have finished pounding, rub it through a clean tammy, add the cream, and salt if necessary ; give one boil, and serve very hot, putting in the barley that was taken **out first.**

Time.—2½ hours. *Average cost,* 1s. per quart, if made with medium stock, or 6d. per quart, with common stock.

Seasonable from September to March.

Sufficient for 8 persons.

SOUP A LA REINE.

I.

183. INGREDIENTS.—1 large fowl, 1 oz. of sweet almonds, the crumb of 1½ French roll, ½ pint of cream, salt to taste, 1 small lump of sugar, 2 quarts of good white veal stock, No. 107.

Mode.—Boil the fowl gently in the stock till quite tender, which will be in about an hour, or rather more ; take out the fowl, pull the meat from the bones, and put it into a mortar with the almonds, and pound very fine. When beaten enough, put the meat back in the stock, with the crumb of the rolls, and let it simmer for an hour ; rub it through a tammy, add the sugar, ½ pint of cream that has boiled, and, if you prefer, cut the crust of the roll into small round pieces, and pour the soup over it, when you serve.

Time.—2 hours, or rather more. *Average cost,* 2s. 7d. per quart.

Seasonable all the year.

Sufficient for 8 persons.

Note.—All white soups should be warmed in a vessel placed in nother of boiling water. (*See* BAIN MARIE, No. 87.)

II.

(*Economical.*)

184. INGREDIENTS.—Any remains of roast chickens, ½ teacupful of rice, salt and pepper to taste, 1 quart of stock No. 106.

Mode.—Take all the white meat and pound it with the rice, which has been slightly cooked, but not much. When it is all well pounded, dilute with the stock, and pass through a sieve. This soup should neither be too clear nor too thick.

Time.—1 hour. *Average cost,* 4*d.* per quart.

Seasonable all the year.

Sufficient for 4 persons.

Note.—If stock is not at hand, put the chicken-bones in water, with an onion, carrot, a few sweet herbs, a blade of mace, pepper and salt, and stew for 3 hours.

STEW SOUP OF SALT MEAT.

185. INGREDIENTS.—Any pieces of salt beef or pork, say 2 lbs.; 4 carrots, 4 parsnips, 4 turnips, 4 potatoes, 1 cabbage, 2 oz. of oatmeal or ground rice, seasoning of salt and pepper, 2 quarts of water.

Mode.—Cut up the meat small, add the water, and let it simmer for 2¾ hours. Now add the vegetables, cut in thin small slices; season, and boil for 1 hour. Thicken with the oatmeal, and serve.

Time.—Nearly 2 hours. *Average cost,* 2*d.* per quart.

Seasonable in winter.

Sufficient for 6 persons.

Note.—If rice is used instead of oatmeal, put it in with the vegetables.

STEW SOUP.

I.

186. INGREDIENTS.—2 lbs. of beef, 5 onions, 5 turnips, ¾ lb. of rice, a large bunch of parsley, a few sweet herbs, pepper and salt, 2 quarts of water.

Mode.—Cut the beef up in small pieces, add the other ingredients, and boil gently for 2½ hours. Oatmeal or potatoes would be a great improvement.

Time.—2½ hours. *Average cost,* 1½*d.* per quart.

Seasonable in winter.

Sufficient for 6 persons.

II.

187. INGREDIENTS.—½ lb. of beef, mutton, or pork; ½ pint of split

peas, 4 turnips, 8 potatoes, 2 onions, 2 oz. of oatmeal or 3 oz. of rice, 2 quarts of water.

Mode.—Cut the meat in small pieces, as also the vegetables, and add them, with the peas, to the water. Boil gently for 3 hours; thicken with the oatmeal, boil for another ¼ hour, stirring all the time, and season with pepper and salt.

Time.—3¼ hours. *Average cost,* 4d. per quart.

Seasonable in winter.

Sufficient for 8 persons.

Note.—This soup may be made of the liquor in which tripe has been boiled, by adding vegetables, seasoning, rice, &c.

TURKEY SOUP (a Seasonable Dish at Christmas).

188. INGREDIENTS.—2 quarts of medium stock, No. 105, the remains of a cold roast turkey, 2 oz. of rice-flour or arrowroot, salt and pepper to taste, 1 tablespoonful of Harvey's sauce or mushroom ketchup.

Mode.—Cut up the turkey in small pieces, and put it in the stock; let it simmer slowly until the bones are quite clean. Take the bones out, and work the soup through a sieve; when cool, skim well. Mix the rice-flour or arrowroot to a batter with a little of the soup; add it with the seasoning and sauce, or ketchup. Give one boil, and serve.

Time.—4 hours. *Average cost,* 10d. per quart.

Seasonable at Christmas.

Sufficient for 8 persons.

Note.—Instead of thickening this soup, vermicelli or macaroni may be served in it.

THE TURKEY.—The common turkey is a native of North America, and was thence introduced to England, in the reign of Henry VIII. According to Tusser's "Five Hundred Points of Good Husbandry," about the year 1585 it began to form a dish at our rural Christmas feasts.

> " Beef, mutton, and pork, shred pies of the best,
> Pig, veal, goose, and capon, and turkey well dress'd,
> Cheese, apples, and nuts, jolly carols to hear,
> As then in the country is counted good cheer."

It is one of the most difficult birds to rear, of any that we have; yet, in its wild state, is found in great abundance in the forests of Canada, where, it might have been imagined that the severity of the climate would be unfavourable to its ever becoming plentiful. They are very fond of the seeds of nettles, and the seeds of the foxglove poison them.

TURTLE SOUP (founded on M. Ude's Recipe).

189. INGREDIENTS.—A turtle, 6 slices of ham, 2 knuckles of veal, 1 large bunch of sweet herbs, 3 bay-leaves, parsley, green onions, 1 onion, 6 cloves, 4 blades of mace, ¼ lb. of fresh butter, 1 bottle of Madeira, 1 lump of sugar. For the *Quenelles à Tortue,* 1 lb. of veal, 1 lb. of bread crumbs, milk, 7 eggs, cayenne, salt, spices, chopped parsley, the juice of 2 lemons.

H

Mode.—To make this soup with less difficulty, cut off the head of the turtle the preceding day. In the morning open the turtle by leaning heavily with a knife on the shell of the animal's back, whilst you cut this off all round. Turn it upright on its end, that all the water, &c. may run out, when the flesh should be cut off along the spine, with the knife sloping towards the bones, for fear of touching the gall, which sometimes might escape the eye. When all the flesh about the members is obtained, wash these clean, and let them drain. Have ready, on the fire, a large vessel full of boiling water, into which put the shells; and when you perceive that they come easily off, take them out of the water, and prick them all, with those of the back, belly, fins, head, &c. Boil the back and belly till the bones can be taken off, without, however, allowing the softer parts to be sufficiently done, as they will be boiled again in the soup. When these latter come off easily, lay them on earthen dishes singly, for fear they should stick together, and put them to cool. Keep the liquor in which you have blanched the softer parts, and let the bones stew thoroughly in it, as this liquor must be used to moisten all the sauces.

All the flesh of the interior parts, the four legs and head, must be drawn down in the following manner:—Lay the slices of ham on the bottom of a very large stewpan, over them the knuckles of veal, according to the size of the turtle; then the inside flesh of the turtle, and over the whole the members. Now moisten with the water in which you are boiling the shell, and draw it down thoroughly. It may now be ascertained if it be thoroughly done by thrusting a knife into the fleshy part of the meat. If no blood appears, it is time to moisten it again with the liquor in which the bones, &c. have been boiling. Put in a large bunch of all such sweet herbs as are used in the cooking of a turtle,—sweet basil, sweet marjoram, lemon thyme, winter savory, 2 or 3 bay-leaves, common thyme, a handful of parsley and green onions, and a large onion stuck with 6 cloves. Let the whole be thoroughly done. With respect to the members, probe them, to see whether they are done, and if so, drain and send them to the larder, as they are to make their appearance only when the soup is absolutely completed. When the flesh is also completely done, strain it through a silk sieve, and make a very thin white *roux;* for turtle soup must not be much thickened. When the flour is sufficiently done on a slow fire, and has a good colour, moisten it with the liquor, keeping it over the fire till it boils. Ascertain that the sauce is neither too thick nor too thin; then draw the stewpan on the side of the stove, to skim off the white scum, and all the fat and oil that rise to the surface of the sauce. By this time all the softer parts will be sufficiently cold; when they must be cut to about the size of one or two inches square, and thrown into the soup, which must now be left to simmer gently. When done, skim off all the fat and froth. Take all the leaves of the herbs from the stock,—sweet basil, sweet marjoram, lemon thyme, winter savory, 2 or 3 bay-leaves, common thyme, a handful of parsley and green onions, and a large onion cut in four pieces, with a few blades of mace. Put these in a stewpan, with about ¼ lb. of fresh butter, and let it simmer on a slow fire till quite melted, when pour in 1 bottle of good Madeira, adding a small bit of sugar, and let it boil gently for 1 hour. When done, rub it through a tammy, and add it to the soup. Let this boil, till no white scum rises; then take with a skimmer all the bits of turtle out of the sauce, and put them in a clean stewpan : when you have all out, pour the soup over the bits of turtle, through a tammy, and proceed as follows :—

QUENELLES A TORTUE.—Make some *quenelles à tortue,* which being substitutes for eggs, do not require to be very delicate. Take out the fleshy part of a leg of veal, about 1 lb., scrape off all the meat, without leaving any sinews or fat, and soak in milk about the same quantity of crumbs of bread. When the bread is well soaked, squeeze it, and put it into a mortar, with the veal, a small quantity of calf's udder, a little butter, the yolks of 4 eggs, boiled hard, a little cayenne pepper, salt, and spices, and pound the whole very fine; then thicken the mixture with 2 whole eggs, and the yolk of another. Next try this *farce* or stuffing in boiling-hot water, to ascertain its consist-ency : if it is too thin, add the yolk of an egg. When the *farce* is perfected, take half of it, and put into it some chopped parsley. Let the whole cool, in order to roll it of the size of the yolk of an egg; poach it in salt and boiling water, and when very hard, drain on a sieve, and put it into the turtle. Before you send up, squeeze the juice of 2 or 3 lemons, with a little cayenne pepper, and pour tha into the soup. THE FINS may be served as a *plat d'entrée* with a little turtle sauce; if not, on the following day you may warm the turtle *au bain marie,* and serve the members entire, with a *matelote* sauce, garnished with mushrooms, cocks' combs, *quenelles,* &c. When either lemon-juice or cayenne pepper has been introduced, no boiling must take place.

Note.—It is necessary to observe, that the turtle prepared a day before it is used, is generally preferable, the flavour being more uniform. Be particular, when you dress a very large turtle, to preserve the green fat (be cautious not to study a very brown colour,—the natural green of the fish is preferred by every epicure and true connoisseur) in a separate stewpan, and likewise when the turtle is entirely done, to have as many tureens as you mean to serve each time. You cannot put the whole in a large vessel, for many reasons: first, it will be long in cooling; secondly, when you take some out, it will break all the rest into rags. If you warm in a *bain marie*, the turtle will always retain the same taste; but if you boil it often, it becomes strong, and loses the delicacy of its flavour.

THE COST OF TURTLE SOUP.—This is the most expensive soup brought to table. It is sold by the quart,—one guinea being the standard price for that quantity. The price of live turtle ranges from 8*d.* to 2*s.* per lb., according to supply and demand. When live turtle is dear, many cooks use the tinned turtle, which is killed when caught, and preserved by being put in hermetically-sealed canisters, and so sent over to England. The cost of a tin, containing 2 quarts, or 4 lbs., is about £2, and for a small one, containing the green fat, 7*s.* 6*d.* From these about 6 quarts of good soup may be made.

THE GREEN TURTLE.—This reptile is found in large numbers on the coasts of all the islands and continents within the tropics, in both the old and new worlds. Their length is often five feet and upwards, and they range in weight from 50 to 500 or 600 lbs. As

THE TURTLE.

turtles find a constant supply of food on the coasts which they frequent, they are not of a quarrelsome disposition, as the submarine meadows in which they pasture, yield plenty for them all. Like other species of amphibia, too, they have the power of living many months without food; so that they live harmlessly and peaceably together, notwithstanding that they seem to have no common bond of association, but merely assemble in the same places as if entirely by accident. England is mostly supplied with them from the West Indies, whence they are brought alive and in tolerable health. The green turtle is highly prized on account of the delicious quality of its flesh, the fat of the upper and lower shields of the animal being esteemed the richest and most delicate parts. The soup, however, is apt to disagree with weak stomachs. As an article of luxury, the turtle has only come into fashion within the last 100 years, and some hundreds of tureens of turtle soup are served annually at the lord mayor's dinner in Guildhall.

A GOOD FAMILY SOUP.

190. INGREDIENTS.—Remains of a cold tongue, 2 lbs. of shin of beef, any cold pieces of meat or beef-bones, 2 turnips, 2 carrots, 2 onions, 1 parsnip, 1 head of celery, 4 quarts of water, ½ teacupful of rice; salt and pepper to taste.

Mode.—Put all the ingredients in a stewpan, and simmer gently for 4 hours, or until all the goodness is drawn from the meat. Strain off the soup, and let it stand to get cold. The kernels and soft parts of the tongue must be saved. When the soup is wanted for use, skim off all the fat, put in the kernels and soft parts of the tongue, slice in a small quantity of fresh carrot, turnip, and onion; stew till the vegetables are tender, and serve with toasted bread.

Time.—5 hours. *Average cost,* 3*d.* per quart.

Seasonable at any time.

Sufficient for 12 persons.

HODGE-PODGE.

191. INGREDIENTS.—2 lbs. of shin of beef, 3 quarts of water, 1 pint of table-beer, 2 onions, 2 carrots, 2 turnips, 1 head of celery; pepper and salt to taste; thickening of butter and flour.

Mode.—Put the meat, beer, and water in a stewpan; simmer for a few minutes, and skim carefully. Add the vegetables and seasoning; stew gently till the meat is tender. Thicken with the butter and flour, and serve with turnips and carrots, or spinach and celery.

Time.—3 hours, or rather more. *Average cost*, 3*d.* per quart.

Seasonable at any time. *Sufficient* for 12 persons.

TABLE BEER.—This is nothing more than a weak ale, and is not made so much with a view to strength, as to transparency of colour and an agreeable bitterness of taste. It is, or ought to be, manufactured by the London professional brewers, from the best pale malt, or amber and malt. Six barrels are usually drawn from one quarter of malt, with which are mixed 4 or 5 lbs. of hops. As a beverage, it is agreeable when fresh; but it is not adapted to keep long.

FISH SOUPS.

FISH STOCK.

192. INGREDIENTS.—2 lbs. of beef or veal (these can be omitted), any kind of white fish trimmings, of fish which are to be dressed for table, 2 onions, the rind of ½ a lemon, a bunch of sweet herbs, 2 carrots, 2 quarts of water.

Mode.—Cut up the fish, and put it, with the other ingredients, into the water. Simmer for 2 hours; skim the liquor carefully, and strain it. When a richer stock is wanted, fry the vegetables and fish before adding the water.

Time.—2 hours. *Average cost*, with meat, 10*d.* per quart; without, 3*d.*

Note.—Do not make fish stock long before it is wanted, as it soon turns sour.

CRAYFISH SOUP.

193. INGREDIENTS.—50 crayfish, ¼ lb. of butter, 6 anchovies, the crumb of 1 French roll, a little lobster-spawn, seasoning to taste, 2 quarts of medium stock, No. 105, or fish stock, No. 192.

Mode.—Shell the crayfish, and put the fish between two plates until they are wanted; pound the shells in a mortar, with the butter and anchovies; when well beaten, add a pint of stock, and simmer for ¾ of an hour. Strain it through a hair sieve, put the remainder of the stock to it, with the crumb of the rolls; give it one boil, and rub it through a tammy, with the lobster-spawn. Put in the fish, but do not let the soup boil, after it has been rubbed through the tammy. If necessary, add seasoning.

CRAYFISH.

Time.—1½ hour. *Average cost*, 2s. 3d. or 1s. 9d. per quart.

Seasonable from January to July.

Sufficient for 8 persons.

THE CRAYFISH.—This is one of those fishes that were highly esteemed by the ancients. The Greeks preferred it when brought from Alexandria, and the Romans ate it boiled with cumin, and seasoned with pepper and other condiments. A recipe tells us, that crayfish can be preserved several days in baskets with fresh grass, such as the nettle, or in a bucket with about three-eighths of an inch of water. More water would kill them, because the large quantity of air they require necessitates the water in which they are kept, to be continually renewed.

EEL SOUP.

194. INGREDIENTS.—3 lbs. of eels, 1 onion, 2 oz. of butter, 3 blades of mace, 1 bunch of sweet herbs, ¼ oz. of peppercorns, salt to taste, 2 tablespoonfuls of flour, ¼ pint of cream, 2 quarts of water.

Mode.—Wash the eels, cut them into thin slices, and put them in the stewpan with the butter; let them simmer for a few minutes, then pour the water to them, and add the onion, cut in thin slices, the herbs, mace, and seasoning. Simmer till the eels are tender, but do not break the fish. Take them out carefully, mix the flour smoothly to a batter with the cream, bring it to a boil, pour over the eels, and serve.

Time.—1 hour, or rather more. *Average cost*, 10d. per quart.

Seasonable from June to March.

Sufficient for 8 persons.

Note.—This soup may be flavoured differently by omitting the cream, and adding a little ketchup or Harvey's sauce.

LOBSTER SOUP.

195. INGREDIENTS.—3 large lobsters, or 6 small ones; the crumb of a French roll, 2 anchovies, 1 onion, 1 small bunch of sweet herbs, 1 strip of lemon-peel, 2 oz. of butter, a little nutmeg, 1 teaspoonful of flour, 1 pint of cream, 1 pint of milk; forcemeat balls, mace, salt and pepper to taste, bread crumbs, 1 egg, 2 quarts of water.

Mode.—Pick the meat from the lobsters, and beat the fins, chine, and small claws in a mortar, previously taking away the brown fin and the bag in the head. Put it in a stewpan, with the crumb of the roll, anchovies, onions, herbs, lemon-peel, and the water; simmer gently till all the goodness is extracted, and strain it off. Pound the spawn in a mortar, with the butter, nutmeg, and flour, and mix with it the cream and milk. Give one boil up, at the same time adding the tails cut in pieces. Make the forcemeat balls with the remainder of the lobster, seasoned with mace, pepper, and salt, adding a little flour, and a few bread crumbs; moisten them with the egg, heat them in the soup, and serve.

Time.—2 hours, or rather more. *Average cost*, 3*s*. 6*d*. per quart.

Seasonable from April to October.

Sufficient for 8 persons.

OYSTER SOUP.

I.

196. INGREDIENTS.—6 dozen of oysters, 2 quarts of white stock, ½ pint of cream, 2 oz. of butter, 1½ oz. of flour; salt, cayenne, and mace to taste.

Mode.—Scald the oysters in their own liquor; take them out, beard them, and put them in a tureen. Take a pint of the stock, put in the beards and the liquor, which must be carefully strained, and simmer for ½ an hour. Take it off the fire, strain it again, and add the remainder of the stock with the seasoning and mace. Bring it to a boil, add the thickening of butter and flour, simmer for 5 minutes, stir in the boiling cream, pour it over the oysters, and serve.

Time.—1 hour. *Average cost*, 2*s*. 8*d*. per quart.

Seasonable from September to April.

Sufficient for 8 persons.

Note.—This soup can be made less rich by using milk instead of cream, and thickening with arrowroot instead of butter and flour.

II.

197. INGREDIENTS.—2 quarts of good mutton broth, 6 dozen oysters, 2 oz. butter, 1 oz. of flour.

Mode.—Beard the oysters, and scald them in their own liquor; then add it, well strained, to the broth; thicken with the butter and flour, and simmer for ¼ of an hour. Put in the oysters, stir well, but do not let it boil, and serve very hot.

Time.—¾ hour. *Average cost*, 2*s*. per quart.

Seasonable from September to April.

Sufficient for 8 persons

SEASON OF OYSTERS.—From April and May to the end of July, oysters are said to be sick; but by the end of August they become healthy, having recovered from the effects of spawning. When they are not in season, the males have a black, and the females a milky substance in the gill. From some lines of Oppian, it would appear that the ancients were ignorant that the oyster is generally found adhering to rocks. The star-fish is one of the most deadly enemies of these bivalves. The poet says :—

> The prickly star creeps on with full deceit
> To force the oyster from his close retreat.
> When gaping lids their widen'd void display,
> The watchful star thrusts in a pointed ray,
> Of all its treasures spoils the rifled case,
> And empty shells the sandy hillock grace.

PRAWN SOUP.

198. INGREDIENTS.—2 quarts of fish stock or water, 2 pints of prawns, the crumbs of a French roll, anchovy sauce or mushroom ketchup to taste, 1 blade of mace, ½ pint of vinegar, a little lemon-juice.

Mode.—Pick out the tails of the prawns, put the bodies in a stew-pan with 1 blade of mace, ½ pint of vinegar, and the same quantity of water; stew them for ¼ hour, and strain off the liquor. Put the fish stock or water into a stewpan; add the strained liquor, pound the prawns with the crumb of a roll moistened with a little of the soup, rub them through a tammy, and mix them by degrees with the soup; add ketchup or anchovy sauce to taste, with a little lemon-juice. When it is well cooked, put in a few picked prawns; let them get thoroughly hot, and serve. If not thick enough, put in a little butter and flour.

Time.—hour. *Average cost,* 1s. 1d. per quart, if made with water.

Seasonable at any time. *Sufficient* for 8 persons.

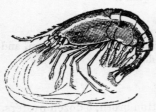

Note.—This can be thickened with tomatoes, and vermicelli served in it, which makes it a very tasteful soup.

THE PRAWN.—This little fish bears a striking resemblance to the shrimp, but is neither so common nor so small. It is to be found on most of the sandy shores of Europe. The Isle of Wight is famous for shrimps, where they are potted; but both the prawns and the shrimps vended in London, are too much salted for the excellence of their natural

THE PRAWN.

flavour to be preserved. They are extremely lively little animals, as seen in their native retreats.

FISH.
CHAPTER VII.
THE NATURAL HISTORY OF FISHES.

199. IN NATURAL HISTORY, FISHES form the fourth class in the system of Linnæus, and are described as having long under-jaws, eggs without white, organs of sense, fins for supporters, bodies covered with concave scales, gills to supply the place of lungs for respiration, and water for the natural element of their existence. Had mankind no other knowledge of animals than of such as inhabit the land and breathe their own atmosphere, they would listen with incredulous wonder, if told that there were other kinds of beings which existed only in the waters, and which would die almost as soon as they were taken from them. However strongly these facts might be attested, they would hardly believe them, without the operation of their own senses, as they would recollect the effect produced on their own bodies when immersed in water, and the impossibility of their sustaining life in it for any lengthened period of time. Experience, however, has taught them, that the "great deep" is crowded with inhabitants of various sizes, and of vastly different constructions, with modes of life entirely distinct from those which belong to the animals of the land, and with peculiarities of design, equally wonderful with those of any other works which have come from the hand of the Creator. The history of these races, however, must remain for ever, more or less, in a state of darkness, since the depths in which they live, are beyond the power of human exploration, and since the illimitable expansion of their domain places them almost entirely out of the reach of human accessibility.

200. IN STUDYING THE CONFORMATION OF FISHES, we naturally conclude that they are, in every respect, well adapted to the element in which they have their existence. Their shape has a striking resemblance to the lower part of a ship; and there is no doubt that the form of the fish originally suggested the form of the ship. The body is in general slender, gradually diminishing towards each of its extremities, and flattened on each of its sides. This is precisely the form of the lower part of the hull of a ship; and it enables both the animal and the vessel, with comparative ease, to penetrate and divide the resisting medium for which they have been adapted. The velocity of a ship, however, in sailing before the wind, is by no means to be compared to that of a fish. It is well known that the largest fishes will, with the greatest ease, overtake a ship in full sail, play round it without effort, and shoot ahead of it at pleasure. This arises from their great flexibility, which, to compete with mocks the labours of art, and enables them to migrate thousands of miles in a season, without the slightest indications of languor or fatigue.

201. THE PRINCIPAL INSTRUMENTS EMPLOYED BY FISHES to accelerate their motion, are their air-bladder, fins, and tail. By means of the air-bladder they enlarge or diminish the specific gravity of their bodies. When they wish to sink, they compress the muscles of the abdomen, and eject the air contained in it; by which, their weight, compared with that of the water, is increased, and they consequently descend. On the other hand, when they wish to rise, they relax the compression of the abdominal muscles, when the air-bladder fills and distends, and the body immediately ascends to the surface. How simply, yet how wonderfully, has the Supreme Being adapted certain means to the attainment of certain ends! Those fishes which are destitute of the air-bladder are heavy in the water, and have no great "alacrity" in rising. The larger proportion of them remain at the bottom, unless they are so formed as to be able to strike their native element downwards with sufficient force to enable them to ascend. When the air-bladder of a fish is burst, its power of ascending to the surface has for ever passed away. From a knowledge of this fact, the fishermen of cod are enabled to preserve them alive for a considerable time in their well-boats. The means they adopt to accomplish this, is to perforate the sound, or air-bladder, with a needle, which disengages the air, when the fishes immediately descend to the bottom of the well, into which they are thrown. Without this operation, it would be impossible to keep the cod under water whilst they had life. In swimming, the *fins* enable fishes to preserve their upright position, especially those of the belly, which act like two feet. Without these, they would swim with their bellies upward, as it is in their backs that the centre of gravity lies. In ascending and descending, these are likewise of great assistance, as they contract and expand accordingly. The *tail* is an instrument of great muscular force, and largely assists the fish in all its motions. In some instances it acts like the rudder of a ship, and enables it to turn sideways; and when moved from side to side with a quick vibratory motion, fishes are made, in the same manner as the "screw" propeller makes

a steamship, to dart forward with a celerity proportioned to the muscular force with which it is employed.

202. THE BODIES OF FISHES are mostly covered with a kind of horny scales; but some are almost entirely without them, or have them so minute as to be almost invisible; as is the case with the eel. The object of these is to preserve them from injury by the pressure of the water, or the sudden contact with pebbles, rocks, or sea-weeds. Others, again, are enveloped in a fatty, oleaginous substance, also intended as a defence against the friction of the water; and those in which the scales are small, are supplied with a larger quantity of slimy matter.

203. THE RESPIRATION OF FISHES is effected by means of those comb-like organs which are placed on each side of the neck, and which are called gills. It is curious to watch the process of breathing as it is performed by the finny tribes. It seems to be so continuous, that it might almost pass for an illustration of the vexed problem which conceals the secret of perpetual motion. In performing it, they fill their mouths with water, which they drive backwards with a force so great as to open the large flap, to allow it to escape behind. In this operation all, or a great portion, of the air contained in the water, is left among the feather-like processes of the gills, and is carried into the body, there to perform its part in the animal economy. In proof of this, it has been ascertained that, if the water in which fishes are put, is, by any means, denuded of its air, they immediately seek the surface, and begin to gasp for it. Hence, distilled water is to them what a vacuum made by an air-pump, is to most other animals. For this reason, when a fishpond, or other aqueous receptacle in which fishes are kept, is entirely frozen over, it is necessary to make holes in the ice, not so especially for the purpose of feeding them, as for that of giving them air to breathe.

204. THE POSITIONS OF THE TEETH OF FISHES are well calculated to excite our amazement; for, in some cases, these are situated in the jaws, sometimes on the tongue or palate, and sometimes even in the throat. They are in general sharp-pointed and immovable; but in the carp they are obtuse, and in the pike so easily moved as to seem to have no deeper hold than such as the mere skin can afford. In the herring, the tongue is set with teeth, to enable it the better, it is supposed, to retain its food.

205. ALTHOUGH NATURALISTS HAVE DIVIDED FISHES into two great tribes, the *osseous* and the *cartilaginous,* yet the distinction is not very precise; for the first have a great deal of cartilage, and the second, at any rate, a portion of calcareous matter in their bones. It may, therefore, be said that the bones of fishes form a kind of intermediate substance between true bones and cartilages. The backbone extends through the whole length of the body, and consists of vertebræ, strong and thick towards the head, but weaker and more slender as it approaches the tail. Each species has a determinate number of vertebræ,

which are increased in size in proportion with the body. The ribs are attached to the processes of the vertebræ, and inclose the breast and abdomen. Some kinds, as the rays, have no ribs; whilst others, as the sturgeon and eel, have very short ones. Between the pointed processes of the vertebræ are situated the bones which support the dorsal (back) and the anal (below the tail) fins, which are connected with the processes by a ligament. At the breast are the sternum or breastbone, clavicles or collar-bones, and the scapulæ or shoulder-blades, on which the pectoral or breast fins are placed. The bones which support the ventral or belly fins are called the *ossa pelvis*. Besides these principal bones, there are often other smaller ones, placed between the muscles to assist their motion.

206. SOME OF THE ORGANS OF SENSE IN FISHES are supposed to be possessed by them in a high degree, and others much more imperfectly. Of the latter kind are the senses of touch and taste, which are believed to be very slightly developed. On the other hand, those of hearing, seeing, and smelling, are ascertained to be acute, but the first in a lesser degree than both the second and third. Their possession of an auditory organ was long doubted, and even denied by some physiologists; but it has been found placed on the sides of the skull, or in the cavity which contains the brain. It occupies a position entirely distinct and detached from the skull, and, in this respect, differs in the local disposition of the same sense in birds and quadrupeds. In some fishes, as in those of the ray kind, the organ is wholly encompassed by those parts which contain the cavity of the skull; whilst in the cod and salmon kind it is in the part within the skull. Its structure is, in every way, much more simple than that of the same sense in those animals which live entirely in the air; but there is no doubt that they have the adaptation suitable to their condition. In some genera, as in the rays, the external orifice or ear is very small, and is placed in the upper surface of the head; whilst in others there is no visible external orifice whatever. However perfect the *sight* of fishes may be, experience has shown that this sense is of much less use to them than that of smelling, in searching for their food. The optic nerves in fishes have this peculiarity,—that they are not confounded with one another in their middle progress between their origin and their orbit. The one passes over the other without any communication; so that the nerve which comes from the left side of the brain goes distinctly to the right eye, and that which comes from the right goes distinctly to the left. In the greater part of them, the eye is covered with the same transparent skin that covers the rest of the head. The object of this arrangement, perhaps, is to defend it from the action of the water, as there are no eyelids. The globe in front is somewhat depressed, and is furnished behind with a muscle, which serves to lengthen or flatten it, according to the necessities of the animal. The crystalline humour, which in quadrupeds is flattened, is, in fishes, nearly globular. The organ of *smelling* in fishes is large, and is endued, at its entry, with a dilating and contracting power, which is employed as the wants of the animal may require. It is mostly by the acuteness of their smell that fishes are enabled to discover their food; for their tongue is not

designed for nice sensation, being of too firm a cartilaginous substance for this purpose.

207. WITH RESPECT TO THE FOOD OF FISHES, this is almost universally found in their own element. They are mostly carnivorous, though they seize upon almost anything that comes in their way : they even devour their own offspring, and manifest a particular predilection for all living creatures. Those, to which Nature has meted out mouths of the greatest capacity, would seem to pursue everything with life, and frequently engage in fierce conflicts with their prey. The animal with the largest mouth is usually the victor ; and he has no sooner conquered his foe than he devours him. Innumerable shoals of one species pursue those of another, with a ferocity which draws them from the pole to the equator, through all the varying temperatures and depths of their boundless domain. In these pursuits a scene of universal violence is the result ; and many species must have become extinct, had not Nature accurately proportioned the means of escape, the production, and the numbers, to the extent and variety of the danger to which they are exposed. Hence the smaller species are not only more numerous, but more productive than the larger ; whilst their instinct leads them in search of food and safety near the shores, where, from the shallowness of the waters, many of their foes are unable to follow them.

208. THE FECUNDITY OF FISHES has been the wonder of every natural philosopher whose attention has been attracted to the subject. They are in general oviparous, or egg-producing ; but there are a few, such as the eel and the blenny, which are viviparous, or produce their young alive. The males have the *milt* and the females the *roe;* but some individuals, as the sturgeon and the cod tribes, are said to contain both. The greater number deposit their spawn in the sand or gravel ; but some of those which dwell in the depths of the ocean attach their eggs to sea-weeds. In every instance, however, their fruitfulness far surpasses that of any other race of animals. According to Lewenhoeck, the cod annually spawns upwards of nine millions of eggs, contained in a single roe. The flounder produces one million ; the mackerel above five hundred thousand ; a herring of a moderate size at least ten thousand ; a carp fourteen inches in length, according to Petit, contained two hundred and sixty-two thousand two hundred and twenty-four ; a perch deposited three hundred and eighty thousand six hundred and forty ; and a female sturgeon seven millions six hundred and fifty-three thousand two hundred. The viviparous species are by no means so prolific ; yet the blenny brings forth two or three hundred at a time, which commence sporting together round their parent the moment they have come into existence.

209. IN-REFERENCE TO THE LONGEVITY OF FISHES, it is affirmed to surpass that of all other created beings ; and it is supposed they are, to a great extent, exempted from the diseases to which the flesh of other animals is heir. In place of suffering from the rigidity of age, which is the cause of the natural

decay of those that "live and move and have their being" on the land, their bodies continue to grow with each succeeding supply of food, and the conduits of life to perform their functions unimpaired. The age of fishes has not been properly ascertained, although it is believed that the most minute of the species has a longer lease of life than man. The mode in which they die has been noted by the Rev. Mr. White, the eminent naturalist of Selbourne. As soon as the fish sickens, the head sinks lower and lower, till the animal, as it were, stands upon it. After this, as it becomes weaker, it loses its poise, till the tail turns over, when it comes to the surface, and floats with its belly upwards. The reason for its floating in this manner is on account of the body being no longer balanced by the fins of the belly, and the broad muscular back preponderating, by its own gravity, over the belly, from this latter being a cavity, and consequently lighter.

210. FISHES ARE EITHER SOLITARY OR GREGARIOUS, and some of them migrate to great distances, and into certain rivers, to deposit their spawn. Of sea-fishes, the cod, herring, mackerel, and many others, assemble in immense shoals, and migrate through different tracts of the ocean ; but, whether considered in their solitary or gregarious capacity, they are alike wonderful to all who look through Nature up to Nature's God, and consider, with due humility, yet exalted admiration, the sublime variety, beauty, power, and grandeur of His productions, as manifested in the Creation.

FISH AS AN ARTICLE OF HUMAN FOOD.

211. AS THE NUTRITIVE PROPERTIES OF FISH are deemed inferior to those of what is called butchers' meat, it would appear, from all we can learn, that, in all ages, it has held only a secondary place in the estimation of those who have considered the science of gastronomy as a large element in the happiness of mankind. Among the Jews of old it was very little used, although it seems not to have been entirely interdicted, as Moses prohibited only the use of such as had neither scales nor fins. The Egyptians, however, made fish an article of diet, notwithstanding that it was rejected by their priests. Egypt, however, is not a country favourable to the production of fish, although we read of the people, when hungry, eating it raw ; of epicures among them having dried it in the sun ; and of its being salted and preserved, to serve as a repast on days of great solemnity.

The modern Egyptians are, in general, extremely temperate in regard to food. Even the richest among them take little pride, and, perhaps, experience as little delight, in the luxuries of the table. Their dishes mostly consist of pilaus, soups, and stews, prepared principally of onions, cucumbers, and other cold vegetables, mixed with a little meat cut into small pieces. On special occasions, however, a whole sheep is placed on the festive board ; but during several of the hottest months of the year, the richest restrict themselves entirely to a vegetable diet. The poor are contented with a little oil or sour milk, in which they may dip their bread.

212. PASSING FROM AFRICA TO EUROPE, we come amongst a people who

have, almost from time immemorial, occupied a high place in the estimation of every civilized country ; yet the Greeks, in their earlier ages, made very little use of fish as an article of diet. In the eyes of the heroes of Homer it had little favour ; for Menelaus complained that "hunger pressed their digestive organs," and they had been obliged to live upon fish. Subsequently, however, fish became one of the principal articles of diet amongst the Hellenes ; and both Aristophanes and Athenæus allude to it, and even satirize their countrymen for their excessive partiality to the turbot and mullet.

So infatuated were many of the Greek gastronomes with the love of fish, that some of them would have preferred death from indigestion to the relinquishment of the precious dainties with which a few of the species supplied them. Philoxenes of Cythera was one of these. On being informed by his physician that he was going to die of indigestion, on account of the quantity he was consuming of a delicious fish, "Be it so," he calmly observed ; "but before I die, let me finish the remainder."

213. THE GEOGRAPHICAL SITUATION OF GREECE was highly favourable for the development of a taste for the piscatory tribes ; and the skill of the Greek cooks was so great, that they could impart every variety of relish to the dish they were called upon to prepare. Athenæus has transmitted to posterity some very important precepts upon their ingenuity in seasoning with salt, oil, and aromatics.

At the present day the food of the Greeks, through the combined influence of poverty and the long fasts which their religion imposes upon them, is, to a large extent, composed of fish, accompanied with vegetables and fruit. Caviare, prepared from the roes of sturgeons, is the national ragout, which, like all other fish dishes, they season with aromatic herbs. Snails dressed in garlic are also a favourite dish.

214. AS THE ROMANS, in a great measure, took their taste in the fine arts from the Greeks, so did they, in some measure, their piscine appetites. The eel-pout and the lotas's liver were the favourite fish dishes of the Roman epicures ; whilst the red mullet was esteemed as one of the most delicate fishes that could be brought to the table.

With all the elegance, taste, and refinement of Roman luxury, it was sometimes promoted or accompanied by acts of great barbarity. In proof of this, the mention of the red mullet suggests the mode in which it was sometimes treated for the, to us, *horrible* entertainment of the *fashionable* in Roman circles. It may be premised, that as England has, Rome, in her palmy days, had, her fops, who had, no doubt, through the medium of their cooks, discovered that when the scales of the red mullet were removed, the flesh presented a fine pink-colour. Having discovered this, it was further observed that at the death of the animal, this colour passed through a succession of beautiful shades, and, in order that these might be witnessed and enjoyed in their fullest perfection, the poor mullet was served alive in a glass vessel.

215. THE LOVE OF FISH among the ancient Romans rose to a real mania. Apicius offered a prize to any one who could invent a new brine compounded of the liver of red mullets ; and Lucullus had a canal cut through a mountain, in the neighbourhood of Naples, that fish might be the more easily transported to the gardens of his villa. Hortensius, the orator, wept over the death of a turbot which he had fed with his own hands ; and the daughter of Druses adorned one that she had, with rings of gold. These were, surely, instances of misplaced affection ; but there is no accounting for tastes. It was but the

other day that we read in the "*Times*" of a wealthy *living* English hermit, who delights in the companionship of rats!

The modern Romans are merged in the general name of Italians, who, with the exception of macaroni, have no specially characteristic article of food.

216. FROM ROME TO GAUL is, considering the means of modern locomotion, no great way; but the ancient sumptuary laws of that kingdom give us little information regarding the ichthyophagous propensities of its inhabitants. Louis XII. engaged six fishmongers to furnish his board with fresh-water animals, and Francis I. had twenty-two, whilst Henry the Great extended his requirements a little further, and had twenty-four. In the time of Louis XIV. the cooks had attained to such a degree of perfection in their art, that they could convert the form and flesh of the trout, pike, or carp, into the very shape and flavour of the most delicious game.

The French long enjoyed a European reputation for their skill and refinement in the preparing of food. In place of plain joints, French cookery delights in the marvels of what are called made dishes, ragouts, stews, and fricassees, in which no trace of the original materials of which they are compounded is to be found.

217. FROM GAUL WE CROSS TO BRITAIN, where it has been asserted, by, at least, one authority, that the ancient inhabitants ate no fish. However this may be, we know that the British shores, particularly those of the North Sea, have always been well supplied with the best kinds of fish, which we may reasonably infer was not unknown to the inhabitants, or likely to be lost upon them for the lack of knowledge as to how they tasted. By the time of Edward II., fish had, in England, become a dainty, especially the sturgeon, which was permitted to appear on no table but that of the king. In the fourteenth century, a decree of King John informs us that the people ate both seals and porpoises; whilst in the days of the Troubadours, whales were fished for and caught in the Mediterranean Sea, for the purpose of being used as human food.

Whatever checks the ancient British may have had upon their piscatory appetites, there are happily none of any great consequence upon the modern, who delight in wholesome food of every kind. Their taste is, perhaps, too much inclined to that which is accounted solid and substantial; but they really eat more moderately, even of animal food, than either the French or the Germans. Roast beef, or other viands cooked in the plainest manner, are, with them, a sufficient luxury; yet they delight in living *well*, whilst it is easy to prove how largely their affections are developed by even the prospect of a substantial cheer. In proof of this we will just observe, that if a great dinner is to be celebrated, it is not uncommon for the appointed stewards and committee to meet and have a preliminary dinner among themselves, in order to arrange the great one, and after that, to have another dinner to discharge the bill which the great one cost. This enjoyable disposition we take to form a very large item in the aggregate happiness of the nation.

218. THE GENERAL USE OF FISH, as an article of human food among civilized nations, we have thus sufficiently shown, and will conclude this portion of our subject with the following hints, which ought to be remembered by all those who are fond of occasionally varying their dietary with a piscine dish :—

I. Fish shortly before they spawn are, in general, best in condition. When the spawning is just over, they are out of season, and unfit for human food.

II. When fish is out of season, it has a transparent, bluish tinge, however much it may be boiled ; when it is in season, its muscles are firm, and boil white and curdy.

III. As food for invalids, white fish, such as the ling, cod, haddock, coal-fish, and whiting, are the best ; flat fish, as soles, skate, turbot, and flounders, are also good.

IV. Salmon, mackerel, herrings, and trout soon spoil or decompose after they are killed ; therefore, to be in perfection, they should be prepared for the table on the day they are caught. With flat fish, this is not of such consequence, as they will keep longer. The turbot, for example, is improved by being kept a day or two.

GENERAL DIRECTIONS FOR DRESSING FISH.

219. In Dressing Fish, of any kind, the first point to be attended to, is to see that it be perfectly clean. It is a common error to wash it too much ; as by doing so the flavour is diminished. If the fish is to be boiled, a little salt and vinegar should be put into the water, to give it firmness, after it is cleaned. Cod-fish, whiting, and haddock, are far better if a little salted, and kept a day ; and if the weather be not very hot, they will be good for two days.

220. When Fish is Cheap and Plentiful, and a larger quantity is purchased than is immediately wanted, the overplus of such as will bear it should be potted, or pickled, or salted, and hung up ; or it may be fried, that it may serve for stewing the next day. Fresh-water fish, having frequently a muddy smell and taste, should be soaked in strong salt and water, after it has been well cleaned. If of a sufficient size, it may be scalded in salt and water, and afterwards dried and dressed.

221. Fish should be put into Cold Water, and set on the fire to do very gently, or the outside will break before the inner part is done. Unless the fishes are small, they should never be put into warm water ; nor should water, either hot or cold, be poured *on* to the fish, as it is liable to break the skin : if it should be necessary to add a little water whilst the fish is cooking, it ought to be poured in gently at the side of the vessel. The fish-plate may be drawn up, to see if the fish be ready, which may be known by its easily separating from the bone. It should then be immediately taken out of the water, or it will become woolly. The fish-plate should be set crossways over the kettle, to keep hot for serving, and a clean cloth over the fish, to prevent its losing its colour.

222. In Garnishing Fish, great attention is required, and plenty of parsley,

I

horseradish, and lemon should be used. If fried parsley be used, it must be washed and picked, and thrown into fresh water. When the lard or dripping boils, throw the parsley into it immediately from the water, and instantly it will be green and crisp, and must be taken up with a slice. When well done, and with very good sauce, fish is more appreciated than almost any other dish. The liver and roe, in some instances, should be placed on the dish, in order that they may be distributed in the course of serving; but to each recipe will be appended the proper mode of serving and garnishing.

223. IF FISH IS TO BE FRIED OR BROILED, it must be dried in a nice soft cloth, after it is well cleaned and washed. If for frying, brush it over with egg, and sprinkle it with some fine crumbs of bread. If done a second time with the egg and bread, the fish will look so much the better. If required to be very nice, a sheet of white blotting-paper must be placed to receive it, that it may be free from all grease. It must also be of a beautiful colour, and all the crumbs appear distinct. Butter gives a bad colour; lard and clarified dripping are most frequently used; but oil is the best, if the expense be no objection. The fish should be put into the lard when boiling, and there should be a sufficiency of this to cover it.

224. WHEN FISH IS BROILED, it must be seasoned, floured, and laid on a very clean gridiron, which, when hot, should be rubbed with a bit of suet, to prevent the fish from sticking. It must be broiled over a very clear fire, that it may not taste smoky; and not too near, that it may not be scorched.

225. IN CHOOSING FISH, it is well to remember that it is possible it may be *fresh,* and yet not *good.* Under the head of each particular fish in this work, are appended rules for its choice and the months when it is in season. Nothing can be of greater consequence to a cook than to have the fish good; as if this important course in a dinner does not give satisfaction, it is rarely that the repast goes off well.

RECESIPES.

CHAPTER VIII.

FISH.

[Nothing is more difficult than to give the average prices of Fish, inasmuch as a few hours of bad weather at sea will, in the space of one day, cause such a difference in its supply, that the same fish—a turbot for instance—which may be bought to-day for six or seven shillings, will, to-morrow, be, in the London markets, worth, perhaps, almost as many pounds. The average costs, therefore, which will be found appended to each recipe, must be understood as about the average price for the different kinds of fish, when the market is supplied upon an average, and when the various sorts are of an average size and quality.

GENERAL RULE IN CHOOSING FISH.—A proof of freshness and goodness in most fishes, is their being covered with scales; for, if deficient in this respect, it is a sign of their being stale, or having been ill-used.]

FRIED ANCHOVIES.

226. INGREDIENTS.—1 tablespoonful of oil, $\frac{1}{2}$ a glass of white wine, sufficient flour to thicken; 12 anchovies.

Mode.—Mix the oil and wine together, with sufficient flour to make them into a thickish paste; cleanse the anchovies, wipe them, dip them in the paste, and fry of a nice brown colour.

Time.—$\frac{1}{2}$ hour. *Average cost* for this quantity, 9d.

Seasonable all the year.

Sufficient for 2 persons.

THE ANCHOVY.—In his book of "British Fishes," Mr. Yarrell states that "the anchovy is a common fish in the Mediterranean, from Greece to Gibraltar, and was well known to the Greeks and Romans, by whom the liquor prepared from it, called *garum*, was in great estimation. Its extreme range is extended into the Black Sea. The fishing for them is carried on during the night, and lights are used with the nets. The anchovy is common on the coasts of Portugal, Spain, and France. It occurs, I have no doubt, at the Channel Islands, and has been taken on the Hampshire coast, and in the Bristol Channel." Other fish, of inferior quality, but resembling the real Gorgona anchovy, are frequently sold for it, and passed off as genuine.

THE ANCHOVY.

ANCHOVY BUTTER OR PASTE.

227. INGREDIENTS.—2 dozen anchovies, ½ lb. of fresh butter.

Mode.—Wash the anchovies thoroughly; bone and dry them, and pound them in a mortar to a paste. Mix the butter gradually with them, and rub the whole through a sieve. Put it by in small pots for use, and carefully exclude the air with a bladder, as it soon changes the colour of anchovies, besides spoiling them.

Average cost for this quantity, 2s.

POTTED ANCHOVIES.

POTTED ANCHOVIES are made in the same way, by adding pounded mace, cayenne, and nutmeg to taste.

ANCHOVY TOAST.

228. INGREDIENTS.—Toast 2 or 3 slices of bread, or, if wanted very savoury, fry them in clarified butter, and spread on them the paste, No. 227. Made mustard, or a few grains of cayenne, may be added to the paste before laying it on the toast.

ANCHOVY PASTE.—"When some delicate zest," says a work just issued on the adulterations of trade, "is required to make the plain English breakfast more palatable, many people are in the habit of indulging in what they imagine to be anchovies. These fish are preserved in a kind of pickling-bottle, carefully corked down, and surrounded by a red-looking liquor, resembling in appearance diluted clay. The price is moderate, one shilling only being demanded for the luxury. When these anchovies are what is termed potted, it implies that the fish have been pounded into the consistency of a paste, and then placed in flat pots, somewhat similar in shape to those used for pomatum. This paste is usually eaten spread upon toast, and is said to form an excellent *bonne bouche*, which enables gentlemen at wine-parties to enjoy their port with redoubled gusto. Unfortunately, in six cases out of ten, the only portion of these preserved delicacies, that contains anything indicative of anchovies, is the paper label pasted on the bottle or pot, on which the word itself is printed. . . . All the samples of anchovy paste, analyzed by different medical men, have been found to be highly and vividly coloured with very large quantities of bole Armenian." The anchovy itself, when imported, is of a dark dead colour, and it is to make it a bright "handsome-looking sauce" that this red earth is used.

BARBEL.

229. INGREDIENTS.—½ pint of port wine, a saltspoonful of salt, 2 tablespoonfuls of vinegar, 2 sliced onions, a faggot of sweet herbs, nutmeg and mace to taste, the juice of a lemon, 2 anchovies; 1 or 2 barbels, according to size.

Mode.—Boil the barbels in salt and water till done; pour off some of the water, and, to the remainder, put the ingredients mentioned above. Simmer gently for ½ hour, or rather more, and strain. Put in the fish; heat it gradually; but do not let it boil, or it will be broken.

Time.—Altogether 1 hour.   *Sufficient* for 4 persons.

Seasonable from September to November.

THE BARBEL.—This fish takes its name from the barbs or wattles at its mouth; and, in England, is esteemed as one of the worst of the fresh-water fish. It was, however, formerly, if not now, a favourite with the Jews, excellent cookers of fish. Others would boil with it a piece of bacon, that it might have a relish. It is to be met with from two to three or four feet long, and is said to live to a great age. From Putney upwards, in the Thames, some are found of large size; but they are valued only as affording sport to the brethren of the angle.

THE BARBEL.

BRILL.

230. INGREDIENTS.—$\frac{1}{4}$ lb. of salt to each gallon of water; a little vinegar.

Mode.—Clean the brill, cut off the fins, and rub it over with a little lemon-juice, to preserve its whiteness. Set the fish in sufficient cold water to cover it; throw in salt, in the above proportions, and a little vinegar, and bring it gradually to boil; simmer very gently till the fish is done, which will be in about 10 minutes; but the time for boiling, of course, depends entirely on the size of the fish. Serve it on a hot napkin, and garnish with cut lemon, parsley, horseradish, and a little lobster coral sprinkled over the fish. Send lobster or shrimp sauce and plain melted butter to table with it.

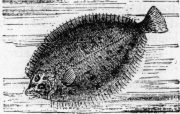

Time.—After the water boils, a small brill, 10 minutes; a large brill, 15 to 20 minutes.

Average cost, from 4s. to 8s.

Seasonable from August to April.

THE BRILL.—This fish resembles the sole, but is broader, and when large, is esteemed by many in a scarcely less degree than the turbot, whilst it is much cheaper. It is a fine fish, and is abundant in the London market.

THE BRILL.

TO CHOOSE BRILL.—The flesh of this fish, like that of turbot, should be of a yellowish tint, and should be chosen on account of its thickness. If the flesh has a bluish tint, it is not good.

CODFISH.

231. Cod may be boiled whole; but a large head and shoulders are quite sufficient for a dish, and contain all that is usually helped, because, when the thick part is done, the tail is insipid and overdone. The latter, cut in slices, makes a very good dish for frying; or it may

be salted down and served with egg sauce and parsnips. Cod, when boiled quite fresh, is watery; salting a little, renders it firmer.

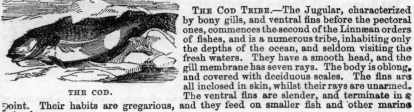

THE COD TRIBE.—The Jugular, characterized by bony gills, and ventral fins before the pectoral ones, commences the second of the Linnæan orders of fishes, and is a numerous tribe, inhabiting only the depths of the ocean, and seldom visiting the fresh waters. They have a smooth head, and the gill membrane has seven rays. The body is oblong, and covered with deciduous scales. The fins are all inclosed in skin, whilst their rays are unarmed. The ventral fins are slender, and terminate in a point. Their habits are gregarious, and they feed on smaller fish and other marine animals.

THE COD.

COD'S HEAD AND SHOULDERS.

232. INGREDIENTS.—Sufficient water to cover the fish; 5 oz. of salt to each gallon of water.

Mode.—Cleanse the fish thoroughly, and rub a little salt over the thick part and inside of the fish, 1 or 2 hours before dressing it, as this very much improves the flavour. Lay it in the fish-kettle, with sufficient cold water to cover it. Be very particular not to pour the water on the fish, as it is liable to break it, and only keep it just simmering. If the water should boil away, add a little by pouring it in at the side of the kettle, and not on the fish. Add salt in the above proportion, and bring it gradually to a boil. Skim very carefully, draw it to the side of the fire, and let it gently simmer till done. Take it out and drain it; serve on a hot napkin, and garnish with cut lemon, horseradish, the roe and liver.

Time.—According to size, ½ an hour, more or less. *Average cost,* from 3*s.* to 6*s.*

Sufficient for 6 or 8 persons.

Seasonable from November to March.

Note.—Oyster sauce and plain melted butter should be served with this.

TO CHOOSE COD.—The cod should be chosen for the table when it is plump and round near the tail, when the hollow behind the head is deep, and when the sides are undulated as if they were ribbed. The glutinous parts about the head lose their delicate flavour, after the fish has been twenty-four hours out of the water. The great point by which the cod should be judged is the firmness of its flesh; and, although the cod is not firm when it is alive, its quality may be arrived at by pressing the finger into the flesh. If this rises immediately, the fish is good; if not, it is stale. Another sign of its goodness is, if the fish, when it is cut, exhibits a bronze appearance, like the silver side of a round of beef. When this is the case, the flesh will be firm when cooked. Stiffness in a cod, or in any other fish, is a sure sign of freshness, though not always of quality. Sometimes, codfish, though exhibiting signs of rough usage, will eat much better than those with red gills, so strongly recommended by many cookery-books. This appearance is generally caused by the fish having been knocked about at sea, in the well-boats, in which they are conveyed from the fishing-grounds to market.

SALT COD, COMMONLY CALLED "SALT-FISH."

233. INGREDIENTS.—Sufficient water to cover the fish.

Mode.—Wash the fish, and lay it all night in water, with a ¼ pint of vinegar. When thoroughly soaked, take it out, see that it is perfectly clean, and put it in the fish-kettle with sufficient cold water to cover it. Heat it gradually, but do not let it boil much, or the fish will be hard. Skim well, and when done, drain the fish and put it on a napkin garnished with hard-boiled eggs cut in rings.

Time.—About 1 hour. *Average cost,* 6*d.* per lb.

Seasonable in the spring.

Sufficient for each person, ¼ lb.

Note.—Serve with egg sauce and parsnips. This is an especial dish on Ash-Wednesday.

PRESERVING COD.—Immediately as the cod are caught, their heads are cut off. They are then opened, cleaned, and salted, when they are stowed away in the hold of the vessel, in beds of five or six yards square, head to tail, with a layer of salt to each layer of fish. When they have lain in this state three or four days, in order that the water may drain from them, they are shifted into a different part of the vessel, and again salted. Here they remain till the vessel is loaded, when they are sometimes cut into thick pieces and packed in barrels for the greater convenience of carriage.

COD SOUNDS

Should be well soaked in salt and water, and thoroughly washed before dressing them. They are considered a great delicacy, and may either be broiled, fried, or boiled: if they are boiled, mix a little milk with the water.

COD SOUNDS, EN POULE.

234. INGREDIENTS.—For forcemeat, 12 chopped oysters, 3 chopped anchovies, ¼ lb. of bread crumbs, 1 oz. of butter, 2 eggs; seasoning of salt, pepper, nutmeg, and mace to taste; 4 cod sounds.

Mode.—Make the forcemeat by mixing the ingredients well together. Wash the sounds, and boil them in milk and water for ½ an hour; take them out and let them cool. Cover each with a layer of forcemeat, roll them up in a nice form, and skewer them. Rub over with lard, dredge with flour, and cook them gently before the fire in a Dutch oven.

Time.—1 hour. *Average cost,* 6*d.* per lb.

Seasonable from November to March.   *Sufficient* for 4 persons.

THE SOUNDS IN CODFISH.—These are the air or swimming bladders, by means of which the fishes are enabled to ascend or descend in the water. In the Newfoundland fishery they are taken out previous to incipient putrefaction, washed from their slime and salted for exportation. The tongues are also cured and packed up in barrels; whilst, from the livers, considerable quantities of oil are extracted, this oil having been found possessed of the most nourishing properties, and particularly beneficial in cases of pulmonary affections.

COD PIE.

(Economical.)

I.

235. INGREDIENTS.—Any remains of cold cod, 12 oysters, sufficient melted butter to moisten it; mashed potatoes enough to fill up the dish.

Mode.—Flake the fish from the bone, and carefully take away all the skin. Lay it in a pie-dish, pour over the melted butter and oysters (or oyster sauce, if there is any left), and cover with mashed potatoes. Bake for ½ an hour, and send to table of a nice brown colour.

Time.— ½ hour.

Seasonable from November to March.

II.

236. INGREDIENTS.—2 slices of cod; pepper and salt to taste; ½ a teaspoonful of grated nutmeg, 1 large blade of pounded mace, 2 oz. of butter, ½ pint of stock No. 107, a paste crust (*see* Pastry). For sauce, 1 tablespoonful of stock, ¼ pint of cream or milk, thickening of flour or butter; lemon-peel chopped very fine to taste; 12 oysters.

Mode.—Lay the cod in salt for 4 hours, then wash it and place it in a dish; season, and add the butter and stock; cover with the crust, and bake for 1 hour, or rather more. Now make the sauce, by mixing the ingredients named above; give it one boil, and pour it into the pie by a hole made at the top of the crust, which can easily be covered by a small piece of pastry cut and baked in any fanciful shape—such as a leaf, or otherwise.

Time.—1½ hour.   *Average cost*, with fresh fish, 2*s.* 6*d.*

Seasonable from November to March.

Sufficient for 6 persons.

Note.—The remains of cold fish may be used for this pie.

CURRIED COD.

237. INGREDIENTS.—2 slices of large cod, or the remains of any cold fish; 3 oz. of butter, 1 onion sliced, a teacupful of white stock, thick-

ening of butter and flour, 1 tablespoonful of curry-powder, ¼ pint of cream, salt and cayenne to taste.

Mode.—Flake the fish, and fry it of a nice brown colour with the butter and onions; put this in a stewpan, add the stock and thickening, and simmer for 10 minutes. Stir the curry-powder into the cream; put it, with the seasoning, to the other ingredients; give one boil, and serve.

Time.—¾ hour. *Average cost*, with fresh fish, 3s.

Seasonable from November to March.

Sufficient for 4 persons.

THE FOOD OF THE COD.—This chiefly consists of the smaller species of the scaly tribes, shell-fish, crabs, and worms. Their voracity is very great, and they will bite at any small body they see moved by the water, even stones and pebbles, which are frequently found in their stomachs. They sometimes attain a great size, but their usual weight is from 14 to 40 lbs.

COD A LA CREME.

238. INGREDIENTS.—1 large slice of cod, 1 oz. of butter, 1 chopped shalot, a little minced parsley, ¼ teacupful of white stock, ¼ pint of milk or cream, flour to thicken, cayenne and lemon-juice to taste, ¼ teaspoonful of powdered sugar.

Mode.—Boil the cod, and while hot, break it into flakes; put the butter, shalot, parsley, and stock into a stewpan, and let them boil for 5 minutes. Stir in sufficient flour to thicken, and pour to it the milk or cream. Simmer for 10 minutes, add the cayenne and sugar, and, when liked, a little lemon-juice. Put the fish in the sauce to warm gradually, but do not let it boil. Serve in a dish garnished with croûtons.

Time.—Rather more than ½ hour. *Average cost*, with cream, 2s.

Seasonable from November to March.

Sufficient for 3 persons.

Note.—The remains of fish from the preceding day answer very well for this dish.

COD A LA BECHAMEL.

239. INGREDIENTS.—Any remains of cold cod, 4 tablespoonfuls of béchamel (*see* Sauces), 2 oz. butter; seasoning to taste of pepper and salt; fried bread, a few bread crumbs.

Mode.—Flake the cod carefully, leaving out all skin and bone; put the béchamel in a stewpan with the butter, and stir it over the fire till the latter is melted; add seasoning, put in the fish, and mix it well with the sauce. Make a border of fried bread round the dish, lay in the fish, sprinkle over with bread crumbs, and baste with butter. Brown either before the fire or with a salamander, and garnish with toasted bread cut in fanciful shapes.

Time.—½ hour.

Average cost, exclusive of the fish, 6*d.*

THE HABITAT OF THE COD.—This fish is found only in the seas of the northern parts of the world, between the latitudes of 45° and 66°. Its great rendezvous are the sand-banks of Newfoundland, Nova Scotia, Cape Breton, and New England. These places are its favourite resorts; for there it is able to obtain great quantities of worms, a food peculiarly grateful to it. Another cause of its attachment to these places has been said to be on account of the vicinity of the Polar seas, where it returns to spawn. Few are taken north of Iceland, and the shoals never reach so far south as the Straits of Gibraltar. Many are taken on the coasts of Norway, in the Baltic, and off the Orkneys, which, prior to the discovery of Newfoundland, formed one of the principal fisheries. The London market is supplied by those taken between the Dogger Bank, the Well Bank, and Cromer, on the east coast of England.

COD A LA MAITRE D'HOTEL.

240. INGREDIENTS.—2 slices of cod, ¼ lb. of butter, a little chopped shalot and parsley; pepper to taste, ¼ teaspoonful of grated nutmeg, or rather less, when the flavour is not liked; the juice of ¼ lemon.

Mode.—Boil the cod, and either leave it whole, or, what is still better, flake it from the bone, and take off the skin. Put it into a stewpan with the butter, parsley, shalot, pepper, and nutmeg. Melt the butter gradually, and be very careful that it does not become like oil. When all is well mixed and thoroughly hot, add the lemon-juice, and serve.

Time.—½ hour. *Average cost,* 2*s.* 6*d.*; with remains of cold fish, 5*d.*

Seasonable from November to March.

Sufficient for 4 persons.

Note.—Cod that has been left will do for this.

THE SEASON FOR FISHING COD.—The best season for catching cod is from the beginning of February to the end of April; and although each fisherman engaged in taking them, catches no more than one at a time, an expert hand will sometimes take four hundred in a day. The employment is excessively fatiguing, from the weight of the fish as well as from the coldness of the climate.

COD A L'ITALIENNE.

241. INGREDIENTS.—2 slices of crimped cod, 1 shalot, 1 slice of ham minced very fine, ½ pint of white stock, No. 107; when liked, ½ teacupful of cream; salt to taste; a few drops of garlic vinegar, a little lemon-juice, ½ teaspoonful of powdered sugar.

Mode.—Chop the shalots, mince the ham very fine, pour on the stock, and simmer for 15 minutes. If the colour should not be good, add cream in the above proportion, and strain it through a fine sieve; season it, and put in the vinegar, lemon-juice, and sugar. Now boil the cod, take out the middle bone, and skin it; put it on the dish without breaking, and pour the sauce over it.

Time.—¾ hour. *Average cost,* 3s. 6d., with fresh fish.
Seasonable from November to March.
Sufficient for 4 persons.

THE FECUNDITY OF THE COD.—In our preceding remarks on the natural history of fishes, we have spoken of the amazing fruitfulness of this fish; but in this we see one more instance of the wise provision which Nature has made for supplying the wants of man. So extensive has been the consumption of this fish, that it is surprising that it has not long ago become extinct; which would certainly have been the case, had it not been for its wonderful powers of reproduction. "So early as 1368," says Dr. Cloquet, "the inhabitants of Amsterdam had dispatched fishermen to the coast of Sweden; and in the first quarter of 1792, from the ports of France only, 210 vessels went out to the cod-fisheries. Every year, however, upwards of 10,000 vessels, of all nations, are employed in this trade, and bring into the commercial world more than 40,000,000 of salted and dried cod. If we add to this immense number, the havoc made among the legions of cod by the larger scaly tribes of the great deep, and take into account the destruction to which the young are exposed by sea-fowls and other inhabitants of the seas, besides the myriads of their eggs destroyed by accident, it becomes a miracle to find that such mighty multitudes of them are still in existence, and ready to continue the exhaustless supply. Yet it ceases to excite our wonder when we remember that the female can every year give birth to more than 9,000,000 at a time."

BAKED CARP.

242. INGREDIENTS.—1 carp, forcemeat, bread crumbs, 1 oz. butter, ½ pint of stock No. 105, ½ pint of port wine, 6 anchovies, 2 onions sliced, 1 bay-leaf, a faggot of sweet herbs, flour to thicken, the juice of 1 lemon; cayenne and salt to taste; ½ teaspoonful of powdered sugar.

Mode.—Stuff the carp with a delicate forcemeat, after thoroughly cleansing it, and sew it up, to prevent the stuffing from falling out. Rub it over with an egg, and sprinkle it with bread crumbs, lay it in a deep earthen dish, and drop the butter, oiled, over the bread crumbs. Add the stock, onions, bay-leaf, herbs, wine, and anchovies, and bake for 1 hour. Put 1 oz. of butter into a stewpan, melt it, and dredge in sufficient flour to dry it up; put in the strained liquor from the carp, stir frequently, and when it has boiled, add the lemon-juice and seasoning. Serve the carp on a dish garnished with parsley and cut lemon, and the sauce in a boat.

Time.—1¼ hour. *Average cost.* Seldom bought.
Seasonable from March to October.
Sufficient for 1 or 2 persons.

THE CARP.—This species of fish inhabit the fresh waters, where they feed on worms, insects, aquatic plants, small fish, clay, or mould. Some of them are migratory. They have very small mouths and no teeth, and the gill membrane has three rays. The body is smooth, and generally whitish. The carp both grows and increases very fast, and is accounted the most valuable of all fish for the stocking of ponds. It has been pronounced the queen of river-fish, and was first introduced to this country about three hundred years ago. Of its sound, or air-bladder, a kind of glue is made, and a green paint of its gall.

THE CARP.

STEWED CARP.

243. INGREDIENTS.—1 carp, salt, stock No. 105, 2 onions, 6 cloves, 12 peppercorns, 1 blade of mace, ¼ pint of port wine, the juice of ½ lemon, cayenne and salt to taste, a faggot of savoury herbs.

Mode.—Scale the fish, clean it nicely, and, if very large, divide it; lay it in the stewpan, after having rubbed a little salt on it, and put in sufficient stock to cover it; add the herbs, onions, and spices, and stew gently for 1 hour, or rather more, should it be very large. Dish up the fish with great care, strain the liquor, and add to it the port wine, lemon-juice, and cayenne; give one boil, pour it over the fish, and serve.

Time.—1¼ hour. *Average cost.* Seldom bought.

Seasonable from March to October.

Sufficient for 1 or 2 persons.

Note.—This fish can be boiled plain, and served with parsley and butter. Chub and Char may be cooked in the same manner as the above, as also Dace and Roach.

THE AGE OF CARP.—This fish has been found to live 150 years. The pond in the garden of Emmanuel College, Cambridge, contained one that had lived there 70 years, and Gesner mentions an instance of one 100 years old. They are, besides, capable of being tamed. Dr. Smith, in his "Tour on the Continent," says, in reference to the prince of Condé's seat at Chantilly, "The most pleasing things about it were the immense shoals of very large carp, silvered over with age, like silver-fish, and perfectly tame; so that, when any passengers approached their watery habitation, they used to come to the shore in such numbers as to heave each other out of the water, begging for bread, of which a quantity was always kept at hand, on purpose to feed them. They would even allow themselves to be handled."

THE CHUB.   THE CHAR.

THE CHUB.—This fish takes its name from its head, not only in England, but in other countries. It is a river-fish, and resembles the carp, but is somewhat longer. Its flesh is not in much esteem, being coarse, and, when out of season, full of small hairy bones. The head and throat are the best parts. The roe is also good.

THE CHAR.—This is one of the most delicious of fish, being esteemed by some superior to the salmon. It is an inhabitant of the deep lakes of mountainous countries. Its flesh is rich and red, and full of fat. The largest and best kind is found in the lakes of Westmoreland, and, as it is considered a rarity, it is often potted and preserved.

THE DACE, OR DARE.—This fish is gregarious, and is seldom above ten inches long; although, according to Linnæus, it grows a foot and a half in length. Its haunts are in deep water, near piles of bridges, where the stream is gentle, over gravelly, sandy, or clayey bottoms; deep holes that are shaded, water-lily leaves, and under the foam caused by an eddy. In the warm months they are to be found in shoals on the shallows near to streams. They are in season about the end of April, and gradually improve till

February, when they attain their highest condition. In that month, when just taken, scotched (crimped), and broiled, they are said to be more palatable than a fresh herring.

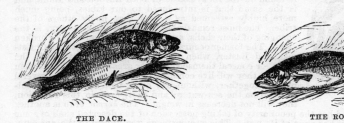

THE DACE.　　　　　　　　　　　　THE ROACH.

THE ROACH.—This fish is found throughout Europe, and the western parts of Asia, in deep still rivers, of which it is an inhabitant. It is rarely more than a pound and a half in weight, and is in season from September till March. It is plentiful in England, and the finest are caught in the Thames. The proverb, "as sound as a roach," is derived from the French name of this fish being *roche*, which also, means rock.

TO DRESS CRAB.

244. INGREDIENTS.—1 crab, 2 tablespoonfuls of vinegar, 1 ditto of oil; salt, white pepper, and cayenne, to taste.

Mode.—Empty the shells, and thoroughly mix the meat with the above ingredients, and put it in the large shell. Garnish with slices of cut lemon and parsley. The quantity of oil may be increased when it is much liked.

Average cost, from 10*d.* to 2*s.*

Seasonable all the year; but not so good in May, June, and July.

Sufficient for 3 persons.

To CHOOSE CRAB.—The middle-sized crab is the best; and the crab, like the lobster, should be judged by its weight; for if light, it is watery.

HOT CRAB.

245. INGREDIENTS.—1 crab, nutmeg, salt and pepper to taste, 3 oz. of butter, ¼ lb. of bread crumbs, 3 tablespoonfuls of vinegar.

Mode.—After having boiled the crab, pick the meat out from the shells, and mix with it the nutmeg and seasoning. Cut up the butter in small pieces, and add the bread crumbs and vinegar. Mix altogether, put the whole in the large shell, and brown before the fire or with a salamander.

Time.—1 hour. *Average cost*, from 10*d.* to 2*s.*

Seasonable all the year; but not so good in May, June, and July.

Sufficient for 3 persons.

THE CRAB TRIBE.—The whole of this tribe of animals have the body covered with a hard and strong shell, and they live chiefly in the sea. Some, however, inhabit fresh waters, and a few live upon land. They feed variously, on aquatic or marine plants, small fish, molluscæ, or dead bodies. The *black-clawed* species is found on the rocky coasts of both Europe and India, and is the same that is introduced to our tables, being much more highly esteemed as a food than many others of the tribe. The most remarkable feature in their history, is the changing of their shells, and the reproduction of their broken claws. The former occurs once a year, usually between Christmas and Easter, when the crabs retire to cavities in the rocks, or conceal themselves under great stones. Fishermen say that they will live confined in a pot or basket for several months together, without any other food than what is collected from the sea-water; and that, even in this situation, they will not decrease in weight. The *hermit* crab is another

THE CRAB.

of the species, and has the peculiarity of taking possession of the deserted shell of some other animal, as it has none of its own. This circumstance was known to the ancients, and is alluded to in the following lines from Oppian :—

> The hermit fish, unarm'd by Nature, left
> Helpless and weak, grow strong by harmless theft.
> Fearful they stroll, and look with panting wish
> For the cast crust of some new-cover'd fish;
> Or such as empty lie, and deck the shore,
> Whose first and rightful owners are no more.
> They make glad seizure of the vacant room,
> And count the borrow'd shell their native home;
> Screw their soft limbs to fit the winding case,
> And boldly herd with the crustaceous race.

CRAYFISH.

246. Crayfish should be thrown into boiling water, to which has been added a good seasoning of salt and a little vinegar. When done, which will be in ¼ hour, take them out and drain them. Let them cool, arrange them on a napkin, and garnish with plenty of double parsley.

Note.—This fish is frequently used for garnishing boiled turkey, boiled fowl, calf's head, turbot, and all kinds of boiled fish.

POTTED CRAYFISH.

247. INGREDIENTS.—100 crayfish; pounded mace, pepper and salt to taste, 2 oz. butter.

Mode.—Boil the fish in salt and water; pick out all the meat and pound it in a mortar to a paste. Whilst pounding, add the butter gradually, and mix in the spice and seasoning. Put it in small pots, and pour over it clarified butter, carefully excluding the air.

Time.—15 minutes to boil the crayfish. *Average cost, 2s. 9d.*

Seasonable all the year.

JOHN DORY.

248. INGREDIENTS.—¼ lb. of salt to each gallon of water.

Mode.—This fish, which is esteemed by most people a great delicacy, is dressed in the same way as a turbot, which it resembles in firmness, but not in richness. Cleanse it thoroughly and cut off the fins; lay it in a fish-kettle, cover with cold water, and add salt in the above proportion. Bring it gradually to a boil, and simmer gently for $\frac{1}{4}$ hour, or rather longer, should the fish be very large. Serve on a hot napkin, and garnish with cut lemon and parsley. Lobster, anchovy, or shrimp sauce, and plain melted butter, should be sent to table with it.

Time.—After the water boils, $\frac{1}{4}$ to $\frac{1}{2}$ hour, according to size.

Average cost, 3s. to 5s.

Seasonable all the year, but best from September to January.

Note.—Small John Dorie are very good, baked.

THE JOHN DORY.

THE DORY, or JOHN DORY.—This fish is of a yellowish golden colour, and is, in general, rare, although it is sometimes taken in abundance on the Devon and Cornish coasts. It is highly esteemed for the table, and its flesh, when dressed, is of a beautiful clear white. When fresh caught, it is tough, and, being a ground fish, it is not the worse for being kept two, or even three days before it is cooked.

BOILED EELS.

249. INGREDIENTS.—4 small eels, sufficient water to cover them; a large bunch of parsley.

Mode.—Choose small eels for boiling; put them in a stewpan with the parsley, and just sufficient water to cover them; simmer till tender. Take them out, pour a little parsley and butter over them, and serve some in a tureen.

Time.—$\frac{1}{2}$ hour. *Average cost*, 6d. per lb.

Seasonable from June to March.

Sufficient for 4 persons.

THE EEL TRIBE.—The Apodal, or bony-gilled and ventral-finned fish, of which the eel forms the first Linnæan tribe, in their general aspect and manners, approach, in some instances, very nearly to serpents. They have a smooth head and slippery skin, are in general naked, or covered with such small, soft, and distant scales, as are scarcely visible. Their bodies are long and slender, and they are supposed to subsist entirely on animal substances. There are about nine species of them, mostly found in the seas. One of them frequents our fresh waters, and three of the others occasionally pay a visit to our shores.

THE EEL.

STEWED EELS.

I.

250. INGREDIENTS.—2 lbs. of eels, 1 pint of rich strong stock,

No. 104, 1 onion, 3 cloves, a piece of lemon-peel, 1 glass of port or Madeira, 3 tablespoonfuls of cream; thickening of flour; cayenne and lemon-juice to taste.

Mode.—Wash and skin the eels, and cut them into pieces about 3 inches long; pepper and salt them, and lay them in a stewpan; pour over the stock, add the onion stuck with cloves, the lemon-peel, and the wine. Stew gently for ½ hour, or rather more, and lift them carefully on a dish, which keep hot. Strain the gravy, stir to the cream sufficient flour to thicken; mix altogether, boil for 2 minutes, and add the cayenne and lemon-juice; pour over the eels and serve.

Time.—¾ hour. *Average cost* for this quantity, 2s. 3d.

Seasonable from June to March.

Sufficient for 5 or 6 persons.

THE COMMON EEL.—This fish is known frequently to quit its native element, and to set off on a wandering expedition in the night, or just about the close of day, over the meadows, in search of snails and other prey. It also, sometimes, betakes itself to isolated ponds, apparently for no other pleasure than that which may be supposed to be found in a change of habitation. This, of course, accounts for eels being found in waters which were never suspected to contain them. This rambling disposition in the eel has been long known to naturalists, and, from the following lines, it seems to have been known to the ancients :—

> " Thus the mail'd tortoise, and the wand'ring eel,
> Oft to the neighbouring beach will silent steal."

II.

251. INGREDIENTS.—2 lbs. of middling-sized eels, 1 pint of medium stock, No. 105, ¼ pint of port wine; salt, cayenne, and mace to taste; 1 teaspoonful of essence of anchovy, the juice of ½ a lemon.

Mode.—Skin, wash, and clean the eels thoroughly; cut them into pieces 3 inches long, and put them into strong salt and water for 1 hour; dry them well with a cloth, and fry them brown. Put the stock on with the heads and tails of the eels, and simmer for ½ hour; strain it, and add all the other ingredients. Put in the eels, and stew gently for ½ hour, when serve.

Time.—2 hours. *Average cost*, 1s. 9d.

Seasonable from June to March.

Sufficient for 5 or 6 persons.

FRIED EELS.

252. INGREDIENTS.—1 lb. of eels, 1 egg, a few bread crumbs, hot lard.

Mode.—Wash the eels, cut them into pieces 3 inches long, trim and wipe them very dry; dredge with flour, rub them over with egg, and cover with bread crumbs; fry of a nice brown in hot lard. If the eels are small, curl them round, instead of cutting them up. Garnish with fried parsley.

Time.—20 minutes, or rather less. *Average cost*, 6*d.* per lb.

Seasonable from June to March.

Note.—Garfish may be dressed like eels, aud either broiled or baked.

THE PRODUCTIVENESS OF THE EEL.—" Having occasion," says Dr. Anderson, in the *Bee*, " to be once on a visit to a friend's house on Dee-side, in Aberdeenshire, I frequently delighted to walk by the banks of the river. I, one day, observed something like a black string moving along the edge of the water, where it was quite shallow. Upon closer inspection, I discovered that this was a shoal of young eels, so closely joined together as to appear, on a superficial view, one continued body, moving briskly up against the stream. To avoid the retardment they experienced from the force of the current, they kept close along the water's edge the whole of the way, following all the bendings and sinuosities of the river. Where they were embayed, and in still water, the shoal dilated in breadth, so as to be sometimes nearly a foot broad ; but when they turned a cape, where the current was strong, they were forced to occupy less space and press close to the shore, struggling very hard till they passed it. This shoal continued to move on, night and day without interruption for several weeks. Their progress might be at the rate of about a mile an hour. It was easy to catch the animals, though they were very active and nimble. They were eels perfectly well formed in every respect, but not exceeding two inches in length. I conceive that the shoal did not contain, on an average, less than from twelve to twenty in breadth ; so that the number that passed, on the whole, must have been very great. Whence they came or whither they went, I know not ; but the place where I saw this, was six miles from the sea."

EEL PIE.

253. INGREDIENTS. — 1 lb. of eels, a little chopped parsley, 1 shalot ; grated nutmeg ; pepper and salt to taste ; the juice of $\frac{1}{2}$ a lemon, small quantity of forcemeat, $\frac{1}{4}$ pint of béchamel (*see* Sauces) ; puff paste.

Mode.—Skin and wash the eels, cut them into pieces 2 inches long, and line the bottom of the pie-dish with forcemeat. Put in the eels, and sprinkle them with the parsley, shalots, nutmeg, seasoning, and lemon-juice, and cover with puff-paste. Bake for 1 hour, or rather more ; make the béchamel hot, and pour it into the pie.

Time.—Rather more than 1 hour.

Seasonable from August to March.

COLLARED EEL.

254. INGREDIENTS.—1 large eel ; pepper and salt to taste ; 2 blades of mace, 2 cloves, a little allspice very finely pounded, 6 leaves of sage, and a small bunch of herbs minced very small.

Mode.—Bone the eel and skin it ; split it, and sprinkle it over with the ingredients, taking care that the spices are very finely pounded, and the herbs chopped very small. Roll it up and bind with a broad piece of tape, and boil it in water, mixed with a little salt and vinegar, till tender. It may either be served whole or cut in slices ;

and when cold, the eel should be kept in the liquor it was boiled in, but with a little more vinegar put to it.

Time.—2 hours.   *Average cost, 6d.* per lb.

Seasonable from August to March.

HAUNTS OF THE EEL.—These are usually in mud, among weeds, under roots or stumps of trees, or in holes in the banks or the bottoms of rivers. Here they often grow to an enormous size, sometimes weighing as much as fifteen or sixteen pounds. They seldom come forth from their hiding-places except in the night; and, in winter, bury themselves deep in the mud, on account of their great susceptibility of cold.

EELS A LA TARTARE.

255. INGREDIENTS.—2 lbs. of eels, 1 carrot, 1 onion, a little flour, 1 glass of sherry; salt, pepper, and nutmeg to taste; bread crumbs, 1 egg, 2 tablespoonfuls of vinegar.

Mode.—Rub the butter on the bottom of the stewpan; cut up the carrot and onion, and stir them over the fire for 5 minutes; dredge in a little flour, add the wine and seasoning, and boil for ½ an hour. Skin and wash the eels, cut them into pieces, put them to the other ingredients, and simmer till tender. When they are done, take them out, let them get cold, cover them with egg and bread crumbs, and fry them of a nice brown. Put them on a dish, pour sauce piquante over, and serve them hot.

Time.—1½ hour.   *Average cost,* 1s. 8d., exclusive of the sauce piquante.

Seasonable from August to March.   *Sufficient* for 5 or 6 persons.

VORACITY OF THE EEL.—We find in a note upon Isaac Walton, by Sir John Hawkins, that he knew of eels, when kept in ponds, frequently destroying ducks. From a canal near his house at Twickenham he himself missed many young ducks; and on draining, in order to clean it, great numbers of large eels were caught in the mud. When some of these were opened, there were found in their stomachs the undigested heads of the quacking tribe which had become their victims.

EELS EN MATELOTE.

256. INGREDIENTS.—5 or 6 young onions, a few mushrooms, when obtainable; salt, pepper, and nutmeg to taste; 1 laurel-leaf, ½ pint of port wine, ⅓ pint of medium stock, No. 105; butter and flour to thicken; 2 lbs. of eels.

Mode.—Rub the stewpan with butter, dredge in a little flour, add the onions cut very small, slightly brown them, and put in all the other ingredients. Wash, and cut up the eels into pieces 3 inches long; put them in the stewpan, and simmer for ½ hour. Make round the dish, a border of croûtons, or pieces of toasted bread; arrange the eels in a pyramid in the centre, and pour over the sauce. Serve very hot.

Time.—¾ hour.   *Average cost,* 1s. 9d. for this quantity.

Seasonable from August to March.   *Sufficient* for 5 or 6 persons.

TENACITY OF LIFE IN THE EEL.—There is no fish so tenacious of life as this. After it is skinned and cut in pieces, the parts will continue to move for a considerable time, and no fish will live so long out of water.

THE LAMPREY.—With the Romans, this fish occupied a respectable rank among the piscine tribes, and in Britain it has at various periods stood high in public favour. It was the cause of the death of Henry I. of England, who ate so much of them, that it brought on an attack of indigestion, which carried him off. It is an inhabitant of the sea, ascending rivers, principally about the end of winter, and, after passing a few months in fresh water, returning again to its oceanic residence. It is most in season in

THE LAMPREY.

March, April, and May, but is, by some, regarded as an unwholesome food, although looked on by others as a great delicacy. They are dressed as eels.

FISH AND OYSTER PIE.

257. INGREDIENTS.—Any remains of cold fish, such as cod or haddock; 2 dozen oysters, pepper and salt to taste, bread crumbs sufficient for the quantity of fish; ½ teaspoonful of grated nutmeg, 1 teaspoonful of finely-chopped parsley.

Mode.—Clear the fish from the bones, and put a layer of it in a pie-dish, which sprinkle with pepper and salt; then a layer of bread crumbs, oysters, nutmeg, and chopped parsley. Repeat this till the dish is quite full. You may form a covering either of bread crumbs, which should be browned, or puff-paste, which should be cut into long strips, and laid in cross-bars over the fish, with a line of the paste first laid round the edge. Before putting on the top, pour in some made melted butter, or a little thin white sauce, and the oyster-liquor, and bake.

Time.—If made of cooked fish, ¼ hour; if made of fresh fish and puff-paste, ¾ hour.

Average cost, 1s. 6d.

Seasonable from September to April.

Note.—A nice little dish may be made by flaking any cold fish, adding a few oysters, seasoning with pepper and salt, and covering with mashed potatoes; ¼ hour will bake it.

FISH CAKE.

258. INGREDIENTS.—The remains of any cold fish, 1 onion, 1 faggot of sweet herbs; salt and pepper to taste, 1 pint of water, equal quantities of bread crumbs and cold potatoes, ½ teaspoonful of parsley, 1 egg, bread crumbs.

Mode.—Pick the meat from the bones of the fish, which latter put, with the head and fins, into a stewpan with the water; add pepper and salt, the onion and herbs, and stew slowly for gravy about 2 hours; chop the fish fine, and mix it well with bread crumbs and cold

K 2

potatoes, adding the parsley and seasoning; make the whole into a cake with the white of an egg, brush it over with egg, cover with bread crumbs, and fry of a light brown; strain the gravy, pour it over, and stew gently for $\frac{1}{4}$ hour, stirring it carefully once or twice. Serve hot, and garnish with slices of lemon and parsley.

Time.—$\frac{1}{2}$ hour, after the gravy is made.

BOILED FLOUNDERS.

259. INGREDIENTS.—Sufficient water to cover the flounders, salt in the proportion of 6 oz. to each gallon, a little vinegar.

Mode.—Put on a kettle with enough water to cover the flounders, lay in the fish, add salt and vinegar in the above proportions, and when it boils, simmer very gently for 5 minutes. They must not boil fast, or they will break. Serve with plain melted butter, or parsley and butter.

FLOUNDERS.

Time.—After the water boils, 5 minutes. *Average cost*, 3d. each.

Seasonable from August to November.

THE FLOUNDER.—This comes under the tribe usually denominated Flat-fish, and is generally held in the smallest estimation of any among them. It is an inhabitant of both the seas and the rivers, while it thrives in ponds. On the English coasts it is very abundant, and the London market consumes it in large quantities. It is considered easy of digestion, and the Thames flounder is esteemed a delicate fish.

FRIED FLOUNDERS.

260. INGREDIENTS.—Flounders, egg, and bread crumbs; boiling lard.

Mode.—Cleanse the fish, and, two hours before they are wanted, rub them inside and out with salt, to render them firm; wash and wipe them very dry, dip them into egg, and sprinkle over with bread crumbs; fry them in boiling lard, dish on a hot napkin, and garnish with crisped parsley.

Time.—From 5 to 10 minutes, according to size.

Average cost, 3d. each.

Seasonable from August to November.

Sufficient, 1 for each person.

GUDGEONS.

261. INGREDIENTS. — Egg and bread crumbs sufficient for the quantity of fish; hot lard.

Mode.—Do not scrape off the scales, but take out the gills and inside, and cleanse thoroughly; wipe them dry, flour and dip them into egg, and sprinkle over with bread crumbs. Fry of a nice brown.

Time.—3 or 4 minutes. *Average cost.* Seldom bought.

Seasonable from March to July.

Sufficient, 3 for each person.

THE GUDGEON.

THE GUDGEON.—This is a fresh-water fish, belonging to the carp genus, and is found in placid streams and lakes. It was highly esteemed by the Greeks, and was, at the beginning of supper, served fried at Rome. It abounds both in France and Germany; and is both excellent and numerous in some of the rivers of England. Its flesh is firm, well-flavoured, and easily digested.

GURNET, or GURNARD.

262. INGREDIENTS.—1 gurnet, 6 oz. of salt to each gallon of water.

Mode.—Cleanse the fish thoroughly, and cut off the fins; have ready some boiling water, with salt in the above proportion; put the fish in, and simmer very gently for ½ hour. Parsley and butter, or anchovy sauce, should be served with it.

Time.—½ hour. *Average cost.* Seldom bought.

Seasonable from October to March, but in perfection in October.

Sufficient, a middling sized one for 2 persons.

Note. — This fish is frequently stuffed with forcemeat and baked.

THE GURNET.

THE GURNET.—"If I be not ashamed of my soldiers, I am a souced gurnet," says Falstaff; which shows that this fish has been long known in England. It is very common on the British coasts, and is an excellent fish as food.

BAKED HADDOCKS.

263. INGREDIENTS.—A nice forcemeat (*see* Forcemeats), butter to taste, egg and bread crumbs.

Mode.—Scale and clean the fish, without cutting it open much; put in a nice delicate forcemeat, and sew up the slit. Brush it over with egg, sprinkle over bread crumbs, and baste frequently with butter. Garnish with parsley and cut lemon, and serve with a nice brown gravy, plain melted butter, or anchovy sauce. The egg and bread crumbs can be omitted, and pieces of butter placed over the fish.

Time.—Large haddock, ¾ hour; moderate size, ¼ hour.

Seasonable from August to February.

Average cost, from 9*d.* upwards.

Note.—Haddocks may be filleted, rubbed over with egg and bread crumbs, and fried a nice brown; garnish with crisped parsley.

THE HADDOCK.

THE HADDOCK.—This fish migrates in immense shoals, and arrives on the Yorkshire coast about the middle of winter. It is an inhabitant of the northern seas of Europe, but does not enter the Baltic, and is not known in the Mediterranean. On each side of the body, just beyond the gills, it has a dark spot, which superstition asserts to be the impressions of the finger and thumb of St. Peter, when taking the tribute money out of a fish of this species.

BOILED HADDOCK.

264. INGREDIENTS.—Sufficient water to cover the fish; ¼ lb. of salt to each gallon of water.

Mode.—Scrape the fish, take out the inside, wash it thoroughly, and lay it in a kettle, with enough water to cover it, and salt in the above proportion. Simmer gently from 15 to 20 minutes, or rather more, should the fish be very large. For small haddocks, fasten the tails in their mouths, and put them into boiling water. 10 to 15 minutes will cook them. Serve with plain melted butter, or anchovy sauce.

Time.—Large haddock, ½ hour; small, ¼ hour, or rather less.

Average cost, from 9*d.* upwards.

Seasonable from August to February.

WEIGHT OF THE HADDOCK.—The haddock seldom grows to any great size. In general, they do not weigh more than two or three pounds, or exceed ten or twelve inches in size. Such are esteemed very delicate eating; but they have been caught three feet long, when their flesh is coarse.

DRIED HADDOCK.

I.

265. Dried haddock should be gradually warmed through, either before or over a nice clear fire. Rub a little piece of butter over, just before sending it to table.

II.

266. INGREDIENTS.—1 large thick haddock, 2 bay-leaves, 1 small bunch of savoury herbs, not forgetting parsley, a little butter and pepper; boiling water.

Mode.—Cut up the haddock into square pieces, make a basin hot by means of hot water, which pour out. Lay in the fish, with the bay-leaves and herbs; cover with boiling water; put a plate over to keep in the steam, and let it remain for 10 minutes. Take out the slices, put them in a hot dish, rub over with butter and pepper, and serve.

Time.—10 minutes. *Seasonable* at any time, but best in winter.

THE FINNAN HADDOCK.—This is the common haddock cured and dried, and takes its name from the fishing-village of Findhorn, near Aberdeen, in Scotland, where the art has long attained to perfection. The haddocks are there hung up for a day or two in the smoke of peat, when they are ready for cooking, and are esteemed, by the Scotch, a great delicacy. In London, an imitation of them is made by washing the fish over with pyroligneous acid, and hanging it up in a dry place for a few days.

RED HERRINGS, or YARMOUTH BLOATERS.

267. The best way to cook these is to make incisions in the skin across the fish, because they do not then require to be so long on the fire, and will be far better than when cut open. The hard roe makes a nice relish by pounding it in a mortar, with a little anchovy, and spreading it on toast. If very dry, soak in warm water 1 hour before dressing.

THE RED HERRING.—*Red* herrings lie twenty-four hours in the brine, when they are taken out and hung up in a smoking-house formed to receive them. A brushwood fire is then kindled beneath them, and when they are sufficiently smoked and dried, they are put into barrels for carriage.

BAKED WHITE HERRINGS.

268. INGREDIENTS.—12 herrings, 4 bay-leaves, 12 cloves, 12 allspice, 2 small blades of mace, cayenne pepper and salt to taste, sufficient vinegar to fill up the dish.

Mode.—Take the herrings, cut off the heads, and gut them. Put them in a pie-dish, heads and tails alternately, and, between each layer, sprinkle over the above ingredients. Cover the fish with the vinegar, and bake for ½ hour, but do not use it till quite cold. The herrings may be cut down the front, the backbone taken out, and closed again. Sprats done in this way are very delicious.

Time.—½ an hour. *Average cost*, 1*d.* each.

TO CHOOSE THE HERRING.—The more scales this fish has, the surer the sign of its freshness. It should also have a bright and silvery look; but if red about the head, it is a sign that it has been dead for some time.

THE HERRING.—The herring tribe are found in the greatest abundance in the highest northern latitudes, where they find a quiet retreat, and security from their numerous enemies. Here they multiply beyond expression, and, in shoals, come forth from their icy region to visit other portions of the great deep. In June they are found about Shetland, whence they proceed down to the Orkneys, where they divide, and surround the islands of Great Britain and Ireland. The principal British herring-fisheries are off the Scotch and Norfolk coasts; and the fishing is always carried on by means of nets, which are usually laid at night; for, if stretched by day, they are supposed to frighten the fish away. The moment the herring is taken out of the water it dies. Hence the origin of the common saying, "dead as a herring."

THE HERRING.

KEGEREE.

269. INGREDIENTS.—Any cold fish, 1 teacupful of boiled rice, 1 oz. of butter, 1 teaspoonful of mustard, 2 soft-boiled eggs, salt and cayenne to taste.

Mode.—Pick the fish carefully from the bones, mix with the other ingredients, and serve very hot. The quantities may be varied according to the amount of fish used.

Time.—¼ hour after the rice is boiled.

Average cost, 5d., exclusive of the fish.

TO BOIL LOBSTERS.

270. INGREDIENTS.—¼ lb. of salt to each gallon of water.

Mode.—Buy the lobsters alive, and choose those that are heavy and full of motion, which is an indication of their freshness. When the shell is incrusted, it is a sign they are old : medium-sized lobsters are the best. Have ready a stewpan of boiling water, salted in the above proportion ; put in the lobster, and keep it boiling quickly from 20 minutes to ¾ hour, according to its size, and do not forget to skim well. If it boils too long, the meat becomes thready, and if not done enough, the spawn is not red : this must be obviated by great attention. Rub the shell over with a little butter or sweet oil, which wipe off again.

Time.—Small lobster, 20 minutes to ½ hour ; large ditto, ½ to ¾ hour.

Average cost, medium size, 1s. 6d. to 2s. 6d.

Seasonable all the year, but best from March to October.

TO CHOOSE LOBSTERS.—This shell-fish, if it has been cooked alive, as it ought to have been, will have a stiffness in the tail, which, if gently raised, will return with a spring. Care, however, must be taken in thus proving it ; for if the tail is pulled straight out, it will not return ; when the fish might be pronounced inferior, which, in reality, may not be the case. In order to be good, lobsters should be weighty for their bulk ; if light, they will be watery ; and those of the medium size, are always the best. Small-sized lobsters are cheapest, and answer very well for sauce. In boiling lobsters, the appearance of the shell will be much improved by rubbing over it a little butter or salad-oil on being immediately taken from the pot.

THE LOBSTER.—This is one of the crab tribe, and is found on most of the rocky coasts of Great Britain. Some are caught with the hand, but the larger number in pots, which serve all the purposes of a trap, being made of osiers, and baited with garbage. They are shaped like a wire mousetrap ; so that when the lobsters once enter them, they cannot get out again. They are fastened to a cord and sunk in the sea, and their place marked by a buoy. The fish is very prolific, and deposits its eggs in the sand, where they are soon hatched. On the coast of Norway, they are very abundant, and it is from there that the English metropolis is mostly supplied. They are rather indigestible, and, as a food, not so nutritive as they are generally supposed to be.

THE LOBSTER.

HOT LOBSTER.

271. INGREDIENTS.—1 lobster, 2 oz. of butter, grated nutmeg ; salt, pepper, and pounded mace, to taste ; bread crumbs, 2 eggs.

Mode.—Pound the meat of the lobster to a smooth paste with the butter and seasoning, and add a few bread crumbs. Beat the eggs, and make the whole mixture into the form of a lobster; pound the spawn, and sprinkle over it. Bake ¼ hour, and just before serving, lay over it the tail and body shell, with the small claws underneath, to resemble a lobster.

Time.—¼ hour. *Average cost,* 2s. 6d.

Seasonable at any time.

Sufficient for 4 or 5 persons.

LOBSTER SALAD.

272. INGREDIENTS.—1 hen lobster, lettuces, endive, small salad (whatever is in season), a little chopped beetroot, 2 hard-boiled eggs, a few slices of cucumber. For dressing, equal quantities of oil and vinegar, 1 teaspoonful of made mustard, the yolks of 2 eggs; cayenne and salt to taste; ¼ teaspoonful of anchovy sauce. These ingredients should be mixed perfectly smooth, and form a creamy-looking sauce.

Mode.—Wash the salad, and thoroughly dry it by shaking it in a cloth. Cut up the lettuces and endive, pour the dressing on them, and lightly throw in the small salad. Mix all well together with the pickings from the body of the lobster; pick the meat from the shell, cut it up into nice square pieces, put half in the salad, the other half reserve for garnishing. Separate the yolks from the whites of 2 hard-boiled eggs; chop the whites very fine, and rub the yolks through a sieve, and afterwards the coral from the inside. Arrange the salad lightly on a glass dish, and garnish, first with a row of sliced cucumber, then with the pieces of lobster, the yolks and whites of the eggs, coral, and beetroot placed alternately, and arranged in small separate bunches, so that the colours contrast nicely.

Average cost, 3s. 6d. *Sufficient* for 4 or 5 persons.

Seasonable from April to October; may be had all the year, but salad is scarce and expensive in winter.

Note.—A few crayfish make a pretty garnishing to lobster salad.

THE SHELL OF THE LOBSTER.—Like the others of its tribe, the lobster annually casts its shell. Previously to its throwing off the old one, it appears sick, languid, and restless, but in the course of a few days it is entirely invested in its new coat of armour. Whilst it is in a defenceless state, however, it seeks some lonely place, where it may lie undisturbed, and escape the horrid fate of being devoured by some of its own species who have the advantage of still being encased in their mail.

LOBSTER (a la Mode Francaise).

273. INGREDIENTS.—1 lobster, 4 tablespoonfuls of white stock, 2 tablespoonfuls of cream, pounded mace, and cayenne to taste; bread crumbs.

Mode.—Pick the meat from the shell, and cut it up into small square pieces ; put the stock, cream, and seasoning into a stewpan, add the lobster, and let it simmer gently for 6 minutes. Serve it in the shell, which must be nicely cleaned, and have a border of puff-paste ; cover it with bread crumbs, place small pieces of butter over, and brown before the fire, or with a salamander.

Time.—¼ hour. *Average cost,* 2s. 6d.

Seasonable at any time.

CELERITY OF THE LOBSTER.—In its element, the lobster is able to run with great speed upon its legs, or small claws, and, if alarmed, to spring, tail foremost, to a considerable distance, "even," it is said, "with the swiftness of a bird flying." Fishermen have seen some of them pass about thirty feet with a wonderful degree of swiftness. When frightened, they will take their spring, and, like a chamois of the Alps, plant themselves upon the very spot upon which they designed to hold themselves.

LOBSTER CURRY (an Entree).

274. INGREDIENTS.—1 lobster, 2 onions, 1 oz. butter, 1 tablespoonful of curry-powder, ½ pint of medium stock, No. 105, the juice of ½ lemon.

Mode.—Pick the meat from the shell, and cut it into nice square pieces ; fry the onions of a pale brown in the butter, stir in the curry-powder · and stock, and simmer till it thickens, when put in the lobster ; stew the whole slowly for ½ hour, and stir occasionally ; and just before sending to table, put in the lemon-juice. Serve boiled rice with it, the same as for other curries.

Time.—Altogether, ¾ hour. *Average cost,* 3s.

Seasonable at any time.

LOBSTER CUTLETS (an Entree).

275. INGREDIENTS.—1 large hen lobster, 1 oz. fresh butter, ½ salt-spoonful of salt, pounded mace, grated nutmeg, cayenne and white pepper to taste, egg, and bread crumbs.

Mode.—Pick the meat from the shell, and pound it in a mortar with the butter, and gradually add the mace and seasoning, well mixing the ingredients ; beat all to a smooth paste, and add a little of the spawn ; divide the mixture into pieces of an equal size, and shape them like cutlets. They should not be very thick. Brush them over with egg, and sprinkle with bread crumbs, and stick a short piece of the small claw in the top of each ; fry them of a nice brown in boiling lard, and drain them before the fire, on a sieve reversed ; arrange them nicely on a dish, and pour béchamel in the middle, but not over the cutlets.

Time.—About 8 minutes after the cutlets are made.

Average cost for this dish, 2s. 9d.

Seasonable all the year. *Sufficient* for 5 or 6 persons.

ANCIENT MODE OF COOKING THE LOBSTER.—When this fish was to be served for the table, among the ancients, it was opened lengthwise, and filled with a gravy composed of coriander and pepper. It was then put on the gridiron and slowly cooked, whilst it was being basted with the same kind of gravy with which the flesh had become impregnated.

TO DRESS LOBSTERS.

276. When the lobster is boiled, rub it over with a little salad-oil, which wipe off again; separate the body from the tail, break off the great claws, and crack them at the joints, without injuring the meat; split the tail in halves, and arrange all neatly in a dish, with the body upright in the middle, and garnish with parsley.

LOBSTER PATTIES (an Entree).

277. INGREDIENTS.—Minced lobster, 4 tablespoonfuls of béchamel, 6 drops of anchovy sauce, lemon-juice, cayenne to taste.

Mode.—Line the patty-pans with puff-paste, and put into each a small piece of bread; cover with paste, brush over with egg, and bake of a light colour. Take as much lobster as is required, mince the meat very fine, and add the above ingredients; stir it over the fire for 5 minutes; remove the lids of the patty-cases, take out the bread, fill with the mixture, and replace the covers.

Seasonable at any time.

LOCAL ATTACHMENT OF THE LOBSTER.—It is said that the attachment of this animal is strong to some particular parts of the sea, a circumstance celebrated in the following lines:—

" Nought like their home the constant lobsters prize,
 And foreign shores and seas unknown despise.
 Though cruel hands the banish'd wretch expel,
 And force the captive from his native cell,
 He will, if freed, return with anxious care,
 Find the known rock, and to his home repair;
 No novel customs learns in different seas,
 But wonted food and home-taught manners please."

POTTED LOBSTER.

278. INGREDIENTS.—2 lobsters; seasoning to taste, of nutmeg, pounded mace, white pepper, and salt; ¼ lb. of butter, 3 or 4 bay-leaves.

Mode.—Take out the meat carefully from the shell, but do not cut it up. Put some butter at the bottom of a dish, lay in the lobster as evenly as possible, with the bay-leaves and seasoning between. Cover with butter, and bake for ¾ hour in a gentle oven. When done, drain the whole on a sieve, and lay the pieces in potting-jars, with the seasoning about them. When cold, pour over it clarified butter, and, if very highly seasoned, it will keep some time.

Time.—¾ hour. *Average cost* for this quantity, 4s. 4d.

Seasonable at any time.

Note.—Potted lobster may be used cold, or as a *fricassee* with cream sauce.

How the Lobster Feeds.—The pincers of the lobster's large claws are furnished with nobs, and those of the other, are always serrated. With the former, it keeps firm hold of the stalks of submarine plants, and with the latter, it cuts and minces its food with great dexterity. The knobbed, or numb claw, as it is called by fishermen, is sometimes on the right and sometimes on the left, indifferently.

BAKED MACKEREL.

279. Ingredients.—4 middling-sized mackerel, a nice delicate forcemeat (*see* Forcemeats), 3 oz. of butter; pepper and salt to taste.

Mode.—Clean the fish, take out the roes, and fill up with forcemeat, and sew up the slit. Flour, and put them in a dish, heads and tails alternately, with the roes; and, between each layer, put some little pieces of butter, and pepper and salt. Bake for ½ an hour, and either serve with plain melted butter or a *maître d'hôtel* sauce.

Time.—½ hour. *Average cost* for this quantity, 1s. 10d.

Seasonable from April to July.

Sufficient for 6 persons.

Note.—Baked mackerel may be dressed in the same way as baked herrings (*see* No. 268), and may also be stewed in wine.

Weight of the Mackerel.—The greatest weight of this fish seldom exceeds 2 lbs., whilst their ordinary length runs between 14 and 20 inches. They die almost immediately after they are taken from their element, and, for a short time, exhibit a phosphoric light.

BOILED MACKEREL.

280. Ingredients.—¼ lb. of salt to each gallon of water.

Mode.—Cleanse the inside of the fish thoroughly, and lay it in the kettle with sufficient water to cover it with salt as above; bring it gradually to boil, skim well, and simmer gently till done; dish them on a hot napkin, heads and tails alternately, and garnish with fennel. Fennel sauce and plain melted butter are the usual accompaniments to boiled mackerel; but caper or anchovy sauce is sometimes served with it.

Time.—After the water boils, 10 minutes; for large mackerel, allow more time. *Average cost*, from 4d.

Seasonable from April to July.

Note.—When variety is desired, fillet the mackerel, boil it, and pour over parsley and butter; send some of this, besides, in a tureen.

BROILED MACKEREL.

281. Ingredients.—Pepper and salt to taste, a small quantity of oil.

Mode.—Mackerel should never be washed when intended to be broiled, but merely wiped very clean and dry, after taking out the gills and insides. Open the back, and put in a little pepper, salt, and oil; **broil it over a clear fire, turn it over on both sides, and also on the back.** When sufficiently cooked, the flesh can be detached from the bone, which will be in about 15 minutes for a small mackerel. Chop a little parsley, work it up in the butter, with pepper and salt to taste, and a squeeze of lemon-juice, and put it in the back. Serve before the butter is quite melted, with a *maître d'hôtel* sauce in a tureen.

Time.—Small mackerel 15 minutes.

Average cost, from 4d.

Seasonable from April to July.

THE MACKEREL.

THE MACKEREL.—This is not only one of the most elegantly-formed, but one of the most beautifully-coloured fishes, when taken out of the sea, that we have. Death, in some degree, impairs the vivid splendour of its colours; but it does not entirely obliterate them. It visits the shores of Great Britain in countless shoals, appearing about March, off the Land's End; in the bays of Devonshire, about April; off Brighton in the beginning of May; and on the coast of Suffolk about the beginning of June. In the Orkneys they are seen till August; but the greatest fishery is on the west coasts of England.

TO CHOOSE MACKEREL.—In choosing this fish, purchasers should, to a great extent, be regulated by the brightness of its appearance. If it have a transparent, silvery hue, the flesh is good; but if it be red about the head, it is stale.

FILLETS OF MACKEREL.

282. INGREDIENTS.—2 large mackerel, 1 oz. butter, 1 small bunch of chopped herbs, 3 tablespoonfuls of medium stock, No. 105, 3 tablespoonfuls of bechamel (*see* Sauces); salt, cayenne, and lemon-juice to taste.

Mode.—Clean the fish, and fillet it; scald the herbs, chop them fine, and put them with the butter and stock into a stewpan. Lay in the mackerel, and simmer very gently for 10 minutes; take them out, and put them on a hot dish. Dredge in a little flour, add the other ingredients, give one boil, and pour it over the mackerel.

Time.— 20 minutes. *Average cost* for this quantity, 1s. 6d.

Seasonable from April to July.

Sufficient for 4 persons.

Note.—Fillets of mackerel may be covered with egg and bread crumbs, and fried of a nice brown. Serve with *maître d'hôtel* sauce and plain melted butter.

THE VORACITY OF THE MACKEREL.—The voracity of this fish is very great, and, from their immense numbers, they are bold in attacking objects of which they might, otherwise, be expected to have a wholesome dread. Pontoppidan relates an anecdote of a sailor belonging to a ship lying in one of the harbours on the coast of Norway, who, having gone into the sea to bathe, was suddenly missed by his companions; in the course of a few minutes, however, he was seen on the surface, with great numbers of mackerel clinging to him by their mouths. His comrades hastened in a boat to his assistance; but when they had struck the fishes from him and got him up, they found he was so severely bitten, that he shortly afterwards expired.

PICKLED MACKEREL.

283. INGREDIENTS.—12 peppercorns, 2 bay-leaves, ½ pint of vinegar, 4 mackerel.

Mode.—Boil the mackerel as in the recipe No. 282, and lay them in a dish; take half the liquor they were boiled in; add as much vinegar, peppercorns, and bay-leaves; boil for 10 minutes, and when cold, pour over the fish.

Time.—½ hour. *Average cost*, 1s. 6d.

MACKEREL GARUM.—This brine, so greatly esteemed by the ancients, was manufactured from various kinds of fishes. When mackerel was employed, a few of them were placed in a small vase, with a large quantity of salt, which was well stirred, and then left to settle for some hours. On the following day, this was put into an earthen pot, which was uncovered, and placed in a situation to get the rays of the sun. At the end of two or three months, it was hermetically sealed, after having had added to it a quantity of old wine, equal to one third of the mixture.

GREY MULLET.

284. INGREDIENTS.—¼ lb. of salt to each gallon of water.

Mode.—If the fish be very large, it should be laid in cold water, and gradually brought to a boil; if small, put it in boiling water, salted in the above proportion. Serve with anchovy sauce and plain melted butter.

Time.—According to size, ¼ to ¾ hour.

Average cost, 8d. per lb.

Seasonable from July to October.

THE GREY MULLET.—This is quite a different fish from the red mullet, is abundant on the sandy coasts of Great Britain, and ascends rivers for miles. On the south coast it is very It improves more than any other salt-water fish

THE GREY MULLET.

plentiful, and is considered a fine fish when kept in ponds.

RED MULLET.

285. INGREDIENTS.—Oiled paper, thickening of butter and flour, ½ teaspoonful of anchovy sauce, 1 glass of sherry; cayenne and salt to taste.

Mode.—Clean the fish, take out the gills, but leave the inside, fold in oiled paper, and bake them gently. When done, take the liquor that flows from the fish, add a thickening of butter kneaded with flour; put in the other ingredients, and let it boil for 2 minutes. Serve the sauce in a tureen, and the fish, either with or without the paper cases.

Time.—About 25 minutes. *Average cost*, 1s. each.

Seasonable at any time, but more plentiful in summer.

Note.—Red mullet may be broiled, and should be folded in oiled paper, the same as in the preceding recipe, and seasoned with pepper and salt. They may be served without sauce; but if any is required, use melted butter, Italian or anchovy sauce. They should never be plain boiled.

THE STRIPED RED MULLET.—This fish was very highly esteemed by the ancients, especially by the Romans, who gave the most extravagant prices for it. Those of 2 lbs. weight were valued at about £15 each; those of 4 lbs. at £60, and, in the reign of Tiberius, three of them were sold for £209. To witness the changing loveliness of their colour during their dying agonies, was one of the principal reasons that such a high price was paid for one of these fishes. It frequents our Cornish and Sussex coasts, and is in high request, the flesh being firm, white, and well flavoured.

THE STRIPED RED MULLET.

FRIED OYSTERS.

286. INGREDIENTS.—3 dozen oysters, 2 oz. butter, 1 tablespoonful of ketchup, a little chopped lemon-peel, ½ teaspoonful of chopped parsley.

Mode.—Boil the oysters for 1 minute in their own liquor, and drain them; fry them with the butter, ketchup, lemon-peel, and parsley; lay them on a dish, and garnish with fried potatoes, toasted sippets, and parsley. This is a delicious delicacy, and is a favourite Italian dish.

Time.—5 minutes. *Average cost* for this quantity, 1s. 9d

Seasonable from September to April.

Sufficient for 4 persons.

THE EDIBLE OYSTER.—This shell-fish is almost universally distributed near the shores of seas in all latitudes, and they especially abound on the coasts of France and Britain. The coasts most celebrated, in England, for them, are those of Essex and Suffolk. Here they are dredged up by means of a net with an iron scraper at the mouth, that is dragged by a rope from a boat over the beds. As soon as taken from their native beds, they are stored in pits, formed for the purpose, furnished with sluices, through which, at the spring tides, the water is suffered to flow. This water, being stagnant, soon becomes green in warm weather; and, in a few days afterwards, the oysters acquire the same tinge, which increases their value in the market. They do not, however, attain their perfection and become fit for sale till the end of six or eight weeks. Oysters are not considered proper for the table till they are about a year and a half old; so that the brood of one spring are not to be taken for sale, till, at least, the September twelvemonth afterwards.

THE EDIBLE OYSTER.

SCALLOPED OYSTERS.

I.

287. INGREDIENTS.—Oysters, say 1 pint, 1 oz. butter, flour, 2 tablespoonfuls of white stock, 2 tablespoonfuls of cream; pepper and salt to taste; bread crumbs, oiled butter.

Mode.—Scald the oysters in their own liquor, take them out, beard them, and strain the liquor free from grit. Put 1 oz. of butter into a stewpan; when melted, dredge in sufficient flour to dry it up; add the stock, cream, and strained liquor, and give one boil. Put in the oysters and seasoning; let them gradually heat through, but not boil. Have ready the scallop-shells buttered; lay in the oysters, and as much of the liquid as they will hold; cover them over with bread crumbs, over which drop a little oiled butter. Brown them in the oven, or before the fire, and serve quickly, and very hot.

Time.—Altogether, ¼ hour.

Average cost for this quantity, 3s. 6d.

Sufficient for 5 or 6 persons.

II.

Prepare the oysters as in the preceding recipe, and put them in a scallop-shell or saucer, and between each layer sprinkle over a few bread crumbs, pepper, salt, and grated nutmeg; place small pieces of butter over, and bake before the fire in a Dutch oven. Put sufficient bread crumbs on the top to make a smooth surface, as the oysters should not be seen.

Time.—About ¼ hour. *Average cost,* 3s. 2d.

Seasonable from September to April.

STEWED OYSTERS.

288. INGREDIENTS.—1 pint of oysters, 1 oz. of butter, flour, ⅓ pint of cream; cayenne and salt to taste; 1 blade of pounded mace.

Mode.—Scald the oysters in their own liquor, take them out, beard them, and strain the liquor; put the butter into a stewpan, dredge in sufficient flour to dry it up, add the oyster-liquor and mace, and stir it over a sharp fire with a wooden spoon; when it comes to a boil, add the cream, oysters, and seasoning. Let all simmer for 1 or 2 minutes, but not longer, or the oysters would harden. Serve on a hot dish, and garnish with croûtons, or toasted sippets of bread. A small piece of lemon-peel boiled with the oyster-liquor, and taken out before the cream is added, will be found an improvement.

Time.—Altogether 15 minutes. *Average cost* for this quantity, 3s. 6d.

Seasonable from September to April.

Sufficient for 6 persons.

THE OYSTER AND THE SCALLOP.—The oyster is described as a bivalve shell-fish, having the valves generally unequal. The hinge is without teeth, but furnished with a somewhat oval cavity, and mostly with lateral transverse grooves. From a similarity in the structure of the hinge, oysters and scallops have been classified as one tribe; but they differ very essentially both in their external appearance and their habits. Oysters adhere to rocks, or, as in two or three species, to roots of trees on the shore; while the scallops are always detached, and usually lurk in the sand.

OYSTER PATTIES (an Entree).

289. INGREDIENTS.—2 dozen oysters, 2 oz. butter, 3 tablespoonfuls of cream, a little lemon-juice, 1 blade of pounded mace; cayenne to taste.

Mode.—Scald the oysters in their own liquor, beard them, and cut each one into 3 pieces. Put the butter into a stewpan, dredge in sufficient flour to dry it up; add the strained oyster-liquor with the other ingredients; put in the oysters, and let them heat gradually, but not boil fast. Make the patty-cases as directed for lobster patties, No. 277: fill with the oyster mixture, and replace the covers.

Time.—2 minutes for the oysters to simmer in the mixture.

Average cost, exclusive of the patty-cases, 1s. 4d.

Seasonable from September to April.

THE OYSTER FISHERY.—The oyster fishery in Britain is esteemed of so much import-ance, that it is regulated by a Court of Admiralty. In the month of May, the fishermen are allowed to take the oysters, in order to separate the spawn from the cultch, the latter of which is thrown in again, to preserve the bed for the future. After this month, it is felony to carry away the cultch, and otherwise punishable to take any oyster, between the shells of which, when closed, a shilling will rattle.

TO KEEP OYSTERS.

290. Put them in a tub, and cover them with salt and water. Let them remain for 12 hours, when they are to be taken out, and allowed to stand for another 12 hours without water. If left without water every alternate 12 hours, they will be much better than if constantly kept in it. Never put the same water twice to them.

OYSTERS FRIED IN BATTER.

291. INGREDIENTS.—$\frac{1}{2}$ pint of oysters, 2 eggs, $\frac{1}{2}$ pint of milk, suffi-cient flour to make the batter; pepper and salt to taste; when liked, a little nutmeg; hot lard.

Mode.—Scald the oysters in their own liquor, beard them, and lay them on a cloth, to drain thoroughly. Break the eggs into a basin, mix the flour with them, add the milk gradually, with nutmeg and seasoning, and put the oysters in the batter. Make some lard hot in a deep frying-pan, put in the oysters, one at a time; when done, take them up with a sharp-pointed skewer, and dish them on a napkin. Fried oysters are frequently used for garnishing boiled fish, and then a few bread crumbs should be added to the flour.

Time.—5 or 6 minutes. *Average cost* for this quantity, 1s. 10d.

Seasonable from September to April.

Sufficient for 3 persons.

L

EXCELLENCE OF THE ENGLISH OYSTER.—The French assert that the English oysters, which are esteemed the best in Europe, were originally procured from Cancalle Bay, near St. Malo; but they assign no proof for this. It is a fact, however, that the oysters eaten in ancient Rome were nourished in the channel which then parted the Isle of Thanet from England, and which has since been filled up, and converted into meadows.

BOILED PERCH.

292. INGREDIENTS.—¼ lb. of salt to each gallon of water.

Mode.—Scale the fish, take out the gills and clean it thoroughly; lay it in boiling water, salted as above, and simmer gently for 10 minutes. If the fish is very large, longer time must be allowed. Garnish with parsley, and serve with plain melted butter, or Dutch sauce. Perch do not preserve so good a flavour when stewed as when dressed in any other way.

Time.—Middling-sized perch, ¼ hour.

Seasonable from September to November.

THE PERCH.

Note.—Tench may be boiled the same way, and served with the same sauces.

THE PERCH.—This is one of the best, as it is one of the most common, of our fresh-water fishes, and is found in nearly all the lakes and rivers in Britain and Ireland, as well as through the whole of Europe within the temperate zone. It is extremely voracious, and it has the peculiarity of being gregarious, which is contrary to the nature of all fresh-water fishes of prey. The best season to angle for it is from the beginning of May to the middle of July. Large numbers of this fish are bred in the Hampton Court and Bushy Park ponds, all of which are well supplied with running water and with plenty of food; yet they rarely attain a large size. In the Regent's Park they are also very numerous; but are seldom heavier than three quarters of a pound.

FRIED PERCH.

293. INGREDIENTS.—Egg and bread crumbs, hot lard.

Mode.—Scale and clean the fish, brush it over with egg, and cover with bread crumbs. Have ready some boiling lard; put the fish in, and fry a nice brown. Serve with plain melted butter or anchovy sauce.

Time.—10 minutes.

Seasonable from September to November.

Note.—Fry tench in the same way.

PERCH STEWED WITH WINE.

294. INGREDIENTS.—Equal quantities of stock No. 105 and sherry, 1 bay-leaf, 1 clove of garlic, a small bunch of parsley, 2 cloves, salt to taste; thickening of butter and flour, pepper, grated nutmeg, ½ teaspoonful of anchovy sauce.

Mode.—Scale the fish and take out the gills, and clean them thoroughly; lay them in a stewpan with sufficient stock and sherry just to cover them. Put in the bay-leaf, garlic, parsley, cloves, and salt, and simmer till tender. When done, take out the fish, strain the liquor, add a thickening of butter and flour, the pepper, nutmeg, and the anchovy sauce, and stir it over the fire until somewhat reduced, when pour over the fish, and serve.

Time.—About 20 minutes.

Seasonable from September to November.

BOILED PIKE.

295. INGREDIENTS.—¼ lb. of salt to each gallon of water; a little vinegar.

Mode.—Scale and clean the pike, and fasten the tail in its mouth by means of a skewer. Lay it in cold water, and when it boils, throw in the salt and vinegar. The time for boiling depends, of course, on the size of the fish; but a middling-sized pike will take about ½ an hour. Serve with Dutch or anchovy sauce, and plain melted butter.

Time.—According to size, ½ to 1 hour.—*Average cost.* Seldom bought.

Seasonable from September to March.

THE PIKE.—This fish is, on account of its voracity, termed the fresh-water shark, and is abundant in most of the European lakes, especially those of the northern parts. It grows to an immense size, some attaining to the measure of eight feet, in Lapland and Russia. The smaller lakes, of this country and Ireland, vary in the kinds of fish they produce; some affording trout, others pike; and so on. Where these happen to be together, however, the trout soon becomes extinct. "Within a short distance of Castlebar," says a writer on sports, "there is a small bog-lake called Derreens. Ten years ago it was celebrated for its numerous well-sized trouts. Accidentally pike effected a passage into the lake from the Minola river, and now the trouts are extinct, or, at least, none of them are caught or seen. Previous to the intrusion

THE PIKE.

of the pikes, half a dozen trouts would be killed in an evening in Derreens, whose collective weight often amounted to twenty pounds." As an eating fish, the pike is in general dry.

BAKED PIKE.

296. INGREDIENTS.—1 or 2 pike, a nice delicate stuffing (*see* Forcemeats), 1 egg, bread crumbs, ¼ lb. butter.

Mode.—Scale the fish, take out the gills, wash, and wipe it thoroughly dry; stuff it with forcemeat, sew it up, and fasten the tail in the mouth by means of a skewer; brush it over with egg, sprinkle with bread crumbs, and baste with butter, before putting it in the oven, which must be well heated. When the pike is of a nice brown colour, cover it with buttered paper, as the outside would become too dry. If 2 are dressed, a little variety may be made by making one of them green with a little chopped parsley mixed with the bread crumbs. Serve anchovy or Dutch sauce, and plain melted butter with it.

Time.—According to size, 1 hour, more or less.

Average cost.—Seldom bought.

Seasonable from September to March.

Note.—Pike *à la génévese* may be stewed in the same manner as salmon *à la génévese.*

FRIED PLAICE.

297.—INGREDIENTS.—Hot lard, or clarified dripping ; egg and bread crumbs.

Mode.—This fish is fried in the same manner as soles. Wash and wipe them thoroughly dry, and let them remain in a cloth until it is time to dress them. Brush them over with egg, and cover with bread crumbs mixed with a little flour. Fry of a nice brown in hot dripping or lard, and garnish with fried parsley and cut lemon. Send them to table with shrimp-sauce and plain melted butter.

Time.—About 5 minutes. *Average cost,* 3d. each.

Seasonable from May to November.

Sufficient, 4 plaice for 4 persons.

Note.—Plaice may be boiled plain, and served with melted butter. Garnish with parsley and cut lemon.

STEWED PLAICE.

298. INGREDIENTS.—4 or 5 plaice, 2 onions, ½ oz. ground ginger, 1 pint of lemon-juice, ¼ pint water, 6 eggs ; cayenne to taste.

Mode.—Cut the fish into pieces about 2 inches wide, salt them, and let them remain ¼ hour. Slice and fry the onions a light brown ; put them in a stewpan, on the top of which put the fish without washing, and add the ginger, lemon-juice, and water. Cook slowly for ½ hour, and do not let the fish boil, or it will break. Take it out, and when the liquor is cool, add 6 well-beaten eggs ; simmer till it thickens, when pour over the fish, and serve.

Time.—¾ hour. *Average cost* for this quantity, 1s. 9d.

Seasonable from May to November.

Sufficient for 4 persons ; according to size.

THE PLAICE.

THE PLAICE.—This fish is found both in the Baltic and the Mediterranean, and is also abundant on the coast of England. It keeps well, and, like all ground-fish, is very tenacious of life. Its flesh is inferior to that of the sole, and, as it is a low-priced fish, it is generally bought by the poor. The best brought to the London market are called *Dowers plaice,* from their being caught in the Dowers, or flats, between Hastings and Folkstone.

TO BOIL PRAWNS OR SHRIMPS.

299. INGREDIENTS.—¼ lb. salt to each gallon of water.

Mode.—Prawns should be very red, and have no spawn under the tail; much depends on their freshness and the way in which they are cooked. Throw them into boiling water, salted as above, and keep them boiling for about 7 or 8 minutes. Shrimps should be done in the same way; but less time must be allowed. It may easily be known when they are done by their changing colour. Care should be taken that they are not over-boiled, as they then become tasteless and indigestible.

Time.—Prawns, about 8 minutes; shrimps, about 5 minutes.

Average cost, prawns, 2s. per lb. ; shrimps, 6d. per pint.

Seasonable all the year.

TO DRESS PRAWNS.

300. Cover a dish with a large cup reversed, and over that lay a small white napkin. Arrange the prawns on it in the form of a pyramid, and garnish with plenty of parsley.

BOILED SALMON.

301. INGREDIENTS.—6 oz. of salt to each gallon of water,—sufficient water to cover the fish.

Mode.—Scale and clean the fish, and be particular that no blood is left inside; lay it in the fish-kettle with sufficient cold water to cover it, adding salt in the above proportion. Bring it quickly to a boil, take off all the scum, and let it simmer gently till the fish is done, which will be when the meat separates easily from the bone. Experience alone can teach the cook to fix the time for boiling fish; but it is especially to be remembered, that it should never be under-dressed, as then nothing is more unwholesome. Neither let it remain in the kettle after it is sufficiently cooked, as that would render it insipid, watery, and colourless. Drain it, and if not wanted for a few minutes, keep it warm by means of warm cloths laid over it. Serve on a hot napkin, garnish with cut lemon and parsley, and send lobster or shrimp sauce, and plain melted butter to table with it. A dish of dressed cucumber usually accompanies this fish.

Time.—8 minutes to each lb. for large thick salmon; 6 minutes for thin fish. *Average cost*, in full season, 1s. 3d. per lb.

Seasonable from April to August.

Sufficient, ½ lb., or rather less, for each person.

Note.—Cut lemon should be put on the table with this fish ; and a little of the juice squeezed over it is considered by many persons a most agreeable addition. Boiled peas are also, by some connoisseurs, considered especially adapted to be served with salmon.

TO CHOOSE SALMON.—To be good, the belly should be firm and thick, which may readily be ascertained by feeling it with the thumb and finger. The circumstance of this fish having *red* gills, though given as a standing rule in most cookery-books, as a sign of its goodness, is not at all to be relied on, as this quality can be easily given them by art.

SALMON AND CAPER SAUCE.

302. INGREDIENTS.—2 slices of salmon, $\frac{1}{4}$ lb. butter, $\frac{1}{2}$ teaspoonful of chopped parsley, 1 shalot ; salt, pepper, and grated nutmeg to taste.

Mode.—Lay the salmon in a baking-dish, place pieces of butter over it, and add the other ingredients, rubbing a little of the seasoning into the fish ; baste it frequently ; when done, take it out and drain for a minute or two ; lay it in a dish, pour caper sauce over it, and serve. Salmon dressed in this way, with tomato sauce, is very delicious.

Time.—About $\frac{3}{4}$ hour. *Average cost,* 1s. 3d. per lb.

Seasonable from April to August.

Sufficient for 4 or 5 persons.

THE MIGRATORY HABITS OF THE SALMON.—The instinct with which the salmon revisits its native river, is one of the most curious circumstances in its natural history. As the swallow returns annually to its nest, so it returns to the same spot to deposit its ova. This fact would seem to have been repeatedly proved. M. De Lande fastened a copper ring round a salmon's tail, and found that, for three successive seasons, it returned to the same place. Dr. Bloch states that gold and silver rings have been attached by eastern princes to salmon, to prove that a communication existed between the Persian Gulf and the Caspian and Northern Seas, and that the experiment succeeded.

COLLARED SALMON.

303. INGREDIENTS.—A piece of salmon, say 3 lbs., a high seasoning of salt, pounded mace, and pepper ; water and vinegar, 3 bay-leaves.

Mode.—Split the fish ; scale, bone, and wash it thoroughly clean ; wipe it, and rub in the seasoning inside and out ; roll it up, and bind firmly ; lay it in a kettle, cover it with vinegar and water ($\frac{1}{3}$ vinegar, in proportion to the water) ; add the bay-leaves and a good seasoning of salt and whole pepper, and simmer till done. Do not remove the lid. Serve with melted butter or anchovy sauce. For preserving the collared fish, boil up the liquor in which it was cooked, and add a little more vinegar. Pour over when cold.

Time.—$\frac{3}{4}$ hour, or rather more.

HABITAT OF THE SALMON.—The salmon is styled by Walton the " king of fresh-water fish," and is found distributed over the north of Europe and Asia, from Britain to

Kamschatka, but is never found in warm latitudes, nor has it ever been caught even so far south as the Mediterranean. It lives in fresh as well as in salt waters, depositing its spawn in the former, hundreds of miles from the mouths of some of those rivers to which it has been known to resort. In 1859, great efforts were made to introduce this fish into the Australian colonies; and it is believed that the attempt, after many difficulties, which were very skilfully overcome, has been successful.

CRIMPED SALMON.

304. Salmon is frequently dressed in this way at many fashionable tables, but must be very fresh, and cut into slices 2 or 3 inches thick. Lay these in cold salt and water for 1 hour; have ready some boiling water, salted, as in recipe No. 301, and well skimmed; put in the fish, and simmer gently for ¼ hour, or rather more; should it be very thick, garnish the same as boiled salmon, and serve with the same sauces.

Time.—¼ hour, more or less, according to size.

Note.—Never use vinegar with salmon, as it spoils the taste and colour of the fish.

THE SALMON.

THE SALMON TRIBE.—This is the Abdominal fish, forming the fourth of the orders of Linnæus. They are distinguished from other fishes by having two dorsal fins, of which the hindmost is fleshy and without rays. They have teeth both on the tongue and in the jaws, whilst the body is covered with round and minutely striated scales.

CURRIED SALMON.

305. INGREDIENTS.—Any remains of boiled salmon, ¾ pint of strong or medium stock (No. 105), 1 onion, 1 tablespoonful of curry-powder, 1 teaspoonful of Harvey's sauce, 1 teaspoonful of anchovy sauce, 1 oz. of butter, the juice of ½ lemon, cayenne and salt to taste.

Mode.—Cut up the onions into small pieces, and fry them of a pale brown in the butter; add all the ingredients but the salmon, and simmer gently till the onion is tender, occasionally stirring the contents; cut the salmon into small square pieces, carefully take away all skin and bone, lay it in the stewpan, and let it gradually heat through; but do not allow it to boil long.

Time.—¾ hour. *Average cost,* exclusive of the cold fish, 9*d.*

GROWTH OF THE SALMON.—At the latter end of the year—some as soon as November—salmon begin to press up the rivers as far as they can reach, in order to deposit their spawn, which they do in the sand or gravel, about eighteen inches deep. Here it lies buried till the spring, when, about the latter end of March, it begins to exclude the young, which gradually increase to four or five inches in length, and are then termed smelts or smouts. About the beginning of May, the river seems to be alive with them, and there is no forming an idea of their numbers without having seen them. A seasonable flood, however, comes, and hurries them to the "great deep;" whence, about the middle of June, they commence their return to the river again. By this time they are twelve or sixteen inches long, and progressively increase, both in number and size, till about the end of July, when they have become large enough to be denominated *grilse*. Early in August they become fewer in numbers, but of greater size, having advanced to a weight of from six to nine pounds. This rapidity of growth appears surprising, and realizes the remark of Walton, that "the salmon becomes a salmon in as short a time as a gosling becomes a goose." Recent writers have, however, thrown considerable doubts on this quick growth of the salmon.

SALMON CUTLETS.

306. Cut the slices 1 inch thick, and season them with pepper and salt; butter a sheet of white paper, lay each slice on a separate piece, with their ends twisted; broil gently over a clear fire, and serve with anchovy or caper sauce. When higher seasoning is required, add a few chopped herbs and a little spice.

Time.—5 to 10 minutes.

SALMON A LA GENEVESE.

307. INGREDIENTS.—2 slices of salmon, 2 chopped shalots, a little parsley, a small bunch of herbs, 2 bay-leaves, 2 carrots, pounded mace, pepper and salt to taste, 4 tablespoonfuls of Madeira, ½ pint of white stock (No. 107), thickening of butter and flour, 1 teaspoonful of essence of anchovies, the juice of 1 lemon, cayenne and salt to taste.

Mode.—Rub the bottom of a stewpan over with butter, and put in the shalots, herbs, bay-leaves, carrots, mace, and seasoning; stir them for 10 minutes over a clear fire, and add the Madeira or sherry; simmer gently for ½ hour, and strain through a sieve over the fish, which stew in this gravy. As soon as the fish is sufficiently cooked, take away all the liquor, except a little to keep the salmon moist, and put it into another stewpan; add the stock, thicken with butter and flour, and put in the anchovies, lemon-juice, cayenne, and salt; lay the salmon on a hot dish, pour over it part of the sauce, and serve the remainder in a tureen.

Time.—1¼ hour. *Average cost* for this quantity, 3s. 6d.

Sufficient for 4 or 5 persons.

PICKLED SALMON.

308. INGREDIENTS.—Salmon, ½ oz. of whole pepper, ½ oz. of whole allspice, 1 teaspoonful of salt, 2 bay-leaves, equal quantities of vinegar and the liquor in which the fish was boiled.

Mode.—After the fish comes from table, lay it in a nice dish with a cover to it, as it should be excluded from the air, and take away the bone; boil the liquor and vinegar with the other ingredients for 10 minutes, and let it stand to get cold; pour it over the salmon, and, in 12 hours this will be fit for the table.

Time, 10 minutes.

To Cure Salmon.—This process consists in splitting the fish, rubbing it with salt, and then putting it into pickle in tubs provided for the purpose. Here it is kept for about six weeks, when it is taken out, pressed and packed in casks, with layers of salt.

POTTED SALMON.

309. Ingredients.—Salmon; pounded mace, cloves, and pepper to taste; 3 bay-leaves, ¼ lb. butter.

Mode.—Skin the salmon, and clean it thoroughly by wiping with a cloth (water would spoil it); cut it into square pieces, which rub with salt; let them remain till thoroughly drained, then lay them in a dish with the other ingredients, and bake. When quite done, drain them from the gravy, press into pots for use, and, when cold, pour over it clarified butter.

Time.—½ hour.

An Aversion in the Salmon.—The salmon is said to have an aversion to anything red; hence, fishermen engaged in catching it do not wear jackets or caps of that colour. Pontoppidan also says, that it has an abhorrence of carrion, and if any happens to be thrown into the places it haunts, it immediately forsakes them. The remedy adopted for this in Norway, is to throw into the polluted water a lighted torch. As food, salmon, when in perfection, is one of the most delicious and nutritive of our fish.

BAKED SEA-BREAM.

310. Ingredients.—1 bream. Seasoning to taste of salt, pepper, and cayenne; ¼ lb. of butter.

Mode.—Well wash the bream, but do not remove the scales, and wipe away all moisture with a nice dry cloth. Season it inside and out with salt, pepper, and cayenne, and lay it in a baking-dish. Place the butter, in small pieces, upon the fish, and bake for rather more than ½ an hour. To stuff this fish before baking, will be found a great improvement.

Time.—Rather more than ½ an hour.

Seasonable in summer.

Note.—This fish may be broiled over a nice clear fire, and served with a good brown gravy or white sauce, or it may be stewed in wine.

The Sea-Bream.—This is an abundant fish in Cornwall, and it is frequently found in the fish-market of Hastings during the summer months, but it is not in much esteem.

THE SEA-BREAM.

MR. YARRELL'S RECIPE.

" When thoroughly cleansed, the fish should be wiped dry, but none of the scales should be taken off. In this state it should be broiled, turning it often, and if the skin cracks, flour it a little to keep the outer case entire. When on table, the whole skin and scales turn off without difficulty, and the muscle beneath, saturated in its own natural juices, which the outside covering has retained, will be of good flavour."

TO DRESS SHAD.

311. INGREDIENTS.—1 shad, oil, pepper, and salt.

Mode.—Scale, empty and wash the fish carefully, and make two or three incisions across the back. Season it with pepper and salt, and let it remain in oil for ½ hour. Broil it on both sides over a clear fire, and serve with caper sauce. This fish is much esteemed by the French, and by them is considered excellent.

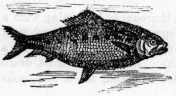

Time.—Nearly 1 hour.

Average cost.—Seldom bought.

Seasonable from April to June.

THE SHAD.

THE SHAD.—This is a salt-water fish, but is held in little esteem. It enters our rivers to spawn in May, and great numbers of them are taken opposite the Isle of Dogs, in the Thames.

POTTED SHRIMPS.

312. INGREDIENTS.—1 pint of shelled shrimps, ¼ lb. of fresh butter, 1 blade of pounded mace, cayenne to taste; when liked, a little nutmeg.

Mode.—Have ready a pint of picked shrimps, and put them, with the other ingredients, into a stewpan; let them heat gradually in the butter, but do not let it boil. Pour into small pots, and when cold, cover with melted butter, and carefully exclude the air.

Time.—¼ hour to soak in the butter.

Average cost for this quantity, 1s. 3d.

BUTTERED PRAWNS OR SHRIMPS.

313. INGREDIENTS.—1 pint of picked prawns or shrimps, ¾ pint of stock No. 104, thickening of butter and flour; salt, cayenne, and nutmeg to taste.

Mode.—Pick the prawns or shrimps, and put them in a stewpan with the stock; add a thickening of butter and flour; season, and simmer gently for 3 minutes. Serve on a dish garnished with fried bread or toasted sippets. Cream sauce may be substituted for the gravy.

Time.—3 minutes.

Average cost for this quantity, 1s. 4d.

THE SHRIMP.

THE SHRIMP.—This shell-fish is smaller than the prawn, and is greatly relished in London as a delicacy. It inhabits most of the sandy shores of Europe, and the Isle of Wight is especially famous for them.

BOILED SKATE.

314. INGREDIENTS.—¼ lb. of salt to each gallon of water.

Mode.—Cleanse and skin the skate, lay it in a fish-kettle, with sufficient water to cover it, salted in the above proportion. Let it simmer very gently till done; then dish it on a hot napkin, and serve with shrimp, lobster, or caper sauce.

Time.—According to size, from ½ to 1 hour. *Average cost,* 4*d.* per lb.

Seasonable from August to April.

CRIMPED SKATE.

315. INGREDIENTS.—½ lb. of salt to each gallon of water.

Mode.—Clean, skin, and cut the fish into slices, which roll and tie round with string. Have ready some water highly salted, put in the fish, and boil till it is done. Drain well, remove the string, dish on a hot napkin, and serve with the same sauces as above. Skate should never be eaten out of season, as it is liable to produce diarrhœa and other diseases. It may be dished without a napkin, and the sauce poured over.

Time.—About 20 minutes. *Average cost,* 4*d.* per lb.

Seasonable from August to April.

TO CHOOSE SKATE.—This fish should be chosen for its firmness, breadth, and thickness, and should have a creamy appearance. When crimped, it should not be kept longer than a day or two, as all kinds of crimped fish soon become sour.

THE SKATE.—This is one of the ray tribe, and is extremely abundant and cheap in the fishing towns of England. The flesh is white, thick, and nourishing; but, we suppose, from its being so plentiful, it is esteemed less than it ought to be on account of its nutritive properties, and the ease with which it is digested. It is much improved by crimping; in which state it is usually sold in London. The THORNBACK differs from the true skate by having large spines in its back, of which the other is destitute. It is taken in great abundance during the spring and summer months, but its flesh is not so good as it is in November. It is, in regard to quality, inferior to that of the true skate.

THORNBACK SKATE.

SKATE WITH CAPER SAUCE (a la Francaise)

316. INGREDIENTS.—2 or 3 slices of skate, ½ pint of vinegar, 2 oz. of salt, ½ teaspoonful of pepper, 1 sliced onion, a small bunch of parsley, 2 bay-leaves, 2 or 3 sprigs of thyme, sufficient water to cover the fish.

Mode.—Put in a fish-kettle all the above ingredients, and simmer the skate in them till tender. When it is done, skin it neatly, and pour over it some of the liquor in which it has been boiling. Drain it, put it on a hot dish, pour over it caper sauce, and send some of the latter to table in a tureen.

Time.—½ hour. *Average cost*, 4*d*. per lb.

Seasonable from August to April.

Note.—Skate may also be served with onion sauce, or parsley and butter.

SMALL SKATE FRIED.

317. INGREDIENTS.—Skate, sufficient vinegar to cover them, salt and pepper to taste, 1 sliced onion, a small bunch of parsley, the juice of ½ lemon, hot dripping.

Mode.—Cleanse the skate, lay them in a dish, with sufficient vinegar to cover them; add the salt, pepper, onion, parsley, and lemon-juice, and let the fish remain in this pickle for 1½ hour. Then drain them well, flour them, and fry of a nice brown, in hot dripping. They may be served either with or without sauce. Skate is not good if dressed too fresh, unless it is crimped; it should, therefore, be kept for a day, but not long enough to produce a disagreeable smell.

Time.—10 minutes. *Average cost*, 4*d*. per lb.

Seasonable from August to April.

OTHER SPECIES OF SKATE.—Besides the true skate, there are several other species found in our seas. These are known as the *white* skate, the long-nosed skate, and the Homelyn ray, which are of inferior quality, though often crimped, and sold for true skate.

TO BAKE SMELTS.

318. INGREDIENTS.—12 smelts, bread crumbs, ¼ lb. of fresh butter, 2 blades of pounded mace; salt and cayenne to taste.

Mode.—Wash, and dry the fish thoroughly in a cloth, and arrange them nicely in a flat baking-dish. Cover them with fine bread crumbs, and place little pieces of butter all over them. Season and bake for 15 minutes. Just before serving, add a squeeze of lemon-juice, and garnish with fried parsley and cut lemon.

Time.—¼ hour. *Average cost*, 2*s*. per dozen.

Seasonable from October to May.

Sufficient for 6 persons.

TO CHOOSE SMELTS.—When good, this fish is of a fine silvery appearance, and when alive, their backs are of a dark brown shade, which, after death, fades to a light fawn. They ought to have a refreshing fragrance, resembling that of a cucumber.

THE ODOUR OF THE SMELT.—This peculiarity in the smelt has been compared, by some, to the fragrance of a cucumber, and by others, to that of a violet. It is a very elegant fish, and formerly abounded in the Thames. The *Atharine*, or sand smelt, is sometimes sold for the true one; but it is an inferior fish, being drier in the quality of its flesh. On the south coast of England, where the true smelt is rare, it is plentiful.

TO FRY SMELTS.

319. INGREDIENTS.—Egg and bread crumbs, a little flour; boiling lard.

Mode.—Smelts should be very fresh, and not washed more than is necessary to clean them. Dry them in a cloth, lightly flour, dip them in egg, and sprinkle over with very fine bread crumbs, and put them into boiling lard. Fry of a nice pale brown, and be careful not to take off the light roughness of the crumbs, or their beauty will be spoiled. Dry them before the fire on a drainer, and serve with plain melted butter. This fish is often used as a garnishing.

Time.—5 minutes.

Average cost, 2s. per dozen.

Seasonable from October to May.

THE SMELT.

THE SMELT.—This is a delicate little fish, and is in high esteem. Mr. Yarrell asserts that the true smelt is entirely confined to the western and eastern coasts of Britain. It very rarely ventures far from the shore, and is plentiful in November, December, and January.

BAKED SOLES.

320. INGREDIENTS.—2 soles, ¼ lb. of butter, egg, and bread crumbs, minced parsley, 1 glass of sherry, lemon-juice; cayenne and salt to taste.

Mode. — Clean, skin, and well wash the fish, and dry them thoroughly in a cloth. Brush them over with egg, sprinkle with bread crumbs mixed with a little minced parsley, lay them in a large flat baking-dish, white side uppermost; or if it will not hold the two soles, they may each be laid on a dish by itself; but they must not be put one on the top of the other. Melt the butter, and pour it over the whole, and bake for 20 minutes. Take a portion of the gravy that flows from the fish, add the wine, lemon-juice, and seasoning, give it one boil, skim, pour it *under* the fish, and serve.

Time.—20 minutes. *Average cost*, 1s. to 2s. per pair.

Seasonable at any time.

Sufficient for 4 or 5 persons.

TO CHOOSE SOLES.—This fish should be both thick and firm. If the skin is difficult to be taken off, and the flesh looks grey, it is good.

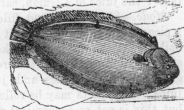

THE SOLE.

THE SOLE.—This ranks next to the turbot in point of excellence among our flat fish. It is abundant on the British coasts, but those of the western shores are much superior in size to those taken on the northern. The finest are caught in Torbay, and frequently weigh 8 or 10 lbs. per pair. Its flesh being firm, white, and delicate, is greatly esteemed.

BOILED SOLES.

321. INGREDIENTS.—$\frac{1}{4}$ lb. salt to each gallon of water.

Mode.—Cleanse and wash the fish carefully, cut off the fins, but do not skin it. Lay it in a fish-kettle, with sufficient cold water to cover it, salted in the above proportion. Let it gradually come to a boil, and keep it simmering for a few minutes, according to the size of the fish. Dish it on a hot napkin after well draining it, and garnish with parsley and cut lemon. Shrimp, or lobster sauce, and plain melted butter, are usually sent to table with this dish.

Time.—After the water boils, 7 minutes for a middling-sized sole.

Average cost, 1s. to 2s. per pair.

Seasonable at any time.

Sufficient,—1 middling-sized sole for 2 persons.

SOLE OR COD PIE.

322. INGREDIENTS.—The remains of cold boiled sole or cod, seasoning to taste of pepper, salt, and pounded mace, 1 dozen oysters to each lb. of fish, 3 tablespoonfuls of white stock, 1 teacupful of cream thickened with flour, puff paste.

Mode.—Clear the fish from the bones, lay it in a pie-dish, and between each layer put a few oysters and a little seasoning; add the stock, and, when liked, a small quantity of butter; cover with puff paste, and bake for $\frac{1}{2}$ hour. Boil the cream with sufficient flour to thicken it; pour in the pie, and serve.

Time.—$\frac{1}{2}$ hour. *Average cost* for this quantity, 10d.

Seasonable at any time.

Sufficient for 4 persons.

SOLES WITH CREAM SAUCE.

323. INGREDIENTS.—2 soles; salt, cayenne, and pounded mace to taste; the juice of $\frac{1}{2}$ lemon, salt and water, $\frac{1}{2}$ pint of cream.

Mode.—Skin, wash, and fillet the soles, and divide each fillet in 2 pieces; lay them in cold salt and water, which bring gradually to a boil. When the water boils, take out the fish, lay it in a delicately clean stewpan, and cover with the cream. Add the seasoning, simmer very gently for ten minutes, and, just before serving, put in the lemon-juice. The fillets may be rolled, and secured by means of a skewer; but this is not so economical a way of dressing them, as double the quantity of cream is required.

Time.—10 minutes in the cream.

Average cost, from 1s. to 2s. per pair.   *Seasonable* at any time.
Sufficient for 4 or 5 persons.

This will be found a most delicate and delicious dish.

THE SOLE A FAVOURITE WITH THE ANCIENT GREEKS.—This fish was much sought after by the ancient Greeks on account of its light and nourishing qualities. The brill, the flounder, the diamond and Dutch plaice, which, with the sole, were known under the general name of *passeres,* were all equally esteemed, and had generally the same qualities attributed to them.

FILLETED SOLES A L'ITALIENNE.

324. INGREDIENTS.—2 soles; salt, pepper, and grated nutmeg to taste; egg and bread crumbs, butter, the juice of 1 lemon.

Mode.—Skin, and carefully wash the soles, separate the meat from the bone, and divide each fillet in two pieces. Brush them over with white of egg, sprinkle with bread crumbs and seasoning, and put them in a baking-dish. Place small pieces of butter over the whole, and bake for ½ hour. When they are nearly done, squeeze the juice of a lemon over them, and serve on a dish, with Italian sauce (*see* Sauces) poured over.

Time.—½ hour. *Average cost,* from 1s. to 2s. per pair.
Seasonable at any time.
Sufficient for 4 or 5 persons.

WHITING may be dressed in the same manner, and will be found very delicious.

THE FLAVOUR OF THE SOLE.—This, as a matter of course, greatly depends on the nature of the ground and bait upon which the animal feeds. Its natural food are small crabs and shell-fish. Its colour also depends on the colour of the ground where it feeds; for if this be white, then the sole is called the white, or lemon sole; but if the bottom be muddy, then it is called the black sole. Small-sized soles, caught in shallow water on the coasts, are the best in flavour.

FRICASSEED SOLES.

325. INGREDIENTS.—2 middling-sized soles, 1 small one, ½ tea-spoonful of chopped lemon-peel, 1 teaspoonful of chopped parsley, a little grated bread; salt, pepper, and nutmeg to taste; 1 egg, 2 oz. butter, ½ pint of good gravy, 2 tablespoonfuls of port wine, cayenne and lemon-juice to taste.

Mode.—Fry the soles of a nice brown, as directed in recipe No. 327, and drain them well from fat. Take all the meat from the small sole, chop it fine, and mix with it the lemon-peel, parsley, bread, and seasoning; work altogether, with the yolk of an egg and the butter; make this into small balls, and fry them. Thicken the gravy with a dessert-spoonful of flour, add the port wine, cayenne, and lemon-juice; lay in the 2 soles and balls; let them simmer gently for 5 minutes; serve hot, and garnish with cut lemon.

Time.—10 minutes to fry the soles.

Average cost for this quantity, 3s.

Seasonable at any time. *Sufficient* for 4 or 5 persons.

HOW SOLES ARE CAUGHT.—The instrument usually employed is a trawl net, which is shaped like a pocket, of from sixty to eighty feet long, and open at the mouth from thirty-two to forty feet, and three deep. This is dragged along the ground by the vessel, and on the art of the fisherman in its employment, in a great measure depends the quality of the fish he catches. If, for example, he drags the net too quickly, all that are caught are swept rapidly to the end of the net, where they are smothered, and sometimes destroyed. A medium has to be observed, in order that as few as possible escape being caught in the net, and as many as possible preserved alive in it.

FRIED FILLETED SOLES.

326. Soles for filleting should be large, as the flesh can be more easily separated from the bones, and there is less waste. Skin and wash the fish, and raise the meat carefully from the bones, and divide it into nice handsome pieces. The more usual way is to roll the fillets, after dividing each one in two pieces, and either bind them round with twine, or run a small skewer through them. Brush over with egg, and cover with bread crumbs; fry them as directed in the foregoing recipe, and garnish with fried parsley and cut lemon. When a pretty dish is desired, this is by far the most elegant mode of dressing soles, as they look much better than when fried whole. (*See* Coloured Plate A.) Instead of rolling the fillets, they may be cut into square pieces, and arranged in the shape of a pyramid on the dish.

Time.—About 10 minutes. *Average cost*, from 1s. to 2s. per pair.

Seasonable at any time.

Sufficient,—2 large soles for 6 persons.

FRIED SOLES.

327. INGREDIENTS.—2 middling-sized soles, hot lard or clarified dripping, egg, and bread crumbs.

Mode.—Skin and carefully wash the soles, and cut off the fins, wipe them very dry, and let them remain in the cloth until it is time to dress them. Have ready some fine bread crumbs and beaten egg; dredge the soles with a little flour, brush them over with egg, and cover with bread crumbs. Put them in a deep pan, with plenty of clarified dripping or lard (when the expense is not objected to, oil is still better) heated, so that it may neither scorch the fish nor make them sodden. When they are sufficiently cooked on one side, turn them carefully, and brown them on the other : they may be considered ready when a thick smoke rises. Lift them out carefully, and lay them before the fire on a reversed sieve and soft paper, to absorb the fat. Particular attention should be paid to this, as nothing is more disagreeable than greasy fish: this may be always avoided by dressing them in good time, and allowing a few minutes for them to get thoroughly crisp, and free from greasy moisture. Dish them on a hot napkin, garnish with cut lemon and fried parsley, and send them to table with shrimp sauce and plain melted butter.

Time.—10 minutes for large soles; less time for small ones.

Average cost, from 1s. to 2s. per pair.

Seasonable at any time.

Sufficient for 4 or 5 persons.

SOLES WITH MUSHROOMS.

328. INGREDIENTS.—1 pint of milk, 1 pint of water, 1 oz. butter, 1 oz. salt, a little lemon-juice, 2 middling-sized soles.

Mode.—Cleanse the soles, but do not skin them, and lay them in a fish-kettle, with the milk, water, butter, salt, and lemon-juice. Bring them gradually to boil, and let them simmer very gently till done, which will be in about 7 minutes. Take them up, drain them well on a cloth, put them on a hot dish, and pour over them a good mushroom sauce. (*See* Sauces.)

Time.—After the water boils, 7 minutes.

Seasonable at any time.

Sufficient for 4 persons.

SPRATS.

329. Sprats should be cooked very fresh, which can be ascertained by their bright and sparkling eyes. Wipe them dry; fasten them in rows by a skewer run through the eyes; dredge with flour, and broil them on a gridiron over a nice clear fire. The gridiron should be rubbed with suet. Serve very hot.

Time.—3 or 4 minutes. *Average cost*, 1d. per lb.

Seasonable from November to March.

TO CHOOSE SPRATS.—Choose these from their silvery appearance, as the brighter they are, so are they the fresher.

SPRATS FRIED IN BATTER.

330. INGREDIENTS.—2 eggs, flour, bread crumbs; seasoning of salt and pepper to taste.

Mode.—Wipe the sprats, and dip them in a batter made of the above ingredients. Fry of a nice brown, serve very hot, and garnish with fried parsley.

Sprats may be baked like herrings. (*See* No. 268.)

M

DRIED SPRATS.

331. Dried sprats should be put into a basin, and boiling water poured over them; they may then be skinned and served, and this will be found a much better way than boiling them.

THE SPRAT.—This migratory fish is rarely found longer than four or five inches, and visits the shores of Britain after the herring and other kinds of fish have taken their departure from them. On the coasts of Suffolk, Essex, and Kent, they are very abundant, and from 400 to 500 boats are employed in catching them during the winter season. Besides plentifully supplying the London market, they are frequently sold at sixpence a bushel to farmers for manuring purposes. They enter the Thames about the beginning of November, and leave it in March. At Yarmouth and Gravesend they are cured like red herrings.

THE SPRAT.

BAKED STURGEON.

332. INGREDIENTS.—1 small sturgeon, salt and pepper to taste, 1 small bunch of herbs, the juice of ½ lemon, ¼ lb. of butter, 1 pint of white wine.

Mode.—Cleanse the fish thoroughly, skin it, and split it along the belly without separating it; have ready a large baking-dish, in which lay the fish, sprinkle over the seasoning and herbs very finely minced, and moisten it with the lemon-juice and wine. Place the butter in small pieces over the whole of the fish, put it in the oven, and baste frequently; brown it nicely, and serve with its own gravy.

Time.—Nearly 1 hour. *Average cost*, 1*s*. to 1*s*. 6*d*. per lb.

Seasonable from August to March.

THE STURGEON.—This fish commences the sixth of the Linnæan order, and all the species are large, seldom measuring, when full-grown, less than three or four feet in length. Its flesh is reckoned extremely delicious, and, in the time of the emperor Severus, was so highly valued by the ancients, that it was brought to table by servants crowned with coronets, and preceded by a band of music. It is an inhabitant of the Baltic, the Mediterranean, the Caspian, and the Black Sea, and of the Danube, the Volga, the Don, and other large rivers. It is abundant in the rivers of North America, and is occasionally taken in the Thames, as well as in the Eske and the Eden. It is one of those fishes considered as royal property. It is from its *roe* that *caviare*, a favourite food of the Russians, is prepared. Its flesh is delicate, firm, and white, but is rare in the London market, where it sells for 1*s*. or 1*s*. 6*d*. per lb.

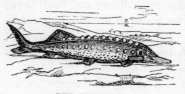

THE STURGEON.

THE STERLET is a smaller species of sturgeon, found in the Caspian Sea and some Russian rivers. It also is greatly prized on account of the delicacy of its flesh.

ROAST STURGEON.

333. INGREDIENTS.—Veal stuffing, buttered paper, the tail-end of a sturgeon.

Mode.—Cleanse the fish, bone and skin it; make a nice veal stuffing (*see* Forcemeats), and fill it with the part where the bones came from ; roll it in buttered paper, bind it up firmly with tape, like a fillet of veal, and roast it in a Dutch oven before a clear fire. Serve with good brown gravy, or plain melted butter.

Time.—About 1 hour. *Average cost*, 1s. to 1s. 6d. per lb.

Seasonable from August to March.

Note.—Sturgeon may be plain-boiled, and served with Dutch sauce. The fish is very firm, and requires long boiling.

ESTIMATE OF THE STURGEON BY THE ANCIENTS.—By the ancients, the flesh of this fish was compared to the ambrosia of the immortals. The poet Martial passes a high eulogium upon it, and assigns it a place on the luxurious tables of the Palatine Mount. If we may credit a modern traveller in China, the people of that country generally entirely abstain from it, and the sovereign of the Celestial Empire confines it to his own kitchen, or dispenses it to only a few of his greatest favourites.

MATELOT OF TENCH.

334. INGREDIENTS.—½ pint of stock No. 105, ½ pint of port wine, 1 dozen button onions, a few mushrooms, a faggot of herbs, 2 blades of mace, 1 oz. of butter, 1 teaspoonful of minced parsley, thyme, 1 shalot, 2 anchovies, 1 teacupful of stock No. 105, flour, 1 dozen oysters, the juice of ½ lemon ; the number of tench, according to size.

Mode.—Scale and clean the tench, cut them into pieces, and lay them in a stewpan ; add the stock, wine, onions, mushrooms, herbs, and mace, and simmer gently for ½ hour. Put into another stewpan all the remaining ingredients but the oysters and lemon-juice, and boil slowly for 10 minutes, when add the strained liquor from the tench, and keep stirring it over the fire until somewhat reduced. Rub it through a sieve, pour it over the tench with the oysters, which must be previously scalded in their own liquor, squeeze in the lemon-juice, and serve. Garnish with croûtons.

Time.—¾ hour.

Seasonable from October to June.

THE TENCH.—This fish is generally found in foul and weedy waters, and in such places as are well supplied with rushes. They thrive best in standing waters, and are more numerous in pools and ponds than in rivers. Those taken in the latter, however, are preferable for the table. It does not often exceed four or five pounds in weight, and is in England esteemed as a delicious and wholesome food. As, however, they are sometimes found in waters where the mud is excessively fetid, their flavour, if cooked immediately on being caught, is often very unpleasant ; but if they are transferred into clear water, they soon recover from the obnoxious taint.

THE TENCH.

TENCH STEWED WITH WINE.

335. INGREDIENTS.—½ pint of stock No. 105, ½ pint of Madeira or

sherry, salt and pepper to taste, 1 bay-leaf, thickening of butter and flour.

Mode.—Clean and crimp the tench; carefully lay it in a stewpan with the stock, wine, salt and pepper, and bay-leaf; let it stew gently for ½ hour; then take it out, put it on a dish, and keep hot. Strain the liquor, and thicken it with butter and flour kneaded together, and stew for 5 minutes. If not perfectly smooth, squeeze it through a tammy, add a very little cayenne, and pour over the fish. Garnish with balls of veal forcemeat.

Time.—Rather more than ½ hour.

Seasonable from October to June.

A SINGULAR QUALITY IN THE TENCH.—It is said that the tench is possessed of such healing properties among the finny tribes, that even the voracious pike spares it on this account.

> The pike, fell tyrant of the liquid plain,
> With ravenous waste devours his fellow train;
> Yet howsoe'er with raging famine pined,
> The tench he spares, a medicinal kind;
> For when by wounds distress'd, or sore disease,
> He courts the salutary fish for ease;
> Close to his scales the kind physician glides,
> And sweats a healing balsam from his sides.

In our estimation, however, this self-denial in the pike may be attributed to a less poetical cause; namely, from the mud-loving disposition of the tench, it is enabled to keep itself so completely concealed at the bottom of its aqueous haunts, that it remains secure from the attacks of its predatory neighbour.

STEWED TROUT.

336. INGREDIENTS.—2 middling-sized trout, ½ onion cut in thin slices, a little parsley, 2 cloves, 1 blade of mace, 2 bay-leaves, a little thyme, salt and pepper to taste, 1 pint of medium stock No. 105, 1 glass of port wine, thickening of butter and flour.

Mode.—Wash the fish very clean, and wipe it quite dry. Lay it in a stewpan, with all the ingredients but the butter and flour, and simmer gently for ½ hour, or rather more, should not the fish be quite done. Take it out, strain the gravy, add the thickening, and stir it over a sharp fire for 5 minutes; pour it over the trout, and serve.

Time.—According to size, ½ hour or more.

Average cost.—Seldom bought.

Seasonable from May to September, and fatter from the middle to the end of August than at any other time.

Sufficient for 4 persons.

Trout may be served with anchovy or caper sauce, baked in buttered paper, or fried whole like smelts. Trout dressed à la Génévese is extremely delicate; for this proceed the same as with salmon, No. 307.

THE TROUT.—This fish, though esteemed by the moderns for its delicacy, was little regarded by the ancients. Although it abounded in the lakes of the Roman empire, it is generally mentioned by writers only on account of the beauty of its colours. About the end of September, they quit the deep water to which they had retired during the hot weather, for the purpose of spawning. This they always do on a gravelly bottom, or where gravel and sand are mixed among stones, towards the end or by the sides of streams. At this period they become black about the head and body, and become soft and unwholesome. They are never good when they are large with roe; but there are in all trout rivers some barren female fish, which continue good throughout the winter. In the common trout, the stomach is uncommonly strong and muscular, shell-fish forming a portion of the food of the animal; and it takes into its stomach gravel or small stones in order to assist in comminuting it.

THE TROUT.

BOILED TURBOT.

337. INGREDIENTS.—6 oz. of salt to each gallon of water.

Mode.—Choose a middling-sized turbot; for they are invariably the most valuable : if very large, the meat will be tough and thready. Three or four hours before dressing, soak the fish in salt and water to take off the slime; then thoroughly cleanse it, and with a knife make an incision down the middle of the back, to prevent the skin of the belly from cracking. Rub it over with lemon, and be particular not to cut off the fins. Lay the fish in a very clean turbot-kettle, with sufficient cold water to cover it, and salt in the above proportion. Let it gradually come to a boil, and skim very carefully; keep it gently simmering, and on no account let it boil fast, as the fish would have a very unsightly appearance. When the meat separates easily from the bone, it is done; then take it out, let it drain well, and dish it on a hot napkin. Rub a little lobster spawn through a sieve, sprinkle it over the fish, and garnish with tufts of parsley and cut lemon. Lobster or shrimp sauce, and plain melted butter, should be sent to table with it.

Time.—After the water boils, about ½ hour for a large turbot; middling size, about 20 minutes.

Average cost,—large turbot, from 10s. to 12s.; middling size, from 12s. to 15s.

Seasonable at any time.

Sufficient, 1 middling-sized turbot for 8 persons.

Note.—An amusing anecdote is related, by Miss Edgeworth, of a bishop, who, descending to his kitchen to superintend the dressing of a turbot, and discovering that his cook had stupidly cut off the fins, immediately commenced sewing them on again with his own episcopal fingers. This dignitary knew the value of a turbot's gelatinous appendages.

GARNISH FOR TURBOT OR OTHER LARGE FISH.

338. Take the crumb of a stale loaf, cut it into small pyramids with flat tops, and on the top of each pyramid, put rather more than a table-spoonful of white of egg beaten to a stiff froth. Over this, sprinkle finely-chopped parsley and fine raspings of a dark colour. Arrange these on the napkin round the fish, one green and one brown alternately.

To CHOOSE TURBOT.—See that it is thick, and of a yellowish white; for if of a bluish tint, it is not good.

THE TURBOT.—This is the most esteemed of all our flat fish. The northern parts of the English coast, and some places off the coast of Holland, produce turbot in great abundance, and in greater excellence than any other parts of the world. The London market is chiefly supplied by Dutch fishermen, who bring to it nearly 90,000 a year. The flesh is firm, white, rich, and gelatinous, and is the better for being kept a day or two previous to cooking it. In many parts of the country, turbot and halibut are indiscriminately sold for each other. They are, however, perfectly distinct; the upper parts of the former being marked with large, unequal, and obtuse tubercles, while those of the other are quite smooth, and covered with oblong soft

THE TURBOT.

scales, which firmly adhere to the body.

TURBOT-KETTLE.

FISH-KETTLES are made in an oblong form, and have two handles, with a movable bottom, pierced full of holes, on which the fish is laid, and on which it may be lifted from the water, by means of two long handles attached to each side of the movable bottom. This is to prevent the liability of breaking the fish, as it would necessarily be if it were cooked in a common saucepan. In the list of Messrs. Richard and John Slack (see 71), the price of two of these is set down at 10s. The turbot-kettle, as will be seen by our cut, is made differently from ordinary fish-kettles, it being less deep, whilst it is wider, and more pointed at the sides; thus exactly answering to the shape of the fish which it is intended should be boiled in it. It may be obtained from the same manufacturers, and its price is £1.

BAKED FILLETS OF TURBOT.

339. INGREDIENTS.—The remains of cold turbot, lobster sauce left from the preceding day, egg, and bread crumbs; cayenne and salt to taste; minced parsley, nutmeg, lemon-juice.

Mode.—After having cleared the fish from all skin and bone, divide it into square pieces of an equal size; brush them over with egg, sprinkle with bread crumbs mixed with a little minced parsley and seasoning. Lay the fillets in a baking-dish, with sufficient butter to baste with. Bake for ¼ hour, and do not forget to keep them well moistened with the butter. Put a little lemon-juice and grated nutmeg to the cold lobster sauce; make it hot, and pour over the fish, which must be well drained from the butter. Garnish with parsley and cut lemon.

Time.—Altogether, ½ hour.

Seasonable at any time.

Note.—Cold turbot thus warmed in the remains of lobster sauce will be found much nicer than putting the fish again in•water.

FILLETS OF TURBOT A L'ITALIENNE.

340. INGREDIENTS.—The remains of cold turbot, Italian sauce. (*See* Sauces.)

Mode.—Clear the fish carefully from the bone, and take away all skin, which gives an unpleasant flavour to the sauce. Make the sauce hot, lay in the fish to warm through, but do not let it boil. Garnish with croûtons.

Time.—5 minutes.

Seasonable all the year.

THE ANCIENT ROMANS' ESTIMATE OF TURBOT.—As this luxurious people compared soles to partridges, and sturgeons to peacocks, so they found a resemblance to the turbot in the pheasant. In the time of Domitian, it is said one was taken of such dimensions as to require, in the imperial kitchen, a new stove to be erected, and a new dish to be made for it, in order that it might be cooked and served whole : not even imperial Rome could furnish a stove or a dish large enough for the monstrous animal. Where it was caught, we are not aware; but the turbot of the Adriatic Sea held a high rank in the " Eternal City."

TURBOT A LA CREME.

341. INGREDIENTS.—The remains of cold turbot. For sauce, 2 oz. of butter, 4 tablespoonfuls of cream ; salt, cayenne, and pounded mace to taste.

Mode.—Clear away all skin. and bone from the flesh of the turbot, which should be done when it comes from table, as it causes less waste when trimmed hot. Cut the flesh into nice square pieces, as equally as possible ; put into a stewpan the butter, let it melt, and add the cream and seasoning; let it just simmer for one minute, but not boil. Lay in the fish to warm, and serve it garnished with croûtons or a paste border.

Time.—10 minutes.

Seasonable at any time.

Note.—The remains of cold salmon may be dressed in this way, and the above mixture may be served in a *vol-au-vent*.

TURBOT AU GRATIN.

342. INGREDIENTS.—Remains of cold turbot, béchamel (*see* Sauces), bread crumbs, butter.

Mode.—Cut the flesh of the turbot into small dice, carefully freeing it from all skin and bone. Put them into a stewpan, and moisten with 4 or 5 tablespoonfuls of béchamel. Let it get thoroughly hot, but do not allow it to boil. Spread the mixture on a dish, cover with finely-grated bread crumbs, and place small pieces of butter over the top. Brown it in the oven, or with a salamander.

Time.—Altogether, ½ hour.   *Seasonable* at any time.

BOILED WHITING.

343. INGREDIENTS.—¼ lb. of salt to each gallon of water.

Mode.—Cleanse the fish, but do not skin them; lay them in a fish-kettle, with sufficient cold water to cover them, and salt in the above proportion. Bring them gradually to a boil, and simmer gently for about 5 minutes, or rather more should the fish be very large. Dish them on a hot napkin, and garnish with tufts of parsley. Serve with anchovy or caper sauce, and plain melted butter.

Time.—After the water boils, 5 minutes.

Average cost for small whitings, 4*d.* each.

Seasonable all the year, but best from October to March.

Sufficient, 1 small whiting for each person.

TO CHOOSE WHITING.—Choose for the firmness of its flesh and the silvery hue of its appearance.

THE WHITING.

THE WHITING.—This fish forms a light, tender, and delicate food, easy of digestion. It appears in our seas in the spring, within three miles of the shores, where it arrives in large shoals to deposit its spawn. It is caught by line, and is usually between ten and twelve inches long, and seldom exceeding a pound and a half in weight. On the edge of the Dogger Bank, however, it has been caught so heavy as to weigh from three to seven or eight pounds. When less than six inches long, it is not allowed to be caught.

BROILED WHITING.

344. INGREDIENTS.—Salt and water, flour.

Mode.—Wash the whiting in salt and water, wipe them thoroughly, and let them remain in the cloth to absorb all moisture. Flour them well, and broil over a very clear fire. Serve with *maître d'hôtel* sauce, or plain melted butter (*see* Sauces). Be careful to preserve the liver, as by some it is considered very delicate.

Time.—5 minutes for a small whiting.   *Average cost,* 4*d.* each.

Seasonable all the year, but best from October to March.

Sufficient, 1 small whiting for each person.

BUCKHORN.—Whitings caught in Cornwall are salted and dried, and in winter taken to the markets, and sold under the singular name of "Buckhorn."

FRIED WHITING.

345. INGREDIENTS.—Egg and bread crumbs, a little flour, hot lard or clarified dripping.

Mode.—Take off the skin, clean, and thoroughly wipe the fish free from all moisture, as this is most essential, in order that the egg and bread crumbs may properly adhere. Fasten the tail in the mouth by means of a small skewer, brush the fish over with egg, dredge with a little flour, and cover with bread crumbs. Fry them in hot lard or clarified dripping of a nice colour, and serve them on a napkin, garnished with fried parsley. Send them to table with shrimp sauce and plain melted butter.

Time.—About 6 minutes. *Average cost*, 4*d.* each.

Seasonable all the year, but best from October to March.

Sufficient, 1 small whiting for each person.

Note.—Large whitings may be filleted, rolled, and served as fried filleted soles. Small fried whitings are frequently used for garnishing large boiled fish, such as turbot, cod, &c.

WHITING AU GRATIN, or BAKED WHITING.

346. INGREDIENTS.—4 whiting, butter, 1 tablespoonful of minced parsley, a few chopped mushrooms when obtainable; pepper, salt, and grated nutmeg to taste; butter, 2 glasses of sherry or Madeira, bread crumbs.

Mode.—Grease the bottom of a baking-dish with butter, and over it, strew some minced parsley and mushrooms. Scale, empty, and wash the whitings, and wipe them thoroughly dry, carefully preserving the livers. Lay them in the dish, sprinkle them with bread crumbs and seasoning, adding a little grated nutmeg, and also a little more minced parsley and mushrooms. Place small pieces of butter over the whiting, moisten with the wine, and bake for 20 minutes in a hot oven. If there should be too much sauce, reduce it by boiling over a sharp fire for a few minutes, and pour under the fish. Serve with a cut lemon, and no other sauce.

Time.—20 minutes. *Average cost*, 4*d.* each.

Seasonable all the year, but best from October to March.

Sufficient.—This quantity for 4 or 5 persons.

WHITING AUX FINES HERBES.

347. INGREDIENTS.—1 bunch of sweet herbs chopped very fine; butter.

Mode.—Clean and skin the fish, fasten the tails in the mouths, and lay them in a baking-dish. Mince the herbs very fine, strew them over the fish, and place small pieces of butter over; cover with another dish, and let them simmer in a Dutch oven for ¼ hour or 20 minutes. Turn the fish once or twice, and serve with the sauce poured over.

Time.—¼ hour or 20 minutes. *Average cost, 4d.* each.

Seasonable all the year, but best from October to March.

Sufficient, 1 small whiting for each person.

THE WHITING POUT, AND POLLACK.—About the mouth of the Thames, and generally all round the English coasts, as well as in the northern seas, the pout is plentiful. It bears a striking resemblance to the whiting, and is esteemed as an excellent fish.— The *pollack* is also taken all round our coasts, and likewise bears a striking resemblance to the whiting; indeed, it is sometimes mistaken by the inexperienced for that fish; its flesh being considered by many equally delicate.

TO DRESS WHITEBAIT.

348. INGREDIENTS.—A little flour, hot lard, seasoning of salt.

Mode.—This fish should be put into iced water as soon as bought, unless they are cooked immediately. Drain them from the water in a colander, and have ready a nice clean dry cloth, over which put 2 good handfuls of flour. Toss in the whitebait, shake them lightly in the cloth, and put them in a wicker sieve to take away the superfluous flour. Throw them into a pan of boiling lard, very few at a time, and let them fry till of a whitey-brown colour. Directly they are done, they must be taken out, and laid before the fire for a minute or two on a sieve reversed, covered with blotting-paper to absorb the fat. Dish them on a hot napkin, arrange the fish very high in the centre, and sprinkle a little salt over the whole.

Time.—3 minutes.

Seasonable from April to August.

WHITEBAIT.

WHITEBAIT. — This highly - esteemed little fish appears in innumerable multitudes in the river Thames, near Greenwich and Blackwall, during the month of July, when it forms a tempting dish to vast numbers of Londoners, who flock to the various taverns of these places, in order to gratify their appetites. The fish has been supposed be the fry of the shad, the sprat, the smelt, or the bleak. Mr. Yarrell, however, maintains that it is a species in itself, distinct from every other fish. When fried with flour, it is esteemed a great delicacy. The ministers of the Crown have had a custom, for many years, of having a "whitebait dinner" just before the close of the session. It is invariably the precursor of the prorogation of Parliament, and the repast is provided by the proprietor of the "Trafalgar," Greenwich.

FISH PIE, WITH TENCH AND EELS.

349. INGREDIENTS.—2 tench, 2 eels, 2 onions, a faggot of herbs, 4 blades of mace, 3 anchovies, 1 pint of water, pepper and salt to taste,

1 teaspoonful of chopped parsley, the yolks of 6 hard-boiled eggs, puff paste.

Mode.—Clean and bone the tench, skin and bone the eels, and cut them into pieces 2 inches long, and leave the sides of the tench whole. Put the bones into a stewpan with the onions, herbs, mace, anchovies, water, and seasoning, and let them simmer gently for 1 hour. Strain it off, put it to cool, and skim off all the fat. Lay the tench and eels in a pie-dish, and between each layer put seasoning, chopped parsley, and hard-boiled eggs; pour in part of the strained liquor, cover in with puff paste, and bake for ½ hour or rather more. The oven should be rather quick, and when done, heat the remainder of the liquor, which pour into the pie.

Time.—½ hour to bake, or rather more if the oven is slow.

FISH SCALLOP.

I.

350. INGREDIENTS.—Remains of cold fish of any sort, ½ pint of cream, ½ tablespoonful of anchovy sauce, ½ teaspoonful of made mustard, ditto of walnut ketchup, pepper and salt to taste (the above quantities are for ½ lb. of fish when picked); bread crumbs.

Mode.—Put all the ingredients into a stewpan, carefully picking the fish from the bones; set it on the fire, let it remain till nearly hot, occasionally stir the contents, but do not allow it to boil. When done, put the fish into a deep dish or scallop shell, with a good quantity of bread crumbs; place small pieces of butter on the top, set in a Dutch oven before the fire to brown, or use a salamander.

Time.—¼ hour. *Average cost*, exclusive of the cold fish, 10*d.*

II.

351. INGREDIENTS.—Any cold fish, 1 egg, milk, 1 large blade of pounded mace, 1 tablespoonful of flour, 1 teaspoonful of anchovy sauce, pepper and salt to taste, bread crumbs, butter.

Mode.—Pick the fish carefully from the bones, and moisten with milk and the egg; add the other ingredients, and place in a deep dish or scallop shells; cover with bread crumbs, butter the top, and brown before the fire; when quite hot, serve.

Time.—20 minutes. *Average cost*, exclusive of the cold fish, 4*d.*

WATER SOUCHY.

352. Perch, tench, soles, eels, and flounders are considered the best fish for this dish. For the souchy, put some water into a stewpan with

a bunch of chopped parsley, some roots, and sufficient salt to make it brackish.   Let these simmer for 1 hour, and then stew the fish in this water.   When they are done, take them out to drain, have ready some finely-chopped parsley, and a few roots cut into slices of about one inch thick and an inch in length.   Put the fish in a tureen or deep dish, strain the liquor over them, and add the minced parsley and roots.   Serve with brown bread and butter.

353. SUPPLY OF FISH TO THE LONDON MARKET.—From Mr. Mayhew's work on "London Labour and the London Poor," and other sources, we are enabled to give the following table of the total annual supply of fish to the London market :—

Description of Fish.	Number of Fish.	Weight of Fish in lbs.
WET FISH.		
Salmon and Salmon-Trout (29,000 boxes, 14 fish per box)	406,000 ...	3,480,000
Turbot, from 2 to 16 lbs. each	800,000 ...	5,600,000
Live Cod, averaging 10 lbs. each	400,000 ...	4,000,000
Soles, averaging ¼ lb. each	97,520,000 ...	26,880,000
Brill and Mullet, averaging 3 lbs. each	1,220,000 ...	3,366,000
Whiting, averaging 6 oz. each	17,920,000 ...	6,720,000
Haddock, averaging 2 lbs. each	2,470,000 ...	4,940,000
Plaice, averaging 1 lb. each	33,600,000 ...	33,600,000
Mackerel, averaging 1 lb. each	23,520,000 ...	23,520,000
Fresh herrings (250,000 barrels, 700 fish per barrel)	175,000,000 ...	42,000,000
Ditto, in bulk	1,050,000,000 ...	252,000,000
Sprats	— ...	4,000,000
Eels (from Holland principally) England & Ireland	9,797,760 ...	1,632,960
Flounders	259,200 ...	43,200
Dabs	270,000 ...	48,750
DRY FISH.		
Barrelled Cod (15,000 barrels, 40 fish per barrel) ...	750,000 ...	4,200,000
Dried Salt Cod, 5 lbs. each	1,600,000 ...	8,000,000
Smoked Haddock (65,000 barrels, 300 fish per barrel)	19,500,000 ...	10,920,000
Bloaters, 265,000 baskets (150 fish per basket) ...	147,000,000 ...	10,600,000
Red Herrings, 100,000 barrels (500 fish per barrel)	50,000,000 ...	14,000,000
Dried Sprats, 9,600 large bundles (30 fish per bundle)	288,000 ..	9,600
SHELL FISH.		
Oysters	495,896,000	
Lobsters, averaging 1 lb. each	1,200,000 ...	1,200,000
Crabs, averaging 1 lb. each	600,000 ...	600,000
Shrimps, 324 to a pint	498,428,648	
Whelks, 227 to a half-bushel	4,943,200	
Mussels, 1,000 to ditto	50,400,000	
Cockles, 2,000 to ditto	67,392,000	
Periwinkles, 4,000 to ditto	304,000,000	

The whole of the above may be, in round numbers, reckoned to amount to the enormous number of 3,000,000,000 fish, with a weight of 300,000 tons.

ADDENDUM AND ANECDOTE.

IT will be seen, from the number and variety of the recipes which we have been enabled to give under the head of FISH, that there exists in the salt ocean, and fresh-water rivers, an abundance of aliment, which the present state of gastronomic art enables the cook to introduce to the table in the most agreeable forms, and oftentimes at a very moderate cost.

Less nutritious as a food than the flesh of animals, more succulent than vegetables, fish may be termed a middle dish, suited to all temperaments and constitutions; and one which those who are recovering from illness may partake of with safety and advantage.

As to which is the best fish, there has been much discussion. The old Latin proverb, however, *de gustibus non disputandum*, and the more modern Spanish one, *sobre los gustos no hai disputa*, declare, with equal force, that where *taste* is concerned, no decision can be arrived at. Each person's palate may be differently affected—pleased or displeased; and there is no standard by which to judge why a red mullet, a sole, or a turbot, should be better or worse than a salmon, trout, pike, or a tiny tench.

Fish, as we have explained, is less nourishing than meat; for it is lighter in weight, size for size, and contains no ozmazome (*see* No. 100). Shell-fish, oysters particularly, furnish but little nutriment; and this is the reason why so many of the latter can be eaten without injury to the system.

In Brillat Savarin's* clever and amusing volume, "The Physiology of Taste," he says, that towards the end of the eighteenth century it was a most common thing for a well-arranged entertainment in Paris to commence with oysters, and that many guests were not contented without swallowing twelve dozen. Being anxious to know the weight of this advanced-guard, he ascertained that a dozen oysters, fluid included, weighed 4 ounces,—thus, the twelve dozen would weigh about 3 lbs.; and there can be no doubt, that the same persons who made no worse a dinner on account of having partaken of the oysters, would have been completely satisfied if they had eaten the same weight of chicken or mutton. An anecdote, perfectly well authenticated, is narrated of a French gentleman (M. Laperte), residing at Versailles, who was extravagantly fond of oysters, declaring he never had enough. Savarin resolved to procure him the satisfaction, and gave him an invitation to dinner, which was duly accepted. The guest arrived, and his host kept company with him in swallowing the delicious bivalves up to the tenth dozen, when, exhausted,

---

* Brillat Savarin was a French lawyer and judge of considerable eminence and great talents, and wrote, under the above title, a book on gastronomy, full of instructive information, enlivened with a fund of pleasantly-told anecdote.

he gave up, and let M. Laperte go on alone. This gentleman managed to eat thirty-two dozen within an hour, and would doubtless have got through more, but the person who opened them is described as not being very skilful. In the interim Savarin was idle, and at length, tired with his painful state of inaction, he said to Laperte, whilst the latter was still in full career, "Mon cher, you will not eat as many oysters to-day as you meant; let us dine." They dined, and the insatiable oyster-eater acted at the repast as if he had fasted for a week.

FISH CARVING.

GENERAL DIRECTIONS FOR CARVING FISH.

IN CARVING FISH, care should be taken to help it in perfect flakes, as, if these are broken, the beauty of the fish is lost. The carver should be acquainted, too, with the choicest parts and morsels; and to give each guest an equal share of these *titbits* should be his maxim. Steel knives and forks should on no account be used in helping fish, as these are liable to impart to it a very disagreeable flavour. Where silver fish-carvers are considered too dear to be bought, good electro-plated ones answer very well, and are inexpensive. The prices set down for them by Messrs. Slack, of the Strand, are from a guinea upwards.

COD'S HEAD AND SHOULDERS.

(For recipe, see No. 232.)

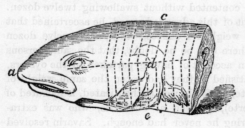

First run the knife along the centre of the side of the fish, namely, from *d* to *b*, down to the bone; then carve it in unbroken slices downwards from *d* to *e*, or upwards from *d* to *c*, as shown in the engraving. The carver should ask the guests if they would like a portion of the roe and liver.

Note.—Of this fish, the parts about the backbone and shoulders are the firmest, and most esteemed by connoisseurs. The sound, which lines the fish beneath the backbone, is considered a delicacy, as are also the gelatinous parts about the head and neck.

SALMON.

(For recipe, see No. 301 ; and for mode of dressing, Coloured Plate B.)

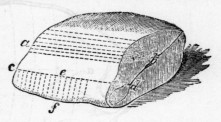

First run the knife quite down to the bone, along the side of the fish, from *a* to *b*, and also from *c* to *d*. Then help the thick part lengthwise, that is, in the direction of the lines from *a* to *b*; and the thin part breadthwise, that is, in the direction of the lines from *e* to *f*, as shown in the engraving. A slice of the thick part should always be accompanied by a smaller piece of the thin from the belly, where lies the fat of the fish.

Note.—Many persons, in carving salmon, make the mistake of slicing the thick part of this fish in the opposite direction to that we have stated ; and thus, by the breaking of the flakes, the beauty of its appearance is destroyed.

BOILED OR FRIED SOLE.

(For recipes, see Nos. 321 and 327.)

The usual way of helping this fish is to cut it quite through, bone and all, distributing it in nice and not too large pieces. A moderately-sized sole will be sufficient for three slices ; namely, the head, middle, and tail. The guests should be asked which of these they prefer. A small one will only give two slices. If the sole is very large, the upper side may be raised from the bone, and then divided into pieces ; and the under side afterwards served in the same way.

In helping FILLETED SOLES, one fillet is given to each person. (For mode of serving, see Coloured Plate A.)

TURBOT.

(For recipe, see No. 337 ; and for mode of serving, Coloured Plate E.)

First run the fish-slice down the thickest part of the fish, quite through to the bone, from *a* to *b*, and then cut handsome and regular slices in the direction of the lines downwards, from *c* to *e*, and upwards from *c* to *d*, as shown in the engraving. When the carver has removed all the meat from the upper side of the fish, the backbone should be raised, put on one side of the dish, and the under side helped as the upper.

A Brill and John Dory are carved in the same manner as a Turbot.

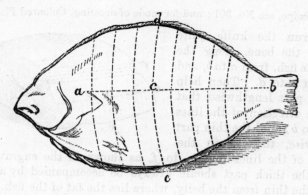

Note.—The thick parts of the middle of the back are the best slices in a turbot; and the rich gelatinous skin covering the fish, as well as a little of the thick part of the fins, are dainty morsels, and should be placed on each plate.

WHITING, &c.

Whiting, pike, haddock, and other fish, when of a sufficiently large size, may be carved in the same manner as salmon. When small, they may be cut through, bone and all, and helped in nice pieces, a middling-sized whiting serving for two slices.

Note.—The THICK part of the EEL is reckoned the best; and this holds good of all flat fish.

The TAIL of the LOBSTER is the prime part, and next to that the CLAWS.

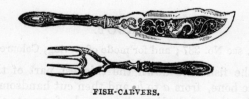

FISH-CARVERS.

SAUCES, PICKLES, GRAVIES, AND FORCEMEATS.

CHAPTER IX.

GENERAL REMARKS.

354. AN ANECDOTE IS TOLD of the prince de Soubise, who, intending to give an entertainment, asked for the bill of fare. His *chef* came, presenting a list adorned with vignettes, and the first article of which, that met the prince's eye, was "fifty hams." "Bertrand," said the prince, "I think you must be extravagant; Fifty hams ! do you intend to feast my whole regiment?" "No, Prince, there will be but one on the table, and the surplus I need for my Espagnole, blondes, garnitures, &c." "Bertrand, you are robbing me : this item will not do." "Monseigneur," said the *artiste*, "you do not appreciate me. Give me the order, and I will put those fifty hams in a crystal flask no longer than my thumb." The prince smiled, and the hams were passed. This was all very well for the prince de Soubise ; but as we do not write for princes and nobles alone, but that our British sisters may make the best dishes out of the least expensive ingredients, we will also pass the hams, and give a few general directions concerning Sauces, &c.

355. THE PREPARATION AND APPEARANCE OF SAUCES AND GRAVIES are of the highest consequence, and in nothing does the talent and taste of the cook more display itself. Their special adaptability to the various viands they are to accompany cannot be too much studied, in order that they may harmonize and blend with them as perfectly, so to speak, as does a pianoforte accompaniment with the voice of the singer.

356. THE GENERAL BASIS OF MOST GRAVIES and some sauces is the same stock as that used for soups (*see* Nos. 104, 105, 106, and 107); and, by the

N

employment of these, with, perhaps, an additional slice of ham, a little spice, a few herbs, and a slight flavouring from some cold sauce or ketchup, very nice gravies may be made for a very small expenditure. A milt (either of a bullock or sheep), the shank-end of mutton that has already been dressed, and the necks and feet of poultry, may all be advantageously used for gravy, where much is not required.   It may, then, be established as a rule, that there exists no necessity for good gravies to be expensive, and that there is no occasion, as many would have the world believe, to buy ever so many pounds of fresh meat, in order to furnish an ever so little quantity of gravy.

357. BROWN SAUCES, generally speaking, should scarcely be so thick as white sauces ; and it is well to bear in mind, that all those which are intended to mask the various dishes of poultry or meat, should be of a sufficient consistency to slightly adhere to the fowls or joints over which they are poured.   For browning and thickening sauces, &c., browned flour may be properly employed.

358. SAUCES SHOULD POSSESS A DECIDED CHARACTER ; and whether sharp or sweet, savoury or plain, they should carry out their names in a distinct manner, although, of course, not so much flavoured as to make them too piquant on the one hand, or too mawkish on the other.

359. GRAVIES AND SAUCES SHOULD BE SENT TO TABLE VERY HOT ; and there is all the more necessity for the cook to see to this point, as, from their being usually served in small quantities, they are more liable to cool quickly than if they were in a larger body.   Those sauces, of which cream or eggs form a component part, should be well stirred, as soon as these ingredients are added to them, and must never be allowed to boil ; as, in that case, they would instantly curdle.

360. ALTHOUGH PICKLES MAY BE PURCHASED at shops at as low a rate as they can usually be made for at home, or perhaps even for less, yet we would advise all housewives, who have sufficient time and convenience, to prepare their own.   The only general rules, perhaps, worth stating here,—as in the recipes all necessary details will be explained, are, that the vegetables and fruits used should be sound, and not over ripe, and that the very best vinegar should be employed.

361. FOR FORCEMEATS, SPECIAL ATTENTION IS NECESSARY.   The points which cooks should, in this branch of cookery, more particularly observe, are the thorough chopping of the suet, the complete mincing of the herbs, the careful grating of the bread-crumbs, and the perfect mixing of the whole. These are the three principal ingredients of forcemeats, and they can scarcely be cut too small, as nothing like a lump or fibre should be anywhere per-ceptible.   To conclude, the flavour of no one spice or herb should be per-mitted to predominate.

RECEIPES

❖

CHAPTER X.

Sauces, Pickles, Gravies, and Forcemeats.

ANCHOVY SAUCE FOR FISH.

362. INGREDIENTS.—4 anchovies, 1 oz. of butter, ½ pint of melted butter, cayenne to taste.

Mode.—Bone the anchovies, and pound them in a mortar to a paste, with 1 oz. of butter. Make the melted butter hot, stir in the pounded anchovies and cayenne; simmer for 3 or 4 minutes; and if liked, add a squeeze of lemon-juice. A more general and expeditious way of making this sauce is to stir in 1½ tablespoonfuls of anchovy essence to ½ pint of melted butter, and to add seasoning to taste. Boil the whole up for 1 minute, and serve hot.

Time.—5 minutes. *Average cost,* 5d. for ½ pint.

Sufficient, this quantity, for a brill, small turbot, 3 or 4 soles, &c.

ANCHOVY BUTTER (*see* No. 227).

CAYENNE.—This is the most acrid and stimulating spice with which we are acquainted. It is a powder prepared from several varieties of the capsicum annual East-India plants, of which there are three so far naturalized in this country as to be able to grow in the open air : these are the Guinea, the Cherry, and the Bell pepper. All the pods of these are extremely pungent to the taste, and in the green state are used by us as a pickle. When ripe, they are ground into cayenne pepper, and sold as a condiment. The best of this, however, is made in the West Indies, from what is called the *Bird* pepper, on account of hens and turkeys being extremely partial to it. It is imported ready for use. Of the capsicum species of plants there are five ; but the principal are,—1. *Capsicum annuum,* the common long-podded capsicum, which is cultivated in our gardens, and of which there are two varieties, one with red, and another with yellow fruit. 2. *Capsicum baccatum,* or bird pepper, which rises with a shrubby stalk four or five feet high, with its berries growing at the division of the branches : this is small, oval-shaped, and of a bright-red colour, from which, as we have said, the best cayenne is made. 3. *Capsicum grossum,* the bell-pepper : the fruit of this is red, and is the only kind fit for pickling.

THE CAPSICUM.

APPLE SAUCE FOR GEESE, PORK, &c.

363. INGREDIENTS.—6 good-sized apples, sifted sugar to taste, a piece of butter the size of a walnut, water.

Mode.—Pare, core, and quarter the apples, and throw them into cold water to preserve their whiteness. Put them in a saucepan, with sufficient water to moisten them, and boil till soft enough to pulp. Beat them up, adding sugar to taste, and a small piece of butter. This quantity is sufficient for a good-sized tureen.

Time.—According to the apples, about ¾ hour. *Average cost,* 4d.

Sufficient, this quantity, for a goose or couple of ducks.

BROWN APPLE SAUCE.

364. INGREDIENTS.—6 good-sized apples, ½ pint of brown gravy, cayenne to taste.

Mode. Put the gravy in a stewpan, and add the apples, after having pared, cored, and quartered them. Let them simmer gently till tender; beat them to a pulp, and season with cayenne. This sauce is preferred by many to the preceding.

Time.—According to the apples, about ¾ hour. *Average cost,* 6d.

ASPARAGUS SAUCE.

365. INGREDIENTS.—1 bunch of green asparagus, salt, 1 oz. of fresh butter, 1 small bunch of parsley, 3 or 4 green onions, 1 large lump of sugar, 4 tablespoonfuls of sauce tournée.

Mode.—Break the asparagus in the tender part, wash well, and put them into boiling salt and water to render them green. When they are tender, take them out, and put them into cold water; drain them on a cloth till all moisture is absorbed from them. Put the butter in a stewpan, with the parsley and onions; lay in the asparagus, and fry the whole over a sharp fire for 5 minutes. Add salt, the sugar and sauce tournée, and simmer for another 5 minutes. Rub all through a tammy, and if not a very good colour, use a little spinach green. This sauce should be rather sweet.

Time.—Altogether 40 minutes.

Average cost for this quantity, 1s. 4d.

ASPIC, or ORNAMENTAL SAVOURY JELLY.

366. INGREDIENTS.—4 lbs. of knuckle of veal, 1 cow-heel, 3 or 4 slices of ham, any poultry trimmings, 2 carrots, 1 onion, 1 faggot of

savoury herbs, 1 glass of sherry, 3 quarts of water; seasoning to taste of salt and whole white pepper; 3 eggs.

Mode.—Lay the ham on the bottom of a stewpan, cut up the veal and cow-heel into small pieces, and lay them on the ham; add the poultry trimmings, vegetables, herbs, sherry, and water, and let the whole simmer very gently for 4 hours, carefully taking away all scum that may rise to the surface; strain through a fine sieve, and pour into an earthen pan to get cold. Have ready a clean stewpan, put in the jelly, and be particular to leave the sediment behind, or it will not be clear. Add the whites of 3 eggs, with salt and pepper, to clarify; keep stirring over the fire, till the whole becomes very white; then draw it to the side, and let it stand till clear. When this is the case, strain it through a cloth or jelly-bag, and use it for moulding poultry, &c. (*See* Explanation of French Terms, page 44.) Tarragon vinegar may be added to give an additional flavour.

Time.—Altogether 4½ hours. *Average cost* for this quantity, 4s.

WHITE PEPPER.—This is the produce of the same plant as that which produces the black pepper, from which it is manufactured by steeping this in lime and water, and rubbing it between the hands till the coats come off. The best berries only will bear this operation; hence the superior qualities of white pepper fetch a higher price than those of the other. It is less acrid than the black, and is much prized among the Chinese. It is sometimes adulterated with rice-flour, as the black is with burnt bread. The berries of the pepper-plant grow in spikes of from twenty to thirty, and are, when ripe, of a bright-red colour. After being gathered, which is done when they are green, they are spread out in the sun, where they dry and become black and shrivelled, when they are ready for being prepared for the market.

BECHAMEL, or FRENCH WHITE SAUCE.

367. INGREDIENTS.—1 small bunch of parsley, 2 cloves, ½ bay-leaf, 1 small faggot of savoury herbs, salt to taste; 3 or 4 mushrooms, when obtainable; 2 pints of white stock, 1 pint of cream, 1 tablespoonful of arrowroot.

Mode.—Put the stock into a stewpan, with the parsley, cloves, bay-leaf, herbs, and mushrooms; add a seasoning of salt, but no pepper, as that would give the sauce a dusty appearance, and should be avoided. When it has boiled long enough to extract the flavour of the herbs, &c., strain it, and boil it up quickly again, until it is nearly half-reduced. Now mix the arrowroot smoothly with the cream, and let it simmer very gently for 5 minutes over a slow fire; pour to it the reduced stock, and continue to simmer slowly for 10 minutes, if the sauce be thick. If, on the contrary, it be too thin, it must be stirred over a sharp fire till it thickens. This is the foundation of many kinds of sauces, especially white sauces. Always make it thick, as you can easily thin it with cream, milk, or white stock.

Time.—Altogether, 2 hours.   *Average cost*, 1*s.* per pint.

THE CLOVE.—The clove-tree is a native of the Molucca Islands, particularly Amboyna, and attains the height of a laurel-tree, and no verdure is ever seen under it. From the extremities of the branches quantities of flowers grow, first white; then they become green, and next red and hard, when they have arrived at their clove state. When they become dry, they assume a yellowish hue, which subsequently changes into a dark brown. As an aromatic, the clove is highly stimulating, and yields an abundance of oil. There are several varieties of the clove; the best is called the *royal clove*, which is scarce, and which is blacker and smaller than the other kinds. It is a curious fact, that the flowers, when fully developed, are quite inodorous, and that the real fruit is not in the least aromatic. The form is that of a nail, having a globular head, formed of the four petals of the corolla, and four leaves of the calyx not expanded, with a nearly cylindrical germen, scarcely an inch in length, situate below.

THE CLOVE.

BECHAMEL MAIGRE, or WITHOUT MEAT.

368. INGREDIENTS.—2 onions, 1 blade of mace, mushroom trimmings, a small bunch of parsley, 1 oz. of butter, flour, ½ pint of water, 1 pint of milk, salt, the juice of ½ lemon, 2 eggs.

Mode.—Put in a stewpan the milk, and ½ pint of water, with the onions, mace, mushrooms, parsley, and salt. Let these simmer gently for 20 minutes. In the mean time, rub on a plate 1 oz. of flour and butter; put it to the liquor, and stir it well till it boils up; then place it by the side of the fire, and continue stirring until it is perfectly smooth. Now strain it through a sieve into a basin, after which put it back in the stewpan, and add the lemon-juice. Beat up the yolks of the eggs with about 4 dessertspoonfuls of milk; strain this to the sauce, keep stirring it over the fire, but do not let it boil, lest it curdle.

Time.—Altogether, ¾ hour.   *Average cost*, 5*d.* per pint.

This is a good sauce to pour over boiled fowls when they are a bad colour.

PICKLED BEETROOT.

369. INGREDIENTS.—Sufficient vinegar to cover the beets, 2 oz. of whole pepper, 2 oz. of allspice to each gallon of vinegar.

Mode.—Wash the beets free from dirt, and be very careful not to prick the outside skin, or they would lose their beautiful colour. Put them into boiling water, let them simmer gently, and when about three parts done, which will be in 1½ hour, take them out and let them cool. Boil the vinegar with pepper and allspice, in the above proportion, for ten minutes, and when cold, pour it on the beets, which must be peeled and cut into slices about ½ inch thick.

Cover with bladder to exclude the air, and in a week they will be fit for use.

Average cost, 3s. per gallon.

BLACK PEPPER.—This well-known aromatic spice is the fruit of a species of climbing vine, and is a native of the East Indies, and is extensively cultivated in Malabar and the eastern islands of Borneo, Sumatra, and Java, and others in the same latitude. It was formerly confined to these countries, but it has now been introduced to Cayenne. It is generally employed as a condiment; but it should never be forgotten, that, even in small quantities, it produces detrimental effects on inflammatory constitutions. Dr. Paris, in his work on Diet, says, "Foreign spices were not intended by Nature for the inhabitants of temperate climes; they are heating, and highly stimulant. I am, however, not anxious to give more weight to this objection than it deserves. Man is no longer the child of Nature, nor the passive inhabitant of any particular region. He ranges over every part of the globe, and elicits nourishment from the productions of every climate. Nature is very kind in favouring the growth of those productions which are most likely to answer our local wants. Those climates, for instance, which engender endemic diseases, are, in general, congenial to the growth of plants that operate as antidotes to them. But if we go to the East for tea, there is no reason why we should not go to the West for sugar. The dyspeptic invalid, however, should be cautious in their use; they may afford temporary benefit, at the expense of permanent mischief. It has been well said,

BLACK PEPPER.

that the best quality of spices is to stimulate the appetite, and their worst to destroy, by insensible degrees, the tone of the stomach. The intrinsic goodness of meats should always be suspected when they require spicy seasonings to compensate for their natural want of sapidity." The quality of pepper is known by rubbing it between the hands: that which withstands this operation is good, that which is reduced to powder by it is bad. The quantity of pepper imported into Europe is very great.

BENTON SAUCE (to serve with Hot or Cold Roast Beef).

370. INGREDIENTS.—1 tablespoonful of scraped horseradish, 1 teaspoonful of made mustard, 1 teaspoonful of pounded sugar, 4 tablespoonfuls of vinegar.

Mode.—Grate or scrape the horseradish very fine, and mix it with the other ingredients, which must be all well blended together; serve in a tureen. With cold meat, this sauce is a very good substitute for pickles.

Average cost for this quantity, 2d.

BREAD SAUCE (to serve with Roast Turkey, Fowl, Game, &c.).

I.

371. INGREDIENTS.—1 pint of milk, ¾ lb. of the crumb of a stale loaf, 1 onion; pounded mace, cayenne, and salt to taste; 1 oz. of butter.

Mode.—Peel and quarter the onion, and simmer it in the milk till perfectly tender. Break the bread, which should be stale, into small pieces, carefully picking out any hard outside pieces; put it in a very clean saucepan, strain the milk over it, cover it up, and let it remain for an hour to soak. Now beat it up with a fork very smoothly, add a seasoning of pounded mace, cayenne, and salt, with 1 oz. of

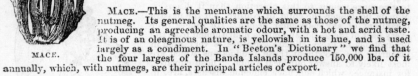

butter; give the whole one boil, and serve. To enrich this sauce, a small quantity of cream may be added just before sending it to table.

Time.—Altogether, 1¾ hour.

Average cost for this quantity, 4*d.*

Sufficient to serve with a turkey, pair of fowls, or brace of partridges.

MACE.—This is the membrane which surrounds the shell of the nutmeg. Its general qualities are the same as those of the nutmeg, producing an agreeable aromatic odour, with a hot and acrid taste. It is of an oleaginous nature, is yellowish in its hue, and is used largely as a condiment. In "Beeton's Dictionary" we find that the four largest of the Banda Islands produce 150,000 lbs. of it annually, which, with nutmegs, are their principal articles of export.

MACE.

II.

372. INGREDIENTS.—Giblets of poultry, ¾ lb. of the crumb of a stale loaf, 1 onion, 12 whole peppers, 1 blade of mace, salt to taste, 2 tablespoonfuls of cream or melted butter, 1 pint of water.

Mode.—Put the giblets, with the head, neck, legs, &c., into a stewpan; add the onion, pepper, mace, salt, and rather more than 1 pint of water. Let this simmer for an hour, when strain the liquor over the bread, which should be previously grated or broken into small pieces. Cover up the saucepan, and leave it for an hour by the side of the fire; then beat the sauce up with a fork until no lumps remain, and the whole is nice and smooth. Let it boil for 3 or 4 minutes; keep stirring it until it is rather thick; when add 3 tablespoonfuls of good melted butter or cream, and serve very hot.

Time.—2¼ hours. *Average cost,* 6*d.*

BROWNING FOR GRAVIES AND SAUCES.

373. The browning for soups (*see* No. 108) answers equally well for sauces and gravies, when it is absolutely necessary to colour them in this manner; but where they can be made to look brown by using ketchup, wine, browned flour, tomatoes, or any colour sauce, it is far preferable. As, however, in cooking, so much depends on appearance, perhaps it would be as well for the inexperienced cook to use the artificial means (No. 108). When no browning is at hand, and you wish to heighten the colour of your gravy, dissolve a lump of sugar in an iron spoon over a sharp fire; when it is in a liquid state, drop it into the sauce or gravy quite hot. Care, however, must be taken not to put in too much, as it would impart a very disagreeable flavour.

BEURRE NOIR, or BROWNED BUTTER (a French Sauce).

374. INGREDIENTS.—¼ lb. of butter, 1 tablespoonful of minced parsley, 3 tablespoonfuls of vinegar, salt and pepper to taste.

Mode.—Put the butter into a fryingpan over a nice clear fire, and when it smokes, throw in the parsley, and add the vinegar and seasoning. Let the whole simmer for a minute or two, when it is ready to serve. This is a very good sauce for skate.

Time.—¼ hour.

CLARIFIED BUTTER.

375. Put the butter in a basin before the fire, and when it melts, stir it round once or twice, and let it settle. Do not strain it unless absolutely necessary, as it causes so much waste. Pour it gently off into a clean dry jar, carefully leaving all sediment behind. Let it cool, and carefully exclude the air by means of a bladder, or piece of wash-leather, tied over. If the butter is salt, it may be washed before melting, when it is to be used for sweet dishes.

MELTED BUTTER.

I.

376. INGREDIENTS. — ¼ lb. of butter, a dessertspoonful of flour, 1 wineglassful of water, salt to taste.

Mode.—Cut the butter up into small pieces, put it in a saucepan, dredge over the flour, and add the water and a seasoning of salt; stir it *one way* constantly till the whole of the ingredients are melted and thoroughly blended. Let it just boil, when it is ready to serve. If the butter is to be melted with cream, use the same quantity as of water, but omit the flour; keep stirring it, but do not allow it to boil.

Time.—1 minute to simmer.

Average cost for this quantity, 4*d.*

II.

(*More Economical.*)

377. INGREDIENTS.—2 oz. of butter, 1 dessertspoonful of flour, salt to taste, ½ pint of water.

Mode.—Mix the flour and water to a smooth batter, which put into a saucepan. Add the butter and a seasoning of salt, keep stirring *one way* till all the ingredients are melted and perfectly smooth; let the whole boil for a minute or two, and serve.

Time.—2 minutes to simmer.

Average cost for this quantity, 2*d.*

MELTED BUTTER (the French Sauce Blanche).

378. INGREDIENTS.—¼ lb. of fresh butter, 1 tablespoonful of flour, salt to taste, ½ gill of water, ½ spoonful of white vinegar, a very little grated nutmeg.

Mode.—Mix the flour and water to a smooth batter, carefully rubbing down with the back of a spoon any lumps that may appear. Put it in a saucepan with all the other ingredients, and let it thicken on the fire, but do not allow it to boil, lest it should taste of the flour.

Time.—1 minute to simmer.

Average cost, 5d. for this quantity.

THE NUTMEG.

NUTMEG.—This is a native of the Moluccas, and was long kept from being spread in other places by the monopolizing spirit of the Dutch, who endeavoured to keep it wholly to themselves by eradicating it from every other island. We find it stated in "Beeton's Dictionary of Universal Information," under the article "Banda Islands," that the four largest are appropriated to the cultivation of nutmegs, of which about 500,000 lbs. are annually produced. The plant, through the enterprise of the British, has now found its way into Penang and Bencoolen, where it flourishes and produces well. It has also been tried to be naturalized in the West Indies, and it bears fruit all the year round. There are two kinds of nutmeg,—one wild, and long and oval-shaped, the other cultivated, and nearly round. The best is firm and hard, and has a strong aromatic odour, with a hot and acrid taste. It ought to be used with caution by those who are of paralytic or apoplectic habits.

THICKENED BUTTER.

379. INGREDIENTS.—¼ pint of melted butter, No. 376, the yolks of 2 eggs, a little lemon-juice.

Mode.—Make the butter quite hot, and be careful not to colour it. Well whisk the yolks of the eggs, pour them to the butter, beating them all the while. Make the sauce hot over the fire, but do not let it boil; add a squeeze of lemon-juice.

MELTED BUTTER MADE WITH MILK.

380. INGREDIENTS.—1 teaspoonful of flour, 2 oz. butter, ⅓ pint of milk, a few grains of salt.

Mode.—Mix the butter and flour smoothly together on a plate, put it into a lined saucepan, and pour in the milk. Keep stirring it *one way* over a sharp fire; let it boil quickly for a minute or two, and it is ready to serve. This is a very good foundation for onion, lobster, or oyster sauce : using milk instead of water makes it look so much whiter and more delicate.

Time.—Altogether, 10 minutes. *Average cost* for this quantity, 3d.

CAMP VINEGAR.

381. INGREDIENTS.—1 head of garlic, ½ oz. cayenne, 2 teaspoonfuls of soy, 2 ditto walnut ketchup, 1 pint of vinegar, cochineal to colour.

Mode.—Slice the garlic, and put it, with all the above ingredients, into a clean bottle. Let it stand to infuse for a month, when strain it off quite clear, and it will be fit for use. Keep it in small bottles well sealed, to exclude the air.

Average cost for this quantity, 8*d.*

CAPER SAUCE FOR BOILED MUTTON.

382. INGREDIENTS.—½ pint of melted butter (No. 376), 3 tablespoonfuls of capers or nasturtiums, 1 tablespoonful of their liquor.

Mode.—Chop the capers twice or thrice, and add them, with their liquor, to ½ pint of melted butter, made very smoothly; keep stirring well; let the sauce just simmer, and serve in a tureen. Pickled nasturtium-pods are fine-flavoured, and by many are eaten in preference to capers. They make an excellent sauce.

Time.—2 minutes to simmer. *Average cost* for this quantity, 8*d.*

Sufficient to serve with a leg of mutton.

CAPER SAUCE FOR FISH.

383. INGREDIENTS.—½ pint of melted butter No. 376, 3 dessertspoonfuls of capers, 1 dessertspoonful of their liquor, a small piece of glaze, if at hand (this may be dispensed with), ¼ teaspoonful of salt, ditto of pepper, 1 tablespoonful of anchovy essence.

Mode.—Cut the capers across once or twice, but do not chop them fine; put them in a saucepan with ½ pint of good melted butter, and add all the other ingredients. Keep stirring the whole until it just simmers, when it is ready to serve.

Time.—1 minute to simmer.

Average cost for this quantity, 5*d.*

Sufficient to serve with a skate, or 2 or 3 slices of salmon.

THE CAPER.

CAPERS.—These are the unopened buds of a low trailing shrub, which grows wild among the crevices of the rocks of Greece, as well as in northern Africa; the plant, however, has come to be cultivated in the south of Europe. After being pickled in vinegar and salt, they are imported from Sicily, Italy, and the south of France. The best are from Toulon.

A SUBSTITUTE FOR CAPER SAUCE.

384. INGREDIENTS.—½ pint of melted butter, No. 376, 2 tablespoonfuls of cut parsley, ⅓ teaspoonful of salt, 1 tablespoonful of vinegar.

Mode.—Boil the parsley slowly to let it become a bad colour; cut, but do not chop it fine. Add it to ½ pint of smoothly-made melted butter, with salt and vinegar in the above proportions. Boil up and serve.

Time.—2 minutes to simmer. *Average cost* for this quantity, 3*d.*

PICKLED CAPSICUMS.

385. INGREDIENTS.—Vinegar, ¼ oz. of pounded mace, and ¼ oz. of grated nutmeg, to each quart; brine.

Mode.—Gather the pods with the stalks on, before they turn red; slit them down the side with a small-pointed knife, and remove the seeds only; put them in a strong brine for 3 days, changing it every morning; then take them out, lay them on a cloth, with another one over them, until they are perfectly free from moisture. Boil sufficient vinegar to cover them, with mace and nutmeg in the above proportions; put the pods in a jar, pour over the vinegar when cold, and exclude them from the air by means of a wet bladder tied over.

CAYENNE VINEGAR, or ESSENCE OF CAYENNE.

386. INGREDIENTS.—½ oz. of cayenne pepper, ½ pint of strong spirit, or 1 pint of vinegar.

Mode.—Put the vinegar, or spirit, into a bottle, with the above proportion of cayenne, and let it steep for a month, when strain off and bottle for use. This is excellent seasoning for soups or sauces, but must be used very sparingly.

CELERY SAUCE, FOR BOILED TURKEY, POULTRY, &c.

387. INGREDIENTS.—6 heads of celery, 1 pint of white stock, No. 107, 2 blades of mace, 1 small bunch of savoury herbs; thickening of butter and flour, or arrowroot, ½ pint of cream, lemon-juice.

Mode.—Boil the celery in salt and water, until tender, and cut it into pieces 2 inches long. Put the stock into a stewpan with the mace and herbs, and let it simmer for ½ hour to extract their flavour. Then strain the liquor, add the celery and a thickening of butter kneaded with flour, or, what is still better, with arrowroot; just before serving, put in the cream, boil it up and squeeze in a little lemon-juice. If necessary, add a seasoning of salt and white pepper.

Time.—25 minutes to boil the celery. *Average cost,* 1s. 3d.

Sufficient, this quantity, for a boiled turkey.

This sauce may be made brown by using gravy instead of white stock, and flavouring it with mushroom ketchup or Harvey's sauce.

ARROWROOT.—This nutritious fecula is obtained from the roots of a plant which is cultivated in both the East and West Indies. When the roots are about a year old, they are dug up, and, after being well washed, are beaten to a pulp, which is afterwards, by means of water, separated from the fibrous part. After being passed through a sieve, once more washed, and then suffered to settle, the sediment is dried in the sun, when it has become arrowroot. The best is obtained from the West Indies, but a large quantity of what is sold in London is adulterated with potato-starch. As a means of knowing arrowroot when it is good, it may be as well to state, that the genuine article, when formed into a jelly, will remain firm for three or four days, whilst the adulterated will become as thin as milk in the course of twelve hours.

ARROWROOT.

CELERY SAUCE (a More Simple Recipe).

388. INGREDIENTS.—4 heads of celery, ½ pint of melted butter, made with milk (No. 380), 1 blade of pounded mace ; salt and white pepper to taste.

Mode.—Wash the celery, boil it in salt and water till tender, and cut it into pieces 2 inches long ; make ½ pint melted butter by recipe No. 380; put in the celery, pounded mace, and seasoning ; simmer for three minutes, when the sauce will be ready to serve.

Time.—25 minutes to boil the celery. *Average cost,* 6d.

Sufficient, this quantity, for a boiled fowl.

CELERY VINEGAR.

389. INGREDIENTS.—¼ oz. of celery-seed, 1 pint of vinegar.

Mode.—Crush the seed by pounding it in a mortar ; boil the vinegar, and when cold, pour it to the seed ; let it infuse for a fortnight, when strain and bottle off for use. This is frequently used in salads.

CHESTNUT SAUCE FOR FOWLS OR TURKEY.

390. INGREDIENTS.—½ lb. of chestnuts, ½ pint of white stock, 2 strips of lemon-peel, cayenne to taste, ¼ pint of cream or milk.

Mode.—Peel off the outside skin of the chestnuts, and put them into boiling water for a few minutes ; take off the thin inside peel, and put them into a saucepan, with the white stock and lemon-peel, and let them simmer for 1½ hour, or until the chestnuts are quite tender. Rub the whole through a hair-sieve with a wooden spoon ; add seasoning and the cream ; let it just simmer, but not boil, and keep stirring all the time. Serve very hot, and quickly. If milk is used instead of cream, a very small quantity of thickening may be required : that, of course, the cook will determine.

Time.—Altogether nearly two hours. *Average cost,* 8*d.*

Sufficient, this quantity, for a turkey.

BROWN CHESTNUT SAUCE.

391. INGREDIENTS.—½ lb. of chestnuts, ½ pink of stock No. 105, 2 lumps of sugar, 4 tablespoonfuls of Spanish sauce (*see* Sauces).

Mode.—Prepare the chestnuts as in the foregoing recipe, by scalding and peeling them ; put them in a stewpan with the stock and sugar, and simmer them till tender. When done, add Spanish sauce in the above proportion, and rub the whole through a tammy. Keep this sauce rather liquid, as it is liable to thicken.

Time.—1½ hour to simmer the chestnuts. *Average cost,* 8*d.*

BENGAL RECIPE FOR MAKING MANGO CHETNEY.

392. INGREDIENTS.—1½ lbs. of moist sugar, ¾ lb. of salt, ¼ lb. of garlic, ¼ lb. of onions, ¾ lb. of powdered ginger, ¼ lb. of dried chilies, ¾ lb. of mustard-seed, ¾ lb. of stoned raisins, 2 bottles of best vinegar, 30 large unripe sour apples.

Mode.—The sugar must be made into syrup ; the garlic, onions, and ginger be finely pounded in a mortar ; the mustard-seed be washed in cold vinegar, and dried in the sun ; the apples be peeled, cored, and sliced, and boiled in a bottle, and a half of the vinegar. When all this is done, and the apples are quite cold, put them into a large pan, and gradually mix the whole of the rest of the ingredients, including the remaining half-bottle of vinegar. It must be well stirred until the whole is thoroughly blended, and then put into bottles for use. Tie a piece of wet bladder over the mouths of the bottles, after they are well corked. This chetney is very superior to any which can be bought, and one trial will prove it to be delicious.

Note.—This recipe was given by a native to an English lady, who had long been a resident in India, and who, since her return to her native country, has become quite celebrated amongst her friends for the excellence of this Eastern relish.

GARLIC.

GARLIC.—The smell of this plant is generally considered offensive, and it is the most acrimonious in its taste of the whole of the alliaceous tribe. In 1548 it was introduced to England from the shores of the Mediterranean, where it is abundant, and in Sicily it grows naturally. It was in greater repute with our ancestors than it is with ourselves, although it is still used as a seasoning herb. On the continent, especially in Italy, it is much used, and the French consider it an essential in many made dishes.

CHILI VINEGAR.

393. INGREDIENTS.—50 fresh red English chilies, 1 pint of vinegar.

Mode.—Pound or cut the chilies in half, and infuse them in the vinegar for a fortnight, when it will be fit for use. This will be found an agreeable relish to fish, as many people cannot eat it without the addition of an acid and cayenne pepper.

CHRISTOPHER NORTH'S SAUCE FOR MEAT OR GAME.

394. INGREDIENTS.—1 glass of port wine, 2 tablespoonfuls of Harvey's sauce, 1 dessertspoonful of mushroom ketchup, ditto of pounded white sugar, 1 tablespoonful of lemon-juice, ½ teaspoonful of cayenne pepper, ditto of salt.

Mode.—Mix all the ingredients thoroughly together, and heat the sauce gradually, by placing the vessel in which it is made in a saucepan of boiling water. Do not allow it to boil, and serve directly it is ready. This sauce, if bottled immediately, will keep good for a fortnight, and will be found excellent.

CONSOMME, or WHITE STOCK FOR MANY SAUCES.

395. Consommé is made precisely in the same manner as stock No. 107, and, for ordinary purposes, will be found quite good enough. When, however, a stronger stock is desired, either put in half the quantity of water, or double that of the meat. This is a very good foundation for all white sauces.

CRAB SAUCE FOR FISH (equal to Lobster Sauce).

396. INGREDIENTS.—1 crab; salt, pounded mace, and cayenne to taste; ½ pint of melted butter made with milk (*see* No. 380).

Mode.—Choose a nice fresh crab, pick all the meat away from the shell, and cut it into small square pieces. Make ½ pint of melted butter by recipe No. 380, put in the fish and seasoning; let it gradually warm through, and simmer for 2 minutes. It should not boil.

Average cost, 1*s*. 2*d*.

CREAM SAUCE FOR FISH OR WHITE DISHES.

397. INGREDIENTS.—⅓ pint of cream, 2 oz. of butter, 1 teaspoonful of flour, salt and cayenne to taste; when liked, a small quantity of pounded mace or lemon-juice.

Mode.—Put the butter in a very clean saucepan, dredge in the flour, and keep shaking round till the butter is melted. Add the seasoning and cream, and stir the whole till it boils; let it just simmer for 5 minutes; when add either pounded mace or lemon-juice to taste, to give it a flavour.

Time.—5 minutes to simmer. *Average cost* for this quantity, 7*d.*

This sauce may be flavoured with very finely-shredded shalot.

CUCUMBER SAUCE.

398. INGREDIENTS.—3 or 4 cucumbers, 2 oz. of butter, 6 tablespoon-fuls of brown gravy.

Mode.—Peel the cucumbers, quarter them, and take out the seeds; cut them into small pieces; put them in a cloth, and rub them well, to take out the water which hangs about them. Put the butter in a saucepan, add the cucumbers, and shake them over a sharp fire until they are of a good colour. Then pour over it the gravy, mix this with the cucumbers, and simmer gently for 10 minutes, when it will be ready to serve.

Time.—Altogether, ½ hour.

PICKLED CUCUMBERS.

399. INGREDIENTS.—1 oz. of whole pepper, 1 oz. of bruised ginger; sufficient vinegar to cover the cucumbers.

Mode.—Cut the cucumbers in thick slices, sprinkle salt over them, and let them remain for 24 hours. The next day, drain them well for 6 hours, put them into a jar, pour boiling vinegar over them, and keep them in a warm place. In a short time, boil up the vinegar again, add pepper and ginger in the above proportion, and instantly cover them up. Tie them down with bladder, and in a few days they will be fit for use.

LONG PEPPER.

LONG PEPPER.—This is the produce of a different plant from that which produces the black, it consisting of the half-ripe flower-heads of what naturalists call *Piper longum* and *chaba.* It is the growth, however, of the same countries; indeed, all the spices are the produce of tropical climates only. Originally, the most valuable of these were found in the Spice Islands, or Moluccas, of the Indian Ocean, and were highly prized by the nations of antiquity. The Romans indulged in them to a most extravagant degree. The long pepper is less aromatic than the black, but its oil is more pungent.

CUCUMBER SAUCE, WHITE.

400. INGREDIENTS.—3 or four cucumbers, ½ pint of white stock, No. 107, cayenne and salt to taste, the yolks of 3 eggs.

Mode.—Cut the cucumbers into small pieces, after peeling them and taking out the seeds. Put them in a stewpan with the white stock and seasoning; simmer gently till the cucumbers are tender, which will be in about ¼ hour. Then add the yolks of the eggs well beaten; stir them to the sauce, but do not allow it to boil, and serve very hot.

Time.—Altogether, ½ hour.

CUCUMBER VINEGAR (a very nice Addition to Salads).

401. INGREDIENTS.—10 large cucumbers, or 12 smaller ones, 1 quart of vinegar, 2 onions, 2 shalots, 1 tablespoonful of salt, 2 tablespoonfuls of pepper, ¼ teaspoonful of cayenne.

Mode.—Pare and slice the cucumbers, put them in a stone jar or wide-mouthed bottle, with the vinegar; slice the onions and shalots, and add them, with all the other ingredients, to the cucumbers. Let it stand 4 or 5 days, boil it all up, and when cold, strain the liquor through a piece of muslin, and store it away in small bottles well sealed. This vinegar is a very nice addition to gravies, hashes, &c., as well as a great improvement to salads, or to eat with cold meat.

GERMAN METHOD OF KEEPING CUCUMBERS FOR WINTER USE.

402. INGREDIENTS.—Cucumbers, salt.

Mode.—Pare and slice the cucumbers (as for the table), sprinkle well with salt, and let them remain for 24 hours; strain off the liquor, pack in jars, a thick layer of cucumbers and salt alternately; tie down closely, and, when wanted for use, take out the quantity required. Now wash them well in fresh water, and dress as usual with pepper, vinegar, and oil.

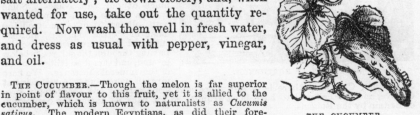

THE CUCUMBER.

THE CUCUMBER.—Though the melon is far superior in point of flavour to this fruit, yet it is allied to the cucumber, which is known to naturalists as *Cucumis sativus*. The modern Egyptians, as did their forefathers, still eat it, and others of its class. Cucumbers were observed, too, by Bishop Heber, beyond the Ganges, in India; and Burckhardt noticed them in Palestine. (*See* No. 127.)

AN EXCELLENT WAY OF PRESERVING CUCUMBERS.

403. INGREDIENTS.—Salt and water; 1 lb. of lump sugar, the rind of 1 lemon, 1 oz. of ginger, cucumbers.

Mode.—Choose the greenest cucumbers, and those that are most free from seeds; put them in strong salt and water, with a cabbage-

leaf to keep them down; tie a paper over them, and put them in a
warm place till they are yellow; then wash them and set them over
the fire in fresh water, with a very little salt, and another cabbage-
leaf over them; cover very closely, but take care they do not boil. If
they are not a fine green, change the water again, cover them as
before, and make them hot. When they are a good colour, take them
off the fire and let them cool; cut them in quarters, take out the seeds
and pulp, and put them into cold water. Let them remain for 2 days,
changing the water twice each day, to draw out the salt. Put the
sugar, with ½ pint of water, in a saucepan over the fire; remove the
scum as it rises, and add the lemon-peel and ginger with the outside
scraped off; when the syrup is tolerably thick, take it off the fire,
and when *cold*, wipe the cucumbers *dry*, and put them in. Boil
the syrup once in 2 or 3 days for 3 weeks; strengthen it if required,
and let it be quite cold before the cucumbers are put in. Great
attention must be paid to the directions in the commencement of this
recipe, as, if these are not properly carried out, the result will be
far from satisfactory.

Seasonable.—This recipe should be used in June, July, or August.

SALT-MINE AT NORTHWICH.

COMMON SALT.—By this we mean
salt used for cooking purposes,
which is found in great abundance
both on land and in the waters of
the ocean. Sea or salt water, as it
is often called, contains, it has been
discovered, about three per cent. of
salt on an average. Solid rocks of
salt are also found in various parts
of the world, and the county of
Chester contains many of these
mines, and it is from there that
much of our salt comes. Some
springs are so highly impregnated
with salt, as to have received the
name of "brine" springs, and are
supposed to have become so by
passing through the salt rocks below
ground, and thus dissolving a portion
of this mineral substance. We here
give an engraving of a salt-mine at
Northwich, Cheshire, where both salt-mines and brine-springs are exceedingly productive, and are believed to have been wrought so far back as during the occupation
of Britain by the Romans.

CUSTARD SAUCE FOR SWEET PUDDINGS OR TARTS.

404. INGREDIENTS.—1 pint of milk, 2 eggs, 3 oz. of pounded sugar,
1 tablespoonful of brandy.

Mode.—Put the milk in a very clean saucepan, and let it boil.
Beat the eggs, stir to them the milk and pounded sugar, and put the
mixture into a jug. Place the jug in a saucepan of boiling water;
keep stirring well until it thickens, but do not allow it to boil, or it

will curdle. Serve the sauce in a tureen, stir in the brandy, and grate a little nutmeg over the top. This sauce may be made very much nicer by using cream instead of milk; but the above recipe will be found quite good enough for ordinary purposes.

Average cost, 6*d.* per pint.

Sufficient, this quantity, for 2 fruit tarts, or 1 pudding.

DUTCH SAUCE FOR FISH.

405. INGREDIENTS.—½ teaspoonful of flour, 2 oz. of butter, 4 table-spoonfuls of vinegar, the yolks of 2 eggs, the juice of ¼ lemon; salt to taste.

Mode.—Put all the ingredients, except the lemon-juice, into a stew-pan; set it over the fire, and keep continually stirring. When it is sufficiently thick, take it off, as it should not boil. If, however, it happens to curdle, strain the sauce through a tammy, add the lemon-juice, and serve. Tarragon vinegar may be used instead of plain, and, by many, is considered far preferable.

Average cost, 6*d.*

Note. — This sauce may be poured hot over salad, and left to get quite cold, when it should be thick, smooth, and somewhat stiff. Excellent salads may be made of hard eggs, or the remains of salt fish flaked nicely from the bone, by pouring over a little of the above mixture when hot, and allowing it to cool.

THE LEMON.—This fruit is a native of Asia, and is mentioned by Virgil as an antidote to poison. It is hardier than the orange, and, as one of the citron tribe, was brought into Europe by the Arabians. The lemon was first cultivated in England in the beginning of the 17th century, and is now often to be found in our green-houses. The kind commonly sold, however, is imported from Portugal, Spain, and the Azores. Some also come from St. Helena; but those from Spain are esteemed the best. Its juice is now an essential for culinary purposes; but as an antiscorbutic its value is still greater. This juice, which is called *citric acid*, may be preserved in bottles for a considerable time, by covering it with a thin stratum of oil. rum and sugar.

THE LEMON.

Shrub is made from it with

GREEN DUTCH SAUCE, or HOLLANDAISE VERTE.

406. INGREDIENTS.—6 tablespoonfuls of Béchamel, No. 367, seasoning to taste of salt and cayenne, a little parsley-green to colour, the juice of ½ a lemon.

Mode.—Put the Béchamel into a saucepan with the seasoning, and bring it to a boil. Make a green colouring by pounding some parsley in a mortar, and squeezing all the juice from it. Let this just simmer,

o 2

when add it to the sauce. A moment before serving, put in the lemon-juice, but not before; for otherwise the sauce would turn yellow, and its appearance be thus spoiled.

Average cost, 4d.

BÉCHAMEL SAUCE.—This sauce takes its name from a Monsieur Béchamel, a rich French financier, who, according to some authorities, invented it; whilst others affirm he only patronized it. Be this as it may, it is one of the most pleasant sauces which come to table, and should be most carefully and intelligently prepared. It is frequently used, as in the above recipe, as a principal ingredient and basis for other sauces.

TO PICKLE EGGS.

407. INGREDIENTS.—16 eggs, 1 quart of vinegar, ½ oz. of black pepper, ½ oz. of Jamaica pepper, ½ oz. of ginger.

Mode.—Boil the eggs for 12 minutes, then dip them into cold water, and take off the shells. Put the vinegar, with the pepper and ginger, into a stewpan, and let it simmer for 10 minutes. Now place the eggs in a jar, pour over them the vinegar, &c., boiling hot, and, when cold, tie them down with bladder to exclude the air. This pickle will be ready for use in a month.

Average cost, for this quantity, 1s. 9d.

GINGER.

Seasonable.—This should be made about Easter, as at this time eggs are plentiful and cheap. A store of pickled eggs will be found very useful and ornamental in serving with many first and second course dishes.

GINGER.—The ginger-plant, known to naturalists as *Zingiber officinale*, is a native of the East and West Indies. It grows somewhat like the lily of the valley, but its height is about three feet. In Jamaica it flowers about August or September, fading about the end of the year. The fleshy creeping roots, which form the ginger of commerce, are in a proper state to be dug when the stalks are entirely withered. This operation is usually performed in January and February; and when the roots are taken out of the earth, each one is picked, scraped, separately washed, and afterwards very carefully dried. Ginger is generally considered as less pungent and heating to the system than might be expected from its effects on the organs of taste, and it is frequently used, with considerable effect, as an anti-spasmodic and carminative.

EGG BALLS FOR SOUPS AND MADE DISHES.

408. INGREDIENTS.—8 eggs, a little flour; seasoning to taste of salt.

Mode.—Boil 6 eggs for 20 minutes, strip off the shells, take the yolks and pound them in a mortar. Beat the yolks of the other 2 eggs; add them, with a little flour and salt, to those pounded; mix all well together, and roll into balls. Boil them before they are put into the soup or other dish they may be intended for.

Time.—20 minutes to boil the eggs. *Average cost*, for this quantity, 8*d*.

Sufficient, 2 dozen balls for 1 tureen of soup.

EGG SAUCE FOR SALT FISH.

409. INGREDIENTS.—4 eggs, ½ pint of melted butter, No. 376; when liked, a very little lemon-juice.

Mode.—Boil the eggs until quite hard, which will be in about 20 minutes, and put them into cold water for ½ hour. Strip off the shells, chop the eggs into small pieces, not, however, too fine. Make the melted butter very smoothly, by recipe No. 376, and, when boiling, stir in the eggs, and serve very hot. Lemon-juice may be added at pleasure.

Time.—20 minutes to boil the eggs. *Average·cost*, 8*d*.

Sufficient.—This quantity for 3 or 4 lbs. of fish.

Note.—When a thicker sauce is required, use one or two more eggs to the same quantity of melted butter.

EPICUREAN SAUCE FOR STEAKS, CHOPS, GRAVIES, OR FISH.

410. INGREDIENTS.—¼ pint of walnut ketchup, ¼ pint of mushroom ditto, 2 tablespoonfuls of Indian soy, 2 tablespoonfuls of port wine; ¼ oz. of white pepper, 2 oz. of shalots, ¼ oz. of cayenne, ¼ oz. of cloves, ¾ pint of vinegar.

Mode.—Put the whole of the ingredients into a bottle, and let it remain for a fortnight in a warm place, occasionally shaking up the contents. Strain, and bottle off for use. This sauce will be found an agreeable addition to gravies, hashes, stews, &c.

Average cost, for this quantity, 1*s*. 6*d*.

SHALOT.

SHALOT, OR ESCHALOT.—This plant is supposed to have been introduced to England by the Crusaders, who found it growing wild in the vicinity of Ascalon. It is a bulbous root, and when full-grown, its leaves wither in July. They ought to be taken up in the autumn, and when dried in the house, will keep till spring. It is called by old authors the "barren onion," and is used in sauces and pickles, soups and made dishes, and as an accompaniment to chops and steaks.

ESPAGNOLE, or BROWN SPANISH SAUCE.

411. INGREDIENTS.—2 slices of lean ham, 1 lb. of veal, 1½ pint of white stock, No. 107; 2 or 3 sprigs of parsley, ½ a bay-leaf, 2 or 3 sprigs of savoury herbs, 6 green onions, 3 shalots, 2 cloves, 1 blade of mace, 2 glasses of sherry or Madeira, thickening of butter and flour.

Mode.—Cut up the ham and veal into small square pieces, and put them into a stewpan. Moisten these with ½ pint of the stock No. 107, and simmer till the bottom of the stewpan is covered with a nicely-coloured glaze, when put in a few more spoonfuls to detach it. Add the remainder of the stock, with the spices, herbs, shalots, and onions, and simmer very gently for 1 hour. Strain and skim off every particle of fat, and when required for use, thicken with butter and flour, or with a little roux. Add the wine, and, if necessary, a seasoning of cayenne; when it will be ready to serve.

Time.—1½ hour. *Average cost,* 2s. per pint.

Note.—The wine in this sauce may be omitted, and an onion sliced and fried of a nice brown substituted for it. This sauce or gravy is used for many dishes, and with most people is a general favourite.

FENNEL SAUCE FOR MACKEREL.

412. INGREDIENTS.—½ pint of melted butter, No. 376, rather more than 1 tablespoonful of chopped fennel.

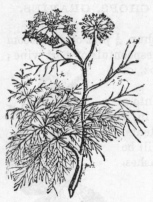

Mode. — Make the melted butter very smoothly, by recipe No. 376; chop the fennel rather small, carefully cleansing it from any grit or dirt, and put it to the butter when this is on the point of boiling. Simmer for a minute or two, and serve in a tureen.

Time.—2 minutes. *Average cost,* 4d.

Sufficient to serve with 5 or 6 mackerel.

FENNEL.—This elegantly-growing plant, of which the Latin name is *Anethum fœniculum*, grows best in chalky soils, where, indeed, it is often found wild. It is very generally cultivated in gardens, and has much improved on its original form. Various dishes are frequently ornamented and garnished with its graceful leaves, and these are sometimes boiled in soups, although it is more usually confined, in English cookery, to the mackerel sauce as here given.

FENNEL.

FISH SAUCE.

413. INGREDIENTS.—1½ oz. of cayenne, 2 tablespoonfuls of walnut ketchup, 2 tablespoonfuls of soy, a few shreds of garlic and shalot, 1 quart of vinegar.

Mode.—Put all the ingredients into a large bottle, and shake well every day for a fortnight. Keep it in small bottles well sealed, and in a few days it will be fit for use.

Average cost, for this quantity, 1s.

FORCEMEAT BALLS FOR FISH SOUPS.

414. INGREDIENTS.—1 middling-sized lobster, ½ an anchovy, 1 head of boiled celery, the yolk of a hard-boiled egg; salt, cayenne, and mace to taste; 4 tablespoonfuls of bread crumbs, 2 oz. of butter, 2 eggs.

Mode.—Pick the meat from the shell of the lobster, and pound it, with the soft parts, in a mortar; add the celery, the yolk of the hard-boiled egg, seasoning, and bread crumbs. Continue pounding till the whole is nicely amalgamated. Warm the butter till it is in a liquid state; well whisk the eggs, and work these up with the pounded lobster-meat. Make into balls of about an inch in diameter, and fry of a nice pale brown.

Sufficient, from 18 to 20 balls for 1 tureen of soup.

FORCEMEAT FOR COLD SAVOURY PIES.

415. INGREDIENTS.—1 lb. of veal, 1 lb. of fat bacon; salt, cayenne, pepper, and pounded mace to taste; a very little nutmeg, the same of chopped lemon-peel, ½ teaspoonful of chopped parsley, ½ teaspoonful of minced savoury herbs, 1 or 2 eggs.

Mode.—Chop the veal and bacon together, and put them in a mortar with the other ingredients mentioned above. Pound well, and bind with 1 or 2 eggs which have been previously beaten and strained. Work the whole well together, and the forcemeat will be ready for use. If the pie is not to be eaten immediately, omit the herbs and parsley, as these would prevent it from keeping. Mushrooms or truffles may be added.

Sufficient for 2 small pies.

MARJORAM.

MARJORAM.—Although there are several species of marjoram, that which is known as the sweet or knotted marjoram, is the one usually preferred in cookery. It is a native of Portugal, and when its leaves are used as a seasoning herb, they have an agreeable aromatic flavour. The winter sweet marjoram used for the same purposes, is a native of Greece, and the pot-marjoram is another variety brought from Sicily. All of them are favourite ingredients in soups, stuffings, &c.

FORCEMEAT FOR PIKE, CARP, HADDOCK, AND VARIOUS KINDS OF FISH.

416. INGREDIENTS.—1 oz. of fresh butter, 1 oz. of suet, 1 oz. of fat bacon, 1 small teaspoonful of minced savoury herbs, including parsley;

a little onion, when liked, shredded very fine; salt, nutmeg, and cayenne to taste; 4 oz. of bread crumbs, 1 egg.

Mode.—Mix all the ingredients well together, carefully mincing them very finely; beat up the egg, moisten with it, and work the whole very smoothly together. Oysters or anchovies may be added to this forcemeat, and will be found a great improvement.

Average cost, 6d.

Sufficient for a moderate-sized haddock or pike.

FORCEMEAT FOR VEAL, TURKEYS, FOWLS, HARE, &c.

417. INGREDIENTS.—2 oz. of ham or lean bacon, ¼ lb. of suet, the rind of half a lemon, 1 teaspoonful of minced parsley, 1 teaspoonful of minced sweet herbs; salt, cayenne, and pounded mace to taste; 6 oz. of bread crumbs, 2 eggs.

Mode.—Shred the ham or bacon, chop the suet, lemon-peel, and herbs, taking particular care that all be very finely minced; add a seasoning to taste, of salt, cayenne, and mace, and blend all thoroughly together with the bread crumbs, before wetting. Now beat and strain the eggs, work these up with the other ingredients, and the force-meat will be ready for use. When it is made into balls, fry of a nice brown, in boiling lard, or put them on a tin and bake for ½ hour in a moderate oven. As we have stated before, no one flavour should predominate greatly, and the forcemeat should be of sufficient body to cut with a knife, and yet not dry and heavy. For very delicate forcemeat, it is advisable to pound the ingredients together before binding with the egg; but for ordinary cooking, mincing very finely answers the purpose.

Average cost, 8d.

Sufficient for a turkey, a moderate-sized fillet of veal, or a hare.

BASIL.

Note.—In forcemeat for HARE, the liver of the animal is sometimes added. Boil for 5 minutes, mince it very small, and mix it with the other ingredients. If it should be in an unsound state, it must be on no account made use of.

SWEET HERBS.—Those most usually employed for purposes of cooking, such as the flavouring of soups, sauces, forcemeats, &c., are thyme, sage, mint, marjoram, savory, and basil. Other sweet herbs are cultivated for purposes of medicine and perfumery: they are most grateful both to the organs of taste and smelling; and to the aroma derived from them is due, in a great measure, the sweet and exhilarating fragrance of our "flowery meads." In town, sweet herbs have to be procured at the greengrocers' or herbalists', whilst, in the country, the garden should furnish all that are wanted, the cook taking great care to have some dried in the autumn for her use throughout the winter months.

FORCEMEAT FOR BAKED PIKE.

418. INGREDIENTS.—3 oz. of bread crumbs, 1 teaspoonful of minced savoury herbs, 8 oysters, 2 anchovies (these may be dispensed with), 2 oz. of suet; salt, pepper, and pounded mace to taste; 6 tablespoonfuls of cream or milk, the yolks of 2 eggs.

Mode.—Beard and mince the oysters, prepare and mix the other ingredients by recipe No. 416, and blend the whole thoroughly together. Moisten with the cream and eggs, put all into a stewpan, and stir it over the fire till it thickens, when put it into the fish, which should have previously been cut open, and sew it up.

Time.—4 or 5 minutes to thicken. *Average cost,* 10*d*.

Sufficient for a moderate-sized pike.

FRENCH FORCEMEAT.

419. It will be well to state, in the beginning of this recipe, that French forcemeat, or quenelles, consist of the blending of three separate processes; namely, panada, udder, and whatever meat you intend using.

Panada.

420. INGREDIENTS.—The crumb of 2 penny rolls, 4 tablespoonfuls of white stock, No. 107, 1 oz. of butter, 1 slice of ham, 1 bay-leaf, a little minced parsley, 2 shalots, 1 clove, 2 blades of mace, a few mushrooms (when obtainable), butter, the yolks of 2 eggs.

Mode.—Soak the crumb of the rolls in milk for about ½ hour, then take it out, and squeeze so as to press the milk from it; put the soaked bread into a stewpan with the above quantity of white stock, and set it on one side; then put into a separate stewpan 1 oz. of butter, a slice of lean ham cut small, with a bay-leaf, herbs, mushrooms, spices, &c., in the above proportions, and fry them gently over a slow fire. When done, moisten with 2 teacupfuls of white stock, boil for 20 minutes, and strain the whole through a sieve over the panada in the other stewpan. Place it over the fire, keep constantly stirring, to prevent its burning, and when quite dry, put in a small piece of butter. Let this again dry up by stirring over the fire; then add the yolks of 2 eggs, mix well, put the panada to cool on a clean plate, and use it when required. Panada should always be well flavoured, as the forcemeat receives no taste from any of the other ingredients used in its preparation.

Boiled Calf's Udder for French Forcemeats.

421. Put the udder into a stewpan with sufficient water to cover it; let it stew gently till quite done, when take it out to cool. Trim all

the upper parts, cut it into small pieces, and pound well in a mortar, till it can be rubbed through a sieve.   That portion which passes through the strainer is one of the three ingredients of which French forcemeats are generally composed; but many cooks substitute butter for this, being a less troublesome and more expeditious mode of preparation.

PESTLE AND MORTAR.

PESTLE AND MORTAR.—No cookery can be perfectly performed without the aid of the useful instruments shown in the engraving. For pounding things sufficiently fine, they are invaluable, and the use of them will save a good deal of time, besides increasing the excellence of the preparations. They are made of iron, and, in that material, can be bought cheap; but as these are not available for all purposes, we should recommend, as more economical in the end, those made of Wedgwood, although these are considerably more expensive than the former.

Veal Quenelles.

422. INGREDIENTS.—Equal quantities of veal, panada (No. 420), and calf's udder (No. 421), 2 eggs; seasoning to taste of pepper, salt, and pounded mace, or grated nutmeg; a little flour.

Mode.—Take the fleshy part of veal, scrape it with a knife, till all the meat is separated from the sinews, and allow about ½ lb. for an entrée. Chop the meat, and pound it in a mortar till reduced to a paste; then roll it into a ball; make another of panada (No. 420), the same size, and another of udder (No. 421), taking care that these three balls be of the same *size*.   It is to be remembered, that equality of *size*, and not of weight, is here necessary.   When the three ingredients are properly prepared, pound them altogether in a mortar for some time; for the more quenelles are pounded, the more delicate they are. Now moisten with the eggs, whites and yolks, and continue pounding, adding a seasoning of pepper, spices, &c.   When the whole is well blended together, mould it into balls, or whatever shape is intended, roll them in flour, and poach in boiling water, to which a little salt should have been added.   If the quenelles are not firm enough, add the yolk of another egg, but omit the white, which only makes them hollow and puffy inside.   In the preparation of this recipe, it would be well to bear in mind that the ingredients are to be well pounded and seasoned, and must be made hard or soft according to the dishes they are intended for.   For brown or white ragoûts they should be firm, and when the quenelles are used very small, extreme delicacy will be necessary in their preparation.   Their flavour may be varied by using the flesh of rabbit, fowl, hare, pheasant, grouse, or an extra quantity of mushroom, parsley, &c.

Time.—About ¼ hour to poach in boiling water.

Sufficient, ½ lb. of veal or other meat, with other ingredients in proportion, for 1 entrée.

Note.—The French are noted for their skill in making forcemeats; one of the principal causes of their superiority in this respect being, that they pound all the ingredients so diligently and thoroughly. Any one with the slightest pretensions to refined cookery, must, in this particular, implicitly follow the example of our friends across the Channel.

FORCEMEAT, or QUENELLES, FOR TURTLE SOUP.

(*See No.* 189.)

423. SOYER'S RECIPE FOR FORCEMEATS.—Take a pound and a half of lean veal from the fillet, and cut it in long thin slices; scrape with a knife till nothing but the fibre remains; put it in a mortar, pound it 10 minutes, or until in a purée; pass it through a wire sieve (use the remainder in stock); then take 1 pound of good fresh beef suet, which skin, shred, and chop very fine; put it in a mortar and pound it; then add 6 oz. of panada (that is, bread soaked in milk and boiled till nearly dry) with the suet; pound them well together, and add the veal; season with a teaspoonful of salt, a quarter one of pepper, half that of nutmeg; work all well together; then add four eggs by degrees, continually pounding the contents of the mortar. When well mixed, take a small piece in a spoon, and poach it in some boiling water; and if it is delicate, firm, and of a good flavour, it is ready for use.

FRIED BREAD CRUMBS.

424. Cut the bread into thin slices, place them in a cool oven overnight, and when thoroughly dry and crisp, roll them down into fine crumbs. Put some lard, or clarified dripping, into a frying-pan; bring it to the boiling-point, throw in the crumbs, and fry them very quickly. Directly they are done, lift them out with a slice, and drain them before the fire from all greasy moisture. When quite crisp, they are ready for use. The fat they are fried in should be clear, and the crumbs should not have the slightest appearance or taste of having been, in the least degree, burnt.

FRIED SIPPETS OF BREAD (for Garnishing many Dishes).

425. Cut the bread into thin slices, and stamp them out in whatever shape you like,—rings, crosses, diamonds, &c. &c. Fry them in the same manner as the bread crumbs, in clear boiling lard, or clarified dripping, and drain them until thoroughly crisp before the fire. When variety is desired, fry some of a pale colour, and others of a darker hue.

FRIED BREAD FOR BORDERS.

426. Proceed as above, by frying some slices of bread cut in any fanciful shape. When quite crisp, dip one side of the sippet into the beaten white of an egg mixed with a little flour, and place it on the edge of the dish. Continue in this manner till the border is completed, arranging the sippets a pale and a dark one alternately.

GENEVESE SAUCE FOR SALMON, TROUT, &c.

427. INGREDIENTS.—1 small carrot, a small faggot of sweet herbs, including parsley, 1 onion, 5 or 6 mushrooms (when obtainable), 1 bay-leaf, 6 cloves, 1 blade of mace, 2 oz. of butter, 1 glass of sherry, 1½ pint of white stock, No. 107, thickening of butter and flour, the juice of half a lemon.

Mode.—Cut up the onion and carrot into small rings, and put them into a stewpan with the herbs, mushrooms, bay-leaf, cloves, and mace; add the butter, and simmer the whole very gently over a slow fire until the onion is quite tender. Pour in the stock and sherry, and stew slowly for 1 hour, when strain it off into a clean saucepan.

Now make a thickening of butter and flour, put it to the sauce, stir it over the fire until perfectly smooth and mellow, add the lemon-juice, give one boil, when it will be ready for table.

Time.—Altogether 2 hours.

Average cost, 1s. 3d per pint.

Sufficient, half this quantity for two slices of salmon.

SAGE.—This was originally a native of the south of Europe, but it has long been cultivated in the English garden. There are several kinds of it, known as the green, the red, the small-leaved, and the broad-leaved balsamic. In cookery, its principal use is for stuffings and sauces, for which purpose the red is the most agreeable, and the green the next. The others are used for medical purposes.

SAGE.

PICKLED GHERKINS.

428. INGREDIENTS.—Salt and water, 1 oz. of bruised ginger, ½ oz of whole black pepper, ¼ oz. of whole allspice, 4 cloves, 2 blades of mace, a little horseradish. This proportion of pepper, spices, &c., for 1 quart of vinegar.

Mode.—Let the gherkins remain in salt and water for 3 or 4 days, when take them out, wipe perfectly dry, and put them into a stone jar. Boil sufficient vinegar to cover them, with spices and pepper, &c., in the above proportion, for 10 minutes; pour it, quite boiling, over the gherkins, cover the jar with vine-leaves, and put over them a plate, setting them near the fire, where they must remain all night. Next day drain off the vinegar, boil it up again, and pour it hot over them. Cover up with fresh leaves, and let the whole remain till quite cold. Now tie down closely with bladder to exclude the air, and in a month or two, they will be fit for use.

Time.—4 days.

Seasonable from the middle of July to the end of August.

GHERKINS.

GHERKINS.—Gherkins are young cucumbers; and the only way in which they are used for cooking purposes is pickling them, as by the recipe here given. Not having arrived at maturity, they have not, of course, so strongly a developed flavour as cucumbers, and, as a pickle, they are very general favourites.

GOOSEBERRY SAUCE FOR BOILED MACKEREL.

429. INGREDIENTS.—1 pint of green gooseberries, 3 tablespoonfuls of Béchamel, No. 367 (veal gravy may be substituted for this), 2 oz. of fresh butter; seasoning to taste of salt, pepper, and grated nutmeg.

Mode.—Boil the gooseberries in water until quite tender; strain them, and rub them through a sieve. Put into a saucepan the Béchamel or gravy, with the butter and seasoning; add the pulp from the gooseberries, mix all well together, and heat gradually through. A little pounded sugar added to this sauce is by many persons considered an improvement, as the saccharine matter takes off the extreme acidity of the unripe fruit.

Time.—Boil the gooseberries from 20 minutes to ½ hour.

Sufficient, this quantity, for a large dish of mackerel.

Seasonable from May to July.

THE GOOSEBERRY.—This useful and wholesome fruit (*Ribes grossularia*) is thought to be indigenous to the British Isles, and may be occasionally found in a wild state in some of the eastern counties, although, when uncultivated, it is but a very small and inferior berry. The high state of perfection to which it has been here brought, is due to the skill of the English gardeners; for in no other country does it attain the same size and flavour. The humidity of the British climate, however, has doubtless something to do with the result; and it is said that gooseberries produced in Scotland as far north as Inverness, are of a very superior character. Malic and citric acid blended with sugar, produce the pleasant flavour of the gooseberry; and upon the proper development of these properties depends the success of all cooking operations with which they are connected.

THE GOOSEBERRY.

GLAZE FOR COVERING COLD HAMS, TONGUES, &c.

430. INGREDIENTS.—Stock No. 104 or 107, doubling the quantity of meat in each.

Mode.—We may remark at the outset, that unless glaze is wanted in very large quantities, it is seldom made expressly. Either of the stocks mentioned above, boiled down and reduced very considerably, will be found to produce a very good glaze. Put the stock into a stewpan, over a nice clear fire; let it boil till it becomes somewhat stiff, when keep stirring, to prevent its burning. The moment it is sufficiently reduced, and comes to a glaze, turn it out into the glaze-pot, of which we have here given an engraving. As, however, this is not to be found in every establishment, a white earthenware jar would answer the purpose; and this may be placed in a vessel of boiling water, to melt the glaze when required. It should never be warmed in a saucepan, except on the principle of the bain marie, lest it should reduce too much, and become black and bitter. If the glaze is wanted of a pale colour, more veal than beef should be used in making the stock; and it is as well to omit turnips and celery, as these impart a disagreeable bitter flavour.

GLAZE-KETTLE.

TO GLAZE COLD JOINTS, &c.—Melt the glaze by placing the vessel which contains it, into the bain marie or saucepan of boiling water; brush it over the meat with a paste-brush, and if in places it is not quite covered, repeat the operation. The glaze should not be too dark a colour. (*See* Coloured Cut of Glazed Ham, P.)

GLAZE-KETTLE.—This is a kettle used for keeping the strong stock boiled down to a jelly, which is known by the name of glaze. It is composed of two tin vessels, as shown in the cut, one of which, the upper,—containing the glaze, is inserted into one of larger diameter and containing boiling water. A brush is put in the small hole at the top of the lid, and is employed for putting the glaze on anything that may require it.

THE BAIN MARIE.—So long ago as the time when emperors ruled in Rome, and the

THE BAIN MARIE.

yellow Tiber passed through a populous and wealthy city, this utensil was extensively employed; and it is frequently mentioned by that profound culinary chemist of the ancients, Apicius. It is an open kind of vessel (as shown in the engraving and explained in our paragraph No. 87, on the French terms used in modern cookery), filled with boiling or nearly boiling water; and into this water should be put all the stewpans containing those ingredients which it is desired to keep hot. The quantity and quality of the contents of these vessels are not at all affected; and if the hour of dinner is uncertain in any establishment, by reason of the nature of the master's business, nothing is so certain a means of preserving the flavour of all dishes as the employment of the bain marie.

GREEN SAUCE FOR GREEN GEESE OR DUCKLINGS.

431. INGREDIENTS.—¼ pint of sorrel-juice, 1 glass of sherry, ½ pint of green gooseberries, 1 teaspoonful of pounded sugar, 1 oz. of fresh butter.

Mode.—Boil the gooseberries in water until they are quite tender; mash them and press them through a sieve; put the pulp into a saucepan with the above ingredients; simmer for 3 or 4 minutes, and serve very hot.

Time.—3 or 4 minutes.

Note.—We have given this recipe as a sauce for green geese, thinking that some of our readers might sometimes require it; but, at the generality of fashionable tables, it is now seldom or never served.

SORREL.—We gather from the pages of Pliny and Apicius, that sorrel was cultivated by the Romans in order to give it more strength and flavour, and that they also partook of it sometimes stewed with mustard, being seasoned with a little oil and vinegar. At the present day, English cookery is not much indebted to this plant (*Rumex Acetosa*), although the French make use of it to a considerable extent. It is found in most parts of Great Britain, and also

SORREL.

on the continent, growing wild in the grass meadows, and, in a few gardens, it is cultivated. The acid of sorrel is very *prononcé*, and is what chemists term a binoxalate of potash; that is, a combination of oxalic acid with potash.

GENERAL STOCK FOR GRAVIES.

432. Either of the stocks, Nos. 104, 105, or 107, will be found to answer very well for the basis of many gravies, unless these are wanted very rich indeed. By the addition of various store sauces, thickening and flavouring, the stocks here referred to may be converted into very good gravies. It should be borne in mind, however, that the goodness and strength of spices, wines, flavourings, &c., evaporate, and that they lose a great deal of their fragrance, if added to the gravy a long time before they are wanted. If this point is attended to, a saving of one half the quantity of these ingredients will be effected, as, with long boiling, the flavour almost entirely passes away. The shank-bones of mutton, previously well soaked, will be found a great assistance in enriching gravies; a kidney or melt, beef skirt, trimmings of meat, &c. &c., answer very well when only a small quantity is wanted, and, as we have before observed, a good gravy need not necessarily be so very expensive; for economically-prepared dishes are oftentimes found as savoury and wholesome as dearer ones. The cook should also remember that the fragrance of gravies should not be overpowered by too much spice, or any strong essences, and that they should always be warmed in a *bain marie*, after

they are flavoured, or else in a jar or jug placed in a saucepan full of boiling water. The remains of roast-meat gravy should always be saved; as, when no meat is at hand, a very nice gravy in haste may be made from it, and when added to hashes, ragoûts, &c., is a great improvement.

GRAVY-KETTLE.

GRAVY-KETTLE. — This is a utensil which will not be found in every kitchen; but it is a useful one where it is necessary to keep gravies hot for the purpose of pouring over various dishes as they are cooking. It is made of copper, and should, consequently, be heated over the hot plate, if there be one, or a charcoal stove. The price at which it can be purchased is set down by Messrs. Slack at 14s.

GRAVY FOR ROAST MEAT.

433. INGREDIENTS.—Gravy, salt.

Mode.—Put a common dish with a small quantity of salt in it under the meat, about a quarter of an hour before it is removed from the fire. When the dish is full, take it away, baste the meat, and pour the gravy into the dish on which the joint is to be served.

SAUCES AND GRAVIES IN THE MIDDLE AGES.—Neither poultry, butcher's meat, nor roast game were eaten dry in the middle ages, any more than fried fish is now. Different sauces, each having its own peculiar flavour, were served with all these dishes, and even with the various *parts* of each animal. Strange and grotesque sauces, as, for example, "eggs cooked on the spit," "butter fried and roasted," were invented by the cooks of those days; but these preparations had hardly any other merit than that of being surprising and difficult to make.

A QUICKLY-MADE GRAVY.

434. INGREDIENTS.—½ lb. of shin of beef, ½ onion, ¼ carrot, 2 or 3 sprigs of parsley and savoury herbs, a piece of butter about the size of a walnut; cayenne and mace to taste, ¾ pint of water.

Mode.—Cut up the meat into very small pieces, slice the onion and carrot, and put them into a small saucepan with the butter. Keep stirring over a sharp fire until they have taken a little colour, when add the water and the remaining ingredients. Simmer for ½ hour, skim well, strain, and flavour, when it will be ready for use.

Time.—½ hour. *Average cost*, for this quantity, 5d.

A HUNDRED DIFFERENT DISHES.—Modern housewives know pretty well how much care, and attention, and foresight are necessary in order to serve well a little dinner for six or eight persons,—a dinner which will give credit to the *ménage*, and satisfaction and pleasure to the guests. A quickly-made gravy, under some circumstances that we have known occur, will be useful to many housekeepers when they have not much time for preparation. But, talking of speed, and time, and preparation, what a combination of all these must have been necessary for the feast at the wedding of Charles VI. of France. On that occasion, as Froissart the chronicler tells us, the art of cooking, with its innumerable paraphernalia of sauces, with gravy, pepper, cinnamon, garlic, scallion, brains, gravy soups, milk *potage*, and ragoûts, had a signal triumph. The skilful *chef-de-cuisine* of the royal household covered the great marble table of the regal palace with no less than a hundred different dishes, prepared in a hundred different ways.

A GOOD BEEF GRAVY FOR POULTRY, GAME, &c.

435. INGREDIENTS.—¼ lb. of lean beef, ½ pint of cold water, 1 shalot or small onion, ½ a teaspoonful of salt, a little pepper, 1 tablespoonful of Harvey's sauce or mushroom ketchup, ½ a teaspoonful of arrowroot.

Mode.—Cut up the beef into small pieces, and put it, with the water, into a stewpan. Add the shalot and seasoning, and simmer gently for 3 hours, taking care that it does not boil fast. A short time before it is required, take the arrowroot, and having mixed it with a little cold water, pour it into the gravy, which keep stirring, adding the Harvey's sauce, and just letting it boil. Strain off the gravy in a tureen, and serve very hot.

Time.—3 hours. *Average cost,* 8*d.* per pint.

BROWN GRAVY.

436. INGREDIENTS.—2 oz. of butter, 2 large onions, 2 lbs. of shin of beef, 2 small slices of lean bacon (if at hand), salt and whole pepper to taste, 3 cloves, 2 quarts of water. For thickening, 2 oz. of butter, 3 oz. of flour.

Mode.—Put the butter into a stewpan; set this on the fire, throw in the onions cut in rings, and fry them a light brown; then add the beef and bacon, which should be cut into small square pieces; season, and pour in a teacupful of water; let it boil for about ten minutes, or until it is of a nice brown colour, occasionally stirring the contents. Now fill up with water in the above proportion; let it boil up, when draw it to the side of the fire to simmer very gently for 1½ hour; strain, and when cold, take off all the fat. In thickening this gravy, melt 3 oz. of butter in a stewpan, add 2 oz. of flour, and stir till of a light-brown colour; when cold, add it to the strained gravy, and boil it up quickly. This thickening may be made in larger quantities, and kept in a stone jar for use when wanted.

Time.—Altogether, 2 hours. *Average cost,* 4*d.* per pint.

CLOVES.—This very agreeable spice is the unexpanded flower-buds of the *Caryophyllus aromaticus,* a handsome branching tree, a native of the Malacca Islands. They take their name from the Latin word *clavus,* or the French *clou,* both meaning a nail, and to which the clove has a considerable resemblance. Cloves were but little known to the ancients, and Pliny appears to be the only writer who mentions them; and he says, vaguely enough, that some were brought to Rome, very similar to grains of pepper, but somewhat longer; that they were only to be found in India, in a wood consecrated to the gods; and that they served in the manufacture of perfumes. The Dutch, as in the case of the nutmeg (*see* 378), endeavoured, when they gained possession of the Spice Islands, to secure a monopoly of cloves, and, so that the cultivation of the tree might be confined to Amboyna, their chief island, bribed the surrounding chiefs to cut down all trees found elsewhere. The Amboyna, or royal clove, is said to be the best, and is rare; but other kinds, nearly equally good, are produced in other parts of the world, and they come to Europe from Mauritius, Bourbon, Cayenne, and Martinique, as also from St. Kitts,

P

St. Vincent's, and Trinidad. The clove contains about 20 per cent. of volatile aromatic oil, to which it owes its peculiar pungent flavour, its other parts being composed of woody fibre, water, gum, and resin.

BROWN GRAVY WITHOUT MEAT.

437. INGREDIENTS.—2 large onions, 1 large carrot, 2 oz. of butter, 3 pints of boiling water, 1 bunch of savoury herbs, a wineglassful of good beer; salt and pepper to taste.

Mode.—Slice, flour, and fry the onions and carrots in the butter until of a nice light-brown colour; then add the boiling water and the remaining ingredients; let the whole stew gently for about an hour; then strain, and when cold, skim off all the fat. Thicken it in the same manner as recipe No. 436, and, if thought necessary, add a few drops of colouring No. 108.

Time.—1 hour. *Average cost,* 2d. per pint.

Note.—The addition of a small quantity of mushroom ketchup or Harvey's sauce very much improves the flavour of this gravy.

RICH GRAVY FOR HASHES, RAGOUTS, &c.

438. INGREDIENTS.—2 lbs. of shin of beef, 1 large onion or a few shalots, a little flour, a bunch of savoury herbs, 2 blades of mace, 2 or 3 cloves, 4 whole allspice, ¼ teaspoonful of whole pepper, 1 slice of lean ham or bacon, ½ a head of celery (when at hand), 2 pints of boiling water; salt and cayenne to taste.

Mode.—Cut the beef into thin slices, as also the onions, dredge them with flour, and fry of a pale brown, but do not allow them to get black; pour in the boiling water, let it boil up; and skim. Add the remaining ingredients, and simmer the whole very gently for 2 hours, or until all the juices are extracted from the meat; put it by to get cold, when take off all the fat. This gravy may be flavoured with ketchup, store sauces, wine, or, in fact, anything that may give additional and suitable relish to the dish it is intended for.

Time.—Rather more than 2 hours.

Average cost, 8d. per pint.

PIMENTO.

ALLSPICE.—This is the popular name given to pimento, or Jamaica pepper, known to naturalists as *Eugenia pimenta,* and belonging to the order of Myrtaceæ. It is the berry of a fine tree in the West Indies and South America, which attains a height of from fifteen to twenty feet: the berries are not allowed to ripen, but, being gathered green, are then dried in the sun, and then become black. It is an inexpensive spice, and is considered more mild and innocent than most other spices; consequently, it is much used for domestic purposes, combining a very agreeable variety of flavours.

GRAVY MADE WITHOUT MEAT FOR FOWLS.

439. INGREDIENTS.—The necks, feet, livers, and gizzards of the fowls, 1 slice of toasted bread, ½ onion, 1 faggot of savoury herbs, salt and pepper to taste, ½ pint of water, thickening of butter and flour, 1 dessertspoonful of ketchup.

Mode.—Wash the feet of the fowls thoroughly clean, and cut them and the neck into small pieces. Put these into a stewpan with the bread, onion, herbs, seasoning, livers, and gizzards; pour the water over them and simmer gently for 1 hour. Now take out the liver, pound it, and strain the liquor to it. Add a thickening of butter and flour, and a flavouring of mushroom ketchup; boil it up and serve.

Time.—1 hour. *Average cost*, 4*d*. per pint.

A CHEAP GRAVY FOR HASHES, &c.

440. INGREDIENTS. — Bones and trimmings of the cooked joint intended for hashing, ¼ teaspoonful of salt, ¼ teaspoonful of whole pepper, ¼ teaspoonful of whole allspice, a small faggot of savoury herbs, ½ head of celery, 1 onion, 1 oz. of butter, thickening, sufficient boiling water to cover the bones.

Mode.—Chop the bones in small pieces, and put them in a stewpan, with the trimmings, salt, pepper, spice, herbs, and celery. Cover with boiling water, and let the whole simmer gently for 1½ or 2 hours. Slice and fry the onion in the butter till it is of a pale brown, and mix it gradually with the gravy made from the bones; boil for ¼ hour, and strain into a basin; now put it back into the stewpan; flavour with walnut pickle or ketchup, pickled-onion liquor, or any store sauce that may be preferred. Thicken with a little butter and flour, kneaded together on a plate, and the gravy will be ready for use. After the thickening is added, the gravy should just boil, to take off the rawness of the flour.

Time.—2 hours, or rather more.

Average cost, 4*d*., exclusive of the bones and trimmings.

JUGGED GRAVY (Excellent).

441. INGREDIENTS.—2 lbs. of shin of beef, ¼ lb. of lean ham, 1 onion or a few shalots, 2 pints of water, salt and whole pepper to taste, 1 blade of mace, a faggot of savoury herbs, ½ a large carrot, ½ a head of celery.

Mode.—Cut up the beef and ham into small pieces, and slice the vegetables; take a jar, capable of holding two pints of water, and arrange therein, in layers, the ham, meat, vegetables, and seasoning, alternately, filling up with the above quantity of water; tie down the jar, or put a plate over the top, so that the steam may not escape; place it in the oven, and let it remain there from 6 to 8 hours; should, however, the oven be very hot, less time will be required. When sufficiently cooked, strain the gravy, and when cold, remove the fat.

It may be flavoured with ketchup, wines, or any other store sauce that may be preferred.

It is a good plan to put the jar in a cool oven over-night, to draw the gravy; and then it will not require so long baking the following day.

Time.— From 6 to 8 hours, according to the oven.

Average cost, 7d. per pint.

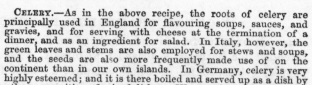

CELERY.

CELERY.—As in the above recipe, the roots of celery are principally used in England for flavouring soups, sauces, and gravies, and for serving with cheese at the termination of a dinner, and as an ingredient for salad. In Italy, however, the green leaves and stems are also employed for stews and soups, and the seeds are also more frequently made use of on the continent than in our own islands. In Germany, celery is very highly esteemed; and it is there boiled and served up as a dish by itself, as well as used in the composition of mixed dishes. We ourselves think that this mild aromatic plant might oftener be cooked than it is; for there are very few nicer vegetable preparations brought to table than a well-dressed plate of stewed celery.

VEAL GRAVY FOR WHITE SAUCES, FRICASSEES, &c.

442. INGREDIENTS.—2 slices of nicely flavoured lean ham, any poultry trimmings, 3 lbs. of lean veal, a faggot of savoury herbs, including parsley, a few green onions (or 1 large onion may be substituted for these), a few mushrooms, when obtainable; 1 blade of mace, salt to taste, 3 pints of water.

Mode.—Cut up the ham and veal into small square pieces, put these in a stewpan, moistening them with a small quantity of water; place them over the fire to draw down. When the bottom of the stewpan becomes covered with a white glaze, fill up with water in the above proportion; add the remaining ingredients, stew very slowly for 3 or 4 hours, and do not forget to skim well the moment it boils. Put it by, and, when cold, take off all the fat. This may be used for Béchamel, sauce tournée, and many other white sauces.

Time.—3 or 4 hours. *Average cost,* 9d. per pint.

CHEAP GRAVY FOR MINCED VEAL.

443. INGREDIENTS.—Bones and trimmings of cold roast or boiled veal, 1½ pint of water, 1 onion, ¼ teaspoonful of minced lemon-peel, ¼ teaspoonful of salt, 1 blade of pounded mace, the juice of ¼ lemon; thickening of butter and flour.

Mode.—Put all the ingredients into a stewpan, except the thickening and lemon-juice, and let them simmer very gently for rather more than 1 hour, or until the liquor is reduced to a pint, when strain through a hair-sieve. Add a thickening of butter and flour, and the lemon-juice; set it on the fire, and let it just boil up, when it will be ready for use. It may be flavoured with a little tomato sauce, and, where a rather dark-coloured gravy is not objected to, ketchup, or Harvey's sauce, may be added at pleasure.

Time.—Rather more than 1 hour. *Average cost, 3d.*

GRAVY FOR VENISON.

444. INGREDIENTS.—Trimmings of venison, 3 or 4 mutton shank-bones, salt to taste, 1 pint of water, 2 teaspoonfuls of walnut ketchup.

Mode.—Brown the trimmings over a nice clear fire, and put them in a stewpan with the shank-bones and water; simmer gently for 2 hours, strain and skim, and add the walnut ketchup and a seasoning of salt. Let it just boil, when it is ready to serve.

Time.—2 hours.

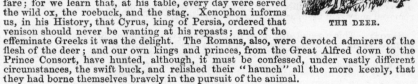

THE DEER.

VENISON.—Far, far away in ages past, our fathers loved the chase, and what it brought; and it is usually imagined that when Isaac ordered his son Esau to go out with his weapons, his quiver and his bow, and to prepare for him savoury meat, such as he loved, that it was venison he desired. The wise Solomon, too, delighted in this kind of fare; for we learn that, at his table, every day were served the wild ox, the roebuck, and the stag. Xenophon informs us, in his History, that Cyrus, king of Persia, ordered that venison should never be wanting at his repasts; and of the effeminate Greeks it was the delight. The Romans, also, were devoted admirers of the flesh of the deer; and our own kings and princes, from the Great Alfred down to the Prince Consort, have hunted, although, it must be confessed, under vastly different circumstances, the swift buck, and relished their "haunch" all the more keenly, that they had borne themselves bravely in the pursuit of the animal.

TO DRY HERBS FOR WINTER USE.

445. On a very dry day, gather the herbs, just before they begin to flower. If this is done when the weather is damp, the herbs will not be so good a colour. (It is very necessary to be particular in little matters like this, for trifles constitute perfection, and herbs nicely dried will be found very acceptable when frost and snow are on the ground. It is hardly necessary, however, to state that the flavour and fragrance of fresh herbs are incomparably finer.) They should be perfectly freed from dirt and dust, and be divided into small bunches, with their roots cut off. Dry them quickly in a very hot oven, or before the fire, as by this means most of their flavour will be preserved, and be careful

not to burn them; tie them up in paper bags, and keep in a dry place. This is a very general way of preserving dried herbs; but we would recommend the plan described in a former recipe.

Seasonable.—From the month of July to the end of September is the proper time for storing herbs for winter use.

HERB POWDER FOR FLAVOURING, when Fresh Herbs are not obtainable.

446. INGREDIENTS.—1 oz. of dried lemon-thyme, 1 oz. of dried winter savory, 1 oz. of dried sweet marjoram and basil, 2 oz. of dried parsley, 1 oz. of dried lemon-peel.

Mode.—Prepare and dry the herbs by recipe No. 445; pick the leaves from the stalks, pound them, and sift them through a hair-sieve; mix in the above proportions, and keep in glass bottles, carefully excluding the air. This, we think, a far better method of keeping herbs, as the flavour and fragrance do not evaporate so much as when they are merely put in paper bags. Preparing them in this way, you have them ready for use at a moment's notice.

Mint, sage, parsley, &c., dried, pounded, and each put into separate bottles, will be found very useful in winter.

CORK WITH WOODEN TOP.

CORKS WITH WOODEN TOPS.—These are the best corks to use when it is indispensable that the air should not be admitted to the ingredients contained in bottles which are in constant use. The top, which, as will be seen by the accompanying little cut, is larger than the cork, is made of wood; and, besides effectually covering the whole top of the bottle, can be easily removed and again used, as no corkscrew is necessary to pull it out.

SAVORY.—This we find described by Columella, a voluminous Roman writer on agriculture, as an odoriferous herb, which, "in the brave days of old," entered into the seasoning of nearly every dish. Verily, there are but few new things under the sun, and we don't find that we have made many discoveries in gastronomy, at least beyond what was known to the ancient inhabitants of Italy. We possess two varieties of this aromatic herb, known to naturalists as *Satureja*. They are called summer and winter savory, according to the time of the year when they are fit for gathering. Both sorts are in general cultivation throughout England.

HORSERADISH SAUCE, to serve with Roast Beef.

447. INGREDIENTS.—4 tablespoonfuls of grated horseradish, 1 teaspoonful of pounded sugar, 1 teaspoonful of salt, ½ teaspoonful of pepper, 2 teaspoonfuls of made mustard; vinegar.

Mode.—Grate the horseradish, and mix it well with the sugar, salt, pepper, and mustard; moisten it with sufficient vinegar to give it the consistency of cream, and serve in a tureen: 3 or 4 tablespoonfuls of cream added to the above, very much improve the appearance and flavour of this sauce. To heat it to serve with hot roast beef, put it in a bain marie or a jar, which place in a saucepan of boiling water; make it hot, but do not allow it to boil, or it will curdle.

Note.—This sauce is a great improvement on the old-fashioned way of serving cold-scraped horse-radish with hot roast beef. The mixing of the cold vinegar with the warm gravy cools and spoils every-thing on the plate. Of course, with cold meat, the sauce should be served cold.

THE HORSERADISH.

THE HORSERADISH.—This has been, for many years, a favourite accompaniment of roast beef, and is a native of England. It grows wild in wet ground, but has long been cultivated in the garden, and is, occasionally, used in winter salads and in sauces. On account of the great volatility of its oil, it should never be preserved by drying, but should be kept moist by being buried in sand. So rapidly does its volatile oil evaporate, that even when scraped for the table, it almost immediately spoils by exposure to the air.

HORSERADISH VINEGAR.

448. INGREDIENTS.—$\frac{1}{4}$ lb. of scraped horseradish, 1 oz. of minced shalot, 1 drachm of cayenne, 1 quart of vinegar.

Mode.—Put all the ingredients into a bottle, which shake well every day for a fortnight. When it is thoroughly steeped, strain and bottle, and it will be fit for use immediately. This will be found an agreeable relish to cold beef, &c.

Seasonable.—This vinegar should be made either in October or November, as horseradish is then in its highest perfection.

INDIAN CURRY-POWDER, founded on Dr. Kitchener's Recipe.

449. INGREDIENTS.—$\frac{1}{4}$ lb. of coriander-seed, $\frac{1}{4}$ lb. of turmeric, 2 oz. of cinnamon-seed, $\frac{1}{2}$ oz. of cayenne, 1 oz. of mustard, 1 oz. of ground ginger, $\frac{1}{2}$ ounce of allspice, 2 oz. of fenugreek-seed.

Mode.—Put all the ingredients in a cool oven, where they should remain one night; then pound them in a mortar, rub them through a sieve, and mix thoroughly together; keep the powder in a bottle, from which the air should be completely excluded.

Note.—We have given this recipe for curry-powder, as some persons prefer to make it at home; but that purchased at any respectable shop is, generally speaking, far superior, and, taking all things into consideration, very frequently more economical.

INDIAN MUSTARD, an excellent Relish to Bread and Butter, or any cold Meat.

450. INGREDIENTS.—$\frac{1}{4}$ lb. of the best mustard, $\frac{1}{4}$ lb. of flour, $\frac{1}{2}$ oz.

of salt, 4 shalots, 4 tablespoonfuls of vinegar, 4 tablespoonfuls of ketchup, ¼ bottle of anchovy sauce.

Mode.—Put the mustard, flour, and salt into a basin, and make them into a stiff paste with boiling water. Boil the shalots with the vinegar, ketchup, and anchovy sauce, for 10 minutes, and pour the whole, *boiling*, over the mixture in the basin ; stir well, and reduce it to a proper thickness ; put it into a bottle, with a bruised shalot at the bottom, and store away for use. This makes an excellent relish, and if properly prepared will keep for years.

MUSTARD.

MUSTARD.—Before the year 1729, mustard was not known at English tables. About that time an old woman, of the name of Clements, residing in Durham, began to grind the seed in a mill, and to pass the flour through several processes necessary to free the seed from its husks. She kept her secret for many years to herself, during which she sold large quantities of mustard throughout the country, but especially in London. Here it was introduced to the royal table, when it received the approval of George I. From the circumstance of Mrs. Clements being a resident at Durham, it obtained the name of Durham mustard. In the county of that name it is still principally cultivated, and the plant is remarkable for the rapidity of its growth. It is the best stimulant employed to impart strength to the digestive organs, and even in its previously coarsely-pounded state, had a high reputation with our ancestors.

INDIAN PICKLE (very Superior).

451. INGREDIENTS.—To each gallon of vinegar allow 6 cloves of garlic, 12 shalots, 2 sticks of sliced horseradish, ¼ lb. of bruised ginger, 2 oz. of whole black pepper, 1 oz. of long pepper, 1 oz. of allspice, 12 cloves, ¼ oz. of cayenne, 2 oz. of mustard-seed, ¼ lb. of mustard, 1 oz. of turmeric ; a white cabbage, cauliflowers, radish-pods, French beans, gherkins, small round pickling-onions, nasturtiums, capsicums, chilies, &c.

Mode.—Cut the cabbage, which must be hard and white, into slices, and the cauliflowers into small branches ; sprinkle salt over them in a large dish, and let them remain two days ; then dry them, and put them into a very large jar, with garlic, shalots, horseradish, ginger, pepper, allspice, and cloves, in the above proportions. Boil sufficient vinegar to cover them, which pour over, and, when cold, cover up to keep them free from dust. As the other things for the pickle ripen at different times, they may be added as they are ready : these will be radish-pods, French beans, gherkins, small onions, nasturtiums, capsicums, chilies, &c. &c. As these are procured, they must, first of all, be washed in a little cold vinegar, wiped, and then simply added to the other ingredients in the large jar, only taking care that they are *covered* by the vinegar. If more vinegar should be wanted to add to the pickle, do not omit first to boil it before adding it to the rest. When you have collected all the things you require, turn all out in a large pan, and thoroughly mix them. Now put the mixed vegetables into smaller jars, without any of the vinegar; then boil the vinegar again, adding as much more as will be required to fill the different jars, and also cayenne, mustard-seed, turmeric, and mustard, which must be well mixed with a little cold vinegar, allowing the quantities named above to each gallon of vinegar. Pour the vinegar, boiling hot, over the pickle, and when cold, tie down with a bladder. If the pickle is wanted for immediate use, the vinegar should be boiled twice more, but the better way is to make it during one season for use during the next. It will keep for years, if care is taken that the vegetables are quite covered by the vinegar.

This recipe was taken from the directions of a lady whose pickle was always pronounced excellent by all who tasted it, and who has, for many years, exactly followed the recipe given above.

Note.—For small families, perhaps the above quantity of pickle will be considered too large; but this may be decreased at pleasure, taking care to properly proportion the various ingredients.

KEEPING PICKLES.—Nothing shows more, perhaps, the difference between a tidy thrifty housewife and a lady to whom these desirable epithets may not honestly be applied, than the appearance of their respective store-closets. The former is able, the moment anything is wanted, to put her hand on it at once; no time is lost, no vexation incurred, no dish spoilt for the want of "just a little something,"—the latter, on the contrary, hunts all over her cupboard for the ketchup the cook requires, or the pickle the husband thinks he should like a little of with his cold roast beef or mutton-chop, and vainly seeks for the Embden groats, or arrowroot, to make one of her little boys some gruel. One plan, then, we strenuously advise all who do not follow, to begin at once, and that is, to label all their various pickles and store sauces, in the same way as the cut here shows. It will occupy a little time at first, but there will be economy of it in the long run.

INDIA PICKLE.

VINEGAR.—This term is derived from the two French words *vin aigre*, 'sour wine,' and should, therefore, be strictly applied to that which is made only from wine. As the acid is the same, however it is procured, that made from ale also takes the same name. Nearly all ancient nations were acquainted with the use of vinegar. We learn in *Ruth*, that the reapers in the East soaked their bread in it to freshen it. The Romans kept large quantities of it in their cellars, using it, to a great extent, in their seasonings and sauces. This people attributed very beneficial qualities to it, as it was supposed to be digestive, antibilious, and antiscorbutic, as well as refreshing. Spartianus, a Latin historian, tells us that, mixed with water, it was the drink of the soldiers, and that, thanks to this beverage, the veterans of the Roman army braved, by its use, the inclemency and variety of all the different seasons and climates of Europe, Asia, and Africa. It is said, the Spanish peasantry, and other inhabitants of the southern parts of Europe, still follow this practice, and add to a gallon of water about a gill of wine vinegar, with a little salt; and that this drink, with a little bread, enables them, under the heat of their burning sun, to sustain the labours of the field.

INDIAN CHETNEY SAUCE.

452. INGREDIENTS.—8 oz. of sharp, sour apples, pared and cored; 8 oz. of tomatoes, 8 oz. of salt, 8 oz. of brown sugar, 8 oz. of stoned

raisins, 4 oz. of cayenne, 4 oz. of powdered ginger, 2 oz. of garlic, 2 oz. of shalots, 3 quarts of vinegar, 1 quart of lemon-juice.

Mode.—Chop the apples in small square pieces, and add to them the other ingredients. Mix the whole well together, and put in a well-covered jar. Keep this in a warm place, and stir every day for a month, taking care to put on the lid after this operation; strain, but do not squeeze it dry; store it away in clean jars or bottles for use, and the liquor will serve as an excellent sauce for meat or fish.

Seasonable.—Make this sauce when tomatoes are in full season, that is, from the beginning of September to the end of October.

PICKLES.—The ancient Greeks and Romans held their pickles in high estimation. They consisted of flowers, herbs, roots, and vegetables, preserved in vinegar, and which were kept, for a long time, in cylindrical vases with wide mouths. Their cooks prepared pickles with the greatest care, and the various ingredients were macerated in oil, brine, and vinegar, with which they were often impregnated drop by drop. Meat, also, after having been cut into very small pieces, was treated in the same manner.

ITALIAN SAUCE (Brown).

453. INGREDIENTS.—A few chopped mushrooms and shalots, $\frac{1}{2}$ pint of stock, No. 105, $\frac{1}{2}$ glass of Madeira, the juice of $\frac{1}{2}$ lemon, $\frac{1}{2}$ teaspoonful of pounded sugar, 1 teaspoonful of chopped parsley.

Mode.—Put the stock into a stewpan with the mushrooms, shalots, and Madeira, and stew gently for $\frac{1}{4}$ hour, then add the remaining ingredients, and let them just boil. When the sauce is done enough, put it in another stewpan, and warm it in a *bain marie*. (*See* No. 430.) The mushrooms should not be chopped long before they are wanted, as they will then become black.

Time.—$\frac{1}{4}$ hour. *Average cost*, for this quantity, 7*d.*

Sufficient for a small dish.

ITALIAN SAUCE (White).

454. INGREDIENTS.—$\frac{1}{2}$ pint of white stock, No. 107; 2 tablespoonfuls of chopped mushrooms, 1 dessertspoonful of chopped shalots, 1 slice of ham, minced very fine; $\frac{1}{4}$ pint of Béchamel, No. 367; salt to taste, a few drops of garlic vinegar, $\frac{1}{2}$ teaspoonful of pounded sugar, a squeeze of lemon-juice.

Mode.—Put the shalots and mushrooms into a stewpan with the stock and ham, and simmer very gently for $\frac{1}{2}$ hour, when add the Béchamel. Let it just boil up, and then strain it through a tammy; season with the above ingredients, and serve very hot. If this sauce should not have retained a nice white colour, a little cream may be added.

Time.—½ hour. *Average cost,* for this quantity, 10*d.*
Sufficient for a moderate-sized dish.

Note.—To preserve the colour of the mushrooms after pickling, throw them into water to which a little lemon-juice has been added.

TO PICKLE LEMONS WITH THE PEEL ON.

455. INGREDIENTS.—6 lemons, 2 quarts of boiling water; to each quart of vinegar allow ½ oz. of cloves, ½ oz. of white pepper, 1 oz. of bruised ginger, ¼ oz. of mace and chilies, 1 oz. of mustard-seed, ½ stick of sliced horseradish, a few cloves of garlic.

Mode.—Put the lemons into a brine that will bear an egg; let them remain in it 6 days, stirring them every day; have ready 2 quarts of boiling water, put in the lemons, and allow them to boil for ¼ hour; take them out, and let them lie in a cloth until perfectly dry and cold. Boil up sufficient vinegar to cover the lemons, with all the above ingredients, allowing the same proportion as stated to each quart of vinegar. Pack the lemons in a jar, pour over the vinegar, &c. boiling hot, and tie down with a bladder. They will be fit for use in about 12 months, or rather sooner.

Seasonable.—This should be made from November to April.

THE LEMON.—In the earlier ages of the world, the lemon does not appear to have been at all known, and the Romans only became acquainted with it at a very late period, and then only used it to keep moths from their garments. Its acidity would seem to have been unpleasant to them; and in Pliny's time, at the commencement of the Christian era, this fruit was hardly accepted, otherwise than as an excellent anti-dote against the effects of poison. Many anecdotes have been related concerning the anti-venomous properties of the lemon; Athenæus, a Latin writer, telling us, that on one occasion, two men felt no effects from the bites of dangerous serpents, because they had previously eaten of this fruit.

TO PICKLE LEMONS WITHOUT THE PEEL.

456. INGREDIENTS.—6 lemons, 1 lb. of fine salt; to each quart of vinegar, the same ingredients as No. 455.

Mode.—Peel the lemons, slit each one down 3 times, so as not to divide them, and rub the salt well into the divisions; place them in a pan, where they must remain for a week, turning them every other day; then put them in a Dutch oven before a clear fire until the salt has become perfectly dry; then arrange them in a jar. Pour over suffi-cient boiling vinegar to cover them, to which have been added the ingredients mentioned in the foregoing recipe; tie down closely, and in about 9 months they will be fit for use.

Seasonable.—The best time to make this is from November to April.

Note.—After this pickle has been made from 4 to 5 months, the liquor may be strained and bottled, and will be found an excellent lemon ketchup.

LEMON-JUICE.—Citric acid is the principal component part of lemon-juice, which, in addition to the agreeableness of its flavour, is also particularly cooling and grateful. It is likewise an antiscorbutic; and this quality enhances its value. In order to combat the fatal effects of scurvy amongst the crews of ships at sea, a regular allowance of lemon-juice is served out to the men; and by this practice, the disease has almost entirely disappeared. By putting the juice into bottles, and pouring on the top sufficient oil to cover it, it may be preserved for a considerable time. Italy and Turkey export great quantities of it in this manner.

LEMON SAUCE FOR BOILED FOWLS.

457. INGREDIENTS.—1 small lemon, $\frac{3}{4}$ pint of melted butter, No. 380.

Mode.—Cut the lemon into very thin slices, and these again into very small dice. Have ready $\frac{3}{4}$ pint of melted butter, made by recipe No. 380; put in the lemon; let it just simmer, but not boil, and pour it over the fowls.

Time.—1 minute to simmer. *Average cost,* 6d.

Sufficient for a pair of large fowls.

LEMON WHITE SAUCE, FOR FOWLS, FRICASSEES, &c.

458. INGREDIENTS.—$\frac{3}{4}$ pint of cream, the rind and juice of 1 lemon, $\frac{1}{2}$ teaspoonful of whole white pepper, 1 sprig of lemon thyme, 3 oz. of butter, 1 dessertspoonful of flour, 1 teacupful of white stock; salt to taste.

Mode.—Put the cream into a very clean saucepan (a lined one is best), with the lemon-peel, pepper, and thyme, and let these infuse for $\frac{1}{2}$ hour, when simmer gently for a few minutes, or until there is a nice flavour of lemon. Strain it, and add a thickening of butter and flour in the above proportions; stir this well in, and put in the lemon-juice at the moment of serving; mix the stock with the cream, and add a little salt. This sauce should not boil after the cream and stock are mixed together.

Time.—Altogether, $\frac{3}{4}$ hour. *Average cost,* 1s. 6d.

LEMON THYME.

Sufficient, this quantity, for a pair of large boiled fowls.

Note.—Where the expense of the cream is objected to, milk may be substituted for it. In this case, an additional dessertspoonful, or rather more, of flour must be added.

LEMON THYME.—Two or three tufts of this species of thyme, *Thymus citriodorus*, usually find a place in the herb compartment of the kitchen-garden. It is a trailing evergreen, is of smaller growth than the common kind (*see* No. 166), and is remarkable for its smell, which closely resembles that of the rind of a lemon. Hence its distinctive name. It is used for some particular dishes, in which the fragrance of the lemon is desired to slightly predominate.

LEAMINGTON SAUCE (an Excellent Sauce for Flavouring Gravies, Hashes, Soups, &c.).

(*Author's Recipe.*)

459. INGREDIENTS.—Walnuts. To each quart of walnut-juice allow 3 quarts of vinegar, 1 pint of Indian soy, 1 oz. of cayenne, 2 oz. of shalots, ¾ oz. of garlic, ½ pint of port wine.

Mode.—Be very particular in choosing the walnuts as soon as they appear in the market; for they are more easily bruised before they become hard and shelled. Pound them in a mortar to a pulp, strew some salt over them, and let them remain thus for two or three days, occasionally stirring and moving them about. Press out the juice, and to *each quart* of walnut-liquor allow the above proportion of vinegar, soy, cayenne, shalots, garlic, and port wine. Pound each ingredient separately in a mortar, then mix them well together, and store away for use in small bottles. The corks should be well sealed.

Seasonable.—This sauce should be made as soon as walnuts are obtainable, from the beginning to the middle of July.

LEMON BRANDY.

460. INGREDIENTS.—1 pint of brandy, the rind of two small lemons, 2 oz. of loaf-sugar, ¼ pint of water.

Mode.—Peel the lemons rather thin, taking care to have none of the white pith. Put the rinds into a bottle with the brandy, and let them infuse for 24 hours, when they should be strained. Now boil the sugar with the water for a few minutes, skim it, and, when cold, add it to the brandy. A dessertspoonful of this will be found an excellent flavouring for boiled custards.

LEMON RIND OR PEEL.—This contains an essential oil of a very high flavour and fragrance, and is consequently esteemed both a wholesome and agreeable stomachic. It is used, as will be seen by many recipes in this book, as an ingredient for flavouring a number of various dishes. Under the name of CANDIED LEMON-PEEL, it is cleared of the pulp and preserved by sugar, when it becomes an excellent sweetmeat. By the ancient medical philosopher Galen, and others, it may be added, that dried lemon-peel was considered as one of the best digestives, and recommended to weak and delicate persons.

LIAISON OF EGGS FOR THICKENING SAUCES.

461. INGREDIENTS.—The yolks of 3 eggs, 8 tablespoonfuls of milk or cream.

Mode.—Beat up the yolks of the eggs, to which add the milk, and strain the whole through a hair-sieve. When the liaison is being added to the sauce it is intended to thicken, care must be exercised to keep stirring it during the whole time, or, otherwise, the eggs will curdle. It should only just simmer, but not boil.

LIVER AND LEMON SAUCE FOR POULTRY.

462. INGREDIENTS.—The liver of a fowl, one lemon, salt to taste, ½ pint of melted butter, No. 376.

Mode.—Wash the liver, and let it boil for a few minutes; peel the lemon very thin, remove the white part and pips, and cut it into very small dice; mince the liver and a small quantity of the lemon rind very fine; add these ingredients to ½ pint of smoothly-made melted butter; season with a little salt, put in the cut lemon, heat it gradually, but do not allow it to boil, lest the butter should oil.

Time,—1 minute to simmer.

Sufficient to serve with a pair of small fowls.

LIVER AND PARSLEY SAUCE FOR POULTRY.

463. INGREDIENTS.—The liver of a fowl, one tablespoonful of minced parsley, ½ pint of melted butter, No. 376.

Mode.—Wash and score the liver, boil it for a few minutes, and mince it very fine; blanch or scald a small bunch of parsley, of which there should be sufficient when chopped to fill a tablespoon; add this, with the minced liver, to ½ pint of smoothly-made melted butter; let it just boil; when serve.

Time.—1 minute to simmer.

Sufficient for a pair of small fowls.

LOBSTER SAUCE, to serve with Turbot, Salmon, Brill, &c.

(*Very Good.*)

464. INGREDIENTS.—1 middling-sized hen lobster, ¾ pint of melted butter, No. 376; 1 tablespoonful of anchovy sauce, ½ oz. of butter, salt and cayenne to taste, a little pounded mace when liked, 2 or 3 tablespoonfuls of cream.

Mode.—Choose a hen lobster, as this is indispensable, in order to render this sauce as good as it ought to be. Pick the meat from the shells, and cut it into small square pieces; put the spawn, which will be found under the tail of the lobster, into a mortar with ½ oz. of butter, and pound it quite smooth; rub it through a hair-sieve, and cover up till wanted. Make ¾ pint of melted butter by recipe No. 376; put in all the ingredients except the lobster-meat, and well mix the sauce before the lobster is added to it, as it should retain its square form, and not come to table shredded and ragged. Put in the meat, let it get thoroughly hot, but do not allow it to boil, as the colour would immediately be spoiled; for it should be remembered that this sauce should always have a bright red appearance. If it is intended to be served with turbot or brill, a little of the spawn (dried and rubbed through a sieve without butter) should be saved to garnish with; but as the goodness, flavour, and appearance of the sauce so much depend on having a proper quantity of spawn, the less used for garnishing the better.

Time.—1 minute to simmer. *Average cost,* for this quantity, 2s.

Seasonable at any time.

Sufficient to serve with a small turbot, a brill, or salmon for 6 persons.

Note.—Melted butter made with milk, No. 380, will be found to answer very well for lobster sauce, as by employing it a nice white colour will be obtained. Less quantity than the above may be made by using a very small lobster, to which add only ½ pint of melted butter, and season as above. Where economy is desired, the cream may be dispensed with, and the remains of a cold lobster left from table, may, with a little care, be converted into a very good sauce.

MAITRE D'HOTEL BUTTER, for putting into Broiled Fish just before it is sent to Table.

465. INGREDIENTS.—¼ lb. of butter, 2 dessertspoonfuls of minced parsley, salt and pepper to taste, the juice of 1 large lemon.

Mode.—Work the above ingredients well together, and let them be thoroughly mixed with a wooden spoon. If this is used as a sauce, it may be poured either under or over the meat or fish it is intended to be served with.

Average cost, for this quantity, 5d.

Note.—4 tablespoonfuls of Béchamel, No. 367, 2 do. of white stock, No. 107, with 2 oz. of the above maître d'hôtel butter stirred into it, and just allowed to simmer for 1 minute, will be found an excellent hot maître d'hôtel sauce.

THE MAÎTRE D'HÔTEL.—The house-steward of England is synonomous with the maître d'hôtel of France; and, in ancient times, amongst the Latins, he was called procurator, or major-domo. In Rome, the slaves, after they had procured the various articles necessary for the repasts of the day, would return to the spacious kitchen laden with meat, game, sea-fish, vegetables, fruit, &c. Each one would then lay his basket at the feet of the major-domo, who would examine its contents and register them on his tablets, placing in the pantry contiguous to the dining-room, those of the provisions which need no preparation, and consigning the others to the more immediate care of the cooks.

MAITRE D'HOTEL SAUCE (HOT), to serve with Calf's Head, Boiled Eels, and different Fish.

466. INGREDIENTS.—1 slice of minced ham, a few poultry-trimmings, 2 shalots, 1 clove of garlic, 1 bay-leaf, ¾ pint of water, 2 oz. of butter, 1 dessertspoonful of flour, 1 heaped tablespoonful of chopped

parsley; salt, pepper, and cayenne to taste; the juice of ½ large lemon, ¼ teaspoonful of pounded sugar.

Mode.—Put at the bottom of a stewpan the minced ham, and over it the poultry-trimmings (if these are not at hand, veal should be substituted), with the shalots, garlic, and bay-leaf. Pour in the water, and let the whole simmer gently for 1 hour, or until the liquor is reduced to a full ½ pint. Then strain this gravy, put it in another saucepan, make a thickening of butter and flour in the above proportions, and stir it to the gravy over a nice clear fire, until it is perfectly smooth and rather thick, care being taken that the butter does not float on the surface. Skim well, add the remaining ingredients, let the sauce gradually heat, but do not allow it to boil. If this sauce is intended for an entrée, it is necessary to make it of a sufficient thickness, so that it may adhere to what it is meant to cover.

Time.—1½ hour. *Average cost*, 1s. 2d. per pint.

Sufficient for re-warming the remains of ½ calf's head, or a small dish of cold flaked turbot, cod, &c.

MAIGRE MAITRE D'HOTEL SAUCE (HOT).
(Made without Meat.)

467. INGREDIENTS.—½ pint of melted butter, No. 376; 1 heaped tablespoonful of chopped parsley, salt and pepper to taste, the juice of ½ large lemon; when liked, 2 minced shalots.

Mode.—Make ½ pint of melted butter, by recipe No. 376; stir in the above ingredients, and let them just boil; when it is ready to serve.

Time.—1 minute to simmer. *Average cost*, 9d. per pint.

MAYONNAISE, a Sauce or Salad-Dressing for cold Chicken, Meat, and other cold Dishes.

468. INGREDIENTS.—The yolks of 2 eggs, 6 tablespoonfuls of salad-oil, 4 tablespoonfuls of vinegar, salt and white pepper to taste, 1 tablespoonful of white stock, No. 107, 2 tablespoonfuls of cream.

Mode.—Put the yolks of the eggs into a basin, with a seasoning of pepper and salt; have ready the above quantities of oil and vinegar, in separate vessels; add them *very gradually* to the eggs; continue stirring and rubbing the mixture with a wooden spoon, as herein consists the secret of having a nice smooth sauce. It cannot be stirred too frequently, and it should be made in a very cool place, or, if ice is at hand, it should be mixed over it. When the vinegar and oil are well incorporated with the eggs, add the stock and cream, stirring all the time, and it will then be ready for use.

For a fish Mayonnaise, this sauce may be coloured with lobster-spawn, pounded; and for poultry or meat, where variety is desired, a little parsley-juice may be used to add to its appearance. Cucumber, Tarragon, or any other flavoured vinegar, may be substituted for plain, where they are liked.

Average cost, for this quantity, 7*d*.

Sufficient for a small salad.

Note.—In mixing the oil and vinegar with the eggs, put in first a few drops of oil, and then a few drops of vinegar, never adding a large quantity of either at one time, By this means, you can be more certain of the sauce not curdling. Patience and practice, let us add, are two essentials for making this sauce good.

MINT SAUCE, to serve with Roast Lamb.

469. INGREDIENTS.—4 dessertspoonfuls of chopped mint, 2 dessert-spoonfuls of pounded white sugar, ¼ pint of vinegar.

Mode.—Wash the mint, which should be young and fresh-gathered, free from grit; pick the leaves from the stalks, mince them very fine, and put them into a tureen; add the sugar and vinegar, and stir till the former is dissolved. This sauce is better by being made 2 or 3 hours before wanted for table, as the vinegar then becomes impregnated with the flavour of the mint. By many persons, the above proportion of sugar would not be considered sufficient; but as tastes vary, we have given the quantity which we have found to suit the general palate.

Average cost, 3*d*.

Sufficient to serve with a middling-sized joint of lamb.

Note.—Where green mint is scarce and not obtainable, mint vinegar may be substituted for it, and will be found very acceptable in early spring.

MINT.

MINT.—The common mint cultivated in our gardens is known as the *Mentha viridis*, and is employed in different culinary processes, being sometimes boiled with certain dishes, and afterwards withdrawn. It has an agreeable aromatic flavour, and forms an ingredient in soups, and sometimes is used in spring salads. It is valuable as a stomachic and antispasmodic; on which account it is generally served at table with pea-soup. Several of its species grow wild in low situations in the country.

MINT VINEGAR.

470. INGREDIENTS.—Vinegar, mint.

Mode.—Procure some nice fresh mint, pick the leaves from the stalks, and fill a bottle or jar with them. Add vinegar to them until the bottle is full; *cover closely* to exclude the air, and let it infuse for a fortnight. Then strain the liquor, and put it into small bottles for use, of which the corks should be sealed.

Seasonable.—This should be made in June, July, or August.

MIXED PICKLE.

(*Very Good.*)

471. INGREDIENTS.—To each gallon of vinegar allow $\frac{1}{4}$ lb. of bruised ginger, $\frac{1}{4}$ lb. of mustard, $\frac{1}{4}$ lb. of salt, 2 oz. of mustard-seed, $1\frac{1}{2}$ oz. of turmeric, 1 oz. of ground black pepper, $\frac{1}{4}$ oz. of cayenne, cauliflowers, onions, celery, sliced cucumbers, gherkins, French beans, nasturtiums, capsicums.

Mode.—Have a large jar, with a tightly-fitting lid, in which put as much vinegar as required, reserving a little to mix the various powders to a smooth paste. Put into a basin the mustard, turmeric, pepper, and cayenne; mix them with vinegar, and stir well until no lumps remain; add all the ingredients to the vinegar, and mix well. Keep this liquor in a warm place, and thoroughly stir every morning for a month with a wooden spoon, when it will be ready for the different vegetables to be added to it. As these come into season, have them gathered on a dry day, and, after merely wiping them with a cloth, to free them from moisture, put them into the pickle. The cauliflowers, it may be said, must be divided into small bunches. Put all these into the pickle raw, and at the end of the season, when there have been added as many of the vegetables as could be procured, store it away in jars, and tie over with bladder. As none of the ingredients are boiled, this pickle will not be fit to eat till 12 months have elapsed. Whilst the pickle is being made, keep a wooden spoon tied to the jar; and its contents, it may be repeated, must be stirred every morning.

Seasonable.—Make the pickle-liquor in May or June, as the season arrives for the various vegetables to be picked.

MUSHROOM KETCHUP.

472. INGREDIENTS.—To each peck of mushrooms $\frac{1}{2}$ lb. of salt; to each quart of mushroom-liquor $\frac{1}{4}$ oz. of cayenne, $\frac{1}{2}$ oz. of allspice, $\frac{1}{2}$ oz. of ginger, 2 blades of pounded mace.

Mode.—Choose full-grown mushroom-flaps, and take care they are perfectly *fresh-gathered* when the weather is tolerably dry; for, if they are picked during very heavy rain, the ketchup from which they are made is liable to get musty, and will not keep long. Put a layer of them in a deep pan, sprinkle salt over them, and then another layer of mushrooms, and so on alternately. Let them remain for a few hours, when break them up with the hand ; put them in a nice cool place for 3 days, occasionally stirring and mashing them well, to extract from them as much juice as possible. Now measure the quantity of liquor without straining, and to each quart allow the above proportion of spices, &c. Put all into a stone jar, cover it up very closely, put it in a saucepan of boiling water, set it over the fire, and let it boil for 3 hours. Have ready a nice clean stewpan ; turn into it the contents of the jar, and let the whole simmer very gently for ½ hour; pour it into a jug, where it should stand in a cool place till the next day ; then pour it off into another jug, and strain it into very dry clean bottles, and do not squeeze the mushrooms. To each pint of ketchup add a few drops of brandy. Be careful not to shake the contents, but leave all the sediment behind in the jug ; cork well, and either seal or rosin the cork, so as perfectly to exclude the air. When a very clear bright ketchup is wanted, the liquor must be strained through a very fine hair-sieve, or flannel bag, *after* it has been very gently poured off; if the operation is not successful, it must be repeated until you have quite a clear liquor. It should be examined occasionally, and if it is spoiling, should be reboiled with a few peppercorns.

Seasonable from the beginning of September to the middle of October, when this ketchup should be made.

Note.—This flavouring ingredient, if genuine and well prepared, is one of the most useful store sauces to the experienced cook, and no trouble should be spared in its preparation. Double ketchup is made by reducing the liquor to half the quantity ; for example, 1 quart must be boiled down to 1 pint. This goes farther than ordinary ketchup, as so little is required to flavour a good quantity of gravy. The sediment may also be bottled for immediate use, and will be found to answer for flavouring thick soups or gravies.

HOW TO DISTINGUISH MUSHROOMS FROM TOADSTOOLS.—The cultivated mushroom, known as *Agaricus campestris*, may be distinguished from other poisonous kinds of fungi by its having pink or flesh-coloured gills, or under-side, and by its invariably having an agreeable smell, which the toadstool has not. When young, mushrooms are like a small round button, both the stalk and head being white. As they grow larger, they expand their heads by degrees into a flat form, the gills underneath being at first of a pale flesh-colour, but becoming, as they stand longer, dark brown or blackish. Nearly all the poisonous kinds are brown, and have in general a rank and putrid smell. Edible mushrooms are found in closely-fed pastures, but seldom grow in woods, where most of the poisonous sorts are to be found.

TO DRY MUSHROOMS.

473. *Mode.*—Wipe them clean, take away the brown part, and peel off the skin ; lay them on sheets of paper to dry, in a cool

oven, when they will shrivel considerably. Keep them in paper bags, which hang in a dry place. When wanted for use, put them into cold gravy, bring them gradually to simmer, and it will be found that they will regain nearly their usual size.

THE MUSHROOM.

THE MUSHROOM.—The cultivated or garden mushroom is a species of fungus, which, in England, is considered the best, and is there usually eaten. The tribe, however, is numerous, and a large proportion of them are poisonous; hence it is always dangerous to make use of mushrooms gathered in their wild state. In some parts of Europe, as in Germany, Russia, and Poland, many species grow wild, and are used as food; but in Britain, two only are generally eaten. These are mostly employed for the flavouring of dishes, and are also dried and pickled. CATSUP, or KETCHUP, is made from them by mixing spices and salt with their juice. The young, called buttons, are the best for pickling when in the globular form.

BROWN MUSHROOM SAUCE, to serve with Roast Meat, &c.

474. INGREDIENTS.—½ pint of button mushrooms, ½ pint of good beef gravy, No. 435, 1 tablespoonful of mushroom ketchup (if at hand), thickening of butter and flour.

Mode.—Put the gravy into a saucepan, thicken it, and stir over the fire until it boils. Prepare the mushrooms by cutting off the stalks and wiping them free from grit and dirt; the large flap mushrooms cut into small pieces will answer for a brown sauce, when the buttons are not obtainable; put them into the gravy, and let them simmer very gently for about 10 minutes; then add the ketchup, and serve.

Time.—Rather more than 10 minutes.

Seasonable from August to October.

Note.—When fresh mushrooms are not obtainable, the powder No. 477 may be used as a substitute for brown sauce.

WHITE MUSHROOM SAUCE, to serve with Boiled Fowls, Cutlets, &c.

I.

475. INGREDIENTS.—Rather more than ½ pint of button mushrooms, lemon-juice and water, 1 oz. of butter, ½ pint of Béchamel, No. 367, ¼ teaspoonful of pounded sugar.

Mode.—Turn the mushrooms white by putting them into lemon-juice and water, having previously cut off the stalks and wiped them perfectly free from grit. Chop them, and put them in a stewpan with the butter. When the mushrooms are softened, add the Béchamel, and simmer for about 5 minutes; should they, however, not be done enough, allow rather more time. They should not boil longer than necessary, as they would then lose their colour and flavour. Rub the whole through a tammy, and serve very hot. After this, it should be warmed in a bain marie.

Time.—Altogether, ¼ hour. *Average cost,* 1s.

Seasonable from August to October.

II.

A More Simple Method.

476. INGREDIENTS.—⅓ pint of melted butter, made with milk, No. 380; ½ pint of button mushrooms, 1 dessertspoonful of mushroom ketchup, if at hand; cayenne and salt to taste.

Mode.—Make the melted butter by recipe No. 380, and add to it the mushrooms, which must be nicely cleaned, and free from grit, and the stalks cut off. Let them simmer gently for about 10 minutes, or until they are quite tender. Put in the seasoning and ketchup; let it just boil, when serve.

Time.—Rather more than 10 minutes. *Average cost,* 8d.

Seasonable from August to October.

GROWTH OF THE MUSHROOM AND OTHER FUNGI.—The quick growth of the mushroom and other fungi is no less wonderful than the length of time they live, and the numerous dangers they resist while they continue in the dormant state. To spring up "like a mushroom in a night" is a scriptural mode of expressing celerity; and this completely accords with all the observations which have been made concerning this curious class of plants. Mr. Sowerby remarks—"I have often placed specimens of the *Phallus caninus* by a window over-night, while in the egg-form, and they have been fully grown by the morning."

MUSHROOM POWDER (a valuable addition to Sauces and Gravies, when fresh Mushrooms are not obtainable).

477. INGREDIENTS.—½ peck of large mushrooms, 2 onions, 12 cloves, ¼ oz. of pounded mace, 2 teaspoonfuls of white pepper.

Mode.—Peel the mushrooms, wipe them perfectly free from grit and dirt, remove the black fur, and reject all those that are at all worm-eaten; put them into a stewpan with the above ingredients, but without water; shake them over a clear fire, till all the liquor is dried up, and be careful not to let them burn; arrange them on tins, and dry them in a slow oven; pound them to a fine powder, which put into small *dry* bottles; cork well, seal the corks, and keep it in a dry place. In using this powder, add it to the gravy just before serving, when it will merely require one boil-up. The flavour imparted by this means to the gravy, ought to be exceedingly good.

Seasonable.—This should be made in September, or at the beginning of October.

Note.—If the bottles in which it is stored away are not perfectly dry, as, also the mushroom powder, it will keep good but a very short time.

PICKLED MUSHROOMS.

478. INGREDIENTS.—Sufficient vinegar to cover the mushrooms; to each quart of mushrooms, 2 blades of pounded mace, 1 oz. of ground pepper, salt to taste.

Mode.—Choose some nice young button mushrooms for pickling, and rub off the skin with a piece of flannel and salt, and cut off the stalks; if very large, take out the red inside, and reject the black ones, as they are too old. Put them in a stewpan, sprinkle salt over them, with pounded mace and pepper in the above proportion; shake them well over a clear fire until the liquor flows, and keep them there until it is all dried up again; then add as much vinegar as will cover them; just let it simmer for 1 minute, and store it away in stone jars for use. When cold, tie down with bladder and keep in a dry place: they will remain good for a length of time, and are generally considered delicious.

Seasonable.—Make this the same time as ketchup, from the beginning of September to the middle of October.

NATURE OF THE MUSHROOM.—Locality has evidently a considerable influence on the nature of the juices of the mushroom; for it has been discovered, after fatal experience, that some species, which are perfectly harmless when raised in open meadows and pasture-lands, become virulently poisonous when they happen to grow in contact with stagnant water or putrescent animal and vegetable substances. What the precise nature of the poison in fungi may be, has not been accurately ascertained.

A VERY RICH AND GOOD MUSHROOM SAUCE, to serve with Fowls or Rabbits.

479. INGREDIENTS.—1 pint of mushroom-buttons, salt to taste, a little grated nutmeg, 1 blade of pounded mace, 1 pint of cream, 2 oz. of butter, flour to thicken.

Mode.—Rub the buttons with a piece of flannel and salt, to take off the skin; cut off the stalks, and put them in a stewpan with the above ingredients, previously kneading together the butter and flour; boil the whole for about ten minutes, stirring all the time. Pour some of the sauce over the fowls, and the remainder serve in a tureen.

Time.—10 minutes. *Average cost,* 2s.

Sufficient to serve with a pair of fowls.

Seasonable from August to October.

HOW TO MIX MUSTARD.

480. INGREDIENTS.—Mustard, salt, and water.

Mode.—Mustard should be mixed with water that has been boiled and allowed to cool; hot water destroys its essential properties, and raw cold water might cause it to ferment. Put the mustard in a cup, with a small pinch of salt, and mix with it very gradually sufficient boiled water to make it drop from the spoon without being watery. Stir and mix well, and rub the lumps well down with the back of a spoon, as well-mixed mustard should be perfectly free from these. The mustard-pot should not be more than half full, or rather less if it will not be used in a day or two, as it is so much better when freshly mixed.

TARTAR MUSTARD.

481. INGREDIENTS.—Horseradish vinegar, cayenne, ½ a teacupful of mustard.

Mode.—Have ready sufficient horseradish vinegar to mix with the above proportion of mustard; put the mustard in a cup, with a slight seasoning of cayenne; mix it perfectly smooth with the vinegar, adding this a little at a time; rub down with the back of a spoon any lumps that may appear, and do not let it be too thin. Mustard may be flavoured in various ways, with Tarragon, shalot, celery, and many other vinegars, herbs, spices, &c.; but this is more customary in France than in England, as there it is merely considered a " vehicle of flavours," as it has been termed.

PICKLED NASTURTIUMS (a very good Substitute for Capers)

482. INGREDIENTS.—To each pint of vinegar, 1 oz. of salt, 6 peppercorns, nasturtiums.

Mode.—Gather the nasturtium-pods on a dry day, and wipe them clean with a cloth; put them in a dry glass bottle, with vinegar, salt, and pepper in the above proportion. If you cannot find enough ripe to fill a bottle, cork up what you have got until you have some more fit: they may be added from day to day. Bung up the bottles, and seal or rosin the tops. They will be fit for use in 10 or 12 months; and the best way is to make them one season for the next.

NASTURTIUMS.

Seasonable.—Look for nasturtium-pods from the end of July to the end of August.

NASTURTIUMS.—The elegant nasturtium-plant, called by naturalists *Tropæolum*, and which sometimes goes by the name of Indian cress, came originally from Peru, but was easily made to grow in these islands. Its young leaves and flowers are of a slightly hot nature, and many consider them a good adjunct to salads, to which they certainly add a pretty appearance. When the beautiful blossoms, which may be employed with great effect in garnishing dishes, are off, then the fruit is used as described in the above recipe.

FRENCH ONION SAUCE, or SOUBISE.

483. INGREDIENTS.—½ pint of Béchamel, No. 367, 1 bay-leaf, seasoning to taste of pounded mace and cayenne, 6 onions, a small piece of ham.

Mode.—Peel the onions and cut them in halves; put them in a stewpan, with just sufficient water to cover them, and add the bay-leaf, ham, cayenne, and mace ; be careful to keep the lid closely shut, and simmer them until tender. Take them out and drain thoroughly ; rub them through a tammy or sieve (an old one does for the purpose) with a wooden spoon, and put them to ½ pint of Béchamel ; keep stirring over the fire until it boils, when serve. If it should require any more seasoning, add it to taste.

Time.—¾ hour to boil the onions.

Average cost, 10d. for this quantity.

Sufficient for a moderate-sized dish.

WHITE ONION SAUCE, for Boiled Rabbits, Roast Shoulder of Mutton, &c.

484. INGREDIENTS.— 9 large onions, or 12 middling-sized ones, 1 pint of melted butter made with milk (No. 380), ½ teaspoonful of salt, or rather more.

Mode.—Peel the onions and put them into water to which a little salt has been added, to preserve their whiteness, and let them remain for ¼ hour. Then put them in a stewpan, cover them with water, and let them boil until tender, and, if the onions should be very strong, change the water after they have been boiling for ¼ hour. Drain them thoroughly, chop them, and rub them through a tammy or sieve. Make 1 pint of melted butter, by recipe No. 380, and when that boils, put in the onions, with a seasoning of salt; stir it till it simmers, when it will be ready to serve. If these directions are carefully attended to, this onion sauce will be delicious.

Time.—From ¾ to 1 hour, to boil the onions.

Average cost, 9d. per pint.

Sufficient to serve with a roast shoulder of mutton, or boiled rabbit.

Seasonable from August to March.

Note.—To make this sauce very mild and delicate, use Spanish onions, which can be procured from the beginning of September to Christmas. 2 or 3 tablespoonfuls of cream added just before serving, will be found to improve its appearance very much. Small onions, when very young, may be cooked whole, and served in melted butter. A sieve or tammy should be kept expressly for onions : an old one answers the purpose, as it is liable to retain the flavour and smell, which of course would be excessively disagreeable in delicate preparations.

BROWN ONION SAUCE.

485. INGREDIENTS.—6 large onions, rather more than ½ pint of good gravy, 2 oz. of butter, salt and pepper to taste.

Mode.—Slice and fry the onions of a pale brown in a stewpan, with the above quantity of butter, keeping them well stirred, that they do not get black. When a nice colour, pour over the gravy, and let them simmer gently until tender. Now skim off every particle of fat, add the seasoning, and rub the whole through a tammy or sieve ; put it back in the saucepan to warm, and when it boils, serve.

Time.—Altogether 1 hour.

Seasonable from August to March.

Note.—Where a very high flavouring is liked, add 1 tablespoonful of mushroom ketchup, or a small quantity of port wine.

HISTORY OF THE ONION.—It is not supposed that any variety of the onion is indigenous to Britain, as when the large and mild roots imported from warmer climates, have been cultivated in these islands a few years, they deteriorate both in size and sweetness. It is therefore most likely that this plant was first introduced into England from continental Europe, and that it originally was produced in a southern climate, and has gradually become acclimatized to a colder atmosphere. (*See* No. 139.)

PICKLED ONIONS (a very Simple Method, and exceedingly Good).

486. INGREDIENTS.—Pickling onions ; to each quart of vinegar, 2 teaspoonfuls of allspice, 2 teaspoonfuls of whole black pepper.

Mode.—Have the onions gathered when quite dry and ripe, and, with the fingers, take off the thin outside skin ; then, with a silver knife (steel should not be used, as it spoils the colour of the onions), remove one more skin, when the onion will look quite clear. Have ready some very dry bottles or jars, and as fast as they are peeled, put them in. Pour over sufficient cold vinegar to cover them, with pepper and allspice in the above proportions, taking care that each jar has its share of the latter ingredients. Tie down with bladder, and put them in a dry place, and in a fortnight they will be fit for use. This is a most simple recipe and very delicious, the onions being nice and crisp. They should be eaten within 6 or 8 months after being done, as the onions are liable to become soft.

Seasonable from the middle of July to the end of August.

PICKLED ONIONS.

487. INGREDIENTS.—1 gallon of pickling onions, salt and water, milk; to each ½ gallon of vinegar, 1 oz. of bruised ginger, ¼ teaspoonful of cayenne, 1 oz. of allspice, 1 oz. of whole black pepper, ¼ oz. of whole nutmeg bruised, 8 cloves, ¼ oz. of mace.

Mode.—Gather the onions, which should not be too small, when they are quite dry and ripe; wipe off the dirt, but do not pare them; make a strong solution of salt and water, into which put the onions, and change this, morning and night, for 3 days, and save the *last* brine they were put in. Then take the outside skin off, and put them into a tin saucepan capable of holding them all, as they are always better done together. Now take equal quantities of milk and the last salt and water the onions were in, and pour this to them; to this add 2 large spoonfuls of salt, put them over the fire, and watch them very attentively. Keep constantly turning the onions about with a wooden skimmer, those at the bottom to the top, and *vice versâ;* and let the milk and water run through the holes of the skimmer. Remember, the onions must never boil, or, if they do, they will be good for nothing; and they should be quite transparent. Keep the onions stirred for a few minutes, and, in stirring them, be particular not to break them. Then have ready a pan with a colander, into which turn the onions to drain, covering them with a cloth to keep in the steam. Place on a table an old cloth, 2 or 3 times double; put the onions on it when quite hot, and over them an old piece of blanket; cover this closely over them, to keep in the steam. Let them remain till the next day, when they will be quite cold, and look yellow and shrivelled; take off the shrivelled skins, when they should be as white as snow. Put them in a pan, make a pickle of vinegar and the remaining ingredients, boil all these up, and pour hot over the onions in the pan. Cover very closely to keep in all the steam, and let them stand till the following day, when they will be quite cold. Put them into jars or bottles well bunged, and a tablespoonful of the best olive-oil on the top of each jar or bottle. Tie them down with bladder, and let them stand in a cool place for a month or six weeks, when they will be fit for use. They should be beautifully white, and eat crisp, without the least softness, and will keep good many months.

Seasonable from the middle of July to the end of August.

ORANGE GRAVY, for Wildfowl, Widgeon, Teal, &c.

488. INGREDIENTS.—½ pint of white stock, No. 107, 1 small onion, 3 or 4 strips of lemon or orange peel, a few leaves of basil, if at hand,

the juice of a Seville orange or lemon, salt and pepper to taste, 1 glass of port wine.

Mode.—Put the onion, cut in slices, into a stewpan with the stock orange-peel, and basil, and let them simmer very gently for ¼ hour or rather longer, should the gravy not taste sufficiently of the peel Strain it off, and add to the gravy the remaining ingredients; let the whole heat through, and, when on the point of boiling, serve very hot in a tureen which should have a cover to it.

Time.—Altogether ½ hour.

Sufficient for a small tureen.

OYSTER FORCEMEAT, for Roast or Boiled Turkey.

489. INGREDIENTS.—½ pint of bread crumbs, 1½ oz. of chopped suet or butter, 1 faggot of savoury herbs, ¼ saltspoonful of grated nutmeg, salt and pepper to taste, 2 eggs, 18 oysters.

Mode.—Grate the bread very fine, and be careful that no large lumps remain; put it into a basin with the suet, which must be very finely minced, or, when butter is used, that must be cut up into small pieces. Add the herbs, also chopped as small as possible, and seasoning; mix all these well together, until the ingredients are thoroughly mingled. Open and beard the oysters, chop them, but not too small, and add them to the other ingredients. Beat up the eggs, and, with the hand, work altogether, until it is smoothly mixed. The turkey should not be stuffed too full: if there should be too much forcemeat, roll it into balls, fry them, and use them as a garnish.

Sufficient for 1 turkey.

OYSTER KETCHUP.

490. INGREDIENTS.—Sufficient oysters to fill a pint measure, 1 pint of sherry, 3 oz. of salt, 1 drachm of cayenne, 2 drachms of pounded mace.

Mode.—Procure the oysters very fresh, and open sufficient to fill a pint measure; save the liquor, and scald the oysters i it with the sherry; strain the oysters, and put them in a mortar with the salt, cayenne, and mace; pound the whole until reduced to a pulp, then add it to the liquor in which they were scalded; boil it again five minutes, and skim well; rub the whole through a sieve, and, when cold, bottle and cork closely. The corks should be sealed.

Seasonable from September to April.

Note.—Cider may be substituted for the sherry.

PICKLED OYSTERS.

491. INGREDIENTS.—100 oysters; to each $\frac{1}{2}$ pint of vinegar, 1 blade of pounded mace, 1 strip of lemon-peel, 12 black peppercorns.

Mode.—Get the oysters in good condition, open them, place them in a saucepan, and let them simmer in their own liquor for about 10 minutes, very gently; then take them out, one by one, and place them in a jar, and cover them, when cold, with a pickle made as follows:—Measure the oyster-liquor; add to it the same quantity of vinegar, with mace, lemon-peel, and pepper in the above proportion, and boil it for 5 minutes; when cold, pour over the oysters, and tie them down very closely, as contact with the air spoils them.

Seasonable from September to April.

Note.—Put this pickle away in small jars; because directly one is opened, its contents should immediately be eaten, as they soon spoil. The pickle should not be kept more than 2 or 3 months.

OYSTER SAUCE, to serve with Fish, Boiled Poultry, &c.

492. INGREDIENTS.—3 dozen oysters, $\frac{1}{2}$ pint of melted butter, made with milk, No. 380.

Mode.—Open the oysters carefully, and save their liquor; strain it into a clean saucepan (a lined one is best), put in the oysters, and let them just come to the boiling-point, when they should look plump. Take them off the fire immediately, and put the whole into a basin. Strain the liquor from them, mix with it sufficient milk to make $\frac{1}{2}$ pint altogether, and follow the directions of No. 380. When the melted butter is ready and very smooth, put in the oysters, which should be previously bearded, if you wish the sauce to be really nice. Set it by the side of the fire to get thoroughly hot, *but do not allow it to boil*, or the oysters will immediately harden. Using cream instead of milk makes this sauce extremely delicious. When liked, add a seasoning of cayenne, or anchovy sauce; but, as we have before stated, a plain sauce *should* be plain, and not be overpowered by highly-flavoured essences; therefore we recommend that the above directions be implicitly followed, and no seasoning added.

Average cost for this quantity, 2s.

Sufficient for 6 persons. Never allow fewer than 6 oysters to 1 person, unless the party is very large.

Seasonable from September to April.

A more economical sauce may be made by using a smaller quantity of oysters, and not bearding them before they are added to the sauce: this may answer the purpose, but we cannot undertake to recommend it as a mode of making this delicious adjunct to fish, &c.

PARSLEY AND BUTTER, to serve with Calf's Head, Boiled Fowls, &c.

493. INGREDIENTS.—2 tablespoonfuls of minced parsley, ½ pint of melted butter, No. 376.

Mode.—Put into a saucepan a small quantity of water, slightly salted, and when it boils, throw in a good bunch of parsley which has been previously washed and tied together in a bunch; let it boil for 5 minutes, drain it, mince the leaves *very fine*, and put the above quantity in a tureen; pour over it ½ pint of smoothly-made melted butter; stir once, that the ingredients may be thoroughly mixed, and serve.

Time.—5 minutes to boil the parsley. *Average cost,* 4*d.*

Sufficient for 1 large fowl; allow rather more for a pair.

Seasonable at any time.

Note.—Sometimes, in the middle of winter, parsley-leaves are not to be had, when the following will be found an excellent substitute:—Tie up a little parsley-seed in a small piece of muslin, and boil it for 10 minutes in a small quantity of water; use this water to make the melted butter with, and throw into it a little boiled spinach, minced rather fine, which will have an appearance similar to that of parsley.

PARSLEY.

PARSLEY.—If there be nothing new under the sun, there are, at any rate, different uses found for the same thing; for this pretty aromatic herb was used in ancient times, as we learn from mythological narrative, to adorn the head of a hero, no less than Hercules; and now—was ever fall so great?—we moderns use it in connection with the head of—a calf. According to Homer's "Iliad," warriors fed their chariot-steeds on parsley; and Pliny acquaints us with the fact that, as a symbol of mourning, it was admitted to furnish the funeral tables of the Romans. Egypt, some say, first produced this herb; thence it was introduced, by some unknown voyager, into Sardinia, where the Carthaginians found it, and made it known to the inhabitants of Marseilles. (*See* No. 123.)

FRIED PARSLEY, for Garnishing.

494. INGREDIENTS.—Parsley, hot lard or clarified dripping.

Mode.—Gather some young parsley; wash, pick, and dry it thorougly in a cloth; put it into the wire basket of which we have given an engraving, and hold it in boiling lard or dripping for a minute or two. Directly it is done, lift out the basket, and let it stand before the fire, that the parsley may become thoroughly crisp; and the quicker it is fried the better. Should the kitchen not be furnished with the

above article, throw the parsley into the frying-pan, and when crisp, lift it out with a slice, dry it before the fire, and when thoroughly crisp, it will be ready for use.

WIRE BASKET.

WIRE BASKET.—For this recipe, a wire basket, as shown in the annexed engraving, will be found very useful. It is very light and handy, and may be used for other similar purposes besides that described above.

PARSLEY JUICE, for Colouring various Dishes.

495. Procure some nice young parsley; wash it and dry it thoroughly in a cloth; pound the leaves in a mortar till all the juice is extracted, and put the juice in a teacup or small jar; place this in a saucepan of boiling water, and warm it on the *bain marie* principle just long enough to take off its rawness; let it drain, and it will be ready for colouring.

TO PRESERVE PARSLEY THROUGH THE WINTER.

496. Use freshly-gathered parsley for keeping, and wash it perfectly free from grit and dirt; put it into boiling water which has been slightly salted and well skimmed, and then let it boil for 2 or 3 minutes; take it out, let it drain, and lay it on a sieve in front of the fire, when it should be dried as expeditiously as possible. Store it away in a very dry place in bottles, and when wanted for use, pour over it a little warm water, and let it stand for about 5 minutes.

Seasonable.—This may be done at any time between June and October.

AN EXCELLENT PICKLE.

497. INGREDIENTS.—Equal quantities of medium-sized onions, cucumbers, and sauce-apples; 1½ teaspoonful of salt, ¾ teaspoonful of cayenne, 1 wineglassful of soy, 1 wineglassful of sherry; vinegar.

Mode.—Slice sufficient cucumbers, onions, and apples to fill a pint stone jar, taking care to cut the slices very thin; arrange them in alternate layers, shaking in as you proceed salt and cayenne in the above proportion; pour in the soy and wine, and fill up with vinegar. It will be fit for use the day it is made.

Seasonable in August and September.

[This recipe was forwarded to the editress of this work by a subscriber to the "Englishwoman's Domestic Magazine." Mrs. Beeton, not having tested it, cannot vouch for its excellence; but the contributor spoke very highly in its favour.]

SOY.—This is a sauce frequently made use of for fish, and comes from Japan, where it is prepared from the seeds of a plant called *Dolichos Soja*. The Chinese also manufacture it; but that made by the Japanese is said to be the best. All sorts of statements have been made respecting the very general adulteration of this article in England, and we fear that many of them are too true. When genuine, it is of an agreeable flavour, thick, and of a clear brown colour.

PICKLED RED CABBAGE.

498. INGREDIENTS.—Red cabbages, salt and water; to each quart of vinegar, ½ oz. of ginger well bruised, 1 oz. of whole black pepper, and, when liked, a little cayenne.

Mode.—Take off the outside decayed leaves of a nice red cabbage, cut it in quarters, remove the stalks, and cut it across in very thin slices. Lay these on a dish, and strew them plentifully with salt, covering them with another dish. Let them remain for 24 hours, turn into a colander to drain, and, if necessary, wipe lightly with a clean soft cloth. Put them in a jar; boil up the vinegar with spices in the above proportion, and, when cold, pour it over the cabbage. It will be fit for use in a week or two, and, if kept for a very long time, the cabbage is liable get soft and to discolour. To be really nice and crisp, and of a good red colour, it should be eaten almost immediately after it is made. A little bruised cochineal boiled with the vinegar adds much to the appearance of this pickle. Tie down with bladder, and keep in a dry place.

Seasonable in July and August, but the pickle will be much more crisp if the frost has just touched the leaves.

RED CABBAGE.—This plant, in its growth, is similar in form to that of the white, but is of a bluish-purple colour, which, however, turns red on the application of acid, as is the case with all vegetable blues. It is principally from the white vegetable that the Germans make their *sauer kraut;* a dish held in such high estimation with the inhabitants of Vaderland, but which requires, generally speaking, with strangers, a long acquaintance in order to become sufficiently impressed with its numerous merits. The large red Dutch is the kind generally recommended for pickling.

PLUM-PUDDING SAUCE.

499. INGREDIENTS.—1 wineglassful of brandy, 2 oz. of very fresh butter, 1 glass of Madeira, pounded sugar to taste.

Mode.—Put the pounded sugar in a basin, with part of the brandy and the butter; let it stand by the side of the fire until it is warm and the sugar and butter are dissolved; then add the rest of the brandy, with the Madeira. Either pour it over the pudding, or serve in a tureen. This is a very rich and excellent sauce.

Average cost, 1s. 3d. for this quantity.

Sufficient for a pudding made for 6 persons.

QUIN'S SAUCE, an excellent Fish Sauce.

500. INGREDIENTS.—½ pint of walnut pickle, ½ pint of port wine,

1 pint of mushroom ketchup, 1 dozen anchovies, 1 dozen shalots, ¼ pint of soy, ½ teaspoonful of cayenne.

Mode.—Put all the ingredients into a saucepan, having previously chopped the shalots and anchovies very small ; simmer for 15 minutes, strain, and, when cold, bottle off for use : the corks should be well sealed to exclude the air.

Time.—¼ hour.

Seasonable at any time.

RAVIGOTTE, a French Salad Sauce.

Mons. Ude's Recipe.

501. INGREDIENTS.—1 teaspoonful of mushroom ketchup, 1 teaspoonful of cavice, 1 teaspoonful of Chili vinegar, 1 teaspoonful of Reading sauce, a piece of butter the size of an egg, 3 tablespoonfuls of thick Béchamel, No. 367, 1 tablespoonful of minced parsley, 3 tablespoonfuls of cream ; salt and pepper to taste.

Mode.—Scald the parsley, mince the leaves very fine, and add it to all the other ingredients ; after mixing the whole together thoroughly, the sauce will be ready for use.

Average cost, for this quantity, 10d.

Seasonable at any time.

READING SAUCE.

502. INGREDIENTS.—2½ pints of walnut pickle, 1½ oz. of shalots, 1 quart of spring water, ¾ pint of Indian soy, ½ oz. of bruised ginger, ½ oz. of long pepper, 1 oz. of mustard-seed, 1 anchovy, ½ oz. of cayenne, ¼ oz. of dried sweet bay-leaves.

Mode.—Bruise the shalots in a mortar, and put them in a stone jar with the walnut-liquor ; place it before the fire, and let it boil until reduced to 2 pints. Then, into another jar, put all the ingredients except the bay-leaves, taking care that they are well bruised, so that the flavour may be thoroughly extracted ; put this also before the fire, and let it boil for 1 hour, or rather more. When the contents of both jars are sufficiently cooked, mix them together, stirring them well as you mix them, and submit them to a slow boiling for ½ hour ; cover closely, and let them stand 24 hours in a cool place ; then open the jar and add the bay-leaves ; let it stand a week longer closed down, when strain through a flannel bag, and it will be ready for use. The above quantities will make ½ gallon.

Time.—Altogether, 3 hours.

Seasonable.—This sauce may be made at any time.

REMOULADE, or FRENCH SALAD-DRESSING.

503. INGREDIENTS. — 4 eggs, ½ tablespoonful of made mustard, salt and cayenne to taste, 3 tablespoonfuls of olive-oil, 1 tablespoonful of tarragon or plain vinegar.

Mode.—Boil 3 eggs quite hard for about ¼ hour, put them into cold water, and let them remain in it for a few minutes; strip off the shells, put the yolks in a mortar, and pound them very smoothly; add to them, very gradually, the mustard, seasoning, and vinegar, keeping all well stirred and rubbed down with the back of a wooden spoon. Put in the oil drop by drop, and when this is thoroughly mixed with the other ingredients, add the yolk of a raw egg, and stir well, when it will be ready for use. This sauce should not be curdled; and to prevent this, the only way is to mix a little of everything at a time, and not to cease stirring. The quantities of oil and vinegar may be increased or diminished according to taste, as many persons would prefer a smaller proportion of the former ingredient.

GREEN REMOULADE is made by using tarragon vinegar instead of plain, and colouring with a little parsley-juice, No. 495. Harvey's sauce, or Chili vinegar, may be added at pleasure.

Time.—¼ hour to boil the eggs.

Average cost, for this quantity, 7d.

Sufficient for a salad made for 4 or 6 persons.

TARRAGON.

TARRAGON.—The leaves of this plant, known to naturalists as *Artemisia dracunculus*, are much used in France as a flavouring ingredient for salads. From it also is made the vinegar known as tarragon vinegar, which is employed by the French in mixing their mustard. It originally comes from Tartary, and does not seed in France.

SAGE-AND-ONION STUFFING, for Geese, Ducks, and Pork.

504. INGREDIENTS.—4 large onions, 10 sage-leaves, ¼ lb. of bread crumbs, 1½ oz. of butter, salt and pepper to taste, 1 egg.

Mode.—Peel the onions, put them into boiling water, let them simmer for 5 minutes or rather longer, and, just before they are taken out, put in the sage-leaves for a minute or two to take off their rawness. Chop both these very fine, add the bread, seasoning, and butter, and work the whole together with the yolk of an egg, when the stuffing will be ready for use. It should be rather highly seasoned, and the sage-leaves should be very finely chopped. Many cooks do not parboil the onions in the manner just stated, but merely use them raw. The stuffing then, however, is not nearly so mild, and, to many tastes, its strong flavour would be very objectionable. When made for goose, a portion of the liver of the bird, simmered for a few minutes and very finely minced, is frequently added to this stuffing; and where economy is studied, the egg may be dispensed with.

Time.—Rather more than 5 minutes to simmer the onions.

Average cost, for this quantity, 4*d*.

Sufficient for 1 goose, or a pair of ducks.

505. SOYER'S RECIPE FOR GOOSE STUFFING.—Take 4 apples, peeled and cored, 4 onions, 4 leaves of sage, and 4 leaves of lemon thyme not broken, and boil them in a stewpan with sufficient water to cover them; when done, pulp them through a sieve, removing the sage and thyme; then add sufficient pulp of mealy potatoes to cause it to be sufficiently dry without sticking to the hand; add pepper and salt, and stuff the bird.

SALAD DRESSING (Excellent).

I.

506. INGREDIENTS.—1 teaspoonsful of mixed mustard, 1 teaspoonful of pounded sugar, 2 tablespoonfuls of salad oil, 4 tablespoonfuls of milk, 2 tablespoonfuls of vinegar, cayenne and salt to taste.

Mode.—Put the mixed mustard into a salad-bowl with the sugar, and add the oil drop by drop, carefully stirring and mixing all these ingredients well together. Proceed in this manner with the milk and vinegar, which must be added very *gradually*, or the sauce will curdle. Put in the seasoning, when the mixture will be ready for use. If this dressing is properly made, it will have a soft creamy appearance, and will be found very delicious with crab, or cold fried fish (the latter cut into dice), as well as with salads. In mixing salad dressings, the ingredients cannot be added *too gradually*, or *stirred too much*.

Average cost, for this quantity, 3*d*.

Sufficient for a small salad.

This recipe can be confidently recommended by the editress, to whom it was given by an intimate friend noted for her salads.

SCARCITY OF SALADS IN ENGLAND.—Three centuries ago, very few vegetables were cultivated in England, and an author writing of the period of Henry VIII.'s reign, tells us that neither salad, nor carrots, nor cabbages, nor radishes, nor any other comestibles of a like nature, were grown in any part of the kingdom: they came from Holland and Flanders. We further learn, that Queen Catharine herself, with all her royalty, could not procure a salad of English growth for her dinner. The king was obliged to mend this sad state of affairs, and send to Holland for a gardener in order to cultivate those pot-herbs, in the growth of which England is now, perhaps, not behind any other country in Europe.

The Olive and Olive Oil.—This tree assumes a high degree of interest from the historical circumstances with which it is connected. A leaf of it was brought into the ark by the dove, when that vessel was still floating on the waters of the great deep, and gave the first token that the deluge was subsiding. Among the Greeks, the prize of the victor in the Olympic games was a wreath of wild olive; and the " Mount of Olives " is rendered familiar to our ears by its being mentioned in the Scriptures as near to Jerusalem. The tree is indigenous in the north of Africa, Syria, and Greece; and the Romans introduced it to Italy. In Spain and the south of France it is now cultivated; and although it grows in England, its fruit does not ripen in the open air. Both in Greece and Portugal the fruit is eaten in its ripe state; but its taste is not agreeable to many palates. To the Italian shepherd, bread and olives, with a little wine, form a nourishing diet; but in England, olives are usually only introduced by way of dessert, to destroy the taste of the viands which have been previously eaten, that the flavour of the wine may be the better enjoyed. There are three kinds of olives imported to London,—the French, Spanish, and Italian: the first are from Provence, and are generally

THE OLIVE.

accounted excellent; the second are larger, but more bitter; and the last are from Lucca, and are esteemed the best. The oil extracted from olives, called olive oil, or salad oil, is, with the continentals, in continual request, more dishes being prepared with than without it, we should imagine. With us, it is principally used in mixing a salad, and when thus employed, it tends to prevent fermentation, and is an antidote against flatulency.

II.

507. Ingredients.—4 eggs, 1 teaspoonful of mixed mustard, ¼ teaspoonful of white pepper, half that quantity of cayenne, salt to taste, 4 tablespoonfuls of cream, vinegar.

Mode.—Boil the eggs until hard, which will be in about ¼ hour or 20 minutes; put them into cold water, take off the shells, and pound the yolks in a mortar to a smooth paste. Then add all the other ingredients, except the vinegar, and stir them well until the whole are thoroughly incorporated one with the other. Pour in sufficient vinegar to make it of the consistency of cream, taking care to add but little at a time. The mixture will then be ready for use.

Average cost, for this quantity, 7*d.*

Sufficient for a moderate-sized salad.

Note.—The whites of the eggs, cut into rings, will serve very well as a garnishing to the salad.

III.

508. Ingredients.—1 egg, 1 teaspoonful of salad oil, 1 teaspoonful of mixed mustard, ¼ teaspoonful of salt, ½ teaspoonful of pounded sugar, 2 tablespoonfuls of vinegar, 6 tablespoonfuls of cream.

Mode.—Prepare and mix the ingredients by the preceding recipe, and be very particular that the whole is well stirred.

Note.—In making salads, the vegetables, &c., should never be added to the sauce very long before they are wanted for table; the dressing, however, may always be prepared some hours before required.   Where salads are much in request, it is a good plan to bottle off sufficient dressing for a few days' consumption, as, thereby, much time and trouble are saved.   If kept in a cool place, it will remain good for 4 or 5 days.

POETIC RECIPE FOR SALAD.—The Rev. Sydney Smith, the witty canon of St. Paul's, who thought that an enjoyment of the good things of this earth was compatible with aspirations for things higher, wrote the following excellent recipe for salad, which we should advise our readers not to pass by without a trial, when the hot weather invites to a dish of cold lamb.   May they find the flavour equal to the rhyme.—

" Two large potatoes, pass'd through kitchen sieve,
   Smoothness and softness to the salad give :
   Of mordent mustard add a single spoon,
   Distrust the condiment that bites too soon ;
   But deem it not, thou man of herbs, a fault,
   To add a double quantity of salt :
   Four times the spoon with oil of Lucca crown,
   And twice with vinegar procured from ' town ;'
   True flavour needs it, and your poet begs,
   The pounded yellow of two well-boil'd eggs.
   Let onion's atoms lurk within the bowl,
   And, scarce suspected, animate the whole ;
   And, lastly, in the flavour'd compound toss
   A magic spoonful of anchovy sauce.
   Oh ! great and glorious, and herbaceous treat,
   'Twould tempt the dying anchorite to eat.
   Back to the world he'd turn his weary soul,
   And plunge his fingers in the salad-bowl."

SAUCE ALLEMANDE, or GERMAN SAUCE.

509. INGREDIENTS.—½ pint of sauce tournée (No. 517), the yolks of 2 eggs.

Mode.—Put the sauce into a stewpan, heat it, and stir to it the beaten yolks of 2 eggs, which have been previously strained.   Let it just simmer, but not boil, or the eggs will curdle ; and after they are added to the sauce, it must be stirred without ceasing.   This sauce is a general favourite, and is used for many made dishes.

Time.—1 minute to simmer.

Average cost, 6d.

SAUCE ARISTOCRATIQUE (a Store Sauce).

510. INGREDIENTS.—Green walnuts.   To every pint of juice, 1 lb. of anchovies, 1 drachm of cloves, 1 drachm of mace, 1 drachm of Jamaica ginger bruised, 8 shalots.   To every pint of the boiled liquor, ¼ pint of vinegar, ¼ pint of port wine, 2 tablespoonfuls of soy.

Mode.—Pound the walnuts in a mortar, squeeze out the juice through a strainer, and let it stand to settle.   Pour off the clear juice, and to every pint of it, add anchovies, spices, and cloves in the above proportion.   Boil all these together till the anchovies are dissolved, then strain the juice again, put in the shalots (8 to every pint), and boil again. To every pint of the boiled liquor add vinegar, wine, and soy, in the above quantities, and bottle off for use. Cork well, and seal the corks.

Seasonable.—Make this sauce from the beginning to the middle of July, when walnuts are in perfection for sauces and pickling.

Average cost, 3s. 6d. for a quart.

MANUFACTURE OF SAUCES.—In France, during the reign of Louis XII., at the latter end of the 14th century, there was formed a company of sauce-manufacturers, who obtained, in those days of monopolies, the exclusive privilege of making sauces. The statutes drawn up by this company inform us that the famous sauce à la cameline, sold by them, was to be composed of "good cinnamon, good ginger, good cloves, good grains of paradise, good bread, and good vinegar." The sauce Tence, was to be made of "good sound almonds, good ginger, good wine, and good verjuice." May we respectfully express a hope—not that we desire to doubt it in the least—that the English sauce-manufacturers of the 19th century are equally considerate and careful in choosing their ingredients for their various well-known preparations.

SAUCE A L'AURORE, for Trout, Soles, &c.

511. INGREDIENTS.—The spawn of 1 lobster, 1 oz. of butter, ½ pint of Béchamel (No. 367), the juice of ½ lemon, a high seasoning of salt and cayenne.

Mode.—Take the spawn and pound it in a mortar with the butter, until quite smooth, and work it through a hair sieve. Put the Béchamel into a stewpan, add the pounded spawn, the lemon-juice, which must be strained, and a plentiful seasoning of cayenne and salt; let it just simmer, but do not allow it to boil, or the beautiful red colour of the sauce will be spoiled. A small spoonful of anchovy essence may be added at pleasure.

Time.—1 minute to simmer. *Average cost*, for this quantity, 1s.

Sufficient for a pair of large soles.

Seasonable at any time.

SAUCE A LA MATELOTE, for Fish.

512. INGREDIENTS.—½ pint of Espagnole (No. 411), 3 onions, 2 table-spoonfuls of mushroom ketchup, ½ glass of port wine, a bunch of sweet herbs, ½ bay-leaf, salt and pepper to taste, 1 clove, 2 berries of allspice, a little liquor in which the fish has been boiled, lemon-juice, and anchovy sauce.

Mode.—Slice and fry the onions of a nice brown colour, and put them into a stewpan with the Espagnole, ketchup, wine, and a little liquor in which the fish has been boiled. Add the seasoning, herbs, and spices, and simmer gently for 10 minutes, stirring well the whole time; strain it through a fine hair sieve, put in the lemon-juice and anchovy sauce, and pour it over the fish. This sauce may be very much enriched by adding a few small quenelles, or forcemeat balls made of fish, and also glazed onions or mushrooms. These, however, should not be added to the matelote till it is dished.

Time.—10 minutes. *Average cost*, 1s. 6d.

Seasonable at any time.

Note.—This sauce originally took its name as being similar to that which the French sailor (*matelot*) employed as a relish to the fish he caught and ate. In some cases, cider and perry were substituted for the wine. The Norman *matelotes* were very celebrated.

THE BAY.—We have already described (*see* No. 180) the difference between the cherry-laurel (*Prunus Laurus cerasus*) and the classic laurel (*Laurus nobilis*), the former only being used for culinary purposes. The latter beautiful evergreen was consecrated by the ancients to priests and heroes, and used in their sacrifices. "A crown of bay" was the earnestly-desired reward for great enterprises, and for the display of uncommon genius in oratory or writing. It was more particularly sacred to Apollo, because, according to the fable, the nymph Daphne was changed into a laurel-tree. The ancients believed, too, that the laurel had the power of communicating the gift of prophecy, as well as poetic genius; and, when they wished to procure pleasant dreams, would place a sprig under the pillow of their bed. It was the symbol, too, of victory, and it was thought that the laurel could never be struck by lightning. From this word comes that of "laureate;" Alfred Tennyson being the present poet laureate, crowned with laurel as the first of living bards.

THE BAY.

SAUCE PIQUANTE, for Cutlets, Roast Meat, &c.

513. INGREDIENTS.—2 oz. of butter, 1 small carrot, 6 shalots, 1 small bunch of savoury herbs, including parsley, ½ a bay-leaf, 2 slices of lean ham, 2 cloves, 6 peppercorns, 1 blade of mace, 3 whole allspice, 4 tablespoonfuls of vinegar, ½ pint of stock (No. 104 or 105), 1 small lump of sugar, ¼ saltspoonful of cayenne, salt to taste.

Mode.—Put into a stewpan the butter, with the carrot and shalots, both of which must be cut into small slices; add the herbs, bay-leaf, spices, and ham (which must be minced rather finely), and let these ingredients simmer over a slow fire, until the bottom of the stewpan is covered with a brown glaze. Keep stirring with a wooden spoon, and put in the remaining ingredients. Simmer very gently for ¼ hour, skim off every particle of fat, strain the sauce through a sieve, and serve very hot. Care must be taken that this sauce be not made too acid, although it should possess a sharpness indicated by its name. Of course the above quantity of vinegar may be increased or diminished at pleasure, according to taste.

Time.—Altogether ½ hour. *Average cost*, 10d.

Sufficient for a medium-sized dish of cutlets.

Seasonable at any time.

A GOOD SAUCE FOR VARIOUS BOILED PUDDINGS.

514. INGREDIENTS.—¼ lb. of butter, ¼ lb. of pounded sugar, a wine-glassful of brandy or rum.

Mode.—Beat the butter to a cream, until no lumps remain ; add the pounded sugar, and brandy or rum ; stir once or twice until the whole is thoroughly mixed, and serve. This sauce may either be poured round the pudding or served in a tureen, according to the taste or fancy of the cook or mistress.

Average cost, 8*d.* for this quantity.

Sufficient for a pudding.

SAUCE ROBERT, for Steaks, &c.

515. INGREDIENTS.—2 oz. of butter, 3 onions, 1 teaspoonful of flour, 4 tablespoonfuls of gravy, or stock No. 105, salt and pepper to taste, 1 teaspoonful of made mustard, 1 teaspoonful of vinegar, the juice of ½ lemon.

Mode.—Put the butter into a stewpan, set it on the fire, and, when browning, throw in the onions, which must be cut into small slices. Fry them brown, but do not burn them ; add the flour, shake the onions in it, and give the whole another fry. Put in the gravy and seasoning, and boil it gently for 10 minutes ; skim off the fat, add the mustard, vinegar, and lemon-juice ; give it one boil, and pour round the steaks, or whatever dish the sauce has been prepared for.

Time.—Altogether ½ hour. *Average cost,* for this quantity, 6*d.*

Seasonable at any time.

Sufficient for about 2 lbs. of steak.

Note.—This sauce will be found an excellent accompaniment to roast goose, pork, mutton cutlets, and various other dishes.

A GOOD SAUCE FOR STEAKS.

516. INGREDIENTS.—1 oz. of whole black pepper, ½ oz. of allspice, 1 oz. of salt, ½ oz. grated horseradish, ½ oz. of pickled shalots, 1 pint of mushroom ketchup or walnut pickle.

Mode.—Pound all the ingredients finely in a mortar, and put them into the ketchup or walnut-liquor. Let them stand for a fortnight, when strain off the liquor and bottle for use. Either pour a little of the sauce over the steaks or mix it in the gravy.

Seasonable.—This can be made at any time.

Note.—In using a jar of pickled walnuts, there is frequently left a large quantity of liquor; this should be converted into a sauce like the above, and will be found a very useful relish.

THE GROWTH OF THE PEPPER-PLANT.—Our readers will see at Nos. 369 and 399, a description, with engravings, of the qualities of black and long pepper, and an account of where these spices are found. We will here say something of the manner of the growth of the pepper-plant. Like the vine, it requires support, and it is usual to plant a thorny tree by its side, to which it may cling. In Malabar, the chief pepper district of India, the jacca-tree (*Artocarpus integrifolia*) is made thus to yield its assistance, the same soil being adapted to the growth of both plants. The stem of the pepper-plant entwines round its support to a considerable height; the flexile branches then droop downwards, bearing at their extremities, as well as at other parts, spikes of green flowers, which are followed by the pungent berries. These hang in large bunches, resembling in shape those of grapes; but the fruit grows distinct, each on a little stalk, like currants. Each berry contains a single seed, of a globular form and brownish colour, but which changes to a nearly black when dried; and this is the pepper of commerce. The leaves are not unlike those of the ivy, but are larger and of rather a lighter colour; they partake strongly of the peculiar smell and pungent taste of the berry.

SAUCE TOURNEE.

517. INGREDIENTS.—1 pint of white stock (No. 107), thickening of flour and butter, or white roux (No. 526), a faggot of savoury herbs, including parsley 6 chopped mushrooms, 6 green onions.

Mode.—Put the stock into a stewpan with the herbs, onions, and mushrooms, and let it simmer very gently for about $\frac{1}{2}$ hour; stir in sufficient thickening to make it of a proper consistency; let it boil for a few minutes, then skim off all the fat, strain and serve. This sauce, with the addition of a little cream, is now frequently called velouté.

Time.—$\frac{1}{2}$ hour. *Average cost*, for this quantity, 6d.

Note.—If poultry trimmings are at hand, the stock should be made of these; and the above sauce should not be made too thick, as it does not then admit of the fat being nicely removed.

SWEET SAUCE, for Venison.

518. INGREDIENTS.—A small jar of red-currant jelly, 1 glass of port wine.

Mode.—Put the above ingredients into a stewpan, set them over the fire, and, when melted, pour in a tureen and serve. It should not be allowed to boil.

Time.—5 minutes to melt the jelly.

Average cost, for this quantity, 1s.

SAUCE FOR WILDFOWL.

519. INGREDIENTS.—1 glass of port wine, 1 tablespoonful of Leamington sauce (No. 459), 1 tablespoonful of mushroom ketchup, 1 tablespoonful of lemon-juice, 1 slice of lemon-peel, 1 large shalot cut in slices, 1 blade of mace, cayenne to taste.

Mode.—Put all the ingredients into a stewpan, set it over the fire, and let it simmer for about 5 minutes; then strain and serve the sauce in a tureen.

Time.—5 minutes. *Average cost*, for this quantity, 8*d*.

SAUSAGE-MEAT STUFFING, for Turkey.

520. INGREDIENTS.—6 oz. of lean pork, 6 oz. of fat pork, both weighed after being chopped (beef suet may be substituted for the latter), 2 oz. of bread crumbs, 1 small tablespoonful of minced sage, 1 blade of pounded mace, salt and pepper to taste, 1 egg.

Mode.—Chop the meat and fat very finely, mix with them the other ingredients, taking care that the whole is thoroughly incorporated. Moisten with the egg, and the stuffing will be ready for use. Equal quantities of this stuffing and forcemeat, No. 417, will be found to answer very well, as the herbs, lemon-peel, &c. in the latter, impart a very delicious flavour to the sausage-meat. As preparations, however, like stuffings and forcemeats, are matters to be decided by individual tastes, they must be left, to a great extent, to the discrimination of the cook, who should study her employer's taste in this, as in every other respect.

Average cost, 9*d*.

Sufficient for a small turkey.

SAVOURY JELLY FOR MEAT PIES.

521. INGREDIENTS.—3 lbs. of shin of beef, 1 calf's-foot, 3 lbs. of knuckle of veal, poultry trimmings (if for game pies, any game trimmings), 2 onions stuck with cloves, 2 carrots, 4 shalots, a bunch of savoury herbs, 2 bay-leaves; when liked, 2 blades of mace and a little spice; 2 slices of lean ham, rather more than 2 quarts of water.

Mode.—Cut up the meat and put it into a stewpan with all the ingredients except the water; set it over a slow fire to draw down, and, when the gravy ceases to flow from the meat, pour in the water. Let it boil up, then carefully take away all scum from the top. Cover the stewpan closely, and let the stock simmer very gently for 4 hours: if rapidly boiled, the jelly will not be clear. When done, strain it through a fine sieve or flannel bag; and when cold, the jelly should be quite transparent. If this is not the case, clarify it with the whites of eggs, as described in recipe No. 109.

Time.—4 hours. *Average cost*, for this quantity, 5*s*.

SHRIMP SAUCE, for Various Kinds of Fish.

522. INGREDIENTS.—⅓ pint of melted butter (No. 376), ¼ pint of picked shrimps, cayenne to taste.

Mode.—Make the melted butter very smoothly by recipe No. 376, shell the shrimps (sufficient to make ¼ pint when picked), and put them into the butter; season with cayenne, and let the sauce just simmer, but do not allow it to boil. When liked, a teaspoonful of anchovy sauce may be added.

Time.—1 minute to simmer. *Average cost, 6d.*

Sufficient for 3 or 4 persons.

SPINACH GREEN FOR COLOURING VARIOUS DISHES.

523. INGREDIENTS.—2 handfuls of spinach.

Mode.—Pick and wash the spinach free from dirt, and pound the leaves in a mortar to extract the juice; then press it through a hair sieve, and put the juice into a small stewpan or jar. Place this in a bain marie, or saucepan of boiling water, and let it set. Watch it closely, as it should not boil; and, as soon as it is done, lay it in a sieve, so that all the water may drain from it, and the green will then be ready for colouring. If made according to this recipe, the spinach-green will be found far superior to that boiled in the ordinary way.

HOT SPICE, a Delicious Adjunct to Chops, Steaks, Gravies, &c.

524. INGREDIENTS.—3 drachms each of ginger, black pepper, and cinnamon, 7 cloves, ½ oz. mace, ¼ oz. of cayenne, 1 oz. grated nutmeg, 1½ oz. white pepper.

Mode.—Pound the ingredients, and mix them thoroughly together, taking care that everything is well blended. Put the spice in a very dry glass bottle for use. The quantity of cayenne may be increased, should the above not be enough to suit the palate.

CINNAMON.

CINNAMON.—The cinnamon-tree (*Laurus Cinnamomum*) is a valuable and beautiful species of the laurel family, and grows to the height of 20 or 30 feet. The trunk is short and straight, with wide-spreading branches, and it has a smooth ash-like bark. The leaves are upon short stalks, and are of an oval shape, and 3 to 5 inches long. The flowers are in panicles, with six small petals, and the fruit is about the size of an olive, soft, insipid, and of a deep blue. This incloses a nut, the kernel of which germinates soon after it falls. The wood of the tree is white and not very solid, and its root is thick and branching, exuding a great quantity of camphor. The inner bark of the tree forms the cinnamon of commerce. Ceylon was thought to be its native island; but it has been found in Malabar, Cochin-China, Sumatra, and the Eastern Islands; also in the Brazils, the Mauritius, Jamaica, and other tropical localities.

BROWN ROUX, a French Thickening for Gravies and Sauces.

525. INGREDIENTS.—6 oz. of butter, 9 oz. of flour.

Mode.—Melt the butter in a stewpan over a slow fire, and

dredge in, very gradually, the flour ; stir it till of a light-brown colour—to obtain this do it very slowly, otherwise the flour will burn and impart a bitter taste to the sauce it is mixed with. Pour it in a jar, and keep it for use : it will remain good some time.

Time.—About ½ hour. *Average cost, 7d.*

WHITE ROUX, for thickening White Sauces.

526. Allow the same proportions of butter and flour as in the preceding recipe, and proceed in the same manner as for brown roux, but do not keep it on the fire too long, and take care not to let it colour. This is used for thickening white sauce. Pour it into a jar to use when wanted.

Time.—¼ hour. *Average cost, 7d.*

Sufficient.—A dessertspoonful will thicken a pint of gravy.

Note.—Besides the above, sauces may be thickened with potato flour, ground rice, baked flour, arrowroot, &c. : the latter will be found far preferable to the ordinary flour for white sauces. A slice of bread, toasted and added to gravies, answers the two purposes of thickening and colouring them.

SPANISH ONIONS—PICKLED.

527. INGREDIENTS.—Onions, vinegar ; salt and cayenne to taste.

Mode.—Cut the onions in thin slices ; put a layer of them in the bottom of a jar ; sprinkle with salt and cayenne ; then add another layer of onions, and season as before. Proceeding in this manner till the jar is full, pour in sufficient vinegar to cover the whole, and the pickle will be fit for use in a month.

Seasonable.—May be had in England from September to February.

STORE SAUCE, or CHEROKEE.

528. INGREDIENTS.—½ oz. of cayenne pepper, 5 cloves of garlic, tablespoonfuls of soy, 1 tablespoonful of walnut ketchup, 1 pint of vinegar.

Mode.—Boil all the ingredients *gently* for about ½ hour ; strain the liquor, and bottle off for use.

Time.—½ hour.

Seasonable.—This sauce can be made at any time.

TOMATO SAUCE—HOT, to serve with Cutlets, Roast Meats, &c

529. INGREDIENTS. — 6 tomatoes, 2 shalots, 1 clove, 1 blade of

mace, salt and cayenne to taste, ¼ pint of gravy, No. 436, or stock No. 104.

Mode.—Cut the tomatoes in two, and squeeze the juice and seeds out; put them in a stewpan with all the ingredients, and let them simmer *gently* until the tomatoes are tender enough to pulp; rub the whole through a sieve, boil it for a few minutes, and serve. The shalots and spices may be omitted when their flavour is objected to.

Time.—1 hour, or rather more, to simmer the tomatoes.

Average cost, for this quantity, 1s.

In full season in September and October.

THE TOMATO.

TOMATO, OR LOVE-APPLE.—The plant which bears this fruit is a native of South America, and takes its name from a Portuguese word. The tomato fruit is about the size of a small potato, and is chiefly used in soups, sauces, and gravies. It is sometimes served to table roasted or boiled, and when green, makes a good ketchup or pickle. In its unripe state, it is esteemed as excellent sauce for roast goose or pork, and when quite ripe, a good store sauce may be prepared from it.

TOMATO SAUCE FOR KEEPING (Excellent).

I.

530. INGREDIENTS.—To every quart of tomato-pulp allow 1 pint of cayenne vinegar (No. 386), ¾ oz. of shalots, ¾ oz. of garlic, peeled and cut in slices; salt to taste. To every six quarts of liquor, 1 pint of soy, 1 pint of anchovy sauce.

Mode.—Gather the tomatoes quite ripe; bake them in a slow oven till tender; rub them through a sieve, and to every quart of pulp add cayenne vinegar, shalots, garlic, and salt, in the above proportion; boil the whole together till the garlic and shalots are quite soft; then rub it through a sieve, put it again into a saucepan, and, to every six quarts of the liquor, add 1 pint of soy and the same quantity of anchovy sauce, and boil altogether for about 20 minutes; bottle off for use, and carefully seal or rosin the corks. This will keep good for 2 or 3 years, but will be fit for use in a week. A useful and less expensive sauce may be made by omitting the anchovy and soy.

Time.—Altogether 1 hour.

Seasonable.—Make this from the middle of September to the end of October.

II.

531. INGREDIENTS.—1 dozen tomatoes, 2 teaspoonfuls of the best powdered ginger, 1 dessertspoonful of salt, 1 head of garlic chopped

fine, 2 tablespoonfuls of vinegar, 1 dessertspoonful of Chili vinegar (a small quantity of cayenne may be substituted for this).

Mode.—Choose ripe tomatoes, put them into a stone jar, and stand them in a cool oven until quite tender ; when cold, take the skins and stalks from them, mix the pulp with the liquor which is in the jar, but do not strain it ; add all the other ingredients, mix well together, and put it into well-sealed bottles. Stored away in a cool dry place, it will keep good for years. It is ready for use as soon as made, but the flavour is better after a week or two. Should it not appear to keep, turn it out, and boil it up with a little additional ginger and cayenne. For immediate use, the skins should be put into a wide-mouthed bottle with a little of the different ingredients, and they will be found very nice for hashes or stews.

Time.—4 or 5 hours in a *cool* oven.

Seasonable from the middle of September to the end of October.

III.

532. INGREDIENTS.—3 dozen tomatoes ; to every pound of tomato-pulp allow 1 pint of Chili vinegar, 1 oz. of garlic, 1 oz. of shalot, 2 oz. of salt, 1 large green capsicum, ½ teaspoonful of cayenne, 2 pickled gherkins, 6 pickled onions, 1 pint of common vinegar, and the juice of 6 lemons.

Mode.—Choose the tomatoes when quite ripe and red ; put them in a jar with a cover to it, and bake them till tender. The better way is to put them in the oven overnight, when it will not be too hot, and examine them in the morning to see if they are tender. Do not allow them to remain in the oven long enough to break them ; but they should be sufficiently soft to skin nicely and rub through the sieve. Measure the pulp, and to each pound of pulp, add the above proportion of vinegar and other ingredients, taking care to chop very fine the garlic, shalot, capsicum, onion, and gherkins. Boil the whole together till everything is tender ; then again rub it through a sieve, and add the lemon-juice. Now boil the whole again till it becomes as thick as cream, and keep continually stirring ; bottle it when quite cold, cork well, and seal the corks. If the flavour of garlic and shalot is very much disliked, diminish the quantities.

Time.—Bake the tomatoes in a *cool* oven all night.

Seasonable from the middle of September to the end of October.

Note.—A quantity of liquor will flow from the tomatoes, which must be put through the sieve with the rest. Keep it well stirred while on the fire, and use a wooden spoon.

UNIVERSAL PICKLE.

533. INGREDIENTS.—To 6 quarts of vinegar allow 1 lb. of salt, ¼ lb. of ginger, 1 oz. of mace, ½ lb. of shalots, 1 tablespoonful of cayenne, oz. of mustard-seed, 1½ oz. of turmeric.

Mode.—Boil all the ingredients together for about 20 minutes; when cold, put them into a jar with whatever vegetables you choose, such as radish-pods, French beans, cauliflowers, gherkins, &c. &c., as these come into season; put them in fresh as you gather them, having previously wiped them perfectly free from moisture and grit. This pickle will be fit for use in about 8 or 9 months.

Time.—20 minutes.

Seasonable.—Make the pickle in May or June, to be ready for the various vegetables.

Note.—As this pickle takes 2 or 3 months to make,—that is to say, nearly that time will elapse before all the different vegetables are added,—care must be taken to keep the jar which contains the pickle well covered, either with a closely-fitting lid, or a piece of bladder securely tied over, so as perfectly to exclude the air.

PICKLED WALNUTS (Very Good).

534. INGREDIENTS.—100 walnuts, salt and water. To each quart of vinegar allow 2 oz. of whole black pepper, 1 oz. of allspice, 1 oz. of bruised ginger.

Mode.—Procure the walnuts while young; be careful they are not woody, and prick them well with a fork; prepare a strong brine of salt and water (4 lbs. of salt to each gallon of water), into which put the walnuts, letting them remain 9 days, and changing the brine every third day; drain them off, put them on a dish, place it in the sun until they become perfectly black, which will be in 2 or 3 days; have ready dry jars, into which place the walnuts, and do not quite fill the jars. Boil sufficient vinegar to cover them, for 10 minutes, with spices in the above proportion, and pour it hot over the walnuts, which must be quite covered with the pickle; tie down with bladder, and keep in a dry place. They will be fit for use in a month, and will keep good 2 or 3 years.

Time.—10 minutes.

Seasonable.—Make this from the beginning to the middle of July, before the walnuts harden.

Note.—When liked, a few shalots may be added to the vinegar, and boiled with it.

WALNUT KETCHUP.

I.

535. INGREDIENTS.—100 walnuts, 1 handful of salt, 1 quart of vinegar, ¼ oz. of mace, ¼ oz. of nutmeg, ¼ oz. of cloves, ¼ oz. of ginger, ¼ oz. of whole black pepper, a small piece of horseradish, 20 shalots, ¼ lb. of anchovies, 1 pint of port wine.

Mode.—Procure the walnuts at the time you can run a pin through them, slightly bruise, and put them into a jar with the salt and vinegar, let them stand 8 days, stirring every day ; then drain the liquor from them, and boil it, with the above ingredients, for about ½ hour. It may be strained or not, as preferred, and, if required, a little more vinegar or wine can be added, according to taste. When bottled well, seal the corks.

Time.—½ hour.

Seasonable.—Make this from the beginning to the middle of July, when walnuts are in perfection for pickling purposes.

II.

536. INGREDIENTS.—½ sieve of walnut-shells, 2 quarts of water, salt, ½ lb. of shalots, 1 oz. of cloves, 1 oz. of mace, 1 oz. of whole pepper, 1 oz. of garlic.

Mode.—Put the walnut-shells into a pan, with the water, and a large quantity of salt ; let them stand for 10 days, then break the shells up in the water, and let it drain through a sieve, putting a heavy weight on the top to express the juice ; place it on the fire, and remove all scum that may arise. Now boil the liquor with the shalots, cloves, mace, pepper, and garlic, and let all simmer till the shalots sink ; then put the liquor into a pan, and, when cold, bottle, and cork closely. It should stand 6 months before using : should it ferment during that time, it must be again boiled and skimmed.

Time.—About ¾ hour.

Seasonable in September, when the walnut-shells are obtainable.

THE WALNUT.

THE WALNUT.—This nut is a native of Persia, and was introduced into England from France. As a pickle, it is much used in the green state ; and grated walnuts in Spain are much employed, both in tarts and other dishes. On the continent it is occasionally employed as a substitute for olive oil in cooking ; but it is apt, under such circumstances, to become rancid. The matter which remains after the oil is extracted is considered highly nutritious for poultry. It is called *mare*, and in Switzerland is eaten under the name of *pain amer* by the poor. The oil is frequently manufactured into a kind of soap, and the leaves and green husks yield an extract, which, as a brown dye, is used to stain hair, wool, and wood.

WHITE SAUCE (Good).

537. Ingredients.—½ pint of white stock (No. 107), ½ pint of cream, 1 dessertspoonful of flour, salt to taste.

Mode.—Have ready a delicately-clean saucepan, into which put the stock, which should be well flavoured with vegetables, and rather savoury ; mix the flour smoothly with the cream, add it to the stock, season with a little salt, and boil all these ingredients very gently for about 10 minutes, keeping them well stirred the whole time, as this sauce is very liable to burn.

Time.—10 minutes. *Average cost,* 1s.

Sufficient for a pair of fowls.

Seasonable at any time.

WHITE SAUCE, made without Meat.

538. Ingredients.—2 oz. of butter, 2 small onions, 1 carrot, ½ a small teacupful of flour, 1 pint of new milk, salt and cayenne to taste.

Mode.—Cut up the onions and carrot very small, and put them into a stewpan with the butter ; simmer them till the butter is nearly dried up ; then stir in the flour, and add the milk ; boil the whole gently until it thickens, strain it, season with salt and cayenne, and it will be ready to serve.

Time.—¼ hour. *Average cost,* 5d.

Sufficient for a pair of fowls.

Seasonable at any time.

WHITE SAUCE (a very Simple and Inexpensive Method).

539. Ingredients.—1½ pint of milk, 1½ oz. of rice, 1 strip of lemon-peel, 1 small blade of pounded mace, salt and cayenne to taste.

Mode.—Boil the milk with the lemon-peel and rice until the latter is perfectly tender, then take out the lemon-peel and pound the milk and rice together ; put it back into the stewpan to warm, add the mace and seasoning, give it one boil, and serve. This sauce should be of the consistency of thick cream.

Time.—About 1½ hour to boil the rice. *Average cost,* 4d.

Sufficient for a pair of fowls.

Seasonable at any time.

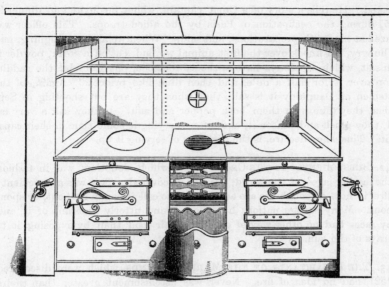

THE LEAMINGTON STOVE, OR KITCHENER.

VARIOUS MODES OF COOKING MEAT.

CHAPTER XI.

GENERAL REMARKS.

540. IN OUR "INTRODUCTION TO COOKERY" (*see* No. 76) we have described
the gradual progress of mankind in the art of cookery, the probability being,
that the human race, for a long period, lived wholly on fruits. Man's means
of attacking animals, even if he had the desire of slaughtering them, were
very limited, until he acquired the use of arms. He, however, made weapons
for himself, and, impelled by a carnivorous instinct, made prey of the animals
that surrounded him. It is natural that man should seek to feed on flesh;
he has too small a stomach to be supported alone by fruit, which has not
sufficient nourishment to renovate him. It is possible he might subsist on
vegetables; but their preparation needs the knowledge of art, only to be
obtained after the lapse of many centuries. Man's first weapons were the
branches of trees, which were succeeded by bows and arrows; and it is
worthy of remark, that these latter weapons have been found with the natives
of all climates and latitudes. It is singular how this idea presented itself to
individuals so differently placed.

S

541. Bríllat Savarin says, that raw flesh has but one inconvenience,—from its viscousness it attaches itself to the teeth. He goes on to say, that it is not, however, disagreeable ; but, when seasoned with salt, that it is easily digested. He tells a story of a Croat captain, whom he invited to dinner in 1815, during the occupation of Paris by the allied troops. This officer was amazed at his host's preparations, and said, " When we are campaigning, and get hungry, we knock over the first animal we find, cut off a steak, powder it with salt, which we always have in the sabretasche, put it under the saddle, gallop over it for half a mile, and then dine like princes." Again, of the huntsmen of Dauphiny it is said, that when they are out shooting in September, they take with them both pepper and salt. If they kill a very fat bird, they pluck and season it, and, after carrying it some time in their caps, eat it. This, they declare, is the best way of serving it up.

542. Subsequently to the Croat Mode, which, doubtless, was in fashion in the earlier ages of the world, fire was discovered. This was an accident ; for fire is not, although we are accustomed to call it so, an element, or spontaneous. Many savage nations have been found utterly ignorant of it, and many races had no other way of dressing their food than by exposing it to the rays of the sun.

543. The Inhabitants of the Marian Islands, which were discovered in 1521, had no idea of fire. Never was astonishment greater than theirs when they first saw it, on the descent of Magellan, the navigator, on one of their isles. At first they thought it a kind of animal, that fixed itself to and fed upon wood. Some of them, who approached too near, being burnt, the rest were terrified, and durst only look upon it at a distance. They were afraid, they said, of being bit, or lest that dreadful animal should wound with his violent respiration and dreadful breath ; for these were the first notions they formed of the heat and flame. Such, too, probably, were the notions the Greeks originally formed of them.

544. Fire having been Discovered, mankind endeavoured to make use of it for drying, and afterwards for cooking their meat ; but they were a considerable time before they hit upon proper and commodious methods of employing it in the preparation of their food.

545. Meat, then, placed on Burning Fuel was found better than when raw : it had more firmness, was eaten with less difficulty, and the ozmazome being condensed by the carbonization, gave it a pleasing perfume and flavour. Still, however, the meat cooked on the coal would become somewhat befouled, certain portions of the fuel adhering to it. This disadvantage was remedied by passing spits through it, and placing it at a suitable height above the burning fuel. Thus grilling was invented ; and it is well known that, simple as is this mode of cookery, yet all meat cooked in this way is richly and pleasantly flavoured. In Homer's time, the art of cookery had not advanced much

beyond this; for we read in the "Iliad," how the great Achilles and his friend Patroclus regaled the three Grecian leaders on bread, wine, and broiled meat. It is noticeable, too, that Homer does not speak of boiled meat anywhere in his poems. Later, however, the Jews, coming out of their captivity in Egypt, had made much greater progress. They undoubtedly possessed kettles; and in one of these, Esau's mess of pottage, for which he sold his birthright, must· have been prepared.

546. HAVING THUS BRIEFLY TRACED A HISTORY OF GASTRONOMICAL PROGRESSES, we will now proceed to describe the various methods of cooking meat, and make a few observations on the chemical changes which occur in each of the operations.

547. IN THIS COUNTRY, plain boiling, roasting, and baking are the usual methods of cooking animal food. To explain the philosophy of these simple culinary operations, we must advert to the effects that are produced by heat on the principal constituents of flesh. When finely-chopped mutton or beef is steeped for some time in a small quantity of clean water, and then subjected to slight pressure, the juice of the meat is extracted, and there is left a white tasteless residue, consisting chiefly of muscular fibres. When this residue is heated to between 158° and 177° Fahrenheit, the fibres shrink together, and become hard and horny. The influence of an elevated temperature on the soluble extract of flesh is not less remarkable. When the watery infusion, which contains all the savoury constituents of the meat, is gradually heated, it soon becomes turbid; and, when the temperature reaches 133°, flakes of whitish matter separate. These flakes are *albumen*, a substance precisely similar, in all its properties, to the white of egg (*see* No. 101). When the temperature of the watery extract is raised to 158°, the colouring matter of the blood coagulates, and the liquid, which was originally tinged red by this substance, is left perfectly clear, and almost colourless. When evaporated, even at a gentle heat, this residual liquid gradually becomes brown, and acquires the flavour of roast meat.

548. THESE INTERESTING FACTS, discovered in the laboratory, throw a flood of light upon the mysteries of the kitchen. The fibres of meat are surrounded by a liquid which contains albumen in its soluble state, just as it exists in the unboiled egg. During the operation of boiling or roasting, this substance coagulates, and thereby prevents the contraction and hardening of the fibres. The tenderness of well-cooked meat is consequently proportioned to the amount of albumen deposited in its substance. Meat is underdone when it has been heated throughout only to the temperature of coagulating albumen: it is thoroughly done when it has been heated through its whole mass to the temperature at which the colouring matter of the blood coagulates: it is overdone when the heat has been continued long enough to harden the fibres.

549. THE JUICE OF FLESH IS WATER, holding in solution many substances

besides albumen, which are of the highest possible value as articles of food. In preparing meat for the table, great care should be taken to prevent the escape of this precious juice, as the succulence and sapidity of the meat depend on its retention. The meat to be cooked should be exposed at first to a quick heat, which immediately coagulates the albumen on and near the surface. A kind of shell is thus formed, which effectually retains the whole of the juice within the meat.

550. DURING THE OPERATIONS OF BOILING, ROASTING, AND BAKING, fresh beef and mutton, when moderately fat, lose, according to Johnston, on an average about—

	In boiling.	In baking.	In roasting.
4 lbs. of beef lose	1 lb.	1 lb. 3 oz.	1 lb. 5 oz.
4 lbs. of mutton lose ...	14 oz.	1 lb. 4 oz.	1 lb. 6 oz.

BAKING.

551. THE DIFFERENCE BETWEEN ROASTING MEAT AND BAKING IT, may be generally described as consisting in the fact, that, in baking it, the fumes caused by the operation are not carried off in the same way as occurs in roasting. Much, however, of this disadvantage is obviated by the improved construction of modern ovens, and of especially those in connection with the Leamington

BAKING-DISH.

kitchener, of which we give an engraving here, and a full description of which will be seen at paragraph No. 65, with the prices at which they can be purchased of Messrs. R. and J. Slack, of the Strand. With meat baked in the generality of ovens, however, which do not possess ventilators on the principle of this kitchener, there is undoubtedly a peculiar taste, which does not at all equal the flavour developed by roasting meat. The chemistry of baking may be said to be the same as that described in roasting.

552. SHOULD THE OVEN BE VERY BRISK, it will be found necessary to cover the joint with a piece of white paper, to prevent the meat from being scorched and blackened outside, before the heat can penetrate into the inside. This paper should be removed half an hour before the time of serving dinner, so that the joint may take a good colour.

553. BY MEANS OF A JAR, many dishes, which will be enumerated under their special heads, may be economically prepared in the oven. The principal of these are soup, gravies, jugged hare, beef tea; and this mode of cooking may be advantageously adopted with a ham, which has previously been covered with a common crust of flour and water.

554. ALL DISHES PREPARED FOR BAKING should be more highly seasoned than when intended to be roasted. There are some dishes which, it may be said, are at least equally well cooked in the oven as by the roaster; thus, a shoulder of mutton and baked potatoes, a fillet or breast of veal, a sucking pig, a hare, well basted, will be received by connoisseurs as well, when baked, as if they had been roasted. Indeed, the baker's oven, or the family oven, may often, as has been said, be substituted for the cook and the spit with greater economy and convenience.

555. A BAKING-DISH, of which we give an engraving, should not be less than 6 or 7 inches deep; so that the meat, which of course cannot be basted, can stew in its own juices. In the recipe for each dish, full explanations concerning any special points in relation to it will be given.

BOILING.

556. BOILING, or the preparation of meat by hot water, though one of the easiest processes in cookery, requires skilful management. Boiled meat should be tender, savoury, and full of its own juice, or natural gravy; but, through the carelessness and ignorance of cooks, it is too often sent to table hard, tasteless, and innutritious. To insure a successful result in boiling flesh, the heat of the fire must be judiciously regulated, the proper quantity of water must be kept up in the pot, and the scum which rises to the surface must be carefully removed.

557. MANY WRITERS ON COOKERY assert that the meat to be boiled should be put into *cold water*, and that the pot should be heated gradually; but Liebig, the highest authority on all matters connected with the chemistry of food, has shown that meat so treated loses some of its most nutritious constituents. "If the flesh," says the great chemist, "be introduced into the boiler when the water is in a state of brisk ebullition, and if the boiling be kept up for a few minutes, and the pot then placed in a warm place, so that the temperature of the water is kept at 158° to 165°, we have the united conditions for giving to the flesh the qualities which best fit it for being eaten." When a piece of meat is plunged into boiling water, the albumen which is near the surface immediately coagulates, forming an envelope, which prevents the escape of the internal juice, and most effectually excludes the water, which, by mixing with this juice, would render the meat insipid. Meat treated thus is juicy and well-flavoured, when cooked, as it retains most of its savoury constituents. On the other hand, if the piece of meat be set on the fire with cold water, and this slowly heated to boiling, the flesh undergoes a loss of soluble and nutritious substances, while, as a matter of course, the soup becomes richer in these matters. The albumen is gradually dissolved from the surface to the centre; the fibre loses, more or less, its quality of shortness or tenderness, and becomes hard and tough: the thinner the piece of meat is, the greater is its loss of savoury constituents. In order to obtain well-flavoured and eatable

meat, we must relinquish the idea of making good soup from it, as that mode of boiling which yields the best soup gives the driest, toughest, and most vapid meat. Slow boiling whitens the meat ; and, we suspect, that it is on this account that it is in such favour with the cooks. The wholesomeness of food is, however, a matter of much greater moment than the appearance it presents on the table. It should be borne in mind, that the whiteness of meat that has been boiled slowly, is produced by the loss of some important alimentary properties.

558. THE OBJECTIONS WE HAVE RAISED to the practice of putting meat on the fire in cold water, apply with equal force to the practice of soaking meat before cooking it, which is so strongly recommended by some cooks. Fresh meat ought never to be soaked, as all its most nutritive constituents are soluble in water. Soaking, however, is an operation that cannot be entirely dispensed with in the preparation of animal food. Salted and dried meats require to be soaked for some time in water before they are cooked.

559. FOR BOILING MEAT, the softer the water is, the better. When spring water is boiled, the chalk which gives to it the quality of hardness, is precipitated. This chalk stains the meat, and communicates to it an unpleasant earthy taste. When nothing but hard water can be procured, it should be softened by boiling it for an hour or two before it is used for culinary purposes.

560. THE FIRE MUST BE WATCHED with great attention during the operation of boiling, so that its heat may be properly regulated. As a rule, the pot should be kept in a simmering state ; a result which cannot be attained without vigilance.

561. THE TEMPERATURE AT WHICH WATER BOILS, under usual circumstances, is 212° Fahr. Water does not become hotter after it has begun to boil, however long or with whatever violence the boiling is continued. This fact is of great importance in cookery, and attention to it will save much fuel. Water made to boil in a gentle way by the application of a moderate heat is just as hot as when it is made to boil on a strong fire with the greatest possible violence. When once water has been brought to the boiling point, the fire may be considerably reduced, as a very gentle heat will suffice to keep the water at its highest temperature.

562. THE SCUM WHICH RISES to the surface of the pot during the operation of boiling must be carefully removed, otherwise it will attach itself to the meat, and thereby spoil its appearance. The cook must not neglect to skim during the whole process, though by far the greater part of the scum rises at first. The practice of wrapping meat in a cloth may be dispensed with if the skimming be skillfully managed. If the scum be removed as fast as it rises, the meat will be cooked clean and pure, and come out of the vessel in which it was boiled, much more delicate and firm than when cooked in a cloth.

563. WHEN TAKEN FROM THE POT, the meat must be wiped with a clean cloth, or, what will be found more convenient, a sponge previously dipped in water and wrung dry. The meat should not be allowed to stand a moment longer than necessary, as boiled meat, as well as roasted, cannot be eaten too hot.

564. THE TIME ALLOWED FOR THE OPERATION OF BOILING must be regulated according to the size and quality of the meat. As a general rule, twenty minutes, reckoning from the moment when the boiling commences, may be allowed for every pound of meat. All the best authorities, however, agree in this, that the longer the boiling the more perfect the operation.

565. A FEW OBSERVATIONS ON THE NUTRITIVE VALUE OF SALTED MEAT may be properly introduced in this place. Every housewife knows that dry salt in contact with fresh meat gradually becomes fluid brine. The application of salt causes the fibres of the meat to contract, and the juice to flow out from its pores: as much as one-third of the juice of the meat is often forced out in this manner. Now, as this juice is pure extract of meat, containing albumen, osmazome, and other valuable principles, it follows that meat which has been preserved by the action of salt can never have the nutritive properties of fresh meat.

566. THE VESSELS USED FOR BOILING should be made of cast-iron, well tinned within, and provided with closely-fitting lids. They must be kept scrupulously clean, otherwise they will render the meat cooked in them unsightly and unwholesome. Copper pans, if used at all, should be reserved for operations that are performed with rapidity; as, by long contact with copper, food may become dangerously contaminated. The kettle in which a joint is dressed should be large enough to allow room for a good supply of water; if the meat be cramped and be surrounded with but little water, it will be stewed, not boiled.

567. IN STEWING, IT IS NOT REQUISITE to have so great a heat as in boiling. A gentle simmering in a small quantity of water, so that the meat is stewed almost in its own juices, is all that is necessary. It is a method much used on the continent, and is wholesome and economical.

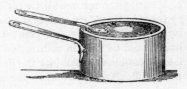

BOILING-POT. STEWPAN.

Two useful culinary vessels are represented above. One is a boiling-pot, in which large joints may be boiled; the other is a stewpan, with a closely-fitting lid, to which is attached a long handle; so the cover that can be removed without scalding the fingers.

568. The Hot-plate is a modern improvement on the old kitchen ranges, being used for boiling and stewing. It is a plate of cast iron, having a closed fire burning beneath it, by which it is thoroughly well heated. On this plate are set the various saucepans, stewpans, &c.; and, by this convenient and economical method, a number of dishes may be prepared at one time. The culinary processes of braising and stewing are, in this manner, rendered more gradual, and consequently the substance acted on becomes more tender, and the gravy is not so much reduced.

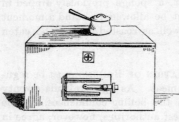

HOT-PLATE.

BROILING.

569. Generally speaking, small dishes only are prepared by this mode of cooking; amongst these, the beef-steak and mutton chop of the solitary English diner may be mentioned as celebrated all the world over. Our beef-steak, indeed, has long crossed the Channel; and, with a view of pleasing the Britons, there is in every *carte* at every French restaurant, by the side of *à la Marengo,* and *à la Mayonnaise,—biftek d'Angleterre.* In order to succeed in a broil, the cook must have a bright, clear fire; so that the surface of the meat may be quickly heated. The result of this is the same as that obtained in roasting; namely, that a crust, so to speak, is formed outside, and thus the juices of the meat are retained. The appetite of an invalid, so difficult to minister to, is often pleased with a broiled dish, as the flavour and sapidity of the meat are so well preserved.

REVOLVING GRIDIRON.

570. The Utensils used for Broiling need but little description. The common gridiron, for which see engraving at No. 68, is the same as it has been for ages past, although some little variety has been introduced into its manufacture, by the addition of grooves to the bars, by means of which the liquid fat is carried into a small trough. One point it is well to bear in mind, viz., that the gridiron should be kept in a direction slanting towards the cook, so that as little fat as possible may fall into the fire. It has been observed, that broiling is the most difficult manual office the general cook has to perform, and one that requires the most unremitting attention; for she may turn her back upon the stewpan or the spit, but the gridiron can never be left with impunity. The revolving gridiron, shown in the engraving, possesses some advantages of convenience, which will be at once apparent.

FRYING.

571. This very favourite Mode of Cooking may be accurately described as boiling in fat or oil. Substances dressed in this way are generally well received, for they introduce an agreeable variety, possessing, as they do, a peculiar flavour. By means of frying, cooks can soon satisfy many requisitions made on them, it being a very expeditious mode of preparing dishes for the table, and one which can be employed when the fire is not sufficiently large for the purposes of roasting and boiling.

SAUTÉ PAN.

The great point to be borne in mind in frying, is that the liquid must be hot enough to act instantaneously, as all the merit of this culinary operation lies in the invasion of the boiling liquid, which carbonizes or burns, at the very instant of the immersion of the body placed in it. It may be ascertained if the fat is heated to the proper degree, by cutting a piece of bread and dipping it in the frying-pan for five or six seconds; and if it be firm and of a dark brown when taken out, put in immediately what you wish to prepare; if it be not, let the fat be heated until of the right temperature. This having been effected, moderate the fire, so that the action may not be too hurried, and that by a continuous heat the juices of the substance may be preserved, and its flavour enhanced.

572. The Philosophy of Frying consists in this, that liquids subjected to the action of fire do not all receive the same quantity of heat. Being differently constituted in their nature, they possess different "capacities for caloric." Thus, you may, with impunity, dip your finger in boiling spirits of wine; you would take it very quickly from boiling brandy, yet more rapidly from water; whilst the effects of the most rapid immersion in boiling oil need not be told. As a consequence of this, heated fluids act differently on the sapid bodies presented to them. Those put in water, dissolve, and are reduced to a soft mass; the result being *bouillon*, stock, &c. (*see* No. 103). Those substances, on the contrary, treated with oil, harden, assume a more or less deep colour, and are finally carbonized. The reason of these different results is, that, in the first instance, water dissolves and extracts the interior juices of the alimentary substances placed in it; whilst, in the second, the juices are preserved; for they are insoluble in oil.

573. It is to be especially remembered, in connection with frying, that all dishes fried in fat should be placed before the fire on a piece of blotting-paper, or sieve reversed, and there left for a few minutes, so that any superfluous greasy moisture may be removed.

574. The Utensils used for the Purposes of Frying are confined to frying-pans, although these are of various sizes; and, for small and delicate dishes, such as collops, fritters, pancakes, &c., the *sauté* pan, of which we give an engraving, is used.

COOKING BY GAS.

575. Gas-Cooking can scarcely now be considered a novelty,—many estab-

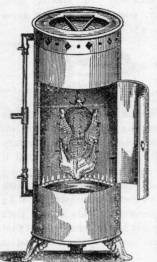

GAS-STOVE.

lishments, both small and large, have been fitted with apparatus for cooking by this mode, which undoubtedly exhibits some advantages. Thus the heat may be more regularly supplied to the substance cooking, and the operation is essentially a clean one, because there can be no cinders or other dirt to be provided for. Some labour and attention necessary, too, with a coal fire or close stove, may be saved; and, besides this, it may, perhaps, be said that culinary operations are reduced, by this means, to something like a certainty.

576. There are, however, we think, many objections to this mode of cooking, more especially when applied to small domestic establishments. For instance, the ingenious machinery necessary for carrying it out, requires cooks perfectly conversant with its use; and if the gas, when the cooking operations are finished, be not turned off, there will be a large increase in the cost of cooking, instead of the economy which it has been supposed to bring. For large establishments, such as some of the immense London warehouses, where a large number of young men have to be catered for daily, it may be well adapted, as it is just possible that a slight increase in the supply of gas necessary for a couple of joints, may serve equally to cook a dozen dishes.

ROASTING.

577. Of the Various Methods of Preparing Meat, Roasting is that which most effectually preserves its nutritive qualities. Meat is roasted by being exposed to the direct influence of the fire. This is done by placing the meat before an open grate, and keeping it in motion to prevent the scorching on any particular part. When meat is properly roasted, the outer layer of its albumen is coagulated, and thus presents a barrier to the exit of the juice. In roasting meat, the heat must be strongest at first, and it should then be much reduced. To have a good juicy roast, therefore, the fire must be red and vigorous at the very commencement of the operation. In the most careful roasting, some of the juice is squeezed out of the meat: this evaporates on the surface of the meat, and gives it a dark brown colour, a rich lustre, and a strong aromatic taste. Besides these effects on the albumen and the expelled juice, roasting converts the cellular tissue of the meat into gelatine, and melts the fat out of the fat-cells.

578. If a Spit is used to support the meat before the fire, it should be kept quite bright. Sand and water ought to be used to scour it with, for brickdust and oil may give a disagreeable taste to the meat. When well scoured, it must be wiped quite dry with a clean cloth; and, in spitting the meat, the prime parts should be left untouched, so as to avoid any great escape of its juices.

579. Kitchens in Large Establishments are usually fitted with what are termed "smoke-jacks." By means of these, several spits, if required, may be turned at the same time. This not being, of course, necessary in smaller establishments, a roasting apparatus, more economical in its consumption of coal, is more frequently in use.

580. The Bottle-jack, of which we here give an illustration, with the wheel and hook, and showing the precise manner of using it, is now commonly used in many kitchens. This consists of a spring inclosed in a brass cylinder, and requires winding up before it is used, and sometimes, also, during the operation of roasting. The joint is fixed to an iron hook, which is suspended by a chain connected with a wheel, and which, in its turn, is connected with the bottle-jack. Beneath it stands the dripping-pan, which we have also engraved, together with the basting-ladle, the use of which latter should not be spared; as there can be no good roast without good basting. "Spare the rod, and spoil the child," might easily be paraphrased into "Spare the basting, and spoil the meat." If the joint is small and light, and so turns unsteadily, this may be remedied by fixing to the wheel one of the kitchen weights. Sometimes this jack is fixed inside a screen; but there is this objection to this apparatus,—that the meat cooked in it resembles the flavour of baked meat. This is derived from its being so completely surrounded with the tin, that no sufficient current of air gets to it. It will be found preferable to make use of a common meat-screen, such as is shown in the woodcut This contains shelves for warming plates and dishes; and with this, the reflection not being so powerful, and more air being admitted to the joint, the roast may be very excellently cooked.

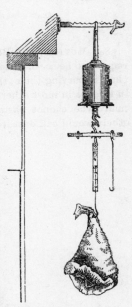

BOTTLE-JACK, WITH WHEEL AND HOOK.

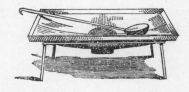

DRIPPING-PAN AND BASTING-LADLE.

581. In Stirring the Fire, or putting fresh coals on it, the dripping-pan should

always be drawn back, so that there may be no danger of the coal, cinders, or ashes falling down into it.

582. UNDER EACH PARTICULAR RECIPE there is stated the time required for roasting each joint; but, as a general rule, it may be here given, that for every pound of meat, in ordinary-sized joints, a quarter of an hour may be allotted.

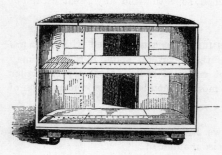

MEAT-SCREEN.

583. WHITE MEATS, AND THE MEAT OF YOUNG ANIMALS, require to be very well roasted, both to be pleasant to the palate and easy of digestion. Thus veal, pork, and lamb, should be thoroughly done to the centre.

584. MUTTON AND BEEF, on the other hand, do not, generally speaking, require to be so thoroughly done, and they should be dressed to the point, that, in carving them, the gravy should just run, but not too freely. Of course in this, as in most other dishes, the tastes of individuals vary; and there are many who cannot partake, with satisfaction, of any joint unless it is what others would call overdressed.

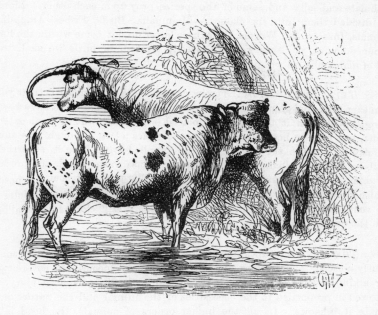

QUADRUPEDS.

CHAPTER XII.

GENERAL OBSERVATIONS ON QUADRUPEDS.

585. BY THE GENERAL ASSENT OF MANKIND, THE EMPIRE OF NATURE has been divided into three kingdoms; the first consisting of minerals, the second of vegetables, and the third of animals. The Mineral Kingdom comprises all substances which are without those organs necessary to locomotion, and the due performance of the functions of life. They are composed of the accidental aggregation of particles, which, under certain circumstances, take a constant and regular figure, but which are more frequently found without any definite conformation. They also occupy the interior parts of the earth, as well as compose those huge masses by which we see the land in some parts guarded against the encroachments of the sea. The Vegetable Kingdom covers and beautifies the earth with an endless variety of form and colour. It consists of organized bodies, but destitute of the power of locomotion. They are nourished by means of roots; they breathe by means of leaves; and propagate by means of seed, dispersed within certain limits. The Animal Kingdom consists of sentient beings, that enliven the external parts of the earth. They possess the powers of voluntary motion, respire air, and are forced into action by the cravings of hunger or the parching of thirst, by the instincts of animal passion, or by pain. Like the vegetable kingdom,

they are limited within the boundaries of certain countries by the conditions of climate and soil ; and some of the species prey upon each other. Linnæus has divided them into six classes ;—Mammalia, Birds, Fishes, Amphibious Animals, Insects, and Worms. The three latter do not come within the limits of our domain ; of fishes we have already treated, of birds we shall treat, and of mammalia we will now treat.

586. THIS CLASS OF ANIMALS embraces all those that nourish their young by means of lacteal glands, or teats, and are so constituted as to have a warm or red blood. In it the whale is placed,—an order which, from external habits, has usually been classed with the fishes ; but, although this animal exclusively inhabits the water, and is supplied with fins, it nevertheless exhibits a striking alliance to quadrupeds. It has warm blood, and produces its young alive ; it nourishes them with milk, and, for that purpose, is furnished with teats. It is also supplied with lungs, and two auricles and two ventricles to the heart ; all of which bring it still closer into an alliance with the quadrupedal species of the animal kingdom.

587. THE GENERAL CHARACTERISTICS OF THE MAMMALIA have been frequently noticed. The bodies of nearly the whole species are covered with hair, a kind of clothing which is both soft and warm, little liable to injury, and bestowed in proportion to the necessities of the animal and the nature of the climate it inhabits. In all the higher orders of animals, the head is the principal seat of the organs of sense. It is there that the eyes, the ears, the nose, and the mouth are placed. Through the last they receive their nourishment. In it are the *teeth*, which, in most of the mammalia, are used not only for the mastication of food, but as weapons of offence. They are inserted into two movable bones called jaws, and the front teeth are so placed that their sharp edges may easily be brought in contact with their food, in order that its fibres may readily be separated. Next to these, on each side, are situated the canine teeth, or tusks, which are longer than the other teeth, and, being pointed, are used to tear the food. In the back jaws are placed another form of teeth, called grinders. These are for masticating the food ; and in those animals that live on vegetables, they are flattened at the top ; but, in carnivora, their upper surfaces are furnished with sharp-pointed protuberances. From the numbers, form, and disposition of the teeth, the various genera of quadrupeds have been arranged. The *nose* is a cartilaginous body, pierced with two holes, which are called nostrils. Through these the animal is affected by the sense of smell ; and in some it is prominent, whilst in others it is flat, compressed, turned upwards, or bent downwards. In beasts of prey, it is frequently longer than the lips ; and in some other animals it is elongated into a movable trunk or proboscis, whilst, in the rhinoceros tribe, it is armed with a horn. The *eyes* of quadrupeds are generally defended by movable lids, on the outer margins of which are fringes of hair, called eyelashes. The opening of the pupil is in general circular ; but in some species, as in those of the Cat and Hare, it is contracted into a

perpendicular line, whilst in the Horse, the Ox, and a few others, it forms a transverse bar. The *ears* are openings, generally accompanied with a cartilage which defends and covers them, called the external ears. In water-animals the latter are wanting; sound, in them, being transmitted merely through orifices in the head, which have the name of auditory-holes. The most defenceless animals are extremely delicate in the sense of hearing, as are likewise most beasts of prey. Most of the mammiferous animals *walk* on four feet, which, at the extremities, are usually divided into toes or fingers. In some, however, the feet end in a single corneous substance called a hoof. The toes of a few end in broad, flat nails, and of most others, in pointed claws. Some, again, have the toes connected by a membrane, which is adapted to those that are destined to pass a considerable portion of their lives in water. Others, again, as in the Bat, have the digitations of the anterior feet greatly elongated, the intervening space being filled by a membrane, which extends round the hinder legs and tail, and by means of which they are enabled to rise into the air. In Man, the hand alone comprises fingers, separate, free, and flexible; but Apes, and some other kinds of animals, have fingers both to the hands and feet. These, therefore, are the only animals that can hold movable objects in a single hand. Others, such as Rats and Squirrels, have the fingers sufficiently small and flexible to enable them to pick up objects; but they are compelled to hold them in both hands. Others, again, have the toes shorter, and must rest on the fore-feet, as is the case with dogs and cats when they wish to hold a substance firmly on the ground with their paws. There are still others that have their toes united and drawn under the skin, or enveloped in corneous hoofs, and are thereby enabled to exercise no prehensile power whatever.

588. ACCORDING TO THE DESIGN AND END OF NATURE, mammiferous animals are calculated, when arrived at maturity, to subsist on various kinds of food,— some to live wholly upon flesh, others upon grain, herbs, or fruits; but in their infant state, milk is the appropriate food of the whole. That this food may never fail them, it is universally ordained, that the young should no sooner come into the world, than the milk should flow in abundance into the members with which the mother is supplied for the secretion of that nutritious fluid. By a wonderful instinct of Nature, too, the young animal, almost as soon as it has come into life, searches for the teat, and knows perfectly, at the first, how, by the process of suction, it will be able to extract the fluid necessary to its existence.

589. IN THE GENERAL ECONOMY OF NATURE, this class of animals seems destined to preserve a constant equilibrium in the number of animated beings that hold their existence on the surface of the earth. To man they are immediately useful in various ways. Some of their bodies afford him food, their skin shoes, and their fleece clothes. Some of them unite with him in participating the dangers of combat with an enemy, and others assist him in the chase, in exterminating wilder sorts, or banishing them from the haunts of civilization

Many, indeed, are injurious to him ; but most of them, in some shape or other, he turns to his service. Of these there is none he has made more subservient to his purposes than the common ox, of which there is scarcely a part that he has not been able to convert into some useful purpose. Of the horns he makes drinking-vessels, knife-handles, combs, and boxes ; and when they are softened by means of boiling water, he fashions them into transparent plates for lanterns. This invention is ascribed to King Alfred, who is said to have been the first to use them to preserve his candle time-measures from the wind. Glue is made of the cartilages, gristles, and the finer pieces of the parings and cuttings of the hides. Their bone is a cheap substitute for ivory. The thinnest of the calf-skins are manufactured into vellum. Their blood is made the basis of Prussian blue, and saddlers use a fine sort of thread prepared from their sinews. The hair is used in various valuable manufactures ; the suet, fat, and tallow, are moulded into candles ; and the milk and cream of the cow yield butter and cheese. Thus is every part of this animal valuable to man, who has spared no pains to bring it to the highest state of perfection.

590. AMONG THE VARIOUS BREEDS OF THE OX, upon which man has bestowed his highest powers of culture, there is now none takes a higher place than that known by the name of SHORT-HORNS. From the earliest ages, Great Britain has been distinguished for the excellence of her native breeds of cattle, and there are none in England that have obtained greater celebrity than those which have this name, and which originated, about seventy years ago, on the banks of the Tees. Thence they have spread into the valleys of the Tweed ; thence to the Lothians, in Scotland ; and southward, into the fine pastures of England. They are now esteemed the

SHORT-HORN COW.   SHORT-HORN BULL.

most profitable breed of cattle, as there is no animal which attains sooner to maturity, and none that supplies meat of a superior quality. The value of some of the improved breeds is something enormous. At the sale of Mr. Charles Colling, a breeder in Yorkshire, in 1810, his bull "Comet" sold for 1,000 guineas. At the sale of Earl Spencer's herd in 1846, 104 cows, heifers, and calves, with nineteen bulls, fetched £8,468. 5s. ; being an average of £68. 17s. apiece. The value of such animals is scarcely to be estimated by those who are unacquainted with the care with which they are tended, and with the anxious attention which is paid to the purity of their breed. A modern writer, well acquainted with this subject, says, "There are now, at least, five hundred herds, large and small, in this kingdom, and from six to seven thousand head registered every alternate year in the herd-book." The necessity for thus recording the breeds is greater than might, at first sight, be imagined, as it tends directly to preserve the character of the cattle, while it sometimes adds to the value and reputation of the animal thus entered. Besides, many of the Americans, and large purchasers for the foreign market, will not look at an animal without the breeder has taken care to qualify him for such reference. Of short-horned stock, there is annually sold from £40,000 to £50,000 worth by public auction, independent of the vast numbers disposed of by private contract. The breed is highly prized in Belgium, Prussia, France, Italy, and Russia; it is imported into most of the British colonies, and is greatly esteemed both for its meat and its dairy produce, wherever it is known. The quickness with which it takes on flesh, and the weight which it frequently makes, are well known; but we may mention that it is not uncommon to see steers of from four to five years old realize a weight of from 800 to 1,000 lbs. Such animals command from the butcher from £30 to £40 per head, according to the quality; whilst others, of two or three years old, and, of course, of less weight, bring as much as £20 apiece.

591. LONG-HORNS.—This is the prevailing breed in our midland counties and in Ireland; but they are greatly inferior to the short-horns, and are fast

LONG-HORN BULL.   LONG-HORN COW.

being supplanted by them. Even where they have been cultivated with the nicest care and brought to the greatest perfection, they are inferior to the others, and must ultimately be driven from the farm.

592. THE ALDERNEY.—Among the dairy breeds of England, the Alderney takes a prominent place, not on account of the quantity of milk which it yields, but on account of the excellent quality of the cream and butter which are produced from it. Its docility is marvellous, and in appearance it greatly resembles the Ayrshire breed of Scotland, the excellence of which is supposed

to be, in some degree, derived from a mixture of the Alderney blood with that breed. The distinction between them, however, lies both in the quantity and

ALDERNEY COW.

ALDERNEY BULL.

quality of the milk which they severally produce ; that of the Alderney being rich in quality, and that of the Ayrshire abundant in quantity. The merit of the former, however, ends with its milk, for as a grazer it is worthless.

593. SCOTTISH BREEDS.—Of these the Kyloe, which belongs to the Highlands of Scotland ; the Galloway, which has been called the Kyloe without horns ; and the Ayrshire, are the breeds most celebrated. The first has kept his place, and on account of the compactness of his form, and the excellent quality of his flesh, he is a great favourite with butchers who have a select family trade. It

GALLOWAY BULL.

GALLOWAY COW.

is alike unsuitable for the dairy and the arable farm ; but in its native High-lands it attains to great perfection, thriving upon the scanty and coarse herbage which it gathers on the sides of the mountains. The Galloway has a larger frame, and when fattened makes excellent beef. But it has given place to the short-horns in its native district, where turnip-husbandry is pursued with advantage. The Ayrshire is peculiarly adapted for the dairy, and for the abundance of its milk cannot be surpassed in its native district. In this it stands unrivalled, and there is no other breed capable of converting the produce of a poor soil into such fine butter and cheese. It is difficult to fatten, however, and its beef is of a coarse quality. We have chosen these as among the principal representative breeds of the ox species; but there are other breeds which, at all events, have a local if not a general celebrity.

594. The general Mode of Slaughtering Oxen in this country is by striking them a smart blow with a hammer or poleaxe on the head, a little above the eyes. By this means, when the blow is skilfully given, the beast is brought down at one blow, and, to prevent recovery, a cane is generally inserted, by which the spinal cord is perforated, which instantly deprives the ox of all sensation of pain. In Spain, and some other countries on the continent, it is also usual to deprive oxen of life by the operation of pithing or dividing the spinal cord in the neck, close to the back part of the head. This is, in effect, the same mode as is practised in the celebrated Spanish bull-fights by the matador, and it is instantaneous in depriving the animal of sensation, if the operator be skilful. We hope and believe that those men whose disagreeable duty it is to slaughter the "beasts of the field" to provide meat for mankind, inflict as little punishment and cause as little suffering as possible.

595. The Manner in which a Side of Beef is cut up in London, is shown in the engraving on this page. In the metropolis, on account of the large number of its population possessing the means to indulge in the "best of everything," the demand for the most delicate joints of meat is great, the price, at the same time, being much higher for these than for the other parts. The consequence is, that in London the carcass is there divided so as to obtain the greatest quantity of meat on the most esteemed joints. In many places,

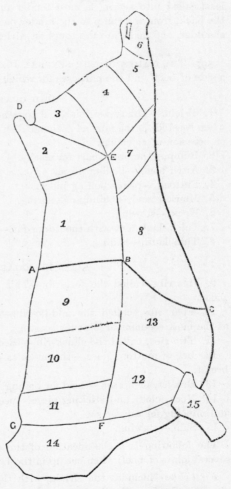

SIDE OF BEEF, SHOWING THE SEVERAL JOINTS.

however, where, from a greater equality in the social condition and habits of the inhabitants, the demand and prices for the different parts of the carcasses are more equalized, there is not the same reason for the butcher to cut the best joints so large.

596. THE MEAT ON THOSE PARTS OF THE ANIMAL in which the muscles are least called into action, is most tender and succulent ; as, for instance, along the back, from the rump to the hinder part of the shoulder ; whilst the limbs, shoulder, and neck, are the toughest, driest, and least-esteemed.

597. THE NAMES OF THE SEVERAL JOINTS in the hind and fore quarters of a side of beef, and the purposes for which they are used, are as follows :—

HIND QUARTER.

1. Sirloin.—The two sirloins, cut together in one joint, form a baron ; this, when roasted, is the famous national dish of Englishmen, at entertainments, on occasion of rejoicing.
2. Rump,—the finest part for steaks.
3. Aitch-bone,—boiling piece.
4. Buttock,—prime boiling piece.
5. Mouse-round,—boiling or stewing.
6. Hock,—stewing.
7. Thick flank, cut with the udder-fat.—primest boiling piece.
8. Thin flank,—boiling.

FORE QUARTER.

9. Five ribs, called the fore-rib.—This is considered the primest roasting piece.
10. Four ribs, called the middle-rib,—greatly esteemed by housekeepers as the most economical joint for roasting.
11. Two ribs, called the chuck-rib,—used for second quality of steaks.
12. Leg-of-mutton piece,—the muscles of the shoulder dissected from the breast.
13. Brisket, or breast,—used for boiling, after being salted.
14. Neck, clod, and sticking-piece,—used for soups, gravies, stocks, pies, and mincing for sausages.
15. Shin,—stewing.

The following is a classification of the qualities of meat, according to the several joints of beef, when cut up in the London manner.

First class—includes the sirloin, with the kidney suet (1), the rump-steak piece (2), the fore-rib (9).

Second class.—The buttock (4), the thick flank (7), the middle-rib (10).

Third class.—The aitch-bone (3), the mouse-round (5), the thin flank (8), the chuck (11), the leg-of-mutton piece (12), the brisket (13).

Fourth class.—The neck, clod, and sticking-piece (14).

Fifth class.—The hock (6), the shin (15).

RECEIPES.

CHAPTER XIII

BAKED BEEF (Cold Meat Cookery).

I.

598. INGREDIENTS.—About 2 lbs. of cold roast beef, 2 small onions, 1 large carrot or two small ones, 1 turnip, a small bunch of savoury herbs, salt and pepper to taste, 4 tablespoonfuls of gravy, 3 tablespoonfuls of ale, crust or mashed potatoes.

Mode.—Cut the beef in slices, allowing a small amount of fat to each slice; place a layer of this in the bottom of a pie-dish, with a portion of the onions, carrots, and turnips, which must be sliced; mince the herbs, strew them over the meat, and season with pepper and salt. Then put another layer of meat, vegetables, and seasoning; and proceed in this manner until all the ingredients are used. Pour in the gravy and ale (water may be substituted for the former, but it is not so nice), cover with a crust or mashed potatoes, and bake for ½ hour, or rather longer.

Time.—Rather more than ½ hour.

Average cost, exclusive of the meat, 6*d.*

Sufficient for 5 or 6 persons.

Seasonable at any time.

Note.—It is as well to parboil the carrots and turnips before adding them to the meat, and to use some of the liquor in which they were boiled as a substitute for gravy; that is to say, when there is no gravy at hand. Be particular to cut the onions in very *thin* slices.

II.

599. INGREDIENTS.—Slices of cold roast beef, salt and pepper to taste, 1 sliced onion, 1 teaspoonful of minced savoury herbs, 5 or 6 tablespoonfuls of gravy or sauce of any kind, mashed potatoes.

Mode.—Butter the sides of a deep dish, and spread mashed potatoes over the bottom of it; on this place layers of beef in thin slices (this may be minced if there is not sufficient beef to cut into slices), well seasoned with pepper and salt, and a very little onion and herbs, which should be previously fried of a nice brown; then put another layer of mashed potatoes, and beef, and other ingredients, as before; pour in the gravy or sauce, cover the whole with another layer of potatoes, and bake for ½ hour. This may be served in the dish, or turned out.

Time.—½ hour. *Average cost*, exclusive of the cold beef, 6d.

Sufficient.—A large pie-dish full for 5 or 6 persons.

Seasonable at any time.

BEEF.—The quality of beef depends on various circumstances; such as the age, the sex, the breed of the animal, and also on the food upon which it has been raised. Bull beef is, in general, dry and tough, and by no means possessed of an agreeable flavour; whilst the flesh of the ox is not only highly nourishing and digestible, but, if not too old, extremely agreeable. The flesh of the cow is, also, nourishing, but it is not so agreeable as that of the ox, although that of a heifer is held in high estimation. The flesh of the smaller breeds is much sweeter than that of the larger, which is best when the animal is about seven years old. That of the smaller breeds is best at about five years, and that of the cow can hardly be eaten too young.

BAKED BEEF-STEAK PUDDING.

600. INGREDIENTS.—6 oz. of flour, 2 eggs, not quite 1 pint of milk, salt to taste, 1½ lb. of rump-steaks, 1 kidney, pepper and salt.

Mode.—Cut the steaks into nice square pieces, with a small quantity of fat, and the kidney divide into small pieces. Make a batter of flour, eggs, and milk in the above proportion; lay a little of it at the bottom of a pie-dish; then put in the steaks and kidney, which should be well seasoned with pepper and salt, and pour over the remainder of the batter, and bake for 1½ hour in a brisk but not fierce oven.

Time.—1½ hour. *Average cost*, 2s.

Sufficient for 4 or 5 persons.

Seasonable at any time.

BEEF A LA MODE.

(*Economical.*)

601. INGREDIENTS.—About 3 lbs. of clod or sticking of beef, 2 oz. of clarified dripping, 1 large onion, flour, 2 quarts of water, 12 berries of allspice, 2 bay-leaves, ½ teaspoonful of whole black pepper, salt to taste.

Mode.—Cut the beef into small pieces, and roll them in flour; put the dripping into a stewpan with the onion, which should be sliced thin. Let it get quite hot; lay in the pieces of beef, and stir them well about. When nicely browned all over, add *by degrees* boiling water in the above proportion, and, as the water is added, keep the whole well stirred. Put in the spice, bay-leaves, and seasoning, cover the stewpan closely, and set it by the side of the fire to stew very *gently,* till the meat becomes quite tender, which will be in about 3 hours, when it will be ready to serve. Remove the bay-leaves before it is sent to table.

Time.—3 hours. *Average cost,* 1s. 3d.

Sufficient for 6 persons.

Seasonable at any time.

BEEF A LA MODE.

602. INGREDIENTS.—6 or 7 lbs. of the thick flank of beef, a few slices of fat bacon, 1 teacupful of vinegar, black pepper, allspice, 2 cloves well mixed and finely pounded, making altogether 1 heaped teaspoonful; salt to taste, 1 bunch of savoury herbs, including parsley, all finely minced and well mixed; 3 onions, 2 large carrots, 1 turnip, 1 head of celery, 1½ pint of water, 1 glass of port wine.

Mode.—Slice and fry the onions of a pale brown, and cut up the other vegetables in small pieces, and prepare the beef for stewing in the following manner:—Choose a fine piece of beef, cut the bacon into long slices, about an inch in thickness, dip them into vinegar, and then into a little of the above seasoning of spice, &c., mixed with the same quantity of minced herbs. With a sharp knife make holes deep enough to let in the bacon; then rub the beef over with the remainder of the seasoning and herbs, and bind it up in a nice shape with tape. Have ready a well-tinned stewpan (it should not be much larger than the piece of meat you are cooking), into which put the beef, with the vegetables, vinegar, and water. Let it simmer *very gently* for 5 hours, or rather longer, should the meat not be extremely tender, and turn it once or twice. When ready to serve, take out the beef, remove the tape, and put it on a hot dish. Skim off every particle of fat from the gravy, add the port wine, just let it boil, pour it over the beef, and it is ready to serve. Great care must be taken that this does not boil fast, or the meat will be tough and tasteless; it should only just bubble. When convenient, all kinds of stews, &c., should be cooked on a hot-plate, as the process is so much more gradual than on an open fire.

Time.—5 hours, or rather more. *Average cost,* 7d. per lb.

Sufficient for 7 or 8 persons.

Seasonable all the year, but more suitable for a winter dish.

GOOD MEAT.—The lyer of meat when freshly killed, and the animal, when slaughtered, being in a state of perfect health, adheres firmly to the bones. Beef of the best quality is of a deep-red colour; and when the animal has approached maturity, and been well fed, the lean is intermixed with fat, giving it the mottled appearance which is so much esteemed. It is also full of juice, which resembles in colour claret wine. The fat of the best beef is of a firm and waxy consistency, of a colour resembling that of the finest grass butter; bright in appearance, neither greasy nor friable to the touch, but moderately unctuous, in a medium degree between the last-mentioned properties.

BEEF-STEAKS AND OYSTER SAUCE.

603. INGREDIENTS.—3 dozen oysters, ingredients for oyster sauce (*see* No. 492), 2 lbs. of rump-steak, seasoning to taste of pepper and salt.

Mode.—Make the oyster sauce by recipe No. 492, and when that is ready, put it by the side of the fire, but do not let it keep boiling. Have the steaks cut of an equal thickness, broil them over a very clear fire, turning them often, that the gravy may not escape. In about 8 minutes they will be done, when put them on a very hot dish ; smother with the oyster sauce, and the remainder send to table in a tureen. Serve quickly.

Time.—About 8 to 10 minutes, according to the thickness of the steak.

Average cost, 1s. per lb.

Sufficient for 4 persons.

Seasonable from September to April.

BEEF-STEAK PIE.

604. INGREDIENTS.—3 lbs. of rump-steak, seasoning to taste of salt, cayenne, and black pepper, crust, water, the yolk of an egg.

Mode.—Have the steaks cut from a rump that has hung a few days, that they may be tender, and be particular that every portion is perfectly sweet. Cut the steaks into pieces about 3 inches long and 2 wide, allowing a *small* piece of fat to each piece of lean, and arrange the meat in layers in a pie-dish. Between each layer sprinkle a seasoning of salt, pepper, and, when liked, a few grains of cayenne. Fill the dish sufficiently with meat to support the crust, and to give

BEEF-STEAK PIE.

it a nice raised appearance when baked, and not to look flat and hollow. Pour in sufficient water to half fill the dish, and border it with paste (*see* Pastry) ; brush it over with a little water, and put on the cover ; slightly press down the edges with the thumb, and trim off close to the dish. Ornament the pie with leaves, or pieces of paste cut in any shape that fancy may direct, brush it over with the beaten yolk of an egg ; make a hole in the top of the crust, and bake in a hot oven for about 1½ hour.

Time.—In a hot oven, 1½ hour. *Average cost*, for this size, 3s. 6d.

Sufficient for 6 or 8 persons.

Seasonable at any time.

Note.—Beef-steak pies may be flavoured in various ways, with oysters and their liquor, mushrooms, minced onions, &c. For family pies, suet may be used instead of butter or lard for the crust, and clarified beef-dripping answers very well where economy is an object. Pieces of underdone roast or boiled meat may in pies be used very advantageously; but always remove the bone from pie-meat, unless it be chicken or game. We have directed that the meat shall be cut smaller than is usually the case; for on trial we have found it much more tender, more easily helped, and with more gravy, than when put into the dish in one or two large steaks.

BEEF-STEAK AND KIDNEY PUDDING.

605. INGREDIENTS.—2 lbs. of rump-steak, 2 kidneys, seasoning to taste of salt and black pepper, suet crust made with milk (*see* Pastry), in the proportion of 6 oz. of suet to each 1 lb. of flour.

Mode.—Procure some tender rump steak (that which has been hung a little time), and divide it into pieces about an inch square, and cut each kidney into 8 pieces. Line the dish (of which we have given an engraving) with crust made with suet and flour in the above proportion, leaving a small piece of crust to overlap the edge. Then cover the bottom with a portion of the steak and a few pieces of kidney; season with salt and pepper (some add a little flour to thicken the gravy, but it is not necessary), and then add another layer of steak, kidney, and seasoning. Proceed in this manner till the dish is full, when pour in sufficient water to come within 2 inches of the top of the basin. Moisten the edges of the crust, cover the pudding over, press the two crusts together, that the gravy may not escape, and turn up the overhanging paste. Wring out a cloth in hot water, flour it,

SUSSEX PUDDING-DISH.

and tie up the pudding; put it into boiling water, and let it boil for at least 4 hours. If the water diminishes, always replenish with some, hot in a jug, as the pudding should be kept covered all the time, and not allowed to stop boiling. When the cloth is removed, cut out a round piece in the top of the crust, to prevent the pudding bursting, and send it to table in the basin, either in an ornamental dish, or with a napkin pinned round it. Serve quickly.

Time.—For a pudding with 2 lbs. of steak and 2 kidneys allow 4 hours.

Average cost, 2s. 8d.

Sufficient for 6 persons.

Seasonable all the year, but more suitable in winter.

Note.—Beef-steak pudding may be very much enriched by adding a few oysters or mushrooms. The above recipe was contributed to this work by a Sussex lady, in which county the inhabitants are noted for their savoury puddings. It differs from the general way of making them, as the meat is cut up into very small pieces and the basin is differently shaped : on trial, this pudding will be found far nicer, and more full of gravy, than when laid in large pieces in the dish.

BAD MEAT.—In the flesh of animals slaughtered whilst suffering acute inflammation or fever, the hollow fibres, or capillaries, as they are called, which form the substance of the lyer, are filled with congested and unassimilated animal fluid, which, from its impurity, gives the lyer a dark colour, and produces a tendency to rapid putrefaction. In a more advanced stage of such disease, serous, and sometimes purulent matter, is formed in the cellular tissues between the muscles of the flesh; and when such is the case, nothing can be more poisonous than such abominable carrion. In the flesh of animals killed whilst under the influence of any disease of an emaciating effect, the lyer adheres but slightly to the bones, with its fibres contracted and dry; and the little fat that there may be is friable, and shrunk within its integuments. The flesh of animals slaughtered whilst under considerable depression of vital energy (as from previous bleeding) has a a diminished tendency to stiffen after death, the feebleness of this tendency being in proportion to the degree of depression. It presents, also, an unnatural blue or pallid appearance, has a faint and slightly sour smell, and soon becomes putrid. When an animal has died otherwise than by slaughtering, its flesh is flaccid and clammy, emits a peculiar faint and disagreeable smell, and, it need scarcely be added, spontaneous decomposition proceeds very rapidly.

BEEF-STEAKS WITH FRIED POTATOES, or BIFTEK AUX POMMES-DE-TERRE (a la mode Francaise).

606. INGREDIENTS.—2 lbs. of steak, 8 potatoes, ¼ lb. of butter, salt and pepper to taste, 1 teaspoonful of minced herbs.

Mode.—Put the butter into a frying or *sauté* pan, set it over the fire, and let it get very hot; peel, and cut the potatoes into long thin slices; put them into the hot butter, and fry them till of a nice brown colour. Now broil the steaks over a bright clear fire, turning them frequently, that every part may be equally done: as they should not be thick, 5 minutes will broil them. Put the herbs and seasoning in the butter the potatoes were fried in, pour it under the steak, and place the fried potatoes round, as a garnish. To have this dish in perfection, a portion of the fillet of the sirloin should be used, as the meat is generally so much more tender than that of the rump, and the steaks should be cut about ⅓ of an inch in thickness.

Time.—5 minutes to broil the steaks, and about the same time to fry the potatoes. *Average cost*, 1s. per lb.

Sufficient for 4 persons.

Seasonable all the year; but not so good in warm weather, as the meat cannot hang to get tender.

BOILED AITCH-BONE OF BEEF.

607. INGREDIENTS.—Beef, water.

Mode.—After this joint has been in salt 5 or 6 days, it will be ready for use, and will not take so long boiling as a round, for it is not so solid. Wash the meat, and, if too salt, soak it for a few hours, changing the water once or twice, till the required freshness is obtained. Put into a saucepan, or boiling-pot, sufficient water to cover the meat; set it over the fire, and when it boils, plunge in the joint (*see* No. 557), and let it boil up quickly. Now draw the pot to the side of the fire, and let the process be very gradual, as the water must only simmer, or the meat will be hard and tough. Carefully remove the scum from the surface of the water, and continue doing this for

AITCH-BONE OF BEEF.

a few minutes after it first boils. Carrots and turnips are served with this dish, and sometimes suet dumplings, which may be boiled with the beef. Garnish with a few of the carrots and turnips, and serve the remainder in a vegetable-dish.

Time.—An aitch-bone of 10 lbs., 2½ hours after the water boils; one of 20 lbs., 4 hours. *Average cost*, 6d. per lb.

Sufficient.—10 lbs. for 7 or 8 persons.

Seasonable all the year, but best from September to March.

Note.—The liquor in which the meat has been boiled may be easily converted into a very excellent pea-soup. It will require very few vegetables, as it will be impregnated with the flavour of those boiled with the meat.

THE ACTION OF SALT ON MEAT.—The manner in which salt acts in preserving meat is not difficult to understand. By its strong affinity, it, in the first place, extracts the juices from the substance of meat in sufficient quantity to form a saturated solution with the water contained in the juice, and the meat then absorbs the saturated brine in place of the juice extracted by the salt. In this way, matter incapable of putrefaction takes the places of that portion in the meat which is most perishable. Such, however, is not the only office of salt as a means of preserving meat; it acts also by its astringency in contracting the fibres of the muscles, and so excludes the action of air on the interior of the substance of the meat. The last-mentioned operation of salt as an antiseptic is evinced by the diminution of the volume of meat to which it is applied. The astringent action of *saltpetre* on meat is much greater than that of salt, and thereby renders meat to which it is applied very hard; but, in small quantities, it considerably assists the antiseptic action of salt, and also prevents the destruction of the florid colour of meat, which is caused by the application of salt. Thus, it will be perceived, from the foregoing statement, that the application of salt and saltpetre diminishes, in a considerable degree, the nutritive, and, to some extent, the wholesome qualities of meat; and, therefore, in their use, the quantity applied should be as small as possible, consistent with the perfect preservation of the meat.

BOILED ROUND OF BEEF.

608. INGREDIENTS.—Beef, water.

Mode.—As a whole round of beef, generally speaking, is too large for small families, and very seldom required, we here give the recipe for dressing a portion of the silver side of the round. Take from 12 to 16 lbs.,

after it has been in salt about 10 days; just wash off the salt, skewer it
up in a nice round-looking form, and bind it with tape to keep the
skewers in their places.   Put it in a saucepan of boiling water, as in
the preceding recipe, set it upon a good fire, and when it begins to boil,
carefully remove all scum from the surface, as, if this is not attended
to, it sinks on to the meat, and when brought to table, presents a
very unsightly appearance.   When it is well skimmed, draw the pot
to the corner of the fire, and let it simmer very gently until done.
Remove the tape and skewers, which should be replaced by a silver
one; pour over a little of the pot-liquor, and garnish with carrots.
(*See* coloured plate 2.)   Carrots, turnips, parsnips, and sometimes suet
dumplings, accompany this dish; and these may all be boiled with
the beef.   The pot-liquor should be saved, and converted into pea-
soup; and the outside slices, which are generally hard, and of an
uninviting appearance, may be cut off before being sent to table, and
potted.   These make an excellent relish for the breakfast or luncheon
table.

Time.—Part of a round of beef weighing 12 lbs., about 3 hours
after the water boils.   *Average cost,* 8*d.* per lb.

Sufficient for 10 persons.

Seasonable all the year, but more suitable for winter.

609. SOYER'S RECIPE FOR PRESERVING THE GRAVY IN SALT MEAT, WHEN IT
IS TO BE SERVED COLD.—Fill two tubs with cold water, into which throw a few
pounds of rough ice; and when the meat is done, put it into one of the tubs
of ice-water; let it remain 1 minute, when take out, and put it into the other
tub.   Fill the first tub again with water, and continue this process for about
20 minutes; then set it upon a dish, and let it remain until quite cold.   When
cut, the fat will be as white as possible, besides having saved the whole of the
gravy.   If there is no ice, spring water will answer the same purpose, but
will require to be more frequently changed.

Note.—The BRISKET and RUMP may be boiled by the above recipe; of course
allowing more or less time, according to the size of the joint.

BEEF CAKE.

610. INGREDIENTS.—The remains of cold roast beef; to each pound
of cold meat allow ¼ lb. of bacon or ham; seasoning to taste of pepper
and salt, 1 small bunch of minced savoury herbs, 1 or 2 eggs.

Mode.—Mince the beef very finely (if underdone it will be better),
add to it the bacon, which must also be chopped very small, and mix
well together.   Season, stir in the herbs, and bind with an egg, or 2
should 1 not be sufficient.   Make it into small square cakes, about

½ inch thick, fry them in hot dripping, and serve in a dish with good gravy poured round them.

Time.—10 minutes. *Average cost*, exclusive of the cold meat, 6*l.*

Seasonable at any time.

BROILED BEEF-STEAKS or RUMP-STEAKS.

611. INGREDIENTS.—Steaks, a piece of butter the size of a walnut, salt to taste, 1 tablespoonful of good mushroom ketchup or Harvey's sauce.

Mode.—As the success of a good broil so much depends on the state of the fire, see that it is bright and clear, and perfectly free from smoke, and do not add any fresh fuel just before you require to use the gridiron. Sprinkle a little salt over the fire, put on the gridiron for a few minutes, to get thoroughly hot through; rub it with a piece of fresh suet, to prevent the meat from sticking, and lay on the steaks, which should be cut of an equal thickness, about ¾ of an inch, or rather thinner, and level them by beating them as *little* as possible with a rolling-pin. Turn them frequently with steak-tongs (if these are not at hand, stick a fork in the edge of the fat, that no gravy escapes), and in from 8 to 10 minutes they will be done. Have ready a very hot dish, into which put the ketchup, and, when liked, a little minced shalot; dish up the steaks, rub them over with butter, and season with pepper and salt. The exact time for broiling steaks must be determined by taste, whether they are liked underdone or well done; more than from 8 to 10 minutes for a steak ¾ inch in thickness, we think, would spoil and dry up the juices of the meat. Great expedition is necessary in sending broiled steaks to table; and, to have them in perfection, they should not be cooked till everything else prepared for dinner has been dished up, as their excellence entirely depends on their being served very hot. Garnish with scraped horseradish, or slices of cucumber. Oyster, tomato, onion, and many other sauces, are frequent accompaniments to rump-steak, but true lovers of this English dish generally reject all additions but pepper and salt.

Time.—8 to 10 minutes. *Average cost*, 1*s.* per lb.

Sufficient.—Allow ½ lb. to each person; if the party consist entirely of gentlemen, ¾ lb. will not be too much.

Seasonable all the year, but not good in the height of summer, as the meat cannot hang long enough to be tender.

DIFFERENT SEASONS FOR BEEF.—We have already stated (*see* No. 593) that the Scots breed of oxen, like the South-down in mutton, stands first in excellence. It should be borne in mind, however, that each county has its particular season, and that the London and other large markets are always supplied by those counties whose meat, from local circumstances, is in the best condition at the time. Thus, the season in Norfolk, from which the Scots come (these being the principal oxen bred by the Norfolk and Suffolk graziers), commences about Christmas and terminates about June, when this breed begins to fall off, their place being taken by grass-fed oxen. A large quantity of most excellent meat is sent to the " dead markets " from Scotland, and some of the best London butchers are supplied from this source.

BROILED BEEF AND MUSHROOM SAUCE
(Cold Meat Cookery).

612. INGREDIENTS.—2 or 3 dozen small button mushrooms, 1 oz. of butter, salt and cayenne to taste, 1 tablespoonful of mushroom ketchup, mashed potatoes, slices of cold roast beef.

Mode.—Wipe the mushrooms free from grit with a piece of flannel, and salt; put them in a stewpan with the butter, seasoning, and ketchup ; stir over the fire until the mushrooms are quite done, when pour it in the middle of mashed potatoes, browned. Then place round the potatoes slices of cold roast beef, nicely broiled, over a clear fire. In making the mushroom sauce, the ketchup may be dispensed with, if there is sufficient gravy.

Time.—¼ hour. *Average cost*, exclusive of the meat, 8d.

Seasonable from August to October.

BROILED BEEF AND OYSTER SAUCE (Cold Meat Cookery).

613. INGREDIENTS.—2 dozen oysters, 3 cloves, 1 blade of mace, 2 oz. of butter, ½ teaspoonful of flour, cayenne and salt to taste, mashed potatoes, a few slices of cold roast beef.

Mode.—Put the oysters in a stewpan, with their liquor strained ; add the cloves, mace, butter, flour, and seasoning, and let them simmer gently for 5 minutes. Have ready in the centre of a dish round walls of mashed potatoes, browned ; into the middle pour the oyster sauce, quite hot, and round the potatoes place, in layers, slices of the beef, which should be previously broiled over a nice clear fire.

Time.—5 minutes. *Average cost*, 1s. 6d., exclusive of the cold meat.

Sufficient for 4 or 5 persons.

Seasonable from September to April.

BROILED BEEF-BONES.

614. INGREDIENTS.—The bones of ribs or sirloin ; salt, pepper, and cayenne.

Mode.—Separate the bones, taking care that the meat on them is not too thick in any part; sprinkle them well with the above seasoning, and broil over a very clear fire. When nicely browned, they are done ; but do not allow them to blacken.

TO DRESS A BULLOCK'S HEART.

615. INGREDIENTS.—1 heart, stuffing of veal forcemeat, No. 417.

Mode.—Put the heart into warm water to soak for 2 hours; then wipe it well with a cloth, and, after cutting off the lobes, stuff the inside with a highly-seasoned forcemeat (No. 417). Fasten it in, by means of a needle and coarse thread; tie the heart up in paper, and set it before a good fire, being very particular to keep it well basted, or it will eat dry, there being very little of its own fat. Two or three minutes before serving, remove the paper, baste well, and serve with good gravy and red-currant jelly or melted butter. If the heart is very large, it will require 2 hours, and, covered with a caul, may be baked as well as roasted.

Time.—Large heart, 2 hours. *Average cost*, 2s. 6d.

Sufficient for 6 or 8 persons.

Seasonable all the year.

Note.—This is an excellent family dish, is very savoury, and, though not seen at many good tables, may be recommended for its cheapness and economy.

BUBBLE-AND-SQUEAK (Cold Meat Cookery).

616. INGREDIENTS.—A few thin slices of cold boiled beef; butter, cabbage, 1 sliced onion, pepper and salt to taste.

Mode.—Fry the slices of beef gently in a little butter, taking care not to dry them up. Lay them on a flat dish, and cover with fried greens. The greens may be prepared from cabbage sprouts or green savoys. They should be boiled till tender, well drained, minced, and placed, till quite hot, in a frying-pan, with butter, a sliced onion, and seasoning of pepper and salt. When the onion is done, it is ready to serve.

Time.—Altogether, ½ hour.

Average cost, exclusive of the cold beef, 3d.

Seasonable at any time.

COLLARED BEEF.

617. INGREDIENTS.—7 lbs. of the thin end of the flank of beef, 2 oz. of coarse sugar, 6 oz. of salt, 1 oz. of saltpetre, 1 large handful of parsley minced, 1 dessertspoonful of minced sage, a bunch of savoury herbs, ½ teaspoonful of pounded allspice; salt and pepper to taste.

Mode.—Choose fine tender beef, but not too fat; lay it in a dish;

rub in the sugar, salt, and saltpetre, and let it remain in the pickle

for a week or ten days, turning and rubbing it every day. Then bone it, remove all the gristle and the coarse skin of the inside part, and sprinkle it thickly with parsley, herbs, spice, and seasoning in the above proportion, taking care that the former are finely minced, and the latter well pounded. Roll the meat up in a cloth as tightly as possible, in the same shape as shown in the engraving; bind it firmly with broad tape, and boil it gently for 6 hours. Immediately on taking it out of the pot, put it under a good weight, without undoing it, and let it remain until cold. This dish is a very nice addition to the breakfast-table.

COLLARED BEEF.

Time.—6 hours. *Average cost*, for this quantity, 4s.

Seasonable at any time.

Note.—During the time the beef is in pickle, it should be kept cool, and regularly rubbed and turned every day.

BEEF-COLLOPS.

618. INGREDIENTS.—2 lbs. of rump-steak, ¼ lb. of butter, 1 pint of gravy (water may be substituted for this), salt and pepper to taste, 1 shalot finely minced, ½ pickled walnut, 1 teaspoonful of capers.

Mode.—Have the steak cut thin, and divide it in pieces about 3 inches long; beat these with the blade of a knife, and dredge with flour. Put them in a frying-pan with the butter, and let them fry for about 3 minutes; then lay them in a small stewpan, and pour over them the gravy. Add a piece of butter, kneaded with a little flour, put in the seasoning and all the other ingredients, and let the whole simmer, but not boil, for 10 minutes. Serve in a hot covered dish.

Time.—10 minutes. *Average cost*, 1s. per lb.

Sufficient for 4 or 5 persons.

Seasonable at any time.

MINCED COLLOPS (an Entree).

619. INGREDIENTS.—1 lb. of rump-steak, salt and pepper to taste, 2 oz. of butter, 1 onion minced, ¼ pint of water, 1 tablespoonful of Harvey's sauce, or lemon-juice, or mushroom ketchup; 1 small bunch of savoury herbs.

Mode.—Mince the beef and onion very small, and fry the latter in butter until of a pale brown. Put all the ingredients together in a stewpan, and boil gently for about 10 minutes; garnish with sippets of toasted bread, and serve very hot.

Time.—10 minutes. *Average cost,* 1s. per lb.

Sufficient for 2 or 3 persons.

Seasonable at any time.

CURRIED BEEF (Cold Meat Cookery).

620. INGREDIENTS.—A few slices of tolerably lean cold roast or boiled beef, 3 oz. of butter, 2 onions, 1 wineglassful of beer, 1 dessert-spoonful of curry powder.

Mode.—Cut up the beef into pieces about 1 inch square, put the butter into a stewpan with the onions sliced, and fry them of a light-brown colour. Add all the other ingredients, and stir gently over a brisk fire for about 10 minutes. Should this be thought too dry, more beer, or a spoonful or two of gravy or water, may be added; but a good curry should not be very thin. Place it in a deep dish, with an edging of dry boiled rice, in the same manner as for other curries.

Time.—10 minutes. *Average cost,* exclusive of the meat, 4d.

Seasonable in winter.

TO CLARIFY BEEF DRIPPING.

I.

621. Good and fresh dripping answers very well for basting everything except game and poultry, and, when well clarified, serves for frying nearly as well as lard; it should be kept in a cool place, and will remain good some time. To clarify it, put the dripping into a basin, pour over it boiling water, and keep stirring the whole to wash away the impurities. Let it stand to cool, when the water and dirty sediment will settle at the bottom of the basin. Remove the dripping, and put it away in jars or basins for use.

ANOTHER WAY.

622. Put the dripping into a clean saucepan, and let it boil for a few minutes over a slow fire, and be careful to skim it well. Let it stand to cool a little, then strain it through a piece of muslin into jars for use. Beef dripping is preferable to any other for cooking purposes, as, with mutton dripping, there is liable to be a tallowy taste and smell.

ROAST FILLET OF BEEF (Larded).

623. INGREDIENTS.—About 4 lbs. of the inside fillet of the sirloin,

U

1 onion, a small bunch of parsley, salt and pepper to taste, sufficient vinegar to cover the meat, glaze, Spanish sauce, No. 411.

Mode.—Lard the beef with bacon, and put it into a pan with sufficient vinegar to cover it, with an onion sliced, parsley, and seasoning, and let it remain in this pickle for 12 hours. Roast it before a nice clear fire for about 1¼ hour, and, when done, glaze it. Pour some Spanish sauce round the beef, and the remainder serve in a tureen. It may be garnished with Spanish onions boiled and glazed.

Time.—1¼ hour. *Average cost*, exclusive of the sauce, 4s.

Sufficient for 6 or 8 persons.

Seasonable at any time.

FRICANDEAU OF BEEF.

624. INGREDIENTS.—About 3 lbs. of the inside fillet of the sirloin (a piece of the rump may be substituted for this), pepper and salt to taste, 3 cloves, 2 blades of mace, 6 whole allspice, 1 pint of stock No. 105, or water, 1 glass of sherry, 1 bunch of savoury herbs, 2 shalots, bacon.

Mode.—Cut some bacon into thin strips, and sprinkle over them a seasoning of pepper and salt, mixed with cloves, mace, and allspice, well pounded. Lard the beef with these, put it into a stewpan with the stock or water, sherry, herbs, shalots, 2 cloves, and more pepper and salt. Stew the meat gently until tender, when take it out, cover it closely, skim off all the fat from the gravy, and strain it. Set it on the fire, and boil, till it becomes a glaze. Glaze the larded side of the beef with this, and serve on sorrel sauce, which is made as follows:—Wash and pick some sorrel, and put it into a stewpan with only the water that hangs about it. Keep stirring, to prevent its burning, and when done, lay it in a sieve to drain. Chop it, and stew it with a small piece of butter and 4 or 5 tablespoonfuls of good gravy, for an hour, and rub it through a tammy. If too acid, add a little sugar; and a little cabbage-lettuce boiled with the sorrel will be found an improvement.

Time.—2 hours to gently stew the meat.

Average cost, for this quantity, 4s.

Sufficient for 6 persons.

Seasonable at any time.

FRIED SALT BEEF (Cold Meat Cookery).

625. INGREDIENTS.—A few slices of cold salt beef, pepper to taste, ¼ lb. of butter, mashed potatoes.

Mode.—Cut any part of cold salt beef into thin slices, fry them gently in butter, and season with a little pepper. Have ready some very hot mashed potatoes, lay the slices of beef on them, and garnish with 3 or 4 pickled gherkins. Cold salt beef, warmed in a little liquor from mixed pickle, drained, and served as above, will be found good.

Time.—About 5 minutes. *Average cost*, exclusive of the meat, 4d. *Seasonable* at any time.

FRIED RUMP-STEAK.

626. INGREDIENTS.—Steaks, butter or clarified dripping.

Mode.—Although broiling is a far superior method of cooking steaks to frying them, yet, when the cook is not very expert, the latter mode may be adopted; and, when properly done, the dish may really look very inviting, and the flavour be good. The steaks should be cut rather thinner than for broiling, and with a small quantity of fat to each. Put some butter or clarified dripping into a frying-pan; let it get quite hot, then lay in the steaks. Turn them frequently until done, which will be in about 8 minutes, or rather more, should the steaks be very thick. Serve on a very hot dish, in which put a small piece of butter and a tablespoonful of ketchup, and season with pepper and salt. They should be sent to table quickly, as, when cold, the steaks are entirely spoiled.

Time.—8 minutes for a medium-sized steak, rather longer for a very thick one.

Average cost, 1s. per lb.

Seasonable all the year, but not good in summer, as the meat cannot hang to get tender.

Note.—Where much gravy is liked, make it in the following manner:—As soon as the steaks are done, dish them, pour a little boiling water into the frying-pan, add a seasoning of pepper and salt, a small piece of butter, and a tablespoonful of Harvey's sauce or mushroom ketchup. Hold the pan over the fire for a minute or two, just let the gravy simmer, then pour on the steak, and serve.

A FRENCHMAN'S OPINION OF BEEF.—The following is translated from a celebrated modern French work, the production of one who in Paris enjoys a great reputation as cook and chemist:—The flesh of the ox, to be in the best condition, should be taken from an animal of from four to six years old, and neither too fat nor too lean. This meat, which possesses in the highest degree the most nutritive qualities, is generally easily digested; stock is made from it, and it is eaten boiled, broiled, roasted, stewed, braised, and in a hundred other different ways. Beef is the foundation of stock, gravies, braises, &c.; its nutritious and succulent gravy gives body and flavour to numberless ragoûts. It is an exhaustless mine in the hands of a skilful artist, and is truly the king of the kitchen. Without it, no soup, no gravy; and its absence would produce almost a famine in the civilized world!

BEEF FRITTERS (Cold Meat Cookery).

627. INGREDIENTS.—The remains of cold roast beef, pepper and

U

salt to taste, $\frac{3}{4}$ lb. of flour, $\frac{1}{2}$ pint of water, 2 oz. of butter, the whites of 2 eggs.

Mode.—Mix very smoothly, and by degrees, the flour with the above proportion of water; stir in 2 oz. of butter, which must be melted, but not oiled, and, just before it is to be used, add the whites of two well-whisked eggs. Should the batter be too thick, more water must be added. Pare down the cold beef into thin shreds, season with pepper and salt, and mix it with the batter. Drop a small quantity at a time into a pan of boiling lard, and fry from 7 to 10 minutes, according to the size. When done on one side, turn and brown them on the other. Let them dry for a minute or two before the fire, and serve on a folded napkin. A small quantity of finely-minced onions, mixed with the batter, is an improvement.

Time.—From 7 to 10 minutes.

Average cost, exclusive of the meat, 6*d.*

Seasonable at any time.

HASHED BEEF (Cold Meat Cookery).

I.

628. INGREDIENTS.—Gravy saved from the meat, 1 teaspoonful of tomato sauce, 1 teaspoonful of Harvey's sauce, 1 teaspoonful of good mushroom ketchup, $\frac{1}{2}$ glass of port wine or strong ale, pepper and salt to taste, a little flour to thicken, 1 onion finely minced, a few slices of cold roast beef.

Mode.—Put all the ingredients but the beef into a stewpan with whatever gravy may have been saved from the meat the day it was roasted; let these simmer gently for 10 minutes, then take the stewpan off the fire; let the gravy cool, and skim off the fat. Cut the beef into thin slices, dredge them with flour, and lay them in the gravy; let the whole simmer gently for 5 minutes, but not boil, or the meat will be tough and hard. Serve very hot, and garnish with sippets of toasted bread.

Time.—20 minutes. *Average cost*, exclusive of the cold meat, 4*d.*

Seasonable at any time.

II.

629. INGREDIENTS.—The remains of ribs or sirloin of beef, 2 onions, 1 carrot, 1 bunch of savoury herbs, pepper and salt to taste, $\frac{1}{2}$ blade of pounded mace, thickening of flour, rather more than 1 pint of water.

Mode.—Take off all the meat from the bones of ribs or sirloin of beef; remove the outside brown and gristle; place the meat on one side, and well stew the bones and pieces, with the above ingredients, for about 2 hours, till it becomes a strong gravy, and is reduced to rather more than ½ pint; strain this, thicken with a teaspoonful of flour, and let the gravy cool; skim off all the fat; lay in the meat, let it get hot through, but do not allow it to boil, and garnish with sippets of toasted bread. The gravy may be flavoured as in the preceding recipe.

Time.—Rather more than 2 hours.

Average cost, exclusive of the cold meat, 2d.

Seasonable at any time.

Note.—Either of the above recipes may be served in walls of mashed potatoes browned; in which case the sippets should be omitted. Be careful that hashed meat does not boil, or it will become tough.

TO PREPARE HUNG BEEF.

630. This is preserved by salting and drying, either with or without smoke. Hang up the beef 3 or 4 days, till it becomes tender, but take care it does not begin to spoil; then salt it in the usual way, either by dry-salting or by brine, with bay-salt, brown sugar, saltpetre, and a little pepper and allspice; afterwards roll it tight in a cloth, and hang it up in a warm, but not hot place, for a fortnight or more, till it is sufficiently hard. If required to have a little of the smoky flavour, it may be hung for some time in a chimney-corner, or smoked in any other way: it will keep a long time.

HUNTER'S BEEF.

631. INGREDIENTS.—For a round of beef weighing 25 lbs. allow 3 oz. of saltpetre, 3 oz. of coarse sugar, 1 oz. of cloves, 1 grated nutmeg, ½ oz. of allspice, 1 lb. of salt, ½ lb. bay-salt.

Mode.—Let the beef hang for 2 or 3 days, and remove the bone. Pound spices, salt, &c. in the above proportion, and let them be reduced to the finest powder. Put the beef into a pan, rub all the ingredients well into it, and turn and rub it every day for rather more than a fortnight. When it has been sufficiently long in pickle, wash the meat, bind it up securely with tape, and put it into a pan with ½ pint of water at the bottom; mince some suet, cover the top of the meat with it, and over the pan put a common crust of flour and water; bake for 6 hours, and, when cold, remove the paste. Save the gravy that flows from it, as it adds greatly to the flavour of hashes, stews, &c. The beef may be glazed and garnished with meat jelly.

Time.—6 hours.

Seasonable all the year.

Note.—In salting or pickling beef or pork for family consumption, it not being generally required to be kept for a great length of time, a less quantity of salt and a larger quantity of other matters more adapted to retain mellowness in meat, may be employed, which could not be adopted by the curer of the immense quantities of meat required to be preserved for victualling the shipping of this maritime country. Sugar, which is well known to possess the preserving principle in a very great degree, without the pungency and astringency of salt, may be, and is, very generally used in the preserving of meat for family consumption. Although it acts without corrugating or contracting the fibres of meat, as is the case in the action of salt, and, therefore, does not impair its mellowness, yet its use in sufficient quantities for preservative effect, without the addition of other antiseptics, would impart a flavour not agreeable to the taste of many persons. It may be used, however, together with salt, with the greatest advantage in imparting mildness and mellowness to cured meat, in a proportion of about one part by weight to four of the mixture; and, perhaps, now that sugar is so much lower in price than it was in former years, one of the obstructions to its more frequent use is removed.

TO DRESS BEEF KIDNEY.

I.

632. INGREDIENTS.—1 kidney, clarified butter, pepper and salt to taste, a small quantity of highly-seasoned gravy, 1 tablespoonful of lemon-juice, $\frac{1}{4}$ teaspoonful of powdered sugar.

Mode.—Cut the kidneys into neat slices, put them into warm water to soak for 2 hours, and change the water 2 or 3 times; then put them on a clean cloth to dry the water from them, and lay them in a frying-pan with some clarified butter, and fry them of a nice brown; season each side with pepper and salt, put them round the dish, and the gravy in the middle. Before pouring the gravy in the dish, add the lemon-juice and sugar.

Time.—From 5 to 10 minutes. *Average cost,* 9*d.* each.

Seasonable at any time.

II.

633. INGREDIENTS.—1 kidney, 1 dessertspoonful of minced parsley, 1 teaspoonful of minced shalot, salt and pepper to taste, $\frac{1}{4}$ pint of gravy, No. 438, 3 tablespoonfuls of sherry.

Mode.—Take off a little of the kidney fat, mince it very fine, and put it in a frying-pan; slice the kidney, sprinkle over it parsley and shalots in the above proportion, add a seasoning of pepper and salt, and fry it of a nice brown. When it is done enough, dredge over a little flour, and pour in the gravy and sherry. Let it just simmer, but not boil any more, or the kidney would harden; serve very hot, and garnish with croûtons. Where the flavour of the shalot is disliked, it may be omitted, and a small quantity of savoury herbs substituted for it.

Time.—From 5 to 10 minutes, according to the thickness of the slices. *Average cost*, 9d. each. *Sufficient* for 3 persons. *Seasonable* at any time.

III.

A more Simple Method.

634. Cut the kidney into thin slices, flour them, and fry of a nice brown. When done, make a gravy in the pan by pouring away the fat, putting in a small piece of butter, ¼ pint of boiling water, pepper and salt, and a tablespoonful of mushroom ketchup. Let the gravy just boil up, pour over the kidney, and serve.

BOILED MARROW-BONES.

635. INGREDIENTS.—Bones, a small piece of common paste, a floured cloth.

Mode.—Have the bones neatly sawed into convenient sizes, and cover the ends with a small piece of common crust, made with flour and water. Over this tie a floured cloth, and place them upright in a saucepan of boiling water, taking care there is sufficient to cover the bones. Boil them for 2 hours, remove the cloth and paste, and serve them upright on a napkin with dry toast. Many persons clear the marrow from the bones after they are cooked, spread it over a slice of toast and add a seasoning of pepper; when served in this manner, it must be very expeditiously sent to table, as it so soon gets cold.

Time.—2 hours.

Seasonable at any time.

Note.—Marrow-bones may be baked after preparing them as in the preceding recipe; they should be laid in a deep dish, and baked for 2 hours.

MARROW-BONES.—Bones are formed of a dense cellular tissue of membranous matter, made stiff and rigid by insoluble earthy salts; of which, phosphate of lime is the most abundant. In a large bone, the insoluble matter is generally deposited in such a manner as to leave a cavity, into which a fatty substance, distinguished by the name of marrow, is thrown. Hollow cylindrical bones possess the qualities of strength and lightness in a remarkable degree. If bones were entirely solid, they would be unnecessarily heavy; and if their materials were brought into smaller compass, they would be weaker, because the strength of a bone is in proportion to the distance at which its fibres are from the centre. Some animals, it must, however, be observed, have no cavities in the centre of their bones; such as the whale tribe, skate, and turtles.

MARROW-BONES.

MINCED BEEF (Cold Meat Cookery).

636. INGREDIENTS.—1 oz. of butter, 1 small onion, 2 tablespoonfuls of gravy left from the meat, 1 tablespoonful of strong ale, ½ a tea

spoonful of flour, salt and pepper to taste, a few slices of lean roast beef.

Mode.—Put into a stewpan the butter with an onion chopped fine ; add the gravy, ale, and ⅓ a teaspoonful of flour to thicken ; season with pepper and salt, and stir these ingredients over the fire until the onion is a rich brown. Cut, but do not chop the meat *very fine,* add it to the gravy, stir till quite hot, and serve. Garnish with sippets of toasted bread. Be careful in not allowing the gravy to boil after the meat is added, as it would render it hard and tough.

Time.—About ½ hour. *Average cost,* exclusive of the meat, 3*d.*

Seasonable at any time.

MIROTON OF BEEF.

637. INGREDIENTS.—A few slices of cold roast beef, 3 oz. of butter, salt and pepper to taste, 3 onions, ⅓ pint of gravy.

Mode.—Slice the onions and put them into a frying-pan with the cold beef and butter ; place it over the fire, and keep turning and stirring the ingredients to prevent them burning. When of a pale brown, add the gravy and seasoning ; let it simmer for a few minutes, and serve very hot. This dish is excellent and economical.

Time.—5 minutes. *Average cost,* exclusive of the meat, 6*d.*

Seasonable at any time.

STEWED OX-CHEEK.

638. INGREDIENTS.—1 cheek, salt and water, 4 or 5 onions, butter and flour, 6 cloves, 3 turnips, 2 carrots, 1 bay-leaf, 1 head of celery, 1 bunch of savoury herbs, cayenne, black pepper and salt to taste, 1 oz. of butter, 2 dessertspoonfuls of flour, 2 tablespoonfuls of Chili vinegar, 2 tablespoonfuls of mushroom ketchup, 2 tablespoonfuls of port wine, 2 tablespoonfuls of Harvey's sauce.

Mode.—Have the cheek boned, and prepare it the day before it is to be eaten, by cleaning and putting it to soak all night in salt and water. The next day, wipe it dry and clean, and put it into a stew-pan. Just cover it with water, skim well when it boils, and let it gently simmer till the meat is quite tender. Slice and fry 3 onions in a little butter and flour, and put them into the gravy ; add 2 whole onions, each stuck with 3 cloves, 3 turnips quartered, 2 carrots sliced, a bay-leaf, 1 head of celery, a bunch of herbs, and seasoning to taste of cayenne, black pepper, and salt. Let these stew till perfectly tender ; then take out the cheek, divide into pieces fit to help at table, skim and strain the gravy, and thicken 1½ pint of it with butter and flour in the above proportions. Add the vinegar, ketchup, and port wine; put in the pieces of cheek; let the whole boil up, and serve quite hot. Send it to table in a ragoût-dish. If the colour of the gravy should not be very good, add a tablespoonful of the browning, No. 108.

Time.—4 hours. *Average cost*, 3*d.* per lb.

Sufficient for 8 persons.

Seasonable at any time.

FRIED OX-FEET, or COW-HEEL.

639. INGREDIENTS.—Ox-feet, the yolk of 1 egg, bread crumbs, parsley, salt and cayenne to taste, boiling butter.

Mode.—Wash, scald, and thoroughly clean the feet, and cut them into pieces about 2 inches long; have ready some fine bread crumbs mixed with a little minced parsley, cayenne, and salt; dip the pieces of heel into the yolk of egg, sprinkle them with the bread crumbs, and fry them until of a nice brown in boiling butter.

Time.—¼ hour. *Average cost*, 6*d.* each.

Seasonable at any time.

Note.—Ox-feet may be dressed in various ways, stewed in gravy or plainly boiled and served with melted butter. When plainly boiled, the liquor will answer for making sweet or relishing jellies, and also to give richness to soups or gravies.

STEWED OX-TAILS.

640. INGREDIENTS.—2 ox-tails, 1 onion, 3 cloves, 1 blade of mace, ¼ teaspoonful of whole black pepper, ¼ teaspoonful of allspice, ½ a teaspoonful of salt, a small bunch of savoury herbs, thickening of butter and flour, 1 tablespoonful of lemon-juice, 1 tablespoonful of mushroom ketchup.

Mode.—Divide the tails at the joints, wash, and put them into a stewpan with sufficient water to cover them, and set them on the fire; when the water boils, remove the scum, and add the onion cut into rings, the spice, seasoning, and herbs. Cover the stewpan closely, and let the tails simmer very gently until tender, which will be in about 2½ hours. Take them out, make a thickening of butter and flour, add it to the gravy, and let it boil for ¼ hour. Strain it through a sieve into a saucepan, put back the tails, add the lemon-juice and ketchup; let the whole just boil up, and serve. Garnish with croûtons or sippets of toasted bread.

Time.—2½ hours to stew the tails.

Average cost, 9*d.* to 1*s.* 6*d.*, according to the season.

Sufficient for 8 persons.

Seasonable all the year.

THE TAILS OF ANIMALS.—In the class Mammalia, the vertebral column or backbone presents only slight modifications, and everywhere shows the same characteristics as in man, who stands at the head of this division of the animal kingdom. The length of this column, however, varies much, and the number of vertebræ of which it is composed is far from being uniform. These numerical differences principally depend on the unequal development of the caudal portion, or tail-end, of the column. Thus, the tail-forming vertebræ sometimes do not exist at all,—amongst certain bats for example; in other instances we reckon forty, fifty, and even upwards of sixty of these bones. Among the greater number of mammals, the tail is of little use for locomotion, except that it acts in many cases as does the rudder of a ship, steadying the animal in his rapid movements, and enabling him to turn more easily and quickly. Among some animals, it becomes a very powerful instrument of progression. Thus, in the kangaroos and jerboas, the tail forms, with the hind feet, a kind of tripod from which the animal makes its spring. With most of the American monkeys it is prehensile, and serves the animal as a fifth hand to suspend itself from the branches of trees; and, lastly, among the whales, it grows to an enormous size, and becomes the principal instrument for swimming.

A PICKLE FOR TONGUES OR BEEF (Newmarket Recipe).

641. INGREDIENTS.—1 gallon of soft water, 3 lbs. of coarse salt, 6 oz. of coarse brown sugar, ½ oz. of saltpetre.

Mode.—Put all the ingredients into a saucepan, and let them boil for ½ hour, clear off the scum as it rises, and when done pour the pickle into a pickling-pan. Let it get cold, then put in the meat, and allow it to remain in the pickle from 8 to 14 days, according to the size. It will keep good for 6 months if well boiled once a fortnight. Tongues will take 1 month or 6 weeks to be properly cured; and, in salting meat, beef and tongues should always be put in separate vessels.

Time.—A moderate-sized tongue should remain in the pickle about a month, and be turned every day.

POTTED BEEF.

I.

642. INGREDIENTS.—2 lbs. of lean beef, 1 tablespoonful of water, ¼ lb. of butter, a seasoning to taste of salt, cayenne, pounded mace, and black pepper.

POTTING-JAR.

Mode.—Procure a nice piece of lean beef, as free as possible from gristle, skin, &c., and put it into a jar (if at hand, one with a lid) with 1 tablespoonful of water. Cover it *closely*, and put the jar into a saucepan of boiling water, letting the water come within 2 inches of the top of the jar. Boil gently for 3½ hours, then take the beef, chop it very small with a chopping-knife, and pound it thoroughly in a mortar. Mix with it by degrees all, or a portion, of the gravy that will have run from it, and a little clarified butter; add the seasoning, put it in small pots for use, and cover with a little butter just warmed and poured over. If much gravy is added to it, it will keep but a short time; on the contrary, if a large proportion of butter is used, it may be preserved for some time.

Time.—3½ hours. *Average cost*, for this quantity, 1s. 8d.

Seasonable at any time.

POTTED BEEF (Cold Meat Cookery).

II.

643. INGREDIENTS.—The remains of cold roast or boiled beef, ¼ lb. of butter, cayenne to taste, 2 blades of pounded mace.

Mode.—As we have stated in recipe No. 608, the outside slices of boiled beef may, with a little trouble, be converted into a very nice addition to the breakfast-table. Cut up the meat into small pieces and pound it well, with a little butter, in a mortar; add a seasoning of cayenne and mace, and be very particular that the latter ingredient is reduced to the finest powder. When all the ingredients are thoroughly mixed, put it into glass or earthen potting-pots, and pour on the top a coating of clarified butter.

Seasonable at any time.

Note.—If cold roast beef is used, remove all pieces of gristle and dry outside pieces, as these do not pound well.

PRESERVED MEATS.—When an organic substance, like the flesh of animals, is heated to the boiling-point, it loses the property of passing into a state of fermentation and decay. Fresh animal milk, as is well known, coagulates, after having been kept for two or three days, into a gelatinous mass; but it may be preserved for an indefinite period, as a perfectly sweet liquid, if it be heated daily to the boiling-point. The knowledge of this effect of an elevated temperature has given rise to a most important branch of industry,—namely, the preparation of preserved meats for the use of the navy and merchant service. At Leith, in the neighbourhood of Edinburgh, at Aberdeen, at Bordeaux, at Marseilles, and in many parts of Germany, establishments of enormous magnitude exist, in which soup, vegetables, and viands of every description are prepared, in such a manner that they retain their freshness for years. The prepared aliments are inclosed in canisters of tinned iron plate, the covers are soldered air-tight, and the canisters exposed to the temperature of boiling water for three or four hours. The aliments thus acquire a stability, which one may almost say is eternal; and when a canister is opened, after the lapse of several years, its contents are found to be unaltered in taste, colour, and smell. We are indebted to the French philosopher Gay-Lussac for this beautiful practical application of the discovery that boiling checks fermentation. An exclusive salt-meat diet is extremely injurious to the health; and, in former times, thousands of mariners lost their lives for the want of fresh aliments during long voyages. We are sorry to say that the preserved meats are sometimes carelessly prepared, and, though the statement seems incredible, sometimes adulterated. Dr. Lankester, who has done so much to expose the frauds of trade, that he ought to be regarded as a public benefactor, says that he has seen things which were utterly unfit for food, shipped as preserved meats. Surely, as he observes, there ought to be some superintendent to examine the so-called articles of food that are taken on board ship, so that the poor men who have been fighting our battles abroad may run no risk of being starved or poisoned on their way home.

RIB OF BEEF BONES.

(*A Pretty Dish.*)

644. INGREDIENTS.—Rib of beef bones, 1 onion chopped fine, a few slices of carrot and turnip, ¼ pint of gravy.

Mode.—The bones for this dish should have left on them a slight covering of meat; saw them into pieces 3 inches long; season them with pepper and salt, and put them into a stewpan with the remaining ingredients. Stew gently, until the vegetables are tender, and serve on a flat dish within walls of mashed potatoes.

Time.—¾ hour. *Average cost*, exclusive of the bones, 2*d.*

Seasonable at any time.

BEEF RISSOLES (Cold Meat Cookery).

645. INGREDIENTS.—The remains of cold roast beef; to each pound of meat allow ¾ lb. of bread crumbs, salt and pepper to taste, a few chopped savoury herbs, ½ a teaspoonful of minced lemon-peel, 1 or 2 eggs, according to the quantity of meat.

Mode.—Mince the beef very fine, which should be rather lean, and mix with this bread crumbs, herbs, seasoning, and lemon-peel, in the above proportion, to each pound of meat. Make all into a thick paste with 1 or 2 eggs; divide into balls or cones, and fry a rich brown. Garnish the dish with fried parsley, and send with them to table some good brown gravy in a tureen. Instead of garnishing with fried parsley, gravy may be poured in the dish, round the rissoles: in this case, it will not be necessary to send any in a tureen.

Time.—From 5 to 10 minutes, according to size.

Average cost, exclusive of the meat, 5*d.*

Seasonable at any time.

ROLLED BEEF, to eat like Hare.

646. INGREDIENTS.—About 5 lbs. of the inside of the sirloin, 2 glasses of port wine, 2 glasses of vinegar, a small quantity of force-meat (No. 417), 1 teaspoonful of pounded allspice.

Mode.—Take the inside of a large sirloin, soak it in 1 glass of port wine and 1 glass of vinegar, mixed, and let it remain for 2 days. Make a forcemeat by recipe No. 417, lay it on the meat, and bind it up securely. Roast it before a nice clear fire, and baste it with 1 glass each of port wine and vinegar, with which mix a teaspoonful of pounded allspice. Serve, with a good gravy in the dish, and send red-currant jelly to table with it.

Time.—A piece of 5 lbs. about 1½ hour before a brisk fire.

Average cost, for this quantity, 5*s.* 4*d.*

Sufficient for 4 persons.

Seasonable at any time.

BEEF ROLLS (Cold Meat Cookery).

647. INGREDIENTS.—The remains of cold roast or boiled beef, seasoning to taste of salt, pepper, and minced herbs ; puff paste.

Mode.—Mince the beef tolerably fine with a small amount of its own fat ; add a seasoning of pepper, salt, and chopped herbs ; put the whole into a roll of puff paste, and bake for ½ hour, or rather longer, should the roll be very large. Beef patties may be made of cold meat, by mincing and seasoning beef as directed above, and baking in a rich puff paste in patty-tins.

Time.—½ hour.

Seasonable at **any** time.

MINIATURE ROUND OF BEEF.

(*An Excellent Dish for a Small Family.*)

648. INGREDIENTS.—From 5 to 10 lbs. of rib of beef, sufficient brine to cover the meat.

Mode.—Choose a fine rib, have the bone removed, rub some salt over the inside, and skewer the meat up into a nice round form, and bind it with tape. Put it into sufficient brine to cover it (the brine should be made by recipe No. 654), and let it remain for 6 days, turning the meat every day. When required to be dressed, drain from the pickle, and put the meat into very hot water ; let it boil rapidly for a few minutes, when draw the pot to the side of the fire, and let it simmer very gently until done. Remove the skewer, and replace it by a plated or silver one. Carrots and turnips should be served with this dish, and may be boiled with the meat.

Time.—A small round of 8 lbs., about 2 hours after the water boils ; one of 12 lbs., about 3 hours.

Average cost, 9d. per lb. *Sufficient* for 6 persons.

Seasonable at any time.

Note.—Should the joint be very small, 4 or 5 days will be sufficient time to salt it.

BRISKET OF BEEF, a la Flamande.

649. INGREDIENTS.—About 6 or 8 lbs. of the brisket of beef, 4 or 5 slices of bacon, 2 carrots, 1 onion, a bunch of savoury herbs, salt and pepper to taste, 4 cloves, 4 whole allspice, 2 blades of mace.

Mode.—Choose that portion of the brisket which contains the gristle, trim it, and put it into a stewpan with the slices of bacon, which should be put under and over the meat. Add the vegetables, herbs, spices, and seasoning, and cover with a little weak stock or water ; close the stewpan as hermetically as possible, and simmer very gently for 4 hours. Strain the liquor, reserve a portion of it for sauce, and the remainder boil quickly over a sharp fire until reduced to a glaze, with which glaze the meat. Garnish the dish with scooped carrots and turnips, and when liked, a little cabbage ; all of which must be cooked separately. Thicken and flavour the liquor that was saved for sauce, pour it round the meat, and serve. The beef may also be garnished with glazed onions, artichoke-bottoms, &c.

Time.—4 hours. *Average cost*, 7*d*. per lb.

Sufficient for 6 or 8 persons.

Seasonable at any time.

FRENCH BEEF.—It has been all but universally admitted, that the beef of France is greatly inferior in quality to that of England, owing to inferiority of pasturage. M. Curmer, however, one of the latest writers on the culinary art, tells us that this is a vulgar error, and that French beef is far superior to that of England. This is mere vaunting on the part of our neighbours, who seem to want *la gloire* in everything ; and we should not deign to notice it, if it had occurred in a work of small pretensions ; but M. Curmer's book professes to be a complete exposition of the scientific principles of cookery, and holds a high rank in the didactic literature of France. We half suspect that M. Curmer obtained his knowledge of English beef in the same way as did the poor Frenchman, whom the late Mr. Mathews, the comedian, so humorously described. Mr. Lewis, in his "Physiology of Common Life," has thus revived the story of the beef-eating son of France :—"A Frenchman was one day blandly remonstrating against the supercilious scorn expressed by Englishmen for the beef of France, which he, for his part, did not find so inferior to that of England. 'I have been two times in England,' he remarked, ' but I nevère find the bif so supérieur to ours. I find it vary conveenient that they bring it you on leetle pieces of stick, fcr one penny ; but I do not find the bif supérieur.' On hearing this, the Englishman, red with astonishment, exclaimed, ' Good heavens, sir ! you have been eating cat's meat.' " No, M. Curmer, we are ready to acknowledge the superiority of your cookery, but we have long since made up our minds as to the inferiority of your raw material.

BEEF OLIVES.

I.

650. INGREDIENTS.—2 lbs. of rump-steak, 1 egg, 1 tablespoonful of minced savoury herbs, pepper and salt to taste, 1 pint of stock, No. 105, 2 or 3 slices of bacon, 2 tablespoonfuls of any store sauce, a slight thickening of butter and flour.

Mode.—Have the steaks cut rather thin, slightly beat them to make them level, cut them into 6 or 7 pieces, brush over with egg, and sprinkle with herbs, which should be very finely minced ; season with pepper and salt, and roll up the pieces tightly, and fasten with a small skewer. Put the stock in a stewpan that will exactly hold them, for by being pressed together, they will keep their shape better ; lay in the rolls of meat, cover them with the bacon, cut in thin slices, and over that put a piece of paper. Stew them very *gently* for full 2 hours ; for the slower they are done the better. Take them out, remove the skewers, thicken the gravy with butter and flour, and flavour with any store sauce that may be preferred. Give one boil, pour over the meat, and serve.

Time.—2 hours. *Average cost,* 1s. per pound.

Sufficient for 4 or 5 persons.

Seasonable at any time.

II.

(*Economical.*)

651. INGREDIENTS.—The remains of underdone cold roast beef, bread crumbs, 1 shalot finely minced, pepper and salt to taste, gravy made from the beef bones, thickening of butter and flour, 1 table-spoonful of mushroom ketchup.

Mode.—Cut some slices of underdone roast beef about half an inch thick ; sprinkle over them some bread crumbs, minced shalot, and a little of the fat and seasoning ; roll them, and fasten with a small skewer. Have ready some gravy made from the beef bones ; put in the pieces of meat, and stew them till tender, which will be in about 1¼ hour, or rather longer. Arrange the meat in a dish, thicken and flavour the gravy, and pour it over the meat, when it is ready to serve.

Time.—1½ hour. *Average cost,* exclusive of the beef, 2d.

Seasonable at any time.

BROILED OX-TAIL (an Entree).

652. INGREDIENTS.—2 tails, 1½ pint of stock, No. 105, salt and cayenne to taste, bread crumbs, 1 egg.

Mode.—Joint and cut up the tails into convenient-sized pieces, and put them into a stewpan, with the stock, cayenne, and salt, and, if liked very savoury, a bunch of sweet herbs. Let them simmer gently for about 2½ hours ; then take them out, drain them, and let them cool. Beat an egg upon a plate ; dip in each piece of tail, and, afterwards, throw them into a dish of bread crumbs ; broil them over a clear fire, until of a brownish colour on both sides, and serve with a good gravy, or any sauce that may be preferred.

Time.—About 2½ hours. *Average cost,* from 9d. to 1s. 6d., according to the season.

Sufficient for 6 persons.

Seasonable at any time.

Note.—These may be more easily prepared by putting the tails in a brisk oven, after they have been dipped in egg and bread-crumb ; and, when brown, they are done. They must be boiled the same time as for broiling.

STRANGE TAILS.—Naturalists cannot explain the uses of some of the strange tails borne by animals. In the Egyptian and Syrian sheep, for instance, the tail grows so large, that it is not unfrequently supported upon a sort of little cart, in order to prevent inconvenience to the animal. This monstrous appendage sometimes attains a weight of seventy, eighty, or even a hundred pounds.

TO DRESS BEEF PALATES (an Entree).

653. INGREDIENTS.—4 palates, sufficient gravy to cover them (No. 438), cayenne to taste, 1 tablespoonful of mushroom ketchup, 1 tablespoonful of pickled-onion liquor, thickening of butter and flour.

Mode.—Wash the palates, and put them into a stewpan, with sufficient water to cover them, and let them boil until perfectly tender, or until the upper skin may be easily peeled off. Have ready sufficient gravy (No. 438) to cover them; add a good seasoning of cayenne, and thicken with roux, No. 525, or a little butter kneaded with flour; let it boil up, and skim. Cut the palates into square pieces, put them in the gravy, and let them simmer gently for ½ hour; add ketchup and onion-liquor, give one boil, and serve.

Time.—From 3 to 5 hours to boil the palates.

Sufficient for 4 persons.

Seasonable at any time.

Note.—Palates may be dressed in various ways with sauce tournée, good onion sauce, tomato sauce, and also served in a vol-au-vent; but the above will be found a more simple method of dressing them.

BEEF PICKLE, which may also be used for any kind of Meat, Tongues, or Hams.

654. INGREDIENTS.—6 lbs. of salt, 2 lbs. of fine sugar, 3 oz. of powdered saltpetre, 3 gallons of spring water.

Mode.—Boil all the ingredients gently together, so long as any scum or impurity arises, which carefully remove; when quite cold, pour it over the meat, every part of which must be covered with the brine. This may be used for pickling any kind of meat, and may be kept for some time, if boiled up occasionally with an addition of the ingredients.

Time.—A ham should be kept in the pickle for a fortnight; a piece of beef weighing 14 lbs., 12 or 15 days; a tongue, 10 days or a fortnight.

Note.—For salting and pickling meat, it is a good plan to rub in only half the quantity of salt directed, and to let it remain for a day or two to disgorge and effectually to get rid of the blood and slime; then rub in the remainder of the salt and other ingredients, and proceed as above. This rule may be applied to all the recipes we have given for salting and pickling meat.

TO PICKLE PART OF A ROUND OF BEEF FOR HANGING.

655. INGREDIENTS.—For 14 lbs. of a round of beef allow 1½ lb. of salt, ½ oz. of powdered saltpetre; or, 1 lb. of salt, ½ lb. of sugar, ½ oz. of powdered saltpetre.

Mode.—Rub in, and sprinkle either of the above mixtures on 14 lbs. of meat. Keep it in an earthenware pan, or a deep wooden tray, and turn twice a week during 3 weeks; then bind up the beef tightly with coarse linen tape, and hang it in a kitchen in which a fire is constantly kept, for 3 weeks. Pork, hams, and bacon may be cured in a similar way, but will require double the quantity of the salting mixture; and, if not smoke-dried, they should be taken down from hanging after 3 or 4 weeks, and afterwards kept in boxes or tubs, amongst dry oat-husks.

Time.—2 or 3 weeks to remain in the brine; to be hung 3 weeks.

Seasonable at any time.

Note.—The meat may be boiled fresh from this pickle, instead of smoking it.

BEEF RAGOUT (Cold Meat Cookery).

656. INGREDIENTS.—About 2 lbs. of cold roast · beef, 6 onions, pepper, salt, and mixed spices to taste; ¼ pint of boiling water, 3 tablespoonfuls of gravy.

Mode.—Cut the beef into rather large pieces, and put them into a stewpan with the onions, which must be sliced. Season well with pepper, salt, and mixed spices, and pour over about ½ pint of boiling water, and gravy in the above proportion (gravy saved from the meat answers the purpose); let the whole stew very gently for about 2 hours, and serve with pickled walnuts, gherkins, or capers, just warmed in the gravy.

Time.—2 hours. *Average cost*, exclusive of the meat, 4d.

Seasonable at any time.

ROAST RIBS OF BEEF.

657. INGREDIENTS.—Beef, a little salt.

Mode.—The fore-rib is considered the primest roasting piece, but the middle-rib is considered the most economical. Let the meat be well hung (should the weather permit), and cut off the thin ends of the bones, which should be salted for a few days, and then boiled. Put the meat down to a nice clear fire, put some clean dripping into the pan, dredge the joint with a little flour, and keep continually basting the whole time. Sprinkle some fine salt over it (this must never be done until the joint is dished, as it draws the juices from the meat); pour the dripping from the pan, put in a little boiling water slightly salted, and *strain* the gravy over the meat. Garnish with tufts of scraped horseradish, and send horseradish sauce to table with it (*see* No. 447). A Yorkshire pudding (*see* Puddings) sometimes accompanies this dish, and, if lightly made and well cooked, will be found a very agreeable addition.

Time.—10 lbs. of beef, 2½ hours; 14 to 16 lbs., from 3½ to 4 hours.

Average cost, 8½*d.* per lb.

Sufficient.—A joint of 10 lbs. sufficient for 8 or 9 persons.

Seasonable at any time.

MEMORANDA IN ROASTING.—The management of the fire is a point of primary importance in roasting. A radiant fire throughout the operation is absolutely necessary to insure a good result. When the article to be dressed is thin and delicate, the fire may be small; but when the joint is large, the fire must fill the grate. Meat must never be put down before a hollow or exhausted fire, which may soon want recruiting : on the other hand, if the heat of the fire becomes too fierce, the meat must be removed to a considerable distance till it is somewhat abated. Some cooks always fail in their roasts, though they succeed in nearly everything else. A French writer on the culinary art says that anybody can learn how to cook, but one must be born a roaster. According to Liebig, beef or mutton cannot be said to be sufficiently roasted until it has acquired, throughout the whole mass, a temperature of 158°; but poultry may be well cooked when the inner parts have attained a temperature of from 130° to 140°. This depends on the greater amount of blood which beef and mutton contain, the colouring matter of blood not being coagulable under 158°.

ROAST RIBS OF BEEF, Boned and Rolled (a very Convenient Joint for a Small Family).

658. INGREDIENTS.—1 or 2 ribs of beef.

Mode.—Choose a fine rib of beef, and have it cut according to the weight you require, either wide or narrow. Bone and roll the meat round, secure it with wooden skewers, and, if necessary, bind it round with a piece of tape. Spit the beef firmly, or, if a bottle-jack is used, put the joint on the hook, and place it *near* a nice clear fire. Let it remain so till the outside of the meat is set, when draw it to a distance, and keep continually basting until the meat is done, which can be ascertained by the steam from it drawing towards the fire. As this joint is solid, rather more than ¼ hour must be allowed for each lb. Remove the skewers, put in a plated or silver one, and send the joint to table with gravy in the dish, and garnish with tufts of horseradish. Horseradish sauce, No. 447, is a great improvement to roast beef.

Time.—For 10 lbs. of the rolled ribs, 3 hours (as the joint is very solid, we have allowed an extra ½ hour); for 6 lbs., 1½ hour.

Average cost, 8½*d.* per lb.

Sufficient.—A joint of 10 lbs. for 6 or 8 persons.

Seasonable all the year.

Note.—When the weight exceeds 10 lbs., we would not advise the above method of boning and rolling; only in the case of 1 or 2 ribs, when the joint cannot stand upright in the dish, and would look awkward. The bones should be put on with a few vegetables and herbs, and made into stock.

ROAST BEEF has long been a national dish in England. In most of our patriotic songs it is contrasted with the fricasseed frogs, popularly supposed to be the exclusive diet of Frenchmen.

"O the roast beef of old England,
And O the old English roast beef."

This national chorus is appealed to whenever a song-writer wishes to account for the valour displayed by Englishmen at sea or on land.

ROAST SIRLOIN OF BEEF.

659. INGREDIENTS.—Beef, a little salt.

Mode.—As a joint cannot be well roasted without a good fire, see that it is well made up about ¾ hour before it is required, so that when the joint is put down, it is clear and bright. Choose a nice sirloin, the weight of which should not exceed 16 lbs., as the outside would be too much done, whilst the inside would not be done enough. Spit it or hook it on to the jack firmly, dredge it slightly with flour, and place it near the fire at first, as directed in the preceding recipe. Then draw it to a distance, and keep continually basting until the meat is done. Sprinkle a small quantity of salt over it, empty the dripping-pan of all the dripping, pour in some boiling water slightly salted, stir it about, and *strain* over the meat. Garnish with tufts of horseradish, and send horseradish sauce and Yorkshire pudding to table with it. For carving, *see* p. 317.

Time.—A sirloin of 10 lbs., 2½ hours; 14 to 16 lbs., about 4 or 4½ hours.

Average cost, 8½d. per lb.

Sufficient.—A joint of 10 lbs. for 8 or 9 persons.

Seasonable at any time.

The rump, round, and other pieces of beef are roasted in the same manner, allowing for solid joints ¼ hour to every lb.

Note.—The above is the usual method of roasting meat; but to have it in perfection and the juices kept in, the meat should at first be laid *close* to the fire, and when the outside is set and firm, drawn away to a good distance, and then left to roast very slowly; where economy is studied, this plan would not answer, as the meat requires to be at the fire double the time of the ordinary way of cooking; consequently, double the quantity of fuel would be consumed.

ORIGIN OF THE WORD "SIRLOIN."—The loin of beef is said to have been knighted by King Charles II., at Friday Hall, Chingford. The "Merry Monarch" returned to this hospitable mansion from Epping Forest literally "as hungry as a hunter," and beheld, with delight, a huge loin of beef steaming upon the table. "A noble joint!" exclaimed the king. "By St. George, it shall have a title!" Then drawing his sword, he raised it above the meat, and cried, with mock dignity, "Loin, we dub thee knight; henceforward be Sir Loin!" This anecdote is doubtless apocryphal, although the oak table upon which the joint was supposed to have received its knighthood, might have been seen by any one who visited Friday-Hill House, a few years ago. It is, perhaps, a pity to spoil so noble a story; but the interests of truth demand that we declare that *sirloin* is probably a corruption of *surloin*, which signifies the upper part of a loin, the prefix *sur* being equivalent to *over* or *above*. In French we find this joint called *sur-longe*, which so closely resembles our *sirloin*, that we may safely refer the two words to a common origin.

SIRLOIN OF BEEF.

TO SALT BEEF.

660. INGREDIENTS.—½ round of beef, 4 oz. of sugar, 1 oz. of powdered saltpetre, 2 oz. of black pepper, ¼ lb. of bay-salt, ½ lb. of common salt.

Mode.—Rub the meat well with salt, and let it remain for a day, to disgorge and clear it from slime. The next day, rub it well with the above ingredients on every side, and let it remain in the pickle for about a fortnight, turning it every day. It may be boiled fresh from the pickle, or smoked.

Time.—½ round of beef to remain in pickle about a fortnight.

Average cost, 7d. per lb.

Seasonable at any time.

Note.—The aitch-bone, flank, or brisket may be salted and pickled by any of the recipes we have given for salting beef, allowing less time for small joints to remain in the pickle; for instance, a joint of 8 or 9 lbs. will be sufficiently salt in about a week.

THE DUTCH WAY TO SALT BEEF.

661. INGREDIENTS.—10 lbs. of lean beef, 1 lb. of treacle, 1 oz. of saltpetre, 1 lb. of common salt.

Mode.—Rub the beef well with the treacle, and let it remain for 3 days, turning and rubbing it often; then wipe it, pound the salt and saltpetre very fine, rub these well in, and turn it every day for 10 days. Roll it up tightly in a coarse cloth, and press it under a large weight; have it smoked, and turn it upside down every day. Boil it, and, on taking it out of the pot, put a heavy weight on it to press it.

Time.—17 days.

Seasonable at any time.

BEEF SAUSAGES.

662. INGREDIENTS.—To every lb. of suet allow 2 lbs. of lean beef; seasoning to taste of salt, pepper, and mixed spices.

Mode.—Clear the suet from skin, and chop that and the beef as finely as possible; season with pepper, salt, and spices, and mix the whole well together. Make it into flat cakes, and fry of a nice brown. Many persons pound the meat in a mortar after it is chopped; but this is not necessary when the meat is minced finely.

Time.—10 minutes. *Average cost*, for this quantity, 1s. 6d.

Seasonable at any time.

BEEF-STEAK, Rolled, Roasted, and Stuffed.

663. INGREDIENTS.—2 lbs. of rump-steak, forcemeat No. 417, pepper and salt to taste, clarified butter.

Mode.—Have the steaks cut rather thick from a well-hung rump of beef, and sprinkle over them a seasoning of pepper and salt. Make a forcemeat by recipe No. 417; spread it over *half* of the steak; roll it up, bind and skewer it firmly, that the forcemeat may not escape, and roast it before a nice clear fire for about 1½ hour, or rather longer, should the roll be very large and thick. Keep it constantly basted with butter, and serve with brown gravy, some of which must be poured round the steak, and the remainder sent to table in a tureen.

Time.—1½ hour. *Average cost*, 1s. per lb.

Sufficient for 4 persons.

Seasonable all the year, but best in winter.

SLICED AND BROILED BEEF—a Pretty Dish (Cold Meat Cookery).

664. INGREDIENTS.—A few slices of cold roast beef, 4 or 5 potatoes, a thin batter, pepper and salt to taste.

Mode.—Pare the potatoes as you would peel an apple; fry the parings in a thin batter seasoned with salt and pepper, until they are of a light brown colour, and place them on a dish over some slices of beef, which should be nicely seasoned and broiled.

Time.—5 minutes to broil the meat.

Seasonable at any time.

SPICED BEEF (to Serve Cold).

665. INGREDIENTS.—14 lbs. of the thick flank or rump of beef, ½ lb. of coarse sugar, 1 oz. of saltpetre, ¼ lb. of pounded allspice, 1 lb. of common salt.

Mode.—Rub the sugar well into the beef, and let it lay for 12 hours; then rub the saltpetre and allspice, both of which should be pounded, over the meat, and let it remain for another 12 hours; then rub in the salt. Turn daily in the liquor for a fortnight, soak it for a few hours in water, dry with a cloth, cover with a coarse paste, put a little water at the bottom of the pan, and bake in a moderate oven for 4 hours. If it is not covered with a paste, be careful to put the beef into a deep vessel, and cover with a plate, or it will be too crisp. During the time the meat is in the oven it should be turned once or twice.

Time.—4 hours. *Average cost, 7d.* per lb.

Seasonable at any time.

BAKING MEAT.—Baking exerts some unexplained influence on meat, rendering it less savoury and less agreeable than meat which has been roasted. "Those who have travelled in Germany and France," writes Mr. Lewis, one of our most popular scientific authors, "must have repeatedly marvelled at the singular uniformity in the flavour, or want of flavour, of the various 'roasts' served up at the *table-d'hôte*." The general explanation is, that the German and French meat is greatly inferior in quality to that of England and Holland, owing to the inferiority of pasturage; and doubtless this is one cause, but it is not the chief cause. The meat is inferior, but the cooking is mainly at fault. The meat is scarcely ever *roasted*, because there is no coal, and firewood is expensive. The meat is therefore *baked;* and the consequence of this baking is, that no meat is eatable or eaten, with its own gravy, but is always accompanied by some sauce more or less piquant. The Germans generally believe that in England we eat our beef and mutton almost raw; they shudder at our gravy, as if it were so much blood.

STEWED BEEF or RUMP STEAK (an Entree).

666. INGREDIENTS.—About 2 lbs. of beef or rump steak, 3 onions, 2 turnips, 3 carrots, 2 or 3 oz. of butter, ½ pint of water, 1 teaspoonful of salt, ½ do. of pepper, 1 tablespoonful of ketchup, 1 tablespoonful of flour.

Mode.—Have the steaks cut tolerably thick and rather lean; divide them into convenient-sized pieces, and fry them in the butter a nice brown on both sides. Cleanse and pare the vegetables, cut the onions and carrots into thin slices, and the turnips into dice, and fry these in the same fat that the steaks were done in. Put all into a saucepan, add ½ pint of water, or rather more should it be necessary, and simmer very gently for 2½ or 3 hours; when nearly done, skim well, add salt, pepper, and ketchup in the above proportions, and thicken with a tablespoonful of flour mixed with 2 of cold water. Let it boil up for a minute or two after the thickening is added, and serve. When a vegetable-scoop is at hand, use it to cut the vegetables in fanciful shapes, and tomato, Harvey's sauce, or walnut-liquor may be used to flavour the gravy. It is less rich if stewed the previous day, so that the fat may be taken off when cold; when wanted for table, it will merely require warming through.

Time.—3 hours. *Average cost,* 1s. per lb.

Sufficient for 4 or 5 persons.

Seasonable at any time.

STEWED BEEF AND CELERY SAUCE (Cold Meat Cookery).

667. INGREDIENTS.—3 roots of celery, 1 pint of gravy, No. 436, 2 onions sliced, 2 lbs. of cold roast or boiled beef.

Mode.—Cut the celery into 2-inch pieces, put them in a stewpan, with the gravy and onions, simmer gently until the celery is tender, when add the beef cut into rather thick pieces; stew gently for 10 minutes, and serve with fried potatoes.

Time.—From 20 to 25 minutes to stew the celery.

Average cost, exclusive of the meat, 6*d.*

Seasonable from September to January.

STEWED BEEF WITH OYSTERS (Cold Meat Cookery).

668. INGREDIENTS.—A few thick steaks of cold ribs or sirloin of beef, 2 oz. of butter, 1 onion sliced, pepper and salt to taste, ½ glass of port wine, a little flour to thicken, 1 or 2 dozen oysters, rather more than ½ pint of water.

Mode.—Cut the steaks rather thick, from cold sirloin or ribs of beef; brown them lightly in a stewpan, with the butter and a little water; add ½ pint of water, the onion, pepper, and salt, and cover the stewpan closely, and let it simmer very gently for ½ hour; then mix about a teaspoonful of flour smoothly with a little of the liquor; add the port wine and oysters, their liquor having been previously strained and put into the stewpan; stir till the oysters plump, and serve. It should not boil after the oysters are added, or they will harden.

Time.—½ hour. *Average cost,* exclusive of the meat, 1*s.* 4*d.*

Seasonable from September to April.

STEWED BRISKET OF BEEF.

669. INGREDIENTS.—7 lbs. of a brisket of beef, vinegar and salt, 6 carrots, 6 turnips, 6 small onions, 1 blade of pounded mace, 2 whole allspice pounded, thickening of butter and flour, 2 tablespoonfuls of ketchup; stock, or water.

Mode.—About an hour before dressing it, rub the meat over with vinegar and salt; put it into a stewpan, with sufficient stock to cover it (when this is not at hand, water may be substituted for it), and be particular that the stewpan is not much larger than the meat. Skim well, and when it has simmered very gently for 1 hour, put in the vegetables, and continue simmering till the meat is perfectly tender. Draw out the bones, dish the meat, and garnish either with tufts of cauliflower or braised cabbage cut in quarters. Thicken as much gravy as required, with a little butter and flour; add spices and ketchup in the above proportion, give one boil, pour some of it over the meat, and the remainder send in a tureen.

Time.—Rather more than 3 hours. *Average cost, 7d.* per lb.

Sufficient for 7 or 8 persons.

Seasonable at any time.

Note.—The remainder of the liquor in which the beef was boiled may be served as a soup, or it may be sent to table with the meat in a tureen.

STEWED RUMP OF BEEF.

670. INGREDIENTS.—½ rump of beef, sufficient stock to cover it (No. 105), 4 tablespoonfuls of vinegar, 2 tablespoonfuls of ketchup, 1 large bunch of savoury herbs, 2 onions, 12 cloves, pepper and salt to taste, thickening of butter and flour, 1 glass of port wine.

Mode.—Cut out the bone, sprinkle the meat with a little cayenne (this must be sparingly used), and bind and tie it firmly up with tape; put it into a stewpan with sufficient stock to cover it, and add vinegar, ketchup, herbs, onions, cloves, and seasoning in the above proportion, and simmer very gently for 4 or 5 hours, or until the meat is perfectly tender, which may be ascertained by piercing it with a thin skewer. When done, remove the tape, lay it into a deep dish, which keep hot; strain and skim the gravy, thicken it with butter and flour, add a glass of port wine and any flavouring to make the gravy rich and palatable; let it boil up, pour over the meat, and serve. This dish may be very much enriched by garnishing with forcemeat balls, or filling up the space whence the bone is taken with a good forcemeat; sliced carrots, turnips, and onions boiled with the meat, are also a great improvement, and, where expense is not objected to, it may be glazed. This, however, is not necessary where a good gravy is poured round and over the meat.

Time.—½ rump stewed gently from 4 to 5 hours.

Average cost, 10d. per lb. *Sufficient* for 8 or 10 persons.

Seasonable at any time.

Note.—A stock or gravy in which to boil the meat, may be made of the bone and trimmings, by boiling them with water, and adding carrots, onions, turnips, and a bunch of sweet herbs. To make this dish richer and more savoury, half-roast the rump, and afterwards stew it in strong stock and a little Madeira. This is an expensive method, and is not, after all, much better than a plainer-dressed joint.

THE BARON OF BEEF.—This noble joint, which consisted of two sirloins not cut asunder, was a favourite dish of our ancestors. It is rarely seen nowadays; indeed, it seems out of place on a modern table, as it requires the grim boar's head and Christmas pie as supporters. Sir Walter Scott has described a feast at which the baron of beef would have appeared to great advantage. We will quote a few lines to remind us of those days when " England was merry England," and when hospitality was thought to be the highest virtue.

" The fire, with well-dried logs supplied,
  Went roaring up the chimney wide ;
  The huge hall-table's oaken face,
  Scrubb'd till it shone, the day to grace,
  Bore then, upon its massive board,
  No mark to part the squire and lord.
  Then was brought in the lusty brawn,
  By old blue-coated serving-man ;
  Then the grim boar's head frown'd on high,
  Crested with bays and rosemary.
  Well can the green-garb'd ranger tell
  How, when, and where the monster fell ;
  What dogs before his death he tore,
  And all the baiting of the boar ;
  While round the merry wassel bowl,
  Garnish'd with ribbons, blithe did trowl.
  There the huge sirloin reek'd ; hard by
  Plum-porridge stood, and Christmas pie ;
  Nor fail'd old Scotland to produce,
  At such high tide, her savoury goose."

When a lord's son came of age, in the olden time, the baron of beef was too small a joint, by many degrees, to satisfy the retainers who would flock to the hall; a whole ox was therefore generally roasted over a fire built up of huge logs. We may here mention, that an ox was roasted entire on the frozen Thames, in the early part of the present century.

STEWED SHIN OF BEEF.

671. INGREDIENTS.—A shin of beef, 1 head of celery, 1 onion, a faggot of savoury herbs, ½ teaspoonful of allspice, ½ teaspoonful of whole black pepper, 4 carrots, 12 button onions, 2 turnips, thickening of butter and flour, 3 tablespoonfuls of mushroom ketchup, 2 tablespoonfuls of port wine ; pepper and salt to taste.

Mode.—Have the bone sawn into 4 or 5 pieces, cover with hot water, bring it to a boil, and remove any scum that may rise to the surface. Put in the celery, onion, herbs, spice, and seasoning, and simmer very gently until the meat is tender. Peel the vegetables, cut them into any shape fancy may dictate, and boil them with the onions until tender ; lift out the beef, put it on a dish, which keep hot, and thicken with butter and flour as much of the liquor as will be wanted for gravy ; keep stirring till it boils, then strain and skim. Put the gravy back in the stewpan, add the seasoning, port wine, and ketchup, give one boil, and pour it over the beef ; garnish with the boiled carrots, turnips, and onions.

Time.—The meat to be stewed about 4 hours. *Average cost*, 4d. per lb. with bone.

Sufficient for 7 or 8 persons.

Seasonable at any time.

TOAD-IN-THE-HOLE (a Homely but Savoury Dish).

672. INGREDIENTS.—1½ lb. of rump-steak, 1 sheep's kidney, pepper

and salt to taste. For the batter, 3 eggs, 1 pint of milk, 4 tablespoonfuls of flour, ½ saltspoonful of salt.

Mode.—Cut up the steak and kidney into convenient-sized pieces,
and put them into a pie-dish, with a good seasoning of salt and pepper;
mix the flour with a small quantity of milk at first, to prevent its
being lumpy; add the remainder, and the 3 eggs, which should be
well beaten; put in the salt, stir the batter for about 5 minutes, and
pour it over the steak.   Place it in a tolerably brisk oven immediately,
and bake for 1½ hour.

Time.—1½ hour.   *Average cost,* 1s. 9d.

Sufficient for 4 or 5 persons.

Seasonable at any time.

Note.—The remains of cold beef, rather underdone, may be substituted for
the steak, and, when liked, the smallest possible quantity of minced onion or
shalot may be added.

BOILED TONGUE.

673. INGREDIENTS.—1 tongue, a bunch of savoury herbs, water.

Mode.—In choosing a tongue, ascertain how long it has been dried
or pickled, and select one with a smooth skin, which denotes its being
young and tender. If a dried one, and rather hard, soak it at least
for 12 hours previous to cooking it; if, however, it is fresh from the
pickle, 2 or 3 hours will be sufficient for it to remain in soak. Put
the tongue into a stewpan with plenty of cold water and a bunch
of savoury herbs; let it gradually come to a boil, skim well, and simmer very gently until tender. Peel off the skin, garnish with tufts
of cauliflowers or Brussels sprouts, and serve. Boiled tongue is
frequently sent to table with boiled poultry, instead of ham, and
is, by many persons, preferred. If to serve cold, peel it, fasten it
down to a piece of board by sticking a fork through the root, and
another through the top, to straighten it. When cold, glaze it,
and put a paper ruche round the root, and garnish with tufts of
parsley.

Time.—A large smoked tongue, 4 to 4½ hours; a small one, 2½ to
3 hours. A large unsmoked tongue, 3 to 3½ hours; a small one, 2 to
2½ hours.

Average cost, for a moderate-sized tongue, 3s. 6d.

Seasonable at any time.

TO CURE TONGUES.

I.

674. INGREDIENTS.—For a tongue of 7 lbs., 1 oz. of saltpetre, ½ oz.
of black pepper, 4 oz. of sugar, 3 oz. of juniper berries, 6 oz. of salt.

Mode.—Rub the above ingredients well into the tongue, and let it remain in the pickle for 10 days or a fortnight; then drain it, tie it up in brown paper, and have it smoked for about 20 days over a· wood fire; or it may be boiled out of this pickle.

Time.—From 10 to 14 days to remain in the pickle; to be smoked 24 days.

Average cost, for a medium-sized uncured tongue, 2s. 6d.

Seasonable at any time.

Note.—If not wanted immediately, the tongue will keep 3 or 4 weeks without being too salt; then it must not be rubbed, but only turned in the pickle.

II.

675. INGREDIENTS.—9 lbs. of salt, 8 oz. of sugar, 9 oz. of powdered saltpetre.

Mode.—Rub the above ingredients well into the tongues, and keep them in this curing mixture for 2 months, turning them every day. Drain them from the pickle, cover with brown paper, and have them smoked for about 3 weeks.

Time.—The tongues to remain in pickle 2 months; to be smoked 3 weeks.

Sufficient.—The above quantity of brine sufficient for 12 tongues, of 5 lbs. each.

Seasonable at any time.

THE TONGUES OF ANIMALS.—The tongue, whether in the ox or in man, is the seat of the sense of taste. This sense warns the animal against swallowing deleterious substances.   Dr. Carpenter says, that, among the lower animals, the instinctive perceptions connected with this sense, are much more remarkable than our own; thus, an omnivorous monkey will seldom touch fruits of a poisonous character, although their taste may be agreeable. However this may be, man's instinct has decided that ox-tongue is better than horse-tongue;

BEEF TONGUE.

nevertheless, the latter is frequently substituted by dishonest dealers for the former. The horse's tongue may be readily distinguished by a spoon-like expansion at its end.

TO PICKLE AND DRESS A TONGUE TO EAT COLD.

676. INGREDIENTS.—6 oz. of salt, 2 oz. of bay-salt, 1 oz. of saltpetre, 3 oz. of coarse sugar; cloves, mace, and allspice to taste; butter, common crust of flour and water.

Mode.—Lay the tongue for a fortnight in the above pickle, turn it every day, and be particular that the spices are well pounded; put it into a small pan just large enough to hold it, place some pieces of butter on it, and cover with a common crust. Bake in a slow oven until so tender that a straw would penetrate it; take off the skin, fasten it down to a piece of board by running a fork through the root and another through the tip, at the same time straightening it and putting it into shape. When cold, glaze it, put a paper ruche round the root, which is generally very unsightly, and garnish with tufts of parsley.

Time.—From 3 or 4 hours in a slow oven, according to size.

Average cost, for a medium-sized uncured tongue, 2s. 6d.

Seasonable at any time.

TO DRESS TRIPE.

677. INGREDIENTS.—Tripe, onion sauce, No. 484, milk and water.

Mode.—Ascertain that the tripe is quite fresh, and have it cleaned and dressed. Cut away the coarsest fat, and boil it in equal proportions of milk and water for ¾ hour. Should the tripe be entirely undressed, more than double that time should be allowed for it. Have ready some onion sauce made by recipe No. 484, dish the tripe, smother it with the sauce, and the remainder send to table in a tureen.

Time.—¾ hour; for undressed tripe, from 2½ to 3 hours.

Average cost, 7d. per lb.

Seasonable at any time.

Note.—Tripe may be dressed in a variety of ways; it may be cut in pieces and fried in batter, stewed in gravy with mushrooms, or cut into collops, sprinkled with minced onion and savoury herbs, and fried a nice brown in clarified butter.

BEEF CARVING.

AITCHBONE OF BEEF.

A boiled aitch-bone of beef is not a difficult joint to carve, as will be seen on reference to the accompanying engraving. By following with the knife the direction of the line from 1 to 2, nice slices will be easily cut. It may be necessary, as in a round of beef, to cut a thick slice off the outside before commencing to serve.

BRISKET OF BEEF.

There is but little description necessary to add, to show the carving of a boiled brisket of beef, beyond the engraving here inserted. The only point to be observed is, that the joint should be cut evenly and firmly quite across the bones, so that, on its reappearance at table, it should not have a jagged and untidy look.

RIBS OF BEEF.

This dish resembles the sirloin, except that it has no fillet or undercut. As explained in the recipes, the end piece is often cut off, salted and boiled. The mode of carving is similar to that of the sirloin, viz., in the direction of the dotted line from 1 to 2. This joint will be the more easily cut if the plan be pursued which is suggested in carving the sirloin; namely, the inserting of the knife immediately between the bone and the meat, before commencing to cut it into slices. All joints of roast beef should be cut in even and thin slices. Horseradish, finely scraped, may be served as a garnish; but horseradish sauce is preferable for eating with the beef.

SIRLOIN OF BEEF.

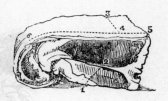

This dish is served differently at various tables, some preferring it to come to table with the fillet, or, as it is usually called, the undercut, uppermost. The reverse way, as shown in the cut, is that most usually adopted. Still the undercut is best eaten when hot; consequently, the carver himself may raise the joint, and cut some slices from the under side, in the direction of from 1 to 2, as the fillet is very much preferred by some eaters. The upper part of the sirloin should be cut in the direction of the line from 5 to 6, and care should be taken to carve it evenly and in thin slices. It will be found a great assistance, in carving this joint well, if the knife be first inserted just above the bone at the bottom, and run sharply along between the bone and meat, and also to divide the meat from the bone in the same way at the side of the joint. The slices will then come away more readily.

Some carvers cut the upper side of the sirloin across, as shown by the line from 3 to 4; but this is a wasteful plan, and one not to be recommended. With the sirloin, very finely-scraped horseradish is usually served, and a little given, when liked, to each guest. Horseradish sauce is preferable, however, for serving on the plate, although the scraped horseradish may still be used as a garnish.

A ROUND OF BEEF.

A round of beef is not so easily carved as many other joints of beef,  and to manage it properly, a thin-bladed and very sharp knife is necessary. Off the outside of the joint, at its top, a thick slice should first be cut, so as to leave the surface smooth; then thin and even slices should be cleverly carved in the direction of the line 1 to 2; and with each slice of the lean a delicate morsel of the fat should be served.

BEEF TONGUE.

Passing the knife down in the direction of from 1 to 2, a not too thin  slice should be helped; and the carving of a tongue may be continued in this way until the best portions of the upper side are served. The fat which lies about the root of the tongue can be served by turning the tongue, and cutting in the direction of from 3 to 4.

CHAPTER XIV.

GENERAL OBSERVATIONS ON THE SHEEP AND LAMB.

678. OF ALL WILD OR DOMESTICATED ANIMALS, the sheep is, without exception, the most useful to man as a food, and the most necessary to his health and comfort; for it not only supplies him with the lightest and most nutritious of meats, but, in the absence of the cow, its udder yields him milk, cream, and a sound though inferior cheese; while from its fat he obtains light, and from its fleece broadcloth, kerseymere, blankets, gloves, and hose. Its bones when burnt make an animal charcoal—ivory black—to polish his boots, and when powdered, a manure for the cultivation of his wheat; the skin, either split or whole, is made into a mat for his carriage, a housing for his horse, or a lining for his hat, and many other useful purposes besides, being extensively employed in the manufacture of parchment; and finally, when oppressed by care and sorrow, the harmonious strains that carry such soothing contentment to the heart, are elicited from the musical strings, prepared almost exclusively from the intestines of the sheep.

679. THIS VALUABLE ANIMAL, of which England is estimated to maintain an average stock of 32,000,000, belongs to the class already indicated under the ox,—the *Mammalia ;* to the order of *Rumenantia,* or cud-chewing animal; to the tribe of *Capridæ,* or horned quadrupeds ; and the genus *Ovis,* or the

" sheep." The sheep may be either with or without horns ; when present, however, they have always this peculiarity, that they spring from a triangular base, are spiral in form, and lateral, at the side of the head, in situation. The fleece of the sheep is of two sorts, either short and harsh, or soft and woolly ; the wool always preponderating in an exact ratio to the care, attention, and amount of domestication bestowed on the animal. The generic peculiarities of the sheep are the triangular and spiral form of the horns, always larger in the male when present, but absent in the most cultivated species ; having sinuses at the base of all the toes of the four feet, with two rudimentary hoofs on the fore legs, two inguinal teats to the udder, with a short tail in the wild breed, but of varying length in the domesticated ; have no incisor teeth in the upper jaw, but in their place a hard elastic cushion along the margin of the gum, on which the animal nips and breaks the herbage on which it feeds ; in the lower jaw there are eight incisor teeth and six molars on each side of both jaws, making in all 32 teeth. The fleece consists of two coats, one to keep the animal warm, the other to carry off the water without wetting the skin. The first is of wool, the weight and fineness of which depend on the quality of the pasture and the care bestowed on the flock ; the other of hair, that pierces the wool and overlaps it, and is in excess in exact proportion to the badness of the keep and inattention with which the animal is treated.

680. THE GREAT OBJECT OF THE GRAZIER is to procure an animal that will yield the greatest pecuniary return in the shortest time ; or, in other words, soonest convert grass and turnips into good mutton and fine fleece. All sheep will not do this alike ; some, like men, are so restless and irritable, that no system of feeding, however good, will develop their frames or make them fat. The system adopted by the breeder to obtain a valuable animal for the butcher, is to enlarge the capacity and functions of the digestive organs, and reduce those of the head and chest, or the mental and respiratory organs. In the first place, the mind should be tranquillized, and those spaces that can never produce animal fibre curtailed, and greater room afforded, as in the abdomen, for those that can. And as nothing militates against the fattening process so much as restlessness, the chief wish of the grazier is to find a dull, indolent sheep, one who, instead of frisking himself, leaping his wattles, or even condescending to notice the butting gambols of his silly companions, silently fills his paunch with pasture, and then seeking a shady nook, indolently and luxuriously chews his cud with closed eyes and blissful satisfaction, only rising when his delicious repast is ended, to proceed silently and without emotion to repeat the pleasing process of laying in more provender, and then returning to his dreamy siesta to renew the delightful task of rumination. Such animals are said to have a *lymphatic* temperament, and are of so kindly a nature, that on good pasturage they may be said to grow daily. The Leicestershire breed is the best example of this lymphatic and contented animal, and the active Orkney, who is half goat in his habits, of the restless and unprofitable. The rich pasture of our midland counties

would take years in making the wiry Orkney fat and profitable, while one day's fatigue in climbing rocks after a coarse and scanty herbage would probably cause the actual death of the pampered and short-winded Leicester.

681. THE MORE REMOVED FROM THE NATURE of the animal is the food on which it lives, the more difficult is the process of assimilation, and the more complex the chain of digestive organs; for it must be evident to all, that the same apparatus that converts *flesh* into *flesh,* is hardly calculated to transmute *grass* into flesh. As the process of digestion in carnivorous animals is extremely simple, these organs are found to be remarkably short, seldom exceeding the length of the animal's body; while, where digestion is more difficult, from the unassimilating nature of the aliment, as in the ruminant order, the alimentary canal, as is the case with the sheep, is *twenty-seven times the length of the body.* The digestive organ in all ruminant animals consists of *four stomachs,* or, rather, a capacious pouch, divided by doorways and valves into four compartments, called, in their order of position, the Paunch, the Reticulum, the Omasum, and the Abomasum. When the sheep nibbles the grass, and is ignorantly supposed to be eating, he is, in fact, only preparing the raw material of his meal, in reality only mowing the pasture, which, as he collects, is swallowed instantly, passing into the first receptacle, the *paunch,* where it is surrounded by a quantity of warm saliva, in which the herbage undergoes a process of maceration or softening, till the animal having filled this compartment, the contents pass through a valve into the second or smaller bag,—the *reticulum,* where, having again filled the paunch with a reserve, the sheep lies down and commences that singular process of chewing the cud, or, in other words, masticating the food he has collected. By the operation of a certain set of muscles, a small quantity of this softened food from the *reticulum,* or second bag, is passed into the mouth, which it now becomes the pleasure of the sheep to grind under his molar teeth into a soft smooth pulp, the operation being further assisted by a flow of saliva, answering the double purpose of increasing the flavour of the aliment and promoting the solvency of the mass. Having completely comminuted and blended this mouthful, it is swallowed a second time; but instead of returning to the paunch or reticulum, it passes through another valve into a side cavity,—the *omasum,* where, after a maceration in more saliva for some hours, it glides by the same contrivance into the fourth pouch,—the *abomasum,* an apartment in all respects analogous to the ordinary stomach of animals, and where the process of digestion, begun and carried on in the previous three, is here consummated, and the nutrient principle, by means of the bile, eliminated from the digestied aliment. Such is the process of digestion in sheep and oxen.

682. NO OTHER ANIMAL, even of the same order, possesses in so remarkable a degree the power of converting pasture into flesh as the Leicestershire sheep; the South Down and Cheviot, the two next breeds in quality, are, in consequence of the greater vivacity of the animal's nature, not equal to it in that respect, though in both the brain and chest are kept subservient to the

Y

greater capacity of the organs of digestion. Besides the advantage of increased bulk and finer fleeces, the breeder seeks to obtain an augmented deposit of tissue in those parts of the carcase most esteemed as food, or, what are called in the trade "prime joints;" and so far has this been effected, that the comparative weight of the hind quarters over the fore has become a test of quality in the breed, the butchers in some markets charging twopence a pound more for that portion of the sheep. Indeed, so superior are the hind quarters of mutton now regarded, that very many of the West-end butchers never deal in any other part of the sheep.

683. THE DIFFERENCE IN THE QUALITY OF THE FLESH in various breeds is a well-established fact, not alone in flavour, but also in tenderness; and that the nature of the pasture on which the sheep is fed influences the flavour of the meat, is equally certain, and shown in the estimation in which those flocks are held which have grazed on the thymy heath of Bamstead in Sussex. It is also a well-established truth, that the *larger* the frame of the animal, the *coarser* is the meat, and that *small bones* are both guarantees for the fineness of the breed and the delicacy of the flesh. The sex too has much to do in determining the quality of the meat; in the males, the lean is closer in fibre, deeper in colour, harder in texture, less juicy, and freer from fat, than in the female, and is consequently tougher and more difficult of digestion; but probably age, and the character of the pasturage on which they are reared, has, more than any other cause, an influence on the quality and tenderness of the meat.

684. THE NUMEROUS VARIETIES of sheep inhabiting the different regions of the earth have been reduced by Cuvier to three, or at most four, species: the *Ovis Ammon,* or the Argali, the presumed parent stock of all the rest; the *Ovis Tragelaphus,* the bearded sheep of Africa; the *Ovis Musmon,* the Musmon of Southern Europe; and the *Ovis montana,* the Mouflon of America; though it is believed by many naturalists that this last is so nearly identical with the Indian Argali as to be undeserving a separate place. It is still a controversy to which of these three we are indebted for the many breeds of modern domestication; the Argali, however, by general belief, has been considered as the most *probable* progenitor of the present varieties.

685. THE EFFECTS PRODUCED BY CHANGE OF CLIMATE, accident, and other causes, must have been great to accomplish so complete a physical alteration as the primitive Argali must have undergone before the Musmon, or Mouflon of Corsica, the *immediate* progenitor of all our European breeds, assumed his present appearance. The Argali is about a fifth larger in size than the ordinary English sheep, and being a native of a tropical clime, his fleece is of hair instead of wool, and of a warm reddish brown, approaching to yellow; a thick mane of darker hair, about seven inches long, commences from two long tufts at the angle of the jaws, and, running *under* the throat and neck, descends down the chest, dividing, at the fore fork, into two parts, one running

down the front of each leg, as low as the shank. The horns, unlike the character of the order generally, have a quadrangular base, and, sweeping inwards, terminate in a sharp point. The tail, about seven inches long, ends in a tuft of stiff hairs. From this remarkable muffler-looking beard, the French have given the species the name of *Mouflon à manchettes*. From the primitive stock *eleven* varieties have been reared in this country, of the domesticated sheep, each supposed by their advocates to possess some one or more special qualities. These eleven, embracing the Shetland or Orkney ; the Dun-woolled ; Black-faced, or heath-bred ; the Moorland, of Devonshire ; the Cheviot ; the Horned, of Norfolk ; the Ryeland ; South-Down ; the Merino ; the Old Leicester, and the Teeswater, or New Leicester, have of late years been epitomized ; and, or all useful and practical purposes, reduced to the following four orders :—

686. THE SOUTH DOWN, the LEICESTER, the BLACK-FACED, and the CHEVIOT.

687. SOUTH DOWNS.—It appears, as far as our investigation can trace the fact, that from the very earliest epoch of agricultural history in England, the breezy range of light chalky hills running through the south-west and

SOUTH-DOWN RAM.

south of Sussex and Hampshire, and known as the South Downs, has been famous for a superior race of sheep ; and we find the Romans early established mills and a cloth-factory at Winchester, where they may be said to terminate, which rose to such estimation, from the fineness of the wool and texture of the cloth, that the produce was kept as only worthy to clothe emperors. From this, it may be inferred that sheep have always been indigenous to this hilly tract. Though boasting so remote a reputation, it is comparatively within late years that the improvement and present state of perfection of this breed has been effected, the South-Down now ranking, for symmetry of shape, constitution, and early maturity, with any stock in the kingdom. The South-Down has no horns, is covered with a fine wool from

Y 2

two to three inches long, has a small head, and legs and face of a grey colour. It is, however, considered deficient in depth and breadth of chest.   A marked

SOUTH-DOWN EWE.

peculiarity of this breed is that its hind quarters stand higher than the fore, the quarters weighing from fifteen to eighteen pounds.

688. THE LEICESTER.—It was not till the year 1755 that Mr. Robert Bakewell directed his attention to the improvement of his stock of sheep, and

LEICESTER RAM.

ultimately effected that change in the character of his flock which has brought the breed to hold so prominent a place.   The Leicester is regarded as the largest example of the improved breeds, very productive, and yielding a good fleece.   He has a small head, covered with short white hairs, a clean muzzle, an open countenance, full eye, long thin ear, tapering neck, well-arched ribs, and straight back.   The meat is indifferent, its flavour not being so good as that of the South-Down, and there is a very large proportion of fat.   Average weight of carcase from 90 to 100 lbs.

689. BLACK-FACED, OR HEATH-BRED SHEEP.—This is the most hardy of all our native breeds, and originally came from Ettrick Forest. The face and legs are black, or sometimes mottled, the horns spiral, and on the top of the

LEICESTER EWE.

orehead it has a small round tuft of lighter-coloured wool than on the face; has the muzzle and lips of the same light hue, and what shepherds call a

HEATH RAM.

mealy mouth; the eye is full of vivacity and fire, and well open; the body long, round, and firm, and the limbs robust. The wool is thin, coarse, and light. Weight of the quarter, from 10 to 16 lbs.

690. THE CHEVIOT.—From the earliest traditions, these hills in the North, like the chalk-ridges in the South, have possessed a race of large-carcased sheep, producing a valuable fleece. To these physical advantages, they added a sound constitution, remarkable vigour, and capability to endure great priva-

tion. Both sexes are destitute of horns, face white, legs long and clean, carries the head erect, has the throat and neck well covered, the ears long and open, and the face animated. The Cheviot is a small-boned sheep, and well covered

HEATH EWE.

with wool to the hough; the only defect in this breed, is in a want of depth in the chest. Weight of the quarter, from 12 to 18 lbs.

691. THOUGH THE ROMNEY MARSHES, that wide tract of morass and low-land moor extending from the Weald (or ancient forest) of Kent into Sussex, has rather been regarded as a general feeding-ground for any kind of sheep to be pastured on, it has yet, from the earliest date, been famous for a breed

ROMNEY-MARSH RAM.

of animals almost peculiar to the locality, and especially for size, length, thickness, and quantity of wool, and what is called thickness of stocking; and on this account for ages held pre-eminence over every other breed in the kingdom. So satisfied were the Kentish men with the superiority of their sheep, that they long resisted any crossing in the breed. At length, however, this was effected, and from the Old Romney and New Leicester a stock was produced that proved, in an eminent degree, the advantage of the cross; and though the breed was actually smaller than the original, it was found that the

ROMNEY-MARSH EWE.

new stock did not consume so much food, the stocking was increased, they were ready for the market a *year* sooner; that the fat formed more on the exterior of the carcase, where it was of most advantage to the grazier, rather than as formerly in the interior, where it went to the butcher as offal; and though the wool was shorter and lighter, it was of a better colour, finer, and possessed of superior felting properties.

692. THE ROMNEY MARSH BREED is a large animal, deep, close, and compact, with white face and legs, and yields a heavy fleece of a good staple quality. The general structure is, however, considered defective, the chest being narrow and the extremities coarse; nevertheless its tendency to fatten, and its early maturity, are universally admitted. The Romney Marsh, therefore, though not ranking as a first class in respect of perfection and symmetry of breed, is a highly useful, profitable, and generally advantageous variety of the English domestic sheep.

693. DIFFERENT NAMES HAVE BEEN GIVEN to sheep by their breeders, according to their age and sex. The male is called a ram, or tup; after weaning, he is said to be a hog, or hogget, or a lamb-hog, tup-hog, or teg; later he is a wether, or wether-hog; after the first shearing, a shearing, or dinmont; and after each succeeding shearing, a two, three, or four-shear ram, tup, or wether, according to circumstances. The female is called a ewe, or gimmer-lamb, till weaned, when she becomes, according to the shepherd's nomenclature, a gimmer-ewe, hog, or teg; after shearing, a gimmer or shearing-ewe, or theave; and in future a two, three, or four-shear ewe, or theave.

694. THE MODE OF SLAUGHTERING SHEEP is perhaps as humane and expeditious a process as could be adopted to attain the objects sought : the animal being laid on its side in a sort of concave stool, the butcher, while pressing the body with his knee, transfixes the throat near the angle of the jaw, passing his knife between the windpipe and bones of the neck ; thus dividing the jugulars, carotids, and large vessels, the death being very rapid from such a hemorrhage.

695. ALMOST EVERY LARGE CITY has a particular manner of cutting up, or, as it is called, dressing the carcase. In London this process is very simple, and as our butchers have found that much skewering back, doubling one part over another, or scoring the inner cuticle or fell, tends to spoil the meat and shorten the time it would otherwise keep, they avoid all such treatment entirely. The carcase when flayed (which operation is performed while yet warm), the sheep when hung up and the head removed, presents the profile shown in our cut ; the small numerals indicating the parts or joints into which one half of the animal is cut. After separating the hind from the fore quarters, with eleven ribs to the latter, the quarters are usually subdivided in the manner shown in the sketch, in which the several joins are defined by the intervening lines and figures. *Hind quarter :* No. 1, the leg ; 2, the loin—the two, when cut in one piece, being called the saddle. *Fore quarter :* No. 3, the shoulder ; 4 and 5 the neck ; No. 5 being called, for distinction, the scrag, which is generally afterwards separated from 4, the lower and better joint ; No. 6, the breast. The haunch of mutton, so often served at public dinners and special entertainments, comprises all the leg and so much of the loin, short of the ribs or lap, as is indicated on the upper part of the carcase by a dotted line.

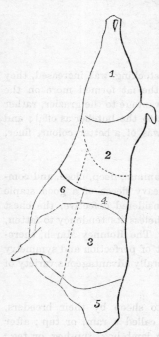

SIDE OF MUTTON, SHOWING THE SEVERAL JOINTS.

696. THE GENTLE AND TIMID DISPOSITION of the sheep, and its defenceless condition, must very early have attached it to man for motives less selfish than either its fleece or its flesh ; for it has been proved beyond a doubt that, obtuse as we generally regard it, it is susceptible of a high degree of domesticity, obedience, and affection. In many parts of Europe, where the flocks are guided by the shepherd's voice alone, it is no unusual thing for a sheep to quit the herd when called by its name, and follow the keeper like a dog. In the mountains of Scotland, when a flock is invaded by a savage dog, the rams have been known to form the herd into a circle, and placing themselves on the

outside line, keep the enemy at bay, or charging on him in a troop, have despatched him with their horns.

697. THE VALUE OF THE SHEEP seems to have been early understood by Adam in his fallen state ; his skin not only affording him protection for his body, but a covering for his tent ; and accordingly, we find Abel intrusted with this portion of his father's stock ; for the Bible tells us that "Abel was a keeper of sheep." What other animals were domesticated at that time we can only conjecture, or at what exact period the flesh of the sheep was first eaten for food by man, is equally, if not uncertain, open to controversy. For though some authorities maintain the contrary, it is but natural to suppose that when Abel brought firstlings of his flock, "and the fat thereof," as a sacrifice, the less dainty portions, not being oblations, were hardly likely to have been flung away as refuse. Indeed, without supposing Adam and his descendants to have eaten animal food, we cannot reconcile the fact of Jubal Cain, Cain's son, and his family, living in tents, as they are reported to have done, knowing that both their own garments and the coverings of the tents, were made from the hides and skins of the animals they bred ; for the number of sheep and oxen slain for oblations only, would not have supplied sufficient material for two such necessary purposes. The opposite opinion is, that animal food was not eaten till after the Flood, when the Lord renewed his covenant with Noah. From Scriptural authority we learn many interesting facts as regards the sheep : the first, that mutton fat was considered the most delicious portion of any meat, and the tail and adjacent part the most exquisite morsel in the whole body ; consequently, such were regarded as especially fit for the offer of sacrifice. From this fact we may reasonably infer that the animal still so often met with in Palestine and Syria, and known as the Fat-tailed sheep, was in use in the days of the patriarchs, though probably not then of the size and weight it now attains to ; a supposition that gains greater strength, when it is remembered that the ram Abraham found in the bush, when he went to offer up Isaac, was a horned animal, being entangled in the brake by his curved horns ; so far proving that it belonged to the tribe of the Capridæ, the fat-tailed sheep appertaining to the same family.

LAMBS.

698. THOUGH THE LAMBING SEASON IN THIS COUNTRY usually commences in March, under the artificial system, so much pursued now to please the appetite of luxury, lambs can be procured at all seasons. When, however, the sheep lambs in mid-winter, or the inclemency of the weather would endanger the lives of mother and young, if exposed to its influence, it is customary to rear the lambs within-doors, and under the shelter of stables or barns, where, foddered on soft hay, and part fed on cow's milk, the little creatures thrive rapidly : to such it is customary to give the name of House Lamb, to distinguish it from that reared in the open air, or grass-fed. The ewe goes five

months with her young, about 152 days, or close on 22 weeks. The weaning season commences on poor lands, about the end of the third month, but on rich pasture not till the close of the fourth—sometimes longer.

699. FROM THE LARGE PROPORTION OF MOISTURE OR FLUIDS contained in the tissues of all young animals, the flesh of lamb and veal is much more prone, in close, damp weather, to become tainted and spoil than the flesh of the more mature, drier, and closer-textured beef and mutton. Among epicures, the most delicious sorts of lamb are those of the South-Down breed, known by their black feet; and of these, those which have been exclusively suckled on the milk of the parent ewe, are considered the finest. Next to these in estimation are those fed on the milk of several dams, and last of all, though the fattest, the grass-fed lamb; this, however, implies an age much greater than either of the others.

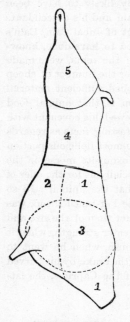

SIDE OF LAMB.

700. LAMB, in the early part of the season, however reared, is in London, and indeed generally, sold in quarters, divided with eleven ribs to the fore-quarter; but, as the season advances, these are sub-divided into two, and the hind-quarter in the same manner; the first consisting of the shoulder, and the neck and breast; the latter, of the leg and the loin,—as shown in the cut illustrative of mutton. As lamb, from the juicy nature of its flesh, is especially liable to spoil in unfavourable weather, it should be frequently wiped, so as to remove any moisture that may form on it.

701. IN THE PURCHASING OF LAMB FOR THE TABLE, there are certain signs by which the experienced judgment is able to form an accurate opinion whether the animal has been lately slaughtered, and whether the joints possess that condition of fibre indicative of good and wholesome meat. The first of these doubts may be solved satisfactorily by the bright and dilated appearance of the eye; the quality of the fore-quarter can always be guaranteed by the blue or healthy ruddiness of the jugular, or vein of the neck; while the rigidity of the knuckle, and the firm, compact feel of the kidney, will answer in an equally positive manner for the integrity of the hind-quarter.

702. MODE OF CUTTING UP A SIDE OF LAMB IN LONDON.—1, 1. Ribs; 2. Breast; 3. Shoulder; 4. Loin; 5. Leg; 1, 2, 3. Fore Quarter.

RECITES.

RECIPES.

CHAPTER XV.

BAKED MINCED MUTTON (Cold Meat Cookery).

703. INGREDIENTS.—The remains of any joint of cold roast mutton, 1 or 2 onions, 1 bunch of savoury herbs, pepper and salt to taste, 2 blades of pounded mace or nutmeg, 2 tablespoonfuls of gravy, mashed potatoes.

Mode.—Mince an onion rather fine, and fry it a light-brown colour; add the herbs and mutton, both of which should be also finely minced and well mixed; season with pepper and salt, and a little pounded mace or nutmeg, and moisten with the above proportion of gravy. Put a layer of mashed potatoes at the bottom of a dish, then the mutton, and then another layer of potatoes, and bake for about ½ hour.

Time.—½ hour. *Average cost*, exclusive of the meat, 4*d.*

Seasonable at any time.

Note.—If there should be a large quantity of meat, use 2 onions instead of 1.

BOILED BREAST OF MUTTON AND CAPER SAUCE.

704. INGREDIENTS.—Breast of mutton, bread crumbs, 2 tablespoonfuls of minced savoury herbs (put a large proportion of parsley), pepper and salt to taste.

Mode.—Cut off the superfluous fat; bone it; sprinkle over a layer of bread crumbs, minced herbs, and seasoning; roll, and bind it up firmly. Boil *gently* for 2 hours, remove the tape, and serve with caper sauce, No. 382, a little of which should be poured over the meat.

Time.—2 hours. *Average cost*, 6*d.* per lb.

Sufficient for 4 or 5 persons.

Seasonable all the year.

BOILED LEG OF MUTTON.

705. INGREDIENTS.—Mutton, water, salt.

Mode.—A leg of mutton for boiling should not hang too long, as it will not look a good colour when dressed. Cut off the shank-bone, trim the knuckle, and wash and wipe it very clean ; plunge it into sufficient boiling water to cover it; let it boil up, then draw the saucepan to the side of the fire, where it should remain till the finger can be borne in the water. Then place it sufficiently near the fire, that the water may gently simmer, and be very careful that it does not boil fast, or the meat will be hard. Skim well, add a little salt, and in about 2¼ hours after the water begins to simmer, a moderate-sized leg of mutton will be done. Serve with carrots and mashed turnips, which may be boiled with the meat, and send caper sauce (No. 382) to table with it in a tureen.

Time.—A moderate-sized leg of mutton of 9 lbs., 2¼ hours after the water boils ; one of 12 lbs., 3 hours.

Average cost, 8½d. per lb.

Sufficient.—A moderate-sized leg of mutton for 6 or 8 persons.

Seasonable nearly all the year, but not so good in June, July, and August.

Note.—When meat is liked very *thoroughly* cooked, allow more time than stated above. The liquor this joint was boiled in should be converted into soup.

THE GOOD SHEPHERD.—The sheep's complete dependence upon the shepherd for protection from its numerous enemies is frequently referred to in the Bible ; thus the Psalmist likens himself to a lost sheep, and prays the Almighty to seek his servant ; and our Saviour, when despatching his twelve chosen disciples to preach the Gospel amongst their unbelieving brethren, compares them to lambs going amongst wolves. The shepherd of the East, by kind treatment, calls forth from his sheep unmistakable signs of affection. The sheep obey his voice and recognize the names by which he calls them, and they follow him in and out of the fold. The beautiful figure of the " good shepherd," which so often occurs in the New Testament, expresses the tenderness of the Saviour for mankind. " The good shepherd giveth his life for the sheep."—*John*, x. 11. " I am the good shepherd, and know my sheep, and am known by mine."—*John*, x. 14. " And other sheep I have which are not of this fold : them also I must bring, and they shall hear my voice : and there shall be one fold and one shepherd."—*John*, x. 16.

BONED LEG OF MUTTON STUFFED.

706. INGREDIENTS.—A small leg of mutton, weighing 6 or 7 lbs., forcemeat, No. 417, 2 shalots finely minced.

Mode.—Make a forcemeat by recipe No. 417, to which add 2 finely-minced shalots. Bone the leg of mutton, without spoiling the skin, and cut off a great deal of the fat. Fill the hole up whence the bone was taken, with the forcemeat, and sew it up underneath, to prevent its falling out. Bind and tie it up compactly, and roast it before a nice clear fire for about 2½ hours or rather longer ; remove the tape and send it to table with a good gravy. It may be glazed or not, as preferred.

Time.—2½ hours, or rather longer. *Average cost,* 4s. 8d.

Sufficient for 6 or 7 persons.

Seasonable at any time.

BRAISED FILLET OF MUTTON, with French Beans.

707. INGREDIENTS.—The chump end of a loin of mutton, buttered paper, French beans, a little glaze, 1 pint of gravy.

Mode.—Roll up the mutton in a piece of buttered paper, roast it for 2 hours, and do not allow it to acquire the least colour. Have ready some French beans, boiled, and drained on a sieve; remove the paper from the mutton, glaze it; just heat up the beans in the gravy, and lay them on the dish with the meat over them. The remainder of the gravy may be strained, and sent to table in a tureen.

Time.—2 hours. *Average cost,* 8½d. per lb.

Sufficient for 4 or 5 persons.

Seasonable at any time.

VARIOUS QUALITIES OF MUTTON.—Mutton is, undoubtedly, the meat most generally used in families; and, both by connoisseurs and medical men, it stands first in favour, whether its fine flavour, digestible qualifications, or general wholesomeness, be considered. Of all mutton, that furnished by the South-Down sheep is the most highly esteemed; it is also the dearest, on account of its scarcity, and the great demand for it. Therefore, if the housekeeper is told by the butcher that he has not any in his shop, it should not occasion disappointment to the purchaser. The London and other markets are chiefly supplied with sheep called half-breeds, which are a cross between the Down and Lincoln or Leicester. These half-breeds make a greater weight of mutton than the true South-Downs, and, for this very desirable qualification, they are preferred by the great sheep-masters. The legs of this mutton range from 7 to 11 lbs. in weight; the shoulders, necks, or loins, about 6 to 9 lbs.; and if care is taken not to purchase it too fat, it will be found the most satisfactory and economical mutton that can be bought.

BRAISED LEG OF MUTTON.

708. INGREDIENTS.—1 small leg of mutton, 4 carrots, 3 onions, 1 faggot of savoury herbs, a bunch of parsley, seasoning to taste of pepper and salt, a few slices of bacon, a few veal trimmings, ½ pint of gravy or water.

Mode.—Line the bottom of a braising-pan with a few slices of bacon, put in the carrots, onions, herbs, parsley, and seasoning, and over these place the mutton. Cover the whole with a few more slices of bacon and the veal trimmings, pour in the gravy or water, and stew very *gently* for 4 hours. Strain the gravy, reduce it to a glaze over a sharp fire, glaze the mutton with it, and send it to table, placed on a dish of white haricot beans boiled tender, or garnished with glazed onions.

Time.—4 hours. *Average cost,* 5s.

Sufficient for 6 or 7 persons.

Seasonable at any time.

THE ORDER OF THE GOLDEN FLEECE.—This order of knighthood was founded by Philip the Good, duke of Burgundy, in 1429, on the day of his marriage with the Princess Isabella of Portugal. The number of the members was originally fixed at thirty-one, including the sovereign, as the head and chief of the institution. In 1516, Pope Leo X. consented to increase the number to fifty-two, including the head. In 1700 the German emperor Charles VI. and King Philip of Spain both laid claim to the order. The former, however, on leaving Spain, which he could not maintain by force of arms, took with him, to Vienna, the archives of the order, the inauguration of which he solemnized there in 1713, with great magnificence ; but Philip V. of Spain declared himself Grand Master, and formally protested, at the congress of Cambrai (1721), against the pretensions of the emperor. The dispute, though subsequently settled by the intercession of France, England, and Holland, was frequently renewed, until the order was tacitly introduced into both countries, and it now passes by the respective names of the Spanish or Austrian " Order of the Golden Fleece," according to the country where it is issued.

AN EXCELLENT WAY TO COOK A BREAST OF MUTTON.

709. INGREDIENTS.—Breast of mutton, 2 onions, salt and pepper to taste, flour, a bunch of savoury herbs, green peas.

Mode.—Cut the mutton into pieces about 2 inches square, and let it be tolerably lean ; put it into a stewpan, with a little fat or butter, and fry it of a nice brown ; then dredge in a little flour, slice the onions, and put it with the herbs in the stewpan ; pour in sufficient water *just* to cover the meat, and simmer the whole gently until the mutton is tender. Take out the meat, strain, and skim off all the fat from the gravy, and put both the meat and gravy back into the stewpan ; add about a quart of young green peas, and let them boil gently until done. 2 or 3 slices of bacon added and stewed with the mutton give additional flavour ; and, to insure the peas being a beautiful green colour, they may be boiled in water separately, and added to the stew at the moment of serving.

Time.—2½ hours. *Average cost,* 6*d.* per lb.

Sufficient for 4 or 5 persons.

Seasonable from June to August.

NAMES OF ANIMALS SAXON, AND OF THEIR FLESH NORMAN.—The names of all our domestic animals are of Saxon origin ; but it is curious to observe that Norman names have been given to the different sorts of flesh which these animals yield. How beautifully this illustrates the relative position of Saxon and Norman after the Conquest. The Saxon hind had the charge of tending and feeding the domestic animals, but only that they might appear on the table of his Norman lord. Thus 'ox,' 'steer,' 'cow,' are Saxon, but 'beef' is Norman ; 'calf' is Saxon, but 'veal' Norman ; 'sheep' is Saxon, but 'mutton' Norman ; so it is severally with 'deer' and 'venison,' 'swine' and 'pork,' 'fowl' and 'pullet.' 'Bacon,' the only flesh which, perhaps, ever came within his reach, is the single exception.

BROILED MUTTON AND TOMATO SAUCE
(Cold Meat Cookery).

710. INGREDIENTS.—A few slices of cold mutton, tomato sauce, No. 529.

Mode.—Cut some nice slices from a cold leg or shoulder of mutton ; season them with pepper and salt, and broil over a clear fire. Make some tomato sauce by recipe No. 529, pour it over the mutton, and serve. This makes an excellent dish, and must be served very hot.

Time.—About 5 minutes to broil the mutton.

Seasonable in September and October, when tomatoes are plentiful and seasonable.

SHEPHERDS AND THEIR FLOCKS.—The shepherd's crook is older than either the husbandman's plough or the warrior's sword. We are told that Abel was a keeper of sheep. Many passages in holy writ enable us to appreciate the pastoral riches of the first eastern nations ; and we can form an idea of the number of their flocks, when we read that Jacob gave the children of Hamor a hundred sheep for the price of a field, and that the king of Israel received a hundred thousand every year from the king of Moab, his tributary, and a like number of rams covered with their fleece. The tendency which most sheep have to ramble, renders it necessary for them to be attended by a shepherd. To keep a flock within bounds is no easy task ; but the watchful shepherd manages to accomplish it without harassing the sheep. In the Highlands of Scotland, where the herbage is scanty, the sheep-farm requires to be very large, and to be watched over by many shepherds. The farms of some of the great Scottish landowners are of enormous extent. "How many sheep have you on your estate ?" asked Prince Esterhazy of the duke of Argyll. "I have not the most remote idea," replied the duke ; "but I know the shepherds number several thousands."

BROILED MUTTON CHOPS.

711. INGREDIENTS.—Loin of mutton, pepper and salt, a small piece of butter.

Mode.—Cut the chops from a well-hung tender loin of mutton, remove a portion of the fat, and trim them into a nice shape; slightly beat and level them ; place the gridiron over a bright clear fire, rub the bars with a little fat, and lay on the chops. Whilst broiling, frequently turn them, and in about 8 minutes they will be done. Season with pepper and salt, dish them on a very hot dish, rub a small piece of butter on each chop, and serve very hot and expeditiously.

Time.—About 8 minutes. *Average cost*, 10*d.* per lb.

Sufficient.—Allow 1 chop to each person.

Seasonable at any time.

CHINA CHILO.

712. INGREDIENTS.—1½ lb. of leg, loin, or neck of mutton, 2 onions, 2 lettuces, 1 pint of green peas, 1 teaspoonful of salt, 1 teaspoonful of pepper, ¼ pint of water, ¼ lb. of clarified butter ; when liked, a little cayenne.

Mode.—Mince the above quantity of undressed leg, loin, or neck of mutton, adding a little of the fat, also minced ; put it into a stewpan with the remaining ingredients, previously shredding the lettuce and onion rather fine ; closely cover the stewpan, after the ingredients have been well stirred, and simmer gently for rather more than 2 hours. Serve in a dish, with a border of rice round, the same as for curry.

Time.—Rather more than 2 hours. *Average cost*, 1*s.* 6*d.*

Sufficient for 3 or 4 persons.

Seasonable from June to August.

CURRIED MUTTON (Cold Meat Cookery).

713. INGREDIENTS.—The remains of any joint of cold mutton, 2 onions, ¼ lb. of butter, 1 dessertspoonful of curry powder, 1 dessert-spoonful of flour, salt to taste, ¼ pint of stock or water.

Mode.—Slice the onions in thin rings, and put them into a stewpan with the butter, and fry of a light brown; stir in the curry powder, flour, and salt, and mix all well together. Cut the meat into nice thin slices (if there is not sufficient to do this, it may be minced), and add it to the other ingredients; when well browned, add the stock or gravy, and stew gently for about ½ hour. Serve in a dish with a border of boiled rice, the same as for other curries.

Time.—½ hour. *Average cost*, exclusive of the meat, 6d.

Seasonable in winter.

CUTLETS OF COLD MUTTON (Cold Meat Cookery).

714. INGREDIENTS.—The remains of cold loin or neck of mutton, 1 egg, bread crumbs, brown gravy (No. 436), or tomato sauce (No. 529).

Mode.—Cut the remains of cold loin or neck of mutton into cutlets, trim them, and take away a portion of the fat, should there be too much; dip them in beaten egg, and sprinkle with bread crumbs, and fry them a nice brown in hot dripping. Arrange them on a dish, and pour round them either a good gravy or hot tomato sauce.

Time.—About 7 minutes.

Seasonable.—Tomatoes to be had most reasonably in September and October.

DORMERS.

715. INGREDIENTS.—½ lb. of cold mutton, 2 oz. of beef suet, pepper and salt to taste, 3 oz. of boiled rice, 1 egg, bread crumbs, made gravy.

Mode.—Chop the meat, suet, and rice finely; mix well together, and add a high seasoning of pepper and salt, and roll into sausages; cover them with egg and bread crumbs, and fry in hot dripping of a nice brown. Serve in a dish with made gravy poured round them, and a little in a tureen.

Time.—¼ hour to fry the sausages.

Average cost, exclusive of the meat, 6d.

Seasonable at any time.

THE GOLDEN FLEECE.—The ancient fable of the Golden Fleece may be thus briefly told:—Phryxus, a son of Athamus, king of Thebes, to escape the persecutions of his stepmother Ino, paid a visit to his friend Æetes, king of Colchis. A ram, whose fleece was of pure gold, carried the youth through the air in a most obliging manner to the court of his friend. When safe at Colchis, Phryxus offered the ram on the altars of Mars, and pocketed the fleece. The king received him with great kindness, and gave him his daughter Chalciope in marriage; but, some time after, he murdered him in order to obtain possession of the precious fleece. The murder of Phryxus was amply revenged by the Greeks. It gave rise to the famous Argonautic expedition, undertaken by Jason and fifty of the most celebrated heroes of Greece. The Argonauts recovered the fleece by the help of the celebrated sorceress Medea, daughter of Æetes, who fell desperately in love with the gallant but faithless Jason. In the story of the voyage of the Argo, a substratum of truth probably exists, though overlaid by a mass of fiction. The ram which carried Phryxus to Colchis is by some supposed to have been the name of the ship in which he embarked. The fleece of gold is thought to represent the immense treasures he bore away from Thebes. The alchemists of the fifteenth century were firmly convinced that the Golden Fleece was a treatise on the transmutation of metals, written on sheepskin.

HARICOT MUTTON.

I.

716. INGREDIENTS.—4 lbs. of the middle or best end of the neck of mutton, 3 carrots, 3 turnips, 3 onions, pepper and salt to taste, 1 tablespoonful of ketchup or Harvey's sauce.

Mode.—Trim off some of the fat, cut the mutton into rather thin chops, and put them into a frying-pan with the fat trimmings. Fry of a pale brown, but do not cook them enough for eating. Cut the carrots and turnips into dice, and the onions into slices, and slightly fry them in the same fat that the mutton was browned in, but do not allow them to take any colour. Now lay the mutton at the bottom of a stewpan, then the vegetables, and pour over them just sufficient boiling water to cover the whole. Give one boil, skim well, and then set the pan on the side of the fire to simmer gently until the meat is tender. Skim off every particle of fat, add a seasoning of pepper and salt, and a little ketchup, and serve. This dish is very much better if made the day before it is wanted for table, as the fat can be so much more easily removed when the gravy is cold. This should be particularly attended to, as it is apt to be rather rich and greasy if eaten the same day it is made. It should be served in rather a deep dish.

Time.—2½ hours to simmer gently. *Average cost,* for this quantity, 3s. *Sufficient* for 6 or 7 persons. *Seasonable* at any time.

II.

717. INGREDIENTS.—Breast or scrag of mutton, flour, pepper and salt to taste, 1 large onion, 3 cloves, a bunch of savoury herbs, 1 blade of mace, carrots and turnips, sugar.

Mode.—Cut the mutton into square pieces, and fry them a nice colour; then dredge over them a little flour and a seasoning of pepper and salt. Put all into a stewpan, and moisten with boiling water, adding the onion, stuck with 3 cloves, the mace, and herbs. Simmer

z

gently till the meat is nearly done, skim off all the fat, and then add the carrots and turnips, which should previously be cut in dice and fried in a little sugar to colour them.   Let the whole simmer again for 10 minutes; take out the onion and bunch of herbs, and serve.

Time.—About 3 hours to simmer.   *Average cost*, 6*d.* per lb.

Sufficient for 4 or 5 persons.

Seasonable at any time.

HARICOT MUTTON (Cold Meat Cookery).

718. INGREDIENTS.—The remains of cold neck or loin of mutton, 2 oz. of butter, 3 onions, 1 dessertspoonful of flour, ½ pint of good gravy, pepper and salt to taste, 2 tablespoonfuls of port wine, 1 tablespoonful of mushroom ketchup, 2 carrots, 2 turnips, 1 head of celery.

Mode.—Cut the cold mutton into moderate-sized chops, and take off the fat; slice the onions, and fry them with the chops, in a little butter, of a nice brown colour; stir in the flour, add the gravy, and let it stew gently nearly an hour. In the mean time boil the vegetables until *nearly* tender, slice them, and add them to the mutton about ¼ hour before it is to be served. Season with pepper and salt, add the ketchup and port wine, give one boil, and serve.

Time.—1 hour.   *Average cost*, exclusive of the cold meat, 9*d.*

Seasonable at any time.

HASHED MUTTON.

719. INGREDIENTS.—The remains of cold roast shoulder or leg of mutton, 6 whole peppers, 6 whole allspice, a faggot of savoury herbs, ½ head of celery, 1 onion, 2 oz. of butter, flour.

Mode.—Cut the meat in nice even slices from the bones, trimming off all superfluous fat and gristle; chop the bones and fragments of the joint, put them into a stewpan with the pepper, spice, herbs, and celery; cover with water, and simmer for 1 hour. Slice and fry the onion of a nice pale-brown colour, dredge in a little flour to make it thick, and add this to the bones, &c. Stew for ¼ hour, strain the gravy, and let it cool; then skim off every particle of fat, and put it, with the meat, into a stewpan. Flavour with ketchup, Harvey's sauce, tomato sauce, or any flavouring that may be preferred, and let the meat gradually warm through, but not boil, or it will harden. To hash meat properly, it should be laid in cold gravy, and only left on the fire just long enough to warm through.

Time.—1½ hour to simmer the gravy.

Average cost, exclusive of the meat, 4*d.*

Seasonable at any time.

HASHED MUTTON.—Many persons express a decided aversion to hashed mutton; and, doubtless, this dislike has arisen from the fact that they have unfortunately never been properly served with this dish. If properly done, however, the meat tender (it ought to be as tender as when first roasted), the gravy abundant and well flavoured, and the sippets nicely toasted, and the whole served neatly; then, hashed mutton is by no means to be despised, and is infinitely more wholesome and appetizing than the cold leg or shoulder, of which fathers and husbands, and their bachelor friends, stand in such natural awe.

HODGE-PODGE (Cold Meat Cookery).

720. INGREDIENTS.—About 1 lb. of underdone cold mutton, 2 lettuces, 1 pint of green peas, 5 or 6 green onions, 2 oz. of butter, pepper and salt to taste, ½ teacupful of water.

Mode.—Mince the mutton, and cut up the lettuces and onions in slices. Put these in a stewpan, with all the ingredients except the peas, and let these simmer very gently for ¾ hour, keeping them well stirred. Boil the peas separately, mix these with the mutton, and serve very hot.

Time.—¾ hour.

Sufficient for 3 or 4 persons.

Seasonable from the end of May to August.

IRISH STEW.

I.

721. INGREDIENTS.—3 lbs. of the loin or neck of mutton, 5 lbs. of potatoes, 5 large onions, pepper and salt to taste, rather more than 1 pint of water.

Mode.—Trim off some of the fat of the above quantity of loin or neck of mutton, and cut it into chops of a moderate thickness. Pare and halve the potatoes, and cut the onions into thick slices. Put a layer of potatoes at the bottom of a stewpan, then a layer of mutton and onions, and season with pepper and salt; proceed in this manner until the stewpan is full, taking care to have plenty of vegetables at the top. Pour in the water, and let it stew very gently for 2½ hours, keeping the lid of the stewpan closely shut the *whole* time, and occasionally shaking it to prevent its burning.

Time.—2½ hours. *Average cost*, for this quantity, 2s. 8d.

Sufficient for 5 or 6 persons.

Seasonable.—More suitable for a winter dish.

II.

722. INGREDIENTS.—2 or 3 lbs. of the breast of mutton, 1½ pint of water, salt and pepper to taste, 4 lbs. of potatoes, 4 large onions.

Mode.—Put the mutton into a stewpan with the water and a little salt, and let it stew gently for an hour; cut the meat into small

z 2

pieces, skim the fat from the gravy, and pare and slice the potatoes and onions. Put all the ingredients into the stewpan in layers, first a layer of vegetables, then one of meat, and sprinkle seasoning of pepper and salt between each layer; cover closely, and let the whole stew very gently for 1 hour or rather more, shaking it frequently to prevent its burning.

Time.—Rather more than 2 hours. *Average cost,* 1s. 6d.

Sufficient for 5 or 6 persons.

Seasonable.—Suitable for a winter dish.

Note.—Irish stew may be prepared in the same manner as above, but baked in a jar instead of boiled. About 2 hours or rather more in a moderate oven will be sufficient time to bake it.

ITALIAN MUTTON CUTLETS.

723. INGREDIENTS.—About 3 lbs. of the neck of mutton, clarified butter, the yolk of 1 egg, 4 tablespoonfuls of bread crumbs, 1 table-spoonful of minced savoury herbs, 1 tablespoonful of minced parsley, 1 teaspoonful of minced shalot, 1 saltspoonful of finely-chopped lemon-peel; pepper, salt, and pounded mace to taste; flour, ½ pint of hot broth or water, 2 teaspoonfuls of Harvey's sauce, 1 teaspoonful of soy, 2 teaspoonfuls of tarragon vinegar, 1 tablespoonful of port wine.

Mode.—Cut the mutton into nicely-shaped cutlets, flatten them, and trim off some of the fat, dip them in clarified butter, and then into the beaten yolk of an egg. Mix well together bread crumbs, herbs, parsley, shalot, lemon-peel, and seasoning in the above propor-tion, and cover the cutlets with these ingredients. Melt some butter in a frying-pan, lay in the cutlets, and fry them a nice brown; take them out, and keep them hot before the fire. Dredge some flour into the pan, and if there is not sufficient butter, add a little more; stir till it looks brown, then pour in the hot broth or water, and the remaining ingredients; give one boil, and pour round the cutlets. If the gravy should not be thick enough, add a little more flour. Mushrooms, when obtainable, are a great improvement to this dish, and when not in season, mushroom-powder may be substituted for them.

Time.—10 minutes;—rather longer, should the cutlets be very thick.

Average cost, 2s. 9d.

Sufficient for 5 or 6 persons.

Seasonable at any time.

THE DOWNS.—The well-known substance chalk, which the chemist regards as a nearly pure carbonate of lime, and the microscopist as an aggregation of inconceivably minute shells and corals, forms the sub-soil of the hilly districts of the south-east of England. The chalk-hills known as the South Downs start from the bold promontory of Beachy Head, traverse the county of Sussex from east to west, and pass through Hampshire into Surrey. The North Downs extend from Godalming, by Godstone, into Kent, and terminate in the line of cliffs which stretches from Dover to Ramsgate. The Downs are clothed with short verdant turf; but the layer of soil which rests upon the chalk is too thin to support trees and shrubs. The hills have rounded summits, and their smooth, undulated outlines are unbroken save by the sepulchral monuments of the early inhabitants of the country. The coombes and furrows, which ramify and extend into deep valleys, appear like dried-up channels of streams and rivulets. From time immemorial, immense flocks of sheep have been reared on these downs. The herbage of these hills is remarkably nutritious; and whilst the natural healthiness of the climate, consequent on the dryness of the air and the moderate elevation of the land, is eminently favourable to rearing a superior race of sheep, the arable land in the immediate neighbourhood of the Downs affords the means of a supply of other food, when the natural produce of the hills fails. The mutton of the South-Down breed of sheep is highly valued for its delicate flavour, and the wool for its fineness; but the best specimens of this breed, when imported from England into the West Indies, become miserably lean in the course of a year or two, and their woolly fleece gives place to a covering of short, crisp, brownish hair.

BROILED KIDNEYS (a Breakfast or Supper Dish).

724. INGREDIENTS.—Sheep kidneys, pepper and salt to taste.

Mode.—Ascertain that the kidneys are fresh, and cut them open very evenly, lengthwise, down to the root, for should one half be thicker than the other, one would be underdone whilst the other would be dried, but do not separate them; skin them, and pass a skewer under the white part of each half to keep them flat, and broil over a nice clear fire, placing the inside downwards; turn them when

KIDNEYS.

done enough on one side, and cook them on the other. Remove the skewers, place the kidneys on a very hot dish, season with pepper and salt, and put a tiny piece of butter in the middle of each; serve very hot and quickly, and send very hot plates to table.

Time.—6 to 8 minutes. *Average cost*, 1½*d*. each.

Sufficient.—Allow 1 for each person.

Seasonable at any time.

Note.—A prettier dish than the above may be made by serving the kidneys each on a piece of buttered toast cut in any fanciful shape. In this case a little lemon-juice will be found an improvement.

FRIED KIDNEYS.

725. INGREDIENTS.—Kidneys, butter, pepper and salt to taste.

Mode.—Cut the kidneys open without quite dividing them, remove the skin, and put a small piece of butter in the frying-pan. When the butter is melted, lay in the kidneys the flat side downwards, and fry them for 7 or 8 minutes, turning them when they are half-done. Serve on a piece of dry toast, season with pepper and salt, and put a small piece of butter in each kidney; pour the gravy from the pan over them, and serve very hot.

Time.—7 or 8 minutes. *Average cost*, 1½*d*. each.

Sufficient.—Allow 1 kidney to each person.

Seasonable at any time.

ROAST HAUNCH OF MUTTON.

726. INGREDIENTS.—Haunch of mutton, a little salt, flour.

Mode.—Let this joint hang as long as possible without becoming tainted, and while hanging dust flour over it, which keeps off the flies, and prevents the air from getting to it. If not well hung, the joint,

HAUNCH OF MUTTON.

when it comes to table, will neither do credit to the butcher or the cook, as it will not be tender. Wash the outside well, lest it should have a bad flavour from keeping; then flour it and put it down to a nice brisk fire, at some distance, so that it may gradually warm through. Keep continually basting, and about ½ hour before it is served, draw it nearer to the fire to get nicely brown. Sprinkle a little fine salt over the meat, pour off the dripping, add a little boiling water slightly salted, and strain this over the joint. Place a paper ruche on the bone, and send red-currant jelly and gravy in a tureen to table with it.

Time.—About 4 hours. *Average cost,* 10*d.* per lb.

Sufficient for 8 to 10 persons.

Seasonable.—In best season from September to March.

HOW TO BUY MEAT ECONOMICALLY.—If the housekeeper is not very particular as to the precise joints to cook for dinner, there is oftentimes an opportunity for her to save as much money in her purchases of meat as will pay for the bread to eat with it. It often occurs, for instance, that the butcher may have a superfluity of certain joints, and these he would be glad to get rid of at a reduction of sometimes as much as 1*d.* or 1½*d.* per lb., and thus, in a joint of 8 or 9 lbs., will be saved enough to buy 2 quartern loaves. It frequently happens with many butchers, that, in consequence of a demand for legs and loins of mutton, they have only shoulders left, and these they will be glad to sell at a reduction.

ROAST LEG OF MUTTON.

727. INGREDIENTS.—Leg of mutton, a little salt.

Mode.—As mutton, when freshly killed, is never tender, hang it

LEG OF MUTTON.

almost as long as it will keep; flour it, and put it in a cool airy place for a few days, if the weather will permit. Wash off the flour, wipe it very dry, and cut off the shank-bone; put it down to a brisk clear fire, dredge with flour, and keep continually basting the whole time it is cooking. About 20 minutes before serving, draw it near the fire to get nicely brown; sprinkle over it a little salt, dish the meat, pour off the dripping, add some boiling water slightly salted, strain it over the joint, and serve.

Time.—A leg of mutton weighing 10 lbs., about 2¼ or 2½ hours ; one of 7 lbs., about 2 hours, or rather less.

Average cost, 8½*d.* per lb.

Sufficient.—A moderate-sized leg of mutton sufficient for 6 or 8 persons.

Seasonable at any time, but not so good in June, July, and August.

ROAST LOIN OF MUTTON.

728. INGREDIENTS.—Loin of mutton, a little salt.

Mode.—Cut and trim off the superfluous fat, and see that the butcher joints the meat properly, as thereby much annoyance is saved to the carver, when it comes to table. Have ready a nice clear fire (it need not be a very wide large one), put down the meat, dredge with flour, and baste well until it is done.

LOIN OF MUTTON.

Make the gravy as for roast leg of mutton, and serve very hot.

Time.—A loin of mutton weighing 6 lbs., 1½ hour, or rather longer.

Average cost, 8½*d.* per lb.   *Sufficient* for 4 or 5 persons.

Seasonable at any time.

ROLLED LOIN OF MUTTON (Very Excellent).

729. INGREDIENTS.—About 6 lbs. of a loin of mutton, ½ teaspoonful of pepper, ¼ teaspoonful of pounded allspice, ¼ teaspoonful of mace, ¼ teaspoonful of nutmeg, 6 cloves, forcemeat No. 417, 1 glass of port wine, 2 tablespoonfuls of mushroom ketchup.

Mode.—Hang the mutton till tender, bone it, and sprinkle over it pepper, mace, cloves, allspice, and nutmeg in the above proportion, all of which must be pounded very fine. Let it remain for a day, then make a forcemeat by recipe No. 417, cover the meat with it, and roll and bind it up firmly. Half bake it in a slow oven, let it grow cold, take off the fat, and put the gravy into a stewpan; flour the meat, put it in the gravy, and stew it till perfectly tender. Now take out the meat, unbind it, add to the gravy wine and ketchup as above, give one boil, and pour over the meat. Serve with red-currant jelly ; and, if obtainable, a few mushrooms stewed for a few minutes in the gravy, will be found a great improvement.

Time.—1½ hour to bake the meat, 1½ hour to stew gently.

Average cost, 4s. 9d.   *Sufficient* for 5 or 6 persons.

Seasonable at any time.

Note.—This joint will be found very nice if rolled and stuffed, as here directed, and plainly roasted. It should be well basted, and served with a good gravy and currant jelly.

BOILED NECK OF MUTTON.

730. INGREDIENTS.—4 lbs. of the middle, or best end of the neck of mutton; a little salt.

Mode.—Trim off a portion of the fat, should there be too much, and if it is to look particularly nice, the chine-bone should be sawn down, the ribs stripped halfway down, and the ends of the bones chopped off; this is, however, not necessary. Put the meat into sufficient *boiling* water to cover it; when it boils, add a little salt and remove all the scum. Draw the saucepan to the side of the fire, and let the water get so cool that the finger may be borne in it; then simmer very *slowly* and gently until the meat is done, which will be in about 1½ hour, or rather more, reckoning from the time that it begins to simmer. Serve with turnips and caper sauce, No. 382, and pour a little of it over the meat. The turnips should be boiled with the mutton; and, when at hand, a few carrots will also be found an improvement. These, however, if very large and thick, must be cut into long thinnish pieces, or they will not be sufficiently done by the time the mutton is ready. Garnish the dish with carrots and turnips placed alternately round the mutton.

Time.—4 lbs. of the neck of mutton, about 1½ hour.

Average cost, 8¼d. per lb.

Sufficient for 6 or 7 persons.

Seasonable at any time.

THE POETS ON SHEEP.—The keeping of flocks seems to have been the first employment of mankind; and the most ancient sort of poetry was probably pastoral. The poem known as the Pastoral gives a picture of the life of the simple shepherds of the golden age, who are supposed to have beguiled their time in singing. In all pastorals, repeated allusions are made to the "fleecy flocks," the "milk-white lambs," and "the tender ewes;" indeed, the sheep occupy a position in these poems inferior only to that of the shepherds who tend them. The "nibbling sheep" has ever been a favourite of the poets, and has supplied them with figures and similes without end. Shakspere frequently compares men to sheep. When Gloster rudely drives the lieutenant from the side of Henry VI., the poor king thus touchingly speaks of his helplessness :—

> "So flies the reckless shepherd from the wolf :
> So first the harmless sheep doth yield his fleece,
> And next his throat, unto the butcher's knife."

In the "Two Gentlemen of Verona," we meet with the following humorous comparison :—

"*Proteus.* The sheep for fodder follow the shepherd, the shepherd for food follows not the sheep : thou for wages followest thy master, thy master for wages follows not thee; therefore, thou art a sheep.

"*Speed.* Such another proof will make me cry *baa.*"

The descriptive poets give us some charming pictures of sheep. Every one is familiar with the sheep-shearing scene in Thomson's " Seasons :"—

> " Heavy and dripping, to the breezy brow
> Slow move the harmless race ; where, as they spread
> Their swelling treasures to the sunny ray,
> Inly disturb'd, and wond'ring what this wild
> Outrageous tumult means, their loud complaints
> The country fill ; and, toss'd from rock to rock,
> Incessant bleatings run around the hills."

What an exquisite idea of stillness is conveyed in the oft-quoted line from Gray's " Elegy :"—

> " And drowsy tinklings lull the distant fold."

From Dyer's quaint poem of " The Fleece " we could cull a hundred passages relating to sheep ; but we have already exceeded our space. We cannot, however, close this brief notice of the allusions that have been made to sheep by our poets, without quoting a couple of verses from Robert Burns's " Elegy on Poor Mailie," his only " pet *yowe :*"—

> " Thro' a' the town she troll'd by him ;
> A lang half-mile she could descry him ;
> Wi' kindly bleat, when she did spy him,
>   She ran wi' speed ;
> A friend mair faithfu' ne'er cam' nigh him
>   Than Mailie dead.

> " I wat she was a sheep o' sense,
> An' could behave hersel' wi' mense ;
> I'll say 't, she never brak a fence,
>   Thro' thievish greed.
> Our bardie, lanely, keeps the spence,
>   Sin' Mailie's dead."

MUTTON COLLOPS (Cold Meat Cookery).

731. INGREDIENTS.—A few slices of a cold leg or loin of mutton, salt and pepper to taste, 1 blade of pounded mace, 1 small bunch of savoury herbs minced very fine, 2 or 3 shalots, 2 or 3 oz. of butter, 1 dessertspoonful of flour, ½ pint of gravy, 1 tablespoonful of lemon-juice.

Mode.—Cut some very thin slices from a leg or the chump end of a loin of mutton ; sprinkle them with pepper, salt, pounded mace, minced savoury herbs, and minced shalot ; fry them in butter, stir in a dessertspoonful of flour, add the gravy and lemon-juice, simmer very gently about 5 or 7 minutes, and serve immediately.

Time.—5 to 7 minutes. *Average cost*, exclusive of the meat, 6*d.*

Seasonable at any time.

MUTTON CUTLETS WITH MASHED POTATOES.

732. INGREDIENTS.—About 3 lbs. of the best end of the neck of mutton, salt and pepper to taste, mashed potatoes.

Mode.—Procure a well-hung neck of mutton, saw off about 3 inches of the top of the bones, and cut the cutlets of a moderate thickness. Shape them by chopping off the thick part of the chine-bone ; beat them flat with a cutlet-chopper, and scrape quite clean, a portion

MUTTON CUTLETS.

of the top of the bone. Broil them over a nice clear fire for about 7 or 8 minutes, and turn them frequently. Have ready some smoothly-mashed white potatoes; place these in the middle of the dish; when the cutlets are done, season with pepper and salt; arrange them round the potatoes, with the thick end of the cutlets downwards, and serve very hot and quickly.

Time.—7 or 8 minutes. *Average cost,* for this quantity, 2s. 4d.

Sufficient for 5 or 6 persons.

Seasonable at any time.

Note.—Cutlets may be served in various ways; with peas, tomatoes, onions, sauce piquante, &c.

MUTTON PIE (Cold Meat Cookery).

733. INGREDIENTS.—The remains of a cold leg, loin, or neck of mutton, pepper and salt to taste, 2 blades of pounded mace, 1 dessert-spoonful of chopped parsley, 1 teaspoonful of minced savoury herbs; when liked, a little minced onion or shalot; 3 or 4 potatoes, 1 teacupful of gravy; crust.

Mode.—Cold mutton may be made into very good pies if well seasoned and mixed with a few herbs; if the leg is used, cut it into very thin slices; if the loin or neck, into thin cutlets. Place some at the bottom of the dish; season well with pepper, salt, mace, parsley, and herbs; then put a layer of potatoes sliced, then more mutton, and so on till the dish is full; add the gravy, cover with a crust, and bake for 1 hour.

Time.—1 hour.

Seasonable at any time.

Note.—The remains of an underdone leg of mutton may be converted into a very good family pudding, by cutting the meat into slices, and putting them into a basin lined with a suet crust. It should be seasoned well with pepper, salt, and minced shalot, covered with a crust, and boiled for about 3 hours.

MUTTON PIE.

734. INGREDIENTS.—2 lbs. of the neck or loin of mutton, weighed after being boned; 2 kidneys, pepper and salt to taste, 2 teacupfuls of gravy or water, 2 tablespoonfuls of minced parsley; when liked, a little minced onion or shalot; puff crust.

Mode.—Bone the mutton, and cut the meat into steaks all of the same thickness, and leave but very little fat. Cut up the kidneys, and arrange these with the meat neatly in a pie-dish; sprinkle over them the minced parsley and a seasoning of pepper and salt; pour in the gravy, and cover with a tolerably good puff crust. Bake for 1½ hour, or rather longer, should the pie be very large, and let the oven be rather brisk. A well-made suet crust may be used instead of puff crust, and will be found exceedingly good.

Time.—1½ hour, or rather longer. *Average cost,* 2s.

Sufficient for 5 or 6 persons.

Seasonable at any time.

MUTTON PUDDING.

735. INGREDIENTS.—About 2 lbs. of the chump end of the loin of mutton, weighed after being boned; pepper and salt to taste, suet crust made with milk (*see* Pastry), in the proportion of 6 oz. of suet to each pound of flour; a very small quantity of minced onion (this may be omitted when the flavour is not liked).

Mode.—Cut the meat into rather thin slices, and season them with pepper and salt; line the pudding-dish with crust; lay in the meat, and nearly, but do not quite, fill it up with water; when the flavour is liked, add a small quantity of minced onion; cover with crust, and proceed in the same manner as directed in recipe No. 605, using the same kind of pudding-dish as there mentioned.

Time.—About 3 hours. *Average cost,* 1s. 9d.

Sufficient for 6 persons.

Seasonable all the year, but more suitable in winter.

RAGOUT OF COLD NECK OF MUTTON (Cold Meat Cookery)

736. INGREDIENTS.—The remains of a cold neck or loin of mutton, 2 oz. of butter, a little flour, 2 onions sliced, ¼ pint of water, 2 small carrots, 2 turnips, pepper and salt to taste.

Mode.—Cut the mutton into small chops, and trim off the greater portion of the fat; put the butter into a stewpan, dredge in a little flour, add the sliced onions, and keep stirring till brown; then put in the meat. When this is quite brown, add the water, and the carrots and turnips, which should be cut into very thin slices; season with pepper and salt, and stew till quite tender, which will be in about ¾ hour. When in season, green peas may be substituted for the carrots and turnips: they should be piled in the centre of the dish, and the chops laid round.

Time.—¾ hour. *Average cost,* exclusive of the meat, 4d.

Seasonable, with peas, from June to August.

ROAST NECK OF MUTTON.

737. INGREDIENTS.—Neck of mutton; a little salt.

Mode.—For roasting, choose the middle, or the best end, of the neck of mutton, and if there is a very large proportion of fat, trim off some of it, and save it for making into suet puddings, which will be found exceedingly good. Let the bones be cut short, and see that it is properly jointed before it is laid down to the fire, as they will be more easily separated when they come to table. Place the joint at a nice brisk fire, dredge it with flour, and keep continually basting until done. A few minutes before serving, draw it nearer the fire to acquire a nice colour, sprinkle over it a little salt, pour off the dripping, add a little boiling water slightly salted; strain this over the meat and serve. Red-currant jelly may be sent to table with it.

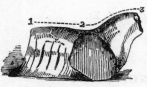

NECK OF MUTTON.
1—2. *Best end.* 2—3. *Scrag.*

Time.—4 lbs. of the neck of mutton, rather more than 1 hour.

Average cost, 8½d. per lb.

Sufficient for 4 or 5 persons. *Seasonable* at any time.

WOOLLEN MANUFACTURES.—The distinction between hair and wool is rather arbitrary than natural, consisting in the greater or less degrees of fineness, softness, and pliability of the fibres. When the fibres possess these properties so far as to admit of their being spun and woven into a texture sufficiently pliable to be used as an article of dress, they are called wool. The sheep, llama, Angora goat, and the goat of Thibet, are the animals from which most of the wool used in manufactures is obtained. The finest of all wools is that from the goat of Thibet, of which the Cashmere shawls are made. Of European wools, the finest is that yielded by the Merino sheep, the Spanish and Saxon breeds taking the precedence. The Merino sheep, as now naturalized in Australia, furnishes an excellent fleece; but all varieties of sheep-wool, reared either in Europe or Australia, are inferior in softness of feel to that grown in India, and to that of the llama of the Andes. The best of our British wools are inferior in fineness to any of the above-mentioned, being nearly twelve times the thickness of the finest Spanish merino; but, for the ordinary purposes of the manufacturer, they are unrivalled.

ROAST SADDLE OF MUTTON.

738. INGREDIENTS.—Saddle of mutton; a little salt.

Mode.—To insure this joint being tender, let it hang for ten days or a fortnight, if the weather permits. Cut off the tail and flaps, and trim away every part that has not indisputable pretensions to be eaten, and have the skin taken off and skewered on again. Put it down to a bright, clear fire, and, when the joint has been cooking for an hour, remove the skin and dredge it with flour. It should not be placed too near

SADDLE OF MUTTON.

the fire, as the fat should not be in the slightest degree burnt. Keep constantly basting, both before and after the skin is removed; sprinkle some salt over the joint. Make a little gravy in the dripping-pan; pour it over the meat, which send to table with a tureen of made gravy and red-currant jelly.

Time.—A saddle of mutton weighing 10 lbs., 2½ hours; 14 lbs., 3¼ hours. When liked underdone, allow rather less time.

Average cost, 10d. per lb.

Sufficient.—A moderate-sized saddle of 10 lbs. for 7 or 8 persons.

Seasonable all the year; not so good when lamb is in full season.

ROAST SHOULDER OF MUTTON.

739. INGREDIENTS.—Shoulder of mutton; a little salt.

Mode.—Put the joint down to a bright, clear fire; flour it well, and keep continually basting. About ¼ hour before serving, draw it near the fire, that the outside may acquire a nice brown colour, but not sufficiently near to blacken the fat. Sprinkle a little fine salt over the meat, empty the dripping-pan of its contents, pour in a little boiling water slightly salted,

SHOULDER OF MUTTON.

and strain this over the joint. Onion sauce, or stewed Spanish onions, are usually sent to table with this dish, and sometimes baked potatoes.

Time.—A shoulder of mutton weighing 6 or 7 lbs., 1½ hour.

Average cost, 8d. per lb.

Sufficient for 5 or 6 persons. *Seasonable* at any time.

Note.—Shoulder of mutton may be dressed in a variety of ways; boiled, and served with onion sauce; boned, and stuffed with a good veal forcemeat; or baked, with sliced potatoes in the dripping-pan.

THE ETTRICK SHEPHERD.—James Hogg was perhaps the most remarkable man that ever wore the *maud* of a shepherd. Under the garb, aspect, and bearing of a rude peasant (and rude enough he was in most of these things, even after no inconsiderable experience of society), the world soon discovered a true poet. He taught himself to write, by copying the letters of a printed book as he lay watching his flock on the hill-side, and believed that he had reached the utmost pitch of his ambition when he first found that his artless rhymes could touch the heart of the ewe-milker who partook the shelter of his mantle during the passing storm. If "the shepherd" of Professor Wilson's "Noctes Ambrosianæ" may be taken as a true portrait of James Hogg, we must admit that, for quaintness of humour, the poet of Ettrick Forest had few rivals. Sir Walter Scott said that Hogg's thousand little touches of absurdity afforded him more entertainment than the best comedy that ever set the pit in a roar. Among the written productions of the shepherd-poet, is an account of his own experiences in sheep-tending, called "The Shepherd's Calender." This work contains a vast amount of useful information upon sheep, their diseases, habits, and management. The Ettrick Shepherd died in 1835.

SHEEP'S BRAINS, EN MATELOTE (an Entrée).

740. INGREDIENTS.—6 sheep's brains, vinegar, salt, a few slices of bacon, 1 small onion, 2 cloves, a small bunch of parsley, sufficient stock or weak broth to cover the brains, 1 tablespoonful of lemon-juice, matelote sauce, No. 512.

Mode.—Detach the brains from the heads without breaking them, and put them into a pan of warm water; remove the skin, and let them remain for two hours. Have ready a saucepan of boiling water, add a little vinegar and salt, and put in the brains. When they are quite firm, take them out and put them into very cold water. Place 2 or 3 slices of bacon in a stewpan, put in the brains, the onion stuck with 2 cloves, the parsley, and a good seasoning of pepper and salt; cover with stock, or weak broth, and boil them gently for about 25 minutes. Have ready some croûtons; arrange these in the dish alternately with the brains, and cover with a matelote sauce, No. 512, to which has been added the above proportion of lemon-juice.

Time.—25 minutes. *Average cost,* 1s. 6d.

Sufficient for 6 persons.

Seasonable at any time.

SHEEP'S FEET or TROTTERS (Soyer's Recipe).

741. INGREDIENTS.—12 feet, $\frac{1}{4}$ lb. of beef or mutton suet, 2 onions, 1 carrot, 2 bay-leaves, 2 sprigs of thyme, 1 oz. of salt, $\frac{1}{4}$ oz. of pepper, 2 tablespoonfuls of flour, $2\frac{1}{2}$ quarts of water, $\frac{1}{4}$ lb. of fresh butter, 1 teaspoonful of salt, 1 teaspoonful of flour, $\frac{1}{4}$ teaspoonful of pepper, a little grated nutmeg, the juice of 1 lemon, 1 gill of milk, the yolks of 2 eggs.

Mode.—Have the feet cleaned, and the long bone extracted from them. Put the suet into a stewpan, with the onions and carrot sliced, the bay-leaves, thyme, salt, and pepper, and let these simmer for 5 minutes. Add 2 tablespoonfuls of flour and the water, and keep stirring till it boils; then put in the feet. Let these simmer for 3 hours, or until perfectly tender, and take them and lay them on a sieve. Mix together, on a plate, with the back of a spoon, butter, salt, flour (1 teaspoonful), pepper, nutmeg, and lemon-juice as above, and put the feet, with a gill of milk, into a stewpan. When very hot, add the butter, &c., and stir continually till melted. Now mix the yolks of 2 eggs with 5 tablespoonfuls of milk; stir this to the other ingredients, keep moving the pan over the fire continually for a minute or two, but do not allow it to boil after the eggs are added.

Serve in a very hot dish, and garnish with croûtons, or sippets of toasted bread.

Time.—3 hours. *Average cost,* 1s. 6d.

Sufficient for 4 persons.

Seasonable at any time.

TO DRESS A SHEEP'S HEAD.

742. INGREDIENTS.—1 sheep's head, sufficient water to cover it, 3 carrots, 3 turnips, 2 or 3 parsnips, 3 onions, a small bunch of parsley, 1 teaspoonful of pepper, 3 teaspoonfuls of salt, $\frac{1}{4}$ lb. of Scotch oatmeal.

Mode.—Clean the head well, and let it soak in warm water for 2 hours, to get rid of the blood; put it into a saucepan, with sufficient cold water to cover it, and when it boils, add the vegetables, peeled and sliced, and the remaining ingredients; before adding the oatmeal, mix it to a smooth batter with a little of the liquor. Keep stirring till it boils up; then shut the saucepan closely, and let it stew gently for $1\frac{1}{2}$ or 2 hours. It may be thickened with rice or barley, but oatmeal is preferable.

Time.—$1\frac{1}{2}$ or 2 hours. *Average cost,* 8d. each.

Sufficient for 3 persons.

Seasonable at any time.

SINGED SHEEP'S HEAD.—The village of Dudingston, which stands "within a mile of Edinburgh town," was formerly celebrated for this ancient and homely Scottish dish. In the summer months, many opulent citizens used to resort to this place to solace themselves over singed sheep's heads, boiled or baked. The sheep fed upon the neighbouring hills were slaughtered at this village, and the carcases were sent to town; but the heads were left to be consumed in the place. We are not aware whether the custom of eating sheep's heads at Dudingston is still kept up by the good folks of Edinburgh.

TOAD-IN-THE-HOLE (Cold Meat Cookery).

743. INGREDIENTS.—6 oz. of flour, 1 pint of milk, 3 eggs, butter, a few slices of cold mutton, pepper and salt to taste, 2 kidneys.

Mode.—Make a smooth batter of flour, milk, and eggs in the above proportion; butter a baking-dish, and pour in the batter. Into this place a few slices of cold mutton, previously well seasoned, and the kidneys, which should be cut into rather small pieces; bake about 1 hour, or rather longer, and send it to table in the dish it was baked in. Oysters or mushrooms may be substituted for the kidneys, and will be found exceedingly good.

Time.—Rather more than 1 hour.

Average cost, exclusive of the cold meat, 8d.

Seasonable at any time.

BREAST OF LAMB AND GREEN PEAS.

744. INGREDIENTS.—1 breast of lamb, a few slices of bacon, ½ pint of stock, No. 105, 1 lemon, 1 onion, 1 bunch of savoury herbs, green peas.

Mode.—Remove the skin from a breast of lamb, put it into a saucepan of boiling water, and let it simmer for 5 minutes. Take it out and lay it in cold water. Line the bottom of a stewpan with a few thin slices of bacon; lay the lamb on these; peel the lemon, cut it into slices, and put these on the meat, to keep it white and make it tender; cover with 1 or 2 more slices of bacon; add the stock, onion, and herbs, and set it on a slow fire to simmer very gently until tender. Have ready some green peas, put these on a dish, and place the lamb on the top of these. The appearance of this dish may be much improved by glazing the lamb, and spinach may be substituted for the peas when variety is desired.

Time.—1½ hour. *Average cost,* 10*d.* per lb.

Sufficient for 3 persons.

Seasonable, grass lamb, from Easter to Michaelmas.

THE LAMB AS A SACRIFICE.—The number of lambs consumed in sacrifices by the Hebrews must have been very considerable. Two lambs "of the first year" were appointed to be sacrificed daily for the morning and evening sacrifice; and a lamb served as a substitute for the first-born of unclean animals, such as the ass, which could not be accepted as an offering to the Lord. Every year, also, on the anniversary of the deliverance of the children of Israel from the bondage of Egypt, every family was ordered to sacrifice a lamb or kid, and to sprinkle some of its blood upon the door-posts, in commemoration of the judgment of God upon the Egyptians. It was to be eaten roasted, with unleavened bread and bitter herbs, in haste, with the loins girded, the shoes on the feet, and the staff in the hand; and whatever remained until the morning was to be burnt. The sheep was also used in the numerous special, individual, and national sacrifices ordered by the Jewish law. On extraordinary occasions, vast quantities of sheep were sacrificed at once; thus Solomon, on the completion of the temple, offered "sheep and oxen that could not be told nor numbered for multitude."

STEWED BREAST OF LAMB.

745. INGREDIENTS.—1 breast of lamb, pepper and salt to taste, sufficient stock, No. 105, to cover it, 1 glass of sherry, thickening of butter and flour.

Mode.—Skin the lamb, cut it into pieces, and season them with pepper and salt; lay these in a stewpan, pour in sufficient stock or gravy to cover them, and stew very gently until tender, which will be in about 1½ hour. Just before serving, thicken the sauce with a little butter and flour; add the sherry, give one boil, and pour it over the meat. Green peas, or stewed mushrooms, may be strewed over the meat, and will be found a very great improvement.

Time.—1½ hour. *Average cost,* 10*d.* per lb.

Sufficient for 3 persons.

Seasonable, grass lamb, from Easter to Michaelmas.

LAMB CHOPS.

746. INGREDIENTS.—Loin of lamb, pepper and salt to taste.

Mode.—Trim off the flap from a fine loin of lamb, and cut it into chops about ¾ inch in thickness. Have ready a bright clear fire : lay the chops on a gridiron, and broil them of a nice pale brown, turning them when required. Season them with pepper and salt ; serve very hot and quickly, and garnish with crisped parsley, or place them on mashed potatoes. Asparagus, spinach, or peas are the favourite accompaniments to lamb chops.

Time.—About 8 or 10 minutes. *Average cost*, 1*s.* per lb.

Sufficient.—Allow 2 chops to each person.

Seasonable from Easter to Michaelmas.

LAMB CUTLETS AND SPINACH (an Entree).

747. INGREDIENTS.—8 cutlets, egg and bread crumbs, salt and pepper to taste, a little clarified butter.

Mode.—Cut the cutlets from a neck of lamb, and shape them by cutting off the thick part of the chine-bone. Trim off most of the fat and all the skin, and scrape the top part of the bones quite clean. Brush the cutlets over with egg, sprinkle them with bread crumbs, and season with pepper and salt. Now dip them into clarified butter, sprinkle over a few more bread crumbs, and fry them over a sharp fire, turning them when required. Lay them before the fire to drain, and arrange them on a dish with spinach in the centre, which should be previously well boiled, drained, chopped, and seasoned.

Time.—About 7 or 8 minutes. *Average cost*, 10*d.* per lb.

Sufficient for 4 persons.

Seasonable from Easter to Michaelmas.

Note.—Peas, asparagus, or French beans, may be substituted for the spinach ; or lamb cutlets may be served with stewed cucumbers, Soubise sauce, &c. &c.

LAMB'S FRY.

748. INGREDIENTS.—1 lb. of lamb's fry, 3 pints of water, egg and bread crumbs, 1 teaspoonful of chopped parsley, salt and pepper to taste.

Mode.—Boil the fry for ¼ hour in the above proportion of water, take it out and dry it in a cloth ; grate some bread down finely, mix with it a teaspoonful of chopped parsley and a high seasoning of pepper and salt. Brush the fry lightly over with the yolk of an egg, sprinkle over the bread crumbs, and fry for 5 minutes. Serve very hot on a napkin in a dish, and garnish with plenty of crisped parsley.

Time.—¼ hour to simmer the fry, 5 minutes to fry it.

Average cost, 10*d.* per lb.

Sufficient for 2 or 3 persons.

Seasonable from Easter to Michaelmas.

HASHED LAMB AND BROILED BLADE-BONE.

749. INGREDIENTS.—The remains of a cold shoulder of lamb, pepper and salt to taste, 2 oz. of butter, about ½ pint of stock or gravy, 1 tablespoonful of shalot vinegar, 3 or 4 pickled gherkins.

Mode.—Take the blade-bone from the shoulder, and cut the meat into collops as neatly as possible. Season the bone with pepper and salt, pour a little oiled butter over it, and place it in the oven to warm through. Put the stock into a stewpan, add the ketchup and shalot vinegar, and lay in the pieces of lamb. Let these heat gradually through, but do not allow them to boil. Take the blade-bone out of the oven, and place it on a gridiron over a sharp fire to brown. Slice the gherkins, put them into the hash, and dish it with the blade-bone in the centre. It may be garnished with croûtons or sippets of toasted bread.

Time.—Altogether ½ hour. *Average cost*, exclusive of the meat, 4*d.*

Seasonable.—House lamb, from Christmas to March; grass lamb, from Easter to Michaelmas.

ROAST FORE-QUARTER OF LAMB.

750. INGREDIENTS.—Lamb, a little salt.

Mode.—To obtain the flavour of lamb in perfection, it should not be long kept; time to cool is all that it requires; and though the meat may be somewhat thready, the juices and flavour will be infinitely superior to that of lamb that has been killed 2 or 3 days. Make up the fire in good time, that it may be clear and brisk when the joint is put down. Place it at a sufficient distance to prevent the fat from burning, and baste it constantly till the moment of serving. Lamb should be very *thoroughly* done without being dried

FORE-QUARTER OF LAMB.

up, and not the slightest appearance of red gravy should be visible, as in roast mutton: this rule is applicable to all young white meats. Serve with a little gravy made in the dripping-pan, the same as for other roasts, and send to table with it a tureen of mint sauce, No. 469, and a fresh salad. A cut lemon, a small piece of fresh butter, and a little cayenne, should also be placed on the table, so that when the carver separates the shoulder from the ribs, they may be ready for his use ; if, however, he should not be very expert, we would recommend that the cook should divide these joints nicely before coming to table.

Time.—Fore-quarter of lamb weighing 10 lbs., 1¾ to 2 hours.

Average cost, 10*d.* to 1*s.* per lb. *Sufficient* for 7 or 8 persons.

Seasonable, grass lamb, from Easter to Michaelmas.

BOILED LEG OF LAMB A LA BECHAMEL.

751. INGREDIENTS.—Leg of lamb, Béchamel sauce, No. 367.

Mode.—Do not choose a very large joint, but one weighing about 5 lbs. Have ready a saucepan of boiling water, into which plunge the lamb, and when it boils up again, draw it to the side of the fire, and let the water cool a little. Then stew very gently for about 1¼ hour, reckoning from the time that the water begins to simmer. Make some Béchamel by recipe No. 367, dish the lamb, pour the sauce over it, and garnish with tufts of boiled cauliflower or carrots. When liked, melted butter may be substituted for the Béchamel : this is a more simple method, but not nearly so nice. Send to table with it some of the sauce in a tureen, and boiled cauliflowers or spinach, with whichever vegetable the dish is garnished.

Time.—1¼ hour after the water simmers.

Average cost, 10*d.* to 1*s.* per lb. *Sufficient* for 4 or 5 persons.

Seasonable from Easter to Michaelmas.

ROAST LEG OF LAMB.

752. INGREDIENTS.—Lamb, a little salt.

Mode.—Place the joint at a good distance from the fire at first, and baste well the whole time it is cooking. When nearly done, draw it nearer the fire to acquire a nice brown colour. Sprinkle a little fine salt over the meat, empty the dripping-pan of its contents; pour in a little boiling water, and strain this over the meat. Serve with mint sauce and a

LEG OF LAMB.

fresh salad, and for vegetables send peas, spinach, or cauliflowers to table with it.

Time.—A leg of lamb weighing 5 lbs., 1½ hour.

Average cost, 10*d.* to 1*s.* per lb. *Sufficient* for 4 or 5 persons.

Seasonable from Easter to Michaelmas.

BRAISED LOIN OF LAMB.

753. INGREDIENTS.—1 loin of lamb, a few slices of bacon, 1 bunch of green onions, 5 or 6 young carrots, a bunch of savoury herbs, 2 blades of pounded mace, 1 pint of stock, salt to taste.

Mode.—Bone a loin of lamb, and line the bottom of a stewpan just capable of holding it, with a few thin slices of fat bacon ; add the remaining ingredients, cover the meat with a few more slices of bacon, pour in the stock, and simmer very *gently* for 2 hours ; take it up, dry it, strain and reduce the gravy to a glaze, with which glaze the meat, and serve it either on stewed peas, spinach, or stewed cucumbers.

LOIN OF LAMB.

Time.—2 hours. *Average cost,* 11*d.* per lb.

Sufficient for 4 or 5 persons.

Seasonable from Easter to Michaelmas.

ROAST SADDLE OF LAMB.

754. INGREDIENTS.—Lamb ; a little salt.

Mode.—This joint is now very much in vogue, and is generally considered a nice one for a small party. Have ready a clear brisk

SADDLE OF LAMB.   RIBS OF LAMB.

fire ; put down the joint at a little distance, to prevent the fat from scorching, and keep it well basted all the time it is cooking. Serve with mint sauce and a fresh salad, and send to table with it, either peas, cauliflowers, or spinach.

Time.—A small saddle, 1½ hour ; a large one, 2 hours.

Average cost, 10*d.* to 1*s.* per lb.

Sufficient for 5 or 6 persons.

Seasonable from Easter to Michaelmas.

Note.—Loin and ribs of lamb are roasted in the same manner, and served with the same sauces as the above. A loin will take about 1¼ hour ; ribs, from 1 to 1¼ hour.

ROAST SHOULDER OF LAMB.

755. INGREDIENTS.—Lamb ; a little salt.

Mode.—Have ready a clear brisk fire, and put down the joint at a sufficient distance from it, that the fat may not burn. Keep constantly basting until done, and serve with a little gravy made in the dripping-pan, and send mint sauce to table with it. Peas, spinach, or cauliflowers are the usual vegetables served with lamb, and also a fresh salad.

Time.—A shoulder of lamb rather more than 1 hour.

Average cost, 10*d.* to 1*s.* per lb.

Sufficient for 4 or 5 persons.

Seasonable from Easter to Michaelmas.

SHOULDER OF LAMB STUFFED.

756. INGREDIENTS.—Shoulder of lamb, forcemeat No. 417, trimmings of veal or beef, 2 onions, ½ head of celery, 1 faggot of savoury herbs, a few slices of fat bacon, 1 quart of stock No. 105.

Mode.—Take the blade-bone out of a shoulder of lamb, fill up its place with forcemeat, and sew it up with coarse thread. Put it into a stewpan with a few slices of bacon under and over the lamb, and add the remaining ingredients. Stew very gently for rather more than 2 hours. Reduce the gravy, with which glaze the meat, and serve with peas, stewed cucumbers, or sorrel sauce.

Time.—Rather more than 2 hours. *Average cost*, 10*d.* to 1*s.* per lb.

Sufficient for 4 or 5 persons.

Seasonable from Easter to Michaelmas.

LAMB'S SWEETBREADS, LARDED, AND ASPARAGUS
(an Entree).

757. INGREDIENTS.—2 or 3 sweetbreads, ½ pint of veal stock, white pepper and salt to taste, a small bunch of green onions, 1 blade of pounded mace, thickening of butter and flour, 2 eggs, nearly ½ pint of cream, 1 teaspoonful of minced parsley, a very little grated nutmeg.

Mode.—Soak the sweetbreads in lukewarm water, and put them into a saucepan with sufficient boiling water to cover them, and let them simmer for 10 minutes; then take them out and put them into cold water. Now lard them, lay them in a stewpan, add the stock, seasoning, onions, mace, and a thickening of butter and flour, and stew gently for ¼ hour or 20 minutes. Beat up the egg with the cream, to which add the minced parsley and a very little grated nutmeg. Put this to the other ingredients; stir it well till quite hot, but do not let it boil after the cream is added, or it will curdle. Have ready some asparagus-tops, boiled; add these to the sweetbreads, and serve.

Time.—Altogether ½ hour. *Average cost*, 2*s.* 6*d.* to 3*s.* 6*d.* each.

Sufficient—3 sweetbreads for 1 entrée.

Seasonable from Easter to Michaelmas.

ANOTHER WAY TO DRESS SWEETBREADS (an Entree).

758. INGREDIENTS.—Sweetbreads, egg and bread crumbs, ⅓ pint of gravy, No. 442, ½ glass of sherry.

Mode.—Soak the sweetbreads in water for an hour, and throw them into boiling water to render them firm. Let them stew gently for about ¼ hour, take them out and put them into a cloth to drain all the water from them. Brush them over with egg, sprinkle them with bread crumbs, and either brown them in the oven or before the fire. Have ready the above quantity of gravy, to which add ½ glass of sherry; dish the sweetbreads, pour the gravy under them, and garnish with water-cresses.

Time.—Rather more than ½ hour. *Average cost*, 2s. 6d. to 3s. 6d. each.
Sufficient—3 sweetbreads for 1 entrée.
Seasonable from Easter to Michaelmas.

MUTTON AND LAMB CARVING.

HAUNCH OF MUTTON.

759. A deep cut should, in the first place, be made quite down to the bone, across the knuckle-end of the joint, along the line 1 to 2. This will let the gravy escape; and then it should be carved, in not too thick slices, along the whole length of the haunch, in the direction of the line from 4 to 3.

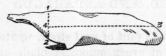

HAUNCH OF MUTTON.

LEG OF MUTTON.

760. This homely, but capital English joint, is almost invariably served at table as shown in the engraving. The carving of it is not very difficult: the knife should be carried sharply down in the direction of the line from 1 to 2, and slices taken from either side, as the guests may desire, some liking the knuckle-end, as well done, and others preferring the more underdone part. The fat should be sought near the line 3 to 4. Some connoisseurs are fond of having this joint dished with the under-side uppermost, so as to get at the finely-grained meat lying under that part of the meat,

LEG OF MUTTON.

known as the Pope's eye; but this is an extravagant fashion, and one that will hardly find favour in the eyes of many economical British housewives and housekeepers.

LOIN OF MUTTON.

761. There is one point in connection with carving a loin of mutton which includes every other; that is, that the joint should be thoroughly well jointed by the butcher before it is cooked. This knack of jointing requires practice and the proper tools; and no one but the butcher is supposed to have these. If the bones be not well jointed, the carving of a loin of mutton is not a gracious business; whereas, if that has been attended to,

LOIN OF MUTTON.

it is an easy and untroublesome task. The knife should be inserted at fig. 1, and after feeling your way between the bones, it should be carried sharply in the direction of the line 1 to 2. As there are some people who prefer the outside cut, while others do not like it, the question as to their choice of this should be asked.

SADDLE OF MUTTON.

762. Although we have heard, at various intervals, growlings expressed at the inevitable "saddle of mutton" at the dinner-parties of our middle classes, yet we doubt whether any other joint is better liked, when it has been well hung and artistically cooked. There is a diversity of opinion respecting the mode of sending this joint to table; but it has only reference to whether or no there shall be any portion of the tail, or, if so, how many

SADDLE OF MUTTON.

joints of the tail. We ourselves prefer the mode as shown in our coloured illustration "O;" but others may, upon equally good grounds, like the way shown in the engraving on this page. Some trim the tail with a paper frill. The carving is not difficult: it is usually cut in the direction of the line from 2 to 1, quite down to the bones, in evenly-sliced pieces. A fashion, however, patronized by some, is to carve it obliquely, in the direction of the line from 4 to 3; in which case the joint would be turned round the other way, having the tail end on the right of the carver.

SHOULDER OF MUTTON.

763. This is a joint not difficult to carve. The knife should be

drawn from the outer edge of the shoulder in the direction of the line

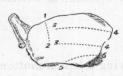

from 1 to 2, until the bone of the shoulder is reached. As many slices as can be carved in this manner should be taken, and afterwards the meat lying on either side of the blade-bone should be served, by carving in the direction of 3 to 4 and 3 to 4. The uppermost side of the shoulder being now finished, the joint should

SHOULDER OF MUTTON.

be turned, and slices taken off along its whole length. There are some who prefer this under-side of the shoulder for its juicy flesh, although the grain of the meat is not so fine as that on the other side.

FORE-QUARTER OF LAMB.

764. We always think that a good and practised carver delights in the manipulation of this joint, for there is a little field for his judg-

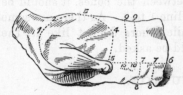

ment and dexterity which does not always occur. The separation of the shoulder from the breast is the first point to be attended to; this is done by passing the knife lightly round the dotted line, as shown by the figures 1, 2, 3, 4, and 5, so as to cut through the skin, and then, by raising with a

FORE-QUARTER OF LAMB.

little force the shoulder, into which the fork should be firmly fixed, it will come away with just a little more exercise of the knife. In dividing the shoulder and breast, the carver should take care not to cut away too much of the meat from the latter, as that would rather spoil its appearance when the shoulder is removed. The breast and shoulder being separated, it is usual to lay a small piece of butter, and sprinkle a little cayenne, lemon-juice, and salt between them; and when this is melted and incorporated with the meat and gravy, the shoulder may, as more convenient, be removed into another dish. The next operation is to separate the ribs from the brisket, by cutting through the meat on the line 5 to 6. The joint is then ready to be served to the guests; the ribs being carved in the direction of the lines from 9 to 10, and the brisket from 7 to 8. The carver should ask those at the table what parts they prefer—ribs, brisket, or a piece of the shoulder.

LEG OF LAMB, LOIN OF LAMB, SADDLE OF LAMB, SHOULDER OF LAMB,

are carved in the same manner as the corresponding joints of Mutton. (*See* Nos. 760, 761, 762, 763.)

CHAPTER XVI.

GENERAL OBSERVATIONS ON THE COMMON HOG.

765. THE HOG belongs to the order *Mammalia*, the genus *Sus scrofa*, and the species *Pachydermata*, or thick-skinned; and its generic characters are, a small head, with long flexible snout truncated; 42 teeth, divided into 4 upper incisors, converging, 6 lower incisors, projecting, 2 upper and 2 lower canine, or tusks,—the former short, the latter projecting, formidable, and sharp, and 14 molars in each jaw; cloven feet furnished with 4 toes, and tail, small, short, and twisted; while, in some varieties, this appendage is altogether wanting.

766. FROM THE NUMBER AND POSITION OF THE TEETH, physiologists are enabled to define the nature and functions of the animal; and from those of the *Sus*, or hog, it is evident that he is as much a *grinder* as a *biter*, or can live as well on vegetable as on animal food; though a mixture of both is plainly indicated as the character of food most conducive to the integrity and health of its physical system.

767. THUS THE PIG TRIBE, though not a ruminating mammal, as might be inferred from the number of its molar teeth, is yet a link between the *herbivorous* and the *carnivorous* tribes, and is consequently what is known as an *omnivorous* quadruped; or, in other words, capable of converting any kind of aliment into nutriment.

768. Though the Hoof in the Hog is, as a general rule, cloven, there are several remarkable exceptions, as in the species native to Norway, Illyria, Sardinia, and *formerly* to the Berkshire variety of the British domesticated pig, in which the hoof is entire and *un*cleft.

769. Whatever Difference in its Physical Nature, climate and soil may produce in this animal, his functional characteristics are the same in whatever part of the world he may be found ; and whether in the trackless forests of South America, the coral isles of Polynesia, the jungles of India, or the spicy brakes of Sumatra, he is everywhere known for his gluttony, laziness, and indifference to the character and quality of his food. And though he occasionally shows an epicure's relish for a succulent plant or a luscious carrot, which he will discuss with all his salivary organs keenly excited, he will, the next moment, turn with equal gusto to some carrion offal that might excite the forbearance of the unscrupulous cormorant. It is this coarse and repulsive mode of feeding that has, in every country and language, obtained for him the opprobrium of being " an unclean animal."

770. In the Mosaical Law, the pig is condemned as an unclean beast, and consequently interdicted to the Israelites, as unfit for human food. "And the swine, though he divideth the hoof and be cloven footed, yet he cheweth not the cud. He is unclean to you."—Lev. xi. 7. Strict, however, as the law was respecting the cud-chewing and hoof-divided animals, the Jews, with their usual perversity and violation of the divine commands, seem afterwards to have ignored the prohibition ; for, unless they ate pork, it is difficult to conceive for what purpose they kept droves of swine, as from the circumstance recorded in Matthew xviii. 32, when Jesus was in Galilee, and the devils, cast out of the two men, were permitted to enter the herd of swine that were feeding on the hills in the neighbourhood of the Sea of Tiberias, it is very evident they did. There is only one interpretation by which we can account for a prohibition that debarred the Jews from so many foods which we regard as nutritious luxuries, that, being fat and the texture more hard of digestion than other meats, they were likely, in a hot dry climate, where vigorous exercise could seldom be taken, to produce disease, and especially cutaneous affections ; indeed, in this light, as a code of sanitary ethics, the book of Leviticus is the most admirable system of moral government ever conceived for man's benefit.

771. Setting his coarse Feeding and slovenly Habits out of the question, there is no domestic animal so profitable or so useful to man as the much-maligned pig, or any that yields him a more varied or more luxurious repast. The prolific powers of the pig are extraordinary, even under the restraint of domestication ; but when left to run wild in favourable situations, as in the islands of the South Pacific, the result, in a few years, from two animals put on shore and left undisturbed, is truly surprising ; for they breed so fast, and have such numerous litters, that unless killed off in

vast numbers both for the use of the inhabitants and as fresh provisions for ships' crews, they would degenerate into vermin. In this country the pig has usually two litters, or farrows, in a year, the breeding seasons being April and October; and the period the female goes with her young is about four months,—16 weeks or 122 days. The number produced at each litter depends upon the character of the breed; 12 being the average number in the small variety, and 10 in the large; in the mixed breeds, however, the average is between 10 and 15, and in some instances has reached as many as 20. But however few, or however many, young pigs there may be to the farrow, there is always one who is the dwarf of the family circle, a poor, little, shrivelled, half-starved anatomy, with a small melancholy voice, a staggering gait, a woe-begone countenance, and a thread of a tail, whose existence the complacent mother ignores, his plethoric brothers and sisters repudiate, and for whose emaciated jaws there is never a spare or supplemental teat, till one of the favoured gormandizers, overtaken by momentary oblivion, drops the lacteal fountain, and gives the little squeaking struggler the chance of a momentary mouthful. This miserable little object, which may be seen bringing up the rear of every litter, is called the Tony pig, or the *Anthony;* so named, it is presumed, from being the one always assigned to the Church, when tithe was taken in kind; and as St. Anthony was the patron of husbandry, his name was given in a sort of bitter derision to the starveling that constituted his dues; for whether there are ten or fifteen farrows to the litter, the Anthony is always the last of the family to come into the world.

772. FROM THE GROSSNESS OF HIS FEEDING, the large amount of aliment he consumes, his gluttonous way of eating it, from his slothful habits, laziness, and indulgence in sleep, the pig is particularly liable to disease, and especially indigestion, heartburn, and affections of the skin.

773. TO COUNTERACT THE CONSEQUENCE OF A VIOLATION OF THE PHYSICAL LAWS, a powerful monitor in the brain of the pig teaches him to seek for relief and medicine. To open the pores of his skin, blocked up with mud, and excite perspiration, he resorts to a tree, a stump, or his trough— anything rough and angular, and using it as a curry-comb to his body, obtains the luxury of a scratch and the benefit of cuticular evaporation; he next proceeds with his long supple snout to grub up antiscorbutic roots, cooling salads of mallow and dandelion, and, greatest treat of all, he stumbles on a piece of chalk or a mouthful of delicious cinder, which, he knows by instinct, is the most sovereign remedy in the world for that hot, unpleasant sensation he has had all the morning at his stomach.

774. IT IS A REMARKABLE FACT that, though every one who keeps a pig knows how prone he is to disease, how that disease injures the quality of the meat, and how eagerly he pounces on a bit of coal or cinder, or any coarse dry substance that will adulterate the rich food on which he lives, and by .

affording soda to his system, correct the vitiated fluids of his body,—yet very few have the judgment to act on what they see, and by supplying the pig with a few shovelfuls of cinders in his sty, save the necessity of his rooting for what is so needful to his health. Instead of this, however, and without supplying the animal with what its instinct craves for, his nostril is bored with a red-hot iron, and a ring clinched in his nose to prevent rooting for what he feels to be absolutely necessary for his health; and ignoring the fact that, in a domestic state at least, the pig lives on the richest of all food,—scraps of cooked animal substances, boiled vegetables, bread, and other items, given in that concentrated essence of aliment for a quadruped called wash, and that he eats to repletion, takes no exercise, and finally sleeps all the twenty-four hours he is not eating, and then, when the animal at last seeks for those medicinal aids which would obviate the evil of such a forcing diet, his keeper, instead of meeting his animal instinct by human reason, and giving him what he seeks, has the inhumanity to torture him by a ring, that, keeping up a perpetual "raw" in the pig's snout, prevents his digging for those corrective drugs which would remove the evils of his artificial existence.

775. Though subject to so many Diseases, no domestic animal is more easily kept in health, cleanliness, and comfort, and this without the necessity of "ringing," or any excessive desire of the hog to roam, break through his sty, or plough up his *pound*. Whatever the kind of food may be on which the pig is being fed or fattened, a teaspoonful or more of salt should always be given in his mess of food, and a little heap of well-burnt cinders, with occasional bits of chalk, should always be kept by the side of his trough, as well as a vessel of clean water; his pound, or the front part of his sty, should be totally free from straw, the brick flooring being every day swept out and sprinkled with a layer of sand. His lair, or sleeping apartment, should be well sheltered by roof and sides from cold, wet, and all changes of weather, and the bed made up of a good supply of clean straw, sufficiently deep to enable the pig to burrow his unprotected body beneath it. All the refuse of the garden, in the shape of roots, leaves, and stalks, should be placed in a corner of his pound or feeding-chamber, for the delectation of his leisure moments; and once a week, on the family washing-day, a pail of warm soap-suds should be taken into his sty, and, by means of a scrubbing-brush and soap, his back, shoulders, and flanks should be well cleaned, a pail of clean warm water being thrown over his body at the conclusion, before he is allowed to retreat to his clean straw to dry himself. By this means, the excessive nutrition of his aliment will be corrected, a more perfect digestion insured, and, by opening the pores of the skin, a more vigorous state of health acquired than could have been obtained under any other system.

776. We have already said that no other animal yields man so *many* kinds and varieties of luxurious food as is supplied to him by the flesh of the hog differently prepared; for almost every part of the animal, either fresh,

salted, or dried, is used for food ; and even those viscera not so employed are of the utmost utility in a domestic point of view.

777. THOUGH DESTITUTE OF THE HIDE, HORNS, AND HOOFS, constituting the offal of most domestic animals, tho pig is not behind the other mammalia in its usefulness to man. Its skin, especially that of the boar, from its extreme closeness of texture, when tanned, is employed for the seats of saddles, to cover powder, shot, and drinking-flasks ; and the hair, according to its colour, flexibility, and stubbornness, is manufactured into tooth, nail, and hair-brushes,—others into hat, clothes, and shoe-brushes ; while the longer and finer qualities are made into long and short brooms and painters' brushes ; and a still more rigid description, under the name of "bristles," are used by the shoemaker as needles for the passage of his wax-end. Besides so many bene-fits and useful services conferred on man by this valuable animal, his fat, in a commercial sense, is quite as important as his flesh, and brings a price equal to the best joints in the carcase. This fat is rendered, or melted out of the caul, or membrane in which it is contained, by boiling water, and, while liquid, run into prepared bladders, when, under the name of *lard*, it becomes an article of extensive trade and value.

778. OF THE NUMEROUS VARIETIES OF THE DOMESTICATED HOG, the fol-lowing list of breeds may be accepted as the best, presenting severally all those qualities aimed at in the rearing of domestic stock, as affecting both the breeder and the consumer. *Native*—Berkshire, Essex, York, and Cumber-land ; *Foreign*—the Chinese. Before, however, proceeding with the con-sideration of the different orders, in the series we have placed them, it will be necessary to make a few remarks relative to the pig generally. In the first place, the *Black Pig* is regarded by breeders as the best and most eligible animal, not only from the fineness and delicacy of the skin, but because it is less affected by the heat in summer, and far less subject to cuticular disease than either the white or brindled hog, but more particularly from its kindlier nature and greater aptitude to fatten.

779. THE GREAT QUALITY FIRST SOUGHT FOR IN A HOG is a capacious stomach, and next, a healthy power of digestion ; for the greater the quantity he can eat, and the more rapidly he can digest what he has eaten, the more quickly will he fatten ; and the faster he can be made to increase in flesh, with-out a material increase of bone, the better is the breed considered, and the more valuable the animal. In the usual order of nature, the development of flesh and enlargement of bone proceed together ; but here the object is to outstrip the growth of the bones by the quicker development of their fleshy covering.

780. THE CHIEF POINTS SOUGHT FOR IN THE CHOICE OF A HOG are breadth of chest, depth of carcase, width of loin, chine, and ribs, compactness of form, docility, cheerfulness, and general beauty of appearance. The head

in a well-bred hog must not be too long, the forehead narrow and convex, cheeks full, snout fine, mouth small, eyes small and quick, ears short, thin, and sharp, pendulous, and pointing forwards; neck full and broad, particularly on the top, where it should join very broad shoulders; the ribs, loin, and haunch should be in a uniform line, and the tail well set, neither too high nor too low; at the same time the back is to be straight or slightly curved, the chest deep, broad, and prominent, the legs short and thick; the belly, when well fattened, should nearly touch the ground, the hair be long, thin, fine, and having few bristles, and whatever the colour, uniform, either white, black, or blue; but not spotted, speckled, brindled, or sandy. Such are the features and requisites that, among breeders and judges, constitute the *beau idéal* of a perfect pig.

781. THE BERKSHIRE PIG IS THE BEST KNOWN AND MOST ESTEEMED of all our English domestic breeds, and so highly is it regarded, that even the

BERKSHIRE SOW.

varieties of the stock are in as great estimation as the parent breed itself. The characteristics of the Berkshire hog are that it has a tawny colour, spotted with black, large ears hanging over the eyes, a thick, close, and well-made body, legs short and small in the bone; feeds up to a great weight, fattens quickly, and is good either for pork or bacon. The New or Improved Berkshire possesses all the above qualities, but is infinitely more prone to fatten, while the objectionable colour has been entirely done away with, being now either all white or completely black.

782. NEXT TO THE FORMER, THE ESSEX takes place in public estimation, always competing, and often successfully, with the Berkshire. The peculiar characters of the Essex breed are that it is tip-eared, has a long sharp head, is roach-backed, with a long flat body, standing high on the legs; is rather bare

of hair, is a quick feeder, has an enormous capacity of stomach and belly, and an appetite to match its receiving capability.   Its colour is white, or else black

ESSEX SOW.

and white, and it has a restless habit and an unquiet disposition.   The present valuable stock has sprung from a cross between the common native animal and either the White Chinese or Black Neapolitan breeds,

783. THE YORKSHIRE, CALLED ALSO THE OLD LINCOLNSHIRE, was at one time the largest stock of the pig family in England, and perhaps, at that time, the

YORKSHIRE SOW.

worst.   It was long-legged, weak in the loins, with coarse white curly hair, and flabby flesh.   Now, however, it has undergone as great a change as any breed in the kingdom, and by judicious crossing has become the most valuable we possess, being a very well-formed pig throughout, with a good head, a pleasant docile countenance, with moderate-sized drooping ears, a broad back, slightly curved, large chine and loins, with deep sides, full chest, and well covered with long thickly-set white hairs. Besides these qualities of form, he is a quick grower, feeds fast, and will easily make from 20 to 25 stone before completing his first year. The quality of the meat is also uncommonly good, the fat and lean being laid on in almost equal proportions. So capable is this species of development, both in flesh and stature, that examples of the Yorkshire breed have been exhibited weighing as much as a Scotch ox.

784. THOUGH ALMOST EVERY COUNTY IN ENGLAND can boast some local variety or other of this useful animal, obtained from the native stock by crossing

CUMBERLAND SOW.

with some of the foreign kinds, Cumberland and the north-west parts of the kingdom have been celebrated for a small breed of white pigs, with a thick, compact, and well-made body, short in the legs, the head and back well formed, ears slouching and a little downwards, and on the whole, a hardy, profitable animal, and one well disposed to fatten.

785. THERE IS NO VARIETY OF THIS USEFUL ANIMAL that presents such peculiar features as the species known to us as the Chinese pig; and as it is the general belief that to this animal and the Neapolitan hog we are indebted for that remarkable improvement which has taken place in the breeds of the English pig, it is necessary to be minute in the description of this, in all respects, singular animal. The Chinese, in the first place, consists of many varieties, and presents as many forms of body as differences of colour; the best kind, however, has a beautiful white skin of singular thinness and delicacy; the hair too is perfectly white, and thinly set over the body, with here and there a few

bristles. He has a broad snout, short head, eyes bright and fiery, very small fine pink ears, wide cheeks, high chine, with a neck of such immense thick-

CHINESE SOW.

ness, that when the animal is fat it looks like an elongated carcase,—a mass of fat, without shape or form, like a feather pillow. The belly is dependent, and almost trailing on the ground, the legs very short, and the tail so small as to be little more than a rudiment. It has a ravenous appetite, and will eat anything that the wonderful assimilating powers of its stomach can digest; and to that capability, there seems no limit in the whole range of animal or vegetable nature. The consequence of this perfect and singularly rapid digestion is an unprecedented proneness to obesity, a process of fattening that, once commenced, goes on with such rapid development, that, in a short time, it loses all form, depositing such an amount of fat, that it in fact ceases to have any refuse part or offal, and, beyond the hair on its back and the callous extremity of the snout, *the whole carcase is eatable.*

786. WHEN JUDICIOUSLY FED ON VEGETABLE DIET, and this obese tendency checked, the flesh of the Chinese pig is extremely delicate and delicious; but when left to gorge almost exclusively on animal food, it becomes oily, coarse, and unpleasant. Perhaps there is no other instance in nature where the effect of rapid and perfect digestion is so well shown as in this animal, which thrives on *everything,* and turns to the benefit of its physical economy, food of the most *opposite nature,* and of the most unwholesome and *offensive* character. When fully fattened, the thin cuticle, that is one of its characteristics, cracks, from the adipose distension beneath, exposing the fatty mass, which discharges a liquid oil from the adjacent tissues. The great fault in this breed is the remarkably small quantity of lean laid down, to the immense proportion of fat. Some idea of the growth of this species may be inferred from the fact of their attaining to 18 stone before two years, and when further advanced, as much

as 40 stone.   In its pure state, except for roasters, the Chinese pig is too
disproportionate for the English market ; but when crossed with some of our
lean stock, the breed becomes almost invaluable.

787. THE WILD BOAR is a much more cleanly and sagacious animal than
the domesticated hog ; he is longer in the snout, has his ears shorter and his
tusks considerably longer, very frequently measuring as much as 10 inches.

WESTPHALIAN BOAR.

They are extremely sharp, and are bent in an upward circle.   Unlike his
domestic brother, who roots up here and there, or wherever his fancy takes,
the wild boar ploughs the ground in continuous lines or furrows.   The boar,
when selected as the parent of a stock, should have a small head, be deep and
broad in the chest ; the chine should be arched, the ribs and barrel well
rounded, with the haunches falling full down nearly to the hock ; and he
should always be more compact and smaller than the female.   The colour of
the wild boar is always of a uniform hue, and generally of an iron grey ;
shading off into a black.   The hair of the boar is of considerable length,
especially about the head and mane ; he stands, in general, from 20 to 30
inches in height at the shoulders, though instances have occurred where he
has reached 42 inches.   The young are of a pale yellowish tint, irregularly
brindled with light brown.   The boar of Germany is a large and formidable
animal, and the hunting of him, with a small species of mastiff, is still a
national sport.   From living almost exclusively on acorns and nuts, his flesh
is held in great esteem, and in Westphalia his legs are made into hams by a
process which, it is said, enhances the flavour and quality of the meat in a
remarkable degree.

788. THERE ARE TWO POINTS to be taken into consideration by all breeders
of pigs—to what ultimate use is the flesh to be put ; for, if meant to be eaten

fresh, or simply salted, the *small* breed of pigs is best suited for the purpose ; if for hams or bacon, the large variety of the animal is necessary. Pigs are usually weaned between six and eight weeks after birth, after which they are fed on soft food, such as mashed potatoes in skimmed or butter-milk. The general period at which the small hogs are killed for the market is from 12 to 16 weeks ; from 4 to 5 months, they are called store pigs, and are turned out to graze till the animal has acquired its full stature. As soon as this point has been reached, the pig should be forced to maturity as quickly as possible ; he should therefore be taken from the fields and farm-yard, and shut up on boiled potatoes, buttermilk, and peas-meal, after a time to be followed by grains, oil-cake, wash, barley, and Indian meal ; supplying his sty at the same time with plenty of water, cinders, and a quantity of salt in every mess of food presented to him.

789. THE ESTIMATED NUMBER OF PIGS IN GREAT BRITAIN is supposed to exceed 20 millions ; and, considering the third of the number as worth £2 apiece, and the remaining two-thirds as of the relative value of 10s. each, would give a marketable estimate of over £20,000,000 for this animal alone.

790. THE BEST AND MOST HUMANE MODE OF KILLING ALL LARGE HOGS is to strike them down like a bullock, with the pointed end of a poleaxe, on the forehead, which has the effect of killing the animal at once ; all the butcher has then to do, is to open the aorta and great arteries, and laying the animal's neck over a trough, let out the blood as quickly as possible. The carcase is then to be scalded, either on a board or by immersion in a tub of very hot water, and all the hair and dirt rapidly scraped off, till the skin is made perfectly white, when it is hung up, opened, and dressed, as it is called, in the usual way. It is then allowed to cool, a sheet being thrown around the carcase, to prevent the air from discolouring the newly-cleaned skin. When meant for bacon, the hair is singed instead of being scalded off.

791. IN THE COUNTRY, where for ordinary consumption the pork killed for sale is usually both larger and fatter than that supplied to the London consumer, it is customary to remove the skin and fat down to the lean, and, salting that, roast what remains of the joint. Pork goes further, and is consequently a more economical food than other meats, simply because the texture is closer, and there is less waste in the cooking, either in roasting or boiling.

792. IN FRESH PORK, the leg is the most economical family joint, and the loin the richest.

793. COMPARATIVELY SPEAKING, very little difference exists between the weight of the live and dead pig, and this, simply because there is neither the head nor the hide to be removed. It has been proved that pork loses in cooking 13½ per cent. of its weight. A salted hand weighing 4 lbs. 5 oz. lost in the cooking 11 oz. ; after cooking, the meat weighing only 3 lbs. 1 oz., and the

bone 9 oz. The original cost was $7\frac{1}{2}d$. a pound ; but by this deduction, the cost rose to $9d$. per pound with the bone, and $10\frac{1}{4}d$. without it.

794. PORK, TO BE PRESERVED, is cured in several ways,—either by covering it with salt, or immersing it in ready-made brine, where it is kept till required : or it is only partially salted, and then hung up to dry, when the meat is called white bacon ; or, after salting, it is hung in wood smoke till the flesh is impregnated with the aroma from the wood. The Wiltshire bacon, which is regarded as the finest in the kingdom, is prepared by laying the sides of a hog in large wooden troughs, and then rubbing into the flesh quantities of powdered bay-salt, made hot in a frying-pan. This process is repeated for four days ; they are then left for three weeks, merely turning the flitches every other day. After that time they are hung up to dry. The hogs usually killed for purposes of bacon in England average from 18 to 20 stone ; on the other hand, the hogs killed in the country for farm-house purposes, seldom weigh less than 26 stone. The legs of boars, hogs, and, in Germany, those of bears, are prepared differently, and called hams.

795. THE PRACTICE IN VOGUE FORMERLY in this country was to cut out the hams and cure them separately ; then to remove the ribs, which were roasted as "spare-ribs," and, curing the remainder of the side, call it a "gammon of bacon."

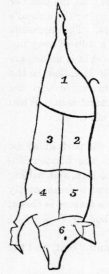

Small pork to cut for table in joints, is cut up, in most places throughout the kingdom, as represented in the engraving. The side is divided with nine ribs to the fore quarter ; and the following is an enumeration of the joints in the two respective quarters :—

HIND QUARTER $\left\{\begin{array}{l} \text{1. The leg.} \\ \text{2. The loin.} \\ \text{3. The spring, or belly.} \end{array}\right.$

FORE QUARTER $\left\{\begin{array}{l} \text{4. The hand.} \\ \text{5. The fore-loin.} \\ \text{6. The cheek.} \end{array}\right.$

The weight of the several joints of a good pork pig of four stone may be as follows ; viz. :—

The leg	8 lbs.
The loin and spring . .	7 ,,
The hand	6 ,,
The chine	7 ,,
The cheek . . from 2 to 3	,,

SIDE OF A PIG, SHOWING THE SEVERAL JOINTS.

Of a bacon pig, the legs are reserved for curing, and when cured are called hams : when the meat is separated from the shoulder-blade and bones and cured, it is called bacon. The bones, with part of the meat left on them, are divided into spare-ribs, griskins, and chines.

RECEIPES.

—◆◇◆—

CHAPTER XVII.

PORK CUTLETS (Cold Meat Cookery).

796. INGREDIENTS.—The remains of cold roast loin of pork, 1 oz. of butter, 2 onions, 1 dessertspoonful of flour, ½ pint of gravy, pepper and salt to taste, 1 teaspoonful of vinegar and mustard.

Mode.—Cut the pork into nice-sized cutlets, trim off most of the fat, and chop the onions. Put the butter into a stewpan, lay in the cutlets and chopped onions, and fry a light brown; then add the remaining ingredients, simmer gently for 5 or 7 minutes, and serve.

Time.—5 to 7 minutes. *Average cost*, exclusive of the meat, 4*d.*

Seasonable from October to March.

AUSTRIAN METHOD OF HERDING PIGS.—In the Austrian empire there are great numbers of wild swine, while, among the wandering tribes peopling the interior of Hungary, and spreading over the vast steppes of that country, droves of swine form a great portion of the wealth of the people, who chiefly live on a coarse bread and wind-dried bacon.

In German Switzerland, the Tyrol, and other mountainous districts of continental Europe, though the inhabitants, almost everywhere, as in England, keep one or more pigs, they are at little or no trouble in feeding them, one or more men being employed by one or several villages as swine-herds; who, at a certain hour, every morning, call for the pig or pigs, and driving them to their feeding-grounds on the mountain-side and in the wood, take custody of the herd till, on the approach of night, they are collected into a compact body and driven home for a night's repose in their several sties.

The amount of intelligence and docility displayed by the pigs in these mountain regions, is much more considerable than that usually allowed to this animal, and the manner in which these immense herds of swine are collected, and again distributed, without an accident or mistake, is a sight both curious and interesting; for it is all done without the assistance of a dog, or the aid even of the human voice, and solely by the crack of the long-lashed and heavily-loaded whip, which the swine-herd carries, and cracks much after the fashion of the French postilion; and which, though he frequently cracks, waking a hundred sharp echoes from the woods and rocks, he seldom has to use correctionally; the animal soon acquiring a thorough knowledge of the meaning of each crack; and once having felt its leaded thong, a lasting remembrance of its power. At early dawn, the swine-herd takes his stand at the outskirts of the first village, and begins flourishing through the misty air his immensely long lash, keeping a sort of rude time with the crack, crack, crack, crack, crack, crack of his whip. The nearest pigs, hearing the well-remembered sound, rouse from their straw, and rush from their sties into the road, followed by all their litters. As soon as a sufficient number are collected, the drove is set in motion, receiving, right and left, as they advance, fresh numbers; whole communities, or solitary individuals, streaming in from all quarters, and taking their place, without distinction, in the general herd; and, as if conscious where their breakfast lay, without wasting a moment on idle investigation, all eagerly push on to the mountains. In this manner village after village is collected, till the drove not unfrequently consists of several thousands. The feeding-ground has, of course, often to be changed, and the drove have sometimes to be driven many miles, and to a considerable height up the mountain, before the whip gives the signal for the dispersion of the body and the order to feed, when the herdsman proceeds to form himself a shelter, and look after his own comfort for the rest of the day. As soon as twilight sets in, the whip is again heard echoing the signal for muster; and in the same order in which they were collected, the swine are driven back, each group tailing off to its respective sty, as the herd approaches the villages, till the last grunter, having found his home, the drover seeks his cottage and repose.

PORK CUTLETS OR CHOPS.

I.

797. INGREDIENTS.—Loin of pork, pepper and salt to taste.

Mode.—Cut the cutlets from a delicate loin of pork, bone and trim them neatly, and cut away the greater portion of the fat. Season them with pepper; place the gridiron on the fire; when quite hot, lay on the chops and broil them for about ¼ hour, turning them 3 or 4 times; and be particular that they are *thoroughly* done, but not dry. Dish them, sprinkle over a little fine salt, and serve plain, or with tomato sauce, sauce piquante, or pickled gherkins, a few of which should be laid round the dish as a garnish.

Time.—About ¼ hour. *Average cost,* 10*d.* per lb. for chops.

Sufficient.—Allow 6 for 4 persons.

Seasonable from October to March.

II.

(*Another Way.*)

798. INGREDIENTS.—Loin, or fore-loin, of pork, egg and bread crumbs, salt and pepper to taste; to every tablespoonful of bread crumbs allow ½ teaspoonful of minced sage; clarified butter.

Mode.—Cut the cutlets from a loin, or fore-loin, of pork; trim them the same as mutton cutlets, and scrape the top part of the bone. Brush them over with egg, sprinkle with bread crumbs, with which have been mixed minced sage and a seasoning of pepper and salt; drop a little clarified butter on them, and press the crumbs well down. Put the frying-pan on the fire, put in some lard; when this is hot, lay in the cutlets, and fry them a light brown on both sides. Take them out, put them before the fire to dry the greasy moisture from them, and dish them on mashed potatoes. Serve with them any sauce that may be preferred; such as tomato sauce, sauce piquante, sauce Robert, or pickled gherkins.

Time.—From 15 to 20 minutes. *Average cost,* 10*d.* per lb. for chops.

Sufficient.—Allow 6 cutlets for 4 persons.

Seasonable from October to March.

Note.—The remains of roast loin of pork may be dressed in the same manner.

PORK CHEESE (an Excellent Breakfast Dish).

799. INGREDIENTS.—2 lbs..of cold roast pork, pepper and salt to taste, 1 dessertspoonful of minced parsley, 4 leaves of sage, a very small bunch of savoury herbs, 2 blades of pounded mace, a little nutmeg, ½ teaspoonful of minced lemon-peel; good strong gravy, sufficient to fill the mould.

Mode.—Cut, but do not chop, the pork into fine pieces, and allow ¼ lb. of fat to each pound of lean. Season with pepper and salt; pound well the spices, and chop finely the parsley, sage, herbs, and lemon-peel, and mix the whole nicely together. Put it into a mould, fill up with good strong well-flavoured gravy, and bake rather more than one hour. When cold, turn it out of the mould.

Time.—Rather more than 1 hour.

Seasonable from October to March.

ROAST LEG OF PORK.

800. INGREDIENTS.—Leg of pork, a little oil for stuffing. (*See* Recipe No. 504.)

Mode.—Choose a small leg of pork, and score the skin across in narrow strips, about ¼ inch apart. Cut a slit in the knuckle, loosen the skin, and fill it with a sage-and-onion stuffing, made by Recipe No. 504. Brush the joint over with a little salad-oil (this makes the crackling crisper, and a better colour), and put it down to a bright, clear fire, not too near,

ROAST LEG OF PORK.

as that would cause the skin to blister. Baste it well, and serve with a little gravy made in the dripping-pan, and do not omit to send to table with it a tureen of well-made apple-sauce. (*See* No. 363.)

Time.—A leg of pork weighing 8 lbs., about 3 hours.

Average cost, 9*d.* per lb.

Sufficient for 6 or 7 persons.

Seasonable from September to March.

ENGLISH MODE OF HUNTING, AND INDIAN PIG-STICKING.—The hunting of the wild boar has been in all times, and in all countries, a pastime of the highest interest and excitement, and from the age of Nimrod, has only been considered second to the more dangerous sport of lion-hunting. The buried treasures of Nineveh, restored to us by Mr. Layard, show us, on their sculptured annals, the kings of Assyria in their royal pastime of boar-hunting. That the Greeks were passionately attached to this sport, we know both from history and the romantic fables of the poets. Marc Antony, at one of his breakfasts with Cleopatra, had *eight wild boars* roasted whole; and though the Romans do not appear to have been addicted to hunting, wild-boar fights formed part of their gladiatorial shows in the amphitheatre. In France, Germany, and Britain, from the earliest time, the boar-hunt formed one of the most exciting of sports; but it was only in this country that the sport was conducted without dogs,—a real hand-to-hand contest of man and beast; the hunter, armed only with a boar-spear, a weapon about four feet long, the ash staff, guarded by plates of steel, and terminating in a long, narrow, and very sharp blade: this, with a hunting-knife, or hanger, completed his offensive arms. Thus equipped, the hunter would either encounter his enemy face to face, confront his desperate charge, as with erect tail, depressed head, and flaming eyes, he rushed with his foamy tusks full against him, who either sought to pierce his vitals through his counter, or driving his spear through his chine, transfix his heart; or failing those more difficult aims, plunge it into his flank, and, without withdrawing the weapon, strike his ready hanger into his throat. But expert as the hunter might be, it was not often the formidable brute was so quickly dispatched; for he would sometimes seize the spear in his powerful teeth, and nip it off like a reed, or, coming full tilt on his enemy, by his momentum and weight bear him to the earth, ripping up, with a horrid gash, his leg or side, and before the writhing hunter could draw his knife, the infuriated beast would plunge his snout in the wound, and rip, with savage teeth, the bowels of his victim. At other times, he would suddenly swerve from his charge, and doubling on his opponent, attack the hunter in the rear. From his speed, great weight, and savage disposition, the wild boar is always a dangerous antagonist, and requires great courage, coolness, and agility on the part of the hunter. The continental sportsman rides to the chase in a cavalcade, with music and dogs,—a kind of small hound or mastiff, and leaving all the honorary part of the contest to them, when the boar is becoming weary, and while beset by the dogs, rides up, and drives his lance home in the beast's back or side. Boar-hunting has been for some centuries obsolete in England, the animal no longer existing in a wild state among us; but in our Indian empire, and especially in Bengal, the pastime is pursued by our countrymen with all the daring of the national character; and as the animal which inhabits the cane-brakes and jungles is a formidable foe, the sport is attended with great excitement. The hunters, mounted on small, active horses, and armed only with long lances, ride, at early daylight, to the skirts of the jungle, and having sent in their attendants to beat the cover, wait till the tusked monster comes crashing from among the canes, when chase is immediately given, till he is come up with, and transfixed by the first weapon. Instead of flight, however, he often turns to bay, and by more than one dead horse and wounded hunter, shows how formidable he is, and what those polished tusks, sharp as pitch-forks, can effect, when the enraged animal defends his life.

TO GLAZE HAM.—(See Recipe No. 430.)

HASHED PORK.

801. INGREDIENTS.—The remains of cold roast pork, 2 onions, 1 teaspoonful of flour, 2 blades of pounded mace, 2 cloves, 1 tablespoonful of vinegar, ½ pint of gravy, pepper and salt to taste.

Mode.—Chop the onions and fry them of a nice brown, cut the pork into thin slices, season them with pepper and salt, and add these to the remaining ingredients. Stew gently for about ½ hour, and serve garnished with sippets of toasted bread.

Time.—½ hour.

Average cost, exclusive of the meat, 3d.

Seasonable from October to March.

FRIED RASHERS OF BACON AND POACHED EGGS.

802. INGREDIENTS.—Bacon; eggs.

Mode.—Cut the bacon into thin slices, trim away the rusty parts, and cut off the rind. Put it into a *cold* frying-pan, that is to say, do not place the pan on the fire before the bacon is in it. Turn it 2 or 3 times, and dish it on a very hot dish. Poach the eggs and slip them on to the bacon without breaking the yolks, and serve quickly.

Time.—3 or 4 minutes. *Average cost*, 10*d*. to 1*s*. per pound for the primest parts.

Sufficient.—Allow 6 eggs for 3 persons.

Seasonable at any time.

Note.—Fried rashers of bacon, curled, serve as a pretty garnish to many dishes; and, for small families, answer very well as a substitute for boiled bacon, to serve with a small dish of poultry, &c.

BROILED RASHERS OF BACON (a Breakfast Dish).

803. Before purchasing bacon, ascertain that it is perfectly free from rust, which may easily be detected by its yellow colour; and for broiling, the streaked part of the thick flank, is generally the most esteemed. Cut it into *thin* slices, take off the rind, and broil over a nice clear fire; turn it 2 or 3 times, and serve very hot. Should there be any cold bacon left from the previous day, it answers very well for breakfast, cut into slices, and broiled or fried.

Time.—3 or 4 minutes.

Average cost, 10*d*. to 1*s*. per pound for the primest parts.

Seasonable at any time.

Note.—When the bacon is cut very thin, the slices may be curled round and fastened by means of small skewers, and fried or toasted before the fire.

BOILED BACON.

804. INGREDIENTS.—Bacon; water.

Mode.—As bacon is frequently excessively salt, let it be soaked in warm water for an hour or two previous to dressing it; then pare off the rusty parts, and scrape the under-side and rind as clean as possible. Put it into a saucepan of cold water, let it come gradually to a boil, and as fast as the scum rises to the surface of the water, remove it.

BOILED BACON.

Let it simmer very gently until it is *thoroughly* done; then take it up, strip off the skin, and sprinkle over the bacon a few bread raspings, and garnish with tufts of cauliflower or Brussels sprouts. When served alone, young and tender broad beans or green peas are the usual accompaniments.

Time.—1 lb. of bacon, ¾ hour; 2 lbs., 1½ hour.

Average cost, 10*d*. to 1*s*. per lb. for the primest parts.

Sufficient.—2 lbs., when served with poultry or veal, sufficient for 10 persons.

Seasonable at any time.

TO CURE BACON IN THE WILTSHIRE WAY.

805. INGREDIENTS.—1½ lb. of coarse sugar, 1½ lb. of bay-salt, 6 oz. of saltpetre, 1 lb. of common salt.

Mode.—Sprinkle each flitch with salt, and let the blood drain off for 24 hours; then pound and mix the above ingredients well together and rub it well into the meat, which should be turned every day for a month; then hang it to dry, and afterwards smoke it for 10 days.

Time.—To remain in the pickle 1 month, to be smoked 10 days.

Sufficient.—The above quantity of salt for 1 pig.

HOW PIGS WERE FORMERLY PASTURED AND FED. — Though unquestionably far greater numbers of swine are now-kept in England than formerly, every peasant having one or more of that useful animal, in feudal times immense droves of pigs were kept by the franklings and barons; in those days the swine-herds being a regular part of the domestic service of every feudal household, their duty consisted in daily driving the herd of swine from the castle-yard, or outlying farm, to the nearest woods, chase, or forest, where the frankling or vavasour had, either by right or grant, what was called *free warren*, or the liberty to feed his hogs off the acorns, beech, and chestnuts that lay in such abundance on the earth, and far exceeded the power of the royal or privileged game to consume. Indeed, it was the license granted the nobles of free warren, especially for their swine, that kept up the iniquitous forest laws to so late a date, and covered so large a portion of the land with such immense tracts of wood and brake, to the injury of agriculture and the misery of the people. Some idea of the extent to which swine were grazed in the feudal times, may be formed by observing the number of pigs still fed in Epping Forest, the Forest of Dean, and the New Forest, in Hampshire, where, for several months of the year, the beech-nuts and acorns yield them so plentiful a diet. In Germany, where the chestnut is so largely cultivated, the amount of food shed every autumn is enormous; and consequently the pig, both wild and domestic, has, for a considerable portion of the year, an unfailing supply of admirable nourishment. Impressed with the value of this fruit for the food of pigs, the Prince Consort has, with great judgment, of late encouraged the collection of chestnuts in Windsor Park, and by giving a small reward to old people and children for every bushel collected, has not only found an occupation for many of the unemployed poor, but, by providing a gratuitous food for their pig, encouraged a feeling of providence and economy.

FOR CURING BACON, AND KEEPING IT FREE FROM RUST (Cobbett's Recipe).

806. THE TWO SIDES THAT REMAIN, and which are called flitches, are to be cured for bacon. They are first rubbed with salt on their insides, or flesh sides, then placed one on the other, the flesh sides uppermost, in a salting-trough which has a gutter round its edges to drain away the brine; for, to have sweet and fine bacon, the flitches must not be sopping in brine, which gives it the sort of vile taste that barrel and sea pork have. Every one knows how different is the taste of fresh dry salt from that of salt in a dissolved state; therefore change the salt often,—once in 4 or 5 days; let it melt and sink in, but not lie too long; twice change the flitches, put that at bottom which was first on the top: this mode will cost you a great deal more in salt than the sopping mode, but without it your bacon will not be so sweet and fine, nor keep so well. As for the time required in making your flitches sufficiently salt, it depends on circumstances. It takes a longer time for a thick than a thin flitch, and longer in dry than in damp weather, or in a dry than in a damp place; but for the flitches of a hog of five score, in weather not very dry or damp, about 6 weeks may do; and as yours is to be fat, which receives little

injury from over-salting, give time enough, for you are to have bacon until Christmas comes again.

807. THE PLACE FOR SALTING SHOULD, like a dairy, always be cool, but well ventilated; confined air, though cool, will taint meat sooner than the mid-day sun accompanied by a breeze. With regard to smoking the bacon, two precautions are necessary: first, to hang the flitches where no rain comes down upon them; and next, that the smoke must proceed from wood, not peat, turf, or coal. As to the time required to smoke a flitch, it depends a good deal upon whether there be a constant fire beneath; and whether the fire be large or small: a month will do, if the fire be pretty constant and rich, as a farm-house fire usually is; but over-smoking, or rather too long hanging in the air, makes the bacon rust; great attention should therefore be paid to this matter. The flitch ought not to be dried up to the hardness of a board, and yet it ought to be perfectly dry. Before you hang it up, lay it on the floor, scatter the flesh side pretty thickly over with bran, or with some fine sawdust, not of deal or fir; rub it on the flesh, or pat it well down upon it: this keeps the smoke from getting into the little openings, and makes a sort of crust to be dried on.

808. TO KEEP THE BACON SWEET AND GOOD, and free from hoppers, sift fine some clean and dry wood ashes. Put some at the bottom of a box or chest long enough to hold a flitch of bacon; lay in one flitch, and then put in more ashes, then another flitch, and cover this with six or eight inches of the ashes. The place where the box or chest is kept ought to be dry, and should the ashes become damp, they should be put in the fireplace to dry, and when cold, put back again. With these precautions, the bacon will be as good at the end of the year as on the first day.

809. FOR SIMPLE GENERAL RULES, these may be safely taken as a guide; and those who implicitly follow the directions given, will possess at the expira-tion of from 6 weeks to 2 months well-flavoured and well-cured bacon.

HOG NOT BACON. ANECDOTE OF LORD BACON.—As Lord Bacon, on one occasion, was about to pass sentence of death upon a man of the name of Hogg, who had just been tried for a long career of crime, the prisoner suddenly claimed to be heard in arrest of judgment, saying, with an expression of arch confidence as he addressed the bench, "I claim indulgence, my lord, on the plea of relationship; for I am convinced your lordship will never be unnatural enough to hang one of your own family."

"Indeed," replied the judge, with some amazement, "I was not aware that I had the honour of your alliance; perhaps you will be good enough to name the degree of our mutual affinity."

"I am sorry, my lord," returned the impudent thief, "I cannot trace the links of consanguinity; but the moral evidence is sufficiently pertinent. My name, my lord, is Hogg, your lordship's is Bacon; and all the world will allow that bacon and hog are very closely allied."

"I am sorry," replied his lordship, "I cannot admit the truth of your instance: hog cannot be bacon till it is hanged; and so, before I can admit your plea, or acknowledge the family compact, Hogg must be hanged to-morrow morning."

TO BAKE A HAM.

810. INGREDIENTS.—Ham; a common crust.

Mode.—As a ham for baking should be well soaked, let it remain in water for at least 12 hours. Wipe it dry, trim away any rusty places underneath, and cover it with a common crust, taking care that this is of sufficient thickness all over to keep the gravy in. Place it in a moderately-heated oven, and bake for nearly 4 hours. Take off the crust, and skin, and cover with raspings, the same as for boiled ham, and garnish the knuckle with a paper frill. This method of cooking a ham is, by many persons, considered far superior to boiling it, as it cuts fuller of gravy and has a finer flavour, besides keeping a much longer time good.

Time.—A medium-sized ham, 4 hours.

Average cost, from 8*d.* to 10*d.* per lb. by the whole ham.

Seasonable all the year.

TO BOIL A HAM.

811. INGREDIENTS.—Ham, water, glaze or raspings.

Mode.—In choosing a ham, ascertain that it is perfectly sweet, by running a sharp knife into it, close to the bone ; and if, when the

BOILED HAM.

knife is withdrawn, it has an agreeable smell, the ham is good ; if, on the contrary, the blade has a greasy appearance and offensive smell, the ham is bad. If it has been long hung, and is very dry and salt, let it remain in soak for 24 hours, changing the water frequently. This length of time is only necessary in the case of its being very hard ; from 8 to 12 hours would be sufficient for a Yorkshire or Westmoreland ham. Wash it thoroughly clean, and trim away from the under-side, all the rusty and smoked parts, which would spoil the appearance. Put it into a boiling-pot, with sufficient cold water to cover it ; bring it gradually to boil, and as the scum rises, carefully remove it. Keep it simmering very gently until tender, and be careful that it does not stop boiling, nor boil too quickly. When done, take it out of the pot, strip off the skin, and sprinkle over it a few fine bread-raspings, put a frill of cut paper round the knuckle, and serve. If to be eaten cold, let the ham remain in the water until nearly cold : by this method the juices are kept in, and it will be found infinitely superior to one taken out of the water hot ; it should, however, be borne in mind that the ham must *not* remain in the saucepan *all* night. When the skin is removed, sprinkle over bread-raspings, or, if wanted particularly nice, glaze it. Place a paper frill round the knuckle, and garnish with parsley or cut vegetable flowers. (*See* Coloured Plate P.)

Time.—A ham weighing 10 lbs., 4 hours to *simmer gently*; 15 lbs.,
5 hours; a very large one, about 6 hours.

Average cost, from 8*d.* to 10*d.* per lb. by the whole ham.

Seasonable all the year.

HOW TO BOIL A HAM TO GIVE IT AN EXCELLENT FLAVOUR.

812. INGREDIENTS.—Vinegar and water, 2 heads of celery, 2 turnips,
3 onions, a large bunch of savoury herbs.

Mode.—Prepare the ham as in the preceding recipe, and let it soak
for a few hours in vinegar and water. Put it on in cold water, and
when it boils, add the vegetables and herbs. Simmer very gently
until tender, take it out, strip off the skin, cover with bread-raspings,
and put a paper ruche or frill round the knuckle.

Time.—A ham weighing 10 lbs., 4 hours.

Average cost, 8*d.* to 10*d.* per lb. by the whole ham.

Seasonable at any time.

HOW TO SILENCE A PIG. ANECDOTE OF CHARLES V.—When the emperor Charles V.
was one day walking in the neighbourhood of Vienna, full of pious considerations,
engendered by the thoughts of the Dominican cloister he was about to visit, he was
much annoyed by the noise of a pig, which a country youth was carrying a little way
before him. At length, irritated by the unmitigated noise, "Have you not learned
how to quiet a pig?" demanded the imperial traveller, tartly.

"Noa," replied the ingenuous peasant, ignorant of the quality of his interrogator;—
"noa; and I should very much like to know how to do it," changing the position
of his burthen, and giving his load a surreptitious pinch of the ear, which immediately
altered the tone and volume of his complaining.

"Why, take the pig by the tail," said the emperor, "and you will see how quiet he
will become."

Struck by the novelty of the suggestion, the countryman at once dangled his noisy
companion by the tail, and soon discovered that, under the partial congestion caused by
its inverted position, the pig had indeed become silent; when, looking with admiration
on his august adviser, he exclaimed,—

"Ah, you must have learned the trade much longer than I, for you understand it a
great deal better."

FRIED HAM AND EGGS (a Breakfast Dish).

813. INGREDIENTS.—Ham; eggs.

Mode.—Cut the ham into slices, and take care that they are of the
same thickness in every part. Cut off the rind, and if the ham should
be particularly hard and salt, it will be found an improvement to
soak it for about 10 minutes in hot water, and then dry it in a cloth.
Put it into a cold frying-pan, set it over the fire, and turn the slices
3 or 4 times whilst they are cooking. When done, place them
on a dish, which should be kept hot in front of the fire during the
time the eggs are being poached. Poach the eggs, slip them on to the
slices of ham, and serve quickly.

Time.—7 or 8 minutes to broil the ham.

Average cost, 8*d*. to 10*d*. per lb. by the whole ham.

Sufficient.—Allow 2 eggs and a slice of ham to each person.

Seasonable at any time.

Note.—Ham may also be toasted or broiled; but, with the latter method, to insure its being well cooked, the fire must be beautifully clear, or it will have a smoky flavour far from agreeable.

POTTED HAM, that will keep Good for some time.

I.

814. INGREDIENTS.—To 4 lbs. of lean ham allow 1 lb. of fat, 2 teaspoonfuls of pounded mace, ½ nutmeg grated, rather more than ½ teaspoonful of cayenne, clarified lard.

Mode.—Mince the ham, fat and lean together in the above proportion, and pound it well in a mortar, seasoning it with cayenne pepper, pounded mace, and nutmeg; put the mixture into a deep baking-dish, and bake for ½ hour; then press it well into a stone jar, fill up the jar with clarified lard, cover it closely, and paste over it a piece of thick paper. If well seasoned, it will keep a long time in winter, and will be found very convenient for sandwiches, &c.

Time.—½ hour.

Seasonable at any time.

II.

(A nice addition to the Breakfast or Luncheon table.)

815. INGREDIENTS.—To 2 lbs. of lean ham allow ½ lb. of fat, 1 teaspoonful of pounded mace, ½ teaspoonful of pounded allspice, ½ nutmeg, pepper to taste, clarified butter.

Mode.—Cut some slices from the remains of a cold ham, mince them small, and to every 2 lbs. of lean, allow the above proportion of fat. Pound the ham in a mortar to a fine paste, with the fat, gradually add the seasoning and spices, and be very particular that all the ingredients are well mixed and the spices well pounded. Press the mixture into potting-pots, pour over clarified butter, and keep it in a cool place.

Average cost for this quantity, 2*s*. 6*d*.

Seasonable at any time.

IMPORTANCE OF THE BOAR'S HEAD, SCOTTISH FEUDS, &c.—The boar's head, in ancient times, formed the most important dish on the table, and was invariably the first placed on the board upon Christmas-day, being preceded by a body of servitors, a flourish of trumpets, and other marks of distinction and reverence, and carried into the hall by the individual of next rank to the lord of the feast. At some of our colleges and inns of court, the serving of the boar's head on a silver platter on Christmas-day is a custom still followed; and till very lately, a boar's head was competed for at Christmas time by the young men of a rural parish in Essex. Indeed, so highly was the grizzly boar's head regarded in former times, that it passed into a cognizance of some of the noblest families in the realm : thus it was not only the crest of the Nevills and Warwicks, with their collateral houses, but it was the cognizance of Richard III., that—

> " Wretched, bloody, and usurping boar,
> That spoil'd your summer fields and fruitful vines,
> Swills your warm blood like wash, and makes his trough
> In your embowell'd bosoms,"—

and whose nature it was supposed to typify; and was universally used as a *sign* to taverns. The Boar's Head in Eastcheap, which, till within the last twenty-five years still stood in all its primitive quaintness, though removed to make way for the London-bridge approaches, will live vividly in the mind of every reader of Shakspeare, as the resort of the prince of Wales, Poins, and his companions, and the residence of Falstaff and his coney-catching knaves, Bardolph, Pistol, and Nym; and whose sign was a boar's head, carved in stone over the door, and a smaller one in wood on each side of the doorway.

The traditions and deeds of savage vengeance recorded in connection with this grim trophy of the chase are numerous in all parts of Europe. But the most remarkable connected with the subject in this country, were two events that occurred in Scotland, about the 11th and 15th centuries.

A border family having been dispossessed of their castle and lands by a more powerful chief, were reduced for many years to great indigence, the expelled owner only living in the hope of wreaking a terrible vengeance, which, agreeably to the motto of his house, he was content to " bide his time" for. The usurper having invited a large number of his kindred to a grand hunt in his new domains, and a feast after in the great hall, returned from the chase, and discovering the feast not spread, vented his wrath in no measured terms on the heads of the tardy servitors. At length a menial approached, followed by a line of servants, and placing the boar's head on the table, the guests rushed forward to begin the meal; when, to their horror, they discovered, not a boar's but a bull's head,—a sign of death. The doors were immediately closed, and the false servants, who were the adherents of the dispossessed chief, threw off their disguise, and falling on the usurper and his friends, butchered them and every soul in the castle belonging to the rival faction.

A tribe of caterans, or mountain robbers, in the Western Highlands, having been greatly persecuted by a powerful chief of the district, waylaid him and his retinue, put them all to the sword, and cutting off the chief's head, repaired to his castle, where they ordered the terrified wife to supply them with food and drink. To appease their savage humour, the lady gave order for their entertainment, and on returning to the hall to see her orders were complied with, discovered, in place of the boar's head that should have graced the board, her husband's bleeding head : the savage caterans, in rude derision, as a substitute for the apple or lemon usually placed between the jaws, having thrust a slice of bread in the dead man's mouth.

FOR CURING HAMS (Mons. Ude's Recipe).

816. INGREDIENTS.—For 2 hams weighing about 16 or 18 lbs. each, allow 1 lb. of moist sugar, 1 lb. of common salt, 2 oz. of saltpetre, 1 quart of good vinegar.

Mode.—As soon as the pig is cold enough to be cut up, take the 2 hams and rub them well with common salt, and leave them in a large pan for 3 days. When the salt has drawn out all the blood, drain the hams, and throw the brine away. Mix sugar, salt, and saltpetre together in the above proportion, rub the hams well with these, and put them into a vessel large enough to hold them, always keeping the salt over them. Let them remain for 3 days, then pour over them a quart of good vinegar. Turn them in the brine every day for a month, then drain them well, and rub them with bran. Have them smoked over a wood fire, and be particular that the hams are hung as high up as possible from the fire; otherwise the fat will melt, and they will become dry and hard.

Time.—To be pickled 1 month ; to be smoked 1 month.

Sufficient for 2 hams of 18 lbs. each.

Seasonable from October to March.

THE PRICE OF A SOW IN AFRICA.—In one of the native states of Africa, a pig one day stole a piece of food from a child as it was in the act of conveying the morsel to its mouth ; upon which the robbed child cried so loud that the mother rushed out of her hovel to ascertain the cause ; and seeing the purloining pig make off munching his booty, the woman in her heat struck the grunter so smart a blow, that the surly rascal took it into his head to go home very much indisposed, and after a certain time resolved to die,—a resolution that he accordingly put into practice ; upon which the owner instituted judicial proceedings before the Star Chamber court of his tribe, against the husband and family of the woman whose rash act had led to such results ; and as the pig happened to be a *sow*, in the very flower of her age, the prospective loss to the owner in unnumbered teems of pigs, with the expenses attending so high a tribunal, swelled the damages and costs to such a sum, that it was found impossible to pay them. And as, in the barbarous justice existing among these rude people, every member of a family is equally liable as the individual who committed the wrong, the father, mother, children, relatives,—an entire community, to the number of *thirty-two souls*, were sold as slaves, and a fearful sum of human misery perpetrated, to pay the value of a thieving old sow.

TO SALT TWO HAMS, about 12 or 15 lbs. each.

817. INGREDIENTS.—2 lbs. of treacle, $\frac{1}{2}$ lb. of saltpetre, 1 lb. of bay-salt, 2 pounds of common salt.

Mode.—Two days before they are put into pickle, rub the hams well with salt, to draw away all slime and blood. Throw what comes from them away, and then rub them with treacle, saltpetre, and salt. Lay them in a deep pan, and let them remain one day; boil the above proportion of treacle, saltpetre, bay-salt, and common salt for $\frac{1}{4}$ hour, and pour this pickle boiling hot over the hams: there should be sufficient of it to cover them. For a day or two rub them well with it ; afterwards they will only require turning. They ought to remain in this pickle for 3 weeks or a month, and then be sent to be smoked, which will take nearly or quite a month to do. An ox-tongue pickled in this way is most excellent, to be eaten either green or smoked.

Time.—To remain in the pickle 3 weeks or a month ; to be smoked about a month.

Seasonable from October to March.

TO CURE SWEET HAMS IN THE WESTMORELAND WAY.

818. INGREDIENTS.—3 lbs. of common salt, 3 lbs. of coarse sugar, 1 lb. of bay-salt, 3 quarts of strong beer.

Mode.—Before the hams are put into pickle, rub them the preceding day well with salt, and drain the brine well from them. Put the above ingredients into a saucepan, and boil for $\frac{1}{4}$ hour; pour over the hams, and let them remain a month in the pickle. Rub and turn them every day, but do not take them out of the pickling-pan ; and have them smoked for a month.

Time.—To be pickled 1 month ; to be smoked 1 month.

Seasonable from October to March.

TO PICKLE HAMS (Suffolk Recipe).

819. INGREDIENTS.—To a ham from 10 to 12 lbs., allow 1 lb. of coarse sugar, $\frac{3}{4}$ lb. of salt, 1 oz. of saltpetre, $\frac{1}{2}$ a teacupful of vinegar.

Mode.—Rub the hams well with common salt, and leave them for a day or two to drain; then rub well in, the above proportion of sugar, salt, saltpetre, and vinegar, and turn them every other day. Keep them in the pickle 1 month, drain them, and send them to be smoked over a wood fire for 3 weeks or a month.

Time.—To remain in the pickle 1 month. To be smoked 3 weeks or 1 month.

Sufficient.—The above proportion of pickle sufficient for 1 ham.

Seasonable.—Hams should be pickled from October to March.

NOVEL WAY OF RECOVERING A STOLEN PIG.—It is a well-known fact, that in Ireland the pig is, in *every* respect, a domesticated animal, sharing often both the bed and the board of the family, and making an outer ring to the domestic circle, as, seated round the pot of potatoes, they partake of the midday meal called dinner. An Irishman upon one occasion having lost an interesting member of his household, in the form of a promising young porker, consulted his priest on the occasion, and having hinted at the person he suspected of purloining the "illegant slip of a pig," he was advised to take no further notice of the matter, but leave the issue to his spiritual adviser. Next Sunday his reverence, after mass, came to the front of the altar-rails, and looking very hard at the supposed culprit, exclaimed, "Who stole Pat Doolan's pig?" To this inquiry there was of course no answer;—the priest did not expect there would be any. The following Sunday the same query was propounded a little stronger—"Who of you was it, I say, who stole *poor* Pat Doolan's pig?" It now became evident that the culprit was a hardened sinner; so on the third Sunday, instead of repeating the unsatisfactory inquiry, the priest, after, as usual, eyeing the obdurate offender, said, in a tone of pious sorrow, "Mike Regan, Mike Regan, you treat me with contempt!" That night, when the family was all asleep, the latch of the door was noiselessly lifted, and the "illegant slip of a pig" cautiously slipped into the cabin.

TO SMOKE HAMS AND FISH AT HOME.

820. Take an old hogshead, stop up all the crevices, and fix a place to put a cross-stick near the bottom, to hang the articles to be smoked on. Next, in the side, cut a hole near the top, to introduce an iron pan filled with sawdust and small pieces of green wood. Having turned the tub upside down, hang the articles upon the cross-stick, introduce the iron pan in the opening, and place a piece of red-hot iron in the pan, cover it with sawdust, and all will be complete. Let a large ham remain 40 hours, and keep up a good smoke.

TO CURE BACON OR HAMS IN THE DEVONSHIRE WAY.

821. INGREDIENTS.—To every 14 lbs. of meat, allow 2 oz. of saltpetre, 2 oz. of salt prunella, 1 lb. of common salt. For the pickle, 3 gallons of water, 5 lbs. of common salt, 7 lbs. of coarse sugar, 3 lbs. of bay-salt.

Mode.—Weigh the sides, hams, and cheeks, and to every 14 lbs. allow the above proportion of saltpetre, salt prunella, and common salt. Pound and mix these together, and rub well into the meat; lay it in a stone trough or tub, rubbing it thoroughly, and turning it daily for 2 successive days. At the end of the second day, pour on it a pickle made as follows :—Put the above ingredients into a saucepan, set it on the fire, and stir frequently; remove all the scum, allow it to boil for $\frac{1}{4}$ hour, and pour it hot over the meat. Let the hams, &c., be well rubbed and turned daily; if the meat is small, a fortnight will be sufficient for the sides and shoulders to remain in the pickle, and the hams 3 weeks; if from 30 lbs. and upwards, 3 weeks will be required for the sides, &c., and from 4 to 5 weeks for the hams. On taking the pieces out, let them drain for an hour, cover with dry sawdust, and smoke from a fortnight to 3 weeks. Boil and carefully skim the pickle after using, and it will keep good, closely corked, for 2 years. When boiling it for use, add about 2 lbs. of common salt, and the same of treacle, to allow for waste. Tongues are excellent put into this pickle cold, having been first rubbed well with saltpetre and salt, and allowed to remain 24 hours, not forgetting to make a deep incision under the thick part of the tongue, so as to allow the pickle to penetrate more readily. A fortnight or 3 weeks, according to the size of the tongue, will be sufficient.

Time.—Small meat to remain in the pickle a fortnight, hams 3 weeks; to be smoked from a fortnight to 3 weeks.

The following is from Morton's " Cyclopædia of Agriculture," and will be found fully worthy of the high character of that publication.

CURING OF HAMS AND BACON.

822. The carcass of the hog, after hanging over-night to cool, is laid on a strong bench or stool, and the head is separated from the body at the neck, close behind the ears; the feet and also the internal fat are removed. The carcass is next divided into two sides in the following manner :—The ribs are divided about an inch from the spine on each side, and the spine, with the ends of the ribs attached, together with the internal flesh between it and the kidneys, and also the flesh above it, throughout the whole length of the sides, are removed. The portion of the carcass thus cut out is in the form of a wedge—the breadth of the interior consisting of the breadth of the spine, and about an inch of the ribs on each side, being diminished to about half an inch at the exterior or skin along the back. The breast-bone, and also the first anterior rib, are also dissected from the side. Sometimes the whole of the ribs are removed; but this, for reasons afterwards to be noticed, is a very bad practice. When the hams are cured separately from the sides, which is generally the case, they are cut out so as to include the hock-bone, in a similar manner to the London mode of cutting a haunch of mutton. The carcass of the hog thus cut up is ready for being salted, which process, in large curing establishments, is generally as

follows. The skin side of the pork is rubbed over with a mixture of fifty parts by weight of salt, and one part of saltpetre in powder and the incised parts of the ham or flitch, and the inside of the flitch covered with the same. The salted bacon, in pairs of flitches with the insides to each other, is piled one pair of flitches above another on benches slightly inclined, and furnished with spouts or troughs to convey the brine to receivers in the floor of the salting-house, to be afterwards used for pickling pork for navy purposes. In this state the bacon remains a fortnight, which is sufficient for flitches cut from hogs of a carcass weight less than 15 stone (14 lbs. to the stone). Flitches of a larger size, at the expiration of that time, are wiped dry and reversed in their place in the pile, having, at the same time, about half the first quantity of fresh, dry, common salt sprinkled over the inside and incised parts; after which they remain on the benches for another week. Hams being thicker than flitches, will require, when less than 20 lbs. weight, 3 weeks; and when above that weight, 4 weeks to remain under the above-described process. The next and last process in the preparation of bacon and hams, previous to being sent to market, is drying. This is effected by hanging the flitches and hams for 2 or 3 weeks in a room heated by stoves, or in a smoke-house, in which they are exposed for the same length of time to the smoke arising from the slow combustion of the sawdust of oak or other hard wood. The latter mode of completing the curing process has some advantages over the other, as by it the meat is subject to the action of *creosote*, a volatile oil produced by the combustion of the sawdust, which is powerfully antiseptic. The process also furnishing a thin covering of a resinous varnish, excludes the air not only from the muscle but also from the fat; thus effectually preventing the meat from becoming rusted; and the principal reasons for condemning the practice of removing the ribs from the flitches of pork are, that by so doing the meat becomes unpleasantly hard and pungent in the process of salting, and by being more opposed to the action of the air, becomes sooner and more extensively rusted. Notwithstanding its superior efficacy in completing the process of curing, the flavour which smoke-drying imparts to meat is disliked by many persons, and it is therefore by no means the most general mode of drying adopted by mercantile curers. A very impure variety of *pyroligneous* acid, or vinegar made from the destructive distillation of wood, is sometimes used, on account of the highly preservative power of the creosote which it contains, and also to impart the smoke-flavour; in which latter object, however, the coarse flavour of tar is given, rather than that derived from the smoke from combustion of wood. A considerable portion of the bacon and hams salted in Ireland is exported from that country packed amongst salt, in bales, immediately from the salting process, without having been in any degree dried. In the process of salting above described, pork loses from eight to ten per cent. of its weight, according to the size and quality of the meat; and a further diminution of weight, to the extent of five to six per cent., takes place in drying during the first fortnight after being taken out of salt; so that the total loss in weight occasioned by the preparation of bacon and hams in a proper state for market, is not less on an average than fifteen per cent. on the weight of the fresh pork.

COLLARED PIG'S FACE (a Breakfast or Luncheon Dish).

823. INGREDIENTS.—1 pig's face; salt. For brine, 1 gallon of spring water, 1 lb. of common salt, ½ handful of chopped juniper-berries, 6 bruised cloves, 2 bay-leaves, a few sprigs of thyme, basil, sage, ¼ oz. of saltpetre. For forcemeat, ½ lb. of ham, ½ lb. bacon, 1 teaspoonful of mixed spices, pepper to taste, ¼ lb. of lard, 1 tablespoonful of minced parsley, 6 young onions.

Mode.—Singe the head carefully, bone it without breaking the skin, and rub it well with salt. Make the brine by boiling the above ingre-

PIG'S FACE.

dients for ¼ hour, and letting it stand to cool. When cold, pour it over the head, and let it steep in this for 10 days, turning and rubbing it often. Then wipe, drain, and dry it. For the forcemeat, pound the ham and bacon very finely, and mix with these the remaining ingredients, taking care that the whole is thoroughly incorporated. Spread this equally over the head, roll it tightly in a cloth, and bind it securely with broad tape. Put it into a saucepan with a few meat trimmings, and cover it with stock; let it simmer gently for 4 hours, and be particular that it does not stop boiling the whole time. When quite tender, take it up, put it between 2 dishes with a heavy weight on the top, and when cold, remove the cloth and tape. It should be sent to table on a napkin, or garnished with a piece of deep white paper with a ruche at the top.

Time.—4 hours. *Average cost*, from 2s. to 2s. 6d.

Seasonable from October to March.

THE WILD AND DOMESTIC HOG.—The domestic hog is the descendant of a race long since banished from this island; and it is remarkable, that while the tamed animal has been and is kept under surveillance, the wild type whence this race sprung, has maintained itself in its ancient freedom, the fierce denizen of the forest, and one of the renowned beasts of the chase. Whatever doubt may exist as to the true origin of the dog, the horse, the ox, and others, or as to whether their original race is yet extant or not, these doubts do not apply to the domestic hog. Its wild source still exists, and is universally recognized: like the wolf, however, it has been expelled from our island; but, like that animal, it still roams through the vast wooded tracts of Europe and Asia.

TO DRESS PIG'S FRY (a Savoury Dish).

824. INGREDIENTS.—1½ lb. of pig's fry, 2 onions, a few sage-leaves, 3 lbs. of potatoes, pepper and salt to taste.

Mode.—Put the lean fry at the bottom of a pie-dish, sprinkle over it some minced sage and onion, and a seasoning of pepper and salt; slice the potatoes; put a layer of these on the seasoning, then the fat fry, then more seasoning, and a layer of potatoes at the top. Fill the dish with boiling water, and bake for 2 hours, or rather longer.

Time.—Rather more than 2 hours. *Average cost*, 6*d*. per lb.
Sufficient for 3 or 4 persons.
Seasonable from October to March.

TO MELT LARD.

825. Melt the inner fat of the pig, by putting it in a stone jar, and
placing this in a saucepan of boiling water, previously stripping off
the skin. Let it simmer gently over a bright fire, and as it melts, pour
it carefully from the sediment. Put it into small jars or bladders for
use, and keep it in a cool place. The flead or inside fat of the pig,
before it is melted, makes exceedingly light crust, and is particularly
wholesome. It may be preserved a length of time by salting it well,
and occasionally changing the brine. When wanted for use, wash
and wipe it, and it will answer for making into paste as well as
fresh lard.

Average cost, 10*d*. per lb.

BOILED LEG OF PORK.

826. INGREDIENTS.—Leg of pork; salt.
Mode.—For boiling, choose a small, compact, well-filled leg, and rub
it well with salt; let it remain in pickle for a week or ten days, turning
and rubbing it every day. An hour before dressing it, put it into
cold water for an hour, which improves the colour. If the pork is
purchased ready salted, ascertain how long the meat has been in
pickle, and soak it accordingly. Put it into a boiling-pot, with sufficient cold water to cover it; let it gradually come to a boil, and remove
the scum as it rises. Simmer it very gently until tender, and do
not allow it to boil fast, or the knuckle will fall to pieces before the
middle of the leg is done. Carrots, turnips, or parsnips may be boiled
with the pork, some of which should be laid round the dish as a garnish,
and a well-made pease-pudding is an indispensable accompaniment.

Time.—A leg of pork weighing 8 lbs., 3 hours after the water boils,
and to be simmered very gently.

Average cost, 9*d*. per lb.

Sufficient for 7 or 8 persons. *Seasonable* from September to March.

Note.—The liquor in which a leg of pork has been boiled, makes excellent
pea-soup.

ANTIQUITY OF THE HOG.—The hog has survived changes which have swept multitudes
of pachydermatous animals from the surface of our earth. It still presents the same
characteristics, both physical and moral, which the earliest writers, whether sacred or pro-
fane, have faithfully delineated. Although the domestic has been more or less modified by
long culture, yet the wild species remains unaltered, insomuch that the fossil relics may
be identified with the bones of their existing descendants.

ROAST GRISKIN OF PORK.

827. INGREDIENTS.—Pork; a little powdered sage.

Mode.—As this joint frequently comes to table hard and dry, particular care should be taken that it is well basted. Put it down to a bright

SPARE-RIB OF PORK.

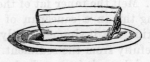

GRISKIN OF PORK.

fire, and flour it. About 10 minutes before taking it up, sprinkle over some powdered sage; make a little gravy in the dripping-pan, strain it over the meat, and serve with a tureen of apple sauce. This joint will be done in far less time than when the skin is left on, consequently, should have the greatest attention that it be not dried up.

Time.—Griskin of pork weighing 6 lbs., 1½ hour.

Average cost, 7*d.* per lb. *Sufficient* for 5 or 6 persons.

Seasonable from September to March.

Note.—A spare-rib of pork is roasted in the same manner as above, and would take 1½ hour for one weighing about 6 lbs.

LARDING.

828. INGREDIENTS.—Bacon and larding-needle.

Mode.—Bacon for larding should be firm and fat, and ought to be cured without any saltpetre, as this reddens white meats. Lay it on

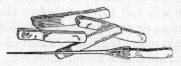

BACON FOR LARDING, AND
LARDING-NEEDLE.

a table, the rinds downwards; trim off any rusty part, and cut it into slices of an equal thickness. Place the slices one on the top of another, and cut them evenly into narrow strips, so arranging it that every piece of bacon is of the same size. Bacon for fricandeaux, poultry, and game, should be about 2 inches in length, and rather more than one-eighth of an inch in width. If for larding fillets of beef or loin of veal, the pieces of bacon must be thicker. The following recipe of Soyer is, we think, very explicit; and any cook, by following the directions here given, may be able to lard, if not well, sufficiently for general use.

"Have the fricandeau trimmed, lay it, lengthwise, upon a clean napkin across your hand, forming a kind of bridge with your thumb at the part you are about to commence at; then with the point of the larding-needle make three distinct lines across, $\frac{1}{2}$ inch apart; run the needle into the third line, at the further side of the fricandeau, and bring it out at the first, placing one of the lardoons in it; draw the needle through, leaving out $\frac{1}{4}$ inch of the bacon at each line; proceed thus to the end of the row; then make another line, $\frac{1}{2}$ inch distant, stick in another row of lardoons, bringing them out at the second line, leaving the ends of the bacon out all the same length; make the next row again at the same distance, bringing the ends out between the lardoons of the first row, proceeding in this manner until the whole surface is larded in chequered rows. Everything else is larded in a similar way; and, in the case of poultry, hold the breast over a charcoal fire for one minute, or dip it into boiling water, in order to make the flesh firm."

ROAST LOIN OF PORK.

829. INGREDIENTS.—Pork; a little salt.

Mode.—Score the skin in strips rather more than $\frac{1}{4}$ inch apart, and place the joint at a good distance from the fire, on account of the

FORE LOIN OF PORK.

HIND LOIN OF PORK.

crackling, which would harden before the meat would be heated through, were it placed too near. If very lean, it should be rubbed over with a little salad oil, and kept well basted all the time it is at the fire. Pork should be very thoroughly cooked, but not dry; and be careful never to send it to table the least underdone, as nothing is more unwholesome and disagreeable than underdressed white meats. Serve with apple sauce, No. 363, and a little gravy made in the dripping-pan. A stuffing of sage and onion may be made separately, and baked in a flat dish: this method is better than putting it in the meat, as many persons have so great an objection to the flavour.

Time.—A loin of pork weighing 5 lbs., about 2 hours: allow more time should it be very fat.

Average cost, 9d. per lb.

Sufficient for 5 or 6 persons.

Seasonable from September to March.

FOSSIL REMAINS OF THE HOG.—In British strata, the oldest fossil remains of the hog which Professor Owen states that he has examined, were from fissures in the red crag (probably miocene) of Newbourne, near Woodbridge, Suffolk. "They were associated with teeth of an extinct *felis* about the size of a leopard, with those of a bear, and with remains of a large cervus. These mammalian remains were found with the ordinary fossils of the red crag: they had undergone the same process of trituration, and were impregnated with the same colouring matter as the associated bones and teeth of fishes acknowledged to be derived from the regular strata of the red crag. These mammaliferous beds have been proved by Mr. Lyell to be older than the fluvio-marine, or Norwich crag, in which remains of the mastodon, rhinoceros, and horse have been discovered; and still older than the fresh-water pleistocene deposits, from which the remains of the mammoth, rhinoceros, &c. are obtained in such abundance. I have met," says the professor, in addition, " with some satisfactory instances of the association of fossil remains of a species of hog with those of the mammoth, in the newer pliocene fresh-water formations of England."

TO DRY PIGS' CHEEKS.

830. INGREDIENTS.—Salt, ½ oz. of saltpetre, 2 oz. of bay-salt, 4 oz. of coarse sugar.

Mode.—Cut out the snout, remove the brains, and split the head, taking off the upper bone to make the jowl a good shape; rub it well with salt; next day take away the brine, and salt it again the following day; cover the head with saltpetre, bay-salt, and coarse sugar, in the above proportion, adding a little common salt. Let the head be often turned, and when it has been in the pickle for 10 days, smoke it for a week or rather longer.

Time.—To remain in the pickle 10 days; to be smoked 1 week.

Seasonable.—Should be made from September to March.

Note.—A pig's cheek, or Bath chap, will take about 2 hours after the water boils.

PIG'S LIVER (a Savoury and Economical Dish).

831. INGREDIENTS.—The liver and lights of a pig, 6 or 7 slices of bacon, potatoes, 1 large bunch of parsley, 2 onions, 2 sage-leaves, pepper and salt to taste, a little broth or water.

Mode.—Slice the liver and lights, and wash these perfectly clean, and parboil the potatoes; mince the parsley and sage, and chop the onion rather small. Put the meat, potatoes, and bacon into a deep tin dish, in alternate layers, with a sprinkling of the herbs, and a seasoning of pepper and salt between each; pour on a little water or broth, and bake in a moderately-heated oven for 2 hours.

Time.—2 hours. *Average cost*, 1s. 6d.

Sufficient for 6 or 7 persons.

Seasonable from September to March.

PIG'S PETTITOES.

832. INGREDIENTS.—A thin slice of bacon, 1 onion, 1 blade of mace, 6 peppercorns, 3 or 4 sprigs of thyme, 1 pint of gravy, pepper and salt to taste, thickening of butter and flour.

Mode.—Put the liver, heart, and pettitoes into a stewpan with the bacon, mace, peppercorns, thyme, onion, and gravy, and simmer these gently for ¼ hour; then take out the heart and liver, and mince them very fine. Keep stewing the feet until quite tender, which will be in from 20 minutes to ½ hour, reckoning from the time that they boiled up first; then put back the minced liver, thicken the gravy with a little butter and flour, season with pepper and salt, and simmer over a gentle fire for 5 minutes, occasionally stirring the contents. Dish the mince, split the feet, and arrange them round alternately with sippets of toasted bread, and pour the gravy in the middle.

Time.—Altogether 40 minutes.

Sufficient for 3 or 4 persons.

Seasonable from September to March.

TO PICKLE PORK.

833. INGREDIENTS.—¼ lb. of saltpetre; salt.

Mode.—As pork does not keep long without being salted, cut it into pieces of a suitable size as soon as the pig is cold. Rub the pieces of pork well with salt, and put them into a pan with a sprinkling of it between each piece : as it melts on the top, strew on more. Lay a coarse cloth over the pan, a board over that, and a weight on the board, to keep the pork down in the brine. If excluded from the air, it will continue good for nearly 2 years.

Average cost, 10*d.* per lb. for the prime parts.

Seasonable.—The best time for pickling meat is late in the autumn,

THE UNIVERSALITY OF THE HOG. — A singular circumstance in the domestic history of the hog, is the extent of its distribution over the surface of the earth; being found even in insulated places, where the inhabitants are semi-barbarous, and where the wild species is entirely unknown. The South-Sea islands, for example, were found on their discovery to be well stocked with a small black hog; and the traditionary belief of the people was that these animals were coeval with the origin of themselves. Yet they possessed no knowledge of the wild boar, or any other animal of the hog kind, from which the domestic breed might be supposed to be derived. In these islands the hog is the principal quadruped, and the fruit of the bread-tree is its principal food, although it is also fed with yams, eddoes, and other vegetables. This nutritious diet, which it has in great abundance, is, according to Foster, the reason of its flesh being so delicious, so full of juice, and so rich in fat, which is not less delicate to the taste than the finest butter.

TO BOIL PICKLED PORK.

834. INGREDIENTS.—Pork ; water.

Mode.—Should the pork be very salt, let it remain in water about 2 hours before it is dressed; put it into a saucepan with sufficient cold water to cover it, let it gradually come to a boil, then gently simmer until quite tender. Allow ample time for it to cook, as nothing is more disagreeable than underdone pork, and when boiled fast, the meat becomes hard. This is sometimes served with boiled poultry

and roast veal, instead of bacon : when tender, and not over salt, it
will be found equally good.

Time.—A piece of pickled pork weighing 2 lbs., 1¼ hour ; 4 lbs.,
rather more than 2 hours.

Average cost, 10*d.* per lb. for the primest parts.

Seasonable at any time.

THE ANTIQUITY OF THE HOG.—By what nation and in what period the hog was
reclaimed, is involved in the deepest obscurity. So far back as we have any records of
history, we find notices of this animal, and of its flesh being used as the food of man.
By some nations, however, its flesh was denounced as unclean, and therefore prohibited
to be used, whilst by others it was esteemed as a great delicacy. By the Mosaic law it
was forbidden to be eaten by the Jews, and the Mahometans hold it in utter abhorrence.   Dr. Kitto, however, says that there does not appear to be any reason in the law
of Moses why the hog should be held in such peculiar abomination.   There seems
nothing to have prevented the Jews, if they had been so inclined, to rear pigs for sale,
or for the use of the land.   In the Talmud there are some indications that this was
actually done ; and it was, probably, for such purposes that the herds of swine mentioned
in the New Testament were kept, although it is usual to consider that they were kept by
the foreign settlers in the land.   Indeed, the story which accounts for the peculiar
aversion of the Hebrews to the hog, assumes that it did not originate until about 130
years before Christ, and that, previously, some Jews were in the habit of rearing hogs
for the purposes indicated.

PORK PIES (Warwickshire Recipe).

835. INGREDIENTS.—For the crust, 5 lbs. of lard to 14 lbs. of flour,
milk, and water. For filling the pies, to every 3 lbs. of meat allow
1 oz. of salt, 2¼ oz. of pepper, a small quantity of cayenne, 1 pint of
water.

Mode.—Rub into the flour a portion of the lard ; the remainder put
with sufficient milk and water to mix the crust, and boil this gently
for ¼ hour. Pour it boiling on the flour, and knead and beat it till
perfectly smooth. Now raise the crust in either a round or oval form,
cut up the pork into pieces the size of a nut, season it in the above
proportion, and press it compactly into the pie, in alternate layers of
fat and lean, and pour in a small quantity of water ; lay on the lid,
cut the edges smoothly round, and pinch them together. Bake in a
brick oven, which should be slow, as the meat is very solid. Very
frequently, the inexperienced cook finds much difficulty in raising the
crust. She should bear in mind that it must not be allowed to get
cold, or it will fall immediately : to prevent this, the operation should
be performed as near the fire as possible. As considerable dexterity
and expertness are necessary to raise the crust with the hand only,
a glass bottle or small jar may be placed in the middle of the paste,
and the crust moulded on this ; but be particular that it is kept warm
the whole time.

Sufficient.—The proportions for 1 pie are 1 lb. of flour and 3 lbs. of
meat.

Seasonable from September to March.

THE FLESH OF SWINE IN HOT CLIMATES.—It is observed by M. Sonini, that the flesh of swine, in hot climates, is considered unwholesome, and therefore may account for its proscription by the legislators and priests of the East. In Egypt, Syria, and even the southern parts of Greece, although both white and delicate, it is so flabby and surcharged with fat, that it disagrees with the strongest stomachs. Abstinence from it in general was, therefore, indispensable to health under the burning suns of Egypt and Arabia. The Egyptians were permitted to eat it only once a year,—on the feast of the moon; and then they sacrificed a number of these animals to that planet. At other seasons, should any one even touch a hog, he was obliged immediately to plunge into the river Nile, as he stood, with his clothes on, in order to purify himself from the supposed contamination he had contracted by the touch.

LITTLE RAISED PORK PIES.

836. INGREDIENTS.—2 lbs. of flour, $\frac{1}{2}$ lb. of butter, $\frac{1}{2}$ lb. of mutton suet, salt and white pepper to taste, 4 lbs. of the neck of pork, 1 dessertspoonful of powdered sage.

Mode.—Well dry the flour, mince the suet, and put these with the butter into a saucepan, to be made hot, and add a little salt. When melted, mix it up into a stiff paste, and put it before the fire with a cloth over it until ready to make up; chop the pork into small pieces, season it with white pepper, salt, and powdered sage; divide the paste into rather small pieces, raise it in a round or oval form, fill with the meat, and bake in a brick oven. These pies will require a fiercer oven than those in the preceding recipe, as they are made so much smaller, and consequently do not require so soaking a heat.

Time.—If made small, about $1\frac{1}{2}$ hour.

Seasonable from September to March.

SWINEHERDS OF ANTIQUITY.—From the prejudice against the hog among the ancients, those who tended them formed an isolated class, and were esteemed as the outcasts of society. However much the flesh of the animal was esteemed by the Greeks and Romans, yet the swineherd is not mentioned by either the classic writers or the poets who, in ancient Greece and Rome, painted rural life. We have no descriptions of gods or heroes descending to the occupation of keeping swine. The swineherd is never introduced into the idyls of Theocritus, nor has Virgil admitted him into his eclogues. The Eumæus of Homer is the only exception that we have of a swineherd meeting with favour in the eyes of a poet of antiquity. This may be accounted for, on the supposition that the prejudices of the Egyptians relative to this class of men, extended to both Greece and Italy, and imparted a bias to popular opinion.

TO MAKE SAUSAGES.
(*Author's Oxford Recipe.*)

837. INGREDIENTS.—1 lb. of pork, fat and lean, without skin or gristle; 1 lb. of lean veal, 1 lb. of beef suet, $\frac{1}{2}$ lb. of bread crumbs, the rind of $\frac{1}{2}$ lemon, 1 small nutmeg, 6 sage-leaves, 1 teaspoonful of pepper, 2 teaspoonfuls of salt, $\frac{1}{2}$ teaspoonful of savory, $\frac{1}{2}$ teaspoonful of marjoram.

Mode.—Chop the pork, veal, and suet finely together, add the bread crumbs, lemon-peel (which should be well minced), and a small nutmeg grated. Wash and chop the sage-leaves very finely; add these with the remaining ingredients to the sausage-meat, and when thoroughly mixed, either put the meat into skins, or, when wanted for table, form it into little cakes, which should be floured and fried.

Average cost, for this quantity, 2s. 6d.

Sufficient for about 30 moderate-sized sausages.

Seasonable from October to March.

THE HOG IN ENGLAND.—From time immemorial, in England, this animal has been esteemed as of the highest importance. In the Anglo-Saxon period, vast herds of swine were tended by men, who watched over their safety, and who collected them under shelter at night. At that time, the flesh of the animal was the staple article of consumption in every family, and a large portion of the wealth of the rich freemen of the country consisted of these animals. Hence it was common to make bequests of swine, with lands for their support; and to these were attached rights and privileges in connection with their feeding, and the extent of woodland to be occupied by a given number was granted in accordance with established rules. This is proved by an ancient Saxon grant, quoted by Sharon Turner, in his "History of the Anglo-Saxons," where the right of pasturage is conveyed in a deed by the following words:—"I give food for seventy swine in that woody allotment which the countrymen call Wolferdinlegh."

FRIED SAUSAGES.

838. INGREDIENTS.—Sausages; a small piece of butter.

Mode.—Prick the sausages with a fork (this prevents them from bursting), and put them into a frying-pan with a small piece of butter.

Keep moving the pan about, and turn the sausages 3 or 4 times. In from 10 to 12 minutes they will be sufficiently cooked, unless they are *very large*, when a little more time should be allowed for them.

FRIED SAUSAGES.

Dish them with or without a piece of toast under them, and serve very hot. In some counties, sausages are boiled and served on toast. They should be plunged into boiling water, and simmered for about 10 or 12 minutes.

Time.—10 to 12 minutes. *Average cost*, 10d. per lb.

Seasonable.—Good from September to March.

Note.—Sometimes, in close warm weather, sausages very soon turn sour; to prevent this, put them in the oven for a few minutes with a small piece of butter to keep them moist. When wanted for table, they will not require so long frying as uncooked sausages.

THE SAXON SWINEHERD.—The men employed in herding swine during the Anglo-Saxon period of our history were, in general, thralls or born slaves of the soil, who were assisted by powerful dogs, capable even of singly contending with the wolf until his master came with his spear to the rescue. In the "Ivanhoe" of Sir Walter Scott, we have an admirable picture, in the character of Gurth, an Anglo-Saxon swineherd, as we also have of his master, a large landed proprietor, a great portion of whose wealth consisted of swine, and whose rude but plentiful board was liberally supplied with the flesh.

SAUSAGE-MEAT CAKES.

839. INGREDIENTS.—To every lb. of lean pork, add ¾ lb. of fat bacon,

½ oz. of salt, 1 saltspoonful of pepper, ¼ teaspoonful of grated nutmeg, 1 teaspoonful of minced parsley.

Mode.—Remove from the pork all skin, gristle, and bone, and chop it finely with the bacon; add the remaining ingredients, and carefully mix altogether. Pound it well in a mortar, make it into convenient-sized cakes, flour these, and fry them a nice brown for about 10 minutes. This is a very simple method of making sausage-meat, and on trial will prove very good, its great recommendation being, that it is so easily made.

Time.—10 minutes.

Seasonable from September to March.

TO SCALD A SUCKING-PIG.

840. Put the pig into cold water directly it is killed; let it remain for a few minutes, then immerse it in a large pan of boiling water for 2 minutes. Take it out, lay it on a table, and pull off the hair as quickly as possible. When the skin looks clean, make a slit down the belly, take out the entrails, well clean the nostrils and ears, wash the pig in cold water, and wipe it thoroughly dry. Take off the feet at the first joint, and loosen and leave sufficient skin to turn neatly over. If not to be dressed immediately, fold it in a wet cloth to keep it from the air.

THE LEARNED PIG.—That the pig is capable of education, is a fact long known to the world; and though, like the ass, naturally stubborn and obstinate, that he is equally amenable with other animals to caresses and kindness, has been shown from very remote time; the best modern evidence of his docility, however, is the instance of the learned pig, first exhibited about a century since, but which has been continued down to our own time by repeated instances of an animal who will put together all the letters or figures that compose the day, month, hour, and date of the exhibition, besides many other unquestioned evidences of memory. The instance already given of breaking a sow into a pointer, till she became more stanch even than the dog itself, though surprising, is far less wonderful than that evidence of education where so generally obtuse an animal may be taught not only to spell, but couple figures and give dates correctly.

ROAST SUCKING-PIG.

841. INGREDIENTS.—Pig, 6 oz. of bread crumbs, 16 sage-leaves, pepper and salt to taste, a piece of butter the size of an egg, salad oil or butter to baste with, about ½ pint of gravy, 1 tablespoonful of lemon-juice.

Mode.—A sucking-pig, to be eaten in perfection, should not be more than three weeks old, and should be dressed the same day that it is killed. After preparing the pig for cooking, as in the preceding recipe, stuff it with finely-grated bread crumbs, minced sage, pepper, salt, and a piece of butter the size of an egg, all of which should be well mixed together, and put into the body of the pig. Sew up the slit neatly, and truss the legs back, to allow the inside to be roasted, and the under part to be crisp. Put the pig down to a bright clear fire, not too near, and let it lay till thoroughly dry ; then have ready

some butter tied up in a piece of thin cloth, and rub the pig with this in every part. Keep it well rubbed with the butter the whole of the time it is roasting, and do not allow the crackling to become blistered or burnt. When half-done, hang a pig-iron before the middle part (if

ROAST SUCKING-PIG.

this is not obtainable, use a flat iron), to prevent its being scorched and dried up before the ends are done. Before it is taken from the fire, cut off the head, and part that and the body down the middle. Chop the brains and mix them with the stuffing ; add $\frac{1}{2}$ pint of good gravy, a tablespoonful of lemon-juice, and the gravy that flowed from the pig ; put a little of this on the dish with the pig, and the remainder send to table in a tureen. Place the pig back to back in the dish, with one half of the head on each side, and one of the ears at each end, and send it to table as hot as possible. Instead of butter, many cooks take salad oil for basting, which makes the crackling *crisp ;* and as this is one of the principal things to be considered, perhaps it is desirable to use it ; but be particular that it is very pure, or it will impart an unpleasant flavour to the meat. The brains and stuffing may be stirred into a tureen of melted butter instead of gravy, when the latter is not liked. Apple sauce and the old-fashioned currant sauce are not yet quite obsolete as an accompaniment to roast pig.

Time.—1½ to 2 hours for a small pig. *Average cost, 5s.* to 6*s.*

Sufficient for 9 or 10 persons.

Seasonable from September to February.

How Roast Pig was discovered.—Charles Lamb, who, in the early part of this century, delighted the reading public by his quaint prose sketches, written under the title of "Essays of Elia," has, in his own quiet humorous way, devoted one paper to the subject of *Roast Pig,* and more especially to that luxurious and toothsome dainty known as "crackling ;" and shows, in a manner peculiarly his own, *how crackling first came into the world.*

According to this erudite authority, man in the golden age, or at all events the primitive age, eat his pork and bacon raw, as, indeed, he did his beef and mutton ; unless, as Hudibras tells us, he was an epicure, when he used to make a saddle of his saddle of mutton, and after spreading it on his horse's back, and riding on it for a few hours till thoroughly warmed, he sat down to the luxury of a dish cooked to a turn. At the epoch of the story, however, a citizen of some Scythian community had the misfortune to have his hut, or that portion of it containing his live stock of pigs, burnt down. In going over the *débris* on the following day, and picking out all the available salvage, the proprietor touched something unusually or unexpectedly hot, which caused him to shake his hand with great energy, and clap the tips of his suffering fingers to his mouth. The act was simple and natural, but the result was wonderful. He rolled his eyes in ecstatic pleasure, his frame distended, and, conscious of a celestial odour, his nostrils widened, and, while drawing in deep inspirations of the ravishing perfume, he sucked his fingers with a gusto he had never, in his most hungry moments, conceived. Clearing away the rubbish from beneath him, he at last brought to view the carcase of one of his pigs, *roasted to death.* Stooping down to examine this curious object, and touching its body, a fragment of the burnt skin was detached, which, with a sort of superstitious dread, he at length, and in a spirit of philosophical inquiry, put into his mouth. Ye gods! the felicity he then enjoyed, no pen can chronicle! Then it was that he—the world—first tasted *crackling.* Like a miser with his gold, the Scythian hid his treasure from the prying eyes of the world, and feasted, in secret, more sumptuously than the gods. When he had eaten up all his pig, the poor man fell into a melancholy ; he refused the most tempting steak, though cooked on the horse's back, and turned every half-hour after his own favourite recipe ; he fell, in fact, from his appetite, and was reduced to a shadow, till, unable longer to endure the torments of memory he hourly suffered, he rose one night and secretly set fire to his hut, and once more was restored to flesh and manhood. Finding it impossible to live in future without roast-pig, he set fire to his house every time his larder became empty ; till at last his neighbours, scandalized by the frequency of these incendiary acts, brought his conduct before the supreme council of the nation. To avert the penalty that awaited him, he brought his judges to the smouldering ruins, and discovering the secret, invited them to eat ; which having done, with tears of gratitude, the august synod embraced him, and, with an overflowing feeling of ecstasy, dedicated a statue to the memory of the man who first *instituted roast pork.*

PORK CARVING.

SUCKING-PIG.

842. A sucking-pig seems, at first sight, rather an elaborate dish, or rather animal, to carve ; but by carefully mastering the details of the business, every difficulty will vanish ; and if a partial failure be at first made, yet all embarrassment will quickly disappear on a second trial. A sucking-pig is usually sent to table in the manner shown in the engraving (and also in coloured plate S), and the first point to be attended to is to

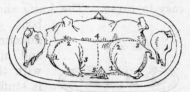

SUCKING-PIG.

separate the shoulder from the carcase, by carrying the knife quickly and neatly round the circular line, as shown by the figures 1, 2, 3 ;—the shoulder will then easily come away. The next step is to take off the leg ; and this is done in the same way, by cutting round this joint in the direction shown by the figures 1, 2, 3, in the same way as the shoulder. The ribs then stand fairly open to the knife, which should be carried down in the direction of the line 4 to 5 ; and two or three helpings will dispose of these. The other half of the pig is served, of course, in the same manner. Different parts of the pig are variously esteemed ; some preferring the flesh of the neck ; others, the ribs ; and others, again, the shoulders. The truth is, the whole of a sucking-pig is delicious, delicate eating ; but, in carving it, the host should consult the various tastes and fancies of his guests, keeping the larger joints, generally, for the gentlemen of the party.

H A M.

843. In cutting a ham, the carver must be guided according as he desires to practise economy, or have, at once, fine slices out of the prime

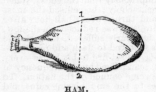

HAM.

part. Under the first supposition, he will commence at the knuckle end, and cut off thin slices towards the thick part of the ham. To reach the choicer portion, the knife, which must be very sharp and thin, should be carried quite down to the bone, in the direction of the line 1 to 2. The slices should be thin and even, and always cut down to the bone. There are some who like to carve a ham by cutting a hole at the top, and then slicing pieces off inside the hole, gradually enlarging the circle; but we think this a plan not to be recommended. A ham, when hot, is usually sent to table with a paper ruffle round the knuckle.

LEG OF PORK.

844. This joint, which is such a favourite one with many people, is easy to carve. The knife should be carried sharply down to the

LEG OF PORK.

bone, clean through the crackling, in the direction of the line 1 to 2. Sage and onion and apple sauce are usually sent to table with this dish,—sometimes the leg of pork is stuffed,—and the guests should be asked if they will have either or both. A frequent plan, and we think a good one, is now pursued, of sending sage and onion to table separately from the joint, as it is not everybody to whom the flavour of this stuffing is agreeable.

Note.—The other dishes of pork do not call for any special remarks as to their carving or helping.

CHAPTER XVIII.

GENERAL OBSERVATIONS ON THE CALF.

845. ANY REMARKS MADE ON THE CALF OR THE LAMB must naturally be in a measure supplementary to the more copious observations made on the parent stock of either. As the calf, at least as far as it is identified with veal, is destined to die young,—to be, indeed, cut off in its comparative infancy,—it may, at first sight, appear of little or no consequence to inquire to what particular variety, or breed of the general stock, his sire or dam may belong. The great art, however, in the modern science of husbandry has been to obtain an animal that shall not only have the utmost beauty of form of which the species is capable, but, at the same time, a constitution free from all taint, a frame that shall rapidly attain bulk and stature, and a disposition so kindly that every *quantum* of food it takes shall, without drawback or procrastination, be eliminated into fat and muscle. The breed, then, is of very considerable consequence in determining, not only the quality of the meat to the consumer, but its commercial value to the breeder and butcher.

846. UNDER THE ARTIFICIAL SYSTEM adopted in the rearing of domestic cattle, and stock in general, to gratify the arbitrary mandates of luxury and fashion, we can have veal, like lamb, at all seasons in the market, though the usual time in the metropolis for veal to make its appearance is about the beginning of February.

847. THE COW GOES WITH YOUNG FOR NINE MONTHS, and the affection and solicitude she evinces for her offspring is more human in its tenderness and intensity than is displayed by any other animal; and her distress when she hears its bleating, and is not allowed to reach it with her distended udders, is often painful to witness, and when the calf has died, or been accidentally killed, her grief frequently makes her refuse to give down her milk. At such times, the breeder has adopted the expedient of flaying the dead carcase, and, distending the skin with hay, lays the effigy before her, and then taking advantage of her solicitude, milks her while she is caressing the skin with her tongue.

848. IN A STATE OF NATURE, the cow, like the deer, hides her young in the tall ferns and brakes, and the most secret places ; and only at stated times, twice or thrice a day, quits the herd, and, hastening to the secret cover, gives suck to her calf, and with the same circumspection returns to the community.

849. IN SOME COUNTRIES, to please the epicurean taste of vitiated appetites, it is the custom to kill the calf for food almost immediately after birth, and any accident that forestalls that event, is considered to enhance its value. We are happy to say, however, that in this country, as far as England and Scotland are concerned, the taste for very young veal has entirely gone out, and "Staggering Bob," as the poor little animal was called in the language of the shambles, is no longer to be met with in such a place.

850. THE WEANING OF CALVES is a process that requires a great amount of care and judgment; for though they are in reality not weaned till between the eighth and the twelfth week, the process of rearing them by hand commences in fact from the birth, the calf never being allowed to suck its dam. As the rearing of calves for the market is a very important and lucrative business, the breeder generally arranges his stock so that ten or a dozen of his cows shall calve about the same time ; and then, by setting aside one or two, to find food for the entire family, gets the remaining eight or ten with their full fountains of milk, to carry on the operations of his dairy. Some people have an idea that skimmed milk, if given in sufficient quantity, is good enough for the weaning period of calf-feeding; but this is a very serious mistake, for the cream, of which it has been deprived, contained nearly all the oleaginous principles, and the azote or nitrogen, on which the vivifying properties of that fluid depends. Indeed, so remarkably correct has this fact proved to be, that a calf reared on one part of new milk mixed with five of water, will thrive and look well ; while another, treated with unlimited skimmed milk, will be poor, thin, and miserable.

851. IT IS SOMETIMES A MATTER OF CONSIDERABLE TROUBLE to induce the blundering calf—whose instinct only teaches him to suck, and that he will do at anything, and with anything—to acquire the knowledge of imbibition, that

for the first few days it is often necessary to fill a bottle with milk, and, opening his mouth, pour the contents down his throat. The manner, however, by which he is finally educated into the mystery of suction, is by putting his allowance of milk into a large wooden bowl; the nurse then puts her hand into the milk, and, by bending her fingers upwards, makes a rude teat for the calf to grasp in his lips, when the vacuum caused by his suction of the fingers, causes the milk to rise along them into his mouth. In this manner one by one the whole family are to be fed three times a day; care being taken, that new-born calves are not, at first, fed on milk from a cow who has some days calved.

852. AS THE CALF PROGRESSES TOWARDS HIS TENTH WEEK, his diet requires to be increased in quantity and quality; for these objects, his milk can be thickened with flour or meal, and small pieces of softened oil-cake are to be slipped into his mouth after sucking, that they may dissolve there, till he grows familiar with, and to like the taste, when it may be softened and scraped down into his milk-and-water. After a time, sliced turnips softened by steam are to be given to him in tolerable quantities; then succulent grasses; and finally, hay may be added to the others. Some farmers, desirous of rendering their calves fat for the butcher in as short a time as possible, forget both the natural weakness of the digestive powers, and the contracted volume of the stomach, and allow the animals either to suck *ad libitum*, or give them, if brought up at the pail or by hand, a larger quantity of milk than they can digest. The idea of overloading the stomach never suggests itself to their minds. They suppose that the more food the young creature consumes, the sooner it will be fat, and they allow it no exercise whatever, for fear it should denude its very bones of their flesh. Under such circumstances, the stomach soon becomes deranged; its functions are no longer capable of acting; the milk, subjected to the acid of the stomach, coagulates, and forms a hardened mass of curd, when the muscles become affected with spasms, and death frequently ensues.

853. THERE WAS NO SPECIES OF SLAUGHTERING practised in this country so inhuman and disgraceful as that, till very lately, employed in killing this poor animal; when, under the plea of making the flesh *white*, the calf was bled day by day, till, when the final hour came, the animal was unable to stand. This inhumanity is, we believe, now everywhere abolished, and the calf is at once killed, and with the least amount of pain; a sharp-pointed knife is run through the neck, severing all the large veins and arteries up to the vertebræ. The skin is then taken off to the knee, which is disjointed, and to the head, which is removed; it is then reflected backwards, and the carcase having been opened and dressed, is kept apart by stretchers, and the thin membrane, the caul, extended over the organs left in the carcase, as the kidneys and sweetbread; some melted fat is then scattered suddenly over the whole interior, giving that white and frosted appearance to the meat, that is thought to add to its beauty; the whole is then hung up to cool and harden.

854. THE MANNER OF CUTTING UP VEAL for the English market is to divide the carcase into four quarters, with eleven ribs to each fore quarter; which are again subdivided into joints as exemplified on the cut.

Hind quarter:—

1. The loin.
2. The chump, consisting of the rump and hock-bone.
3. The fillet.
4. The hock, or hind knuckle.

Fore quarter:—

5. The shoulder.
6. The neck.
7. The breast.
8. The fore knuckle.

SIDE OF A CALF, SHOWING
THE SEVERAL JOINTS.

855. THE SEVERAL PARTS OF A MODERATELY-SIZED WELL-FED CALF, about eight weeks old, are nearly of the following weights:—loin and chump 18 lbs., fillet 12½ lbs., hind knuckle 5½ lbs., shoulder 11 lbs., neck 11 lbs., breast 9 lbs., and fore knuckle 5 lbs.; making a total of 144 lbs. weight. The London mode of cutting the carcase is considered better than that pursued in Edinburgh, as giving three roasting joints, and one boiling, in each quarter; besides the pieces being more equally divided, as regards flesh, and from the handsomer appearance they make on the table.

RECIPES.

——◆◇◆——

CHAPTER XIX.

BAKED VEAL (Cold Meat Cookery).

856. INGREDIENTS.—½ lb. of cold roast veal, a few slices of bacon, 1 pint of bread crumbs, ½ pint of good veal gravy, ½ teaspoonful of minced lemon-peel, 1 blade of pounded mace, cayenne and salt to taste, 4 eggs.

Mode.—Mince finely the veal and bacon; add the bread crumbs, gravy, and seasoning, and stir these ingredients well together. Beat up the eggs thoroughly; add these, mix the whole well together, put into a dish, and bake from ¾ to 1 hour. When liked, a little good gravy may be served in a tureen as an accompaniment.

Time.—From ¾ to 1 hour.

Average cost, exclusive of the cold meat, 6*d.*

Sufficient for 3 or 4 persons.

Seasonable from March to October.

ROAST BREAST OF VEAL.

857. INGREDIENTS.—Veal; a little flour.

Mode.—Wash the veal, well wipe it, and dredge it with flour; put it down to a bright fire, not too near, as it should not be scorched. Baste it plentifully until done; dish it, pour over the meat some good melted butter, and send to table with it a piece of boiled bacon and a cut lemon.

BREAST OF VEAL.

Time.—From 1½ to 2 hours.

Average cost, 8½*d.* per lb.   *Sufficient* for 5 or 6 persons.

Seasonable from March to October.

STEWED BREAST OF VEAL AND PEAS.

858. INGREDIENTS.—Breast of veal, 2 oz. of butter, a bunch of savoury herbs, including parsley ; 2 blades of pounded mace, 2 cloves, 5 or 6 young onions, 1 strip of lemon-peel, 6 allspice, ¼ teaspoonful of pepper, 1 teaspoonful of salt, thickening of butter and flour, 2 tablespoonfuls of sherry, 2 tablespoonfuls of tomato sauce, 1 tablespoonful of lemon-juice, 2 tablespoonfuls of mushroom ketchup, green peas.

Mode.—Cut the breast in half, after removing the bone underneath, and divide the meat into convenient-sized pieces. Put the butter into a frying-pan, lay in the pieces of veal, and fry until of a nice brown colour. Now place these in a stewpan with the herbs, mace, cloves, onions, lemon-peel, allspice, and seasoning ; pour over them just sufficient boiling water to cover the meat ; well close the lid, and let the whole simmer very gently for about 2 hours. Strain off as much gravy as is required, thicken it with butter and flour, add the remaining ingredients, skim well, let it simmer for about 10 minutes, then pour it over the meat. Have ready some green peas, boiled separately ; sprinkle these over the veal, and serve. It may be garnished with forcemeat balls, or rashers of bacon curled and fried. Instead of cutting up the meat, many persons prefer it dressed whole ;—in that case it should be half-roasted before the water, &c. are put to it.

Time.—2¼ hours. *Average cost,* 8½d. per lb.

Sufficient for 5 or 6 persons.

Seasonable from March to October.

BREEDING OF CALVES.—The forwarding of calves to maturity, whether intended to be reared for stock, or brought to an early market as veal, is always a subject of great importance, and requires a considerable amount of intelligence in the selection of the best course, to adopt for either end. When meant to be reared as stock, the breeding should be so arranged that the cow shall calve about the middle of May. As our subject, however, has more immediate reference to the calf as *meat* than as *stock*, we shall confine our remarks to the mode of procedure adopted in the former case ; and here, the first process adopted is that of weaning; which consists in separating the calf *entirely* from the cow, but, at the same time, rearing it on the mother's milk. As the business of the dairy would be suspended if every cow were allowed to rear its young, and butter, cheese, and cream become *desiderata*,—things to be desired, but not possessed, a system of economical husbandry becomes necessary, so as to retain our dairy produce, and yet, for some weeks at least, nourish the calf on its mother's milk, but without allowing the animal to draw that supply for itself : this, with the proper substituted food on which to rear the young animal, is called weaning.

VEAL CAKE (a Convenient Dish for a Picnic).

859. INGREDIENTS.—A few slices of cold roast veal, a few slices of cold ham, 2 hard-boiled eggs, 2 tablespoonfuls of minced parsley, a little pepper, good gravy.

Mode.—Cut off all the brown outside from the veal, and cut the eggs into slices. Procure a pretty mould ; lay veal, ham, eggs, and parsley in layers, with a little pepper between each, and when the mould is full, get some *strong* stock, and fill up the shape. Bake for ½ hour, and when cold, turn it out.

Time.—½ hour.

Seasonable at any time.

BOILED CALF'S FEET AND PARSLEY AND BUTTER.

860. INGREDIENTS.—2 calf's feet, 2 slices of bacon, 2 oz. of butter, 2 tablespoonfuls of lemon-juice, salt and whole pepper to taste, 1 onion, a bunch of savoury herbs, 4 cloves, 1 blade of mace, water, parsley and butter No. 493.

Mode.—Procure 2 white calf's feet; bone them as far as the first joint, and put them into warm water to soak for 2 hours. Then put the bacon, butter, lemon-juice, onion, herbs, spices, and seasoning into a stewpan; lay in the feet, and pour in just sufficient water to cover the whole. Stew gently for about 3 hours; take out the feet, dish them, and cover with parsley and butter, made by recipe No. 493. The liquor they were boiled in should be strained and put by in a clean basin for use: it will be found very good as an addition to gravies, &c. &c.

Time.—Rather more than 3 hours.

Average cost, in full season, 9*d.* each.   *Sufficient* for 4 persons.

Seasonable from March to October.

WHEN A CALF SHOULD BE KILLED.—The age at which a calf ought to be killed should not be under four weeks : before that time the flesh is certainly not wholesome, wanting firmness, due development of muscular fibre, and those animal juices on which the flavour and nutritive properties of the flesh depend, whatever the unhealthy palate of epicures may deem to the contrary. In France, a law exists to prevent the slaughtering of calves under *six weeks* of age. The calf is considered in prime condition at ten weeks, when he will weigh from sixteen to eighteen stone, and sometimes even twenty.

FRICASSEED CALF'S FEET.

861. INGREDIENTS.—A set of calf's feet; for the batter allow for each egg 1 tablespoonful of flour, 1 tablespoonful of bread crumbs, hot lard or clarified dripping, pepper and salt to taste.

Mode.—If the feet are purchased uncleaned, dip them into warm water repeatedly, and scrape off the hair, first one foot and then the other, until the skin looks perfectly clean, a saucepan of water being kept by the fire until they are finished. After washing and soaking in cold water, boil them in just sufficient water to cover them, until the bones come easily away. Then pick them out, and after straining the liquor into a clean vessel, put the meat into a pie-dish until the next day. Now cut it down in slices about ½ inch thick, lay on them a stiff batter made of egg, flour, and bread crumbs in the above proportion ; season with pepper and salt, and plunge them into a pan of boiling lard.   Fry the slices a nice brown, dry them before the fire for a minute or two, dish them on a napkin, and garnish with tufts of parsley.   This should be eaten with melted butter, mustard, and vinegar.   Be careful to have the lard boiling to *set* the batter, or the pieces of feet will run about the pan.   The liquor they were boiled in should be saved, and will be found useful for enriching gravies, making jellies, &c. &c.

Time.—About 3 hours to stew the feet, 10 or 15 minutes to fry them.

Average cost, in full season, 9*d.* each.

Sufficient for 8 persons.

Seasonable from March to October.

Note.—This dish can be highly recommended to delicate persons.

COLOUR OF VEAL.—As whiteness of flesh is considered a great advantage in veal, butchers, in the selection of their calves, are in the habit of examining the inside of its mouth, and noting the colour of the calf's eyes ; alleging that, from the signs they there see, they can prognosticate whether the veal will be white or florid.

COLLARED CALF'S HEAD.

862. INGREDIENTS.—A calf's head, 4 tablespoonfuls of minced parsley, 4 blades of pounded mace, ½ teaspoonful of grated nutmeg, white pepper to taste, a few thick slices of ham, the yolks of 6 eggs boiled hard.

Mode.—Scald the head for a few minutes ; take it out of the water, and with a blunt knife scrape off all the hair.   Clean it nicely, divide the head and remove the brains.   Boil it tender enough to take out the bones, which will be in about 2 hours.   When the head is boned, flatten it on the table, sprinkle over it a thick layer of parsley, then a layer of ham, and then the yolks of the eggs cut into thin rings and put a seasoning of pounded mace, nutmeg, and white pepper between each layer ; roll the head up in a cloth, and tie it up as tightly as possible.   Boil it for 4 hours, and when it is taken out of the pot, place a heavy weight on the top, the same as for other collars. Let it remain till cold ; then remove the cloth and binding, and it will be ready to serve.

Time.—Altogether 6 hours.   *Average cost, 5s.* to *7s.* each.

Seasonable from March to October.

FEEDING A CALF.—The amount of milk necessary for a calf for some time, will be about four quarts a day, though, after the first fortnight, that quantity should be gradually increased, according to its development of body, when, if fed exclusively on milk, as much as three gallons a day will be requisite for the due health and requirements of the animal. If the weather is fine and genial, it should be turned into an orchard or small paddock for a few hours each day, to give it an opportunity to acquire a relish for the fresh pasture, which, by the tenth or twelfth week, it will begin to nibble and enjoy. After a certain time, the quantity of milk may be diminished, and its place supplied by water thickened with meal. Hay-tea and linseed-jelly are also highly nutritious substances, and may be used either as adjuncts or substitutes.

FRICASSEED CALF'S HEAD (an Entree).

863. INGREDIENTS.—The remains of a boiled calf's head, 1½ pint of the liquor in which the head was boiled, 1 blade of pounded mace, 1 onion minced, a bunch of savoury herbs, salt and white pepper to taste, thickening of butter and flour, the yolks of 2 eggs, 1 tablespoonful of lemon-juice, forcemeat balls.

Mode.—Remove all the bones from the head, and cut the meat into nice square pieces. Put 1½ pint of the liquor it was boiled in into a saucepan, with mace, onion, herbs, and seasoning in the above proportion; let this simmer gently for ¾ hour, then strain it and put in the meat. When quite hot through, thicken the gravy with a little butter rolled in flour, and, just before dishing the fricassee, put in the beaten yolks of eggs and lemon-juice; but be particular, after these two latter ingredients are added, that the sauce does not boil, or it will curdle. Garnish with forcemeat balls and curled slices of broiled bacon. To insure the sauce being smooth, it is a good plan to dish the meat first, and then to add the eggs to the gravy: when these are set, the sauce may be poured over the meat.

Time.—Altogether, 1¼ hour.

Average cost, exclusive of the meat, 6d.

CALF'S HEAD a la Maître d'Hotel.

864. INGREDIENTS.—The remains of a cold calf's head, rather more than ½ pint of Maître d'hôtel sauce No. 466.

Mode.—Make the sauce by recipe No. 466, and have it sufficiently thick that it may nicely cover the meat; remove the bones from the head, and cut the meat into neat slices. When the sauce is ready, lay in the meat; let it *gradually* warm through, and, after it boils up, let it simmer very gently for 5 minutes, and serve.

Time.—Rather more than 1½ hour.

Average cost, exclusive of the meat, 1s. 2d.

Seasonable from March to October.

THE CALF IN AMERICA.—In America, the calf is left with the mother for three or four days, when it is removed, and at once fed on barley and oats ground together and made into a gruel, 1 quart of the meal being boiled for half an hour in 12 quarts of water. One quart of this certainly nutritious gruel, is to be given, lukewarm, morning and evening. In ten days, a bundle of soft hay is put beside the calf, which he soon begins to eat, and, at the same time, some of the dry meal is placed in his manger for him to lick. This process, gradually increasing the quantity of gruel twice a day, is continued for two months, till the calf is fit to go to grass, and, as it is said, with the best possible success. But, in this country, the mode pointed out in No. 862 has received the sanction of the best experience.

CURRIED VEAL (Cold Meat Cookery).

865. INGREDIENTS.—The remains of cold roast veal, 4 onions, 2 apples sliced, 1 tablespoonful of curry-powder, 1 dessertspoonful of flour, ½ pint of broth or water, 1 tablespoonful of lemon-juice.

Mode.—Slice the onions and apples, and fry them in a little butter; then take them out, cut the meat into neat cutlets, and fry these of a pale brown; add the curry-powder and flour, put in the onion, apples, and a little broth or water, and stew gently till quite tender; add the lemon-juice, and serve with an edging of boiled rice. The curry may be ornamented with pickles, capsicums, and gherkins arranged prettily on the top.

Time.—¾ hour. *Average cost,* exclusive of the meat, 4*d.*

Seasonable from March to October.

VEAL CUTLETS (an Entree).

866. INGREDIENTS.—About 3 lbs. of the prime part of the leg of veal, egg and bread crumbs, 3 tablespoonfuls of minced savoury herbs, salt and pepper to taste, a small piece of butter.

Mode.—Have the veal cut into slices about ¾ of an inch in thickness, and, if not cut perfectly even, level the meat with a cutlet-bat or rolling-pin. Shape and trim the cutlets, and brush them over with egg. Sprinkle with bread crumbs, with which have been mixed minced herbs and a seasoning of pepper and salt, and press the crumbs down. Fry them of a delicate brown in fresh lard or butter, and be careful not to burn them. They should be very thoroughly done, but not dry. If the cutlets be thick, keep the pan covered for a few minutes at a good distance from the fire, after they have acquired a good colour: by this means, the meat will be done through. Lay the cutlets in a dish, keep them hot, and make a gravy in the pan as follows: Dredge in a little flour, add a piece of butter the size of a walnut, brown it, then pour as much boiling water as is required over it, season with pepper and salt, add a little lemon-juice, give one boil, and pour it over the cutlets. They should be garnished with slices of broiled bacon, and a few forcemeat balls will be found a very excellent addition to this dish.

VEAL CUTLETS.

Time.—For cutlets of a moderate thickness, about 12 minutes; if very thick, allow more time.

Average cost, 10*d.* per lb. *Sufficient* for 6 persons.

Seasonable from March to October.

Note.—Veal cutlets may be merely floured and fried of a nice brown ; the gravy and garnishing should be the same as in the preceding recipe. They may also be cut from the loin or neck, as shown in the engraving.

BROILED VEAL CUTLETS a l'Italienne (an Entree).

867. INGREDIENTS.—Neck of veal, salt and pepper to taste, the yolk of 1 egg, bread crumbs, ½ pint of Italian sauce No. 453.

Mode.—Cut the veal into cutlets, flatten and trim them nicely ; powder over them a little salt and pepper ; brush them over with the yolk of an egg, dip them into bread crumbs, then into clarified butter, and, afterwards, in the bread crumbs again ; broil or fry them over a clear fire, that they may acquire a good brown colour. Arrange them in the dish alternately with rashers of broiled ham, and pour the sauce, made by recipe No. 453, in the middle.

Time.—10 to 15 minutes, according to the thickness of the cutlets.

Average cost, 10*d.* per lb.

Seasonable from March to October.

THE CALF'S-HEAD CLUB.—When the restoration of Charles II. took the strait waistcoat off the minds and morose religion of the Commonwealth period, and gave a loose rein to the long-compressed spirits of the people, there still remained a large section of society wedded to the former state of things. The elders of this party retired from public sight, where, unoffended by the reigning saturnalia, they might dream in seclusion over their departed Utopia. The young bloods of this school, however, who were compelled to mingle in the world, yet detesting the politics which had become the fashion, adopted a novel expedient to keep alive their republican sentiments, and mark their contempt of the reigning family. They accordingly met, in considerable numbers, at some convenient inn, on the 30th of January in each year,—the anniversary of Charles's death, and dined together off a feast prepared from *calves' heads,* dressed in every possible variety of way, and with an abundance of wine drank toasts of defiance and hatred to the house of Stuart, and glory to the memory of old Holl Cromwell ; and having lighted a large bonfire in the yard, the club of fast young Puritans, with their white handkerchiefs stained *red* in wine, and one of the party in a mask, bearing an axe, followed by the chairman, carrying a *calf's head* pinned up in a napkin, marched in mock procession to the bonfire, into which, with great shouts and uproar, they flung the enveloped head. This odd custom was continued for some time, and even down to the early part of this century it was customary for men of republican politics always to dine off calf's head on the 30th of January.

VEAL CUTLETS a la Maintenon (an Entree).

868. INGREDIENTS.—2 or 3 lbs. of veal cutlets, egg and bread crumbs, 2 tablespoonfuls of minced savoury herbs, salt and pepper to taste, a little grated nutmeg.

Mode.—Cut the cutlets about ¾ inch in thickness, flatten them, and brush them over with the yolk of an egg ; dip them into bread crumbs and minced herbs, season with pepper and salt and grated nutmeg, and fold each cutlet in a piece of buttered paper. Broil them, and send them to table with melted butter or a good gravy.

Time.—From 15 to 18 minutes. *Average cost*, 10*d*. per lb.

Sufficient for 5 or 6 persons.

Seasonable from March to October.

VEAL A LA BOURGEOISE.
(*Excellent.*)

869. INGREDIENTS.—2 to 3 lbs. of the loin or neck of veal, 10 or 12 young carrots, a bunch of green onions, 2 slices of lean bacon, 2 blades of pounded mace, 1 bunch of savoury herbs, pepper and salt to taste, a few new potatoes, 1 pint of green peas.

Mode.—Cut the veal into cutlets, trim them, and put the trimmings into a stewpan with a little butter; lay in the cutlets and fry them a nice brown colour on both sides. Add the bacon, carrots, onions, spice, herbs, and seasoning; pour in about a pint of boiling water, and stew gently for 2 hours on a very slow fire. When done, skim off the fat, take out the herbs, and flavour the gravy with a little tomato sauce and ketchup. Have ready the peas and potatoes, boiled *separately*; put them with the veal, and serve.

Time.—2 hours. *Average cost*, 2*s*. 9*d*.

Sufficient for 5 or 6 persons.

Seasonable from June to August with peas;—rather earlier when these are omitted.

SCOTCH COLLOPS (Cold Meat Cookery).

870. INGREDIENTS.—The remains of cold roast veal, a little butter, flour, ½ pint of water, 1 onion, 1 blade of pounded mace, 1 tablespoonful of lemon-juice, ½ teaspoonful of finely-minced lemon-peel, 2 tablespoonfuls of sherry, 1 tablespoonful of mushroom ketchup.

Mode.—Cut the veal the same thickness as for cutlets, rather larger than a crown-piece; flour the meat well, and fry a light brown in butter; dredge again with flour, and add ½ pint of water, pouring it in by degrees; set it on the fire, and when it boils, add the onion and mace, and let it simmer very gently about ¾ hour; flavour the gravy with lemon-juice, peel, wine, and ketchup, in the above proportion; give one boil, and serve.

Time.—¾ hour.

Seasonable from March to October.

SCOTCH COLLOPS, WHITE (Cold Meat Cookery).

871. INGREDIENTS.—The remains of cold roast veal, ½ teaspoonful of grated nutmeg, 2 blades of pounded mace, cayenne and salt to taste,

a little butter, 1 dessertspoonful of flour, ¼ pint of water, 1 teaspoonful of anchovy sauce, 1 tablespoonful of lemon-juice, ¼ teaspoonful of lemon-peel, 1 tablespoonful of mushroom ketchup, 3 tablespoonfuls of cream, 1 tablespoonful of sherry.

Mode.—Cut the veal into thin slices about 3 inches in width; hack them with a knife, and grate on them the nutmeg, mace, cayenne, and salt, and fry them in a little butter. Dish them, and make a gravy in the pan by putting in the remaining ingredients. Give one boil, and pour it over the collops; garnish with lemon and slices of toasted bacon, rolled. Forcemeat balls may be added to this dish. If cream is not at hand, substitute the yolk of an egg beaten up well with a little milk.

Time.—About 5 or 7 minutes.

Seasonable from May to October.

COOKING COLLOPS.—Dean Ramsay, who tells us, in his "Reminiscences of Scottish Life and Character," a number of famous stories of the strong-headed, warm-hearted, and plain-spoken old dames of the north, gives, amongst them, the following:—A strong-minded lady of this class was inquiring the character of a cook she was about to hire. The lady who was giving the character entered a little upon the cook's moral qualifications, and described her as a very decent woman; to which the astounding reply—this was 60 years ago, and a Dean tells the story—"Oh, d——n her decency; can she make good collops?"

ROAST FILLET OF VEAL.

872. INGREDIENTS.—Veal, forcemeat No. 417, melted butter.

Mode.—Have the fillet cut according to the size required; take out the bone, and after raising the skin from the meat, put under the flap a nice forcemeat, made by recipe No. 417. Prepare sufficient of this, as there should be some left to eat cold, and to season and flavour a mince if required. Skewer and bind the veal up in a round form; dredge well with flour, put it down at some distance from the fire at first, and baste con-

FILLET OF VEAL.

tinually. About ½ hour before serving, draw it nearer the fire, that it may acquire more colour, as the outside should be of a rich brown, but not burnt. Dish it, remove the skewers, which replace by a silver one; pour over the joint some good melted butter, and serve with either boiled ham, bacon, or pickled pork. Never omit to send a cut lemon to table with roast veal.

Time.—A fillet of veal weighing 12 lbs., about 4 hours.

Average cost, 9d. per lb.

Sufficient for 9 or 10 persons.

Seasonable from March to October.

STEWED FILLET OF VEAL.

873. INGREDIENTS.—A small fillet of veal, forcemeat No. 417, thickening of butter and flour, a few mushrooms, white pepper to taste, 2 tablespoonfuls of lemon-juice, 2 blades of pounded mace, ½ glass of sherry.

Mode.—If the whole of the leg is purchased, take off the knuckle to stew, and also the square end, which will serve for cutlets or pies. Remove the bone, and fill the space with a forcemeat No. 417. Roll and skewer it up firmly; place a few skewers at the bottom of a stew-pan to prevent the meat from sticking, and cover the veal with a little weak stock. Let it simmer very *gently* until tender, as the more slowly veal is stewed, the better. Strain and thicken the sauce, flavour it with lemon-juice, mace, sherry, and white pepper; give one boil, and pour it over the meat. The skewers should be removed, and replaced by a silver one, and the dish garnished with slices of cut lemon.

Time.—A fillet of veal weighing 6 lbs., 3 hours' very gentle stewing.
Average cost, 9*d.* per lb.
Sufficient for 5 or 6 persons.
Seasonable from March to October.

THE GOLDEN CALF.—We are told in the book of Genesis, that Aaron, in the lengthened absence of Moses, was constrained by the impatient people to make them an image to worship; and that Aaron, instead of using his delegated power to curb this sinful expression of the tribes, and appease the discontented Jews, at once complied with their demand, and, telling them to bring to him their rings and trinkets, fashioned out of their willing contributions a calf of gold, before which the multitude fell down and worshipped. Whether this image was a solid figure of gold, or a wooden effigy merely, coated with metal, is uncertain. To suppose the former,—knowing the size of the image made from such trifling articles as *rings*, we must presuppose the Israelites to have spoiled the Egyptians most unmercifully: the figure, however, is of more consequence than the weight or size of the idol. That the Israelites brought away more from Goshen than the plunder of the Egyptians, and that they were deeply imbued with Egyptian superstition, the golden calf is only one, out of many, instances of proof; for a gilded ox, covered with a pall, was in that country an emblem of Osiris, one of the gods of the Egyptian trinity. Besides having a sacred cow, and many varieties of the holy bull, this priest-ridden people worshipped the ox as a symbol of the sun, and offered to it divine honours, as the emblem of frugality, industry, and husbandry. It is therefore probable that, in borrowing so familiar a type, the Israelites, in their calf-worship, meant, under a well-understood cherubic symbol, to acknowledge the full force of those virtues, under an emblem of divine power and goodness. The prophet Hosea is full of denunciations against calf-worship in Israel, and alludes to the custom of kissing these idols, Hosea, viii. 4—6.

FRICANDEAU OF VEAL (an Entree).

874. INGREDIENTS.—A piece of the fat side of a leg of veal (about 3 lbs.), lardoons, 2 carrots, 2 large onions, a faggot of savoury herbs, 2 blades of pounded mace, 6 whole allspice, 2 bay-leaves, pepper to taste, a few slices of fat bacon, 1 pint of stock No. 107.

Mode.—The veal for a fricandeau should be of the best quality, or it will not be good. It may be known by the meat being white and not thready. Take off the skin, flatten the veal on the table, then at one stroke of the knife, cut off as much as is required, for a fricandeau with an uneven surface never looks well. Trim it, and with a sharp knife make two or three slits in the middle, that it may taste more of the seasoning. Now lard it thickly with fat bacon, as lean gives a red colour to the fricandeau. Slice the vegetables, and put these, with the herbs and spices, in the *middle* of a stewpan, with a few slices of bacon

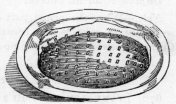

FRICANDEAU OF VEAL.

at the top: these should form a sort of mound in the centre for the veal to rest upon. Lay the fricandeau over the bacon, sprinkle over it a little salt, and pour in just sufficient stock to cover the bacon, &c., without touching the veal. Let it gradually come to a boil; then put it over a slow and equal fire, and let it *simmer very* gently for about 2½ hours, or longer should it be very large. Baste it frequently with the liquor, and a short time before serving, put it into a brisk oven, to make the bacon firm, which otherwise would break when it was glazed. Dish the fricandeau, keep it hot, skim off the fat from the liquor, and reduce it quickly to a glaze, with which glaze the fricandeau, and serve with a purée of whatever vegetable happens to be in season—spinach, sorrel, asparagus, cucumbers, peas, &c.

Time.—2½ hours. If very large, allow more time.

Average cost, 3s. 6d.

Sufficient for an entrée.

Seasonable from March to October.

FRICANDEAU OF VEAL.

(*More economical.*)

875. INGREDIENTS.—The best end of a neck of veal (about 2½ lbs.), lardoons, 2 carrots, 2 onions, a faggot of savoury herbs, 2 blades of mace, 2 bay-leaves, a little whole white pepper, a few slices of fat bacon.

Mode.—Cut away the lean part of the best end of a neck of veal with a sharp knife, scooping it from the bones. Put the bones in with a little water, which will serve to moisten the fricandeau: they should stew about 1½ hour. Lard the veal, proceed in the same way as in the preceding recipe, and be careful that the gravy does not touch the fricandeau. Stew very gently for 3 hours; glaze, and serve it on sorrel, spinach, or with a little gravy in the dish.

Time.—3 hours. *Average cost*, 2s. 6d.

Sufficient for an entrée. *Seasonable* from March to October.

Note.—When the prime part of the leg is cut off, it spoils the whole; consequently, to use this for a fricandeau is rather extravagant. The best end of the neck answers the purpose nearly or quite as well.

BOILED CALF'S HEAD (with the Skin on).

876. INGREDIENTS.—Calf's head, boiling water, bread crumbs, 1 large bunch of parsley, butter, white pepper and salt to taste, 4 tablespoonfuls of melted butter, 1 tablespoonful of lemon-juice, 2 or 3 grains of cayenne.

Mode.—Put the head into boiling water, and let it remain by the side of the fire for 3 or 4 minutes; take it out, hold it by the ear, and with the back of a knife, scrape off the hair (should it not come off easily, dip the head again into boiling water). When perfectly clean, take the eyes out, cut off the ears, and remove the brain, which soak for an hour in warm water. Put the head into hot water to soak for a few minutes, to make it look white, and then have ready a stewpan, into which lay the head; cover it with cold water, and bring it gradually to boil. Remove the scum, and add a little salt, which assists to throw it up. Simmer it very gently from 2½ to 3 hours, and when nearly done, boil the brains for ¼ hour; skin and chop them, not too finely, and add a tablespoonful of minced parsley which has been previously scalded. Season with pepper and salt, and stir the brains, parsley, &c., into about 4 tablepoonsfuls of melted butter; add the lemon-juice and cayenne, and keep these hot by the side of the fire. Take up the head, cut out the tongue, skin it, put it on a small dish with the brains round it; sprinkle over the head a few bread crumbs mixed with a little minced parsley; brown these before the fire, and serve with a tureen of parsley and butter, and either boiled bacon, ham, or pickled pork as an accompaniment.

Time.—2½ to 3 hours.

Average cost, according to the season, from 3s. to 7s. 6d.

Sufficient for 8 or 9 persons.

Seasonable from March to October.

BOILED CALF'S HEAD (without the Skin).

877. INGREDIENTS.—Calf's head, water, a little salt, 4 tablespoonfuls of melted butter, 1 tablespoonful of minced parsley, pepper and salt to taste, 1 tablespoonful of lemon-juice.

Mode.—After the head has been thoroughly cleaned, and the brains removed, soak it in warm water to blanch it. Lay the brains also into warm water to soak, and let them remain for about an hour. Put the head into a stewpan, with sufficient cold water to cover it, and

CALF'S HEAD.

HALF A CALF'S HEAD.

when it boils, add a little salt; take off every particle of scum as it rises, and boil the head until perfectly tender. Boil the brains, chop them, and mix with them melted butter, minced parsley, pepper, salt, and lemon-juice in the above proportion. Take up the head, skin the tongue, and put it on a small dish with the brains round it. Have ready some parsley and butter, smother the head with it, and the remainder send to table in a tureen. Bacon, ham, pickled pork, or a pig's cheek, are indispensable with calf's head. The brains are sometimes chopped with hard-boiled eggs, and mixed with a little Béchamel or white sauce.

Time.—From 1½ to 2¼ hours.

Average cost, according to the season, from 3s. to 5s.

Sufficient for 6 or 7 persons.

Seasonable from March to October.

Note.—The liquor in which the head was boiled should be saved : it makes excellent soup, and will be found a nice addition to gravies, &c. Half a calf's head is as frequently served as a whole one, it being a more convenient-sized joint for a small family. It is cooked in the same manner, and served with the same sauces, as in the preceding recipe.

HASHED CALF'S HEAD (Cold Meat Cookery).

878. INGREDIENTS.—The remains of a cold boiled calf's head, 1 quart of the liquor in which it was boiled, a faggot of savoury herbs, 1 onion, 1 carrot, a strip of lemon-peel, 2 blades of pounded mace, salt and white pepper to taste, a very little cayenne, rather more than 2 tablespoonfuls of sherry, 1 tablespoonful of lemon-juice, 1 tablespoonful of mushroom ketchup, forcemeat balls.

Mode.—Cut the meat into neat slices, and put the bones and trimmings into a stewpan with the above proportion of liquor that the head was boiled in. Add a bunch of savoury herbs, 1 onion, 1 carrot, a strip of lemon-peel, and 2 blades of pounded mace, and let these

2 E

boil for 1 hour, or until the gravy is reduced nearly half. Strain it into a clean stewpan, thicken it with a little butter and flour, and add a flavouring of sherry, lemon-juice, and ketchup, in the above proportion; season with pepper, salt, and a little cayenne; put in the meat, let it *gradually* warm through, but not boil more than *two* or *three* minutes. Garnish the dish with forcemeat balls and pieces of bacon rolled and toasted, placed alternately, and send it to table very hot.

Time.—Altogether 1½ hour.

Average cost, exclusive of the remains of the head, 6*d*.

Seasonable from March to October.

VEAL COLLOPS (an Entree).

879. INGREDIENTS.—About 2 lbs. of the prime part of the leg of veal, a few slices of bacon, forcemeat No. 417, cayenne to taste, egg and bread crumbs, gravy.

Mode.—Cut the veal into long thin collops, flatten them, and lay on each a piece of thin bacon of the same size; have ready some force-meat, made by recipe No. 417, which spread over the bacon, sprinkle over all a little cayenne, roll them up tightly, and do not let them be more than 2 inches long. Skewer each one firmly, egg and bread crumb them, and fry them a nice brown in a little butter, turning them occasionally, and shaking the pan about. When done, place them on a dish before the fire; put a small piece of butter in the pan, dredge in a little flour, add ¼ pint of water, 2 tablespoonfuls of lemon-juice, a seasoning of salt, pepper, and pounded mace; let the whole boil up, and pour it over the collops.

Time.—From 10 to 15 minutes. *Average cost*, 10*d*. per lb.

Sufficient for 5 or 6 persons.

Seasonable from March to October.

CALF'S LIVER AUX FINES HERBES & SAUCE PIQUANTE.

880. INGREDIENTS.—A calf's liver, flour, a bunch of savoury herbs, including parsley; when liked, 2 minced shalots; 1 teaspoonful of flour, 1 tablespoonful of vinegar, 1 tablespoonful of lemon-juice, pepper and salt to taste, ¼ pint water.

Mode.—Procure a calf's liver as white as possible, and cut it into slices of a good and equal shape. Dip them in flour, and fry them of a good colour in a little butter. When they are done, put them on a dish, which keep hot before the fire. Mince the herbs very fine, put them in the frying-pan with a little more butter, add the remaining ingredients, simmer gently until the herbs are done, and pour over the liver.

Time.—According to the thickness of the slices, from 5 to 10 minutes.

Average cost, 10*d.* per lb.   *Sufficient* for 7 or 8 persons.

Seasonable from March to October.

CALF'S LIVER AND BACON.

881. INGREDIENTS.—2 or 3 lbs. of liver, bacon, pepper and salt to taste, a small piece of butter, flour, 2 tablespoonfuls of lemon-juice, ¼ pint of water.

Mode.—Cut the liver in thin slices, and cut as many slices of bacon as there are of liver; fry the bacon first, and put that on a hot dish before the fire. Fry the liver in the fat which comes from the bacon, after seasoning it with pepper and salt and dredging over it a very little flour. Turn the liver occasionally to prevent its burning, and when done, lay it round the dish with a piece of bacon between each. Pour away the bacon fat, put in a small piece of butter, dredge in a little flour, add the lemon-juice and water, give one boil, and pour it in the *middle* of the dish. It may be garnished with slices of cut lemon, or forcemeat balls.

Time.—According to the thickness of the slices, from 5 to 10 minutes.

Average cost, 10*d.* per lb.   *Sufficient* for 6 or 7 persons.

Seasonable from March to October.

CALF'S LIVER LARDED AND ROASTED (an Entree).

882. INGREDIENTS.—A calf's liver, vinegar, 1 onion, 3 or 4 sprigs of parsley and thyme, salt and pepper to taste, 1 bay-leaf, lardoons, brown gravy.

Mode.—Take a fine white liver, and lard it the same as a fricandeau; put it into vinegar with an onion cut in slices, parsley, thyme, bay-leaf, and seasoning in the above proportion. Let it remain in this pickle for 24 hours, then roast and baste it frequently with the vinegar, &c.; glaze it, serve under it a good brown gravy, or sauce piquante, and send it to table very hot.

Time.—Rather more than 1 hour. *Average cost,* 10*d.* per lb.

Sufficient for 7 or 8 persons.

Seasonable from March to October.

Note.—Calf's liver stuffed with forcemeat No. 417, to which has been added a little fat bacon, will be found a very savoury dish. It should be larded or wrapped in buttered paper, and roasted before a clear fire. Brown gravy and currant jelly should be served with it.

FILLET OF VEAL AU BECHAMEL (Cold Meat Cookery).

883. INGREDIENTS.—A small fillet of veal, 1 pint of Béchamel sauce No. 367, a few bread crumbs, clarified butter.

Mode.—A fillet of veal that has been roasted the preceding day will answer very well for this dish. Cut the middle out rather deep, leaving a good margin round, from which to cut nice slices, and if there should be any cracks in the veal, fill them up with forcemeat. Mince finely the meat that was taken out, mixing with it a little of the forcemeat to flavour, and stir to it sufficient Béchamel to make it of a proper consistency. Warm the veal in the oven for about an hour, taking care to baste it well, that it may not be dry; put the mince in the place where the meat was taken out, sprinkle a few bread crumbs over it, and drop a little clarified butter on the bread crumbs; put it into the oven for ¼ hour to brown, and pour Béchamel round the sides of the dish.

Time.—Altogether 1½ hour.

Seasonable from March to October.

TO RAGOUT A KNUCKLE OF VEAL.

884. INGREDIENTS.—Knuckle of veal, pepper and salt to taste, flour, 1 onion, 1 head of celery, or a little celery-seed, a faggot of savoury herbs, 2 blades of pounded mace, thickening of butter and flour, a few young carrots, 1 tablespoonful of ketchup, 1 tablespoonful of tomato sauce, 3 tablespoonfuls of sherry, the juice of ½ lemon.

Mode.—Cut the meat from a knuckle of veal into neat slices, season with pepper and salt, and dredge them with flour. Fry them in a little butter of a pale brown, and put them into a stewpan with the bone (which should be chopped in several places); add the celery, herbs, mace, and carrots; pour over all about 1 pint of hot water, and let it simmer very gently for 2 hours, over a slow but clear fire. Take out the slices of meat and carrots, strain and thicken the gravy with a little butter rolled in flour; add the remaining ingredients, give one boil, put back the meat and carrots, let these get hot through, and serve. When in season, a few green peas, *boiled separately*, and added to this dish at the moment of serving, would be found a very agreeable addition.

Time.—2 hours. *Average cost, 5d.* to *6d.* per lb.

Sufficient for 4 or 5 persons.

STEWED KNUCKLE OF VEAL AND RICE.

885. INGREDIENTS.—Knuckle of veal, 1 onion, 2 blades of mace, 1 teaspoonful of salt, ½ lb. of rice.

Mode.—Have the knuckle cut small, or cut some cutlets from it, that it may be just large enough to be eaten the same day it is dressed, as cold boiled veal is not a particularly tempting dish. Break the shank-bone, wash it clean, and put the meat into a stewpan with sufficient water to cover it. Let it gradually come to a boil, put in the salt, and remove the scum as fast as it rises. When it has simmered

KNUCKLE OF VEAL.

gently for about ¾ hour, add the remaining ingredients, and stew the whole gently for 2¼ hours. Put the meat into a deep dish, pour over it the rice, &c., and send boiled bacon, and a tureen of parsley and butter to table with it.

Time.—A knuckle of veal weighing 6 lbs., 3 hours' gentle stewing.
Average cost, 5*d.* to 6*d.* per lb.
Sufficient for 5 or 6 persons.
Seasonable from March to October.

Note.—Macaroni, instead of rice, boiled with the veal, will be found good ; or the rice and macaroni may be omitted, and the veal sent to table smothered in parsley and butter.

ROAST LOIN OF VEAL.

886. INGREDIENTS.—Veal ; melted butter.
Mode.—Paper the kidney fat ; roll in and skewer the flap, which makes the joint a good shape ; dredge it well with flour, and put it down to a bright fire. Should the loin be very large, skewer the kidney back for a time to roast thoroughly. Keep it well basted, and a short time before serving, remove the paper from the kid-ney, and allow it to acquire a nice brown colour, but it should not be burnt. Have

LOIN OF VEAL.

ready some melted butter, put it into the dripping-pan after it is emptied of its contents, pour it over the veal, and serve. Garnish the dish with slices of lemon and forcemeat balls, and send to table with it, boiled bacon, ham, pickled pork, or pig's cheek.

Time.—A large loin, 3 hours. *Average cost,* 9¼*d.* per lb.
Sufficient for 7 or 8 persons.
Seasonable from March to October.

Note.—A piece of toast should be placed under the kidney when the veal is dished.

LOIN OF VEAL AU BECHAMEL (Cold Meat Cookery).

887. INGREDIENTS.—Loin of veal, ½ teaspoonful of minced lemon-peel, rather more than ½ pint of Béchamel or white sauce.

Mode.—A loin of veal which has come from table with very little taken off, answers very well for this dish. Cut off the meat from the inside, mince it, and mix with it some minced lemon-peel; put it into sufficient Béchamel to warm through. In the mean time, wrap the joint in buttered paper, and place it in the oven to warm. When thoroughly hot, dish the mince, place the loin above it, and pour over the remainder of the Béchamel.

Time.—1½ hour to warm the meat in the oven.

Seasonable from March to October.

LOIN OF VEAL, a la Daube.

888. INGREDIENTS.—The chump end of a loin of veal, forcemeat No. 417, a few slices of bacon, a bunch of savoury herbs, 2 blades of mace, ½ teaspoonful of whole white pepper, 1 pint of veal stock or water, 5 or 6 green onions.

Mode.—Cut off the chump from a loin of veal, and take out the bone; fill the cavity with forcemeat No. 417, tie it up tightly, and lay it in a stewpan with the bones and trimmings, and cover the veal with a few slices of bacon. Add the herbs, mace, pepper, and onions, and stock or water; cover the pan with a closely-fitting lid, and simmer for 2 hours, shaking the stewpan occasionally. Take out the bacon, herbs, and onions; reduce the gravy, if not already thick enough, to a glaze, with which glaze the meat, and serve with tomato, mushroom, or sorrel sauce.

Time.—2 hours. *Average cost,* 9d. per lb.

Sufficient for 4 or 5 persons.

Seasonable from March to October.

MINCED VEAL, with Bechamel Sauce (Cold Meat Cookery).
(*Very Good.*)

889. INGREDIENTS.—The remains of a fillet of veal, 1 pint of Béchamel sauce No. 367, ½ teaspoonful of minced lemon-peel, forcemeat balls.

Mode.—Cut—but do not *chop*—a few slices of cold roast veal as finely as possible, sufficient to make rather more than 1 lb., weighed after being minced. Make the above proportion of Béchamel, by recipe No. 367; add the lemon-peel, put in the veal, and let the whole gradually warm through. When it is at the point of simmering, dish it, and garnish with forcemeat balls and fried sippets of bread.

Time.—To simmer 1 minute.

Average cost, exclusive of the cold meat, 1s. 4d.

Sufficient for 5 or 6 persons.

Seasonable from March to October.

MINCED VEAL.
(*More Economical.*)

890. INGREDIENTS.—The remains of cold roast fillet or loin of veal, rather more than 1 pint of water, 1 onion, ½ teaspoonful of minced lemon-peel, salt and white pepper to taste, 1 blade of pounded mace, 2 or 3 young carrots, a faggot of sweet herbs, thickening of butter and flour, 1 tablespoonful of lemon-juice, 3 tablespoonfuls of cream or milk.

Mode.—Take about 1 lb. of veal, and should there be any bones, dredge them with flour, and put them into a stewpan with the brown outside, and a few meat trimmings; add rather more than a pint of water, the onion cut in slices, lemon-peel, seasoning, mace, carrots, and herbs; simmer these well for rather more than 1 hour, and strain the liquor. Rub a little flour into some butter; add this to the gravy, set it on the fire, and, when it boils, skim well. Mince the veal finely by *cutting*, and not chopping it; put it in the gravy; let it get warmed through gradually; add the lemon-juice and cream, and, when it is on the point of boiling, serve. Garnish the dish with sippets of toasted bread and slices of bacon rolled and toasted. Forcemeat balls may also be added. If more lemon-peel is liked than is stated above, put a little very finely minced to the veal, after it is warmed in the gravy.

Time.—1 hour to make the gravy.

Average cost, exclusive of the cold meat, 6d.

Seasonable from March to October.

THE CALF A SYMBOL OF DIVINE POWER.—A singular symbolical ceremony existed among the Hebrews, in which the calf performed a most important part. The calf being a type or symbol of Divine power, or what was called the *Elohim*,—the Almighty intelligence that brought them out of Egypt,—was looked upon much in the same light by the Jews, as the cross subsequently was by the Christians, a mystical emblem of the Divine passion and goodness. Consequently, an oath taken on either the calf or the cross was considered equally solemn and sacred by Jew or Nazarene, and the breaking of it a soul-staining perjury on themselves, and an insult and profanation directly offered to the Almighty. To render the oath more impressive and solemn, it was customary to slaughter a dedicated calf in the temple, when, the priests having divided the carcase into a certain number of parts, and with intervening spaces, arranged the severed limbs on the marble pavement, the one, or all the party, if there were many individuals, to be bound by the oath, repeating the words of the compact, threaded their way in and out through the different spaces, till they had taken the circuit of each portion of the divided calf, when the ceremony was concluded. To avert the anger of the Lord, when Jerusalem was threatened by Nebuchadnezzar and his Babylonian host, the Jews had made a solemn vow to God, ratified by the ceremony of the calf, if He released them from their dreaded foe, to cancel the servitude of their Hebrew brethren. After investing the city for some time, and reducing the inhabitants to dreadful suffering and privation, the Babylonians, hearing that Pharaoh, whom the Jews had solicited for aid, was rapidly approaching with a powerful army, hastily raised the siege, and, removing to a distance, took up a position where they could intercept the Egyptians, and still cover the city. No sooner did the Jews behold the retreat of the enemy, than they believed all danger was past, and, with their usual turpitude, they repudiated their oath, and refused to liberate their oppressed countrymen. For this violation of their covenant with the Lord, they were given over to all the horrors of the sword, pestilence, and famine.—Jeremiah, xxxiv. 15—17.

MINCED VEAL AND MACARONI.

(*A pretty side or corner dish.*)

891. INGREDIENTS.—¾ lb. of minced cold roast veal, 3 oz. of ham, 1 tablespoonful of gravy, pepper and salt to taste, ¼ teaspoonful of grated nutmeg, ¼ lb. of bread crumbs, ¼ lb. of macaroni, 1 or 2 eggs to bind, a small piece of butter.

Mode.—Cut some nice slices from a cold fillet of veal, trim off the brown outside, and mince the meat finely with the above proportion of ham : should the meat be very dry, add a spoonful of good gravy. Season highly with pepper and salt, add the grated nutmeg and bread crumbs, and mix these ingredients with 1 or 2 eggs well beaten, which should bind the mixture and make it like forcemeat. In the mean time, boil the macaroni in salt and water, and drain it ; butter a mould, put some of the macaroni at the bottom and sides of it, in whatever form is liked ; mix the remainder with the forcemeat, fill the mould up to the top, put a plate or small dish on it, and steam for ½ hour. Turn it out carefully, and serve with good gravy poured round, but not over, the meat.

Time.—½ hour. *Average cost*, exclusive of the cold meat, 10*d.*

Seasonable from March to October.

Note.—To make a variety, boil some carrots and turnips separately in a little salt and water ; when done, cut them into pieces about ⅛ inch in thickness ; butter an oval mould, and place these in it, in white and red stripes alternately, at the bottom and sides. Proceed as in the foregoing recipe, and be very careful in turning it out of the mould.

MOULDED MINCED VEAL (Cold Meat Cookery).

892. INGREDIENTS.—¾ lb. of cold roast veal, a small slice of bacon, ⅓ teaspoonful of minced lemon-peel, ½ onion chopped fine, salt, pepper, and pounded mace to taste, a slice of toast soaked in milk, 1 egg.

Mode.—Mince the meat very fine, after removing from it all skin and outside pieces, and chop the bacon ; mix these well together, adding the lemon-peel, onion, seasoning, mace, and toast. When all the ingredients are thoroughly incorporated, beat up an egg, with which bind the mixture. Butter a shape, put in the meat, and bake for ¾ hour; turn it out of the mould carefully, and pour round it a good brown gravy. A sheep's head dressed in this manner is an economical and savoury dish.

Time.—¾ hour. *Average cost,* exclusive of the meat, 6d.
Seasonable from March to October.

BRAISED NECK OF VEAL.

893. INGREDIENTS.—The best end of the neck of veal (from 3 to 4 lbs.), bacon, 1 tablespoonful of minced parsley, salt, pepper, and grated nutmeg to taste; 1 onion, 2 carrots, a little celery (when this is not obtainable, use the seed), ½ glass of sherry, thickening of butter and flour, lemon-juice, 1 blade of pounded mace.

Mode.—Prepare the bacon for larding, and roll it in minced parsley, salt, pepper, and grated nutmeg; lard the veal, put it into a stewpan with a few slices of lean bacon or ham, an onion, carrots, and celery; and do not quite cover it with water. Stew it gently for 2 hours, or until it is quite tender; strain off the liquor; stir together over the fire, in a stewpan, a little flour and butter until brown; lay the veal in this, the upper side to the bottom of the pan, and let it remain till of a nice brown colour. Place it in the dish; pour into the stewpan as much gravy as is required, boil it up, skim well, add the wine, pounded mace, and lemon-juice; simmer for 3 minutes, pour it over the meat, and serve.

Time.—Rather more than 2 hours. *Average cost,* 8d. per lb.
Sufficient for 5 or 6 persons.
Seasonable from March to October.

BIRTH OF CALVES.—The cow seldom produces more than a single calf; sometimes, twins, and, very rarely, three. A French newspaper, however,—the "Nouveau Bulletin des Sciences,"—gave a trustworthy but extraordinary account of a cow which produced nine calves in all, at three successive births, in three successive years. The first year, four cow calves; the second year, three calves, two of them females; the third year, two calves, both females. With the exception of two belonging to the first birth, all were suckled by the mother.

ROAST NECK OF VEAL.

894. INGREDIENTS.—Veal, melted butter, forcemeat balls.
Mode.—Have the veal cut from the best end of the neck; dredge it with flour, and put it down to a bright clear fire; keep it well basted; dish it, pour over it some melted butter, and garnish the dish with fried forcemeat balls; send to table with a cut lemon. The scrag

may be boiled or stewed in various ways, with rice, onion-sauce, or parsley-and butter.

Time.—About 2 hours.   *Average cost,* 8*d.* per lb.

Sufficient.—4 or 5 lbs. for 5 or 6 persons.

Seasonable from March to October.

VEAL OLIVE PIE (Cold Meat Cookery).

895. INGREDIENTS.—A few thin slices of cold fillet of veal, a few thin slices of bacon, forcemeat No. 417, a cupful of gravy, 4 table-spoonfuls of cream, puff-crust.

Mode.—Cut thin slices from a fillet of veal, place on them thin slices of bacon, and over them a layer of forcemeat, made by recipe No. 417, with an additional seasoning of shalot and cayenne ; roll them tightly, and fill up a pie-dish with them ; add the gravy and cream, cover with a puff-crust, and bake for 1 to 1½ hour : should the pie be very large, allow 2 hours.   The pieces of rolled veal should be about 3 inches in length, and about 3 inches round.

Time.—Moderate-sized pie, 1 to 1½ hour.

Seasonable from March to October.

FRIED PATTIES (Cold Meat Cookery).

896. INGREDIENTS.—Cold roast veal, a few slices of cold ham, 1 egg boiled hard, pounded mace, pepper and salt to taste, gravy, cream, 1 teaspoonful of minced lemon-peel, good puff-paste.

Mode.—Mince a little cold veal and ham, allowing one-third ham to two-thirds veal; add an egg boiled hard and chopped, and a seasoning of pounded mace, salt, pepper, and lemon-peel; moisten with a little gravy and cream.   Make a good puff-paste; roll rather thin, and cut it into round or square pieces ; put the mince between two of them, pinch the edges to keep in the gravy, and fry a light brown.   They may be also baked in patty-pans : in that case, they should be brushed over with the yolk of an egg before they are put in the oven.   To make a variety, oysters may be substituted for the ham.

Time.—15 minutes to fry the patties.

Seasonable from March to October.

VEAL PIE.

897. INGREDIENTS.—2 lbs. of veal cutlets, 1 or 2 slices of lean bacon or ham, pepper and salt to taste, 2 tablespoonfuls of minced savoury herbs, 2 blades of pounded mace, crust, 1 teacupful of gravy.

Mode.—Cut the cutlets into square pieces, and season them with pepper, salt, and pounded mace; put them in a pie-dish with the savoury herbs sprinkled over, and 1 or 2 slices of lean bacon or ham placed at the top: if possible, this should be previously cooked, as undressed bacon makes the veal red, and spoils its appearance. Pour in a little water, cover with crust, ornament it in any way that is approved; brush it over with the yolk of an egg, and bake in a well-heated oven for about 1½ hour. Pour in a good gravy after baking, which is done by removing the top ornament, and replacing it after the gravy is added.

Time.—About 1½ hour. *Average cost,* 2s. 6d.

Sufficient for 5 or 6 persons.

Seasonable from March to October.

A VERY VEAL DINNER.—At a dinner given by Lord Polkemmet, a Scotch nobleman and judge, his guests saw, when the covers were removed, that the fare consisted of veal broth, a roasted fillet of veal, veal cutlets, a calf's head, and calf's-foot jelly. The judge, observing the surprise of his guests, volunteered an explanation.— "Ou, ay, it's a' cauf; when we kill a beast, we just eat up ae side, and doun the tither."

VEAL AND HAM PIE.

898. INGREDIENTS.—2 lbs. of veal cutlets, ½ lb. of boiled ham, 2 tablespoonfuls of minced savoury herbs, ¼ teaspoonful of grated nutmeg, 2 blades of pounded mace, pepper and salt to taste, a strip of lemon-peel finely minced, the yolks of 2 hard-boiled eggs, ½ pint of water, nearly ½ pint of good strong gravy, puff-crust.

Mode.—Cut the veal into nice square pieces, and put a layer of them at the bottom of a pie-dish; sprinkle over these a portion of the herbs, spices, seasoning, lemon-peel, and the yolks of the eggs cut in slices; cut the ham very thin, and put a layer of this in. Proceed in this manner until the dish is full, so arranging it that the ham comes at the top. Lay a puff-paste on the edge of the dish, and pour in about ½ pint of water; cover with crust, ornament it with leaves, brush it over with the yolk of an egg, and bake in a well-heated oven for 1 to 1½ hour, or longer, should the pie be very large. When it is taken out of the oven, pour in at the top, through a funnel, nearly ½ pint of strong gravy: this should be made sufficiently good that, when cold, it may cut in a firm jelly. This pie may be very much enriched by adding a few mushrooms, oysters, or sweetbreads; but it will be found very good without any of the last-named additions.

Time.—1½ hour, or longer, should the pie be very large.

Average cost, 3s.

Sufficient for 5 or 6 persons.

Seasonable from March to October.

POTTED VEAL (for Breakfast).

899. INGREDIENTS.—To every lb. of veal allow ¼ lb. of ham, cayenne and pounded mace to taste, 6 oz. of fresh butter; clarified butter.

Mode.—Mince the veal and ham together as finely as possible, and pound well in a mortar, with cayenne, pounded mace, and fresh butter in the above proportion. When reduced to a perfectly smooth paste, press it into potting-pots, and cover with clarified butter. If kept in a cool place, it will remain good some days.

Seasonable from March to October.

NAMES OF CALVES, &c.—During the time the young male calf is suckled by his mother, he is called a bull- or ox-calf; when turned a year old, he is called a stirk, stot, or yearling; on the completion of his second year, he is called a two-year-old bull or steer (and in some counties a twinter); then, a three-year-old steer; and at four, an ox or a bullock, which latter names are retained till death. It may be here remarked, that the term ox is used as a general or common appellation for neat cattle, in a specific sense, and irrespective of sex; as the British ox, the Indian ox. The female is termed cow, but while sucking the mother, a cow-calf; at the age of a year, she is called a yearling quey; in another year, a heifer, or twinter; then, a three-year-old quey or twinter; and, at four years old, a cow. Other names, to be regarded as provincialisms, may exist in different districts.

RAGOUT OF COLD VEAL (Cold Meat Cookery).

900. INGREDIENTS.—The remains of cold veal, 1 oz. of butter, ½ pint of gravy, thickening of butter and flour, pepper and salt to taste, 1 blade of pounded mace, 1 tablespoonful of mushroom ketchup, 1 tablespoonful of sherry, 1 dessertspoonful of lemon-juice, forcemeat balls.

Mode.—Any part of veal will make this dish. Cut the meat into nice-looking pieces, put them in a stewpan with 1 oz. of butter, and fry a light brown; add the gravy (hot water may be substituted for this), thicken with a little butter and flour, and stew gently about ¼ hour; season with pepper, salt, and pounded mace; add the ketchup, sherry, and lemon-juice; give one boil, and serve. Garnish the dish with forcemeat balls and fried rashers of bacon.

Time.—Altogether ½ hour.

Average cost, exclusive of the cold meat, 6d.

Seasonable from March to October.

Note.—The above recipe may be varied, by adding vegetables, such as peas, cucumbers, lettuces, green onions cut in slices, a dozen or two of green gooseberries (not seedy), all of which should be fried a little with the meat, and then stewed in the gravy.

VEAL RISSOLES (Cold Meat Cookery).

901. INGREDIENTS.—A few slices of cold roast veal, a few slices of

ham or bacon, 1 tablespoonful of minced parsley, 1 tablespoonful of minced savoury herbs, 1 blade of pounded mace, a very little grated nutmeg, cayenne and salt to taste, 2 eggs well beaten, bread crumbs.

Mode.—Mince the veal very finely with a little ham or bacon ; add the parsley, herbs, spices, and seasoning ; mix into a paste with an egg ; form into balls or cones ; brush these over with egg, sprinkle with bread crumbs, and fry a rich brown. Serve with brown gravy, and garnish the dish with fried parsley.

Time.—About 10 minutes to fry the rissoles.

Seasonable from March to October.

VEAL ROLLS (Cold Meat Cookery).

902. INGREDIENTS.—The remains of a cold fillet of veal, egg and bread crumbs, a few slices of fat bacon, forcemeat No. 417.

Mode.—Cut a few slices from a cold fillet of veal ½ inch thick ; rub them over with egg ; lay a thin slice of fat bacon over each piece of veal ; brush these with the egg, and over this spread the forcemeat thinly ; roll up each piece tightly, egg and bread crumb them, and fry them a rich brown. Serve with mushroom sauce or brown gravy.

Time.—10 to 15 minutes to fry the rolls.

Seasonable from March to October.

SHOULDER OF VEAL, Stuffed and Stewed.

903. INGREDIENTS.—A shoulder of veal, a few slices of ham or bacon, forcemeat No. 417, 3 carrots, 2 onions, salt and pepper to taste, a faggot of savoury herbs, 3 blades of pounded mace, water, thickening of butter and flour.

Mode.—Bone the joint by carefully detaching the meat from the blade-bone on one side, and then on the other, being particular not to pierce the skin ; then cut the bone from the knuckle, and take it out. Fill the cavity whence the bone was taken with a forcemeat made by recipe No. 417. Roll and bind the veal up tightly ; put it into a stew-pan with the carrots, onions, seasoning, herbs, and mace ; pour in just sufficient water to cover it, and let it stew *very gently* for about 5 hours. Before taking it up, try if it is properly done by thrusting a larding-needle in it : if it penetrates easily, it is sufficiently cooked. Strain and skim the gravy, thicken with butter and flour, give one boil, and pour it round the meat. A few young carrots may be boiled and placed round the dish as a garnish, and, when in season, green peas should always be served with this dish.

Time.—5 hours. *Average cost,* 7*d.* per lb.

Sufficient for 8 or 9 persons. *Seasonable* from March to October.

THE FATTENING OF CALVES.—The fattening of calves for the market is an important business in Lanarkshire or Clydesdale, and numbers of newly-dropped calves are regularly carried there from the farmers of the adjacent districts, in order to be prepared for the butcher. The mode of feeding them is very simple ; milk is the chief article of their diet, and of this the calves require a sufficient supply from first to last. Added to this, they must be kept in a well-aired place, neither too hot nor too cold, and freely supplied with dry litter. It is usual to exclude the light,—at all events to a great degree, and to put within their reach a lump of chalk, which they are very fond of licking. Thus fed, calves, at the end of 8 or 9 weeks, often attain a very large size ; viz., 18 to 20 stone, exclusive of the offal. Far heavier weights have occurred, and without any deterioration in the delicacy and richness of the flesh. This mode of feeding upon milk alone at first appears to be very expensive, but it is not so, when all things are taken into consideration ; for at the age of 9 or 10 weeks a calf, originally purchased for 8 shillings, will realize nearly the same number of pounds. For 4, or even 6 weeks, the milk of one cow is sufficient,—indeed half that quantity is enough for the first fortnight ; but after the 5th or 6th week it will consume the greater portion of the milk of two moderate cows ; but then it requires neither oil-cake nor linseed, nor any other food. Usually, however, the calves are not kept beyond the age of 6 weeks, and will then sell for 5 or 6 pounds each : the milk of the cow is then ready for a successor. In this manner a relay of calves may be prepared for the markets from early spring to the end of summer, a plan more advantageous than that of overfeeding one to a useless degree of corpulency.

VEAL SAUSAGES.

904. INGREDIENTS.—Equal quantities of fat bacon and lean veal ; to every lb. of meat, allow 1 teaspoonful of minced sage, salt and pepper to taste.

Mode.—Chop the meat and bacon finely, and to every lb. allow the above proportion of very finely-minced sage ; add a seasoning of pepper and salt, mix the whole well together, make it into flat cakes, and fry a nice brown.

Seasonable from March to October.

STEWED VEAL, with Peas, young Carrots, and new Potatoes.

905. INGREDIENTS.—3 or 4 lbs. of the loin or neck of veal, 15 young carrots, a few green onions, 1 pint of green peas, 12 new potatoes, a bunch of savoury herbs, pepper and salt to taste, 1 tablespoonful of lemon-juice, 2 tablespoonfuls of tomato sauce, 2 tablespoonfuls of mushroom ketchup.

Mode.—Dredge the meat with flour, and roast or bake it for about ¾ hour : it should acquire a nice brown colour. Put the meat into a stewpan with the carrots, onions, potatoes, herbs, pepper, and salt ; pour over it sufficient boiling water to cover it, and stew gently for 2 hours. Take out the meat and herbs, put it in a deep dish, skim off all the fat from the gravy, and flavour it with lemon-juice, tomato sauce, and mushroom ketchup in the above proportion. Have ready a pint of green peas boiled *separately ;* put these with the meat, pour over it the gravy, and serve. The dish may be garnished with a few forcemeat balls. The meat, when preferred, may be cut into chops, and floured and fried instead of being roasted; and any part of veal dressed in this way will be found extremely savoury and good.

Time.—3 hours.   *Average cost,* 9*d.* per lb.

Sufficient for 6 or 7 persons.

Seasonable, with peas, from June to August.

BAKED SWEETBREADS (an Entree).

906. INGREDIENTS.—3 sweetbreads, egg and bread crumbs, oiled butter, 3 slices of toast, brown gravy.

Mode.—Choose large white sweetbreads; put them into warm water to draw out the blood, and to improve their colour; let them remain for rather more than 1 hour; then put them into boiling water, and allow them to simmer for about 10 minutes, which renders them firm. Take them up, drain them, brush over with egg, sprinkle

SWEETBREADS.

with bread crumbs; dip them in egg again, and then into more bread crumbs. Drop on them a little oiled butter, and put the sweetbreads into a moderately-heated oven, and let them bake for nearly ¾ hour. Make 3 pieces of toast; place the sweetbreads on the toast, and pour round, but not over them, a good brown gravy.

Time.—To soak 1 hour, to be boiled 10 minutes, baked 40 minutes.

Average cost, 1*s.* to 5*s.*   *Sufficient* for an entrée.

Seasonable.—In full season from May to August.

FRIED SWEETBREADS a la Maitre d'Hotel (an Entree).

907. INGREDIENTS.—3 sweetbreads, egg and bread crumbs, ¼ lb. of butter, salt and pepper to taste, rather more than ½ pint of Maître d'hôtel sauce No. 466.

Mode.—Soak the sweetbreads in warm water for an hour; then boil them for 10 minutes; cut them in slices, egg and bread crumb them, season with pepper and salt, and put them into a frying-pan, with the above proportion of butter. Keep turning them until done, which will be in about 10 minutes; dish them, and pour over them a Maître d'hôtel sauce, made by recipe No. 466. The dish may be garnished with slices of cut lemon.

Time.—To soak 1 hour, to be broiled 10 minutes, to be fried about 10 minutes.

Average cost, 1*s.* to 5*s.*, according to the season.

Sufficient for an entrée.

Seasonable.—In full season from May to August.

Note.—The egg and bread crumb may be omitted, and the slices of sweet-bread dredged with a little flour instead, and a good gravy may be substituted for the maître d'hôtel sauce. This is a very simple method of dressing them.

STEWED SWEETBREADS (an Entree).

908. INGREDIENTS.—3 sweetbreads, 1 pint of white stock No. 107, thickening of butter and flour, 6 tablespoonfuls of cream, 1 table-spoonful of lemon-juice, 1 blade of pounded mace, white pepper and salt to taste.

Mode.—Soak the sweetbreads in warm water for 1 hour, and boil them for 10 minutes; take them out, put them into cold water for a few minutes; lay them in a stewpan with the stock, and simmer them gently for rather more than ½ hour. Dish them; thicken the gravy with a little butter and flour; let it boil up, add the remaining ingredients, allow the sauce to get quite *hot*, but *not boil*, and pour it over the sweetbreads.

Time.—To soak 1 hour, to be boiled 10 minutes, stewed rather more than ½ hour.

Average cost, from 1s. to 5s., according to the season.

Sufficient for an entrée.

Seasonable.—In full season from May to August.

Note.—A few mushrooms added to this dish, and stewed with the sweet-breads, will be found an improvement.

SEASON AND CHOICE OF VEAL.—Veal, like all other meats, has its season of plenty. The best veal, and the largest supply, are to be had from March to the end of July. It comes principally from the western counties, and is generally of the Alderney breed. In purchasing veal, its whiteness and fineness of grain should be considered, the colour being especially of the utmost consequence. Veal may be bought at all times of the year, and of excellent quality, but is generally very dear, except in the months of plenty.

STEWED TENDRONS DE VEAU (an Entree).

909. INGREDIENTS.—The gristles from 2 breasts of veal, stock No. 107, 1 faggot of savoury herbs, 2 blades of pounded mace, 4 cloves, 2 carrots, 2 onions, a strip of lemon-peel.

Mode.—The *tendrons* or gristles, which are found round the front of a breast of veal, are now very frequently served as an entrée, and when well dressed, make a nice and favourite dish. Detach the gristles from the bone, and cut them neatly out, so as not to spoil the joint for roasting or stewing. Put them into a stewpan, with sufficient stock, No. 107, to cover them; add the herbs, mace, cloves, carrots, onions, and lemon, and simmer these for nearly, or quite, 4 hours. They should be stewed until a fork will enter the meat easily. Take them up, drain them, strain the gravy, boil it down to a glaze, with which glaze the meat. Dish the *tendrons* in a circle, with croûtons fried of a nice colour placed between each; and put mushroom sauce, or a purée of green peas or tomatoes, in the middle.

Time.—4 hours.　*Sufficient* for one entrée.

Seasonable.—With peas, from June to August.

Cow-Pox, or Variola.—It is to Dr. Jenner, of Berkeley, Gloucestershire, who died in 1823, that we owe the practice of vaccination, as a preservative from the attack of that destructive scourge of the human race, the small-pox. The experiments of this philosophic man were begun in 1797, and published the next year. He had observed that cows were subject to a certain infectious eruption of the teats, and that those persons who became affected by it, while milking the cattle, escaped the small-pox raging around them. This fact, known to farmers from time immemorial, led him to a course of experiments, the result of which all are acquainted with.

TENDRONS DE VEAU (an Entree).

910. Ingredients.—The gristles from 2 breasts of veal, stock No. 107, 1 faggot of savoury herbs, 1 blade of pounded mace, 4 cloves, 2 carrots, 2 onions, a strip of lemon-peel, egg and bread crumbs, 2 tablespoonfuls of chopped mushrooms, salt and pepper to taste, 2 tablespoonfuls of sherry, the yolk of 1 egg, 3 tablespoonfuls of cream.

Mode.—After removing the gristles from a breast of veal, stew them for 4 hours, as in the preceding recipe, with stock, herbs, mace, cloves, carrots, onions, and lemon-peel. When perfectly tender, lift them out and remove any bones or hard parts remaining. Put them between two dishes, with a weight on the top, and when cold, cut them into slices. Brush these over with egg, sprinkle with bread crumbs, and fry a pale brown. Take ½ pint of the gravy they were boiled in, add 2 tablespoonfuls of chopped mushrooms, a seasoning of salt and pepper, the sherry, and the yolk of an egg beaten with 3 tablespoonfuls of cream. Stir the sauce over the fire until it thickens; when it is on the *point of boiling*, dish the tendrons in a circle, and pour the sauce in the middle. Tendrons are dressed in a variety of ways,—with sauce à l'Espagnole, vegetables of all kinds: when they are served with a purée, they should always be glazed.

Time.—4½ hours. *Average cost.*—Usually bought with breast of veal. *Sufficient* for an entrée.

Seasonable from March to October.

TETE DE VEAU EN TORTUE (an Entree).

911. Ingredients.—Half a calf's head, or the remains of a cold boiled one; rather more than 1 pint of good white stock, No. 107, 1 glass of sherry or Madeira, cayenne and salt to taste, about 12 mushroom-

2 F

buttons (when obtainable), 6 hard-boiled eggs, 4 gherkins, 8 quenelles or forcemeat balls, No. 422 or 423, 12 crayfish, 12 croûtons.

Mode.—Half a calf's head is sufficient to make a good entrée, and if there are any remains of a cold one left from the preceding day, it will answer very well for this dish. After boiling the head until tender, remove the bones, and cut the meat into neat pieces ; put the stock into a stewpan, add the wine, and a seasoning of salt and cayenne ; fry the mushrooms in butter for 2 or 3 minutes, and add these to the gravy. Boil this quickly until somewhat reduced ; then put in the yolks of the hard-boiled eggs *whole*, the whites cut in small pieces, and the gherkins chopped. Have ready a few veal quenelles, made by recipe No. 422 or 423 ; add these, with the slices of head, to the other ingredients, and let the whole get thoroughly hot, *without boiling*. Arrange the pieces of head as high in the centre of the dish as possible ; pour over them the ragoût, and garnish with the crayfish and croûtons placed alternately. A little of the gravy should also be served in a tureen.

Time.—About ½ hour to reduce the stock.

Sufficient for 6 or 7 persons.

Average cost, exclusive of the calf's head, 2*s.* 9*d.*

Seasonable from March to October.

A FRENCHMAN'S OPINION OF VEAL.—A great authority in his native Paris tells us, that veal, as a meat, is but little nourishing, is relaxing, and sufficiently difficult of digestion. Lending itself, as it does, he says, in all the flowery imagery of the French tongue and manner, " to so many metamorphoses, it may be called, without exaggeration, the chameleon of the kitchen. Who has not eaten calf's head *au naturel*, simply boiled with the skin on, its flavour heightened by sauce just a little sharp ? It is a dish as wholesome as it is agreeable, and one that the most inexperienced cook may serve with success. Calf's feet *à la poulette*, *au gratin*, fried, &c. ; *les cervelles*, served in the same manner, and under the same names ; sweetbreads *en fricandeau*, *piqués en fin*,—all these offer most satisfactory entrées, which the art of the cook, more or less, varies for the grati- fication of his glory and the well-being of our appetites. We have not spoken, in the above catalogue, either of the liver, or of the *fraise*, or of the ears, which also share the honour of appearing at our tables. Where is the man not acquainted with calf's liver *à la bourgeoise*, the most frequent and convenient dish at unpretentious tables ? The *fraise*, cooked in water, and eaten with vinegar, is a wholesome and agreeable dish, and contains a mucilage well adapted for delicate persons. Calf's ears have, in common with the feet and *cervelles*, the advantage of being able to be eaten either fried or *à la poulette ;* and besides, can be made into a *farce*, with the addition of peas, onions, cheese, &c. Neither is it confined to the calf's tongue, or even the eyes, that these shall dispute alone the glory of awakening the taste of man ; thus, the *fressure* (which, as is known, comprises the heart, the *mcu*, and the *rate*), although not a very recherché dish, lends itself to all the caprices of an expert artist, and may, under various marvellous disguises, deceive, and please, and even awaken our appetite."—Verily, we might say, after this rhapsody of our neighbour, that his country's weal will not suffer in him as an able and eloquent exponent and admirer.

VEAL CARVING.

BREAST OF VEAL.

912. The carving of a breast of veal is not dissimilar to that of a fore-quarter of lamb, when the shoulder has been taken off. The breast of veal consists of two parts,— the rib-bones and the gristly brisket. These two parts should first be separated by sharply passing the knife in the direction of the lines 1, 2; when they are entirely divided, the rib-bones should be carved in the

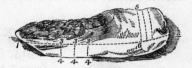

BREAST OF VEAL.

direction of the lines 5 to 6; and the brisket can be helped by cutting pieces in the direction 3 to 4. The carver should ask the guests whether they have a preference for the brisket or ribs; and if there be a sweetbread served with the dish, as it often is with roast breast of veal, each person should receive a piece.

CALF'S HEAD.

913. This is not altogether the most easy-looking dish to cut when it is put before a carver for the first time; there is not much real difficulty in the operation, however, when the head has been attentively examined, and, after the manner of a phrenologist, you get to know its bumps, good and bad. In the first place, inserting the knife quite down to the bone, cut slices in the direction of the line 1 to 2; with

CALF'S HEAD.

each of these should be helped a piece of what is called the throat sweetbread, cut in the direction of from 3 to 4. The eye, and the flesh round, are favourite morsels with many, and should be given to those at the table who are known to be the greatest connoisseurs. The jawbone being removed, there will then be found some nice lean; and the palate, which is reckoned by some a tit-bit, lies under the head. On a separate dish there is always served the tongue and brains, and each guest should be asked to take some of these.

2 F 2

FILLET OF VEAL.

FILLET OF VEAL.

914. The carving of this joint is similar to that of a round of beef. Slices, not too thick, in the direction of the line 1 to 2 are cut; and the only point to be careful about is, that the veal be *evenly* carved. Between the flap and the meat the stuffing is inserted, and a small portion of this should be served to every guest. The persons whom the host wishes most to honour should be asked if they like the delicious brown outside slice, as this, by many, is exceedingly relished.

KNUCKLE OF VEAL.

KNUCKLE OF VEAL.

915. The engraving, showing the dotted line from 1 to 2, sufficiently indicates the direction which should be given to the knife in carving this dish. The best slices are those from the thickest part of the knuckle, that is, outside the line 1 to 2.

LOIN OF VEAL.

916. As is the case with a loin of mutton, the careful jointing of a loin of veal is more than half the battle in carving it. If the butcher

LOIN OF VEAL.

be negligent in this matter, he should be admonished; for there is nothing more annoying or irritating to an inexperienced carver than to be obliged to turn his knife in all directions to find the exact place where it should be inserted in order to divide the bones. When the jointing is properly performed, there is little difficulty in carrying the knife down in the direction of the line 1 to 2. To each guest should be given a piece of the kidney and kidney fat, which lie underneath, and are considered great delicacies.

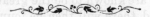

CHAPTER XX.

GENERAL OBSERVATIONS ON BIRDS.

"Birds, the free tenants of land, air, and ocean,
   Their forms all symmetry, their motions grace;
In plumage delicate and beautiful;
Thick without burthen, close as fishes' scales,
Or loose as full-blown poppies to the breeze."

The Pelican Island.

917. THE DIVISIONS OF BIRDS are founded principally on their habits of life, and the natural resemblance which their external parts, especially their bills, bear to each other. According to Mr. Vigors, there are five orders, each of which occupies its peculiar place on the surface of the globe; so that the air, the forest, the land, the marsh, and the water, has each its appropriate kind of inhabitants. These are respectively designated as BIRDS OF PREY, PERCHERS, WALKERS, WADERS, and SWIMMERS; and, in contemplating their variety, lightness, beauty, and wonderful adaptation to the regions they severally inhabit, and the functions they are destined to perform in the grand scheme of creation, our hearts are lifted with admiration at the exhaustless ingenuity, power, and wisdom of HIM who has, in producing them, so strikingly "manifested His handiwork." Not only these, however, but all classes of animals, have their peculiar ends to fulfil; and, in order that this may be effectually performed, they are constructed in such a manner as will enable them to carry out their conditions. Thus the quadrupeds, that are formed to

tread the earth in common with man, are muscular and vigorous; and, whether they have passed into the servitude of man, or are permitted to range the forest or the field, they still retain, in a high degree, the energies with which they were originally endowed. Birds, on the contrary, are generally feeble, and, therefore, timid. Accordingly, wings have been given them to enable them to fly through the air, and thus elude the force which, by nature, they are unable to resist. Notwithstanding the natural tendency of all bodies towards the centre of the earth, birds, when raised in the atmosphere, glide through it with the greatest ease, rapidity, and vigour. There, they are in their natural element, and can vary their course with the greatest promptitude—can mount or descend with the utmost facility, and can light on any spot with the most perfect exactness, and without the slightest injury to themselves.

918. THE MECHANISM WHICH ENABLES BIRDS to wing their course through the air, is both singular and instructive. Their bodies are covered with feathers, which are much lighter than coverings of hair, with which quadrupeds are usually clothed. The feathers are so placed as to overlap each other, like the slates or the tiles on the roof of a house. They are also arranged from the fore-part backwards; by which the animals are enabled the more conveniently to cut their way through the air. Their bones are tubular or hollow, and extremely light compared with those of terrestrial animals. This greatly facilitates their rising from the earth, whilst their heads, being comparatively small, their bills shaped like a wedge, their bodies slender, sharp below, and round above,—all these present a union of conditions, favourable, in the last degree, to cutting their way through the aërial element to which they are considered as more peculiarly to belong. With all these conditions, however, birds could not fly without wings. These, therefore, are the instruments by which they have the power of rapid locomotion, and are constructed in such a manner as to be capable of great expansion when struck in a downward direction. If we except, in this action, the slight hollow which takes place on the under-side, they become almost two planes. In order that the downward action may be accomplished to the necessary extent, the muscles which move the wings have been made exceedingly large; so large, indeed, that, in some instances, they have been estimated at not less than a sixth of the weight of the whole body. Therefore, when a bird is on the ground and intends to fly, it takes a leap, and immediately stretching its wings, strikes them out with great force. By this act these are brought into an oblique direction, being turned partly upwards and partly horizontally forwards. That part of the force which has the upward tendency is neutralized by the weight of the bird, whilst the horizontal force serves to carry it forward. The stroke being completed, it moves upon its wings, which, being contracted and having their edges turned upwards, obviate, in a great measure, the resistance of the air. When it is sufficiently elevated, it makes a second stroke downwards, and the impulse of the air again moves it forward. These successive strokes may be regarded as so many leaps taken in the air. When

the bird desires to direct its course to the right or the left, it strikes strongly with the opposite wing, which impels it to the proper side. In the motions of the animal, too, the tail takes a prominent part, and acts like the rudder of a ship, except that, instead of sideways, it moves upwards and downwards. If the bird wishes to rise, it raises its tail; and if to fall, it depresses it; and, whilst in a horizontal position, it keeps it steady. There are few who have not observed a pigeon or a crow preserve, for some time, a horizontal flight without any apparent motion of the wings. This is accomplished by the bird having already acquired sufficient velocity, and its wings being parallel to the horizon, meeting with but small resistance from the atmosphere. If it begins to fall, it can easily steer itself upward by means of its tail, till the motion it had acquired is nearly spent, when it must be renewed by a few more strokes of the wings. On alighting, a bird expands its wings and tail fully against the air, as a ship, in tacking round, backs her sails, in order that they may meet with all the resistance possible.

919. In the Construction of the Eyes of birds, there is a peculiarity necessary to their condition. As they pass a great portion of their lives among thickets and hedges, they are provided for the defence of their eyes from external injuries, as well as from the effects of the light, when flying in opposition to the rays of the sun, with a nictating or winking membrane, which can, at pleasure, be drawn over the whole eye like a curtain. This covering s neither opaque nor wholly pellucid, but is somewhat transparent; and it is by its means that the eagle is said to be able to gaze at the sun. "In birds," says a writer on this subject, "we find that the sight is much more piercing, extensive, and exact, than in the other orders of animals. The eye is much larger in proportion to the bulk of the head, than in any of these. This is a superiority conferred upon them not without a corresponding utility: it seems even indispensable to their safety and subsistence. Were this organ in birds dull, or in the least degree opaque, they would be in danger, from the rapidity of their motion, of striking against various objects in their flight. In this case their celerity, instead of being an advantage, would become an evil, and their flight be restrained by the danger resulting from it. Indeed we may consider the velocity with which an animal moves, as a sure indication of the perfection of its vision. Among the quadrupeds, the sloth has its sight greatly limited; whilst the hawk, as it hovers in the air, can espy a lark sitting on a clod, perhaps at twenty times the distance at which a man or a dog could perceive it."

920. Amongst the many peculiarities in the Construction of Birds, not the least is the mode by which their respiration is accomplished. This is effected by means of air-vessels, which extend throughout the body, and adhere to the under-surface of the bones. These, by their motion, force the air through the true lungs, which are very small, and placed in the uppermost part of the chest, and closely braced down to the back and ribs. The lungs, which are never expanded by air, are destined to the sole purpose of oxidizing

the blood. In the experiments made by Mr. John Hunter, to discover the use of this general diffusion of air through the bodies of birds, he found that it prevents their respiration from being stopped or interrupted by the rapidity of their motion through a resisting medium. It is well known that, in proportion to celerity of motion, the air becomes resistive ; and were it possible for a man to move with the swiftness of a swallow, as he is not provided with an internal construction similar to that of birds, the resistance of the air would soon suffocate him.

921. BIRDS ARE DISTRIBUTED OVER EVERY PART OF THE GLOBE, being found in the coldest as well as the hottest regions, although some species are restricted to particular countries, whilst others are widely dispersed. At certain seasons of the year, many of them change their abodes, and migrate to climates better adapted to their temperaments or modes of life, for a time, than those which they leave. Many of the birds of Britain, directed by an unerring instinct, take their departure from the island before the commencement of winter, and proceed to the more congenial warmth of Africa, to return with the next spring. The causes assigned by naturalists for this peculiarity are, either a deficiency of food, or the want of a secure asylum for the incubation and nourishment of their young. Their migrations are generally performed in large companies, and, in the day, they follow a leader, which is occasionally changed. During the night, many of the tribes send forth a continual cry, to keep themselves together ; although one would think that the noise which must accompany their flight would be sufficient for that purpose. The flight of birds across the Mediterranean was noticed three thousand years ago, as we find it said in the book of Numbers, in the Scriptures, that "There went forth a wind from the Lord, and brought quails from the sea, and let them fall upon the camp, and a day's journey round about it, to the height of two cubits above the earth."

922. IF THE BEAUTY OF BIRDS were not a recommendation to their being universally admired, their general liveliness, gaiety, and song would endear them to mankind. It appears, however, from accurate observations founded upon experiment, that the notes peculiar to different kinds of birds are altogether acquired, and that they are not innate, any more than language is to man. The attempt of a nestling bird to sing has been compared to the endeavour of a child to talk. The first attempts do not seem to possess the slightest rudiments of the future song; but, as the bird grows older and becomes stronger, it is easily perceived to be aiming at acquiring the art of giving utterance to song. Whilst the scholar is thus endeavouring to form his notes, when he is once sure of a passage, he usually raises his tone, but drops it again when he finds himself unequal to the voluntary task he has undertaken. "Many well-authenticated facts," says an ingenious writer, "seem decisively to prove that birds have no innate notes, but that, like mankind, the language of those to whose care they have been committed at their birth, will be their language in after-life." It would appear, however,

somewhat unaccountable why, in a wild state, they adhere so steadily to the song of their own species only, when the notes of so many others are to be heard around them. This is said to arise from the attention paid by the nestling bird to the instructions of its own parent only, generally disregarding the notes of all the rest. Persons, however, who have an accurate ear, and who have given their attention to the songs of birds, can frequently distinguish some which have their notes mixed with those of another species ; but this is in general so trifling, that it can hardly be considered as more than the mere varieties of provincial dialects.

923. IN REFERENCE TO THE FOOD OF BIRDS, we find that it varies, as it does in quadrupeds, according to the species. Some are altogether carnivorous ; others, as so many of the web-footed tribes, subsist on fish ; others, again, on insects and worms ; and others on grain and fruit. The extraordinary powers of the gizzard of the granivorous tribes, in comminuting their food so as to prepare it for digestion, would, were they not supported by incontrovertible facts founded on experiment, appear to exceed all credibility. Tin tubes, full of grain, have been forced into the stomachs of turkeys, and in twenty-four hours have been found broken, compressed, and distorted into every shape. Twelve small lancets, very sharp both at the point and edges, have been fixed in a ball of lead, covered with a case of paper, and given to a turkey-cock, and left in its stomach for eight hours. After that time the stomach was opened, when nothing appeared except the naked ball. The twelve lancets were broken to pieces, whilst the stomach remained perfectly sound and entire. From these facts, it is concluded that the stones, so frequently found in the stomachs of the feathered tribes, are highly useful in assisting the gastric juices to grind down the grain and other hard substances which constitute their food. The stones, themselves, being also ground down and separated by the powerful action of the gizzard, are mixed with the food, and, no doubt, contribute very greatly to the health, as well as to the nourishment of the animals.

924. ALL BIRDS BEING OVIPAROUS, the eggs which they produce after the process of incubation, or sitting for a certain length of time, are, in the various species, different both in figure and colour, as well as in point of number. They contain the elements of the future young, for the perfecting of which in the incubation a bubble of air is always placed at the large end, between the shell and the inside skin. It is supposed that from the heat communicated by the sitting bird to this confined air, its spring is increased beyond its natural tenor, and, at the same time, its parts are put into motion by the gentle rarefaction. By this means, pressure and motion are communicated to the parts of the egg, which, in some inscrutable way, gradually promote the formation and growth of the young, till the time comes for its escaping from the shell. To preserve an egg perfectly fresh, and even fit for incubation, for 5 or 6 months after it has been laid, Réaumur, the French naturalist, has shown that it is only necessary to stop up its pores with a slight coating of varnish or mutton-suet.

925. BIRDS, HOWEVER, DO NOT LAY EGGS before they have some place to put them ; accordingly, they construct nests for themselves with astonishing art. As builders, they exhibit a degree of architectural skill, niceness, and propriety, that would seem even to mock the imitative talents of man, however greatly these are marked by his own high intelligence and ingenuity.

> "Each circumstance
> Most artfully contrived to favour warmth.
> Here read the reason of the vaulted roof;
> How Providence compensates, ever kind,
> The enormous disproportion that subsists
> Between the mother and the numerous brood
> Which her small bulk must quicken into life."

In building their nests, the male and female generally assist each other, and they contrive to make the outside of their tenement bear as great a resemblance as possible to the surrounding foliage or branches ; so that it cannot very easily be discovered even by those who are in search of it. This art of nidification is one of the most wonderful contrivances which the wide field of Nature can show, and which, of itself, ought to be sufficient to compel mankind to the belief, that they and every other part of the creation, are constantly under the protecting power of a superintending Being, whose benign dispensations seem as exhaustless as they are unlimited.

RECIPES.

————◆————

CHAPTER XXI.

CHICKEN CUTLETS (an Entree).

926. INGREDIENTS.—2 chickens; seasoning to taste of salt, white pepper, and cayenne ; 2 blades of pounded mace, egg and bread crumbs, clarified butter, 1 strip of lemon-rind, 2 carrots, 1 onion, 2 tablespoonfuls of mushroom ketchup, thickening of butter and flour, 1 egg.

Mode.—Remove the breast and leg bones of the chickens; cut the meat into neat pieces after having skinned it, and season the cutlets with pepper, salt, pounded mace, and cayenne. Put the bones, trimmings, &c., into a stewpan with 1 pint of water, adding carrots, onions, and lemon-peel in the above proportion ; stew gently for 1½ hour, and strain the gravy. Thicken it with butter and flour, add the ketchup and 1 egg well beaten ; stir it over the fire, and bring it to the simmering-point, but do not allow it to boil. In the mean time, egg and bread-crumb the cutlets, and give them a few drops of clarified butter ; fry them a delicate brown, occasionally turning them ; arrange them pyramidically on the dish, and pour over them the sauce.

Time.—10 minutes to fry the cutlets. *Average cost,* 2s. each.

Sufficient for an entrée.

Seasonable from April to July.

FOWLS AS FOOD.—Brillat Savarin, pre-eminent in gastronomic taste, says that he believes the whole gallinaceous family was made to enrich our larders and furnish our tables; for, from the quail to the turkey, he avers their flesh is a light aliment, full of flavour, and fitted equally well for the invalid as for the man of robust health. The fine flavour, however, which Nature has given to all birds coming under the definition of poultry, man has not been satisfied with, and has used many means—such as keeping them in solitude and darkness, and forcing them to eat—to give them an unnatural state of fatness or fat. This fat, thus artificially produced, is doubtless delicious, and the taste and succulence of the boiled and roasted bird draw forth the praise of the guests around the table. Well-fattened and tender, a fowl is to the cook what the canvas is to the painter; for do we not see it served boiled, roasted, fried, fricasseed, hashed, hot, cold, whole, dismembered, boned, broiled, stuffed, on dishes, and in pies,—always handy and ever acceptable?

THE COMMON OR DOMESTIC FOWL.—From time immemorial, the common or domestic fowl has been domesticated in England, and is supposed to be originally the offspring of some wild species which abound in the forests of India. It is divided into a variety of breeds, but the most esteemed are, the Poland or Black, the Dorking, the Bantam, the Game Fowl, and the Malay or Chittagong. The common, or barn-door fowl, is one of the most delicate of the varieties; and at Dorking, in Surrey, the breed is brought to great perfection. Till they are four months old, the term chicken is applied to the young female; after that age they are called pullets, till they begin to lay, when they are called hens. The English counties most productive in poultry are Surrey, Sussex, Norfolk, Herts, Devon, and Somerset.

FRENCH CHICKEN CUTLETS (Cold Meat Cookery).

927. INGREDIENTS.—The remains of cold roast or boiled fowl, fried bread, clarified butter, the yolk of 1 egg, bread crumbs, ½ teaspoonful of finely-minced lemon-peel; salt, cayenne, and mace to taste. For sauce,—1 oz. of butter, 2 minced shalots, a few slices of carrot, a small bunch of savoury herbs, including parsley, 1 blade of pounded mace, 6 peppercorns, ½ pint of gravy.

Mode.—Cut the fowls into as many nice cutlets as possible; take a corresponding number of sippets about the same size, all cut one shape; fry them a pale brown, put them before the fire, then dip the cutlets into clarified butter mixed with the yolk of an egg, cover with bread crumbs seasoned in the above proportion, with lemon-peel, mace, salt, and cayenne; fry them for about 5 minutes, put each piece on one of the sippets, pile them high in the dish, and serve with the following sauce, which should be made ready for the cutlets. Put the butter into a stewpan, add the shalots, carrot, herbs, mace, and peppercorns; fry for 10 minutes or rather longer; pour in ½ pint of good gravy, made of the chicken bones, stew gently for 20 minutes, strain it, and serve.

Time.— 5 minutes to fry the cutlets; 35 minutes to make the gravy.

Average cost, exclusive of the chicken, 9d.

Seasonable from April to July.

EGGS FOR HATCHING.—Eggs intended for hatching should be removed as soon as laid, and placed in bran in a dry, cool place. Choose those that are near of a size; and, as a rule, avoid those that are equally thick at both ends,—such, probably, contain a double yolk, and will come to no good. Eggs intended for hatching should never be stored longer than a month, as much less the better. Nine eggs may be placed under a Bantam hen, and as many as fifteen under a Dorking. The odd number is considered preferable, as more easily packed. It will be as well to mark the eggs you give the hen to sit on, so that you may know if she lays any more: if she does, you must remove them; for, if hatched at all, they would be too late for the brood. If during incubation an egg should be broken, remove it, and take out the remainder, and cleanse them in luke-warm water, or it is probable the sticky nature of the contents of the broken egg will make the others cling to the hen's feathers; and they, too, may be fractured.

HENS SITTING.—Some hens are very capricious as regards sitting; they will make a great fuss, and keep pining for the nest, and, when they are permitted to take to it, they will sit just long enough to addle the eggs, and then they're off again. The safest way to guard against such annoyance, is to supply the hen with some hard-boiled eggs; if she sits on them a reasonable time, and seems steadily inclined, like a good matron, you may then give her proper eggs, and let her set about the business in earnest.

CHICKEN OR FOWL PATTIES.

928. INGREDIENTS.—The remains of cold roast chicken or fowl; to every $\frac{1}{4}$ lb. of meat allow 2 oz. of ham, 3 tablespoonfuls of cream, 2 tablespoonfuls of veal gravy, $\frac{1}{2}$ teaspoonful of minced lemon-peel; cayenne, salt, and pepper to taste; 1 tablespoonful of lemon-juice, 1 oz. of butter rolled in flour; puff paste.

Mode.—Mince very small the white meat from a cold roast fowl, after removing all the skin; weigh it, and to every $\frac{1}{4}$ lb. of meat allow the above proportion of minced ham. Put these into a stewpan with the remaining ingredients, stir over the fire for 10 minutes or $\frac{1}{4}$ hour, taking care that the mixture does not burn. Roll out some puff paste about $\frac{1}{4}$ inch in thickness; line the patty-pans with this, put upon each a small piece of bread, and cover with another layer of paste; brush over with the yolk of an egg, and bake in a brisk oven for about $\frac{1}{4}$ hour. When done, cut a round piece out of the top, and, with a small spoon, take out the bread (be particular in not breaking the outside border of the crust), and fill the patties with the mixture.

Time.—$\frac{1}{4}$ hour to prepare the meat; not quite $\frac{1}{4}$ hour to bake the crust.

Seasonable at any time.

HATCHING.—Sometimes the chick within the shell is unable to break away from its prison; for the white of the egg will occasionally harden in the air to the consistence of joiners' glue, when the poor chick is in a terrible fix. An able writer says, " Assistance in hatching must not be rendered prematurely, and thence unnecessarily, but only in the case of the chick being plainly unable to release itself; then, indeed, an addition may probably be made to the brood, as great numbers are always lost in this way. The chick makes a circular fracture at the big end of the egg, and a section of about one-third of the length of the shell being separated, delivers the prisoner, provided there is no obstruction from adhesion of the body to the membrane which lines the shell. Between the body of the chick and the membrane of the shell there exists a viscous fluid, the white of the egg thickened with the intense heat of incubation, until it becomes a positive glue. When this happens, the feathers stick fast to the shell, and the chicks remain confined, and must perish, if not released."
The method of assistance to be rendered to chicks which have a difficulty in releasing themselves from the shell, is to take the egg in the hand, and dipping the finger or a piece of linen rag in warm water, to apply it to the fastened parts until they are loosened by the gluey substance becoming dissolved and separated from the feathers. The chick, then, being returned to the nest, will extricate itself,—a mode generally to be observed, since, if violence were used, it would prove fatal. Nevertheless, breaking the shell may sometimes be necessary; and separating with the fingers, as gently as may be, the membrane from the feathers, which are still to be moistened as mentioned above, to facilitate the operation. The points of small scissors may be useful, and when there is much resistance, as also apparent pain to the bird, the process must be conducted in the gentlest manner, and the shell separated into a number of small pieces. The signs of a need of assistance are the egg being partly pecked and chipped, and the chick discontinuing its efforts for five or six hours. Weakness from cold may disable the chicken from commencing the operation of pecking the shell, which must then be artificially performed with a circular fracture, such as is made by the bird itself.

CHICKEN OR FOWL PIE.

929. INGREDIENTS.—2 small fowls or 1 large one, white pepper and salt to taste, ½ teaspoonful of grated nutmeg, ½ teaspoonful of pounded mace, forcemeat No. 417, a few slices of ham, 3 hard-boiled eggs, ⅓ pint of water, puff crust.

Mode.—Skin and cut up the fowls into joints, and put the neck, leg, and backbones in a stewpan, with a little water, an onion, a bunch of savoury herbs, and a blade of mace; let these stew for about an hour, and, when done, strain off the liquor: this is for gravy. Put a layer of fowl at the bottom of a pie-dish, then a layer of ham, then one of forcemeat and hard-boiled eggs cut in rings; between the layers put a seasoning of pounded mace, nutmeg, pepper, and salt. Proceed in this manner until the dish is full, and pour in about ⅓ pint of water; border the edge of the dish with puff crust, put on the cover, ornament the top, and glaze it by brushing over it the yolk of an egg. Bake from 1¼ to 1½ hour, should the pie be very large, and, when done, pour in, at the top, the gravy made from the bones. If to be eaten cold, and wished particularly nice, the joints of the fowls should be boned, and placed in the dish with alternate layers of forcemeat; sausage-meat may also be substituted for the forcemeat, and is now very much used. When the chickens are boned, and mixed with sausage-meat, the pie will take about 2 hours to bake. It should be covered with a piece of paper when about half-done, to prevent the paste from being dried up or scorched.

Time.—For a pie with unboned meat, 1¼ to 1½ hour; with boned meat and sausage or forcemeat, 1½ to 2 hours.

Average cost, with 2 fowls, 6s. 6d.

Sufficient for 6 or 7 persons.

Seasonable at any time.

THE YOUNG CHICKS.—The chicks that are hatched first should be taken from underneath the hen, lest she might think her task at an end, and leave the remaining eggs to spoil. As soon as the young birds are taken from the mother, they must be placed in a basket lined with soft wool, flannel, or hay, and stood in the sunlight if it be summer time, or by the fire if the weather be cold. It is a common practice to cram young chicks with food as soon as they are born. This is quite unnecessary. They will, so long as they are kept warm, come to no harm if they take no food for twenty-four hours following their birth. Should the whole of the brood not be hatched by that time, those that are born may be fed with bread soaked in milk, and the yolk of a hard-boiled egg.

POTTED CHICKEN OR FOWL (a Luncheon or Breakfast Dish).

930. INGREDIENTS.—The remains of cold roast chicken; to every lb. of meat allow ¼ lb. of fresh butter, salt and cayenne to taste, 1 teaspoonful of pounded mace, ½ small nutmeg.

Mode.—Strip the meat from the bones of cold roast fowl; when it is freed from gristle and skin, weigh it, and, to every lb. of meat, allow the above proportion of butter, seasoning, and spices. Cut the meat into small pieces, pound it well with the fresh butter, sprinkle in the spices gradually, and keep pounding until reduced to a perfectly smooth paste. Put it into potting-pots for use, and cover it with clarified butter, about $\frac{1}{4}$ inch in thickness, and, if to be kept for some time, tie over a bladder : 2 or 3 slices of ham, minced and pounded with the above ingredients, will be found an improvement. It should be kept in a dry place.

Seasonable at any time.

FEEDING AND COOPING THE CHICKS.—When all the chicks are hatched, they should be placed along with the mother under a coop in a warm dry spot. If two hens happen to have their broods at the same time, their respective chicks should be carefully kept separate ; as, if they get mixed, and so go under the wrong coop, the hens will probably maim and destroy those who have mistaken their dwelling. After being kept snug beneath the coop for a week (the coop should be placed under cover at nightfall), the chicks may be turned loose for an hour or so in the warmest part of the day. They should be gradually weaned from the soaked bread and chopped egg, instead of which grits or boiled barley should be given ; in 8 or 10 days their stomachs will be strong enough to receive bruised barley, and at the end of 3 weeks, if your chicks be healthy, they will be able to take care of themselves. It will be well, however, to keep your eye on them a week or so longer, as the elder chickens may drive them from their food. Great care should be taken that the very young chicks do not run about the wet ground or on damp grass, as this is the most prominent and fatal cause of disease. While under the coop with their mother, a shallow pan or plate of water should be supplied to the chicks, as in a deeper vessel they are liable to drench themselves and take cold, or possibly to get drowned.

CHICKEN OR FOWL SALAD.

931. INGREDIENTS.—The remains of cold roast or boiled chicken, 2 lettuces, a little endive, 1 cucumber, a few slices of boiled beetroot, salad-dressing No. 506.

Mode.—Trim neatly the remains of the chicken ; wash, dry, and slice the lettuces, and place in the middle of a dish; put the pieces of fowl on the top, and pour the salad-dressing over them. Garnish the edge of the salad with hard-boiled eggs cut in rings, sliced cucumber, and boiled beetroot cut in slices. Instead of cutting the eggs in rings, the yolks may be rubbed through a hair sieve, and the whites chopped very finely, and arranged on the salad in small bunches, yellow and white alternately. This should not be made long before it is wanted for table.

Average cost, exclusive of the cold chicken, 8*d*.

Sufficient for 4 or 5 persons.

Seasonable at any time.

AGE AND FLAVOUR OF CHICKENS.—It has been the opinion of the medical faculty of all ages and all countries, that the flesh of the young chicken is the most delicate and easy to digest of all animal food. It is less alkalescent than the flesh of any other animal, and its entire freedom from any irritating quality renders it a fit dish for the ailing, or those whose stomachs are naturally weak. In no animal, however, does age work such a change, in regard to the quality of its flesh, as it does in domestic fowls. In their infancy, cocks and hens are equally tender and toothsome ; but as time overtakes them, it is the cock whose flesh toughens first. A year-old cock, indeed, is fit for little else than to be converted into soup, while a hen at the same age, although sufficiently substantial, is not callous to the insinuations of a carving-knife. As regards capons, however, the rule respecting age does not hold good. There is scarcely to be found a more delicious animal than a well-fed, well-dressed capon. Age does not dry up his juices; indeed, like wine, he seems but to mellow. At three years old, even, he is as tender as a chick, with the additional advantage of his proper chicken flavour being fully developed. The above remarks, however, concerning the capon, only apply to such as are *naturally* fed, and not crammed. The latter process may produce a handsome-*looking* bird, and it may weigh enough to satisfy the whim or avarice of its stuffer; but, when before the fire, it will reveal the cruel treatment to which it has been subjected, and will weep a drippingpan-ful of fat tears. You will never find heart enough to place such a grief-worn guest at the head of your table. It should be borne in mind as a rule, that small-boned and short-legged poultry are likely to excel the contrary sort in delicacy of colour, flavour, and fineness of flesh.

HASHED DUCK (Cold Meat Cookery).

932. INGREDIENTS.—The remains of cold roast duck, rather more than 1 pint of weak stock or water, 1 onion, 1 oz. of butter, thickening of butter and flour, salt and cayenne to taste, ½ teaspoonful of minced lemon-peel, 1 dessertspoonful of lemon-juice, ½ glass of port wine.

Mode.—Cut the duck into nice joints, and put the trimmings into a stewpan; slice and fry the onion in a little butter; add these to the trimmings, pour in the above proportion of weak stock or water, and stew gently for 1 hour. Strain the liquor, thicken it with butter and flour, season with salt and cayenne, and add the remaining ingredients; boil it up and skim well; lay in the pieces of duck, and let them get thoroughly hot through by the side of the fire, but do not allow them to boil: they should soak in the gravy for about ½ hour. Garnish with sippets of toasted bread. The hash may be made richer by using a stronger and more highly-flavoured gravy; a little spice or pounded mace may also be added, when their flavour is liked.

Time.—1½ hour. *Average cost,* exclusive of the cold duck, 4d.

Seasonable from November to February; ducklings from May to August.

THE DUCK.—This bird belongs to the order of *Natatores,* or Swimmers; the most familiar tribes of which are ducks, swans, geese, auks, penguins, petrels, pelicans, guillemots, gulls, and terns. They mostly live in the water, feeding on fish, worms, and aquatic plants. They are generally polygamous, and make their nests among reeds, or in moist places. The flesh of many of the species is eatable, but that of some is extremely rank and oily. The duck is a native of Britain, but is found on the margins of most of the European lakes. It is excessively greedy, and by no means a nice feeder. It requires a mixture of vegetable and animal food; but aquatic insects, corn, and vegetables, are its proper food. Its flesh, however, is savoury, being not so gross as that of the goose, and of easier digestion. In the green-pea season it is usually found on an English table; but, according to Ude, "November is its proper season, when it is plump and fat."

TO RAGOUT A DUCK WHOLE.

933. INGREDIENTS.—1 large duck, pepper and salt to taste, good beef gravy, 2 onions sliced, 4 sage-leaves, a few leaves of lemon thyme, thickening of butter and flour.

Mode.—After having emptied and singed the duck, season it inside with pepper and salt, and truss it. Roast it before a clear fire for about 20 minutes, and let it acquire a nice brown colour. Put it into a stewpan with sufficient well-seasoned beef gravy to cover it; slice and fry the onions, and add these, with the sage-leaves and lemon thyme, both of which should be finely minced, to the stock. Simmer gently until the duck is tender; strain, skim, and thicken the gravy with a little butter and flour; boil it up, pour over the duck, and serve. When in season, about 1½ pint of young green peas, boiled separately, and put in the ragoût, very much improve this dish.

Time.—20 minutes to roast the duck; 20 minutes to stew it.

Average cost, from 2s. 3d. to 2s. 6d. each.

Sufficient for 4 or 5 persons.

Seasonable from November to February; ducklings from April to August.

THE BUENOS AYRES DUCK.—The Buenos Ayres duck is of East-Indian birth, and is chiefly valuable as an ornament; for we suppose one would as soon think of picking a Chinese teal for luncheon, or a gold fish for breakfast, as to consign the handsome Buenos Ayres to the spit. The prevailing colour of this bird is black, with a metallic lustre, and a gleaming of blue steel about its breast and wings.

VARIETIES OF DUCKS.—Naturalists count nearly a hundred different species of ducks; and there is no doubt that the intending keeper of these harmless and profitable birds may easily take his choice from amongst twenty different sorts. There is, however, so little difference in the various members of the family, either as regards hardiness, laying,

BUENOS AYRES DUCKS.

or hatching, that the most incompetent fancier or breeder may indulge his taste without danger of making a bad bargain. In connection with their value for table, light-coloured ducks are always of milder flavour than those that are dark-coloured, the white Aylesbury's being general favourites. Ducks reared exclusively on vegetable diet will have a whiter and more delicate flesh than those allowed to feed on animal offal; while the flesh of birds fattened on the latter food, will be firmer than that of those which have only partaken of food of a vegetable nature.

ROAST DUCKS.

934. INGREDIENTS.—A couple of ducks; sage-and-onion stuffing No. 504; a little flour.

Choosing and Trussing.—Choose ducks with plump bellies, and with thick and yellowish feet. They should be trussed with the feet on, which should be scalded, and the skin peeled off, and then turned up close to the legs. Run a skewer through the middle of each leg, after having drawn them as close as possible to the body, to plump up the breast, passing the same quite through the body. Cut off the heads and necks, and the pinions at the first joint; bring these close to the sides, twist the feet round, and truss them at the back of the bird. After the duck is stuffed, both ends should be secured with string, so as to keep in the seasoning.

Mode.—To insure ducks being tender, never dress them the same day they are killed; and if the weather permits, they should hang a day or two. Make a stuffing of sage and onion sufficient for one duck, and leave the other unseasoned, as the flavour is not liked by every-

ROAST DUCK.

body. Put them down to a brisk clear fire, and keep them well basted the whole of the time they are cooking. A few minutes before serving, dredge them lightly with flour, to make them froth and look plump; and when the steam draws towards the fire, send them to table hot and quickly, with a good brown gravy poured *round*, but not *over* the ducks, and a little of the same in a tureen. When in season, green peas should invariably accompany this dish.

Time.— Full-grown ducks from ¾ to 1 hour; ducklings from 25 to 35 minutes.

Average cost, from 2s. 3d. to 2s. 6d. each.

Sufficient.—A couple of ducks for 6 or 7 persons.

Seasonable.—Ducklings from April to August; ducks from November to February.

Note.—Ducklings are trussed and roasted in the same manner, and served with the same sauces and accompaniments. When in season, serve apple sauce.

THE ROUEN DUCK.—The Rouen, or Rhone duck, is a large and handsome variety, of French extraction. The plumage of the Rouen duck is somewhat sombre; its flesh is

ROUEN DUCKS.

also much darker, and, though of higher flavour, not near so delicate as that of our own Aylesbury. It is with this latter breed that the Rouen duck is generally mated; and the result is said to be in-crease of size and strength. In Nor-mandy and Brittany these ducks, as well as other sorts, greatly abound; and the "duck-liver *pâtés*" are there almost as popular as the *pâté de foie gras* of Stras-burg. In order to bring the livers of the wretched duck to the fashionable and unnatural size, the same diabolical cruelty is resorted to as in the case of the Stras-burg goose. The poor birds are *nailed* by the feet to a board placed close to a fire, and, in that position, plentifully sup-plied with food and water. In a few days, the carcase is reduced to a mere shadow, while the liver has grown monstrously. We would rather abstain from the acquaintance of a man who ate *pâté de foie gras*, knowing its component parts.

DUCK'S EGGS.—The ancient notion that ducks whose beaks have a tendency to curve upwards, are better layers than those whose beaks do not thus point, is, we need hardly say, simply absurd: all ducks are good layers, if they are carefully fed and tended. Ducks generally lay at night, or early in the morning. While they are in perfect health, they will do this; and one of the surest signs of indisposition, among birds of this class, is irregularity in laying. The eggs laid will approach nearly the colour of the layer,—light-coloured ducks laying white eggs, and brown ducks greenish-blue eggs; dark-coloured birds laying the largest eggs. One time of day the notion was prevalent that a duck would hatch no other eggs than her own; and although this is not true, it will be, nevertheless, as well to match the duck's own eggs as closely as possible; for we have known instances wherein the duck has turned out of the nest and destroyed eggs differing from her own in size and colour.

DUCKS.—The Mallard, or Wild Duck, from which is derived the domestic species, is prevalent throughout Europe, Asia, and America. The mallard's most remarkable characteristic is one which sets at defiance the speculations of the most profound ornithologist. The female bird is extremely plain, but the male's plumage is a splendour of greens and browns, and browns and blues. In the spring, however, the plumage of the male begins to fade, and in two months, every vestige of his finery has departed, and he is not to be distinguished from his soberly-garbed wife. Then the greens, and the blues, and the browns begin to bud out again, and by October he is once more a gorgeous drake. It is to be regretted that domestication has seriously deteriorated the moral character of the duck. In a wild state, he is a faithful husband, desiring but one wife, and devoting himself to her; but no sooner is he domesticated than he becomes polygamous, and makes nothing of owning ten or a dozen wives at a time. As regards the females, they are much more solicitous for the welfare of their progeny in a wild state than a tame. Should a tame duck's duckling get into mortal trouble, its mother will just signify her sorrow by an extra "quack," or so and a flapping of her wings; but touch a wild duck's little one if you dare! she will buffet you with her broad wings, and dash boldly at your face with her stout beak. If you search for her nest amongst the long grass, she will try no end of manœuvres to lure you from it, her favourite *ruse* being to pretend lameness, to delude you into the notion that you have only to pursue her vigorously, and her capture is certain; so you persevere for half a mile or so, and then she is up and away, leaving you to find your way back to the nest if you can. Among the ancients, opinion was at variance respecting the wholesomeness and digestibility of goose flesh, but concerning the excellence of the duck all parties were agreed; indeed, they not only assigned to duck-meat the palm for exquisite flavour and delicacy, they even attributed to it medicinal powers of the highest order. Not only the Roman medical writers of the time make mention of it, but likewise the philosophers of the period. Plutarch assures us that Cato preserved his whole household in health, in a season when plague and disease were rife, through dieting them on roast duck.

STEWED DUCK AND PEAS (Cold Meat Cookery).

935. INGREDIENTS.—The remains of cold roast duck, 2 oz. of butter, 3 or 4 slices of lean ham or bacon, 1 tablespoonful of flour, 2 pints of thin gravy, 1, or a small bunch of green onions, 3 sprigs of parsley, 3 cloves, 1 pint of young green peas, cayenne and salt to taste, 1 teaspoonful of pounded sugar.

Mode.—Put the butter into a stewpan; cut up the duck into joints, lay them in with the slices of lean ham or bacon; make it brown, then dredge in a tablespoonful of flour, and stir this well in before adding the gravy. Put in the onion, parsley, cloves, and gravy, and when it has simmered for $\frac{1}{4}$ hour, add a pint of young green peas, and stew gently for about $\frac{1}{2}$ hour. Season with cayenne, salt, and sugar; take out the duck, place it round the dish, and the peas in the middle.

Time.—$\frac{3}{4}$ hour.

Average cost, exclusive of the cold duck, 1s.

Seasonable from June to August.

DUCKS HATCHING.—Concerning incubation by ducks, a practised writer says, "The duck requires a secret and safe place, rather than any attendance, and will, at nature's call, cover her eggs and seek her food. On hatching, there is not often a necessity for taking away any of the brood; and, having hatched, let the mother retain her young ones upon the nest her own time. On her moving with her brood, let a coop be prepared upon the short grass, if the weather be fine, and under shelter, if otherwise."

COOPING AND FEEDING DUCKLINGS.—Brood ducks should be cooped at some distance from any other. A wide and flat dish of water, to be often renewed, should stand just outside the coop, and barley, or any other meal, be the first food of the ducklings. It will be needful, if it be wet weather, to clip their tails, lest these draggle, and so weaken the bird. The period of the duck's confinement to the coop will depend on the weather, and on the strength of the ducklings. A fortnight is usually the extent of time necessary, and they may even be sometimes permitted to enjoy the luxury of a swim at the end of a week. They should not, however, be allowed to stay too long in the water at first; for they will then become ill, their feathers get rough, and looseness of the bowels ensue. In the latter case, let them be closely cooped for a few days, and bean-meal or oatmeal be mixed with their ordinary food.

THE AYLESBURY DUCK.—The white Aylesbury duck is, and deservedly, a universal favourite. Its snowy plumage and comfortable comportment make it a credit to the poultry-yard, while its broad and deep breast, and its ample back, convey the assurance that your satisfaction will not cease at its death. In parts of Buckinghamshire, this member of the duck family is bred on an extensive scale; not on plains and commons, however, as might be naturally imagined, but in the abodes of the cottagers. Round the walls of the living-rooms, and of the bedroom even, are fixed rows of wooden boxes, lined with hay; and it is the business of the wife and children to nurse and comfort the feathered lodgers, to feed the little ducklings, and to take the old ones out for an airing. Sometimes the "stock" ducks are the cottager's own property, but it more frequently happens that they are intrusted to his care by a wholesale breeder, who pays him so much *per* score for all ducklings properly raised. To be perfect, the Aylesbury duck should be plump, pure white, with yellow feet, and a flesh-coloured beak.

AYLESBURY DUCKS.

STEWED DUCK AND PEAS (Cold Meat Cookery).

936. INGREDIENTS.—The remains of cold roast duck, ½ pint of good gravy, cayenne and salt to taste, ½ teaspoonful of minced lemon-peel, 1 teaspoonful of pounded sugar, 2 oz. of butter rolled in flour, 1½ pint of green peas.

Mode.—Cut up the duck into joints, lay it in the gravy, and add a seasoning of cayenne, salt, and minced lemon-peel; let this gradually warm through, but not boil. Throw the peas into boiling water slightly salted, and boil them rapidly until tender. Drain them, stir in the pounded sugar, and the butter rolled in flour; shake them over the fire for two or three minutes, and serve in the centre of the dish, with the duck laid round.

Time.—15 minutes to boil the peas, when they are full grown.

Average cost, exclusive of the cold duck, 10*d*.

Seasonable from June to August.

FATTENING DUCKS.—Many duck-keepers give their birds nothing in the shape of food, letting them wander about and pick up a living for themselves; and they will seem to get fat even upon this precarious feeding. Unless, however, ducks are supplied with, besides chance food, a liberal feed of solid corn, or grain, morning and evening, their flesh will become flabby and insipid. The simple way to fatten ducks is to let them have as much substantial food as they will eat, bruised oats and pea-meal being the standard fattening food for them. No cramming is required, as with the turkey and some other poultry: they will cram themselves to the very verge of suffocation. At the same time, plenty of exercise and clean water should be at their service.

AMERICAN MODE OF CAPTURING DUCKS.—On the American rivers, the modes of capture are various. Sometimes half a dozen artificial birds are fastened to a little raft, and which is so weighted that the sham birds squat naturally on the water. This is quite sufficient to attract the notice of a passing flock, who descend to cultivate the acquaintance of the isolated few, when the concealed hunter, with his fowling-piece, scatters a deadly leaden shower amongst them. In the winter, when the water is covered with rubble ice, the fowler of the Delaware paints his canoe entirely white, lies flat in the bottom of it, and floats with the broken ice; from which the aquatic inhabitants fail to distinguish it. So floats the canoe till he within it understands, by the quacking, and fluttering, and whirring of wings, that he is in the midst of a flock, when he is up in a moment with the murderous piece, and dying quacks and lamentations rend the still air.

Bow-bill Ducks, &c.—Every one knows how awkward are the *Anatidæ*, waddling along on their unelastic webbed toes, and their short legs, which, being placed considerably backward, make the fore part of the body preponderate. Some, however, are formed more adapted to terrestrial habits than others, and notably amongst these may be named *Dendronessa sponsa*, the summer duck of America. This beautiful bird rears her young in the holes of trees, generally overhanging the water. When strong enough, the young scramble to the mouth of the hole, launch into the air with their little wings and feet spread out, and drop into their favourite element. Whenever their birthplace is at some distance from the water, the mother carries them to it, one by one, in her bill, holding them so as not to injure their yet tender frame. On several occasions, however, when the hole was 30, 40, or more yards from a piece of water, Audubon observed that the mother suffered the young to fall on the grass and dried leaves beneath the tree, and afterwards led them directly to the nearest edge of the next pool or creek. There are some curious varieties of the domestic duck, which only appear interesting from their singularity, for there does not seem to be anything of use or value in the unusual characteristics which distinguish them; thus, the bow-bill duck, as shown in the engraving, called by some writers the hook-bill, is remarkable for the peculiarly strange distortion of its beak, and the tuft on the top of its head. The penguin duck, again, waddles in an upright position, like the penguin, on account of the unnatural situation of its legs. These odd peculiarities add nothing of value to the various breeds, and may be set down as only the result of accidental malformation, transmitted from generation to generation.

BOW-BILL DUCKS.

STEWED DUCK AND TURNIPS (Cold Meat Cookery).

937. Ingredients.—The remains of cold roast duck, ¼ pint of good gravy, 4 shalots, a few slices of carrot, a small bunch of savoury herbs, 1 blade of pounded mace, 1 lb. of turnips, weighed after being peeled, 2 oz. of butter, pepper and salt to taste.

Mode.—Cut up the duck into joints, fry the shalots, carrots, and herbs, and put them, with the duck, into the gravy; add the pounded mace, and stew gently for 20 minutes or ½ hour. Cut about 1 lb. of turnips, weighed after being peeled, into ½-inch squares, put the butter into a stewpan, and stew them till quite tender, which will be in about ½ hour, or rather more; season with pepper and salt, and serve in the centre of the dish, with the duck, &c. laid round.

Time.—Rather more than ½ hour to stew the turnips.

Average cost, exclusive of the cold duck, 1s.

Seasonable from November to February.

The Wild Duck.—In many parts of England the wild duck is to be found, especially in those desolate fenny parts where water abounds. In Lincolnshire they are plentiful, and are annually taken in the decoys, which consist of ponds situate in the marshes, and surrounded with wood or reeds to prevent the birds which frequent them from. being disturbed. In these the birds sleep during the day; and as soon as evening sets in, the *decoy rises,* and the wild fowl feed during the night. Now is the time for the decoy ducks to entrap the others. From the ponds diverge, in different directions, certain canals, at the end of which funnel nets are placed; along these the *decoy ducks,* trained

CALL-DUCKS.

for the purpose, lead the others in search of food. After they have got a certain length, a decoy-man appears, and drives them further on, until they are finally taken in the nets. It is from these decoys, in Lincolnshire, that the London market is mostly supplied. The Chinese have a singular mode of catching these ducks. A person wades in the water up to the chin, and, having his head covered with an empty calabash, approaches the place where the ducks are. As the birds have no suspicion of the nature of the object which is concealed under the calabash, they suffer its approach, and allow it to move at will among their flock. The man, accordingly, walks about in the midst of his game, and, whenever he pleases, pulls them by the legs under the water, and fixes them to his belt, until he has secured as many as he requires, and then moves off as he went amongst them, without exciting the slightest suspicion of the trick he has been playing them. This singular mode of duck-hunting is also practised on the Ganges, the earthen vessels of the Hindoos being used instead of calabashes. These vessels, being those in which the inhabitants boil their rice, are considered, after once being used, as defiled, and are accordingly thrown into the river. The duck-takers, finding them suitable for their purpose, put them on their heads; and as the ducks, from seeing them constantly floating down the stream, are familiar with their appearance, they regard them as objects from which no danger is to be expected.

DUCK-SNARES IN THE LINCOLNSHIRE FENS.—The following interesting account of how duck-snaring used to be managed in the Lincolnshire fens, was published some years ago, in a work entitled the "Feathered Tribes."—"In the lakes to which they resorted, their favourite haunts were observed, and in the most sequestered part of a haunt, a pipe or ditch was cut across the entrance, decreasing gradually in width from the entrance to the further end, which was not more than two feet wide. The ditch was of a circular form, but did not bend much for the first ten yards. The banks of the lake on each side of the ditch were kept clear of weeds and close herbage, in order that the ducks might get on them to sit and dress themselves. Along the ditch, poles were driven into the ground close to the edge on each side, and the tops were bent over across the ditch and tied together. The poles then bent forward at the entrance to the ditch, and formed an arch, the top of which was ten feet distant from the surface of the water; the arch was made to decrease in height as the ditch decreased in width, so that the remote end was not more than eighteen inches in height. The poles were placed about six feet from each other, and connected by poles laid lengthwise across the arch, and tied together. Over the whole was thrown a net, which was made fast to a reed fence at the entrance and nine or ten yards up the ditch, and afterwards strongly pegged to the ground. At the end of the ditch furthest from the entrance, was fixed what was called a tunnel-net, of about four yards in length, of a round form, and kept open by a number of hoops about eighteen inches in diameter, placed at a small distance from each other to keep it distended. Supposing the circular bend of the ditch to be to the right, when one stands with his back to the lake, then on the left-hand side, a number of reed fences were constructed, called shootings, for the purpose of screening the decoy-man from observation, and, in such a manner, that the fowl in the decoy would not be alarmed while he was driving those that were in the pipe. These shootings, which were ten in number, were about four yards in length and about six feet high. From the end of the last shooting a person could not see the lake, owing to the bend of the ditch; and there was then no further occasion for shelter. Were it not for these shootings, the fowl that remained about the mouth of the ditch would have been alarmed, if the person driving the fowl already under the net should have been exposed, and would have become so shy as entirely to forsake the place."

THE DECOY-MAN, DOG, AND DUCKS.—"The first thing the decoy-man did, on approaching the ditch, was to take a piece of lighted peat or turf, and to hold it near his mouth, to prevent the birds from smelling him. He was attended by a dog trained to render him assistance. He walked very silently about halfway up the shootings, where a small piece of wood was thrust through the reed fence, which made an aperture just large enough to enable him to see if there were any fowl within; if not, he walked to see if any were about the entrance to the ditch. If there were, he stopped, made a motion to his dog, and gave him a piece of cheese to eat, when the dog went directly to a hole through the reed fence, and the birds immediately flew off the bank into the water. The dog returned along the bank between the reed fences, and came out to his master at another hole. The man then gave the dog something more to encourage him, and the dog repeated his rounds, till the birds were attracted by his motions, and followed him into the mouth of the ditch—an operation which was called 'working them.' The man now retreated further back, working the dog at different holes, until the ducks were sufficiently under the net. He then commanded his dog to lie down under the fence, and going himself forward to the end of the ditch next the lake, he took off his hat, and gave it a wave between the shootings. All the birds that were under the net could then see him, but none that were in the lake could. The former flew forward, and the man then ran to the next shooting, and waved his hat, and so on, driving them along until they came into the tunnel-net, into which they crept. When they were all in, the man gave the net a twist, so as to prevent them getting back. He then took the net off from the end of the ditch, and taking out, one by one, the ducks that were in it, dislocated their necks."

BOILED FOWLS OR CHICKENS.

938. INGREDIENTS.—A pair of fowls ; water.

Choosing and Trussing.—In choosing fowls for boiling, it should be borne in mind that those that are not black-legged are generally much whiter when dressed. Pick, draw, singe, wash, and truss them in the following manner, without the livers in the wings ; and, in drawing, be careful not to break the gall-bladder :—Cut off the neck, leaving sufficient skin to skewer back. Cut the feet off to the first joint, tuck the stumps into a slit made on each side of the belly, twist the wings over the back of the fowl, and secure the top of the leg and the bottom of the wing together by running a skewer through them and the body. The other side must be done in the same manner. Should the fowl be very large and old, draw the sinews of the legs before tucking them in. Make a slit in the apron of the fowl, large enough to admit the parson's nose, and tie a string on the tops of the legs to keep them in their proper place.

Mode.—When they are firmly trussed, put them into a stewpan with plenty of hot water; bring it to boil, and carefully remove all the scum as it rises. *Simmer very gently* until the fowl is tender, and bear in mind that the slower it boils, the plumper and whiter will the fowl be. Many cooks wrap them in a floured cloth to preserve the colour, and to prevent the scum from clinging to them ; in this

BOILED FOWL.

case, a few slices of lemon should be placed on the breasts ; over these a sheet of buttered paper, and then the cloth ; cooking them in this manner renders the flesh very white. Boiled ham, bacon, boiled tongue, or pickled pork, are the usual accompaniments to boiled fowls, and they may be served with Béchamel, white sauce, parsley and butter, oyster, lemon, liver, celery, or mushroom sauce. A little should be poured over the fowls, after the skewers are removed, and the remainder sent in a tureen to table.

Time.—Large fowl, 1 hour; moderate-sized one, ¾ hour; chicken, from 20 minutes to ¼ hour. *Average cost*, in full season, 5s. the pair.

Sufficient for 7 or 8 persons.

Seasonable all the year, but scarce in early spring.

THE GAME FOWL.—Respecting the period at which this well-known member of the *Gallus* family became domesticated, history is silent. There is little doubt, however, that, like the dog, it has been attached to mankind ever since mankind were attached to civilization. Although the social position of this bird is, at the present time, highly respectable, it is nothing to what it was when Rome was mistress of the world. Writing at that period, Pliny says, respecting the domestic cock, "The gait of the cock is proud and commanding; he walks with head erect and elevated crest; alone, of all birds, he habitually looks up to the sky, raising, at the same time, his curved and scythe-formed tail, and inspiring terror in the lion himself, that most intrepid of animals. * * They regulate the conduct of our magistrates, and open or close to them their own houses. They prescribe rest or movement to the Roman fasces: they command or prohibit battles. In a word, they lord it over the masters of the world." As well among the ancient Greeks as the Romans, was the cock regarded with respect, and even awe. The former people practised divinations by means of this bird. Supposing there to be a doubt in the camp as to the fittest day to fight a battle, the letter of every day in the week would be placed face downwards, and a grain of corn placed on each; then the sacred cock would be let loose, and, according to the letters he pecked his corn from, so would the battle-time be regulated. On one momentous occasion, however, a person inimical to priestly interest officiously examined the grain, and found that those lying on the letters not wanted were made of wax, and the birds, preferring the true grain, left these untouched. It is needless to add that, after this, divination through the medium of cocks and grain fell out of fashion. Whether or no the learned fowl above alluded to were of the "game" breed, is unknown; but that the birds were bred for the inhuman sport of fighting many hundred years before the Christian era, there can be no doubt. Themistocles, the Athenian king, who flourished more than two thousand years ago, took advantage of the sight of a pitched battle between two cocks to harangue his soldiers on courage. "Observe," said he, "with what intrepid valour they fight, inspired by no other motive than love of victory; whereas you have to contend for your religion and your liberty, for your wives and children, and for the tombs of your ancestors." And to this day his courage has not degenerated. He still preserves his bold and elegant gait, his sparkling eye, while his wedge-shaped beak and cruel spurs are ever ready to support his defiant crow. It is no wonder that the breed is not plentiful—first, on account of the few eggs laid by the hen; and, secondly, from the incurable pugnacity of the chicks. Half-fledged broods may be found blind as bats from fighting, and only waiting for the least glimmer of sight to be at it again. Without doubt, the flesh of game fowls is every way superior to that of every chicken of the family.

GAME FOWLS.

BROILED FOWL AND MUSHROOM SAUCE.

939. INGREDIENTS.—A large fowl, seasoning, to taste, of pepper and salt, 2 handfuls of button mushrooms, 1 slice of lean ham, ¾ pint of thickened gravy, 1 teaspoonful of lemon-juice, ½ teaspoonful of pounded sugar.

Mode.—Cut the fowl into quarters, roast it until three-parts done, and keep it well basted whilst at the fire. Take the fowl up, broil it for a few minutes over a clear fire, and season it with pepper and salt. Have ready some mushroom sauce made in the following manner. Put the mushrooms into a stewpan with a small piece of butter, the ham, a seasoning of pepper and salt, and the gravy; simmer these gently for ½ hour, add the lemon-juice and sugar, dish the fowl, and pour the sauce round them.

Time.—To roast the fowl, 35 minutes; to broil it, 10 to 15 minutes.

Average cost, in full season, 2s. 6d.

Sufficient for 4 or 5 persons.

Seasonable.—In full season from May to January.

THE BANTAM.—No one will dispute that for beauty, animation, plumage, and courage, the Bantam is entitled to rank next to the game fowl. As its name undoubtedly implies, the bird is of Asiatic origin. The choicest sorts are the buff-coloured, and those that are entirely black. A year-old Bantam cock of pure breed will not weigh more than sixteen ounces. Despite its small size, however, it is marvellously bold, especially in defence of its progeny. A friend of the writer's, residing at Kensington, possessed a pair of thorough-bred Bantams, that were allowed the range of a yard where a fierce bull-terrier was kennelled. The hen had chicks; and, when about three weeks old, one of them strayed into the dog-kennel. The grim beast within took no notice of the tiny fledgeling; but, when the anxious mother ventured in to fetch out the truant, with a growl the dog

BLACK BANTAMS.

woke, and nearly snapped her asunder in his great jaws. The cock bird saw the tragic fate of its partner; but, nothing daunted, flew at the dog with a fierce cry, and pecked savagely at its face. The odds, however, were too great; and, when the terrier had sufficiently recovered from the astonishment caused by the sudden and unexpected attack, he seized the audacious Bantam, and shook him to death; and, in five minutes, the devoted couple were entombed in *Pincher's* capacious maw.

BOILED FOWL AND RICE.

940. INGREDIENTS.—1 fowl, mutton broth, 2 onions, 2 small blades of pounded mace, pepper and salt to taste, ¼ pint of rice, parsley and butter.

Mode.—Truss the fowl as for boiling, and put it into a stewpan with sufficient clear well-skimmed mutton broth to cover it; add the onion, mace, and a seasoning of pepper and salt; stew very gently for about 1 hour, should the fowl be large, and about ½ hour before it is ready put in the rice, which should be well washed and soaked. When the latter is tender, strain it from the liquor, and put it on a sieve reversed to dry before the fire, and, in the mean time, keep the fowl hot. Dish it, put the rice round as a border, pour a little parsley and butter over the fowl, and the remainder send to table in a tureen.

Time.—A large fowl, 1 hour. *Average cost,* in full season, 2*s.* 6*d.*

Sufficient for 3 or 4 persons.

Seasonable all the year, but scarce in early spring.

THE DORKING.—This bird takes its name from that of a town in Surrey, where the breed is to be found in greater numbers, and certainly in greater perfection, than else-where. It is generally believed that this particular branch of poultry was found in the town above mentioned as long ago as the Roman era. The Dorking's chief characteristic is that he has five claws on each foot; the extra claw, however, is never of sufficient length to encumber the foot, or to cause it to "drag" its nest, or scratch out the eggs. The colour of the true Dorking is pure white; long in the body, short in the legs, and a prolific layer. Thirty years ago, there was much controversy respecting the origin of the Dorking. The men of Sussex declared that the bird belonged to them, and brought birds indigenous to their weald, and possessing all the Dorking fine points and peculiarities, in proof of the declaration. Others inclined to the

DORKINGS.

belief that the Poland bird was the father of the Dorking, and not without at least a show of reason, as the former bird much resembles the latter in shape; and, despite its sombre hue, it is well known that the Poland cock will occasionally beget thorough white stock from white English hens. The commotion has, however, long ago subsided, and Dorking still retains its fair reputation for fowl.

CURRIED FOWL.

941. INGREDIENTS.—1 fowl, 2 oz. of butter, 3 onions sliced, 1 pint of white veal gravy, 1 tablespoonful of curry-powder, 1 tablespoonful of flour, 1 apple, 4 tablespoonfuls of cream, 1 tablespoonful of lemon-juice.

Mode.—Put the butter into a stewpan, with the onions sliced, the fowl cut into small joints, and the apple peeled, cored, and minced. Fry of a pale brown, add the stock, and stew gently for 20 minutes; rub down the curry-powder and flour with a little of the gravy, quite smoothly, and stir this to the other ingredients; simmer for rather more than ½ hour, and just before serving, add the above proportion of hot cream and lemon-juice. Serve with boiled rice, which may either be heaped lightly on a dish by itself, or put round the curry as a border.

Time.—50 minutes. *Average cost,* 3*s.* 3*d.*

Sufficient for 3 or 4 persons.

Seasonable in the winter.

Note.—This curry may be made of cold chicken, but undressed meat will be found far superior.

THE POLAND.—This bird, a native of Holland, is a great favourite with fowl-keepers, especially those who have an eye to profit rather than to amusement. Those varieties known as the "silver spangled" and the "gold spangled" are handsome enough to please the most fastidious; but the common black breed, with the bushy crown of white feathers, is but a plain bird. The chief value of the common Poland lies in the great number of eggs they produce; indeed, in many parts, they are as well known as "everlasting layers" as by their proper name. However, the experienced breeder would take good care to send the eggs of his everlasting layers to market, and not use them for home consumption, as, although they may be as large as those laid by other hens, the amount of nutriment contained in them is not nearly so great. Mr. Mowbray once kept an account of the number of eggs produced by this prolific bird, with the following result:—From the 25th of October to the 25th of the following September five hens laid 503 eggs; the average weight of each egg was one ounce five drachms, and the total weight of the whole, exclusive of the shells, 50¼ pounds. Taking the weight of the birds at the fair average of five pounds each, we thus see them producing within a year double their weight of egg alone; and, supposing every egg to contain a chick, and allowing the chick to grow, in less than eighteen months from the laying of the first egg, *two thousand five hundred pounds* of chicken-meat would be the result. The Poland is easily fattened, and its flesh is generally considered juicier and of richer flavour than most others.

SPANGLED POLANDS.

CURRIED FOWL OR CHICKEN (Cold Meat Cookery).

942. INGREDIENTS.—The remains of cold roast fowls, 2 large onions, 1 apple, 2 oz. of butter, 1 dessertspoonful of curry-powder, 1 teaspoonful of flour, ½ pint of gravy, 1 tablespoonful of lemon-juice.

Mode.—Slice the onions, peel, core, and chop the apple, and cut the fowl into neat joints; fry these in the butter of a nice brown; then add the curry-powder, flour, and gravy, and stew for about 20 minutes. Put in the lemon-juice, and serve with boiled rice, either placed in a ridge round the dish or separately. Two or three shalots or a little garlic may be added, if approved.

Time.—Altogether ½ hour. *Av. cost*, exclusive of the cold fowl, 6d.

Seasonable in the winter.

THE COCHIN-CHINA.—About fifteen years ago, the arrival of this distinguished Asiatic created in England as great a sensation as might be expected from the landing of an invading host. The first pair that ever made their appearance here were natives of Shanghai, and were presented to the queen, who exhibited them at the Dublin poultry-show of 1846. Then began the "Cochin" *furor.* As soon as it was discovered, despite the most strenuous endeavours to keep the tremendous secret, that a certain dealer was possessed of a pair of these birds, straightway the avenues to that dealer's shop were blocked by broughams, and chariots, and hack cabs, until the shy poulterer had been tempted by a sufficiently high sum to part with his treasure. Bank-notes were exchanged for Cochin chicks, and Cochin eggs were in as great demand as though they had been laid by the fabled golden goose.

COCHIN-CHINAS.

The reign of the Cochin China was, however, of inconsiderable duration. The bird that, in 1847, would fetch thirty guineas, is now counted but ordinary chicken-meat, and its price is regulated according to its weight when ready for the spit. As for the precious buff eggs, against which, one time of day, guineas were weighed,—send for sixpenn'orth at the cheesemonger's, and you will get at least five; which is just as it should be. For elegance of shape or quality of flesh, the Cochin cannot for a moment stand comparison with our handsome dunghill; neither can the indescribable mixture of growling and braying, peculiar to the former, vie with the musical trumpeting of our own morning herald: yet our poultry-breeders have been immense gainers by the introduction of the ungainly celestial, inasmuch as *new blood* has been infused into the English chicken family. Of this incalculable advantage we may be sure; while, as to the Cochin's defects, they are certain to be lost in the process of " cross and cross " breeding.

BOILED FOWLS A LA BECHAMEL.

943. INGREDIENTS.—A pair of fowls, 1 pint of Béchamel, No. 367, a few bunches of boiled brocoli or cauliflower.

Mode.—Truss and boil the fowls by recipe No. 938 ; make a pint of Béchamel sauce by recipe No. 367; pour some of this over the fowls, and the remainder send to table in a tureen. Garnish the dish with bunches of boiled cauliflowers or brocoli, and serve very hot. The sauce should be made sufficiently thick to adhere to the fowls ; that for the tureen should be thinned by adding a spoonful or two of stock.

Time.—From ½ to 1 hour, according to size.

Average cost, in full season, 5s. a pair.

Sufficient for 6 or 7 persons.

Seasonable all the year, but scarce in early spring.

SPACE FOR FOWLS.—We are no advocates for converting the domestic fowl into a cage-bird. We have known amateur fowl-keepers—worthy souls, who would butter the very barley they gave their pets, if they thought they would the more enjoy it—coop up a male bird and three or four hens in an ordinary egg-chest placed on its side, and with the front closely barred with iron hooping! This system will not do. Every animal, from man himself to the guinea-pig, *must* have what is vulgarly, but truly, known as " elbow-room ;" and it must be self-evident how emphatically this rule applies to winged animals. It may be urged, in the case of domestic fowls, that from constant disuse, and from clipping and plucking, and other sorts of maltreatment, their wings can hardly be regarded as instruments of flight; we maintain, however, that you may pluck a fowl's wing-joints as bare as a pumpkin, but you will not erase from his memory that he *is* a fowl, and that his proper sphere is the open air. If he likewise reflects that he is an ill-used fowl—a prison-bird—he will then come to the conclusion, that there is not the least use, under such circumstances, for his existence; and you must admit that the decision is only logical and natural.

BOILED FOWL, with Oysters.
(*Excellent.*)

944. INGREDIENTS.—1 young fowl, 3 dozen oysters, the yolks of 2 eggs, ¼ pint of cream.

Mode.—Truss a young fowl as for boiling ; fill the inside with oysters which have been bearded and washed in their own liquor ; secure the ends of the fowl, put it into a jar, and plunge the jar into a saucepan of boiling water. Keep it boiling for 1½ hour, or rather longer ; then take the gravy that has flowed from the oysters and fowl, of which there will be a good quantity ; stir in the cream and yolks of eggs, add a few oysters scalded in their liquor; let the sauce get quite *hot*, but do not allow it to *boil ;* pour some of it over the fowl, and the remainder send to table in a tureen. A blade of pounded mace added to the sauce, with the cream and eggs, will be found an improvement.

Time.—1½ hour. *Average cost,* 4s. 6d.

Sufficient for 3 or 4 persons.

Seasonable from September to April.

THE FOWL-HOUSE.—In building a fowl-house, take care that it be, if possible, built against a wall or fence that faces the *south*, and thus insure its inmates against many cold winds, driving rains, and sleets they will otherwise suffer. Let the floor of the house slope half an inch to the foot from back to front, so as to insure drainage; let it also be close, hard, and perfectly smooth; so that it may be cleanly swept out. A capital plan is to mix a few bushels of chalk and dry earth, spread it over the floor, and pay a paviour's labourer a trifle to hammer it level with his rammer. The fowl-house should be seven feet high, and furnished with perches at least two feet apart. The perches must be level, and not one above the other, or unpleasant consequences may ensue to the undermost row. The perches should be ledged (not fixed—just dropped into sockets, that they may be easily taken out and cleaned) not lower than five feet from the ground, convenient slips of wood being driven into the wall, to render the ascent as easy as possible. The front of the fowl-house should be latticed, taking care that the interstices be not wide enough even to tempt a chick to crawl through. Nesting-boxes, containing soft hay, and fitted against the walls, so as to be easily reached by the perch-ladder, should be supplied. It will be as well to keep by you a few portable doors, so that you may hang one before the entrance to a nesting-box, when the hen goes in to sit. This will prevent other hens from intruding, a habit to which some are much addicted.

FRICASSEED FOWL OR CHICKEN (an Entree).

945. INGREDIENTS.—2 small fowls or 1 large one, 3 oz. of butter, a bunch of parsley and green onions, 1 clove, 2 blades of mace, 1 shalot, 1 bay-leaf, salt and white pepper to taste, ¼ pint of cream, the yolks of 3 eggs.

Mode.—Choose a couple of fat plump chickens, and, after drawing, singeing, and washing them, skin, and carve them into joints; blanch these in boiling water for 2 or 3 minutes; take them out, and immerse them in cold water to render them white. Put the trimmings, with the necks and legs, into a stewpan ; add the parsley, onions, clove, mace, shalot, bay-leaf, and a seasoning of pepper and salt; pour to these the water that the chickens were blanched in, and simmer gently for rather more than 1 hour. Have ready another stewpan ; put in the joints of fowl, with the above proportion of butter; dredge them with flour, let them get hot, but do not brown them much; then moisten the fricassee with the gravy made from the trimmings, &c., and stew very gently for ½ hour. Lift the fowl into another stewpan, skim the sauce, reduce it quickly over the fire, by letting it boil fast, and strain it over them. Add the cream, and a seasoning of pounded mace and cayenne ; let it boil up, and when ready to serve, stir to it the well-beaten yolks of 3 eggs : these should not be put in till the last moment, and the sauce should be made *hot*, but must *not boil*, or it will instantly curdle. A few button-mushrooms stewed with the fowl are by many persons considered an improvement.

Time.—1 hour to make the gravy, ⅓ hour to simmer the fowl.

Average cost, 5s. the pair.

Sufficient.—1 large fowl for one entrée.

Seasonable at any time.

STOCKING THE FOWL-HOUSE.—Take care that the birds with which you stock your house are *young*. The surest indications of old age are fading of the comb and gills from brilliant red to a dingy brick-colour, general paleness of plumage, brittleness of the feathers, length and size of the claws, and the scales of the legs and feet assuming a ragged and *corny* appearance. Your cock and hens should be as near two years old as possible. Hens will lay at a year old, but the eggs are always insignificant in size, and the layers giddy and unsteady sitters. The hen-bird is in her prime for breeding at three years old, and will continue so, under favourable circumstances, for two years longer ; after which she will decline. Crowing hens, and those that have large combs, are generally looked on with mistrust ; but this is mere silliness and superstition—though it is possible that a spruce young cock would as much object to a spouse with such peculiar addictions, as a young fellow of our own species would to a damsel who whistled and who wore whiskers. Fowls with yellow legs should be avoided ; they are generally of a tender constitution, loose-fleshed, and of indifferent flavour.

FRICASSEED FOWL (Cold Meat Cookery).

946. INGREDIENTS.—The remains of cold roast fowl, 1 strip of lemon-peel, 1 blade of pounded mace, 1 bunch of savoury herbs, 1 onion, pepper and salt to taste, 1 pint of water, 1 teaspoonful of flour, ¼ pint of cream, the yolks of 2 eggs.

Mode.—Carve the fowls into nice joints ; make gravy of the trimmings and legs, by stewing them with the lemon-peel, mace, herbs, onion, seasoning, and water, until reduced to ½ pint ; then strain, and put in the fowl. Warm it through, and thicken with a teaspoonful of flour ; stir the yolks of the eggs into the cream ; add these to the sauce, let it get thoroughly hot, but do not allow it to boil, or it will curdle.

Time.—1 hour to make the gravy, ¼ hour to warm the fowl.

Average cost, exclusive of the cold chicken, 8d.

Seasonable at any time.

CHARACTERISTICS OF HEALTH AND POWER.—The chief characteristics of health in a fowl are brightness and dryness of eye and nostrils, the comb and wattles firm and ruddy, the feathers elastic and glossy. The most useful cock is generally the greatest tyrant, who struts among his hens despotically, with his head erect and his eyes ever watchful. There is likely to be handsomer and stronger chicks in a house where a bold, active— even savage—bird reigns, than where the lord of the hen-house is a weak, meek creature, who bears the abuse and peckings of his wives without a remonstrance. I much prefer dark-coloured cock-birds to those of light plumage. A cock, to be handsome, should be of middling size ; his bill should be short, comb bright-red, wattles large, breast broad, and wings strong. His head should be rather small than otherwise, his legs short and sturdy, and his spurs well-formed ; his feathers should be short and close, and the more frequently and heartily he crows, the better father he is likely to become. The common error of choosing hens *above* the ordinary stature of their respective varieties should be avoided, as the best breeding-hens are those of medium size.

FRIED FOWLS (Cold Meat Cookery).

I.

947. INGREDIENTS.—The remains of cold roast fowls, vinegar, salt and cayenne to taste, 3 or 4 minced shalots. For the batter,—½ lb. of flour, ½ pint of hot water, 2 oz. of butter, the whites of 2 eggs.

Mode.—Cut the fowl into nice joints; steep them for an hour in a little vinegar, with salt, cayenne, and minced shalots. Make the batter by mixing the flour and water smoothly together; melt in it the butter, and add the whites of egg beaten to a froth; take out the pieces of fowl, dip them in the batter, and fry, in boiling lard, a nice brown. Pile them high in the dish, and garnish with fried parsley or rolled bacon. When approved, a sauce or gravy may be served with them.

Time.—10 minutes to fry the fowl.

Average cost, exclusive of the cold fowl, 8*d.*

Seasonable at any time.

CHANTICLEER AND HIS COMPANIONS.—On bringing the male and female birds together, for the first time, it will be necessary to watch the former closely, as it is a very common occurrence with him to conceive a sudden and violent dislike for one or more of his wives, and not allow the obnoxious ones to approach within some distance of the others; indeed, I know many cases where the capricious tyrant has set upon the innocent cause of his resentment and killed her outright. In all such cases, the hen objected to should be removed and replaced by another. If the cock should, by any accident, get killed, considerable delicacy is required in introducing a new one. The hens may mope, and refuse to associate with their new husband, clustering in corners, and making odious comparisons between him and the departed; or the cock may have his own peculiar notions as to what a wife should be, and be by no means satisfied with those you have provided him. The plan is, to keep him by himself nearly the whole day, supplying him plentifully with exhilarating food, then to turn him loose among the hens, and to continue this practice, allowing him more of the society of his wives each day, until you suffer him to abide with them altogether.

II.

948. INGREDIENTS.—The remains of cold roast fowl, vinegar, salt and cayenne to taste, 4 minced shalots, yolk of egg; to every teacupful of bread crumbs allow 1 blade of pounded mace, ½ teaspoonful of minced lemon-peel, 1 saltspoonful of salt, a few grains of cayenne.

Mode.—Steep the pieces of fowl as in the preceding recipe, then dip them into the yolk of an egg or clarified butter; sprinkle over bread crumbs with which have been mixed salt, mace, cayenne, and lemon-peel in the above proportion. Fry a light brown, and serve with or without gravy, as may be preferred.

Time.—10 minutes to fry the fowl.

Average cost, exclusive of the cold fowl, 6*d.*

Seasonable at any time.

VARIOUS MODES OF FATTENING FOWLS.—It would, I think, be a difficult matter to find, among the entire fraternity of fowl-keepers, a dozen whose mode of fattening "stock" is the same. Some say that the grand secret is to give them abundance of saccharine food; others say nothing beats heavy corn steeped in milk; while another breeder, celebrated in his day, and the recipient of a gold medal from a learned society, says, " The best method is as follows :—The chickens are to be taken from the hen the night after they are hatched, and fed with eggs hard-boiled, chopped, and mixed with crumbs of bread, as larks and other small birds are fed, for the first fortnight ; after which give them oatmeal and treacle mixed so as to crumble, of which the chickens are very fond, and thrive so fast that, at the end of two months, they will be as large as full-grown fowls."   Others there are who insist that nothing beats oleaginous diet, and cram their birds with ground oats and suet.   But, whatever the course of diet favoured, on one point they seem agreed ; and that is, that, while fattening, the fowls *should be kept in the dark*.   Supposing the reader to be a dealer,—a breeder of gross chicken-meat for the market (against which supposition the chances are 10,000 to 1), and beset with as few scruples as generally trouble the huckster, the advice is valuable.   " Laugh and grow fat " is a good maxim enough ; but " Sleep and grow fat " is, as is well known to folks of porcine attributes, a better.   The poor birds, immured in their dark dungeons, ignorant that there is life and sunshine abroad, tuck their heads under their wings and make a long night of it ; while their digestive organs, having no harder work than to pile up fat, have an easy time enough.   But, unless we are mistaken, he who breeds poultry for his own eating, bargains for a more substantial reward than the questionable pleasure of burying his carving-knife in chicken grease.   Tender, delicate, and nutritious *flesh* is the great aim ; and these qualities, I can affirm without fear of contradiction, were never attained by a dungeon-fatted chicken : perpetual gloom and darkness is as incompatible with chicken life as it is with human.   If you wish to be convinced of the absurdity of endeavouring to thwart nature's laws, plant a tuft of grass, or a cabbage-plant, in the darkest corner of your coal-cellar.   The plant or the tuft may increase in length and breadth, but its colour will be as wan and pale, almost, as would be your own face under the circumstances.

POULET A LA MARENGO.

949. INGREDIENTS.—1 large fowl, 4 tablespoonfuls of salad oil, 1 tablespoonful of flour, 1 pint of stock No. 105, or water, about 20 mushroom-buttons, salt and pepper to taste, 1 teaspoonful of powdered sugar, a very small piece of garlic.

Mode.—Cut the fowl into 8 or 10 pieces ; put them with the oil into a stewpan, and brown them over a moderate fire ; dredge in the above proportion of flour ; when that is browned, pour in the stock or water ; let it simmer very slowly for rather more than ½ hour, and skim off the fat as it rises to the top ; add the mushrooms ; season with salt, pepper, garlic, and sugar ; take out the fowl, which arrange pyramidically on the dish, with the inferior joints at the bottom. Reduce the sauce by boiling it quickly over the fire, keeping it stirred until sufficiently thick to adhere to the back of a spoon ; pour over the fowl, and serve.

Time.—Altogether 50 minutes.   *Average cost*, 3s. 6d.

Sufficient for 3 or 4 persons.

Seasonable at any time.

A FOWL À LA MARENGO.—The following is the origin of the well-known dish Poulet à la Marengo :—On the evening of the battle the first consul was very hungry after the agitation of the day, and a fowl was ordered with all expedition.   The fowl was procured, but there was no butter at hand, and unluckily none could be found in the neighbourhood.   There was oil in abundance, however ; and the cook having poured a certain quantity into his skillet, put in the fowl, with a clove of garlic and other seasoning, with a little white wine, the best the country afforded ; he then gar-nished it with mushrooms, and served it up hot.   This dish proved the second conquest of the day, as the first consul found it most agreeable to his palate, and expressed his satisfaction.   Ever since, a fowl à la Marengo is a favourite dish with all lovers of good cheer.

MINCED FOWL A LA BECHAMEL.

950. INGREDIENTS.—The remains of cold roast fowl, 6 tablespoon-fuls of Béchamel sauce No. 367, 6 tablespoonfuls of white stock No. 107, the white of 1 egg, bread crumbs, clarified butter.

Mode.—Take the remains of roast fowls, mince the white meat very small, and put it into a stewpan with the Béchamel and stock ; stir it well over the fire, and just let it boil up. Pour the mince into a dish, beat up the white of egg, spread it over, and strew on it a few grated bread crumbs ; pour a very little clarified butter on the whole, and brown either before the fire or with a salamander. This should be served in a silver dish, if at hand.

Time.—2 or 3 minutes to simmer in the sauce.

Seasonable at any time.

THE BEST WAY TO FATTEN FOWLS.—The barn-door fowl is in itself a complete refutation of the cramming and dungeon policy of feeding practised by some. This fowl, which has the common run of the farm-yard, living on dairy-scraps and offal from the stable, begins to grow fat at threshing-time. He has his fill of the finest corn ; he has his fill of fresh air and natural exercise, and at last he comes smoking to the table,— a dish for the gods. In the matter of unnaturally stuffing and confining fowls, Mowbray is exactly of our opinion. He says : "The London chicken-butchers, as they are termed, are said to be, of all others, the most expeditious and dexterous feeders, putting up a coop of fowls, and making them thoroughly fat within the space of a fortnight, using much grease, and that perhaps not of the most delicate kind, in the food. In this way I have no boasts to make, having always found it necessary to allow a considerable number of weeks for the purpose of making fowls fat in coops. In the common way this business is often badly managed, fowls being huddled together in a small coop, tearing each other to pieces, instead of enjoying that repose which alone can insure the wished-for object—irregularly fed and cleaned, until they become so stenched and poisoned in their own excrement, that their flesh actually smells and tastes when smoking upon the table." Sussex produces the fattest and largest poultry of any county in England, and the fatting process there most common is to give them a gruel made of pot-liquor and bruised oats, with which are mixed hog's grease, sugar, and milk. The fowls are kept very warm, and crammed morning and night. They are put into the coop, and kept there two or three days before the cramming begins, and then it is con-tinued for a fortnight, and the birds are sent to market.

RAGOUT OF FOWL.

951. INGREDIENTS.—The remains of cold roast fowls, 3 shalots, 2 blades of mace, a faggot of savoury herbs, 2 or three slices of lean ham, 1 pint of stock or water, pepper and salt to taste, 1 onion, 1 dessertspoonful of flour, 1 tablespoonful of lemon-juice, $\frac{1}{2}$ teaspoonful of pounded sugar, 1 oz. of butter.

Mode.—Cut the fowls up into neat pieces, the same as for a fricassee ; put the trimmings into a stewpan with the shalots, mace, herbs, ham, onion, and stock (water may be substituted for this). Boil it slowly for 1 hour, strain the liquor, and put a small piece of butter into à stewpan ; when melted, dredge in sufficient flour to dry up the butter, and stir it over the fire. Put in the strained liquor, boil for a few minutes, and strain it again over the pieces of fowl. Squeeze in the lemon-juice, add the sugar and a seasoning of pepper and salt, make it hot, but do not allow it to boil; lay the fowl neatly on the dish, and garnish with croûtons.

Time.—Altogether 1½ hour.　*Average cost,* exclusive of the cold fowl, 9*d*.

Seasonable at any time.

THE BEST FOWLS TO FATTEN, &c.—The chicks most likely to fatten well are those first hatched in the brood, and those with the shortest legs.　Long-legged fowls, as a rule, are by far the most difficult to fatten.　The most delicate sort are those which are put up to fatten as soon as the hen forsakes them; for, as says an old writer, "then they will be in fine condition, and full of flesh, which flesh is afterwards expended in the exercise of foraging for food, and in the increase of stature; and it may be a work of some weeks to recover it,—especially with young cocks."　But whether you take them in hand as chicks, or not till they are older, the three prime rules to be observed are, sound and various food, warmth, and cleanliness.　There is nothing that a fatting fowl grows so fastidious about as his water.　If water any way foul be offered him, he will not drink it, but sulk with his food, and pine, and you all the while wondering the reason why.　Keep them separate, allowing to each bird as much space as you can spare.　Spread the ground with sharp sandy gravel; take care that they are not disturbed.　In addition to their regular diet of good corn, make them a cake of ground oats or beans, brown sugar, milk, and mutton suet.　Let the cake lie till it is stale, then crumble it, and give each bird a gill-measureful morning and evening.　No entire grain should be given to fowls during the time they are fattening; indeed, the secret of success lies in supplying them with the most nutritious food without stint, and in such a form that their digestive mills shall find no difficulty in grinding it.

ROAST FOWLS.

952. INGREDIENTS.—A pair of fowls; a little flour.

Mode.—Fowls to be tender should be killed a couple of days before they are dressed; when the feathers come out easily, then let them be picked and cooked.　In drawing them, be careful not to break the gall-bag, as, wherever it touches, it would impart a very bitter taste; the liver and gizzard should also be preserved.　Truss them in the following manner :—After having carefully picked them, cut off the

ROAST FOWL.

head, and skewer the skin of the neck down over the back.　Cut off the claws; dip the legs in boiling water, and scrape them; turn the pinions under, run a skewer through them and the middle of the legs, which should be passed through the body to the pinion and leg on the other side, one skewer securing the limbs on both sides.　The liver and gizzard should be placed in the wings, the liver on one side and the gizzard on the other.　Tie the legs together by passing a trussing-needle, threaded with twine, through the backbone, and secure it on the other side.　If trussed like a capon, the legs are placed more apart.　When firmly trussed, singe them all over; put them down to a bright clear fire, paper the breasts with a sheet of buttered paper, and keep the fowls well basted.　Roast them for ¾ hour, more or less, according to the size, and 10 minutes before serving, remove the paper, dredge the fowls with a little fine flour, put a piece of butter into the basting-ladle, and as it melts, baste the fowls with it; when nicely frothed and of a rich colour, serve with good brown gravy, a little of which should be poured over the fowls, and a tureen of well-made bread sauce, No. 371. Mushroom, oyster, or egg sauce are very suitable accompaniments to roast fowl.—Chicken is roasted in the same manner.

Time.—A very large fowl, quite 1 hour, medium-sized one ¾ hour, chicken ½ hour, or rather longer.

Average cost, in full season, 5*s*. a pair; when scarce, 7*s*. 6*d*. the pair.

Sufficient for 6 or 7 persons.

Seasonable all the year, but scarce in early spring.

THE DISEASES OF FOWLS, AND HOW TO CURE THEM.—The diseases to which *Gallus domesticus* is chiefly liable, are roup, pip, scouring, and chip. The first-mentioned is the most common of all, and results from cold. The ordinary symptoms,—swollen eyes, running at the nostrils, and the purple colour of the wattles. Part birds so affected from the healthy ones, as, when the disease is at its height it is as contagious as glanders among horses. Wash out the nostrils with warm water, give daily a peppercorn inclosed in dough; bathe the eyes and nostrils with warm milk and water. If the head is much swollen, bathe with warm brandy and water. When the bird is getting well, put half a spoonful of sulphur in his drinking-water. Some fanciers prescribe for this disease half a spoonful of table salt, dissolved in half a gill of water, in which rue has been steeped; others, pills composed of ground rice and fresh butter: but the remedy first mentioned will be found far the best. As there is a doubt respecting the wholesomeness of the eggs laid by roupy hens, it will be as well to throw them away. The pip is a white horny skin growing on the tip of the bird's tongue. It should be removed with the point of a penknife, and the place rubbed with salt.

FOWL AND RICE CROQUETTES (an Entree).

953. INGREDIENTS.—½ lb. of rice, 1 quart of stock or broth, 3 oz. of butter, minced fowl, egg, and bread crumbs.

Mode.—Put the rice into the above proportion of cold stock or broth, and let it boil very gently for ½ hour; then add the butter, and simmer it till quite dry and soft. When cold, make it into balls, hollow out the inside, and fill with minced fowl made by recipe No. 956. The mince should be rather thick. Cover over with rice, dip the balls into egg, sprinkle them with bread crumbs, and fry a nice brown. Dish them, and garnish with fried parsley. Oysters, white sauce, or a little cream, may be stirred into the rice before it cools.

Time.—½ hour to boil the rice, 10 minutes to fry the croquettes.

Average cost, exclusive of the fowl, 8*d*.

Seasonable at any time.

CHIP.—If the birds are allowed to paddle about on wet soil, or to be much out in the rain, they will get "chip." Young chicks are especially liable to this complaint. They will sit shivering in out-of-the-way corners, perpetually uttering a dolorous "chip, chip;" seemingly frozen with cold, though, on handling them, they are found to be in high fever. A wholesale breeder would take no pains to attempt the cure of fowls so afflicted; but they who keep chickens for the pleasure, and not for the profit they yield, will be inclined to recover them if possible. Give them none but warm food, half a peppercorn rolled in a morsel of dough every night, and a little nitre in their water. Above all, keep them warm; a corner in the kitchen fender, for a day or two, will do more to effect a cure than the run of a druggist's warehouse.

CROQUETTES OF FOWL (an Entree).

954. INGREDIENTS.—3 or 4 shalots, 1 oz. of butter, 1 teaspoonful of flour, white sauce; pepper, salt, and pounded mace to taste; ½ teaspoonful of pounded sugar, the remains of cold roast fowls, the yolks of 2 eggs, egg, and bread crumbs.

Mode.—Mince the fowl, carefully removing all skin and bone, and fry the shalots in the butter; add the minced fowl, dredge in the flour, put in the pepper, salt, mace, pounded sugar, and sufficient white sauce to moisten it; stir to it the yolks of 2 well-beaten eggs, and set it by to cool. Then make the mixture up into balls, egg and bread-crumb them, and fry a nice brown. They may be served on a border of mashed potatoes, with gravy or sauce in the centre.

Time.—10 minutes to fry the balls.

Seasonable at any time.

THE TURN.—What is termed "turrling" with song-birds, is known, as regard fowls, as the "turn." Its origin is the same in both cases,—over-feeding and want of exercise. Without a moment's warning, a fowl so afflicted will totter and fall from its perch, and unless assistance be at hand, speedily give up the ghost. The veins of the palate should be opened, and a few drops of a mixture composed of six parts of sweet nitre and one of ammonia, poured down its throat. I have seen ignorant keepers plunge a bird, stricken with the "turn," into cold water; but I never saw it taken out again alive; and for a good reason: the sudden chill has the effect of driving the blood to the head,—of aggravating the disease indeed, instead of relieving it.

HASHED FOWL—an Entree (Cold Meat Cookery).

955. INGREDIENTS.—The remains of cold roast fowl, 1 pint of water, 1 onion, 2 or three small carrots, 1 blade of pounded mace, pepper and salt to taste, 1 small bunch of savoury herbs, thickening of butter and flour, 1½ tablespoonful of mushroom ketchup.

Mode.—Cut off the best joints from the fowl, and the remainder make into gravy, by adding to the bones and trimmings a pint of water, an onion sliced and fried of a nice brown, the carrots, mace, seasoning, and herbs. Let these stew gently for 1½ hour, strain the liquor, and thicken with a little flour and butter. Lay in the fowl, thoroughly warm it through, add the ketchup, and garnish with sippets of toasted bread.

Time.—Altogether 1¾ hour.

Average cost, exclusive of the cold fowl, 4*d.*

Seasonable at any time.

SKIN-DISEASE IN FOWLS.—Skin-disease is, nine times out of ten, caused by the feathers being swarmed by parasites. Poor feeding will induce this, even if cleanliness be observed; uncleanliness, however liberal the bill of fare, will be taken as an invitation by the little biting pests, and heartily responded to. Mix half a teaspoonful of hydro-oxalic acid with twelve teaspoonfuls of water,—apply to the itching parts with an old shaving-brush.

OBSTRUCTION OF THE CROP.—Obstruction of the crop is occasioned by weakness or greediness. You may know when a bird is so afflicted by his crop being distended almost to bursting. Mowbray tells of a hen of his in this predicament ; when the crop was opened, a quantity of new beans were discovered in a state of vegetation. The crop should be slit from the *bottom* to the *top* with a sharp pair of scissors, the contents taken out, and the slit sewed up again with fine white thread.

MINCED FOWL—an Entree (Cold Meat Cookery).

956. INGREDIENTS.—The remains of cold roast fowl, 2 hard-boiled eggs, salt, cayenne, and pounded mace, 1 onion, 1 faggot of savoury herbs, 6 tablespoonfuls of cream, 1 oz. of butter, two teaspoonfuls of flour, ½ teaspoonful of finely-minced lemon-peel, 1 tablespoonful of lemon-juice.

Mode.—Cut out from the fowl all the white meat, and mince it finely without any skin or bone ; put the bones, skin, and trimmings into a stewpan with an onion, a bunch of savoury herbs, a blade of mace, and nearly a pint of water ; let this stew for an hour, then strain the liquor. Chop the eggs small ; mix them with the fowl ; add salt, cayenne, and pounded mace, put in the gravy and remaining ingredients ; let the whole just boil, and serve with sippets of toasted bread.

Time.—Rather more than 1 hour.

Average cost, exclusive of the fowl, 8*d.*

Seasonable at any time.

Note.—Another way to make this is to mince the fowl, and warm it in white sauce or Béchamel. When dressed like this, 3 or 4 poached eggs may be placed on the top : oysters, or chopped mushrooms, or balls of oyster forcemeat, may be laid round the dish.

THE MOULTING SEASON.—During the moulting season, beginning properly at the end of September, the fowls will require a little extra attention. Keep them dry and warm, and feed them liberally on warm and satisfying food. If in any fowl the moult should seem protracted, examine it for broken feather-stumps still bedded in the skin : if you find any, extract them carefully with a pair of tweezers. If a fowl is hearty and strong, six weeks will see him out of his trouble ; if he is weakly, or should take cold during the time, he will not thoroughly recover in less than three months. It is seldom or ever that hens will lay during the moult ; while the cock, during the same period, will give so little of his consideration to the frivolities of love, that you may as well, nay, much better, keep him by himself till he perfectly recovers. A moulting chicken makes but a sorry dish.

HASHED FOWL, Indian Fashion (an Entree).

957. INGREDIENTS.—The remains of cold roast fowl, 3 or 4 sliced onions, 1 apple, 2 oz. of butter, pounded mace, pepper and salt to taste, 1 tablespoonful of curry-powder, 2 tablespoonfuls of vinegar, 1 table-spoonful of flour, 1 teaspoonful of pounded sugar, 1 pint of gravy.

Mode.—Cut the onions into slices, mince the apple, and fry these in the butter; add pounded mace, pepper, salt, curry-powder, vinegar, flour, and sugar in the above proportions; when the onion is brown, put in the gravy, which should be previously made from the bones and trimmings of the fowls, and stew for ¾ hour; add the fowl cut into nice-sized joints, let it warm through, and when quite tender, serve. The dish should be garnished with an edging of boiled rice.

Time.—1 hour. *Average cost*, exclusive of the fowl, 8*d*.

Seasonable at any time.

THE SCOUR OR DYSENTERY.—The scour, or dysentery, or diarrhœa, is induced variously. A sudden alteration in diet will cause it, as will a superabundance of green food. The best remedy is a piece of toasted biscuit sopped in ale. If the disease has too tight a hold on the bird to be quelled by this, give six drops of syrup of white poppies and six drops of castor-oil, mixed with a little oatmeal or ground rice. Restrict the bird's diet, for a few days, to dry food,—crushed beans or oats, stale bread-crumbs, &c.

FOWL SCOLLOPS (Cold Meat Cookery).

958. INGREDIENTS.—The remains of cold roast or boiled fowl, ½ pint of Béchamel, No. 367, or white sauce, No. 537 or 539.

Mode.—Strip off the skin from the fowl; cut the meat into thin slices, and warm them in about ½ pint, or rather more, of Béchamel, or white sauce. When quite hot, serve, and garnish the dish with rolled ham or bacon toasted.

Time.—1 minute to simmer the slices of fowl.

Seasonable at any time.

THE FEATHER-LEGGED BANTAM.—Since the introduction of the Bantam into Europe, it has ramified into many varieties, none of which are destitute of elegance, and some, indeed, remarkable for their beauty. All are, or ought to be, of small size, but lively and vigorous, exhibiting in their movements both grace and stateliness. The variety shown in the engraving is remarkable for the *tarsi*, or beams of the legs, being plumed to the toes, with stiff, long feathers, which brush the ground. Owing, possibly, to the little care taken to preserve this variety from admixture, it is now not frequently seen. Another variety is often red, with a black breast and single dentated comb. The *tarsi* are smooth, and of a dusky blue. When this sort of Bantam is pure, it yields in courage and spirit to none, and is, in fact, a game-fowl in miniature, being as beautiful and graceful as it is spirited. A pure white Bantam, possessing all the qualifications just named, is also bred in the royal aviary at Windsor.

FEATHER-LEGGED BANTAMS.

AN INDIAN DISH OF FOWL (an Entree).

959. INGREDIENTS.—The remains of cold roast fowl, 3 or 4 sliced onions, 1 tablespoonful of curry-powder, salt to taste.

Mode.—Divide the fowl into joints; slice and fry the onions in a little butter, taking care not to burn them; sprinkle over the fowl a little curry-powder and salt; fry these nicely, pile them high in the centre of the dish, cover with the onion, and serve with a cut lemon on a plate. Care must be taken that the onions are not greasy: they should be quite dry, but not burnt.

Time.—5 minutes to fry the onions, 10 minutes to fry the fowl.

Average cost, exclusive of the fowl, 4*d.*

Seasonable during the winter months.

THE SPECKLED HAMBURG.—Of the speckled, or spangled Hamburg, which is a favourite breed with many persons, there are two varieties,—the golden-speckled and the silver-speckled. The general colour of the former is golden, or orange-yellow, each feather having a glossy dark brown or black tip, particularly remarkable on the hackles of the cock and the wing-coverts, and also on the darker feathers of the breast. The female is yellow, or orange-brown, the feathers in like manner being margined with black. The silver-speckled variety is distinguished by the ground-colour of the plumage being of a silver-white, with perhaps a tinge of straw-yellow, every feather being margined with a semi-lunar mark of glossy black. Both of these varieties are extremely beautiful, the hens laying freely. First-rate birds command a high price.

SPECKLED HAMBURGS.

FOWL SAUTE WITH PEAS (an Entree).

960. INGREDIENTS.—The remains of cold roast fowl, 2 oz. of butter, pepper, salt, and pounded mace to taste, 1 dessertspoonful of flour, ½ pint of weak stock, 1 pint of green peas, 1 teaspoonful of pounded sugar.

Mode.—Cut the fowl into nice pieces; put the butter into a stewpan; sautez or fry the fowl a nice brown colour, previously sprinkling it with pepper, salt, and pounded mace. Dredge in the flour, shake the ingredients well round, then add the stock and peas, and stew till the latter are tender, which will be in about 20 minutes; put in the pounded sugar, and serve, placing the chicken round, and the peas in the middle of the dish. When liked, mushrooms may be substituted for the peas.

Time.—Altogether 40 minutes.

Average cost, exclusive of the fowl, 7*d.*

Seasonable from June to August.

BOUDIN A LA REINE (an Entree).

(*M. Ude's Recipe.*)

961. INGREDIENTS.—The remains of cold roast fowls, 1 pint of Béchamel No. 367, salt and cayenne to taste, egg and bread crumbs.

Mode.—Take the breasts and nice white meat from the fowls; cut it into small dice of an equal size, and throw them into some good Béchamel, made by recipe No. 367; season with salt and cayenne, and put the mixture into a dish to cool. When this preparation is quite cold, cut it into 2 equal parts, which should be made into *boudins* of a long shape, the size of the dish they are intended to be served on; roll them in flour, egg and bread-crumb them, and be careful that the ends are well covered with the crumbs, otherwise they would break in the frying-pan; fry them a nice colour, put them before the fire to drain the greasy moisture from them, and serve with the remainder of the Béchamel poured round: this should be thinned with a little stock.

Time.—10 minutes to fry the boudins.

Average cost, exclusive of the fowl, 1*s.* 3*d.*

Sufficient for 1 entrée.

SIR JOHN SEBRIGHT'S BANTAMS.—Above all Bantams is placed, the celebrated and beautiful breed called Sir John Sebright's Silver Bantams. This breed, which Sir John brought to perfection after years of careful trials, is very small, with un-feathered legs, and a rose comb and short hackles. The plumage is gold or silver, span-gled, every feather being of a golden orange, or of a silver white, with a glossy jet-black margin; the cocks have the tail folded like that of a hen, with the sickle feathers short-ened straight, or nearly so, and broader than usual. The term *hen-cocks* is, in consequence, often applied to them; but although the sickle feathers are thus modified, no bird possesses higher courage, or a more gallant carriage. The attitude of the cock is, indeed, singularly proud; and he is often seen to bear himself so haughtily, that his head, thrown back as if in disdain, nearly touches the two upper feathers—

SEBRIGHT BANTAMS.

sickles they can scarcely be called—of his tail. Half-bred birds of this kind are not un-common, but birds of the pure breed are not to be obtained without trouble and expense; indeed, some time ago, it was almost impossible to procure either a fowl or an egg. "The finest," says the writer whom we have consulted as to this breed, "we have ever seen, were in Sir John's poultry-yard, adjacent to Turnham-Green Common, in the byroad leading to Acton."

FOWL A LA MAYONNAISE.

962. INGREDIENTS.—A cold roast fowl, Mayonnaise sauce No. 468, 4 or 5 young lettuces, 4 hard-boiled eggs, a few water-cresses, endive.

Mode.—Cut the fowl into neat joints, lay them in a deep dish, piling them high in the centre, sauce the fowl with Mayonnaise made by recipe No. 468, and garnish the dish with young lettuces cut in halves, water-cresses, endive, and hard-boiled eggs: these may be sliced in rings, or laid on the dish whole, cutting off at the bottom a piece of the white, to make the egg stand. All kinds of cold meat and solid fish may be dressed à la Mayonnaise, and make excellent luncheon or supper dishes. The sauce should not be poured over the fowls until the moment of serving. Should a very large Mayonnaise be required, use 2 fowls instead of 1, with an equal proportion of the remaining ingredients.

Average cost, with one fowl, 3s. 6d.

Sufficient for a moderate-sized dish.

Seasonable from April to September.

BLACK SPANISH.—The real Spanish fowl is recognized by its uniformly black colour, burnished with tints of green; its peculiar white face, and the large development of its comb and wattle. The hens are excellent layers, and their eggs are of a very large size. They are, however, bad nurses; consequently, their eggs should be laid in the nest of other varieties to be hatched. "In purchasing Spanish," says an authority, "blue legs, the entire absence of white or coloured feathers in the plumage, and a large white face, with a very large high comb, which should be erect in the cock, though pendent in the hens, should be insisted on." The flesh of this fowl is esteemed; but, from the smallness of its body when compared with that of the Dorking, it is not placed on an equality with it for the table. Otherwise, however, they are profitable birds, and their handsome carriage, and striking contrast of colour

BLACK SPANISH.

in the comb, face, and plumage, are a high recommendation to them as kept fowls. For a town fowl, they are perhaps better adapted than any other variety.

FOWL PILLAU, based on M. Soyer's Recipe (an Indian Dish).

963. INGREDIENTS.—1 lb. of rice, 2 oz. of butter, a fowl, 2 quarts of stock or good broth, 40 cardamum-seeds, ½ oz. of coriander-seed, ¼ oz. of cloves, ¼ oz. of allspice, ¼ oz. of mace, ¼ oz. of cinnamon, ½ oz. of peppercorns, 4 onions, 6 thin slices of bacon, 2 hard-boiled eggs.

Mode.—Well wash 1 lb. of the best Patna rice, put it into a frying-pan with the butter, which keep moving over a slow fire until the rice is lightly browned. Truss the fowl as for boiling, put it into a stewpan with the stock or broth; pound the spices and seeds thoroughly in a mortar, tie them in a piece of muslin, and put them in with the fowl. Let it boil slowly until it is nearly done; then add the rice, which should stew until quite tender and almost dry; cut the onions into slices, sprinkle them with flour, and fry, without breaking them, of a nice brown colour. Have ready the slices of bacon curled and grilled, and the eggs boiled hard. Lay the fowl in the form of a pyramid upon a dish, smother with the rice, garnish with the bacon, fried onions, and the hard-boiled eggs cut into quarters, and serve very hot. Before taking the rice out, remove the spices.

Time.—½ hour to stew the fowl without the rice; ½ hour with it.

Average cost, 4s. 3d.   *Sufficient* for 4 or 5 persons.
Seasonable at any time.

THE SERAI TA-OOK, OR FOWLS OF THE SULTAN.—This fowl is the size of our English Polands, and is the latest species introduced to England. They have a white and flowing plumage, a full-sized, compact Poland tuft on the head, are muffed, have a full flowing tail, short legs well feathered, and five toes upon each foot. Their comb consists merely of two little points, and their wattles are very small: their colour is that of a pure white. In January, 1854, they arrived in this country from Constantinople; and they take their name from *sarai,* the Turkish word for sultan's palace, and *ta-ook,* the Turkish for fowl. They are thus called the "fowls of the sultan," a name which has the twofold advantage of being the nearest to be found to that by which they have been known in their own country, and of designating the country whence they come. Their habits are described as being generally brisk and

SULTANS.

happy-tempered, but not so easily kept in as Cochin-Chinas. They are excellent layers; but they are non-sitters and small eaters: their eggs are large and white. Brahmas or Cochins will clear the crop of a grass-run long before they will, and, with scattered food, they soon satisfy themselves and walk away.

POULET AUX CRESSONS.

964. INGREDIENTS.—A fowl, a large bunch of water-cresses, 3 tablespoonfuls of vinegar, ¼ pint of gravy.

Mode.—Truss and roast a fowl by recipe No. 952, taking care that it is nicely frothed and brown. Wash and dry the water-cresses, pick them nicely, and arrange them in a flat layer on a dish. Sprinkle over a little salt and the above proportion of vinegar; place over these the fowl, and pour over it the gravy. A little gravy should be served in a tureen. When not liked, the vinegar may be omitted.

Time.—From ½ to 1 hour, according to size.
Average cost, in full season, 2s. 6d. each.
Sufficient for 3 or 4 persons.
Seasonable at any time.

ROAST FOWL, Stuffed.

965. INGREDIENTS.—A large fowl, forcemeat No. 417, a little flour.

Mode.—Select a large plump fowl, fill the breast with forcemeat, made by recipe No. 417, truss it firmly, the same as for a plain roast fowl, dredge it with flour, and put it down to a bright fire. Roast it for nearly or quite an hour, should it be very large; remove the skewers, and serve with a good brown gravy and a tureen of bread sauce.

Time.—Large fowl, nearly or quite 1 hour.

Average cost, in full season, 2*s.* 6*d.* each.

Sufficient for 4 or 5 persons.

Seasonable all the year, but scarce in early spring.

Note.—Sausage-meat stuffing may be substituted for the above : this is now a very general mode of serving fowl.

PENCILLED HAMBURG.—This variety of the Hamburg fowl is of two colours, golden and silver, and is very minutely marked. The hens of both should have the body clearly pencilled across with several bars of black, and the hackle in both sexes should be perfectly free from dark marks. The cocks do not exhibit the pencillings, but are white or brown in the golden or silver birds respectively. Their form is compact, and their attitudes graceful and sprightly. The hens do not sit, but lay extremely well; hence one of their common names, that of Dutch every-day layers. They are also known in different parts of the country, as Chitteprats, Creoles, or Corals, Bolton bays and grays, and, in some parts of Yorkshire, by the wrong name of Corsican fowls. They are imported in large numbers from Holland, but those bred in this country are greatly superior in size.

PENCILLED HAMBURGS.

GIBLET PIE.

966. INGREDIENTS.—A set of duck or goose giblets, 1 lb. of **rump-steak**, 1 onion, ½ teaspoonful of whole black pepper, a bunch of savoury herbs, plain crust.

Mode.—Clean, and put the giblets into a stewpan with an onion, whole pepper, and a bunch of savoury herbs; add rather more than a pint of water, and simmer gently for about 1½ hour. Take them out, let them cool, and cut them into pieces; line the bottom of a pie-dish with a few pieces of rump-steak; add a layer of giblets and a few more pieces of steak; season with pepper and salt, and pour in the gravy (which should be strained), that the giblets were stewed in; cover with a plain crust, and bake for rather more than 1½ hour in a brisk oven. Cover a piece of paper over the pie, to prevent the crust taking too much colour.

Time.—1½ hour to stew the giblets, about 1 hour to bake the pie.

Average cost, exclusive of the giblets, 1*s.* 4*d.*

Sufficient for 5 or 6 persons.

THE BRENT GOOSE.—This is the smallest and most numerous species of the geese which visit the British islands. It makes its appearance in winter, and ranges over the whole of the coasts and estuaries frequented by other migrant geese. Mr. Selby states that a vary large body of these birds annually resort to the extensive sandy and muddy flats which lie between the mainland and Holy Island, on the Northumbrian coast, and which are covered by every flow of the tide. This part of the coast appears to have been a favourite resort of these birds from time immemorial, where they have always received the name of Ware geese, no doubt from their continually feeding on marine vegetables. Their flesh is very agreeable. .

HASHED GOOSE.

967. INGREDIENTS.—The remains of cold roast goose, 2 onions, 2 oz. of butter, 1 pint of boiling water, 1 dessertspoonful of flour, pepper and salt to taste, 1 tablespoonful of port wine, 2 tablespoonfuls of mushroom ketchup.

Mode.—Cut up the goose into pieces of the size required; the inferior joints, trimmings, &c., put into a stewpan to make the gravy; slice and fry the onions in the butter of a very pale brown; add these to the trimmings, and pour over about a pint of boiling water; stew these gently for ¾ hour, then skim and strain the liquor. Thicken it with flour, and flavour with port wine and ketchup, in the above proportion; add a seasoning of pepper and salt, and put in the pieces of goose; let these get thoroughly hot through, but do not allow them to boil, and serve with sippets of toasted bread.

Time.—Altogether, rather more than 1 hour.

Average cost, exclusive of the cold goose, 4d.

Seasonable from September to March.

THE WILD GOOSE.—This bird is sometimes called the "Gray-lag" and is the original of the domestic goose. It is, according to Pennant, the only species which the Britons could take young, and familiarize. "The Gray-lag," says Mr. Gould, "is known to inhabit all the extensive marshy districts throughout the temperate regions of Europe generally; its range northwards not extending further than the fifty-third degree of latitude, while southwards it extends to the northern portions of Africa, easterly to Persia, and we believe it is generally dispersed over Asia Minor." It is the bird that saved the Capitol by its vigilance, and by the Romans was cherished accordingly.

ROAST GOOSE.

968. INGREDIENTS.—Goose, 4 large onions, 10 sage-leaves, ¼ lb. of bread crumbs, 1½ oz. of butter, salt and pepper to taste, 1 egg.

Choosing and Trussing.—Select a goose with a clean white skin, plump breast, and yellow feet: if these latter are red, the bird is old. Should the weather permit, let it hang for a few days: by so doing, the flavour will be very much improved. Pluck, singe, draw, and carefully wash and wipe the goose; cut off the neck close to the back, leaving the skin long enough to turn over; cut off the feet at the first joint, and separate the pinions at the first joint. Beat the breast-bone flat with a rolling-pin, put a skewer through the under part of each wing, and having drawn up the legs closely, put a skewer into the middle of each, and pass the same quite through the body. Insert another skewer into the small of the leg, bring it close down to the side bone, run it through, and do the same to the other side. Now cut off the end of the vent, and make a hole in the skin sufficiently large for the passage of the rump, in order to keep in the seasoning.

Mode.—Make a sage-and-onion stuffing of the above ingredients, by recipe No. 504 ; put it into the body of the goose, and secure it firmly at both ends, by passing the rump through the hole made in the skin, and the other end by tying the skin of the neck to the back ; by this means the seasoning will not escape. Put it down to a brisk fire, keep it well basted, and roast from 1½ to 2 hours, according to the size. Remove the skewers, and serve with a tureen of good gravy, and one of well-made apple-sauce. Should a very

ROAST GOOSE.

highly-flavoured seasoning be preferred, the onions should not be parboiled, but minced raw : of the two methods, the mild seasoning is far superior. A ragoût, or pie, should be made of the giblets, or they may be stewed down to make gravy. Be careful to serve the goose before the breast falls, or its appearance will be spoiled by coming flattened to table. As this is rather a troublesome joint to carve, a *large* quantity of gravy should not be poured round the goose, but sent in a tureen.

Time.—A large goose, 1¾ hour ; a moderate-sized one, 1¼ to 1½ hour.

Seasonable from September to March; but in perfection from Michaelmas to Christmas.

Average cost, 5s. 6d. each. *Sufficient* for 8 or 9 persons.

Note.—A teaspoonful of made mustard, a saltspoonful of salt, a few grains of cayenne, mixed with a glass of port wine, are sometimes poured into the goose by a slit made in the apron. This sauce is, by many persons, considered an improvement.

THE GOOSE.—This bird is pretty generally distributed over the face of the globe, being met with in North America, Lapland, Iceland, Arabia, and Persia. Its varieties are numerous ; but in England there is only one species, which is supposed to be a native breed. The best geese are found on the borders of Suffolk, and in Norfolk and Berkshire; but the largest flocks are reared in the fens of Lincolnshire and Cambridge. They thrive best where they have an easy access to water, and large herds of them are sent every year to London, to be fattened by the metropolitan poulterers. "A Michaelmas goose," says Dr. Kitchener, "is as famous in the mouths of the million as the minced-pie at Christmas; yet for those who eat with delicacy, it is, at that time, too full-grown. The true period when the goose is in the highest perfection is when it has just acquired

EMDEN GOOSE.

its full growth, and not begun to harden; if the March goose is insipid, the Michaelmas goose is rank. The fine time is between both; from the second week in June to the first in September." It is said that the Michaelmas goose is indebted to Queen Elizabeth for its origin on the table at that season. Her majesty happened to dine on one at the table of an English baronet, when she received the news of the discomfiture of the Spanish Armada. In commemoration of this event, she commanded the goose to make its appearance at table on every Michaelmas. We here give an engraving of the Emden goose.

TO DRESS A GREEN GOOSE.

969. INGREDIENTS.—Goose, 3 oz. of butter, pepper and salt to taste.

Mode.—Geese are called green till they are about four months old, and should not be stuffed. After it has been singed and trussed, the same as in the preceding recipe, put into the body a seasoning of pepper and salt, and the butter to moisten it inside. Roast before a clear fire for about $\frac{3}{4}$ hour, froth and brown it nicely, and serve with a brown gravy, and, when liked, gooseberry-sauce. This dish should be garnished with water-cresses.

Time.—About $\frac{3}{4}$ hour. *Average cost,* 4s. 6d. each.

Sufficient for 5 or 6 persons.

Seasonable in June, July, and August.

THE EGYPTIAN GOOSE.—Especial attention has been directed to this bird by Herodotus, who says it was held sacred by the ancient Egyptians, which has been partially confirmed by modern travellers. Mr. Salt remarks, "Horus Apollo says the old geese stay with their young in the most imminent danger, at the risk of their own lives, which I have myself frequently witnessed. Vielpanser is the goose of the Nile, and wherever this goose is represented on the walls of the temples in colours, the resemblance may be clearly traced." The goose is also said to have been a bird under the care of Isis. It has been placed by Mr. Gould amongst the birds of Europe; not from the number of half-reclaimed individuals which are annually shot in Britain, but from the circumstance of its occasionally visiting the southern parts of the continent from its native country, Africa. The Toulouse goose, of which we give an engraving, is a well-known bird.

TOULOUSE GOOSE.

ROAST GUINEA-FOWL, Larded.

970. INGREDIENTS.—A Guinea-fowl, lardoons, flour, and salt.

Mode.—When this bird is larded, it should be trussed the same as a pheasant; if plainly roasted, truss it like a turkey. After larding and trussing it, put it down to roast at a brisk fire; keep it well basted, and a short time before serving, dredge it with a little flour, and let it froth nicely. Serve with a little gravy in the dish, and a tureen of the same, and one of well-made bread-sauce.

Time.—Guinea-fowl, larded, 1¼ hour; plainly roasted, about 1 hour.

Sufficient for 6 persons.

Seasonable in winter.

Note.—The breast, if larded, should be covered with a piece of paper, and removed about 10 minutes before serving.

THE GUINEA-FOWL.—The bird takes its name from Guinea, in Africa, where it is found wild, and in great abundance. It is gregarious in its habits, associating in flocks of two or three hundred, delighting in marshy grounds, and at night perching upon trees, or on high situations. Its size is about the same as that of a common hen, but it stands higher on its legs. Though domesticated, it retains much of its wild nature, and is apt to wander. The hens lay abundantly, and the eggs are excellent. In their flesh, however, they are not so white as the common fowl, but more inclined to the colour of the pheasant, for which it frequently makes a good substitute at table. The flesh is both savoury and easy of digestion, and is in season when game is out of season.

GUINEA-FOWLS.

LARK PIE (an Entree).

971. INGREDIENTS.—A few thin slices of beef, the same of bacon, 9 larks, flour; for stuffing, 1 teacupful of bread crumbs, ½ teaspoonful of minced lemon-peel, 1 teaspoonful of minced parsley, 1 egg, salt and pepper to taste, 1 teaspoonful of chopped shalot, ½ pint of weak stock or water, puff-paste.

Mode.—Make a stuffing of bread crumbs, minced lemon-peel, parsley, and the yolk of an egg, all of which should be well mixed together; roll the larks in flour, and stuff them. Line the bottom of a pie-dish with a few slices of beef and bacon; over these place the larks, and season with salt, pepper, minced parsley, and chopped shalot, in the above proportion. Pour in the stock or water, cover with crust, and bake for an hour in a moderate oven. During the time the pie is baking, shake it 2 or 3 times, to assist in thickening the gravy, and serve very hot.

Time.—1 hour. *Average cost,* 1s. 6d. a dozen.

Sufficient for 5 or 6 persons.

Seasonable.—In full season in November.

ROAST LARKS.

972. INGREDIENTS.—Larks, egg and bread crumbs, fresh butter.

Mode.—These birds are by many persons esteemed a great delicacy, and may be either roasted or broiled. Pick, gut, and clean them;

when they are trussed, brush them over with the yolk of an egg; sprinkle with bread crumbs, and roast them before a quick fire; baste them continually with fresh butter, and keep sprinkling with the bread crumbs until the birds are well covered. Dish them on bread crumbs fried in clarified butter, and garnish the dish with slices of lemon. Broiled larks are also very excellent: they should be cooked over a clear fire, and would take about 10 minutes or $\frac{1}{4}$ hour.

Time.—$\frac{1}{4}$ hour to roast; 10 minutes to broil.

Seasonable.—In full season in November.

Note.—Larks may also be plainly roasted, without covering them with egg and bread crumbs; they should be dished on fried crumbs.

BROILED PIGEONS.

973. INGREDIENTS.—Pigeons, 3 oz. of butter, pepper and salt to taste.

Mode.—Take care that the pigeons are quite fresh, and carefully pluck, draw, and wash them; split the backs, rub the birds over with butter, season them with pepper and salt, and broil them over a moderate fire for $\frac{1}{4}$ hour or 20 minutes. Serve very hot, with either mushroom-sauce or a good gravy. Pigeons may also be plainly boiled, and served with parsley and butter; they should be trussed like boiled fowls, and take from $\frac{1}{4}$ hour to 20 minutes to boil.

Time.—To broil a pigeon, from $\frac{1}{4}$ hour to 20 minutes; to boil one, the same time.

Average cost, from 6d. to 9d. each.

Seasonable from April to September, but in the greatest perfection from midsummer to Michaelmas.

THE POUTER PIGEON.—This is a very favourite pigeon, and, without doubt, the most curious of his species. He is a tall strong bird, as he had need be to carry about his great inflated crop, frequently as large and as round as a middling-sized turnip. A perfect pouter, seen on a windy day, is certainly a ludicrous sight: his feathered legs have the appearance of white trousers; his tapering tail looks like a swallow-tailed coat; his head is entirely concealed by his immense windy protuberance; and, altogether, he reminds you of a little "swell" of a past century, staggering under a bale of linen. The most common pouters are the blues, buffs, and whites, or an intermixture of all these various colours. The pouter is not a prolific breeder, is a bad nurse, and more likely to degenerate, if not repeatedly crossed and re-crossed with fresh stock, than any other pigeon: nevertheless, it is a useful bird to keep if you are founding a new colony, as it is much attached to its home, and little apt to stray; consequently it is calculated to induce more restless birds to settle down and make themselves comfortable. If you wish to breed pouters, you cannot do worse than intrust them with the care of their own eggs.

POUTER PIGEON.

ROAST PIGEONS.

974. INGREDIENTS.—Pigeons, 3 oz. of butter, pepper and salt to taste.

Trussing.—Pigeons, to be good, should be eaten fresh (if kept a little, the flavour goes off), and they should be drawn as soon as killed. Cut off the heads and necks, truss the wings over the backs, and cut off the toes at the first joint: previous to trussing, they should be carefully cleaned, as no bird requires so much washing.

Mode.—Wipe the birds very dry, season them inside with pepper and salt, and put about ¾ oz. of butter into the body of each: this makes them moist. Put them down to a bright fire, and baste them well ·the whole of the time they are cooking (they will be done enough in from 20 to 30 minutes); garnish with fried parsley, and serve with a tureen of parsley and butter. Bread-sauce and gravy, the same as for roast fowl, are exceedingly nice accompaniments to roast pigeons, as also egg-sauce.

ROAST PIGEON.

Time.—From 20 minutes to ½ hour. *Average cost,* 6*d.* to 9*d.* each.

Seasonable from April to September; but in the greatest perfection from Midsummer to Michaelmas.

THE PIGEON.—The pigeon tribe forms a connecting link between the passerine birds and poultry. They are widely distributed over the world, some of the species being found even in the arctic regions. Their chief food is grain, and they drink much; not at intervals, like other birds, but by a continuous draught, like quadrupeds. The wild pigeon, or stockdove, is the parent whence all the varieties of the domestic pigeon are derived. In the wild state it is still found in many parts of this island, making its nest in the holes of rocks, in the hollows of trees, or in old towers, but never, like the ringdove, on branches. The blue house-pigeon is the variety principally reared for the table in this country, and is produced from our farmyards in great numbers. When young, and still fed by their parents, they are most preferable for the table, and are called *squabs;* under six months they are denominated *squeakers,* and at six months they begin to breed. Their flesh is accounted savoury, delicate, and stimulating, and the dark-coloured birds are considered to have the highest flavour, whilst the light are esteemed to have the more delicate flesh.

THE PIGEON-HOUSE, OR DOVECOT.—The first thing to be done towards keeping pigeons is to provide a commodious place for their reception; and the next is, to provide the pigeons themselves. The situation or size of the dovecot will necessarily depend on convenience; but there is one point which must invariably be observed, and that is, that every pair of pigeons has two holes or rooms to nest in. This is indispensable, as, without it, there will be no security, but the constant prospect of confusion, breaking of eggs, and the destruction of young. The proper place for the pigeon-house is the poultry-yard; but it does very well near dwellings, stables, brewhouses, bakehouses, or such offices. Some persons keep pigeons in rooms, and have them making their nests on the floor. The object is to escape the danger of the young falling out; but in such cases, there is a great risk of rats or other vermin getting at the pigeons.

ASPECT OF THE PIGEON-HOUSE.—The front of the pigeon-house should have a south-west aspect, and, if a room be selected for the purpose, it is usual to break a hole in the roof of the building for the passage of the pigeons, but which can be closed at convenience. A platform ought to be laid at the entrance for the pigeons to perch upon, with some kind of defence against strange cats, which will frequently depopulate a whole dovecot. Yet, although cats are dangerous neighbours for the birds, they are necessary to defend them from the approach of rats and mice, which will not only suck the eggs, but destroy the birds. The platform should be painted white, and renewed as the paint wears off, white being a favourite colour with pigeons, and also most conspicuous as a mark to enable them to find their house. The boxes ought also to be similarly painted, and renewed when necessary, for which purpose lime and water will do very well.

THE NECESSITY OF CLEANLINESS.—As cleanliness in human habitations is of the first importance, so is it in the pigeon-house. There the want of it will soon render the place a nuisance not to be approached, and the birds, both young and old, will be so covered with vermin and filth, that they will neither enjoy health nor comfort, whilst early mortality amongst them will be almost certain. In some cases, the pigeon-house is cleaned daily; but it should always be done, at any rate, once a week, and the floor covered with sifted gravel, frequently renewed. Pigeons being exceedingly fond of water, and having a prescience of the coming of rain, they may be seen upon the house-tops waiting upon it until late in the evening, and then spreading their wings to receive the luxury of the refreshing shower. When they are confined in a room, therefore, they should be allowed a wide pan of water, to be often renewed. This serves them for a bath, which cools, refreshes, and assists them to keep their bodies clear of vermin.

BREEDING PIGEONS.—In breeding pigeons, it is necessary to match a cock and hen, and shut them up together, or place them near to each other, and in the course of a day or two there is little doubt of their mating. Various rules have been laid down for the purpose of assisting to distinguish the cock from the hen pigeon; but the masculine forwardness and action of the cock is generally so remarkable, that he is easily ascertained. The pigeon being monogamous, the male attaches and confines himself to one female, and the attachment is reciprocal, and the fidelity of the dove to its mate is proverbial. At the age of six months, young pigeons are termed squeakers, and then begin to breed, when properly managed. Their courtship, and the well-known tone of voice in the cock, just then acquired and commencing, are indications of their approaching union. Nestlings, while fed by cock and hen, are termed squabs, and are, at that age, sold and used for the table. The dove-house pigeon is said to breed monthly, when well supplied with food. At all events, it may be depended on, that pigeons of almost any healthy and well-established variety will breed eight or ten times in the year; whence it may readily be conceived how vast are the numbers that may be raised.

THE CARRIER PIGEON.—Without doubt the carrier is entitled to rank first in the pigeon family, with the exception, perhaps, of the blue-rock pigeons. No domestic fowl can be traced to so remote an antiquity. When Greece was in its glory, carrier pigeons were used to convey to distant parts the names of the victors at the Olympian games. During the holy war, when Acre was besieged by King Richard, Saladin habitually corresponded with the besieged by means of carrier pigeons. A shaft from an English crossbow, however, happened to bring one of these feathered messengers to the ground, and the stratagem was discovered, the design of the Saracens revealed, and so turned against the designers, that Acre was in the hands of the Christians

CARRIER PIGEONS.

before the wily Saladin dreamt of such a thing.

PIGEON PIE (Epsom Grand-Stand Recipe).

975. INGREDIENTS.—1½ lb. of rump-steak, 2 or 3 pigeons, 3 slices of ham, pepper and salt to taste, 2 oz. of butter, 4 eggs, puff crust.

Mode.—Cut the steak into pieces about 3 inches square, and with it line the bottom of a pie-dish, seasoning it well with pepper and salt. Clean the pigeons, rub them with pepper and salt inside and out, and put into the body of each rather more than ½ oz. of butter; lay them on the steak, and a piece of ham on each pigeon. Add the yolks of 4 eggs, and half fill the dish with stock; place a border of puff paste round the edge of the dish, put on the cover, and ornament it in any way that may be preferred. Clean three of the feet, and place them in a hole made in the crust at the top: this shows what kind of pie it is. Glaze the crust,—that is to say, brush it over with the yolk of an egg,—and bake it in a well-heated oven for about $1\frac{1}{4}$ hour. When liked, a seasoning of pounded mace may be added.

Time.—$1\frac{1}{4}$ hour, or rather less. *Average cost, 5s. 3d.*

Sufficient for 5 or 6 persons. *Seasonable* at any time.

TUMBLER PIGEONS.—The smaller the size of this variety, the greater its value. The head should be round and smooth, the neck thin, and the tail similar to that of the turbit. Highly-bred birds of this variety will attain an elevation in their flight beyond that of any other pigeons; and it is in seeing these little birds wing themselves so far into the skies that the fanciers take such delight. For four or five hours tumblers have been known to keep on the wing; and it is when they are almost lost to the power of human vision that they exhibit those pantomimic feats which give them their name, and which are marked by a tumbling over-and-over process, which suggests the idea of their having suddenly become giddy, been deprived of their self-control, or overtaken by some calamity. This acrobatic propensity in these pigeons has been ascribed by some to the absence

TUMBLER PIGEONS.

of a proper power in the tail; but it is nothing more than a natural habit, for which no adequate reason can be assigned. Of this variety, the Almond Tumbler is the most beautiful; and the greater the variation of the colour in the flight and tail, the greater their value.

THE RUNT PIGEON.—This is generally esteemed among the largest of the pigeon varieties, and being possessed of proportionate strength, with a strong propensity to exercise it, they keep the dovecot in a state of almost continual commotion by domineering over the weaker inmates. They breed tolerably well, however, and are valuable for the table. There is both the Leghorn and the Spanish Runt, variously plumaged; but when red, white, or black mottled, are most highly esteemed. One of the great advantages connected with the Runt is, that he is not likely to fly away from home. Being heavy birds, they find it difficult, when well fed, to mount even to a low housetop. Again, they require no loft, or special dwelling-place, but, if properly tended, will be perfectly satisfied, and thrive as well, in a rabbit-hutch as anywhere. Their flavour is very good; and it is not an uncommon thing for a squeaker Runt to exceed a pound and a quarter in weight.

RUNT PIGEONS.

THE NUN PIGEON.—The Tumbler bears a strong resemblance to this variety, which is characterized by a tuft of feathers rising from the back of the head, and which, on the whole, is an extremely pretty little bird. According to the colour of the head, it is called the red, black, or yellow-headed Nun. To be a perfect bird, it should have a small head and beak; and the larger the tuft at the back of his head, the handsomer the bird is esteemed, and proportianately valuable in the eyes of pigeon-fanciers.

NUN PIGEONS.

THE TRUMPETER PIGEON.—From the circumstance of this bird imitating the sound

TRUMPETER PIGEONS.

of a trumpet, instead of cooing, like other pigeons, it has received its designation. It is of the middle size, having its legs and feet covered with feathers, and its plumage generally of a mottled black-and-white. It has a tuft springing from the root of its beak, and the larger this topknot is, the higher the estimation in which the breed is held. In their powers of trumpeting some are more expert than others; and whether this has any effect in influencing their own estimate of themselves, we cannot say; but they are rather select in the choice of their company. If two of them are put in a pigeon-house with other doves, it will be found that they confine their association almost entirely to each other. As much as two guineas have been paid for a well-trained docile bird of this kind.

THE WOOD, OR WILD PIGEON.—Buffon enumerates upwards of thirty varieties of the

WOOD-PIGEON.

pigeon, which he derives from one root,—viz. the stockdove, or common wild pigeon. All the varieties of colour and form which we witness, he attributes to human contrivance and fancy. Nevertheless, there exist essentially specific differences in these birds, which would appear to be attributable rather to the nature of the region, soil, and climate to which they are indigenous, than to the art and ingenuity of man. The stockdove, in its wild state, is still found in some parts of Britain, forming its nest in the holes of rocks, old towers, and in the hollows of trees; it never, however, like the ringdove, nestles in the branches. Multitudes of wild pigeons still visit our shores in the winter, coming from their more northerly retreats, making their appearance about November, and retiring again in the spring. When forests of beechwood covered large tracts of the ground of this country, these birds used to haunt them in myriads, frequently covering a mile of ground in extent when they went out in the morning to feed.

STEWED PIGEONS.

976. INGREDIENTS.—6 pigeons, a few slices of bacon, 3 oz. of butter, 2 tablespoonfuls of minced parsley, sufficient stock No. 104 to cover the pigeons, thickening of butter and flour, 1 tablespoonful of mushroom ketchup, 1 tablespoonful of port wine.

Mode.—Empty and clean the pigeons thoroughly, mince the livers, add to these the parsley and butter, and put it into the insides of the birds. Truss them with the legs inward, and put them into a stewpan, with a few slices of bacon placed under and over them; add the stock, and stew gently for rather more than ½ hour. Dish the pigeons, strain the gravy, thicken it with butter and flour, add the ketchup and port wine, give one boil, pour over the pigeons, and serve.

Time.—Rather more than ½ hour. *Average cost*, 6*d.* to 9*d.* each.

Sufficient for 4 or 5 persons.

Seasonable from April to September.

THE FANTAIL PIGEON.—This curious variety is inferior in point of size to most of the other varieties, and is characterized by having a short, slender bill, pendent wings, and naked legs and feet. It has the power of erecting its tail in the manner of a turkey-cock; during which action, especially when paying court to its mate, it trembles or shakes, like the peacock when moving about with his train expanded and in full display. This power of erecting and spreading the tail is not confined to the male bird alone: the female possesses the same power to an equal extent, and otherwise resembles the male in every respect. It is not very prolific, and seldom succeeds so well in the aviary or pigeon-house as most of the other kinds.

FANTAIL PIGEONS.

THE JACOBIN PIGEON.—This variety, having the power to transmit to posterity a form precisely similar, with all its peculiar characters undiminished, is, among pigeon-fanciers, designated as of a pure or permanent race. It is distinguished by a remarkable ruff or frill of raised feathers, which, commencing behind the head and proceeding down the neck and breast, forms a kind of hood, not unlike that worn by a monk. From this circumstance, it has obtained its Gallic name of *nonnain capuchin*. In size it is one of the smallest of the domestic pigeons, and its form is light and elegant. It is a very productive species, and, having its flight considerably impeded by the size and form of its hooded frill, keeps much at home, and is well adapted for the aviary or other buildings where pigeons are confined.

JACOBIN PIGEONS.

THE TURBIT PIGEON.—This variety bears a strong resemblance to the Jacobin, having a kind of frill in the fore part of its neck, occasioned by the breast-feathers lying contrariwise and standing straight out. The species is classed in accordance with the colour of the shoulders, similarly as the Nuns are by the colour of their heads. Their characteristics of excellence are a full frill, short bill, and small round head. In Germany it is called the ruffle pigeon, in allusion to the feathers on its breast; and it has rarely any feathers on its feet. There is a peculiarity connected with this bird, which somewhat lowers it in the estimation of fanciers: it seldom rears more than one at a time, which, therefore, marks it as a bird rather for amusement than profit.

TURBIT PIGEONS.

THE BARB PIGEON.—The name of this variety is a contraction of Barbary, from which country it originally comes. It is both prolific and has excellent qualities as a nurse. The kind most esteemed is that of one uniform colour, that of blue-black being preferable to any other. Speckled or mottled Barbs are esteemed the most common of all pigeons. It is not unlike the Carrier pigeon, and, at a small distance, might easily be mistaken for the latter. It has a short beak and a small wattle. A spongy, pinky skin round the eyes is its chief characteristic, however, and this increases in size till the bird is three or four years old. This peculiarity is hardly distinguishable in very young birds.

BARB PIGEONS.

THE ROCK PIGEON.—This variety, in its wild state, is found upon the rocky parts of the west of Scotland, and the bold shores of the Western Isles, more abundant than in any other parts of the British islands. As the shores of the mainland are exposed to the muds of the Atlantic, and the comparatively small islands are surrounded by that ocean, the low grounds exposed to the west are seldom covered with snow for any length of time, and thus the birds easily find a supply of food. The numbers which there congregate are often very great, and the din of their united cry is sometimes very loud and even alarming. The love of home and the certainty of returning to it is very conspicuous in the rock-pigeon or *biset*, as it is called by the French. Flocks from different parts of the coasts often meet on the feeding-

BLUE ROCK-PIGEON.

grounds; but when the time of returning to rest comes round, each one keeps to its own party.

OWL PIGEONS.

THE OWL PIGEON.—This pigeon does not seem to be so well known as it formerly was, if we may judge from the fact that few modern writers mention it. Like the Turbit pigeon, the Owl has a remarkable tuft of feathers on the breast, it having been compared by some to the frill of a shirt, and by others to a full-blown white rose. In size, it is not quite so large a pigeon as the Jacobin. It is said to be preferred in France, above other varieties, as a bird to rear and kill for the table. In England it is very far from being common; indeed, we have applied to several keepers of pigeons, who have fancied themselves acquainted with all the varieties of this bird, and they have been able to tell us nothing of it. Mr. Harrison Weir, our artist, however, has made his portrait from the life.

BOILED RABBIT.

977. INGREDIENTS.—Rabbit; water.

Mode.—For boiling, choose rabbits with smooth and sharp claws, as that denotes they are young: should these be blunt and rugged, the ears dry and tough, the animal is old. After emptying and

BOILED RABBIT.

skinning it, wash it well in cold water, and let it soak for about $\frac{1}{4}$ hour in warm water, to draw out the blood. Bring the head round to the side, and fasten it there by means of a skewer run through that and the body. Put the rabbit into sufficient hot water to cover it, let it boil very gently until tender, which will be in from $\frac{1}{2}$ to $\frac{3}{4}$ hour, according to its size and age. Dish it, and smother it either with onion, mushroom, or liver sauce, or parsley-and-butter; the former is, however, generally preferred to any of the last-named sauces. When liver-sauce is preferred, the liver should be boiled for a few minutes, and minced very finely, or rubbed through a sieve before it is added to the sauce.

Time.—A very young rabbit, ½ hour; a large one, ¾ hour; an old one, 1 hour or longer.

Average cost, from 1s. to 1s. 6d. each.

Sufficient for 4 persons.

Seasonable from September to February.

THE RABBIT.—Though this animal is an inhabitant of most temperate climates, it does not reach so far north as the hare. The wild rabbit is a native of Great Britain, and is found in large numbers in the sandy districts of Norfolk and Cambridgeshire. Its flesh is, by some, considered to have a higher flavour than that of the tame rabbit, although it is neither so white nor so delicate. The animal, however, becomes larger and fatter in the tame than in the wild state; but it is not desirable to have it so fat as it can be made.

CURRIED RABBIT.

978. INGREDIENTS.—1 rabbit, 2 oz. of butter, 3 onions, 1 pint of stock No. 104, 1 tablespoonful of curry powder, 1 tablespoonful of flour, 1 teaspoonful of mushroom powder, the juice of ½ lemon, ½ lb. of rice.

Mode.—Empty, skin, and wash the rabbit thoroughly, and cut it neatly into joints. Put it into a stewpan with the butter and sliced onions, and let them acquire a nice brown colour, but do not allow them to blacken. Pour in the stock, which should be boiling; mix the curry powder and flour smoothly with a little water, add it to the stock, with the mushroom powder, and simmer gently for rather more than ½ hour; squeeze in the lemon-juice, and serve in the centre of a dish, with an edging of boiled rice all round. Where economy is studied, water may be substituted for the stock; in this case, the meat and onions must be very nicely browned. A little sour apple and rasped cocoa-nut stewed with the curry will be found a great improvement.

Time.—Altogether ¾ hour.

Average cost, from 1s. to 1s. 6d. each.

Sufficient for 4 persons.

Seasonable in winter.

THE COMMON OR WILD RABBIT.—Warrens, or inclosures, are frequently made in favourable localities, and some of them are so large as to comprise 2,000 acres. The common wild rabbit is of a grey colour, and is esteemed the best for the purposes of food. Its skin is valuable as an article of commerce, being used for the making of hats. Another variety of the rabbit, however, called the "silver-grey," has been lately introduced to this country, and is still more valuable. Its colour is a black ground, thickly interspersed with grey hairs; and its powers as a destroyer and consumer of vegetable food are well known to be enormous, especially by those who have gardens in the vicinity of a rabbit-warren.

WILD RABBITS.

FRIED RABBIT.

979. INGREDIENTS.—1 rabbit, flour, dripping, 1 oz. of butter, 1 teaspoonful of minced shalot, 2 tablespoonfuls of mushroom ketchup.

Mode.—Cut the rabbit into neat joints, and flour them well; make the dripping boiling in a fryingpan, put in the rabbit, and fry it a nice brown. Have ready a very hot dish, put in the butter, shalot, and ketchup; arrange the rabbit pyramidically on this, and serve as quickly as possible.

Time.—10 minutes. *Average cost,* from 1s. to 1s. 6d. each.

Sufficient for 4 or 5 persons.

Seasonable from September to February.

Note.—The rabbit may be brushed over with egg, and sprinkled with bread crumbs, and fried as above. When cooked in this manner, make a gravy in the pan by recipe No. 866, and pour it round, but not over, the pieces of rabbit.

VARIETIES IN RABBITS.—Almost everybody knows that a rabbit is a furry animal, that lives on plants, and burrows in the ground; that it has its varieties as well as other animals, and that it is frequently an especial favourite with boys. Among its varieties, the short-legged, with width and substance of loin, is the most hardy, and fattens the most expeditiously. It has, besides, the soundest liver, rabbits generally being subject to defects of that part. It is also the smallest variety. There is a very large species of the hare-colour, having much bone, length and depth of carcase, large and long ears, with full eyes, resembling those of the hare: it might readily be taken for a hybrid or mule, but for the objection to its breeding. Its flesh is high-coloured, substantial, and more savoury than that of the common rabbit; and, cooked like the hare, it makes a good dish. The large white, and yellow and white species, have whiter and more delicate flesh, and, cooked in the same way, will rival the turkey. Rabbits are divided into four kinds, distinguished as warreners, parkers, hedgehogs, and sweethearts. The warrener, as his name implies, is a member of a subterranean community, and is less effeminate than his kindred who dwell *upon* the earth and have "the world at their will," and his fur is the most esteemed. After him, comes the parker, whose favourite resort is a gentleman's pleasure-ground, where he usually breeds in great numbers, and from which he frequently drives away the hares. The hedgehog is a sort of vagabond rabbit, that, tinker like, roams about the country, and would have a much better coat on his back if he was more settled in his habits, and remained more at home. The sweetheart is a tame rabbit, with its fur so sleek, soft, and silky, that it is also used to some extent in the important branch of hat-making.

RABBIT A LA MINUTE.

980. INGREDIENTS.—1 rabbit, ¼ lb. of butter, salt and pepper to taste, 2 blades of pounded mace, 3 dried mushrooms, 2 tablespoonfuls of minced parsley, 2 teaspoonfuls of flour, 2 glasses of sherry, 1 pint of water.

Mode.—Empty, skin, and wash the rabbit thoroughly, and cut it into joints. Put the butter into a stewpan with the pieces of rabbit: add salt, pepper, and pounded mace, and let it cook until three parts done; then put in the remaining ingredients, and boil for about 10 minutes: it will then be ready to serve. Fowls or hare may be dressed in the same manner.

Time.—Altogether, 35 minutes. *Average cost,* from 1s. to 1s. 6d. each.

Sufficient for 4 or 5 persons.

Seasonable from September to February.

RABBIT PIE.

981. INGREDIENTS.—1 rabbit, a few slices of ham, salt and white pepper to taste, 2 blades of pounded mace, ½ teaspoonful of grated nutmeg, a few forcemeat balls, 3 hard-boiled eggs, ⅓ pint of gravy, puff crust.

Mode.—Cut up the rabbit (which should be young), remove the breastbone, and bone the legs. Put the rabbit, slices of ham, forcemeat balls, and hard eggs, by turns, in layers, and season each layer with pepper, salt, pounded mace, and grated nutmeg. Pour in about ½ pint of water, cover with crust, and bake in a well-heated oven for about 1½ hour. Should the crust acquire too much colour, place a piece of paper over it to prevent its burning. When done, pour in at the top, by means of the hole in the middle of the crust, a little good gravy, which may be made of the breast- and leg-bones of the rabbit and 2 or 3 shank-bones, flavoured with onion, herbs, and spices.

Time.—1½ hour. *Average cost,* from 1s. to 1s. 6d. each.

Sufficient for 5 or 6 persons.

Seasonable from September to February.

Note.—The liver of the rabbit may be boiled, minced, and mixed with the forcemeat balls, when the flavour is liked.

FECUNDITY OF THE RABBIT.—The fruitfulness of this animal has been the subject of wonder to all naturalists. It breeds seven times in the year, and generally begets seven or eight young ones at a time. If we suppose this to happen regularly for a period of four years, the progeny that would spring from a single pair would amount to more than a million. As the rabbit, however, has many enemies, it can never be permitted to increase in numbers to such an extent as to prove injurious to mankind; for it not only furnishes man with an article of food, but is, by carnivorous animals of every description, mercilessly sacrificed. Notwithstanding this, however, in the time of the Roman power, they once infested the Balearic islands to such an extent, that the inhabitants were obliged to implore the assistance of a military force from Augustus to exterminate them.

RAGOUT OF RABBIT OR HARE.

982. INGREDIENTS.—1 rabbit, 3 teaspoonfuls of flour, 3 sliced onions, 2 oz. of butter, a few thin slices of bacon, pepper and salt to taste, 2 slices of lemon, 1 bay-leaf, 1 glass of port wine.

Mode.—Slice the onions, and put them into a stewpan with the flour and butter; place the pan near the fire, stir well as the butter melts, till the onions become a rich brown colour, and add, by degrees, a little water or gravy till the mixture is of the consistency of cream. Cut some thin slices of bacon; lay in these with the rabbit, cut into neat joints; add a seasoning of pepper and salt, the lemon and bay-leaf, and let the whole simmer until tender. Pour in the port wine, give one boil, and serve.

Time.—About ½ hour to simmer the rabbit.

Average cost, from 1s. to 1s. 6d. each.   *Sufficient* for 4 or 5 persons.
Seasonable from September to February.

THE RABBIT-HOUSE.—Rabbit-keeping is generally practised by a few individuals in almost every town, and by a few in almost every part of the country. Forty years ago, there were in the metropolis one or two considerable feeders, who, according to report, kept from 1,500 to 2,000 breeding does. These large establishments, however, have ceased to exist, and London receives the supply of tame as well as wild rabbits chiefly from the country. Where they are kept, however, the rabbit-house should be placed upon a dry foundation, and be well ventilated. Exposure to rain, whether externally or internally, is fatal to rabbits, which, like sheep, are liable to the rot, springing from the same causes. Thorough ventilation and good air are indispensable where many rabbits are kept, or they will neither prosper nor remain healthy for any length of time. A thorough draught or passage for the air is, therefore, absolutely necessary, and should be so contrived as to be checked in cold or wet weather by the closing or shutting of opposite doors or windows.

ROAST OR BAKED RABBIT.

983. INGREDIENTS.—1 rabbit, forcemeat No. 417, buttered paper, sausage-meat.

Mode.—Empty, skin, and thoroughly wash the rabbit; wipe it dry, line the inside with sausage-meat and forcemeat made by recipe No. 417, and to which has been added the minced liver. Sew the stuffing inside,

ROAST RABBIT.

skewer back the head between the shoulders, cut off the fore-joints of the shoulders and legs, bring them close to the body, and secure them by means of a skewer. Wrap the rabbit in buttered paper, and put it down to a bright clear fire; keep it well basted, and a few minutes before it is done remove the paper, flour and froth it, and let it acquire a nice brown colour. Take out the skewers, and serve with brown gravy and red-currant jelly. To bake the rabbit, proceed in the same manner as above: in a good oven, it will take about the same time as roasting.

Time.—A young rabbit, 35 minutes; a large one, about ¾ hour.

Average cost, from 1s. to 1s. 6d. each.   *Sufficient* for 4 persons.

Seasonable from September to February.

THE HUTCH.—Hutches are generally placed one above another to the height required by the number of rabbits and the extent of the room. Where a large stock is kept, to make the most of room, the hutches may be placed in rows, with a sufficient interval between for feeding and cleaning, instead of being, in the usual way, joined to the wall. It is preferable to rest the hutches upon stands, about a foot above the ground, for the convenience of cleaning under them. Each of the hutches intended for breeding should have two rooms,—a feeding and a bed-room. Those are single for the use of the weaned rabbits, or for the bucks, which are always kept separate. The floors should be planed smooth, that wet may run off, and a common hoe, with a short handle, and a short broom, are most convenient implements for cleaning these houses.

STEWED RABBIT.

984. INGREDIENTS.—1 rabbit, 2 large onions, 6 cloves; 1 small teaspoonful of chopped lemon-peel, a few forcemeat balls, thickening of butter and flour, 1 large tablespoonful of mushroom ketchup.

Mode.—Cut the rabbit into small joints; put them into a stewpan, add the onions sliced, the cloves, and minced lemon-peel. Pour in sufficient water to cover the meat, and, when the rabbit is nearly done, drop in a few forcemeat balls, to which has been added the liver, finely chopped. Thicken the gravy with flour and butter, put in the ketchup, give one boil, and serve.

Time.—Rather more than $\frac{1}{2}$ hour.   *Average cost*, 1s. to 1s. 6d. each.

Sufficient for 4 or 5 persons.

Seasonable from September to February.

FANCY RABBITS.—The graceful fall of the ears is the first thing that is looked to by the fancier; next, the dewlap, if the animal is in its prime; then the colours and marked points, and, lastly, the shape and general appearance. The ears of a fine rabbit should extend not less than seven inches, measured from tip to tip in a line across the skull; but even should they exceed this length, they are admitted with reluctance into a fancy stock, unless they have a uniform and graceful droop. The dewlap, which is a fold of skin under the neck and throat, is only seen in fancy rabbits, after they have attained their full growth: it commences immediately under the jaw, and adds greatly to the beauty of their appearance. It goes down the throat and between the fore legs, and is so broad that it projects beyond the chin.

LOP-EARED RABBIT.

The difference between the fancy and common rabbit in the back, independent of the ears, is sufficient to strike the common observer. Fancy rabbits fetch a very high price; so much as five and ten guineas, and even more, is sometimes given for a first-rate doe. If young ones are first procured from a good family, the foundation of an excellent stock can be procured for a much smaller sum. Sometimes the ears, instead of drooping down, slope backwards: a rabbit with this characteristic is scarcely admitted into a fancy lot, and is not considered worth more than the common variety. The next position is when one ear lops outwards, and the other stands erect: rabbits of this kind possess but little value, however fine the shape and beautiful the colour, although they sometimes breed as good specimens as finer ones.

The forward or horn-lop is one degree nearer perfection than the half-lop: the ears, in this case, slope forward and down over the forehead. Rabbits with this peculiarity are often perfect in other respects, with the exception of the droop of the ears, and often become the parents of perfect young ones: does of this kind often have the power of lifting an ear erect. In the ear-lop, the ears spread out in an horizontal position, like the wings of a bird in flight, or the arms of a man swimming. A great many excellent does have this characteristic, and some of the best-bred bucks in the fancy are entirely so. Sometimes a rabbit drops one ear completely, but raises the other so nearly horizontally as to constitute an ear-lop: this is superior to all others, except the perfect fall, which is so rarely to be met with, that those which are merely ear-lopped are considered as valuable rabbits, if well bred and with other good qualities.

"The real lop has ears that hang down by the side of the cheek, slanting somewhat outward in their descent, with the open part of the ear inward, and sometimes either backwards or forwards instead of perpendicular: when the animals stand in an easy position, the tips of the ears touch the ground. The hollows of the ears, in a fancy rabbit of a first-rate kind, should be turned so completely backwards that only the outer part of them should remain in front: they should match exactly in their descent, and should slant outwards as little as possible."

The same authority asserts that perfect lops are so rare, that a breeder possessing twenty of the handsomest and most perfect does would consider himself lucky if, in the course of a year, he managed to raise twelve full-lopped rabbits out of them all. As regards variety and purity of colour, an experienced breeder says :—

"The fur of fancy rabbits may be blue, or rather lead-colour, and white, or black and white, or tawny and white, that is, tortoiseshell-coloured. But it is not of so much importance what colours the coat of a rabbit displays, as it is that those colours shall be arranged in a particular manner, forming imaginary figures or fancied resemblances to certain objects. Hence the peculiarities of their markings have been denoted by dis tinctive designations. What is termed 'the blue butterfly smut' was, for some time, considered the most valuable of fancy rabbits. It is thus named on account of having bluish or lead-coloured spots on either side of the nose, having some resemblance to the spread wings of a butterfly, what may be termed the groundwork of the rabbit's face being white. A black and white rabbit may also have the face marked in a similar manner, constituting a 'black butterfly smut.'

"But a good fancy rabbit must likewise have other marks, without which it cannot be considered a perfect model of its kind. There should be a black or blue patch on its back, called the saddle; the tail must be of the same colour with the back and snout; while the legs should be all white; and there ought to be dark stripes on both sides of the body in front, passing backwards to meet the saddle, and uniting on the top of the shoulders at the part called the withers in a horse. These stripes form what is termed the 'chain,' having somewhat the appearance of a chain or collar hanging round the neck.

"Among thorough-bred fancy rabbits, perhaps not one in a hundred will have all these markings clearly and exactly displayed on the coat; but the more nearly the figures on the coat of a rabbit approach to the pattern described, the greater will be its value, so far, at least, as relates to colour. The beauty and consequent worth of a fancy rabbit, however, depends a good deal on its shape, or what is styled its carriage. A rabbit is said to have a good carriage when its back is finely arched, rising full two inches above the top of its head, which must be held so low as for the muzzle and the points of the ears to reach almost to the ground.''

STEWED RABBIT, Larded.

985. INGREDIENTS.—1 rabbit, a few strips of bacon, rather more than 1 pint of good broth or stock, a bunch of savoury herbs, salt and pepper to taste, thickening of butter and flour, 1 glass of sherry.

Mode.—Well wash the rabbit, cut it into quarters, lard them with slips of bacon, and fry them; then put them into a stewpan with the broth, herbs, and a seasoning of pepper and salt; simmer gently until the rabbit is tender, then strain the gravy, thicken it with butter and flour, add the sherry, give one boil, pour it over the rabbit, and serve. Garnish with slices of cut lemon.

Time.—Rather more than ½ hour. *Average cost,* 1s. to 1s. 6d. each.

Sufficient for 4 or 5 persons.

Seasonable from September to February.

THE HARE-RABBIT.—There has been lately introduced to French tables an animal called the "Hare-rabbit," partaking of the nature, characteristics, and qualifications of both the hare and the rabbit. It is highly spoken of, both as regards flesh and flavour; and it is said to be the only hybrid which is able to perpetuate its race. We hope that some enterprising individual will soon secure for English tables what would seem to be a really valuable addition to our other game and poultry dishes; although it will be rather difficult to exactly assign its proper position, as within or without the meaning of "game," as by law established. Only a few specimens have been seen in England at present, but there is no reason to doubt that our rabbit-fanciers will prove equal to the occasion, and cope successfully with our neighbours across the Channel in introducing a new animal serviceable in the kitchen.

THE HARE-RABBIT.

THE ANGORA RABBIT.—This is one of the handsomest of all rabbits. It takes its name from being an inhabitant of Angora, a city and district of Asia Minor. Like the well-known Angora goat and cat, both of which are valuable on account of the fineness of their wool and fur, this rabbit is prized for its long, waved, silky fur, which, as an article of commerce, is highly esteemed. We are not aware whether it is eaten by the inhabitants, and but few specimens have been introduced into England, where, doubtless, the beauty of its coat would materially suffer from the more humid and less genial character of the climate. To the rabbits of the ancient and mountainous district of Angora the words of the wise man would seem most to apply, "The conies are but feeble folk, yet make they their houses in the rocks."

ANGORA RABBIT.

THE HIMALAYA RABBIT.—Amidst the mighty Himalaya mountains, whose peaks are the highest on the globe, the pretty rabbit here portrayed is found; and his colour seems to be like the snow, which, above the altitude of from 13,000 to 16,000 feet, perpetually crowns the summits of these monarchs of the world. It is, at present, a very rare animal in England, but will, doubtless, be more extensively known in the course of a few years. From the earth-tunnelling powers of this little animal, Martial declares that mankind learned the art of fortification, mining, and covered roads.

HIMALAYA RABBITS.

BOILED TURKEY.

986. INGREDIENTS.—Turkey; forcemeat No. 417.

Choosing and Trussing.—Hen turkeys are preferable for boiling, on account of their whiteness and tenderness, and one of moderate size should be selected, as a large one is not suitable for this mode of cooking. They should not be dressed until they have been killed 3 or 4 days, as they will neither look white, nor will they be tender. Pluck the bird, carefully draw, and singe it with a piece of white paper; wash it inside and out, and wipe it thoroughly dry with a cloth. Cut off the head and neck, draw the strings or sinews of the thighs, and cut off the legs at the first joint; draw the legs into the body, fill the breast with forcemeat made by recipe No. 417; run a skewer through the wing and the middle joint of the leg, quite into the leg and wing on the opposite side; break the breastbone, and make the bird look as round and as compact as possible.

Mode.—Put the turkey into sufficient *hot* water to cover it; let it come to a boil, then carefully remove all the scum : if this is attended to, there is no occasion to boil the bird in a floured cloth; but it should be well covered with the water. Let it simmer very gently for about 1½ hour to 1¾ hour, according

BOILED TURKEY.

to the size, and serve with either white, celery, oyster, or mushroom sauce, or parsley-and-butter, a little of which should be poured over the turkey. Boiled ham, bacon, tongue, or pickled pork, should always accompany this dish; and when oyster sauce is served, the turkey should be stuffed with oyster forcemeat.

Time.—A small turkey, 1½ hour; a large one, 1¾ hour.

Average cost, 5s. 6d. to 7s. 6d. each, but more expensive at Christmas, on account of the great demand.

Sufficient for 7 or 8 persons.

Seasonable from December to February.

THE TURKEY.—The turkey, for which fine bird we are indebted to America, is certainly one of the most glorious presents made by the New World to the Old. Some, indeed, assert that this bird was known to the ancients, and that it was served at the wedding-feast of Charlemagne. This opinion, however, has been controverted by first-rate authorities, who declare that the French name of the bird, *dindon*, proves its origin; that the form of the bird is altogether foreign, and that it is found in America alone in a wild state. There is but little doubt, from the information which has been gained at considerable trouble, that it appeared, generally, in Europe about the end of the 17th century; that it was first imported into France by Jesuits, who had been sent out missionaries to the West; and that from France it spread over Europe. To this day, in many localities in France, a turkey is called a jesuit. On the farms of N. America, where turkeys are very common, they are raised either from eggs which have been found, or from young ones caught in the woods: they thus preserve almost entirely their original plumage. The turkey only became gradually acclimated, both on the continent and in England: in the middle of the 18th century, scarcely 10 out of 20 young turkeys lived; now, generally speaking, 15 out of the same number arrive at maturity.

CROQUETTES OF TURKEY (Cold Meat Cookery).

987. INGREDIENTS.—The remains of cold turkey; to every ½ lb. of meat allow 2 oz. of ham or bacon, 2 shalots, 1 oz. of butter, 1 tablespoonful of flour, the yolks of 2 eggs, egg and bread crumbs.

Mode.—The smaller pieces, that will not do for a fricassée or hash, answer very well for this dish. Mince the meat finely with ham or bacon in the above proportion; make a gravy of the bones and trimmings, well seasoning it; mince the shalots, put them into a stewpan with the butter, add the flour; mix well, then put in the mince, and about ½ pint of the gravy made from the bones. (The proportion of the butter must be increased or diminished according to the quantity of mince.) When just boiled, add the yolks of 2 eggs; put the mixture out to cool, and then shape it in a wineglass. Cover the croquettes with egg and bread crumbs, and fry them a delicate brown. Put small pieces of parsley-stems for stalks, and serve with rolled bacon cut very thin.

Time.—8 minutes to fry the croquettes.

Seasonable from December to February.

THE WILD TURKEY.—In its wild state, the turkey is gregarious, going together in extensive flocks, numbering as many as five hundred. These frequent the great swamps of America, where they roost; but, at sunrise, leave these situations to repair to the dry woods, in search of berries and acorns. They perch on the boughs of trees, and, by rising from branch to branch, attain the height they desire. They usually mount to the highest tops, apparently from an instinctive conception that the loftier they are the further they are out of danger. They fly awkwardly, but run with great swiftness, and about the month of March become so fat as not to be able to take a flight beyond three or four hundred yards, and are then, also, easily run down by a horseman. Now, however, it rarely happens that wild turkeys are seen in the inhabited parts of America. It is only in the distant and more unfrequented parts that they are found in great numbers.

FRICASSEED TURKEY (Cold Meat Cookery).

988. INGREDIENTS.—The remains of cold roast or boiled turkey ; a strip of lemon-peel, a bunch of savoury herbs, 1 onion, pepper and salt to taste, 1 pint of water, 4 tablespoonfuls of cream, the yolk of an egg.

Mode.—Cut some nice slices from the remains of a cold turkey, and put the bones and trimmings into a stewpan, with the lemon-peel, herbs, onion, pepper, salt, and the water ; stew for an hour, strain the gravy, and lay in the pieces of turkey. When warm through, add the cream and the yolk of an egg ; stir it well round, and, when getting thick, take out the pieces, lay them on a hot dish, and pour the sauce over. Garnish the fricassée with sippets of toasted bread. Celery or cucumbers, cut into small pieces, may be put into the sauce ; if the former, it must be boiled first.

Time.—1 hour to make the gravy.

Average cost, exclusive of the cold turkey, 4*d.*

Seasonable from December to February.

THE TURKEY.—This is one of the gallinaceous birds, the principal genera of which are Pheasants, Turkeys, Peacocks, Bustards, Pintatoes, and Grouse. They live mostly on the ground, scraping the earth with their feet, and feeding on seeds and grains, which, previous to digestion, are macerated in their crops. They usually associate in families, consisting of one male and several females. Turkeys are particularly fond of the seeds of nettles, whilst the seeds of the foxglove will poison them. The common turkey is a native of North America, and, in the reign of Henry VIII., was introduced into England. According to Tusser's "Five Hundred Points of Good Husbandry," it began about the year 1585 to form a dish at our rural Christmas feasts :—

> " Beefe, mutton, and pork, shred pies of the best,
> Pig, veal, goose, and capon, and turkey well drest ;
> Cheese, apples, and nuts, jolly carols to hear,
> As then in the country is counted good cheer."

The turkey is one of the most difficult birds to rear, and its flesh is much esteemed.

THE DISPOSITION OF THE TURKEY.—Among themselves, turkeys are extremely furious, whilst amongst other animals they are usually both weak and cowardly. The domestic cock frequently makes them keep at a distance, whilst they will rarely attack him but in a united body, when the cock is rather crushed by their weight than defeated by their prowess. The disposition of the female is in general much more gentle than that of the male. When leading forth her young to collect their food, though so large and apparently so powerful a bird, she gives them very slight protection from the attacks of any rapacious animal which may appear against them. She rather warns them of their danger than offers to defend them ; yet she is extremely affectionate to her young.

HASHED TURKEY.

989. INGREDIENTS.—The remains of cold roast turkey, 1 onion, pepper and salt to taste, rather more than 1 pint of water, 1 carrot, 1

turnip, 1 blade of mace, a bunch of savoury herbs, 1 tablespoonful of mushroom ketchup, 1 tablespoonful of port wine, thickening of butter and flour.

Mode.—Cut the turkey into neat joints; the best pieces reserve for the hash, the inferior joints and trimmings put into a stewpan with an onion cut in slices, pepper and salt, a carrot, turnip, mace, herbs, and water in the above proportion; simmer these for an hour, then strain the gravy, thicken it with butter and flour, flavour with ketchup and port wine, and lay in the pieces of turkey to warm through; if there is any stuffing left, put that in also, as it so much improves the flavour of the gravy. When it boils, serve, and garnish the dish with sippets of toasted bread.

Time.—1 hour to make the gravy.

Seasonable from December to February.

HUNTING TURKEYS.—Formerly, in Canada, hunting turkeys was one of the principal diversions of the natives of that country. When they discovered the retreat of the birds, which was generally near a field of nettles, or where grain of any kind was plentiful, they would send a well-trained dog into the midst of the flock. The turkeys no sooner perceived their enemy than they would run off at full speed, and with such swiftness that they would leave the dog far behind. He, however, would follow in their wake, and as they could not, for a great length of time, continue at their speed, they were at last forced to seek shelter in the trees. There they would sit, spent with fatigue, till the hunters would approach, and, with long poles, knock them down one after the other.

ROAST TURKEY.

990. INGREDIENTS.—Turkey; forcemeat No. 417.

Choosing and Trussing.—Choose cock turkeys by their short spurs and black legs, in which case they are young; if the spurs are long, and the legs pale and rough, they are old. If the bird has been long killed, the eyes will appear sunk and the feet very dry; but, if fresh, the contrary will be the case. Middling-sized fleshy turkeys are by many persons considered superior to those of an immense growth, as they are, generally speaking, much more tender. They should never be dressed the same day they are killed; but, in cold weather, should hang at least 8 days; if the weather is mild, 4 or 5 days will be found sufficient. Carefully pluck the bird, singe it with white paper, and wipe it thoroughly with a cloth; draw it, preserve the liver and gizzard, and be particular not to break the gall-bag, as no washing will remove the bitter taste it imparts where it once touches. Wash it *inside* well, and wipe it thoroughly dry with a cloth; the *outside* merely requires nicely wiping, as we have just stated. Cut off the neck close to the back, but leave enough of the crop-skin to turn over; break the leg-bone close below the knee, draw out the strings from the thighs, and flatten the breastbone to make it look plump. Have ready a forcemeat made by recipe No. 417; fill the breast with this, and, if a trussing-needle is used, sew the neck over to the back; if a needle is not at hand, a skewer will answer the purpose. Run a skewer through the pinion and thigh into the body to the pinion and thigh on the other side, and press the legs as much as possible between the breast and the side bones, and put the liver under one pinion and the gizzard under the other. Pass a string across the back of the bird, catch it over the points of the skewer, tie

ROAST TURKEY.

it in the centre of the back, and be particular that the turkey is very firmly trussed. This may be more easily accomplished with a needle and twine than with skewers.

Mode.—Fasten a sheet of buttered paper on to the breast of the bird, put it down to a bright fire, at some little distance *at first* (afterwards draw it nearer), and keep it well basted the whole of the time it is cooking. About ¼ hour before serving, remove the paper, dredge the turkey lightly with flour, and put a piece of butter into the basting-ladle; as the butter melts, baste the bird with it. When of a nice brown and well frothed, serve with a tureen of good brown gravy and one of bread sauce. Fried sausages are a favourite addition to roast turkey; they make a pretty garnish, besides adding very much to the flavour. When these are not at hand, a few forcemeat balls should be placed round the dish as a garnish. Turkey may also be stuffed with sausage-meat, and a chestnut forcemeat with the same sauce is, by many persons, much esteemed as an accompaniment to this favourite dish.—See coloured plate, A 1.

Time.—Small turkey, 1½ hour; moderate-sized one, about 10 lbs., 2 hours; large turkey, 2½ hours, or longer.

Average cost, from 10s. to 12s., but expensive at Christmas, on account of the great demand.

Sufficient.—A moderate-sized turkey for 7 or 8 persons.

Seasonable from December to February.

ENGLISH TURKEYS.—These are reared in great numbers in Suffolk, Norfolk, and several other counties, whence they were wont to be driven to the London market in flocks of several hundreds; the improvements in our modes of travelling now, however, enable them to be brought by railway. Their drivers used to manage them with great facility, by means of a bit of red rag tied to the end of a long stick, which, from the antipathy these birds have to that colour, effectually answered the purpose of a scourge. There are three varieties of the turkey in this country,—the black, the white, and the speckled, or copper-coloured. The black approaches nearest to the original stock, and is esteemed the best. Its flesh is white and tender, delicate, nourishing, and of excellent flavour; it greatly deteriorates with age, however, and is then good for little but stewing.

ROAST TURKEY POULTS.

991. INGREDIENTS.—Turkey poult; butter.

Choosing and Trussing.—Choose a plump bird, and truss it in the following manner:—After it has been carefully plucked, drawn, and singed, skin the neck, and fasten the head under the wing; turn the legs at the first joint, and bring the feet close to the thighs, as a woodcock should be trussed, *and do not stuff it.*

Mode.—Put it down to a bright fire, keep it well basted, and at first place a piece of paper on the breast to prevent its taking too much colour. About 10 minutes before serving, dredge it lightly with flour, and baste well; when nicely frothed, send it to table immediately, with a little gravy in the dish, and some in a tureen. If at hand, a few water-cresses may be placed round the turkey as a garnish, or it may be larded.

Time.—About 1 hour. *Average cost,* 7s. to 8s. each.

Sufficient for 6 or 7 persons.

Seasonable.—In full season from June to October.

THE FEATHERS OF THE TURKEY.—Human ingenuity subjects almost every material to the purposes of ornament or use, and the feathers of turkeys have been found adapted for more ends than one. The American Indians convert them into an elegant clothing, and, by twisting the inner ribs into a strong double string, with hemp or the inner bark of the mulberry-tree, work it like matting. This fabric has a very rich and glossy appearance, and is as fine as silk shag. The natives of Louisiana used to make fans of the tail; and four of that appendage joined together was formerly constructed into a parasol by the French.

TO BONE A TURKEY OR FOWL WITHOUT OPENING IT.

(*Miss Acton's Recipe.*)

992. After the fowl has been drawn and singed, wipe it inside and out with a clean cloth, but do not wash it. Take off the head, cut through the skin all round the first joint of the legs, and pull them from the fowl, to draw out the large tendons. Raise the flesh first from the lower part of the backbone, and a little also from the end of the breastbone, if necessary; work the knife gradually to the socket of the thigh; with the point of the knife detach the joint from it, take the end of the bone firmly in the fingers, and cut the flesh clean from it down to the next joint, round which pass the point of the knife carefully, and when the skin is loosened from it in every part, cut round the next bone, keeping the edge of the knife close to it, until the whole of the leg is done. Remove the bones of the other leg in the same manner; then detach the flesh from the back- and breast-bone sufficiently to enable you to reach the upper joints of the wings; proceed with these as with the legs, but be especially careful

not to pierce the skin of the second joint : it is usual to leave the pinions unboned, in order to give more easily its natural form to the fowl when it is dressed. The merrythought and neck-bones may now easily be cut away, the back- and side-bones taken out without being divided, and the breastbone separated carefully from the flesh (which, as the work progresses, must be turned back from the bones upon the fowl, until it is completely inside out). After the one remaining bone is removed, draw the wings and legs back to their proper form, and turn the fowl right side outwards.

993. A turkey is boned exactly in the same manner; but as it requires a very large proportion of forcemeat to fill it entirely, the legs and wings are sometimes drawn into the body, to diminish the expense of this. If very securely trussed, and sewn, the bird may be either boiled, or stewed in rich gravy, as well as roasted, after being boned and forced ; but it must be most gently cooled, or it may burst.

ANOTHER MODE OF BONING A TURKEY OR FOWL.
(*Miss Acton's Recipe.*)

994. Cut through the skin down the centre of the back, and raise the flesh carefully on either side with the point of a sharp knife, until the sockets of the wings and thighs are reached. Till a little practice has been gained, it will perhaps be better to bone these joints before proceeding further ; but after they are once detached from it, the whole of the body may easily be separated from the flesh and taken out entire : only the neck-bones and merrythought will then remain to be removed. The bird thus prepared may either be restored to its original form, by filling the legs and wings with forcemeat, and the body with the livers of two or three fowls, mixed with alternate layers of parboiled tongue freed from the rind, fine sausage-meat, or veal forcemeat, or thin slices of the nicest bacon, or aught else of good flavour, which will give a marbled appearance to the fowl when it is carved ; and then be sewn up and trussed as usual ; or the legs and wings may be drawn inside the body, and the bird being first flattened on a table, may be covered with sausage-meat, and the various other ingredients we have named, so placed that it shall be of equal thickness in every part ; then tightly rolled, bound firmly together with a fillet of broad tape, wrapped in a thin pudding-cloth, closely tied at both ends, and dressed as follows :—Put it into a braising-pan, stew-pan, or thick iron saucepan, bright in the inside, and fitted as nearly as may be to its size; add all the chicken-bones, a bunch of sweet herbs, two carrots, two bay-leaves, a large blade of mace, twenty-four

white peppercorns, and any trimmings or bones of undressed veal which may be at hand; cover the whole with good veal broth, add salt, if needed, and stew it very softly, from an hour and a quarter to an hour and a half; let it cool in the liquor in which it was stewed; and after it is lifted out, boil down the gravy to a jelly and strain it; let it become cold, clear off the fat, and serve it cut into large dice or roughed, and laid round the fowl, which is to be served cold. If restored to its form, instead of being rolled, it must be stewed gently for an hour, and may then be sent to table hot, covered with mushroom, or any other good sauce that may be preferred; or it may be left until the following day, and served garnished with the jelly, which should be firm, and very clear and well-flavoured: the liquor in which a calf's foot has been boiled down, added to the broth, will give it the necessary degree of consistence.

TO BONE FOWLS FOR FRICASSEES, CURRIES, & PIES.

995. First carve them entirely into joints, then remove the bones, beginning with the legs and wings, at the head of the largest bone; hold this with the fingers, and work the knife as directed in the recipe above. The remainder of the birds is too easily done to require any instructions.

TO DRESS WHEATEARS.

996. INGREDIENTS.—Wheatears; fresh butter.

Mode.—After the birds are picked, gutted, and cleaned, truss them like larks, put them down to a quick fire, and baste them well with fresh butter. When done, which will be in about 20 minutes, dish them on fried bread crumbs, and garnish the dish with slices of lemon.

Time.—20 minutes.

Seasonable from July to October.

THE WHEATEAR.—The wheatear is an annual visitor of England: it arrives about the middle of March and leaves in September. The females come about a fortnight before the males, and continue to arrive till the middle of May. They are in season from July to October, and are taken in large numbers on the South Downs, in the neighbourhood of Eastbourne, Brighton, and other parts of Sussex. They are taken by means of snares and nets, and numbers of them are eaten on the spot by the inhabitants. The larger ones are sent to London and potted, where they are by many as much esteemed as the ortolans of the continent. Mr. Pennant assigns as the reason of their abounding on the downs about Eastbourne, the existence of a species of fly which forms their favourite food, and which feeds on the wild thyme on the adjacent hills.

997. THE GUINEA-PIG.—This common hutch-companion of the rabbit, although originally a native of Brazil, propagates freely in England and other European countries. Were it not that they suffer cruelly from cats, and numerous other enemies, and that it is the habit of the males to devour their own offspring, their numbers would soon become overwhelming. Rats, however, it is said, carefully avoid them; and for this reason they are

frequently bred by rabbit-fanciers, by way of protection for their young stock against those troublesome vermin. The lower tier of a rabbit-hutch is esteemed excellent quarters by the guinea-pig : here, as he runs loose, he will devour the waste food of his more admired companion. Some naturalists assert that the guinea-pig will breed at two months old, the litter varying from four to twelve at a time. It is varied in colour,—white, fawn, and black, and a mixture of the three colours, forming a tortoiseshell, which is the more generally admired hue. Occasionally, the white ones have red eyes, like those of the ferret and the white rabbit. Their flesh, although eatable, is decidedly unfit for food; they have been tasted, however, we presume by some enthusiast eager to advance the cause of science, or by some eccentric epicure in search of a new pleasure for his palate. Unless it has been that they deter rats from intruding within the rabbit-hutch, they are as useless as they are harmless. The usual ornament of an animal's hind quarters is denied them ; and were it not for this fact, and also for their difference in colour, the Shaksperean locution, "a rat without a tail," would designate them very properly.

THE GUINEA-PIG.

998. THE CYGNET.—The Cygnet, or the young Swan, was formerly much esteemed ; but it has "fallen from its high estate," and is now rarely seen upon the table. We are not sure that it is not still fattened in Norwich for the corporation of that place. Persons who have property on the river there, take the young birds, and send them to some one who is employed by the corporation, to be fed ; and for this trouble he is paid, or was wont to be paid, about half a guinea a bird. It is as the future bird of elegance and grace that the young swan is mostly admired ; when it has become old enough to grace the waters, then it is that all admire her, when she with

"Archèd neck,
Between her white wings mantling,
        proudly rows
Her state with oary feet."

THE CYGNET.

POULTRY CARVING.

ROAST DUCK.

999. No dishes require so much knowledge and skill in their carving as do game and poultry ; for it is necessary to be well acquainted with the anatomy of the bird and animal in order to place the knife at exactly the proper point. A tough fowl and an old goose are sad triers of a carver's powers and temper, and, indeed, sometimes of the good humour of those in the neighbourhood of the carver ; for a sudden tilt of the

ROAST DUCK.

dish may eventuate in the placing a quantity of the gravy in the lap of the right or left-hand supporter of the host. We will endeavour to assist those who are unacquainted with the "gentle art of carving," and also those who are but slightly acquainted with it, by simply describing the rules to follow, and referring to the distinctly-marked illustrations of each dish, which will further help to bring light to the minds of the uninitiated. If the bird be a young duckling, it may be carved like a fowl, viz., by first taking off the leg and the wing on either side, as described at No. 1000; but in cases where the duckling is very small, it will be as well not to separate the leg from the wing, as they will not then form too large a portion for a single

LEG, WING,
AND NECKBONE
OF DUCK.

serving. After the legs and wings are disposed of, the remainder of the duck will be also carved in the same manner as a fowl; and not much difficulty will be experienced, as ducklings are tender, and the joints are easily broken by a little gentle forcing, or penetrated by the knife. In cases where the duck is a large bird, the better plan to pursue is then to carve it like a goose, that is, by cutting pieces from the breast in the direction indicated by the lines marked from 1 to 2, commencing to carve the slices close to the wing, and then proceeding upwards from that to the breastbone. If more should be wanted than can be obtained from both sides of the breast, then the legs and wings must be attacked, in the same way as is described in connection with carving a fowl. It may be here remarked, that as the legs of a duck are placed far more backward than those of a fowl, their position causing the waddling motion of the bird, the thigh-bones will be found considerably nearer towards the backbone than in a chicken: this is the only difference worth mentioning. The carver should ask each guest if a portion of stuffing would be agreeable; and in order to get at this, a cut should be made below the breast, as shown by the line from 3 to 4, at the part called the "apron," and the spoon inserted. (As described in the recipe, it is an excellent plan, when a couple of ducks are served, to have one with, and the other without stuffing.) As to the prime parts of a duck, it has been said that "the wing of a flier and the leg of a swimmer" are severally the best portions. Some persons are fond of the feet of the duck; and, in trussing, these should never be taken off. The leg, wing, and neckbone are here shown; so that it will be easy to see the shape they should be when cut off.

BOILED FOWL.

1000. This will not be found a very difficult member of the poultry family to carve, unless, as may happen, a very old farmyard occupant, useless for egg-laying purposes, has, by some unlucky mischance, been introduced into the kitchen as a "fine young chicken." Skill, however, and the application of a small amount of strength, combined with a fine keeping of the temper, will even get over that

BOILED FOWL.

difficulty. Fixing the fork firmly in the breast, let the knife be sharply passed along the line shown from 1 to 2; then cut downwards from that line to fig. 3; and the wing, it will be found, can be easily withdrawn. The shape of the wing should be like the accompanying engraving. Let the fork be placed inside the leg, which should be gently forced away from the body of the fowl; and the joint, being thus discovered, the carver can readily cut through it, and the leg can be served. When the leg is displaced, it should be of the same shape as that shown in the annexed woodcut. The legs and wings on either side having been taken off, the carver should draw his knife through the flesh in the direction of the line 4 to 5: by this means the knife can be slipped underneath the merrythought, which, being lifted up and pressed backward, will immediately come off. The collar- or neck-bones are

LEG, WING, AND NECKBONE OF FOWL.

the next to consider: these lie on each side of the merrythought, close under the upper part of the wings; and, in order to free these from the fowl, they must also be raised by the knife at their broad end, and turned from the body towards the breastbone, until the shorter piece of the bone, as shown in the cut, breaks off. There will now be left only the breast, with the ribs. The breast can be, without difficulty, disengaged from the ribs by cutting through the latter, which will offer little impediment. The side-bones are now to be taken off; and to do this, the lower end of the back should be turned from the carver, who should press the point of the knife through the top of the backbone, near the centre, bringing it down towards the end of the back completely through the bone. If the knife is now turned in the opposite direction, the joint will be easily separated from the vertebræ. The backbone being now uppermost, the fork should be pressed firmly down on it, whilst at the same time the knife should be employed in raising up the lower small end of the fowl towards the fork, and thus the back will be dislocated about its middle. The wings, breast, and merrythought are esteemed the prime parts of a fowl, and are usually served to the ladies of the company, to whom legs, except as a matter of paramount necessity, should not be given. Byron gave it as one reason why he did not like dining with ladies, that they always had the wings of the fowls, which he himself preferred. We heard a gentleman who, when he might have had a wing, declare his partiality for a leg, saying that he had been obliged to eat legs for so long a time, that he had at last come to like them better than the other more prized parts. If the fowl is, capon-like, very large, slices may be carved from its breast in the same manner as from a turkey's.

ROAST FOWL.

ROAST FOWL.

1001. Generally speaking, it is not necessary so completely to cut up a fowl as we have described in the preceding paragraphs, unless, indeed, a large family party is assembled, and there are a number of "little mouths" to be filled, or some other such circumstances prevail. A roast fowl is carved in the same manner as a boiled fowl, No. 1000; viz., by cutting along the line from 1 to 2, and then round the leg between it and the wing. The markings and detached pieces, as shown in the engravings under the heading of "Boiled Fowl," supersede the necessity of our lengthily again describing the operation. It may be added, that the liver, being considered a delicacy, should be divided, and one half served with each wing. In the case of a fowl being stuffed, it will be proper to give each guest a portion, unless it be not agreeable to some one of the party.

ROAST GOOSE.

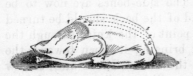

ROAST GOOSE.

1002. It would not be fair to say that this dish bodes a great deal of happiness to an inexperienced carver, especially if there is a large party to serve, and the slices off the breast should not suffice to satisfy the desires and cravings of many wholesome appetites, produced, may be, by the various sports in vogue at Michaelmas and Christmas. The beginning of the task, however, is not in any way difficult. Evenly-cut slices, not too thick or too thin, should be carved from the breast in the direction of the line from 2 to 3; after the first slice has been cut, a hole should be made with the knife in the part called the apron, passing it round the line, as indicated by the figures 1, 1, 1: here the stuffing is located, and some of this should be served on each plate, unless it is discovered that it is not agreeable to the taste of some one guest. If the carver manages cleverly, he will be able to cut a very large number of fine slices off the breast, and the more so if he commences close down by the wing, and carves upwards towards the ridge of the breastbone. As many slices as can be taken from the breast being carved, the wings should be cut off; and the same process as described in carving boiled fowl, is made use of in this in-

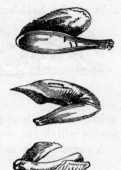

LEG, WING, AND NECK-BONE OF GOOSE.

stance, only more dexterity and greater force will most probably be required: the shape of the leg, when disengaged from the body of the goose, should be like that shown in the accompanying engraving. It will be necessary, perhaps, in taking off the leg, to turn the goose on its side, and then, pressing down the small end of the leg, the knife should be passed under it from the top quite down to the joint; the leg being now turned back by the fork, the knife must cut through the joint, loosening the thigh-bone from its socket. The merrythought, which in a goose is not so large as might be expected, is disengaged in the same way as that of a fowl—by passing the knife under it, and pressing it backwards towards the neck. The neck-bones, of which we give a cut, are freed by the same process as are those of a fowl; and the same may be said of all the other parts of this bird. The breast of a goose is the part most esteemed; all parts, however, are good, and full of juicy flavour.

PIGEON.

1003. A very straightforward plan is adopted in carving a pigeon: the knife is carried sharply in the direction of the line as shown from 1 to 2, entirely through the bird, cutting it into two precisely equal and similar parts. If it is necessary to make three pieces of it, a small wing should be cut off with the leg on either side, thus serving two guests; and, by this means, there will be sufficient meat left on the breast to send to the third guest.

PIGEON.

RABBITS.

1004. In carving a boiled rabbit, let the knife be drawn on each side of the backbone, the whole length of the rabbit, as shown by

BOILED RABBIT.

the dotted line 3 to 4 : thus the rabbit will be in three parts. Now let the back be divided into two equal parts in the direction of the line from 1 to 2 ; then let the leg be taken off, as shown by the line 5 to 6, and the shoulder, as shown by the line 7 to 8. This, in our opinion, is the best plan to carve a rabbit, although there are other modes which are preferred by some.

A roast rabbit is rather differently trussed from one that is meant

ROAST RABBIT.

to be boiled ; but the carving is nearly similar, as will be seen by the cut. The back should be divided into as many pieces as it will give, and the legs and shoulders can then be disengaged in the same manner as those of the boiled animal.

ROAST TURKEY.

1005. A noble dish is a turkey, roast or boiled. A Christmas dinner, with the middle classes of this empire, would scarcely be a Christmas dinner without its turkey ; and we can

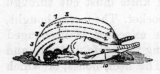

ROAST TURKEY.

hardly imagine an object of greater envy than is presented by a respected portly pater-familias carving, at the season devoted to good cheer and genial charity, his own fat turkey, and carving it well. The only art consists, as in the carving of a goose, in getting from the breast as many fine slices as possible ; and all must have remarked the very great difference in the large number of people whom a good carver will find slices for, and the comparatively few that a bad carver will succeed in serving. As we have stated in both the carving of a duck and goose, the carver should commence cutting slices close to the wing from, 2 to 3, and then proceed upwards towards the ridge of the breastbone : this is not the usual plan, but, in practice, will be found the best. The breast is the only part which is looked on as fine in a turkey, the legs being very seldom cut off and eaten at table : they are usually removed to the kitchen, where they are taken off, as here marked, to appear only in a form which seems to have a special attraction at a bachelor's supper-table,—we mean devilled : served in this way, they are especially liked and relished.

A boiled turkey is carved in the same manner as when roasted.

CHAPTER XXII.

GENERAL OBSERVATIONS ON GAME.

1006. THE COMMON LAW OF ENGLAND has a maxim, that goods, in which no person can claim any property, belong, by his or her prerogative, to the king or queen. Accordingly, those animals, those *feræ naturæ*, which come under the denomination of game, are, in our laws, styled his or her majesty's, and may therefore, as a matter of course, be granted by the sovereign to another; in consequence of which another may prescribe to possess the same within a certain precinct or lordship. From this circumstance arose the right of lords of manors or others to the game within their respective liberties; and to protect these species of animals, the game laws were originated, and still remain in force. There are innumerable acts of parliament inflicting penalties on persons who may illegally kill game, and some of them are very severe; but they cannot be said to answer their end, nor can it be expected that they ever will, whilst there are so many persons of great wealth who have not otherwise the means of procuring game, except by purchase, and who will have it. These must necessarily encourage poaching, which, to a very large extent, must continue to render all game laws nugatory as to their intended effects upon the rustic population.

1007. THE OBJECT OF THESE LAWS, however, is not wholly confined to the restraining of the illegal sportsman. Even qualified or privileged persons must not kill game at all seasons. During the day, the hours allowed for sporting are from one hour before sunrise till one hour after sunset ; whilst the time of killing certain species is also restricted to certain seasons. For example, the season for bustard-shooting is from December 1 to March 1 ; for grouse, or red grouse, from August 12 to December 10 ; heath-fowl, or black-game, from August 20 to December 20 ; partridges from September 1 to February 12 ; pheasants from October 1 to February 1 ; widgeons, wild ducks, wild geese, wild fowls, at any time but in June, July, August, and September. Hares may be killed at any time of the year, under certain restrictions defined by an act of parliament of the 10th of George III.

1008. THE EXERCISE OR DIVERSION OF PURSUING FOUR-FOOTED BEASTS OF GAME is called hunting, which, to this day, is followed in the field and the forest, with gun and greyhound. Birds, on the contrary, are not hunted, but shot in the air, or taken with nets and other devices, which is called fowling ; or they are pursued and taken by birds of prey, which is called hawking, a species of sport now fallen almost entirely into desuetude in England, although, in some parts, showing signs of being revived.

1009. IN PURSUING FOUR-FOOTED BEASTS, such as deer, boars, and hares, properly termed hunting, mankind were, from the earliest ages, engaged. It was the rudest and the most obvious manner of acquiring human support before the agricultural arts had in any degree advanced. It is an employment, however, requiring both art and contrivance, as well as a certain fearlessness of character, combined with the power of considerable physical endurance. Without these, success could not be very great ; but, at best, the occupation is usually accompanied with rude and turbulent habits ; and, when combined with these, it constitutes what is termed the savage state of man. As culture advances, and as the soil proportionably becomes devoted to the plough or to the sustenance of the tamer or more domesticated animals, the range of the huntsman is proportionably limited ; so that when a country has attained to a high state of cultivation, hunting becomes little else than an amusement of the opulent. In the case of fur-bearing animals, however, it is somewhat different ; for these continue to supply the wants of civilization with one of its most valuable materials of commerce.

1010. THE THEMES WHICH FORM THE MINSTRELSY OF THE EARLIEST AGES, either relate to the spoils of the chase or the dangers of the battle-field. Even the sacred writings introduce us to Nimrod, the first mighty hunter before the Lord, and tell us that Ishmael, in the solitudes of Arabia, became a skilful bowman ; and that David, when yet young, was not afraid to join in combat with the lion or the bear. The Greek mythology teems with hunting exploits. Hercules overthrows the Nemæan lion, the Erymanthean boar, and the hydra of Lerna ; Diana descends to the earth, and pursues the stag ; whilst Æsculapius, Nestor, Theseus, Ulysses, and Achilles are all followers of the chase. Aristotle, sage as he was, advises young men to apply themselves early to it ; and Plato finds in it something divine. Horace exalts it as a preparative exercise for the path of glory, and several of the heroes of Homer are its ardent votaries. The Romans followed the hunting customs of the Greeks, and the ancient Britons were hunters before Julius Cæsar invaded their shores.

1011. ALTHOUGH THE ANCIENT BRITONS FOLLOWED HUNTING, however, they did not confine themselves solely to its pursuit. They bred cattle and tilled the ground, and, to some extent, indicated the rudimentary state of a pastoral and agricultural life; but, in every social change, the sports of the field maintained their place. After the expulsion of the Danes, and during the brief restoration of the Saxon monarchy, these were still followed : even Edward the Confessor, who would join in no other secular amusements, took the greatest delight, says William of Malmesbury, " to follow a pack of swift hounds in pursuit of game, and to cheer them with his voice."

1012. NOR WAS EDWARD the only English sovereign who delighted in the pleasures of the chase. William the Norman, and his two sons who succeeded him, were passionately fond of the sport, and greatly circumscribed the liberties of their subjects in reference to the killing of game. The privilege of hunting in the royal forests was confined to the king and his favourites ; and in order that these umbrageous retreats might be made more extensive, whole villages were depopulated, places of worship levelled with the ground, and every means adopted that might give a sufficient amplitude of space, in accordance with the royal pleasure, for the beasts of the chase. King John was likewise especially attached to the sports of the field ; whilst Edward III. was so enamoured of the exercise, that even during his absence at the wars in France, he took with him sixty couples of stag-hounds and as many hare-hounds, and every day amused himself either with hunting or hawking. Great in wisdom as the Scotch Solomon, James I., conceited himself to be, he was much addicted to the amusements of hunting, hawking, and shooting. Yea, it is even asserted that his precious time was divided between hunting, the bottle, and his standish : to the first he gave his fair weather, to the second his dull, and to the third his cloudy. From his days down to the present, the sports of the field have continued to hold their high reputation, not only for the promotion of health, but for helping to form that manliness of character which enters so largely into the composition of the sons of the British soil. That it largely helps to do this there can be no doubt. The late duke of Grafton, when hunting, was, on one occasion, thrown into a ditch. A young curate, engaged in the same chase, cried out, " Lie still, my lord !" leapt over him, and pursued his sport. Such an apparent want of feeling might be expected to have been resented by the duke ; but not so. On his being helped up by his attendant, he said, " That man shall have the first good living that falls to my disposal : had he stopped to have given me his sympathy, I never would have given him anything." Such was the manly sentiment of the duke, who delighted in the exemplification of a spirit similarly ardent as his own in the sport, and above the baseness of an assumed sorrow.

1013. THAT HUNTING HAS IN MANY INSTANCES BEEN CARRIED TO AN EXCESS is well known, and the match given by the Prince Esterhazy, regent of Hungary, on the signing of the treaty of peace with France, is not the least extraordinary upon record. On that occasion, there were killed 160 deer, 100 wild boars, 300 hares, and 80 foxes : this was the achievement of one day. Enormous, however, as this slaughter may appear, it is greatly inferior to that made by the contemporary king of Naples on a hunting expedition. That sovereign had a larger extent of ground at his command, and a longer period for the exercise of his talents ; consequently, his sport, if it can so be called, was proportionably greater. It was pursued during his journey to Vienna, in Austria, Bohemia, and Moravia ; when he killed 5 bears, 1,820 boars, 1,950 deer, 1,145 does, 1,625 roebucks, 11,121 rabbits, 13 wolves, 17 badgers, 16,354 hares, and 354 foxes. In birds, during the same expedition, he killed 15,350 pheasants and 12,335 partridges. Such an amount of destruction can hardly be called sport ; it resembles more the indiscriminate slaughter of a battle-field, where the scientific engines of civilized warfare are brought to bear upon defenceless savages.

1014. DEER AND HARES may be esteemed as the only four-footed animals now hunted in Britain for the table ; and even these are not followed with the same ardour as they were wont to be. Still, there is no country in the world where the sport of hunting on horseback is carried to such an extent as in Great Britain, and where the pleasures of the chase are so well understood, and conducted on such purely scientific principles. The Fox, of all " the beasts of the field," is now considered to afford the best sport. For this, it is infinitely superior to the stag ; for the real sportsman can only enjoy that chase when the deer is sought for and found like other game which are pursued with hounds. In the case of finding an outlying fallow-deer, which is unharboured, in this manner, great sport is frequently obtained ; but this is now rarely to be met with in Britain. In reference to hare-hunting, it is much followed in many parts of this and the sister island ; but, by the true foxhunter, it is considered as a sport only fit to be pursued by women and old men. Although it is less dangerous and exciting than the fox-chase, however, it has great charms for those who do not care for the hard riding which the other requires.

1015. THE ART OF TAKING OR KILLING BIRDS is called "fowling," and is either practised as an amusement by persons of rank or property, or for a livelihood by persons who use nets and other apparatus. When practised as an amusement, it principally consists of killing them with a light firearm called a " fowling-piece," and the sport is secured to those who pursue it by the game laws. The other means by which birds are taken, consist in imitating their voices, or leading them, by other artifices, into situations where they become entrapped by nets, birdlime, or otherwise. For taking large numbers of birds, the pipe or call is the most common means employed ; and this is done during the months of September and October. We will here briefly give a description of the *modus operandi* pursued in this sport. A thin wood is usually the spot chosen, and, under a tree at a little distance from the others, a cabin is erected, and there are only such branches left on the tree as are necessary for the placing of the birdlime, and which are covered with it. Around the cabin are placed avenues with twisted perches, also covered with' birdlime. Having thus prepared all that is necessary, the birdcatcher places himself in the cabin, and, at sunrise and sunset, imitates the cry of a small bird calling the others to its assistance. Supposing that the cry of the owl is imitated, immediately different kinds of birds will flock together at the cry of their common enemy, when, at every instant, they will be seen falling to the ground, their wings being of no use to them, from their having come in contact with the birdlime. The cries of those which are thus situated now attract others, and thus are large numbers taken in a short space of time. If owls were themselves desired to be taken, it is only during the night that this can be done, by counterfeiting the squeak of the mouse. Larks, other birds, and water-fowl, are sometimes taken by nets ; but to describe fully the manner in which this is done, would here occupy too much space.

1016. Feathered Game have from time immemorial given gratification to the palate of man. With the exception of birds of prey, and some other species, Moses permitted his people to eat them ; and the Egyptians made offerings to their priests of their most delicate birds. The ancient Greeks commenced their repasts with little roasted birds ; and feathered game, amongst the Romans, was served as the second course. Indeed, several of the ancient *gourmands* of the "imperial city" were so fond of game, that they brought themselves to ruin by eating flamingoes and pheasants. "Some modern nations, the French among others," says Monsieur Soyer, "formerly ate the heron, crane, crow, stork, swan, cormorant, and bittern. The first three especially were highly esteemed ; and Laillevant, cook of Charles VII., teaches us how to prepare these meagre, tough birds. Belon says, that in spite of its revolting taste when unaccustomed to it, the bittern is, however, among the delicious treats of the French. This writer also asserts, that a falcon or a vulture, either roasted or boiled, is excellent eating ; and that if one of these birds happened to kill itself in flying after game, the falconer instantly cooked it. Lebaut calls the heron a royal viand."

1017. The Heron was hunted by the Hawk, and the sport of hawking is usually placed at the head of those amusements that can only be practised in the country. This precedency it probably obtained from its being a pastime so generally followed by the nobility, not in Great Britain only, but likewise on the continent. In former times, persons of high rank rarely appeared in public without their dogs and their hawks : the latter they carried with them when they journeyed from one country to another, and sometimes even took them to battle with them, and would not part with them when taken prisoners, even to obtain their own liberty. Such birds were esteemed as the ensigns of nobility, and no action was reckoned more dishonourable in a man of rank than that of giving up his hawk.   We have already alluded to the hunting propensities of our own Edward III., and we may also allude to his being equally addicted to hawking.   According to Froissart, when this sovereign invaded France, he took with him thirty falconers on horseback, who had charge of his hawks, and every day, as his royal fancy inclined him, he either hunted, or went to the river for the purpose of hawking.   In the great and powerful, the pursuit of game as a sport is allowable, but in those who have to earn their bread by the sweat of their brow, it is to be condemned.   In Burton's "Anatomy of Melancholy" we find a humorous story, told by Poggius, the Florentine, who reprobates this folly in such persons.   It is this.   A physician of Milan, that cured madmen, had a pit of water in his house, in which he kept his patients, some up to the knees, some to the girdle, some to the chin, *pro modo insaniæ*, as they were more or less affected.   One of them by chance, that was well recovered, stood in the door, and seeing a gallant pass by with a hawk on his fist, well mounted, with his spaniels after him, would needs know to what use all this preparation served.   He made answer, To kill certain fowl.   The patient demanded again, what his fowl might be worth which he killed in a year?   He replied, Five or ten crowns ; and when he urged him further, what his dogs, horse, and hawks stood him in, he told him four hundred crowns.   With that the patient bade him begone, as he loved his life and welfare ; "for if our master come and find thee here, he will put thee in the pit, amongst the madmen, up to the chin."   Thus reproving the madness of such men as will spend themselves in those vain sports, to the neglect of their business and necessary affairs.

1018. As the inevitable Result of Social Progress is, at least to limit, if not entirely to suppress, such sports as we have here been treating of, much of the romance of country life has passed away.   This is more especially the case with falconry, which had its origin about the middle of the fourth century, although, lately, some attempts have been rather successfully made to institute a revival of the "gentle art" of hawking.   Julius Firmicus, who lived about that time, is, so far as we can find, the first Latin author who speaks of falconers, and the art of teaching one species of birds to fly after and catch others.   The occupation of these functionaries has now, however, all but ceased.   New and nobler efforts characterize the aims of mankind in the development of their civilization, and the sports of the field have, to a large extent, been superseded by other exercises, it may be less healthful and invigorating, but certainly more elegant, intellectual, and humanizing.

RECIPES.

CHAPTER XXIII.

ROAST BLACK-COCK.

1019. INGREDIENTS.—Black-cock, butter, toast.

Mode.—Let these birds hang for a few days, or they will be tough and tasteless, if not well kept. Pluck and draw them, and wipe the insides and outsides with a damp cloth, as washing spoils the flavour. Cut off the heads, and truss them, the same as a roast fowl, cutting off the toes, and scalding and peeling the feet. Trussing them with the head on, as shown in the engraving, is still practised by many cooks, but the former method is

ROAST BLACK-COCK.

now considered the best. Put them down to a brisk fire, well baste them with butter, and serve with a piece of toast under, and a good gravy and bread sauce. After trussing, some cooks cover the breast with vine-leaves and slices of bacon, and then roast them. They should be served in the same manner and with the same accompaniments as with the plainly-roasted birds.

Time.—45 to 50 minutes.

Average cost, from 5s. to 6s. the brace; but seldom bought.

Sufficient,—2 or 3 for a dish.

Seasonable from the middle of August to the end of December.

THE BLACK-COCK, HEATH-COCK, MOOR-FOWL, OR HEATH-POULT.—This bird sometimes weighs as much as four pounds, and the hen about two. It is at present confined to the more northern parts of Britain, culture and extending population having united in driving it into more desolate regions, except, perhaps, in a few of the more wild and less-frequented portions of England. It may still be found in the New Forest, in Hampshire, Dartmoor, and Sedgmoor, in Devonshire, and among the hills of Somersetshire, contiguous to the latter. It may also be found in Staffordshire, in North Wales, and again in the north of England; but nowhere so plentiful as in some parts of the Highlands of Scotland. The males are hardly distinguishable from the females until they are about half-grown, when the black

BLACK-COCK.

feathers begin to appear, first about the sides and breast. Their food consists of the tops of birch and heath, except when the mountain berries are ripe, at which period they eagerly and even voraciously pick the bilberries and cranberries from the bushes. Large numbers of these birds are found in Norway, almost rivalling the turkey in point of size. Some of them have begun to be imported into London, where they are vended in the shops; but the flavour of their flesh is not equal to that of the Scotch bird.

HASHED WILD DUCK.

1020. INGREDIENTS.—The remains of cold roast wild duck, 1 pint of good brown gravy, 2 tablespoonfuls of bread crumbs, 1 glass of claret, salt, cayenne, and mixed spices to taste; 1 tablespoonful of lemon or Seville orange-juice.

Mode.—Cut the remains of the duck into neat joints, put them into a stewpan, with all the above ingredients; let them get gradually hot by the side of the fire, and occasionally stir the contents; when on the point of boiling, serve, and garnish the dish with sippets of toasted bread.

Time.—About ¼ hour.

Seasonable from November to February.

RAGOUT OF WILD DUCK.

1021. INGREDIENTS.—2 wild ducks, 4 shalots, 1 pint of stock No. 105, 1 glass of port wine, 1 oz. of butter, a little flour, the juice of ½ lemon, cayenne and salt to taste.

Mode.—Ducks that have been dressed and left from the preceding day will answer for this dish. Cut them into joints, reserve the legs, wings, and breasts until wanted; put the trimmings into a stewpan with the shalots and stock, and let them simmer for about ½ hour, and strain the gravy. Put the butter into a stewpan; when melted, dredge in a little flour, and pour in the gravy made from the bones; give it one boil, and strain it again; add the wine, lemon-juice, and cayenne; lay in the pieces of duck, and let the whole gradually warm through, but do not allow it to boil, or the duck will be hard. The gravy should not be too thick, and should be very highly seasoned. The squeeze of a Seville orange is a great improvement to this dish.

Time.—About ½ hour to make the gravy; ¼ hour for the duck gradually to warm through.

Seasonable from November to February.

ROAST WILD DUCK.

1022. INGREDIENTS.—Wild duck, flour, butter.

Mode.—Carefully pluck and draw them; cut off the heads close to the necks, leaving sufficient skin to turn over, and do not cut off the feet; some twist each leg at the knuckle, and rest the claws on each side of the breast; others truss them as shown in our illustration. Roast the birds before a quick fire, and, when they are first put down, let them remain for 5 minutes without basting (this will keep the gravy in); afterwards baste plen-tifully with butter, and a few minutes before serving dredge them lightly with flour; baste well, and send them to table nicely frothed, and full of gravy. If overdone, the birds will lose their flavour.

ROAST WILD DUCK.

Serve with a good gravy in the dish, or orange gravy, No. 488; and send to table with them a cut lemon. To take off the fishy taste which wild fowl sometimes have, baste them for a few minutes with hot water to which have been added an onion and a little salt; then take away the pan, and baste with butter.

Time.—When liked underdressed, 20 to 25 minutes; well done, 25 to 35 minutes.

Average cost, 4s. to 5s. the couple.

Sufficient,—2 for a dish.

Seasonable from November to February.

THE WILD DUCK.—The male of the wild duck is called a mallard; and the young ones are called flappers. The time to try to find a brood of these is about the month of July, among the rushes of the deepest and most retired parts of some brook or stream, where, if the old bird is sprung, it may be taken as a certainty that its brood is not far off. When once found, flappers are easily killed, as they attain their full growth before their wings are fledged. Consequently, the sport is more like hunting water-rats than shoot-ing birds. When the flappers take wing, they assume the name of wild ducks, and about the month of August repair to the corn-fields, where they remain until they are disturbed by the harvest-peole. They then frequent the rivers pretty early in the evening, and give excellent sport to those who have pa-tience to wait for them. In order to know a wild duck, it is necessary only to look at the claws, which should be black.

THE WILD DUCK.

HASHED GAME (Cold Meat Cookery).

1023. INGREDIENTS.—The remains of cold game, 1 onion stuck with 3 cloves, a few whole peppers, a strip of lemon-peel, salt to taste, thickening of butter and flour, 1 glass of port wine, 1 tablespoonful of lemon-juice, 1 tablespoonful of ketchup, 1 pint of water or weak stock.

Mode.—Cut the remains of cold game into joints, reserve the best pieces, and the inferior ones and trimmings put into a stewpan with the onion, pepper, lemon-peel, salt, and water or weak stock; stew these for about an hour, and strain the gravy; thicken it with butter and flour; add the wine, lemon-juice, and ketchup; lay in the pieces of game, and let them gradually warm through by the side of the fire; do not allow it to boil, or the game will be hard. When on the point of simmering, serve, and garnish the dish with sippets of toasted bread.

Time.—Altogether 1¼ hour.

Seasonable from August to March.

Note.—Any kind of game may be hashed by the above recipe, and the flavour may be varied by adding flavoured vinegars, curry powder, &c.; but we cannot recommend these latter ingredients, as a dish of game should really have a gamy taste; and if too many sauces, essences, &c., are added to the gravy, they quite overpower and destroy the flavour the dish should possess.

GROUSE PIE.

1024. INGREDIENTS.—Grouse; cayenne, salt, and pepper to taste; 1 lb. of rump-steak, ½ pint of well-seasoned broth, puff paste.

Mode.—Line the bottom of a pie-dish with the rump-steak cut into neat pieces, and, should the grouse be large, cut them into joints; but, if small, they may be laid in the pie whole; season highly with salt, cayenne, and black pepper; pour in the broth, and cover with a puff paste; brush the crust over with the yolk of an egg, and bake from ¾ to 1 hour. If the grouse is cut into joints, the backbones and trimmings will make the gravy, by stewing them with an onion, a little sherry, a bunch of herbs, and a blade of mace: this should be poured in after the pie is baked.

Time.—¾ to 1 hour.

Average cost, exclusive of the grouse, which are seldom bought, 1s. 9d.

Seasonable from the 12th of August to the beginning of December.

ROAST GROUSE.

1025. INGREDIENTS.—Grouse, butter, a thick slice of toasted bread.

Mode.—Let the birds hang as long as possible; pluck and draw them; wipe, but do not wash them, inside and out, and truss them without the head, the same as for a roast fowl. Many persons still continue to truss them with the head under the wing, but

ROAST GROUSE.

the former is now considered the most approved method. Put them down to a sharp clear fire; keep them well basted the whole of the time they are cooking, and serve them on a buttered toast, soaked in the dripping-pan, with a little melted butter poured over them, or with bread-sauce and gravy.

Time.—½ hour; if liked very thoroughly done, 35 minutes.

Average cost, 2s. to 2s. 6d. the brace; but seldom bought.

Sufficient,—2 for a dish.

Seasonable from the 12th of August to the beginning of December.

GROUSE.—These birds are divided into wood grouse, black grouse, red grouse, and white grouse. The wood grouse is further distinguished as the cock of the wood, or capercalzie, and is as large as the turkey, being about two feet nine inches in length, and weighing from twelve to fifteen pounds. The female is considerably less than the male, and, in the colour of her feathers, differs widely from the other. This beautiful species is found principally in lofty, mountainous regions, and is very rare in Great Britain; but in the pine forests of Russia, Sweden, and other northern countries, it is very common. In these it has its habitat, feeding on the cones of the trees, and the fruits of various kinds of plants, especially the berry of the juniper. Black grouse is also distinguished as black-game, or the black-cock. It is not larger than the common hen, and weighs only about four pounds. The female is about one-third

RED GROUSE.

less than the male, and also differs considerably from him in point of colour. Like the former, they are found chiefly in high situations, and are common in Russia, Siberia, and other northern countries. They are also found in the northern parts of Great Britain, feeding in winter on the various berries and fruits belonging to mountainous countries, and, in summer, frequently descending to the lower lands, to feed upon corn. The red grouse, gorcock, or moor-cock, weighs about nineteen ounces, and the female somewhat less. In the wild heathy tracts of the northern counties of England it is plentiful, also in Wales and the Highlands of Scotland. Mr. Pennant considered it peculiar to Britain, those found in the mountainous parts of Spain, France, and Italy, being only varieties of the same bird. White grouse, white game, or ptarmigan, is nearly the same size as the red grouse, and is found in lofty situations, where it supports itself in the severest weather. It is to be met with in most of the northern countries of Europe, and appears even in Greenland. In the Hebrides, Orkneys, and the Highlands of Scotland, it is also found; and sometimes, though rarely, among the fells of Northumberland and Cumberland. In winter they fly in flocks, and are so little familiar with the sight of man, that they are easily shot, and even snared. They feed on the wild produce of the hills, which sometimes imparts to their flesh a bitter but not unpalatable taste. According to Buffon, it is dark-coloured, and somewhat flavoured like the hare.

GROUSE SALAD.

(*Soyer's Recipe.*)

1026. INGREDIENTS.—8 eggs, butter, fresh salad, 1 or 2 grouse; for the sauce, 1 teaspoonful of minced shalot, 1 teaspoonful of pounded sugar, the yolk of 1 egg, 1 teaspoonful of minced parsley, ¼ oz. of salt, 4 tablespoonfuls of oil, 2 tablespoonfuls of Chili vinegar, 1 gill of cream.

Mode.—Boil the eggs hard, shell them, throw them into cold water cut a thin slice off the bottom to facilitate the proper placing of them in the dish, cut each one into four lengthwise, and make a very thin flat border of butter, about one inch from the edge of the dish the salad is to be served on; fix the pieces of egg upright close to each other, the yolk outside, or the yolk and white alternately; lay in the centre a fresh salad of whatever is in season, and, having previously roasted the grouse rather underdone, cut it into eight or ten pieces, and prepare the sauce as follows:—Put the shalots into a basin, with the sugar, the yolk of an egg, the parsley, and salt, and mix in by degrees the oil and vinegar; when these ingredients are well mixed, put the sauce on ice or in a cool place. When ready to serve, whip the cream rather thick, which lightly mix with it; then lay the inferior parts of the grouse on the salad, sauce over so as to cover each piece, then lay over the salad and the remainder of the grouse, pour the rest of the sauce over, and serve. The eggs may be ornamented with a little dot of radishes or beetroot on the point. Anchovy and gherkin, cut into small diamonds, may be placed between, or cut gherkins in slices, and a border of them laid round. Tarragon or chervil-leaves are also a pretty addition. The remains of cold black-game, pheasant, or partridge may be used in the above manner, and will make a very delicate dish.

Average cost, 2s. 6d.

Seasonable from the 12th of August to the beginning of December.

THE CAPERCALZIE.—This bird was to be met with formerly both in Ireland and Scotland, but is now extinct. The male lives separate from the females, except in the breeding season. Its manners and habits are very like those of black grouse, except that it seems to be wholly confined to forests of pine, on the tender shoots of which it feeds. It is by no means uncommon in the woods of Norway, whence we received it. It is also found abundant in Russia, Siberia, Italy, and in some portions of the Alps. It was, in 1760, last seen in Scotland, in the woods of Strathglass. Recent attempts have been made to re-introduce it into that country, but without success; principally owing, as we should imagine, to the want of sufficient food suitable for its sustenance.

THE CAPERCALZIE.

GROUSE.—Under this general term are included several species of game birds, called black, red, woodland, and white grouse. The black is larger than the red (see No. 1025), and is not so common, and therefore held in higher estimation. The red, however, is a bird of exquisite flavour, and is a native of the mountainous districts of Scotland and the north of England. It feeds on the tops of the heath and the berries that grow amongst them: its colour is a rich chestnut, striped with black. The woodland, or cock of the wood, is the largest among the bird tribes which pass under the denomination of game. It is smaller than the turkey, and was originally common in our mountains; but it is now to be found only in the mountains of Scotland, though it still abounds in the north of Europe, Germany, and in the Alps. It is esteemed as delicious eating, and its plumage is extremely beautiful. The white grouse, or ptarmigan, is not a plentiful bird in Britain; but it is still found in the islands, and weighs about half a pound. The London market is supplied by Norway and Scotland; those from the former country being esteemed the best. When young, it is held in high estimation, being considered as little different from common grouse.

ROAST HARE.

1027. INGREDIENTS.—Hare, forcemeat No. 417, a little milk, butter.

Choosing and Trussing.—Choose a young hare; which may be known by its smooth and sharp claws, and by the cleft in the lip not being much spread. To be eaten in perfection, it must hang for some time; and, if properly taken care of, it may be kept for several days. It is better to hang without being paunched; but should it be previously emptied, wipe the inside every day, and sprinkle over it a little pepper and ginger, to prevent the musty taste which long keeping in the damp occasions, and which also affects the stuffing. After it is skinned, wash it well, and soak for an hour in warm water to draw out the blood; if old, let it lie in vinegar for a short time, but wash it well afterwards in several waters. Make a forcemeat by recipe No. 417, wipe the hare dry, fill the belly with it, and sew it up. Bring the hind and fore legs close to

ROAST HARE.

the body towards the head, run a skewer through each, fix the head between the shoulders by means of another skewer, and be careful to leave the ears on. Put a string round the body from skewer to skewer, and tie it above the back.

Mode.—The hare should be kept at a distance from the fire when it is first laid down, or the outside will become dry and hard before the inside is done. Baste it well with milk for a short time, and afterwards with butter; and particular attention must be paid to the basting, so as to preserve the meat on the back juicy and nutritive. When it is almost roasted enough, flour the hare, and baste well with butter. When nicely frothed, dish it, remove the skewers, and send it to table with a little gravy in the dish, and a tureen of the same. Red-currant jelly must also not be forgotten, as this is an indispensable accompaniment to roast hare. For economy, good beef dripping may be substituted for the milk and butter to baste with; but the basting, as we have before stated, must be continued without intermission. If the liver is good, it may be parboiled, minced, and mixed with the stuffing; but it should not be used unless quite fresh.

Time.—A middling-sized hare, 1¼ hour; a large hare, 1½ to 2 hours.

Average cost, from 4s. to 6s.

Sufficient for 5 or 6 persons.

Seasonable from September to the end of February.

THE HARE.—This little animal is found generally distributed over Europe, and, indeed, in most parts of the northern world. Its extreme timidity is the endowment which Providence has bestowed upon it as a means of defence; it is therefore attentive to every sound, and is supplied with ears both long and tubular, with which it can hear with great acuteness. Its eyes, also, are so constructed, and placed so prominent in its head, that it can see both before and behind it. It lives entirely upon vegetables, but its flesh is considered dry, notwithstanding that it is deemed, in many respects, superior to that of the rabbit, being more savoury, and of a much higher flavour. Its general time of feeding is the evening; but during the day, if not disturbed, it adheres closely to its *form*.

THE HARE.

POTTED HARE (a Luncheon or Breakfast Dish).

1028. INGREDIENTS.—1 hare, a few slices of bacon, a large bunch of savoury herbs, 4 cloves, ½ teaspoonful of whole allspice, 2 carrots, 2 onions, salt and pepper to taste, 1 pint of water, 2 glasses of sherry.

Mode.—Skin, empty, and wash the hare; cut it down the middle, and put it into a stewpan, with a few slices of bacon under and over it; add the remaining ingredients, and stew very gently until the hare is tender, and the flesh will separate easily from the bones. When done enough, take it up, remove the bones, and pound the meat, *with the bacon*, in a mortar, until reduced to a perfectly smooth paste. Should it not be sufficiently seasoned, add a little cayenne, salt, and pounded mace, but be careful that these are well mixed with the other ingredients. Press the meat into potting-pots, pour over clarified butter, and keep in a dry place. The liquor that the hare was stewed in, should be saved for hashes, soups, &c. &c.

Time.—About 2½ hours to stew the hare.

Seasonable from September to the end of February.

BROILED HARE (a Supper or Luncheon Dish).

1029. INGREDIENTS.—The leg and shoulders of a roast hare, cayenne and salt to taste, a little butter.

Mode.—Cut the legs and shoulders from a roast hare, season them highly with salt and cayenne, and broil them over a very clear fire for 5 minutes. Dish them on a hot dish, rub over them a little cold butter, and send to table very quickly.

Time.—5 minutes.

Seasonable from September to the end of February.

HASHED HARE.

1030. INGREDIENTS.—The remains of cold roast hare, 1 blade of pounded mace, 2 or 3 allspice, pepper and salt to taste, 1 onion, a bunch of savoury herbs, 3 tablespoonfuls of port wine, thickening of butter and flour, 2 tablespoonfuls of mushroom ketchup.

Mode.—Cut the cold hare into neat slices, and put the head, bones, and trimmings into a stewpan, with ¾ pint of water; add the mace, allspice, seasoning, onion, and herbs, and stew for nearly an hour, and strain the gravy; thicken it with butter and flour, add the wine and ketchup, and lay in the pieces of hare, with any stuffing that may be left. Let the whole gradually heat by the side of the fire, and, when it has simmered for about 5 minutes, serve, and garnish the dish with sippets of toasted bread. Send red-currant jelly to table with it.

Time.—Rather more than 1 hour.

Average cost, exclusive of the cold hare, 6*d.*

Seasonable from September to the end of February.

JUGGED HARE.

(*Very Good.*)

1031. INGREDIENTS.—1 hare, 1½ lb. of gravy beef, ½ lb. of butter, 1 onion, 1 lemon, 6 cloves; pepper, cayenne, and salt to taste; ½ pint of port wine.

Mode.—Skin; paunch, and wash the hare, cut it into pieces, dredge them with flour, and fry in boiling butter. Have ready 1½ pint of gravy, made from the above proportion of beef, and thickened with a little flour. Put this into a jar; add the pieces of fried hare, an onion stuck with six cloves, a lemon peeled and cut in half, and a good seasoning of pepper, cayenne, and salt; cover the jar down tightly, put it up to the neck into a stewpan of boiling water, and let it stew until the hare is quite tender, taking care to keep the water boiling. When nearly done, pour in the wine, and add a few force-meat balls, made by recipe No. 417: these must be fried or baked in the oven for a few minutes before they are put to the gravy. Serve with red-currant jelly.

Time.—3½ to 4 hours. If the hare is very old, allow 4½ hours.

Average cost, 7*s.*

Sufficient for 7 or 8 persons.

Seasonable from September to the end of February

II.

(*A Quicker and more Economical Way.*)

1032. INGREDIENTS.—1 hare, a bunch of sweet herbs, 2 onions, each stuck with 3 cloves, 6 whole allspice, ½ teaspoonful of black pepper, a strip of lemon-peel, thickening of butter and flour, 2 tablespoonfuls of mushroom ketchup, ¼ pint of port wine.

Mode.—Wash the hare nicely, cut it up into joints (not too large), and flour and brown them as in the preceding recipe ; then put them into a stewpan with the herbs, onions, cloves, allspice, pepper, and lemon-peel ; cover with hot water, and when it boils, carefully remove all the scum, and let it simmer gently till tender, which will be in about 1¾ hour, or longer, should the hare be very old. Take out the pieces of hare, thicken the gravy with flour and butter, add the ketchup and port wine, let it boil for about 10 minutes, strain it through a sieve over the hare, and serve. A few fried forcemeat balls should be added at the moment of serving, or instead of frying them, they may be stewed in the gravy, about 10 minutes before the hare is wanted for table. Do not omit to serve red-currant jelly with it.

Time.—Altogether 2 hours. *Average cost,* 5s. 6d.

Sufficient for 7 or 8 persons.

Seasonable from September to the end of February.

Note.—Should there be any left, rewarm it the next day by putting the hare, &c. into a covered jar, and placing this jar in a saucepan of boiling water : this method prevents a great deal of waste.

ROAST LANDRAIL, OR CORN-CRAKE.

1033. INGREDIENTS.—3 or 4 birds, butter, fried bread crumbs.

Mode.—Pluck and draw the birds, wipe them inside and out with damp cloths, and truss them in the following manner :—Bring the head round under the wing, and the thighs close to the sides ; pass a skewer through them and the body, and keep the legs straight. Roast them before a clear fire, keep them well basted, and serve on fried bread crumbs, with a tureen of brown gravy. When liked, bread-sauce may also be sent to table with them.

LANDRAILS.

Time.—12 to 20 minutes., *Average cost.*—Seldom bought.

Sufficient.—Allow 4 for a dish.

Seasonable from August 12th to the middle of September.

THE LANDRAIL, OR CORN-CRAKE.—This bird is migratory in its habits, yet from its formation, it seems ill adapted for long aërial passages, its wings being short, and placed so forward out of the centre of gravity, that it flies in an extremely heavy and embarrassed manner, and with its legs hanging down. When it alights, it can hardly be sprung a second time, as it runs very fast, and seems to depend for its safety more on the swiftness of its feet than the celerity of its wings. It makes its appearance in England about the same time as the quail, that is, in the months of April and May, and frequents the same places. Its singular cry is first heard when the grass becomes long enough to shelter it, and it continues to be heard until the grass is cut. The bird, however, is seldom seen, for it constantly skulks among the thickest portions of the herbage, and runs so nimbly through it, doubling and winding in every direction, that it is difficult to get near it. It leaves this island before the winter, and repairs to other countries in search of its food, which principally consists of slugs, large numbers of which it destroys. It is very common in Ireland, and, whilst migrating to this country, is seen in great numbers in the island of Anglesea. On its first arrival in England, it is so lean as scarcely to weigh above five or six ounces; before its departure, however, it has been known to exceed eight ounces, and is then most delicious eating.

THE LANDRAIL.

TO DRESS A LEVERET.

1034. INGREDIENTS.—2 leverets, butter, flour.

Mode.—Leverets should be trussed in the same manner as a hare, but they do not require stuffing. Roast them before a clear fire, and keep them well basted all the time they are cooking. A few minutes before serving, dredge them lightly with flour, and froth them nicely. Serve with plain gravy in the dish, and send to table red-currant jelly with them.

Time.—½ to ¾ hour. *Average cost*, in full season, 4s. each.

Sufficient for 5 or 6 persons.

Seasonable from May to August, but cheapest in July and August.

BROILED PARTRIDGE (a Luncheon, Breakfast, or Supper Dish).

1035. INGREDIENTS.—3 partridges, salt and cayenne to taste, a small piece of butter, brown gravy or mushroom sauce.

Mode.—Pluck, draw, and cut the partridges in half, and wipe the inside thoroughly with a damp cloth. Season them with salt and cayenne, broil them over a very clear fire, and dish them on a hot dish; rub a small piece of butter over each half, and send them to table with brown gravy or mushroom sauce.

Time.— About ¼ hour. *Average cost*, 1s. 6d. to 2s. a brace.

Sufficient for 3 or 4 persons.

Seasonable from the 1st of September to the beginning of February.

PARTRIDGE PIE.

1036. INGREDIENTS.—3 partridges, pepper and salt to taste, 1 tea-spoonful of minced parsley (when obtainable, a few mushrooms), ¾ lb. of veal cutlet, a slice of ham, ½ pint of stock, puff paste.

Mode.—Line a pie-dish with a veal cutlet; over that place a slice of ham and a seasoning of pepper and salt. Pluck, draw, and wipe the partridges; cut off the legs at the first joint, and season them inside with pepper, salt, minced parsley, and a small piece of butter; place them in the dish, and pour over the stock; line the edges of the dish with puff paste, cover with the same, brush it over with the yolk of an egg, and bake for ¾ to 1 hour.

Time.—¾ to 1 hour. *Average cost*, 1s. 6d. to 2s. a brace.

Sufficient for 4 or 5 persons.

Seasonable from the 1st of September to the beginning of February.

Note.—Should the partridges be very large, split them in half; they will then lie in the dish more compactly. When at hand, a few mushrooms should always be added.

POTTED PARTRIDGE.

1037. INGREDIENTS.—Partridges; seasoning to taste of mace, allspice white pepper, and salt; butter, coarse paste.

Mode.—Pluck and draw the birds, and wipe them inside with a damp cloth. Pound well some mace, allspice, white pepper, and salt; mix together, and rub every part of the partridges with this. Pack the birds as closely as possible in a baking-pan, with plenty of butter over them, and cover with a coarse flour and water crust. Tie a paper over this, and bake for rather more than 1½ hour; let the birds get cold, then cut them into pieces for keeping, pack them closely into a large potting-pot, and cover with clarified butter. This should be kept in a cool dry place. The butter used for potted things will answer for basting, or for paste for meat pies.—See coloured plate, D 1.

Time.—1½ hour.

Seasonable from the 1st of September to the beginning of February.

SALMI DE PERDRIX, or HASHED PARTRIDGES.

1038. INGREDIENTS.—3 young partridges, 3 shalots, a slice of lean ham, 1 carrot, 3 or 4 mushrooms, a bunch of savoury herbs, 2 cloves, 6 whole peppers, ¾ pint of stock, 1 glass of sherry or Madeira, a small lump of sugar.

Mode.—After the partridges are plucked and drawn, roast them rather underdone, and cover them with paper, as they should not be browned; cut them into joints, take off the skin from the wings, legs, and breasts; put these into a stewpan, cover them up, and set by until the gravy is ready. Cut a slice of ham into small pieces, and put them, with the carrots sliced, the shalots, mushrooms, herbs, cloves, and pepper, into a stewpan; fry them lightly in a little butter, pour in the stock, add the bones and trimming from the partridges, and simmer for ¼ hour. Strain the gravy, let it cool, and skim off every particle of fat; put it to the legs, wings, and breasts, add a glass of sherry or Madeira and a small lump of sugar, let all gradually warm through by the side of the fire, and when on the point of boiling, serve, and garnish the dish with croûtons. The remains of roast partridge answer very well dressed in this way, although not so good as when the birds are in the first instance only half-roasted. This recipe is equally suitable for pheasants, moor-game, &c.; but care must be taken always to skin the joints.

Time.—Altogether 1 hour.

Sufficient.—2 or 3 partridges for an entrée.

Seasonable from the 1st of September to the beginning of February.

ROAST PARTRIDGE.

1039. INGREDIENTS.—Partridge; butter.

Choosing and Trussing.—Choose young birds, with dark-coloured bills and yellowish legs, and let them hang a few days, or there will be no flavour to the flesh, nor will it be tender. The time they should be kept, entirely depends on the taste of those for whom they are intended, as what some persons would consider delicious, would be to others disgusting and offensive. They may be trussed with or without the head, the latter mode being now considered the most fashionable. Pluck, draw, and wipe the partridge carefully inside and out; cut off the head, leaving sufficient skin on the neck to

ROAST PARTRIDGE.

skewer back; bring the legs close to the breast, between it and the side-bones, and pass a skewer through the pinions and the thick part of the thighs. When the head is left on, it should be brought round and fixed on to the point of the skewer.

Mode.—When the bird is firmly and plumply trussed, roast it before a nice bright fire; keep it well basted, and a few minutes before serving, flour and froth it well. Dish it, and serve with gravy and bread sauce, and send to table hot and quickly. A little of the gravy should be poured over the bird.

Time.—25 to 35 minutes.   *Average cost,* 1s. 6d. to 2s. a brace.

Sufficient,—2 for a dish.

Seasonable from the 1st of September to the beginning of February.

THE PARTRIDGE.—This bird is to be found in nearly all the temperate countries of Europe, but is most abundant in the Ukraine, although it is unable to bear the extremes of climate, whether hot or cold. It was formerly very common in France, and is considered a table luxury in England. The instinct of this bird is frequently exemplified in a remarkable manner, for the preservation of its young. " I have seen it often," says a very celebrated writer, and an accurate observer of nature, " and once in particular, I saw an extraordinary instance of an old bird's solicitude to save its brood. As I was hunting with a young pointer, the dog ran on a brood of very small partridges ; the old bird cried, fluttered, and ran tumbling along just before the dog's nose, till she had drawn him to a considerable distance, when she took wing, and flew still further off, but not out of the

PARTRIDGES.

field ; on this the dog returned to me, near the place where the young ones lay concealed in the grass, which the old bird no sooner perceived than she flew back to us, settled just before the dog's nose again, and by rolling and tumbling about, drew off his attention from her young, and thus preserved her brood a second time. I have also seen, when a kite has been hovering over a covey of young partridges, the old birds fly up at the bird of prey, screaming and fighting with all their might to preserve their brood." Partridges should be chosen young ; if old, they are valueless. The young ones are generally known by their yellow legs and dark-coloured bills.

PHEASANT CUTLETS.

1040. INGREDIENTS.—2 or 3 pheasants, egg and bread crumbs, cayenne and salt to taste, brown gravy.

Mode.—Procure 3 young pheasants that have been hung a few days ; pluck, draw, and wipe them inside ; cut them into joints ; remove the bones from the best of these ; and the backbones, trimmings, &c., put into a stewpan, with a little stock, herbs, vegetables, seasoning, &c., to make the gravy. Flatten and trim the cutlets of a good shape, egg and bread crumb them, broil them over a clear fire, pile them high in the dish, and pour under them the gravy made from the bones, which should be strained, flavoured, and thickened. One of the small bones should be stuck on the point of each cutlet.

Time.—10 minutes.   *Average cost,* 2s. 6d. to 3s. each.

Sufficient for 2 entrées.

Seasonable from the 1st of October to the beginning of February.

ROAST PHEASANT.

1041. INGREDIENTS.—Pheasant, flour, butter.

Choosing and Trussing.—Old pheasants may be known by the length and sharpness of their spurs; in young ones they are short and blunt. The cock bird is generally reckoned the best, except when the hen is with egg. They should hang some time before they are dressed, as, if they are cooked fresh, the flesh will be exceedingly dry and tasteless. After the bird is plucked and drawn, wipe the inside with a damp cloth, and truss it in the same

ROAST PHEASANT.

manner as partridge, No. 1039. If the head is left on, as shown in the engraving, bring it round under the wing, and fix it on to the point of the skewer.

Mode.—Roast it before a brisk fire, keep it well basted, and flour and froth it nicely. Serve with brown gravy, a little of which should be poured round the bird, and a tureen of bread sauce. 2 or 3 of the pheasant's best tail-feathers are sometimes stuck in the tail as an ornament; but the fashion is not much to be commended.—See coloured plate, F 1.

Time.—½ to 1 hour, according to the size.

Average cost, 2s. 6d. to 3s. each. *Sufficient*,—1 for a dish.

Seasonable from the 1st of October to the beginning of February.

THE PHEASANT.—This beautiful bird is said to have been discovered by the Argonauts on the banks of the Phasis, near Mount Ararat, in their expedition to Colchis. It is common, however, in almost all the southern parts of the European continent, and has been long naturalized in the warmest and most woody counties of England. It is very common in France; indeed, so common as to be esteemed a nuisance by the farmers. Although it has been domesticated, this is not easily accomplished, nor is its flesh so palatable then as it is in the wild state. Mr. Ude says—"It is not often that pheasants are met with possessing that exquisite taste which is acquired only by long keeping, as the damp of this climate prevents their being kept as long as they are in other countries. The hens, in general, are the most delicate. The cocks show their age by their spurs. They are only fit to be eaten when the blood begins to run from the bill, which is commonly six days or a

THE PHEASANT.

week after they have been killed. The flesh is white, tender, and has a good flavour, if you keep it long enough; if not, it is not much different from that of a common fowl or hen."

BRILLAT SAVARIN'S RECIPE FOR ROAST PHEASANT,
a la Sainte Alliance.

1042. When the pheasant is in good condition to be cooked (*see* No. 1041), it should be plucked, and not before. The bird should then be stuffed in the following manner :—Take two snipes, and draw them, putting the bodies on one plate, and the livers, &c., on another. Take off the flesh, and mince it finely with a little beef, lard, a few truffles, pepper and salt to taste, and stuff the pheasant carefully with this. Cut a slice of bread, larger considerably than the bird, and cover it with the liver, &c., and a few truffles : an anchovy and a little fresh butter added to these will do no harm. Put the bread, &c., into the dripping-pan, and, when the bird is roasted, place it on the preparation, and surround it with Florida oranges.

Do not be uneasy, Savarin adds, about your dinner ; for a pheasant served in this way is fit for beings better than men. The pheasant itself is a very good bird ; and, imbibing the dressing and the flavour of the truffle and snipe, it becomes thrice better.

BROILED PHEASANT (a Breakfast or Luncheon Dish).

1043. INGREDIENTS.—1 pheasant, a little lard, egg and bread crumbs, salt and cayenne to taste.

Mode.—Cut the legs off at the first joint, and the remainder of the bird into neat pieces ; put them into a fryingpan with a little lard, and when browned on both sides, and about half done, take them out and drain them ; brush the pieces over with egg, and sprinkle with bread crumbs with which has been mixed a good seasoning of cayenne and salt. Broil them over a moderate fire for about 10 minutes, or rather longer, and serve with mushroom-sauce, sauce piquante, or brown gravy, in which a few game-bones and trimmings have been stewed.

Time.—Altogether ½ hour. *Sufficient* for 4 or 5 persons.

Seasonable from the 1st of October to the beginning of February.

THE HEIGHT OF EXCELLENCE IN A PHEASANT.—Things edible have their degrees of excellence under various circumstances : thus, asparagus, capers, peas, and partridges are best when young. Perfection in others is only reached when they attain maturity : let us say, for example, melons and nearly all fruits (we must except, perhaps, the medlar), with the majority of those animals whose flesh we eat. But others, again, are not good until decomposition is about to set in ; and here we may mention particularly the snipe and the pheasant. If the latter bird be eaten so soon as three days after it has been killed, it then has no peculiarity of flavour ; a pullet would be more relished, and a quail would surpass it in aroma. Kept, however, a proper length of time,—and this can be ascertained by a slight smell and change of colour,—then it becomes a highly-flavoured dish, occupying, so to speak, the middle distance between chicken and venison. It is difficult to define any exact time to "hang" a pheasant ; but any one possessed of the instincts of gastronomical science, can at once detect the right moment when a pheasant should be taken down, in the same way as a good cook knows whether a bird should be removed from the spit, or have a turn or two more.

TO DRESS PLOVERS.

1044. INGREDIENTS.—3 plovers, butter, flour, toasted bread.

Choosing and Trussing.—Choose those that feel hard at the vent, as that shows their fatness. There are three sorts,—the grey, green, and bastard plover, or lapwing. They will keep good for some time, but if very stale, the feet will be very dry. Plovers are scarcely fit for anything but roasting ; they are, however, sometimes stewed, or made into a ragoût, but this mode of cooking is not to be recommended.

Mode.—Pluck off the feathers, wipe the outside of the birds with a damp cloth, and do not draw them; truss with the head under the wing, put them down to a clear fire, and lay slices of moistened toast in the dripping-pan, to catch the trail. Keep them *well basted*, dredge them lightly with flour a few minutes before they are done, and let them be nicely frothed. Dish them on the toasts, over which the *trail* should be equally spread. Pour round the toast a little good gravy, and send some to table in a tureen.

Time.—10 minutes to ¼ hour.

Average cost, 1s. 6d. the brace, if plentiful.

Sufficient for 2 persons.

Seasonable.—In perfection from the beginning of September to the end of January.

THE PLOVER.—There are two species of this bird, the grey and the green, the former being larger than the other, and somewhat less than the woodcock. It has generally been classed with those birds which chiefly live in the water; but it would seem only to seek its food there, for many of the species breed upon the loftiest mountains. Immense flights of these birds are to be seen in the Hebrides, and other parts of Scotland; and, in the winter, large numbers are sent to the London market, which is sometimes so much glutted with them that they are sold very cheap. Previous to dressing, they are kept till they have a game flavour; and although their flesh is a favourite with many, it is not universally relished. The green is preferred to

THE PLOVER.

the grey, but both are inferior to the woodcock. Their eggs are esteemed as a great delicacy. Birds of this kind are migratory. They arrive in England in April, live with us all the spring and summer, and at the beginning of autumn prepare to take leave by getting together in flocks. It is supposed that they then retire to Spain, and frequent the sheep-walks with which that country abounds.

TO DRESS THE PTARMIGAN.

1045. INGREDIENTS.—2 or 3 birds; butter, flour, fried bread crumbs.

Mode.—The ptarmigan, or white grouse, when young and tender, are exceedingly fine eating, and should be kept as long as possible, to be good. Pluck, draw, and truss them in the same manner as grouse, No. 1025, and roast them before a brisk fire. Flour and froth them nicely, and serve on buttered toast, with a tureen of brown gravy. Bread sauce, when liked, may be sent to table with them, and fried bread crumbs substituted for the toasted bread.

Time.—About ½ hour. *Sufficient,*—2 for a dish.

Seasonable from the beginning of February to the end of April.

THE PTARMIGAN, OR WHITE GROUSE.—This bird is nearly the same size as red grouse, and is fond of lofty situations, where it braves the severest weather, and is found in most parts of Europe, as well as in Greenland. At Hudson's Bay they appear in such multitudes that so many as sixty or seventy are frequently taken at once in a net. As they are as tame as chickens, this is done without difficulty. Buffon says that the Ptarmigan avoids the solar heat, and prefers the frosts of the summits of the mountains; for, as the snow melts on the sides of the mountains, it ascends till it gains the top, where it makes a hole, and burrows in the snow. In winter, it flies in flocks, and feeds on the wild vegetation of the hills, which imparts to its flesh a bitter, but not altogether an unpalatable taste. It is dark-coloured, and has something of the flavour of the hare,

THE PTARMIGAN.

and is greatly relished, and much sought after by some sportsmen.

TO DRESS QUAILS.

1046. INGREDIENTS.—Quails, butter, toast.

Mode.—These birds keep good several days, and should be roasted without drawing. Truss them in the same manner as woodcocks, No. 1062; roast them before a clear fire, keep them well basted, and serve on toast.

Time.—About 20 minutes.   *Average cost.*—Seldom bought.

Sufficient 2 for a dish.

Seasonable from October to December.

THE QUAIL.—Quails are almost universally diffused over Europe, Asia, and Africa. Being birds of passage, they are seen in immense flocks, traversing the Mediterranean Sea from Europe to Africa, in the autumn, and returning again in the spring, frequently alighting in their passage on many of the islands of the Archipelago, which, with their vast numbers, they almost completely cover. On the western coasts of the kingdom of Naples, they have appeared in such prodigious numbers, that, within the compass of four or five miles, as many as a hundred thousand have been taken in a day. "From these circumstances," says a writer on natural history, "it appears highly probable that the quails which supplied the Israelites with food during their journey through the wilderness, were sent thither, on their passage

THE QUAIL.

to the north, by a wind from the south-west, sweeping over Egypt and Ethiopia towards the shores of the Red Sea." In England they are not very numerous, although they breed in it; and many of them are said to remain throughout the year, changing their quarters from the interior parts of the country for the seacoast.

TO DRESS SNIPES.

1047. INGREDIENTS.—Snipes, butter, flour, toast.

Mode.—These, like woodcocks, should be dressed without being drawn. Pluck, and wipe them outside, and truss them with the head under the wing, having previously skinned that and the neck. Twist the legs at the first joint, press the feet upon the thighs, and pass a skewer through these and the body. Place four on a skewer, tie them on to the jack or spit, and roast before a clear fire for about ¼ hour. Put some pieces of buttered

ROAST SNIPE.

toast into the dripping-pan to catch the trails; flour and froth the birds nicely, dish the pieces of toast with the snipes on them, and pour round, but not over them, a little good brown gravy. They should be sent to table very hot and expeditiously, or they will not be worth eating.

Time.—About ¼ hour. *Average cost*, 1s. 6d. to 2s. the brace.

Sufficient,—4 for a dish.

Seasonable from November to February.

Note.—Ortolans are trussed and dressed in the same manner.

THE SNIPE.—This is a migratory bird, and is generally distributed over Europe. It is found in most parts of England, in the high as well as the low lands, depending much on the weather. In very wet seasons it resorts to the hills, but at other times frequents marshes, where it can penetrate the earth with its bill, hunting for worms, which form its principal food. In the Hebrides and the Orkneys snipes are plentiful, and they are fattest in frosty weather. In the breeding season the snipe changes its note entirely from that which it has in the winter. The male will keep on wing for an hour together, mounting like a lark, and uttering a shrill piping noise; then, with a bleating sound, not unlike that made by an old goat, it will descend with great velocity, espe-

THE SNIPE.

cially if the female be sitting in her nest, from which it will not wander far.

ROAST TEAL.

1048. INGREDIENTS.—Teal, butter, a little flour.

Mode.—Choose fat plump birds, after the frost has set in, as they are generally better flavoured; truss them in the same manner as wild duck, No. 1022; roast them before a brisk fire, and keep them well basted. Serve with brown or orange gravy, water-cresses, and a cut lemon. The remains of teal make excellent hash.

Time.—From 9 to 15 minutes.

Average cost, 1s. each; but seldom bought.

Sufficient,—2 for a dish.

Seasonable from October to February.

ROAST HAUNCH OF VENISON.

1049. INGREDIENTS. — Venison, coarse flour-and-water paste, a little flour.

Mode.—Choose a haunch with clear, bright, and thick fat, and the cleft of the hoof smooth and close; the greater quantity of fat there is, the better quality will the meat be. As many people object to venison when it has too much *haut goût*, ascertain how long it has been kept, by running a sharp skewer into the meat close to the bone: when this is withdrawn, its sweetness can be judged of. With care and attention, it will keep good a fortnight, unless the weather is very mild. Keep it perfectly dry by wiping it with clean cloths till not the least damp remains, and sprinkle over powdered ginger or pepper, as a preventative against the fly. When required for use, wash it in warm water, and *dry* it *well* with a cloth; butter a sheet of white

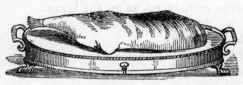

paper, put it over the fat, lay a coarse paste, about ⅓ inch in thickness, over this, and then a sheet or two of strong paper. Tie the whole firmly on to the haunch with twine, and put the joint down to a strong

ROAST HAUNCH OF VENISON.

close fire; baste the venison immediately, to prevent the paper and string from burning, and continue this operation, without intermission, the whole of the time it is cooking. About 20 minutes before it is done, carefully remove the paste and paper, dredge the joint with flour, and baste well with *butter* until it is nicely frothed, and of a nice pale-brown colour; garnish the knuckle-bone with a frill of white paper, and serve with a good, strong, but unflavoured gravy, in a tureen, and currant jelly; or melt the jelly with a little port wine, and serve that also in a tureen. As the principal object in roasting venison is to preserve the fat, the above is the best mode of doing so where expense is not objected to; but, in ordinary cases, the paste may be dispensed with, and a double paper placed over the roast instead: it will not require so long cooking without the paste. Do not omit to send very hot plates to table, as the venison fat so soon freezes: to be thoroughly enjoyed by epicures, it should be eaten on hot-water plates. The neck and shoulder may be roasted in the same manner.

Time.—A large haunch of buck venison, with the paste, 4 to 5 hours; haunch of doe venison, 3¼ to 3¾ hours. Allow less time without the paste.

Average cost, 1s. 4d. to 1s. 6d. per lb.

Sufficient for 18 persons.

Seasonable.—Buck venison in greatest perfection from June to Michaelmas; doe venison from November to the end of January.

THE DEER.—This active tribe of animals principally inhabit wild and woody regions. In their contentions, both with each other and the rest of the brute creation, these animals not only use their horns, but strike very furiously with their fore feet. Some of the species are employed as beasts of draught, whilst the flesh of the whole is wholesome, and that of some of the kinds, under the name of " venison," is considered very delicious. Persons fond of hunting have invented peculiar terms by which the objects of their pursuit are characterized : thus the stag is called, the first year, a *calf,* or *hind-calf;* the second, a *knobber;* the third, a *brock;* the fourth, a *staggard;* the fifth, a *stag;* and the sixth, a *hart.* The female is, the first year, called a *calf;* the second, a *hearse;* and the third, a *hind.* In Britain, the stag has become scarcer than it formerly was ; but, in the High-lands of Scotland, herds of four or five hundred may still be seen, ranging over the vast mountains of the north ; and some of the stags of a great size. In former times, the great feudal chieftains used to hunt with all the pomp of eastern sovereigns, assembling some thousands of their clans, who drove the deer into the toils, or to such stations as were occupied by their chiefs. As this sport, however, was occasionally used as a means for collecting their vassals together for the purpose of concocting rebellion, an act was passed prohibitory of such assemblages. In the "Waverley" of Sir Walter Scott, a deer-hunting scene of this kind is admirably described.

VENISON.—This is the name given to the flesh of some kinds of deer, and is esteemed as very delicious. Different species of deer are found in warm as well as cold climates, and are in several instances invaluable to man. This is especially the case with the Laplander, whose reindeer constitutes a large proportion of his wealth. There—

> " The reindeer unharness'd in freedom can play,
> And safely o'er Odin's steep precipice stray,
> Whilst the wolf to the forest recesses may fly,
> And howl to the moon as she glides through the sky."

In that country it is the substitute for the horse, the cow, the goat, and the sheep. From its milk is produced cheese ; from its skin, clothing ; from its tendons, bowstrings and thread ; from its horns, glue ; from its bones, spoons ; and its flesh furnishes food. In England we have the stag, an animal of great beauty, and much admired. He is a native of many parts of Europe, and is supposed to have been originally introduced into this country from France. About a century back he was to be found wild in some of the rough and mountainous parts of Wales, as well as in the forests of Exmoor, in Devonshire, and the woods on the banks of the Tamar. In the middle ages the deer formed food for the not over abstemious monks, as represented by Friar Tuck's larder, in the admirable fiction of "Ivanhoe;" and at a later period it was a deer-stealing adventure that drove the "ingenious" William Shakspeare to London, to become a common player, and the greatest dramatist that ever lived.

HASHED VENISON.

1050. INGREDIENTS.—The remains of roast venison, its own or mutton gravy, thickening of butter and flour.

Mode.—Cut the meat from the bones in neat slices, and, if there is sufficient of its own gravy left, put the meat into this, as it is prefer-able to any other. Should there not be enough, put the bones and trimmings into a stewpan, with about a pint of mutton gravy ; let them stew gently for an hour, and strain the gravy. Put a little flour and butter into the stewpan, keep stirring until brown, then add the strained gravy, and give it a boil up ; skim and strain again, and, when a little cool, put in the slices of venison. Place the stewpan by the side of the fire, and, when on the point of simmering, serve : do not allow it to boil, or the meat will be hard. Send red-currant jelly to table with it.

Time.—Altogether, 1½ hour.

Seasonable.—Buck venison, from June to Michaelmas ; doe venison, from November to the end of January.

Note.—A small quantity of Harvey's sauce, ketchup, or port wine, may be added to enrich the gravy: these ingredients must, however, be used very sparingly, or they will overpower the flavour of the venison.

THE FALLOW-DEER.—This is the domestic or park deer; and no two animals can make a nearer approach to each other than the stag and it, and yet no two animals keep more distinct, or avoid each other with a more inveterate animosity. They never herd or intermix together, and consequently never give rise to an intermediate race: it is even rare, unless they have been transported thither, to find fallow-deer in a

FALLOW-DEER (DOE).

FALLOW-DEER (BUCK).

country where stags are numerous. He is very easily tamed, and feeds upon many things which the stag refuses: he also browzes closer than the stag, and preserves his venison better. The doe produces one fawn, sometimes two, but rarely three. In short, they resemble the stag in all his natural habits, and the greatest difference between them is the duration of their lives: the stag, it is said, lives to the age of thirty-five or forty years, and the fallow-deer does not live more than twenty. As they are smaller than the stag, it is probable that their growth is sooner completed.

STEWED VENISON.

1051. INGREDIENTS.—A shoulder of venison, a few slices of mutton fat, 2 glasses of port wine, pepper and allspice to taste, 1½ pint of weak stock or gravy, ½ teaspoonful of whole pepper, ½ teaspoonful of whole allspice.

Mode.—Hang the venison till tender; take out the bone, flatten the meat with a rolling-pin, and place over it a few slices of mutton fat, which have been previously soaked for 2 or 3 hours in port wine; sprinkle these with a little fine allspice and pepper, roll the meat up, and bind and tie it securely. Put it into a stewpan with the bone and the above proportion of weak stock or gravy, whole allspice, black pepper, and port wine; cover the lid down closely, and simmer, very gently, from 3½ to 4 hours. When quite tender, take off the tape, and dish the meat; strain the gravy over it, and send it to table with red-currant jelly. Unless the joint is very fat, the above is the best mode of cooking it.

Time.—3½ to 4 hours.

Average cost, 1s. 4d. to 1s. 6d. per lb.

Sufficient for 10 or 12 persons.

Seasonable.—Buck venison, from June to Michaelmas; doe venison, from November to the end of January.

THE ROEBUCK.—This is the *Cervus capreolus*, or common roe, and is of a reddish-brown colour. It is an inhabitant of Asia, as well as of Europe. It has great grace in its

THE ROEBUCK.

movements, and stands about two feet seven inches high, and has a length of about three feet nine. The extent of its horns is from six to eight inches.

THE STAG.—The stag, or hart, is the male of the red deer, and the hind is the female. He is much larger than the fallow-deer, and his age is indicated by his horns, which are round instead of being palmated, like those of the fallow-deer. During the first year he has no horns, but a horny excrescence, which is short and rough, and covered with

THE HIND.

THE STAG.

a thin hairy skin. The next year, the horns are single and straight; and in the third they have two antlers, three the fourth, four the fifth, and five the sixth year; although this number is not always certain, for sometimes they are more, and often less. After the sixth year, the antlers do not always increase; and, although in number they may amount to six or seven on each side, yet the animal's age is then estimated rather by the size of the antlers and the thickness of the branch which sustains them, than by their variety. Large as these horns seem, however, they are shed every year, and their place supplied by new ones. This usually takes place in the spring. When the old horns have fallen off, the new ones do not make their appearance immediately; but the bones of the skull are seen covered with a transparent periosteum, or skin, which enwraps the bones of all animals. After a short time, however, the skin begins to swell, and to form a sort of tumour. From this, by-and-by, rising from the head, shoot forth the antlers from each side; and, in a short time, in proportion as the animal is in condition, the entire horns are completed. The solidity of the extremities, however, is not perfect until the horns have arrived at their full growth. Old stags usually shed their horns first, which generally happens towards the latter end of February or the beginning of March. Such as are between five and six years old shed them about the middle or latter end of March; those still younger in the month of April; and the youngest of all not till the middle or latter end of May. These rules, though generally true, are subject to variations; for a severe winter will retard the shedding of the horns.—The HIND has no horns, and is less fitted for being hunted than the male. She takes the greatest care of her young, and secretes them in the most obscure thickets, lest they become a prey to their numerous enemies. All the rapacious family of the cat kind, with the wolf, the dog, the eagle, and the falcon, are continually endeavouring to find her retreat, whilst the stag himself is the foe of his own offspring. When she has young, therefore, it would seem that the courage of the male is transferred to the female, for she defends them with the most resolute bravery. If pursued by the hunter, she will fly before the hounds for half the day, and then return to her young, whose life she has thus preserved at the hazard of her own.

THE NEW VENISON.—The deer population of our splendid English parks was, until a few years since, limited to two species, the fallow and the red. But as the fallow-deer itself was an acclimated animal, of comparatively recent introduction, it came to be a question why might not the proprietor of any deer-park in England have the luxury of at least half a dozen species of deer and antelopes, to adorn the hills, dales, ferny brakes, and rich pastures of his domain? The temperate regions of the whole world might be made to yield specimens of the noble ruminant, valuable either for their individual beauty, or for their availability to gastronomic purposes.

During the last four or five years a few spirited English noblemen have made the experiment of breeding foreign deer in their parks, and have obtained such a decided

ELAND (BULL).   ELAND (COW).

success, that it may be hoped their example will induce others to follow in a course which will eventually give to England's rural scenery a new element of beauty, and to English tables a fresh viand of the choicest character.

A practical solution of this interesting question was made by Viscount Hill, at Hawkestone Park, Salop, in January, 1859. On that occasion a magnificent eland, an acclimated scion of the species whose native home is the South African wilderness, was killed for the table. The noble beast was thus described:—" He weighed 1,176 lbs. as he dropped; huge as a short-horn, but with bone not half the size; active as a deer, stately in all his paces, perfect in form, bright in colour, with a vast dewlap, and strong sculptured horn. This eland in his lifetime strode majestic on the hill-side, where he dwelt with his mates and their progeny, all English-born, like himself." Three pairs of the same species of deer were left to roam at large on the picturesque slopes throughout the day, and to return to their home at pleasure. "Here, during winter, they are assisted with roots and hay, but in summer they have nothing but the pasture of the park; so that, in point of expense, they cost no more than cattle of the best description." Travellers and sportsmen say that the male eland is unapproached in the quality of his flesh by any ruminant in South Africa; that it grows to an enormous size, and lays on fat with as great facility as a true short-horn; while in texture and flavour it is infinitely superior. The lean is remarkably fine, the fat firm and delicate. It was tried in every fashion,—braised brisket, roasted ribs, broiled steaks, filet sauté, boiled aitchbone, &c.,—and in all, gave evidence of the fact, that a new meat of surpassing value had been added to the products of the English park.

When we hear such a gratifying account of the eland, it is pleasing to record that Lord Hastings has a herd of the Canadian wapiti, a herd of Indian nylghaus, and another of the small Indian hog-deer; that the Earl of Ducie has been successful in breeding the magnificent Persian deer. The eland was first acclimated in England by the late Earl of Derby, between the years 1835—1851, at his menagerie at Knowsley. On his death, in 1851, he bequeathed to the Zoological Society his breed of elands, consisting of two males and three females. Here the animals have been treated with the greatest success, and from the year 1853 to the present time, the females have regularly reproduced, without the loss of a single calf.

ROAST WIDGEON.

1052. INGREDIENTS.—Widgeons, a little flour, butter.

Mode.—These are trussed in the same manner as wild duck, No. 1022, but must not be kept so long before they are dressed. Put them down to a brisk fire; flour, and baste them continually with butter, and, when browned and nicely frothed, send them to table hot and quickly. Serve with brown gravy, or orange gravy, No. 488, and a cut lemon.

Time.—$\frac{1}{4}$ hour; if liked well done, 20 minutes.

Average cost, 1s. each; but seldom bought.

Sufficient,—2 for a dish.

Seasonable from October to February.

ROAST WOODCOCK.

1053. INGREDIENTS.—Woodcocks; butter, flour, toast.

Mode.—Woodcocks should not be drawn, as the trails are, by epicures, considered a great delicacy. Pluck, and wipe them well outside; truss them with the legs close to the body, and the feet pressing upon the thighs; skin the neck and head, and bring the beak round under the wing. Place some slices of toast in the dripping-pan to catch the trails, allowing a piece of toast for each bird. Roast before a clear fire from 15 to 25 minutes; keep them well basted, and flour and froth them nicely. When done, dish the pieces of toast with the birds upon them, and pour round a very little gravy; send some more to table in a tureen. These are most delicious birds when well cooked, but they should not be kept too long: when the feathers drop, or easily come out, they are fit for table.

ROAST WOODCOCK.

Time.—When liked underdone, 15 to 20 minutes; if liked well done, allow an extra 5 minutes.

Average cost.—Seldom bought.

Sufficient,—2 for a dish.

Seasonable from November to February.

THE WOODCOCK.—This bird being migratory in its habits, has, consequently, no settled habitation; it cannot be considered as the property of any one, and is, therefore, not game by law. It breeds in high northern lati-

THE WOODCOCK.

tudes, and the time of its appearance and disappearance in Sweden coincides exactly with that of its arrival in and return from Great Britain. On the coast of Suffolk its vernal and autumnal visits have been accurately observed. In the first week of October it makes its appearance in small numbers, but in November and December it appears in larger numbers, and always after sunset, and most gregariously. In the same manner as woodcocks take their leave of us, they quit France, Germany, and Italy, making the northern and colder climates their summer rendezvous. They visit Burgundy in the latter part of October, but continue there only a few weeks, the country being hard, and unable to supply them with such sustenance as they require. In the winter, they are found as far south as Smyrna and Aleppo, and, during the same season, in Barbary, where the Africans name them "the ass of the partridge." It has been asserted that they have been seen as far south as Egypt, which is the most remote region to which they can be traced on that side of the eastern world; on the other side, they are common in Japan. Those which resort to the countries of the Levant are supposed to come from the mountains of Armenia, or the deserts of Tartary or Siberia. The flesh of the woodcock is held in high estimation; hence the bird is eagerly sought after by the sportsman.

GAME CARVING.

BLACKCOCK.

1054. Skilful carving of game undoubtedly adds to the pleasure of the guests at a dinner-table; for game seems pre-eminently to be composed of such delicate limbs and tender flesh that an inapt practitioner appears to more disadvantage when mauling these pretty and favourite dishes, than larger and more robust *pièces de résistance*. As described at recipe No. 1019, this bird is variously served with or without the head on; and although we do not personally object to the appearance of the head as shown in the woodcut, yet it seems to be

BLACKCOCK.

more in vogue to serve it without. The carving is not difficult, but should be elegantly and deftly done. Slices from the breast, cut in the direction of the dotted line from 2 to 1, should be taken off, the merrythought displaced, and the leg and wing removed by running the knife along from 3 to 4, and following the directions given under the head of boiled fowl, No. 1000, reserving the thigh, which is considered a great delicacy, for the most honoured guests, some of whom may also esteem the brains of this bird.

WILD DUCK.

1055. As game is almost universally served as a dainty, and not as a dish to stand the assaults of an altogether fresh appetite, these dishes are not usually cut up entirely, but only those parts are served of each, which are considered the best-flavoured and the primest. Of wild-fowl, the breast alone is considered by epicures worth eat-

WILD DUCK.

ing, and slices are cut from this, in the direction indicated by the lines, from 1 to 2 ; if necessary, the leg and wing can be taken off by passing the knife from 3 to 4, and by generally following the directions described for carving boiled fowl, No. 1000.

ROAST HARE.

1056. The " Grand Carver " of olden times, a functionary of no ordinary dignity, was pleased when he had a hare to manipulate, for his skill and grace had an opportunity of display. *Diners à la Russe* may possibly, erewhile, save modern gentlemen the necessity of learning the art which was in auld lang syne one of the necessary accomplishments of the youthful squire ; but, until

ROAST HARE.

side-tables become universal, or till we see the office of " grand carver " once more instituted, it will be well for all to learn how to assist at the carving of this dish, which, if not the most elegant in appearance, is a very general favourite. The hare, having its head to the left, as shown in the woodcut, should be first served by cutting slices from each side of the backbone, in the direction of the lines from 3 to 4. After these prime parts are disposed of, the leg should next be disengaged by cutting round the line indicated by the figures 5 to 6. The shoulders will then be taken off by passing the knife round from 7 to 8. The back of the hare should now be divided by cutting quite through its spine, as shown by the line 1 to 2, taking care to feel with the point of the knife for a joint where the back may be readily penetrated. It is the usual plan not to serve any bone in helping hare ; and thus the flesh should be sliced from the legs and placed alone on the plate. In large establishments, and where men-cooks are kept, it is often the case that the backbone of the hare, especially in old animals, is taken out, and then the process of carving is, of course, considerably facilitated. A great point to be remembered in connection with carving hare is, that plenty of gravy should accompany each helping; otherwise this dish, which is naturally dry, will lose half its flavour, and so become a failure. Stuffing is also served with it; and the ears, which should be nicely crisp, and the brains of the hare, are esteemed as delicacies by many connoisseurs.

PARTRIDGES.

1057. There are several ways of carving this most familiar game bird. The more usual and summary mode is to carry the knife

ROAST PARTRIDGES.

sharply along the top of the breastbone of the bird, and cut it quite through, thus dividing it into two precisely equal and similar parts, in the same manner as carving a pigeon, No. 1003. Another plan is to cut it into three pieces; viz., by severing a small wing and leg on either side from the body, by following the line 1 to 2 in the upper woodcut; thus making 2 helpings, when the breast will remain for a third plate. The most elegant manner is that of thrusting back the body from the legs, and then cutting through the breast in the direction shown by the line 1 to 2: this plan will give 4 or more small helpings. A little bread-sauce should be served to each guest.

GROUSE.

1058. GROUSE may be carved in the way first described in carving partridge. The backbone of the grouse is highly esteemed by many, and this part of many game birds is considered the finest flavoured.

PHEASANT.

1059. Fixing the fork in the breast, let the carver cut slices from it in the direction of the lines from 2 to 1: these are the prime pieces. If

ROAST PHEASANT.

there be more guests to satisfy than these slices will serve, then let the legs and wings be disengaged in the same manner as described in carving boiled fowl, No. 1000, the point where the wing joins the neckbone being carefully found. The merrythought will come off in the same way as that of a fowl. The most valued parts are the same as those which are most considered in a fowl.

SNIPE.

1060. One of these small but delicious birds may be given, whole, to a gentleman; but, in helping a lady, it will be better to cut them quite through the centre, from 1 to 2, completely dividing them into equal and like portions, and put only one half on the plate.

SNIPE.

HAUNCH OF VENISON.

1061. Here is a grand dish for a knight of the carving-knife to exercise his skill upon, and, what will be pleasant for many to know, there is but little difficulty in the performance. An incision being made completely down to the bone, in the direction of the line 1 to 2, the gravy will then be able easily to flow; when slices, not too thick,

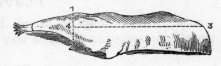

HAUNCH OF VENISON.

should be cut along the haunch, as indicated by the line 4 to 3; that end of the joint marked 3 having been turned towards the carver, so that he may have a more complete command over the joint. Although some epicures affect to believe that some parts of the haunch are superior to others, yet we doubt if there is any difference between the slices cut above and below the line. It should be borne in mind to serve each guest with a portion of fat; and the most expeditious carver will be the best carver; as, like mutton, venison soon begins to chill, when it loses much of its charm.

WOODCOCK.

1062. This bird, like a partridge, may be carved by cutting it exactly into two like portions, or made into three helpings, as described in carving partridge (No. 1057). The backbone is considered the tit-bit of a woodcock, and by many the thigh is also thought a great delicacy. This bird is served in the manner advised by Brillat Savarin, in connection with the pheasant, viz., on toast which has received its drippings whilst roasting; and a piece of this toast should invariably accompany each plate.

WOODCOCK.

LANDRAIL.

1063. LANDRAIL, being trussed like Snipe, with the exception of its being drawn, may be carved in the same manner.—See No. 1060.

PTARMIGAN.

1064. PTARMIGAN, being of much the same size, and trussed in the same manner, as the red-bird, may be carved in the manner described in Partridge and Grouse carving, Nos. 1057 and 1058.

QUAILS.

1065. QUAILS, being trussed and served like Woodcock, may be similarly carved.—See No. 1062.

PLOVERS.

1066. PLOVERS may be carved like Quails or Woodcock, being trussed and served in the same way as those birds.—See No. 1055.

TEAL.

1067. TEAL, being of the same character as Widgeon and Wild Duck, may be treated, in carving, in the same style.

WIDGEON.

1068. WIDGEON may be carved in the same way as described in regard to Wild Duck, at No. 1055.

CHAPTER XXIV.

GENERAL OBSERVATIONS ON VEGETABLES.

"Strange there should be found
Who, self-imprison'd in their proud saloons,
Renounce the odours of the open field
For the unscented fictions of the loom ;
Who, satisfied with only pencilled scenes,
Prefer to the performance of a God,
Th' inferior wonders of an artist's hand !
Lovely, indeed, the mimic works of art,
But Nature's works far lovelier."—COWPER.

1069. "THE ANIMAL AND VEGETABLE KINGDOMS," says Hogg, in his Natural History of the Vegetable Kingdom, "may be aptly compared to the primary colours of the prismatic spectrum, which are so gradually and intimately blended, that we fail to discover where the one terminates and where the other begins. If we had to deal with yellow and blue only, the eye would easily distinguish the one from the other ; but when the two are blended, and form green, we cannot tell where the blue ends and the yellow begins. And so it is in the animal and vegetable kingdoms. If our powers of observation were limited to the highest orders of animals and plants, if there were only mammals, birds, reptiles, fishes, and insects in the one, and trees, shrubs, and herbs in the other, we should then be able with facility to define the bounds of the two kingdoms ; but as we descend the scale of each, and arrive at the lowest forms of animals and plants, we there meet with bodies of the simplest structure, sometimes a mere cell, whose organization, modes of development and reproduction, are so anomalous, and partake so much of the character of both, that we cannot distinguish whether they are plants or whether they are animals."

1070. WHILST IT IS THUS DIFFICULT TO DETERMINE where the animal begins and the vegetable ends, it is as difficult to account for many of the singularities by which numbers of plants are characterized. This, however, can hardly be regarded as a matter of surprise, when we recollect that, so far as it is at present known, the vegetable kingdom is composed of upwards of 92,000 species of plants. Of this amazing number the lichens and the mosses are of the simplest and hardiest kinds. These, indeed, may be considered as the very creators of the soil : they thrive in the coldest and most sterile regions, many of them commencing the operations of nature in the growth of vegetables on the barest rocks, and receiving no other nourishment than such as may be supplied to them by the simple elements of air and rain. When they have exhausted their period in such situations as have been assigned them, they pass into a state of decay, and become changed into a very fine mould, which, in the active spontaneity of nature, immediately begins to produce other species, which in their turn become food for various mosses, and also rot. This process of growth and decay, being, from time to time, continued, by-and-by forms a soil sufficient for the maintenance of larger plants, which also die and decay, and so increase the soil, until it becomes deep enough to sustain an oak, or even the weight of a tropical forest. To create soil amongst rocks, however, must not be considered as the only end of the lichen ; different kinds of it minister to the elegant arts, in the form of beautiful dyes ; thus the *lichen rocella* is used to communicate to silk and wool, various shades of purple and crimson, which greatly enhance the value of these materials. This species is chiefly imported from the Canary Islands, and, when scarce, as an article of commerce has brought as much as £1,000 per ton.

1071. IN THE VICINITY OF LICHENS, THE MUSCI, OR MOSSES, are generally to be found. Indeed, wherever vegetation can be sustained, there they are, affording protection to the roots and seeds of more delicate vegetables, and, by their spongy texture, retaining a moisture which preserves other plants from the withering drought of summer. But even in winter we find them enlivening, by their verdure, the cold bosom of Nature. We see them abounding in our pastures and our woods, attaching themselves to the living, and still more abundantly to the dead, trunks and branches of trees. In marshy places they also abound, and become the medium of their conversion into fruitful fields. This is exemplified by the manner in which peat-mosses are formed : on the surface of these we find them in a state of great life and vigour ; immediately below we discover them, more or less, in a state of decomposition ; and, still deeper, we find their stems and branches consolidated into a light brown peat. Thus are extensive tracts formed, ultimately to be brought into a state of cultivation, and rendered subservient to the wants of man.

1072. WHEN NATURE HAS FOUND A SOIL, her next care is to perfect the growth of her seeds, and then to disperse them. Whilst the seed remains confined in its capsule, it cannot answer its purpose ; hence, when it is sufficiently ripe, the pericardium opens, and lets it out. What must strike every observer with surprise is, how nuts and shells, which we can hardly crack with our teeth, or even with a hammer, will divide of themselves, and make way for the little tender sprout which proceeds from the kernel. There are instances, it is said, such as in the Touch-me-not (*impatiens*), and the Cuckooflower (*cardamine*), in which the seed-vessels, by an elastic jerk at the moment of their explosion, cast the seeds to a distance. We are all aware, however, that many seeds—those of the most composite flowers, as of the thistle and dandelion—are endowed with, what have not been inappropriately called, wings. These consist of a beautiful silk-looking down, by which they are enabled to float in the air, and to be transported, sometimes, to considerable distances from the parent plant that produced them. The swelling of this downy tuft within the seed-vessel is the means by which the seed is enabled to overcome the resistance of its coats, and to force for itself a passage by which it escapes from its little prison-house.

1073. BIRDS, AS WELL AS QUADRUPEDS, are likewise the means of dispersing the seeds of plants, and placing them in situations where they ultimately grow. Amongst the latter is the squirrel, which is an extensive planter of oaks ; nay, it may be regarded as having, in some measure, been one of the creators of the British navy. We have read of a gentleman who was walking one day in some woods belonging to the Duke of Beaufort, near Troy House, in Monmouthshire, when his attention was arrested by a squirrel, sitting very composedly upon the ground. He stopped to observe its motions, when, in a short time, the little animal suddenly quitted its position, and darted to the top of the tree beneath which it had been sitting. In an instant it returned with an acorn in its mouth, and with its paws began to burrow in the earth. After digging a small hole, it therein deposited an acorn, which it hastily covered, and then darted up the tree again. In a moment it was down with another, which it buried in the same manner ; and so continued its labour, gathering and burying, as long as the gentleman had patience to watch it. This industry in the squirrel is an instinct which directs it to lay up a store of provision for the winter ; and as it is probable that its memory is not sufficiently retentive to enable it to recollect all the spots in which it deposits its acorns, it no doubt makes some slips in the course of the season, and loses some of them. These few spring up, and are, in time, destined to supply the place of the parent tree. Thus may the sons of Britain, in some degree, consider themselves to be indebted to the industry and defective memory of this little animal for the production of some of those " wooden walls " which have, for centuries, been the national pride, and which have so long " braved the battle and the breeze " on the broad bosom of the great deep, in every quarter of the civilized globe. As with the squirrel, so with jays and pies, which plant among the grass and moss, horse-beans, and probably forget where they have secreted them. Mr. White, the naturalist, says, that both horse-beans and peas sprang up in his field-walks in the autumn ; and he attributes the sowing of them to birds. Bees, he also observes, are much the best setters of cucumbers. If they do not happen to take kindly to the frames, the best way is to tempt them by a little honey put on the male and female bloom. When they are once induced to haunt the frames, they set all the fruit, and will hover with impatience round the lights in a morning till the glasses are opened.

1074. SOME OF THE ACORNS PLANTED BY THE SQUIRREL OF MONMOUTHSHIRE may be now in a fair way to become, at the end of some centuries, venerable trees ; for not the least remarkable quality of oaks is the strong principle of life with which they are endued. In Major Rooke's " Sketch of the Forest of Sherwood " we find it stated that, on some timber cut down in Berkland and Bilhaugh, letters were found stamped in the bodies of the trees, denoting the king's reign in which they were marked. The bark appears to have been cut off, and then the letters to have been cut in, and the next year's wood to have grown over them without adhering to where the bark had been cut out. The ciphers were found to be of James I., William and Mary, and one of King John. One of the ciphers of James was about one foot within the tree, and one foot from the centre. It was cut down in 1786. The tree must have been two feet in diameter, or two yards in circumference, when the mark was cut. A tree of this size is generally estimated at 120 years' growth; which number being subtracted from the middle year of the reign of James, would carry the year back to 1492, which would be about the period of its being planted. The tree with the cipher of William and Mary displayed its mark about nine inches within the tree, and three feet three inches from the centre. This tree was felled in 1786. The cipher of John was eighteen inches within the tree, and rather more than a foot from the centre. The middle year of the reign of that monarch was 1207. By subtracting from this 120, the number of years requisite for a tree's growth to arrive at the diameter of two feet, the date of its being planted would seem to have been 1085, or about twenty years after the Conquest.

1075. CONSIDERING THE GREAT ENDURANCE OF THESE TREES, we are necessarily led to inquire into the means by which they are enabled to arrive at such strength and maturity ; and whether it may be considered as a humiliation we will not determine, but, with all the ingenious mechanical contrivances of man, we are still unable to define the limits of the animal and vegetable kingdoms. " Plants have been described by naturalists, who would determine the limits of the two kingdoms, as organized living bodies, without volition or locomotion, destitute of a mouth or intestinal cavity, which, when detached from their place of growth, die, and, in decay, ferment, but do not putrefy, and which, on being subjected to analysis, furnish an excess of carbon and no nitrogen. The powers of chemistry, and of the microscope, however, instead of confirming these views, tend more and more to show that a still closer affinity exists between plants and animals ; for it is now ascertained that nitrogen, which was believed to be present only in animals, enters largely into the composition of plants also. When the microscope is brought to aid our powers of observation, we find that there are organized bodies belonging to the vegetable kingdom which possess very evident powers of locomotion, and which change about in so very remarkable a manner, that no other cause than that of volition can be assigned to it." Thus it would seem that, in this particular at least, some vegetables bear a very close resemblance to animal life; and when we consider the manner in which they are supplied with nourishment, and perform the functions of their existence, the resemblance would seem still closer. If, for example, we take a thin transverse slice of the stem of any plant, or a slice cut across its stem, and immerse it in a little pure water, and place it under a microscope, we will find that it consists principally of cells, more or less regular, and resembling those of a honeycomb,

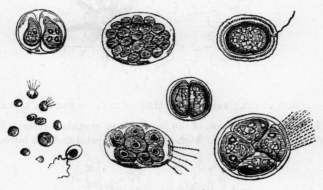

CELLULAR DEVELOPMENT.

or a network of cobweb. The size of these varies in different plants, as it does in different parts of the same plant, and they are sometimes so minute as to require a million to cover a square inch of surface. This singular structure, besides containing water and air, is the repository or storehouse of various secretions. Through it, the sap, when produced, is diffused sideways through the plant, and by it numerous changes are effected in the juices which fill its cells. The forms of the cells are various; they are also subject to various transformations. Sometimes a number of cylindrical cells are laid end to end, and, by the absorption of the transverse partitions, form a continuous tube, as in the sap-vessels of plants, or in muscular and nervous fibre; and when cells are thus woven together, they are called cellular tissue, which, in the human body, forms a fine net-like membrane, enveloping or connecting most of its structures. In pulpy fruits, the cells may be easily separated one from the other; and within the cells are smaller cells, commonly known as pulp. Among the cell-contents of some plants are beautiful crystals, called *raphides*. The term is derived from ῥαφις, a *needle*, on account of the resemblance of the crystal to a needle. They are composed of the phosphate and oxalate of lime ; but there is great difference of opinion as to their use in the economy of the plant, and one of the French philosophers endeavoured to prove that crys-

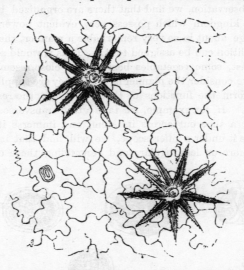

SILICEOUS CUTICLE FROM UNDER-SIDE OF LEAF OF DEUTZIA SCABRA.

tals are the possible transition of the inorganic to organic matter. The differences, however, between the highest form of crystal and the lowest form of

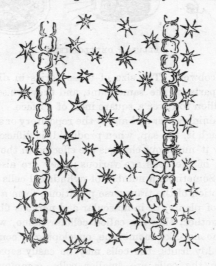

SILICEOUS CUTICLE OF GRASS.

organic life known, viz., a simple reproductive cell, are so manifold and striking, that the attempt to make crystals the bridge over which inorganic matter passes into organic, is almost totally regarded as futile. In a layer of an onion, a fig, a section of garden rhubarb, in some species of aloe, in the bark of many trees, and in portions of the cuticle of the medicinal squill, bundles of these needle-shaped crystals are to be found. Some of them are as large as 1-40th of an inch, others are as small as the 1-1000th. They are found in all parts of the plant,—in the stem, bark, leaves, stipules, petals, fruit, roots, and even in the pollen, with some few exceptions, and they are always situated in the interior of cells. Some plants, as many of the *cactus* tribe, are made up almost entirely of these needle-crystals; in some instances, every cell of the cuticle contains a stellate mass of crystals; in others, the whole interior is full of them, rendering the plant so exceedingly brittle, that the least touch will occasion a fracture; so much so, that some specimens of *Cactus senilis*, said to be a thousand years old, which were sent a few years since to Kew, from South America, were obliged to be packed in cotton, with all the care of the most delicate jewellery, to preserve them during transport.

1076. BESIDES THE CELLULAR TISSUE, there is what is called a vascular system, which consists of another set of small vessels. If, for example, we, early in the spring, cut a branch transversely, we will perceive the sap oozing out from numerous points over the whole of the divided surface, except on that part occupied by the pith and the bark; and if a twig, on which the leaves are already unfolded, be cut from the tree, and placed with its cut end in a watery solution of Brazil-wood, the colouring matter will be found to ascend into the leaves and to the top of the twig. In both these cases, a close examination with a powerful microscope, will discover the sap perspiring from the divided portion of the stem, and the colouring matter rising through real tubes to the top of the twig: these are the sap or conducting vessels of the plant. If, however, we examine a transverse section of the vine, or of any other tree, at a later period of the season, we find that the wood is apparently dry, whilst the bark, particularly that part next the wood, is swelled with fluid. This is contained in vessels of a different kind from those in which the sap rises. They are found in the *bark* only in trees, and may be called returning vessels, from their carrying the sap downwards after its preparation in the leaf. It is believed that the passage of the sap in plants is conducted in a manner precisely similar to that of the blood in man, from the regular contraction and expansion of the vessels; but, on account of their extreme minuteness, it is almost an impossibility to be certain upon this point. Numerous observations made with the microscope show that their diameter seldom exceeds a 290th part of a line, or a 3,000th part of an inch. Leuwenhoeck reckoned 20,000 vessels in a morsel of oak about one nineteenth of an inch square.

1077. IN THE VASCULAR SYSTEM OF A PLANT, we at once see the great analogy which it bears to the veins and arteries in the human system; but neither it, nor the cellular tissue combined, is all that is required to perfect the production of a vegetable. There is, besides, a tracheal system, which is composed of very minute elastic spiral tubes, designed for the purpose of conveying air both to and from the plant. There are also fibres, which consist of collections of these cells and vessels closely united together. These form the root and the stem. If we attempt to cut them transversely, we meet with difficulty, because we have to force our way across the tubes, and break them; but if we slit the wood lengthwise, the vessels are separated without breaking. The layers of wood, which appear in the stem or branch of a tree cut transversely, consist of different zones of fibres, each the produce of one year's growth, and separated by a coat of cellular tissue, without which they could not be well distinguished. Besides all these, there is the cuticle, which extends over every part of the plant, and covers the bark with three distinct coats. The *liber*, or inner bark, is said to be formed of hollow tubes, which convey the sap downwards to increase the solid diameter of the tree.

1078. THE ROOT AND THE STEM NOW DEMAND A SLIGHT NOTICE. The former is designed, not only to support the plant by fixing it in the soil, but also to fulfil the functions of a channel for the conveyance of nourishment: it is therefore furnished with pores, or spongioles, as they are called, from their resemblance to a sponge, to suck up whatever comes within its reach. It is found in a variety of forms, and hence its adaptation to a great diversity of soils and circumstances. We have heard of a willow-tree being dug up and its head planted where its roots were, and these suffered to spread out in the air like naked branches. In course of time, the roots became branches, and the branches roots, or rather, roots rose from the branches beneath the ground, and branches shot from the roots above. Some roots last one year, others two, and others, like the shrubs and trees which they produce, have an indefinite period of existence; but they all consist of a collection of fibres, composed of vascular and cellular tissue, without tracheæ, or breathing-vessels. The stem is the grand distributor of the nourishment taken up by the roots, to the several parts of the plant. The seat of its vitality is said to be in the point or spot called the neck, which separates the stem from the root. If the root of a young plant be cut off, it will shoot out afresh; if even the stem be taken away, it will be renewed; but if this part be injured, the plant will assuredly die.

1079. IN ACCORDANCE WITH THE PLAN OF THIS WORK, special notices of culinary vegetables will accompany the various recipes in which they are spoken of; but here we cannot resist the opportunity of declaring it as our conviction, that he or she who introduces a useful or an ornamental plant into our island, ought justly to be considered, to a large extent, a benefactor to the country. No one can calculate the benefits which may spring from this very vegetable, after its qualities have become thoroughly known. If viewed in no other light, it is pleasing to consider it as bestowing upon us a share of the blessings of other climates, and enabling us to participate in the luxury which a more genial sun has produced.

RECIPES.

CHAPTER XXV.

BOILED ARTICHOKES.

1080. INGREDIENTS.—To each ½ gallon of water, allow 1 heaped tablespoonful of salt, a piece of soda the size of a shilling ; artichokes.

Mode.—Wash the artichokes well in several waters ; see that no insects remain about them, and trim away the leaves at the bottom. Cut off the stems and put them into *boiling* water, to which have been added salt and soda in the above proportion. Keep the saucepan uncovered, and let them boil quickly until tender ; ascertain when they are done by thrusting a fork in them, or by trying if the leaves can be easily removed. Take them out, let them drain for a minute or two, and serve in a napkin, or with a little

ARTICHOKES.

white sauce poured over. A tureen of melted butter should accompany them. This vegetable, unlike any other, is considered better for being gathered two or three days ; but they must be well soaked and washed previous to dressing.

Time.—20 to 25 minutes, after the water boils.

Sufficient,—a dish of 5 or 6 for 4 persons.

Seasonable from July to the beginning of September.

THE COMPOSITÆ, OR COMPOSITE FLOWERS.—This family is so extensive, as to contain nearly a twelfth part of the whole of the vegetable kingdom. It embraces about 9,000 species, distributed over almost every country ; and new discoveries are constantly being made and added to the number. Towards the poles their numbers diminish, and slightly, also, towards the equator ; but they abound in the tropical and sub-tropical islands, and in the tracts of continent not far from the seashore. Among esculent vegetables, the Lettuce, Salsify, Scorzonera, Cardoon, and Artichoke belong to the family.

CARDOON ARTICHOKE.

FRIED ARTICHOKES.

(Entremets, or Small Dish to be served with the Second Course.)

1081. INGREDIENTS.—5 or 6 artichokes, salt and water : for the batter,—¼ lb. of flour, a little salt, the yolk of 1 egg, milk.

Mode.—Trim and boil the artichokes by recipe No. 1080, and rub them over with lemon-juice, to keep them white. When they are quite tender, take them up, remove the chokes, and divide the bottoms; dip each piece into batter, fry them in hot lard or dripping, and garnish the dish with crisped parsley. Serve with plain melted butter.

Time.—20 minutes to boil the artichokes, 5 to 7 minutes to fry them.
Sufficient,—5 or 6 for 4 or 5 persons.
Seasonable from July to the beginning of September.

A FRENCH MODE OF COOKING ARTICHOKES.

1082. INGREDIENTS.—5 or 6 artichokes; to each ½ gallon of water allow 1 heaped tablespoonful of salt, ¼ teaspoonful of pepper, 1 bunch of savoury herbs, 2 oz. of butter.

Mode.—Cut the ends of the leaves, as also the stems; put the artichokes into boiling water, with the above proportion of salt, pepper, herbs, and butter; let them boil quickly until tender, keeping the lid of the saucepan off, and when the leaves come out easily, they are cooked enough. To keep them a beautiful green, put a large piece of cinder into a muslin bag, and let it boil with them. Serve with plain melted butter.

Time.—20 to 25 minutes.
Sufficient,—5 or 6 sufficient for 4 or 5 persons.
Seasonable from July to the beginning of September.

ARTICHOKES A L'ITALIENNE.

1083. INGREDIENTS.—4 or 5 artichokes, salt and butter, about ½ pint of good gravy.

Mode.—Trim and cut the artichokes into quarters, and boil them until tender in water mixed with a little salt and butter. When done, drain them well, and lay them all round the dish, with the leaves outside. Have ready some good gravy, highly flavoured with mushrooms; reduce it until quite thick, and pour it round the artichokes, and serve.

Time.—20 to 25 minutes to boil the artichokes.
Sufficient for one side-dish.
Seasonable from July to the beginning of September.

CONSTITUENT PROPERTIES OF THE ARTICHOKE.—According to the analysis of Braconnet, the constituent elements of an artichoke are,—starch 30, albumen 10, uncrystallizable sugar 148, gum 12, fixed oil 1, woody fibre 12, inorganic matter 27, and water 770.

BOILED JERUSALEM ARTICHOKES.

1084. INGREDIENTS.—To each ½ gallon of water allow 1 heaped tablespoonful of salt; artichokes.

Mode.—Wash, peel, and shape the artichokes in a round or oval form, and put them into a saucepan with sufficient *cold* water to cover them, salted in the above proportion. Let them boil gently until tender; take them up, drain them, and serve them in a napkin, or plain, whichever mode is preferred; send to table with them a tureen of melted butter or cream sauce, a little of which may be poured over the artichokes when they are *not* served in a napkin.

JERUSALEM ARTICHOKES.

Time.—About 20 minutes after the water boils.

Average cost, 2*d.* per lb.

Sufficient,—10 for a dish for 6 persons.

Seasonable from September to June.

USES OF THE JERUSALEM ARTICHOKE.—This being a tuberous-rooted plant, with leafy stems from four to six feet high, it is alleged that its tops will afford as much fodder per acre as a crop of oats, or more, and its roots half as many tubers as an ordinary crop of potatoes. The tubers, being abundant in the market-gardens, are to be had at little more than the price of potatoes. The fibres of the stems may be separated by maceration, and manufactured into cordage or cloth; and this is said to be done in some parts of the north and west of France, as about Hagenau, where this plant, on the poor sandy soils, is an object of field culture.

MASHED JERUSALEM ARTICHOKES.

1085. INGREDIENTS.—To each ½ gallon of water allow 1 oz. of salt; 15 or 16 artichokes, 1 oz. butter, pepper and salt to taste.

Mode.—Boil the artichokes as in the preceding recipe until tender; drain and press the water from them, and beat them up with a fork. When thoroughly mashed and free from lumps, put them into a saucepan with the butter and a seasoning of *white* pepper and salt; keep stirring over the fire until the artichokes are quite hot, and serve.

Time.—About 20 minutes. *Average cost,* 2*d.* per lb.

Sufficient for 6 or 7 persons.

Seasonable from September to June.

JERUSALEM ARTICHOKES WITH WHITE SAUCE.

(Entremets, or to be served with the Second Course as a Side-dish.)

1086. INGREDIENTS.—12 to 15 artichokes, 12 to 15 Brussels sprouts, ½ pint of white sauce, No. 538.

Mode.—Peel and cut the artichokes in the shape of a pear; cut a piece off the bottom of each, that they may stand upright in the dish, and boil them in salt and water until tender. Have ready ½ pint of white sauce, made by recipe No. 538; dish the artichokes, pour over them the sauce, and place between each a fine Brussels sprout: these should be boiled separately, and not with the artichokes.

Time.—About 20 minutes. *Average cost*, 2*d.* per lb.

Sufficient for 6 or 7 persons.

Seasonable from September to June.

THE JERUSALEM ARTICHOKE.—This plant is well known, being, for its tubers, cultivated not only as a garden vegetable, but also as an agricultural crop. By many it is much esteemed as an esculent, when cooked in various ways; and the domesticated animals eat both the fresh foliage and the tubers with great relish. By some, they are not only considered nourishing, but even fattening.

BOILED ASPARAGUS.

1087. INGREDIENTS.—To each ½ gallon of water allow 1 heaped tablespoonful of salt; asparagus.

Mode.—Asparagus should be dressed as soon as possible after it is cut, although it may be kept for a day or two by putting the stalks into cold water; yet, to be good, like every other vegetable, it cannot be cooked too fresh. Scrape the white part of the stems, *beginning* from the *head*, and throw them into cold water; then tie them into

ASPARAGUS ON TOAST.

ASPARAGUS TONGS.

bundles of about 20 each, keeping the heads all one way, and cut the stalks evenly, that they may all be the same length; put them into *boiling* water, with salt in the above proportion; keep them boiling quickly until tender, with the saucepan uncovered. When the asparagus is done, dish it upon toast, which should be dipped in the water it was cooked in, and leave the white ends outwards each way, with the points meeting in the middle. Serve with a tureen of melted butter.

Time.—15 to 18 minutes after the water boils.

Average cost, in full season, 2*s.* 6*d.* the 100 heads.

Sufficient.—Allow about 50 heads for 4 or 5 persons.

Seasonable.—May be had, forced, from January, but cheapest in May, June, and July.

ASPARAGUS.

ASPARAGUS.—This plant belongs to the variously-featured family of the order *Liliaceæ*, which, in the temperate regions of both hemispheres, are most abundant, and, between the tropics, gigantic in size and arborescent in form. Asparagus is a native of Great Britain, and is found on various parts of the seacoast, and in the fens of Lincolnshire. At Kynarve Cove, in Cornwall, there is an island called "Asparagus Island," from the abundance in which it is there found. The uses to which the young shoots are applied, and the manure in which they are cultivated in order to bring them to the highest state of excellence, have been a study with many kitchen-gardeners.

ASPARAGUS PEAS.

(Entremets, or to be served as a Side-dish with the Second Course.)

1088. INGREDIENTS.—100 heads of asparagus, 2 oz. of butter, a small bunch of parsley, 2 or 3 green onions, flour, 1 lump of sugar, the yolks of 2 eggs, 4 tablespoonfuls of cream, salt.

Mode.—Carefully scrape the asparagus, cut it into pieces of an equal size, avoiding that which is in the least hard or tough, and throw them into cold water. Then boil the asparagus in salt and water until three-parts done ; take it out, drain, and place it on a cloth to dry the moisture away from it. Put it into a stewpan with the butter, parsley, and onions, and shake over a brisk fire for 10 minutes. Dredge in a little flour, add the sugar, and moisten with boiling water. When boiled a short time and reduced, take out the parsley and onions, thicken with the yolks of 2 eggs beaten with the cream ; add a seasoning of salt, and, when the whole is on the point of simmering, serve. Make the sauce sufficiently thick to adhere to the vegetable.

Time.—Altogether, ½ hour. *Average cost,* 1s. 6d. a pint.

Seasonable in May, June, and July.

MEDICINAL USES OF ASPARAGUS.—This plant not only acts as a wholesome and nutritious vegetable, but also as a diuretic, aperient, and deobstruent. The chemical analysis of its juice discovers its composition to be a peculiar crystallizable principle, called asparagin, albumen, mannite, malic acid, and some salts. Thours says, the cellular tissue contains a substance similar to sago. The berries are capable of undergoing vinous fermentation, and affording alcohol by distillation. In their unripe state they possess the same properties as the roots, and probably in a much higher degree.

ASPARAGUS PUDDING.

(A delicious Dish, to be served with the Second Course.)

1089. INGREDIENTS.—½ pint of asparagus peas, 4 eggs, 2 tablespoonfuls of flour, 1 tablespoonful of *very finely* minced ham, 1 oz. of butter, pepper and salt to taste, milk.

Mode.—Cut up the nice green tender parts of asparagus, about the size of peas ; put them into a basin with the eggs, which should be well beaten, and the flour, ham, butter, pepper, and salt. Mix all these ingredients well together, and moisten with sufficient milk to make the pudding of the consistency of thick batter ; put it into a pint buttered mould, tie it down tightly with a floured cloth, place it in *boiling water*, and let it boil for 2 hours ; turn it out of the mould on to a hot dish, and pour plain melted butter *round,* but not over, the pudding. Green peas pudding may be made in exactly the same manner, substituting peas for the asparagus.

Time.—2 hours. *Average cost,* 1s. 6d. per pint.

Seasonable in May, June, and July.

BOILED FRENCH BEANS.

1090. INGREDIENTS.—To each ½ gallon of water allow 1 heaped tablespoonful of salt, a *very small* piece of soda.

Mode.—This vegetable should always be eaten young, as, when allowed to grow too long, it tastes stringy and tough when cooked. Cut off the heads and tails, and a thin strip on each side of the beans, to remove the strings. Then divide each bean into 4 or 6 pieces, according to size, cutting them lengthways in a slanting direction, and, as they are cut, put them into cold water, with a small quantity of salt dissolved in it. Have ready a saucepan of boiling water, with salt and soda in the above proportion; put in the beans, keep them boiling quickly, with the lid uncovered, and be careful that they do not get smoked. When tender,

SCARLET RUNNER.   which may be ascertained by their sinking to

the bottom of the saucepan, take them up, throw them into a colander; and when drained, dish and serve with plain melted butter. When very young, beans are sometimes served whole: when they are thus dressed, their colour and flavour are much better preserved; but the more general way of dressing them is to cut them into thin strips.

Time.—Very young beans, 10 to 12 minutes; moderate size, 15 to 20 minutes, after the water boils.

Average cost, in full season, 1s. 4d. a peck; but, when forced, very expensive.

Sufficient.—Allow ½ peck for 6 or 7 persons.

Seasonable from the middle of July to the end of September; but may be had, forced, from February to the beginning of June.

FRENCH MODE OF COOKING FRENCH BEANS.

1091. INGREDIENTS.—A quart of French beans, 3 oz. of fresh butter, pepper and salt to taste, the juice of ½ lemon.

Mode.—Cut and boil the beans by the preceding recipe, and when tender, put them into a stewpan, and shake over the fire, to dry away the moisture from the beans. When quite dry and hot, add the butter, pepper, salt, and lemon-juice; keep moving the stewpan, without using a spoon, as that would break the beans; and when the butter is melted, and all is thoroughly hot, serve. If the butter should not mix well, add a tablespoonful of gravy, and serve very quickly.

Time.—About ¼ hour to boil the beans; 10 minutes to shake them over the fire.

Average cost, in full season, about 1*s.* 4*d.* a peck.

Sufficient for 4 or 5 persons.

Seasonable from the middle of July to the end of September.

BOILED BROAD OR WINDSOR BEANS.

1092. INGREDIENTS.—To each ½ gallon of water, allow 1 heaped tablespoonful of salt; beans.

Mode.—This is a favourite vegetable with many persons, but to be nice, should be young and freshly gathered. After shelling the beans, put them into *boiling* water, salted in the above proportion, and let them boil rapidly until tender. Drain them well in a colander; dish, and serve with them separately a tureen of parsley and butter. Boiled bacon should always accompany this vegetable, but the beans should be cooked separately. It is usually served with the beans laid round, and the parsley and butter in a tureen. Beans also make an excellent garnish to a ham, and when used for this purpose, if very old, should have their skins removed.

BROAD BEAN.

Time.—Very young beans, 15 minutes; when of a moderate size, 20 to 25 minutes, or longer.

Average cost, unshelled, 6*d.* per peck.

Sufficient.—Allow one peck for 6 or 7 persons.

Seasonable in July and August.

NUTRITIVE PROPERTIES OF THE BEAN.—The produce of beans in meal is, like that of peas, more in proportion to the grain than in any of the cereal grasses. A bushel of beans is supposed to yield fourteen pounds more of flour than a bushel of oats; and a bushel of peas eighteen pounds more, or, according to some, twenty pounds. A thousand parts of bean flour were found by Sir H. Davy to yield 570 parts of nutritive matter, of which 426 were mucilage or starch, 103 gluten, and 41 extract, or matter rendered insoluble during the process.

BROAD BEANS A LA POULETTE.

1093. INGREDIENTS.—2 pints of broad beans, ½ pint of stock or broth, a small bunch of savoury herbs, including parsley, a small lump of sugar, the yolk of 1 egg, ¼ pint of cream, pepper and salt to taste.

Mode.—Procure some young and freshly-gathered beans, and shell sufficient to make 2 pints; boil them, as in the preceding recipe, until nearly done; then drain them and put them into a stewpan, with the stock, finely-minced herbs, and sugar. Stew the beans until perfectly tender, and the liquor has dried away a little; then beat up the yolk of an egg with the cream, add this to the beans, let the whole get thoroughly hot, and when on the point of simmering, serve. Should the beans be very large, the skin should be removed previously to boiling them.

Time.—10 minutes to boil the beans, 15 minutes to stew them in the stock.

Average cost, unshelled, 6*d.* per peck.

Seasonable in July and August.

ORIGIN AND VARIETIES OF THE BEAN.—This valuable plant is said to be a native of Egypt, but, like other plants which have been domesticated, its origin is uncertain. It has been cultivated in Europe and Asia from time immemorial, and has been long known in Britain. Its varieties may be included under two general heads,—the white, or garden beans, and the grey, or field beans. Of the former, sown in the fields, the mazagan and long-pod are almost the only sorts; of the latter, those known as the horse-bean, the small or ticks, and the prolific of Heligoland, are the principal sorts. New varieties are procured in the same manner as in other plants.

BOILED BEETROOT.

1094. INGREDIENTS.—Beetroot; boiling water.

Mode.—When large, young, and juicy, this vegetable makes a very excellent addition to winter salads, and may easily be converted into an economical and quickly-made pickle. (*See* No. 369.) Beetroot is more frequently served cold than hot: when the latter mode is preferred, melted butter should be sent to table with it. It may also be stewed with button onions, or boiled and served with roasted onions. Wash the beets thoroughly; but do not prick or break the skin before they are cooked, or they would lose their beautiful colour in boiling. Put them into boiling water, and let them boil until tender, keeping them well covered. If to be served hot, remove the peel quickly, cut the beetroot into thick slices, and send to table melted butter. For salads, pickle, &c., let the root cool, then peel, and cut it into slices.

Time.—Small beetroot, 1½ to 2 hours; large, 2½ to 3 hours.

Average cost, in full season, 2*d.* each.

Seasonable.—May be had at any time.

BEETROOT.

BEETROOT.—The geographical distribution of the order Saltworts (*Salsolaceæ*), to which beetroot belongs, is most common in extra-tropical and temperate regions, where they are common weeds, frequenting waste places, among rubbish, and on marshes by the seashore. In the tropics they are rare. They are characterized by the large quantity of mucilage, sugar, starch, and alkaline salts which are found in them. Many of them are used as potherbs, and some are emetic and vermifuge in their medicinal properties. The *root* of *garden* or red beet is exceedingly wholesome. and nutritious, and Dr. Lyon Playfair has recommended that a good brown bread may be made by rasping down this root with an equal quantity of flour. He says that the average quality of flour contains about 12 per cent. of azotized principles adapted for the formation of flesh, and the average quality of beet contains about 2 per cent. of the same materials.

BOILED BROCOLI.

1095. INGREDIENTS.—To each ½ gallon of water allow 1 heaped tablespoonful of salt ; brocoli.

Mode.—Strip off the dead outside leaves, and the inside ones cut off level with the flower ; cut off the stalk close at the bottom, and put the brocoli into cold salt and water, with the heads downwards. When they have remained in this for about ¾ hour, and they are *perfectly* free from insects, put them into a saucepan of *boiling* water, salted in the above

BOILED BROCOLI.

proportion, and keep them boiling quickly over a brisk fire, with the saucepan uncovered. Take them up with a slice the moment they are done ; drain them well, and serve with a tureen of melted butter, a *little* of which should be poured over the brocoli. If left in the water after it is done, it will break, its colour will be spoiled, and its crispness gone.

Time.—Small brocoli, 10 to 15 minutes ; large one, 20 to 25 minutes.

Average cost, 2*d.* each.

Sufficient,—2 for 4 or 5 persons.

Seasonable from October to March ; plentiful in February and March.

BROCOLI.

THE KOHL-RABI, OR TURNIP-CABBAGE.—This variety presents a singular development, inasmuch as the stem swells out like a large turnip on the surface of the ground, the leaves shooting from it all round, and the top being surmounted by a cluster of leaves issuing from it. Although not generally grown as a garden vegetable, if used when young and tender, it is wholesome, nutritious, and very palatable.

BOILED BRUSSELS SPROUTS.

1096. INGREDIENTS.—To each ½ gallon of water allow 1 heaped tablespoonful of salt ; a *very small* piece of soda.

Mode.—Clean the sprouts from insects, nicely wash them, and pick off any dead or discoloured leaves from the outsides ; put them into a saucepan of *boiling* water, with salt and soda in the above proportion ; keep the pan uncovered, and let them boil quickly over a brisk fire until tender ; drain, dish, and serve with a tureen of melted butter, or with a maître d'hôtel sauce poured over them. Another mode of serving is, when they are dished, to stir in about 1½ oz. of butter and a seasoning of pepper and salt. They must, however, be sent to table very quickly, as, being so very small, this vegetable soon cools. Where the cook is very expeditious, this vegetable, when cooked, may be arranged on the dish in the form of a pineapple, and, so served, has a very pretty appearance.

Time.—From 9 to 12 minutes after the water boils.

Average cost, 1s. 4d. per peck.

Sufficient.—Allow between 40 and 50 for 5 or 6 persons.

Seasonable from November to March.

SAVOYS AND BRUSSELS SPROUTS.—When the Green Kale, or Borecóle, has been advanced a step further in the path of improvement, it assumes the headed or hearting character, with blistered leaves; it is then known by the name of Savoys and Brussels Sprouts. Another of its headed forms, but with smooth glaucous leaves, is the cultivated Cabbage of our gardens (the *Borecole oleracea capitula* of science); and all its varieties of green, red, dwarf, tall, early, late, round, conical, flat, and all the forms into which it is possible to put it.

TO BOIL YOUNG GREENS OR SPROUTS.

1097. INGREDIENTS.—To each ½ gallon of water allow 1 heaped tablespoonful of salt; a *very small* piece of soda.

Mode.—Pick away all the dead leaves, and wash the greens well in cold water; drain them in a colander, and put them into fast-boiling water, with salt and soda in the above proportion. Keep them boiling quickly, with the lid uncovered, until tender; and the moment they are done, take them up, or their colour will be spoiled; when well drained, serve. The great art in cooking greens properly, and to have them a good colour, is to put them into *plenty* of *fast-boiling* water, to let them boil very quickly, and to take them up the moment they become tender.

BRUSSELS SPROUTS.

Time.—Brocoli sprouts, 10 to 12 minutes; young greens, 10 to 12 minutes; sprouts, 12 minutes, after the water boils.

Seasonable.—Sprouts of various kinds may be had all the year.

GREEN KALE, OR BORECOLE.—When Colewort, or Wild Cabbage, is brought into a state of cultivation, its character becomes greatly improved, although it still retains the loose open leaves, and in this form it is called Green Kale, or Borecole. The scientific name is *Borecole oleracea acephala,* and of it there are many varieties, both as regards the form and colour of the leaves, as well as the height which the plants attain. We may observe, that among them, are included the Thousand-headed, and the Cow or Tree Cabbage.

BOILED CABBAGE.

1098. INGREDIENTS.—To each ½ gallon of water allow 1 heaped tablespoonful of salt; a *very small* piece of soda.

Mode.—Pick off all the dead outside leaves, cut off as much of the stalk as possible, and cut the cabbages across twice, at the stalk end; if they should be very large, quarter them. Wash them well in cold water, place them in a colander, and drain; then put them into *plenty* of *fast-boiling* water, to which have been added salt and soda in the above proportions. Stir them down once or twice in the water, keep the pan uncovered, and let them boil quickly until tender. The instant they are done, take them up into a colander, place a plate over them, let them thoroughly drain, dish, and serve.

Time.—Large cabbages, or savoys, $\frac{1}{2}$ to $\frac{3}{4}$ hour, young summer cabbage, 10 to 12 minutes, after the water boils.

Average cost, 2d. each in full season.

Sufficient,—2 large ones for 4 or 5 persons.

Seasonable.—Cabbages and sprouts of various kinds at any time.

THE CABBAGE TRIBE; THEIR ORIGIN.—Of all the tribes of the *Cruciferæ* this is by far the most important. Its scientific name is *Brassiceæ*, and it contains a collection of plants which, both in themselves and their products, occupy a prominent position in agriculture, commerce, and domestic economy. On the cliffs of Dover, and in many places on the coasts of Dorsetshire, Cornwall, and Yorkshire, there grows a wild plant, with variously-indented, much-waved, and loose spreading leaves, of a sea-green colour, and large yellow flowers. In spring, the leaves of this plant are collected by the inhabitants, who, after boiling them in two waters, to remove the saltness, use them as a vegetable along with their meat. This is the *Brassica oleracea* of science, the Wild Cabbage, or Colewort, from which have originated all the varieties of Cabbage, Cauliflower, Greens, and Brocoli.

STEWED RED CABBAGE.

1099. INGREDIENTS.—1 red cabbage, a small slice of ham, $\frac{1}{2}$ oz. of fresh butter, 1 pint of weak stock or broth, 1 gill of vinegar, salt and pepper to taste, 1 tablespoonful of pounded sugar.

Mode.—Cut the cabbage into very thin slices, put it into a stewpan, with the ham cut in dice, the butter, $\frac{1}{2}$ pint of stock, and the vinegar; cover the pan closely, and let it stew for 1 hour. When it is very tender, add the remainder of the stock, a seasoning of salt and pepper, and the pounded sugar; mix all well together, stir over the fire until nearly all the liquor is dried away, and serve. Fried sausages are usually sent to table with this dish: they should be laid round and on the cabbage, as a garnish.

Time.—Rather more than 1 hour. *Average cost*, 4d. each.

Sufficient for 4 persons.

Seasonable from September to January.

THE WILD CABBAGE, OR COLEWORT.—This plant, as it is found on the sea-cliffs of England, presents us with the origin of the cabbage tribe in its simplest and normal form. In this state it is the true Collet, or Colewort, although the name is now applied to any young cabbage which has a loose and open heart.

BOILED CARROTS.

1100. INGREDIENTS.—To each $\frac{1}{2}$ gallon of water, allow 1 heaped tablespoonful of salt; carrots.

Mode.—Cut off the green tops, wash and scrape the carrots, and

2 o

should there be any black specks, remove them. If very large, cut them in halves, divide them lengthwise into four pieces, and put them into boiling water, salted in the above proportion; let them boil until tender, which may be ascertained by thrusting a fork into them: dish, and serve very hot. This vegetable is an indispensable accompaniment to boiled beef. When thus served, it is usually boiled with the beef; a few carrots are placed round the dish as a garnish, and the remainder sent to table in a vegetable-dish. Young carrots do not require nearly so much boiling, nor should they be divided: these make a nice addition to stewed veal, &c.

CARROTS.

Time.—Large carrots, 1¾ to 2¼ hours; young ones, about ½ hour.

Average cost, 6*d.* to 8*d.* per bunch of 18.

Sufficient,—4 large carrots for 5 or 6 persons.

Seasonable.—Young carrots from April to June, old ones at any time.

ORIGIN OF THE CARROT.—In its wild state, this vegetable is found plentifully in Britain, both in cultivated lands and by waysides, and is known by the name of birds-nest, from its umbels of fruit becoming incurved from a hollow cup, like a birds-nest. In this state its root is whitish, slender, and hard, with an acrid, disagreeable taste, and a strong aromatic smell, and was formerly used as an aperient. When cultivated, it is reddish, thick, fleshy, with a pleasant odour, and a peculiar, sweet, mucilaginous taste. The carrot is said by naturalists not to contain much nourishing matter, and, generally speaking, is somewhat difficult of digestion.

TO DRESS CARROTS IN THE GERMAN WAY.

1101. INGREDIENTS.—8 large carrots, 3 oz. of butter, salt to taste, a very little grated nutmeg, 1 tablespoonful of finely-minced parsley, 1 dessertspoonful of minced onion, rather more than 1 pint of weak stock or broth, 1 tablespoonful of flour.

Mode.—Wash and scrape the carrots, and cut them into rings of about ¼ inch in thickness. Put the butter into a stewpan; when it is melted, lay in the carrots, with salt, nutmeg, parsley, and onion in the above proportions. Toss the stewpan over the fire for a few minutes, and when the carrots are well saturated with the butter, pour in the stock, and simmer gently until they are nearly tender. Then put into another stewpan a small piece of butter; dredge in about a tablespoonful of flour; stir this over the fire, and when of a nice brown colour, add the liquor that the carrots have been boiling in; let this just boil up, pour it over the carrots in the other stewpan, and let them finish simmering until quite tender. Serve very hot.

This vegetable, dressed as above, is a favourite accompaniment of roast pork, sausages, &c. &c.

Time.—About ¾ hour. *Average cost,* 6*d.* to 8*d.* per bunch of 18.

Sufficient for 6 or 7 persons.

Seasonable.—Young carrots from April to June, old ones at any time.

CONSTITUENTS OF THE CARROT.—These are crystallizable and uncrystallizable sugar, a little starch, extractive, gluten, albumen, volatile oil, vegetable jelly, or pectin, saline matter, malic acid, and a peculiar crystallizable ruby-red neuter principle, without odour or taste, called carotin. This vegetable jelly, or pectin, so named from its singular property of gelatinizing, is considered by some as another form of gum or mucilage, combined with vegetable acid. It exists more or less in all vegetables, and is especially abundant in those roots and fruits from which jellies are prepared.

STEWED CARROTS.

1102. INGREDIENTS.—7 or 8 large carrots, 1 teacupful of broth, pepper and salt to taste, ½ teacupful of cream, thickening of butter and flour.

Mode.—Scrape the carrots nicely; half-boil, and slice them into a stewpan; add the broth, pepper and salt, and cream; simmer till tender, and be careful the carrots are not broken. A few minutes before serving, mix a little flour with about 1 oz. of butter; thicken the gravy with this; let it just boil up, and serve.

Time.—About ¾ hour to parboil the carrots, about 20 minutes to cook them after they are sliced.

Average cost, 6*d.* to 8*d.* per bunch of 18.

Sufficient for 5 or 6 persons.

Seasonable.—Young carrots from April to June, old ones at any time.

NUTRITIVE PROPERTIES OF THE CARROT.—Sir H. Davy ascertained the nutritive matter of the carrot to amount to ninety-eight parts in one thousand; of which ninety-five are sugar and three are starch. It is used in winter and spring in the dairy to give colour and flavour to butter; and it is excellent in stews, haricots, soups, and, when boiled whole, with salt beef. In the distillery, owing to the great proportion of sugar in its composition, it yields more spirit than the potato. The usual quantity is twelve gallons per ton.

SLICED CARROTS.

(Entremets, or to be served with the Second Course, as a Side-dish.)

1103. INGREDIENTS.—5 or 6 large carrots, a large lump of sugar, 1 pint of weak stock, 3 oz. of fresh butter, salt to taste.

Mode.—Scrape and wash the carrots, cut them into slices of an equal size, and boil them in salt and water, until half done; drain them well, put them into a stewpan with the sugar and stock, and let them boil over a brisk fire. When reduced to a glaze, add the fresh butter and a seasoning of salt; shake the stewpan about well, and when the butter is well mixed with the carrots, serve. There should be no sauce in the dish when it comes to table, but it should all adhere to the carrots.

Time.—Altogether, ¾ hour.

Average cost, 6*d.* to 8*d.* per bunch of 18.

Sufficient for 1 dish.

Seasonable.—Young carrots from April to June, old ones at any time.

THE SEED OF THE CARROT.—In order to save the seed of carrots, the plan is, to select annually the most perfect and best-shaped roots in the taking-up season, and either preserve them in sand in a cellar till spring, or plant them immediately in an open airy part of the garden, protecting them with litter during severe frost, or earthing them over, and uncovering them in March following. The seed is in no danger from being injured by any other plant. In August it is fit to gather, and is best preserved on the stalks till wanted.

BOILED CAULIFLOWERS.

1104. INGREDIENTS.—To each ½ gallon of water allow 1 heaped tablespoonful of salt.

Mode.—Choose cauliflowers that are close and white; trim off the decayed outside leaves, and cut the stalk off flat at the bottom. Open the flower a little in places to remove the insects, which generally are found about the stalk, and let the cauliflowers lie in salt and water for an hour previous to dressing them, with their heads downwards: this will effectually draw out all the

BOILED CAULIFLOWER.

CAULIFLOWER.

vermin. Then put them into fast-boiling water, with the addition of salt in the above proportion, and let them boil briskly over a good fire, keeping the saucepan uncovered. The water should be well skimmed; and, when the cauliflowers are tender, take them up with a slice; let them drain, and, if large enough, place them upright in the dish. Serve with plain melted butter, a little of which may be poured over the flower.

Time.—Small cauliflower, 12 to 15 minutes, large one, 20 to 25 minutes, after the water boils.

Average cost, for large cauliflowers, 6*d.* each.

Sufficient.—Allow 1 large cauliflower for 3 persons.

Seasonable from the beginning of June to the end of September.

CAULIFLOWERS A LA SAUCE BLANCHE.

(Entremets, or Side-dish, to be served with the Second Course.)

1105. INGREDIENTS.—3 cauliflowers, ½ pint of sauce blanche, or French melted butter, No. 378; 3 oz. of butter; salt and water.

Mode.—Cleanse the cauliflowers as in the preceding recipe, and cut the stalks off flat at the bottom; boil them until tender in salt and water, to which the above proportion of butter has been added, and be careful to take them up the moment they are done, or they will break, and the appearance of the dish will be spoiled. Drain them well, and dish them in the shape of a large cauliflower. Have ready ½ pint of sauce, made by recipe No. 378, pour it over the flowers, and serve hot and quickly.

Time.—Small cauliflowers, 12 to 15 minutes, large ones, 20 to 25 minutes, after the water boils.

Average cost,—large cauliflowers, in full season, 6*d*. each.

Sufficient,—1 large cauliflower for 3 or 4 persons.

Seasonable from the beginning of June to the end of September.

CAULIFLOWER AND BROCOLI.—These are only forms of the wild Cabbage in its culti-vated state. They are both well known; but we may observe, that the purple and white Brocoli are only varieties of the Cauliflower.

CAULIFLOWERS WITH PARMESAN CHEESE.

(Entremets, or Side-dish, to be served with the Second Course.)

1106. INGREDIENTS.—2 or 3 cauliflowers, rather more than ½ pint of white sauce No. 378, 2 tablespoonfuls of grated Parmesan cheese, 2 oz. of fresh butter, 3 tablespoonfuls of bread crumbs.

Mode.—Cleanse and boil the cauliflowers by recipe No. 1104, and drain them and dish them with the flowers standing upright. Have ready the above proportion of white sauce; pour sufficient of it over the cauliflowers just to cover the top; sprinkle over this some rasped Parmesan cheese and bread crumbs, and drop on these the butter, which should be melted, but not oiled. Brown with a salamander, or before the fire, and pour round, but not over, the flowers the remainder of the sauce, with which should be mixed a small quantity of grated Parmesan cheese.

Time.—Altogether, ½ hour.   *Average cost,* for large cauliflowers, 6*d*. each.

Sufficient,—3 small cauliflowers for 1 dish.

Seasonable from the beginning of June to the end of September.

CELERY.

1107. With a good heart, and nicely blanched, this vegetable is  generally eaten raw, and is usually served with the cheese. Let the roots be washed free from dirt, all the decayed and outside leaves being cut off, preserving as much of the stalk as possible, and all specks or blemishes being carefully removed. Should the celery be large, divide it lengthwise into quarters, and place it, root downwards, in a celery-glass, which should be rather more than half filled with water. The top leaves may be curled, by shredding them in narrow strips with the point of a clean skewer, at a distance of about 4 inches from the top.

CELERY IN GLASS.

Average cost, 2*d*. per head.

Sufficient.—Allow 2 heads for 4 or 5 persons.

Seasonable from October to April.

Note.—This vegetable is exceedingly useful for flavouring soups, sauces, &c., and makes a very nice addition to winter salad.

STEWED CELERY A LA CREME.

1108. INGREDIENTS.—6 heads of celery; to each ½ gallon of water allow 1 heaped tablespoonful of salt, 1 blade of pounded mace, ⅓ pint of cream.

Mode.—Wash the celery thoroughly; trim, and boil it in salt and water until tender. Put the cream and pounded mace into a stewpan; shake it over the fire until the cream thickens, dish the celery, pour over the sauce, and serve.

Time.—Large heads of celery, 25 minutes; small ones, 15 to 20 minutes.

Average cost, 2*d*. per head.

Sufficient for 5 or 6 persons.

Seasonable from October to April.

ALEXANDERS.—This plant is the *Smyrnium olustratum* of science, and is used in this country in the same way in which celery is. It is a native of Great Britain, and is found in its wild state near the seacoast. It received its name from the Italian "herba Alexandrina," and is supposed to have been originally brought from Alexandria; but, be this as it may, its cultivation is now almost entirely abandoned.

STEWED CELERY (with White Sauce).

I.

1109. INGREDIENTS.—6 heads of celery, 1 oz. of butter; to each

½ gallon of water allow 1 heaped tablespoonful of salt, ½ pint of white sauce, No. 537 or 538.

Mode.—Have ready sufficient boiling water just to cover the celery, with salt and butter in the above proportion. Wash the celery well; cut off the decayed outside leaves, trim away the green tops, and shape the root into a point; put it into the boiling water; let it boil rapidly until tender; then take it out, drain well, place it upon a dish, and pour over about ½ pint of white sauce, made by either of the recipes No. 537 or 538. It may also be plainly boiled as above, placed on toast, and melted butter poured over, the same as asparagus is dished.

Time.—Large heads of celery, 25 minutes, small ones, 15 to 20 minutes, after the water boils.

Average cost, 2*d.* per head.

Sufficient for 5 or 6 persons.

Seasonable from October to April.

ORIGIN OF CELERY.—In the marshes and ditches of this country there is to be found a very common plant, known by the name of Smallage. This is the wild form of celery; but, by being subjected to cultivation, it loses its acrid nature, and becomes mild and sweet. In its natural state, it has a peculiar rank, coarse taste and smell, and its root was reckoned by the ancients as one of the "five greater aperient roots." There is a variety of this in which the root becomes turnip-shaped and large. It is called *Celeriæ,* and is extensively used by the Germans, and preferred by them to celery. In a raw state, this plant does not suit weak

CELERY.

stomachs; cooked, it is less difficult of digestion, although a large quantity should not be taken.

II.

1110. INGREDIENTS.—6 heads of celery, ½ pint of white stock or weak broth, 4 tablespoonfuls of cream, thickening of butter and flour, 1 blade of pounded mace, a *very little* grated nutmeg; pepper and salt to taste.

Mode.—Wash the celery, strip off the outer leaves, and cut it into lengths of about 4 inches. Put these into a saucepan, with the broth, and stew till tender, which will be in from 20 to 25 minutes; then add the remaining ingredients, simmer altogether for 4 or 5 minutes, pour into a dish, and serve. It may be garnished with sippets of toasted bread.

Time.—Altogether, ½ hour. *Average cost,* 2*d.* per head.

Sufficient for 5 or 6 persons.

Seasonable from October to April.

Note.—By cutting the celery into smaller pieces, by stewing it a little longer, and, when done, by pressing it through a sieve, the above stew may be converted into a purée of celery.

TO DRESS CUCUMBERS.

1111. INGREDIENTS.—3 tablespoonfuls of salad-oil, 4 tablespoonfuls of vinegar, salt and pepper to taste ; cucumber.

Mode.—Pare the cucumber, cut it equally into *very thin* slices, and *commence* cutting from the *thick end ;* if commenced at the stalk, the cucumber will most likely have an exceedingly bitter taste, far from agreeable. Put the slices into a dish, sprinkle over salt and pepper,

SLICED CUCUMBERS.

and pour over oil and vinegar in the above proportion; turn the cucumber about, and it is ready to serve. This is a favourite accompaniment to boiled salmon, is a nice addition to all descriptions of salads, and makes a pretty garnish to lobster salad.

Average cost, when scarce, 1*s.* to 2*s.* 6*d.*; when cheapest, may be had for 4*d.* each.

Seasonable.—Forced from the beginning of March to the end of June; in full season in July, August, and September.

CUCUMBER.

GEOGRAPHICAL DISTRIBUTION OF CUCUMBERS.—This family is not known in the frigid zone, is somewhat rare in the temperate, but in the tropical and warmer regions throughout the world they are abundant. They are most plentiful in the continent of Hindostan; but in America are not near so plentiful. Many of the kinds supply useful articles of consumption for food, and others are actively medicinal in their virtues. Generally speaking, delicate stomachs should avoid this plant, for it is cold and indigestible.

CUCUMBERS A LA POULETTE.

1112. INGREDIENTS.—2 or 3 cucumbers, salt and vinegar, 2 oz. of butter, flour, ½ pint of broth, 1 teaspoonful of minced parsley, a lump of sugar, the yolks of 2 eggs, salt and pepper to taste.

Mode.—Pare and cut the cucumbers into slices of an equal thickness, and let them remain in a pickle of salt and vinegar for ½ hour ; then drain them in a cloth, and put them into a stewpan with the butter. Fry them over a brisk fire, but do not brown them, and then dredge over them a little flour ; add the broth, skim off all the fat, which will rise to the surface, and boil gently until the gravy is somewhat reduced ; but the cucumber should not be broken. Stir in the yolks of the eggs, add the parsley, sugar, and a seasoning of pepper and salt ; bring the whole to the *point of boiling,* and serve.

Time.—Altogether, 1 hour.

Average cost, when cheapest, 4*d.* each.

Sufficient for 5 or 6 persons.

Seasonable in July, August, and September ; but may be had, forced, from the beginning of March.

FRIED CUCUMBERS.

1113. INGREDIENTS.—2 or 3 cucumbers, pepper and salt to taste, flour, oil or butter.

Mode.—Pare the cucumbers and cut them into slices of an equal thickness, commencing to slice from the thick, and not the stalk end of the cucumber. Wipe the slices dry with a cloth, dredge them with flour, and put them into a pan of boiling oil or butter; keep turning them about until brown; lift them out of the pan, let them drain, and serve, piled lightly in a dish. These will be found a great improvement to rump-steak: they should be placed on a dish with the steak on the top.

Time.—5 minutes. *Average cost,* when cheapest, 4*d.* each.

Sufficient for 4 or 5 persons.

Seasonable.—Forced from the beginning of March to the end of June; in full season in July and August.

PROPERTIES AND USES OF THE CUCURBITS.—The common cucumber is the *C. sativus* of science, and although the whole of the family have a similar action in the animal economy, yet there are some which present us with great anomalies. The roots of those which are perennial contain, besides fecula, which is their base, a resinous, acrid, and bitter principle. The fruits of this family, however, have in general a sugary taste, and are more or less dissolving and perfumed, as we find in the melons, gourds, cucumbers, vegetable-marrows, and squashes. But these are slightly laxative if partaken of largely. In tropical countries, this order furnishes the inhabitants with a large portion of their food, which, even in the most arid deserts and most barren islands, is of the finest quality. In China, Cashmere, and Persia, they are cultivated on the lakes on the floating collections of weeds common in these localities. In India they are everywhere abundant, either in a cultivated or wild state, and the seeds of all the family are sweet and mucilaginous.

STEWED CUCUMBERS.

1114. INGREDIENTS.—3 large cucumbers, flour, butter, rather more than ½ pint of good brown gravy.

Mode.—Cut the cucumbers lengthwise the size of the dish they are intended to be served in; empty them of the seeds, and put them into boiling water with a little salt, and let them simmer for 5 minutes; then take them out, place them in another stewpan, with the gravy, and let them boil over a brisk fire until the cucumbers are tender. Should these be bitter, add a lump of sugar; carefully dish them, skim the sauce, pour over the cucumbers, and serve.

Time.—Altogether, 20 minutes.

Average cost, when cheapest, 1*d.* each.

Sufficient for 3 or 4 persons.

Seasonable in June, July, and August; but may be had, forced, from the beginning of March.

THE CHATE.—This cucumber is a native of Egypt and Arabia, and produces a fruit of almost the same substance as that of the Melon. In Egypt it is esteemed by the upper class natives, as well as by Europeans, as the most pleasant fruit they have.

STEWED CUCUMBERS WITH ONIONS.

1115. INGREDIENTS.—6 cucumbers, 3 moderate-sized onions, not quite 1 pint of white stock, cayenne and salt to taste, the yolks of 2 eggs, a very little grated nutmeg.

Mode.—Pare and slice the cucumbers, take out the seeds, and cut the onions into thin slices; put these both into a stewpan, with the stock, and let them boil for ¼ hour or longer, should the cucumbers be very large. Beat up the yolks of 2 eggs; stir these into the sauce; add the cayenne, salt, and grated nutmeg; bring it to the point of boiling, and serve. Do not allow the sauce to boil, or it will curdle. This is a favourite dish with lamb or mutton chops, rump-steaks, &c.

Time.—Altogether, 20 minutes.

Average cost, when cheapest, 4*d.* each.

Sufficient for 6 or 7 persons.

Seasonable in July, August, and September; but may be had, forced, from the beginning of March.

THE MELON.—This is another species of the cucumber, and is highly esteemed for its rich and delicious fruit. It was introduced to this country from Jamaica, in 1570; since which period it has continued to be cultivated. It was formerly called the Musk Melon.

ENDIVE.

1116. This vegetable, so beautiful in appearance, makes an excellent addition to winter salad, when lettuces and other salad herbs are not  obtainable. It is usually placed in the centre of the dish, and looks remarkably pretty with slices of beetroot, hard-boiled eggs, and curled celery placed round it, so that the colours contrast nicely. In preparing it, carefully wash and cleanse it free from insects, which are generally found near the heart; remove any decayed or dead leaves, and dry it thoroughly by shaking in a cloth. This vegetable may also be served hot, stewed in cream, brown gravy, or butter; but when dressed thus, the sauce it is stewed in should not be very highly seasoned, as that would destroy and overpower the flavour of the vegetable.

ENDIVE.

Average cost, 1*d.* per head.

Sufficient,—1 head for a salad for 4 persons.

Seasonable from November to March.

ENDIVE.—This is the *C. endivium* o' science, and is much used as a salad. It belongs to the family of the *Compositæ*, with Chicory, common Goats-beard, and others of the same genus. Withering states, that before the stems of the common Goats-beard shoot up, the roots, boiled like asparagus, have the same flavour, and are nearly as nutritious. We are also informed by Villars that the children in Dauphiné universally eat the stems and leaves of the young plant before the flowers appear, with great avidity. The fresh juice of these tender herbs is said to be the best solvent of bile.

STEWED ENDIVE.

1117. INGREDIENTS.—6 heads of endive, salt and water, 1 pint of broth, thickening of butter and flour, 1 tablespoonful of lemon-juice, a small lump of sugar.

Mode.—Wash and free the endive thoroughly from insects, remove the green part of the leaves, and put it into boiling water, slightly salted. Let it remain for 10 minutes; then take it out, drain it till there is no water remaining, and chop it very fine. Put it into a stewpan with the broth; add a little salt and a lump of sugar, and boil until the endive is perfectly tender. When done, which may be ascertained by squeezing a piece between the thumb and finger, add a thickening of butter and flour and the lemon-juice: let the sauce boil up, and serve.

Time.—10 minutes to boil, 5 minutes to simmer in the broth.

Average cost, 1*d.* per head.

Sufficient for 3 or 4 persons.

Seasonable from November to March.

ENDIVE A LA FRANCAISE.

1118. INGREDIENTS.—6 heads of endive, 1 pint of broth, 3 oz. of fresh butter; salt, pepper, and grated nutmeg to taste.

Mode.—Wash and boil the endive as in the preceding recipe; chop it rather fine, and put into a stewpan with the broth; boil over a brisk fire until the sauce is all reduced; then put in the butter, pepper, salt, and grated nutmeg (the latter must be very sparingly used); mix all well together, bring it to the boiling point, and serve very hot.

Time.—10 minutes to boil, 5 minutes to simmer in the broth.

Average cost, 1*d.* per head.

Sufficient for 3 or 4 persons.

Seasonable from November to March.

TO BOIL HARICOTS BLANCS, or WHITE HARICOT BEANS.

1119. INGREDIENTS.—1 quart of white haricot beans, 2 quarts of soft water, 1 oz. of butter, 1 heaped tablespoonful of salt.

Mode.—Put the beans into cold water, and let them soak from 2 to

4 hours, according to their age; then put them into cold water, salted in the above proportion, bring them to boil, and let them simmer very slowly until tender; pour the water away from them, let them stand by the side of the fire, with the lid of the saucepan partially off, to allow the beans to dry; then add 1 oz. of butter and a seasoning of pepper and salt. Shake the beans about for a minute or two, and serve: do not stir them with a spoon, for fear of breaking them to pieces.

Time.—After the water boils, from 2 to 2½ hours.

Average cost, 4*d*. per quart.

Sufficient for 4 or 5 persons.

Seasonable in winter, when other vegetables are scarce.

Note.—Haricots blancs, when new and fresh, should be put into boiling water, and do not require any soaking previous to dressing.

HARICOTS AND LENTILS.—Although these vegetables are not much used in this country, yet in France, and other Catholic countries, from their peculiar constituent properties, they form an excellent substitute for animal food during Lent and *maigre* days. At the time of the prevalence of the Roman religion in this country, they were probably much more generally used than at present. As reformations are often carried beyond necessity, possibly lentils may have fallen into disuse, as an article of diet amongst Protestants, for fear the use of them might be considered a sign of popery.

HARICOTS BLANCS A LA MAITRE D'HOTEL.

1120. INGREDIENTS.—1 quart of white haricot beans, ¼ lb. of fresh butter, 1 tablespoonful of minced parsley, pepper and salt to taste, the juice of ½ lemon.

Mode.—Should the beans be very dry, soak them for an hour or two

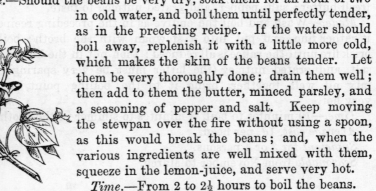

in cold water, and boil them until perfectly tender, as in the preceding recipe. If the water should boil away, replenish it with a little more cold, which makes the skin of the beans tender. Let them be very thoroughly done; drain them well; then add to them the butter, minced parsley, and a seasoning of pepper and salt. Keep moving the stewpan over the fire without using a spoon, as this would break the beans; and, when the various ingredients are well mixed with them, squeeze in the lemon-juice, and serve very hot.

Time.—From 2 to 2½ hours to boil the beans.

Average cost, 4*d*. per quart.

HARICOT BEANS.

Sufficient for 4 or 5 persons.

Seasonable in winter.

HARICOT BEANS.—This is the *haricot blanc* of the French, and is a native of India. It ripens readily, in dry summers, in most parts of Britain, but its culture has hitherto been confined to gardens in England; but in Germany and Switzerland it is grown in fields. It is usually harvested by pulling up the plants, which, being dried, are stacked and thrashed. The haulm is both of little bulk and little use, but the seed is used in making the esteemed French dish called haricot, with which it were well if the working classes of this country were acquainted. There is, perhaps, no other vegetable dish so cheap and easily cooked, and, at the same time, so agreeable and nourishing. The beans are boiled, and then mixed with a little fat or salt butter, and a little milk or water and flour. From 3,840 parts of kidney-bean Einhoff obtained 1,805 parts of matter analogous to starch, 351 of vegeto-animal matter, and 799 parts of mucilage.

HARICOT BEANS AND MINCED ONIONS.

1121. INGREDIENTS.—1 quart of white haricot beans, 4 middling-sized onions, ¼ pint of good brown gravy, pepper and salt to taste, a little flour.

Mode.—Peel and mince the onions not too finely, and fry them in butter of a light brown colour; dredge over them a little flour, and add the gravy and a seasoning of pepper and salt. Have ready a pint of haricot beans well boiled and drained; put them with the onions and gravy, mix all well together, and serve very hot.

Time.—From 2 to 2½ hours to boil the beans; 5 minutes to fry the onions.

Average cost, 4*d.* per quart.

Sufficient for 4 or 5 persons. *Seasonable* in winter.

HORSERADISH.

1122. This root, scraped, is always served with hot roast beef, and is used for garnishing many kinds of boiled fish. Let the horseradish remain in cold water for an hour; wash it well, and with a sharp knife scrape it into very thin shreds, commencing from the thick end of the root. Arrange some of it lightly in a small glass dish, and the remainder use for garnishing the joint: it should be placed in tufts round the border of the dish, with 1 or 2 bunches on the meat.

Average cost, 2*d.* per stick.

Seasonable from October to June.

THE HORSERADISH.—This belongs to the tribe *Alyssidæ,* and is highly stimulant and exciting to the stomach. It has been recommended in chronic rheumatism, palsy, dropsical complaints, and in cases of enfeebled digestion. Its principal use, however, is as a condiment to promote appetite and excite the digestive organs. The horseradish contains sulphur to the extent of thirty per cent. in the number of its elements; and it is to the presence of this quality that the metal vessels in which the radish is sometimes distilled, are turned into a black colour. It is one of the most powerful excitants and antiscorbutics we have, and forms the basis of several medical preparations, in the form of wines, tinctures, and syrups.

HORSERADISH.

LETTUCES.

1123. These form one of the principal ingredients to summer salads; should be nicely blanched, and be eaten young. They are seldom served in any other way, but may be stewed and sent to table in a good brown gravy flavoured with lemon-juice. In preparing them for a salad, carefully wash them free from dirt, pick off all the decayed and outer leaves, and dry them thoroughly by shaking them in a cloth. Cut off the stalks, and either halve or cut the lettuces into small pieces. The manner of cutting them up entirely depends on the salad for which they are intended. In France the lettuces are sometimes merely wiped with a cloth and not washed, the cooks there declaring that the act of washing them injuriously affects the pleasant crispness of the plant: in this case scrupulous attention must be paid to each leaf, and the grit thoroughly wiped away.

Average cost, when cheapest, 1*d.* each.

Sufficient.—Allow 2 lettuces for 4 or 5 persons.

Seasonable from March to the end of August, but may be had all the year.

LETTUCE.

THE LETTUCE.—All the varieties of the garden lettuce have originated from the *Lactuca sativa* of science, which has never yet been found in a wild state. Hence it may be concluded that it is merely another form of some species, changed through the effects of cultivation. In its young state, the lettuce forms a well-known and wholesome salad, containing a bland pellucid juice, with little taste or smell, and having a cooling and soothing influence on the system. This arises from the large quantities of water and mucilage it contains, and not from any narcotic principle which it is supposed to possess. During the period of flowering, it abounds in a peculiar milky juice, which flows from the stem when wounded, and which has been found to be possessed of decided medicinal properties.

BAKED MUSHROOMS.

(A Breakfast, Luncheon, or Supper Dish.)

1124. INGREDIENTS.—16 to 20 mushroom-flaps, butter, pepper to taste.

Mode.—For this mode of cooking, the mushroom flaps are better than the buttons, and should not be too large. Cut off a portion of the stalk, peel the top, and wipe the mushrooms carefully with a piece of flannel and a little fine salt. Put them into a tin baking-dish, with a very small piece of butter placed on each mushroom; sprinkle over a little pepper, and let them bake for about 20 minutes, or longer should the mushrooms be very large. Have ready a *very hot* dish, pile the mushrooms high in the centre, pour the gravy round, and send them to table quickly, with very *hot* plates.

Time.—20 minutes ; large mushrooms, ½ hour.

Average cost, 1*d.* each for large mushroom-flaps.

Sufficient for 5 or 6 persons.

Seasonable.—Meadow mushrooms in September and October ; cultivated mushrooms may be had at any time.

FUNGI. — These are common parasitical plants, originating in the production of copious filamentous threads, called the mycelium, or spawn. Rounded tubers appear on the mycelium ; some of these enlarge rapidly, burst an outer covering, which is left at the base, and protrude a thick stalk, bearing at its summit a rounded body, which in a short time expands into the pileus or cap. The gills, which occupy its lower surface, consist of parallel plates, bearing naked sporules over their whole surface. Some of the cells, which are visible by the microscope, produce four small cells at their free summit, apparently by germination and constriction. These are the sporules, and this is the development of the Agarics.

BROILED MUSHROOMS.
(A Breakfast, Luncheon, or Supper Dish.)

1125. INGREDIENTS.—Mushroom-flaps, pepper and salt to taste, butter, lemon-juice.

Mode.—Cleanse the mushrooms by wiping them with a piece of flannel and a little salt ; cut off a portion of the stalk, and peel the tops : broil them over a clear fire, turning them once, and arrange them on a very hot dish. Put a small piece of butter on each mushroom, season with pepper and salt, and squeeze over them a few drops of lemon-juice. Place the

BROILED MUSHROOMS.

dish before the fire, and when the butter is melted, serve very hot and quickly. Moderate-sized flaps are better suited to this mode of cooking than the buttons : the latter are better in stews.

Time.—10 minutes for medium-sized mushrooms.

Average cost, 1*d.* each for large mushrooms.

Sufficient.—Allow 3 or 4 mushrooms to each person.

Seasonable.—Meadow mushrooms in September and October ; cultivated mushrooms may be had at any time.

VARIETIES OF THE MUSHROOM.—The common mushroom found in our pastures is the *Agaricus campestris* of science, and another edible British species is *A. Georgii* ; but *A. primulus* is affirmed to be the most delicious mushroom. The morel is *Morchella esculenta*, and *Tuber cibarium* is the common truffle. There is in New Zealand a long fungus, which grows from the head of a caterpillar, and which forms a horn, as it were, and is called *Sphæria Robertsii*.

MUSHROOMS.

TO PRESERVE MUSHROOMS.

1126. INGREDIENTS.—To each quart of mushrooms, allow 3 oz. of butter, pepper and salt to taste, the juice of 1 lemon, clarified butter.

Mode.—Peel the mushrooms, put them into cold water, with a little lemon-juice; take them out and *dry* them very carefully in a cloth. Put the butter into a stewpan capable of holding the mushrooms; when it is melted, add the mushrooms, lemon-juice, and a seasoning of pepper and salt; draw them down over a slow fire, and let them remain until their liquor is boiled away, and they have become quite dry, but be careful in not allowing them to stick to the bottom of the stewpan. When done, put them into pots, and pour over the top clarified butter. If wanted for immediate use, they will keep good a few days without being covered over. To re-warm them, put the mushrooms into a stewpan, strain the butter from them, and they will be ready for use.

Average cost, 1*d.* each.

Seasonable.—Meadow mushrooms in September and October; cultivated mushrooms may be had at any time.

LOCALITIES OF THE MUSHROOM.—Mushrooms are to be met with in pastures, woods, and marshes, but are very capricious and uncertain in their places of growth, multitudes being obtained in one season where few or none were to be found in the preceding. They sometimes grow solitary, but more frequently they are gregarious, and rise in a regular circular form. Many species are employed by man as food; but, generally speaking, they are difficult of digestion, and by no means very nourishing. Many of them are also of suspicious qualities. Little reliance can be placed either on their taste, smell, or colour, as much depends on the situation in which they vegetate; and even the same plant, it is affirmed, may be innocent when young, but become noxious when advanced in age.

STEWED MUSHROOMS.

1127. INGREDIENTS.—1 pint mushroom-buttons, 3 oz. of fresh butter, white pepper and salt to taste, lemon-juice, 1 teaspoonful of flour, cream or milk, ¼ teaspoonful of grated nutmeg.

Mode.—Cut off the ends of the stalks, and pare neatly a pint of mushroom-buttons; put them into a basin of water, with a little lemon-juice, as they are done. When all are prepared, take them from the water with the hands, to avoid the sediment, and put them into a stewpan with the fresh butter, white pepper, salt, and the juice of ½ lemon; cover the pan closely, and let the mushrooms stew gently from 20 to 25 minutes; then thicken the butter with the above proportion of flour, add gradually sufficient cream, or cream and milk, to make the sauce of a proper consistency, and put in the grated nutmeg. If the mushrooms are not perfectly tender, stew them for 5 minutes longer, remove every particle of butter which may be floating on the top, and serve.

Time.—½ hour.   *Average cost,* from 9d. to 2s. per pint.

Sufficient for 5 or 6 persons.

Seasonable.—Meadow mushrooms in September and October.

To PROCURE MUSHROOMS.—In order to obtain mushrooms at all seasons, several methods of propagation have been had recourse to. It is said that, in some parts of Italy, a species of stone is used for this purpose, which is described as being of two different kinds; the one is found in the chalk hills near Naples, and has a white, porous, stalactical appearance; the other is a hardened turf from some volcanic mountains near Florence. These stones are kept in cellars, and occasionally moistened with water which has been used in the washing of mushrooms, and are thus supplied with their minute seeds. In this country, gardeners provide themselves with what is called *spawn,* either from the old manure of cucumber-beds, or purchase it from those whose business it is to propagate it. When thus procured, it is usually made up for sale in quadrils, consisting of numerous white fibrous roots, having a strong smell of mushrooms. This is planted in rows, in a dry situation, and carefully attended to for five or six weeks, when the bed begins to produce, and continues to do so for several months.

STEWED MUSHROOMS IN GRAVY.

1128. INGREDIENTS.—1 pint of mushroom-buttons, 1 pint of brown gravy No. 436, ¼ teaspoonful of grated nutmeg, cayenne and salt to taste.

Mode.—Make a pint of brown gravy by recipe 436; cut nearly all the stalks away from the mushrooms and peel the tops; put them into a stewpan, with the gravy, and simmer them gently from 20 minutes to ½ hour. Add the nutmeg and a seasoning of cayenne and salt, and serve very hot.

Time.—20 minutes to ½ hour.

Average cost, 9d. to 2s. per pint.

Sufficient for 5 or 6 persons.

Seasonable.—Meadow mushrooms in September and October.

ANALYSIS OF FUNGI.—The fungi have been examined chemically with much care, both by MM. Bracannot and Vauquelin, who designate the insoluble spongy matter by the name of fungin, and the soluble portion is found to contain the bolotic and the fungic acids.

BAKED SPANISH ONIONS.

1129. INGREDIENTS.—4 or 5 Spanish onions, salt, and water.

Mode.—Put the onions, with their skins on, into a saucepan of boiling water slightly salted, and let them boil quickly for an hour. Then take them out, wipe them thoroughly, wrap each one in a piece of paper separately, and bake them in a moderate oven for 2 hours, or longer, should the onions be very large. They may be served in their skins, and eaten with a piece of cold butter and a seasoning of pepper and salt; or they may be peeled, and a good brown gravy poured over them.

ONION.

Time.—1 hour to boil, 2 hours to bake.

Average cost, medium-sized, 2*d.* each.

Sufficient for 5 or 6 persons.

Seasonable from September to January.

THE GENUS ALLIUM.—The Onion, like the Leek, Garlic, and Shalot, belongs to the genus *Allium*, which is a numerous species of vegetable; and every one of them possesses, more or less, a volatile and acrid penetrating principle, pricking the thin transparent membrane of the eyelids; and all are very similar in their properties. In the whole of them the bulb is the most active part, and any one of them may supply the place of the other; for they are all irritant, excitant, and vesicant. With many, the onion is a very great favourite, and is considered an extremely nutritive vegetable. The Spanish kind is frequently taken for supper, it being simply boiled, and then seasoned with salt, pepper, and butter. Some dredge on a little flour, but many prefer it without this.

BURNT ONIONS FOR GRAVIES.

1130. INGREDIENTS.—½ lb. of onions, ½ pint of water, ½ lb. of moist sugar, ⅓ pint of vinegar.

Mode.—Peel and chop the onions fine, and put them into a stewpan (not tinned), with the water; let them boil for 5 minutes, then add the sugar, and simmer gently until the mixture becomes nearly black and throws out bubbles of smoke. Have ready the above proportion of boiling vinegar, strain the liquor gradually to it, and keep stirring with a wooden spoon until it is well incorporated. When cold, bottle for use.

Time.—Altogether, 1 hour.

PROPERTIES OF THE ONION.—The onion is possessed of a white, acrid, volatile oil, holding sulphur in solution, albumen, a good deal of uncrystallizable sugar and mucilage; phosphoric acid, both free and combined with lime; acetic acid, citrate of lime, and lignine. Of all the species of allium, the onion has the volatile principle in the greatest degree; and hence it is impossible to separate the scales of the root without the eyes being affected. The juice is sensibly acid, and is capable of being, by fermentation, converted into vinegar, and, mixed with water or the dregs of beer, yields, by distillation, an alcoholic liquor. Although used as a common esculent, onions are not suited to all stomachs; there are some who cannot eat them either fried or roasted, whilst others prefer them boiled, which is the best way of using them, as, by the process they then undergo, they are deprived of their essential oil. The pulp of roasted onions, with oil, forms an excellent anodyne and emollient poultice to suppurating tumours.

STEWED SPANISH ONIONS.

1131. INGREDIENTS.—5 or 6 Spanish onions, 1 pint of good broth or gravy.

Mode.—Peel the onions, taking care not to cut away too much of the tops or tails, or they would then fall to pieces; put them into a stewpan capable of holding them at the bottom without piling them one on the top of another; add the broth or gravy, and simmer *very gently* until the onions are perfectly tender. Dish them, pour the gravy round, and serve. Instead of using broth, Spanish onions may be stewed with a large piece of butter: they must be done very gradually over a slow fire or hot-plate, and will produce plenty of gravy.

Time.—To stew in gravy, 2 hours, or longer if very large.

Average cost,—medium-sized, 2*d.* each.

Sufficient for 6 or 7 persons.

Seasonable from September to January.

Note.—Stewed Spanish onions are a favourite accompaniment to roast shoulder of mutton.

ORIGIN OF THE ONION.—This vegetable is thought to have originally come from India, through Egypt, where it became an object of worship. Thence it was transmitted to Greece, thence to Italy, and ultimately it was distributed throughout Europe, in almost every part of which it has, from time immemorial, been cultivated. In warm climates it is found to be less acrid and much sweeter than in colder latitudes; and in Spain it is not at all unusual to see a peasant munching an onion, as an Englishman would an apple. Spanish onions, which are imported to this country during the winter months, are, when properly roasted, perfectly sweet, and equal to many preserves.

BOILED PARSNIPS.

1132. INGREDIENTS.—Parsnips; to each ½ gallon of water allow 1 heaped tablespoonful of salt.

Mode.—Wash the parsnips, scrape them thoroughly, and, with the point of the knife, remove any black specks about them, and, should they be very large, cut the thick part into quarters. Put them into a saucepan of boiling water salted in the above proportion, boil them rapidly until tender, which may be ascertained by thrusting a fork in them; take them up, drain them, and serve in a vegetable-dish. This vegetable is usually served with salt fish, boiled pork, or boiled beef: when sent to table with the latter, a few should be placed alternately with carrots round the dish, as a garnish.

Time.—Large parsnips, 1 to 1½ hour; small ones, ½ to 1 hour.

Average cost, 1*d.* each.

Sufficient.—Allow 1 for each person.

Seasonable from October to May.

PARSNIP.

THE PARSNIP.—This vegetable is found wild in meadows all over Europe, and, in England, is met with very frequently on dry banks in a chalky soil. In its wild state, the root is white, mucilaginous, aromatic, and sweet, with some degree of acrimony: when old, it has been known to cause vertigo. Willis relates that a whole family fell into delirium from having eaten of its roots, and cattle never touch it in its wild state. In domestic economy the parsnip is much used, and is found to be a highly nutritious vegetable. In times of scarcity, an excellent bread has been made from the roots, and they also furnish an excellent wine, resembling the malmsey of Madeira and the Canaries: a spirit is also obtained from them in as great quantities as from carrots. The composition of the parsnip-root has been found to be 79·4 of water, 6·9 starch and fibre, 6·1 gum, 5·5 sugar, and 2·1 of albumen.

BOILED GREEN PEAS.

1133. INGREDIENTS.—Green peas; to each ½ gallon of water allow 1 *small* teaspoonful of moist sugar, 1 heaped tablespoonful of salt.

Mode.—This delicious vegetable, to be eaten in perfection, should be young, and not *gathered* or *shelled* long before it is dressed. Shell the peas, wash them well in cold water, and drain them; then put them into a saucepan with plenty of *fast-boiling* water, to which salt and *moist sugar* have been added in the above proportion; let them boil quickly over a brisk fire, with the lid of the saucepan uncovered, and be careful that the smoke does not draw in. When tender, pour them into a colander; put them into a hot vegetable-dish, and quite in the centre of the peas place a piece of butter, the size of a walnut. Many cooks boil a small bunch of mint *with* the *peas*, or garnish them with it, by boiling a few sprigs in a saucepan by themselves. Should the peas be very old, and difficult to boil a good colour, a very tiny piece of soda may be thrown in the water previous to putting them in; but this must be very sparingly used, as it causes the peas, when boiled, to have a smashed and broken appearance. With young peas, there is not the slightest occasion to use it.

Time.—Young peas, 10 to 15 minutes; the large sorts, such as marrowfats, &c., 18 to 24 minutes; old peas, ½ hour.

Average cost, when cheapest, 6d. per peck; when first in season, 1s. to 1s. 6d. per peck.

Sufficient.—Allow 1 peck of unshelled peas for 4 or 5 persons.

Seasonable from June to the end of August.

ORIGIN OF THE PEA.—All the varieties of garden peas which are cultivated have originated from the *Pisum sativum*, a native of the south of Europe; and field peas are varieties of *Pisum arvense*. The Everlasting Pea is *Lathyrus latifolius*, an old favourite in flower-gardens. It is said to yield an abundance of honey to bees, which are remarkably fond of it. In this country the pea has been grown from time immemorial; but its culture seems to have diminished since the more general introduction of herbage, plants, and roots.

GREEN PEAS A LA FRANCAISE.

1134. INGREDIENTS.—2 quarts of green peas, 3 oz. of fresh butter, a bunch of parsley, 6 green onions, flour, a small lump of sugar, ½ teaspoonful of salt, a teaspoonful of flour.

Mode.—Shell sufficient fresh-gathered peas to fill 2 quarts; put them into cold water, with the above proportion of butter, and stir them about until they are well covered with the butter; drain them in a colander, and put them in a stewpan, with the parsley and onions; dredge over them a little flour, stir the peas well, and moisten them with boiling water; boil them quickly over a large fire for 20 minutes, or until there is no liquor remaining. Dip a small lump of sugar into some water, that it may soon melt; put it with the peas, to which add ½ teaspoonful of salt. Take a piece of butter the size of a walnut, work it together with a teaspoonful of flour; and add this to the peas, which should be boiling when it is put in. Keep shaking the stewpan, and, when the peas are nicely thickened, dress them high in the dish, and serve.

Time.—Altogether, ¾ hour. *Average cost,* 6*d.* per peck.

Sufficient for 4 or 5 persons.

Seasonable from June to the end of August.

VARIETIES OF THE PEA.—The varieties of the Pea are numerous; but they may be divided into two classes—those grown for the ripened seed, and those grown for gathering in a green state. The culture of the latter is chiefly confined to the neighbourhoods of large towns, and may be considered as in part rather to belong to the operations of the gardener than to those of the agriculturist. The grey varieties are the early grey, the late grey, and the purple grey; to which some add the Marlborough grey and the horn grey. The white varieties grown in fields are the pearl, early Charlton, golden hotspur, the common white, or Suffolk, and other Suffolk varieties.

STEWED GREEN PEAS.

1135. INGREDIENTS.—1 quart of peas, 1 lettuce, 1 onion, 2 oz. of butter, pepper and salt to taste, 1 egg, ½ teaspoonful of powdered sugar.

Mode.—Shell the peas, and cut the onion and lettuce into slices; put these into a stewpan, with the butter, pepper, and salt, but with no more water than that which hangs round the lettuce from washing. Stew the whole very gently for rather more than 1 hour; then stir to it a well-beaten egg, and about ½ teaspoonful of powdered sugar. When the peas, &c., are nicely thickened, serve; but, after the egg is added, do not allow them to boil.

Time.—1¼ hour. *Average cost,* 6*d.* per peck.

Sufficient for 3 or 4 persons.

Seasonable from June to the end of August.

GREEN PEA.

THE SWEET-PEA AND THE HEATH OR WOOD-PEA. —The well-known sweet-pea forms a fine covering to a trellis, or lattice-work in a flower-garden. Its gay and fragrant flowers, with its rambling habit, render it peculiarly adapted for such a purpose. The wood-pea, or heath-pea, is found in the heaths of Scotland, and the Highlanders of that country are extremely partial to them, and dry and chew them to give a greater relish to their whiskey. They also regard them as good against chest complaints, and say that by the use of them they are enabled to withstand hunger and thirst for a long time. The peas have a sweet taste, somewhat like the root of liquorice, and, when boiled, have an agreeable flavour, and are nutritive. In times of scarcity they have served as an article of food. When well boiled, a fork will pass through them; and, slightly dried, they are roasted, and in Holland and Flanders served up like chestnuts.

BAKED POTATOES.

1136. INGREDIENTS.—Potatoes.

Mode.—Choose large potatoes, as much of a size as possible; wash them in lukewarm water, and scrub them well, for the browned skin of a baked potato is by many persons considered the better part of it.

BAKED POTATOES SERVED
IN NAPKIN.

Put them into a moderate oven, and bake them for about 2 hours, turning them three or four times whilst they are cooking. Serve them in a napkin immediately they are done, as, if kept a long time in the oven, they have a shrivelled appearance. Potatoes may also be roasted before the fire, in an American oven; but when thus cooked, they must be done very slowly. Do not forget to send to table with them a piece of cold butter.

Time.—Large potatoes, in a hot oven 1½ hour to 2 hours; in a cool oven, 2 to 2½ hours.

Average cost, 4s. per bushel.

Sufficient.—Allow 2 to each person.

Seasonable all the year, but not good just before and whilst new potatoes are in season.

POTATO-SUGAR.—This sugary substance, found in the tubers of potatoes, is obtained in the form of syrup or treacle, and has not yet been crystallized. It resembles the sugar of grapes, has a very sweet taste, and may be used for making sweetmeats, and as a substitute for honey. Sixty pounds of potatoes, yielding eight pounds of dry starch, will produce seven and a half pounds of sugar. In Russia it is extensively made, as good, though of less consistency than the treacle obtained from cane-sugar. A spirit is also distilled from the tubers, which resembles brandy, but is milder, and has a flavour as if it were charged with the odour of violets or raspberries. In France this manufacture is carried on pretty extensively, and five hundred pounds of the tubers will produce twelve quarts of spirit, the pulp being given to cattle.

TO BOIL POTATOES.

1137. INGREDIENTS.—10 or 12 potatoes; to each ½ gallon of water allow 1 heaped tablespoonful of salt.

Mode.—Choose potatoes of an equal size, pare them, take out all the eyes and specks, and as they are peeled, throw them into cold water. Put them into a saucepan, with sufficient *cold* water to cover them, with salt in the above proportion, and let them *boil gently* until tender. Ascertain when they are done by thrusting a fork in them, and take them up the moment they feel soft through; for if they are left in the water afterwards, they become waxy or watery. Drain away the water, put the saucepan by the side of the fire, with the lid partially uncovered, to allow the steam to escape, and let the potatoes get thoroughly dry, and do not allow them to get burnt. Their superfluous moisture will evaporate, and the potatoes, if a good sort, should be perfectly mealy and dry. Potatoes vary so much in quality and size, that it is difficult to give the exact time for boiling; they should be attentively watched, and probed with a fork, to ascertain when they are cooked. Send them to table quickly, and very hot, and with an opening in the cover of the dish, that a portion of the steam may evaporate, and not fall back on the potatoes.

Time.—Moderate-sized old potatoes, 15 to 20 minutes after the water boils; large ones, ½ hour to 35 minutes.

Average cost, 4s. per bushel.

Sufficient for 6 persons.

Seasonable all the year, but not good just before and whilst new potatoes are in season.

Note.—To keep potatoes hot, after draining the water from them, put a folded cloth or flannel (kept for the purpose) on the top of them, keeping the saucepan-lid partially uncovered. This will absorb the moisture, and keep them hot some time without spoiling.

THE POTATO.—The potato belongs to the family of the *Solanaceæ*, the greater number of which inhabit the tropics, and the remainder are distributed over the temperate regions of both hemispheres, but do not extend to the arctic and antarctic zones. The whole of the family are suspicious; a great number are narcotic, and many are deleterious. The roots partake of the properties of the plants, and are sometimes even more active. The tubercles of such as produce them, are amylaceous and nutritive, as in those of the potato. The leaves are generally narcotic; but they lose this principle in boiling, as is the case with the *Solanum nigrum*, which are used as a vegetable when cooked.

TO BOIL POTATOES IN THEIR JACKETS.

1138. INGREDIENTS.—10 or 12 potatoes; to each ½ gallon of water, allow 1 heaped tablespoonful of salt.

Mode.—To obtain this wholesome and delicious vegetable cooked in perfection, it should be boiled and sent to table with the skin on. In Ireland, where, perhaps, the cooking of potatoes is better understood than in any country, they are always served so. Wash the potatoes well, and if necessary, use a clean scrubbing-brush to remove the dirt from them; and if possible, choose the potatoes so that they may all be as nearly the same size as possible. When thoroughly cleansed, fill the saucepan half full with them, and just cover the potatoes with cold water, salted in the above proportion: they are more quickly boiled with a small quantity of water, and, besides, are more savoury than when drowned in it. Bring them to boil, then draw the pan to the side of the fire, and let them simmer gently until tender. Ascertain when they are done by probing them with a fork; then pour off the water, uncover the saucepan, and let the potatoes dry by the side of the fire, taking care not to let them burn. Peel them quickly, put them in a very hot vegetable-dish, either with or without a napkin, and serve very quickly. After potatoes are cooked, they should never be entirely covered up, as the steam, instead of escaping, falls down on them, and makes them watery and insipid. In Ireland they are usually served up with the skins on, and a small plate is placed by the side of each guest.

Time.—Moderate-sized potatoes, with their skins on, 20 to 25 minutes after the water boils; large potatoes, 25 minutes to $\frac{3}{4}$ hour, or longer; 5 minutes to dry them.

Average cost, 4s. per bushel. *Sufficient* for 6 persons.

Seasonable all the year, but not good just before and whilst new potatoes are in season.

ANALYSIS OF THE POTATO.—Next to the cereals, the potato is the most valuable plant for the production of human food. Its tubers, according to analysis conducted by Mr. Fromberg, in the laboratory of the Agricultural Chemical Association in Scotland, contain the following ingredients:—75·52 per cent. of water, 15·72 starch, 0·55 dextrine, 3·3 of impure saccharine matter, and 3·25 of fibre with coagulated albumen. In a dried state the tuber contains 64·2 per cent. of starch, 2·25 of dextrine, 13·47 of impure saccharine matter, 5·77 of caseine, gluten, and albumen, 1 of fatty matter, and 13·31 of fibre with coagulated albumen.

TO BOIL NEW POTATOES.

1139. INGREDIENTS.—Potatoes; to each $\frac{1}{2}$ gallon of water allow 1 heaped tablespoonful of salt.

Mode.—Do not have the potatoes dug long before they are dressed, as they are never good when they have been out of the ground some time. Well wash them, rub off the skins with a coarse cloth, and put them into *boiling* water salted in the above proportion. Let them boil until tender; try them with a fork, and when done, pour the water away from them; let them stand by the side of the fire with the lid of the saucepan partially uncovered, and when the potatoes are thoroughly dry, put them into a hot vegetable-dish, with a piece of butter the size of a walnut; pile the potatoes over this, and serve. If the potatoes are too old to have the skins rubbed off, boil them in their jackets; drain, peel, and serve them as above, with a piece of butter placed in the midst of them.

Time.—$\frac{1}{4}$ to $\frac{1}{2}$ hour, according to the size.

Average cost, in full season, 1d. per lb.

Sufficient.—Allow 3 lbs. for 5 or 6 persons.

Seasonable in May and June, but may be had, forced, in March.

POTATO STARCH.—This fecula has a beautiful white crystalline appearance, and is inodorous, soft to the touch, insoluble in cold, but readily soluble in boiling water. It is on this starch that the nutritive properties of the tubers depend. As an aliment, it is well adapted for invalids and persons of delicate constitution. It may be used in the form of arrow-root, and eaten with milk or sugar. For pastry of all kinds it is more light and easier of digestion than that made with flour of wheat. In confectionery it serves to form creams and jellies, and in cookery may be used to thicken soups and sauces. It accommodates itself to the chest and stomach of children, for whom it is well adapted; and it is an aliment that cannot be too generally used, as much on account of its wholesomeness as its cheapness, and the ease with which it is kept, which are equal, if not superior, to all the much-vaunted exotic feculæ; as, salep, tapioca, sago, and arrow-root.

TO STEAM POTATOES.

1140. INGREDIENTS.—Potatoes; boiling water.

Mode.—This mode of cooking potatoes is now much in vogue, particularly where they are wanted on a large scale, it being so very convenient. Pare the potatoes, throw them into cold water as they are peeled, then put them into a steamer. Place the steamer over a saucepan of boiling water, and steam the potatoes from 20 to 40 minutes, according to the size and sort. When a fork goes easily through them, they are done; then take them up, dish, and serve very quickly.

Time.—20 to 40 minutes. *Average cost,* 4s. per bushel.

Sufficient.—Allow 2 large potatoes to each person.

Seasonable all the year, but not so good whilst new potatoes are in season.

USES OF THE POTATO.—Potatoes boiled and beaten along with sour milk form a sort of cheese, which is made in Saxony; and, when kept in close vessels, may be preserved for several years. It is generally supposed that the water in which potatoes are boiled is injurious; and as instances are recorded where cattle having drunk it were seriously affected, it may be well to err on the safe side, and avoid its use for any alimentary purpose. Potatoes which have been exposed to the air and become green, are very unwholesome. Cadet de Vaux asserts that potatoes will clean linen as well as soap; and it is well known that the berries of the *S. saponaceum* are used in Peru for the same purpose.

HOW TO USE COLD POTATOES.

1141. INGREDIENTS.—The remains of cold potatoes; to every lb. allow 2 tablespoonfuls of flour, 2 ditto of minced onions, 1 oz. of butter, milk.

Mode.—Mash the potatoes with a fork until perfectly free from lumps; stir in the other ingredients, and add sufficient milk to moisten them well; press the potatoes into a mould, and bake in a moderate oven until nicely brown, which will be in from 20 minutes to ½ hour. Turn them out of the mould, and serve.

Time.—20 minutes to ½ hour.

Seasonable at any time.

POTATO BREAD.—The manner in which this is made is very simple. The adhesive tendency of the flour of the potato acts against its being baked or kneaded without being mixed with wheaten flour or meal; it may, however, be made into cakes in the following manner :—A small wooden frame, nearly square, is laid on a pan like a frying-pan, and is grooved, and so constructed that, by means of a presser or lid introduced into the groove, the cake is at once fashioned, according to the dimensions of the mould. The frame containing the farina may be almost immediately withdrawn after the mould is formed upon the pan; because, from the consistency imparted to the incipient cake by the heat, it will speedily admit of being safely handled : it must not, however, be fried too hastily. It will then eat very pulatably, and might from time to time be soaked for puddings, like tapioca, or might be used like the cassada-cake, for, when well buttered and toasted, it will be found an excellent accompaniment to breakfast. In Scotland, cold boiled potatoes are frequently squeezed up and mixed with flour or oatmeal, and an excellent cake, or *scon,* obtained.

FRIED POTATOES (French Fashion).

1142. INGREDIENTS.—Potatoes, hot butter or clarified dripping, salt.

Mode.—Peel and cut the potatoes into thin slices, as nearly the same size as possible ; make some butter or dripping quite hot in a frying-pan ; put in the potatoes, and fry them on both sides of a nice brown. When they are crisp and done, take them up, place them on a cloth before the fire to drain the grease from them, and serve very hot, after sprinkling them with salt. These are delicious with rump-steak, and, in France, are frequently served thus as a breakfast dish. The remains of cold potatoes may also be sliced and fried by the above recipe, but the slices must be cut a little thicker.

Time.—Sliced raw potatoes, 5 minutes ; cooked potatoes, 5 minutes.

Average cost, 4s. per bushel.

Sufficient,—6 sliced potatoes for 3 persons.

Seasonable at any time.

A GERMAN METHOD OF COOKING POTATOES.

1143. INGREDIENTS.—8 to 10 middling-sized potatoes, 3 oz. of butter, 2 tablespoonfuls of flour, ½ pint of broth, 2 tablespoonfuls of vinegar.

Mode.—Put the butter and flour into a stewpan ; stir over the fire until the butter is of a nice brown colour, and add the broth and vinegar ; peel and cut the potatoes into long thin slices, lay them in the gravy, and let them simmer gently until tender, which will be in from 10 to 15 minutes, and serve very hot. A laurel-leaf simmered with the potatoes is an improvement.

Time.—10 to 15 minutes.

Seasonable at any time.

PRESERVING POTATOES.—In general, potatoes are stored or preserved in pits, cellars, pies, or camps ; but, whatever mode is adopted, it is essential that the tubers be perfectly dry ; otherwise, they will surely rot ; and a few rotten potatoes will contaminate a whole mass. The pie, as it is called, consists of a trench, lined and covered with straw ; the potatoes in it being piled in the shape of a house roof, to the height of about three feet. The camps are shallow pits, filled and ridged up in a similar manner, covered up with the excavated mould of the pit. In Russia and Canada, the potato is preserved in boxes, in houses or cellars, heated, when necessary, to a temperature one or two degrees above the freezing-point, by stoves. To keep potatoes for a considerable time, the best way is to place them in thin layers on a platform suspended in an ice-cellar : there, the temperature being always below that of active vegetation, they will not sprout ; while, not being above one or two degrees below the freezing-point, the tubers will not be frostbitten. Another mode is to scoop out the eyes with a very small scoop, and keep the roots buried in earth ; a third mode is to destroy the vital principle, by kiln-drying, steaming, or scalding ; a fourth is to bury them so deep in dry soil, that no change of temperature will reach them ; and thus, being without air, they will remain upwards of a year without vegetating.

POTATOES A LA MAITRE D'HOTEL.

1144. INGREDIENTS.—Potatoes, salt and water ; to every 6 potatoes allow 1 tablespoonful of minced parsley, 2 oz. of butter, pepper and salt to taste, 4 tablespoonfuls of gravy, 2 tablespoonfuls of lemon-juice.

Mode.—Wash the potatoes clean, and boil them in salt and water by recipe No. 1138 ; when they are done, drain them, let them cool ; then peel and cut the potatoes into thick slices : if these are too thin, they would break in the sauce. Put the butter into a stewpan with the pepper, salt, gravy, and parsley ; mix these ingredients well together, put in the potatoes, shake them two or three times, that they may be well covered with the sauce, and, when quite hot through, squeeze in the lemon-juice, and serve.

Time.—½ to ¾ hour to boil the potatoes ; 10 minutes for them to heat in the sauce.

Average cost, 4s. per bushel.

Sufficient for 3 persons. *Seasonable* all the year.

MASHED POTATOES.

1145. INGREDIENTS.—Potatoes ; to every lb. of mashed potatoes allow 1 oz. of butter, 2 tablespoonfuls of milk, salt to taste.

Mode.—Boil the potatoes in their skins ; when done, drain them, and let them get thoroughly dry by the side of the fire ; then peel them, and, as they are peeled, put them into a clean saucepan, and with a *large fork* beat them to a light paste ; add butter, milk, and salt in the above proportion, and stir all the ingredients well over the fire. When thoroughly hot, dish them lightly, and draw the fork backwards over the potatoes to make the surface rough, and serve. When dressed in this manner, they may be browned at the top with a salamander, or before the fire. Some cooks press the potatoes into moulds, then turn them out, and brown them in the oven : this is a pretty mode of serving, but it makes them heavy. In whatever way they are sent to table, care must be taken to have them quite free from lumps.

Time.—From ½ to ¾ hour to boil the potatoes.

Average cost, 4s. per bushel.

Sufficient,—1 lb. of mashed potatoes for 3 persons.

Seasonable at any time.

PUREE DE POMMES DE TERRE, or, Very Thin-mashed Potatoes.

1146. INGREDIENTS.—To every lb. of mashed potatoes allow ¼ pint of good broth or stock, 2 oz. of butter.

Mode.—Boil the potatoes, well drain them, and pound them smoothly in a mortar, or beat them up with a fork ; add the stock or broth, and rub the potatoes through a sieve. Put the purée into a very clean saucepan with the butter; stir it well over the fire until thoroughly hot, and it will then be ready to serve. A purée should be rather thinner than mashed potatoes, and is a delicious accompaniment to delicately broiled mutton cutlets. Cream or milk may be substituted for the broth when the latter is not at hand. A casserole of potatoes, which is often used for ragoûts instead of rice, is made by mashing potatoes rather thickly, placing them on a dish, and making an opening in the centre. After having browned the potatoes in the oven, the dish should be wiped clean, and the ragoût or fricassée poured in.

Time.—About ½ hour to boil the potatoes ; 6 or 7 minutes to warm the purée.

Average cost, 4s. per bushel.

Sufficient.—Allow 1 lb. of cooked potatoes for 3 persons.

Seasonable at any time.

VARIETIES OF THE POTATO.—These are very numerous. "They differ," says an

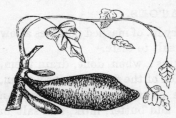

SWEET POTATO.

authority, "in their leaves and bulk of haulm ; in the colour of the skin of the tubers; in the colour of the interior, compared with that of the skin ; in the time of ripening ; in being farinaceous, glutinous, or watery ; in tasting agreeably or disagreeably ; in cooking readily or tediously ; in the length of the subterraneous *stolones* to which the tubers are attached ; in blossoming or not blossoming ; and, finally, in the soil which they prefer." The earliest varieties grown in fields are,—the Early Kidney, the Nonsuch, the Early Shaw, and the Early Champion. This last is the most generally cultivated round London : it is both mealy and hardy. The sweet potato is but rarely eaten in Britain; but in America it is often served at table, and is there very highly esteemed.

POTATO RISSOLES.

1147. INGREDIENTS.—Mashed potatoes, salt and pepper to taste ; when liked, a very little minced parsley, egg, and bread crumbs.

Mode.—Boil and mash the potatoes by recipe No. 1145 ; add a

POTATO RISSOLES.

seasoning of pepper and salt, and, when liked, a little minced parsley. Roll the potatoes into small balls, cover them with egg and bread crumbs, and fry in hot lard for about 10 minutes ; let them drain before the fire, dish them on a napkin, and serve.

Time.—10 minutes to fry the rissoles.

Seasonable at any time.

Note.—The flavour of these rissoles may be very much increased by adding finely-minced tongue or ham, or even chopped onions, when these are liked.

QUALITIES OF POTATOES.—In making a choice from the many varieties of potatoes which are everywhere found, the best way is to get a sample and taste them, and then fix upon the kind which best pleases your palate. The Shaw is one of the most esteemed of the early potatoes for field culture; and the Kidney and Bread-fruit are also good sorts. The Lancashire Pink is also a good potato, and is much cultivated in the neighbourhood of Liverpool. As late or long-keeping potatoes, the Tartan or Red-apple stands very high in favour.

POTATO SNOW.

1148. INGREDIENTS.—Potatoes, salt, and water.

Mode.—Choose large white potatoes, as free from spots as possible; boil them in their skins in salt and water until perfectly tender; drain and *dry them thoroughly* by the side of the fire, and peel them. Put a hot dish before the fire, rub the potatoes through a coarse sieve on to this dish; do not touch them afterwards, or the flakes will fall, and serve as hot as possible.

Time.—$\frac{1}{2}$ to $\frac{3}{4}$ hour to boil the potatoes.

Average cost, 4s. per bushel.

Sufficient,—6 potatoes for 3 persons.

Seasonable at any time.

THE POTATO AS AN ARTICLE OF HUMAN FOOD.—This valuable esculent, next to wheat, is of the greatest importance in the eye of the political economist. From no other crop that can be cultivated does the public derive so much benefit; and it has been demonstrated that an acre of potatoes will feed double the number of people that can be fed from an acre of wheat.

TO DRESS SALSIFY.

1149. INGREDIENTS.—Salsify; to each $\frac{1}{2}$ gallon of water allow 1 heaped tablespoonful of salt, 1 oz. of butter, 2 tablespoonfuls of lemon-juice.

Mode.—Scrape the roots gently, so as to strip them only of their outside peel; cut them into pieces about 4 inches long, and, as they are peeled, throw them into water with which has been mixed a little lemon-juice, to prevent their discolouring. Put them into boiling water, with salt, butter, and lemon-juice in the above proportion, and let them boil rapidly until tender; try them with a fork; and, when it penetrates easily, they are done. Drain the salsify, and serve with a good white sauce or French melted butter.

Time.—30 to 50 minutes. *Seasonable* in winter.

Note.—This vegetable may be also boiled, sliced, and fried in batter of a nice brown. When crisp and a good colour, they should be served with fried parsley in the centre of the dish, and a little fine salt sprinkled over the salsify.

SALSIFY.—This esculent is, for the sake of its roots, cultivated in gardens. It belongs to the Composite class of flowers, which is the most extensive family in the vegetable kingdom. This family is not only one of the most natural and most uniform in structure, but there is also a great similarity existing in the properties of the plants of which it is composed. Generally speaking, all composite flowers are tonic or stimulant in their medical virtues.

BOILED SEA-KALE.

1150. INGREDIENTS.—To each ½ gallon of water allow 1 heaped tablespoonful of salt.

Mode.—Well wash the kale, cut away any wormeaten pieces, and tie it into small bunches; put it into *boiling* water, salted in the above proportion, and let it boil quickly until tender.

BOILED SEA-KALE.

Take it out, drain, untie the bunches, and serve with plain melted butter or white sauce, a little of which may be poured over the kale. Sea-kale may also be parboiled and stewed in good brown gravy: it will then take about ½ hour altogether.

Time.—15 minutes; when liked very thoroughly done, allow an extra 5 minutes.

Average cost, in full season, 9*d*. per basket.

Sufficient.—Allow 12 heads for 4 or 5 persons.

Seasonable from February to June.

SEA-KALE.

SEA-KALE.—This plant belongs to the Asparagus tribe, and grows on seashores, especially in the West of England, and in the neighbourhood of Dublin. Although it is now in very general use, it did not come into repute till 1794. It is easily cultivated, and is esteemed as one of the most valuable esculents indigenous to Britain. As a vegetable, it is stimulating to the appetite, easily digestible, and nutritious. It is so light that the most delicate organizations may readily eat it. The flowers form a favourite resort for bees, as their petals contain a great amount of saccharine matter.

BOILED SALAD.

1151. INGREDIENTS.—2 heads of celery, 1 pint of French beans, lettuce, and endive.

Mode.—Boil the celery and beans separately until tender, and cut the celery into pieces about 2 inches long. Put these into a salad-

FRENCH BEANS.

CHERVIL.

bowl or dish; pour over either of the sauces No. 506, 507, or 508, and garnish the dish with a little lettuce finely chopped, blanched endive, or a few tufts of boiled cauliflower. This composition, if less agreeable than vegetables in their raw state, is more wholesome; for salads, however they may be compounded, when eaten uncooked, prove to some people indigestible. Tarragon, chervil, burnet, and boiled onion, may be added to the above salad with advantage, as also slices of cold meat, poultry, or fish.

Seasonable from July to October.

ACETARIOUS VEGETABLES.—By the term Acetarious vegetables, is expressed a numerous class of plants, of various culture and habit, which are principally used as salads, pickles, and condiments. They are to be considered rather as articles of comparative luxury than as ordinary food, and are more desirable for their coolness, or their agreeable flavour, than for their nutritive powers.

CAULIFLOWER.—The cauliflower is less indigestible than the cabbage; it possesses a most agreeable flavour, and is sufficiently delicate to be served at the tables of the wealthy. It is a wholesome vegetable, but should be eaten moderately, as it induces flatulence. Persons of ·weak constitutions and delicate stomachs should abstain from cauliflower as much as possible. They may be prepared in a variety of ways; and, in selecting them, the whitest should be chosen; those tinged with green or yellow being of indifferent quality.

SUMMER SALAD.

1152. INGREDIENTS.—3 lettuces, 2 handfuls of mustard-and-cress, 10 young radishes, a few slices of cucumber.

Mode.—Let the herbs be as fresh as possible for a salad, and, if at all stale or dead-looking, let them lie in water for an hour or two, which will very much refresh them. Wash and carefully pick them over, remove any decayed or wormeaten leaves, and drain them thoroughly by swinging them gently in a clean cloth. With a silver knife, cut the lettuces into small pieces, and the radishes and cucumbers into thin slices; arrange all these ingredients lightly on a dish, with the mustard-

SALAD IN BOWL.

and-cress, and pour under, but not over the salad, either of the sauces No. 506, 507, or 508, and do not stir it up until it is to be eaten. It may be garnished with hard-boiled eggs, cut in slices, sliced cucumbers, nasturtiums, cut vegetable-flowers, and many other things that taste will always suggest to make a pretty and elegant dish. In making a good salad, care must be taken to have the herbs freshly gathered, and *thoroughly drained* before the sauce is added to them, or it will be watery and thin. Young spring onions, cut small, are by many persons considered an improvement to salads; but, before these are added, the cook should always consult the taste of her employer. Slices of cold meat or poultry added to a salad make a convenient and quickly-made summer luncheon-dish; or cold fish, flaked, will also be found exceedingly nice, mixed with it.

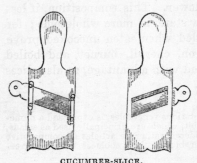

CUCUMBER-SLICE.

Average cost, 9*d.* for a salad for 5 or 6 persons; but more expensive when the herbs are forced.

Sufficient for 5 or 6 persons.

Seasonable from May to September.

CUCUMBERS.—The cucumber is refreshing, but neither nutritious nor digestible, and should be excluded from the regimen of the delicate. There are various modes of preparing cucumbers. When gathered young, they are called gherkins: these, pickled, are much used in seasonings.

RADISHES.—This is the common name given to the root of the *Raphanus sativus,* one of the varieties of the cultivated horseradish. There are red and white radishes; and the French have also what they call violet and black ones, of which the black are the larger. Radishes are composed of nearly the same constituents as turnips, that is to say, mostly fibre and nitrogen; and, being generally eaten raw, it is on the last of these that their flavour depends. They do not agree with people, except those who are in good health,

TURNIP RADISHES.

LONG RADISHES.

and have active digestive powers; for they are difficult of digestion, and cause flatulency and wind, and are the cause of headaches when eaten to excess. Besides being eaten raw, they are sometimes, but rarely, boiled; and they also serve as a pretty garnish for salads. In China, the radish may be found growing naturally, without cultivation; and may be occasionally met with in England as a weed, in similar places to where the wild turnip grows; it, however, thrives best in the garden, and the ground it likes best is a deep open loam, or a well-manured sandy soil.

WINTER SALAD.

1153. INGREDIENTS.—Endive, mustard-and-cress, boiled beetroot, 3 or 4 hard-boiled eggs, celery.

Mode.—The above ingredients form the principal constituents of a winter salad, and may be converted into a very pretty dish, by nicely contrasting the various colours, and by tastefully garnishing it. Shred the celery into thin pieces, after having carefully washed and cut away all wormeaten pieces; cleanse the endive and mustard-and-cress free from grit, and arrange these high in the centre of a salad-bowl or dish; garnish with the hard-boiled eggs and beetroot, both of which should be cut in slices; and pour into the dish, but not over the salad, either of the sauces No. 506, 507, or 508. Never dress a salad long before it is required for table, as, by standing, it loses its freshness and pretty crisp and light appearance; the sauce, however, may always be prepared a few hours beforehand, and when required for use, the herbs laid lightly over it.

Average cost, 9*d*. for a salad for 5 or 6 persons.

Sufficient for 5 or 6 persons.

Seasonable from the end of September to March.

SALADS.—Salads are raw vegetables, of which, among us, the lettuce is the most generally used; several others, however, such as cresses, celery, onions, beetroot, &c., are occasionally employed. As vegetables eaten in a raw state are apt to ferment on the stomach, and as they have very little stimulative power upon that organ, they are usually dressed with some condiments, such as pepper, vinegar, salt, mustard, and oil. Respecting the use of these, medical men disagree, especially in reference to oil, which is condemned by some and recommended by others.

POTATO SALAD.

1154. INGREDIENTS.—10 or 12 cold boiled potatoes, 4 tablespoonfuls of tarragon or plain vinegar, 6 tablespoonfuls of salad-oil, pepper and salt to taste, 1 teaspoonful of minced parsley.

Mode.—Cut the potatoes into slices about ½ inch in thickness; put these into a salad-bowl with oil and vinegar in the above proportion; season with pepper, salt, and a teaspoonful of minced parsley; stir the salad well, that all the ingredients may be thoroughly incorporated, and it is ready to serve. This should be made two or three hours before it is wanted for table. Anchovies, olives, or pickles may be added to this salad, as also slices of cold beef, fowl, or turkey.

Seasonable at any time.

CHICKEN SALAD.—(See No. 931.)

GROUSE SALAD.—(See No. 1026.)

LOBSTER SALAD.—(See No. 272.)

TO BOIL SPINACH (English Mode).

1155. INGREDIENTS.—2 pailfuls of spinach, 2 heaped tablespoonfuls of salt, 1 oz. of butter, pepper to taste.

Mode.—Pick the spinach carefully, and see that no stalks or weeds are left amongst it; wash it in several waters, and, to prevent it being gritty, act in the following manner:—
Have ready two large pans or tubs filled with water; put the spinach into one of these, and thoroughly wash it; then, *with the hands*, take

SPINACH GARNISHED WITH CROÛTONS.

out the spinach, and put it into the *other tub* of water (by this means all the grit will be left at the bottom of the tub); wash it again, and, should it not be perfectly free from dirt, repeat the process. Put it into a very large saucepan, with about ½ pint of water, just sufficient to keep the spinach from burning, and the above proportion of salt. Press it down frequently with a wooden spoon, that it may be done equally;

2 Q

and when it has boiled for rather more than 10 minutes, or until it is perfectly tender, drain it in a colander, squeeze it quite dry, and chop it finely. Put the spinach into a clean stewpan, with the butter and a seasoning of pepper; stir the whole over the fire until quite hot; then put it on a hot dish, and garnish with sippets of toasted bread.

Time.—10 to 15 minutes to boil the spinach, 5 minutes to warm with the butter.

Average cost for the above quantity, 8*d.*

Sufficient for 5 or 6 persons.

Seasonable.—Spring spinach from March to July; winter spinach from November to March.

Note.—Grated nutmeg, pounded mace, or lemon-juice may also be added to enrich the flavour; and poached eggs are also frequently served with spinach: they should be placed on the top of it, and it should be garnished with sippets of toasted bread.—See coloured plate U.

VARIETIES OF SPINACH.—These comprise thé Strawberry spinach, which, under that name, was wont to be grown in our flower-gardens; the Good King Harry, the Garden Oracle, the Prickly, and the Round, are the varieties commonly used. The Oracle is a hardy sort, much esteemed in France, and is a native of Tartary, introduced in 1548. The common spinach has its leaves round, and is softer and more succulent than any of the Brassica tribe.

SPINACH DRESSED WITH CREAM, a la Francaise.

1156. INGREDIENTS.—2 pailfuls of spinach, 2 tablespoonfuls of salt, 2 oz. of butter, 8 tablespoonfuls of cream, 1 small teaspoonful of pounded sugar, a very little grated nutmeg.

Mode.—Boil and drain the spinach as in recipe No. 1155; chop it finely, and put it into a stewpan with the butter; stir over a gentle fire, and, when the butter has dried away, add the remaining ingredients, and simmer for about 5 minutes. Previously to adding the cream, boil it first, in case it should curdle. Serve on a hot dish, and garnish either with sippets of toasted bread or leaves of puff-paste.

SPINACH.

Time.—10 to 15 minutes to boil the spinach; 10 minutes to stew with the cream.

Average cost for the above quantity, 8*d.*

Sufficient for 5 or 6 persons.

Seasonable. — Spring spinach from March to July; winter spinach from November to March.

SPINACH.—This is a Persian plant. It has been cultivated in our gardens about two hundred years, and is the most wholesome of vegetables. It is not very nutritious, but is very easily digested. It is very light and laxative. Wonderful properties have been ascribed to spinach. It is an excellent vegetable, and very beneficial to health. Plainly dressed, it is a resource for the poor; prepared luxuriantly, it is a choice dish for the rich.

SPINACH.—This vegetable belongs to a sub-order of the *Salsolaceæ*, or saltworts, and is classified under the head of *Spirolobeæ*, with leaves shaped like worms, and of a succulent kind. In its geographical distribution it is commonly found in extratropical and temperate regions, where they grow as weeds in waste places, and among rubbish, and in marshes by the seashore. In the tropics the order is rarely found. Many of them are used as potherbs, and some of them are emetic and vermifuge in their medicinal properties.

FRENCH MODE OF DRESSING SPINACH.

1157. INGREDIENTS.—2 pailfuls of spinach, 2 tablespoonfuls of salt, 2 oz. of butter, 1 teaspoonful of flour, 8 tablespoonfuls of good gravy ; when liked, a very little grated nutmeg.

Mode.—Pick, wash, and boil the spinach, as in recipe No. 1155, and when quite tender, drain and squeeze it perfectly dry from the water that hangs about it. Chop it very fine, put the butter into a stewpan, and lay the spinach over that; stir it over a gentle fire, and dredge in the flour. Add the gravy, and let it boil *quickly* for a few minutes, that it may not discolour. When the flavour of nutmeg is liked, grate some to the spinach, and when thoroughly hot, and the gravy has dried away a little, serve. Garnish the dish with sippets of toasted bread.

Time.—10 to 15 minutes to boil the spinach ; 10 minutes to simmer in the gravy.

Average cost for the above quantity, 8*d.*

Sufficient for 5 or 6 persons.

Seasonable.—Spring spinach from March to July ; winter spinach from October to February.

Note.—For an entremets or second-course dish, spinach dressed by the above recipe may be pressed into a hot mould ; it should then be turned out quickly, and served very hot.

BAKED TOMATOES.
(*Excellent.*)

1158. INGREDIENTS.—8 or 10 tomatoes, pepper and salt to taste, 2 oz. of butter, bread crumbs.

Mode.—Take off the stalks from the tomatoes ; cut them into thick slices, and put them into a deep baking-dish ; add a plentiful season-ing of pepper and salt, and butter in the above proportion ; cover the whole with bread crumbs ; drop over these a little clarified butter ; bake in a moderate oven from 20 minutes to ½ hour, and serve very hot. This vegetable, dressed as above, is an exceedingly nice accompani-ment to all kinds of roast meat. The tomatoes, instead of being cut in slices, may be baked whole; but they will take rather longer time to cook.

Time.—20 minutes to ½ hour.

Average cost, in full season, 9*d.* per basket.

Sufficient for 5 or 6 persons.

THE TOMATO.

Seasonable in August, September, and October; but may be had, forced, much earlier.

TOMATOES.—The Tomato is a native of tropical countries, but is now cultivated considerably both in France and England. Its skin is of a brilliant red, and its flavour, which is somewhat sour, has become of immense importance in the culinary art. It is used both fresh and preserved. When eaten fresh, it is served as an *entremets;* but its principal use is in sauce and gravy; its flavour stimulates the appetite, and is almost universally approved. The Tomato is a wholesome fruit, and digests easily. From July to September, they gather the tomatoes green in France, not breaking them away from the stalk; they are then hung, head downwards, in a dry and not too cold place; and there they ripen.

HOT TOMATO SAUCE, or PUREE OF TOMATOES.
(See No. 529.)

STEWED TOMATOES.
I.

1159. INGREDIENTS.—8 tomatoes, pepper and salt to taste, 2 oz. of butter, 2 tablespoonfuls of vinegar.

Mode.—Slice the tomatoes into a *lined* saucepan; season them with pepper and salt, and place small pieces of butter on them. Cover

STEWED TOMATOES.

the lid down closely, and stew from 20 to 25 minutes, or until the tomatoes are perfectly tender; add the vinegar, stir two or three times, and serve with any kind of roast meat, with which they will be found a delicious accompaniment.

Time.—20 to 25 minutes.

Average cost, in full season, 9*d.* per basket

Sufficient for 4 or 5 persons.

Seasonable from August to October; but may be had, forced, much earlier.

ANALYSIS OF THE TOMATO.—The fruit of the love-apple is the only part used as an esculent, and it has been found to contain a particular acid, a volatile oil, a brown, very fragrant extracto-resinous matter, a vegeto-mineral matter, muco-saccharine, some salts, and, in all probability, an alkaloid. The whole plant has a disagreeable odour, and its juice, subjected to the action of the fire, emits a vapour so powerful as to cause vertigo and vomiting.

II.

1160. INGREDIENTS.—8 tomatoes, about ½ pint of good gravy, thickening of butter and flour, cayenne and salt to taste.

Mode.—Take out the stalks of the tomatoes; put them into a wide stewpan, pour over them the above proportion of good brown gravy, and stew gently until they are tender, occasionally *carefully* turning them, that they may be equally done. Thicken the gravy with a little butter and flour worked together on a plate; let it just boil up after the thickening is added, and serve. If it be at hand, these should be served on a silver or plated vegetable-dish.

Time.—20 to 25 minutes, very gentle stewing.

Average cost, in full season, 9*d.* per basket.

Sufficient for 4 or 5 persons.

Seasonable in August, September, and October; but may be had, forced, much earlier.

THE TOMATO, OR LOVE-APPLE.—This vegetable is a native of Mexico and South America, but is also found in the East Indies, where it is supposed to have been introduced by the Spaniards. In this country it is much more cultivated than it formerly was; and the more the community becomes acquainted with the many agreeable forms in which the fruit can be prepared, the more widely will its cultivation be extended. For ketchup, soups, and sauces, it is equally applicable, and the unripe fruit makes one of the best pickles.

TRUFFLES AU NATUREL.

1161. INGREDIENTS.—Truffles, buttered paper.

Mode.—Select some fine truffles; cleanse them, by washing them in several waters with a brush, until not a particle of sand or grit remains on them; wrap each truffle in buttered paper, and bake in a hot oven for quite an hour; take off the paper, wipe the truffles, and serve them in a hot napkin.

Time.—1 hour. *Average cost.*—Not often bought in this country.

Seasonable from November to March.

THE COMMON TRUFFLE.—This is the *Tuber cibarium* of science, and belongs to that numerous class of esculent fungi distinguished from other vegetables not only by the singularity of their forms, but by their chemical composition. Upon analysis, they are found not only to contain the usual components of the vegetable kingdom, such as carbon, oxygen, and hydrogen, but likewise a large proportion of nitrogen; from which they approach more nearly to the nature of animal flesh. It was long ago observed by Dr. Darwin, that all the mushrooms cooked at our tables, as well as those used for ketchup, possessed an animal flavour; and soup enriched by mushrooms only has sometimes been supposed to contain meat.

TRUFFLES.

TO DRESS TRUFFLES WITH CHAMPAGNE.

1162. INGREDIENTS.—12 fine black truffles, a few slices of fat bacon, 1 carrot, 1 turnip, 2 onions, a bunch of savoury herbs, including parsley, 1 bay-leaf, 2 cloves, 1 blade of pounded mace, 2 glasses of champagne, ½ pint of stock.

Mode.—Carefully select the truffles, reject those that have a musty smell, and wash them well with a brush, in cold water only, until perfectly clean. Put the bacon into a stewpan, with the truffles and the remaining ingredients; simmer these gently for an hour, and let the whole cool in the stewpan. When to be served, rewarm them, and drain them on a clean cloth; then arrange them on a delicately-white napkin, that it may contrast as strongly as possible with the truffles, and serve.   The trimmings of truffles are used to flavour gravies, stock, sauces, &c.; and are an excellent addition to ragoûts, made dishes of fowl, &c.

Time.—1 hour.   *Average cost.*—Not often bought in this country.

Seasonable from November to March.

THE TRUFFLE.—The Truffle belongs to the family of the Mushroom.   It is certain that the truffle must possess, equally with other plants, organs of reproduction; yet, notwithstanding all the efforts of art and science, it has been impossible to subject it to a regular culture.   Truffles grow at a considerable depth under the earth, never appearing on the surface.   They are found in many parts of France those of Périgord and Magny are the most esteemed for their odour.   There are three varieties of the species, —the black, the red, and the white : the latter are of little value.   The red are very rare, and their use is restricted.   The black has the highest repute, and its consumption is enormous.   When the peasantry go to gather truffles, they take a pig with them to scent out the spot where they grow.   When that is found, the pig turns up the surface with his snout, and the men then dig until they find the truffles.   Good truffles are easily distinguished by their agreeable perfume ; they should be light in proportion to their size, and elastic when pressed by the finger.   To have them in perfection, they should be quite fresh, as their aroma is considerably diminished by any conserving process.   Truffles are stimulating and heating.   Weak stomachs digest them with difficulty. Some of the culinary uses to which they are subjected render them more digestible ; but they should always be eaten sparingly.   Their chief use is in seasoning and garnitures. In short, a professor has said, "Meats with truffles are the most distinguished dishes that opulence can offer to the epicure."   The Truffle grows in clusters, some inches below the surface of the soil, and is of an irregular globular form.   Those which grow wild in England are about the size of a hen's egg, and have no roots.   As there is nothing to indicate the places where they are, dogs have been trained to discriminate their scent, by which they are discovered.   Hogs are very fond of them, and frequently lead to their being found, from their rutting up the ground in search of them.

ITALIAN MODE OF DRESSING TRUFFLES.

1163. INGREDIENTS.—10 truffles, ¼ pint of salad-oil, pepper and salt to taste, 1 tablespoonful of minced parsley, a very little finely-minced garlic, 2 blades of pounded mace, 1 tablespoonful of lemon-juice.

Mode.—After cleansing and brushing the truffles, cut them into thin slices, and put them in a baking-dish, on a seasoning of oil, pepper, salt, parsley, garlic, and mace in the above proportion.   Bake them for nearly an hour, and, just before serving, add the lemon-juice, and send them to table very hot.

Time.—Nearly 1 hour.

Average cost.—Not often bought in this country.

Seasonable from November to March.

WHERE TRUFFLES ARE FOUND.—In this country, the common truffle is found on the downs of Hampshire, Wiltshire, and Kent; and they abound in dry light soils, and more especially in oak and chestnut forests.   In France they are plentiful, and many are imported from the south of that country and Italy, where they are much larger and in greater perfection : they lose, however, much of their flavour by drying.   Truffles have in England been tried to be propagated artificially, but without success.

TRUFFLES A L'ITALIENNE.

1164. INGREDIENTS.—10 truffles, 1 tablespoonful of minced parsley, 1 minced shalot, salt and pepper to taste, 2 oz. of butter, 2 tablespoonfuls of good brown gravy, the juice of ½ lemon, cayenne to taste.

Mode.—Wash the truffles and cut them into slices about the size of a penny-piece; put them into a sauté pan, with the parsley, shalot, salt, pepper, and 1 oz. of butter; stir them over the fire, that they may all be equally done, which will be in about 10 minutes, and drain off some of the butter; then add a little more fresh butter, 2 table-spoonfuls of good gravy, the juice of ½ lemon, and a little cayenne; stir over the fire until the whole is on the point of boiling, when serve.

Time.—Altogether, 20 minutes.

Average cost.—Not often bought in this country.

Seasonable from November to March.

USES OF THE TRUFFLE.—Like the Morel, truffles are seldom eaten alone, but are much used in gravies, soups, and ragoûts. They are likewise dried for the winter months, and, when reduced to powder, form a useful culinary ingredient; they, however, have many virtues attributed to them which they do not possess. Their wholesomeness is, perhaps, questionable, and they should be eaten with moderation.

BOILED TURNIPS.

1165. INGREDIENTS.—Turnips; to each ½ gallon of water allow 1 heaped tablespoonful of salt.

Mode.—Pare the turnips, and, should they be very large, divide them into quarters; but, unless this is the case, let them be cooked whole. Put them into a saucepan of boiling water, salted in the above proportion, and let them boil gently until tender. Try them with a fork, and, when done, take them up in a colander; let them thoroughly drain, and serve. Boiled turnips are usually sent to table with boiled mutton, but are infinitely nicer when mashed than served whole: unless nice and young, they are scarcely worth the trouble of dressing plainly as above.

Time.—Old turnips, ¾ to 1¼ hour; young ones, about 18 to 20 minutes.

Average cost, 4d. per bunch.

Sufficient.—Allow a bunch of 12 turnips for 5 or 6 persons.

Seasonable.—May be had all the year; but in spring only useful for flavouring gravies, &c.

THE TURNIP.—This vegetable is the *Brassica Rapa* of science, and grows wild in England, but cannot be brought exactly to resemble what it becomes in a cultivated state. It is said to have been originally introduced from Hanover, and forms an excellent culinary vegetable, much used all over Europe, where it is either eaten alone or mashed and cooked in soups and stews. They do not thrive in a hot climate; for in India they, and many more of our garden vegetables, lose their flavour and become comparatively tasteless. The Swede is the largest variety, but it is too coarse for the table.

TURNIPS.

MASHED TURNIPS.

1166. INGREDIENTS.—10 or 12 large turnips; to each ½ gallon of water allow 1 heaped tablespoonful of salt, 2 oz. of butter, cayenne or white pepper to taste.

Mode.—Pare the turnips, quarter them, and put them into boiling water, salted in the above proportion; boil them until tender; then drain them in a colander, and squeeze them as dry as possible by pressing them with the back of a large plate. When quite free from water, rub the turnips with a wooden spoon through the colander, and put them into a very clean saucepan; add the butter, white pepper, or cayenne, and, if necessary, a little salt. Keep stirring them over the fire until the butter is well mixed with them, and the turnips are thoroughly hot; dish, and serve. A little cream or milk added after the turnips are pressed through the colander, is an improvement to both the colour and flavour of this vegetable.

Time.—From ¼ to ¾ hour to boil the turnips; 10 minutes to warm them through.

Average cost, 4*d.* per bunch.

Sufficient for 4 or 5 persons.

Seasonable.—May be had all the year; but in spring only good for flavouring gravies.

VEGETABLES REDUCED TO PURÉE.—Persons in the flower of youth, having healthy stomachs, and leading active lives, may eat all sorts of vegetables, without inconvenience, save, of course, in excess. The digestive functions possess, great energy during the period of youth: the body, to develop itself, needs nourishment. Physical exercise gives an appetite, which it is necessary to satisfy, and vegetables cannot resist the vigorous action of the gastric organs. An old proverb says, "At twenty one can digest iron." But for aged persons, the sedentary, or the delicate, it is quite otherwise. Then the gastric power has considerably diminished, the digestive organs have lost their energy, the process of digestion is consequently slower, and the least excess at table is followed by derangement of the stomach for several days. Those who generally digest vegetables with difficulty, should eat them reduced to a pulp or purée, that is to say, with their skins and tough fibres removed. Subjected to this process, vegetables which, when entire, would create flatulence and wind, are then comparatively harmless. Experience has established the rule, that nourishment is not complete without the alliance of meat with vegetables. We would also add, that the régime most favourable to health is found in variety: variety pleases the senses, monotony is disagreeable. The eye is fatigued by looking always on one object, the ear by listening to one sound, and the palate by tasting one flavour. It is the same with the stomach: consequently, variety of food is one of the essentials for securing good digestion.

GERMAN MODE OF COOKING TURNIPS.

1167. INGREDIENTS.—8 large turnips, 3 oz. of butter, pepper and salt to taste, rather more than ½ pint of weak stock or broth, 1 tablespoonful of flour.

Mode.—Make the butter hot in a stewpan, lay in the turnips, after having pared and cut them into dice, and season them with pepper and salt. Toss them over the fire for a few minutes, then add the broth, and simmer the whole gently till the turnips are tender. Brown the above proportion of flour with a little butter; add this to the turnips, let them simmer another 5 minutes, and serve. Boiled mutton is usually sent to table with this vegetable, and may be cooked with the turnips by placing it in the midst of them: the meat would then be very delicious, as, there being so little liquid with the turnips, it would almost be steamed, and consequently very tender.

Time.—20 minutes. *Average cost,* 4*d.* per bunch.

Sufficient for 4 persons.

Seasonable.—May be had all the year.

TURNIPS.—Good turnips are delicate in texture, firm, and sweet. The best sorts contain a sweet juicy mucilage, uniting with the aroma a slightly acid quality, which is completely neutralized in cooking. The turnip is prepared in a variety of ways. Ducks stuffed with turnips have been highly appreciated. It is useful in the regimen of persons afflicted with chronic visceral irritations. The turnip only creates flatulency when it is soft, porous, and stringy. It is then, consequently, bad.

TURNIPS IN WHITE SAUCE.

(An Entremets, or to be served with the Second Course as a Side-dish.)

1168. INGREDIENTS.—7 or 8 turnips, 1 oz. of butter, ½ pint of white sauce, No. 538 or 539.

Mode.—Peel and cut the turnips in the shape of pears or marbles; boil them in salt and water, to which has been added a little butter, until tender; then take them out, drain, arrange them on a dish, and pour over the white sauce made by recipe No. 538 or 539, and to which has been added a small lump of sugar. In winter, when other vegetables are scarce, this will be found a very good and pretty-looking dish: when approved, a little mustard may be added to the sauce.

Time.—About ¾ hour to boil the turnips.

Average cost, 4*d.* per bunch.

Sufficient for 1 side-dish.   *Seasonable* in winter.

THE FRENCH NAVET.—This is a variety of the turnip; but, instead of being globular, has more the shape of the carrot. Its flavour being excellent, it is much esteemed on the Continent for soups and made dishes. Two or three of them will impart as much flavour as a dozen of the common turnips will. Accordingly, when stewed in gravy, they are greatly relished. This flavour resides in the rind, which is not cut off, but scraped. This variety was once grown in England, but now it is rarely found in our gardens, though highly deserving of a place there. It is of a yellowish-white colour, and is sometimes imported to the London market.

BOILED TURNIP GREENS.

1169. INGREDIENTS.—To each ½ gallon of water, allow 1 heaped tablespoonful of salt; turnip-greens.

Mode.—Wash the greens well in two or three waters, and pick off all the decayed and dead leaves; tie them in small bunches, and put them into plenty of boiling water, salted in the above proportion. Keep them boiling quickly, with the lid of the saucepan uncovered, and when tender, pour them into a colander; let them drain, arrange them in a vegetable-dish, remove the string that the greens were tied with, and serve.

Time.—15 to 20 minutes. *Average cost,* 4d. for a dish for 3 persons.

Seasonable in March, April, and May.

CABBAGE, TURNIP-TOPS, AND GREENS.—All the cabbage tribe, which comprises cole-worts, brocoli, cauliflower, sprouts, and turnip-tops, in order to be delicate, should be dressed young, when they have a rapid growth; but, if they have stood the summer, in order to be tender, they should be allowed to have a touch of frost. The cabbage contains much vegetable albumen, and several parts sulphur and nitrate of potass. Cabbage is heavy, and a long time digesting, which has led to a belief that it is very nourishing. It is only fit food for robust and active persons; the sedentary or delicate should carefully avoid it. Cabbage may be prepared in a variety of ways: it serves as a garniture to several recherché dishes,—partridge and cabbage for example. Bacon and cabbage is a very favourite dish; but only a good stomach can digest it.

BOILED VEGETABLE MARROW.

1170. INGREDIENTS.—To each ½ gallon of water, allow 1 heaped tablespoonful of salt; vegetable marrows.

Mode.—Have ready a saucepan of boiling water, salted in the above proportion; put in the marrows after peeling them, and boil them

VEGETABLE MARROW
ON TOAST.

until quite tender. Take them up with a slice, halve, and, should they be very large, quarter them. Dish them on toast, and send to table with them a tureen of melted butter, or, in lieu of this, a small pat of salt butter. Large vegetable marrows may be preserved throughout the winter by storing them in a dry place; when wanted for use, a few slices should be cut and boiled in the same manner as above; but, when once begun, the marrow must be eaten quickly, as it keeps but a short time after it is cut. Vegetable marrows are also very delicious mashed: they should be boiled, then drained, and mashed smoothly with a wooden spoon. Heat them in a saucepan, add a seasoning of salt and pepper, and a small piece of butter, and dish with a few sippets of toasted bread placed round as a garnish.

Time.—Young vegetable marrows 10 to 20 minutes; old ones, ½ to ¾ hour.

Average cost, in full season, 1s. per dozen.

Sufficient.—Allow 1 moderate-sized marrow for each person.

Seasonable in July, August, and September; but may be preserved all the winter.

FRIED VEGETABLE MARROW.

1171. INGREDIENTS.—3 medium-sized vegetable marrows, egg and bread crumbs, hot lard.

Mode.—Peel, and boil the marrows until tender in salt and water; then drain them and cut them in quarters, and take out the seeds.

When thoroughly drained, brush the marrows over with egg, and sprinkle with bread crumbs; have ready some hot lard, fry the marrow in this, and, when of a nice brown, dish; sprinkle over a little salt and pepper, and serve.

Time.—About ½ hour to boil the marrow, 7 minutes to fry it.

Average cost, in full season, 1s. per dozen.

Sufficient for 4 persons.

Seasonable in July, August, and September.

VEGETABLE MARROW.

THE VEGETABLE MARROW.—This vegetable is now extensively used, and belongs to the Cucurbits. It is the *C. ovifera* of science, and, like the melon, gourd, cucumber, and squash, is widely diffused in the tropical or warmer regions of the globe. Of the nature of this family we have already spoken when treating of the cucumber.

CUT VEGETABLES FOR SOUPS, &c.

1172. The annexed engraving represents a cutter for shaping vegetables for soups, ragoûts, stews, &c.; carrots and turnips being the usual vegetables for which this utensil is used. Cut the vegetables into slices about ¼ inch in thickness, stamp them out with the cutter, and boil them for a few minutes in salt and water, until tender. Turnips should be cut in rather thicker slices than carrots, on account of the former boiling more quickly to a pulp than the latter.

VEGETABLE-CUTTER.

CARROTS.—Several species of carrots are cultivated,—the red, the yellow, and the white. Those known as the Creey carrots are considered the best, and are very sweet. The carrot has been classed by hygienists among flatulent vegetables, and as difficult of digestion. When the root becomes old, it is almost as hard as wood; but the young carrot, which has not reached its full growth, is tender, relishing, nutritious, and digests well when properly cooked.

VEGETABLE MARROWS IN WHITE SAUCE.

1173. INGREDIENTS.—4 or 5 moderate-sized marrows, ½ pint of white sauce, No. 539.

Mode.—Pare the marrows; cut them in halves, and shape each half at the top in a point, leaving the bottom end flat for it to stand upright in the dish. Boil the marrows in salt and water until tender; take them up very carefully, and arrange them on a hot dish. Have ready ½ pint of white sauce, made by recipe No. 539; pour this over the marrows, and serve.

VEGETABLE MARROW IN WHITE SAUCE.

Time.—From 15 to 20 minutes to boil the marrows.

Average cost, in full season, 1*s.* per dozen.

Sufficient for 5 or 6 persons.

Seasonable in July, August, and September.

BOILED INDIAN WHEAT or MAIZE.

1174. INGREDIENTS.—The ears of young and green Indian wheat ; to every ½ gallon of water allow 1 heaped tablespoonful of salt.

Mode.—This vegetable, which makes one of the most delicious dishes brought to table, is unfortunately very rarely seen in Britain ; and we wonder that, in the gardens of the wealthy, it is not invariably cultivated. Our sun, it is true, possesses hardly power sufficient to ripen maize ; but, with well-prepared ground, and in a favourable position, it might be sufficiently advanced by the beginning of autumn to serve as a vegetable. The outside sheath being taken off and the waving fibres removed, let the ears be placed in boiling water, where they should remain for about 25 minutes (a longer time may be necessary for larger ears than ordinary) ; and, when sufficiently boiled and well drained, they may be sent to table whole, and with a piece of toast underneath them. Melted butter should be served with them.

Time.—25 to 35 minutes. *Average cost.*—Seldom bought.

Sufficient,—1 ear for each person. *Seasonable* in autumn.

Note.—William Cobbett, the English radical writer and politician, was a great cultivator and admirer of maize, and constantly ate it as a vegetable, boiled. We believe he printed a special recipe for it, but we have been unable to lay our hands on it. Mr. Buchanan, the present president of the United States, was in the habit, when ambassador here, of receiving a supply of Indian corn from America in hermetically-sealed cases ; and the publisher of this work remembers, with considerable satisfaction, his introduction to a dish of this vegetable, when in America. He found it to combine the excellences of the young green pea and the finest asparagus ; but he felt at first slightly awkward in holding the large ear with one hand, whilst the other had to be employed in cutting off with a knife the delicate green grains.

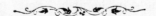

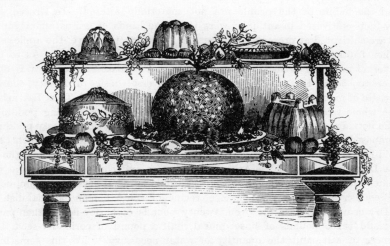

CHAPTER XXVI.

GENERAL OBSERVATIONS ON PUDDINGS AND PASTRY.

1175. PUDDINGS AND PASTRY, familiar as they may be, and unimportant as they may be held in the estimation of some, are yet intimately connected with the development of agricultural resources in reference to the cereal grasses. When they began to be made is uncertain; but we may safely presume, that a simple form of pudding was amongst the first dishes made after discovering a mode of grinding wheat into flour. Traditional history enables us to trace man back to the time of the Deluge. After that event he seems to have recovered himself in the central parts of Asia, and to have first risen to eminence in the arts of civilization on the banks of the Nile. From this region, Greece, Carthage, and some other parts along the shores of the Mediterranean Sea, were colonized. In process of time, Greece gave to the Romans the arts which she had thus received from Egypt, and these subsequently diffused them over Europe. How these were carried to or developed in India and China, is not so well ascertained; and in America their ancient existence rests only on very indistinct traditions. As to who was the real discoverer of the use of corn, we have no authentic knowledge. The traditions of different countries ascribe it to various fabulous personages, whose names it is here unnecessary to introduce. In Egypt, however, corn must have grown abundantly; for Abraham, and after him Jacob, had recourse to that country for supplies during times of famine.

1176. THE HABITS OF A PEOPLE, to a great extent, are formed by the climate in which they live, and by the native or cultivated productions in which their country abounds. Thus we find that the agricultural produce of the ancient Egyptians is pretty much the same as that of the present day, and the habits of the people are not materially altered. In Greece, the products cultivated in antiquity were the same kinds of grains and legumes as are cultivated at present, with the vine, the fig, the olive, the apple, and other fruits. So with the Romans, and so with other nations. As to the different modes of artificially preparing these to please the taste, it is only necessary to say that they arise from the universal desire of novelty, characteristic of man in the development of his social conditions. Thus has arisen the whole science of cookery, and thus arose the art of making puddings. The porridge of the Scotch is nothing more than a species of hasty pudding, composed of oatmeal, salt, and water ; and the "red pottage" for which Esau sold his birthright, must have been something similar. The barley-gruel of the Lacedæmonians, of the Athenian gladiators and common people, was the same, with the exception of the slight seasoning it had beyond the simplicity of Scottish fare. Here is the ancient recipe for the Athenian national dish :— "Dry near the fire, in the oven, twenty pounds of barley-flour ; then parch it ; add three pounds of linseed-meal, half a pound of coriander-seed, two ounces of salt, and the quantity of water necessary." To this sometimes a little millet was added, in order to give the paste greater cohesion and delicacy.

1177. OATMEAL AMONGST THE GREEKS AND ROMANS was highly esteemed, as was also rice, which they considered as beneficial to the chest. They also held in high repute the Irion, or Indian wheat of the moderns. The flour of this cereal was made into a kind of hasty pudding, and, parched or roasted, was eaten with a little salt. The Spelt, or Red wheat, was likewise esteemed, and its flour formed the basis of the Carthaginian pudding, for which we here give the scientific recipe :—"Put a pound of red-wheat flour into water, and when it has steeped some time, transfer it to a wooden bowl. Add three pounds of cream cheese, half a pound of honey, and one egg. Beat the whole together, and cook it on a slow fire in a stewpan." Should this be considered unpalatable, another form has been recommended. "Sift the flour, and, with some water, put it into a wooden vessel, and, for ten days, renew the water twice each day. At the end of that period, press out the water and place the paste in another vessel. It is now to be reduced to the consistence of thick lees, and passed through a piece of new linen. Repeat this last operation, then dry the mass in the sun and boil it in milk. Season according to taste." These are specimens of the puddings of antiquity, and this last recipe was held in especial favour by the Romans.

1178. HOWEVER GREAT MAY HAVE BEEN THE QUALIFICATIONS of the ancients, however, in the art of pudding-making, we apprehend that such preparations as gave gratification to their palates, would have generally found little favour amongst the insulated inhabitants of Great Britain. Here, from the simple suet dumpling up to the most complicated Christmas production. the grand feature of substantiality is primarily attended to. Variety in the ingredients, we think, is held only of secondary consideration with the great body of the people, provided that the whole is agreeable and of sufficient abundance.

1179. ALTHOUGH FROM PUDDINGS TO PASTRY is but a step, it requires a higher degree of art to make the one than to make the other. Indeed, pastry is one of the most important branches of the culinary science. It unceasingly occupies itself with ministering pleasure to the sight as well as to the taste; with erecting graceful monuments, miniature fortresses, and all kinds of architectural imitations, composed of the sweetest and most agreeable products of all climates and countries. At a very early period, the Orientals were acquainted with the art of manipulating in pastry, but they by no means attained to the taste, variety, and splendour of design, by which it is characterized amongst the moderns. At first it generally consisted of certain mixtures of flour, oil, and honey, to which it was confined for centuries, even among the southern nations of the European continent. At the commencement of the middle ages, a change began to take place in the art of mixing it. Eggs, butter, and salt came into repute in the making of paste, which was forthwith used as an inclosure for meat, seasoned with spices. This advance attained, the next step was to inclose cream, fruit, and marmalades; and the next, to build pyramids and castles; when the summit of the art of the pastry-cook may be supposed to have been achieved.

DIRECTIONS IN CONNECTION WITH THE MAKING OF PUDDINGS AND PASTRY.

1180. A few general remarks respecting the various ingredients of which puddings and pastry are composed, may be acceptable as preliminary to the recipes in this department of Household Management.

1181. *Flour* should be of the best quality, and perfectly dry, and sifted before being used; if in the least damp, the paste made from it will certainly be heavy.

1182. *Butter*, unless fresh is used, should be washed from the salt, and well squeezed and wrung in a cloth, to get out all the water and buttermilk, which, if left in, assists to make the paste heavy.

1183. *Lard* should be perfectly sweet, which may be ascertained by cutting the bladder through, and, if the knife smells sweet, the lard is good.

1184. *Suet* should be finely chopped, perfectly free from skin, and quite sweet; during the process of chopping, it should be lightly dredged with flour, which prevents the pieces from sticking together. Beef suet is considered the best; but veal suet, or the outside fat of a loin or neck of mutton, makes good crusts; as also the skimmings in which a joint of mutton has been boiled, but *without* vegetables.

1185. *Clarified Beef Dripping*, directions for which will be found in recipes Nos. 621 and 622, answers very well for kitchen pies, puddings, cakes, or for family use. A very good short crust may be made by mixing with it a small quantity of moist sugar; but care must be taken to use the dripping sparingly, or a very disagreeable flavour will be imparted to the paste.

1186. Strict cleanliness must be observed in pastry-making; all the utensils used should be perfectly free from dust and dirt, and the things required for pastry, kept entirely for that purpose.

PASTE-BOARD AND ROLLING-PIN.

1187. In mixing paste, add the water very gradually, work the whole together with the knife-blade, and knead it until perfectly smooth. Those who are inexperienced in pastry-making, should work the butter in by breaking it in small pieces and covering the paste rolled out. It should then be dredged with flour, and the ends folded over and rolled out very thin again: this process must be repeated until all the butter is used.

PASTE-PINCERS AND JAGGER, FOR ORNAMENTING THE EDGES OF PIE-CRUSTS.

1188. The art of making paste requires much practice, dexterity, and skill: it should be touched as lightly as possible, made with cool hands and in a cool place (a marble slab is better than a board for the purpose), and the coolest part of the house should be selected for the process during warm weather.

1189. To insure rich paste being light, great expedition must be used in the making and baking; for if it stand long before it is put in the oven, it becomes flat and heavy.

PASTE-CUTTER AND CORNER-CUTTER.   ORNAMENTAL-PASTE CUTTER.

1190. *Puff-paste* requires a brisk oven, but not too hot, or it would blacken the crust; on the other hand, if the oven be too slack, the paste will be soddened, and will not rise, nor will it have any colour.

PATTY-PANS, PLAIN AND FLUTED.   PIE-DISH.

Tart-tins, cake-moulds, dishes for baked puddings, pattypans, &c., should all be buttered before the article intended to be baked is put in them : things to be baked on sheets should be placed on buttered

RAISED-PIE MOULD.   RAISED-PIE MOULD, OPEN.

paper. Raised-pie paste should have a soaking heat, and paste glazed must have rather a slack oven, that the icing be not scorched. It is better to ice tarts, &c. when they are three-parts baked.

1191. To ascertain when the oven is heated to the proper degree for puff-paste, put a small piece of the paste in previous to baking the whole, and then the heat can thus be judged of.

1192. The freshness of all pudding ingredients is of much importance, as one bad article will taint the whole mixture.

1193. When the *freshness* of eggs is *doubtful*, break each one

2 R

separately in a cup, before mixing them altogether. Should there be a bad one amongst them, it can be thrown away; whereas, if mixed with the good ones, the entire quantity would be spoiled. The yolks and whites beaten separately make the articles they are put into much lighter.

1194. Raisins and dried fruits for puddings should be carefully picked, and, in many cases, stoned. Currants should be well washed, pressed in a cloth, and placed on a dish before the fire to get thoroughly dry; they should then be picked carefully over, and *every piece of grit or stone* removed from amongst them. To plump them, some cooks pour boiling water over them, and then dry them before the fire.

1195. Batter pudding should be smoothly mixed and free from lumps. To insure this, first mix the flour with a very small proportion of milk, and add the remainder by degrees. Should the pudding be very lumpy, it may be strained through a hair sieve.

1196. *All boiled puddings* should be put on in *boiling water*, which must not be allowed to stop simmering, and the pudding must always be covered with the water; if requisite, the saucepan should be kept filled up.

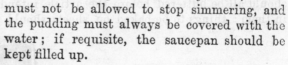

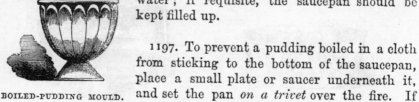

1197. To prevent a pudding boiled in a cloth from sticking to the bottom of the saucepan, place a small plate or saucer underneath it, and set the pan *on a trivet* over the fire. If a mould is used, this precaution is not neces-

BOILED-PUDDING MOULD.

sary; but care must be taken to keep the pudding well covered with water.

1198. For dishing a boiled pudding as soon as it comes out of the pot, dip it into a basin of cold water, and the cloth will then not adhere to it. Great expedition is necessary in sending puddings to table, as, by standing, they quickly become heavy, batter puddings particularly.

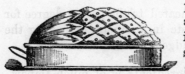

BOILED-PUDDING MOULD.

1199. For baked or boiled puddings, the moulds, cups, or basins, should be always buttered before the mixture is put in them, and they should be put into the saucepan directly they are filled.

1200. Scrupulous attention should be paid to the cleanliness of pudding-cloths, as, from neglect in this particular, the outsides of boiled puddings frequently taste very dis-agreeably. As soon as possible after it is taken off the pudding, it should be soaked in water, and then well washed, without soap, unless it be very greasy. It should be dried out of doors, then folded up and kept in a dry place. When wanted for

PUDDING-BASIN.

use, dip it in boiling water, and dredge it slightly with flour.

1201. *The dry ingredients* for puddings are better for being mixed some time before they are wanted; the liquid portion should only be added just before the pudding is put into the saucepan.

1202. A pinch of salt is an improvement to the generality of puddings; but this ingredient should be added very sparingly, as the flavour should not be detected.

1203. When baked puddings are sufficiently solid, turn them out of the dish they were baked in, bottom uppermost, and strew over them fine sifted sugar.

1204. When pastry or baked puddings are not done through, and yet the outside is sufficiently brown, cover them over with a piece of white paper until thoroughly cooked : this prevents them from getting burnt.

RECIPES.

CHAPTER XXVII.

VERY GOOD PUFF-PASTE.

1205. INGREDIENTS.—To every lb. of flour allow 1 lb. of butter, and not quite ½ pint of water.

Mode.—Carefully weigh the flour and butter, and have the exact proportion; squeeze the butter well, to extract the water from it, and afterwards wring it in a clean cloth, that no moisture may remain. Sift the flour; see that it is perfectly dry, and proceed in the following manner to make the paste, using a very *clean* paste-board and rolling-pin:—Supposing the quantity to be 1 lb. of flour, work the whole into a smooth paste, with not quite ½ pint of water, using a knife to mix it with: the proportion of this latter ingredient must be regulated by the discretion of the cook; if too much be added, the paste, when baked, will be tough. Roll it out until it is of an equal thickness of about an inch; break 4 oz. of the butter into small pieces; place these on the paste, sift over it a little flour, fold it over, roll out again, and put another 4 oz. of butter. Repeat the rolling and buttering until the paste has been rolled out 4 times, or equal quantities of flour and butter have been used. Do not omit, every time the paste is rolled out, to dredge a little flour over that and the rolling-pin, to prevent both from sticking. Handle the paste as lightly as possible, and do not press heavily upon it with the rolling-pin. The next thing to be considered is the oven, as the baking of pastry requires particular attention. Do not put it into the oven until it is sufficiently hot to raise the paste; for the best-prepared paste, if not properly baked, will be good for nothing. Brushing the paste as often as rolled out, and the pieces of butter placed thereon, with the white of an egg, assists it to rise in *leaves* or *flakes*. As this is the great beauty of puff-paste, it is as well to try this method.

Average cost, 1s. 4d. per lb.

BUTTER.—About the second century of the Christian era, butter was placed by Galen amongst the useful medical agents; and about a century before him, Dioscorides mentioned that he had noticed that fresh butter, made of ewes' and goats' milk, was served at meals instead of oil, and that it took the place of fat in making pastry. Thus we have undoubted authority that, eighteen hundred years ago, there existed a knowledge of the useful qualities of butter. The Romans seem to have set about making it much as we do; for Pliny tells us, "Butter is made from milk; and the use of this aliment, so much sought after by barbarous nations, distinguished the rich from the common people. It is obtained principally from cows' milk; that from ewes is the fattest; goats also supply some. It is produced by agitating the milk in long vessels with narrow openings: a little water is added."

MEDIUM PUFF-PASTE.

1206. INGREDIENTS.—To every lb. of flour allow 8 oz. of butter, 4 oz. of lard, not quite ½ pint of water.

Mode.—This paste may be made by the directions in the preceding recipe, only using less butter and substituting lard for a portion of it. Mix the flour to a smooth paste with not quite ½ pint of water; then roll it out 3 times, the first time covering the paste with butter, the second with lard, and the third with butter. Keep the rolling-pin and paste slightly dredged with flour, to prevent them from sticking, and it will be ready for use.

Average cost, 1s. per lb.

BUTTER IN HASTE.—In his "History of Food," Soyer says that to obtain butter instantly, it is only necessary, in summer, to put new milk into a bottle, some hours after it has been taken from the cow, and shake it briskly. The clots which are thus formed should be thrown into a sieve, washed and pressed together, and they constitute the finest and most delicate butter that can possibly be made.

COMMON PASTE, for Family Pies.

1207. INGREDIENTS.—1¼ lb. of flour, ½ lb. of butter, rather more than ½ pint of water.

Mode.—Rub the butter lightly into the flour, and mix it to a smooth paste with the water; roll it out 2 or 3 times, and it will be ready for use. This paste may be converted into an excellent short crust for sweet tart, by adding to the flour, after the butter is rubbed in, 2 tablespoonfuls of fine-sifted sugar.

Average cost, 8d. per lb.

TO KEEP BUTTER FRESH.—One of the best means to preserve butter fresh is, first to completely press out all the buttermilk, then to keep it under water, renewing the water frequently, and to remove it from the influence of heat and air, by wrapping it in a wet cloth.

FRENCH PUFF-PASTE, or FEUILLETAGE.
(*Founded on M. Ude's Recipe.*)

1208. INGREDIENTS.—Equal quantities of flour and butter — say 1 lb. of each; ½ saltspoonful of salt, the yolks of 2 eggs, rather more than ¼ pint of water.

Mode.—Weigh the flour; ascertain that it is perfectly *dry*, and sift it; squeeze all the water from the butter, and wring it in a clean cloth till there is no moisture remaining. Put the flour on the paste-board, work lightly into it 2 oz. of the butter, and then make a hole in the centre; into this well put the yolks of 2 eggs, the salt, and about

¼ pint of water (the quantity of this latter ingredient must be regulated by the cook, as it is impossible to give the exact proportion of it); knead up the paste quickly and lightly, and, when quite smooth, roll it out square to the thickness of about ½ inch. Presuming that the butter is perfectly free from moisture, and *as cool* as possible, roll it into a ball, and place this ball of butter on the paste; fold the paste over the butter all round, and secure it by wrapping it well all over. Flatten the paste by rolling it lightly with the rolling-pin until it is quite thin, but not thin enough to allow the butter to break through, and keep the board and paste dredged lightly with flour during the process of making it. This rolling gives it the *first* turn. Now fold the paste in three, and roll out again, and, should the weather be very warm, put it in a cold place on the ground to cool between the several turns; for, unless this is particularly attended to, the paste will be spoiled. Roll out the paste again *twice*, put it by to cool, then roll it out *twice* more, which will make 6 *turnings* in all. Now fold the paste in two, and it will be ready for use. If properly baked and well made, this crust will be delicious, and should rise in the oven about 5 or 6 inches. The paste should be made rather firm in the first instance, as the ball of butter is liable to break through. Great attention must also be paid to keeping the butter very cool, as, if this is in a liquid and soft state, the paste will not answer at all. Should the cook be dexterous enough to succeed in making this, the paste will have a much better appearance than that made by the process of dividing the butter into 4 parts, and placing it over the rolled-out paste; but, until experience has been acquired, we recommend puff-paste made by recipe No. 1205. The above paste is used for vols-au-vent, small articles of pastry, and, in fact, everything that requires very light crust.

Average cost, 1s. 6d. per lb.

WHAT TO DO WITH RANCID BUTTER.—When butter has become very rancid, it should be melted several times by a moderate heat, with or without the addition of water, and as soon as it has been well kneaded, after the cooling, in order to extract any water it may have retained, it should be put into brown freestone pots, sheltered from the contact of the air. The French often add to it, after it has been melted, a piece of toasted bread, which helps to destroy the tendency of the butter to rancidity.

SOYER'S RECIPE FOR PUFF-PASTE.

1209. INGREDIENTS.—To every lb. of flour allow the yolk of 1 egg, the juice of 1 lemon, ½ saltspoonful of salt, cold water, 1 lb. of fresh butter.

Mode.—Put the flour on to the paste-board; make a hole in the centre, into which put the yolk of the egg, the lemon-juice, and salt; mix the whole with cold water (this should be iced in summer, if convenient) into a soft flexible paste, with the right hand, and handle it as little as possible; then squeeze all the buttermilk from the butter, wring it in a cloth, and roll out the paste; place the butter on this, and fold the edges of the paste over, so as to hide it; roll it out again to the thickness of $\frac{1}{4}$ inch; fold over one third, over which again pass the rolling-pin; then fold over the other third, thus forming a square; place it with the ends, top, and bottom before you, shaking a little flour both under and over, and repeat the rolls and turns twice again, as before. Flour a baking-sheet, put the paste on this, and let it remain on ice or in some cool place for $\frac{1}{2}$ hour; then roll twice more, turning it as before; place it again upon the ice for $\frac{1}{4}$ hour, give it 2 more rolls, making 7 in all, and it is ready for use when required.

Average cost, 1s. 6d. per lb.

VERY GOOD SHORT CRUST FOR FRUIT TARTS.

1210. INGREDIENTS.—To every lb. of flour allow $\frac{3}{4}$ lb. of butter, 1 tablespoonful of sifted sugar, $\frac{1}{3}$ pint of water.

Mode.—Rub the butter into the flour, after having ascertained that the latter is perfectly dry; add the sugar, and mix the whole into a stiff paste, with about $\frac{1}{3}$ pint of water. Roll it out two or three times, folding the paste over each time, and it will be ready for use.

Average cost, 1s. 1d. per lb.

ANOTHER GOOD SHORT CRUST.

1211. INGREDIENTS.—To every lb. of flour allow 8 oz. of butter, the yolks of 2 eggs, 2 oz. of sifted sugar, about $\frac{1}{4}$ pint of milk.

Mode.—Rub the butter into the flour, add the sugar, and mix the whole as lightly as possible to a smooth paste, with the yolks of eggs well beaten, and the milk. The proportion of the latter ingredient must be judged of by the size of the eggs: if these are large, so much will not be required, and more if the eggs are smaller.

Average cost, 1s. per lb.

SUGAR AND BEETROOT.—There are two sorts of Beet,—white and red; occasionally, in the south, a yellow variety is met with. Beetroot contains twenty parts sugar. Everybody knows that the beet has competed with the sugar-cane, and a great part of the French sugar is manufactured from beet. Beetroot has a refreshing, composing, and slightly purgative quality. The young leaves, when cooked, are a substitute for spinach; they are also useful for mixing with sorrel, to lessen its acidity. The large ribs of the leaves are serviceable in various culinary preparations; the root also may be prepared in several ways, but its most general use is in salad. Some writers upon the subject have expressed their opinion that beetroot is easily digested, but those who have taken pains to carefully analyze its qualities make quite a contrary statement. Youth, of course, can digest it; but to persons of a certain age beet is very indigestible, or rather, it does not digest at all. It is not the sugary pulp which is indigestible, but its fibrous network that resists the action of the gastric organs. Thus, when the root is reduced to a purée, almost any person may eat it.

FRENCH SUGAR.—It had long been thought that tropical heat was not necessary to form sugar, and, about 1740, it was discovered that many plants of the temperate zone, and amongst others the beet, contained it. Towards the beginning of the 19th century, circumstances having, in France, made sugar scarce, and consequently dear, the government caused inquiries to be instituted as to the possibility of finding a substitute for it. Accordingly, it was ascertained that sugar exists in the whole vegetable kingdom; that it is to be found in the grape, chestnut, potato; but that, far above all, the beet contains it in a large proportion. Thus the beet became an object of the most careful culture; and many experiments went to prove that in this respect the old world was independent of the new. Many manufactories came into existence in all parts of France, and the making of sugar became naturalized in that country.

COMMON SHORT CRUST.

1212. INGREDIENTS.—To every pound of flour allow 2 oz. of sifted sugar, 3 oz. of butter, about ½ pint of boiling milk.

Mode.—Crumble the butter into the flour as finely as possible, add the sugar, and work the whole up to a smooth paste with the boiling milk. Roll it out thin, and bake in a moderate oven.

Average cost, 6d. per lb.

QUALITIES OF SUGAR.—Sugars obtained from various plants are, in fact, of the same nature, and have no intrinsic difference when they have become equally purified by the same processes. Taste, crystallization, colour, weight, are absolutely identical; and the most acute observer cannot distinguish the one from the other.

BUTTER CRUST, for Boiled Puddings.

1213. INGREDIENTS.—To every lb. of flour allow 6 oz. of butter, ½ pint of water.

Mode.—With a knife, work the flour to a smooth paste with ½ pint of water; roll the crust out rather thin; place the butter over it in small pieces; dredge lightly over it some flour, and fold the paste over; repeat the rolling once more, and the crust will be ready for use. It may be enriched by adding another 2 oz. of butter; but, for ordinary purposes, the above quantity will be found quite sufficient.

Average cost, 6d. per lb.

DRIPPING CRUST, for Kitchen Puddings, Pies, &c.

1214. INGREDIENTS.—To every lb. of flour allow 6 oz. of clarified beef dripping, ½ pint of water.

Mode.—After having clarified the dripping, by either of the recipes No. 621 or 622, weigh it, and to every lb. of flour allow the above proportion of dripping. With a knife, work the flour into a smooth paste with the water, rolling it out 3 times, each time placing on the crust 2 oz. of the dripping, broken into small pieces. If this paste is lightly made, if good dripping is used, and *not too much* of it, it will be found good; and by the addition of two tablespoonfuls of fine moist sugar, it may be converted into a common short crust for fruit pies.

Average cost, 4d. per pound.

WATER:—WHAT THE ANCIENTS THOUGHT OF IT.—All the nations of antiquity possessed great veneration for water: thus, the Egyptians offered prayers and homage to water, and the Nile was an especial object of their adoration; the Persians would not wash their hands; the Scythians honoured the Danube; the Greeks and Romans erected altars to the fountains and rivers; and some of the architectural embellishments executed for fountains in Greece were remarkable for their beauty and delicacy. The purity of the water was a great object of the care of the ancients; and we learn that the Athenians appointed four officers to keep watch and ward over the water in their city. These men had to keep the fountains in order and clean the reservoirs, so that the water might be preserved pure and limpid. Like officers were appointed in other Greek cities.

SUET CRUST, for Pies or Puddings.

1215. INGREDIENTS.—To every lb. of flour allow 5 or 6 oz. of beef suet, ½ pint of water.

Mode.—Free the suet from skin and shreds; chop it extremely fine, and rub it well into the flour; work the whole to a smooth paste with the above proportion of water; roll it out, and it is ready for use. This crust is quite rich enough for ordinary purposes, but when a better one is desired, use from ½ to ¾ lb. of suet to every lb. of flour. Some cooks, for rich crusts, pound the suet in a mortar, with a small quantity of butter. It should then be laid on the paste in small pieces, the same as for puff-crust, and will be found exceedingly nice for hot tarts. 5 oz. of suet to every lb. of flour will make a very good crust; and even ¼ lb. will answer very well for children, or where the crust is wanted very plain.

Average cost, 5d. per lb.

PATE BRISEE, or FRENCH CRUST, for Raised Pies.

1216. INGREDIENTS.—To every lb. of flour allow ½ saltspoonful of salt, 2 eggs, ⅓ pint of water, 6 oz. of butter.

Mode.—Spread the flour, which should be sifted and thoroughly dry, on the paste-board; make a hole in the centre, into which put the butter; work it lightly into the flour, and when quite fine, add the salt; work the whole into a smooth paste with the eggs (yolks and whites) and water, and make it very firm. Knead the paste well, and let it be rather stiff, that the sides of the pie may be easily raised, and that they do not afterwards tumble or shrink.

Average cost, 1s. per lb.

Note.—This paste may be very much enriched by making it with equal quantities of flour and butter; but then it is not so easily raised as when made plainer.

WATER SUPPLY IN ROME.—Nothing in Italy is more extraordinary than the remains of the ancient aqueducts. At first, the Romans were contented with the water from the Tiber. Ancus Martius was the first to commence the building of aqueducts destined to convey the water of the fountain of Piconia from Tibur to Rome, a distance of some 33,000 paces. Appius Claudius continued the good work, and to him is due the completion of the celebrated Appian Way. In time, the gigantic waterways greatly multiplied, and, by the reign of Nero, there were constructed nine principal aqueducts, the pipes of which were of bricks, baked tiles, stone, lead, or wood. According to the calculation of Vigenerus, half a million hogsheads of water were conveyed into Rome every day, by upwards of 10,000 small pipes not one-third of an inch in diameter. The water was received in large closed basins, above which rose splendid monuments: these basins supplied other subterranean conduits, connected with various quarters of the city, and these conveyed water to small reservoirs furnished with taps for the exclusive use of certain streets. The water which was not drinkable ran out, by means of large pipes, into extensive inclosures, where it served to water cattle. At these places the people washed their linen; and here, too, was a supply of the necessary element in case of fire.

COMMON CRUST FOR RAISED PIES.

1217. INGREDIENTS.—To every lb. of flour allow ½ pint of water, 1½ oz. of butter, 1½ oz. of lard, ½ saltspoonful of salt.

Mode.—Put into a saucepan the water; when it boils, add the butter and lard; and when these are melted, make a hole in the middle of the flour; pour in the water gradually; beat it well with a wooden spoon, and be particular in not making the paste too soft. When it is well mixed, knead it with the hands until quite stiff, dredging a little flour over the paste and board, to prevent them from sticking. When it is well kneaded, place it before the fire, with a cloth covered over it, for a few minutes; it will then be more easily worked into shape. This paste does not taste so nicely as the preceding one, but is worked with greater facility, and answers just as well for raised pies, for the crust is seldom eaten.

Average cost, 5d. per lb.

LARD OR FLEAD CRUST.

1218. INGREDIENTS.—To every lb. of flour allow ½ lb. of lard or flead, ½ pint of water, ½ saltspoonful of salt.

Mode.—Clear the flead free from skin, and slice it into thin flakes; rub it into the flour, add the salt, and work the whole into a smooth paste, with the above proportion of water; fold the paste over two or three times, beat it well with the rolling-pin, roll it out, and it will be ready for use. The crust made from this will be found extremely light, and may be made into cakes or tarts; it may also be very much enriched by adding more flead to the same proportion of flour.

Average cost, 8d. per lb.

NUTRITIOUS QUALITIES OF FLOUR.—The gluten of grain and the albumen of vegetable juices are identical in composition with the albumen of blood. Vegetable caseine has also the composition of animal caseine. The finest wheat flour contains more starch than the coarser; the bran of wheat is proportionably richer in gluten. Rye and rye-bread contain a substance resembling starch-gum (or dextrine, as it is called) in its properties, which is very easily converted into sugar. The starch of barley approaches in many properties to cellulose, and is, therefore, less digestible. Oats are particularly rich in plastic substances; Scotch oats are richer than those grown in England or in Germany. This kind of grain contains in its ashes, after deduction of the silica of the husks, very nearly the same ingredients as are found in the ashes of the juice of flesh. Fine American flour is one of the varieties which is richest in gluten, and is consequently one of the most nutritious.

ALMOND CHEESECAKES.

1219. INGREDIENTS.—¼ lb. of sweet almonds, 4 bitter ones, 3 eggs, 2 oz. of butter, the rind of ¼ lemon, 1 tablespoonful of lemon-juice, 3 oz. of sugar.

Mode.—Blanch and pound the almonds smoothly in a mortar, with a little rose- or spring-water ; stir in the eggs, which should be well beaten, and the butter, which should be warmed ; add the grated lemon-peel and -juice, sweeten, and stir well until the whole is thoroughly mixed.   Line some pattypans with puff-paste, put in the mixture, and bake for 20 minutes, or rather less in a quick oven.

Time.—20 minutes, or rather less.

Average cost, 10d.

Sufficient for about 12 cheesecakes.

Seasonable at any time.

ALMONDS.—Almonds are the fruit of the *Amygdalus communis,* and are cultivated throughout the whole of the south of Europe, Syria, Persia, and Northern Africa ; but England is mostly supplied with those which are grown in Spain and the south of France. They are distinguished into Sweet and Bitter, the produce of different varieties. Of the sweet, there are two varieties, distinguished in commerce by the names of Jordan and Valentia almonds. The former are imported from Malaga, and are longer, narrower, more pointed, and more highly esteemed than the latter, which are imported from Valentia.   Bitter almonds are principally obtained from Morocco, and are exported from Mogador.

ALMOND AND BLOSSOM

ALMOND PASTE, for Second-Course Dishes.

1220. INGREDIENTS.—1 lb. of sweet almonds, 6 bitter ones, 1 lb. of very finely sifted sugar, the whites of 2 eggs.

Mode.—Blanch the almonds, and dry them thoroughly ; put them into a mortar, and pound them well, wetting them gradually with the whites of 2 eggs. When well pounded, put them into a small preserving-pan, add the sugar, and place the pan on a small but clear fire (a hot-plate is better) ; keep stirring until the paste is dry, then take it out of the pan, put it between two dishes, and, when cold, make it into any shape that fancy may dictate.

Time.—½ hour.   *Average cost,* 2s. for the above quantity.

Sufficient for 3 small dishes of pastry.

Seasonable at any time.

BITTER ALMONDS.—The Bitter Almond is a variety of the common almond, and is injurious to animal life, on account of the great quantity of hydrocyanic acid it contains, and is consequently seldom used in domestic economy, unless it be to give flavour to confectionery ; and even then it should be used with great caution. A single drop of the essential oil of bitter almonds is sufficient to destroy a bird, and four drops have caused the death of a middle-sized dog.

BAKED ALMOND PUDDING.

(*Very rich.*)

1221. INGREDIENTS.—¼ lb. of almonds, 4 bitter ditto, 1 glass of sherry, 4 eggs, the rind and juice of ½ lemon, 3 oz. of butter, 1 pint of cream, 2 tablespoonfuls of sugar.

Mode.—Blanch and pound the almonds to a smooth paste with the water; mix these with the butter, which should be melted; beat up the eggs, grate the lemon-rind, and strain the juice; add these, with the cream, sugar, and wine, to the other ingredients, and stir them well together. When well mixed, put it into a pie-dish lined with puff-paste, and bake for ½ hour.

Time.—½ hour. *Average cost,* 2s. 3d.

Sufficient for 4 or 5 persons.

Seasonable at any time.

Note.—To make this pudding more economically, substitute milk for the cream; but then add rather more than 1 oz. of finely-grated bread.

USES OF THE SWEET ALMOND.—The kernels of the sweet almond are used either in a green or ripe state, and as an article in the dessert. Into cookery, confectionery, perfumery, and medicine, they largely enter, and in domestic economy, should always be used in preference to bitter almonds. The reason for advising this, is because the kernels do not contain any hydrocyanic or prussic acid, although it is found in the leaves, flowers, and bark of the tree. When young and green, they are preserved in sugar, like green apricots. They furnish the almond-oil; and the farinaceous matter which is left after the oil is expressed, forms the *pâte d'amandes* of perfumers. In the arts, the oil is employed for the same purposes as the olive-oil, and forms the basis of kalydor, macassar oil, Gowland's lotion, and many other articles of that kind vended by perfumers. In medicine, it is considered a nutritive, laxative, and an emollient.

SMALL ALMOND PUDDINGS.

1222. INGREDIENTS.—½ lb. of sweet almonds, 6 bitter ones, ¼ lb. of butter, 4 eggs, 2 tablespoonfuls of sifted sugar, 2 tablespoonfuls of cream, 1 tablespoonful of brandy.

Mode.—Blanch and pound the almonds to a smooth paste with a spoonful of water; warm the butter, mix the almonds with this, and  add the other ingredients, leaving out the whites of 2 eggs, and be particular that these are well beaten. Mix well, butter some cups,

ALMOND PUDDINGS.

half fill them, and bake the puddings from 20 minutes to ½ hour. Turn them out on a dish, and serve with sweet sauce.

Time.—20 minutes to ½ hour. *Average cost,* 1s.

Sufficient for 4 or 5 persons. *Seasonable* at any time.

THE HUSKS OF ALMONDS.—In the environs of Alicante, the husks of almonds are ground to a powder, and enter into the composition of common soap, the large quantity of alkaline principle they contain rendering them suitable for this purpose. It is said that in some parts of the south of France, where they are extensively grown, horses and mules are fed on the green and dry husks; but, to prevent any evil consequences arising from this practice, they are mixed with chopped straw or oats.

ALMOND PUFFS.

1223. INGREDIENTS.—2 tablespoonfuls of flour, 2 oz. of butter, 2 oz. of pounded sugar, 2 oz. of sweet almonds, 4 bitter almonds.

Mode.—Blanch and pound the almonds in a mortar to a smooth paste; melt the butter, dredge in the flour, and add the sugar and pounded almonds. Beat the mixture well, and put it into cups or very tiny jelly-pots, which should be well buttered, and bake in a moderate oven for about 20 minutes, or longer should the puffs be large. Turn them out on a dish, the bottom of the puff uppermost, and serve.

Time.—20 minutes. *Average cost,* 6d.

Sufficient for 2 or 3 persons. *Seasonable* at any time.

AUNT NELLY'S PUDDING.

1224. INGREDIENTS.—½ lb. of flour, ½ lb. of treacle, ½ lb. of suet, the rind and juice of 1 lemon, a few strips of candied lemon-peel, 3 tablespoonfuls of cream, 2 eggs.

Mode.—Chop the suet finely; mix with it the flour, treacle, lemon-peel minced, and candied lemon-peel; add the cream, lemon-juice, and 2 well-beaten eggs; beat the pudding well, put it into a buttered basin, tie it down with a cloth, and boil from 3½ to 4 hours.

Time.—3½ to 4 hours. *Average cost,* 1s. 2d.

Sufficient for 5 or 6 persons.

Seasonable at any time, but more suitable for a winter pudding.

TREACLE, OR MOLASSES.—Treacle is the uncrystallizable part of the saccharine juice drained from the Muscovado sugar, and is either naturally so or rendered uncrystallizable through some defect in the process of boiling. As it contains a large quantity of sweet or saccharine principle and is cheap, it is of great use as an article of domestic economy. Children are especially fond of it; and it is accounted wholesome. It is also useful for making beer, rum, and the very dark syrups.

BAKED APPLE DUMPLINGS (a Plain Family Dish).

1225. INGREDIENTS.—6 apples, ¾ lb. of suet-crust No. 1215, sugar to taste.

Mode.—Pare and take out the cores of the apples without dividing them, and make ½ lb. of suet-crust by recipe No. 1215; roll the apples in the crust, previously sweetening them with moist sugar, and taking care to join the paste nicely. When they are formed into round balls, put them on a tin, and bake them for about ½ hour, or longer should the apples be very large; arrange them pyramidically on a dish, and sift over them some pounded white sugar. These may be made richer by using one of the puff-pastes instead of suet.

Time.—From ½ to ¾ hour, or longer. *Average cost,* 1½d. each.

Sufficient for 4 persons.

Seasonable from August to March, but flavourless after the end of January.

USES OF THE APPLE.—It is well known that this fruit forms a very important article of food, in the form of pies and puddings, and furnishes several delicacies, such as sauces, marmalades, and jellies, and is much esteemed as a dessert fruit. When flattened in the form of round cakes, and baked in ovens, they are called beefings; and large quantities are annually dried in the sun in America, as well as in Normandy, and stored for use during winter, when they may be stewed or made into pies. In a roasted state they are remarkably wholesome, and, it is said, strengthening to a weak stomach. In putrid and malignant fevers, when used with the juice of lemons and currants, they are considered highly efficacious.

APPLE CHEESECAKES.

1226. INGREDIENTS.—½ lb. of apple pulp, ¼ lb. of sifted sugar, ¼ lb. of butter, 4 eggs, the rind and juice of 1 lemon.

Mode.—Pare, core, and boil sufficient apples to make ½ lb. when cooked; add to these the sugar, the butter, which should be melted; the eggs, leaving out 2 of the whites, and the grated rind and juice of

1 lemon; stir the mixture well; line some pattypans with puff-paste, put in the mixture, and bake about 20 minutes.

Time.—About 20 minutes.

Average cost, for the above quantity, with the paste, 1s. 2d.

Sufficient for about 18 or 20 cheesecakes.

Seasonable from August to March.

APPLE AND BLOSSOM.

THE APPLE.—The most useful of all the British fruits is the apple, which is a native of Britain, and may be found in woods and hedges, in the form of the common wild crab, of which all our best apples are merely seminal varieties, produced by culture or particular circumstances. In most temperate climates it is very extensively cultivated, and in England, both as regards variety and quantity, it is excellent and abundant. Immense supplies are also imported from the United States and from France. The apples grown in the vicinity of New York are universally admitted to be the finest of any; but unless selected and packed with great care, they are apt to spoil before reaching England.

BOILED APPLE DUMPLINGS.

1227. INGREDIENTS.—6 apples, ¾ lb. of suet-crust No. 1215, sugar to taste.

Mode.—Pare and take out the cores of the apples without dividing them; sweeten, and roll each apple in a piece of crust, made by recipe No. 1211; be particular that the paste is nicely joined; put the dumplings into floured cloths, tie them securely, and put them into boiling water. Keep them boiling from ½ to ¾ hour; remove the cloths, and send them hot and quickly to table. Dumplings boiled in knitted cloths have a very pretty appearance when they come to table. The cloths should be made square, just large enough to hold one dumpling, and should be knitted in plain knitting, with *very coarse* cotton.

Time.—$\frac{3}{4}$ to 1 hour, or longer should the dumplings be very large.

Average cost, 1$\frac{1}{2}$d. each.   *Sufficient* for 4 persons.

Seasonable from August to March, but flavourless after the end of January.

LAMBSWOOL, or LAMASOOL.—This old English beverage is composed of apples mixed with ale, and seasoned with sugar and spice. It takes its name from *Lamœs abhal,* which, in ancient British, signifies the day of apple fruit, from being drunk on the apple feast in autumn. In France, a beverage, called by the Parisians *raisinée*, is made by boiling any given quantity of new wine, skimming it as often as fresh scum rises, and, when it is boiled to half its bulk, straining it. To this apples, pared and cut into quarters, are added ; the whole is then allowed to simmer gently, stirring it all the time with a long wooden spoon, till the apples are thoroughly mixed with the liquor, and the whole forms a species of marmalade, which is extremely agreeable to the taste, having a slight flavour of acidity, like lemon mixed with honey.

RICH BAKED APPLE PUDDING.

I.

1228. INGREDIENTS.—$\frac{1}{2}$ lb. of the pulp of apples, $\frac{1}{2}$ lb. of loaf sugar, 6 oz. of butter, the rind of 1 lemon, 6 eggs, puff-paste.

Mode.—Peel, core, and cut the apples, as for sauce ; put them into a stewpan, with only just sufficient water to prevent them from burning, and let them stew until reduced to a pulp. Weigh the pulp, and to every $\frac{1}{2}$ lb. add sifted sugar, grated lemon-rind, and 6 well-beaten eggs. Beat these ingredients well together ; then melt the butter, stir it to the other things, put a border of puff-paste round the dish, and bake for rather more than $\frac{1}{2}$ hour. The butter should not be added until the pudding is ready for the oven.

Time.—$\frac{1}{2}$ to $\frac{3}{4}$ hour.   *Average cost*, 1s. 10d.

Sufficient for 5 or 6 persons.

Seasonable from August to March.

II.

(*More Economical.*)

1229. INGREDIENTS.—12 large apples, 6 oz. of moist sugar, $\frac{1}{4}$ lb. of butter, 4 eggs, 1 pint of bread crumbs.

Mode.—Pare, core, and cut the apples, as for sauce, and boil them until reduced to a pulp ; then add the butter, melted, and the eggs, which should be well whisked. Beat up the pudding for 2 or 3 minutes ; butter a pie-dish ; put in a layer of bread crumbs, then the apple, and then another layer of bread crumbs ; flake over these a few tiny pieces of butter, and bake for about $\frac{1}{2}$ hour.

Time.—About $\frac{1}{2}$ hour.   *Average cost*, 1s. 3d.

Sufficient for 5 or 6 persons.

Seasonable from August to March.

Note.—A very good economical pudding may be made merely with apples, boiled and sweetened, with the addition of a few strips of lemon-peel. A layer of bread crumbs should be placed above and below the apples, and the pudding baked for $\frac{1}{2}$ hour.

CONSTITUENTS OF THE APPLE.—All apples contain sugar, malic acid, or the acid of apples; mucilage, or gum; woody fibre, and water; together with some aroma, on which their peculiar flavour depends. The hard acid kinds are unwholesome if eaten raw; but by the process of cooking, a great deal of this acid is decomposed and converted into sugar. The sweet and mellow kinds form a valuable addition to the dessert. A great part of the acid juice is converted into sugar as the fruit ripens, and even after it is gathered, by a natural process, termed maturation; but, when apples decay, the sugar is changed into a bitter principle, and the mucilage becomes mouldy and offensive. Old cheese has a remarkable effect in meliorating the apple when eaten; probably from the volatile alkali or ammonia of the cheese neutralizing its acid.

RICH SWEET APPLE PUDDING.

1230. INGREDIENTS.—$\frac{1}{2}$ lb. of bread crumbs, $\frac{1}{2}$ lb. of suet, $\frac{1}{2}$ lb. of currants, $\frac{1}{2}$ lb. of apples, $\frac{1}{2}$ lb. of moist sugar, 6 eggs, 12 sweet almonds, $\frac{1}{2}$ saltspoonful of grated nutmeg, 1 wineglassful of brandy.

Mode.—Chop the suet very fine; wash the currants, dry them, and pick away the stalks and pieces of grit; pare, core, and chop the apple, and grate the bread into fine crumbs, and mince the almonds. Mix all these ingredients together, adding the sugar and nutmeg; beat up the eggs, omitting the whites of three; stir these to the pudding, and when all is well mixed, add the brandy, and put the pudding into a buttered mould; tie down with a cloth, put it into boiling water, and let it boil for 3 hours.

Time.—3 hours.   *Average cost*, 2s.

Sufficient for 5 or 6 persons.

Seasonable from August to March.

To PRESERVE APPLES.—The best mode of preserving apples is to carry them at once to the fruit-room, where they should be put upon shelves, covered with white paper, after gently wiping each of the fruit. The room should be dry, and well aired, but should not admit the sun. The finer and larger kinds of fruit should not be allowed to touch each other, but should be kept separate. For this purpose, a number of shallow trays should be provided, supported by racks or stands above each other. In very cold frosty weather, means should be adopted for warming the room.

BAKED APPLE PUDDING.
(*Very Good.*)

1231. INGREDIENTS.—5 moderate-sized apples, 2 tablespoonfuls of finely-chopped suet, 3 eggs, 3 tablespoonfuls of flour, 1 pint of milk, a little grated nutmeg.

Mode.—Mix the flour to a smooth batter with the milk; add the eggs, which should be well whisked, and put this batter into a well-buttered pie-dish. Wipe the apples clean, but do not pare them; cut them in halves, and take out the cores; lay them in the batter, rind uppermost; shake the suet on the top, over which also grate a little nutmeg; bake in a moderate oven for an hour, and cover, when served, with sifted loaf sugar. This pudding is also very good with the apples pared, sliced, and mixed with the batter.

Time.—1 hour. *Average cost*, 9*d.*

Sufficient for 5 or 6 persons.

BOILED APPLE PUDDING.

1232. INGREDIENTS.—Crust No. 1215, apples, sugar to taste, 1 small teaspoonful of finely-minced lemon-peel, 2 tablespoonfuls of lemon-juice.

Mode.—Make a butter-crust by recipe No. 1213, or a suet one by recipe No. 1215, using for a moderate-sized pudding from ¾ to 1 lb. of flour, with the other ingredients in proportion. Butter a basin; line it with some of the paste; pare, core, and cut the apples into slices, and fill the basin with these; add the sugar, the lemon-peel and juice, and cover with crust; pinch the edges together, flour the cloth, place it over the pudding, tie it securely, and put it into plenty of fast-boiling water. Let it boil from 1½ to 2½ hours, according to the size; then turn it out of the basin and send to table quickly. Apple puddings may also be boiled in a cloth without a basin; but, when made in this way, must be served without the least delay, as the crust so soon becomes heavy. Apple pudding is a very convenient dish to have when the dinner-hour is rather uncertain, as it does not spoil by being boiled an extra hour; care, however, must be taken to keep it well covered with the water all the time, and not to allow it to stop boiling.

Time.—From 1½ to 2½ hours, according to the size of the pudding and the quality of the apples.

Average cost, 10*d.*

Sufficient, made with 1 lb. of flour, for 7 or 8 persons.

Seasonable from August to March; but the apples become flavourless and scarce after February.

APPLE TART OR PIE.

1233. INGREDIENTS.—Puff-paste No. 1205 or 1206, apples; to every lb. of unpared apples allow 2 oz. of moist sugar, ½ teaspoonful of finely-minced lemon-peel, 1 tablespoonful of lemon-juice.

Mode.—Make ½ lb. of puff-paste by either of the above-named recipes, place a border of it round the edge of a pie-dish, and fill it with apples pared, cored, and cut into slices; sweeten with moist sugar, add the lemon-peel and juice, and 2 or 3 tablespoonfuls of water; cover with crust, cut it evenly round close to the edge of the pie-dish, and bake in a hot oven from ½ to ¾ hour, or rather longer, should the pie be

2 s

very large. When it is three-parts done, take it out of the oven, put the white of an egg on a plate, and, with the blade of a knife, whisk it to a froth; brush the pie over with this, then sprinkle upon it some sifted sugar, and then a few drops of water. Put the pie back into the oven, and finish baking, and be particularly careful that it does not catch or burn, which it is very liable to do after the crust is iced. If made with a plain crust, the icing may be omitted.

Time.—½ hour before the crust is iced; 10 to 15 minutes afterwards.

Average cost, 9*d.*

Sufficient.—Allow 2 lbs. of apples for a tart for 6 persons.

Seasonable from August to March; but the apples become flavourless after February.

Note.—Many things are suggested for the flavouring of apple pie; some say 2 or 3 tablespoonfuls of beer, others the same quantity of sherry, which very much improve the taste; whilst the old-fashioned addition of a few cloves is, by many persons, preferred to anything else, as also a few slices of quince.

QUINCES.—The environs of Corinth originally produced the most beautiful quinces, but the plant was subsequently introduced into Gaul with the most perfect success. The ancients preserved the fruit by placing it, with its branches and leaves, in a vessel filled with honey or sweet wine, which was reduced to half the quantity by ebullition. Quinces may be profitably cultivated in this country as a variety with other fruit-trees, and may be planted in espaliers or as standards. A very fine-flavoured marmalade may be prepared from quinces, and a small portion of quince in apple pie much improves its flavour. The French use quinces for flavouring many sauces. This fruit has the remarkable peculiarity of exhaling an agreeable odour, taken singly; but when in any quantity, or when they are stowed away in a drawer or close room, the pleasant aroma becomes an intolerable stench, although the fruit may be perfectly sound; it is therefore desirable that, as but a few quinces are required for keeping, they should be kept in a high and dry loft, and out of the way of the rooms used by the family.

QUINCE.

CREAMED APPLE TART.

1234. INGREDIENTS.—Puff-crust No. 1205 or 1206, apples; to every lb. of pared and cored apples, allow 2 oz. of moist sugar, ½ teaspoonful of minced lemon-peel, 1 tablespoonful of lemon juice, ½ pint of boiled custard.

Mode.—Make an apple tart by the preceding recipe, with the exception of omitting the icing. When the tart is baked, cut out the middle of the lid or crust, leaving a border all round the dish. Fill up with a nicely-made boiled custard, grate a little nutmeg over the top, and the pie is ready for table. This tart is usually eaten cold; is rather an old-fashioned dish, but, at the same time, extremely nice.

Time.—½ to ¾ hour. *Average cost,* 1*s.* 3*d.*

Sufficient for 5 or 6 persons. *Seasonable* from August to March.

APPLE SNOWBALLS.

1235. INGREDIENTS.—2 teacupfuls of rice, apples, moist sugar, cloves.

Mode.—Boil the rice in milk until three-parts done; then strain it off, and pare and core the apples without dividing them. Put a small quantity of sugar and a clove into each apple, put the rice round them, and tie each ball separately in a cloth. Boil until the apples are tender; then take them up, remove the cloths, and serve.

Time.—½ hour to boil the rice separately; ½ to 1 hour with the apple.

Seasonable from August to March.

APPLE TOURTE OR CAKE.
(*German Recipe.*)

1236. INGREDIENTS.—10 or 12 apples, sugar to taste, the rind of 1 small lemon, 3 eggs, ¼ pint of cream or milk, ¼ lb. of butter, ¾ lb. of good short crust No. 1211, 3 oz. of sweet almonds.

Mode.—Pare, core, and cut the apples into small pieces; put sufficient moist sugar to sweeten them into a basin; add the lemon-peel, which should be finely minced, and the cream; stir these ingredients well, whisk the eggs, and melt the butter; mix altogether, add the sliced apple, and let these be well stirred into the mixture. Line a large round plate with the paste, place a narrow rim of the same round the outer edge, and lay the apples thickly in the middle. Blanch the almonds, cut them into long shreds, and strew over the top of the apples, and bake from ½ to ¾ hour, taking care that the almonds do not get burnt: when done, strew some sifted sugar over the top, and serve. This tourte may be eaten either hot or cold, and is sufficient to fill 2 large-sized plates.

Time.—½ to ¾ hour. *Average cost,* 2s. 2d.

Sufficient for 2 large-sized tourtes.

Seasonable from August to March.

APPLES.—No fruit is so universally popular as the apple. It is grown extensively for cider, but many sorts are cultivated for the table. The apple, uncooked, is less digestible than the pear; the degree of digestibility varying according to the firmness of its texture and flavour. Very wholesome and delicious jellies, marmalades, and sweetmeats are prepared from it. Entremets of apples are made in great variety. Apples, when peeled, cored, and well cooked, are a most grateful food for the dyspeptic.

ALMA PUDDING.

1237. INGREDIENTS.—½ lb. of fresh butter, ½ lb. of powdered sugar, ½ lb. of flour, ¼ lb. of currants, 4 eggs.

Mode.—Beat the butter to a thick cream, strew in, by degrees, the sugar, and mix both these well together; then dredge the flour in

2 s 2

gradually, add the currants, and moisten with the eggs, which should be well beaten. When all the ingredients are well stirred and mixed, butter a mould that will hold the mixture exactly, tie it down with a cloth, put the pudding into boiling water, and boil for 5 hours; when turned out, strew some powdered sugar over it, and serve.

Time.—6 hours. *Average cost,* 1s. 6d.

Sufficient for 5 or 6 persons.

Seasonable at any time.

BAKED APRICOT PUDDING.

1238. INGREDIENTS.—12 large apricots, ¾ pint of bread crumbs, 1 pint of milk, 3 oz. of pounded sugar, the yolks of 4 eggs, 1 glass of sherry.

Mode.—Make the milk boiling hot, and pour it on to the bread crumbs; when half cold, add the sugar, the well-whisked yolks of the eggs, and the sherry. Divide the apricots in half, scald them until they are soft, and break them up with a spoon, adding a few of the kernels, which should be well pounded in a mortar; then mix the fruit and other ingredients together, put a border of paste round the dish, fill with the mixture, and bake the pudding from ½ to ¾ hour.

Time.—½ to ¾ hour. *Average cost,* in full season, 1s. 6d.

Sufficient for 4 or 5 persons.

Seasonable in August, September, and October.

APRICOT TART.

1239. INGREDIENTS.—12 or 14 apricots, sugar to taste, puff-paste or short crust.

Mode.—Break the apricots in half, take out the stones, and put them into a pie-dish, in the centre of which place a very small cup or jar, bottom uppermost; sweeten with good moist sugar, but add no water. Line the edge of the dish with paste, put on the cover, and ornament the pie in any of the usual modes. Bake from ½ to ¾ hour, according to size; and if puff-paste is used, glaze it about 10 minutes before the pie is done, and put it into the oven again to set the glaze. Short crust merely requires a little sifted sugar sprinkled over it before being sent to table.

Time.—½ to ¾ hour. *Average cost,* in full season, 1s.

Sufficient for 4 or 5 persons.

Seasonable in August, September, and October; green ones rather earlier.

Note.—Green apricots make very good tarts, but they should be boiled with a little sugar and water before they are covered with the crust.

APRICOTS.—The apricot is indigenous to the plains of Armenia, but is now cultivated in almost every climate, temperate or tropical. There are several varieties. The skin of this fruit has a perfumed flavour, highly esteemed. A good apricot, when perfectly ripe, is an excellent fruit. It has been somewhat condemned for its laxative qualities, but this has possibly arisen from the fruit having been eaten unripe, or in too great excess. Delicate persons should not eat the apricot uncooked, without a liberal allowance of powdered sugar. The apricot makes excellent jam and marmalade, and there are several foreign preparations of it which are considered great luxuries.

BAKED OR BOILED ARROWROOT PUDDING.

1240. INGREDIENTS.—2 tablespoonfuls of arrowroot, 1½ pint of milk, 1 oz. of butter, the rind of ½ lemon, 2 heaped tablespoonfuls of moist sugar, a little grated nutmeg.

Mode.—Mix the arrowroot with as much cold milk as will make it into a smooth batter, moderately thick; put the remainder of the milk into a stewpan with the lemon-peel, and let it infuse for about ½ hour; when it boils, strain it gently to the batter, stirring it all the time to keep it smooth; then add the butter; beat this well in until thoroughly mixed, and sweeten with moist sugar. Put the mixture into a pie-dish, round which has been placed a border of paste, grate a little nutmeg over the top, and bake the pudding from 1 to 1¼ hour, in a moderate oven, or boil it the same length of time in a well-buttered basin. To enrich this pudding, stir to the other ingredients, just before it is put in the oven, 3 well-whisked eggs, and add a table-spoonful of brandy. For a nursery pudding, the addition of the latter ingredients will be found quite superfluous, as also the paste round the edge of the dish.

Time.—1 to 1¼ hour, baked or boiled. *Average cost, 7d.*

Sufficient for 5 or 6 persons. *Seasonable* at any time.

ARROWROOT.—In India, and in the colonies, by the process of rasping, they extract from a vegetable (*Maranta arundinacea*) a sediment nearly resembling tapioca. The grated pulp is sifted into a quantity of water, from which it is afterwards strained and dried, and the sediment thus produced is called arrowroot. Its qualities closely resemble those of tapioca.

A BACHELOR'S PUDDING.

1241. INGREDIENTS.—4 oz. of grated bread, 4 oz. of currants, 4 oz. of apples, 2 oz. of sugar, 3 eggs, a few drops of essence of lemon, a little grated nutmeg.

Mode.—Pare, core, and mince the apples very finely, sufficient, when minced, to make 4 oz.; add to these the currants, which should be well washed, the grated bread, and sugar; whisk the eggs, beat these up with the remaining ingredients, and, when all is thoroughly mixed, put the pudding into a buttered basin, tie it down with a cloth, and boil for 3 hours.

Time.—3 hours. *Average cost, 9d.*

Sufficient for 4 or 5 persons. *Seasonable* from August to March.

BAKEWELL PUDDING.
(*Very Rich.*)
I.

1242. INGREDIENTS.—$\frac{1}{4}$ lb. of puff-paste, 5 eggs, 6 oz. of sugar, $\frac{1}{4}$ lb. of butter, 1 oz. of almonds, jam.

Mode.—Cover a dish with thin paste, and put over this a layer of any kind of jam, $\frac{1}{2}$ inch thick; put the yolks of 5 eggs into a basin with the white of 1, and beat these well; add the sifted sugar, the butter, which should be melted, and the almonds, which should be well pounded; beat all together until well mixed, then pour it into the dish over the jam, and bake for an hour in a moderate oven.

Time.—1 hour. *Average cost*, 1s. 6d.

Sufficient for 4 or 5 persons. *Seasonable* at any time.

II.

1243. INGREDIENTS.—$\frac{3}{4}$ pint of bread crumbs, 1 pint of milk, 4 eggs, 2 oz. of sugar, 3 oz. of butter, 1 oz. of pounded almonds, jam.

Mode.—Put the bread crumbs at the bottom of a pie-dish, then over them a layer of jam of any kind that may be preferred; mix the milk and eggs together; add the sugar, butter, and pounded almonds; beat all well together; pour it into the dish, and bake in a moderate oven for 1 hour.

Time.—1 hour. *Average cost*, 1s. 3d. to 1s. 6d.

Sufficient for 4 or 5 persons. *Seasonable* at any time.

BARONESS PUDDING.
(*Author's Recipe.*)

1244. INGREDIENTS.—$\frac{3}{4}$ lb. of suet, $\frac{3}{4}$ lb. of raisins weighed after being stoned, $\frac{3}{4}$ lb. of flour, $\frac{1}{2}$ pint of milk, $\frac{1}{4}$ saltspoonful of salt.

Mode.—Prepare the suet, by carefully freeing it from skin, and chop it finely; stone the raisins, and cut them in halves, and mix both these ingredients with the salt and flour; moisten the whole with the above proportion of milk, stir the mixture well, and tie the pudding in a floured cloth, which has been previously wrung out in boiling water. Put the pudding into a saucepan of boiling water, and let it boil, without ceasing, 4$\frac{1}{2}$ hours. Serve merely with plain sifted sugar, a little of which may be sprinkled over the pudding.

Time.—4$\frac{1}{2}$ hours. *Average cost*, 1s. 4d.

Sufficient for 7 or 8 persons.

Seasonable in winter, when fresh fruit is not obtainable.

Note.—This pudding the editress cannot too highly recommend. The recipe was kindly given to her family by a lady who bore the title here prefixed to it; and with all who have partaken of it, it is an especial favourite. Nothing is of greater consequence, in the above directions, than attention to the time of boiling, which should never be *less* than that mentioned.

BARBERRY TART.

1245. INGREDIENTS.—To every lb. of barberries allow ¾ lb. of lump sugar; paste.

Mode.—Pick the barberries from the stalks, and put the fruit into a stone jar; place this jar in boiling water, and let it simmer very slowly until the fruit is soft; then put it into a preserving-pan with the sugar, and boil gently for 15 minutes; line a tartlet-pan with paste, bake it, and, when the paste is cold, fill with the barberries, and ornament the tart with a few baked leaves of paste, cut out, as shown in the engraving.

LEAF IN PUFF-PASTE.

Time.—¼ hour to bake the tart.

Average cost, 4d. per pint.

Seasonable in autumn.

BARBERRY.

BARBERRIES (*Berberis vulgaris*).—A fruit of such great acidity, that even birds refuse to eat it. In this respect, it nearly approaches the tamarind. When boiled with sugar, it makes a very agreeable preserve or jelly, according to the different modes of preparing it. Barberries are also used as a dry sweetmeat, and in sugarplums or comfits; are pickled with vinegar, and are used for various culinary purposes. They are well calculated to allay heat and thirst in persons afflicted with fevers. The berries, arranged on bunches of nice curled parsley, make an exceedingly pretty garnish for supper-dishes, particularly for white meats, like boiled fowl à la Béchamel, the three colours, scarlet, green, and white, contrasting so well, and producing a very good effect.

BAKED BATTER PUDDING.

1246. INGREDIENTS.—1½ pint of milk, 4 tablespoonfuls of flour, 2 oz. of butter, 4 eggs, a little salt.

Mode.—Mix the flour with a small quantity of cold milk; make the remainder hot, and pour it on to the flour, keeping the mixture well stirred; add the butter, eggs, and salt; beat the whole well, and put the pudding into a buttered pie-dish; bake for ¾ hour, and serve with sweet sauce, wine sauce, or stewed fruit. Baked in small cups, this makes very pretty little puddings, and should be eaten with the same accompaniments as above.

Time.—¾ hour. *Average cost*, 9d.

Sufficient for 5 or 6 persons. *Seasonable* at any time.

BAKED BATTER PUDDING, with Dried or Fresh Fruit.

1247. INGREDIENTS.—1½ pint of milk, 4 tablespoonfuls of flour, 3 eggs, 2 oz. of finely-shredded suet, ¼ lb. of currants, a pinch of salt.

Mode.—Mix the milk, flour, and eggs to a smooth batter; add a little salt, the suet, and the currants, which should be well washed, picked, and dried; put the mixture into a buttered pie-dish, and bake in a moderate oven for 1¼ hour. When fresh fruits are in season, this pudding is exceedingly nice, with damsons, plums, red currants, gooseberries, or apples; when made with these, the pudding must be thickly sprinkled over with sifted sugar. Boiled batter pudding, with fruit, is made in the same manner, by putting the fruit into a buttered basin, and filling it up with batter made in the above proportion, but omitting the suet. It must be sent quickly to table, and covered plentifully with sifted sugar.

Time.—Baked batter pudding, with fruit, 1¼ to 1½ hour; boiled ditto, 1½ to 1¾ hour, allowing that both are made with the above proportion of batter. Smaller puddings will be done enough in ¾ or 1 hour.

Average cost, 10*d.*

Sufficient for 7 or 8 persons.

Seasonable at any time, with dried fruits.

BOILED BATTER PUDDING.

1248. INGREDIENTS.—3 eggs, 1 oz. of butter, 1 pint of milk, 3 tablespoonfuls of flour, a little salt.

Mode.—Put the flour into a basin, and add sufficient milk to moisten it; carefully rub down all the lumps with a spoon, then pour in the remainder of the milk, and stir in the butter, which should be previously melted; keep beating the mixture, add the eggs and a pinch of salt, and when the batter is quite smooth, put it into a well-buttered basin, tie it down very tightly, and put it into boiling water; move the basin about for a few minutes after it is put into the water, to prevent the flour settling in any part, and boil for 1¼ hour. This pudding may also be boiled in a floured cloth that has been wetted in hot water; it will then take a few minutes less than when boiled in a basin. Send these puddings very quickly to table, and serve with sweet sauce, wine sauce, stewed fruit, or jam of any kind: when the latter is used, a little of it may be placed round the dish in small quantities, as a garnish.

Time.—1¼ hour in a basin, 1 hour in a cloth. *Average cost,* 7*d.*

Sufficient for 5 or 6 persons. *Seasonable* at any time.

ORANGE BATTER PUDDING.

1249. INGREDIENTS.—4 eggs, 1 pint of milk, 1½ oz. of loaf sugar, 3 tablespoonfuls of flour.

Mode.—Make the batter with the above ingredients, put it into a well-buttered basin, tie it down with a cloth, and boil for 1 hour. As soon as it is turned out of the basin, put a small jar of orange marmalade all over the top, and send the pudding very quickly to table.

Time.—1 hour. *Average cost,* with the marmalade, 1s. 3d.

Sufficient for 5 or 6 persons.

Seasonable at any time; but more suitable for a winter pudding.

BAKED BREAD PUDDING.

1250. INGREDIENTS.—½ lb. of grated bread, 1 pint of milk, 4 eggs, 4 oz. of butter, 4 oz. of moist sugar, 2 oz. of candied peel, 6 bitter almonds, 1 tablespoonful of brandy.

Mode.—Put the milk into a stewpan, with the bitter almonds; let it infuse for ¼ hour; bring it to the boiling point; strain it on to the bread crumbs, and let these remain till cold; then add the eggs, which should be well whisked, the butter, sugar, and brandy, and beat the pudding well until all the ingredients are thoroughly mixed; line the bottom of a pie-dish with the candied peel sliced thin, put in the mixture, and bake for nearly ¾ hour.

Time.—Nearly ¾ hour. *Average cost,* 1s. 4d.

Sufficient for 5 or 6 persons.

Seasonable at any time.

Note.—A few currants may be substituted for the candied peel, and will be found an excellent addition to this pudding: they should be beaten in with the mixture, and not laid at the bottom of the pie-dish.

VERY PLAIN BREAD PUDDING.

1251. INGREDIENTS.—Odd pieces of crust or crumb of bread; to every quart allow ½ teaspoonful of salt, 1 teaspoonful of grated nutmeg, 3 oz. of moist sugar, ½ lb. of currants, 1½ oz. of butter.

Mode.—Break the bread into small pieces, and pour on them as much boiling water as will soak them well. Let these stand till the water is cool; then press it out, and mash the bread with a fork until it is quite free from lumps. Measure this pulp, and to every quart stir in salt, nutmeg, sugar, and currants in the above proportion; mix all well together, and put it into a well-buttered pie-dish. Smooth the surface with the back of a spoon, and place the butter in small pieces over the top; bake in a moderate oven for 1½ hour, and serve very hot.   Boiling milk substituted for the boiling water would very much improve this pudding.

Time.—1½ hour.   *Average cost*, 6d., exclusive of the bread.

Sufficient for 6 or 7 persons.   *Seasonable* at any time.

BOILED BREAD PUDDING.

1252. INGREDIENTS.—1½ pint of milk, ¾ pint of bread crumbs, sugar to taste, 4 eggs, 1 oz. of butter, 3 oz. of currants, ¼ teaspoonful of grated nutmeg.

Mode.—Make the milk boiling, and pour it on the bread crumbs; let these remain till cold; then add the other ingredients, taking care that the eggs are well beaten and the currants well washed, picked, and dried.   Beat the pudding well, and put it into a buttered basin; tie it down tightly with a cloth, plunge it into boiling water, and boil for 1¼ hour; turn it out of the basin, and serve with sifted sugar.   Any odd pieces or scraps of bread answer for this pudding; but they should be soaked overnight, and, when wanted for use, should have the water well squeezed from them.

Time.—1¼ hour.   *Average cost*, 1s.

Sufficient for 6 or 7 persons.   *Seasonable* at any time.

BREAD.—Bread contains, in its composition, in the form of vegetable albumen and vegetable fibrine, two of the chief constituents of flesh, and, in its incombustible constituents, the salts which are indispensable for sanguification, of the same quality and in the same proportion as flesh.   But flesh contains, besides these, a number of substances which are entirely wanting in vegetable food; and on these peculiar constituents of flesh depend certain effects, by which it is essentially distinguished from other articles of food.

BROWN-BREAD PUDDING.

1253. INGREDIENTS.—¾ lb. of brown-bread crumbs, ½ lb. of currants, ½ lb. of suet, ¼ lb. of moist sugar, 4 eggs, 2 tablespoonfuls of brandy, 2 tablespoonfuls of cream, grated nutmeg to taste.

Mode.—Grate ¾ lb. of crumbs from a stale brown loaf; add to these the currants and suet, and be particular that the latter is finely chopped.   Put in the remaining ingredients; beat the pudding well for a few minutes; put it into a buttered basin or mould; tie it down tightly, and boil for nearly 4 hours.   Send sweet sauce to table with it.

Time.—Nearly 4 hours.   *Average cost*, 1s. 6d.

Sufficient for 6 or 7 persons.

Seasonable at any time; but more suitable for a winter pudding.

MINIATURE BREAD PUDDINGS.

1254. INGREDIENTS.—1 pint of milk, ½ lb. of bread crumbs, 4 eggs, 2 oz. of butter, sugar to taste, 2 tablespoonfuls of brandy, 1 teaspoonful of finely-minced lemon-peel.

Mode.—Make the milk boiling, pour it on to the bread crumbs, and let them soak for about ½ hour. Beat the eggs, mix these with the bread crumbs, add the remaining ingredients, and stir well until all is thoroughly mixed. Butter some small cups; rather more than half fill them with the mixture, and bake in a moderate oven from 20 minutes to ½ hour, and serve with sweet sauce. A few currants may be added to these puddings: about 3 oz. will be found sufficient for the above quantity.

Time.—20 minutes to ½ hour. *Average cost,* 10*d.*

Sufficient for 7 or 8 small puddings.

Seasonable at any time.

BAKED BREAD-AND-BUTTER PUDDING.

1255. INGREDIENTS.—9 thin slices of bread and butter, 1½ pint of milk, 4 eggs, sugar to taste, ¼ lb. of currants, flavouring of vanilla, grated lemon-peel or nutmeg.

Mode.—Cut 9 slices of bread and butter not very thick, and put them into a pie-dish, with currants between each layer and on the top. Sweeten and flavour the milk, either by infusing a little lemon-peel in it, or by adding a few drops of essence of vanilla; well whisk the eggs, and stir these to the milk. *Strain* this over the bread and butter, and bake in a moderate oven for 1 hour, or rather longer. This pudding may be very much enriched by adding cream, candied peel, or more eggs than stated above. It should not be turned out, but sent to table in the pie-dish, and is better for being made about 2 hours before it is baked.

Time.—1 hour, or rather longer. *Average cost,* 9*d.*

Sufficient for 6 or 7 persons.

Seasonable at any time.

BUTTER.—Butter is indispensable in almost all culinary preparations. Good fresh butter, used in moderation, is easily digested; it is softening, nutritious, and fattening, and is far more easily digested than any other of the oleaginous substances sometimes used in its place.

CABINET or CHANCELLOR'S PUDDING.

1256. INGREDIENTS.—1½ oz. of candied peel, 4 oz. of currants, 4 dozen sultanas, a few slices of Savoy cake, sponge cake, a French roll, 4 eggs, 1 pint of milk, grated lemon-rind, ¼ nutmeg, 3 table-spoonfuls of sugar.

Mode.—Melt some butter to a paste, and with it, well grease the mould or basin in which the pudding is to be boiled, taking care that it is buttered in every part. Cut the peel into thin slices, and place

CABINET PUDDING.

these in a fanciful device at the bottom of the mould, and fill in the spaces between with currants and sultanas; then add a few slices of sponge cake or French roll; drop a few drops of melted butter on these, and between each layer sprinkle a few currants. Proceed in this manner until the mould is nearly full; then flavour the milk with nutmeg and grated lemon-rind; add the sugar, and stir to this the eggs, which should be well beaten. Beat this mixture for a few minutes; then strain it into the mould, which should be quite full; tie a piece of buttered paper over it, and let it stand for 2 hours; then tie it down with a cloth, put it into boiling water, and let it boil slowly for 1 hour. In taking it up, let it stand for a minute or two before the cloth is removed; then quickly turn it out of the mould or basin, and serve with sweet sauce separately. The flavouring of this pudding may be varied by substituting for the lemon-rind essence of vanilla or bitter almonds; and it may be made much richer by using cream; but this is not at all necessary.

Time.—1 hour. *Average cost*, 1s. 3d.

Sufficient for 5 or 6 persons. *Seasonable* at any time.

A PLAIN CABINET or BOILED BREAD-AND-BUTTER PUDDING.

1257. INGREDIENTS.—2 oz. of raisins, a few thin slices of bread and butter, 3 eggs, 1 pint of milk, sugar to taste, ¼ nutmeg.

Mode.—Butter a pudding-basin, and line the inside with a layer of raisins that have been previously stoned; then nearly fill the basin with slices of bread and butter with the crust cut off, and, in another basin, beat the eggs; add to them the milk, sugar, and grated nutmeg; mix all well together, and pour the whole on to the bread and butter; let it stand ½ hour, then tie a floured cloth over it; boil for 1 hour, and serve with sweet sauce. Care must be taken that the basin is quite full before the cloth is tied over.

Time.—1 hour. *Average cost*, 9d.

Sufficient for 5 or 6 persons. *Seasonable* at any time.

CANARY PUDDING.

1258. INGREDIENTS.—The weight of 3 eggs in sugar and butter, the weight of 2 eggs in flour, the rind of 1 small lemon, 3 eggs.

Mode.—Melt the butter to a liquid state, but do not allow it to oil; stir to this the sugar and finely-minced lemon-peel, and gradually dredge in the flour, keeping the mixture well stirred; whisk the eggs;

add these to the pudding; beat all the ingredients until thoroughly blended, and put them into a buttered mould or basin; boil for 2 hours, and serve with sweet sauce.

Time.—2 hours. *Average cost,* 9d.

Sufficient for 4 or 5 persons. *Seasonable* at any time.

BAKED OR BOILED CARROT PUDDING.

1259. INGREDIENTS.—$\frac{1}{2}$ lb. of bread crumbs, 4 oz. of suet, $\frac{1}{4}$ lb. of stoned raisins, $\frac{3}{4}$ lb. of carrot, $\frac{1}{4}$ lb. of currants, 3 oz. of sugar, 3 eggs, milk, $\frac{1}{4}$ nutmeg.

Mode.—Boil the carrots until tender enough to mash to a pulp; add the remaining ingredients, and moisten with sufficient milk to make the pudding of the consistency of thick batter. If to be boiled, put the mixture into a buttered basin, tie it down with a cloth, and boil for 2$\frac{1}{2}$ hours : if to be baked, put it into a pie-dish, and bake for nearly an hour ; turn it out of the dish, strew sifted sugar over it, and serve.

Time.—2$\frac{1}{2}$ hours to boil ; 1 hour to bake. *Average cost,* 1s. 2d.

Sufficient for 5 or 6 persons.

Seasonable from September to March.

CARROTS, says Liebig, contain the same kind of sugar as the juice of the sugar-cane.

ROYAL COBURG PUDDING.

1260. INGREDIENTS.—1 pint of new milk, 6 oz. of flour, 6 oz. of sugar, 6 oz. of butter, 6 oz. of currants, 6 eggs, brandy and grated nutmeg to taste.

Mode.—Mix the flour to a smooth batter with the milk, add the remaining ingredients *gradually,* and when well mixed, put it into four basins or moulds half full ; bake for $\frac{3}{4}$ hour, turn the puddings out on a dish, and serve with wine sauce.

Time.—$\frac{3}{4}$ hour. *Average cost,* 1s. 9d.

Sufficient for 7 or 8 persons. *Seasonable* at any time.

CHERRY TART.

1261. INGREDIENTS.—1$\frac{1}{2}$ lb. of cherries, 2 small tablespoonfuls of moist sugar, $\frac{1}{2}$ lb. of short crust, No. 1210 or 1211.

Mode.—Pick the stalks from the cherries, put them, with the sugar, into a *deep* pie-dish just capable of holding them, with a small cup placed upside down in the midst of them. Make a short crust with $\frac{1}{2}$ lb. of flour, by either of the recipes 1210 or 1211 ; lay a border round the edge of the dish ; put on the cover, and ornament the edges ; bake in a brisk oven from $\frac{1}{4}$ hour to 40 minutes ; strew finely-sifted sugar over, and serve hot or cold, although the latter is the more usual mode. It is more economical to make two or three tarts at one time, as the trimmings from one tart answer for lining the edges of the dish for another, and so much paste is not required as when they are made singly. Unless for family use, never make fruit pies in very *large* dishes; select them, however, as *deep* as possible.

Time.—½ hour to 40 minutes.

Average cost, in full season, 8*d*.

Sufficient for 5 or 6 persons.

Seasonable in June, July, and August.

Note.—A few currants added to the cherries will be found to impart a nice piquant taste to them.

CHERRY.

CHERRIES.—According to Lucullus, the cherry-tree was known in Asia in the year of Rome 680. Seventy different species of cherries, wild and cultivated, exist, which are distinguishable from each other by the difference of their form, size, and colour. The French distil from cherries a liqueur named *kirsch-waser* (*eau de cérises*) ; the Italians prepare, from a cherry called marusca, the liqueur named *marasquin*, sweeter and more agreeable than the former. The most wholesome cherries have a tender and delicate skin; those with a hard skin should be very carefully masticated. Sweetmeats, syrups, tarts, entremets, &c., of cherries, are universally approved.

COLD PUDDING.

1262. INGREDIENTS.—4 eggs, 1 pint of milk, sugar to taste, a little grated lemon-rind, 2 oz. of raisins, 4 tablespoonfuls of marmalade, a few slices of sponge cake.

Mode.—Sweeten the milk with lump sugar, add a little grated lemon-rind, and stir to this the eggs, which should be well whisked ; line a buttered mould with the raisins, stoned and cut in half; spread the slices of cake with the marmalade, and place them in the mould ; then pour in the custard, tie the pudding down with paper and a cloth, and boil gently for 1 hour : when cold, turn it out, and serve.

Time.—1 hour. *Average cost*, 1*s*. 2*d*.

Sufficient for 5 or 6 persons.

Seasonable at any time.

COLLEGE PUDDINGS.

1263. INGREDIENTS.—1 pint of bread crumbs, 6 oz. of finely-chopped suet, ¼ lb. of currants, a few thin slices of candied peel, 3 oz. of sugar, ¼ nutmeg, 3 eggs, 4 tablespoonfuls of brandy.

Mode.—Put the bread crumbs into a basin; add the suet, currants, candied peel, sugar, and nutmeg, grated, and stir these ingredients until they are thoroughly mixed. Beat up the eggs, moisten the pudding with these, and put in the brandy ; beat well for a few minutes, then form the mixture into round balls or egg-shaped pieces ; fry these in hot butter or lard, letting them stew in it until thoroughly done, and turn them two or three times, till of a fine light brown ; drain them on a piece of blotting-paper before the fire ; dish, and serve with wine sauce.

Time.—15 to 20 minutes. *Average cost*, 1s.

Sufficient for 7 or 8 puddings. *Seasonable* at any time.

CURRANT DUMPLINGS.

1264. INGREDIENTS.—1 lb. of flour, 6 oz. of suet, ½ lb. of currants, rather more than ½ pint of water.

Mode.—Chop the suet finely, mix it with the flour, and add the currants, which should be nicely washed, picked, and dried ; mix the whole to a limp paste with the water (if wanted very nice, use milk) ; divide it into 7 or 8 dumplings ; tie them in cloths, and boil for 1¼ hour. They may be boiled without a cloth : they should then be made into round balls, and dropped into boiling water, and should be moved about at first, to prevent them from sticking to the bottom of the saucepan. Serve with a cut lemon, cold butter, and sifted sugar.

Time.—In a cloth, 1¼ hour ; without, ¾ hour.

Average cost, 9d.

Sufficient for 6 or 7 persons.

Seasonable at any time.

ZANTE CURRANTS.—The dried fruit which goes by the name of currants in grocers' shops is not a currant really, but a small kind of grape, chiefly cultivated in the Morea and the Ionian Islands, Corfu, Zante, &c. Those of Zante are cultivated in an immense plain, under the shelter of mountains, on the shore of the island, where the sun has great power, and brings them to maturity. When gathered and dried by the sun and air, on mats, they are conveyed to magazines, heaped together, and left to cake, until ready for shipping. They are then dug out by iron crowbars, trodden into casks, and exported. The fertile vale of "Zante the woody" produces about 9,000,000 lbs. of currants annually. In cakes and puddings this delicious little grape is most extensively used ; in fact, we could not make a *plum* pudding without the currant.

ZANTE CURRANTS.

BOILED CURRANT PUDDING.

(Plain and Economical.)

1265. INGREDIENTS.—1 lb. of flour, ½ lb. of suet, ½ lb. of currants, milk.

Mode.—Wash the currants, dry them thoroughly, and pick away any stalks or grit ; chop the suet finely ; mix all the ingredients together, and moisten with sufficient milk to make the pudding into a stiff batter ; tie it up in a floured cloth, put it into boiling water, and boil for 3½ hours ; serve with a cut lemon, cold butter, and sifted sugar.

Time.—3½ hours. *Average cost,* 10*d.*

Sufficient for 7 or 8 persons. *Seasonable* at any time.

BLACK or RED CURRANT PUDDING.

1266. INGREDIENTS.—1 quart of red or black currants, measured with the stalks, ¼ lb. of moist sugar, suet crust No. 1215, or butter crust No. 1213.

Mode.—Make, with ¾ lb. of flour, either a suet crust or butter crust (the former is usually made); butter a basin, and line it with part of the crust; put in the currants, which should be stripped from the stalks, and sprinkle the sugar over them; put the cover of the pudding on; make the edges very secure, that the juice does not escape; tie it down with a floured cloth, put it into boiling water, and boil from 2½ to 3 hours. Boiled without a basin, allow ½ hour less. We have allowed rather a large proportion of sugar; but we find fruit puddings are so much more juicy and palatable when *well sweetened* before they are boiled, besides being more economical. A few raspberries added to red-currant pudding are a very nice addition: about ½ pint would be sufficient for the above quantity of fruit. Fruit puddings are very delicious if, when they are turned out of the basin, the crust is browned with a salamander, or put into a very hot oven for a few minutes to colour it: this makes it crisp on the surface.

Time.—2½ to 3 hours; without a basin, 2 to 2½ hours.

Average cost, in full season, 8*d.*

Sufficient for 6 or 7 persons.

Seasonable in June, July, and August.

CURRANTS.

CURRANTS.—The utility of currants, red, black, or white, has long been established in domestic economy. The juice of the red species, if boiled with an equal weight of loaf sugar, forms an agreeable substance called *currant jelly,* much employed in sauces, and very valuable in the cure of sore throats and colds. The French mix it with sugar and water, and thus form an agreeable beverage. The juice of currants is a valuable remedy in obstructions of the bowels; and, in febrile complaints, it is useful on account of its readily quenching thirst, and for its cooling effect on the stomach. White and flesh-coloured currants have, with the exception of the fullness of flavour, in every respect, the same qualities as the red species. Both white and red currants are pleasant additions to the dessert, but the black variety is mostly used for culinary and medicinal purposes, especially in the form of jelly for quinsies. The leaves of the black currant make a pleasant tea.

RED-CURRANT AND RASPBERRY TART.

1267. INGREDIENTS.—1½ pint of picked currants, ½ pint of raspberries, 3 heaped tablespoonfuls of moist sugar, ½ lb. of short crust.

Mode.—Strip the currants from the stalks, and put them into a deep pie-dish, with a small cup placed in the midst, bottom upwards ; add the raspberries and sugar ; place a border of paste round the edge of the dish, cover with crust, ornament the edges, and bake from ½ to ¾ hour : strew some sifted sugar over before being sent to table. This tart is more generally served cold than hot.

Time.—½ to ¾ hour.

Average cost,

Sufficient for 5 or 6 persons.

Seasonable in June, July, and August.

RASPBERRIES.—There are two sorts of raspberries, the red and the white. Both the scent and flavour of this fruit are very refreshing, and the berry itself is exceedingly wholesome, and invaluable to people of a nervous or bilious temperament. We are not aware, however, of its being cultivated with the same amount of care which is bestowed upon some other of the berry tribe, although it is far from improbable that a more careful cultivation would not be repaid by a considerable improvement in the size and flavour of the berry; neither, as an eating fruit, is it so universally esteemed as the strawberry, with whose lusciousness and peculiarly agreeable flavour it can bear no comparison. In Scotland, it is found in large quantities, growing wild, and is eagerly sought after, in the woods, by children. Its juice is rich and abundant, and to many, extremely agreeble.

RASPBERRY.

BAKED CUSTARD PUDDING.

1268. INGREDIENTS.—1½ pint of milk, the rind of ¼ lemon, ¼ lb. of moist sugar, 4 eggs.

Mode.—Put the milk into a saucepan with the sugar and lemon-rind, and let this infuse for about ½ hour, or until the milk is well flavoured ; whisk the eggs, yolks and whites ; pour the milk to them, stirring all the while ; then have ready a pie-dish, lined at the edge with paste ready baked ; strain the custard into the dish, grate a little nutmeg over the top, and bake in a *very slow* oven for about ½ hour, or rather longer. The flavour of this pudding may be varied by substituting bitter almonds for the lemon-rind ; and it may be very much enriched by using half cream and half milk, and doubling the quantity of eggs.

Time.—½ to ¾ hour. *Average cost,* 9*d.*

Sufficient for 5 or 6 persons. *Seasonable* at any time.

Note.—This pudding is usually served cold with fruit tarts.

BOILED CUSTARD PUDDING.

1269. INGREDIENTS.—1 pint of milk, 1 tablespoonful of flour, 4 eggs, flavouring to taste.

2 T

Mode.—Flavour the milk by infusing in it a little lemon-rind or cinnamon; whisk the eggs, stir the flour gradually to these, and pour over them the milk, and stir the mixture well. Butter a basin that will exactly hold it; put in the custard, and tie a floured cloth over; plunge it into boiling water, and turn it about for a few minutes, to prevent the flour from settling in one part. Boil it slowly for ½ hour; turn it out of the basin, and serve. The pudding may be garnished with red-currant jelly, and sweet sauce may be sent to table with it.

Time.—½ hour. *Average cost,* 7d.

Sufficient for 5 or 6 persons. *Seasonable* at any time.

DAMSON TART.

1270. INGREDIENTS.—1½ pint of damsons, ¼ lb. of moist sugar, ½ lb. of short or puff crust.

Mode.—Put the damsons, with the sugar between them, into a deep pie-dish, in the midst of which, place a small cup or jar turned upside down; pile the fruit high in the middle, line the edges of the dish with short or puff crust, whichever may be preferred; put on the cover, ornament the edges, and bake from ½ to ¾ hour in a good oven. If puff-crust is used, about 10 minutes before the pie is done, take it out of the oven, brush it over with the white of an egg beaten to a froth with the blade of a knife; strew some sifted sugar over, and a few drops of water, and put the tart back to finish baking: with short crust, a little plain sifted sugar, sprinkled over, is all that will be required.

DAMSONS.

Time.—½ to ¾ hour.

Average cost, 10d.

Sufficient for 5 or 6 persons.

Seasonable in September and October.

DAMSONS.—Whether for jam, jelly, pie, pudding, water, ice, wine, dried fruit or preserved, the damson, or *damascene* (for it was originally brought from Damascus, whence its name), is invaluable. It combines sugary and acid qualities in happy proportions, when full ripe. It is a fruit easily cultivated; and, if budded nine inches from the ground on vigorous stocks, it will grow several feet high in the first year, and make fine standards the year following. Amongst the list of the best sorts of baking plums, the damson stands first, not only on account of the abundance of its juice, but also on account of its soon softening. Because of the roughness of its flavour, it requires a large quantity of sugar.

DAMSON PUDDING.

1271. INGREDIENTS.—1½ pint of damsons, ¼ lb. of moist sugar, ¾ lb. of suet or butter crust.

Mode.—Make a suet crust with ¾ lb. of flour by recipe No. 1215;

line a buttered pudding-basin with a portion of it; fill the basin with the damsons, sweeten them, and put on the lid; pinch the edges of the crust together, that the juice does not escape; tie over a floured cloth, put the pudding into boiling water, and boil from 2½ to 3 hours.

Time.—2½ to 3 hours. *Average cost,* 8*d.*

Sufficient for 6 or 7 persons.

Seasonable in September and October.

DELHI PUDDING.

1272. INGREDIENTS.—4 large apples, a little grated nutmeg, 1 teaspoonful of minced lemon-peel, 2 large tablespoonfuls of sugar, 6 oz. of currants, ¾ lb. of suet crust No. 1215.

Mode.—Pare, core, and cut the apples into slices; put them into a saucepan, with the nutmeg, lemon-peel, and sugar; stir them over the fire until soft; then have ready the above proportion of crust, roll it out thin, spread the apples over the paste, sprinkle over the currants, roll the pudding up, closing the ends properly, tie it in a floured cloth, and boil for 2 hours.

Time.—2 hours. *Average cost,* 1*s.*

Sufficient for 5 or 6 persons. *Seasonable* from August to March.

EMPRESS PUDDING.

1273. INGREDIENTS.—½ lb. of rice, 2 oz. of butter, 3 eggs, jam, sufficient milk to soften the rice.

Mode.—Boil the rice in the milk until very soft; then add the butter; boil it for a few minutes after the latter ingredient is put in, and set it by to cool. Well beat the eggs, stir these in, and line a dish with puff-paste; put over this a layer of rice, then a thin layer of any kind of jam, then another layer of rice, and proceed in this manner until the dish is full; and bake in a moderate oven for ¾ hour. This pudding may be eaten hot or cold; if the latter, it will be much improved by having a boiled custard poured over it.

Time.—¾ hour. *Average cost,* 1*s.*

Sufficient for 6 or 7 persons. *Seasonable* at any time.

EXETER PUDDING.

(*Very rich.*)

1274. INGREDIENTS.—10 oz. of bread crumbs, 4 oz. of sago, 7 oz. of finely-chopped suet, 6 oz. of moist sugar, the rind of ½ lemon, ¼ pint of rum, 7 eggs, 4 tablespoonfuls of cream, 4 small sponge cakes, 2 oz. of ratafias, ½ lb. of jam.

Mode.—Put the bread crumbs into a basin with the sago, suet, sugar, minced lemon-peel, rum, and 4 eggs; stir these ingredients well together, then add 3 more eggs and the cream, and let the mixture be well beaten. Then butter a mould, strew in a few bread crumbs, and cover the bottom with a layer of ratafias; then put in a layer of the mixture, then a layer of sliced sponge cake spread thickly with any kind of jam; then add some ratafias, then some of the mixture and sponge cake, and so on until the mould is full, taking care that a layer of the mixture is on the top of the pudding. Bake in a good oven from ¾ to 1 hour, and serve with the following sauce:—Put 3 tablespoonfuls of black-currant jelly into a stewpan, add 2 glasses of sherry, and, when warm, turn the pudding out of the mould, pour the sauce over it, and serve hot.

Time.—From 1 to 1¼ hour. *Average cost,* 2s. 6d.

Sufficient for 7 or 8 persons. *Seasonable* at any time.

FIG PUDDING.

I.

1275. INGREDIENTS.—2 lbs. of figs, 1 lb. of suet, ½ lb. of flour, ½ lb. of bread crumbs, 2 eggs, milk.

Mode.—Cut the figs into small pieces, grate the bread finely, and chop the suet very small; mix these well together, add the flour, the eggs, which should be well beaten, and sufficient milk to form the whole into a stiff paste; butter a mould or basin, press the pudding into it very closely, tie it down with a cloth, and boil for 3 hours, or rather longer; turn it out of the mould, and serve with melted butter, wine-sauce, or cream.

Time.—3 hours, or longer. *Average cost,* 2s.

Sufficient for 7 or 8 persons.

Seasonable.—Suitable for a winter pudding.

II.

(*Staffordshire Recipe.*)

1276. INGREDIENTS.—1 lb. of figs, 6 oz. of suet, ¾ lb. of flour, milk.

Mode.—Chop the suet finely, mix with it the flour, and make these into a smooth paste with milk; roll it out to the thickness of about ½ inch, cut the figs in small pieces, and strew them over the paste; roll it up, make the ends secure, tie the pudding in a cloth, and boil it from 1½ to 2 hours.

Time.—1½ to 2 hours. *Average cost,* 1s. 1d.

Sufficient for 5 or 6 persons. *Seasonable* at any time.

FOLKESTONE PUDDING-PIES.

1277. INGREDIENTS.—1 pint of milk, 3 oz. of ground rice, 3 oz. of butter, ¼ lb. of sugar, flavouring of lemon-peel or bay-leaf, 6 eggs, puff-paste, currants.

Mode.—Infuse 2 laurel or bay leaves, or the rind of ½ lemon, in the milk, and when it is well flavoured, strain it, and add the rice; boil these for ¼ hour, stirring all the time; then take them off the fire, stir in the butter, sugar, and eggs, and let these latter be well beaten before they are added to the other ingredients; when nearly cold, line some patty-pans with puff-paste, fill with the custard, strew over each a few currants, and bake from 20 to 25 minutes in a moderate oven.

Time.—20 to 25 minutes. *Average cost*, 1s. 1d.

Sufficient to fill a dozen patty-pans.

Seasonable at any time.

FRUIT TURNOVERS (suitable for Pic-Nics).

1278. INGREDIENTS.—Puff-paste No. 1206, any kind of fruit, sugar to taste.

Mode.—Make some puff-paste by recipe No. 1206; roll it out to the thickness of about ¼ inch, and cut it out in pieces of a circular form; pile the fruit on half of the paste, sprinkle over some sugar, wet the edges and turn the paste over. Press the edges together, ornament them, and brush the turnovers over with the white of an egg; sprinkle over sifted sugar, and bake on tins, in a brisk oven, for about 20 minutes. Instead of putting the fruit in raw, it may be boiled down with a little sugar first, and then inclosed in the crust; or jam, of any kind, may be substituted for fresh fruit.

Time.—20 minutes.

Sufficient—½ lb. of puff-paste will make a dozen turnovers.

Seasonable at any time.

GERMAN PUDDING.

1279. INGREDIENTS.—2 teaspoonfuls of flour, 1 teaspoonful of arrow-root, 1 pint of milk, 2 oz. of butter, sugar to taste, the rind of ½ lemon, 4 eggs, 3 tablespoonfuls of brandy.

Mode.—Boil the milk with the lemon-rind until well flavoured; then strain it, and mix with it the flour, arrowroot, butter, and sugar. Boil these ingredients for a few minutes, keeping them well stirred; then take them off the fire and mix with them the eggs, yolks and whites, beaten separately and added separately. Boil some sugar to candy; line a mould with this, put in the brandy, then the mixture; tie down with a cloth, and boil for rather more than 1 hour. When turned out, the brandy and sugar make a nice sauce.

Time.—Rather more than 1 hour. *Average cost*, 1s.

Sufficient for 4 or 5 persons. *Seasonable* at any time.

DAMPFNUDELN, or GERMAN PUDDINGS.

1280. INGREDIENTS.—1 lb. of flour, ¼ lb. of butter, 5 eggs, 2 small tablespoonfuls of yeast, 2 tablespoonfuls of finely-pounded sugar, milk, a very little salt.

Mode.—Put the flour into a basin, make a hole in the centre, into which put the yeast, and rather more than ¼ pint of warm milk ; make this into a batter with the middle of the flour, and let the sponge rise in a warm temperature. When sufficiently risen, mix the eggs, butter, sugar, and salt with a little more warm milk, and knead the whole well together with the hands, beating the dough until it is perfectly smooth, and it drops from the fingers. Then cover the basin with a cloth, put it in a warm place, and when the dough has nicely risen, knead it into small balls ; butter the bottom of a deep sauté-pan, strew over some pounded sugar, and let the dampfnudeln be laid in, but do not let them touch one another ; then pour over sufficient milk to cover them, put on the lid, and let them rise to twice their original size by the side of the fire. Now place them in the oven for a few minutes, to acquire a nice brown colour, and serve them on a napkin, with custard sauce flavoured with vanilla, or a *compôte* of any fruit that may be preferred.

Time.—½ to ¾ hour for the sponge to rise ; 10 to 15 minutes for the puddings to rise ; 10 minutes to bake them in a brisk oven.

Sufficient for 10 or 12 dampfnudeln.

Seasonable at any time.

GINGER PUDDING.

1281. INGREDIENTS.—½ lb. of flour, ¼ lb. of suet, ¼ lb. of moist sugar, 2 large teaspoonfuls of grated ginger.

Mode.—Shred the suet very fine, mix it with the flour, sugar, and ginger ; stir all well together ; butter a basin, and put the mixture in *dry ;* tie a cloth over, and boil for 3 hours.

Time.—3 hours. *Average cost*, 6d.

Sufficient for 5 or 6 persons. *Seasonable* at any time.

GOLDEN PUDDING.

1282. INGREDIENTS.—¼ lb. of bread crumbs, ¼ lb. of suet, ¼ lb. of marmalade, ¼ lb. of sugar, 4 eggs.

Mode.—Put the bread crumbs into a basin; mix with them the suet, which should be finely minced, the marmalade, and the sugar; stir all these ingredients well together, beat the eggs to a froth, moisten the pudding with these, and when well mixed, put it into a mould or buttered basin; tie down with a floured cloth, and boil for 2 hours. When turned out, strew a little fine-sifted sugar over the top, and serve.

Time.—2 hours. *Average cost,* 11*d.*

Sufficient for 5 or 6 persons. *Seasonable* at any time.

Note.—The mould may be ornamented with stoned raisins, arranged in any fanciful pattern, before the mixture is poured in, which would add very much to the appearance of the pudding. For a plainer pudding, double the quantities of the bread crumbs, and if the eggs do not moisten it sufficiently, use a little milk.

BAKED GOOSEBERRY PUDDING.

1283. INGREDIENTS.—Gooseberries, 3 eggs, 1½ oz. of butter, ½ pint of bread crumbs, sugar to taste.

Mode.—Put the gooseberries into a jar, previously cutting off the tops and tails; place this jar in boiling water, and let it boil until the gooseberries are soft enough to pulp; then beat them through a coarse sieve, and to every pint of pulp add 3 well-whisked eggs, 1½ oz. of butter, ½ pint of bread crumbs, and sugar to taste; beat the mixture well, put a border of puff-paste round the edge of a pie-dish, put in the pudding, bake for about 40 minutes, strew sifted sugar over, and serve.

Time.—About 40 minutes. *Average cost,* 10*d.*

Sufficient for 4 or 5 persons. *Seasonable* from May to July.

BOILED GOOSEBERRY PUDDING.

1284. INGREDIENTS.—¾ lb. of suet crust No. 1215, 1½ pint of green gooseberries, ¼ lb. of moist sugar.

Mode.—Line a pudding-basin with suet crust No. 1215, rolled out to about ½ inch in thickness, and, with a pair of scissors, cut off the tops and tails of the gooseberries; fill the basin with the fruit, put in the sugar, and cover with crust. Pinch the edges of the pudding together, tie over it a floured cloth, put it into boiling water, and boil from 2½ to 3 hours; turn it out of the basin, and serve with a jug of cream.

BOILED FRUIT PUDDING.

Time.—2½ to 3 hours. *Average cost,* 10*d.*

Sufficient for 6 or 7 persons. *Seasonable* from May to July.

GOOSEBERRY TART.

1285. Ingredients.—1½ pint of gooseberries, ½ lb. of short crust No. 1211, ¼ lb. of moist sugar.

Mode.—With a pair of scissors cut off the tops and tails of the gooseberries; put them into a deep pie-dish, pile the fruit high in the centre, and put in the sugar; line the edge of the dish with short crust, put on the cover, and ornament the edges of the tart; bake in a good oven for about ¾ hour, and before being sent to table, strew over it some fine-sifted sugar. A jug of cream, or a dish of boiled or baked custards, should always accompany this dish.

Time.—¾ hour.

Average cost, 9d.

Sufficient for 5 or 6 persons.

Seasonable from May to July.

GOOSEBERRY.

Gooseberries.—The red and the white are the two principal varieties of gooseberries. The red are rather the more acid; but, when covered with white sugar, are most wholesome, because the sugar neutralizes their acidity. Red gooseberries make an excellent jelly, which is light and refreshing, but not very nourishing. It is good for bilious and plethoric persons, and to invalids generally who need light and digestible food. It is a fruit from which many dishes might be made. All sorts of gooseberries are agreeable when stewed, and, in this country especially, there is no fruit so universally in favour. In Scotland, there is scarcely a cottage-garden without its gooseberry-bush. Several of the species are cultivated with the nicest care.

HALF-PAY PUDDING.

1286. Ingredients.—¼ lb. of suet, ¼ lb. of currants, ¼ lb. of raisins, ¼ lb. of flour, ¼ lb. of bread crumbs, 2 tablespoonfuls of treacle, ½ pint of milk.

Mode.—Chop the suet finely; mix with it the currants, which should be nicely washed and dried, the raisins, which should be stoned, the flour, bread crumbs, and treacle; moisten with the milk, beat up the ingredients until all are thoroughly mixed, put them into a buttered basin, and boil the pudding for 3½ hours.

Time.—3½ hours. *Average cost,* 8d.

Sufficient for 5 or 6 persons. *Seasonable* at any time.

HERODOTUS PUDDING.

1287. Ingredients.—½ lb. of bread crumbs, ½ lb. of good figs, 6 oz. of suet, 6 oz. of moist sugar, ½ saltspoonful of salt, 3 eggs, nutmeg to taste.

Mode.—Mince the suet and figs very finely; add the remaining ingredients, taking care that the eggs are well whisked; beat the mixture for a few minutes, put it into a buttered mould, tie it down with a floured cloth, and boil the pudding for 5 hours. Serve with wine sauce.

Time.—5 hours. *Average cost,* 10*d.*

Sufficient for 5 or 6 persons. *Seasonable* at any time.

HUNTER'S PUDDING.

1288. INGREDIENTS.—1 lb. of raisins, 1 lb. of currants, 1 lb. of suet, 1 lb. of bread crumbs, ½ lb. of moist sugar, 8 eggs, 1 tablespoonful of flour, ¼ lb. of mixed candied peel, 1 glass of brandy, 10 drops of essence of lemon, 10 drops of essence of almonds, ½ nutmeg, 2 blades of mace, 6 cloves.

Mode.—Stone and shred the raisins rather small, chop the suet finely, and rub the bread until all lumps are well broken; pound the spice to powder, cut the candied peel into thin shreds, and mix all these ingredients well together, adding the sugar. Beat the eggs to a strong froth, and as they are beaten, drop into them the essence of lemon and essence of almonds; stir these to the dry ingredients, mix well, and add the brandy. Tie the pudding firmly in a cloth, and boil it for 6 hours at the least: 7 or 8 hours would be still better for it. Serve with boiled custard, or red-currant jelly, or brandy sauce.

Time.—6 to 8 hours. *Average cost,* 3*s.* 6*d.*

Sufficient for 9 or 10 persons. *Seasonable* in winter.

ICED PUDDING.
(*Parisian Recipe.*)

1289. INGREDIENTS.—½ lb. of sweet almonds, 2 oz. of bitter ones, ¾ lb. of sugar, 8 eggs, 1½ pint of milk.

Mode.—Blanch and dry the almonds thoroughly in a cloth, then pound them in a mortar until re-duced to a smooth paste; add to these the well-beaten eggs, the sugar, and milk; stir these ingredients over the fire until they thicken, but do not allow them to boil; then strain and put the mixture into the freezing-pot; surround it with ice, and freeze it as directed in recipe 1290. When quite frozen, fill an iced-pudding mould, put on the lid, and keep the pudding in ice until

ICED-PUDDING MOULD.

required for table; then turn it out on the dish, and garnish it with a *compôte* of any fruit that may be preferred, pouring a little over the top of the pudding. This pudding may be flavoured with vanilla, Curaçoa, or Maraschino.

Time.—¼ hour to freeze the mixture.

Seasonable.—Served all the year round.

ICED APPLE PUDDING.
(*French Recipe, after Carême.*)

1290. INGREDIENTS.—2 dozen apples, a small pot of apricot-jam, ½ lb. of sugar, 1 Seville orange, ¼ pint of preserved cherries, ¼ lb. of raisins, 1 oz. of citron, 2 oz. of almonds, 1 gill of Curaçoa, 1 gill of Maraschino, 1 pint of cream.

Mode.—Peel, core, and cut the apples into quarters, and simmer them over the fire until soft; then mix with them the apricot-jam and the sugar, on which the rind of the orange should be previously rubbed; work all these ingredients through a sieve, and put them into the freezing-pot. Stone the raisins, and simmer them in a little syrup for a few minutes; add these, with the sliced ci-tron, the almonds cut in dice, and the cherries drained from their syrup, to the ingredients in the freezing-pot; put in the Curaçoa and Maraschino, and freeze again; add as much whipped cream as will be required, freeze again, and fill the mould. Put the lid on, and plunge the mould into the ice-pot; cover it with a wet cloth and pounded ice and saltpetre, where it should remain until wanted for table. Turn the pudding out of the mould on to a clean and neatly-folded napkin, and serve, as sauce, a little iced whipped cream, in a sauce-tureen or glass dish.

ICE-SPATTLE.

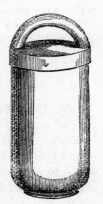

ICE-FREEZING PAIL.

Time.—½ hour to freeze the mixture.

Seasonable from August to March.

Method of working the freezing Apparatus.—Put into the outer pail some pounded ice, upon which strew some saltpetre; then fix the pewter freezing-pot upon this, and surround it entirely with ice and saltpetre. Wipe the cover and edges of the pot, pour in the pre-paration, and close the lid; a quarter of an hour after, begin turning the freezing-pan from right to left, and when the mixture begins to be firm round the sides of the pot, stir it about with the slice or spattle, that the preparation may be equally congealed. Close the lid again, keep working from right to left, and, from time to time, remove the mixture from the sides, that it may be smooth; and when perfectly frozen, it is ready to put in the mould; the mould should then be placed in the ice again, where it should remain until wanted for table.

ROLY-POLY JAM PUDDING.

1291. INGREDIENTS.—¾ lb of suet-crust No. 1215, ¾ lb. of any kind of jam.

Mode.—Make a nice light suet-crust by recipe No. 1215, and roll it out to the thickness of about ½ inch. Spread the jam equally over it, leaving a small margin of paste without any, where the pudding joins. Roll it up, fasten the ends securely, and tie it in a floured cloth; put the pudding into boiling water, and boil for 2 hours. Mincemeat or marmalade may be substituted for the jam, and makes excellent puddings.

Time.—2 hours. *Average cost,* 9d.

Sufficient for 5 or 6 persons.

Seasonable.—Suitable for winter puddings, when fresh fruit is not obtainable.

LEMON CHEESECAKES.

1292. INGREDIENTS.—¼ lb. of butter, 1 lb. of loaf sugar, 6 eggs, the rind of 2 lemons and the juice of 3.

Mode.—Put all the ingredients into a stewpan, carefully grating the lemon-rind and straining the juice. Keep stirring the mixture over the fire until the sugar is dissolved, and it begins to thicken : when of the consistency of honey, it is done ; then put it into small jars, and keep in a dry place. This mixture will remain good 3 or 4 months. When made into cheesecakes, add a few pounded almonds, or candied peel, or grated sweet biscuit; line some patty-pans with good puff-paste, rather more than half fill them with the mixture, and bake for about ¼ hour in a good brisk oven.

Time.—¼ hour. *Average cost,* 1s. 4d.

Sufficient for 24 cheesecakes. *Seasonable* at any time.

LEMON MINCEMEAT.

1293. INGREDIENTS.—2 large lemons, 6 large apples, ½ lb. of suet, 1 lb. of currants, ½ lb. of sugar, 2 oz. of candied lemon-peel, 1 oz. of citron, mixed spice to taste.

Mode.—Pare the lemons, squeeze them, and boil the peel until tender enough to mash. Add to the mashed lemon-peel the apples, which should be pared, cored, and minced; the chopped suet, currants, sugar, sliced peel, and spice. Strain the lemon-juice to these ingredients, stir the mixture well, and put it in a jar with a closely-fitting lid. Stir occasionally, and in a week or 10 days the mincemeat will be ready for use.

Average cost, 2s.

Sufficient for 18 large or 24 small pies.

Seasonable.—Make this about the beginning of December.

LEMON DUMPLINGS.

1294. INGREDIENTS.—½ lb. of grated bread, ¼ lb. of chopped suet, ¼ lb. of moist sugar, 2 eggs, 1 large lemon.

Mode.—Mix the bread, suet, and moist sugar well together, adding the lemon-peel, which should be very finely minced. Moisten with

the eggs and strained lemon-juice; stir well, and put the mixture into small buttered cups. Tie them down and boil for ¾ hour. Turn them out on a dish, strew sifted sugar over them, and serve with wine sauce.

LEMON DUMPLINGS.

Time.—¾ hour. *Average cost*, 7d.

Sufficient for 6 dumplings. *Seasonable* at any time.

BAKED LEMON PUDDING.

I.

1295. INGREDIENTS.—The yolks of 4 eggs, 4 oz. of pounded sugar, 1 lemon, ¼ lb. of butter, puff-crust.

Mode.—Beat the eggs to a froth; mix with them the sugar and warmed butter; stir these ingredients well together, putting in the grated rind and strained juice of the lemon-peel. Line a shallow dish with puff-paste; put in the mixture, and bake in a moderate oven for 40 minutes; turn the pudding out of the dish, strew over it sifted sugar, and serve.

Time.—40 minutes. *Average cost*, 10d.

Sufficient for 5 or 6 persons. *Seasonable* at any time.

II.

1296. INGREDIENTS.—10 oz. of bread crumbs, 2 pints of milk, 2 oz. of butter, 1 lemon, ¼ lb. of pounded sugar, 4 eggs, 1 tablespoonful of brandy.

Mode.—Bring the milk to the boiling point, stir in the butter, and pour these hot over the bread crumbs; add the sugar and very finely-minced lemon-peel; beat the eggs, and stir these in with the brandy to the other ingredients; put a paste round the dish, and bake for ¾ hour.

Time.—¾ hour. *Average cost,* 1s. 2d.

Sufficient for 6 or 7 persons.

Seasonable at any time.

LEMON.—The lemon is a variety of the citron. The juice of this fruit makes one of our most popular and refreshing beverages—lemonade, which is gently stimulating and cooling, and soon quenches the thirst. It may be freely partaken by bilious and sanguine temperaments; but persons with irritable stomachs should avoid it, on account of its acid qualities. The fresh rind of the lemon is a gentle tonic, and, when dried and grated, is used in flavouring a variety of culinary preparations. Lemons appear in company with the orange in most orange-growing countries. They were only known to the Romans at a very late period, and, at first, were used only to keep the moths from their garments: their acidity was unpleasant to them. In the time of Pliny, the lemon was hardly known otherwise than as an excellent counter-poison.

LEMON.

III.
(*Very rich.*)

1297. INGREDIENTS.—The rind and juice of 2 large lemons, ½ lb. of loaf sugar, ¼ pint of cream, the yolks of 8 eggs, 2 oz. of almonds, ½ lb. of butter, melted.

Mode.—Mix the pounded sugar with the cream, and add the yolks of eggs and the butter, which should be previously warmed. Blanch and pound the almonds, and put these, with the grated rind and strained juice of the lemons, to the other ingredients. Stir all well together; line a dish with puff-paste, put in the mixture, and bake for 1 hour.

Time.—1 hour. *Average cost,* 2s.

Sufficient for 6 or 7 persons. *Seasonable* at any time.

BOILED LEMON PUDDING.

1298. INGREDIENTS.—½ lb. of chopped suet, ¾ lb. of bread crumbs, 2 small lemons, 6 oz. of moist sugar, ¼ lb. of flour, 2 eggs, milk.

Mode.—Mix the suet, bread crumbs, sugar, and flour well together, adding the lemon-peel, which should be very finely minced, and the juice, which should be strained. When these ingredients are well mixed, moisten with the eggs and sufficient milk to make the pudding of the consistency of thick batter; put it into a well-buttered mould, and boil for 3½ hours; turn it out, strew sifted sugar over, and serve with wine sauce, or not, at pleasure.

Time.—3½ hours. *Average cost,* 1s.

Sufficient for 7 or 8 persons. *Seasonable* at any time.

Note.—This pudding may also be baked, and will be found very good. It will take about 2 hours.

PLAIN LEMON PUDDING.

1299. INGREDIENTS.—¾ lb. of flour, 6 oz. of lard or dripping, the juice of 1 large lemon, 1 teaspoonful of flour, sugar.

Mode.—Make the above proportions of flour and lard into a smooth paste, and roll it out to the thickness of about ½ inch. Squeeze the lemon-juice, strain it into a cup, stir the flour into it, and as much moist sugar as will make it into a stiff and thick paste; spread this mixture over the paste, roll it up, secure the ends, and tie the pudding in a floured cloth. Boil for 2 hours.

Time.—2 hours. *Average cost,* 7*d.*

Sufficient for 5 or 6 persons. *Seasonable* at any time.

MANCHESTER PUDDING (to eat Cold).

1300. INGREDIENTS.—3 oz. of grated bread, ½ pint of milk, a strip of lemon-peel, 4 eggs, 2 oz. of butter, sugar to taste, puff-paste, jam, 3 tablespoonfuls of brandy.

Mode.—Flavour the milk with lemon-peel, by infusing it in the milk for ½ hour; then strain it on to the bread crumbs, and boil it for 2 or 3 minutes; add the eggs, leaving out the whites of 2, the butter, sugar, and brandy; stir all these ingredients well together; cover a pie-dish with puff-paste, and at the bottom put a thick layer of any kind of jam; pour the above mixture, cold, on the jam, and bake the pudding for an hour. Serve cold, with a little sifted sugar sprinkled over.

Time.—1 hour. *Average cost,* 1*s.*

Sufficient for 5 or 6 persons. *Seasonable* at any time.

SWEET MACARONI PUDDING.

1301. INGREDIENTS.—2½ oz. of macaroni, 2 pints of milk, the rind of ¼ lemon, 3 eggs, sugar and grated nutmeg to taste, 2 tablespoonfuls of brandy.

Mode.—Put the macaroni, with a pint of the milk, into a saucepan with the lemon-peel, and let it simmer gently until the macaroni is tender; then put it into a pie-dish without the peel; mix the other pint of milk with the eggs; stir these well together, adding the sugar and brandy, and pour the mixture over the macaroni. Grate a little nutmeg over the top, and bake in a moderate oven for ½ hour. To make this pudding look nice, a paste should be laid round the edges of the dish, and, for variety, a layer of preserve or marmalade may be placed on the macaroni: in this case omit the brandy.

Time.—$\frac{3}{4}$ hour to simmer the macaroni; $\frac{1}{2}$ hour to bake the pudding.

Average cost, 11*d.*

Sufficient for 5 or 6 persons.

Seasonable at any time.

MACARONI.

MACARONI is composed of wheaten flour, flavoured with other articles, and worked up with water into a paste, to which, by a peculiar process, a tubular or pipe form is given, in order that it may cook more readily in hot water. That of smaller diameter than macaroni (which is about the thickness of a goose-quill) is called *vermicelli;* and when smaller still, *fidelini.* The finest is made from the flour of the hard-grained Black-Sea wheat. Macaroni is the principal article of food in many parts of Italy, particularly Naples, where the best is manufactured, and from whence, also, it is exported in considerable quantities. In this country, macaroni and vermicelli are frequently used in soups.

MANNA KROUP PUDDING.

1302. INGREDIENTS.—3 tablespoonfuls of manna kroup, 12 bitter almonds, 1 pint of milk, sugar to taste, 3 eggs.

Mode.—Blanch and pound the almonds in a mortar; mix them with the manna kroup; pour over these a pint of boiling milk, and let them steep for about $\frac{1}{4}$ hour. When nearly cold, add sugar and the well-beaten eggs; mix all well together; put the pudding into a buttered dish, and bake for $\frac{1}{2}$ hour.

Time.—$\frac{1}{2}$ hour. *Average cost,*

Sufficient for 4 or 5 persons. *Seasonable* at any time.

MANNA KROUP, SEMORA, or SEMOLINA, are three names given to a flour made from ground wheat and rice. The preparation is white when it is made only of these materials; the yellow colour which it usually has, is produced by a portion of saffron and yolks of eggs. Next to vermicelli, this preparation is the most useful for thickening either meat or vegetable soups. As a food, it is light, nutritious, wholesome, and easily digested. The best preparation is brought from Arabia, and, next to that, from Italy.

MANSFIELD PUDDING.

1303. INGREDIENTS.—The crumb of 2 rolls, 1 pint of milk, sugar to taste, 4 eggs, 2 tablespoonfuls of brandy, 6 oz. of chopped suet, 2 tablespoonfuls of flour, $\frac{1}{2}$ lb. of currants, $\frac{1}{2}$ teaspoonful of grated nutmeg, 2 tablespoonfuls of cream.

Mode.—Slice the roll very thin, and pour upon it a pint of boiling milk; let it remain covered close for $\frac{1}{4}$ hour, then beat it up with a fork, and sweeten with moist sugar; stir in the chopped suet, flour, currants, and nutmeg. Mix these ingredients well together, moisten with the eggs, brandy, and cream; beat the mixture for 2 or 3 minutes, put it into a buttered dish or mould, and bake in a moderate oven for $1\frac{1}{4}$ hour. Turn it out, strew sifted sugar over, and serve.

Time.—$1\frac{1}{4}$ hour. *Average cost,* 1*s.* 3*d.*

Sufficient for 6 or 7 persons. *Seasonable* at any time.

MARLBOROUGH PUDDING.

1304. INGREDIENTS.—¼ lb. of butter, ¼ lb. of powdered lump sugar, 4 eggs, puff-paste, a layer of any kind of jam.

Mode.—Beat the butter to a cream, stir in the powdered sugar, whisk the eggs, and add these to the other ingredients. When these are well mixed, line a dish with puff-paste, spread over a layer of any kind of jam that may be preferred, pour in the mixture, and bake the pudding for rather more than ½ hour.

Time.— Rather more than ½ hour. *Average cost,* 1s.

Sufficient for 5 or 6 persons. *Seasonable* at any time.

MARMALADE AND VERMICELLI PUDDING.

1305. INGREDIENTS.—1 breakfastcupful of vermicelli, 2 tablespoonfuls of marmalade, ¼ lb. of raisins, sugar to taste, 3 eggs, milk.

Mode.—Pour some boiling milk on the vermicelli, and let it remain covered for 10 minutes; then mix with it the marmalade, stoned raisins, sugar, and beaten eggs. Stir all well together, put the mixture into a buttered mould, boil for 1½ hour, and serve with custard sauce.

Time.—1½ hour. *Average cost.* 1s.

Sufficient for 5 or 6 persons. *Seasonable* at any time.

MARROW DUMPLINGS, to serve with Roast Meat, in Soup, with Salad, &c.

(*German Recipe.*)

1306. INGREDIENTS.—1 oz. of beef marrow, 1 oz. of butter, 2 eggs, 2 penny rolls, 1 teaspoonful of minced onion, 1 teaspoonful of minced parsley, salt and grated nutmeg to taste.

Mode.—Beat the marrow and butter together to a cream; well whisk the eggs, and add these to the other ingredients. When they are well stirred, put in the rolls, which should previously be well soaked in boiling milk, strained, and beaten up with a fork. Add the remaining ingredients, omitting the minced onion where the flavour is very much disliked, and form the mixture into small round dumplings. Drop these into boiling broth, and let them simmer for about 20 minutes or ⅓ hour. They may be served in soup, with roast meat, or with salad, as in Germany, where they are more frequently sent to table than in this country. They are very good.

Time.—20 minutes to ½ hour. *Average cost,* 6d.

Sufficient for 7 or 8 dumplings. *Seasonable* at any time.

BAKED OR BOILED MARROW PUDDING.

1307. INGREDIENTS.—½ pint of bread crumbs, 1½ pint of milk, 6 oz.

of marrow, 4 eggs, ¼ lb. of raisins or currants, or 2 oz. of each; sugar and grated nutmeg to taste.

Mode.—Make the milk boiling, pour it hot on to the bread crumbs, and let these remain covered for about ½ hour; shred the marrow, beat up the eggs, and mix these with the bread crumbs; add the remaining ingredients, beat the mixture well, and either put it into a buttered mould and boil it for 2½ hours, or put it into a pie-dish edged with puff-paste, and bake for rather more than ¾ hour. Before sending it to table, sift a little pounded sugar over, after being turned out of the mould or basin.

Time.—2½ hours to boil, ¾ hour to bake. *Average cost*, 1s. 2d.

Sufficient for 5 or 6 persons. *Seasonable* at any time.

MILITARY PUDDINGS.

1308. INGREDIENTS.—½ lb. of suet, ½ lb. of bread crumbs, ½ lb. of moist sugar, the rind and juice of 1 large lemon.

Mode.—Chop the suet finely, mix it with the bread crumbs and sugar, and mince the lemon-rind and strain the juice; stir these into the other ingredients, mix well, and put the mixture into small buttered cups, and bake for rather more than ½ hour; turn them out on the dish, and serve with lemon-sauce. The above ingredients may be made into small balls, and boiled for about ½ hour; they should then be served with the same sauce as when baked.

Time.—Rather more than ½ hour. *Average cost*, 9d.

Sufficient to fill 6 or 7 moderate-sized cups. *Seasonable* at any time.

MINCEMEAT.

1309. INGREDIENTS.—2 lbs. of raisins, 3 lbs. of currants, 1½ lb. of lean beef, 3 lbs. of beef suet, 2 lbs. of moist sugar, 2 oz. of citron, 2 oz. of candied lemon-peel, 2 oz. of candied orange-peel, 1 small nutmeg, 1 pottle of apples, the rind of 2 lemons, the juice of 1, ½ pint of brandy.

Mode.—Stone and *cut* the raisins once or twice across, but do not chop them; wash, dry, and pick the currants free from stalks and grit, and mince the beef and suet, taking care that the latter is chopped very fine; slice the citron and candied peel, grate the nutmeg, and pare, core, and mince the apples; mince the lemon-peel, strain the juice, and when all the ingredients are thus prepared, mix them well together, adding the brandy when the other things are well blended; press the whole into a jar, carefully exclude the air, and the mincemeat will be ready for use in a fortnight.

Average cost for this quantity, 8d.

Seasonable.—Make this about the beginning of December.

EXCELLENT MINCEMEAT.

1310. INGREDIENTS.—3 large lemons, 3 large apples, 1 lb. of stoned raisins, 1 lb. of currants, 1 lb. of suet, 2 lbs. of moist sugar, 1 oz. of sliced candied citron, 1 oz. of sliced candied orange-peel, and the same quantity of lemon-peel, 1 teacupful of brandy, 2 tablespoonfuls of orange marmalade.

Mode.—Grate the rinds of the lemons ; squeeze out the juice, strain it, and boil the remainder of the lemons until tender enough to pulp or chop very finely. Then add to this pulp the apples, which should be baked, and their skins and cores removed ; put in the remaining ingredients one by one, and, as they are added, mix everything very thoroughly together. Put the mincemeat into a stone jar with a closely-fitting lid, and in a fortnight it will be ready for use.

Seasonable.—This should be made the first or second week in December.

MINCE PIES.

1311. INGREDIENTS.—Good puff-paste No. 1205, mincemeat No. 1309.

Mode.—Make some good puff-paste by recipe No. 1205 ; roll it out to the thickness of about $\frac{1}{4}$ inch, and line some good-sized pattypans

MINCE PIES.

with it ; fill them with mincemeat, cover with the paste, and cut it off all round close to the edge of the tin. Put the pies into a brisk oven, to draw the paste up, and bake for 25 minutes, or longer, should the pies be very large ; brush them over with the white of an egg, beaten with the blade of a knife to a stiff froth ; sprinkle over pounded sugar, and put them into the oven for a minute or two, to dry the egg ; dish the pies on a white d'oyley, and serve hot. They may be merely sprinkled with pounded sugar instead of being glazed, when that mode is preferred. To re-warm them, put the pies on the pattypans, and let them remain in the oven for 10 minutes or $\frac{1}{4}$ hour, and they will be almost as good as if freshly made.

Time.—25 to 30 minutes ; 10 minutes to re-warm them.

Average cost, 4d. each.

Sufficient—$\frac{1}{2}$ lb. of paste for 4 pies. *Seasonable* at Christmas time.

MONDAY'S PUDDING.

1312. INGREDIENTS.—The remains of cold plum-pudding, brandy, custard made with 5 eggs to every pint of milk.

Mode.—Cut the remains of a *good* cold plum-pudding into finger-pieces, soak them in a little brandy, and lay them cross-barred in a mould until full. Make a custard with the above proportion of milk and eggs, flavouring it with nutmeg or lemon-rind; fill up the mould with it; tie it down with a cloth, and boil or steam it for an hour. Serve with a little of the custard poured over, to which has been added a tablespoonful of brandy.

Time.—1 hour. *Average cost*, exclusive of the pudding, 6d.

Sufficient for 5 or 6 persons. *Seasonable* at any time.

NESSELRODE PUDDING.

(*A fashionable iced pudding—Carême's Recipe.*)

1313. INGREDIENTS.—40 chestnuts, 1 lb. of sugar, flavouring of vanilla, 1 pint of cream, the yolks of 12 eggs, 1 glass of Maraschino, 1 oz. of candied citron, 2 oz. of currants, 2 oz. of stoned raisins, ½ pint of whipped cream, 3 eggs.

Mode.—Blanch the chestnuts in boiling water, remove the husks, and pound them in a mortar until perfectly smooth, adding a few spoonfuls of syrup. Then rub them through a fine sieve, and mix them in a basin with a pint of syrup made from 1 lb. of sugar, clarified, and flavoured with vanilla, 1 pint of cream, and the yolks of 12 eggs. Set this mixture over a slow fire, stirring it *without ceasing*, and just as it begins to boil, take it off and pass it through a tammy. When it is cold, put it into a freezing-pot, adding the Maraschino, and make the mixture set; then add the sliced citron, the currants, and stoned raisins (these two latter should be soaked the day previously in Maraschino and sugar pounded with vanilla); the whole thus mingled, add a plateful of whipped cream mixed with the whites of 3 eggs, beaten to a froth with a little syrup. When the pudding is perfectly frozen, put it into a pineapple-shaped mould; close the lid, place it again in the freezing-pan, covered over with pounded ice and saltpetre, and let it remain until required for table; then turn the pudding out, and serve.

Time.—½ hour to freeze the mixture.

Seasonable from October to February.

BAKED ORANGE PUDDING.

1314. INGREDIENTS.—6 oz. of stale sponge cake or bruised ratafias, 6 oranges, 1 pint of milk, 6 eggs, ¼ lb. of sugar.

Mode.—Bruise the sponge cake or ratafias into fine crumbs, and pour upon them the milk, which should be boiling. Rub the rinds of 2 of the oranges on sugar, and add this, with the juice of the remainder, to the other ingredients. Beat up the eggs, stir them in, sweeten to taste, and put the mixture into a pie-dish previously lined with puff-paste. Bake for rather more than ½ hour; turn it out of the dish, strew sifted sugar over, and serve.

Time.—Rather more than ½ hour.   *Average cost*, 1s. 6d.

Sufficient for 3 or 4 persons.   *Seasonable* from November to May.

ORANGE (*Citrus Aurantium*).—The principal varieties are the sweet, or China orange, and the bitter, or Seville orange; the Maltese is also worthy of notice, from its red

blood-like pulp. The orange is extensively cultivated in the south of Europe, and in Devonshire, on walls with a south aspect, it bears an abundance of fruit. So great is the increase in the demand for the orange, and so ample the supply, that it promises to rival the apple in its popularity. The orange-tree is considered young at the age of a hundred years. The pulp of the orange consists of a collection of oblong vesicles filled with a sugary and refreshing juice. The orange blossom is proverbially chosen for the bridal wreath, and, from the same flower, an essential oil is extracted hardly less esteemed than the celebrated ottar of roses. Of all marmalades, that made from the Seville orange is the best. The peel and juice of the orange are much used in culinary preparations. From oranges are made preserves, comfitures, jellies, glacés, sherbet, liqueurs, and syrups. The juice of the orange in a glass *d'eau sucrée* makes a refreshing and wholesome drink.

ORANGE.

From the clarified pulp of the orange the French make a delicious jelly, which they serve in small pots, and call *crème*. The rasped peel of the orange is used in several sweet *entremets*, to which it communicates its perfume. The confectioner manufactures a variety of dainties from all parts of the orange. Confections of orange-peel are excellent tonics and stomachics. Persons with delicate stomachs should abstain from oranges at dessert, because their acidity is likely to derange the digestive organs.

SMALL DISHES OF PASTRY FOR ENTREMETS, SUPPER-DISHES, &c.

FANCHONNETTES, or CUSTARD TARTLETS.

1315. INGREDIENTS.—For the custard, 4 eggs, ¾ pint of milk, 2 oz. of butter, 2 oz. of pounded sugar, 3 dessertspoonfuls of flour, flavouring to taste; the whites of 2 eggs, 2 oz. of pounded sugar.

Mode.—Well beat the eggs; stir to them the milk, the butter, which should be beaten to a cream, the sugar, and flour; mix these ingredients well together, put them into a very clean saucepan, and bring them to the simmering point, but do not allow them to boil. Flavour with essence of vanilla, bitter almonds, lemon, grated chocolate, or any flavouring ingredient that may be preferred. Line some round tartlet-pans with good puff-paste; fill them with the custard, and bake in a moderate oven for about 20 minutes; then take them out of the pans; let them cool, and in the mean time whisk the whites of the eggs to a stiff froth; stir into this the pounded sugar, and spread smoothly over the tartlets a little of this mixture. Put them in the oven again to set the icing, but be particular that they do not scorch:

when the icing looks crisp, they are done. Arrange them, piled high in the centre, on a white napkin, and garnish the dish, and in between the tartlets, with strips of bright jelly, or very firmly-made preserve.

Time.—20 minutes to bake the tartlets; 5 minutes after being iced.
Average cost, exclusive of the paste, 1s.
Sufficient to fill 10 or 12 tartlets. *Seasonable* at any time.

Note.—The icing may be omitted on the top of the tartlets, and a spoonful of any kind of preserve put at the bottom of the custard instead: this varies both the flavour and appearance of this dish.

ALMOND FLOWERS.

1316. INGREDIENTS.—Puff-paste No. 1205; to every ½ lb. of paste allow 3 oz. of almonds, sifted sugar, the white of an egg.

Mode.—Roll the paste out to the thickness of ¼ inch, and, with a round fluted cutter, stamp out as many pieces as may be required. Work the paste up again, roll it out, and, with a smaller cutter, stamp out some pieces the size of a shilling. Brush the larger pieces over with the white of an egg, and place one of the smaller pieces on each. Blanch and cut the almonds into strips lengthwise; press them slanting into the paste closely round the rings; and when they are all completed, sift over some pounded sugar, and bake for about ¼ hour or 20 minutes. Garnish between the almonds with strips of apple jelly, and place in the centre of the ring a small quantity of strawberry jam; pile them high on the dish, and serve.

Time.—¼ hour or 20 minutes.
Sufficient.—18 or 20 for a dish. *Seasonable* at any time.

FLUTED ROLLS.

1317. INGREDIENTS.—Puff-paste, the white of an egg, sifted sugar, jelly or preserve.

Mode.—Make some good puff-paste by recipe No. 1205 (trimmings answer very well for little dishes of this sort); roll it out to the thickness of ¼ inch, and, with a round fluted paste-cutter, stamp out as many round pieces as may be required; brush over the upper side with the white of an egg; roll up the pieces, pressing the paste lightly together where it joins; place the rolls on a baking-sheet, and bake for about ¼ hour. A few minutes before they are done, brush them over with the white of an egg; strew over sifted sugar, put them back in the oven; and when the icing is firm and of a pale brown colour, they are done. Place a strip of jelly or preserve across each roll, dish them high on a napkin, and serve cold.

Time.—¼ hour before being iced ; 5 to 10 minutes after.
Average cost, 1s. 3d.
Sufficient.—½ lb. of puff-paste for 2 dishes.
Seasonable at any time.

PASTRY SANDWICHES.

1318. INGREDIENTS.—Puff-paste, jam of any kind, the white of an egg, sifted sugar.

Mode.—Roll the paste out thin ; put half of it on a baking-sheet or tin, and spread equally over it apricot, greengage, or any preserve that may be preferred. Lay over this preserve another thin paste ; press the edges together all round ; and mark the paste in lines with a knife on the surface, to show where to cut it when baked. Bake from 20 minutes to ¼ hour ; and, a short time before being done, take the pastry out of the oven, brush it over with the white of an egg, sift over pounded sugar, and put it back in the oven to colour. When cold, cut it into strips ; pile these on a dish pyramidically, and serve. These strips, cut about 2 inches long, piled in circular rows, and a plateful of flavoured whipped cream poured in the middle, make a very pretty dish.

Time.—20 minutes to ½ hour. *Average cost,* with ½ lb. of paste, 1s.
Sufficient.—½ lb. of paste will make 2 dishes of sandwiches.
Seasonable at any time.

PETITES BOUCHEES.

1319. INGREDIENTS.—6 oz. of sweet almonds, ¼ lb. of sifted sugar, the rind of ½ lemon, the white of 1 egg, puff-paste.

Mode.—Blanch the almonds, and chop them fine ; rub the sugar on the lemon-rind, and pound it in a mortar ; mix this with the almonds and the white of the egg. Roll some puff-paste out ; cut it in any shape that may be preferred, such as diamonds, rings, ovals, &c., and spread the above mixture over the paste. Bake the bouchées in an oven, not too hot, and serve cold.

Time.—¼ hour, or rather more. *Average cost,* 1s.
Sufficient for ½ lb. of puff-paste. *Seasonable* at any time.

POLISH TARTLETS.

1320. INGREDIENTS.—Puff-paste, the white of an egg, pounded sugar.

Mode.—Roll some good puff-paste out thin, and cut it into 2½-inch squares ; brush each square over with the white of an egg, then fold down the corners, so that they all meet in the middle of each piece of paste ; slightly press the two pieces together, brush them over with the egg, sift over sugar, and bake in a nice quick oven for about ¼ hour. When they are done, make a little hole in the middle of the paste, and fill it up with apricot jam, marmalade, or red-currant jelly. Pile them high in- the centre of a dish, on a napkin, and garnish with the same preserve the tartlets are filled with.

Time.—¼ hour or 20 minutes.

Average cost, with ½ lb. of puff-paste, 1s.

Sufficient for 2 dishes of pastry. *Seasonable* at any time.

Note.—It should be borne in mind, that, for all dishes of small pastry, such as the preceding, trimmings of puff-paste, left from larger tarts, answer as well as making the paste expressly.

PUITS d'AMOUR, or PUFF-PASTE RINGS.

1321. INGREDIENTS.—Puff-paste No. 1205, the white of an egg, sifted loaf sugar.

Mode.—Make some good puff-paste by recipe No. 1205 ; roll it out to the thickness of about ¼ inch, and, with a round fluted paste-cutter, stamp out as many pieces as may be required ; then work the paste up again, and roll it out to the same thickness, and with a *smaller* cutter, stamp out sufficient pieces to correspond with the larger ones. Again stamp out the centre of these smaller rings ; brush over the others with the white of an egg, place a small ring on the top of every large circular piece of paste, egg over the tops, and bake from 15 to 20 minutes. Sift over sugar, put them back in the oven to colour them ; then fill the rings with preserve of any bright colour. Dish them high on a napkin, and serve. So many pretty dishes of pastry may be made by stamping puff-paste out with fancy cutters, and filling the pieces, when baked, with jelly or preserve, that our space will not allow us to give a separate recipe for each of them ; but, as they are all made from one paste, and only the shape and garnishing varied, perhaps it is not necessary, and by exercising a little ingenuity, variety may always be obtained. Half-moons, leaves, diamonds, stars, shamrocks, rings, &c., are the most appropriate shapes for fancy pastry.

Time.—15 to 25 minutes. *Average cost*, with ½ lb. of paste, 1s.

Sufficient for 2 dishes of pastry. *Seasonable* at any time.

PARADISE PUDDING.

1322. INGREDIENTS.—3 eggs, 3 apples, ¼ lb. of bread crumbs, 3 oz. of sugar, 3 oz. of currants, salt and grated nutmeg to taste, the rind of ½ lemon, ½ wineglassful of brandy.

Mode.—Pare, core, and mince the apples into small pieces, and mix them with the other dry ingredients; beat up the eggs, moisten the mixture with these, and beat it well; stir in the brandy, and put the pudding into a buttered mould; tie it down with a cloth, boil for 1½ hour, and serve with sweet sauce.

Time.—1½ hour.   *Average cost*, 1s.

Sufficient for 4 or 5 persons.

PEASE PUDDING.

1323. INGREDIENTS.—1½ pint of split peas, 2 oz. of butter, 2 eggs, pepper and salt to taste.

Mode.—Put the peas to soak over-night, in rain-water, and float off any that are wormeaten or discoloured.   Tie them loosely in a clean cloth, leaving a little room for them to swell, and put them on to boil in cold rain-water, allowing 2½ hours after the water has simmered up.   When the peas are tender, take them up and drain; rub them through a colander with a wooden spoon; add the butter, eggs, pepper, and salt; beat all well together for a few minutes, until the ingredients are well incorporated; then tie them tightly in a floured cloth; boil the pudding for another hour, turn it on to the dish, and serve very hot.   This pudding should always be sent to table with boiled leg of pork, and is an exceedingly nice accompaniment to boiled beef.

Time.—2½ hours to boil the peas, tied loosely in the cloth; 1 hour for the pudding.

Average cost, 6d.

Sufficient for 7 or 8 persons.

Seasonable from September to March.

BAKED PLUM-PUDDING.

1324. INGREDIENTS.—2 lbs. of flour, 1 lb. of currants, 1 lb. of raisins, 1 lb. of suet, 2 eggs, 1 pint of milk, a few slices of candied peel.

Mode.—Chop the suet finely; mix with it the flour, currants, stoned raisins, and candied peel; moisten with the well-beaten eggs, and add sufficient milk to make the pudding of the consistency of very thick batter.   Put it into a buttered dish, and bake in a good oven from 2¼ to 2½ hours; turn it out, strew sifted sugar over, and serve.   For a very plain pudding, use only half the quantity of fruit, omit the eggs, and substitute milk or water for them.   The above ingredients make a large family pudding; for a small one, half the quantity would be found ample; but it must be baked quite 1½ hour.

Time.—Large pudding, 2¼ to 2½ hours; half the size, 1½ hour.

Average cost, 2s. 6d.

Sufficient for 9 or 10 persons.

Seasonable in winter.

RAISIN-GRAPE.—All the kinds of raisins have much the same virtues; they are nutritive and balsamic, but they are very subject to fermentation with juices of any kind; and hence, when eaten immoderately, they often bring on colics. There are many varieties of grape used for raisins; the fruit of Valencia is that mostly dried for culinary purposes, whilst most of the table kinds are grown in Malaga, and called Muscatels. The finest of all table raisins come from Provence or Italy; the most esteemed of all are those of Roquevaire; they are very large and very sweet. This sort is rarely eaten by any but the most wealthy. The dried Malaga, or Muscatel raisins, which come to this country packed in small boxes, and nicely preserved in bunches, are variable in their quality, but mostly of a rich flavour, when new, juicy, and of a deep purple hue.

RAISIN-GRAPE.

AN EXCELLENT PLUM-PUDDING, made without Eggs.

1325. INGREDIENTS.—½ lb. of flour, 6 oz. of raisins, 6 oz. of currants, ¼ lb. of chopped suet, ¼ lb. of brown sugar, ¼ lb. of mashed carrot, ¼ lb. of mashed potatoes, 1 tablespoonful of treacle, 1 oz. of candied lemon-peel, 1 oz. of candied citron.

Mode.—Mix the flour, currants, suet, and sugar well together; have ready the above proportions of mashed carrot and potato, which stir into the other ingredients; add the treacle and lemon-peel; but put no liquid in the mixture, or it will be spoiled. Tie it loosely in a cloth, or, if put in a basin, do not quite fill it, as the pudding should have room to swell, and boil it for 4 hours. Serve with brandy-sauce. This pudding is better for being mixed over-night.

Time.—4 hours. *Average cost,* 1s. 6d.

Sufficient for 6 or 7 persons. *Seasonable* in winter.

AN UNRIVALLED PLUM-PUDDING.

1326. INGREDIENTS.—1½ lb. of muscatel raisins, 1¾ lb. of currants, 1 lb. of sultana raisins, 2 lbs. of the finest moist sugar, 2 lbs. of bread crumbs, 16 eggs, 2 lbs. of finely-chopped suet, 6 oz. of mixed candied peel, the rind of 2 lemons, 1 oz. of ground nutmeg, 1 oz. of ground cinnamon, ½ oz. of pounded bitter almonds, ¼ pint of brandy.

Mode.—Stone and cut up the raisins, but do not chop them; wash and dry the currants, and cut the candied peel into thin slices. Mix all the dry ingredients well together, and moisten with the eggs, which should be well beaten and strained, to the pudding; stir in the brandy, and, when all is thoroughly mixed, well butter and flour a stout new pudding-cloth; put in the pudding, tie it down very tightly and closely, boil from 6 to 8 hours, and serve with brandy-sauce. A few sweet almonds, blanched and cut in strips, and stuck on the pudding, ornament it prettily. This quantity may be divided and boiled in buttered moulds. For small families this is the most desirable way; as the above will be found to make a pudding of rather large dimensions.

Time.—6 to 8 hours. *Average cost, 7s. 6d.*

Seasonable in winter. *Sufficient* for 12 or 14 persons.

Note.—The muscatel raisins can be purchased at a cheap rate loose (not in bunches): they are then scarcely higher in price than the ordinary raisins, and impart a much richer flavour to the pudding.

SULTANA GRAPE.

SULTANA GRAPE.—We have elsewhere stated that the small black grape grown in Corinth and the Ionian Isles is, when dried, the common currant of the grocers' shops; the white or yellow grape, grown in the same places, is somewhat larger than the black variety, and is that which produces the Sultana raisin. It has been called Sultana from its delicate qualities and unique growth: the finest are those of Smyrna. They have not sufficient flavour and sugary properties to serve alone for puddings and cakes, but they are peculiarly valuable for mixing, that is to say, for introducing in company with the richer sorts of Valencias or Muscatels. In white puddings, or cakes, too, where the whiteness must be preserved, the Sultana raisin should be used. But the greatest value of this fruit in the *cuisine* is that of its saving labour; for it has no stones. Half Muscatels and half Sultanas are an admirable mixture for general purposes.

A PLAIN CHRISTMAS PUDDING FOR CHILDREN.

1327. INGREDIENTS.—1 lb. of flour, 1 lb. of bread crumbs, $\frac{3}{4}$ lb. of stoned raisins, $\frac{3}{4}$ lb. of currants, $\frac{3}{4}$ lb. of suet, 3 or 4 eggs, milk, 2 oz. of candied peel, 1 teaspoonful of powdered allspice, $\frac{1}{2}$ saltspoonful of salt.

Mode.—Let the suet be finely chopped, the raisins stoned, and the currants well washed, picked, and dried. Mix these with the other dry ingredients, and stir all well together; beat and strain the eggs to the pudding, stir these in, and add just sufficient milk to make it mix properly. Tie it up in a well-floured cloth, put it into boiling water, and boil for at least 5 hours. Serve with a sprig of holly placed in the middle of the pudding, and a little pounded sugar sprinkled over it.

Time.—5 hours. *Average cost, 1s. 9d.*

Sufficient for 9 or 10 children. *Seasonable* at Christmas.

RAISINS.—Raisins are grapes, prepared by suffering them to remain on the vine until they are perfectly ripe, and then drying them in the sun or by the heat of an oven. The sun-dried grapes are sweet, the oven-dried of an acid flavour. The common way of drying grapes for raisins is to tie two or three bunches of them together, whilst yet on the vine, and dip them into a hot lixivium of wood-ashes mixed with a little of the oil of olives: this disposes them to shrink and wrinkle, after which they are left on the vine three or four days, separated, on sticks in a horizontal situation, and then dried in the sun at leisure, after being cut from the tree.

CHRISTMAS PLUM-PUDDING.
(*Very Good.*)

1328. INGREDIENTS.—1½ lb. of raisins, ½ lb. of currants, ½ lb. of mixed peel, ¾ lb. of bread crumbs, ¾ lb. of suet, 8 eggs, 1 wineglassful of brandy.

Mode.—Stone and cut the raisins in halves, but do not chop them; wash, pick, and dry the currants, and mince the suet finely; cut the candied peel into thin slices, and grate down the bread into fine crumbs. When all these dry ingredients are prepared, mix them well together; then moisten the mixture with the eggs, which should be well beaten, and the brandy; stir well, that everything may be very thoroughly blended, and *press* the pudding into a buttered mould; tie it down tightly with a floured cloth, and boil for 5 or 6 hours. It may be boiled in a cloth without a

CHRISTMAS PLUM-PUDDING IN MOULD

mould, and will require the same time allowed for cooking. As Christmas puddings are usually made a few days before they are required for table, when the pudding is taken out of the pot, hang it up immediately, and put a plate or saucer underneath to catch the water that may drain from it. The day it is to be eaten, plunge it into boiling water, and keep it boiling for at least 2 hours; then turn it out of the mould, and serve with brandy-sauce. On Christmas-day a sprig of holly is usually placed in the middle of the pudding, and about a wineglassful of brandy poured round it, which, at the moment of serving, is lighted, and the pudding thus brought to table encircled in flame.

Time.—5 or 6 hours the first time of boiling; 2 hours the day it is to be served.

Average cost, 4s.

Sufficient for a quart mould for 7 or 8 persons.

Seasonable on the 25th of December, and on various festive occasions till March.

Note.—Five or six of these puddings should be made at one time, as they will keep good for many weeks, and in cases where unexpected guests arrive, will be found an acceptable, and, as it only requires warming through, a quickly-prepared dish. Moulds of every shape and size are manufactured for these puddings, and may be purchased of Messrs. R. & J. Slack, 336, Strand.

BRANDY is the alcoholic or spirituous portion of wine, separated from the aqueous part, the colouring matter, &c., by distillation. The word is of German origin, and in its German form, *brantwein*, signifies burnt wine, or wine that has undergone the action of fire; brandies, so called, however, have been made from potatoes, carrots, beetroot, pears, and other vegetable substances; but they are all inferior to true brandy. Brandy is prepared in most wine countries, but that of France is the most esteemed. It is procured not only by distilling the wine itself, but also by fermenting and distilling the *marc*, or residue of the pressings of the grape. It is procured indifferently from red or white wine, and different wines yield very different proportions of it, the strongest, of course, giving the largest quantity. Brandy obtained from marc has a more acrid taste than that from wine. The celebrated brandy of Cognac, a town in the department of Charente, and that brought from Andraye, seem to owe their excellence from being made from white wine. Like other spirit, brandy is colourless when recently distilled; by mere keeping, however, owing, probably, to some change in the soluble matter contained in it, it acquires a slight colour, which is much increased by keeping in casks, and is made of the required intensity by the addition of burnt sugar or other colouring matter. What is called *British brandy* is not, in fact, brandy, which is the name, as we have said, of a spirit distilled from *wine*; but is a spirit made chiefly from malt spirit, with the addition of mineral acids and various flavouring ingredients, the exact composition being kept secret. It is distilled somewhat extensively in this country; real brandy scarcely at all. The brandies imported into England are chiefly from Bordeaux, Rochelle, and Cognac.

A POUND PLUM-PUDDING.

1329. INGREDIENTS.—1 lb. of suet, 1 lb. of currants, 1 lb. of stoned raisins, 8 eggs, ½ grated nutmeg, 2 oz. of sliced candied peel, 1 teaspoonful of ground ginger, ½ lb. of bread crumbs, ½ lb. of flour, ½ pint of milk.

Mode.—Chop the suet finely; mix with it the dry ingredients; stir these well together, and add the well-beaten eggs and milk to moisten with. Beat up the mixture well, and should the above proportion of milk not be found sufficient to make it of the proper consistency, a little more should be added. Press the pudding into a mould, tie it in a floured cloth, and boil for 5 hours, or rather longer, and serve with brandy-sauce.

BAKED PUDDING- OR CAKE-MOULD.

Time.—5 hours, or longer. *Average cost*, 3s.
Sufficient for 7 or 8 persons. *Seasonable* in winter.

Note.—The above pudding may be baked instead of boiled; it should be put into a buttered mould or tin, and baked for about 2 hours; a smaller one would take about 1¼ hour.

CITRON.—The fruit of the citron-tree (*Citrus medica*) is acidulous, antiseptic, and antiscorbutic: it excites the appetite, and stops vomiting, and, like lemon-juice, has been greatly extolled in chronic rheumatism, gout, and scurvy. Mixed with cordials, it is used as an antidote to the *machineel poison*. The candied peel is prepared in the same manner as orange or lemon-peel; that is to say, the peel is boiled in water until quite soft, and then suspended in concentrated syrup (in the cold), after which it is either dried in a current of warm air, or in a stove, at a heat not exceeding 120° Fahrenheit. The syrup must be kept fully saturated with sugar by reboiling it once or twice during the process. It may be dusted with powdered lump sugar, if necessary. The citron is supposed to be the Median, Assyrian, or Persian apple of the Greeks. It is described by Risso as having a majestic appearance, its shining leaves and rosy flowers being succeeded by fruit whose beauty and size astonish the observer, whilst their odour gratifies his senses. In China there is an enormous variety, but the citron is cultivated in all orange-growing countries.

PLUM-PUDDING OF FRESH FRUIT.

1330. INGREDIENTS.—$\frac{3}{4}$ lb. of suet crust No. 1215, 1$\frac{1}{2}$ pint of Orleans or any other kind of plum, $\frac{1}{4}$ lb. of moist sugar.

Mode.—Line a pudding-basin with suet crust rolled out to the thickness of about $\frac{1}{2}$ inch; fill the basin with the fruit, put in the sugar, and cover with crust. Fold the edges over, and pinch them together, to prevent the juice escaping. Tie over a floured cloth, put the pudding into boiling water, and boil from 2 to 2$\frac{1}{2}$ hours. Turn it out of the basin, and serve quickly.

Time.—2 to 2$\frac{1}{2}$ hours.
Average cost, 10*d.*
Sufficient for 6 or 7 persons.
Seasonable, with various kinds of plums, from the beginning of August to the beginning of October.

PLUM.—Almost all the varieties of the cultivated plum are agreeable and refreshing: it is not a nourishing fruit, and if indulged in to excess, when unripe, is almost certain to cause diarrhœa and cholera. Weak and delicate persons had better abstain from plums altogether. The modes of preparing plums are as numerous as the varieties of the fruit. The objections raised against raw plums do not apply to the cooked fruit, which even the invalid may eat in moderation.

PLUM.

PLUM TART.

1331. INGREDIENTS.—$\frac{1}{2}$ lb. of good short crust No. 1211, 1$\frac{1}{2}$ pint of plums, $\frac{1}{4}$ lb. of moist sugar.

Mode.—Line the edges of a deep tart-dish with crust made by recipe No. 1211; fill the dish with plums, and place a small cup or jar, upside down, in the midst of them. Put in the sugar, cover the pie with crust, ornament the edges, and bake in a good oven from $\frac{1}{2}$ to $\frac{3}{4}$ hour. When puff-crust is preferred to short crust, use that made by

PLUM TART.

recipe No. 1206, and glaze the top by brushing it over with the white of an egg beaten to a stiff froth with a knife; sprinkle over a little sifted sugar, and put the pie in the oven to set the glaze.

Time.—½ to ¾ hour.   *Average cost*, 1s.

Sufficient for 5 or 6 persons.

Seasonable, with various kinds of plums, from the beginning of August to the beginning of October.

POTATO PASTY.

1332. INGREDIENTS.—1½ lb. of rump-steak or mutton cutlets, pepper and salt to taste, ⅓ pint of weak broth or gravy, 1 oz. of butter, mashed potatoes.

Mode.—Place the meat, cut in small pieces, at the bottom of the pan; season it with pepper and salt, and add the gravy and butter

POTATO-PASTY PAN.

broken into small pieces. Put on the perforated plate, with its valve-pipe screwed on, and fill up the whole space to the top of the tube with nicely-mashed potatoes mixed with a little milk, and finish the surface of them in any ornamental manner. If carefully baked, the potatoes will be covered with a delicate brown crust, retaining all the savoury steam rising from the meat. Send it to table as it comes from the oven, with a napkin folded round it.

Time.—40 to 60 minutes.   *Average cost*, 2s.

Sufficient for 4 or 5 persons.   *Seasonable* at any time.

POTATO PUDDING.

1333. INGREDIENTS.—½ lb. of mashed potatoes, 2 oz. of butter, 2 eggs, ¼ pint of milk, 3 tablespoonfuls of sherry, ¼ saltspoonful of salt, the juice and rind of 1 small lemon, 2 oz. of sugar.

Mode.—Boil sufficient potatoes to make ½ lb. when mashed; add to these the butter, eggs, milk, sherry, lemon-juice, and sugar; mince the lemon-peel very finely, and beat all the ingredients well together. Put the pudding into a buttered pie-dish, and bake for rather more than ½ hour. To enrich it, add a few pounded almonds, and increase the quantity of eggs and butter.

Time.—½ hour, or rather longer.   *Average cost*, 8d.

Sufficient for 5 or 6 persons.   *Seasonable* at any time.

TO ICE OR GLAZE PASTRY.

1334. To glaze pastry, which is the usual method adopted for meat or raised pies, break an egg, separate the yolk from the white, and beat the former for a short time. Then, when the pastry is nearly baked, take it out of the oven, brush it over with this beaten yolk of egg, and put it back in the oven to set the glaze.

1335. To ice pastry, which is the usual method adopted for fruit tarts and sweet dishes of pastry, put the white of an egg on a plate, and with the blade of a knife beat it to a stiff froth. When the pastry is nearly baked, brush it over with this, and sift over some pounded sugar; put it back into the oven to set the glaze, and, in a few minutes, it will be done. Great care should be taken that the paste does not catch or burn in the oven, which it is very liable to do after the icing is laid on.

Sufficient.—Allow 1 egg and 1½ oz. of sugar to glaze 3 tarts.

SUGAR has been happily called "the honey of reeds." The sugar-cane appears to be originally a native of the East Indies. The Chinese have cultivated it for 2,000 years. The Egyptians, Phœnicians, and Jews knew nothing about it. The Greek physicians are the first who speak of it. It was not till the year 1471 that a Venetian discovered the method of purifying brown sugar and making loaf sugar. He gained an immense fortune by this discovery. Our supplies are now obtained from Barbadoes, Jamaica, Mauritius, Ceylon, the East and West Indies generally, and the United States; but the largest supplies come from Cuba. Sugar is divided into the following classes:—Refined sugar, white clayed, brown clayed, brown raw, and molasses. The sugar-cane grows to the height of six, twelve, or even sometimes twenty feet. It is propagated from cuttings, requires much hoeing and weeding, giving employment to thousands upon thousands of slaves in the slave countries, and attains maturity in twelve or thirteen months. When ripe, it is cut down close to the stole, the stems are divided into lengths of about three feet, which are made up into bundles, and carried to the mill, to be crushed between rollers. In the process of crushing, the juice runs down into a reservoir, from which, after a while, it is drawn through a siphon; that is to say, the clear fluid is taken from the scum. This fluid undergoes

SUGAR-CANES.

several processes of drying and refining; the methods varying in different manufactories. There are some large establishments engaged in sugar-refining in the neighbourhoods of Blackwall and Bethnal Green, London. The process is mostly in the hands of German workmen. Sugar is adulterated with fine sand and sawdust. Pure sugar is highly nutritious, adding to the fatty tissue of the body; but it is not easy of digestion.

BAKED RAISIN PUDDING.

(*Plain and Economical.*)

1336. INGREDIENTS.—1 lb. of flour, ¾ lb. of stoned raisins, ½ lb. of suet, a pinch of salt, 1 oz. of sugar, a little grated nutmeg, milk.

Mode.—Chop the suet finely; stone the raisins and cut them in halves; mix these with the suet, add the salt, sugar, and grated nutmeg, and moisten the whole with sufficient milk to make it of the consistency of thick batter. Put the pudding into a buttered pie-dish, and bake for 1½ hour, or rather longer. Turn it out of the dish, strew sifted sugar over, and serve. This is a very plain recipe, and suitable where there is a family of children. It, of course, can be much improved by the addition of candied peel, currants, and rather a larger proportion of suet : a few eggs would also make the pudding richer.

Time.—1½ hour. *Average cost*, 9*d*.

Sufficient for 7 or 8 persons. *Seasonable* in winter.

INTRODUCTION OF SUGAR.—Sugar was first known as a drug, and used by the apothecaries, and with them was a most important article. At its first appearance, some said it was heating; others, that it injured the chest; others, that it disposed persons to apoplexy; the truth, however, soon conquered these fancies, and the use of sugar has increased every day, and there is no household in the civilized world which can do without it.

BOILED RAISIN PUDDING.

(*Plain and Economical.*)

1337. INGREDIENTS.—1 lb. of flour, ½ lb. of stoned raisins, ½ lb. of chopped suet, ½ saltspoonful of salt, milk.

Mode.—After having stoned the raisins and chopped the suet finely, mix them with the flour, add the salt, and when these dry ingredients are thoroughly mixed, moisten the pudding with sufficient milk to make it into rather a stiff paste. Tie it up in a floured cloth, put it into boiling water, and boil for 4 hours : serve with sifted sugar. This pudding may, also, be made in a long shape, the same as a rolled jam-pudding, and will then not require so long boiling ;—2½ hours would then be quite sufficient.

Time.—Made round, 4 hours ; in a long shape, 2½ hours.

Average cost, 9*d*.

Sufficient for 8 or 9 persons. *Seasonable* in winter.

BOILED RHUBARB PUDDING.

1338. INGREDIENTS.—4 or 5 sticks of fine rhubarb, ¼ lb. of moist sugar, ¾ lb. of suet-crust No. 1215.

Mode.—Make a suet-crust with ¾ lb. of flour, by recipe No. 1215, and line a buttered basin with it. Wash and wipe the rhubarb, and, if old, string it—that is to say, pare off the outside skin. Cut it into inch lengths, fill the basin with it, put in the sugar, and cover with crust. Pinch the edges of the pudding together, tie over it a floured cloth, put it into boiling water, and boil from 2 to 2½ hours. Turn it out of the basin, and serve with a jug of cream and sifted sugar.

Time.—2 to 2½ hours. *Average cost*, 7*d*.

Sufficient for 6 or 7 persons. *Seasonable* in spring.

RHUBARB TART.

1339. INGREDIENTS.—½ lb. of puff-paste No. 1206, about 5 sticks of large rhubarb, ¼ lb. of moist sugar.

Mode.—Make a puff-crust by recipe No. 1206; line the edges of a deep pie-dish with it, and wash, wipe, and cut the rhubarb into pieces about 1 inch long. Should it be old and tough, string it, that is to say, pare off the outside skin. Pile the fruit high in the dish as it shrinks very much in the cooking; put in the sugar, cover with crust, ornament the edges, and bake the tart in a well-heated oven from ½ to ¾ hour. If wanted very nice, brush it over with the white of an egg beaten to a stiff froth, then sprinkle on it some sifted sugar, and put it in the oven just to set the glaze: this should be done when the tart is nearly baked. A small quantity of lemon-juice, and a little of the peel minced, are by many persons considered an improvement to the flavour of rhubarb tart.

Time.—½ to ¾ hour. *Average cost,* 9d.

Sufficient for 4 or 5 persons.

Seasonable in spring.

RHUBARB.—This is one of the most useful of all garden productio. s that are put into pies and puddings. It was comparatively little known till within the last twenty or thirty years, but it is now cultivated in almost every British garden. The part used is the footstalks of the leaves, which, peeled and cut into small pieces, are put into tarts, either mixed with apples or alone. When quite young, they are much better not peeled. Rhubarb comes in season when apples are going out. The common rhubarb is a native of Asia; the scarlet variety has the finest flavour. Turkey rhubarb, the well-known medicinal drug, is the root of a very elegant plant (*Rheum palmatum*), coming to greatest perfection in Tartary. For culinary purposes, all kinds of rhubarb are the better for being blanched.

RHUBARB.

RAISED PIE OF POULTRY OR GAME.

1340. INGREDIENTS.—To every lb. of flour allow ½ lb. of butter, ½ pint of water, the yolks of 2 eggs, ½ teaspoonful of salt (these are for the crust); 1 large fowl or pheasant, a few slices of veal cutlet, a few slices of dressed ham, forcemeat, seasoning of nutmeg, allspice, pepper and salt, gravy.

Mode.—Make a stiff short crust with the above proportion of butter, flour, water, and eggs, and work it up very smoothly; butter a raised-pie mould, as shown in No. 1190, and line it with the paste. Previously to making the crust, bone the fowl, or whatever bird is intended to be used, lay it, breast downwards, upon a cloth, and season the inside well with pounded mace, allspice, pepper, and salt; then spread over it a layer of forcemeat, then a layer of seasoned

2 x

veal, and then one of ham, and then another layer of forcemeat, and roll the fowl over, making the skin meet at the back. Line the pie with forcemeat, put in the fowl, and fill up the cavities with slices of seasoned veal and ham and forcemeat; wet the edges of the pie, put on the cover, pinch the edges together with the paste-pincers, and

decorate it with leaves; brush it over with beaten yolk of egg, and bake in a moderate oven for 4 hours. In the mean time, make a good strong gravy from the bones, pour it through a funnel into the hole at the top; cover this hole with a small leaf, and the pie, when cold, will be ready for use. Let

RAISED PIE.

it be remembered that the gravy must be considerably reduced before it is poured into the pie, as, when cold, it should form a firm jelly, and not be the least degree in a liquid state. This recipe is suitable for all kinds of poultry or game, using one or more birds, according to the size of the pie intended to be made; but the birds must always be boned. Truffles, mushrooms, &c., added to this pie, make it much nicer; and, to enrich it, lard the fleshy parts of the poultry or game with thin strips of bacon. This method of forming raised pies in a mould is generally called a *timbale*, and has the advantage of being more easily made than one where the paste is raised by the hands; the crust, besides, being eatable. (*See* coloured plate N 1.)

Time.—Large pie, 4 hours. *Average cost*, 6s. 6d.

Seasonable, with poultry, all the year; with game, from September to March.

RAISED PIE OF VEAL AND HAM.

1341. INGREDIENTS.—3 or 4 lbs. of veal cutlets, a few slices of bacon or ham, seasoning of pepper, salt, nutmeg, and allspice, forcemeat No. 415, 2 lbs. of hot-water paste No. 1217, ½ pint of good strong gravy.

Mode.—To raise the crust for a pie with the hands is a very difficult task, and can only be accomplished by skilled and experienced cooks. The process should be seen to be satisfactorily learnt, and plenty of practice given to the making of raised pies, as by that means only will success be insured. Make a hot-water paste by recipe No. 1217, and from the mass raise the pie with the hands; if this cannot be accomplished, cut out pieces for the top and bottom, and a long piece for the sides; fasten the bottom and side-piece together by means of egg, and pinch the edges well together; then line the pie with forcemeat made by recipe No. 415, put in a layer of veal, and a plentiful seasoning of salt, pepper, nutmeg, and allspice, as, let it be remembered, these pies taste very insipid unless highly seasoned. Over the seasoning place a layer of sliced bacon or cooked ham, and then a layer of forcemeat, veal seasoning, and bacon, and so on until the meat rises to about an inch above the paste; taking care to finish with a layer of forcemeat, to fill all the cavities of the pie, and to lay in the meat firmly and compactly. Brush the top edge of the pie with beaten egg, put on the cover, press the edges, and pinch them round with paste-pincers. Make a hole in the middle of the lid, and ornament the pie with leaves, which should be stuck on with the white of an egg; then brush it all over with the beaten yolk of an egg, and bake the pie in an oven with a soaking heat from 3 to 4 hours. To ascertain when it is done, run a sharp-pointed knife or skewer through the hole at the top into the middle of the pie, and if the meat feels tender, it is sufficiently baked. Have ready about ½ pint of very strong gravy, pour it through a funnel into the hole at the top, stop up the hole with a small leaf of baked paste, and put the pie away until wanted for use. Should it acquire too much colour in the baking, cover it with white paper, as the crust should not in the least degree be burnt. Mushrooms, truffles, and many other ingredients, may be added to enrich the flavour of these pies, and the very fleshy parts of the meat may be larded. These pies are more frequently served cold than hot, and form excellent dishes for cold suppers or breakfasts. The cover of the pie is sometimes carefully removed, leaving the perfect edges, and the top decorated with square pieces of very bright aspic jelly: this has an exceedingly pretty effect.

Time.—About 4 hours. *Average cost, 6s. 6d.*

Sufficient for a very large pie. *Seasonable* from March to October.

BAKED RICE PUDDING.

I.

1342. INGREDIENTS.—1 small teacupful of rice, 4 eggs, 1 pint of milk, 2 oz. of fresh butter, 2 oz. of beef marrow, ¼ lb. of currants, 2 tablespoonfuls of brandy, nutmeg, ¼ lb. of sugar, the rind of ½ lemon.

Mode.—Put the lemon-rind and milk into a stewpan, and let it infuse till the milk is well flavoured with the lemon; in the mean time, boil the rice until tender in water, with a very small quantity of salt, and, when done, let it be thoroughly drained. Beat the eggs, stir to them the milk, which should be strained, the butter, marrow, currants, and remaining ingredients; add the rice, and mix all well together. Line the edges of the dish with puff-paste, put in the pud-

2 x 2

ding, and bake for about ¾ hour in a slow oven. Slices of candied-peel may be added at pleasure, or Sultana raisins may be substituted for the currants.

Time.—¾ hour. *Average cost,* 1s. 3d.

Sufficient for 5 or 6 persons.

Seasonable.—Suitable for a winter pudding, when fresh fruits are not obtainable.

RICE, with proper management in cooking it, forms a very valuable and cheap addition to our farinaceous food, and, in years of scarcity, has been found eminently useful in lessening the consumption of flour. When boiled, it should be so managed that the grains, though soft, should be as little broken and as dry as possible. The water in which it is dressed should only simmer, and not boil hard. Very little water should be used, as the grains absorb a great deal, and, consequently, swell much; and if they take up too much at first, it is difficult to get rid of it. Baking it in puddings is the best mode of preparing it.

II.
(*Plain and Economical; a nice Pudding for Children.*)

1343. INGREDIENTS.—1 teacupful of rice, 2 tablespoonfuls of moist sugar, 1 quart of milk, ½ oz. of butter or 2 small tablespoonfuls of chopped suet, ½ teaspoonful of grated nutmeg.

Mode.—Wash the rice, put it into a pie-dish with the sugar, pour in the milk, and stir these ingredients well together; then add the butter cut up into very small pieces, or, instead of this, the above proportion of finely-minced suet; grate a little nutmeg over the top, and bake the pudding, in a *moderate* oven, from 1½ to 2 hours. As the rice is not previously cooked, care must be taken that the pudding be very slowly baked, to give plenty of time for the rice to swell, and for it to be very thoroughly done.

Time.—1½ to 2 hours. *Average cost,* 7d.

Sufficient for 5 or 6 children. *Seasonable* at any time.

PLAIN BOILED RICE PUDDING.

1344. INGREDIENTS.—½ lb. of rice.

Mode.—Wash the rice, tie it in a pudding-cloth, allowing room for the rice to swell, and put it into a saucepan of cold water; boil it gently for 2 hours, and if, after a time, the cloth seems tied too loosely, take the rice up and tighten the cloth. Serve with sweet melted butter, or cold butter and sugar, or stewed fruit, jam, or marmalade; any of which accompaniments are suitable for plain boiled rice.

Time.—2 hours after the water boils. *Average cost,* 2d.

Sufficient for 4 or 5 persons. *Seasonable* at any time.

BOILED RICE PUDDING.
I.

1345. INGREDIENTS.—¼ lb. of rice, 1½ pint of new milk, 2 oz. of butter, 4 eggs, ½ saltspoonful of salt, 4 large tablespoonfuls of moist sugar, flavouring to taste.

Mode.—Stew the rice very gently in the above proportion of new milk, and, when it is tender, pour it into a basin; stir in the butter, and let it stand to cool; then beat the eggs, add these to the rice with the sugar, salt, and any flavouring that may be approved, such as nutmeg, powdered cinnamon, grated lemon-peel, essence of bitter almonds, or vanilla. When all is well stirred, put the pudding into a buttered basin, tie it down with a cloth, plunge it into boiling water, and boil for 1¼ hour.

Time.—1¼ hour. *Average cost,* 1s.

Sufficient for 5 or 6 persons. *Seasonable* at any time.

VARIETIES OF RICE.—Of the varieties of rice brought to our market, that from Bengal is chiefly of the species denominated *cargo* rice, and is of a coarse reddish-brown cast, but peculiarly sweet and large-grained; it does not readily separate from the husk, but it is preferred by the natives to all the others. *Patna* rice is more esteemed in Europe, and is of very superior quality; it is small-grained, rather long and wiry, and is remarkably white. The *Carolina* rice is considered as the best, and is likewise the dearest in London.

II.

(With Dried or Fresh Fruit; a nice dish for the Nursery.)

1346. INGREDIENTS.—½ lb. of rice, 1 pint of any kind of fresh fruit that may be preferred, or ½ lb. of raisins or currants.

Mode.—Wash the rice, tie it in a cloth, allowing room for it to swell, and put it into a saucepan of cold water; let it boil for an hour, then take it up, untie the cloth, stir in the fruit, and tie it up again tolerably tight, and put it into the water for the remainder of the time. Boil for another hour, or rather longer, and serve with sweet sauce, if made with dried fruit, and with plain sifted sugar and a little cream or milk, if made with fresh fruit.

Time.—1 hour to boil the rice without the fruit; 1 hour, or longer, afterwards.

Average cost, 6d.

Sufficient for 6 or 7 children. *Seasonable* at any time.

Note.—This pudding is very good made with apples: they should be pared, cored, and cut into thin slices.

BOILED RICE FOR CURRIES, &c.

1347. INGREDIENTS.—¾ lb. of rice, water, salt.

Mode.—Pick, wash, and soak the rice in plenty of cold water; then have ready a saucepan of boiling water, drop the rice into it, and keep it boiling quickly, with the lid uncovered, until it is tender, but not soft. Take it up, drain it, and put it on a dish before the fire to dry: do not handle it much with a spoon, but shake it about a little with two forks, that it may all be equally dried, and strew over a little salt. It is now ready to serve, and may be heaped lightly on a dish by itself, or be laid round the dish as a border, with a curry or fricassee in the centre. Some cooks smooth the rice with the back of a spoon, and then brush it over with the yolk of an egg, and set it in the oven to colour; but the rice well boiled, white, dry, and with every grain distinct, is by far the more preferable mode of dressing it. During the process of boiling, the rice should be attentively watched, that it be not overdone, as, if this is the case, it will have a mashed and soft appearance.

Time.—15 to 25 minutes, according to the quality of the rice.

Average cost, 3*d.*

Sufficient for a large dish of curry. *Seasonable* at any time.

RICE, in the native rough state, with the husk on, is called *paddy*, both in India and America, and it will keep better, and for a much longer time, in this state, than after the husk has been removed; besides which, prepared rice is apt to become dirty from rubbing about in the voyage on board ship, and in the warehouses. It is sometimes brought to England in the shape of paddy, and the husk detached here. Paddy pays less duty than shelled rice.

TO BOIL RICE FOR CURRIES, &c.

(*Soyer's Recipe.*)

1348. INGREDIENTS.—1 lb. of the best Carolina rice, 2 quarts of water, 1½ oz. of butter, a little salt.

Mode.—Wash the rice well in two waters; make 2 quarts of water boiling, and throw the rice into it; boil it until three-parts done, then drain it on a sieve. Butter the bottom and sides of a stewpan, put in the rice, place the lid on tightly, and set it by the side of the fire until the rice is perfectly tender, occasionally shaking the pan to prevent its sticking. Prepared thus, every grain should be separate and white. Either dish it separately, or place it round the curry as a border.

Time.—15 to 25 minutes. *Average cost*, 7*d.*

Sufficient for 2 moderate-sized curries. *Seasonable* at any time.

BUTTERED RICE.

1349. INGREDIENTS:—¼ lb. of rice, 1½ pint of milk, 2 oz. of butter, sugar to taste, grated nutmeg or pounded cinnamon.

Mode.—Wash and pick the rice, drain and put it into a saucepan with the milk; let it swell gradually, and, when tender, pour off the milk; stir in the butter, sugar, and nutmeg or cinnamon, and, when the butter is thoroughly melted, and the whole is quite hot, serve. After the milk is poured off, be particular that the rice does not burn: to prevent this, do not cease stirring it.

Time.—About ¾ hour to swell the rice. *Average cost,* 7*d.*
Sufficient for 4 or 5 persons. *Seasonable* at any time.

RICE was held in great esteem by the ancients : they considered it as a very beneficial food for the chest ; therefore it was recommended in cases of consumption, and to persons subject to spitting of blood.

SAVOURY CASSEROLE OF RICE,

Or Rice Border, for Ragouts, Fricassees, &c. (an Entree).

1350. INGREDIENTS.—1½ lb. of rice, 3 pints of weak stock or broth, 2 slices of fat ham, 1 teaspoonful of salt.

Mode.—A casserole of rice, when made in a mould, is not such a difficult operation as when it is moulded by the hand. It is an elegant and inexpensive entrée, as the remains of cold fish, flesh, or fowl may be served as ragoûts, fricassees, &c., inclosed in the casserole. It requires great
nicety in its preparation, the principal
thing to attend to being the boiling of the
rice, as, if this is not sufficiently cooked,

CASSEROLE OF RICE.

the casserole, when moulded, will have a rough appearance, which would entirely spoil it. After having washed the rice in two or three waters, drain it well, and put it into a stewpan with the stock, ham, and salt ; cover the pan closely, and let the rice gradually swell over a slow fire, occasionally stirring, to prevent its sticking. When it is quite soft, strain it, pick out the pieces of ham, and, with the back of a large wooden spoon, mash the rice to a perfectly smooth paste. Then well grease a mould (moulds are made purposely for rice borders), and turn it upside down for a minute or two, to drain away the fat, should there be too much ; put some rice all round the bottom and sides of it ; place a piece of soft bread in the middle, and cover it with rice ; press it in equally with the spoon, and let it cool. Then dip the mould into hot water, turn the casserole carefully on to a dish, mark where the lid is to be formed on the top, by making an incision with the point of a knife about an inch from the edge all round, and put it into a *very hot* oven. Brush it over with a little clarified butter, and bake about ½ hour, or rather longer ; then carefully remove the lid, which will be formed by the incision having been made all round, and remove the bread, in small pieces, with the point of a penknife, being careful not to injure the casserole. Fill the centre with the ragoût or fricassee, which should be made thick ; put on the cover, glaze it, place it in the oven to set the glaze, and serve as hot as possible. The casserole should not be emptied too much, as it is liable to crack from the weight of whatever is put in ;

and in baking it, let the oven be very hot, or the casserole will probably break.

Time.—About ¾ hour to swell the rice.

Sufficient for 2 moderate-sized casseroles.

Seasonable at any time.

SWEET CASSEROLE OF RICE (an Entremets).

1351. INGREDIENTS.—1½ lb. of rice, 3 pints of milk, sugar to taste, flavouring of bitter almonds, 3 oz. of butter, the yolks of 3 eggs.

Mode.—This is made in precisely the same manner as a savoury casserole, only substituting the milk and sugar for the stock and salt. Put the milk into a stewpan, with sufficient essence of bitter almonds to flavour it well; then add the rice, which should be washed, picked, and drained, and let it swell gradually in the milk over a slow fire. When it is tender, stir in the sugar, butter, and yolks of eggs; butter a mould, press in the rice, and proceed in exactly the same manner as in recipe No. 1350. When the casserole is ready, fill it with a compôte of any fruit that may be preferred, or with melted apricot-jam, and serve.

Time.—From ¾ to 1 hour to swell the rice, ½ to ¾ hour to bake the casserole.

Average cost, exclusive of the compôte or jam, 1s. 9d.

Sufficient for 2 casseroles. *Seasonable* at any time.

FRENCH RICE PUDDING, or GATEAU DE RIZ.

1352. INGREDIENTS.—To every ¼ lb. of rice allow 1 quart of milk, the rind of 1 lemon, ½ teaspoonful of salt, sugar to taste, 4 oz. of butter, 6 eggs, bread crumbs.

Mode.—Put the milk into a stewpan with the lemon-rind, and let it infuse for ½ hour, or until the former is well flavoured; then take out the peel; have ready the rice washed, picked, and drained; put it into the milk, and let it gradually swell over a very slow fire. Stir in the butter, salt, and sugar, and when properly sweetened, add the yolks of the eggs, and then the whites, both of which should be well beaten, and added separately to the rice. Butter a mould, strew in some fine bread crumbs, and let them be spread equally over it; then carefully pour in the rice, and bake the pudding in a *slow* oven for 1 hour. Turn it out of the mould, and garnish the dish with preserved cherries, or any bright-coloured jelly or jam. This pudding would be exceedingly nice, flavoured with essence of vanilla.

Time.—$\frac{3}{4}$ to 1 hour for the rice to swell; to be baked 1 hour in a slow oven.

Average cost, 1s. 8d.

Sufficient for 5 or 6 persons. *Seasonable* at any time.

BAKED OR BOILED GROUND RICE PUDDING.

1353. INGREDIENTS.—2 pints of milk, 6 tablespoonfuls of ground rice, sugar to taste, 4 eggs, flavouring of lemon-rind, nutmeg, bitter almonds or bay-leaf.

Mode.—Put 1½ pint of the milk into a stewpan, with any of the above flavourings, and bring it to the boiling-point, and, with the other ½ pint of milk, mix the ground rice to a smooth batter; strain the boiling milk to this, and stir over the fire until the mixture is tolerably thick; then pour it into a basin, leave it uncovered, and when nearly or quite cold, sweeten it to taste, and add the eggs, which should be previously well beaten, with a little salt. Put the pudding into a well-buttered basin, tie it down with a cloth, plunge it into boiling water, and boil for 1½ hour. For a baked pudding, proceed in precisely the same manner, only using half the above proportion of ground rice, with the same quantity of all the other ingredients : an hour will bake the pudding in a moderate oven. Stewed fruit, or preserves, or marmalade, may be served with either the boiled or baked pudding, and will be found an improvement.

Time.—1½ hour to boil, 1 hour to bake. *Average cost*, 10d.

Sufficient for 5 or 6 persons. *Seasonable* at any time.

ICED RICE PUDDING.

1354. INGREDIENTS.—6 oz. of rice, 1 quart of milk, ½ lb. of sugar, the yolks of 6 eggs, 1 small teaspoonful of essence of vanilla.

Mode.—Put the rice into a stewpan, with the milk and sugar, and let these simmer over a gentle fire until the rice is sufficiently soft to break up into a smooth mass, and should the milk dry away too much, a little more may be added. Stir the rice occasionally, to prevent its burning, then beat it to a smooth mixture; add the yolks of the eggs, which should be well whisked, and the vanilla (should this flavouring not be liked, essence of bitter almonds may be substituted for it); put this rice custard into the freezing-pot, and proceed as directed in recipe No. 1290. When wanted for table, turn the pudding out of the mould, and pour over the top, and round it, a *compôte* of oranges, or any other fruit that may be preferred, taking care that the flavouring in the pudding harmonizes well with the fruit that is served with it.

Time.—½ hour to freeze the mixture.

Average cost, 1s. 6d. ; exclusive of the *compôte,* 1s. 4d.

Seasonable.—Served all the year round.

MINIATURE RICE PUDDINGS.

1355. INGREDIENTS.—¼ lb. of rice, 1½ pint of milk, 2 oz. of fresh butter, 4 eggs, sugar to taste ; flavouring of lemon-peel, bitter almonds, or vanilla ; a few strips of candied peel.

Mode.—Let the rice swell in 1 pint of the milk over a slow fire, putting with it a strip of lemon-peel ; stir to it the butter and the other ½ pint of milk, and let the mixture cool. Then add the well-beaten eggs, and a few drops of essence of almonds or essence of vanilla, whichever may be preferred ; butter well some small cups or moulds, line them with a few pieces of candied peel sliced very thin, fill them three parts full, and bake for about 40 minutes ; turn them out of the cups on to a white d'oyley, and serve with sweet sauce. The flavouring and candied peel might be omitted, and stewed fruit or preserve served instead, with these puddings.

Time.—40 minutes. *Average cost,* 1s.

Sufficient for 6 puddings. *Seasonable* at any time.

ARROWROOT SAUCE FOR PUDDINGS.

1356. INGREDIENTS.—2 small teaspoonfuls of arrowroot, 4 dessert-spoonfuls of pounded sugar, the juice of 1 lemon, ¼ teaspoonful of grated nutmeg, ½ pint of water.

Mode.—Mix the arrowroot smoothly with the water ; put this into a stewpan ; add the sugar, strained lemon-juice, and grated nutmeg. Stir these ingredients over the fire until they boil, when the sauce is ready for use. A small quantity of wine, or any liqueur, would very much improve the flavour of this sauce : it is usually served with bread, rice, custard, or any dry pudding that is not very rich.

Time.—Altogether, 15 minutes. *Average cost,* 4d.

Sufficient for 6 or 7 persons.

CHERRY SAUCE FOR SWEET PUDDINGS.
(*German Recipe.*)

1357. INGREDIENTS.—1 lb. of cherries, 1 tablespoonful of flour, 1 oz. of butter, ½ pint of water, 1 wineglassful of port wine, a little grated lemon-rind, 4 pounded cloves, 2 tablespoonfuls of lemon-juice, sugar to taste.

Mode.—Stone the cherries, and pound the kernels in a mortar to a smooth paste ; put the butter and flour into a saucepan ; stir them over the fire until of a pale brown; then add the cherries, the pounded kernels, the wine, and the water. Simmer these gently for ¼ hour, or until the cherries are quite cooked, and rub the whole through a hair sieve; add the remaining ingredients, let the sauce boil for another 5 minutes, and serve. This is a delicious sauce to serve with boiled batter pudding, and when thus used, should be sent to table poured over the pudding.

Time.—20 minutes to ½ hour.   *Average cost*, 1s. 2d.

Sufficient for 4 or 5 persons.   *Seasonable* in June, July, and August.

LEMON SAUCE FOR SWEET PUDDINGS.

1358. INGREDIENTS.—The rind and juice of 1 lemon, 1 tablespoonful of flour, 1 oz. of butter, 1 large wineglassful of sherry, 1 wineglassful of water, sugar to taste, the yolks of 4 eggs.

Mode.—Rub the rind of the lemon on to some lumps of sugar; squeeze out the juice, and strain it; put the butter and flour into a saucepan, stir them over the fire, and when of a pale brown, add the wine, water, and strained lemon-juice. Crush the lumps of sugar that were rubbed on the lemon; stir these into the sauce, which should be very sweet. When these ingredients are well mixed, and the sugar is melted, put in the beaten yolks of 4 eggs; keep stirring the sauce until it thickens, when serve: Do not, on any account, allow it to boil, or it will curdle, and be entirely spoiled.

Time.—Altogether, 15 minutes.   *Average cost*, 1s. 2d.

Sufficient for 7 or 8 persons.

SOYER'S SAUCE FOR PLUM-PUDDING.

1359. INGREDIENTS.—The yolks of 3 eggs, 1 tablespoonful of powdered sugar, 1 gill of milk, a very little grated lemon-rind, 2 small wineglassfuls of brandy.

Mode.—Separate the yolks from the whites of 3 eggs, and put the former into a stewpan; add the sugar, milk, and grated lemon-rind, and stir over the fire until the mixture thickens; but do *not* allow it to *boil*. Put in the brandy; let the sauce stand by the side of the fire, to get quite hot; keep stirring it, and serve in a boat or tureen separately, or pour it over the pudding.

Time.—Altogether, 10 minutes.   *Average cost*, 1s.

Sufficient for 6 or 7 persons.

SWEET SAUCE FOR PUDDINGS.

1360. INGREDIENTS.—½ pint of melted butter made with milk, 3 heaped teaspoonfuls of pounded sugar, flavouring of grated lemon-rind, or nutmeg, or cinnamon.

Mode.—Make ½ pint of melted butter by recipe No. 380, omitting the salt; stir in the sugar, add a little grated lemon-rind, nutmeg, or powdered cinnamon, and serve. Previously to making the melted butter, the milk can be flavoured with bitter almonds, by infusing about half a dozen of them in it for about ½ hour; the milk should then be strained before it is added to the other ingredients. This simple sauce may be served for children with rice, batter, or bread pudding.

Time.—Altogether, 15 minutes. *Average cost,* 4d.

Sufficient for 6 or 7 persons.

VANILLA CUSTARD SAUCE, to serve with Puddings.

1361. INGREDIENTS.—½ pint of milk, 2 eggs, 2 oz. of sugar, 10 drops of essence of vanilla.

Mode.—Beat the eggs, sweeten the milk; stir these ingredients well together, and flavour them with essence of vanilla, regulating the proportion of this latter ingredient by the strength of the essence, the size of the eggs, &c. Put the mixture into a small jug, place this jug in a saucepan of boiling water, and stir the sauce *one way* until it thickens; but do not allow it to boil, or it will instantly curdle. Serve in a boat or tureen separately, with plum, bread, or any kind of dry pudding. Essence of bitter almonds or lemon-rind may be substituted for the vanilla, when they are more in accordance with the flavouring of the pudding with which the sauce is intended to be served.

Time.—To be stirred in the jug from 8 to 10 minutes.

Average cost, 4d.

Sufficient for 4 or 5 persons.

AN EXCELLENT WINE SAUCE FOR PUDDINGS.

1362. INGREDIENTS.—The yolks of 4 eggs, 1 teaspoonful of flour, 2 oz. of pounded sugar, 2 oz. of fresh butter, ¼ saltspoonful of salt, ½ pint of sherry or Madeira.

Mode.—Put the butter and flour into a saucepan, and stir them over the fire until the former thickens; then add the sugar, salt, and wine, and mix these ingredients well together. Separate the yolks from the whites of 4 eggs; beat up the former, and stir them briskly to the sauce; let it remain over the fire until it is on the point of simmering; but do not allow it to boil, or it will instantly curdle. This sauce is delicious with plum, marrow, or bread puddings; but should be served separately, and not poured over the pudding.

Time.—From 5 to 7 minutes to thicken the butter; about 5 minutes to stir the sauce over the fire.

Average cost, 1s. 10d.   *Sufficient* for 7 or 8 persons.

WINE OR BRANDY SAUCE FOR PUDDINGS.

1363. INGREDIENTS.—½ pint of melted butter No. 377, 3 heaped teaspoonfuls of pounded sugar; 1 *large* wineglassful of port or sherry, or ¾ of a *small* glassful of brandy.

Mode.—Make ½ pint of melted butter by recipe No. 377, omitting the salt; then stir in the sugar and wine or spirit in the above-proportion, and bring the sauce to the point of boiling. Serve in a boat or tureen separately, and, if liked, pour a little of it over the pudding. To convert this into punch sauce, add to the sherry and brandy a small wineglassful of rum and the juice and grated rind of ½ lemon. Liqueurs, such as Maraschino or Curaçoa, substituted for the brandy, make excellent sauces.

Time.—Altogether, 15 minutes. *Average cost*, 8d.

Sufficient for 6 or 7 persons.

WINE SAUCE FOR PUDDINGS.

1364. INGREDIENTS.—½ pint of sherry, ¼ pint of water, the yolks of 5 eggs, 2 oz. of pounded sugar, ½ teaspoonful of minced lemon-peel, a few pieces of candied citron cut thin.

Mode.—Separate the yolks from the whites of 5 eggs; beat them, and put them into a very clean saucepan (if at hand, a lined one is best); add all the other ingredients, place them over a sharp fire, and keep stirring until the sauce begins to thicken; then take it off and serve. If it is allowed to boil, it will be spoiled, as it will immediately curdle.

Time.—To be stirred over the fire 3 or 4 minutes; but it must not boil. *Average cost*, 2s.

Sufficient for a large pudding; allow half this quantity for a moderate-sized one.

Seasonable at any time.

OPEN TART OF STRAWBERRY OR ANY OTHER KIND OF PRESERVE.

1365. INGREDIENTS.—Trimmings of puff-paste, any kind of jam.

Mode.—Butter a tart-pan of the shape shown in the engraving;

OPEN TART.

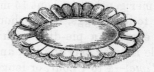

OPEN-TART MOULD.

roll out the paste to the thickness of ½ an inch, and line the pan with it; prick a few holes at the bottom with a fork, and bake the tart in a brisk oven from 10 to 15 minutes. Let the paste cool a little; then fill it with preserve, place a few stars or leaves on it, which have been previously cut out of the paste and baked, and the tart is ready for table. By making it in this manner, both the flavour and colour of the jam are preserved, which would otherwise be lost, were it baked in the oven on the paste; and, besides, so much jam is not required.

Time.—10 to 15 minutes. *Average cost,* 8d.

Sufficient.—1 tart for 3 persons. *Seasonable* at any time.

STRAWBERRY.—The name of this favourite fruit is said to be derived from an ancient custom of putting straw beneath the fruit when it began to ripen, which is very useful to keep it moist and clean. The strawberry belongs to temperate and rather cold climates; and no fruit of these latitudes, that ripens without the aid of artificial heat, is at all comparable with it in point of flavour. The strawberry is widely diffused, being found in most parts of the world, particularly in Europe and America.

QUICKLY-MADE PUDDINGS.

1366. INGREDIENTS.—¼ lb. of butter, ½ lb. of sifted sugar, ¼ lb. of flour, 1 pint of milk, 5 eggs, a little grated lemon-rind.

Mode.—Make the milk hot; stir in the butter, and let it cool before the other ingredients are added to it; then stir in the sugar, flour, and eggs, which should be well whisked, and omit the whites of 2; flavour with a little grated lemon-rind, and beat the mixture well. Butter some small cups, rather more than half fill them; bake from 20 minutes to ½ hour, according to the size of the puddings, and serve with fruit, custard, or wine sauce, a little of which may be poured over them.

Time.—20 minutes to ½ hour. *Average cost,* 1s. 2d.

Sufficient for 6 puddings. *Seasonable* at any time.

SAGO PUDDING.

1367. INGREDIENTS.—1½ pint of milk, 3 tablespoonfuls of sago, the rind of ½ lemon, 3 oz. of sugar, 4 eggs, 1½ oz. of butter, grated nutmeg, puff-paste.

Mode.—Put the milk and lemon-rind into a stewpan, place it by the side of the fire, and let it remain until the milk is well flavoured with the lemon; then strain it, mix with it the sago and sugar, and simmer gently for about 15 minutes. Let the mixture cool a little, and stir to it the eggs, which should be well beaten, and the butter. Line the edges of a pie-dish with puff-paste, pour in the pudding, grate a little nutmeg over the top, and bake from ¾ to 1 hour.

Time.—¾ to 1 hour, or longer if the oven is very slow.

Average cost, 1s.

Sufficient for 5 or 6 persons. *Seasonable* at any time.

Note.—The above pudding may be boiled instead of baked; but then allow 2 extra tablespoonfuls of sago, and boil the pudding in a buttered basin from 1¼ to 1¾ hour.

SAGO.—Sago is the pith of a species of palm (*Cycas circinalis*). Its form is that of a small round grain. There are two sorts of sago,—the white and the yellow; but their properties are the same. Sago absorbs the liquid in which it is cooked, becomes transparent and soft, and retains its original shape. Its alimentary properties are the same as those of tapioca and arrowroot.

SAGO SAUCE FOR SWEET PUDDINGS.

1368. INGREDIENTS.—1 tablespoonful of sago, ⅓ pint of water, ¼ pint of port or sherry, the rind and juice of 1 small lemon, sugar to taste; when the flavour is liked, a little pounded cinnamon.

Mode.—Wash the sago in two or three waters; then put it into a saucepan, with the water and lemon-peel; let it simmer gently by the side of the fire for 10 minutes; then take out the lemon-peel, add the remaining ingredients, give one boil, and serve. Be particular to strain the lemon-juice before adding it to the sauce. This, on trial, will be found a delicious accompaniment to various boiled puddings, such as those made of bread, raisins, rice, &c.

Time.—10 minutes. *Average cost*, 9*d.*

Sufficient for 7 or 8 persons.

BAKED SEMOLINA PUDDING.

1369. INGREDIENTS.—3 oz. of semolina, 1½ pint of milk, ¼ lb. of sugar, 12 bitter almonds, 3 oz. of butter, 4 eggs.

Mode.—Flavour the milk with the bitter almonds, by infusing them in it by the side of the fire for about ½ hour; then strain it, and mix with it the semolina, sugar, and butter. Stir these ingredients over the fire for a few minutes; then take them off, and gradually mix in the eggs, which should be well beaten. Butter a pie-dish, line the edges with puff-paste, put in the pudding, and bake in rather a slow oven from 40 to 50 minutes. Serve with custard sauce or stewed fruit, a little of which may be poured over the pudding.

Time.—40 to 50 minutes. *Average cost*, 1*s.* 2*d.*

Sufficient for 5 or 6 persons. *Seasonable* at any time.

SEMOLINA.—After vermicelli, semolina is the most useful ingredient that can be used for thickening soups, meat or vegetable, of rich or simple quality. Semolina is softening, light, wholesome, easy of digestion, and adapted to the infant, the aged, and the invalid. That of a clear yellow colour, well dried and newly made, is the fittest for use.

TAPIOCA PUDDING.

1370. INGREDIENTS.—3 oz. of tapioca, 1 quart of milk, 2 oz. of butter, ¼ lb. of sugar, 4 eggs, flavouring of vanilla, grated lemon-rind, or bitter almonds.

Mode.—Wash the tapioca, and let it stew gently in the milk by the side of the fire for ¼ hour, occasionally stirring it; then let it cool a little; mix with it the butter, sugar, and eggs, which should be well beaten, and flavour with either of the above ingredients, putting in about 12 drops of the essence of almonds or vanilla, whichever is preferred. Butter a pie-dish, and line the edges with puff-paste; put in the pudding, and bake in a moderate oven for an hour. If the pudding is boiled, add a little more tapioca, and boil it in a buttered basin 1½ hour.

Time.—1 hour to bake, 1½ hour to boil. *Average cost,* 1s. 2d.

Sufficient for 5 or 6 persons. *Seasonable* at any time.

TAPIOCA.—Tapioca is recommended to the convalescent, as being easy of digestion. It may be used in soup or broth, or mixed with milk or water, and butter. It is excellent food for either the healthy or sick, for the reason that it is so quickly digested without fatigue to the stomach.

TARTLETS.

1371. INGREDIENTS.—Trimmings of puff-paste, any jam or marmalade that may be preferred.

Mode.—Roll out the paste to the thickness of about ½ inch; butter some small round patty-pans, line them with it, and cut off the superfluous paste close to the edge of the pan. Put a small piece of bread

into each tartlet (this is to keep them in shape), and bake in a brisk oven for about 10 minutes, or rather longer. When they are done, and are of a nice colour, take the pieces of bread out

DISH OF TARTLETS. carefully, and replace them by a spoonful of jam or marmalade. Dish them high on a white d'oyley, piled high in the centre, and serve.

Time.—10 to 15 minutes. *Average cost,* 1d. each.

Sufficient.—1 lb. of paste will make 2 dishes of tartlets.

Seasonable at any time.

ROLLED TREACLE PUDDING.

1372. INGREDIENTS.—1 lb. of suet crust No. 1215, ¼ lb. of treacle, ½ teaspoonful of grated ginger.

Mode.—Make, with 1 lb. of flour, a suet crust by recipe No. 1215; roll it out to the thickness of ½ inch, and spread the treacle equally over it, leaving a small margin where the paste joins; close the ends securely, tie the pudding in a floured cloth, plunge it into boiling water, and boil for 2 hours. We have inserted this pudding, being economical, and a favourite one with children; it is, of course, only suitable for a nursery, or very plain family dinner. Made with a lard instead of a suet crust, it would be very nice baked, and would be sufficiently done in from 1½ to 2 hours.

Time.—Boiled pudding, 2 hours; baked pudding, 1½ to 2 hours.

Average cost, 7d.

Sufficient for 5 or 6 persons. *Seasonable* at any time.

MEAT OR SAUSAGE ROLLS.

1373. INGREDIENTS.—1 lb. of puff-paste No. 1206, sausage-meat No. 837, the yolk of 1 egg.

Mode.—Make 1 lb. of puff-paste by recipe No. 1206; roll it out to the thickness of about ½ inch, or rather less, and divide it into 8, 10, or 12 squares, according to the size the rolls are intended to be. Place some sausage-meat on one-half of each square, wet the edges of the paste, and fold it over the meat; slightly press the edges together, and trim them neatly with a knife. Brush the rolls over with the yolk of an egg, and bake them in a well-heated oven for about ½ hour, or longer should they be very large. The remains of cold chicken and ham, minced and seasoned, as also cold veal or beef, make very good rolls.

Time.—½ hour, or longer if the rolls are large.

Average cost, 1s. 6d.

Sufficient.—1 lb. of paste for 10 or 12 rolls.

Seasonable, with sausage-meat, from September to March or April.

SOMERSETSHIRE PUDDINGS.

1374. INGREDIENTS.—3 eggs, their weight in flour, pounded sugar and butter, flavouring of grated lemon-rind, bitter almonds, or essence of vanilla.

Mode.—Carefully weigh the various ingredients, by placing on one side of the scales the eggs, and on the other the flour; then the sugar, and then the butter. Warm the butter, and with the hands beat it to a cream; gradually dredge in the flour and pounded sugar, and keep stirring and beating the mixture without ceasing until it is perfectly smooth. Then add the eggs, which should be well whisked, and either of the above flavourings that may be preferred; butter some small cups, rather more than half-fill them, and bake in a brisk oven for about ½ hour. Turn them out, dish them on a napkin, and serve custard or wine-sauce with them. A pretty little supper-dish may be made of these puddings cold, by cutting out a portion of the inside with the point of a knife, and putting into the cavity a little whipped cream or delicate preserve, such as apricot, greengage, or very bright marmalade. The paste for these puddings requires a great deal of mixing, as the more it is beaten, the better will the puddings be. When served cold, they are usually called *gâteaux à la Madeleine.*

Time.—½ hour. *Average cost,* 10*d.*

Sufficient for 6 or 7 puddings. *Seasonable* at any time.

SUET PUDDING, to serve with Roast Meat.

1375. INGREDIENTS.—1 lb. of flour, 6 oz. of finely-chopped suet, ½ saltspoonful of salt, ½ saltspoonful of pepper, ½ pint of milk or water.

Mode.—Chop the suet very finely, after freeing it from skin, and mix it well with the flour; add the salt and pepper (this latter ingredient may be omitted if the flavour is not liked), and make the whole into a smooth paste with the above proportion of milk or water. Tie the pudding in a floured cloth, or put it into a buttered basin, and boil from 2½ to 3 hours. To enrich it, substitute 3 beaten eggs for some of the milk or water, and increase the proportion of suet.

Time.—2½ to 3 hours. *Average cost,* 6*d.*

Sufficient for 5 or 6 persons. *Seasonable* at any time.

Note.—When there is a joint roasting or baking, this pudding may be boiled in a long shape, and then cut into slices a few minutes before dinner is served: these slices should be laid in the dripping-pan for a minute or two, and then browned before the fire. Most children like this accompaniment to roast meat. Where there is a large family of children, and the means of keeping them are limited, it is a most economical plan to serve up the pudding before the meat: as, in this case, the consumption of the latter article will be much smaller than it otherwise would be.

SUSSEX, or HARD DUMPLINGS.

1376. INGREDIENTS.—1 lb. of flour, ½ pint of water, ¼ saltspoonful of salt.

Mode.—Mix the flour and water together to a smooth paste, previously adding a small quantity of salt. Form this into small round dumplings; drop them into boiling water, and boil from ½ to ¾ hour. They may be served with roast or boiled meat; in the latter case they may be cooked with the meat, but should be dropped into the water when it is quite boiling.

Time.—½ to ¾ hour.

Sufficient for 10 or 12 dumplings. *Seasonable* at any time.

VERMICELLI PUDDING.

1377. INGREDIENTS.—4 oz. of vermicelli, 1½ pint of milk, ¼ pint of cream 3 oz. of butter, 3 oz. of sugar, 4 eggs.

Mode.—Boil the vermicelli in the milk until it is tender; then stir in the remaining ingredients, omitting the cream, if not obtainable. Flavour the mixture with grated lemon-rind, essence of bitter almonds. or vanilla; butter a pie-dish; line the edges with puff-paste, put in the pudding, and bake in a moderate oven for about $\frac{3}{4}$ hour.

Time.—$\frac{3}{4}$ hour. *Average cost,* 1s. 2d. without cream.

Sufficient for 5 or 6 persons. *Seasonable* at any time.

VERMICELLI.—The finest vermicelli comes from Marseilles, Nîmes, and Montpellier. It is a nourishing food, and owes its name to its peculiar thread-like form. Vermicelli means, little worms.

VICARAGE PUDDING.

1378. INGREDIENTS.—$\frac{1}{4}$ lb. of flour, $\frac{1}{4}$ lb. of chopped suet, $\frac{1}{4}$ lb. of currants, $\frac{1}{4}$ lb. of raisins, 1 tablespoonful of moist sugar, $\frac{1}{2}$ teaspoonful of ground ginger, $\frac{1}{2}$ saltspoonful of salt.

Mode.—Put all the ingredients into a basin, having previously stoned the raisins, and washed, picked, and dried the currants; mix well with a clean knife; dip the pudding-cloth into boiling water, wring it out, and put in the mixture. Have ready a saucepan of boiling water, plunge in the pudding, and boil for 3 hours. Turn it out on the dish, and serve with sifted sugar.

Time.—3 hours. *Average cost,* 8d.

Sufficient for 5 or 6 persons.

Seasonable.—Suitable for a winter pudding.

VOL-AU-VENT (an Entree).

1379. INGREDIENTS.—$\frac{3}{4}$ to 1 lb. of puff-paste No. 1208, fricasseed chickens, rabbits, ragoûts, or the remains of cold fish, flaked and warmed in thick white sauce.

Mode.—Make from $\frac{3}{4}$ to 1 lb. of puff-paste, by recipe No. 1208, taking care that it is very evenly rolled out each time, to insure its rising properly; and if the paste is not extremely light, and put into a good hot oven, this cannot be accomplished, and the *vol-au-vent* will look very badly. Roll out the paste to the thickness of about 1$\frac{1}{2}$ inch, and, with a fluted cutter, stamp it out to the desired shape, either round or oval, and, with the point of a small knife, make a slight incision in the paste all round the top, about an inch from the edge, which, when baked, forms the lid. Put the *vol-au-vent* into a good brisk oven, and keep the door shut for a few minutes after it is put in. Particular attention should be paid to the heating of the oven, for the paste *cannot* rise without a tolerable degree of heat.

VOL-AU-VENT.

When of a nice colour, without being scorched, withdraw it from the oven, instantly remove the cover where it was marked, and detach all the soft crumb from the centre : in doing this, be careful not to break the edges of the *vol-au-vent'*; but should they look thin in places, stop them with small flakes of the inside paste, stuck on with the white of an egg.   This precaution is necessary to prevent the fricassee or ragoût from bursting the case, and so spoiling the appearance of the dish. Fill the *vol-au-vent* with a rich mince, or fricassee, or ragoût, or the remains of cold fish flaked and warmed in a good white sauce, and do not make them very-liquid, for fear of the gravy bursting the crust : replace the lid, and serve. To improve the appearance of the crust, brush it over with the yolk of an egg *after* it has risen properly.

Time.—¾ hour to bake the *vol-au-vent*.

Average cost, exclusive of interior, 1s. 6d.

Seasonable at any time.

SMALL VOL-AU-VENTS.

Note.—Small *vol-au-vents* may be made like those shown in the engraving, and filled with minced veal, chicken, &c. They should be made of the same paste as the larger ones, and stamped out with a small fluted cutter.

SWEET VOL-AU-VENT OF PLUMS, APPLES, OR ANY OTHER FRESH FRUIT.

1380. INGREDIENTS.—¾ lb. of puff-paste No. 1208, about 1 pint of fruit compôte.

Mode.—Make ½ lb. of puff-paste by recipe No. 1208, taking care to bake it in a good brisk oven, to draw it up nicely and make it look light. Have ready sufficient stewed fruit, the syrup of which must be boiled down until very thick ; fill the *vol-au-vent* with this, and pile it high in the centre; powder a little sugar over it, and put it back in the oven to glaze, or use a salamander for the purpose : the *vol-au-vent* is then ready to serve. They may be made with any fruit that is in season, such as rhubarb, oranges, gooseberries, currants, cherries, apples. &c. ; but care must be taken not to have the syrup too thin, for fear of its breaking through the crust.

Time.—½ hour to 40 minutes to bake the *vol-au-vent*.

Average cost, exclusive of the compôte, 1s. 1d.

Sufficient for 1 entremets.

VOL-AU-VENT OF FRESH STRAWBERRIES WITH WHIPPED CREAM.

1381. INGREDIENTS.—¾ lb. of puff-paste No. 1208, 1 pint of freshly-gathered strawberries, sugar to taste, a plateful of whipped cream.

Mode.—Make a *vol-au-vent* case by recipe No. 1379, only not quite so large nor so high as for a savoury one. When nearly done, brush the paste over with the white of an egg, then sprinkle on it some pounded sugar, and put it back in the oven to set the glaze. Remove the interior, or soft crumb, and, at the moment of serving, fill it with the strawberries, which should be picked, and broken up with sufficient sugar to sweeten them nicely. Place a few spoonfuls of whipped cream on the top, and serve.

Time.—½ hour to 40 minutes to bake the *vol-au-vent*.

Average cost, 2s. 3d.

Sufficient for 1 *vol-au-vent*.

Seasonable in June and July.

STRAWBERRY.—Among the Greeks, the name of the strawberry indicated its tenuity, this fruit forming hardly a mouthful. With the Latins, the name reminded one of the delicious perfume of this plant. Both nations were equally fond of it, and applied the same care to its cultivation. Virgil appears to place it in the same rank with flowers; and Ovid gives it a tender epithet, which delicate palates would not disavow. Neither does this luxurious poet forget the wild strawberry, which disappears beneath its modest foliage, but whose presence the scented air reveals.

WEST-INDIAN PUDDING.

1382. INGREDIENTS.—1 pint of cream, ¼ lb. of loaf-sugar, ½ lb. of Savoy or sponge-cakes, 8 eggs, 3 oz. of preserved green ginger.

Mode.—Crumble down the cakes, put them into a basin, and pour over them the cream, which should be previously sweetened and brought to the boiling-point; cover the basin, well beat the eggs, and when the cream is soaked up, stir them in. Butter a mould, arrange the ginger round it, pour in the pudding carefully, and tie it down with a cloth; steam or boil it slowly for 1½ hour, and serve with the syrup from the ginger, which should be warmed, and poured over the pudding.

Time.—1½ hour. *Average cost,* with cream at 1s. per pint, 2s. 8d.

Sufficient for 5 or 6 persons. *Seasonable* at any time.

YEAST DUMPLINGS.

1383. INGREDIENTS.—½ quartern of dough, boiling water.

Mode.—Make a very light dough as for bread, using to mix it, milk, instead of water; divide it into 7 or 8 dumplings; plunge them into boiling water, and boil them for 20 minutes. Serve the instant they are taken up, as they spoil directly, by falling and becoming heavy; and in eating them do not touch them with a knife, but tear them apart with two forks. They may be eaten with meat gravy, or cold butter and sugar, and if not convenient to make the dough at home, a little from the baker's answers as well, only it must be placed for a few minutes near the fire, in a basin with a cloth over it, to let it rise again before it is made into dumplings.

Time.—20 minutes. *Average cost,* 4d.

Sufficient for 5 or 6 persons. *Seasonable* at any time.

YEAST consists principally of a substance very similar in composition, and in many of its sensible properties, to gluten; and, when new or fresh, it is inflated and rendered frothy by a large quantity of carbonic acid. When mixed with wort, this substance acts upon the saccharine matter; the temperature rises, carbonic acid is disengaged, and the result is *ale*, which always contains a considerable proportion of alcohol, or spirit. The quantity of yeast employed in brewing ale being small, the saccharine matter is but imperfectly decomposed: hence a considerable portion of it remains in the liquor, and gives it that viscid quality and body for which it is remarkable. The fermenting property of yeast is weakened by boiling for ten minutes, and is entirely destroyed by continuing the boiling. Alcohol poured upon it likewise renders it inert; on which account its power lessens as the alcohol is formed during fermentation.

YORKSHIRE PUDDING, to serve with hot Roast Beef.

1384. INGREDIENTS.—1½ pint of milk, 6 *large* tablespoonfuls of flour, 3 eggs, 1 saltspoonful of salt.

Mode.—Put the flour into a basin with the salt, and stir gradually to this enough milk to make it into a stiff batter. When this is per-

YORKSHIRE PUDDING.

fectly smooth, and all the lumps are well rubbed down, add the remainder of the milk and the eggs, which should be well beaten. Beat the mixture for a few minutes, and pour it into a shallow tin, which has been previously well rubbed with beef dripping. Put the pudding into the oven, and bake it for an hour; then, for another ½ hour, place it under the meat, to catch a little of the gravy that flows from it. Cut the pudding into small square pieces, put them on a hot dish, and serve. If the meat is baked, the pudding may at once be placed under it, resting the former on a small three-cornered stand.

Time.—1½ hour. *Average cost,* 7d.

Sufficient for 5 or 6 persons. *Seasonable* at any time.

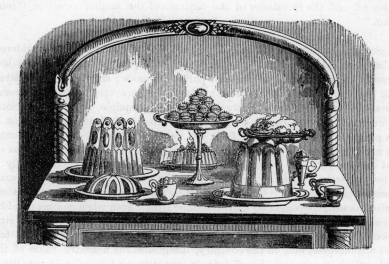

CHAPTER XXVIII.

GENERAL OBSERVATIONS ON CREAMS, JELLIES, SOUFFLES, OMELETS, & SWEET DISHES.

1385. CREAMS.—The yellowish-white, opaque fluid, smooth and unctuous to the touch, which separates itself from new milk, and forms a layer on its surface, when removed by skimming, is employed in a variety of culinary preparations. The analyses of the contents of cream have been decided to be, in 100 parts—butter, 3·5 ; curd, or matter of cheese, 3·5 ; whey, 92·0. That cream contains an oil, is evinced by its staining clothes in the manner of oil ; and when boiled for some time, a little oil floats upon the surface. The thick animal oil which it contains, the well-known *butter*, is separated only by agitation, as in the common process of *churning*, and the cheesy matter remains blended with the whey in the state of *buttermilk*. Of the several kinds of cream, the principal are the Devonshire and Dutch clotted creams, the Costorphin cream, and the Scotch sour cream. The Devonshire cream is produced by nearly boiling the milk in shallow tin vessels over a charcoal fire, and kept in that state until the whole of the cream is thrown up. It is used for eating with fruits and tarts. The cream from Costorphin, a village of that name near Edinburgh, is accelerated in its separation from three or four days' old milk, by a certain degree of heat ; and the Dutch clotted cream—a coagulated mass in which a spoon will stand upright—is manufactured from fresh-drawn milk, which is put into a pan, and stirred with a spoon two or three times a day, to prevent the cream from separating from the milk. The Scotch " sour cream " is a misnomer ; for it is a material produced without cream. A small tub filled with skimmed milk is put into a larger one, containing hot water, and after remaining there all night, the thin milk (called *wigg*) is drawn off, and the remainder of the contents of the smaller vessel is "sour cream."

1386. JELLIES are not the nourishing food they were at one time considered to be, and many eminent physicians are of opinion that they are less digestible than the flesh, or muscular part of animals ; still, when acidulated with lemon-juice and flavoured with wine, they are very suitable for some convalescents. Vegetable jelly is a distinct principle, existing in fruits, which possesses the property of gelatinizing when boiled and cooled ; but it is a principle entirely different from the gelatine of animal bodies, although the name of jelly, common to both, sometimes leads to an erroneous idea on that subject. Animal jelly, or gelatine, is glue, whereas vegetable jelly is rather analogous to gum. Liebig places gelatine very low indeed in the scale of usefulness. He says, " Gelatine, which by itself is tasteless, and when eaten, excites nausea, possesses no nutritive value ; that, even when accompanied by the savoury constituents of flesh, it is not capable of supporting the vital process, and when added to the usual diet as a substitute for plastic matter, does not increase, but, on the contrary, diminishes the nutritive value of the food, which it renders insufficient in quantity and inferior in quality." It is this substance which is most frequently employed in the manufacture of the jellies supplied by the confectioner ; but those prepared at home from calves' feet do possess some nutrition, and are the only sort that should be given to invalids. Isinglass is the purest variety of gelatine, and is prepared from the sounds or swimming-bladders of certain fish, chiefly the sturgeon. From its whiteness it is mostly used for making blanc-mange and similar dishes.

1387. THE WHITE OF EGGS is perhaps the best substance that can be employed in clarifying jelly, as well as some other fluids, for the reason that when albumen (and the white of eggs is nearly pure albumen) is put into a liquid that is muddy, from substances suspended in it, on boiling the liquid, the albumen coagulates in a flocculent manner, and, entangling with it the impurities, rises with them to the surface as a scum, or sinks to the bottom, according to their weight.

1388. SOUFFLES, OMELETS, AND SWEET DISHES, in which eggs form the principal ingredient, demand, for their successful manufacture, an experienced cook. They are the prettiest, but most difficult of all entremets. The most essential thing to insure success is to secure the best ingredients from an honest tradesman. The entremets coming within the above classification, are healthy, nourishing, and pleasant to the taste, and may be eaten with safety by persons of the most delicate stomachs.

RECIPES.

CHAPTER XXIX.

BAKED APPLE CUSTARD.

1389. INGREDIENTS.—1 dozen large apples, moist sugar to taste, 1 small teacupful of cold water, the grated rind of one lemon, 1 pint of milk, 4 eggs, 2 oz. of loaf sugar.

Mode.—Peel, cut, and core the apples ; put them into a lined sauce-pan with the cold water, and as they heat, bruise them to a pulp ; sweeten with moist sugar, and add the grated lemon-rind. When cold, put the fruit at the bottom of a pie-dish, and pour over it a custard, made with the above proportion of milk, eggs, and sugar ; grate a little nutmeg over the top, place the dish in a moderate oven, and bake from 25 to 35 minutes. The above proportions will make rather a large dish.

Time.—25 to 35 minutes. *Average cost,* 1s. 4d.

Sufficient for 6 or 7 persons. *Seasonable* from July to March.

BUTTERED APPLES (Sweet Entremets).

1390. INGREDIENTS.—Apple marmalade No. 1395, 6 or 7 good boiling apples, ½ pint of water, 6 oz. of sugar, 2 oz. of butter, a little apricot jam.

Mode.—Pare the apples, and take out the cores without dividing them ; boil up the sugar and water for a few minutes ; then lay in the apples, and simmer them very gently until tender, taking care not to let them break. Have ready sufficient marmalade made by recipe No. 1395, and flavoured with lemon, to cover the bottom of the dish ; arrange the apples on this with a piece of butter placed in each, and in between them a few spoonfuls of apricot jam or marmalade ; place the dish in the oven for 10 minutes, then sprinkle over the top sifted sugar ; either brown it before the fire or with a salamander, and serve hot.

Time.—From 20 to 30 minutes to stew the apples very gently, 10 minutes in the oven.

Average cost, 1s. 6d.　*Sufficient* for 1 entremets.

Note.—The syrup that the apples were boiled in should be saved for another occasion.

FLANC OF APPLES, or APPLES IN A RAISED CRUST.
(*Sweet Entremets.*)

1391. INGREDIENTS.—¾ lb. of short crust No. 1211 or 1212, 9 moderate-sized apples, the rind and juice of ½ lemon, ½ lb. of white sugar, ¾ pint of water, a few strips of candied citron.

Mode.—Make a short crust by either of the above recipes; roll it out to the thickness of ½ inch, and butter an oval mould; line it with the crust, and press it carefully all round the sides, to obtain the form of the mould, but be particular not to break the paste. Pinch the part that just rises above the mould with the paste-pincers, and fill the case with flour; bake it for about ¾ hour; then take it out of the oven, remove the flour, put the case back in the oven for another ¼ hour, and do not allow it to get scorched. It is now ready for the apples, which should be prepared in the following manner: peel, and take out the cores with a small knife, or a cutter for the purpose, without dividing the apples; put them into a small lined saucepan, just capable of holding them, with sugar, water, lemon juice and rind, in the above proportion. Let them simmer very gently until tender; then take out the apples, let them cool, arrange them in the flanc or case, and boil down the syrup until reduced to a thick jelly; pour it over the apples, and garnish them with a few slices of candied citron.

1392. A MORE SIMPLE FLANC may be made by rolling out the paste, cutting the bottom of a round or oval shape, and then a narrow strip for the sides: these should be stuck on with the white of an egg, to the bottom piece, and the flanc then filled with raw fruit, with sufficient sugar to sweeten it nicely. It will not require so long baking as in a mould; but the crust must be made everywhere of an equal thickness, and so perfectly joined, that the juice does not escape. This dish may also be served hot, and should be garnished in the same manner, or a little melted apricot jam may be poured over the apples, which very much improves their flavour.

Time.—Altogether, 1 hour to bake the flanc, from 30 to 40 minutes to stew the apples very gently.

Average cost, 1s. 6d.

Sufficient for 1 entremets or side-dish.

Seasonable from July to March.

APPLE FRITTERS.

1393. INGREDIENTS.—For the batter, $\frac{1}{2}$ lb. of flour, $\frac{1}{2}$ oz. of butter, $\frac{1}{2}$ saltspoonful of salt, 2 eggs, milk, apples, hot lard or clarified beef-dripping.

Mode.—Break the eggs; separate the whites from the yolks, and beat them separately. Put the flour into a basin, stir in the butter, which should be melted to a cream; add the salt, and moisten with sufficient warm milk to make it of a proper consistency, that is to say, a batter that will drop from the spoon. Stir this well, rub down any lumps that may be seen, and add the whites of the eggs, which have been previously well whisked; beat up the batter for a few minutes, and it is ready for use. Now peel and cut the apples into rather thick whole slices, without dividing them, and stamp out the middle of each slice, where the core is, with a cutter. Throw the slices into the batter; have ready a pan of boiling lard or clarified dripping; take out the pieces of apple one by one, put them into the hot lard, and fry a nice brown, turning them when required. When done, lay them on a piece of blotting-paper before the fire, to absorb the greasy moisture; then dish on a white d'oyley, piled one above the other; strew over them some pounded sugar, and serve very hot. The flavour of the fritters would be very much improved by soaking the pieces of apple in a little wine, mixed with sugar and lemon-juice, for 3 or 4 hours before wanted for table; the batter, also, is better for being mixed some hours before the fritters are made.

Time.—About 10 minutes to fry them; 5 minutes to drain them.

Average cost, 9d.

Sufficient for 4 or 5 persons.

Seasonable from July to March.

ICED APPLES, or APPLE HEDGEHOG.

1394. INGREDIENTS.—About 3 dozen good boiling apples, $\frac{1}{2}$ lb. of sugar, $\frac{1}{2}$ pint of water, the rind of $\frac{1}{4}$ lemon minced very fine, the whites of 2 eggs, 3 tablespoonfuls of pounded sugar. a few sweet almonds.

Mode.—Peel and core a dozen of the apples without dividing them, and stew them very gently in a lined saucepan with $\frac{1}{2}$ lb. of sugar and $\frac{1}{2}$ pint of water, and when tender, lift them carefully on to a dish. Have ready the remainder of the apples pared, cored, and cut into thin slices; put them into the same syrup with the lemon-peel, and boil gently until they are reduced to a marmalade: they must be kept stirred, to prevent them from burning. Cover the bottom of a dish with some of the marmalade, and over that a layer of the stewed apples, in the insides of which, and between each, place some of the marmalade ; then place another layer of apples, and fill up the cavities with marmalade as before, forming the whole into a raised oval shape. Whip the whites of the eggs to a stiff froth, mix with them the pounded sugar, and cover the apples very smoothly all over with the icing ; blanch and cut each almond into 4 or 5 strips ; place these strips at equal distances over the icing sticking up ; strew over a little rough pounded sugar, and place the dish in a very slow oven, to colour the almonds, and for the apples to get warm through. This entremets may also be served cold, and makes a pretty supper-dish.

Time.—From 20 to 30 minutes to stew the apples.

Average cost, 1s. 9d. to 2s.

Sufficient for 5 or 6 persons. *Seasonable* from July to March.

THICK APPLE JELLY OR MARMALADE, for Entremets or Dessert Dishes.

1395. INGREDIENTS.—Apples ; to every lb. of pulp allow ¾ lb. of sugar, ½ teaspoonful of minced lemon-peel.

Mode.—Peel, core, and boil the apples with only sufficient water to prevent them from burning ; beat them to a pulp, and to every lb. of

APPLE JELLY STUCK WITH ALMONDS.

pulp allow the above proportion of sugar in lumps. Dip the lumps into water ; put these into a saucepan, and boil till the syrup is thick and can be well skimmed ; then add this syrup to the apple pulp, with the minced lemon-peel, and stir it over a quick fire for about 20 minutes, or until the apples cease to stick to the bottom of the pan. The jelly is then done, and may be poured into moulds which have been previously dipped in water, when it will turn out nicely for dessert or a side-dish ; for the latter a little custard should be poured round, and it should be garnished with strips of citron or stuck with blanched almonds.

Time.—From ½ to ¾ hour to reduce the apples to a pulp ; 20 minutes to boil after the sugar is added.

Sufficient.—1½ lb. of apples sufficient for a small mould.

Seasonable from July to March ; but is best in September, October, or November.

CLEAR APPLE JELLY.

1396. INGREDIENTS.—2 dozen apples, 1½ pint of spring-water ; to every pint of juice allow ½ lb. of loaf sugar, ½ oz. of isinglass, the rind of ¼ lemon.

Mode.—Pare, core, and cut the apples into quarters, and boil them, with the lemon-peel, until tender; then strain off the apples, and run the juice through a jelly-bag; put the strained juice, with the sugar and isinglass, which has been previously boiled in ½ pint of water, into a lined saucepan or preserving-pan; boil all together for about ¼ hour, and put the jelly into moulds. When this jelly is nice and clear, and turned out well, it makes a pretty addition to the supper-table, with a little custard or whipped cream round it: the addition of a little lemon-juice improves the flavour, but it is apt to render the jelly muddy and thick. If required to be kept any length of time, rather a larger proportion of sugar must be used.

Time.—From 1 to 1½ hour to boil the apples; ¼ hour the jelly.

Average cost, 1s. 6d.

Sufficient for a 1½-pint mould. *Seasonable* from July to March.

A PRETTY DISH OF APPLES AND RICE.

1397. INGREDIENTS.—6 oz. of rice, 1 quart of milk, the rind of ½ lemon, sugar to taste, ½ saltspoonful of salt, 8 apples, ¼ lb. of sugar, ¼ pint of water, ½ pint of boiled custard No. 1423.

Mode.—Flavour the milk with lemon-rind, by boiling them together for a few minutes; then take out the peel, and put in the rice, with sufficient sugar to sweeten it nicely, and boil gently until the rice is quite soft; then let it cool. In the mean time pare, quarter, and core the apples, and boil them until tender in a syrup made with sugar and water in the above proportion; and, when soft, lift them out on a sieve to drain. Now put a middling-sized gallipot in the centre of a dish; lay the rice all round till the top of the gallipot is reached; smooth the rice with the back of a spoon, and stick the apples into it in rows, one row sloping to the right and the next to the left. Set it in the oven to colour the apples; then, when required for table, remove the gallipot, garnish the rice with preserved fruits, and pour in the middle sufficient custard, made by recipe No. 1423, to be level with the top of the rice, and serve hot.

Time.—From 20 to 30 minutes to stew the apples; ¾ hour to simmer the rice; ¼ hour to bake. *Average cost*, 1s. 6d.

Sufficient for 5 or 6 persons. *Seasonable* from July to March.

APPLES A LA PORTUGAISE.

1398. INGREDIENTS.—8 good boiling apples, ½ pint of water, 6 oz. of sugar, a layer of apple marmalade No. 1395, 8 preserved cherries, garnishing of apricot jam.

Mode.—Peel the apples, and, with a vegetable-cutter, push out the cores; boil them in the above proportion of sugar and water, without being too much done, and take care they do not break. Have ready a white apple marmalade, made by recipe No. 1395; cover the bottom of the dish with this, level it, and lay the apples in a sieve to drain; pile them neatly on the marmalade, making them high in the centre, and place a preserved cherry in the middle of each. Garnish with strips of candied citron or apricot jam, and the dish is ready for table.

Time.—From 20 to 30 minutes to stew the apples.

Average cost, 1s. 3d.

Sufficient for 1 entremets. *Seasonable* from July to March.

APPLES IN RED JELLY.
(*A pretty Supper Dish.*)

1399. INGREDIENTS.—6 good-sized apples, 12 cloves, pounded sugar, 1 lemon, 2 teacupfuls of water, 1 tablespoonful of gelatine, a few drops of prepared cochineal.

Mode.—Choose rather large apples; peel them and take out the cores, either with a scoop or a small silver knife, and put into each apple 2 cloves and as much sifted sugar as they will hold. Place them, without touching each other, in a large pie-dish; add more white sugar, the juice of 1 lemon, and 2 teacupfuls of water. Bake in the oven, with a dish over them, until they are done. Look at them frequently, and, as each apple is cooked, place it in a glass dish. They must not be left in the oven after they are done, or they will break, and so would spoil the appearance of the dish. When the apples are neatly arranged in the dish without touching each other, strain the liquor in which they have been stewing, into a lined saucepan; add to it the rind of the lemon, and a tablespoonful of gelatine which has been previously dissolved in cold water, and, if not sweet, a little more sugar, and 6 cloves. Boil till quite clear; colour with a few drops of prepared cochineal, and strain the jelly through a double muslin into a jug; let it cool *a little;* then pour it into the dish round the apples. When quite cold, garnish the tops of the apples with a bright-coloured marmalade, a jelly, or the white of an egg, beaten to a strong froth, with a little sifted sugar.

Time.—From 30 to 50 minutes to bake the apples.

Average cost, 1s., with the garnishing.

Sufficient for 4 or 5 persons. *Seasonable* from July to March.

APPLES AND RICE.
(*A Plain Dish.*)

1400. INGREDIENTS.—8 good-sized apples, 3 oz. of butter, the rind of ½ lemon minced very fine, 6 oz. of rice, 1½ pint of milk, sugar to taste, ⅓ teaspoonful of grated nutmeg, 6 tablespoonfuls of apricot jam.

Mode.—Peel the apples, halve them, and take out the cores; put them into a stewpan with the butter, and strew sufficient sifted sugar over to sweeten them nicely, and add the minced lemon-peel. Stew the apples very gently until tender, taking care they do not break. Boil the rice, with the milk, sugar, and nutmeg, until soft, and, when thoroughly done, dish it, piled high in the centre; arrange the apples on it, warm the apricot jam, pour it over the whole, and serve hot.

Time.—About 30 minutes to stew the apples very gently; about ¾ hour to cook the rice.

Average cost, 1s. 6d.

Sufficient for 5 or 6 persons. *Seasonable* from July to March.

APPLE SNOW.

(*A pretty Supper Dish.*)

1401. INGREDIENTS.—10 good-sized apples, the whites of 10 eggs, the rind of 1 lemon, ½ lb. of pounded sugar.

Mode.—Peel, core, and cut the apples into quarters, and put them into a saucepan with the lemon-peel and sufficient water to prevent them from burning,—rather less than ½ pint. When they are tender, take out the peel, beat them to a pulp, let them cool, and stir them to the whites of the eggs, which should be previously beaten to a strong froth. Add the sifted sugar, and continue the whisking until the mixture becomes quite stiff; and either heap it on a glass dish, or serve it in small glasses. The dish may be garnished with preserved barberries, or strips of bright-coloured jelly; and a dish of custards should be served with it, or a jug of cream.

Time.—From 30 to 40 minutes to stew the apples.

Average cost, 1s. 6d.

Sufficient to fill a moderate-sized glass dish.

Seasonable from July to March.

APPLE SOUFFLE.

1402. INGREDIENTS.—6 oz. of rice, 1 quart of milk, the rind of ½ lemon, sugar to taste, the yolks of 4 eggs, the whites of 6, 1½ oz. of butter, 4 tablespoonfuls of apple marmalade No. 1395.

Mode.—Boil the milk with the lemon-peel until the former is well flavoured; then strain it, put in the rice, and let it gradually swell over a slow fire, adding sufficient sugar to sweeten it nicely. Then crush the rice to a smooth pulp with the back of a wooden spoon; line the bottom and sides of a round cake-tin with it, and put it into the oven to set; turn it out of the tin carefully, and be careful that the border of rice is firm in every part. Mix with the marmalade the beaten yolks of eggs and the butter, and stir these over the fire until the mixture thickens. Take it off the fire; to this add the whites of the eggs, which should be previously beaten to a strong froth; stir all together, and put it into the rice border. Bake in a moderate oven for about ½ hour, or until the soufflé rises very light. It should be watched, and served instantly, or it will immediately fall after it is taken from the oven.

Time.—½ hour. *Average cost,* 1s. 6d.

Sufficient for 4 or 5 persons. *Seasonable* from July to March.

STEWED APPLES AND CUSTARD.
(*A pretty Dish for a Juvenile Supper.*)

1403. INGREDIENTS.—7 good-sized apples, the rind of ½ lemon or 4 cloves, ½ lb. of sugar, ¾ pint of water, ½ pint of custard No. 1423.

Mode.—Pare and take out the cores of the apples, without dividing them, and, if possible, leave the stalks on; boil the sugar and water together for 10 minutes; then put in the apples with the lemon-rind or cloves, whichever flavour may be preferred, and simmer gently until they are tender, taking care not to let them break. Dish them neatly on a glass dish, reduce the syrup by boiling it quickly for a few minutes, let it cool a little; then pour it over the apples. Have ready quite ½ pint of custard made by recipe No. 1423; pour it round, but not over, the apples when they are quite cold, and the dish is ready for table. A few almonds blanched and cut into strips, and stuck in the apples, would improve their appearance.—See coloured plate Q 1.

Time.—From 20 to 30 minutes to stew the apples.

Average cost, 1s.

Sufficient to fill a large glass dish. *Seasonable* from July to March.

APPLE TRIFLE.
(*A Supper Dish.*)

1404. INGREDIENTS.—10 good-sized apples, the rind of ½ lemon, 6 oz. of pounded sugar, ½ pint of milk, ½ pint of cream, 2 eggs, whipped cream.

Mode.—Peel, core, and cut the apples into thin slices, and put them into a saucepan with 2 tablespoonfuls of water, the sugar, and minced lemon-rind. Boil all together until quite tender, and pulp the apples through a sieve; if they should not be quite sweet enough, add a little more sugar, and put them at the bottom of the dish to form a thick layer. Stir together the milk, cream, and eggs, with a little sugar, over the fire, and let the mixture thicken, but do not allow it to reach the boiling-point. When thick, take it off the fire; let it cool a little, then pour it over the apples. Whip some cream with sugar, lemon-peel, &c., the same as for other trifles; heap it high over the custard, and the dish is ready for table. It may be garnished as fancy dictates, with strips of bright apple jelly, slices of citron, &c.

Time.—From 30 to 40 minutes to stew the apples; 10 minutes to stir the custard over the fire.

Average cost, 1s. 6d.

Sufficient for a moderate-sized trifle.

Seasonable from July to March.

APRICOT CREAM.

1405. INGREDIENTS.—12 to 16 ripe apricots, $\frac{1}{2}$ lb. of sugar, $1\frac{1}{2}$ pint of milk, the yolks of 8 eggs, 1 oz. of isinglass.

Mode.—Divide the apricots, take out the stones, and boil them in a syrup made with $\frac{1}{4}$ lb. of sugar and $\frac{1}{4}$ pint of water, until they form a thin marmalade, which rub through a sieve. Boil the milk with the other $\frac{1}{4}$ lb. of sugar, let it cool a little, then mix with it the yolks of eggs which have been previously well beaten; put this mixture into a jug, place this jug in boiling water, and stir it one way over the fire until it thickens; but on no account let it boil. Strain through a sieve, add the isinglass, previously boiled with a small quantity of water, and keep stirring it till nearly cold; then mix the cream with the apricots; stir well, put it into an oiled mould, and, if convenient, set it on ice; at any rate, in a very cool place. It should turn out on the dish without any difficulty.

Time.—From 20 to 30 minutes to boil the apricots. *Average cost*, 2s.

Sufficient to fill a quart mould.

Seasonable in August, September, and October.

Note.—In winter-time, when fresh apricots are not obtainable, a little jam may be substituted for them.

FLANC OF APRICOTS, or Compote of Apricots in a Raised Crust.
(*Sweet Entremets.*)

1406. INGREDIENTS.—$\frac{3}{4}$ lb. of short crust No. 1212, from 9 to 12 good-sized apricots, $\frac{3}{4}$ pint of water, $\frac{1}{2}$ lb. of sugar.

Mode.—Make a short crust by recipe No. 1212, and line a mould with it as directed in recipe No. 1391. Boil the sugar and water

2 z

together for 10 minutes; halve the apricots, take out the stones, and simmer them in the syrup until tender; watch them carefully, and take them up the moment they are done, for fear they break. Arrange them neatly in the flanc or case; boil the syrup until reduced to a jelly, pour it over the fruit, and serve either hot or cold. Greengages, plums of all kinds, peaches, &c., may be done in the same manner, as also currants, raspberries, gooseberries, strawberries, &c.; but with the last-named fruits, a little currant-juice added to them will be found an improvement.

Time.—Altogether, 1 hour to bake the flanc, about 10 minutes to simmer the apricots.

Average cost, 1s. 6d.

Sufficient for 1 entremets or side-dish.

Seasonable in July, August, and September.

ARROWROOT BLANC-MANGE.

(*An inexpensive Supper Dish.*)

1407. INGREDIENTS.—4 heaped tablespoonfuls of arrowroot, 1¼ pint of milk, 3 laurel-leaves or the rind of ½ lemon, sugar to taste.

Mode.—Mix to a smooth batter the arrowroot with ½ pint of the milk; put the other pint on the fire, with laurel-leaves or lemon-peel, whichever may be preferred, and let the milk steep until it is well flavoured. Then strain the milk, and add it, boiling, to the mixed arrowroot; sweeten it with sifted sugar, and let it boil, stirring it all the time, till it thickens sufficiently to come from the saucepan. Grease a mould with pure salad-oil, pour in the blanc-mange, and when quite set, turn it out on a dish, and pour round it a compôte of any kind of fruit, or garnish it with jam. A tablespoonful of brandy, stirred in just before the blanc-mange is moulded, very much improves the flavour of this sweet dish. .

Time.—Altogether, ½ hour.

Average cost, 6d. without the garnishing.

Sufficient for 4 or 5 persons. *Seasonable* at any time.

BLANC-MANGE.

(*A Supper Dish.*)

1408. INGREDIENTS.—1 pint of new milk, 1¼ oz. of isinglass, the rind of ½ lemon, ¼ lb. of loaf sugar, 10 bitter almonds, ½ oz. of sweet almonds, 1 pint of cream.

Mode.—Put the milk into a saucepan, with the isinglass, lemon-rind, and sugar, and let these ingredients stand by the side of the fire until the milk is well flavoured; add the almonds, which should be blanched and pounded in a mortar to a paste, and let the milk just boil up; strain it through a fine sieve or muslin into a jug, add the cream, and stir the mixture occasionally until nearly cold. Let it stand for a few minutes, then pour it into the mould, which should be previously oiled with the purest salad-oil, or dipped in cold water. There will be a sediment

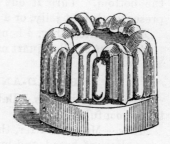

BLANC-MANGE MOULD.

at the bottom of the jug, which must not be poured into the mould, as, when turned out, it would very much disfigure the appearance of the blanc-mange. This blanc-mange may be made very much richer by using 1½ pint of cream, and melting the isinglass in ½ pint of boiling water. The flavour may also be very much varied by adding bay-leaves, laurel-leaves, or essence of vanilla, instead of the lemon-rind and almonds. Noyeau, Maraschino, Curaçoa, or any favourite liqueur, added in small proportions, very much enhances the flavour of this always favourite dish. In turning it out, just loosen the edges of the blanc-mange from the mould, place a dish on it, and turn it quickly over: it should come out easily, and the blanc-mange have a smooth glossy appearance when the mould is oiled, which it frequently has not when it is only dipped in water. It may be garnished as fancy dictates.

Time.—About 1½ hour to steep the lemon-rind and almonds in the milk.

Average cost, with cream at 1s. per pint, 1s. 8d.

Sufficient to fill a quart mould. *Seasonable* at any time.

CHEAP BLANC-MANGE.

1409. INGREDIENTS.—¼ lb. of sugar, 1 quart of milk, 1½ oz. of isinglass, the rind of ½ lemon, 4 laurel-leaves.

Mode.—Put all the ingredients into a lined saucepan, and boil gently until the isinglass is dissolved; taste it occasionally, to ascertain when it is sufficiently flavoured with the laurel-leaves; then take them out, and keep stirring the mixture over the fire for about

BLANC-MANGE.

2 z 2

10 minutes. Strain it through a fine sieve into a jug, and, when nearly cold, pour it into a well-oiled mould, omitting the sediment at the bottom. Turn it out carefully on a dish, and garnish with preserves, bright jelly, or a compôte of fruit.

Time.—Altogether, ½ hour. *Average cost,* 8*d.*

Sufficient to fill a quart mould. *Seasonable* at any time.

BREAD-AND-BUTTER FRITTERS.

1410. INGREDIENTS.—Batter, 8 slices of bread and butter, 3 or 4 tablespoonfuls of jam.

Mode.—Make a batter, the same as for apple fritters No. 1393; cut some slices of bread and butter, not very thick; spread half of them with any jam that may he preferred, and cover with the other slices; slightly press them together, and cut them out in square, long, or round pieces. Dip them in the batter, and fry in boiling lard for about 10 minutes; drain them before the fire on a piece of blotting-paper or cloth. Dish them, sprinkle over sifted sugar, and serve.

Time.—About 10 minutes.

Average cost, 1*s.*

Sufficient for 4 or 5 persons. *Seasonable* at any time.

TO MAKE THE STOCK FOR JELLY, AND TO CLARIFY IT.

1411. INGREDIENTS.—2 calf's feet, 6 pints of water.

Mode.—The stock for jellies should always be made the day before it is required for use, as the liquor has time to cool, and the fat can be so much more easily and effectually removed when thoroughly set. Procure from the butcher's nice calf's feet; scald them, to take off

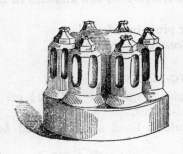

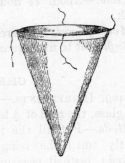

JELLY-MOULD.   JELLY-BAG.

the hair; slit them in two, remove the fat from between the claws, and wash the feet well in warm water; put them into a stewpan, with the above proportion of cold water, bring it gradually to boil, and remove every particle of scum as it rises. When it is well skimmed, boil it very gently for 6 or 7 hours, or until the liquor is reduced rather more than half; then strain it through a sieve into a basin, and put it in a cool place to set. As the liquor is strained, measure it, to ascertain the proportion for the jelly, allowing something for the sediment and fat at the top. To clarify it, carefully remove all the fat from the top, pour over a little warm water, to wash away any that may remain, and wipe the jelly with a clean cloth; remove the jelly from the sediment, put it into a saucepan, and, supposing the quantity to be a quart, add to it 6 oz. of loaf sugar, the shells and well-whisked whites of 5 eggs, and stir these ingredients together cold; set the saucepan on the fire, but *do not stir the jelly after it begins to warm.* Let it boil about 10 minutes after it rises to a head, then throw in a teacupful of cold water; let it boil 5 minutes longer, then take the saucepan off, cover it closely, and let it remain ½ hour near the fire. Dip the jelly-bag into hot water, wring it out quite dry, and fasten it on to a stand or the back of a chair, which must be placed near the fire, to prevent the jelly from setting before it has run through the bag. Place a basin underneath to receive the jelly; then pour it into the bag, and should it not be clear the first time, run it through the bag again. This stock is the foundation of all *really good* jellies, which may be varied in innumerable ways, by colouring and flavouring with liqueurs, and by moulding it with fresh and preserved fruits. To insure the jelly being firm when turned out, ½ oz. of isinglass clarified might be added to the above proportion of stock. Substitutes for calf's feet are now frequently used in making jellies, which lessen the expense and trouble in preparing this favourite dish; isinglass and gelatine being two of the principal materials employed; but, although they may *look* as nicely as jellies made from good stock, they are never so delicate, having very often an unpleasant flavour, somewhat resembling glue, particularly when made with gelatine.

Time.—About 6 hours to boil the feet for the stock; to clarify it,— ¼ hour to boil, ½ hour to stand in the saucepan covered.

Average cost.—Calf's feet may be purchased for 6*d.* each when veal is in full season, but more expensive when it is scarce.

Sufficient.—2 calf's feet should make 1 quart of stock.

Seasonable from March to October, but may be had all the year.

How to make a Jelly-bag.—The very stout flannel called double-mill, used for ironing-blankets, is the best material for a jelly-bag: those of home manufacture are the only ones to be relied on for thoroughly clearing the jelly. Care should be taken that the seam of the bag be stitched twice, to secure it against unequal filtration. The most convenient mode of using the bag is to tie it upon a hoop the exact size of the outside of its mouth; and, to do this, strings should be sewn round it at equal distances. The jelly-bag may, of course, be made any size; but one of twelve or fourteen inches deep, and seven or eight across the mouth, will be sufficient for ordinary use. The form of a jelly-bag is the fool's cap.

COW-HEEL STOCK FOR JELLIES.

(More Economical than Calf's Feet.)

1412. INGREDIENTS.—2 cow-heels, 3 quarts of water.

Mode.—Procure 2 heels that have only been scalded, and not boiled; split them in two, and remove the fat between the claws; wash them well in warm water, and put them into a saucepan with the above proportion of cold water; bring it gradually to boil, remove all the scum as it rises, and simmer the heels gently from 7 to 8 hours, or until the liquor is reduced one-half; then strain it into a basin, measuring the quantity, and put it in a cool place. Clarify it in the same manner as calf's-feet stock No. 1411, using, with the other ingredients, about ½ oz. of isinglass to each quart. This stock should be made the day before it is required for use. Two dozen shank-bones of mutton, boiled for 6 or 7 hours, yield a quart of strong firm stock. They should be put on in 2 quarts of water, which should be reduced one-half. Make this also the day before it is required.

Time.—7 to 8 hours to boil the cow-heels, 6 to 7 hours to boil the shank-bones.

Average cost, from 4d. to 6d. each.

Sufficient.—2 cow-heels should make 3 pints of stock.

Seasonable at any time.

ISINGLASS OR GELATINE JELLY.

(Substitutes for Calf's Feet.)

1413. INGREDIENTS.—3 oz. of isinglass or gelatine, 2 quarts of water.

Mode.—Put the isinglass or gelatine into a saucepan with the above proportion of cold water; bring it quickly to boil, and let it boil very fast, until the liquor is reduced one-half. Carefully remove the scum as it rises, then strain it through a jelly-bag, and it will be ready for use. If not required very clear, it may be merely strained through a fine sieve, instead of being run through a bag. Rather more than ½ oz. of isinglass is about the proper quantity to use for a quart of strong calf's-feet stock, and rather more than 2 oz. for the same quantity of fruit juice. As isinglass varies so much in quality and strength, it is difficult to give the exact proportions. The larger the mould, the stiffer should be the jelly; and where there is no ice, more isinglass must be used than if the mixture were frozen. This forms a stock for all kinds of jellies, which may be flavoured in many ways.

Time.—1½ hour.

Sufficient, with wine, syrup, fruit, &c., to fill two moderate-sized moulds.

Seasonable at any time.

Note.—The above, when boiled, should be perfectly clear, and may be mixed warm with wine, flavourings, fruits, &c., and then run through the bag.

ISINGLASS.—The best isinglass is brought from Russia; some of an inferior kind is brought from North and South America and the East Indies : the several varieties may be had from the wholesale dealers in isinglass in London. In choosing isinglass for domestic use, select that which is whitest, has no unpleasant odour, and which dissolves most readily in water. The inferior kinds are used for fining beer, and similar purposes. Isinglass is much adulterated : to test its purity, take a few threads of the substance, drop some into boiling water, some into cold water, and some into vinegar. In the boiling water the isinglass will dissolve, in cold water it will become white and " cloudy," and in vinegar it will swell and become jelly-like. If the isinglass is adulterated with gelatine (that is to say, the commoner sorts of gelatine,—for isinglass is classed amongst gelatines, of all which varieties it is the very purest and best), in boiling water the gelatine will not so completely dissolve as the isinglass; in cold water it becomes clear and jelly-like; and in vinegar it will harden.

HOW TO MOULD BOTTLED JELLIES.

1414. UNCORK the bottle; place it in a saucepan of hot water until the jelly is reduced to a liquid state; taste it, to ascertain whether it is sufficiently flavoured, and if not, add a little wine. Pour the jelly into moulds which have been soaked in water; let it set, and turn it out by placing the mould in hot water for a minute; then wipe the outside, put a dish on the top, and turn it over quickly. The jelly should then slip easily away from the mould, and be quite firm. It may be garnished as taste dictates.

TO CLARIFY SYRUP FOR JELLIES.

1415. INGREDIENTS.—To every quart of water allow 2 lbs. of loaf sugar; the white of 1 egg.

Mode.—Put the sugar and water into a stewpan; set it on the fire, and, when the sugar is dissolved, add the white of the egg, whipped up with a little water. Whisk the whole well together, and simmer very gently until it has thrown up all the scum. Take this off as it rises, strain the syrup through a fine sieve or cloth into a basin, and keep it for use.

CALF'S-FEET JELLY.

1416. INGREDIENTS.—1 quart of calf's-feet stock No. 1411, ¼ lb. of sugar, ½ pint of sherry, 1 glass of brandy, the shells and whites of 5 eggs, the rind and juice of 2 lemons, ½ oz. of isinglass.

Mode.—Prepare the stock as directed in recipe No. 1411, taking care to leave the sediment, and to remove all the fat from the surface.

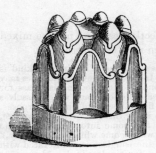

JELLY-MOULD.

Put it into a saucepan, cold, without clarifying it; add the remaining ingredients, and stir them well together before the saucepan is placed on the fire. Then simmer the mixture gently for ¼ hour, *but do not stir it after it begins to warm.* Throw in a teacupful of cold water, boil for another 5 minutes, and keep the saucepan covered by the side of the fire for about ½ hour, but do not let it boil again. In simmering, the head or scum may be carefully removed as it rises; but particular attention must be given to the jelly, that it be not stirred in the slightest degree after it is heated. The isinglass should be added when the jelly begins to boil: this assists to clear it, and makes it firmer for turning out. Wring out a jelly-bag in hot water; fasten it on to a stand, or the back of a chair; place it near the fire with a basin underneath it, and run the jelly through it. Should it not be perfectly clear the first time, repeat the process until the desired brilliancy is obtained. Soak the moulds in water, drain them for half a second, pour in the jelly, and put it in a cool place to set. If ice is at hand, surround the moulds with it, and the jelly will set sooner, and be firmer when turned out. In summer it is necessary to have ice in which to put the moulds, or the cook will be, very likely, disappointed, by her jellies being in too liquid a state to turn out properly, unless a great deal of isinglass is used. When wanted for table, dip the moulds in hot water for a minute, wipe the outside with a cloth, lay a dish on the top of the mould, turn it quickly over, and the jelly should slip out easily. It is sometimes served broken into square lumps, and piled high in glasses. Earthenware moulds are preferable to those of pewter or tin, for red jellies, the colour and transparency of the composition being often spoiled by using the latter.

To make this jelly more economically, raisin wine may be substituted for the sherry and brandy, and the stock made from cow-heels, instead of calf's feet.

Time.—20 minutes to simmer the jelly, ½ hour to stand covered.

Average cost, reckoning the feet at 6*d.* each, 3*s.* 6*d.*

Sufficient to fill two 1½-pint moulds. *Seasonable* at any time.

Note.—As lemon-juice, unless carefully strained, is liable to make the jelly muddy, see that it is clear before it is added to the other ingredients. Omit the brandy when the flavour is objected to.

SHERRY.—There are several kinds of sherry, as pale and brown, and there are various degrees of each. Sherry is, in general, of an amber-colour, and, when good, has a fine aromatic odour, with something of the agreeable bitterness of the peach kernel. When new, it is harsh and fiery, and requires to be mellowed in the wood for four or five years. Sherry has of late got much into fashion in England, from the idea that it is more free from acid than other wines; but some careful experiments on wines do not fully confirm this opinion.

CANNELONS, or FRIED PUFFS.

(Sweet Entremets.)

1417. INGREDIENTS.—½ lb. of puff-paste No. 1205; apricot, or any kind of preserve that may be preferred; hot lard.

Mode.—Cannelons which are made of puff-paste rolled very thin, with jam inclosed, and cut out in long narrow rolls or puffs, make a very pretty and elegant dish. Make some good puff-paste, by recipe No. 1205; roll it out very thin, and cut it into pieces of an equal size, about 2 inches wide and 8 inches long; place upon each piece a spoonful of jam, wet the edges with the white of egg, and fold the paste over *twice;* slightly press the edges together, that the jam may not escape in the frying; and when all are prepared, fry them in boiling lard until of a nice brown, letting them remain by the side of the fire after they are coloured, that the paste may be thoroughly done. Drain them before the fire, dish on a d'oyley, sprinkle over them sifted sugar, and serve. These cannelons are very delicious made with fresh instead of preserved fruit, such as strawberries, raspberries, or currants: it should be laid in the paste, plenty of pounded sugar sprinkled over, and folded and fried in the same manner as stated above.

Time.—About 10 minutes. *Average cost, 1s.*

Sufficient,—½ lb. of paste for a moderate-sized dish of cannelons.

Seasonable, with jam, at any time.

CHARLOTTE-AUX-POMMES.

1418. INGREDIENTS.—A few slices of rather stale bread ½ inch thick, clarified butter, apple marmalade made by recipe No. 1395, with about 2 dozen apples, ½ glass of sherry.

Mode.—Cut a slice of bread the same shape as the bottom of a plain round mould, which has been well buttered, and a few strips the height of the mould, and about 1½ inch wide; dip the bread in clarified butter (or spread it with cold butter, if not wanted quite so rich); place the round piece at the bottom of the mould, and set the narrow strips up the sides of it, overlapping each other a little, that no juice from the apples may escape, and that they may hold firmly to the mould. Brush the *interior* over with

CHARLOTTE-AUX-POMMES.

white of egg (this will assist to make the case firmer); fill it with apple marmalade made by recipe No. 1395, with the addition of a little sherry, and cover them with a round piece of bread, also brushed over with egg, the same as the bottom; slightly press the bread down, to make it adhere to the other pieces; put a plate on the top, and bake the *charlotte* in a brisk oven, of a light colour. Turn it out on the dish, strew sifted sugar over the top, and pour round it a little melted apricot jam.

Time.—40 to 50 minutes. *Average cost*, 1s. 9d.

Sufficient for 5 or 6 persons. *Seasonable* from July to March.

AN EASY METHOD OF MAKING A CHARLOTTE-AUX-POMMES.

1419. INGREDIENTS.—½ lb. of flour, ¼ lb. of butter, ¼ lb. of powdered sugar, ½ teaspoonful of baking-powder, 1 egg, milk, 1 glass of raisin-wine, apple marmalade No. 1395, ¼ pint of cream, 2 dessertspoonfuls of pounded sugar, 2 tablespoonfuls of lemon-juice.

Mode.—Make a cake with the flour, butter, sugar, and baking-powder; moisten with the egg and sufficient milk to make it the proper consistency, and bake it in a round tin. When cold, scoop out the middle, leaving a good thickness all round the sides, to prevent them breaking; take some of the scooped-out pieces, which should be trimmed into neat slices; lay them in the cake, and pour over sufficient raisin-wine, with the addition of a little brandy, if approved, to soak them well. Have ready some apple marmalade, made by recipe No. 1395; place a layer of this over the soaked cake, then a layer of cake and a layer of apples; whip the cream to a froth, mixing with it the sugar and lemon-juice; pile it on the top of the *charlotte*, and garnish it with pieces of clear apple jelly. This dish is served cold, but may be eaten hot, by omitting the cream, and merely garnishing the top with bright jelly just before it is sent to table.

Time.—1 hour to bake the cake. *Average cost*, 2s.

Sufficient for 5 or 6 persons. *Seasonable* from July to March.

A VERY SIMPLE APPLE CHARLOTTE.

1420. INGREDIENTS.—9 slices of bread and butter, about 6 good-sized apples, 1 tablespoonful of minced lemon-peel, 2 tablespoonfuls of juice, moist sugar to taste.

Mode.—Butter a pie-dish; place a layer of bread and butter, without the crust, at the bottom; then a layer of apples, pared, cored, and cut into thin slices; sprinkle over these a portion of the lemon-peel and juice, and sweeten with moist sugar. Place another layer of bread and butter, and then one of apples, proceeding in this manner until the dish is full ; then cover it up with the peel of the apples, to preserve the top from browning or burning ; bake in a brisk oven for rather more than $\frac{3}{4}$ hour ; turn the charlotte on a dish, sprinkle sifted sugar over, and serve.

Time.—$\frac{3}{4}$ hour.   *Average cost,* 9*d*.

Sufficient for 5 or 6 persons.   *Seasonable* from July to March.

CHARLOTTE RUSSE.
(*An Elegant Sweet Entremets.*)

1421. INGREDIENTS.—About 18 Savoy biscuits, $\frac{3}{4}$ pint of cream, flavouring of vanilla, liqueurs, or wine, 1 tablespoonful of pounded sugar, $\frac{1}{2}$ oz. of isinglass.

Mode.—Procure about 18 Savoy biscuits, or ladies'-fingers, as they are sometimes called ; brush the edges of them with the white of an egg, and line the bottom of a plain round mould, placing them like a star or rosette. Stand them upright all round the edge ; carefully put them so closely together that the white of the egg connects them firmly, and place this case in the oven for about 5 minutes, just to dry the egg. Whisk the cream to a stiff froth, with the sugar, flavouring, and melted isinglass ; fill the charlotte with it, cover with a slice of sponge-cake cut in the shape of the mould ; place it in ice, where let it remain till ready for table ; then turn it on a dish, remove the mould, and serve. 1 tablespoonful of liqueur of any kind, or 4 tablespoonfuls of wine, would nicely flavour the above proportion of cream. For arranging the biscuits in the mould, cut them to the shape required, so that they fit in nicely, and level them with the mould at the top, that, when turned out, there may be something firm to rest upon. Great care and attention is required in the turning out of this dish, that the cream does not burst the case ; and the edges of the biscuits must have the smallest quantity of egg brushed over them, or it would stick to the mould, and so prevent the charlotte from coming away properly.

Time.—5 minutes in the oven.

Average cost, with cream at 1*s*. per pint, 1*s*. 6*d*.

Sufficient for 1 charlotte.   *Seasonable* at any time.

CREAM A LA VALOIS.

1422. INGREDIENTS.—4 sponge-cakes, jam, $\frac{3}{4}$ pint of cream, sugar to taste, the juice of $\frac{1}{2}$ lemon, $\frac{1}{4}$ glass of sherry, $1\frac{1}{4}$ oz. of isinglass.

Mode.—Cut the sponge-cakes into thin slices ; place two together, with preserve between them, and pour over them a small quantity of sherry mixed with a little brandy. Sweeten and flavour the cream with the lemon-juice and sherry; add the isinglass, which should be dissolved in a little water, and beat up the cream well. Place a little in an oiled mould; arrange the pieces of cake in the cream; then fill the mould with the remainder; let it cool, and turn it out on a dish. By oiling the mould, the cream will have a much smoother appearance, and will turn out more easily than when merely dipped in cold water.

Average cost, 2s.

Sufficient to fill a 1½-pint mould. *Seasonable* at any time.

BOILED CUSTARDS.

1423. INGREDIENTS.—1 pint of milk, 5 eggs, 3 oz. of loaf sugar, 3 laurel-leaves, or the rind of ½ lemon, or a few drops of essence of vanilla, 1 tablespoonful of brandy

Mode.—Put the milk into a *linea* saucepan, with the sugar, and whichever of the above flavourings may be preferred (the lemon-rind

CUSTARDS IN GLASSES.

flavours custards most deliciously), and let the milk steep by the side of the fire until it is well flavoured. Bring it to the point of boiling, then strain it into a basin; whisk the eggs well, and, when the milk has cooled a little, stir in the eggs, and *strain* this mixture into a jug. Place this jug in a saucepan of boiling water over the fire; keep stirring the custard *one way* until it thickens; but on no account allow it to reach the boiling-point, as it will instantly curdle and be full of lumps. Take it off the fire, stir in the brandy, and, when this is well mixed with the custard, pour it into glasses, which should be rather more than three-parts full; grate a little nutmeg over the top, and the dish is ready for table. To make custards look and eat better, ducks' eggs should be used, when obtainable; they add very much to the flavour and richness, and so many are not required as of the ordinary eggs, 4 ducks' eggs to the pint of milk making a delicious custard. When desired extremely rich and good, cream should be substituted for the milk, and double the quantity of eggs used, to those mentioned, omitting the whites.

Time.—½ hour to infuse the lemon-rind, about 10 minutes to stir the custard. *Average cost,* 8d.

Sufficient to fill 8 custard-glasses. *Seasonable* at any time.

GINGER APPLES.

(A pretty Supper or Dessert Dish.)

1424. INGREDIENTS.—1½ oz. of whole ginger, ¼ pint of whiskey, 3 lbs. of apples, 2 lbs. of white sugar, the juice of 2 lemons.

Mode.—Bruise the ginger, put it into a small jar, pour over sufficient whiskey to cover it, and let it remain for 3 days; then cut the apples into thin slices, after paring and coring them; add the sugar and the lemon-juice, which should be strained; and simmer all together *very gently* until the apples are transparent, but not broken. Serve cold, and garnish the dish with slices of candied lemon-peel or preserved ginger.

Time.—3 days to soak the ginger; about ¾ hour to simmer the apples very gently.

Average cost, 2s. 6d.

Sufficient for 3 dishes. *Seasonable* from July to March.

FRENCH PANCAKES.

1425. INGREDIENTS.—2 eggs, 2 oz. of butter, 2 oz. of sifted sugar, 2 oz. of flour, ½ pint of new milk.

Mode.—Beat the eggs thoroughly, and put them into a basin with the butter, which should be beaten to a cream; stir in the sugar and flour, and when these ingredients are well mixed, add the milk; keep stirring and beating the mixture for a few minutes; put it on buttered plates, and bake in a quick oven for 20 minutes. Serve with a cut lemon and sifted sugar, or pile the pancakes high on a dish, with a layer of preserve or marmalade between each.

Time.—20 minutes. *Average cost,* 7d.

Sufficient for 3 or 4 persons. *Seasonable* at any time.

DUTCH FLUMMERY.

1426. INGREDIENTS.—1½ oz. of isinglass, the rind and juice of 1 lemon, 1 pint of water, 4 eggs, 1 pint of sherry, Madeira, or raisin-wine; sifted sugar to taste.

Mode.—Put the water, isinglass, and lemon-rind into a lined saucepan, and simmer gently until the isinglass is dissolved; strain this into a basin, stir in the eggs, which should be well beaten, the lemon-juice, which should be strained, and the wine; sweeten to taste with pounded sugar, mix all well together, pour it into a jug, set this jug in a saucepan of boiling water over the fire, and keep stirring it one way until it thickens; but *take care that it does not boil.* Strain it into a mould that has been oiled or laid in water for a short time, and put it in a cool place to set. A tablespoonful of brandy stirred in just before it is poured into the mould, improves the flavour of this dish: it is better if made the day before it is required for table.

Time.—¼ hour to simmer the isinglass; about ¼ hour to stir the mixture over the fire.

Average cost, 2s., if made with sherry; less with raisin-wine.

Sufficient to fill a quart mould. *Seasonable* at any time.

PALE SHERRIES are made from the same grapes as brown. The latter are coloured by an addition of some cheap must, or wine which has been boiled till it has acquired a deep-brown tint. Pale sherries were, some time ago, preferred in England, being supposed most pure; but the brown are preferred by many people. The inferior sherries exported to England are often mixed with a cheap and light wine called Moguer, and are strengthened in the making by brandy; but too frequently they are adulterated by the London dealers.

CHOCOLATE SOUFFLE.

1427. INGREDIENTS.—4 eggs, 3 teaspoonfuls of pounded sugar, 1 teaspoonful of flour, 3 oz. of the best chocolate.

Mode.—Break the eggs, separating the whites from the yolks, and put them into different basins; add to the yolks the sugar, flour, and chocolate, which should be very finely grated, and stir these ingredients for 5 minutes. Then well whisk the whites of the eggs in the other basin, until they are stiff, and, when firm, mix lightly with the yolks, till the whole forms a smooth and light substance; butter a round cake-tin, put in the mixture, and bake in a moderate oven from 15 to 20 minutes. Pin a white napkin round the tin, strew sifted sugar over the top of the soufflé, and send it immediately to table. The proper appearance of this dish depends entirely on the expedition with which it is served, and some cooks, to preserve its lightness, hold a salamander over the soufflé until it is placed on the table. If allowed to stand after it comes from the oven, it will be entirely spoiled, as it falls almost immediately.

Time.—15 to 20 minutes. *Average cost*, 1s.

Sufficient for a moderate-sized soufflé. *Seasonable* at any time.

DARIOLES A LA VANILLE.
(*Sweet Entremets.*)

1428. INGREDIENTS.—¼ pint of milk, ½ pint of cream, 2 oz. of flour, 3 oz. of pounded sugar, 6 eggs, 2 oz. of butter, puff-paste, flavouring of essence of vanilla.

Mode.—Mix the flour to a smooth batter, with the milk; stir in the cream, sugar, the eggs, which should be well whisked, and the butter, which should be beaten to a cream. Put in some essence of vanilla, drop by drop, until the mixture is well flavoured; line some dariole-moulds with puff-paste, three-parts fill them with the batter, and bake in a good oven from 25 to 35 minutes. Turn them out of the moulds on a dish, without breaking them; strew over sifted sugar, and serve. The flavouring of the darioles may be varied by substituting lemon, cinnamon, or almonds, for the vanilla.

Time.— 25 to 35 minutes. *Average cost*, 1s. 8d.

Sufficient to fill 6 or 7 dariole-moulds. *Seasonable* at any time.

CURRANT FRITTERS.

1429. INGREDIENTS.—½ pint of milk, 2 tablespoonfuls of flour, 4 eggs, 3 tablespoonfuls of boiled rice, 3 tablespoonfuls of currants, sugar to taste, a very little grated nutmeg, hot lard or clarified dripping.

Mode.—Put the milk into a basin with the flour, which should previously be rubbed to a smooth batter with a little cold milk ; stir these ingredients together ; add the well-whisked eggs, the rice, currants, sugar, and nutmeg. Beat the mixture for a few minutes, and, if not sufficiently thick, add a little more boiled rice ; drop it, in small quantities, into a pan of boiling lard or clarified dripping ; fry the fritters a nice brown, and, when done, drain them on a piece of blotting-paper, before the fire Pile them on a white d'oyley, strew over sifted sugar, and serve them very hot. Send a cut lemon to table with them.

Time.—From 8 to 10 minutes to fry the fritters.
Average cost, 9d.
Sufficient for 3 or 4 persons. *Seasonable* at any time.

CHOCOLATE CREAM.

1430. INGREDIENTS.—3 oz. of grated chocolate, ¼ lb. of sugar, 1½ pint of cream, 1½ oz. of clarified isinglass, the yolks of 6 eggs.

Mode.—Beat the yolks of the eggs well ; put them into a basin with the grated chocolate, the sugar, and 1 pint of the cream ; stir these ingredients well together, pour them into a jug, and set this jug in a sauce-pan of boiling water ; stir it one way until the mixture thickens, but *do not allow it to boil,* or it will curdle. Strain the cream through a sieve into a basin ; stir in the isinglass and the other ½ pint of cream, which should be well whipped ; mix all well together, and pour it into a mould which has been

CREAM-MOULD.

previously oiled with the purest salad-oil, and, if at hand, set it in ice until wanted for table.

Time.—About 10 minutes to stir the mixture over the fire.
Average cost, 3s., with cream at 1s. per pint.
Sufficient to fill a quart mould. *Seasonable* at any time.

GENEVA WAFERS.

1431. INGREDIENTS.—2 eggs, 3 oz. of butter, 3 oz. of flour, 3 oz. of pounded sugar.

Mode.—Well whisk the eggs; put them into a basin, and stir to them the butter, which should be beaten to a cream; add the flour and sifted sugar gradually, and then mix all well together. Butter a baking-sheet, and drop on it a teaspoonful of the mixture at a time, leaving a space between each. Bake in a cool oven; watch the pieces of paste, and, when half done, roll them up like wafers, and put in a small wedge of bread or piece of wood, to keep them in shape. Return them to the oven until crisp. Before serving, remove the bread, put a spoonful of preserve in the widest end, and fill up with whipped cream. This is a very pretty and ornamental dish for the supper-table, and is very nice and very easily made.

Time.—Altogether 20 to 25 minutes.

Average cost, exclusive of the preserve and cream, 7*d.*

Sufficient for a nice-sized dish. *Seasonable* at any time.

GINGER CREAM.

1432. INGREDIENTS.—The yolks of 4 eggs, 1 pint of cream, 3 oz. of preserved ginger, 2 dessertspoonfuls of syrup, sifted sugar to taste, 1 oz. of isinglass.

Mode.—Slice the ginger finely; put it into a basin with the syrup, the well-beaten yolks of eggs, and the cream; mix these ingredients well together, and stir them over the fire for about 10 minutes, or until the mixture thickens; then take it off the fire, whisk till nearly cold, sweeten to taste, add the isinglass, which should be melted and strained, and serve the cream in a glass dish. It may be garnished with slices of preserved ginger or candied citron.

Time.—About 10 minutes to stir the cream over the fire.

Average cost, with cream at 1*s.* per pint, 2*s.* 3*d.*

Sufficient for a good-sized dish. *Seasonable* at any time.

PRESERVED GINGER comes to us from the West Indies. It is made by scalding the roots when they are green and full of sap, then peeling them in cold water, and putting them into jars, with a rich syrup; in which state we receive them. It should be chosen of a bright-yellow colour, with a little transparency: what is dark-coloured, fibrous, and stringy, is not good. Ginger roots, fit for preserving, and in size equal to West Indian, have been produced in the Royal Agricultural Garden in Edinburgh.

TO MAKE GOOSEBERRY FOOL.

1433. INGREDIENTS.—Green gooseberries; to every pint of pulp add 1 pint of milk, or ½ pint of cream and ½ pint of milk; sugar to taste.

Mode.—Cut the tops and tails off the gooseberries; put them into a jar, with 2 tablespoonfuls of water and a little good moist sugar; set this jar in a saucepan of boiling water, and let it boil until the fruit is soft enough to mash. When done enough, beat it to a pulp, work this pulp through a colander, and stir to every pint the above proportion of milk, or equal quantities of milk and cream. Ascertain if the mixture is sweet enough, and put in plenty of sugar, or it will not be eatable; and in mixing the milk and gooseberries, add the former very gradually to these: serve in a glass dish, or in small glasses. This, although a very old-fashioned and homely dish, is, when well made, very delicious, and, if properly sweetened, a very suitable preparation for children.

Time.—From ¾ to 1 hour. *Average cost*, 6*d*. per pint, with milk.

Sufficient.—A pint of milk and a pint of gooseberry pulp for 5 or 6 children.

Seasonable in May and June.

GOOSEBERRY TRIFLE.

1434. INGREDIENTS.—1 quart of gooseberries, sugar to taste 1 pint of custard No. 1423, a plateful of whipped cream.

Mode.—Put the gooseberries into a jar, with sufficient moist sugar to sweeten them, and boil them until reduced to a pulp. Put this pulp at the bottom of a trifle-dish; pour over it a pint of custard made by recipe No. 1423, and, when cold, cover with whipped cream. The cream should be whipped the day before it is wanted for table, as it will then be so much firmer and more solid. The dish may be garnished as fancy dictates.

Time.—About ¾ hour to boil the gooseberries.

Average cost, 1*s*. 6*d*.

Sufficient for 1 trifle. *Seasonable* in May and June.

INDIAN FRITTERS.

1435. INGREDIENTS.—3 tablespoonfuls of flour, boiling water, the yolks of 4 eggs, the whites of 2, hot lard or clarified dripping, jam.

Mode.—Put the flour into a basin, and pour over it sufficient *boiling* water to make it into a stiff paste, taking care to stir and beat it well, to prevent it getting lumpy. Leave it a little time to cool, and then break into it (*without beating them at first*) the yolks of 4 eggs and the whites of 2, and stir and beat all well together. Have ready some boiling lard or butter; drop a dessertspoonful of batter in at a time, and fry the fritters of a light brown. They should rise so much as to be almost like balls. Serve on a dish, with a spoonful of preserve

3 A

or marmalade dropped in between each fritter. This is an excellent
dish for a hasty addition to dinner, if a guest unexpectedly arrives,
it being so easily and quickly made, and it is always a great
favourite.

Time.—From 5 to 8 minutes to fry the fritters.

Average cost, exclusive of the jam, 5*d.*

Sufficient for 4 or 5 persons. *Seasonable* at any time.

INDIAN TRIFLE.

1436. INGREDIENTS.—1 quart of milk, the rind of ½ large lemon,
sugar to taste, 5 heaped tablespoonfuls of rice-flour, 1 oz. of sweet
almonds, ½ pint of custard.

Mode.—Boil the milk and lemon-rind together until the former is
well flavoured; take out the lemon-rind and stir in the rice-flour, which
should first be moistened with cold milk, and add sufficient loaf sugar
to sweeten it nicely. Boil gently for about 5 minutes, and keep the
mixture stirred; take it off the fire, let it cool *a little*, and pour it
into a glass dish. When cold, cut the rice out in the form of a star,
or any other shape that may be preferred; take out the spare rice,
and fill the space with boiled custard. Blanch and cut the almonds
into strips; stick them over the trifle, and garnish it with pieces of
bright-coloured jelly, or preserved fruits, or candied citron.

Time.—¼ hour to simmer the milk, 5 minutes after the rice is added.

Average cost, 1*s.*

Sufficient for 1 trifle.

Seasonable at any time.

THE CITRON.

THE CITRON belongs to the same species as the lemon,
being considered only as a variety, the distinction between them not being very great. It is larger, and is
less succulent, but more acid: with a little artificial heat,
the citron comes to as great perfection in England as in
Spain and Italy. The fruit is oblong, and about five or
six inches in length. The tree is thorny. The juice
forms an excellent lemonade with sugar and water; its
uses in punch, negus, and in medicine, are well known.
The rind is very thick, and, when candied with sugar,
forms an excellent sweetmeat. There are several varieties
cultivated in England, one of which is termed the Forbidden Fruit.

ITALIAN CREAM.

1437. INGREDIENTS.—½ pint of milk, ½ pint of cream, sugar to
taste, 1 oz. of isinglass, 1 lemon, the yolks of 4 eggs.

Mode.—Put the cream and milk into a saucepan, with sugar to
sweeten, and the lemon-rind. Boil until the milk is well flavoured;

then strain it into a basin, and add the beaten yolks of eggs. Put this mixture into a jug; place the jug in a saucepan of boiling water over the fire, and stir the contents until they thicken, but do not allow them to boil. Take the cream off the fire, stir in the lemon-juice and isinglass, which should be melted, and whip well; fill a mould, place it in ice if at hand, and, when set, turn it out on a dish, and garnish as taste may dictate. The mixture may be whipped and drained, and then put into small glasses, when this mode of serving is preferred.

Time.—From 5 to 8 minutes to stir the mixture in the jug.

Average cost, with the best isinglass, 2s. 6d.

Sufficient to fill 1½-pint mould. *Seasonable* at any time.

THE HIDDEN MOUNTAIN.

(*A pretty Supper Dish.*)

1438. INGREDIENTS.—6 eggs, a few slices of citron, sugar to taste, ¼ pint of cream, a layer of any kind of jam.

Mode.—Beat the whites and yolks of the eggs separately; then mix them and beat well again, adding a few thin slices of citron, the cream, and sufficient pounded sugar to sweeten it nicely. When the mixture is well beaten, put it into a buttered pan, and fry the same as a pancake; but it should be three times the thickness of an ordinary pancake. Cover it with jam, and garnish with slices of citron and holly-leaves. This dish is served cold.

Time.—About 10 minutes to fry the mixture.

Average cost, with the jam, 1s. 4d.

Sufficient for 3 or 4 persons. *Seasonable* at any time.

JAUNEMANGE.

1439. INGREDIENTS.—1 oz. of isinglass, 1 pint of water, ½ pint of white wine, the rind and juice of 1 large lemon, sugar to taste, the yolks of 6 eggs.

Mode.—Put the isinglass, water, and lemon-rind into a saucepan, and boil gently until the former is dissolved; then add the strained lemon-juice, the wine, and sufficient white sugar to sweeten the whole nicely. Boil for 2 or 3 minutes, strain the mixture into a jug, and add the yolks of the eggs, which should be well beaten; place the jug in a saucepan of boiling water; keep stirring the mixture *one way* until it thickens, *but do not allow it to boil;* then take it off the fire, and keep stirring until nearly cold. Pour it into a mould, omitting the sediment at the bottom of the jug, and let it remain until quite firm.

Time.—¼ hour to boil the isinglass and water; about 10 minutes to stir the mixture in the jug.

Average cost, with the best isinglass, 2s. 9d.

Sufficient to fill a quart mould.   *Seasonable* at any time.

JELLY MOULDED WITH FRESH FRUIT, or MACEDOINE DE FRUITS.

1440. INGREDIENTS.—Rather more than 1½ pint of jelly, a few nice strawberries, or red or white currants, or raspberries, or any fresh fruit that may be in season.

Mode.—Have ready the above proportion of jelly, which must be very clear and rather sweet, the raw fruit requiring an additional quantity of sugar.   Select ripe, nice-looking fruit; pick off the stalks, unless currants are used, when they are laid in the jelly as they come

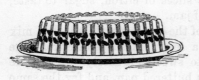

JELLY MOULDED WITH CHERRIES.

from the tree. Begin by putting a little jelly at the bottom of the mould, which must harden; then arrange the fruit round the sides of the mould, recollecting that *it will be reversed when turned out;* then pour in some more jelly to make the fruit adhere, and, when that layer is set, put another row of fruit and jelly until the mould is full.   If convenient, put it in ice until required for table, then wring a cloth in boiling water, wrap it round the mould for a minute, and turn the jelly carefully out.   Peaches, apricots, plums, apples, &c., are better for being boiled in a little clear syrup before they are laid in the jelly; strawberries, raspberries, grapes, cherries, and currants are put in raw.   In winter, when fresh fruits are not obtainable, a very pretty jelly may be made with preserved fruits or brandy cherries: these, in a bright and clear jelly, have a very pretty effect; of course, unless the jelly be *very clear*, the beauty of the dish will be spoiled.   It may be garnished with the same fruit as is laid in the jelly; for instance, an open jelly with straw-berries might have, piled in the centre a few of the same fruit prettily arranged, or a little whipped cream might be substituted for the fruit.

Time.—One layer of jelly should remain 2 hours in a very cool place, before another layer is added.   *Average cost*, 2s. 6d.

Sufficient, with fruit, to fill a quart mould.

Seasonable, with fresh fruit, from June to October; with dried, at any time.

JELLY OF TWO COLOURS.

1441. INGREDIENTS.—1½ pint of calf's-feet jelly No. 1416, a few drops of prepared cochineal.

Mode.—Make 1½ pint of jelly by recipe No. 1416, or, if wished more economical, of clarified syrup and gelatine, flavouring it in any way that may be preferred. Colour one-half of the jelly with a few drops of prepared cochineal, and the other half leave as pale as possible. Have

ready a mould well wetted in every part; pour in a small quantity of the red jelly, and let this set; when quite firm, pour on it the same quantity of the pale jelly, and let this set; then proceed in this manner until the mould is full, always taking care to let one

JELLY OF TWO COLOURS.

jelly set before the other is poured in, or the colours would run one into the other. When turned out, the jelly should have a striped appearance. For variety, half the mould may be filled at once with one of the jellies, and, when firm, filled up with the other: this, also, has a very pretty effect, and is more expeditiously prepared than when the jelly is poured in small quantities into the mould. Blancmange and red jelly, or blancmange and raspberry cream, moulded in the above manner, look very well. The layers of blancmange and jelly should be about an inch in depth, and each layer should be perfectly hardened before another is added. Half a mould of blancmange and half a mould of jelly are frequently served in the same manner. A few pretty dishes may be made, in this way, of jellies or blancmanges left from the preceding day, by melting them separately in a jug placed in a saucepan of boiling water, and then moulding them by the foregoing directions.

Time.—¾ hour to make the jelly.

Average cost, with calf's-feet jelly, 2s.; with gelatine and syrup, more economical.

Sufficient to fill 1½-pint mould. *Seasonable* at any time.

Note.—In making the jelly, use for flavouring a very pale sherry, or the colour will be too dark to contrast nicely with the red jelly.

LEMON BLANCMANGE.

1442. INGREDIENTS.—1 quart of milk, the yolks of 4 eggs, 3 oz. of ground rice, 6 oz. of pounded sugar, 1½ oz. of fresh butter, the rind of 1 lemon, the juice of 2, ½ oz. of gelatine.

Mode.—Make a custard with the yolks of the eggs and ½ pint of the milk, and, when done, put it into a basin; put half the remainder of

the milk into a saucepan with the ground rice, fresh butter, lemon-rind, and 3 oz. of the sugar, and let these ingredients boil until the mixture is stiff, stirring them continually; when done, pour it into the bowl where the custard is, mixing both well together. Put the gelatine with the rest of the milk into a saucepan, and let it stand by the side of the fire to dissolve; boil for a minute or two, stir carefully into the basin, adding 3 oz. more of

BLANCMANGE MOULD.

pounded sugar. When cold, stir in the lemon-juice, which should be carefully strained, and pour the mixture into a well-oiled mould, leaving out the lemon-peel, and set the mould in a pan of cold water until wanted for table. Use eggs that have rich-looking yolks; and, should the weather be very warm, rather a larger proportion of gelatine must be allowed.

Time.—Altogether, ½ hour. *Average cost,* 1s. 6d.

Sufficient to fill 2 small moulds. *Seasonable* at any time.

LEMON CREAM.

1443. INGREDIENTS.—1 pint of cream, the yolks of 2 eggs, ¼ lb. of white sugar, 1 large lemon, 1 oz. of isinglass.

Mode.—Put the cream into a *lined* saucepan with the sugar, lemon-peel, and isinglass, and simmer these over a gentle fire for about

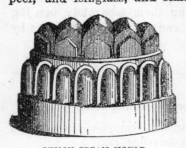

10 minutes, stirring them all the time. Strain the cream into a jug, add the yolks of eggs, which should be well beaten, and put the jug into a saucepan of boiling water; stir the mixture one way until it thickens, *but do not allow it to boil;* take it off the fire, and keep stirring it until nearly cold. Strain the lemon-juice into a basin, gradually pour on it the cream, and

LEMON-CREAM MOULD.

stir it well until the juice is well mixed with it. Have ready a well-oiled mould, pour the cream into it, and let it remain until perfectly set. When required for table, loosen the edges with a small blunt knife, put a dish on the top of the mould, turn it over quickly, and the cream should easily slip away.

Time.—10 minutes to boil the cream; about 10 minutes to stir it over the fire in the jug.

Average cost, with cream at 1*s.* per pint, and the best isinglass, 2*s.* 6*d.*

Sufficient to fill 1½-pint mould. *Seasonable* at any time.

ECONOMICAL LEMON CREAM.

1444. INGREDIENTS.—1 quart of milk, 8 bitter almonds, 2 oz. of gelatine, 2 large lemons, ¾ lb. of lump sugar, the yolks of 6 eggs.

Mode.—Put the milk into a lined saucepan with the almonds, which should be well pounded in a mortar, the gelatine, lemon-rind, and lump sugar, and boil these ingredients for about 5 minutes. Beat up the yolks of the eggs, strain the milk into a jug, add the eggs, and pour the mixture backwards and forwards a few times, until nearly cold; then stir briskly to it the lemon-juice, which should be strained, and keep stirring until the cream is almost cold: put it into an oiled mould, and let it remain until perfectly set. The lemon-juice must not be added to the cream when it is warm, and should be well stirred after it is put in.

Time.—5 minutes to boil the milk. *Average cost*, 2*s.* 5*d.*

Sufficient to fill two 1½-pint moulds. *Seasonable* at any time.

LEMON CREAMS.
(*Very good.*)

1445. INGREDIENTS.—1 pint of cream, 2 dozen sweet almonds, 3 glasses of sherry, the rind and juice of 2 lemons, sugar to taste.

Mode.—Blanch and chop the almonds, and put them into a jug with the cream; in another jug put the sherry, lemon-rind, strained juice, and sufficient pounded sugar to sweeten the whole nicely. Pour rapidly from one jug to the other till the mixture is well frothed; then pour it into jelly-glasses, omitting the lemon-rind. This is a very cool and delicious sweet for summer, and may be made less rich by omitting the almonds and substituting orange or raisin wine for the sherry.

Time.—Altogether, ½ hour.

Average cost, with cream at 1*s.* per pint, 3*s.*

Sufficient to fill 12 glasses. *Seasonable* at any time.

LEMON CREAMS OR CUSTARDS.

1446. INGREDIENTS.—5 oz. of loaf sugar, 2 pints of boiling water, the rind of 1 lemon and the juice of 3, the yolks of 8 eggs.

Mode.—Make a quart of lemonade in the following manner:—Dissolve the sugar in the boiling water, having previously, with part of the sugar, rubbed off the lemon-rind, and add the strained juice. Strain the lemonade into a saucepan, and add the yolks of the eggs, which should be well beaten ; stir this *one way* over the fire until the mixture thickens, but do not allow it to boil, and serve in custard-glasses, or on a glass dish. After the boiling water is poured on the sugar and lemon, it should stand covered for about ½ hour before the eggs are added to it, that the flavour of the rind may be extracted.

Time.—½ hour to make the lemonade ; about 10 minutes to stir the custard over the fire.

Average cost, 1s.

Sufficient to fill 12 to 14 custard-glasses. *Seasonable* at any time.

LEMON JELLY.

1447. INGREDIENTS.—6 lemons, ¾ lb. of lump sugar, 1 pint of water, 1¼ oz. of isinglass, ¼ pint of sherry.

Mode.—Peel 3 of the lemons, pour ½ pint of boiling water on the rind, and let it infuse for ½ hour ; put the sugar, isinglass, and ½ pint of water into a lined saucepan, and boil these ingredients for 20 minutes ; then put in the strained lemon-juice, the strained infusion of the rind, and bring the whole to the point of boiling ; skim well, add the wine, and run the jelly through a bag ; pour it into a mould that has been wetted or soaked in water ; put it in ice, if convenient, where let it remain until required for table. Previously to adding the lemon-juice to the other ingredients, ascertain that it is very nicely strained, as, if this is not properly attended to, it is liable to make the jelly thick and muddy. As this jelly is very pale, and almost colourless, it answers very well for moulding with a jelly of any bright hue ; for instance, half a jelly bright red, and the other half made of the above, would have a very good effect. Lemon jelly may also be made with calf's-feet stock, allowing the juice of 3 lemons to every pint of stock.

Time.—Altogether, 1 hour.

Average cost, with the best isinglass, 2s. 9d.

Sufficient to fill 1½-pint mould. *Seasonable* at any time.

LEMON SPONGE.

1448. INGREDIENTS.—2 oz. of isinglass, 1¾ pint of water, ¾ lb. of pounded sugar, the juice of 5 lemons, the rind of 1, the whites of 3 eggs.

Mode.—Dissolve the isinglass in the water, strain it into a saucepan, and add the sugar, lemon-rind, and juice. Boil the whole from 10 to 15 minutes ; strain it again, and let it stand till it is cold and begins to stiffen. Beat the whites of the eggs, put them to it, and whisk the mixture till it is quite white; put it into a mould which has been previously wetted, and let it remain until perfectly set; then turn it out, and garnish it according to taste.

Time.—10 to 15 minutes. *Average cost*, with the best isinglass, 3*s.* 6*d.* *Sufficient* to fill a quart mould. *Seasonable* at any time.

LIQUEUR JELLY.

1449. INGREDIENTS.—1 lb. of lump sugar, 2 oz. of isinglass, 1½ pint of water, the juice of 2 lemons, ¼ pint of liqueur.

Mode.—Put the sugar, with 1 pint of the water, into a stewpan, and boil them gently by the side of the fire until there is no scum remaining, which must be carefully re-moved as fast as it rises. Boil the isinglass with the other ½ pint of water, and skim it carefully in the same manner. Strain the lemon-juice, and add it, with the clarified isinglass, to the syrup; put in the liqueur, and bring the whole to the boiling-point. Let the saucepan remain covered by the side of the

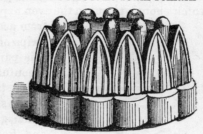

OVAL JELLY-MOULD.

fire for a few minutes; then pour the jelly through a bag, put it into a mould, and set the mould in ice until required for table. Dip the mould in hot water, wipe the outside, loosen the jelly by passing a knife round the edges, and turn it out carefully on a dish. Noyeau, Maraschino, Curaçoa, brandy, or any kind of liqueur, answers for this jelly; and, when made with isinglass, liqueur jellies are usually prepared as directed above.

Time.—10 minutes to boil the sugar and water.

Average cost, with the best isinglass, 3*s.* 6*d.*

Sufficient to fill a quart mould. *Seasonable* at any time.

A SWEET DISH OF MACARONI.

1450. INGREDIENTS.—¼ lb. of macaroni, 1½ pint of milk, the rind of ½ lemon, 3 oz. of lump sugar, ¾ pint of custard No. 1423.

Mode.—Put the milk into a saucepan, with the lemon-peel and sugar; bring it to the boiling-point, drop in the macaroni, and let it gradually swell over a gentle fire, but do not allow the pipes to break. The form should be entirely preserved; and, though tender, should be firm, and not soft, with no part beginning to melt. Should the milk dry away before the macaroni is sufficiently swelled, add a little more. Make a custard by recipe No. 1423; place the macaroni on a dish, and pour the custard over the hot macaroni ; grate over it a little nut-meg, and, when cold, garnish the dish with slices of candied citron.

Time.—From 40 to 50 minutes to swell the macaroni.

Average cost, with the custard, 1s.

Sufficient for 4 or 5 persons.   *Seasonable* at any time.

MERINGUES.

1451. INGREDIENTS.—½ lb. of pounded sugar, the whites of 4 eggs.

Mode.—Whisk the whites of the eggs to a stiff froth, and, with a wooden spoon, stir in *quickly* the pounded sugar ; and have some boards thick enough to put in the oven to prevent the bottom of the meringues

MERINGUES.

from acquiring too much colour. Cut some strips of paper about 2 inches wide ; place this paper on the board, and drop a table-spoonful at a time of the mixture on the paper, taking care to let all the meringues be the same size. In dropping it from the spoon, give the mixture the form of an egg, and keep the meringues about 2 inches apart from each other on the paper. Strew over them some sifted sugar, and bake in a moderate oven for ½ hour. As soon as they begin to colour, remove them from the oven ; take each slip of paper by the two ends, and turn it gently on the table, and, with a small spoon, take out the soft part of each meringue. Spread some clean paper on the board, turn the meringues upside down, and put them into the oven to harden and brown on the other side. When required for table, fill them with whipped cream, flavoured with liqueur or vanilla, and sweetened with pounded sugar. Join two of the merin-gues together, and pile them high in the dish, as shown in the annexed drawing. To vary their appearance, finely-chopped almonds or cur-rants may be strewn over them before the sugar is sprinkled over ; and they may be garnished with any bright-coloured preserve. Great expedition is necessary in making this sweet dish ; as, if the me-ringues are not put into the oven as soon as the sugar and eggs are mixed, the former melts, and the mixture would run on the paper, instead of keeping its egg-shape. The sweeter the meringues are made, the crisper will they be ; but, if there is not sufficient sugar mixed with them, they will most likely be tough. They are some-times coloured with cochineal ; and, if kept well covered in a dry place, will remain good for a month or six weeks.

Time.—Altogether, about ½ hour.

Average cost, with the cream and flavouring, 1s.

Sufficient to make 2 dozen meringues.   *Seasonable* at any time.

NOYEAU CREAM.

1452. INGREDIENTS.—1½ oz. of isinglass, the juice of 2 lemons, noyeau and pounded sugar to taste, 1½ pint of cream.

Mode.—Dissolve the isinglass in a little boiling water, add the lemon-juice, and strain this to the cream, putting in sufficient noyeau and sugar to flavour and sweeten the mixture nicely; whisk the cream well, put it into an oiled mould, and set the mould in ice or in a cool place; turn it out, and garnish the dish to taste.

Time.—Altogether, ½ hour.

Average cost, with cream at 1s. per pint and the best isinglass, 4s.

Sufficient to fill a quart mould.   *Seasonable* at any time.

OPEN JELLY WITH WHIPPED CREAM.

(A very pretty dish.)

1453. INGREDIENTS.—1½ pint of jelly, ½ pint of cream, 1 glass of sherry, sugar to taste.

Mode.—Make the above proportion of calf's-feet or isinglass jelly, colouring and flavouring it in any way that may be preferred; soak a mould, open in the centre, for about ½ hour in cold water; fill it with the jelly, and let it remain in a cool place until perfectly set; then turn it out on a dish; fill the centre with whipped cream, flavoured with sherry and sweetened with pounded sugar; pile this cream high in the centre, and

OPEN JELLY WITH WHIPPED CREAM.

serve.   The jelly should be made of rather a dark colour, to contrast nicely with the cream.

Time.—¾ hour.   *Average cost*, 3s. 6d.

Sufficient to fill 1½-pint mould.   *Seasonable* at any time.

ORANGE JELLY.

1454. INGREDIENTS.—1 pint of water, 1½ to 2 oz. of isinglass, ¼ lb. of loaf sugar, 1 Seville orange, 1 lemon, about 9 China oranges.

Mode.—Put the water into a saucepan, with the isinglass, sugar, and the rind of 1 orange, and the same of ½ lemon, and stir these over

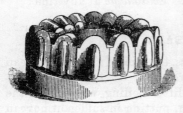

OPEN MOULD.

the fire until the isinglass is dissolved, and remove the scum; then add to this the juice of the Seville orange, the juice of the lemon, and sufficient juice of China oranges to make in all 1 pint: from 8 to 10 oranges will yield the desired quantity. Stir all together over the fire until it is just on the point of boiling; skim well; then strain the jelly through a very fine sieve or jelly-bag, and when nearly cold, put it into a mould previously wetted, and, when quite set, turn it out on a dish, and garnish it to taste. To insure this jelly being clear, the orange- and lemon-juice should be well strained, and the isinglass clarified, before they are added to the other ingredients, and, to heighten the colour, a few drops of prepared cochineal may be added.

Time.—5 minutes to boil without the juice; 1 minute after it is added.

Average cost, with the best isinglass, 3s. 6d.

Sufficient to fill a quart mould. *Seasonable* from November to May.

ORANGE JELLY MOULDED WITH SLICES OF ORANGE.

1455. INGREDIENTS.—1½ pint of orange jelly No. 1454, 4 oranges, ½ pint of clarified syrup.

Mode.—Boil ½ lb. of loaf sugar with ½ pint of water until there is no scum left (which must be carefully removed as fast as it rises), and carefully peel the oranges; divide them into thin slices, without breaking the thin skin, and put these pieces of orange into the syrup, where let them remain for about 5 minutes; then take them out, and use the syrup for the jelly, which should be made by recipe No. 1454. When the oranges are well drained, and the jelly is nearly cold, pour a little of the latter into the bottom of the mould; then lay in a few pieces of orange; over these pour a little jelly, and when this is set, place another layer of oranges, proceeding in this manner until the mould is full. Put it in ice, or in a cool place, and, before turning it out, wrap a cloth round the mould for a minute or two, which has been wrung out in boiling water.

Time.—5 minutes to simmer the oranges. *Average cost*, 3s. 6d.

Sufficient, with the slices of orange, to fill a quart mould.

Seasonable from November to May.

TO MAKE A PLAIN OMELET.

1456. INGREDIENTS.—6 eggs, 1 saltspoonful of salt, ½ saltspoonful of pepper, ¼ lb. of butter.

Mode.—Break the eggs into a basin, omitting the whites of 3, and beat them up with the salt and pepper until extremely light; then add 2 oz. of the butter broken into small pieces, and stir this into the mixture. Put the other 2 oz. of butter into a frying-pan, make it quite hot, and, as soon as it begins to bubble, whisk the eggs, &c. very

OMELET.

briskly for a minute or two, and pour them into the pan; stir the omelet with a spoon one way until the mixture thickens and becomes firm, and when the whole is set, fold the edges over, so that the omelet assumes an oval form; and when it is nicely brown on one side, and quite firm, it is done. To take off the rawness on the upper side, hold the pan before the fire for a minute or two, and brown it with a salamander or hot shovel. Serve very expeditiously on a very hot dish, and never cook it until it is just wanted. The flavour of this omelet may be very much enhanced by adding minced parsley, minced onion or eschalot, or grated cheese, allowing 1 tablespoonful of the former, and half the quantity of the latter, to the above proportion of eggs. Shrimps or oysters may also be added : the latter should be scalded in their liquor, and then bearded and cut into small pieces. In making an omelet, be particularly careful that it is not too thin, and, to avoid this, do not make it in too large a frying-pan, as the mixture would then spread too much, and taste of the outside. It should also not be greasy, burnt, or too much done, and should be cooked over a gentle fire, that the whole of the substance may be heated without drying up the outside. Omelets are sometimes served with gravy; but *this should never be poured over them*, but served in a tureen, as the liquid causes the omelet to become heavy and flat, instead of eating light and soft. In making the gravy, the flavour should not overpower that of the omelet, and should be thickened with arrowroot or rice flour.

Time.—With 6 eggs, in a frying-pan 18 or 20 inches round, 4 to 6 minutes. *Average cost, 9d.*

Sufficient for 4 persons. *Seasonable* at any time.

HAM OMELET.

(*A delicious Breakfast Dish.*)

1457. INGREDIENTS.—6 eggs, 4 oz. of butter, ½ saltspoonful of pepper, 2 tablespoonfuls of minced ham.

Mode.—Mince the ham very finely, without any fat, and fry it for 2 minutes in a little butter; then make the batter for the omelet, stir in the ham, and proceed as directed in recipe No. 1456. Do not add any salt to the batter, as the ham is usually sufficiently salt to impart a flavour to the omelet. Good lean bacon, or tongue, answers equally well for this dish; but they must also be slightly cooked previously to mixing them with the batter. Serve very hot and quickly, without gravy.

Time.—From 4 to 6 minutes. *Average cost,* 1s.

Sufficient for 4 persons. *Seasonable* at any time.

KIDNEY OMELET.

(*A favourite French dish.*)

1458. INGREDIENTS.—6 eggs, 1 saltspoonful of salt, ½ saltspoonful of pepper, 2 sheep's kidneys, or 2 tablespoonfuls of minced veal kidney, 5 oz. of butter.

Mode.—Skin the kidneys, cut them into small dice, and toss them in a frying-pan, in 1 oz. of butter, over the fire for 2 or 3 minutes.

Mix the ingredients for the omelet the same as in recipe No. 1456, and when the eggs are well whisked, stir in the pieces of kidney. Make the butter hot in the frying-pan, and when it bubbles, pour in

OMELET-PAN.

the omelet, and fry it over a gentle fire from 4 to 6 minutes. When the eggs are set, fold the edges over, so that the omelet assumes an oval form, and be careful that it is not too much done: to brown the top, hold the pan before the fire for a minute or two, or use a salamander until the desired colour is obtained, but never turn an omelet in the pan. Slip it carefully on to a *very hot* dish, or, what is a much safer method, put a dish on the omelet, and turn the pan quickly over. It should be served the instant it comes from the fire.

Time.—4 to 6 minutes. *Average cost,* 1s.

Sufficient for 4 persons. *Seasonable* at any time.

TO MAKE A PLAIN SWEET OMELET.

1459. INGREDIENTS.—6 eggs, 4 oz. of butter, 2 oz. of sifted sugar.

Mode.—Break the eggs into a basin, omitting the whites of 3; whisk them well, adding the sugar and 2 oz. of the butter, which should be broken into small pieces, and stir all these ingredients well together. Make the remainder of the butter quite hot in a small frying-pan, and when it commences to bubble, pour in the eggs, &c. Keep stirring them until they begin to set; then turn the edges of the omelet over, to make it an oval shape, and finish cooking it. To brown the top, hold the pan before the fire, or use a salamander, and turn it carefully on to a *very hot* dish : sprinkle sifted sugar over, and serve.

Time.—From 4 to 6 minutes. *Average cost*, 10*d*.

Sufficient for 4 persons. *Seasonable* at any time.

OMELETTE AUX CONFITURES, or JAM OMELET.

1460. INGREDIENTS.—6 eggs, 4 oz. of butter, 3 tablespoonfuls of apricot, strawberry, or any jam that may be preferred.

Mode.—Make the omelet by recipe No. 1459, only instead of doubling it over, leave it flat in the pan. When quite firm, and nicely brown on one side, turn it carefully on to a hot dish, spread over the middle of it the jam, and fold the omelet over on each side ; sprinkle sifted sugar over, and serve very quickly. A pretty dish of small omelets may be made by dividing the batter into 3 or 4 portions, and frying them separately ; they should then be spread each one with a different kind of preserve, and the omelets rolled over. Always sprinkle sweet omelets with sifted sugar before being sent to table.

Time.—4 to 6 minutes. *Average cost*, 1*s*. 2*d*.

Sufficient for 4 persons. *Seasonable* at any time.

OMELETTE SOUFFLE.

1461. INGREDIENTS.—6 eggs, 5 oz. of pounded sugar, flavouring of vanilla, orange-flower water, or lemon-rind, 3 oz. of butter, 1 dessert-spoonful of rice-flour.

Mode.—Separate the yolks from the whites of the eggs, add to the former the sugar, the rice-flour, and either of the above flavourings that may be preferred, and stir these ingredients well together. Whip the whites of the eggs, mix them lightly with the batter, and put the butter into a small frying-pan. As soon as it begins to bubble, pour the batter into it, and set the pan over a bright but gentle fire ; and when the omelet is set, turn the edges over to make it an oval shape, and slip it on to a silver dish, which has been previously well buttered. Put it in the oven, and bake from 12 to 15 minutes ; sprinkle finely-powdered sugar over the soufflé, and *serve it immediately*.

Time.—About 4 minutes in the pan ; to bake, from 12 to 15 minutes. *Average cost*, 1*s*.

Sufficient for 3 or 4 persons. *Seasonable* at any time.

BACHELOR'S OMELET.

1462. INGREDIENTS.—2 or 3 eggs, 2 oz. of butter, 1 teaspoonful of flour, ½ teacupful of milk.

Mode.—Make a thin cream of the flour and milk; then beat up the eggs, mix all together, and add a pinch of salt and a few grains of cayenne. Melt the butter in a small frying-pan, and, when very hot, pour in the batter. Let the pan remain for a few minutes over a clear fire; then sprinkle upon the omelet some chopped herbs and a few shreds of onion; double the omelet dexterously, and shake it out of the pan on to a hot dish. A simple sweet omelet can be made by the same process, substituting sugar or preserve for the chopped herbs.

Time.—2 minutes. *Average cost,* 6d.

Sufficient for 2 persons. *Seasonable* at any time.

ORANGE CREAM.

1463. INGREDIENTS.—1 oz. of isinglass, 6 large oranges, 1 lemon, sugar to taste, water, ½ pint of good cream.

Mode.—Squeeze the juice from the oranges and lemon; strain it, and put it into a saucepan with the isinglass, and sufficient water to

OPEN MOULD.

make in all 1½ pint. Rub the sugar on the orange and lemon-rind, add it to the other ingredients, and boil all together for about 10 minutes. Strain through a muslin bag, and, when cold, beat up with it ½ pint of thick cream. Wet a mould, or soak it in cold water; pour in the cream, and put it in a cool place to set. If the weather is very cold, 1 oz. of isinglass will be found sufficient for the above proportion of ingredients.

Time.—10 minutes to boil the juice and water.

Average cost, with the best isinglass, 3s.

Sufficient to fill a quart mould. *Seasonable* from November to May.

ORANGE CREAMS.

1464. INGREDIENTS.—1 Seville orange, 1 tablespoonful of brandy, ¼ lb. of loaf sugar, the yolks of 4 eggs, 1 pint of cream.

Mode.—Boil the rind of the Seville orange until tender, and beat it in a mortar to a pulp; add to it the brandy, the strained juice of the orange, and the sugar, and beat all together for about 10 minutes, adding the well-beaten yolks of eggs. Bring the cream to the boiling-point, and pour it very gradually to the other ingredients, and beat the mixture till nearly cold; put it into custard-cups, place the cups in a deep dish of boiling water, where let them remain till quite cold.

Take the cups out of the water, wipe them, and garnish the tops of the creams with candied orange-peel or preserved chips.

Time.—Altogether, ¾ hour.

Average cost, with cream at 1*s.* per pint, 1*s.* 7*d.*

Sufficient to make 7 or 8 creams.

Seasonable from November to May.

Note.—To render this dish more economical, substitute milk for the cream, but add a small pinch of isinglass to make the creams firm.

SEVILLE ORANGE (*Citrus vulgaris*).—This variety, called also *bitter orange*, is of the same species as the sweet orange, and grows in great abundance on the banks of the Guadal-quiver, in Andalusia, whence this fruit is chiefly obtained. In that part of Spain there are very extensive orchards of these oranges, which form the chief wealth of the monasteries. The pulp of the bitter orange is not eaten raw. In the yellow rind, separated from the white spongy substance immediately below it, is contained an essential oil, which is an agreeable warm aromatic, much superior for many purposes to that of the common orange. The best marmalade and the richest wine are made from this orange; and from its flowers the best orange-flower water is distilled. Seville oranges are also preserved whole as a sweetmeat.

ORANGE FRITTERS.

1465. INGREDIENTS.—For the batter, ½ lb. of flour, ½ oz. of butter, ½ saltspoonful of salt, 2 eggs, milk, oranges, hot lard or clarified dripping.

Mode.—Make a nice light batter with the above proportion of flour, butter, salt, eggs, and sufficient milk to make it the proper consistency; peel the oranges, remove as much of the white skin as possible, and divide each orange into eight pieces, without breaking the thin skin, unless it be to remove the pips; dip each piece of orange in the batter. Have ready a pan of boiling lard or clarified dripping; drop in the oranges, and fry them a delicate brown from 8 to 10 minutes. When done, lay them on a piece of blotting-paper before the fire, to drain away the greasy moisture, and dish them on a white d'oyley; sprinkle over them plenty of pounded sugar, and serve quickly.

Time.—8 to 10 minutes to fry the fritters; 5 minutes to drain them.

Average cost, 9*d.*

Sufficient for 4 or 5 persons. *Seasonable* from November to May.

A PRETTY DISH OF ORANGES.

1466. INGREDIENTS.—6 large oranges, ¼ lb. of loaf sugar, ¼ pint of water, ½ pint of cream, 2 tablespoonfuls of any kind of liqueur, sugar to taste.

Mode.—Put the sugar and water into a saucepan, and boil them until the sugar becomes brittle, which may be ascertained by taking up a small quantity in a spoon, and dipping it in cold water; if the sugar is sufficiently boiled, it will easily snap. Peel the oranges, remove as much of the white pith as possible, and divide them into nice-sized slices, without breaking the thin white skin which surrounds the juicy pulp. Place the pieces of orange on small skewers, dip them into the hot sugar, and arrange them in layers round a plain mould, which should be well oiled with the purest salad-oil. The sides of the mould only should be lined with the oranges, and the centre left open for the cream. Let the sugar become firm by cooling ; turn the oranges carefully out on a dish, and fill the centre with whipped cream, flavoured with any kind of liqueur, and sweetened with pounded sugar. This is an exceedingly ornamental and nice dish for the supper-table.

Time.—10 minutes to boil the sugar. *Average cost*, 1s. 8d.

Sufficient for 1 mould. *Seasonable* from November to May.

TO MAKE PANCAKES.

1467. INGREDIENTS.—Eggs, flour, milk ; to every egg allow 1 oz. of flour, about 1 gill of milk, ⅛ saltspoonful of salt.

Mode.—Ascertain that the eggs are fresh ; break each one separately in a cup ; whisk them well, put them into a basin, with the flour, salt, and a few drops of milk, and beat the whole to a perfectly *smooth* batter ; then add by degrees the remainder of the milk. The proportion of this latter ingredient must be regulated by the size of the eggs, &c. &c. ; but the batter, when ready for frying; should be of the consistency of thick cream. Place a small frying-pan on the fire

PANCAKES.

to get hot ; let it be delicately clean, or the pancakes will stick, and, when quite hot, put into it a small piece of butter, allowing about ½ oz. to each pancake. When it is melted, pour in the batter, about ½ teacupful to a pan 5 inches in diameter, and fry it for about 4 minutes, or until it is nicely brown on one side. By only pouring in a small quantity of batter, and so making the pancakes thin, the necessity of turning them (an operation rather difficult to unskilful cooks) is obviated. When the pancake is done, sprinkle over it some pounded sugar, roll it up in the pan, and take it out with a large slice, and place it on a dish before the fire. Proceed in this manner until sufficient are cooked for a dish ; then send them quickly· to table, and continue to send in a further quantity, as pancakes are never good unless eaten almost immediately they come from the frying-pan. The batter may be flavoured with a little grated lemon-rind, or the pancakes may have preserve rolled in them instead of sugar. Send sifted sugar and a cut lemon to table with them. To render the pancakes very light, the yolks and whites of the eggs should be beaten separately, and the whites added the last thing to the batter before frying.

Time.—From 4 to 5 minutes for a pancake that does not require turning; from 6 to 8 minutes for a thicker one.

Average cost, for 3 persons, 6*d*.

Sufficient.—Allow 3 eggs, with the other ingredients in proportion, for 3 persons.

Seasonable at any time, but specially served on Shrove Tuesday.

RICHER PANCAKES.

1468. INGREDIENTS.—6 eggs, 1 pint of cream, ¼ lb. of loaf sugar, 1 glass of sherry, ½ teaspoonful of grated nutmeg, flour.

Mode.—Ascertain that the eggs are extremely fresh, beat them well, strain and mix with them the cream, pounded sugar, wine, nutmeg, and as much flour as will make the batter nearly as thick as that for ordinary pancakes. Make the frying-pan hot, wipe it with a clean cloth, pour in sufficient batter to make a thin pancake, and fry it for about 5 minutes. Dish the pancakes piled one above the other, strew sifted sugar between each, and serve.

Time.—About 5 minutes.

Average cost, with cream at 1*s*. per pint, 2*s*. 3*d*.

Sufficient to make 8 pancakes.

Seasonable at any time, but specially served on Shrove Tuesday.

PEACH FRITTERS.

1469. INGREDIENTS.—For the batter: ½ lb. of flour, ½ oz. of butter, ½ saltspoonful of salt, 2 eggs, milk;—peaches, hot lard or clarified dripping.

Mode.—Make a nice smooth batter in the same manner as directed in recipe No. 1393, and skin, halve, and stone the peaches, which should be quite ripe; dip them in the batter, and fry the pieces in hot lard or clarified dripping, which should be brought to the boiling-point before the peaches are put in. From 8 to 10 minutes will be required to fry them, and, when done, drain them before the fire, and dish them on a white d'oyley. Strew over plenty of pounded sugar, and serve.

Time.—From 8 to 10 minutes to fry the fritters, 5 minutes to drain them. *Average cost*, 1*s*.

Sufficient for 4 or 5 persons.

Seasonable in July, August, and September.

PEACH.—The peach and nectarine are amongst the most delicious of our fruits, and are considered as varieties of the same species produced by cultivation. The former is characterized by a very delicate down, while the latter is smooth; but, as a proof of their identity as to species, trees have borne peaches in one part and nectarines in another; and even a single fruit has had down on one side and the other smooth. The trees are almost exactly alike, as well as the blossoms. Pliny states that the peach was originally brought from Persia, where it grows naturally, from which the name of *Persica* was bestowed upon it by the Romans; and some modern botanists apply this as the generic name, separating them from *Amygdalus*, or Almond, to which Linnæus had united them. Although they are not tropical, they require a great deal of warmth to bring them to perfection: hence they seldom ripen in this country, in ordinary seasons, without the use of walls or glass; consequently, they bear a high price. In a good peach, the flesh is firm, the skin thin, of a deep bright colour next the sun, and of a yellowish green next to the wall; the pulp is yellowish, full of highly-flavoured juice, the fleshy part thick, and the stone small. Too much down is a sign of inferior quality. This fruit is much used at the dessert, and makes a delicious preserve.

PEACH.

PEARS A L'ALLEMANDE.

1470. INGREDIENTS.—6 to 8 pears, water, sugar, 2 oz. of butter, the yolk of an egg, ½ oz. of gelatine.

Mode.—Peel and cut the pears into any form that may be preferred, and steep them in cold water to prevent them turning black; put them into a saucepan with sufficient cold water to cover them, and boil them with the butter and enough sugar to sweeten them nicely, until tender; then brush the pears over with the yolk of an egg, sprinkle them with sifted sugar, and arrange them on a dish. Add the gelatine to the syrup, boil it up quickly for about 5 minutes, strain it over the pears, and let it remain until set. The syrup may be coloured with a little prepared cochineal, which would very much improve the appearance of the dish.

Time.—From 20 minutes to ½ hour to stew the pears; 5 minutes to boil the syrup.

Average cost, 1s. 3d.

Sufficient for a large dish.

Seasonable from August to February.

MOULDED PEARS.

1471. INGREDIENTS.—4 large pears or 6 small ones, 8 cloves, sugar to taste, water, a small piece of cinnamon, ¼ pint of raisin wine, a strip of lemon-peel, the juice of ½ lemon, ½ oz. of gelatine.

Mode.—Peel and cut the pears into quarters; put them into a jar with ¾ pint of water, cloves, cinnamon, and sufficient sugar to sweeten the whole nicely; cover down the top of the jar, and bake the pears in a gentle oven until perfectly tender, but do not allow them to break. When done, lay the pears in a plain mould, which should be well wetted, and boil ½ pint of the liquor the pears were baked in with the wine, lemon-peel, strained juice, and gelatine. Let these ingredients boil quickly for 5 minutes, then strain the liquid warm over the pears; put the mould in a cool place, and when the jelly is firm, turn it out on a glass dish.

Time.—2 hours to bake the pears in a cool oven.

Average cost, 1s. 3d.

Sufficient for a quart mould. *Seasonable* from August to February.

PINEAPPLE FRITTERS.
(*An elegant Dish.*)

1472. INGREDIENTS.—A small pineapple, a small wineglassful of brandy or liqueur, 2 oz. of sifted sugar; batter as for apple fritters No. 1393.

Mode.—This elegant dish, although it may appear extravagant, is really not so if made when pineapples are plentiful. We receive them now in such large quantities from the West Indies, that at times they may be purchased at an exceedingly low rate : it would not, of course, be economical to use the pines which are grown in our English pineries for the purposes of fritters. Pare the pine with as little waste as possible, cut it into rather thin slices, and soak these slices in the above proportion of brandy or liqueur and pounded sugar for 4 hours ; then make a batter the same as for apple fritters, substituting cream for the milk, and using a smaller quantity of flour ; and, when this is ready, dip in the pieces of pine, and fry them in boiling lard from 5 to 8 minutes ; turn them when sufficiently brown on one side, and, when done, drain them from the lard before the fire, dish them on a white d'oyley, strew over them sifted sugar, and serve quickly.

Time.—5 to 8 minutes.

Average cost, when cheap and plentiful, 1s. 6d. for the pine.

Sufficient for 3 or 4 persons. *Seasonable* in July and August.

PINEAPPLE.—The pineapple has not been known in Europe above two hundred years, and has not been cultivated in England much above a century. It is stated that the first pineapples raised in Europe were by M. La Cour, of Leyden, about the middle of the 17th century ; and it is said to have been first cultivated in England by Sir Matthew Decker, of Richmond. In Kensington Palace, there is a picture in which Charles II. is represented as receiving a pineapple from his gardener Rose, who is presenting it on his knees.

PLAIN FRITTERS.

1473. INGREDIENTS.—3 oz. of flour, 3 eggs, ⅓ pint of milk.

Mode.—Mix the flour to a smooth batter with a small quantity of the milk ; stir in the eggs, which should be well whisked, and then the remainder of the milk; beat the whole to a perfectly smooth batter, and should it be found not quite thin enough, add two or

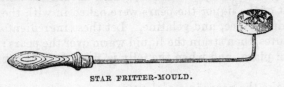

STAR FRITTER-MOULD.

three tablespoonfuls more milk. Have ready a frying-pan, with plenty of boiling lard in it; drop in rather more than a tablespoonful at a time of the batter, and fry the fritters a nice brown, turning them when sufficiently cooked on one side. Drain them well from the greasy moisture by placing them upon a piece of blotting-paper before the fire; dish them on a white d'oyley, sprinkle over them sifted sugar, and send to table with them a cut lemon and plenty of pounded sugar.

Time.—From 6 to 8 minutes.   Average cost, 4d.

Sufficient for 3 or 4 persons.   Seasonable at any time.

POTATO FRITTERS.

1474. INGREDIENTS.—2 large potatoes, 4 eggs, 2 tablespoonfuls of cream, 2 ditto of raisin or sweet wine, 1 dessertspoonful of lemon-juice, ½ teaspoonful of grated nutmeg, hot lard.

Mode.—Boil the potatoes, and beat them up lightly with a fork, but do not use a spoon, as that would make them heavy. Beat the eggs well, leaving out one of the whites; add the other ingredients, and beat all together for at least 20 minutes, or until the batter is extremely light. Put plenty of good lard into a frying-pan, and drop a tablespoonful of the batter at a time into it, and fry the fritters a nice brown. Serve them with the following sauce :—A glass of sherry mixed with the strained juice of a lemon, and sufficient white sugar

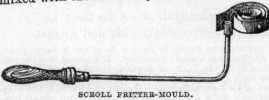

SCROLL FRITTER-MOULD.

to sweeten the whole nicely. Warm these ingredients, and serve the sauce separately in a tureen. The fritters should be neatly dished on a white d'oyley, and pounded sugar sprinkled over them; and they should be well drained on a piece of blotting-paper before the fire previously to being dished.

Time.—From 6 to 8 minutes.   Average cost, 9d.

Sufficient for 3 or 4 persons.   Seasonable at any time.

RASPBERRY CREAM.

1475. INGREDIENTS.—$\frac{3}{4}$ pint of milk, $\frac{3}{4}$ pint of cream, 1$\frac{1}{2}$ oz. of isinglass, raspberry jelly, sugar to taste, 2 tablespoonfuls of brandy.

Mode.—Boil the milk, cream, and isinglass together for $\frac{1}{4}$ hour, or until the latter is melted, and strain it through a hair sieve into a basin. Let it cool a little; then add to it sufficient raspberry jelly, which, when melted, would make $\frac{1}{8}$ pint, and stir well till the ingredients are thoroughly mixed. If not sufficiently sweet, add a little pounded sugar with the brandy; whisk the mixture well until nearly cold, put it into a well-oiled mould, and set it in a cool place till perfectly set. Raspberry jam may

RASPBERRY-CREAM MOULD.

be substituted for the jelly, but must be melted, and rubbed through a sieve, to free it from seeds: in summer, the juice of the fresh fruit may be used, by slightly mashing it with a wooden spoon, and sprinkling sugar over it; the juice that flows from the fruit should then be used for mixing with the cream. If the colour should not be very good, a few drops of prepared cochineal may be added to improve its appearance.

Time.—$\frac{1}{4}$ hour to boil the cream and isinglass.

Average cost, with cream at 1*s.* per pint, and the best isinglass, 3*s.*

Sufficient to fill a quart mould.

Seasonable, with jelly, at any time.

Note.—Strawberry cream may be made in precisely the same manner, substituting strawberry jam or jelly for the raspberry.

RICE BLANCMANGE.

1476. INGREDIENTS.—$\frac{1}{4}$ lb. of ground rice, 3 oz. of loaf sugar, 1 oz. of fresh butter, 1 quart of milk, flavouring of lemon-peel, essence of almonds or vanilla, or laurel-leaves.

Mode.—Mix the rice to a smooth batter with about $\frac{1}{2}$ pint of the milk, and the remainder put into a saucepan, with the sugar, butter, and whichever of the above flavourings may be preferred; bring the milk to the boiling-point, quickly stir in the rice, and let it boil for about 10 minutes, or until it comes easily away from the saucepan, keeping it well stirred the whole time. Grease a mould with pure salad-oil; pour in the rice, and let it get perfectly set, when it should turn out quite easily; garnish it with jam, or pour round a compôte of any kind of fruit, just before it is sent to table. This blancmange is better for being made the day before it is wanted, as it then has time to become firm. If laurel-leaves are used for flavouring, steep 3 of them in the milk, and take them out before the rice is added : about 8 drops of essence of almonds, or from 12 to 16 drops of essence of vanilla, would be required to flavour the above proportion of milk.

Time.—From 10 to 15 minutes to boil the rice.

Average cost, 9*d.*

Sufficient to fill a quart mould.   *Seasonable* at any time.

RICE CROQUETTES.

1477. INGREDIENTS.—¼ lb. of rice, 1 quart of milk, 6 oz. of pounded sugar, flavouring of vanilla, lemon-peel, or bitter almonds, egg and bread crumbs, hot lard.

Mode.—Put the rice, milk, and sugar into a saucepan, and let the former gradually swell over a gentle fire until all the milk is dried up ; and just before the rice is done, stir in a few drops of essence of any of the above flavourings. Let the rice get cold ; then form it into small round balls, dip them into yolk of egg, sprinkle them with bread crumbs, and fry them in boiling lard for about 10 minutes, turning them about, that they may get equally browned. Drain the greasy moisture from them, by placing them on a cloth in front of the fire for a minute or two ; pile them on a white d'oyley, and send them quickly to table. A small piece of jam is sometimes introduced into the middle of each croquette, which adds very much to the flavour of this favourite dish.

Time.—From ¾ to 1 hour to swell the rice ; about 10 minutes to fry the croquettes.

Average cost, 10*d.*

Sufficient to make 7 or 8 croquettes.   *Seasonable* at any time.

RICE FRITTERS.

1478. INGREDIENTS.—6 oz. of rice, 1 quart of milk, 3 oz. of sugar, 1 oz. of fresh butter, 6 oz. of orange marmalade, 4 eggs.

Mode.—Swell the rice in the milk, with the sugar and butter, over a slow fire until it is perfectly tender, which will be in about ¾ hour. When the rice is done, strain away the milk, should there be any left, and mix with it the marmalade and well-beaten eggs ; stir the whole over the fire until the eggs are set ; then spread the mixture on a dish to the thickness of about ½ inch, or rather thicker. When it is perfectly cold, cut it into long strips, dip them in a batter the same as for apple fritters, and fry them a nice brown. Dish them on a white d'oyley, strew sifted sugar over, and serve quickly.

Time.—About ¾ hour to swell the rice; from 7 to 10 minutes to fry the fritters.

Average cost, 1s. 6d.

Sufficient to make 7 or 8 fritters. *Seasonable* at any time.

RICE SNOWBALLS.
(*A pretty dish for Juvenile Suppers.*)

1479. INGREDIENTS.—6 oz. of rice, 1 quart of milk, flavouring of essence of almonds, sugar to taste, 1 pint of custard made by recipe No. 1423.

Mode.—Boil the rice in the milk, with sugar and a flavouring of essence of almonds, until the former is tender, adding, if necessary, a little more milk, should it dry away too much. When the rice is quite soft, put it into teacups, or *small* round jars, and let it remain until cold; then turn the rice out on a deep glass dish, pour over a custard made by recipe No. 1423, and, on the top of each ball place a small piece of bright-coloured preserve or jelly. Lemon-peel or vanilla may be boiled with the rice instead of the essence of almonds, when either of these is preferred; but the flavouring of the custard must correspond with that of the rice.

Time.—About ¾ hour to swell the rice in the milk.

Average cost, with the custard, 1s. 6d.

Sufficient for 5 or 6 children. *Seasonable* at any time.

RICE SOUFFLE.

1480. INGREDIENTS.—3 tablespoonfuls of ground rice, 1 pint of milk, 5 eggs, pounded sugar to taste, flavouring of lemon-rind, vanilla, coffee, chocolate, or anything that may be preferred, a piece of butter the size of a walnut.

Mode.—Mix the ground rice with 6 tablespoonfuls of the milk quite smoothly, and put it into a saucepan with the remainder of the milk and butter, and keep stirring it over the fire for about ¼ hour, or until the mixture thickens. Separate the yolks from the whites of the eggs, beat the former in a basin, and stir to them the rice and sufficient pounded sugar to sweeten the soufflé; but add this latter ingredient as sparingly as possible, as, the less sugar there is used, the lighter will be the soufflé. Now whisk the whites of the eggs to a stiff froth or snow; mix them with the other preparation, and pour the whole into a soufflé-dish, and put it instantly into the oven; bake it about ½ hour in a moderate oven; take it out, hold a salamander or hot

shovel over the top, sprinkle sifted sugar over it, and send the soufflé
to table in the dish it was baked in, either with a napkin pinned
round, or inclosed in a more ornamental dish. The excellence of this
fashionable dish entirely depends on the proper whisking of the whites
of the eggs, the manner of baking, and the expedition with which it
is sent to table. Soufflés should be served *instantly* from the oven, or
they will sink, and be nothing more than an ordinary pudding.

Time.—About ½ hour. *Average cost,* 1s.

Sufficient for 3 or 4 persons. *Seasonable* at any time.

TO MAKE A SOUFFLE.

1481. INGREDIENTS.—3 heaped tablespoonfuls of potato-flour, rice-
flour, arrowroot, or tapioca, 1 pint of milk, 5 eggs, a piece of butter
the size of a walnut, sifted sugar to taste, ¼ saltspoonful of salt,
flavouring.

Mode.—Mix the potato-flour, or whichever one of the above ingredients is used, with a little of the milk ; put it into a saucepan, with the
remainder of the milk, the butter, salt, and sufficient pounded sugar
to sweeten the whole nicely. Stir these ingredients over the fire until
the mixture thickens ; then take it off the fire, and let it cool a little.
Separate the whites from the yolks of the eggs, beat the latter, and
stir them into the soufflé batter. Now whisk the whites of the eggs
to the firmest possible froth, for on this depends the excellence of the

SOUFFLÉ-PAN.

dish ; stir them to the other ingredients, and
add a few drops of essence of any flavouring that
may be preferred ; such as vanilla, lemon, orange,
ginger, &c. &c. Pour the batter into a soufflé-
dish, put it immediately into the oven, and bake
for about ½ hour ; then take it out, put the dish
into another more ornamental one, such as is made for the purpose ;
hold a salamander or hot shovel over the soufflé, strew it with sifted
sugar, and send it instantly to table. The secret of making a soufflé
well, is to have the eggs well whisked, but particularly the whites,
the oven not too hot, and to send it to table the moment it comes from
the oven. If the soufflé be ever so well made, and it is allowed to
stand before being sent to table, its appearance and goodness will be
entirely spoiled. Soufflés may be flavoured in various ways, but must
be named accordingly. Vanilla is one of the most delicate and recherché flavourings that can be used for this very fashionable dish.

Time.—About ½ hour in the oven ; 2 or 3 minutes to hold the salamander over. *Average cost,* 1s.

Sufficient for 3 or 4 persons. *Seasonable* at any time.

SNOW EGGS, or ŒUFS A LA NEIGE.

(*A very pretty Supper Dish.*)

1482. INGREDIENTS.—4 eggs, ¾ pint of milk, pounded sugar to taste, flavouring of vanilla, lemon-rind, or orange-flower water.

Mode.—Put the milk into a saucepan with sufficient sugar to sweeten it nicely, and the rind of ½ lemon. Let this steep by the side of the fire for ½ hour, when take out the peel; separate the whites from the yolks of the eggs, and whisk the former to a perfectly stiff froth, or until there is no liquid remaining; bring the milk to the boiling-point, and drop in the snow a tablespoonful at a time, and keep turning the eggs until sufficiently cooked. Then place them on a glass dish, beat up the yolks of the eggs, stir to them the milk, add a little more sugar, and strain this mixture into a jug; place the jug in a saucepan of boiling water, and stir it one way until the mixture thickens, but do not allow it to boil, or it will curdle. Pour this custard over the eggs, when they should rise to the surface. They make an exceedingly pretty addition to a supper, and should be put in a cold place after being made. When they are flavoured with vanilla or orange-flower water, it is not necessary to steep the milk. A few drops of the essence of either may be poured in the milk just before the whites are poached. In making the custard, a little more flavouring and sugar should always be added.

Time.—About 2 minutes to poach the whites; 8 minutes to stir the custard.

Average cost, 8*d.*

Sufficient for 4 or 5 persons. *Seasonable* at any time.

STONE CREAM OF TOUS LES MOIS.

1483. INGREDIENTS.—½ lb. of preserve, 1 pint of milk, 2 oz. of lump sugar, 1 heaped tablespoonful of tous les mois, 3 drops of essence of cloves, 3 drops of almond-flavouring.

Mode.—Place the preserve at the bottom of a glass dish; put the milk into a lined saucepan, with the sugar, and make it boil. Mix to a smooth batter the tous les mois, with a very little cold milk; stir it briskly into the boiling milk, add the flavouring, and simmer for 2 minutes. When rather cool, but before turning solid, pour the cream over the jam, and ornament it with strips of red-currant jelly or preserved fruit.

Time.—2 minutes. *Average cost*, 10*d.*

Sufficient for 4 or 5 persons. *Seasonable* at any time.

STRAWBERRY JELLY.

1484. INGREDIENTS.—Strawberries, pounded sugar; to every pint of juice allow 1¼ oz. of isinglass.

Mode.—Pick the strawberries, put them into a pan, squeeze them well with a wooden spoon, add sufficient pounded sugar to sweeten them nicely, and let them remain for 1 hour, that the juice may be extracted; then add ½ pint of water to every pint of juice. Strain the strawberry-juice and water through a bag; measure it, and to every pint allow 1¼ oz. of isinglass, melted and clarified in ¼ pint of water. Mix this with the juice; put the jelly into a mould, and set the mould in ice. A little lemon-juice added to the strawberry-juice improves the flavour of the jelly, if the fruit is very ripe; but it must be well strained before it is put to the other ingredients, or it will make the jelly muddy.

Time.—1 hour to draw the juice.

Average cost, with the best isinglass, 3s.

Sufficient.—Allow 1½ pint of jelly for 5 or 6 persons.

Seasonable in June, July, and August.

SWISS CREAM.

1485. INGREDIENTS.—¼ lb. of macaroons or 6 small sponge-cakes, sherry, 1 pint of cream, 5 oz. of lump sugar, 2 large tablespoonfuls of arrowroot, the rind of 1 lemon, the juice of ½ lemon, 3 tablespoonfuls of milk.

Mode.—Lay the macaroons or sponge-cakes in a glass dish, and pour over them as much sherry as will cover them, or sufficient to soak them well. Put the cream into a lined saucepan, with the sugar and lemon-rind, and let it remain by the side of the fire until the cream is well flavoured, when take out the lemon-rind. Mix the arrowroot smoothly with the cold milk; add this to the cream, and let it boil gently for about 3 minutes, keeping it well stirred. Take it off the fire, stir till nearly cold, when add the lemon-juice, and pour the whole over the cakes. Garnish the cream with strips of angelica, or candied citron cut thin, or bright-coloured jelly or preserve. This cream is exceedingly delicious, flavoured with vanilla instead of lemon: when this flavouring is used, the sherry may be omitted, and the mixture poured over the *dry* cakes.

Time.—About ½ hour to infuse the lemon-rind; 5 minutes to boil the cream.

Average cost, with cream at 1s. per pint, 3s.

Sufficient for 5 or 6 persons. *Seasonable* at any time.

TO MAKE SYLLABUB.

1486. INGREDIENTS.—1 pint of sherry or white wine, ½ grated nutmeg, sugar to taste, 1½ pint of milk.

Mode.—Put the wine into a bowl, with the grated nutmeg and plenty of pounded sugar, and milk into it the above proportion of milk frothed up. Clouted cream may be laid on the top, with pounded cinnamon or nutmeg and sugar; and a little brandy may be added to the wine before the milk is put in. In some counties, cider is substituted for the wine: when this is used, brandy must always be added. Warm milk may be poured on from a spouted jug or teapot; but it must be held very high.

Average cost, 2s.

Sufficient for 5 or 6 persons. *Seasonable* at any time.

TIPSY CAKE.

1487. INGREDIENTS.—1 moulded sponge- or Savoy-cake, sufficient sweet wine or sherry to soak it, 6 tablespoonfuls of brandy, 2 oz. of sweet almonds, 1 pint of rich custard.

Mode.—Procure a cake that is three or four days old,—either sponge, Savoy, or rice answering for the purpose of a tipsy cake. Cut the bottom of the cake level, to make it stand firm in the dish; make a small hole in the centre, and pour in and over the cake sufficient sweet wine or sherry, mixed with the above proportion of brandy, to soak it nicely. When the cake is well soaked, blanch and cut the almonds into strips, stick them all over the cake, and pour round it a good custard, made by recipe No. 1423, allowing 8 eggs instead of 5 to the pint of milk. The cakes are sometimes crumbled and soaked, and a whipped cream heaped over them, the same as for trifles.

TIPSY CAKE.

Time.—About 2 hours to soak the cake. *Average cost*, 4s. 6d.

Sufficient for 1 dish. *Seasonable* at any time.

ALMOND.—The almond-tree is a native of warmer climates than Britain, and is indigenous to the northern parts of Africa and Asia; but it is now commonly cultivated in Italy, Spain, and the south of France. It is not usually grown in Britain, and the fruit seldom ripens in this country: it is much admired for the beauty of its blossoms. In the form of its leaves and blossoms it strongly resembles the peach-tree, and is included in the same genus by botanists; but the fruit, instead of presenting a delicious pulp like the peach, shrivels up as it ripens, and becomes only a tough coriaceous covering to the stone inclosing the eatable kernel, which is surrounded by a thin bitter skin. It flowers early in the spring, and produces fruit in August. There are two sorts of almonds,—sweet and bitter; but they are considered to be only varieties of the species; and though the qualities of the kernels are very different, they are not distinguishable by their appearance.

AN EASY WAY OF MAKING A TIPSY CAKE.

1488. INGREDIENTS.—12 stale small sponge-cakes, raisin wine, ¼ lb. of jam, 1 pint of custard No. 1423.

Mode.—Soak the sponge-cakes, which should be stale (on this account they should be cheaper), in a little raisin wine; arrange them on a deep glass dish in four layers, putting a layer of jam between each, and pour round them a pint of custard, made by recipe No. 1423, decorating the top with cut preserved fruit.

Time.—2 hours to soak the cakes. *Average cost,* 2s. 6d.

Sufficient for 1 dish. *Seasonable* at any time.

TO MAKE A TRIFLE.

1489. INGREDIENTS.—For the whip, 1 pint of cream, 3 oz. of pounded sugar, the whites of 2 eggs, a small glass of sherry or raisin wine. For the trifle, 1 pint of custard, made with 8 eggs to a pint of milk; 6 small sponge-cakes, or 6 slices of sponge-cake; 12 macaroons, 2 dozen ratafias, 2 oz. of sweet almonds, the grated rind of 1 lemon, a layer of raspberry or strawberry jam, ½ pint of sherry or sweet wine, 6 tablespoonfuls of brandy.

Mode.—The whip to lay over the top of the trifle should be made the day before it is required for table, as the flavour is better, and it is

TRIFLE.

much more solid than when prepared the same day. Put into a large bowl the pounded sugar, the whites of the eggs, which should be beaten to a stiff froth, a glass of sherry or sweet wine, and the cream. Whisk these ingredients well in a cool place, and take off the froth with a skimmer as fast as it rises, and put it on a sieve to drain; continue the whisking till there is sufficient of the whip, which must be put away in a cool place to drain. The next day, place the sponge-cakes, macaroons, and ratafias at the bottom of a trifle-dish; pour over them ½ pint of sherry or sweet wine, mixed with 6 tablespoonfuls of brandy, and, should this proportion of wine not be found quite sufficient, add a little more, as the cakes should be well soaked. Over the cakes put the grated lemon-rind, the sweet almonds, blanched and cut into strips, and a layer of raspberry or strawberry jam. Make a good custard by recipe No. 1423, using 8 instead of 5 eggs to the pint of milk, and let this cool a little; then pour it over the cakes, &c. The whip being made the day previously, and the trifle prepared, there remains nothing to do now but heap the whip lightly over the top : this should stand as high as possible, and it may be garnished with strips of bright currant jelly, crystallized sweetmeats, or flowers ; the small coloured comfits are sometimes used for the purpose of garnishing a trifle, but they are now considered rather old-fashioned.

Average cost, with cream at 1s. per pint, 5s. 6d.

Sufficient for 1 trifle.   *Seasonable* at any time.

VANILLA CREAM.

1490. INGREDIENTS.—1 pint of milk, the yolks of 8 eggs, 6 oz. of sugar, 1 oz. of isinglass, flavouring to taste of essence of vanilla.

Mode.—Put the milk and sugar into a saucepan, and let it get hot over a slow fire ; beat up the yolks of the eggs, to which add gradually the sweetened milk ; flavour the whole with essence of vanilla, put the mixture into a jug, and place this jug in a saucepan of boiling water. Stir the contents with a wooden spoon one way until the mixture thickens, but do not allow it to boil, or it will be full of lumps. Take it off the fire ; stir in the isinglass, which should be previously dissolved in about ¼ pint of water, and boiled for 2 or 3 minutes ; pour the

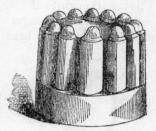

VANILLA-CREAM MOULD.

cream into an oiled mould, put it in a cool place to set, and turn it out carefully on a dish. Instead of using the essence of vanilla, a pod may be boiled in the milk instead, until the flavour is well extracted. A pod, or a pod and a half, will be found sufficient for the above proportion of ingredients.

Time.—About 10 minutes to stir the mixture.

Average cost, with the best isinglass, 2s. 6d.

Sufficient to fill a quart mould.   *Seasonable* at any time.

VANILLE, or VANILLA, is the fruit of the vanillier, a parasitical herbaceous plant, which flourishes in Brazil, Mexico, and Peru. The fruit is a long capsule, thick and fleshy. Certain species of this fruit contain a pulp with a delicious perfume and flavour. Vanilla is principally imported from Mexico. The capsules for export are always picked at perfect maturity. The essence is the form in which it is used generally and most conveniently. Its properties are stimulating and exciting. It is in daily use for ices, chocolates, and flavouring confections generally.

VICTORIA SANDWICHES.

1491. INGREDIENTS.—4 eggs ; their weight in pounded sugar, butter, and flour ; ¼ saltspoonful of salt, a layer of any kind of jam or marmalade.

Mode.—Beat the butter to a cream ; dredge in the flour and pounded sugar ; stir these ingredients well together, and add the eggs, which should be previously thoroughly whisked. When the mixture has been well beaten for about 10 minutes, butter a Yorkshire-pudding tin, pour in the batter, and bake it in a moderate oven for 20 minutes. Let it cool, spread one half of the cake with a layer of nice preserve, place over it the other half of the cake, press the pieces slightly together, and then cut it into long finger-pieces; pile them in cross-bars on a glass dish, and serve.

Time.—20 minutes.   *Average cost*, 1s. 3d.

Sufficient for 5 or 6 persons.   *Seasonable* at any time.

WHIPPED CREAM, for putting on Trifles, serving in Glasses, &c.

1492. INGREDIENTS.—To every pint of cream allow 3 oz. of pounded sugar, 1 glass of sherry or any kind of sweet white wine, the rind of ½ lemon, the white of 1 egg.

Mode.—Rub the sugar on the lemon-rind, and pound it in a mortar until quite fine, and beat up the white of the egg until quite stiff;

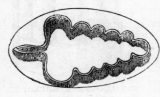

PASTRY LEAF.

put the cream into a large bowl, with the sugar, wine, and beaten egg, and whip it to a froth; as fast as the froth rises, take it off with a skimmer, and put it on a sieve to drain, in a cool place. This should be made the day before it is wanted, as the whip is then so much firmer. The cream should be whipped in a cool place, and in summer, over ice, if it is obtainable. A plain whipped cream may be served on a glass dish, and garnished with strips of angelica, or pastry leaves, or pieces of bright-coloured jelly: it makes a very pretty addition to the supper-table.

Time.—About 1 hour to whip the cream.

Average cost, with cream at 1s. per pint, 1s. 9d.

Sufficient for 1 dish or 1 trifle.   *Seasonable* at any time.

WHIPPPED SYLLABUBS.

1493. INGREDIENTS.—½ pint of cream, ¼ pint of sherry, half that quantity of brandy, the juice of ½ lemon, a little grated nutmeg, 3 oz. of pounded sugar, whipped cream the same as for trifle No. 1489.

Mode.—Mix all the ingredients together, put the syllabub into glasses, and over the top of them heap a little whipped cream, made in the same manner as for trifle No. 1489. Solid syllabub is made by whisking or milling the mixture to a stiff froth, and putting it in the glasses, without the whipped cream at the top.

Average cost, 1s. 8d.

Sufficient to fill 8 or 9 glasses.   *Seasonable* at any time.

THE CURE'S OMELET.

"Every one knows," says Brillat Savarin, in his "Physiology of Taste," "that for twenty years Madame Récamier was the most beautiful woman in Paris. It is also well known that she was exceedingly charitable, and took a great interest in every benevolent work. Wishing to consult the Curé of ———— respecting the working of an institution, she went to his house at five o'clock in the afternoon, and was much astonished at finding him already at his dinner-table.

" Madame Récamier wished to retire, but the Curé would not hear of it. A neat white cloth covered the table ; some good old wine sparkled in a crystal decanter ; the porcelain was of the best ; the plates had heaters of boiling water beneath them ; a neatly-costumed maid-servant was in attendance. The repast was a compromise between frugality and luxury. The crawfish-soup had just been removed, and there was on the table a salmon-trout, an omelet, and a salad.

" 'My dinner will tell you,' said the worthy Curé, with a smile, 'that it is fast-day, according to our Church's regulations.' Madame Récamier and her host attacked the trout, the sauce served with which betrayed a skilful hand, the countenance of the Curé the while showing satisfaction.

"And now they fell upon the omelet, which was round, sufficiently thick, and cooked, so to speak, to a hair's-breadth.

"As the spoon entered the omelet, a thick rich juice issued from it, pleasant to the eye as well as to the smell ; the dish became full of it ; and our fair friend owns that, between the perfume and the sight, it made her mouth water.

" 'It is an *omelette au thon*' (that is to say, a tunny omelet), said the Curé, noticing, with the greatest delight, the emotion of Madame Récamier, ' and few people taste it without lavishing praises on it.'

" ' It surprises me not at all,' returned the beauty ; ' never has so enticing an omelet met my gaze at any of our lay tables.'

" ' My cook understands them well, I think.'

" ' Yes,' added Madame, ' I never ate anything so delightful.' "

Then came the salad, which Savarin recommends to all who place confidence in him. It refreshes without exciting ; and he has a theory that it makes people younger.

Amidst pleasant converse the dessert arrived. It consisted of three apples, cheese, and a plate of preserves ; and then upon a little round table was served the Mocha coffee, for which France has been, and is, so justly famous.

" ' I never,' said the Curé, ' take spirits ; I always offer liqueurs to my guests, but reserve the use of them, myself, to my old age, if it should please Providence to grant me that.'

" Finally, the charming Madame Récamier took her leave, and told all her friends of the delicious omelet which she had seen and partaken of."

And Brillat Savarin, in his capacity as the Layard of the concealed

3 c

treasures of Gastronòmia, has succeeded in withdrawing from obscurity the details of the preparation of which so much had been said, and which he imagines to be as wholesome as it was agreeable.

Here follows the recipe : —

OMELETTE AU THON.

1494. TAKE, for 6 persons, the roes of 2 carp ;* bleach them, by putting them, for 5 minutes, in boiling water slightly salted. Take a piece of fresh tunny about the size of a hen's egg, to which add a small shalot already chopped ; hash up together the roe and the tunny, so as to mix them well, and throw the whole into a saucepan, with a sufficient quantity of very good butter : whip it up until the butter is melted ! This constitutes the specialty of the omelet. Take a second piece of butter, *à discrétion*, mix it with parsley and herbs, place it in a long-shaped dish destined to receive the omelet ; squeeze the juice of a lemon over it, and place it on hot embers. Beat up 12 eggs (the fresher the better) ; throw up the sauté of roe and tunny, stirring it so as to mix all well together ; then make your omelet in the usual manner, endeavouring to turn it out long, thick, and soft. Spread it carefully on the dish prepared for it, and serve at once. This dish ought to be reserved for recherché déjeûners, or for assemblies where amateurs meet who know how to eat well : washed down with a good old wine, it will work wonders.

Note. — The roe and the tunny must be beaten up (sauté) without allowing them to boil, to prevent their hardening, which would prevent them mixing well with the eggs. Your dish should be hollowed towards the centre, to allow the gravy to concentrate, that it may be helped with a spoon. The dish ought to be slightly heated, otherwise the cold china will extract all the heat from the omelet.

* An American writer says he has followed this recipe, substituting pike, shad, &c., in the place of carp, and can recommend all these also, with a quiet conscience. Any fish, indeed, may be used with success.

CHAPTER XXX.

GENERAL OBSERVATIONS ON PRESERVES, CONFECTIONARY, ICES, AND DESSERT DISHES.

PRESERVES.

1495. FROM the nature of vegetable substances, and chiefly from their not passing so rapidly into the putrescent state as animal bodies, the mode of preserving them is somewhat different, although the general principles are the same. All the means of preservation are put in practice occasionally for fruits and the various parts of vegetables, according to the nature of the species, the climate, the uses to which they are applied, &c. Some are dried, as nuts, raisins, sweet herbs, &c.; others are preserved by means of sugar, such as many fruits whose delicate juices would be lost by drying; some are preserved by means of vinegar, and chiefly used as condiments or pickles; a few also by salting, as French beans; while others are preserved in spirits. We have, however, in this place to treat of the best methods of preserving fruits. Fruit is a most important item in the economy of health; the epicurean can scarcely be said to have any luxuries without it; therefore, as it is so invaluable, when we cannot have it fresh, we must have it preserved. It has long been a desideratum to preserve fruits by some cheap method, yet by such as would keep them fit for the various culinary purposes, as making tarts and other similar dishes. The expense of preserving them with sugar is a serious objection; for, except the sugar is used in considerable quantities, the success is very uncertain. Sugar also overpowers and destroys the sub-acid taste so desirable in many fruits: those which are preserved in this manner are chiefly intended for the dessert. Fruits intended for preservation should be gathered in the morning, in dry weather, with the morning sun upon them, if possible; they will then have their fullest flavour, and keep in good condition longer than when gathered at any other time. Until fruit can be used, it should be placed in the dairy, an ice-house, or a refrigerator. In an ice-house it will remain fresh and plump for several days. Fruit gathered in wet or foggy weather will soon be mildewed, and be of no service for preserves.

1496. Having secured the first and most important contribution to the manufacture of preserves,—the fruit, the next consideration is the preparation of the syrup in which the fruit is to be suspended; and this requires much care. In the confectioner's art there is a great nicety in proportioning the degree of concentration of the syrup very exactly to each particular case; and they know this by signs, and express it by certain technical terms. But to distinguish these properly requires very great attention and considerable experience. The principal thing to be acquainted with is the fact, that, in proportion as the syrup is longer boiled, its water will become evaporated, and its consistency will be thicker. Great care must be taken in the management of the fire, that the syrup does not boil over, and that the boiling is not carried to such an extent as to burn the sugar.

1497. The first degree of consistency is called *the thread,* which is subdivided into the little and great thread. If you dip the finger into the syrup and apply it to the thumb, the tenacity of the syrup will, on separating the finger and thumb, afford a thread, which shortly breaks: this is the little thread. If the thread, from the greater tenacity, and, consequently, greater strength of the syrup, admits of a greater extension of the finger and thumb, it is called the great thread. There are half a dozen other terms and experiments for testing the various thickness of the boiling sugar towards the consistency called *caramel;* but that degree of sugar-boiling belongs to the confectioner. A solution of sugar prepared by dissolving two parts of double-refined sugar (the best sugar is the most economical for preserves) in one of water, and boiling this a little, affords a syrup of the right degree of strength, and which neither ferments nor crystallizes. This appears to be the degree called *smooth* by the confectioners, and is proper to be used for the purposes of preserves. The syrup employed should sometimes be clarified, which is done in the following manner:—Dissolve 2 lbs. of loaf sugar in a pint of water; add to this solution the white of an egg, and beat it well. Put the preserving-pan upon the fire with the solution; stir it with a wooden spatula, and, when it begins to swell and boil up, throw in some cold water or a little oil, to damp the boiling; for, as it rises suddenly, if it should boil over, it would take fire, being of a very inflammable nature. Let it boil up again; then take it off, and remove carefully the scum that has risen. Boil the solution again, throw in a little more cold water, remove the scum, and so on for three or four times successively; then strain it. It is considered to be sufficiently boiled when some taken up in a spoon pours out like oil.

1498. Although sugar passes so easily into the state of fermentation, and is, in fact, the only substance capable of undergoing the vinous stage of that process, yet it will not ferment at all if the quantity be sufficient to constitute a very strong syrup : hence, syrups are used to preserve fruits and other vegetable substances from the changes they would undergo if left to themselves. Before sugar was in use, honey was employed to preserve many vegetable productions, though this substance has now given way to the juice of the sugar-cane.

1499. The fruits that are the most fit for preservation in syrup are, apricots, peaches, nectarines, apples, greengages, plums of all kinds, and pears. As an example, take some apricots not too ripe, make a small slit at the stem end, and push out the stone ; simmer them in water till they are softened and about half done, and afterwards throw them into cold water. When they have cooled, take them out and drain them. Put the apricots into the preserving-pan with sufficient syrup to cover them ; let them boil up three or four times, and then skim them ; remove them from the fire, pour them into an earthen pan, and let them cool till next day. Boil them up three days successively, skimming each time, and they will then be finished and in a state fit to be put into pots for use. After each boiling, it is proper to examine into the state of the syrup when cold ; if too thin, it will bear additional boiling ; if too thick, it may be lowered with more syrup of the usual standard. The reason why the fruit is emptied out of the preserving-pan into an earthen pan is, that the acid of the fruit acts upon the copper, of which the preserving-pans are usually made. From this example the process of preserving fruits by syrup will be easily comprehended. The first object is to soften the fruit by blanching or boiling it in water, in order that the syrup by which it is preserved may penetrate through its substance.

1500. Many fruits, when preserved by boiling, lose much of their peculiar and delicate flavour, as, for instance, pine-apples ; and this inconvenience may, in some instances, be remedied by preserving them without heat. Cut the fruit in slices about one fifth of an inch thick, strew powdered loaf sugar an eighth of an inch thick on the bottom of a jar, and put the slices on it. Put more sugar on this, and then another layer of the slices, and so on till the jar is full. Place the jar with the fruit up to the neck in boiling water, and keep it there till the sugar is completely dissolved, which may take half an hour, removing the scum as it rises. Lastly, tie a wet bladder over the mouth of the jar, or cork and wax it.

1501. Any of the fruits that have been preserved in syrup may be converted into dry preserves, by first draining them from the syrup, and then drying them in a stove or very moderate oven, adding to them a quantity of powdered loaf sugar, which will gradually penetrate the fruit, while the fluid parts of the syrup gently evaporate. They should be dried in the stove or oven on a sieve, and turned every six or eight hours, fresh powdered sugar being sifted over them every time they are turned.   Afterwards, they are to be kept in a dry situation, in drawers or boxes.   Currants and cherries preserved whole in this manner, in bunches, are extremely elegant, and have a fine flavour.   In this way it is, also, that orange and lemon chips are preserved.

1502. Marmalades, jams, and fruit pastes are of the same nature, and are now in very general request.   They are prepared without difficulty, by attending to a very few directions ; they are somewhat expensive, but may be kept without spoiling for a considerable time.   Marmalades and jams differ little from each other : they are preserves of a half-liquid consistency, made by boiling the pulp of fruits, and sometimes part of the rinds, with sugar.   The appellation of marmalade is applied to those confitures which are composed of the firmer fruits, as pineapples or the rinds of oranges ; whereas jams are made of the more juicy berries, such as strawberries, raspberries, currants, mulberries, &c.   Fruit pastes are a kind of marmalades, consisting of the pulp of fruits, first evaporated to a proper consistency, and afterwards boiled with sugar.   The mixture is then poured into a mould, or spread on sheets of tin, and subsequently dried in the oven or stove till it has acquired the state of a paste.   From a sheet of this paste, strips may be cut and formed into any shape that may be desired, as knots, rings, &c.   Jams require the same care and attention in the boiling as marmalade ; the slightest degree of burning communicates a disagreeable empyreumatic taste, and if they are not boiled sufficiently, they will not keep.   That they may keep, it is necessary not to be sparing of sugar.

1503. In all the operations for preserve-making, when the preserving-pan is used, it should not be placed on the fire, but on a trivet, unless the jam is made on a hot plate, when this is not necessary.   If the pan is placed close on to the fire, the preserve is very liable to burn, and the colour and flavour be consequently spoiled.

1504. Fruit jellies are compounds of the juices of fruits combined with sugar, concentrated, by boiling, to such a consistency that the liquid, upon cooling, assumes the form of a tremulous jelly.

1505. Before fruits are candied, they must first be boiled in syrup, after which they are taken out and dried on a stove, or before the fire ; the syrup is then to be concentrated, or boiled to a candy height, and the fruit dipped in it, and again laid on the stove to dry and candy : they are then to be put into boxes, and kept dry.

1506. Conserves consist of fresh vegetable matters beat into a uniform mass with refined sugar, and they are intended to preserve the virtues and properties of recent flowers, leaves, roots, peels, or fruits, unaltered, and as near as possible to what they were when fresh gathered, and to give them an agreeable taste.

1507. The last mentioned, but not the least-important preparation of fruit, is the *compôte*, a confiture made at the moment of need, and with much less sugar than would be ordinarily put to preserves. They are most wholesome things, suitable to most stomachs which cannot accommodate themselves to raw fruit or a large portion of sugar : they are the happy medium, and far better than ordinary stewed fruit.

CONFECTIONARY.

1508. In speaking of confectionary, it should be remarked that all the various preparations above named come, strictly speaking, under that head ; for the various fruits, flowers, herbs, roots, and juices, which, when boiled with sugar, were formerly employed in pharmacy as well as for sweetmeats, were called *confections,* from the Latin word *conficere,* 'to make up ;' but the term confectionary embraces a very large class indeed of sweet food, many kinds of which should not be attempted in the ordinary cuisine. The thousand and one ornamental dishes that adorn the tables of the wealthy should be purchased from the confectioner : they cannot profitably be made at home. Apart from these, cakes, biscuits, and tarts, &c., the class of sweetmeats called confections may be thus classified :—1. Liquid confects, or fruits either whole or in pieces, preserved by being immersed in a fluid transparent syrup ; as the liquid confects of apricots, green citrons, and many foreign fruits. 2. Dry confects are those which, after having been boiled in the syrup, are taken out and put to dry in an oven, as citron and orange-peel, &c. 3. Marmalade, jams, and pastes, a kind of soft compounds made of the pulp of fruits or other vegetable substances, beat up with sugar or honey ; such as oranges, apricots, pears, &c. 4. Jellies are the juices of fruits boiled with sugar to a pretty thick consistency, so as, upon cooling, to form a trembling jelly ; as currant, gooseberry, apple jelly, &c. 5. Conserves are a kind of dry confects, made by beating up flowers, fruits, &c., with sugar, not dissolved. 6. Candies are fruits candied over with sugar after having been boiled in the syrup.

DESSERT DISHES.

1509. With moderns the dessert is not so profuse, nor does it hold the same relationship to the dinner that it held with the ancients,—the Romans more especially. On ivory tables they would spread hundreds of different kinds of raw, cooked, and preserved fruits, tarts and cakes, as substitutes for the more substantial comestibles with which the guests were satiated. However, as late as the reigns of our two last Georges, fabulous sums were often expended upon fanciful desserts. The dessert certainly repays, in its general effect, the expenditure upon it of much pains ; and it may be said, that if there be any poetry at all in meals, or the process of feeding, there is poetry in the dessert, the materials for which should be selected with taste, and, of course, must depend, in a great measure, upon the season. Pines, melons, grapes, peaches, nectarines, plums, strawberries, apples, pears, oranges, almonds, raisins, figs, walnuts, filberts, medlars, cherries, &c. &c., all kinds of dried fruits, and choice and delicately-flavoured cakes and biscuits, make up the dessert, together with the most costly and *recherché* wines. The shape of the dishes varies at different periods, the prevailing fashion at present being oval and circular dishes on stems. The patterns and colours are also subject to changes of fashion ; some persons selecting china, chaste in pattern and colour ; others, elegantly-shaped glass dishes on stems, with gilt edges. The beauty of the dessert services at the tables of the wealthy tends to enhance the splendour of the plate. The general mode of putting a dessert on table, now the elegant tazzas are fashionable, is, to place them down the middle of the table, a tall and short dish alternately ; the fresh fruits being arranged on the tall dishes, and dried fruits, bon-bons, &c., on small round or oval glass plates. The garnishing needs especial attention, as the contrast of the brilliant-coloured fruits with nicely-arranged foliage is very charming. The garnish *par excellence* for dessert is the ice-plant ; its crystallized dewdrops producing a marvellous effect in the height of summer, giving a most inviting sense of coolness to the fruit it encircles. The double-edged mallow, strawberry, and vine leaves have a pleasing effect ; and for winter desserts, the bay, cuba, and laurel are sometimes used. In town, the expense and difficulty of obtaining natural foliage is great, but paper and composite leaves are to be purchased at an almost nominal price. Mixed fruits of the larger sort are now frequently served on one dish. This mode admits of the display of much taste in the arrangement of the fruit : for instance, a pine in the centre of the dish, surrounded with large plums of various sorts and colours, mixed with pears, rosy-cheeked apples, all arranged with a due regard to colour, have a very good effect. Again, apples and pears look well mingled with plums and grapes, hanging from the border of the dish in a *négligé* sort of manner, with a large bunch of the same fruit lying on the top of the apples. A dessert would not now be considered complete without candied and preserved fruits and confections. The candied fruits may be purchased at a less cost than they can be manufactured at home. They are preserved abroad in most ornamental and elegant forms. And since, from the facilities of travel, we have become so familiar with the tables of the French, chocolate in different forms is indispensable to our desserts.

ICES.

1510. Ices are composed, it is scarcely necessary to say, of congealed cream or water, combined sometimes with liqueurs or other flavouring ingredients, or more generally with the juices of fruits. At desserts, or at some evening parties, ices are scarcely to be dispensed with. The principal utensils required for making ice-creams are ice-tubs, freezing-pots, spaddles, and a cellaret. The tub must be large enough to contain about a bushel of ice, pounded small, when brought out of the ice-house, and mixed very carefully with either *salt, nitre,* or *soda.* The freezing-pot is best made of pewter. If it be of tin, as is sometimes the case, the congelation goes on too rapidly in it for the thorough intermingling of its contents, on which the excellence of the ice greatly depends. The spaddle is generally made of copper, kept bright and clean. The cellaret is a tin vessel, in which ices are kept for a short time from dissolving. The method to be pursued in the freezing process must be attended to. When the ice-tub is prepared with fresh-pounded ice and salt, the freezing-pot is put into it up to its cover. The articles to be congealed are then poured into it and covered over; but to prevent the ingredients from separating and the heaviest of them from falling to the bottom of the mould, it is requisite to turn the freezing-pot round and round by the handle, so as to keep its contents moving until the congelation commences. As soon as this is perceived (the cover of the pot being occasionally taken off for the purpose of noticing when freezing takes place), the cover is immediately closed over it, ice is put upon it, and it is left in this state till it is served. The use of the spaddle is to stir up and remove from the sides of the freezing-pot the cream, which in the shaking may have washed against it, and by stirring it in with the rest, to prevent waste of it occurring. Any negligence in stirring the contents of the freezing-pot before congelation takes place, will destroy the whole: either the sugar sinks to the bottom and leaves the ice insufficiently sweetened, or lumps are formed, which disfigure and discolour it.

1511. The aged, the delicate, and children should abstain from ices or iced beverages; even the strong and healthy should partake of them in moderation. They should be taken immediately after the repast, or some hours after, because the taking these substances *during* the process of digestion is apt to provoke indisposition. It is necessary, then, that this function should have scarcely commenced, or that it should be completely finished, before partaking of ices. It is also necessary to abstain from them when persons are very warm, or immediately after taking violent exercise, as in some cases they have produced illnesses which have ended fatally.

[Do ladies know to whom they are indebted for the introduction of ices, which all the fair sex are passionately fond of?—To Catherine de' Medici. Will not this fact cover a multitude of sins committed by the instigator of St. Bartholomew?]

RECIPES.

—◆—

CHAPTER XXXI.

TO MAKE SYRUP FOR COMPOTES, &c.

1512. INGREDIENTS.—To every lb. of sugar allow 1½ pint of water.

Mode.—Boil the sugar and water together for ¼ hour, carefully removing the scum as it rises : the syrup is then ready for the fruit. The articles boiled in this syrup will not keep for any length of time, it being suitable only for dishes intended to be eaten immediately. A larger proportion of sugar must be added for a syrup intended to keep.

Time.—¼ hour.

TO CLARIFY SUGAR OR SYRUP.

1513. INGREDIENTS.—To every lb. of sugar allow ½ pint of water and ½ the white of an egg.

Mode.—Put the sugar, water, and the white of the egg, which should be well beaten, into a preserving-pan or lined saucepan ; and do not put it on the fire till the sugar is dissolved. Then place it on the fire, and when it boils, throw in a teacupful of cold water, and do not stir the sugar after this is added. Bring it to the boiling-point again, and then place the pan by the side of the fire, for the preparation to settle. Remove all the scum, and the sugar will be ready for use. The scum should be placed on a sieve, so that what syrup runs from it may be boiled up again : this must also be well skimmed.

Time.—20 minutes for the sugar to dissolve ; 5 minutes to boil.

Note.—The above two recipes are those used in the preparation of dishes usually made at home. There are many degrees of boiling sugar, which process requires great care, attention, and experience. Caramel sugar, which makes an elegant cover for sweetmeats, is difficult to prepare, and is best left to an experienced confectioner. We give the recipe, for those of our readers who care to attempt the operation.

TO BOIL SUGAR TO CARAMEL.

1514. INGREDIENTS.—To every lb. of lump sugar allow 1 gill of spring water.

Mode.—Boil the sugar and water together very quickly over a clear fire, skimming it very carefully as soon as it boils. Keep it boiling until the sugar snaps when a little of it is dropped in a pan of cold water. If it remains hard, the sugar has attained the right degree; then squeeze in a little lemon-juice, and let it remain an instant on the fire. Set the pan into another of cold water, and the caramel is then ready for use. The insides of well-oiled moulds are often ornamented with this sugar, which with a fork should be spread over them in fine threads or network. A dish of light pastry, tastefully arranged, looks very prettily with this sugar spun lightly over it. The sugar must be carefully watched, and taken up the instant it is done. Unless the cook is very experienced and thoroughly understands her business, it is scarcely worth while to attempt to make this elaborate ornament, as it may be purchased quite as economically at a confectioner's, if the failures in the preparation are taken into consideration.

COMPOTE OF APPLES.

(*Soyer's Recipe,—a Dessert Dish.*)

1515. INGREDIENTS.—6 ripe apples, 1 lemon, ½ lb. of lump sugar, ½ pint of water.

Mode.—Select the apples of a moderate size, peel them, cut them in halves, remove the cores, and rub each piece over with a little lemon. Put the sugar and water together into a lined saucepan, and let them boil until forming a thickish syrup, when lay in the apples with the rind of the lemon cut thin, and the juice of the same. Let the apples simmer till tender; then take them out very carefully, drain them on a sieve, and reduce the syrup by boiling it quickly for a few minutes.

COMPÔTE OF APPLES.

When both are cold, arrange the apples neatly on a glass dish, pour over the syrup, and garnish with strips of green angelica or candied citron. Smaller apples may be dressed in the same manner: they should not be divided in half, but peeled and the cores pushed out with a vegetable-cutter.

Time.—10 minutes to boil the sugar and water together; from 15 to 25 minutes to simmer the apples.

Average cost, 6d.

Sufficient for 4 or 5 persons. *Seasonable* from July to March.

APPLE GINGER.

(A Dessert Dish.)

1516. INGREDIENTS.—2 lbs. of any kind of hard apples, 2 lbs. of loaf sugar, 1½ pint of water, 1 oz. of tincture of ginger.

Mode.—Boil the sugar and water until they form a rich syrup, adding the ginger when it boils up. Pare, core, and cut the apples into pieces; dip them in cold water to preserve the colour, and boil them in the syrup until transparent; but be careful not to let them break. Put the pieces of apple into jars, pour over the syrup, and carefully exclude the air, by well covering them. It will remain good some time, if kept in a dry place.

Time.—From 5 to 10 minutes to boil the syrup; about ½ hour to simmer the apples.

Average cost, 2s.

Sufficient for 7 or 8 persons.

Seasonable.—Make this in September, October, or November.

APPLE JAM.

1517. INGREDIENTS.—To every lb. of fruit weighed after being pared, cored, and sliced, allow ¾ lb. of preserving-sugar, the grated rind of 1 lemon, the juice of ½ lemon.

Mode.—Peel the apples, core and slice them very thin, and be particular that they are all the same sort. Put them into a jar, stand this in a saucepan of boiling water, and let the apples stew until quite tender. Previously to putting the fruit into the jar, weigh it, to ascertain the proportion of sugar that may be required. Put the apples into a preserving-pan, crush the sugar to small lumps, and add it, with the grated lemon-rind and juice, to the apples. Simmer these over the fire for ½ hour, reckoning from the time the jam begins to simmer properly; remove the scum as it rises, and when the jam is done, put it into pots for use. Place a piece of oiled paper over the jam, and to exclude the air, cover the pots with tissue-paper dipped in the white of an egg, and stretched over the top. This jam will keep good for a long time.

Time.—About 2 hours to stew in the jar; ½ hour to boil after the jam begins to simmer.

Average cost, for this quantity, 5s.

Sufficient.—7 or 8 lbs. of apples for 6 pots of jam.

Seasonable.—Make this in September, October, or November.

APPLE JELLY.

I.

1518. INGREDIENTS.—To 6 lbs. of apples allow 3 pints of water ; to every quart of juice allow 2 lbs. of loaf sugar ;—the juice of ½ lemon.

Mode.—Pare, core, and cut the apples into slices, and put them into a jar, with water in the above proportion. Place them in a cool oven, with the jar well covered, and when the juice is thoroughly drawn and the apples are quite soft, strain them through a jelly-bag. To every quart of juice allow 2 lbs. of loaf sugar, which should be crushed to small lumps, and put into a preserving-pan with the juice. Boil these together for rather more than ½ hour, remove the scum as it rises, add the lemon-juice just before it is done, and put the jelly into pots for use. This preparation is useful for garnishing sweet dishes, and may be turned out for dessert.

Time.—The apples to be put in the oven over-night, and left till morning ; rather more than ½ hour to boil the jelly.

Average cost, for this quantity, 3s.

Sufficient for 6 small pots of jelly.

Seasonable.—This should be made in September, October, or November.

II.

1519. INGREDIENTS.—Apples, water ; to every pint of syrup allow ¾ lb. of loaf sugar.

Mode.—Pare and cut the apples into pieces, remove the cores, and put them in a preserving-pan with sufficient cold water to cover them. Let them boil for an hour ; then drain the syrup from them through a hair sieve or jelly-bag, and measure the juice ; to every pint allow ¾ lb. of loaf sugar, and boil these together for ¾ hour, removing every particle of scum as it rises, and keeping the jelly well stirred, that it may not burn. A little lemon-rind may be boiled with the apples, and a small quantity of strained lemon-juice may be put in the jelly just before it is done, when the flavour is liked. This jelly may be ornamented with preserved greengages, or any other preserved fruit, and will turn out very prettily for dessert. It should be stored away in small pots.

Time.—1 hour to boil the fruit and water ; ¾ hour to boil the juice with the sugar.

Average cost, for 6 lbs. of apples, with the other ingredients in proportion, 3s.

Sufficient for 6 small pots of jelly.

Seasonable.—Make this in September, October, or November.

TO PRESERVE APPLES IN QUARTERS, in imitation of Ginger.

1520. INGREDIENTS.—To every lb. of apples allow ¾ lb. of sugar, 1½ oz. of the best white ginger; 1 oz. of ginger to every ½ pint of water.

Mode.—Peel, core, and quarter the apples, and put the fruit, sugar, and ginger in layers into a wide-mouthed jar, and let them remain for 2 days; then infuse 1 oz. of ginger in ⅓ pint of boiling water, and cover it closely, and let it remain for 1 day: this quantity of ginger and water is for 3 lbs. of apples, with the other ingredients in proportion. Put the apples, &c., into a preserving-pan with the water strained from the ginger, and boil till the apples look clear and the syrup is rich, which will be in about an hour. The rind of a lemon may be added just before the apples have finished boiling; and great care must be taken not to break the pieces of apple in putting them into the jars. Serve on glass dishes for dessert.

Time.—2 days for the apples to remain in the jar with sugar, &c.; 1 day to infuse the ginger; about 1 hour to boil the apples.

Average cost, for 3 lbs. of apples, with the other ingredients in proportion, 2s. 3d.

Sufficient.—3 lbs. should fill 3 moderate-sized jars.

Seasonable.—This should be made in September, October, or November.

COMPOTE OF APRICOTS.

(An elegant Dish.)

1521. INGREDIENTS.—½ pint of syrup No. 1512, 12 green apricots.

Mode.—Make the syrup by recipe No. 1512, and, when it is ready, put in the apricots whilst the syrup is boiling. Simmer them very gently until tender, taking care not to let them break; take them out carefully, arrange them on a glass dish, let the syrup cool a little, pour it over the apricots, and, when cold, serve.

Time.—From 15 to 20 minutes to simmer the apricots.

Average cost, 9d.

Sufficient for 4 or 5 persons.

Seasonable in June and July, with green apricots.

APRICOT JAM or MARMALADE.

1522. INGREDIENTS.—To every lb. of ripe apricots, weighed after being skinned and stoned, allow 1 lb. of sugar.

Mode.—Pare the apricots, which should be ripe, as thinly as possible, break them in half, and remove the stones. Weigh the fruit, and to every lb. allow the same proportion of loaf sugar. Pound the sugar very finely in a mortar, strew it over the apricots, which should be placed on dishes, and let them remain for 12 hours. Break the stones, blanch the kernels, and put them with the sugar and fruit into a preserving-pan. Let these simmer very gently until clear; take out the pieces of apricot singly as they become so, and, as fast as the scum rises, carefully remove it. Put the apricots into small jars, pour over them the syrup and kernels, cover the jam with pieces of paper dipped in the purest salad-oil, and stretch over the top of the jars tissue-paper, cut about 2 inches larger and brushed over with the white of an egg: when dry, it will be perfectly hard and air-tight.

Time.—12 hours sprinkled with sugar; about ¾ hour to boil the jam.

Average cost.—When cheap, apricots may be purchased for preserving at about 1s. 6d. per gallon.

Sufficient,—10 lbs. of fruit for 12 pots of jam.

Seasonable.—Make this in August or September.

BARBERRIES IN BUNCHES.

1523. INGREDIENTS.—1 pint of syrup No. 1513, barberries.

Mode.—Prepare some small pieces of clean white wood, 3 inches long and ¼ inch wide, and tie the fruit on to these in nice bunches. Have ready some clear syrup, made by recipe No. 1513; put in the barberries, and simmer them in it for 2 successive days, boiling them for nearly ½ hour each day, and covering them each time with the syrup when cold. When the fruit looks perfectly clear, it is sufficiently done, and should be stored away in pots, with the syrup poured over, or the fruit may be candied.

Time.—½ hour to simmer each day.

Seasonable in autumn.

Note.—The berries in their natural state make a very pretty garnishing for dishes, and may even be used for the same purpose, preserved as above, and look exceedingly nice on sweet dishes.

TO MAKE BARLEY-SUGAR.

1524. INGREDIENTS.—To every lb. of sugar allow ½ pint of water, ½ the white of an egg.

Mode.—Put the sugar into a well-tinned saucepan, with the water, and, when the former is dissolved, set it over a moderate fire, adding the well-beaten egg before the mixture gets warm, and stir it well together. When it boils, remove the scum as it rises, and keep it boiling until no more appears, and the syrup looks perfectly clear; then strain it through a fine sieve or muslin bag, and put it back into the saucepan. Boil it again like caramel, until it is brittle, when a little is dropped in a basin of cold water: it is then sufficiently boiled. Add a little lemon-juice and a few drops of essence of lemon, and let it stand for a minute or two. Have ready a marble slab or large dish, rubbed over with salad-oil; pour on it the sugar, and cut it into strips with a pair of scissors: these strips should then be twisted, and the barley-sugar stored away in a very dry place. It may be formed into lozenges or drops, by dropping the sugar in a very small quantity at a time on to the oiled slab or dish.

Time.—¼ hour. *Average cost, 7d.*

Sufficient for 5 or 6 sticks.

CARROT JAM TO IMITATE APRICOT PRESERVE.

1525. INGREDIENTS.—Carrots; to every lb. of carrot pulp allow 1 lb. of pounded sugar, the grated rind of 1 lemon, the strained juice of 2, 6 chopped bitter almonds, 2 tablespoonfuls of brandy.

Mode.—Select young carrots; wash and scrape them clean, cut them into round pieces, put them into a saucepan with sufficient water to cover them, and let them simmer until perfectly soft; then beat them through a sieve. Weigh the pulp, and to every lb. allow the above ingredients. Put the pulp into a preserving-pan with the sugar, and let this boil for 5 minutes, stirring and skimming all the time. When cold, add the lemon-rind and juice, almonds and brandy; mix these well with the jam; then put it into pots, which must be well covered and kept in a dry place. The brandy may be omitted, but the preserve will then not keep: with the brandy it will remain good for months.

Time.—About ¾ hour to boil the carrots; 5 minutes to simmer the pulp.

Average cost, 1s. 2d. for 1 lb. of pulp, with the other ingredients in proportion.

Sufficient to fill 3 pots. *Seasonable* from July to December.

TO MAKE CHERRY BRANDY.

1526. INGREDIENTS.—Morella cherries, good brandy; to every lb. of cherries allow 3 oz. of pounded sugar.

Mode.—Have ready some glass bottles, which must be perfectly dry. Ascertain that the cherries are not too ripe and are freshly gathered, and cut off about half of the stalks. Put them into the bottles, with the above proportion of sugar to every lb. of fruit; strew this in between the cherries, and, when the bottles are nearly full, pour in sufficient brandy to reach just below the cork. A few peach or apricot kernels will add much to their flavour, or a few blanched bitter almonds. Put corks or bungs into the bottles, tie over them a piece of bladder, and store away in a dry place. The cherries will be fit to eat in 2 or 3 months, and will remain good for years. They are liable to shrivel and become tough if too much sugar be added to them.

Average cost, 1s. to 1s. 6d. per lb.

Sufficient.—1 lb. of cherries and about ¼ pint of brandy for a quart bottle.

Seasonable in August and September.

DRIED CHERRIES.

1527. CHERRIES may be put in a slow oven and thoroughly dried before they begin to change colour. They should then be taken out of the oven, tied in bunches, and stored away in a dry place. In the winter, they may be cooked with sugar for dessert, the same as Normandy pippins. Particular care must be taken that the oven be not too hot. Another method of drying cherries is to stone them, and to put them into a preserving-pan, with plenty of loaf sugar strewed amongst them. They should be simmered till the fruit shrivels, when they should be strained from the juice. The cherries should then be placed in an oven, cool enough to dry without baking them. About 5 oz. of sugar would be required for 1 lb. of cherries, and the same syrup may be used again to do another quantity of fruit.

CHERRY JAM.

1528. INGREDIENTS.—To every lb. of fruit, weighed before stoning, allow ½ lb. of sugar; to every 6 lbs. of fruit allow 1 pint of red-currant juice, and to every pint of juice 1 lb. of sugar.

Mode.—Weigh the fruit before stoning, and allow half the weight of sugar; stone the cherries, and boil them in a preserving-pan until nearly all the juice is dried up; then add the sugar, which should be crushed to powder, and the currant-juice, allowing 1 pint to every 6 lbs. of cherries (original weight), and 1 lb. of sugar to every pint of juice. Boil all together until it jellies, which will be in from 20 minutes to ½ hour; skim the jam well, keep it well stirred, and, a few minutes before it is done, crack some of the stones, and add the kernels: these impart a very delicious flavour to the jam.

Time.—According to the quality of the cherries, from ¾ to 1 hour to boil them; 20 minutes to ½ hour with the sugar.

Average cost, from 7d. to 8d. per lb. pot.

Sufficient.—1 pint of fruit for a lb. pot of jam.

Seasonable.—Make this in July or August.

3 D

TO PRESERVE CHERRIES IN SYRUP.

(*Very delicious.*)

1529. INGREDIENTS.—4 lbs. of cherries, 3 lbs. of sugar, 1 pint of white-currant juice.

Mode.—Let the cherries be as clear and as transparent as possible, and perfectly ripe; pick off the stalks, and remove the stones, damaging the fruit as little as you can. Make a syrup with the above proportion of sugar, by recipe No. 1512; mix the cherries with it, and boil them for about 15 minutes, carefully skimming them; turn them gently into a pan, and let them remain till the next day; then drain the cherries on a sieve, and put the syrup and white-currant juice into the preserving-pan again. Boil these together until the syrup is somewhat reduced and rather thick; then put in the cherries, and let them boil for about 5 minutes; take them off the fire, skim the syrup, put the cherries into small pots or wide-mouthed bottles; pour the syrup over, and when quite cold, tie them down carefully, so that the air is quite excluded.

Time.—15 minutes to boil the cherries in the syrup; 10 minutes to boil the syrup and currant-juice; 5 minutes to boil the cherries the second time.

Average cost for this quantity, 3s. 6d.

Seasonable.—Make this in July or August.

BLACK-CURRANT JAM.

1530. INGREDIENTS.—To every lb. of fruit, weighed before being stripped from the stalks, allow ¾ lb. of loaf sugar, 1 gill of water.

Mode.—Let the fruit be very ripe, and gathered on a dry day. Strip it from the stalks, and put it into a preserving-pan, with a gill of water to each lb. of fruit; boil these together for 10 minutes; then add the sugar, and boil the jam again for 30 minutes, reckoning from the time when the jam simmers equally all over, or longer, should it not appear to set nicely when a little is poured on to a plate. Keep stirring it to prevent it from burning, carefully remove all the scum, and when done, pour it into pots. Let it cool, cover the top of the jam with oiled paper, and the top of the jars with a piece of tissue-paper brushed over on both sides with the white of an egg: this, when cold, forms a hard stiff cover, and perfectly excludes the air. Great attention must be paid to the stirring of this jam, as it is very liable to burn, on account of the thickness of the juice.

Time.—10 minutes to boil the fruit and water; 30 minutes with the sugar, or longer.

Average cost, from 6*d*. to 8*d*. for a pot capable of holding 1 lb.

Sufficient.—Allow from 6 to 7 quarts of currants to make 1 dozen pots of jam, each pot to hold 1 lb.

Seasonable.—Make this in July.

BLACK-CURRANT JELLY.

1531. INGREDIENTS.—Black currants; to every pint of juice allow ¼ pint of water, 1 lb. of loaf sugar.

Mode.—Strip the currants from the stalks, which may be done in an expeditious manner, by holding the bunch in one hand, and passing a small silver fork down the currants : they will then readily fall from the stalks. Put them into a jar, place this jar in a saucepan of boiling water, and simmer them until their juice is extracted ; then strain them, and to every pint of juice allow the above proportion of sugar and water ; stir these ingredients together cold until the sugar is dissolved ; place the preserving-pan on the fire, and boil the jelly for about ½ hour, reckoning from the time it commences to boil all over, and carefully remove the scum as it rises. If the jelly becomes firm when a little is put on a plate, it is done ; it should then be put into *small* pots, and covered the same as the jam in the preceding recipe. If the jelly is wanted very clear, the fruit should not be squeezed dry ; but, of course, so much juice will not be obtained. If the fruit is not much squeezed, it may be converted into a jam for immediate eating, by boiling it with a little common sugar : this answers very well for a nursery preserve.

Time.—About ¾ hour to extract the juice ; ½ hour to boil the jelly.

Average cost, from 8*d*. to 10*d*. per ½-lb. pot.

Sufficient.—From 3 pints to 2 quarts of fruit should yield a pint of juice.

Seasonable.—Make this in July.

RED-CURRANT JAM.

1532. INGREDIENTS.—To every lb. of fruit allow ¾ lb. of loaf sugar.

Mode.—Let the fruit be gathered on a fine day ; weigh it, and then strip the currants from the stalks ; put them into a preserving-pan with sugar in the above proportion ; stir them, and boil them for about ¾ hour. Carefully remove the scum as it rises. Put the jam into pots, and, when cold, cover with oiled papers ; over these put a piece of tissue-paper brushed over on both sides with the white of an egg ; press the paper round the top of the pot, and, when dry, the covering will be quite hard and air-tight.

JAM-POT.

Time.—½ to ¾ hour, reckoning from the time the jam boils all over.
Average cost, for a lb. pot, from 6*d.* to 8*d.*

Sufficient.—Allow from 6 to 7 quarts of currants to make 12 1-lb. pots of jam.

Seasonable.—Make this in July.

RED-CURRANT JELLY.

1533. INGREDIENTS.—Red currants; to every pint of juice allow ¾ lb. of loaf sugar.

Mode.—Have the fruit gathered in fine weather; pick it from the stalks, put it into a jar, and place this jar in a saucepan of boiling water over the fire, and let it simmer gently until the juice is well drawn from the currants; then strain them through a jelly-bag or fine cloth, and, if the jelly is wished very clear, do not squeeze them *too much*, as the skin and pulp from the fruit will be pressed through with the juice, and so make the jelly muddy. Measure the juice, and to each pint allow ¾ lb. of loaf sugar; put these into a preserving-pan, set it over the fire, and keep stirring the jelly until it is done, carefully removing every particle of scum as it rises, using a wooden or silver spoon for the purpose, as metal or iron ones would spoil the colour of the jelly. When it has boiled from 20 minutes to ½ hour, put a little of the jelly on a plate, and if firm when cool, it is done. Take it off the fire, pour it into small gallipots, cover each of the pots with an oiled paper, and then with a piece of tissue-paper brushed over on both sides with the white of an egg. Label the pots, adding the year when the jelly was made, and store it away in a dry place. A jam may be made with the currants, if they are not squeezed too dry, by adding a few fresh raspberries, and boiling all together, with sufficient sugar to sweeten it nicely. As this preserve is not worth storing away, but is only for immediate eating, a smaller proportion of sugar than usual will be found enough: it answers very well for children's puddings, or for a nursery preserve.

Time.—From ¾ to 1 hour to extract the juice; 20 minutes to ½ hour to boil the jelly.

Average cost, from 8*d.* to 10*d.* per ½-lb. pot.

Sufficient.—8 quarts of currants will make from 10 to 12 pots of jelly.

Seasonable.—Make this in July.

Note.—Should the above proportion of sugar not be found sufficient for some tastes, add an extra ¼ lb. to every pint of juice, making altogether 1 lb.

WHITE-CURRANT JELLY.

1534. INGREDIENTS.—White currants; to every pint of juice allow ¾ lb. of good loaf sugar.

Mode.—Pick the currants from the stalks, and put them into a jar; place this jar in a saucepan of boiling water, and simmer until the juice is well drawn from the fruit, which will be in from $\frac{3}{4}$ to 1 hour. Then strain the currants through a fine cloth or jelly-bag; do not squeeze them too much, or the jelly will not be clear, and put the juice into a very clean preserving-pan, with the sugar. Let this simmer gently over a clear fire until it is firm, and keep stirring and skimming until it is done; then pour it into small pots, cover them, and store away in a dry place.

Time.—$\frac{3}{4}$ hour to draw the juice; $\frac{1}{2}$ hour to boil the jelly.

Average cost, from 8*d.* to 10*d.* per $\frac{1}{2}$-lb. pot.

Sufficient.—From 3 pints to 2 quarts of fruit should yield 1 pint of juice.

Seasonable in July and August.

BAKED DAMSONS FOR WINTER USE.

1535. INGREDIENTS.—To every lb. of fruit allow 6 oz. of pounded sugar; melted mutton suet.

Mode.—Choose sound fruit, not too ripe; pick off the stalks, weigh it, and to every lb. allow the above proportion of pounded sugar. Put the fruit into large dry stone jars, sprinkling the sugar amongst it; cover the jars with saucers, place them in a rather cool oven, and bake the fruit until it is quite tender. When cold, cover the top of the fruit with a piece of white paper cut to the size of the jar; pour over this melted mutton suet about an inch thick, and cover the tops of the jars with thick brown paper, well tied down. Keep the jars in a cool dry place, and the fruit will remain good till the following Christmas, but not much longer.

Time.—From 5 to 6 hours to bake the damsons, in a very cool oven.

Seasonable in September and October.

DAMSON CHEESE.

1536. INGREDIENTS.—Damsons; to every lb. of fruit pulp allow $\frac{1}{2}$ lb. of loaf sugar.

Mode.—Pick the stalks from the damsons, and put them into a preserving-pan; simmer them over the fire until they are soft, occasionally stirring them; then beat them through a coarse sieve, and put the pulp and juice into the preserving-pan, with sugar in the above proportion, having previously carefully weighed them. Stir the sugar well in, and simmer the damsons slowly for 2 hours. Skim well; then boil the preserve quickly for $\frac{1}{2}$ hour, or until it looks firm and hard in the spoon; put it quickly into shallow pots, or very tiny earthenware moulds, and, when cold, cover it with oiled papers, and the jars with tissue-paper brushed over on both sides with the white of an egg. A few of the stones may be cracked, and the kernels boiled with the damsons, which very much improves the flavour of the cheese.

Time.—1 hour to boil the damsons without the sugar; 2 hours to simmer them slowly, ½ hour quickly.

Average cost, from 8*d.* to 10*d.* per ¼-lb. pot.

Sufficient.—1 pint of damsons to make a *very small* pot of cheese.

Seasonable.—Make this in September or October.

COMPOTE OF DAMSONS.

1537. INGREDIENTS.—1 quart of damsons, 1 pint of syrup No. 1512.

Mode.—Procure sound ripe damsons; pick the stalks from them, and put them into boiling syrup, made by recipe No. 1512. Simmer them gently until the fruit is tender, but not sufficiently soft to break; take them up, boil the syrup for 5 minutes; pour it over the damsons, and serve. This should be sent to table in a glass dish.

Time.—About ¼ hour to simmer the damsons; 5 minutes to boil the syrup.

Average cost, 9*d.*

Sufficient for 4 or 5 persons. *Seasonable* in September and October.

DAMSON JAM.

1538. INGREDIENTS.—Damsons; to every lb. of fruit allow ¾ lb. of loaf sugar.

Mode.—Have the fruit gathered in dry weather; pick it over, and reject any that is at all blemished. Stone the damsons, weigh them, and to every lb. allow ¾ lb. of loaf sugar. Put the fruit and sugar into a preserving-pan; keep stirring them gently until the sugar is dissolved, and carefully remove the scum as it rises. Boil the jam for about an hour, reckoning from the time it commences to simmer all over alike: it must be well stirred all the time, or it will be liable to burn and stick to the pan, which will cause the jam to have a very disagreeable flavour. When the jam looks firm, and the juice appears to set, it is done. Then take it off the fire, put into pots, cover it down, when quite cold, with oiled and egged papers, the same as in recipe No. 1530, and store it away in a dry place.

Time.—1 hour after the jam simmers all over.

Average cost, from 6*d.* to 8*d.* per lb. pot.

Sufficient.—1½ pint of damsons for a lb. pot.

Seasonable.—Make this in September or October.

A VERY NICE PRESERVE OF DAMSONS.

1539. INGREDIENTS.—To every quart of damsons allow ½ lb. of loaf sugar.

Mode.—Put the damsons (which should be picked from the stalks and quite free from blemishes) into a jar, with pounded sugar sprinkled amongst them in the above proportion; tie the jar closely down, set it in a saucepan of cold water; bring it gradually to boil, and simmer gently until the damsons are soft, without being broken. Let them stand till cold; then strain the juice from them, boil it up well, strain it through a jelly-bag, and pour it over the fruit. Let it cool, cover with oiled papers, and the jars with tissue-paper brushed over on both sides with the white of an egg, and store away in a dry cool place.

Time.—About ¾ hour to simmer the fruit after the water boils; ¼ hour to boil the juice.

Seasonable.—Make this in September or October.

TO PRESERVE DAMSONS, OR ANY KIND OF PLUMS.
(*Useful in Winter.*)

1540. INGREDIENTS.—Damsons or plums; boiling water.

Mode.—Pick the fruit into clean dry stone jars, taking care to leave out all that are broken or blemished. When full, pour boiling water on the plums, until it stands one inch above the fruit; cut a piece of paper to fit the inside of the jar, over which pour melted mutton-suet; cover down with brown paper, and keep the jars in a dry cool place. When used, the suet should be removed, the water poured off, and the jelly at the bottom of the jar used and mixed with the fruit.

Seasonable in September and October.

COMPOTE OF GREEN FIGS.

1541. INGREDIENTS.—1 pint of syrup No. 1512, 1½ pint of green figs, the rind of ½ lemon.

Mode.—Make a syrup by recipe No. 1512, boiling with it the lemon-rind, and carefully remove all the scum as it rises. Put in the figs, and simmer them very slowly until tender; dish them on a glass dish; reduce the syrup

COMPÔTE OF FIGS.

by boiling it quickly for 5 minutes; take out the lemon-peel, pour the syrup over the figs; and the compôte, when cold, will be ready for table. A little port wine, or lemon-juice, added just before the figs are done, will be found an improvement.

Time.—2 to 3 hours to stew the figs.

Average cost, figs, 2*s.* to 3*s.* per dozen.

Seasonable in August and September.

TO BOTTLE FRESH FRUIT.

(*Very useful in Winter.*)

I.

1542. INGREDIENTS.—Fresh fruits, such as currants, raspberries, cherries, gooseberries, plums of all kinds, damsons, &c.; wide-mouthed glass bottles, new corks to fit them tightly.

Mode.—Let the fruit be full grown, but not too ripe, and gathered in dry weather. Pick it off the stalks without bruising or breaking the skin, and reject any that is at all blemished: if gathered in the damp, or if the skins are cut at all, the fruit will mould. Have ready some *perfectly dry* glass bottles, and some nice *new* soft corks or bungs; burn a match in each bottle, to exhaust the air, and quickly place the fruit in to be preserved; gently cork the bottles, and put them into a very *cool* oven, where let them remain until the fruit has shrunk away a fourth part. Then take the bottles out; *do not open them*, but immediately beat the corks in tight, cut off the tops, and cover them with melted resin. If kept in a dry place, the fruit will remain good for months; and on this principally depends the success of the preparation; for if stored away in a place that is in the least damp, the fruit will soon spoil.

Time.—From 5 to 6 hours in a very slow oven.

II.

1543. INGREDIENTS.—Any kind of fresh fruit, such as currants, cherries, gooseberries, all kinds of plums, &c.; wide-mouthed glass bottles, new corks to fit them tightly.

Mode.—The fruit must be full-grown, not too ripe, and gathered on a fine day. Let it be carefully picked and put into the bottles, which must be clean and perfectly dry. Tie over the tops of the bottles pieces of bladder; stand the bottles in a large pot, copper, or boiler, with cold water to reach to their necks; kindle a fire under, let the water boil, and as the bladders begin to rise and puff, prick them. As soon as the water boils, extinguish the fire, and let the bottles remain where they are, to become cold. The next day remove the bladders, and strew over the fruit a thick layer of pounded sugar; fit the bottles with corks, and let each cork lie close at hand to its own bottle. Hold for a few moments, in the neck of the bottle, two or three lighted matches, and when they have filled the bottle neck with gas, and before they go out, remove them very quickly; instantly cork the bottle closely, and dip it in bottle cement.

Time.—Altogether about 8 hours.

TO BOTTLE FRESH FRUIT WITH SUGAR.
(*Very useful in Winter.*)

1544. INGREDIENTS.—Any kind of fresh fruit; to each quart bottle allow ¼ lb. of pounded sugar.

Mode.—Let the fruit be gathered in dry weather. Pick it carefully, and drop it into *clean* and *very dry* quart glass bottles, sprinkling over it the above proportion of pounded sugar to each quart. Put the corks in the bottles, and place them in a copper of cold water up to their necks, with small hay-wisps round them, to prevent the bottles from knocking together. Light the fire under, bring the water gradually to boil, and let it simmer gently until the fruit in the bottles is reduced nearly one third. Extinguish the fire, *and let the bottles remain in the water until it is perfectly cold;* then take them out, make the corks secure, and cover them with melted resin or wax.

Time.—About ½ hour from the time the water commences to boil.

TO FROST HOLLY-LEAVES, for garnishing and decorating Dessert and Supper Dishes.

1545.—INGREDIENTS.—Sprigs of holly, oiled butter, coarsely-powdered sugar.

Mode.—Procure some nice sprigs of holly; pick the leaves from the stalks, and wipe them with a clean cloth free from all moisture; then place them on a dish near the fire, to get thoroughly dry, but not too near to shrivel the leaves; dip them into oiled butter, sprinkle over them some coarsely-powdered sugar, and dry them before the fire They should be kept in a dry place, as the least damp would spoil their appearance.

Time.—About 10 minutes to dry before the fire.

Seasonable.—These may be made at any time; but are more suitable for winter garnishes, when fresh flowers are not easily obtained.

COMPOTE OF GOOSEBERRIES.

1546. INGREDIENTS.—Syrup made by recipe No. 1512; to 1 pint of syrup allow nearly a quart of gooseberries.

Mode.—Top and tail the gooseberries, which should not be very ripe, and pour over them some boiling water; then take them out, and plunge them into cold water, with which has been mixed a tablespoonful of vinegar, which will assist to keep the fruit a good colour. Make a pint of syrup by recipe No. 1512, and when it boils, drain the gooseberries and put them in; simmer them gently until the fruit is nicely pulped and tender, without being broken; then dish the gooseberries on a glass dish, boil the syrup for 2 or 3 minutes, pour over the gooseberries, and serve cold.

Time.—About 5 minutes to boil the gooseberries in the syrup; 3 minutes to reduce the syrup.

Average cost, 9d.

Sufficient,—a quart of gooseberries for 5 or 6 persons.

Seasonable in June.

GOOSEBERRY JAM.

I.

1547. INGREDIENTS.—To every lb. of fruit allow ¾ lb. of loaf sugar; currant-juice.

Mode.—Select red hairy gooseberries; have them gathered in dry weather, when quite ripe, without being too soft. Weigh them; with a pair of scissors, cut off the tops and tails, and to every 6 lbs. of fruit have ready ½ pint of red-currant juice, drawn as for jelly. Put the gooseberries and currant-juice into a preserving-pan; let them boil tolerably quickly, keeping them well stirred; when they begin to break, add to them the sugar, and keep simmering until the jam becomes firm, carefully skimming and stirring it, that it does not burn at the bottom. It should be boiled rather a long time, or it will not keep. Put it into pots (not too large); let it get perfectly cold; then cover the pots down with oiled and egged papers, as directed for red-currant jelly No. 1533.

Time.—About 1 hour to boil the gooseberries in the currant-juice; from ½ to ¾ hour with the sugar.

Average cost, per lb. pot, from 6d. to 8d.

Sufficient.—Allow 1½ pint of fruit for a lb. pot.

Seasonable.—Make this in June or July.

II.

1548. INGREDIENTS.—To every 8 lbs. of red, rough, ripe gooseberries allow 1 quart of red-currant juice, 5 lbs. of loaf sugar.

Mode.—Have the fruit gathered in dry weather, and cut off the tops and tails. Prepare 1 quart of red-currant juice, the same as for red-currant jelly No. 1533; put it into a preserving-pan with the sugar, and keep stirring until the latter is dissolved. Keep it boiling for about 5 minutes; skim well; then put in the gooseberries, and let them boil from ½ to ¾ hour; then turn the whole into an earthen pan, and let it remain for 2 days. Boil the jam up again until it looks clear; put it into pots, and when cold, cover with oiled paper, and over the jars put tissue-paper brushed over on both sides with the white of an egg, and store away in a dry place. Care must be taken, in making this, to keep the jam well stirred and well skimmed, to prevent it burning at the bottom of the pan, and to have it very clear.

Time.—5 minutes to boil the currant-juice and sugar after the latter is dissolved; from ½ to ¾ hour to simmer the gooseberries the first time, ¼ hour the second time of boiling.

Average cost, from 8*d.* to 10*d.* per lb. pot.

Sufficient.—Allow 1½ pint of fruit for a lb. pot.

Seasonable.—Make this in June or July.

WHITE OR GREEN GOOSEBERRY JAM.

1549. INGREDIENTS.—Equal weight of fruit and sugar.

Mode.—Select the gooseberries not very ripe, either white or green, and top and tail them. Boil the sugar with water (allowing ½ pint to every lb.) for about ¼ hour, carefully removing the scum as it rises; then put in the gooseberries, and simmer gently till clear and firm: try a little of the jam on a plate; if it jellies when cold, it is done, and should then be poured into pots. When cold, cover with oiled paper, and tissue-paper brushed over on both sides with the unbeaten white of an egg, and store away in a dry place.

Time.—¼ hour to boil the sugar and water, ¾ hour the jam.

Average cost, from 6*d.* to 8*d.* per lb. pot.

Sufficient.—Allow 1½ pint of fruit for a lb. pot.

Seasonable.—Make this in June.

GOOSEBERRY JELLY.

1550. INGREDIENTS.—Gooseberries; to every pint of juice allow ¾ lb. of loaf sugar.

Mode.—Put the gooseberries, after cutting off the tops and tails, into a preserving-pan, and stir them over the fire until they are quite soft; then strain them through a sieve, and to every pint of juice allow ¾ lb. of sugar. Boil the juice and sugar together for nearly ¾ hour, stirring and skimming all the time; and if the jelly appears firm when a little of it is poured on to a plate, it is done, and should then be taken up and put into small pots. Cover the pots with oiled and egged papers, the same as for currant jelly No. 1533, and store away in a dry place.

Time.—¾ hour to simmer the gooseberries without the sugar; ¾ hour to boil the juice.

Average cost, from 8*d.* to 10*d.* per ½-lb. pot.

Seasonable in July.

COMPOTE OF GREENGAGES.

1551. INGREDIENTS.—1 pint of syrup made by recipe No. 1512, 1 quart of greengages.

Mode.—Make a syrup by recipe No. 1512, skim it well, and put in the greengages when the syrup is boiling, having previously removed the stalks and stones from the fruit. Boil gently for ¼ hour, or until the fruit is tender; but take care not to let it break, as the appearance of the dish would be spoiled were the fruit reduced to a pulp. Take the greengages carefully out, place them on a glass dish, boil the syrup for another 5 minutes, let it cool a little, pour over the fruit, and, when cold, it will be ready for use.

Time.—¼ hour to simmer the fruit, 5 minutes the syrup.

Average cost, in full season, 10*d.*

Sufficient for 4 or 5 persons.

Seasonable in July, August, and September.

GREENGAGE JAM.

1552. INGREDIENTS.—To every lb. of fruit, weighed before being stoned, allow ¾ lb. of lump sugar.

Mode.—Divide the greengages, take out the stones, and put them into a preserving-pan. Bring the fruit to a boil, then add the sugar, and keep stirring it over a gentle fire until it is melted. Remove all the scum as it rises, and, just before the jam is done, boil it rapidly for 5 minutes. To ascertain when it is sufficiently boiled, pour a little on a plate, and if the syrup thickens and appears firm, it is done. Have ready half the kernels blanched; put them into the jam, give them one boil, and pour the preserve into pots. When cold, cover down with oiled papers, and, over these, tissue-paper brushed over on both sides with the white of an egg.

Time.—¾ hour after the sugar is added.

Average cost, from 6*d.* to 8*d.* per lb. pot.

Sufficient.—Allow about 1½ pint of fruit for every lb. pot of jam.

Seasonable.—Make this in August or September.

TO PRESERVE AND DRY GREENGAGES.

1553. INGREDIENTS.—To every lb. of sugar allow 1 lb. of fruit, ¼ pint of water.

Mode.—For this purpose, the fruit must be used before it is quite ripe, and part of the stalk must be left on. ·Weigh the fruit, rejecting all that is in the least degree blemished, and put it into a lined saucepan with the sugar and water, which should have been previously boiled together to a rich syrup. Boil the fruit in this for 10 minutes, remove it from the fire, and drain the greengages. The next day, boil up the syrup and put in the fruit again, and let it simmer for 3 minutes, and drain the syrup away. Continue this process for 5 or 6 days, and the last time place the greengages, when drained, on a hair sieve, and put them in an oven or warm spot to dry; keep them in a box, with paper between each layer, in a place free from damp.

Time.—10 minutes the, first time of boiling.

Seasonable.—Make this in August or September.

PRESERVED GREENGAGES IN SYRUP.

1554. INGREDIENTS.—To every lb. of fruit allow 1 lb. of loaf sugar ¼ pint of water.

Mode.—Boil the sugar and water together for about 10 minutes; divide the greengages, take out the stones, put the fruit into the syrup, and let it simmer gently until nearly tender. Take it off the fire, put it into a large pan, and, the next day, boil it up again for about 10 minutes with the kernels from the stones, which should be blanched. Put the fruit carefully into jars, pour over it the syrup, and, when cold, cover down, so that the air is quite excluded. Let the syrup be well skimmed both the first and second day of boiling, otherwise it will not be clear.

Time.—10 minutes to boil the syrup; ¼ hour to simmer the fruit the first day, 10 minutes the second day.

Average cost, from 6*d.* to 8*d.* per lb. pot.

Sufficient.—Allow about 1 pint of fruit to fill a 1-lb. pot.

Seasonable.—Make this in August or September.

TO MAKE FRUIT ICE-CREAMS.

1555. INGREDIENTS.—To every pint of fruit-juice allow 1 pint of cream; sugar to taste.

Mode.—Let the fruit be well ripened; pick it off the stalks, and put it into a large earthen pan. Stir it about with a wooden spoon, breaking it until it is well mashed; then, with the back of the spoon, rub it through a hair sieve. Sweeten it nicely with pounded sugar; whip the cream for a few minutes, add it to the fruit, and whisk the whole again for another 5 minutes. Put the mixture into the freezing-pot, and freeze in the same manner as directed for Ice Pudding, No. 1290, taking care to stir the cream, &c., two or three times, and to remove it from the sides of the vessel, that the mixture may be equally frozen and smooth. Ices are usually served in glasses, but if moulded, as they sometimes are for dessert, must have a small quantity of melted isinglass added to them, to enable them to keep their shape. Raspberry, strawberry, currant, and all fruit ice-creams, are made in the same manner. A little pounded sugar sprinkled over the fruit before it is mashed assists to extract the juice. In winter, when fresh fruit is not obtainable, a little jam may be substituted for it : it should be melted and worked through a sieve before being added to the whipped cream ; and if the colour should not be good, a little prepared cochineal or beetroot may be put in to improve its appearance.

Time.—½ hour to freeze the mixture.

Average cost, with cream at 1s. per pint, 4d. each ice.

Seasonable, with fresh fruit, in June, July, and August.

TO MAKE FRUIT-WATER ICES.

1556. INGREDIENTS.—To every pint of fruit-juice allow 1 pint of syrup made by recipe No. 1513.

Mode.—Select nice ripe fruit ; pick off the stalks, and put it into a large earthen pan, with a little pounded sugar strewed over ; stir it

DISH OF ICES.

about with a wooden spoon until it is well broken, then rub it through a hair sieve. Make the syrup by recipe No. 1513, omitting the white of the egg ; let it cool, add the fruit-juice, mix well together, and put the mixture into the freezing-pot. Proceed as directed for Ice Puddings, No. 1290, and when the mixture is equally frozen, put it into small glasses. Raspberry, strawberry, currant, and other fresh-fruit-water ices, are made in the same manner.

Time.—½ hour to freeze the mixture.

Average cost, 3d. to 4d. each.

Seasonable, with fresh fruit, in June, July, and August.

LEMON-WATER ICE.

1557. INGREDIENTS.—To every pint of syrup, made by recipe No. 1513, allow ⅓ pint of lemon-juice ; the rind of 4 lemons.

Mode.—Rub the sugar on the rinds of the lemons, and with it make the syrup by recipe No. 1513, omitting the white of egg. Strain the lemon-juice, add it to the other ingredients, stir well, and put the mixture into a freezing-pot. Freeze as directed for Ice Pudding, No.

1290, and, when the mixture is thoroughly and equally frozen, put it into ice-glasses.

Time.—½ hour to freeze the mixture. *Average cost,* 3*d.* to 4*d.* each. *Seasonable* at any time.

ICED CURRANTS, for Dessert.

1558. INGREDIENTS.—¼ pint of water, the whites of 2 eggs, currants, pounded sugar.

Mode.—Select very fine bunches of red or white currants, and well beat the whites of the eggs. Mix these with the water; then take the currants, a bunch at a time, and dip them in; let them drain for a minute or two, and roll them in very fine pounded sugar. Lay them to dry on paper, when the sugar will crystallize round each currant, and have a very pretty effect. All fresh fruit may be prepared in the same manner; and a mixture of various fruits iced in this manner, and arranged on one dish, looks very well for a summer dessert.

Time.—¼ day to dry the fruit.

Average cost, 8*d.* for a pint of iced currants. *Seasonable* in summer.

MELONS.

1559. This fruit is rarely preserved or cooked in any way, and should be sent to table on a dish garnished with leaves or flowers, as fancy dictates. A border of any other kind of small fruit, arranged round the melon, has a pretty effect, the colour of the former contrasting nicely with the melon. Plenty of pounded sugar should be served with it; and the fruit should be cut lengthwise, in moderate-sized slices. In America, it is frequently eaten with pepper and salt.

Average cost,—English, in full season, 3*s.* 6*d.* to 5*s.* each; when scarce, 10*s.* to 15*s.*; *seasonable,* June to August. French, 2*s.* to 3*s.* 6*d.* each; *seasonable,* June and July. Dutch, 9*d.* to 2*s.* each; *seasonable,* July and August.

MELON.—The melon is a most delicious fruit, succulent, cool, and high-flavoured. With us, it is used only at the dessert, and is generally eaten with sugar, ginger, or pepper; but, in France, it is likewise served up at dinner as a sauce for boiled meats. It grows wild in Tartary, and has been lately found in abundance on the sandy plains of Jeypoor. It was brought originally from Asia by the Romans, and is said to have been common in England in the time of Edward III., though it is supposed that it was lost again, as well as the cucumber, during the wars of York and Lancaster. The best kind, called the *Cantaloupe,* from the name of a place near Rome where it was first cultivated in Europe, is a native of Armenia, where it grows so plentifully that a horse-load may be bought for a crown.

PRESERVED MULBERRIES.

1560. INGREDIENTS.—To 2 lbs. of fruit and 1 pint of juice allow 2½ lbs. of loaf sugar.

Mode.—Put some of the fruit into a preserving-pan, and simmer it gently until the juice is well drawn. Strain it through a bag, measure it, and to every pint allow the above proportion of sugar and fruit. Put the sugar into the preserving-pan, moisten it with the juice, boil it up, skim well, and then add the mulberries, which should be ripe, but not soft enough to break to a pulp. Let them stand in the syrup till warm through, then set them on the fire to boil gently; when half done, turn them carefully into an earthen pan, and let them remain till the next day; then boil them as before, and when the syrup is thick, and becomes firm when cold, put the preserve into pots. In making this, care should be taken not to break the mulberries: this may be avoided by very gentle stirring, and by simmering the fruit very slowly.

Time.—¾ hour to extract the juice; ¼ hour to boil the mulberries the first time, ¼ hour the second time.

Seasonable in August and September.

MULBERRY.

MULBERRY.—Mulberries are esteemed for their highly aromatic flavour, and their sub-acid nature. They are considered as cooling, laxative, and generally wholesome. This fruit was very highly esteemed by the Romans, who appear to have preferred it to every other. The mulberry-tree is stated to have been introduced into this country in 1548, being first planted at Sion House, where the original trees still thrive. The planting of them was much encouraged by King James I. about 1605; and considerable attempts were made at that time to rear silkworms on a large scale for the purpose of making silk; but these endeavours have always failed, the climate being scarcely warm enough.

TO PRESERVE MORELLO CHERRIES.

1561. INGREDIENTS.—To every lb. of cherries allow 1¼ lb. of sugar, 1 gill of water.

Mode.—Select ripe cherries; pick off the stalks, and reject all that have any blemishes. Boil the sugar and water together for 5 minutes; put in the cherries, and boil them for 10 minutes, removing the scum as it rises. Then turn the fruit, &c. into a pan, and let it remain until the next day, when boil it all again for another 10 minutes, and, if necessary, skim well. Put the cherries into small pots; pour over them the syrup, and, when cold, cover down with oiled papers, and the tops of the jars with tissue-paper brushed over on both sides with the white of an egg, and keep in a dry place.

Time.—Altogether, 25 minutes to boil.

Average cost, from 8d. to 10d. per lb. pot.

Seasonable.—Make this in July or August.

THE CHERRY-TREE IN ROME.—The Cherry-tree was introduced into Rome by Lucullus, about seventy years before the Christian era; but the capital of the world knew not at first how to appreciate this present as it deserved ; for the cherry-tree was propagated so slowly in Italy, that more than a century after its introduction it was far from being generally cultivated: The Romans distinguished three principal species of cherries—the *Apronian*, of a bright red, with a firm and delicate pulp ; the *Lutatian*, very black and sweet ; the *Cæcilian*, round and stubby, and much esteemed. The cherry embellished the third course in Rome and the second at Athens.

PRESERVED NECTARINES.

1562. INGREDIENTS.—To every lb. of sugar allow ¼ pint of water ; nectarines.

Mode.—Divide the nectarines in two, take out the stones, and make a strong syrup with sugar and water in the above proportion. Put in the nectarines, and boil them until they have thoroughly imbibed the sugar. Keep the fruit as whole as possible, and turn it carefully into a pan. The next day boil it again for a few minutes, take out the nectarines, put them into jars, boil the syrup quickly for 5 minutes, pour it over the fruit, and, when cold, cover the preserve down. The syrup and preserve must be carefully skimmed, or it will not be clear.

Time.—10 minutes to boil the sugar and water ; 20 minutes to boil the fruit the first time, 10 minutes the second time ; 5 minutes to boil the syrup.

Seasonable in August and September, but cheapest in September.

STEWED NORMANDY PIPPINS.

1563. INGREDIENTS.—1 lb. of Normandy pippins, 1 quart of water, ½ teaspoonful of powdered cinnamon, ½ teaspoonful of ground ginger, 1 lb. of moist sugar, 1 lemon.

Mode.—Well wash the pippins, and put them into 1 quart of water with the above proportion of cinnamon and ginger, and let them stand 12 hours ; then put these all together into a stewpan, with the lemon sliced thinly, and half the moist sugar. Let them boil slowly until the pippins are half done ; then add the remainder of the sugar, and simmer until they are quite tender. Serve on glass dishes for dessert.

Time.—2 to 3 hours. *Average cost*, 1s. 6d.

Seasonable.—Suitable for a winter dish.

ICED ORANGES.

1564. INGREDIENTS.—Oranges ; to every lb. of pounded loaf sugar allow the whites of 2 eggs.

Mode.—Whisk the whites of the eggs well, stir in the sugar, and beat this mixture for ¼ hour. Skin the oranges, remove as much of the white pith as possible without injuring the pulp of the fruit ; pass a thread through the centre of each orange, dip them into the sugar, and tie them to a stick. Place this stick across the oven, and let the oranges remain until dry, when they will have the appearance of balls of ice. They make a pretty dessert or supper dish. Care must be taken not to have the oven too fierce, or the oranges would scorch and acquire a brown colour, which would entirely spoil their appearance.

Time.—From ½ to 1 hour to dry in a moderate oven.

Average cost, 1½*d.* each.

Sufficient.— ½ lb. of sugar to ice 12 oranges.

Seasonable from November to May.

THE FIRST ORANGE-TREE IN FRANCE.—The first Orange-tree cultivated in the centre of France was to be seen a few years ago at Fontainebleau. It was called *Le Connétable* (the Constable), because it had belonged to the Connétable de Bourbon, and had been confiscated, together with all property belonging to that prince, after his revolt against his sovereign.

COMPOTE OF ORANGES.

1565. INGREDIENTS.—1 pint of syrup No. 1512, 6 oranges.

Mode.—Peel the oranges, remove as much of the white pith as possible, and divide them into small pieces without breaking the thin skin with which they are surrounded. Make the syrup by recipe No. 1512, adding the rind of the orange cut into thin narrow strips. When the syrup has been well skimmed, and is quite clear, put in the pieces of orange, and simmer them for 5 minutes. Take them out carefully with a spoon without breaking them, and arrange them on a glass dish. Reduce the syrup by boiling it quickly until thick; let it cool a little, pour it over the oranges, and, when cold, they will be ready for table.

COMPÔTE OF ORANGES.

Time.—10 minutes to boil the syrup; 5 minutes to simmer the oranges; 5 minutes to reduce the syrup.

Average cost, 9*d.*

Sufficient for 5 or 6 persons.

Seasonable from November to May.

THE ORANGE IN PORTUGAL.—The Orange known under the name of "Portugal Orange" comes originally from China. Not more than two centuries ago, the Portuguese brought thence the first scion, which has multiplied so prodigiously that we now see entire forests of orange-trees in Portugal.

ORANGE AND CLOVES.—It appears to have been the custom formerly, in England, to make new year's presents with oranges stuck full with cloves. We read in one of Ben Jonson's pieces,—the "Christmas Masque,"—"He has an orange and rosemary, but not a clove to stick in it."

ORANGE MARMALADE.

I.

1566. INGREDIENTS.—Equal weight of fine loaf sugar and Seville oranges; to 12 oranges allow 1 pint of water.

Mode.—Let there be an equal weight of loaf sugar and Seville oranges, and allow the above proportion of water to every dozen oranges. Peel them carefully, remove a little of the white pith, and boil the rinds in water 2 hours, changing the water three times to take off a little of the bitter taste. Break the pulp into small pieces, take out all the pips, and cut the boiled rind into chips. Make a syrup with the sugar and water; boil this well, skim it, and, when clear, put in the pulp and chips. Boil all together from 20 minutes to ½ hour; pour it into pots, and, when cold, cover down with bladders or tissue-paper brushed over on both sides with the white of an egg. The juice and grated rind of 2 lemons to every dozen of oranges, added with the pulp and chips to the syrup, are a very great improvement to this marmalade.

Time.—2 hours to boil the orange-rinds; 10 minutes to boil the syrup; 20 minutes to ½ hour to boil the marmalade.

Average cost, from 6*d.* to 8*d.* per lb. pot.

Seasonable.—This should be made in March or April, as Seville oranges are then in perfection.

II.

1567. INGREDIENTS.—Equal weight of Seville oranges and sugar; to every lb. of sugar allow ½ pint of water.

Mode.—Weigh the sugar and oranges, score the skin across, and take it off in quarters. Boil these quarters in a muslin bag in water until they are quite soft, and they can be pierced easily with the head of a pin; then cut them into chips about 1 inch long, and as thin as possible. Should there be a great deal of white stringy pulp, remove it before cutting the rind into chips. Split open the oranges, scrape out the best part of the pulp, with the juice, rejecting the white pith and pips. Make a syrup with the sugar and water; boil it until clear; then put in the chips, pulp, and juice, and boil the marmalade from 20 minutes to ½ hour, removing all the scum as it rises. In boiling the syrup, clear it carefully from scum before the oranges are added to it.

Time.—2 hours to boil the rinds, 10 minutes the syrup, 20 minutes to ½ hour the marmalade.

Average cost, 6*d.* to 8*d.* per lb. pot.

Seasonable.—Make this in March or April, when Seville oranges are in perfection.

AN EASY WAY OF MAKING ORANGE MARMALADE.

1568. INGREDIENTS.—To every lb. of pulp allow 1½ lb. of loaf sugar.

Mode.—Choose some fine Seville oranges; put them whole into a stewpan with sufficient water to cover them, and stew them until they become perfectly tender, changing the water 2 or 3 times; drain them, take off the rind, remove the pips from the pulp, weigh it, and to every lb. allow 1½ of loaf sugar and ½ pint of the water the oranges were last boiled in. Boil the sugar and water together for 10 minutes; put in the pulp, boil for another 10 minutes; then add the peel cut into strips, and boil the marmalade for another 10 minutes, which completes the process. Pour it into jars; let it cool; then cover down with bladders, or tissue-paper brushed over on both sides with the white of an egg.

Time.—2 hours to boil the oranges; altogether ½ hour to boil the marmalade.

Average cost, from 6*d*. to 8*d*. per lb. pot.

Seasonable.—Make this in March or April.

ORANGE MARMALADE MADE WITH HONEY.

1569. Ingredients.—To 1 quart of the juice and pulp of Seville oranges allow 2 lbs. of honey, 1 lb. of the rind.

Mode.—Peel the oranges and boil the rind in water until tender, and cut it into strips. Take away the pips from the juice and pulp, and put it with the honey and chips into a preserving-pan; boil all together for about ½ hour, or until the marmalade is of the proper consistency; put it into pots, and, when cold, cover down with bladders.

Time.—2 hours to boil the rind, ½ hour the marmalade.

Average cost, from 7*d*. to 9*d*. per lb. pot.

Seasonable.—Make this in March or April.

TO PRESERVE ORANGES.

1570. Ingredients.—Oranges; to every lb. of juice and pulp allow 2 lbs. of loaf sugar; to every pint of water ¼ lb. of loaf sugar.

Mode.—Wholly grate or peel the oranges, taking off only the thin outside portion of the rind. Make a small incision where the stalk is taken out, squeeze out as much of the juice as can be obtained, and preserve it in a basin with the pulp that accompanies it. Put the oranges into cold water; let them stand for 3 days, changing the water twice; then boil them in fresh water till they are very tender, and put them to drain. Make a syrup with the above proportion of sugar and water, sufficient to cover the oranges; let them stand in it for 2 or 3 days; then drain them well. Weigh the juice and pulp, allow double their weight of sugar, and boil them together until the scum ceases to rise, which must all be carefully removed; put in the oranges, boil them for 10 minutes, place them in jars, pour over them the syrup, and, when cold, cover down. They will be fit for use in a week.

Time.—3 days for the oranges to remain in water, 3 days in the syrup; ½ hour to boil the pulp, 10 minutes the oranges.

Seasonable.—This preserve should be made in February or March, when oranges are plentiful.

ORANGE SALAD.

1571. INGREDIENTS.—6 oranges, ¼ lb. of muscatel raisins, 2 oz. of pounded sugar, 4 tablespoonfuls of brandy.

Mode.—Peel 5 of the oranges; divide them into slices without breaking the pulp, and arrange them on a glass dish. Stone the raisins, mix them with the sugar and brandy, and mingle them with the oranges. Squeeze the juice of the other orange over the whole, and the dish is ready for table. A little pounded spice may be put in when the flavour is liked; but this ingredient must be added very sparingly.

Average cost, 1s.

Sufficient for 5 or 6 persons.

Seasonable from November to May.

COMPOTE OF PEACHES.

1572. INGREDIENTS.—1 pint of syrup No. 1512, about 15 small peaches.

Mode.—Peaches that are not very large, and that would not look well for dessert, answer very nicely for a compôte. Divide the peaches, take out the stones, and pare the fruit; make a syrup by recipe No. 1512, put in the peaches, and stew them gently for about 10 minutes. Take them out without breaking, arrange them on a glass dish, boil the syrup for 2 or 3 minutes, let it cool, pour it over the fruit, and, when cold, it will be ready for table.

Time.—10 minutes. *Average cost*, 1s. 2d.

Sufficient for 5 or 6 persons. *Seasonable* in August and September.

PEACH AND NECTARINE.—The peach and nectarine, which are among the most delicious of our fruits, are considered as varieties of the same species, produced by cultivation. The former is characterized by a very delicate down, while the latter is smooth; but, as a proof of their identity as to species, trees have borne peaches on one part and nectarines on another; and even a single fruit has had down on one side, and on the other none: the trees are almost exactly alike, as well as the blossoms. Pliny states that the peach was originally brought from Persia, where it grows naturally. At Montreuil, a village near Paris, almost the whole population is employed in the cultivation of peaches; and this occupation has maintained the inhabitants for ages, and, in consequence, they raise better peaches than anywhere else in France. In Maryland and Virginia, peaches grow nearly wild in orchards resembling forests; but the fruit is of little value for the table, being employed only in fattening hogs and for the distillation of peach brandy. On the east side of the Andes, peaches grow wild among the cornfields and in the mountains, and are dried as an article of food. The young leaves of the peach are sometimes used in cookery, from their agreeable flavour ; and a liqueur resembling the fine noyeau of Martinique may be made by steeping them in brandy sweetened with sugar and fined with milk : gin may also be flavoured in the same manner. The kernels of the fruit have the same flavour. The nectarine is said to have received its name from nectar, the particular drink of the gods. Though it is considered as the same species as the peach, it is not known which of the varieties come from the other : the nectarine is by some considered as the superior fruit.

PEACHES PRESERVED IN BRANDY.

1573. INGREDIENTS.—To every lb. of fruit weighed before being stoned, allow ¼ lb. of finely-pounded loaf sugar ; brandy.

Mode.—Let the fruit be gathered in dry weather ; wipe and weigh it, and remove the stones as carefully as possible, without injuring the peaches much. Put them into a jar, sprinkle amongst them pounded loaf sugar in the above proportion, and pour brandy over the fruit. Cover the jar down closely, place it in a saucepan of boiling water over the fire, and bring the brandy to the simmering-point, but do not allow it to boil. Take the fruit out carefully, without breaking it ; put it into small jars, pour over it the brandy, and, when cold, exclude the air by covering the jars with bladders, or tissue-paper brushed over on both sides with the white of an egg. Apricots may be done in the same manner, and, if properly prepared, will be found delicious.

Time —From 10 to 20 minutes to bring the brandy to the simmering-point.

Seasonable in August and September.

BAKED PEARS.

1574. INGREDIENTS.—12 pears, the rind of 1 lemon, 6 cloves, 10 whole allspice ; to every pint of water allow ½ lb. of loaf sugar.

Mode.—Pare and cut the pears into halves, and, should they be very large, into quarters ; leave the stalks on, and carefully remove the cores. Place them in a clean baking-jar, with a closely-fitting lid ; add to them the lemon-rind cut in strips, the juice of ½ lemon, the cloves, pounded allspice, and sufficient water just to cover the whole, with sugar in the above proportion. Cover the jar down closely, put it into a very cool oven, and bake the pears from 5 to 6 hours, but be very careful that the oven is not too hot. To improve the colour of the fruit, a few drops of prepared cochineal may be added ; but this will not be found necessary if the pears are very gently baked.

Time.—Large pears, 5 to 6 hours, in a very slow oven.

Average cost, 1*d.* to 2*d.* each.

Sufficient for 7 or 8 persons.

Seasonable from September to January.

PEAR.—The pear, like the apple, is indigenous to this country ; but the wild pear is a very unsatisfactory fruit. The best varieties were brought from the East by the Romans, who cultivated them with care, and probably introduced some of their best sorts into this island, to which others were added by the inhabitants of the monasteries. The Dutch and Flemings, as well as the French, have excelled in the cultivation of the pear, and most of the late varieties introduced are from France and Flanders. The pear is a hardy tree, and a longer liver than the apple: it has been known to exist for centuries. There are now about 150 varieties of this fruit. Though perfectly wholesome when ripe, the pear is not so when green; but in this state it is fit for stewing. An agreeable beverage, called perry, is made from pears, and the varieties which are least fit for eating make the best perry.

PRESERVED PEARS.

1575. INGREDIENTS.—Jargonelle pears; to every lb. of sugar allow ½ pint of water.

Mode.—Procure some Jargonelle pears, not too ripe; put them into a stewpan with sufficient water to cover them, and simmer them till rather tender, but do not allow them to break; then put them into cold water. Boil the sugar and water together for 5 minutes, skim well, put in the pears, and simmer them gently for 5 minutes. Repeat the simmering for 3 successive days, taking care not to let the fruit break. The last time of boiling, the syrup should be made rather richer, and the fruit boiled for 10 minutes. When the pears are done, drain them from the syrup, and dry them in the sun, or in a cool oven; or they may be kept in the syrup, and dried as they are wanted.

Time.—½ hour to simmer the pears in water, 20 minutes in the syrup. *Average cost*, 1d. to 2d. each.

Seasonable.—Most plentiful in September and October.

STEWED PEARS.

1576. INGREDIENTS.—8 large pears, 5 oz. of loaf sugar, 6 cloves, 6 whole allspice, ½ pint of water, ¼ pint of port wine, a few drops of prepared cochineal.

Mode.—Pare the pears, halve them, remove the cores, and leave the stalks on; put them into a *lined* saucepan with the above ingredients, and let them simmer very gently until tender, which will be in from 3 to 4 hours, according to the quality of the pears. They should be watched, and, when done, carefully lifted out on to a glass dish without breaking them. Boil up the syrup quickly for 2 or 3 minutes;

STEWED PEARS.

allow it to cool a little, pour it over the pears, and let them get perfectly cold. To improve the colour of the fruit, a few drops of prepared cochineal may be added, which rather enhances the beauty of this dish. The fruit must not be boiled fast, but only simmered, and watched that it be not too much done.

Time.—3 to 4 hours.　*Average cost,* 1s. 6d.

Sufficient for 5 or 6 persons.　*Seasonable* from September to January.

THE BON CHRETIEN PEAR.—The valuable variety of pear called *Bon Chrétien,* which comes to our tables in winter, either raw or cooked, received its name through the following incident :—Louis XI., king of France, had sent for Saint François de Paule from the lower part of Calabria, in the hopes of recovering his health through his intercession. The saint brought with him the seeds of this pear; and, as he was called at court *Le Bon Chrétien,* this fruit obtained the name of him to whom France owed its introduction.

PINEAPPLE CHIPS.

1577. INGREDIENTS.—Pineapples ; sugar to taste.

Mode.—Pare and slice the fruit thinly, put it on dishes, and strew over it plenty of pounded sugar. Keep it in a hot closet, or very slow oven, 8 or 10 days, and turn the fruit every day until dry ; then put the pieces of pine on tins, and place them in a quick oven for 10 minutes. Let them cool, and store them away in dry boxes, with paper between each layer.

Time.—8 to 10 days.

Seasonable.—Foreign pines, in July and August.

PRESERVED PINEAPPLE.

1578. INGREDIENTS.—To every lb. of fruit, weighed after being pared, allow 1 lb. of loaf sugar ; ¼ pint of water.

Mode.—The pines for making this preserve should be perfectly sound but ripe. Cut them into rather thick slices, as the fruit shrinks very much in the boiling. Pare off the rind carefully, that none of the pine be wasted ; and, in doing so, notch it in and out, as the edge cannot be smoothly cut without great waste. Dissolve a portion of the sugar in a preserving-pan with ¼ pint of water ; when this is melted, gradually add the remainder of the sugar, and boil it until it forms a clear syrup, skimming well. As soon as this is the case, put in the pieces of pine, and boil well for at least ½ hour, or until it looks nearly transparent. Put it into pots, cover down when cold, and store away in a dry place.

Time.—½ hour to boil the fruit.　*Average cost,* 10d. to 1s. per lb. pot.

Seasonable.—Foreign pines, in July and August.

THE PINEAPPLE IN HEATHENDOM.—Heathen nations invented protective divinities for their orchards (such as Pomona, Vertumnus, Priapus, &c.), and benevolent patrons for their fruits : thus, the olive-tree grew under the auspices of Minerva ; the Muses cherished the palm-tree, Bacchus the fig and grape, and *the pine and its cone were consecrated to the great Cybele.*

PRESERVED PINEAPPLE, for Present Use.

1579. INGREDIENTS.—Pineapple, sugar, water.

Mode.—Cut the pine into slices ¼ inch in thickness ; peel them, and remove the hard part from the middle. Put the parings and hard pieces into a stewpan with sufficient water to cover them, and boil for ¼ hour. Strain the liquor, and put in the slices of pine. Stew them for 10 minutes, add sufficient sugar to sweeten the whole nicely, and boil again for another ¼ hour; skim well, and the preserve will be ready for use. It must be eaten soon, as it will keep but a very short time.

Time.—¼ hour to boil the parings in water; 10 minutes to boil the pine without sugar, ¼ hour with sugar.

Average cost.—Foreign pines, 1s. to 3s. each; English, from 2s. to 12s. per lb.

Seasonable.—Foreign, in July and August; English, all the year.

PLUM JAM.

1580. INGREDIENTS.—To every lb. of plums, weighed before being stoned, allow ¾ lb. of loaf sugar.

Mode.—In making plum jam, the quantity of sugar for each lb. of fruit must be regulated by the quality and size of the fruit, some plums requiring much more sugar than others. Divide the plums, take out the stones, and put them on to large dishes, with roughly-pounded sugar sprinkled over them in the above proportion, and let them remain for one day; then put them into a preserving-pan, stand them by the side of the fire to simmer gently for about ½ hour, and then boil them rapidly for another 15 minutes. The scum must be carefully removed as it rises, and the jam must be well stirred all the time, or it will burn at the bottom of the pan, and so spoil the colour and flavour of the preserve. Some of the stones may be cracked, and a few kernels added to the jam just before it is done : these impart a very delicious flavour to the plums. The above proportion of sugar would answer for Orleans plums; the Impératrice, Magnum-bonum, and Winesour would not require quite so much.

Time.—½ hour to simmer gently, ¼ hour to boil rapidly.

Best plums for preserving.—Violets, Mussels, Orleans, Impératrice, Magnum-bonum, and Winesour.

Seasonable from the end of July to the beginning of October.

PLUMS.—The Damson, or Damascene plum, takes its name from Damascus, where it grows in great quantities, and whence it was brought into Italy about 114 B.C. The Orleans plum is from France. The Greengage is called after the Gage family, who first brought it into England from the monastery of the Chartreuse, at Paris, where it still bears the name of Reine Claude. The Magnum-bonum is our largest plum, and greatly esteemed for preserves and culinary purposes. The best sorts of plums are agreeable at the dessert, and, when perfectly ripe, are wholesome; but some are too astringent. They lose much of their bad qualities by baking, and are extensively used, from their cheapness, when in full season, in tarts and preserves; but they are not a very wholesome fruit, and should be eaten in moderation.

PRESERVED PLUMS.

1581. INGREDIENTS.—To every lb. of fruit allow ¾ lb. of loaf sugar; for the thin syrup, ¼ lb. of sugar to each pint of water.

Mode.—Select large ripe plums; slightly prick them, to prevent them from bursting, and simmer them very gently in a syrup made with the above proportion of sugar and water. Put them carefully into a pan, let the syrup cool, pour it over the plums, and allow them to remain for two days. Having previously weighed the other sugar, dip the lumps quickly into water, and put them into a preserving-pan with no more water than hangs about them; and boil the sugar to a syrup, carefully skimming it. Drain the plums from the first syrup; put them into the fresh syrup, and simmer them very gently until they are clear; lift them out singly into pots, pour the syrup over, and when cold, cover down to exclude the air. This preserve will remain good some time, if kept in a dry place, and makes a very nice addition to a dessert. The magnum-bonum plums answer for this preserve better than any other kind of plum. Greengages are also very delicious done in this manner.

Time.—¼ hour to 20 minutes to simmer the plums in the first syrup; 20 minutes to ½ hour very gentle simmering in the second.

Seasonable from August to October.

TO PRESERVE PLUMS DRY.

1582. INGREDIENTS.—To every lb. of sugar allow ¼ pint of water.

Mode.—Gather the plums when they are full-grown and just turning colour; prick them, put them into a saucepan of cold water, and set them on the fire until the water is on the point of boiling. Then take them out, drain them, and boil them gently in syrup made with the above proportion of sugar and water; and if the plums shrink, and will not take the sugar, prick them as they lie in the pan; give them another boil, skim, and set them by. The next day add some more sugar, boiled almost to candy, to the fruit and syrup; put all together into a wide-mouthed jar, and place them in a cool oven for 2 nights; then drain the plums from the syrup, sprinkle a little powdered sugar over, and dry them in a cool oven.

Time.—15 to 20 minutes to boil the plums in the syrup.

Seasonable from August to October.

PLUMS.—The wild sloe is the parent of the plum, but the acclimated kinds come from the East. The cultivation of this fruit was probably attended to very early in England, as Gerrard informs us that, in 1597, he had in his garden, in Holborn, threescore sorts. The sloe is a shrub common in our hedgerows, and belongs to the natural order *Amygdaleæ;* the fruit is about the size of a large pea, of a black colour, and covered with a bloom of a bright blue. It is one of the few indigenous to our island. The juice is extremely sharp and astringent, and was formerly employed as a medicine, where astringents were necessary. It now assists in the manufacture of a red wine made to imitate port, and also for adulteration. The leaves have been used to adulterate tea: the fruit, when ripe, makes a good preserve.

STEWED FRENCH PLUMS.

(A Dessert Dish.)

1583. INGREDIENTS. — 1½ lb. of French plums, ¾ pint of syrup No. 1512, 1 glass of port wine, the rind and juice of 1 lemon.

Mode.—Stew the plums gently in water for 1 hour; strain the water, and with it make the syrup. When it is clear, put in the plums with the port wine, lemon-juice, and rind, and simmer very gently for 1½ hour. Arrange the plums on a glass dish, take out the lemon-rind, pour the syrup over the plums, and, when cold, they will be ready for table. A little allspice stewed with the fruit is by many persons considered an improvement.

Time.—1 hour to stew the plums in water, 1½ hour in the syrup.

Average cost,—plums sufficiently good for stewing, 1s. per lb.

Sufficient for 7 or 8 persons. *Seasonable* in winter.

PRESERVED PUMPKIN.

1584. INGREDIENTS.—To each lb. of pumpkin allow 1 lb. of roughly-pounded loaf sugar, 1 gill of lemon-juice.

Mode.—Obtain a good sweet pumpkin; halve it, take out the seeds, and pare off the rind; cut it into neat slices, or into pieces about the size of a five-shilling piece. Weigh the pumpkin, put the slices in a pan or deep dish in layers, with the sugar sprinkled between them; pour the lemon-juice over the top, and let the whole remain for 2 or 3 days. Boil altogether, adding ½ pint of water to every 3 lbs. of sugar used until the pumpkin becomes tender; then turn the whole into a pan, where let it remain for a week; then drain off the syrup, boil it until it is quite thick; skim, and pour it, boiling, over the pumpkin. A little bruised ginger and lemon-rind, thinly pared, may be boiled in the syrup to flavour the pumpkin.

Time.—From ½ to ¾ hour to boil the pumpkin tender.

Average cost, 5d. to 7d. per lb. pot.

Seasonable in September and October; but better when made in the latter month, as the pumpkin is then quite ripe.

Note.—Vegetable marrows are very good prepared in the same manner, but are not quite so rich.

QUINCE JELLY.

585. INGREDIENTS.—To every pint of juice allow 1 lb. of loaf sugar.

Mode.—Pare and slice the quinces, and put them into a preserving-pan with sufficient water to float them. Boil them until tender, and the fruit is reduced to a pulp; strain off the clear juice, and to each pint allow the above proportion of loaf sugar. Boil the juice and sugar together for about ¾ hour; remove all the scum as it rises, and, when the jelly appears firm when a little is poured on a plate, it is done. The residue left on the sieve will answer to make a common marmalade, for immediate use, by boiling it with ⅓ lb. of common sugar to every lb. of pulp.

Time.—3 hours to boil the quinces in water; ¾ hour to boil the jelly.

Average cost, from 8*d.* to 10*d.* per lb. pot.

Seasonable from August to October.

QUINCE MARMALADE.

1586. INGREDIENTS.—To every lb. of quince pulp allow ¾ lb. of loaf sugar.

Mode.—Slice the quinces into a preserving-pan, adding sufficient water for them to float ; place them on the fire to stew, until reduced to a pulp, keeping them stirred occasionally from the bottom, to prevent their burning ; then pass the pulp through a hair sieve, to keep back the skin and seeds. Weigh the pulp, and to each lb. add lump sugar in the above proportion, broken very small. Place the whole on the fire, and keep it well stirred from the bottom of the pan with a wooden spoon, until reduced to a marmalade, which may be known by dropping a little on a cold plate, when, if it jellies, it is done. Put it into jars whilst hot; let it cool, and cover with pieces of oiled paper cut to the size of the mouths of the jars. The tops of them may be afterwards covered with pieces of bladder, or tisssue-paper brushed over on both sides with the white of an egg.

Time.—3 hours to boil the quinces without the sugar ; ¾ hour to boil the pulp with the sugar.

Average cost, from 8*d.* to 9*d.* per lb. pot.

Sufficient.—Allow 1 pint of sliced quinces for a lb. pot.

Seasonable in August, September, and October.

RAISIN CHEESE.

1587. INGREDIENTS.—To every lb. of raisins allow ⅓ lb. of loaf sugar ; pounded cinnamon and cloves to taste.

Mode.—Stone the raisins ; put them into a stewpan with the sugar, cinnamon, and cloves, and let them boil for 1½ hour, stirring all the time. Let the preparation cool a little, pour it into a glass dish, and garnish with strips of candied lemon-peel and citron. This will remain good some time, if kept in a dry place.

Time.—1½ hour. *Average cost,* 9*d.*

Sufficient.—1 lb. for 4 or 5 persons. *Seasonable* at any time.

RASPBERRY JAM.

1588. INGREDIENTS.—To every lb. of raspberries allow 1 lb. of sugar, ¼ pint of red-currant juice.

Mode.—Let the fruit for this preserve be gathered in fine weather, and used as soon after it is picked as possible. Take off the stalks, put the raspberries into a preserving-pan, break them well with a wooden spoon, and let them boil for ¼ hour, keeping them well stirred. Then add the currant-juice and sugar, and boil again for ½ hour. Skim the jam well after the sugar is added, or the preserve will not be clear. The addition of the currant juice is a very great improvement to this preserve, as it gives it a piquant taste, which the flavour of the raspberries seems to require.

Time.—¼ hour to simmer the fruit without the sugar; ½ hour after it is added.

Average cost, from 6*d.* to 8*d.* per lb. pot.

Sufficient.—Allow about 1 pint of fruit to fill a 1-lb. pot.

Seasonable in July and August.

RASPBERRY JELLY.

1589. INGREDIENTS.—To each pint of juice allow ¾ lb. of loaf sugar.

Mode.—Let the raspberries be freshly gathered, quite ripe, and picked from the stalks; put them into a large jar, after breaking the fruit a little with a wooden spoon, and place this jar, covered, in a saucepan of boiling water. When the juice is well drawn, which will be in from ¾ to 1 hour, strain the fruit through a fine hair sieve or cloth; measure the juice, and to every pint allow the above proportion of loaf sugar. Put the juice and sugar into a preserving-pan, place it over the fire, and boil gently until the jelly thickens when a little is poured on a plate; carefully remove all the scum as it rises, pour the jelly into small pots, cover down, and keep in a dry place. This jelly answers for making raspberry cream, and for flavouring various sweet dishes, when, in winter, the fresh fruit is not obtainable.

Time.—¾ to 1 hour to draw the juice.

Average cost, from 9*d.* to 1*s.* per lb. pot.

Sufficient.—From 3 pints to 2 quarts of fruit should yield 1 pint of juice.

Seasonable.—This should be made in July or August.

RHUBARB JAM.

1590 INGREDIENTS.—To every lb. of rhubarb allow 1 lb. of loaf sugar, the rind of ½ lemon.

Mode.—Wipe the rhubarb perfectly dry, take off the string or peel, and weigh it; put it into a preserving-pan, with sugar in the above proportion; mince the lemon-rind very finely, add it to the other ingredients, and place the preserving-pan by the side of the fire; keep stirring to prevent the rhubarb from burning, and when the sugar is well dissolved, put the pan more over the fire, and let the jam boil until it is done, taking care to keep it well skimmed and stirred with a wooden or silver spoon. Pour it into pots, and cover down with oiled and egged papers.

Time.—If the rhubarb is young and tender, $\frac{3}{4}$ hour, reckoning from the time it simmers equally; old rhubarb, $1\frac{1}{4}$ to $1\frac{1}{2}$ hour.

Average cost, 5*d.* to 7*d.* per lb. pot.

Sufficient.—About 1 pint of sliced rhubarb to fill a lb. pot.

Seasonable from February to April.

RHUBARB AND ORANGE JAM, to resemble Scotch Marmalade.

1591. INGREDIENTS.—1 quart of finely-cut rhubarb, 6 oranges, $1\frac{1}{2}$ lb. of loaf sugar.

Mode.—Peel the oranges; remove as much of the white pith as possible, divide them, and take out the pips; slice the pulp into a preserving-pan, add the rind of half the oranges cut into thin strips, and the loaf sugar, which should be broken small. Peel the rhubarb, cut it into thin pieces, put it to the oranges, and stir altogether over a gentle fire until the jam is done. Remove all the scum as it rises, put the preserve into pots, and, when cold, cover down. Should the rhubarb be very old, stew it alone for $\frac{1}{4}$ hour before the other ingredients are added.

Time.—$\frac{3}{4}$ to 1 hour. *Average cost,* from 6*d.* to 8*d.* per lb. pot.

Seasonable from February to April.

RASPBERRY AND CURRANT, or any Fresh Fruit Salad.
(*A Dessert Dish.*)

1592. *Mode.*—Fruit salads are made by stripping the fruit from the stalks, piling it on a dish, and sprinkling over it finely-pounded sugar. They may be made of strawberries, raspberries, currants, or any of these fruits mixed; peaches also make a very good salad. After the sugar is sprinkled over, about 6 large tablespoonfuls of wine or brandy, or 3 tablespoonfuls of liqueur, should be poured in the middle of the fruit; and, when the flavour is liked, a little pounded cinnamon may be added. In helping the fruit, it should be lightly stirred, that the wine and sugar may be equally distributed.

Sufficient.—1½ pint of fruit, with 3 oz. of pounded sugar, for 4 or 5 persons.

Seasonable in summer.

STRAWBERRIES AND CREAM.

1593. INGREDIENTS.—To every pint of picked strawberries allow ⅓ pint of cream, 2 oz. of finely-pounded sugar.

Mode.—Pick the stalks from the fruit, place it on a glass dish, sprinkle over it pounded sugar, and slightly stir the strawberries, that they may all be equally sweetened; pour the cream over the top, and serve. Devonshire cream, when it can be obtained, is exceedingly delicious for this dish; and, if very thick indeed, may be diluted with a little thin cream or milk.

Average cost for this quantity, with cream at 1s. per pint, 1s.

Sufficient for 2 persons. *Seasonable* in June and July.

STRAWBERRY JAM.

1594. INGREDIENTS.—To every lb. of fruit allow ½ pint of red-currant juice, 1¼ lb. of loaf sugar.

Mode.—Strip the currants from the stalks, put them into a jar; place this jar in a saucepan of boiling water, and simmer until the juice is well drawn from the fruit; strain the currants, measure the juice, put it into a preserving-pan, and add the sugar. Select well-ripened but sound strawberries; pick them from the stalks, and when the sugar is dissolved in the currant juice, put in the fruit. Simmer the whole over a moderate fire, from ½ to ¾ hour, carefully removing the scum as it rises. Stir the jam only enough to prevent it from burning at the bottom of the pan, as the fruit should be preserved as whole as possible. Put the jam into jars, and when cold, cover down.

Time.—½ to ¾ hour, reckoning from the time the jam simmers all over.

Average cost, from 7d. to 8d. per lb. pot.

Sufficient.—12 pints of strawberries will make 12 lb. pots of jam.

Seasonable in June and July.

PRESERVED STRAWBERRIES IN WINE.

1595. INGREDIENTS.—To every quart bottle allow ¼ lb. of finely-pounded loaf sugar; sherry or Madeira.

Mode.—Let the fruit be gathered in fine weather, and used as soon as picked. Have ready some perfectly dry glass bottles, and some nice soft corks or bungs. Pick the stalks from the strawberries, drop them into the bottles, sprinkling amongst them pounded sugar in the above proportion, and when the fruit reaches to the neck of the bottle, fill up with sherry or Madeira. Cork the bottles down with new corks, and dip them into melted resin.

Seasonable.—Make this in June or July.

TO PRESERVE STRAWBERRIES WHOLE.

1596. INGREDIENTS.—To every lb. of fruit allow 1¼ lb. of good loaf sugar, 1 pint of red-currant juice.

Mode.—Choose the strawberries not too ripe, of a fine large sort and of a good colour. Pick off the stalks, lay the strawberries in a dish, and sprinkle over them half the quantity of sugar, which must be finely pounded. Shake the dish gently, that the sugar may be equally distributed and touch the under-side of the fruit, and let it remain for 1 day. Then have ready the currant-juice, drawn as for red-currant jelly No. 1533; boil it with the remainder of the sugar until it forms a thin syrup, and in this simmer the strawberries and sugar, until the whole is sufficiently jellied. Great care must be taken not to stir the fruit roughly, as it should be preserved as whole as possible. Strawberries prepared in this manner are very good served in glasses and mixed with thin cream.

Time.—¼ hour to 20 minutes to simmer the strawberries in the syrup.

Seasonable in June and July.

TO MAKE EVERTON TOFFEE.

1597. INGREDIENTS.—1 lb. of powdered loaf sugar, 1 teacupful of water, ¼ lb. of butter, 6 drops of essence of lemon.

Mode.—Put the water and sugar into a brass pan, and beat the butter to a cream. When the sugar is dissolved, add the butter, and keep stirring the mixture over the fire until it sets, when a little is poured on to a buttered dish; and just before the toffee is done, add the essence of lemon. Butter a dish or tin, pour on it the mixture, and when cool, it will easily separate from the dish. Butter-Scotch, an excellent thing for coughs, is made with brown, instead of white sugar, omitting the water, and flavoured with ½ oz. of powdered ginger. It is made in the same manner as toffee.

Time.—18 to 35 minutes. *Average cost,* 10*d.*

Sufficient to make a lb. of toffee.

DESERT DISHES.

1598. The tazza, or dish with stem, the same as that shown in our illustrations, is now the favourite shape for dessert-dishes. The fruit can be arranged and shown to better advantage on these tall high dishes than on the short flat ones. All the dishes are now usually placed down the centre of the table, dried and fresh fruit alternately, the former being arranged on small round or oval glass plates, and the latter on the dishes with stems. The fruit should always be gathered on the same day that it is required for table, and should be tastefully arranged on the dishes, with leaves between and round it. By purchasing fruits that *are in season*, a dessert can be supplied at a very moderate cost. These, with a few fancy biscuits, crystallized fruit, bon-bons, &c., are sufficient for an ordinary dessert.

DISH OF NUTS.

BOX OF FRENCH PLUMS.

DISH OF MIXED FRUIT.

When fresh fruit cannot be obtained, dried and foreign fruits, compôtes, baked pears, stewed Normandy pippins, &c. &c., must supply its place, with the addition of preserves, bon-bons, cakes, biscuits, &c. At fashionable tables, forced fruit is served growing in pots, these pots being hidden in more ornamental ones, and arranged with the other dishes.

A few vases of fresh flowers, tastefully arranged, add very much to the appearance of the dessert; and, when these are not obtainable, a few paper ones, mixed with green leaves, answer very well as a substitute. In decorating a table, whether for luncheon, dessert, or supper, a vase or two of flowers should

3 F

never be forgotten, as they add so much to the elegance of the *tout ensemble*. In summer and autumn, ladies residing in the country can always manage to have a few freshly-gathered flowers on their tables, and should never be without this inexpensive luxury. On the continent, vases or epergnes filled with flowers are invariably placed down the centre of the dinner-table at regular distances. Ices for dessert are usually moulded : when this is not the case, they are handed round in glasses with wafers to accompany them. Preserved ginger is frequently handed round after ices, to prepare the palate for the delicious dessert wines. A basin or glass of finely-pounded lump sugar must never be omitted at a dessert, as also a glass jug of fresh cold water (iced, if possible), and two goblets by its side. Grape-

BOX OF CHOCOLATE.

DISH OF APPLES.

DISH OF MIXED SUMMER FRUIT.

ALMONDS AND RAISINS.

DISH OF STRAWBERRIES.

scissors, a melon-knife and fork, and nutcrackers, should always be put on table, if there are dishes of fruit requiring them. Zests are sometimes served at the close of the dessert; such as anchovy toasts or biscuits. The French often serve plain or grated cheese with a dessert of fresh or dried fruits. At some tables, finger-glasses are placed at the right of each person, nearly half filled with cold spring water, and in winter with tepid water. These precede the dessert. At other tables, a glass or vase is simply handed round, filled with perfumed water, into which each guest dips the corner of his napkin, and, when needful, refreshes his lips and the tips of his fingers. After the dishes are placed, and every one is provided with plates, glasses, spoons, &c., the wine should be put at each end of the table, cooled or otherwise, according to the season. If the party be small, the wine may be placed only at the top of the table, near the host.

DISH OF NUTS.

1599. These are merely arranged piled high in the centre of the dish, as shown in the engraving, with or without leaves round the edge. Filberts should always be served with the outer skin or husk on them; and walnuts should be well wiped with a damp cloth, and then with a dry one, to remove the unpleasant sticky feeling the shells frequently have.

Seasonable.—Filberts from September to March, good; may be had after that time, but are generally shrivelled and dry. Walnuts from September to January.

HAZEL NUT AND FILBERT.—The common Hazel is the wild, and the Filbert the cultivated state of the same tree. The hazel is found wild, not only in forests and hedges, in dingles and ravines, but occurs in extensive tracts in the more northern and mountainous parts of the country. It was formerly one of the most abundant of those trees which are indigenous in this island. It is seldom cultivated as a fruit-tree, though perhaps its nuts are superior in flavour to the others. The Spanish nuts imported are a superior kind, but they are somewhat oily and rather indigestible. Filberts, both the red and the white, and the cob-nut, are supposed to be merely varieties of the common hazel, which have been produced, partly by the superiority of soil and climate, and partly by culture. They were originally brought out of Greece to Italy, whence they have found their way to Holland, and from that country to England. It is supposed that, within a few miles of Maidstone, in Kent, there are more filberts grown than in all England besides; and it is from that place that the London market is supplied. The filbert is longer than the common nut, though of the same thickness, and has a larger kernel. The cob-nut is a still larger variety, and is roundish. Filberts are more esteemed at the dessert than common nuts, and are generally eaten with salt. They are very free from oil, and disagree with few persons.

. WALNUTS.—The Walnut is a native of Persia, the Caucasus, and China, but was introduced to this kingdom from France. The ripe kernel is brought to the dessert on account of its agreeable flavour; and the fruit is also much used in the green state, before the stone hardens, as a pickle. In Spain, grated walnuts are employed in tarts and other dishes. The walnut abounds in oil, which is expressed, and which, being of a highly drying nature, and very limpid, is much employed for delicate painting. This, on the continent, is sometimes used as a substitute for olive-oil in cooking, but is very apt to turn rancid. It is also manufactured into a kind of soap. The marc, or refuse matter after the oil is extracted, proves very nutritious for poultry or other domestic animals. In Switzerland, this is eaten by poor people under the name of *pain amer*.

BOX OF FRENCH PLUMS.

1600. If the box which contains them is exceedingly ornamental, it may be placed on the table; if small, on a glass dish; if large, without one. French plums may also be arranged on a glass plate, and garnished with bright-coloured sweetmeats, which make a very good effect. All fancy boxes of preserved and crystallized fruit may be put on the table or not, at pleasure. These little matters of detail must, of course, be left to individual taste.

Seasonable.—May be purchased all the year; but are in greater perfection in the winter, and are more suitable for that season, as fresh fruit cannot be obtained.

DISH OF MIXED FRUIT.

1601. For a centre dish, a mixture of various fresh fruits has a remarkably good effect, particularly if a pine be added to the list. A high raised appearance should be given to the fruit, which is done in the following manner. Place a tumbler in the centre of the dish. and, in this tumbler, the pine, crown uppermost; round the tumbler put a thick layer of moss, and, over this, apples, pears, plums, peaches, and such fruit as is simultaneously in season. By putting a layer of moss underneath, so much fruit is not required, besides giving a better shape to the dish. Grapes should be placed on the top of the fruit, a portion of some of the bunches hanging over the sides of the dish in a négligé kind of manner, which takes off the formal look of the dish. In arranging the plums, apples, &c., let the colours contrast well.

Seasonable.—Suitable for a dessert in September or October.

GRAPES.—France produces about a thousand varieties of the grape, which is cultivated more extensively in that country than in any other. Hygienists agree in pronouncing grapes as among the best of fruits. The grape possesses several rare qualities: it is nourishing and fattening, and its prolonged use has often overcome the most obstinate cases of constipation. The skins and pips of grapes should not be eaten.

BOX OF CHOCOLATE.

1602. This is served in an ornamental box. placed on a glass plate or dish.

Seasonable.—May be purchased at any time.

DISH OF APPLES.

1603. The apples should be nicely wiped with a dry cloth, and arranged on a dish, piled high in the centre, with evergreen leaves between each layer. The inferior apples should form the bottom layer, with the bright-coloured large ones at the top. The leaves of the laurel, bay, holly, or any shrub green in winter, are suitable for garnishing dessert dishes. Oranges may be arranged in the same manner; they should also be wiped with a dry cloth before being sent to table.

DISH OF MIXED SUMMER FRUIT.

1604. This dish consists of cherries, raspberries, currants, and strawberries, piled in different layers, with plenty of leaves between each layer; so that each fruit is well separated. The fruit should be arranged with a due regard to colour, so that they contrast nicely one with the other. Our engraving shows a layer of white cherries at the bottom, then one of red raspberries; over that a layer of white currants, and at the top some fine scarlet strawberries.

Seasonable in June, July, and August.

ALMONDS AND RAISINS.

1605. These are usually served on glass dishes, the fruit piled high in the centre, and the almonds blanched, and strewn over. To blanch the almonds, put them into a small mug or teacup, pour over them boiling water, let them remain for 2 or 3 minutes, and the skins may then be easily removed. Figs, dates, French plums, &c., are all served on small glass plates or oval dishes, but without the almonds. .

Seasonable at any time, but more suitable in winter, when fresh fruit is not obtainable.

DATES.—Dates are imported into Britain, in a dried state, from Barbary and Egypt, and, when in good condition, they are much esteemed. An inferior kind has lately become common, which are dried hard, and have little or no flavour. They should be chosen large, softish, not much wrinkled, of a reddish-yellow colour on the outside, with a whitish membrane between the fruit and the stone.

DISH OF STRAWBERRIES.

1606. Fine strawberries, arranged in the manner shown in the engraving, look exceedingly well. The inferior ones should be placed at the bottom of the dish, and the others put in rows pyramidically, with the stalks downwards; so that when the whole is completed, nothing but the red part of the fruit is visible. The fruit should be gathered with rather long stalks, as there is then something to support it, and it can be placed more upright in each layer. A few of the finest should be reserved to crown the top.

TO HAVE WALNUTS FRESH THROUGHOUT THE SEASON.

1607. INGREDIENTS.—To every pint of water allow 1 teaspoonful of salt.

Mode.—Place the walnuts in the salt and water for 24 hours at least; then take them out, and rub them dry. Old nuts may be freshened in this manner; or walnuts, when first picked, may be put into an earthen pan with salt sprinkled amongst them, and with damped hay placed on the top of them, and then covered down with a lid. They must be well wiped before they are put on table.

Seasonable.—Should be stored away in September or October.

CHAPTER XXXII.

GENERAL OBSERVATIONS ON MILK, BUTTER, CHEESE, AND EGGS.

MILK.

1608. MILK is obtained only from the class of animals called Mammalia, and is intended by Nature for the nourishment of their young. The milk of each animal is distinguished by some peculiarities ; but as that of the cow is by far the most useful to us in this part of the world, our observations will be confined to that variety.

1609. Milk, when drawn from the cow, is of a yellowish-white colour, and is the most yellow at the beginning of the period of lactation. Its taste is agreeable, and rather saccharine. The viscidity and specific gravity of milk are somewhat greater than that of water ; but these properties vary somewhat in the milk procured from different individuals. On an average, the specific gravity of milk is 1.035, water being 1. The small cows of the Alderney breed afford the richest milk.

1610. Milk which is carried to a considerable distance, so as to be much agitated, and cooled before it is put into pans to settle for cream, never throws up so much, nor such rich cream, as if the same milk had been put into pans directly after it was milked.

1611. Milk, considered as an aliment, is of such importance in domestic economy as to render all the improvements in its production extremely valuable. To enlarge upon the antiquity of its use is unnecessary ; it has always been a favourite food in Britain. "Lacte et carne vivunt," says Cæsar, in his Commentaries ; the English of which is, "the inhabitants subsist upon flesh and milk." The breed of the cow has received great improvement in modern times, as regards the quantity and quality of the milk which she affords ; the form of milch-cows, their mode of nourishment, and progress, are also manifest in the management of the dairy.

1612. Although milk in its natural state be a fluid, yet, considered as an aliment, it is both solid and fluid : for no sooner does it enter the stomach, than it is coagulated by the gastric juice, and separated into curd and whey, the first of these being extremely nutritive.

1613. Milk of the *human subject* is much thinner than cow's milk ; *Ass's milk* comes the nearest to human milk of any other ; *Goat's milk* is something thicker and richer than cow's milk ; *Ewe's milk* has the appearance of cow's milk, and affords a larger quantity of cream ; *Mare's milk* contains more sugar than that of the ewe ; *Camel's milk* is used only in Africa ; *Buffalo's milk* is employed in India.

1614. From no other substance, solid or fluid, can so great a number of distinct kinds of aliment be prepared as from milk ; some forming food, others drink ; some of them delicious, and deserving the name of luxuries ; all of them wholesome, and some medicinal : indeed, the variety of aliments that seems capable of being produced from milk, appears to be quite endless. In every age this must have been a subject for experiment, and every nation has added to the number by the invention of some peculiarity of its own.

BUTTER.

1615. BECKMAN, in his "History of Inventions," states that butter was not used either by the Greeks or Romans in cooking, nor was it brought upon their tables at certain meals, as is the custom at present. In England it has been made from time immemorial, though the art of making cheese is said not to have been known to the ancient Britons, and to have been learned from their conquerors.

1616. The taste of butter is peculiar, and very unlike any other fatty substance. It is extremely agreeable when of the best quality ; but its flavour depends much upon the food given to the cows : to be good, it should not adhere to the knife.

1617. Butter, with regard to its dietetic properties, may be regarded nearly in the light of vegetable oils and animal fats ; but it becomes sooner rancid than most other fat oils. When fresh, it cannot but be considered as very wholesome ; but it should be quite free from rancidity. If slightly salted when it is fresh, its wholesomeness is probably not at all impaired ; but should it begin to turn rancid, salting will not correct its unwholesomeness. When salt butter is put into casks, the upper part next the air is very apt to become rancid, and this rancidity is also liable to affect the whole cask.

1618. *Epping butter* is the kind most esteemed in London. *Fresh butter* comes to London from Buckinghamshire, Suffolk, Oxfordshire, Yorkshire, Devonshire, &c. *Cambridge butter* is esteemed next to fresh ; *Devonshire butter* is nearly similar in quality to the latter ; *Irish butter* sold in London is all salted, but is generally good. The number of firkins exported annually from Ireland amounts to 420,000, equal to a million of money. *Dutch butter* is in good repute all over Europe, America, and even India ; and no country in the world is so successful in the manufacture of this article, Holland supplying more butter to the rest of the world than any country whatever.

1619. There are two methods pursued in the manufacture of butter. In one, the cream is separated from the milk, and in that state it is converted into butter by churning, as is the practice about Epping ; in the other, milk is subjected to the same process, which is the method usually followed in Cheshire. The first method is generally said to give the richest butter, and the latter the largest quantity, though some are of opinion that there is little difference either in quality or quantity.

CHEESE.

1620. CHEESE is the curd formed from milk by artificial coagulation, pressed and dried for use. Curd, called also casein and caseous matter, or the basis of cheese, exists in the milk, and not in the cream, and requires only to be separated by coagulation. The coagulation, however, supposes some alteration of the curd. By means of the substance employed to coagulate it, it is rendered insoluble in water. When the curd is freed from the whey, kneaded and pressed to expel it entirely, it becomes cheese. This assumes a degree of transparency, and possesses many of the properties of coagulated albumen. If it be well dried, it does not change by exposure to the air ; but if it contain moisture, it soon putrefies. It therefore requires some salt to preserve it, and this acts likewise as a kind of seasoning. All our cheese is coloured more or less, except that made from skim milk. The colouring substances employed are arnatto, turmeric, or marigold, all perfectly harmless unless they are adulterated ; and it is said that arnatto sometimes contains red lead.

1621. Cheese varies in quality and richness according to the materials of which it is composed. It is made—1. Of entire milk, as in Cheshire ; 2. of milk and cream, as at Stilton ; 3. of new milk mixed with skimmed milk, as in Gloucestershire ; 4. of skimmed milk only, as in Suffolk, Holland, and Italy.

1622. The principal varieties of cheese used in England are the following :— *Cheshire cheese*, famed all over Europe for its rich quality and fine piquant flavour. It is made of entire new milk, the cream not being taken off. *Gloucester cheese* is much milder in its taste than the Cheshire. There are two kinds of Gloucester cheese,—single and double. *Single Gloucester* is made of skimmed milk, or of the milk deprived of half the cream ; *Double Gloucester* is a cheese that pleases almost every palate : it is made of the whole milk and cream. *Stilton cheese* is made by adding the cream of one day to the entire milk of the next : it was first made at Stilton, in Leicestershire. *Sage cheese* is so called from the practice of colouring some curd with bruised sage, marigold-leaves, and parsley, and mixing this with some uncoloured curd. With the Romans, and during the middle ages, this practice was extensively adopted. *Cheddar cheese* much resembles Parmesan. It has a very agreeable taste and flavour, and has a spongy appearance. *Brickbat cheese* has nothing remarkable except its form. It is made by turning with rennet a mixture of cream and new milk. The curd is put into a wooden vessel the shape of a brick, and is then pressed and dried in the usual way. *Dunlop cheese* has a peculiarly mild and rich taste : the best is made entirely from new milk. *New cheese* (as it is called in London) is made chiefly in Lincolnshire, and is either made of all cream, or, like Stilton, by adding the cream of one day's milking to the milk that comes immediately from the cow : they are extremely thin, and are compressed gently two or three times, turned for a few days, and then eaten new with radishes, salad, &c. *Skimmed Milk cheese* is made for sea voyages principally. *Parmesan cheese* is made in Parma and Piacenza. It is the most celebrated of all cheese : it is made entirely of skimmed cow's milk. The high flavour which it has, is supposed to be owing to the rich herbage of the meadows of the Po, where the cows are pastured. The best Parmesan is kept for three or four years, and none is carried to market till it is at least six months old. *Dutch cheese* derives its peculiar pungent taste from the practice adopted in Holland of coagulating the milk with muriatic acid instead of rennet. *Swiss cheeses* in their several varieties are all remarkable for their fine flavour. That from *Gruyère*, a bailiwick in the canton of Fribourg, is best known in England. It is flavoured by the dried herb of *Melilotos officinalis* in powder. Cheese from milk and potatoes is manufactured in Thuringia and Saxony. *Cream cheese*, although so called, is not properly cheese, but is nothing more than cream dried sufficiently to be cut with a knife.

EGGS.

1623. THERE is only one opinion as to the nutritive properties of eggs, although the qualities of those belonging to different birds vary somewhat. Those of the common hen are most esteemed as delicate food, particularly when "new-laid." The quality of eggs depends much upon the food given to the hen. Eggs in general are considered most easily digestible when little subjected to the art of cookery. The lightest way of dressing them is by poaching, which is effected by putting them for a minute or two into brisk boiling water : this coagulates the external white, without doing the inner part too much. Eggs are much better when new-laid than a day or two afterwards. The usual time allotted for boiling eggs in the shell is 3 to $3\frac{3}{4}$ minutes : less time than that in boiling water will not be sufficient to solidify the white, and more will make the yolk hard and less digestible : it is very difficult to *guess* accurately as to the time. Great care should be employed in putting them into the water, to prevent cracking the shell, which inevitably causes a portion of the white to exude, and lets water into the egg. Eggs are often beaten up raw in nutritive beverages.

1624. Eggs are employed in a very great many articles of cookery, entrées, and entremets, and they form an essential ingredient in pastry, creams, flip, &c. It is particularly necessary that they should be quite fresh, as nothing is worse than stale eggs. Cobbett justly says, stale, or even preserved eggs, are things to be run from, not after.

1625. The Metropolis is supplied with eggs from all parts of the kingdom, and they are likewise largely imported from various places on the continent ; as France, Holland, Belgium, Guernsey, and Jersey. It appears from official statements mentioned in McCulloch's "Commercial Dictionary," that the number imported from France alone amounts to about 60,000,000 a year ; and supposing them on an average to cost fourpence a dozen, it follows that we pay our continental neighbours above £83,000 a year for eggs.

1626. The eggs of different birds vary much in size and colour. Those of the ostrich are the largest : one laid in the menagerie in Paris weighed 2 lbs. 14 oz., held a pint, and was six inches deep : this is about the usual size of those brought from Africa. Travellers describe *ostrich eggs* as of an agreeable taste : they keep longer than hen's eggs. Drinking-cups are often made of the shell, which is very strong. The eggs of the *turkey* are almost as mild as those of the hen ; the egg of the *goose* is large, but well-tasted. *Duck's eggs* have a rich flavour ; the albumen is slightly transparent, or bluish, when set or coagulated by boiling, which requires less time than hen's eggs. *Guinea-fowl eggs* are smaller and more delicate than those of the hen. Eggs of *wild fowl* are generally coloured, often spotted ; and the taste generally partakes somewhat of the flavour of the bird they belong to. Those of land birds that are eaten, as the *plover, lapwing, ruff*, &c., are in general much esteemed ; but those of *sea-fowl* have, more or less, a strong fishy taste. The eggs of the *turtle* are very numerous : they consist of yolk only, without shell, and are delicious.

RECIPES.

CHAPTER XXXIII.

SEPARATION OF MILK AND CREAM.

1627. IF it be desired that the milk should be freed entirely from cream, it should be poured into a very shallow broad pan or dish, not more than 1½ inch deep, as cream cannot rise through a great depth of milk. In cold and wet weather, milk is not so rich as it is in summer and warm weather, and the morning's milk is always richer than the evening's. The last-drawn milk of each milking, at all times and seasons, is richer than the first-drawn, and on that account should be set apart for cream. Milk should be shaken as little as possible when carried from the cow to the dairy, and should be poured into the pans very gently. Persons not keeping cows, may always have a little cream, provided the milk they purchase be pure and unadulterated. As soon as it comes in, it should be poured into very shallow open pie-dishes, and set by in a very cool place, and in 7 or 8 hours a nice cream should have risen to the surface.

MILK is one of the most complete of all articles of food: that is to say, it contains a very large number of the elements which enter into the composition of the human body. It "disagrees" with fat, heavy, languid people, of slow circulation; and, at first, with many people of sedentary habits, and stomachs weakened by stimulants of different kinds. But, if exercise can be taken and a little patience shown, while the system accommodates itself to a new regimen, this bland and soothing article of diet is excellent for the majority of thin, nervous people; especially for those who have suffered much from emotional disturbances, or have relaxed their stomachs by too much tea or coffee, taken too hot. Milk is, in fact, a nutrient and a sedative at once. Stomachs, however, have their idiosyncrasies, and it sometimes proves an unwelcome and ill-digested article of food. As milk, when good, contains a good deal of respiratory material (fat),—material which *must* either be burnt off, or derange the liver, and be rejected in other ways, it may disagree because the lungs are not sufficiently used in the open air. But it is very probable that there are really "constitutions" which cannot take to it; and *they* should not be forced.

TO KEEP MILK AND CREAM IN HOT WEATHER.

1628. When the weather is very warm, and it is very difficult to prevent milk from turning sour and spoiling the cream, it should be scalded, and it will then remain good for a few hours. It must on no account be allowed to boil, or there will be a skin instead of a cream upon the milk; and the slower the process, the safer will it be. A very good plan to scald milk, is to put the pan that contains it into a saucepan or wide kettle of boiling water.   When the surface looks thick, the milk is sufficiently scalded, and it should then be put away in a cool place in the same vessel that it was scalded in.   Cream may be kept for 24 hours, if scalded without sugar ; and by the addition of the latter ingredient, it will remain good double the time, if kept in a cool place.   All pans, jugs, and vessels intended for milk, should be kept beautifully clean, and well scalded before the milk is put in, as any negligence in this respect may cause large quantities of it to be spoiled ; and milk should never be kept in vessels of zinc or copper. Milk may be preserved good in hot weather, for a few hours, by placing the jug which contains it in ice, or very cold water ; or a pinch of bicarbonate of soda may be introduced into the liquid.

MILK, when of good quality, is of an opaque white colour : the cream always comes to the top; the well-known milky odour is strong; it will boil without altering its appearance in these respects; the little bladders which arise on the surface will renew themselves if broken by the spoon. To boil milk is, in fact, the simplest way of testing its quality. The commonest adulterations of milk are not of a hurtful character. It is a good deal thinned with water, and sometimes thickened with a little starch, or coloured with yolk of egg, or even saffron; but these processes have nothing murderous in them.

CURDS AND WHEY.

1629. INGREDIENTS.—A very small piece of rennet, ½ gallon of milk.

Mode.—Procure from the butcher's a small piece of rennet, which is the stomach of the calf, taken as soon as it is killed, scoured, and well rubbed with salt, and stretched on sticks to dry.   Pour some boiling water on the rennet, and let it remain for 6 hours ; then use the liquor to turn the milk.   The milk should be warm and fresh from the cow : if allowed to cool, it must be heated till it is of a degree quite equal to new milk ; but do not let it be too hot.   About a tablespoonful, or rather more, would be sufficient to turn the above proportion of milk into curds and whey ; and whilst the milk is turning, let it be kept in rather a warm place.

Time.—From 2 to 3 hours to turn the milk.

Seasonable at any time.

DEVONSHIRE CREAM.

1630. The milk should stand 24 hours in the winter, half that time when the weather is very warm.   The milkpan is then set on a stove, and should there remain until the milk is quite hot ; but it must not boil, or there will be a thick skin on the surface.   When it is sufficiently done, the undulations on the surface look thick, and small rings appear.   The time required for scalding cream depends on the size of the pan and the heat of the fire ; but the slower it is done, the better. The pan should be placed in the dairy when the cream is sufficiently scalded, and skimmed the following day. This cream is so much esteemed that it is sent to the London markets in small square tins, and is exceedingly delicious eaten with fresh fruit. In Devonshire, butter is made from this cream, and is usually very firm.

DEVONSHIRE JUNKET.

1631. INGREDIENTS.—To every pint of new milk allow 2 dessert-spoonfuls of brandy, 1 dessertspoonful of sugar, and 1½ dessertspoonful of prepared rennet; thick cream, pounded cinnamon, or grated nutmeg.

Mode.—Make the milk blood-warm; put it into a deep dish with the brandy, sugar, and rennet; stir it altogether, and cover it over until it is set. Then spread some thick or clotted cream over the top, grate some nutmeg, and strew some sugar over, and the dish will be ready to serve.

Time.—About 2 hours to set the milk. *Seasonable* at any time.

TO KEEP AND CHOOSE FRESH BUTTER.

1632. Fresh butter should be kept in a dark, cool place, and in as large a mass as possible. Mould as much only as is required, as the more surface is exposed, the more liability there will be to spoil; and the outside very soon becomes rancid. Fresh butter should be kept covered with white paper. For small larders, butter-coolers of red brick are now very much used for keeping fresh butter in warm weather. These coolers are made with a large bell-shaped cover, into the top of which a little cold water should be poured, and in summer time very frequently changed; and the butter must be kept covered. These coolers keep butter remarkably firm in hot weather, and are extremely convenient for those whose larder accommodation is limited.

In choosing fresh butter, remember it should smell deliciously, and be of an equal colour all through: if it smells sour, it has not been sufficiently washed from the buttermilk; and if veiny and open, it has probably been worked with a staler or an inferior sort.

BUTTER-DISH.

TO PRESERVE AND TO CHOOSE SALT BUTTER.

1633. In large families, where salt butter is purchased a tub at a time, the first thing to be done is to turn the whole of the butter out.

and, with a clean knife, to scrape the outside; the tub should then be wiped with a clean cloth, and sprinkled all round with salt, the butter replaced, and the lid kept on to exclude the air. It is necessary to take these precautions, as sometimes a want of proper cleanliness in the dairymaid causes the outside of the butter to become rancid, and if the scraping be neglected, the whole mass would soon become spoiled. To choose salt butter, plunge a knife into it, and if, when drawn out, the blade smells rancid or unpleasant, the butter is bad. The layers in tubs will vary greatly, the butter being made at different times; so, to try if the whole tub be good, the cask should be unhooped, and the butter tried between the staves.

It is not necessary to state that butter is extracted from cream, or from unskimmed milk, by the churn. Of course it partakes of the qualities of the milk, and winter butter is said not to be so good as spring butter.

A word of caution is necessary about *rancid* butter. Nobody eats it on bread, but it is sometimes used in cooking, in forms in which the acidity can be more or less disguised. So much the worse; it is almost poisonous, disguise it as you may. Never, under any exigency whatever, be tempted into allowing butter with even a *soupçon* of "turning" to enter into the composition of any dish that appears on your table. And, in general, the more you can do without the employment of butter that has been subjected to the influence of heat, the better. The woman of modern times is not a "leech;" but she might often keep the "leech" from the door, if she would give herself the trouble to invent *innocent* sauces.

BUTTER-MOULDS, for Moulding Fresh Butter.

1634. Butter-moulds, or wooden stamps for moulding fresh butter, are much used, and are made in a variety of forms and shapes. In

DISH OF ROLLED BUTTER.

using them, let them be kept scrupulously clean, and before the butter is pressed in, the interior should be well wetted with cold water; the butter must then be pressed in, the mould opened, and the perfect shape taken out. The butter may be then dished, and garnished with a wreath of parsley, if for a cheese course; if for breakfast, put it into an ornamental butter-dish, with a little water at the bottom, should the weather be very warm.

CURLED BUTTER.

1635. Tie a strong cloth by two of the corners to an iron hook in the wall; make a knot with the other two ends, so that a stick might pass through. Put the butter into the cloth; twist it tightly over a dish, into which the butter will fall through the knot, so forming small and pretty little strings. The butter may then be garnished with parsley, if to serve with a cheese course; or it may be sent to table plain for breakfast, in an ornamental dish. Squirted butter for garnishing hams, salads, eggs, &c., is made by forming a piece of stiff paper in the shape of a cornet, and squeezing the butter in fine strings from the hole at the bottom. Scooped butter is made by dipping a teaspoon or scooper in warm water, and then scooping the butter quickly and thin. In warm weather, it would not be necessary to heat the spoon.

BUTTER may be kept fresh for ten or twelve days by a very simple process. Knead it well in cold water till the buttermilk is extracted; then put it in a glazed jar, which invert in another, putting into the latter a sufficient quantity of water to exclude the air. Renew the water every day.

FAIRY BUTTER.

1636. INGREDIENTS.—The yolks of 2 hard-boiled eggs, 1 table-spoonful of orange-flower water, 2 tablespoonfuls of pounded sugar, $\frac{1}{4}$ lb. of good fresh butter.

Mode.—Beat the yolks of the eggs smoothly in a mortar, with the orange-flower water and the sugar, until the whole is reduced to a fine paste; add the butter, and force all through an old but clean cloth by wringing the cloth and squeezing the butter very hard. The butter will then drop on the plate in large and small pieces, according to the holes in the cloth. Plain butter may be done in the same manner, and is very quickly prepared, besides having a very good effect.

BUTTER.—White-coloured butter is said not to be so good as the yellow; but the yellow colour is often artificially produced, by the introduction of colouring matter into the churn.

ANCHOVY BUTTER.

1637. INGREDIENTS.—To every lb. of butter allow 6 anchovies, 1 small bunch of parsley.

Mode.—Wash, bone, and pound the anchovies well in a mortar; scald the parsley, chop it, and rub through a sieve; then pound all the ingredients together, mix well, and make the butter into pats immediately. This makes a pretty dish, if fancifully moulded, for breakfast or supper, and should be garnished with parsley.

Average cost, 1s. 8d.

Sufficient to make 2 dishes, with 4 pats each.

Seasonable at any time.

CHEESE.

1638. In families where much cheese is consumed, and it is bought in large quantities, a piece from the whole cheese should be cut, the larger quantity spread with a thickly-buttered sheet of white paper, and the outside occasionally wiped. To keep cheeses moist that are in daily use, when they come from table a damp cloth should be wrapped round them, and the cheese put into a pan with a cover to it, in a cool but not very dry place. To ripen cheeses, and bring them forward, put them into a damp cellar; and, to check too large a production of mites, spirits may be poured into the parts affected. Pieces of cheese which are too near the rind, or too dry to put on table, may be made into Welsh rare-bits, or grated down and mixed with macaroni. Cheeses may be preserved in a perfect state for years, by covering them with parchment made pliable by soaking in water, or by rubbing them over with a coating of melted fat. The cheeses selected should be free from cracks or bruises of any kind.

CHEESE.—It is well known that some persons like cheese in a state of decay, and even "alive." There is no accounting for tastes, and it may be hard to show why mould, which is vegetation, should not be eaten as well as salad, or maggots as well as eels. But, generally speaking, decomposing bodies are not wholesome eating, and the line must be drawn somewhere.

STILTON CHEESE.

1639. Stilton cheese, or British Parmesan, as it is sometimes called, is generally preferred to all other cheeses by those whose authority

few will dispute. Those made in May or June are usually served at Christmas; or, to be in prime order, should be kept from 10 to 12 months, or even longer. An artificial ripeness in Stilton cheese is sometimes produced by inserting a small piece of decayed Cheshire into an aperture at the top. From 3 weeks to a month is sufficient time to ripen the cheese. An additional flavour

STILTON CHEESE.

may also be obtained by scooping out a piece from the top, and pouring therein port, sherry, Madeira, or old ale, and letting the cheese absorb these for 2 or 3 weeks. But that cheese is the finest which is ripened without any artificial aid, is the opinion of those who are judges in these matters. In serving a Stilton cheese, the top of it should be cut off to form a lid, and a napkin or piece of white paper, with a frill at the top, pinned round. When the cheese goes from table, the lid should be replaced.

MODE OF SERVING CHEESE.

1640. The usual mode of serving cheese at good tables is to cut a small quantity of it into neat square pieces, and to put them into a glass cheese-dish, this dish being handed round. Should the cheese crumble much, of course this method is rather wasteful, and it may then be put on the table in the piece, and the host may cut from it. When served thus, the

CHEESE-GLASS.

cheese must always be carefully scraped, and laid on a white d'oyley or napkin, neatly folded. Cream cheese is often served in a cheese course, and, sometimes, grated Parmesan: the latter should be put into a covered glass dish. Rusks, cheese-biscuits, pats or slices of butter, and salad, cucumber, or water-cresses, should always form part of a cheese course.

SMOKING CHEESES.—The Romans smoked their cheeses, to give them a sharp taste. They possessed public places expressly for this use, and subject to police regulations which no one could evade.

A celebrated gourmand remarked that a dinner without cheese is like a woman with one eye.

CHEESE SANDWICHES.

1641. INGREDIENTS.—Slices of brown bread-and-butter, thin slices of cheese.

Mode.—Cut from a nice fat Cheshire, or any good rich cheese, some slices about ½ inch thick, and place them between some slices of brown bread-and-butter, like sandwiches. Place them on a plate in the oven, and, when the bread is toasted, serve on a napkin very hot and very quickly.

Time.—10 minutes in a brisk oven.

Average cost, 1½d. each sandwich.

Sufficient.—Allow a sandwich for each person.

Seasonable at any time.

CHEESE.—One of the most important products of coagulated milk is cheese. Unfermented, or cream-cheese, when quite fresh, is good for subjects with whom milk does not disagree; but cheese, in its commonest shape, is only fit for sedentary people, as an after-dinner stimulant; and in very small quantity. Bread and cheese, as a meal, is only fit for soldiers on march or labourers in the open air, who like it because it "holds the stomach a long time."

CAYENNE CHEESES.

1642. INGREDIENTS.—⅓ lb. of butter, ⅓ lb. of flour, ½ lb. of grated cheese, ⅛ teaspoonful of cayenne, ⅛ teaspoonful of salt; water.

Mode.—Rub the butter in the flour; add the grated cheese, cayenne and salt; and mix these ingredients well together. Moisten with sufficient water to make the whole into a paste; roll out, and cut into fingers about 4 inches in length. Bake them in a moderate oven a very light colour, and serve very hot.

Time.—15 to 20 minutes. *Average cost*, 1s. 4d.

Sufficient for 6 or 7 persons. *Seasonable* at any time.

TO MAKE A FONDUE.

1643. INGREDIENTS.—4 eggs, the weight of 2 in Parmesan or good Cheshire cheese, the weight of 2 in butter; pepper and salt to taste.

Mode.—Separate the yolks from the whites of the eggs; beat the former in a basin, and grate the cheese, or cut it into *very thin* flakes. Parmesan or Cheshire cheese may be used, whichever is the most convenient, although the former is considered more suitable for this dish; or an equal quantity of each may be used. Break the butter into small pieces, add it to the other ingredients, with sufficient pepper and salt to season nicely, and beat the mixture thoroughly. Well whisk the whites of the eggs, stir them lightly in, and either bake the fondue in a soufflé-dish or small round cake-tin. Fill the dish only half full, as the fondue should rise very much. Pin a napkin round the tin or dish, and serve very hot and very quickly. If allowed to stand after it is withdrawn from the oven, the beauty and lightness of this preparation will be entirely spoiled.

Time.—From 15 to 20 minutes. *Average cost*, 10d.

Sufficient for 4 or 5 persons. *Seasonable* at any time.

BRILLAT SAVARIN'S FONDUE.

(*An excellent Recipe.*)

1644. INGREDIENTS.—Eggs, cheese, butter, pepper and salt.

Mode.—Take the same number of eggs as there are guests; weigh the eggs in the shell, allow a third of their weight in Gruyère cheese, and a piece of butter one-sixth of the weight of the cheese. Break the eggs into a basin, beat them well; add the cheese, which should be grated, and the butter, which should be broken into small pieces. Stir these ingredients together with a wooden spoon; put the mixture into a lined saucepan, place it over the fire, and stir until the substance is thick and soft. Put in a little salt, according to the age of the cheese, and a good sprinkling of pepper, and serve the fondue on a very hot silver or metal plate. Do not allow the fondue to remain on the fire after the mixture is set, as, if it boils, it will be entirely spoiled. Brillat Savarin recommends that some choice Burgundy should be handed round with this dish. We have given this recipe exactly as he recommends it to be made; but we have tried it with good Cheshire cheese, and found it answer remarkably well.

Time.—About 4 minutes to set the mixture.

Average cost for 4 persons, 10*d.*

Sufficient.—Allow 1 egg, with the other ingredients in proportion, for one person.

Seasonable at any time.

MACARONI, as usually served with the CHEESE COURSE.

I.

1645. INGREDIENTS.—½ lb. of pipe macaroni, ¼ lb. of butter, 6 oz. of Parmesan or Cheshire cheese, pepper and salt to taste, 1 pint of milk, 2 pints of water, bread crumbs.

Mode.—Put the milk and water into a saucepan with sufficient salt to flavour it; place it on the fire, and, when it boils quickly, drop in the macaroni. Keep the water boiling until it is quite tender; drain the macaroni, and put it into a deep dish. Have ready the grated cheese, either Parmesan or Cheshire; sprinkle it amongst the macaroni and some of the butter cut into small pieces, reserving some of the cheese for the top layer. Season with a little pepper, and cover the top layer of cheese with some very fine bread crumbs. Warm, without oiling, the remainder of the butter, and pour it gently over the bread crumbs. Place the dish before a bright fire to brown the crumbs; turn it once or twice, that it may be equally coloured, and serve very hot. The top of the macaroni may be browned with a salamander, which is even better than placing it before the fire, as the process is more expeditious; but it should never be browned in the oven, as the butter would oil, and so impart a very disagreeable flavour to the dish. In boiling the macaroni, let it be perfectly tender but firm, no part beginning to melt, and the form entirely preserved. It may be boiled in plain water, with a little salt instead of using milk, but should then have a small piece of butter mixed with it.

Time.—1½ to 1¾ hour to boil the macaroni, 5 minutes to brown it before the fire.

Average cost, 1*s.* 6*d.*

Sufficient for 6 or 7 persons. *Seasonable* at any time.

Note.—Riband macaroni may be dressed in the same manner, but does not require boiling so long a time.

II.

1646. INGREDIENTS.—¼ lb. of pipe or riband macaroni, ½ pint of milk, ½ pint of veal or beef gravy, the yolks of 2 eggs, 4 tablespoonfuls of cream, 3 oz. of grated Parmesan or Cheshire cheese, 1 oz. of butter.

Mode.—Wash the macaroni, and boil it in the gravy and milk until quite tender, without being broken. Drain it, and put it into rather a deep dish. Beat the yolks of the eggs with the cream and 2 table-spoonfuls of the liquor the macaroni was boiled in; make this sufficiently hot to thicken, but do not allow it to boil; pour it over the macaroni, over which sprinkle the grated cheese and the butter broken into small pieces; brown with a salamander, or before the fire, and serve.

Time.—1½ to 1¾ hour to boil the macaroni, 5 minutes to thicken the eggs and cream, 5 minutes to brown.

Average cost, 1s. 2d.

Sufficient for 3 or 4 persons. *Seasonable* at any time.

III.

1647. INGREDIENTS.—¼ lb. of pipe macaroni, ½ pint of brown gravy No. 436, 6 oz. of grated Parmesan cheese.

Mode.—Wash the macaroni, and boil it in salt and water until quite tender; drain it, and put it into rather a deep dish. Have ready a pint of good brown gravy, pour it hot over the macaroni, and send it to table with grated Parmesan served on a separate dish. When the flavour is liked, a little pounded mace may be added to the water in which the macaroni is boiled; but this must always be sparingly added, as it will impart a very strong flavour.

Time.—1½ to 1¾ hour to boil the macaroni.

Average cost, with the gravy and cheese, 1s. 3d.

Sufficient for 3 or 4 persons. *Seasonable* at any time.

POUNDED CHEESE.

1648. INGREDIENTS.—To every lb. of cheese allow 3 oz. of fresh butter.

Mode.—To pound cheese is an economical way of using it, if it has become dry; it is exceedingly good spread on bread, and is the best way of eating it for those whose digestion is weak. Cut up the cheese into small pieces, and pound it smoothly in a mortar, adding butter in the above proportion. Press it down into a jar, cover with clarified butter, and it will keep for several days. The flavour may be very much increased by adding mixed mustard (about a teaspoonful to every lb.), or cayenne, or pounded mace. Curry-powder is also not unfrequently mixed with it.

RAMAKINS, to serve with the CHEESE COURSE.

1649. INGREDIENTS.—¼ lb. of Cheshire cheese, ¼ lb. of Parmesan cheese, ¼ lb. of fresh butter, 4 eggs, the crumb of a small roll; pepper, salt, and pounded mace to taste.

Mode.—Boil the crumb of the roll in milk for 5 minutes; strain, and put it into a mortar; add the cheese, which should be finely scraped, the butter, the yolks of the eggs, and seasoning, and pound these ingredients well together. Whisk the whites of the eggs, mix them with the paste, and put it into small pans or saucers, which should not be more than half filled. Bake them from 10 to 12 minutes, and serve them very hot and very quickly. This batter answers equally well for macaroni after it is boiled tender.

Time.—10 to 12 minutes. *Average cost,* 1s. 4d.

Sufficient for 7 or 8 persons. *Seasonable* at any time.

PASTRY RAMAKINS, to serve with the CHEESE COURSE.

1650. INGREDIENTS.—Any pieces of very good light puff-paste Cheshire, Parmesan, or Stilton cheese.

Mode.—The remains or odd pieces of paste left from large tarts, &c. answer for making these little dishes. Gather up the pieces of paste; roll it out evenly, and sprinkle it with grated cheese of a nice flavour. Fold the paste in three, roll it out again, and sprinkle more cheese over; fold the paste, roll it out, and with a paste-cutter shape it in any way that may be desired. Bake the ramakins in a brisk oven from 10 to 15 minutes, dish them on a hot napkin, and serve quickly The appearance of this dish may be very much improved by brushing the ramakins over with yolk of egg before they are placed in the oven. Where expense is not objected to, Parmesan is the best kind of cheese to use for making this dish.

Time.—10 to 15 minutes. *Average cost,* with ½ lb. of paste, 10d.

Sufficient for 6 or 7 persons. *Seasonable* at any time.

TOASTED CHEESE, or SCOTCH RARE-BIT.

1651. INGREDIENTS.—A few slices of rich cheese, toast, mustard, and pepper.

Mode.—Cut some nice rich sound cheese into rather thin slices; melt it in a chéese-toaster on a hot plate, or over steam, and, when melted, add a small quantity of mixed mustard and a seasoning of pepper; stir the cheese until it is completely dissolved, then brown it before the fire, or with a salamander. Fill the bottom of the cheese-toaster with hot

HOT-WATER CHEESE-DISH.

water, and serve with dry or buttered toasts, whichever may be preferred. Our engraving illustrates a cheese-toaster with hot-water reservoir: the cheese is melted in the upper tin, which is placed in another vessel of boiling water, so keeping the preparation beautifully hot. A small quantity of porter, or port wine, is sometimes mixed with the cheese; and, if it be not very rich, a few pieces of butter may be mixed with it to great advantage. Sometimes the melted cheese is spread on the toasts, and then laid in the cheese-dish at the top of the hot water. Whichever way it is served, it is highly necessary that the mixture be very hot, and very quickly sent to table, or it will be worthless.

Time.—About 5 minutes to melt the cheese.

Average cost, 1½d. per slice.

Sufficient.—Allow a slice to each person. *Seasonable* at any time.

TOASTED CHEESE, or WELSH RARE-BIT.

1652. INGREDIENTS.—Slices of bread, butter, Cheshire or Gloucester cheese, mustard, and pepper.

Mode.—Cut the bread into slices about ½ inch in thickness; pare off the crust, toast the bread slightly without hardening or burning it, and spread it with butter. Cut some slices, not quite so large as the bread, from a good rich fat cheese; lay them on the toasted bread in a cheese-toaster; be careful that the cheese does not burn, and let it be equally melted. Spread over the top a little made mustard and a seasoning of pepper, and serve very hot, with very hot plates. To facilitate the melting of the cheese, it may be cut into thin flakes or toasted on one side before it is laid on the bread. As it is so essential to send this dish hot to table, it is a good plan to melt the cheese in small round silver or metal pans, and to send these pans to table, allowing one for each guest. Slices of dry or buttered toast should always accompany them, with mustard, pepper, and salt.

Time.—About 5 minutes to melt the cheese.

Average cost, 1½d. each slice.

Sufficient.—Allow a slice to each person. *Seasonable* at any time.

Note.—Should the cheese be dry, a little butter mixed with it will be an improvement.

"Cow Cheese."—It was only fifty years after Aristotle—the fourth century before Christ—that butter began to be noticed as an aliment. The Greeks, in imitation of the Parthians and Scythians, who used to send it to them, had it served upon their tables, and called it at first "oil of milk," and later, *bouturos*, "cow cheese."

SCOTCH WOODCOCK.

1653. INGREDIENTS.—A few slices of hot buttered toast; allow 1 anchovy to each slice. For the sauce,—¼ pint of cream, the yolks of 3 eggs.

Mode.—Separate the yolks from the whites of the eggs; beat the former, stir to them the cream, and bring the sauce to the boiling-

point, but do not allow it to boil, or it will curdle. Have ready some
hot buttered toast, spread with anchovies pounded to a paste; pour a
little of the hot sauce on the top, and serve very hot and very quickly.

Time.—5 minutes to make the sauce hot.

Sufficient.—Allow ½ slice to each person. *Seasonable* at any time.

TO CHOOSE EGGS.

1654. In choosing eggs, apply the tongue to the large end of the
egg, and, if it feels warm, it is new, and may be relied on as a fresh
egg. Another mode of ascertaining their freshness is to hold them
before a lighted candle, or to the light, and if the egg looks clear, it
will be tolerably good; if thick, it is stale; and if there is a black
spot attached to the shell, it is worthless. No egg should be used for
culinary purposes with the slightest taint in it, as it will render
perfectly useless those with which it has been mixed. Eggs that are
purchased, and that cannot be relied on, should always be broken in
a cup, and then put into a basin: by this means stale or bad eggs
may be easily rejected, without wasting the others.

Eggs contain, for their volume, a greater quantity of nutriment than any other article
of food. But it does not follow that they are always good for weak stomachs; quite the
contrary; for it is often a great object to give the stomach a large surface to work upon,
a considerable volume of *ingesta*, over which the nutritive matter is diffused, and so
exposed to the action of the gastric juice at many points. There are many persons who
cannot digest eggs, however cooked. It is said, however, that their digestibility decreases
in proportion to the degree in which they are hardened by boiling.

TO KEEP EGGS FRESH FOR SEVERAL WEEKS.

1655. Have ready a large saucepan, capable of holding 3 or 4 quarts,
full of boiling water. Put the eggs into a cabbage-net, say 20 at a
time, and hold them in the water (which must be kept boiling) *for* 20
seconds. Proceed in this manner till you have done as many eggs as
you wish to preserve; then pack them away in sawdust. We have
tried this method of preserving eggs, and can vouch for its excellence:
they will be found, at the end of 2 or 3 months, quite good enough
for culinary purposes; and although the white may be a little tougher
than that of a new-laid egg, the yolk will be nearly the same. Many
persons keep eggs for a long time by smearing the shells with butter
or sweet oil: they should then be packed in plenty of bran or sawdust,
and the eggs not allowed to touch each other. Eggs for storing should
be collected in fine weather, and should not be more than 24 hours
old when they are packed away, or their flavour, when used, cannot
be relied on. Another simple way of preserving eggs is to immerse
them in lime-water soon after they have been laid, and then to put
the vessel containing the lime-water in a cellar or cool outhouse.

Seasonable.—The best time for preserving eggs is from July to September.

EGGS.—The quality of eggs is said to be very much affected by the food of the fowls who lay them. Herbs and grain together make a better food than grain only. When the hens eat too many insects, the eggs have a disagreeable flavour.

TO BOIL EGGS FOR BREAKFAST, SALADS, &c.

1656. Eggs for boiling cannot be too fresh, or boiled too soon after they are laid; but rather a longer time should be allowed for boiling a new-laid egg than for one that is three or four days old. Have ready a saucepan of boiling water; put the eggs into it gently with a spoon, letting the spoon touch the bottom of the saucepan before it is withdrawn, that the egg may not fall, and consequently crack. For those who like eggs lightly boiled, 3 minutes will be found sufficient; 3¾ to 4 minutes will be ample time to set the white nicely; and, if liked hard, 6 to 7 minutes will not be found too long. Should the eggs be unusually large, as those of black Spanish fowls sometimes are, allow an extra ½ minute for them. Eggs for salads should be boiled from 10 minutes to ¼ hour, and should be placed in a basin of cold water for a few minutes; they should then be rolled on the table with the hand, and the shell will peel off easily.

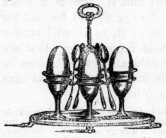

EGG-STAND FOR THE BREAKFAST-TABLE.

Time.—To boil eggs lightly, for invalids or children, 3 minutes; to boil eggs to suit the generality of tastes, 3¾ to 4 minutes; to boil eggs hard, 6 to 7 minutes; for salads, 10 to 15 minutes.

Note.—Silver or plated egg-dishes, like that shown in our engraving, are now very much used. The price of the one illustrated is £2. 2s., and may be purchased of Messrs. R. & J. Slack, 336, Strand.

EGGS.—When fresh eggs are dropped into a vessel *full* of boiling water, they crack, because the eggs being well filled, the shells give way to the efforts of the interior fluids, dilated by heat. If the volume of hot water be small, the shells do not crack, because its temperature is reduced by the eggs before the interior dilation can take place. Stale eggs, again, do not crack, because the air inside is easily compressed.

BUTTERED EGGS.

1657. INGREDIENTS.—4 new-laid eggs, 2 oz. of butter.

Mode.—Procure the eggs new-laid if possible; break them into a basin, and beat them well; put the butter into another basin, which place in boiling water, and stir till the butter is melted. Pour that and the eggs into a lined saucepan; hold it over a gentle fire, and, as the mixture begins to warm, pour it two or three times into the basin, and back again, that the two ingredients may be well incorporated. Keep stirring the eggs and butter one way until they are hot, *without boiling,* and serve on hot buttered toast. If the mixture is allowed to boil, it will curdle, and so be entirely spoiled.

Time.—About 5 minutes to make the eggs hot. *Average cost,* 7d.

Sufficient.—Allow a slice to each person. *Seasonable* at any time.

DUCKS' EGGS.

1658. Ducks' eggs are usually so strongly flavoured that, plainly boiled, they are not good for eating ; they answer, however, very well for various culinary preparations where eggs are required ; such as custards, &c. &c. Being so large and highly-flavoured, 1 duck's egg will go as far as 2 small hen's eggs ; besides making whatever they are mixed with exceedingly rich. They also are admirable when used in puddings.

PRIMITIVE METHOD OF COOKING EGGS.—The shepherds of Egypt had a singular manner of cooking eggs without the aid of fire. They placed them in a sling, which they turned so rapidly that the friction of the air heated them to the exact point required for use.

FRIED EGGS.

1659. INGREDIENTS.—4 eggs, ¼ lb. of lard, butter or clarified dripping.

Mode.—Place a delicately-clean frying-pan over a gentle fire ; put in the fat, and allow it to come to the boiling-point. Break the eggs into cups, slip them into the boiling fat, and let them remain until the whites are delicately set ; and, whilst they are frying, ladle a little of the fat over them. Take them up with a slice, drain them for a minute from

FRIED EGGS ON BACON.

their greasy moisture, trim them neatly, and serve on slices of fried bacon or ham ; or the eggs may be placed in the middle of the dish, with the bacon put round as a garnish.

Time.—2 to 3 minutes. *Average cost,* 1d. each ; 2d. when scarce.

Sufficient for 2 persons. *Seasonable* at any time.

VENERATION FOR EGGS.—Many of the most learned philosophers held eggs in a kind of respect, approaching to veneration, because they saw in them the emblem of the world and the four elements. The shell, they said, represented the earth ; the white, water ; the yolk, fire ; and air was found under the shell at one end of the egg.

EGGS A LA MAITRE D'HOTEL.

1660. INGREDIENTS.—¼ lb. of fresh butter, 1 tablespoonful of flour, ½ pint of milk, pepper and salt to taste, 1 tablespoonful of minced parsley, the juice of ½ lemon, 6 eggs.

Mode.—Put the flour and half the butter into a stewpan; stir them over the fire until the mixture thickens; pour in the milk, which should be boiling; add a seasoning of pepper and salt, and simmer the whole for 5 minutes. Put the remainder of the butter into the sauce, and add the minced parsley; then boil the eggs hard, strip off the shells, cut the eggs into quarters, and put them on a dish. Bring the sauce to the boiling-point, add the lemon-juice, pour over the eggs, and serve.

Time.—5 minutes to boil the sauce; the eggs, 10 to 15 minutes.

Average cost, 1s.

Sufficient for 4 or 5 persons. *Seasonable* at any time.

ŒUFS AU PLAT, or AU MIROIR, served on the Dish in which they are Cooked.

1661. INGREDIENTS.—4 eggs, 1 oz. of butter, pepper and salt to taste.

Mode.—Butter a dish rather thickly with good fresh butter; melt it, break the eggs into it the same as for poaching, sprinkle them with white pepper and fine salt, and put the remainder of the butter, cut into very small pieces, on the top of them. Put the dish on a hot plate, or in the oven, or before the fire, and let it remain until the whites become set, but not hard, when serve immediately, placing the dish they were cooked in on another. To hasten the cooking of the eggs, a salamander may be held over them for a minute; but great care must be taken that they are not too much done. This is an exceedingly nice dish, and one very easily prepared for breakfast.

Time.—3 minutes. *Average cost,* 5d.

Sufficient for 2 persons. *Seasonable* at any time.

PLOVERS' EGGS.

1662. Plovers' eggs are usually served boiled hard, and sent to table in a napkin, either hot or cold. They may also be shelled, and served the same as eggs à la Tripe, with a good Béchamel sauce, or brown gravy, poured over them. They are also used for decorating salads, the beautiful colour of the white being generally so much admired.

POACHED EGGS.

1663. INGREDIENTS.—Eggs, water. To every pint of water allow 1 tablespoonful of vinegar.

Mode.—Eggs for poaching should be perfectly fresh, but not quite new-laid; those that are about 36 hours old are the best for the purpose. If quite new-laid, the white is so milky it is almost impossible to set it ; and, on the other hand, if the egg be at all stale, it is equally difficult to poach it nicely. Strain some boiling water into a deep clean frying-pan ; break the egg into a cup without damaging the yolk, and, when the water boils, remove the pan to the side of the fire, and gently slip the egg into it. Place the pan over a gentle fire, and keep the water simmering until the white looks nicely set, when the egg is ready. Take it up gently with a slice, cut away the ragged edges of the white, and serve either on toasted bread or on slices of ham or bacon, or on spinach, &c. A poached egg should not be overdone, as its appearance and taste will be quite spoiled if the yolk be allowed to harden. When the egg is slipped into the water, the white should be gathered together, to keep it a little

EGGS POACHED ON TOAST.

TIN EGG-POACHER.

in form, or the cup should be turned over it for ½ minute. To poach an egg to perfection is rather a difficult operation ; so, for inexperienced cooks, a tin egg-poacher may be purchased, which greatly facilitates this manner of dressing eggs. Our illustration clearly shows what it is: it consists of a tin plate with a handle, with a space for three perforated cups. An egg should be broken into each cup, and the machine then placed in a stewpan of boiling water, which has been previously strained. When the whites of the eggs appear set, they are done, and should then be carefully slipped on to the toast or spinach, or with whatever they are served. In poaching eggs in a frying-pan, never do more than four at a time ; and, when a little vinegar is liked mixed with the water in which the eggs are done, use the above proportion.

Time.—2½ to 3½ minutes, according to the size of the egg.

Sufficient.—Allow 2 eggs to each person.

Seasonable at any time, but less plentiful in winter.

POACHED EGGS, WITH CREAM.

1664. INGREDIENTS.—1 pint of water, 1 teaspoonful of salt, 4 teaspoonfuls of vinegar, 4 fresh eggs, ½ gill of cream, salt, pepper, and pounded sugar to taste, 1 oz. of butter.

Mode.—Put the water, vinegar, and salt into a frying-pan, and break each egg into a separate cup ; bring the water, &c. to boil, and slip the eggs gently into it without breaking the yolks. Simmer them from 3 to 4 minutes, but not longer, and, with a slice, lift them out on to a hot dish, and trim the edges.   Empty the pan of its contents, put in the cream, add a seasoning to taste of pepper, salt, and pounded sugar ; bring the whole to the boiling-point; then add the butter, broken into small pieces ; toss the pan round and round till the butter is melted ; pour it over the eggs, and serve.   To insure the eggs not being spoiled whilst the cream, &c., is preparing, it is a good plan to warm the cream with the butter, &c., before the eggs are poached, so that it may be poured over them immediately after they are dished.

Time.—3 to 4 minutes to poach the eggs, 5 minutes to warm the cream.

Average cost for the above quantity, 9*d.*

Sufficient for 2 persons.   *Seasonable* at any time.

1665. COMPARATIVE SIZES OF EGGS.

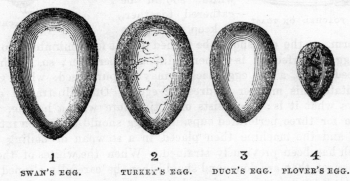

1   **2**   **3**   **4**

SWAN'S EGG.   TURKEY'S EGG.   DUCK'S EGG. PLOVER'S EGG.

SCOTCH EGGS.

1666. INGREDIENTS.—6 eggs, 6 tablespoonfuls of forcemeat No. 417, hot lard, ½ pint of good brown gravy.

Mode.—Boil the eggs for 10 minutes ; strip them from the shells, and cover them with forcemeat made by recipe No. 417 ; or substitute pounded anchovies for the ham. Fry the eggs a nice brown in boiling lard, drain them before the fire from their greasy moisture, dish them, and pour round from ¼ to ½ pint of good brown gravy. To enhance the appearance of the eggs, they may be rolled in beaten egg and sprinkled with bread crumbs ; but this is scarcely necessary if they are carefully fried. The flavour of the ham or anchovy in the force-meat must preponderate, as it should be very relishing.

Time.—10 minutes to boil the eggs, 5 to 7 minutes to fry them.

Average cost, 1*s.* 4*d.*

Sufficient for 3 or 4 persons.   *Seasonable* at any time.

EGGS A LA TRIPE.

1667. INGREDIENTS.—8 eggs, ¾ pint of Béchamel sauce No. 368, 1 dessertspoonful of finely-minced parsley.

Mode.—Boil the eggs hard; put them into cold water, peel them, take out the yolks whole, and shred the whites. Make ¾ pint of Béchamel sauce by recipe No. 368; add the parsley, and, when the sauce is quite hot, put the yolks of the eggs into the middle of the dish, and the shred whites round them; pour over the sauce, and garnish with leaves of puff-paste or fried croûtons. There is no necessity for putting the eggs into the saucepan with the Béchamel; the sauce, being quite hot, will warm the eggs sufficiently.

Time.—10 minutes to boil the eggs. *Average cost*, 1s.

Sufficient for 5 or 6 persons. *Seasonable* at any time.

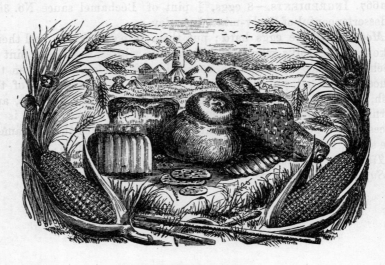

CHAPTER XXXIV.

GENERAL OBSERVATIONS ON BREAD, BISCUITS, AND CAKES.

BREAD AND BREAD-MAKING.

1668. AMONG the numerous vegetable products yielding articles of food for man, the Cereals hold the first place. By means of skilful cultivation, mankind have transformed the original forms of these growths, poor and ill-flavoured as they perhaps were, into various fruitful and agreeable species, which yield an abundant and pleasant supply. Classified according to their respective richness in alimentary elements, the Cereals stand thus :—Wheat, and its varieties, Rye, Barley, Oats, Rice, Indian Corn. Everybody knows it is wheat flour which yields the best bread. Rye-bread is viscous, hard, less easily soluble by the gastric juice, and not so rich in nutritive power. Flour produced from barley, Indian corn, or rice, is not so readily made into bread ; and the article, when made, is heavy and indigestible.

1669. On examining a grain of corn from any of the numerous cereals* used in the preparation of flour, such as wheat, maize, rye, barley, &c., it will be found to consist of two parts,—the husk, or exterior covering, which is generally of a dark colour, and the inner, or albuminous part, which is more or less

---

* *Cereal*, a corn-producing plant ; from Ceres, the goddess of agriculture.

white. In grinding, these two portions are separated, and the husk being blown away in the process of winnowing, the flour remains in the form of a light brown powder, consisting principally of starch and gluten. In order to render it white, it undergoes a process called "bolting." It is passed through a series of fine sieves, which separate the coarser parts, leaving behind fine white flour,—the "fine firsts" of the corn-dealer. The process of bolting, as just described, tends to deprive flour of its gluten, the coarser and darker portion containing much of that substance; while the lighter part is peculiarly rich in starch. Bran contains a large proportion of gluten; hence it will be seen why brown bread is so much more nutritious than white; in fact, we may lay it down as a general rule, that the whiter the bread the less nourishment it contains. Majendie proved this by feeding a dog for forty days with white wheaten bread, at the end of which time he died; while another dog, fed on brown bread made with flour mixed with bran, lived without any disturbance of his health. The "bolting" process, then, is rather injurious than beneficial in its result; and is one of the numerous instances where fashion has chosen a wrong standard to go by. In ancient times, down to the Emperors, no bolted flour was known. In many parts of Germany the entire meal is used; and in no part of the world are the digestive organs of the people in a better condition. In years of famine, when corn is scarce, the use of bolted flour is most culpable, for from 18 to 20 per cent. is lost in bran. Brown bread has, of late years, become very popular; and many physicians have recommended it to invalids with weak digestions with great success. This rage for white bread has introduced adulterations of a very serious character, affecting the health of the whole community. Potatoes are added for this purpose; but this is a comparatively harmless cheat, only reducing the nutritive property of the bread; but bone-dust and alum are also put in, which are far from harmless.

1670. Bread-making is a very ancient art indeed. The Assyrians, Egyptians, and Greeks, used to make bread, in which oil, with aniseed and other spices, was an element; but this was unleavened. Every family used to prepare the bread for its own consumption, the *trade* of baking not having yet taken shape. It is said, that somewhere about the beginning of the thirtieth Olympiad, the slave of an archon, at Athens, made leavened bread by accident. He had left some wheaten dough in an earthen pan, and forgotten it; some days afterwards, he lighted upon it again, and found it turning sour. His first thought was to throw it away; but, his master coming up, he mixed this now acescent dough with some fresh dough, which he was working at. The bread thus produced, by the introduction of dough in which alcoholic fermentation had begun, was found delicious by the archon and his friends; and the slave, being summoned and catechised, told the secret. It spread all over Athens; and everybody wanting leavened bread at once, certain persons set up as bread-makers, or bakers. In a short time bread-baking became quite an art, and "Athenian bread" was quoted all over Greece as the best bread, just as the honey of Hymettus was celebrated as the best honey.

1671. In our own times, and among civilized peoples, bread has become an article of food of the first necessity ; and properly so, for it constitutes of itself a complete life-sustainer, the gluten, starch, and sugar, which it contains, representing azotized and hydro-carbonated nutrients, and combining the sustaining powers of the animal and vegetable kingdoms in one product.

1672. WHEATEN BREAD.—The finest, wholesomest, and most savoury bread is made from wheaten flour. There are, of wheat, three leading qualities,—the soft, the medium, and the hard wheat ; the last of which yields a kind of bread that is not so white as that made from soft wheat, but is richer in gluten, and, consequently, more nutritive.

1673. RYE BREAD.—This comes next to wheaten bread : it is not so rich in gluten, but is said to keep fresh longer, and to have some laxative qualities.

1674. BARLEY BREAD, INDIAN-CORN BREAD, &c.—Bread made from barley, maize, oats, rice, potatoes, &c. "rises" badly, because the grains in question contain but little gluten, which makes the bread heavy, close in texture, and difficult of digestion ; in fact, corn-flour has to be added before panification can take place. In countries where wheat is scarce and maize abundant, the people make the latter a chief article of sustenance, when prepared in different forms.

BREAD-MAKING.

1675. PANIFICATION, or bread-making, consists of the following processes, in the case of Wheaten Flour. Fifty or sixty per cent. of water is added to the flour, with the addition of some leavening matter, and, preferably, of yeast from malt and hops. All kinds of leavening matter have, however, been, and are still used in different parts of the world : in the East Indies, "toddy," which is a liquor that flows from the wounded cocoa-nut tree ; and, in the West Indies, "dunder," or the refuse of the distillation of rum. The dough then undergoes the well-known process called *kneading*. The yeast produces fermentation, a process which may be thus described :—The dough reacting upon the leavening matter introduced, the starch of the flour is transformed into saccharine matter, the saccharine matter being afterwards changed into alcohol and carbonic acid. The dough must be well "bound," and yet allow the escape of the little bubbles of carbonic acid which accompany the fermentation, and which, in their passage, cause the numerous little holes which are seen in light bread.

1676. The yeast must be good and fresh, if the bread is to be digestible and nice. Stale yeast produces, instead of vinous fermentation, an acetous fermentation, which flavours the bread and makes it disagreeable. A poor thin yeast produces an imperfect fermentation, the result being a heavy unwholesome loaf.

1677. When the dough is well kneaded, it is left to stand for some time, and then, as soon as it begins to swell, it is divided into loaves; after which it is again left to stand, when it once more swells up, and manifests, for the last time, the symptoms of fermentation. It is then put into the oven, where the water contained in the dough is partly evaporated, and the loaves swell up again, while a yellow crust begins to form upon the surface. When the bread is sufficiently baked, the bottom crust is hard and resonant if struck with the finger, while the crumb is elastic, and rises again after being pressed down with the finger. The bread is, in all probability, baked sufficiently if, on opening the door of the oven, you are met by a cloud of steam which quickly passes away.

1678. One word as to the unwholesomeness of new bread and hot rolls. When bread is taken out of the oven, it is full of moisture; the starch is held together in masses, and the bread, instead of being crusted so as to expose each grain of starch to the saliva, actually prevents their digestion by being formed by the teeth into leathery poreless masses, which lie on the stomach like so many bullets. Bread should always be at least a day old before it is eaten; and, if properly made, and kept in a *cool dry* place, ought to be perfectly soft and palatable at the end of three or four days. Hot rolls, swimming in melted butter, and new bread, ought to be carefully shunned by everybody who has the slightest respect for that much-injured individual—the Stomach.

1679. AERATED BREAD.—It is not unknown to some of our readers that Dr. Dauglish, of Malvern, has recently patented a process for making bread "light" without the use of leaven. The ordinary process of bread-making by fermentation is tedious, and much labour of human hands is requisite in the kneading, in order that the dough may be thoroughly interpenetrated with the leaven. The new process impregnates the bread, by the application of machinery, with carbonic acid gas, or fixed air. Different opinions are expressed about the bread; but it is curious to note, that, as corn is now reaped by machinery, and dough is baked by machinery, the whole process of bread-making is probably in course of undergoing changes which will emancipate both the housewife and the professional baker from a large amount of labour.

1680. In the production of Aërated Bread, wheaten flour, water, salt, and carbonic acid gas (generated by proper machinery), are the only materials employed. We need not inform our readers that carbonic acid gas is the source of the effervescence, whether in common water coming from a depth, or in lemonade, or any aërated drink. Its action, in the new bread, takes the place of fermentation in the old.

1681. In the patent process, the dough is mixed in a great iron ball, inside which is a system of paddles, perpetually turning, and doing the kneading part of the business. Into this globe the flour is dropped till it is full, and then the common atmospheric air is pumped out, and the pure gas turned on. The gas is followed by the water, which has been aërated for the purpose, and then begins the churning or kneading part of the business.

1682. Of course, it is not long before we have the dough, and very "light" and nice it looks. This is caught in tins, and passed on to the floor of the oven, which is an endless floor, moving slowly through the fire. Done to a turn, the loaves emerge at the other end of the apartment,—and the Aërated Bread is made.

1683. It may be added, that it is a good plan to change one's baker from time to time, and so secure a change in the quality of the bread that is eaten.

1684. MIXED BREADS.—Rye bread is hard of digestion, and requires longer and slower baking than wheaten bread. It is better when made with leaven of wheaten flour rather than yeast, and turns out lighter. It should not be eaten till two days old. It will keep a long time.

1685. A good bread may be made by mixing rye-flour, wheat-flour, and rice-paste in equal proportions; also by mixing rye, wheat, and barley. In Norway, it is said that they only bake their barley bread once a year, such is its "keeping" quality.

1686. Indian-corn flour mixed with wheat-flour (half with half) makes a nice bread; but it is not considered very digestible, though it keeps well.

1687. Rice cannot be made into bread, nor can potatoes; but one-third potato-flour to three-fourths wheaten flour makes a tolerably good loaf.

1688. A very good bread, better than the ordinary sort, and of a delicious flavour, is said to be produced by adopting the following recipe:—Take ten parts of wheat-flour, five parts of potato-flour, one part of rice-paste; knead together, add the yeast, and bake as usual. This is, of course, cheaper than wheaten bread.

1689. Flour, when freshly ground, is too glutinous to make good bread, and should therefore not be used immediately, but should be kept dry for a few weeks, and stirred occasionally, until it becomes dry, and crumbles easily between the fingers.

1690. Flour should be perfectly dry before being used for bread or cakes; if at all damp, the preparation is sure to be heavy. Before mixing it with the other ingredients, it is a good plan to place it for an hour or two before the fire, until it feels warm and dry.

1691. Yeast from home-brewed beer is generally preferred to any other : it is very bitter, and, on that account, should be well washed, and put away until the thick mass settles. If it still continues bitter, the process should be repeated ; and, before being used, all the water floating at the top must be poured off. German yeast is now very much used, and should be moistened, and thoroughly mixed with the milk or water with which the bread is to be made.

1692. The following observations are extracted from a valuable work on Bread-making,* and will be found very useful to our readers :—

1693. The first thing required for making wholesome bread is the utmost cleanliness ; the next is the soundness and sweetness of all the ingredients used for it ; and, in addition to these, there must be attention and care through the whole process.

1694. An almost certain way of spoiling dough is to leave it half-made, and to allow it to become cold before it is finished. The other most common causes of failure are using yeast which is no longer sweet, or which has been frozen, or has had hot liquid poured over it.

1695. Too small a proportion of yeast, or insufficient time allowed for the dough to rise, will cause the bread to be heavy.

1696. Heavy bread will also most likely be the result of making the dough very hard, and letting it become quite cold, particularly in winter.

1697. If either the sponge or the dough be permitted to overwork itself, that is to say, if the mixing and kneading be neglected when it has reached the proper point for either, sour bread will probably be the consequence in warm weather, and bad bread in any. The goodness will also be endangered by placing it so near a fire as to make any part of it hot, instead of main-taining the gentle and equal degree of heat required for its due fermentation.

1698. MILK OR BUTTER.—Milk which is not perfectly sweet will not only injure the flavour of the bread, but, in sultry weather, will often cause it to be quite uneatable ; yet either of them, if *fresh and good*, will materially improve its quality.

1699. To keep bread sweet and fresh, as soon as it is cold it should be put into a clean earthen pan, with a cover to it : this pan should be placed at a little distance from the ground, to allow a current of air to pass underneath. Some persons prefer keeping bread on clean wooden shelves, without being covered, that the crust may not soften. Stale bread may be freshened by warming it through in a gentle oven. Stale pastry, cakes, &c., may also be improved by this method.

---

* "The English Bread-Book." By Eliza Acton. London : Longman.

1700. The utensils required for making bread, on a moderate scale, are a kneading-trough or pan, sufficiently large that the dough may be kneaded freely without throwing the flour over the edges, and also to allow for its rising; a hair sieve for straining yeast, and one or two strong spoons.

1701. Yeast must always be good of its kind, and in a fitting state to produce ready and proper fermentation. Yeast of strong beer or ale produces more effect than that of milder kinds; and the fresher the yeast, the smaller the quantity will be required to raise the dough.

1702. As a general rule, the oven for baking bread should be rather quick, and the heat so regulated as to penetrate the dough without hardening the outside. The oven door should not be opened after the bread is put in until the dough is set, or has become firm, as the cool air admitted will have an unfavourable effect on it.

1703. Brick ovens are generally considered the best adapted for baking bread: these should be heated with wood faggots, and then swept and mopped out, to cleanse them for the reception of the bread. Iron ovens are more difficult to manage, being apt to burn the surface of the bread before the middle is baked. To remedy this, a few clean bricks should be set at the bottom of the oven, close together, to receive the tins of bread. In many modern stoves the ovens are so much improved that they bake admirably; and they can always be brought to the required temperature, when it is higher than is needed, by leaving the door open for a time.

A FEW HINTS respecting the Making and Baking of CAKES.

1704. *Eggs* should always be broken into a cup, the whites and yolks separated, and they should always be strained. Breaking the eggs thus, the bad ones may be easily rejected without spoiling the others, and so cause no waste. As eggs are used instead of yeast, they should be very thoroughly whisked; they are generally sufficiently beaten when thick enough to carry the drop that falls from the whisk.

1705. *Loaf Sugar* should be well pounded, and then sifted through a fine sieve.

1706. *Currants* should be nicely washed, picked, dried in a cloth, and then carefully examined, that no pieces of grit or stone may be left amongst them. They should then be laid on a dish before the fire, to become thoroughly dry; as, if added damp to the other ingredients, cakes will be liable to be heavy.

1707. *Good Butter* should always be used in the manufacture of cakes; and if beaten to a cream, it saves much time and labour to warm, but not melt, it before beating.

1708. Less butter and eggs are required for cakes when yeast is mixed with the other ingredients.

1709. The heat of the oven is of great importance, especially for large cakes. If the heat be not tolerably fierce, the batter will not rise. If the oven is too quick, and there is any danger of the cake burning or catching, put a sheet of clean paper over the top. Newspaper, or paper that has been printed on, should never be used for this purpose.

1710. To know when a cake is sufficiently baked, plunge a clean knife into the middle of it ; draw it quickly out, and if it looks in the least sticky, put the cake back, and close the oven door until the cake is done.

1711. Cakes should be kept in closed tin canisters or jars, and in a dry place. Those made with yeast do not keep so long as those made without it.

BISCUITS.

1712. SINCE the establishment of the large modern biscuit manufactories, biscuits have been produced both cheap and wholesome, in, comparatively speaking, endless variety. Their actual component parts are, perhaps, known only to the various makers ; but there are several kinds of biscuits which have long been in use, that may here be advantageously described.

1713. BISCUITS belong to the class of unfermented bread, and are, perhaps, the most wholesome of that class. In cases where fermented bread does not agree with the human stomach, they may be recommended: in many instances they are considered lighter, and less liable to create acidity and flatulence. The name is derived from the French *bis cuit*, "twice-baked," because, originally, that was the mode of entirely depriving them of all moisture, to insure their keeping ; but, although that process is no longer employed, the name is retained. The use of this kind of bread on land is pretty general, and some varieties are luxuries ; but, at sea, biscuits are articles of the first necessity.

1714. SEA, or SHIP BISCUITS, are made of wheat-flour from which only the coarsest bran has been separated. The dough is made up as stiff as it can be worked, and is then formed into shapes, and baked in an oven ; after which, the biscuits are exposed in lofts over the oven until perfectly dry, to prevent them from becoming mouldy when stored.

1715. CAPTAINS' BISCUITS are made in a similar manner, only of fine flour.

RECIPES.

CHAPTER XXXV.

TO MAKE YEAST FOR BREAD.

1716. INGREDIENTS.—1½ oz. of hops, 3 quarts of water, 1 lb. of bruised malt, ½ pint of yeast.

Mode.—Boil the hops in the water for 20 minutes; let it stand for about 5 minutes, then add it to 1 lb. of bruised malt prepared as for brewing. Let the mixture stand covered till about lukewarm; then put in not quite ½ pint of yeast; keep it warm, and let it work 3 or 4 hours; then put it into small ½-pint bottles (ginger-beer bottles are the best for the purpose), cork them well, and tie them down. The yeast is now ready for use; it will keep good for a few weeks, and 1 bottle will be found sufficient for 18 lbs. of flour. When required for use, boil 3 lbs. of potatoes without salt, mash them in the same water in which they were boiled, and rub them through a colander. Stir in about ½ lb. of flour; then put in the yeast, pour it in the middle of the flour, and let it stand warm on the hearth all night, and in the morning let it be quite warm when it is kneaded. The bottles of yeast require very careful opening, as it is generally exceedingly ripe.

Time.—20 minutes to boil the hops and water, the yeast to work 3 or 4 hours.

Sufficient.—½ pint sufficient for 18 lbs. of flour.

KIRKLEATHAM YEAST.

1717. INGREDIENTS.—2 oz. of hops, 4 quarts of water, ½ lb. of flour, ½ pint of yeast.

Mode.—Boil the hops and water for 20 minutes; strain, and mix with the liquid ½ lb. of flour and not quite ½ pint of yeast. Bottle it up, and tie the corks down. When wanted for use, boil potatoes according to the quantity of bread to be made (about 3 lbs. are sufficient for about a peck of flour); mash them, add to them ½ lb. of flour, and mix about ½ pint of the yeast with them; let this mixture stand all day, and lay the bread to rise the night before it is wanted.

Time.—20 minutes to boil the hops and water.

Sufficient.—½ pint of this yeast sufficient for a peck of flour, or rather more.

TO MAKE GOOD HOME-MADE BREAD.

(*Miss Acton's Recipe.*)

1718. INGREDIENTS.—1 quartern of flour, 1 large tablespoonful of solid brewer's yeast, or nearly 1 oz. of fresh German yeast, 1¼ to 1½ pint of warm milk-and-water.

Mode.—Put the flour into a large earthenware bowl or deep pan; then, with a strong metal or wooden spoon, hollow out the middle; but do not clear it entirely away from the bottom of the pan, as, in

COTTAGE LOAF.

TIN BREAD.

that case, the sponge (or leaven, as it was formerly termed) would stick to it, which it ought not to do. Next take either a large table-spoonful of brewer's yeast which has been rendered solid by mixing it with plenty of cold water, and letting it afterwards stand to settle for a day and night; or nearly an ounce of German yeast; put it into a large basin, and proceed to mix it, so that it shall be as smooth as cream, with ¾ pint of warm milk-and-water, or with water only; though even a very little milk will much improve the bread. Pour the yeast into the hole made in the flour, and stir into it as much of that which lies round it as will make a thick batter, in which there must be no lumps. Strew plenty of flour on the top; throw a thick clean cloth over, and set it where the air is warm; but do not place it upon the kitchen fender, for it will become too much heated there. Look at it from time to time: when it has been laid for nearly an hour, and when the yeast has risen and broken through the flour, so that bubbles appear in it, you will know that it is ready to be made up into dough. Then place the pan on a strong chair, or dresser, or table, of convenient height; pour into the sponge the remainder of the warm milk-and-water; stir into it as much of the flour as you can with the spoon; then wipe it out clean with your fingers, and lay it aside. Next take plenty of the remaining flour, throw it on the top of the leaven, and begin, with the knuckles of both hands, to knead it well. When the flour is nearly all kneaded in, begin to draw the edges of the dough towards the middle, in order to mix the whole thoroughly; and when it is free from flour and lumps and crumbs, and does not stick to the hands when touched, it will be done, and may again be covered with the cloth, and left to rise a second time. In ¾ hour look at it, and should it have swollen very much, and begin to crack, it will be light enough to bake. Turn it then on to a paste-board or very clean dresser, and with a large sharp knife divide it in two; make it up quickly into loaves, and dispatch it to the oven: make one or two incisions across the tops of the loaves, as they will rise more easily if this be done. If baked in tins or pans, rub them with a tiny piece of butter laid on a piece of clean paper, to prevent the dough from sticking to them. All bread should be turned upside down, or on its side, as soon as it is drawn from the oven: if this be neglected, the under part of the loaves will become wet and blistered from the steam, which cannot then escape from them. *To make the dough without setting a sponge*, merely mix the yeast with the greater part of the warm milk-and-water, and wet up the whole of the flour at once after a little salt has been stirred in,

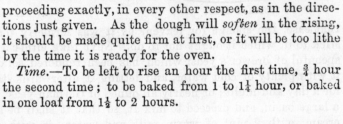

proceeding exactly, in every other respect, as in the directions just given. As the dough will *soften* in the rising, it should be made quite firm at first, or it will be too lithe by the time it is ready for the oven.

Time.—To be left to rise an hour the first time, ¾ hour the second time; to be baked from 1 to 1¼ hour, or baked in one loaf from 1½ to 2 hours.

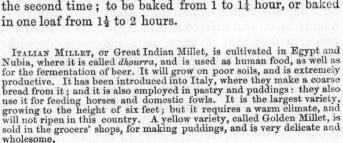

ITALIAN MILLET, or Great Indian Millet, is cultivated in Egypt and Nubia, where it is called *dhourra*, and is used as human food, as well as for the fermentation of beer. It will grow on poor soils, and is extremely productive. It has been introduced into Italy, where they make a coarse bread from it; and it is also employed in pastry and puddings: they also use it for feeding horses and domestic fowls. It is the largest variety, growing to the height of six feet; but it requires a warm climate, and will not ripen in this country. A yellow variety, called Golden Millet, is sold in the grocers' shops, for making puddings, and is very delicate and wholesome.

ITALIAN MILLET.

TO MAKE A PECK OF GOOD BREAD.

1719. INGREDIENTS.—3 lbs. of potatoes, 6 pints of cold water, ½ pint of good yeast, a peck of flour, 2 oz. of salt.

Mode.—Peel and boil the potatoes; beat them to a cream while warm; then add 1 pint of cold water, strain through a colander, and add to it ½ pint of good yeast, which should have been put in water over-night, to take off its bitterness. Stir all well together with a wooden spoon, and pour the mixture into the centre of the flour; mix it to the substance of cream, cover it over closely, and let it remain near the fire for an hour; then add the 5 pints of water, milk-warm, with 2 oz. of salt; pour this in, and mix the whole to a nice light dough. Let it remain for about 2 hours; then make it into 7 loaves, and bake for about 1½ hour in a good oven. When baked, the bread should weigh nearly 20 lbs.

Time.—About 1½ hour.

RED WINTER WHEAT.

THE RED VARIETIES OF WHEAT are generally hardier and more easily grown than the white sorts, and, although of less value to the miller, they are fully more profitable to the grower, in consequence of the better crops which they produce. Another advantage the red wheats possess is their comparative immunity from the attacks of mildew and fly. The best English wheat comes from the counties of Kent and Essex; the qualities under these heads always bearing a higher price than others, as will be seen by the periodical lists in the journals.

RICE BREAD.

1720. INGREDIENTS.—To every lb. of rice allow 4 lbs. of wheat flour, nearly 3 tablespoonfuls of yeast, ¼ oz. of salt.

Mode.—Boil the rice in water until it is quite tender; pour off the water, and put the rice, before it is cold, to the flour. Mix these well together with the yeast, salt, and sufficient warm water to make the whole into a smooth dough; let it rise by the side of the fire, then form it into loaves, and bake them from 1½ to 2 hours, according to their size. If the rice is boiled in milk instead of water, it makes very delicious bread or cakes. When boiled in this manner, it may be mixed with the flour without straining the liquid from it.

Time.—1½ to 2 hours.

INDIAN-CORN-FLOUR BREAD.

1721. INGREDIENTS.—To 4 lbs. of flour allow 2 lbs. of Indian-corn flour, 2 tablespoonfuls of yeast, 3 pints of warm water, ¼ oz. of salt.

Mode.—Mix the two flours well together, with the salt; make a hole in the centre, and stir the yeast up well with ½ pint of the warm water; put this into the middle of the flour, and mix enough of it with the yeast to make a thin batter; throw a little flour over the surface of this batter, cover the whole with a thick cloth, and set it to rise in a warm place. When the batter has nicely risen, work the whole to a nice smooth dough, adding the water as required; knead it well, and mould the dough into loaves; let them rise for nearly

$\frac{1}{2}$ hour, then put them into a well-heated oven. If made into 2 loaves, they will require from $1\frac{1}{2}$ to 2 hours' baking.

Time.—$1\frac{1}{2}$ to 2 hours.

MAIZE.—Next to wheat and rice, maize is the grain most used in the nourishment of man. In Asia, Africa, and America, it is the principal daily food of a large

portion of the population, especially of the colonists. In some of the provinces of France, too, it is consumed in large quantities. There are eight varieties of the maize; the most productive is the maize of Cusco. The flour of maize is yellow, and it contains an oily matter, which, when fresh, gives it an agreeable flavour and odour; but the action of the air on it soon develops rancidity. If carried any distance, it should be stored away in air-tight vessels. An excellent soup is prepared with meat and maize-flour. The inhabitants of some countries, where wheat is scarce, make, with maize and water, or milk and salt, a kind of biscuit, which is pleasant in taste, but indigestible. Some of the preparations of maize-flour are very good, and, when partaken in moderation, suitable food for almost everybody.

MAIZE PLANT.   EAR OF MAIZE.

SODA BREAD.

1722. INGREDIENTS.—To every 2 lbs. of flour allow 1 teaspoonful of tartaric acid, 1 teaspoonful of salt, 1 teaspoonful of carbonate of soda, 2 breakfast-cupfuls of cold milk.

Mode.—Let the tartaric acid and salt be reduced to the finest possible powder; then mix them well with the flour. Dissolve the soda in the milk, and pour it several times from one basin to another, before adding it to the flour. Work the whole quickly into a light dough, divide it into 2 loaves, and put them into a well-heated oven immediately, and bake for an hour. Sour milk or buttermilk may be used, but then a little less acid will be needed.

Time.—1 hour.

POLISH AND POMERANIAN WHEAT are accounted by authorities most excellent. Large raft-like barges convey this grain down the rivers, from the interior of the country to the seaports. This corn is described as being white, hard, and thin-skinned; and it yields a large quantity of flour, having a small proportion of bran.

POLISH WHEAT.

EXCELLENT ROLLS.

1723. INGREDIENTS.—To every lb. of flour allow 1 oz. of butter, $\frac{1}{4}$ pint of milk, 1 large teaspoonful of yeast, a little salt.

Mode.—Warm the butter in the milk, add to it the yeast and salt, and mix these ingredients well together. Put the flour into a pan, stir in the above ingredients, and let the dough rise, covered in a warm place. Knead it well, make it into rolls, let them rise again for a few minutes, and bake in a quick oven.

ROLLS.

Richer rolls may be made by adding 1 or 2 eggs and a larger proportion of butter, and their appearance improved by brushing the tops over with yolk of egg or a little milk.

Time.—1 lb. of flour, divided into 6 rolls, from 15 to 20 minutes.

HOT ROLLS.

1724. This dish, although very unwholesome and indigestible, is nevertheless a great favourite, and eaten by many persons. As soon as the rolls come from the baker's, they should be put into the oven, which, in the early part of the morning, is sure not to be very hot; and the rolls must not be buttered until wanted. When they are quite hot, divide them lengthwise into three; put some thin flakes of good butter between the slices, press the rolls together, and put them in the oven for a minute or two, but not longer, or the butter would oil; take them out of the oven, spread the butter equally over, divide the rolls in half, and put them on to a very hot clean dish, and send them instantly to table.

TO MAKE DRY TOAST.

1725. To make dry toast properly, a great deal of attention is required; much more, indeed, than people generally suppose. Never use new bread for making any kind of toast, as it eats heavy, and, besides, is very extravagant. Procure a loaf of household bread about two days old; cut off as many slices as may be required, not quite $\frac{1}{4}$ inch in thickness; trim off the crusts and ragged edges, put the bread on a toasting-fork, and hold it before a very clear fire. Move it backwards and forwards until the bread is nicely coloured; then turn it and toast the other side, and do not place it so near the fire that it blackens. Dry toast should be more gradually made than buttered toast, as its great beauty consists in its crispness, and this cannot be attained unless the process is slow and the bread is allowed gradually to colour. It should never be made long before it is wanted, as it soon becomes tough, unless placed on the fender in front of the fire. As soon as each piece is ready, it should be put into a rack, or stood upon its edges, and sent quickly to table.

TO MAKE HOT BUTTERED TOAST.

1726. A loaf of household bread about two days old answers for making toast better than cottage bread, the latter not being a good shape, and too crusty for the purpose. Cut as many nice even slices as may be required, rather more than $\frac{1}{4}$ inch in thickness, and toast them before a very bright fire, without allowing the bread to blacken, which spoils the appearance and flavour of all toast. When of a nice colour on both sides, put it on a hot plate; divide some good butter into small pieces, place them on the toast, set this before the fire, and when the butter is just beginning to melt, spread it lightly over the toast. Trim off the crust and ragged edges, divide each round into 4 pieces, and send the toast quickly to table. Some persons cut the slices of toast across from corner to corner, so making the pieces of a three-cornered shape. Soyer recommends that each slice should be cut into pieces as soon as it is buttered, and when all are ready, that they should be piled lightly on the dish they are intended to be served on. He says that by cutting through 4 or 5 slices at a time, all the butter is squeezed out of the upper ones, while the bottom one is swimming in fat liquid. It is highly essential to use good butter for making this dish.

MUFFINS.

1727. INGREDIENTS.—To every quart of milk allow 1½ oz. of German yeast, a little salt; flour.

Mode.—Warm the milk, add to it the yeast, and mix these well together; put them into a pan, and stir in sufficient flour to make the whole into a dough of rather a soft consistence; cover it over with a cloth, and place it in a warm place to rise, and, when light and nicely risen, divide the dough into pieces, and round them to the proper shape with the hands; place them, in a layer of flour about two inches thick, on wooden trays, and let them rise again; when this is effected, they each will exhibit a semi-globular shape. Then place them carefully on a hot-plate or stove, and bake them until they are slightly browned, turning them when they are done on one side. Muffins are not easily made, and are more generally purchased than manufactured at home. *To toast them*, divide the edge of the muffin all round, by pulling it open, to the depth of about an inch, with the fingers. Put it on a toasting-fork, and hold it before a very clear fire until one side is nicely browned, but not burnt; turn, and toast it on the other. Do not toast them too quickly, as, if this is done, the middle of the

MUFFINS.

muffin will not be warmed through. When done, divide them by pulling them open; butter them slightly on both sides, put them together again, and cut them into halves: when sufficient are toasted and buttered, pile them on a very hot dish, and send them very quickly to table.

Time.—From 20 minutes to ½ hour to bake them.

Sufficient.—Allow 1 muffin to each person.

CRUMPETS.

1728. These are made in the same manner as muffins; only, in making the mixture, let it be more like batter than dough. Let it rise for about ½ hour; pour it into iron rings, which should be ready on a hot-plate; bake them, and when one side appears done, turn them quickly on the other. *To toast them,* have ready a very *bright clear* fire; put the crumpet

CRUMPETS.

on a toasting-fork, and hold it before the fire, *not too close,* until it is nicely brown on one side, but do not allow it to blacken. Turn it, and brown the other side; then spread it with good butter, cut it in half, and, when all are done, pile them on a hot dish, and send them quickly to table. Muffins and crumpets should always be served on separate dishes, and both toasted and served as expeditiously as possible.

Time.—From 10 to 15 minutes to bake them.

Sufficient.—Allow 2 crumpets to each person.

PLAIN BUNS.

1729. INGREDIENTS.—To every 2 lbs. of flour allow 6 oz. of moist sugar, ½ gill of yeast, ½ pint of milk, ½ lb. of butter, warm milk.

Mode.—Put the flour into a basin, mix the sugar well with it, make a hole in the centre, and stir in the yeast and milk (which should be lukewarm), with enough of the flour to make it the thickness of cream. Cover the basin over with a cloth, and let the sponge rise in a warm place, which will be accomplished in about 1½ hour. Melt the butter, but do not allow it to oil; stir it into the other ingredients, with enough warm milk to make the whole into a soft dough; then mould it into buns about the size of an egg; lay them in rows quite 3 inches apart; set them again in a warm place, until they have risen to double their size; then put them into a good brisk oven, and just before they are done, wash them over with a little milk. From 15 to 20 minutes will be required to bake them nicely. These buns may be varied by adding a few currants, candied peel, or caraway seeds to the other ingredients; and the above mixture answers for hot cross buns, by putting in a little ground allspice; and by pressing a tin mould in the form of a cross in the centre of the bun.

Time.—15 to 20 minutes.   *Average cost,* 1*d.* each.

Sufficient to make 18 buns.

TO MAKE GOOD PLAIN BUNS.

1730. INGREDIENTS.—1 lb. of flour, 6 oz. of good butter, ¼ lb. of sugar, 1 egg, nearly ¼ pint of milk, 2 small teaspoonfuls of baking-powder, a few drops of essence of lemon.

Mode.—Warm the butter, without oiling it; beat it with a wooden spoon; stir the flour in gradually with the sugar, and mix these ingredients well together. Make the milk lukewarm, beat up with it the yolk of the egg and the essence of lemon, and stir these to the flour, &c. Add the baking-powder, beat the dough well for about 10 minutes, divide it into 24 pieces, put them into buttered tins or cups, and bake in a brisk oven from 20 to 30 minutes.

Time.—20 to 30 minutes.   *Average cost,* 1*s.*

Sufficient to make 12 buns.   *Seasonable* at any time.

LIGHT BUNS.

1731. INGREDIENTS.—½ teaspoonful of tartaric acid, ½ teaspoonful of bicarbonate of soda, 1 lb. of flour, 2 oz. of butter, 2 oz. of loaf sugar, ¼ lb. of currants or raisins,—when liked, a few caraway seeds, ½ pint of cold new milk, 1 egg.

Mode.—Rub the tartaric acid, soda, and flour all together through a hair sieve; work the butter into the flour; add the sugar, currants, and

BUNS.

caraway seeds, when the flavour of the latter is liked. Mix all these ingredients well together; make a hole in the middle of the flour, and pour in the milk, mixed with the egg, which should be well beaten; mix quickly, and set the dough, with a fork, on baking-tins, and bake the buns for about 20 minutes. This mixture makes a very good cake, and if put into a tin, should be baked 1½ hour. The same quantity of flour, soda, and tartaric acid, with ½ pint of milk and a little salt, will make either bread or teacakes, if wanted quickly.

Time.—20 minutes for the buns; if made into a cake, 1½ hour.

Sufficient to make about 12 buns.

VICTORIA BUNS.

1732. INGREDIENTS.—2 oz. of pounded loaf sugar, 1 egg, 1½ oz. of ground rice, 2 oz. of butter, 1½ oz. of currants, a few thin slices of candied peel; flour.

Mode.—Whisk the egg, stir in the sugar, and beat these ingredients well together; beat the butter to a cream, stir in the ground rice, currants, and candied peel, and as much flour as will make it of such a consistency that it may be rolled into 7 or 8 balls. Put these on to a buttered tin, and bake them from ½ to ¾ hour. They should be put into the oven immediately, or they will become heavy; and the oven should be tolerably brisk.

Time.—½ to ¾ hour. *Average cost,* 6d.

Sufficient to make 7 or 8 buns. *Seasonable* at any time.

ITALIAN RUSKS.

1733. A stale Savoy or lemon cake may be converted into very good rusks in the following manner. Cut the cake into slices, divide each slice in two; put them on a baking-sheet, in a slow oven, and when they are of a nice brown and quite hard, they are done. They should be kept in a closed tin canister in a dry place, to preserve their crispness.

PANNICLED MILLET.—This is the smallest-seeded of the corn-plants, being a true grass; but the number of the seeds in each ear makes up for their size. It grows in sandy soils that will not do for the cultivation of many other kinds of grain, and forms the chief sustenance in the arid districts of Arabia, Syria, Nubia, and parts of India. It is not cultivated in England, being principally confined to the East. The nations who make use of it grind it, in the primitive manner, between two stones, and make it into a diet which cannot be properly called bread, but rather a kind of soft thin cake half-baked. When we take into account that the Arabians are fond of lizards and locusts as articles of food, their *cuisine,* altogether, is scarcely a tempting one.

PANNICLED MILLET.

TO MAKE RUSKS.

(*Suffolk Recipe.*)

1734. INGREDIENTS.—To every lb. of flour allow 2 oz. of butter, ¼ pint of milk, 2 oz. of loaf sugar, 3 eggs, 1 tablespoonful of yeast.

Mode.—Put the milk and butter into a saucepan, and keep shaking it round until the latter is melted. Put the flour into a basin with the sugar, mix these well together, and beat the eggs. Stir them with the yeast to the milk and butter, and with this liquid work the flour into a smooth dough. Cover a cloth over the

RUSKS.

basin, and leave the dough to rise by the side of the fire; then knead it, and divide it into 12 pieces; place them in a brisk oven, and bake for about 20 minutes. Take the rusks out, break them in half, and then set them in the oven to get crisp on the other side. When cold, they should be put into tin canisters to keep them dry; and, if intended for the cheese course, the sifted sugar should be omitted.

Time.—20 minutes to bake the rusks; 5 minutes to render them crisp after being divided.

Average cost, 8*d.*

Sufficient to make 2 dozen rusks. *Seasonable* at any time.

ALMOND ICING FOR CAKES.

1735. INGREDIENTS.—To every lb. of finely-pounded loaf sugar allow 1 lb. of sweet almonds, the whites of 4 eggs, a little rose-water.

Mode.—Blanch the almonds, and pound them (a few at a time) in a mortar to a paste, adding a little rose-water to facilitate the operation. Whisk the whites of the eggs to a strong froth; mix them with the pounded almonds, stir in the sugar, and beat altogether. When the cake is sufficiently baked, lay on the almond icing, and put it into the oven to dry. Before laying this preparation on the cake, great care must be taken that it is nice and smooth, which is easily accomplished by well beating the mixture.

SUGAR ICING FOR CAKES.

1736. INGREDIENTS.—To every lb. of loaf sugar allow the whites of 4 eggs, 1 oz. of fine starch.

Mode.—Beat the eggs to a strong froth, and gradually sift in the sugar, which should be reduced to the finest possible powder, and gradually add the starch, also finely powdered. Beat the mixture well until the sugar is smooth; then with a spoon or broad knife lay the icing equally over the cakes. These should then be placed in a very cool oven, and the icing allowed to dry and harden, but not to colour. The icing may be coloured with strawberry or currant-juice, or with prepared cochineal. If it be put on the cakes as soon as they are withdrawn from the oven, it will become firm and hard by the time the cakes are cold. On very rich cakes, such as wedding, christening cakes, &c., a layer of almond icing, No. 1735, is usually spread over the top, and over that the white icing as described. All iced cakes should be kept in a very dry place.

BISCUIT POWDER, generally used for Infants' Food.

1737. This powder may be purchased in tin canisters, and may also be prepared at home. Dry the biscuits well in a slow oven; roll them and grind them with a rolling-pin on a clean board, until they are reduced to powder; sift it through a close hair sieve, and it is fit for use. It should be kept in well-covered tins, and in a dry place.

ARROWROOT BISCUITS OR DROPS.

1738. INGREDIENTS.—½ lb. of butter, 6 eggs, ½ lb. of flour, 6 oz. of arrowroot, ½ lb. of pounded loaf sugar.

Mode.—Beat the butter to a cream; whisk the eggs to a strong froth, add them to the butter, stir in the flour a little at a time, and beat the mixture well. Break down all the lumps from the arrowroot, and add that with the sugar to the other ingredients. Mix all well together, drop the dough on a buttered tin, in pieces the size of a shilling, and bake the biscuits about ¼ hour in a slow oven.

Time.—¼ hour. *Average cost*, 2s. 6d.

Sufficient to make from 3 to 4 dozen biscuits.

Seasonable at any time.

NICE BREAKFAST CAKES.

1739. INGREDIENTS.—1 lb. of flour, ½ teaspoonful of tartaric acid, ½ teaspoonful of salt, ½ teaspoonful of carbonate of soda, 1½ breakfast-cupful of milk, 1 oz. of sifted loaf sugar, 2 eggs.

Mode.—These cakes are made in the same manner as the soda bread No. 1722, with the addition of eggs and sugar. Mix the flour, tartaric acid, and salt well together, taking care that the two latter ingredients are reduced to the finest powder, and stir in the sifted sugar, which should also be very fine. Dissolve the soda in the milk, add the eggs, which should be well whisked, and with this liquid work the flour, &c. into a light dough. Divide it into small cakes, put them into the oven immediately, and bake for about 20 minutes.

Time.—20 minutes.

COCOA-NUT BISCUITS OR CAKES.

1740. INGREDIENTS.—10 oz. of sifted sugar, 3 eggs, 6 oz. of grated cocoa-nut.

Mode.—Whisk the eggs until they are very light; add the sugar gradually; then stir in the cocoa-nut. Roll a tablespoonful of the paste at a time in your hands in the form of a pyramid; place the

3 I

pyramids on paper, put the paper on tins, and bake the biscuits in rather a cool oven until they are just coloured a light brown.

Time. About ¼ hour.　*Seasonable* at any time.

CRISP BISCUITS.

1741. INGREDIENTS.—1 lb. of flour, the yolk of 1 egg, milk.

Mode.—Mix the flour and the yolk of the egg with sufficient milk to make the whole into a very stiff paste; beat it well, and knead it until it is perfectly smooth. Roll the paste out *very thin;* with a round cutter shape it into small biscuits, and bake them a nice brown in a slow oven from 12 to 18 minutes.

Time.—12 to 18 minutes.　*Average cost,* 4d.

Seasonable at any time.

DESSERT BISCUITS, which may be flavoured with Ground Ginger, Cinnamon, &c. &c.

1742. INGREDIENTS.—1 lb. of flour, ½ lb. of butter, ½ lb. of sifted sugar, the yolks of 6 eggs, flavouring to taste.

Mode.—Put the butter into a basin; warm it, but do not allow it to oil; then with the hand beat it to a cream. Add the flour by degrees, then the sugar and flavouring, and moisten the whole with the yolks of the eggs, which should previously be well beaten. When all the ingredients are thoroughly incorporated, drop the mixture from a spoon on to a buttered paper, leaving a distance between each cake, as they spread as soon as they begin to get warm. Bake in rather a slow oven from 12 to 18 minutes, and do not let the biscuits acquire too much colour. In making the above quantity, half may be flavoured with ground ginger and the other half with essence of lemon or currants, to make a variety. With whatever the preparation is flavoured, so are the biscuits called; and an endless variety may be made in this manner.

Time.—12 to 18 minutes, or rather longer, in a very slow oven.

Average cost, 1s. 6d.

Sufficient to make from 3 to 4 dozen cakes.

Seasonable at any time.

LEMON BISCUITS.

1743. INGREDIENTS.—1¼ lb. of flour, ¾ lb. of loaf sugar, 6 oz. of fresh butter, 4 eggs, 1 oz. of lemon-peel, 2 dessertspoonfuls of lemon-juice.

Mode.—Rub the flour into the butter; stir in the pounded sugar and very finely-minced lemon-peel, and when these ingredients are thoroughly mixed, add the eggs, which should be previously well whisked, and the lemon-juice. Beat the mixture well for a minute or two, then drop it from a spoon on to a buttered tin, about 2 inches apart, as the cakes will spread when they get warm; place the tin in the oven, and bake the cakes of a pale brown from 15 to 20 minutes.

Time.—15 to 20 minutes. *Average cost,* 1s. 6d.

Seasonable at any time.

MACAROONS.

1744. INGREDIENTS.—½ lb. of sweet almonds, ½ lb. of sifted loaf sugar, the whites of 3 eggs, wafer-paper.

Mode.—Blanch, skin, and dry the almonds, and pound them well with a little orange-flower water or plain water; then add to them the sifted sugar and the whites of the eggs, which should be beaten to a stiff froth, and mix all the ingredients well together. When the paste looks soft, drop it at equal distances from a biscuit-syringe on to sheets of wafer-paper; put a strip

MACAROONS.

of almond on the top of each; strew some sugar over, and bake the macaroons in rather a slow oven, of a light brown colour. When hard and set, they are done, and must not be allowed to get very brown, as that would spoil their appearance. If the cakes, when baked, appear heavy, add a little more white of egg, but let this always be well whisked before it is added to the other ingredients. We have given a recipe for making these cakes, but we think it almost or quite as economical to purchase such articles as these at a good confectioner's.

Time.—From 15 to 20 minutes, in a slow oven.

Average cost, 1s. 8d. per lb.

RATAFIAS.

1745. INGREDIENTS.—½ lb. of sweet almonds, ¼ lb. of bitter ones, ¾ lb. of sifted loaf sugar, the whites of 4 eggs.

Mode.—Blanch, skin, and dry the almonds, and pound them in a mortar with the white of an egg; stir in the sugar, and gradually add the remaining whites of eggs, taking care that they are very thoroughly whisked. Drop the mixture through a small biscuit-syringe on to cartridge paper, and bake the cakes from 10 to 12 minutes in rather a quicker oven than for

RATAFIAS.

macaroons. A very small quantity should be dropped on the paper to form one cake, as, when baked, the ratafias should be about the size of a large button.

Time.—10 to 12 minutes. *Average cost,* 1s. 8d. per lb.

RICE BISCUITS OR CAKES.

1746. INGREDIENTS.—To every ½ lb. of rice-flour allow ¼ lb. of. pounded lump sugar, ¼ lb. of butter, 2 eggs.

Mode.—Beat the butter to a cream, stir in the rice-flour and pounded sugar, and moisten the whole with the eggs, which should be previously well beaten. Roll out the paste, shape it with a round paste-cutter into small cakes, and bake them from 12 to 18 minutes in a very slow oven.

Time.—12 to 18 minutes. *Average cost,* 9d.

Sufficient to make about 18 cakes. *Seasonable* at any time.

GROUND RICE, or rice-flour, is used for making several kinds of cakes, also for thickening soups, and for mixing with wheaten flour in producing Manna Kroup. The Americans make rice-bread, and prepare the flour for it in the following manner :— When the rice is thoroughly cleansed, the water is drawn off, and the rice, while damp, bruised in a mortar : it is then dried, and passed through a hair sieve.

ROCK BISCUITS.

1747. INGREDIENTS.—6 eggs, 1 lb. of sifted sugar, ½ lb. of flour, a few currants.

Mode.—Break the eggs into a basin, beat them well until very light, add the pounded sugar, and when this is well mixed with the eggs, dredge in the flour gradually, and add the currants. Mix all well together, and put the dough, with a fork, on the tins, making it look as rough as possible. Bake the cakes in a moderate oven from 20 minutes to ½ hour; when they are done, allow them to get cool, and store them away in a tin canister, in a dry place.

Time.—20 minutes to ½ hour. *Average cost,* 1s. 2d.

Seasonable at any time.

SAVOY BISCUITS OR CAKES.

1748. INGREDIENTS.—4 eggs, 6 oz. of pounded sugar, the rind of 1 lemon, 6 oz. of flour.

Mode.—Break the eggs into a basin, separating the whites from the yolks; beat the yolks well, mix with them the pounded sugar and grated lemon-rind, and beat these ingredients together for ¼ hour. Then dredge in the flour gradually, and when the whites of the eggs have been whisked to a solid froth, stir them to the flour, &c.; beat the mixture well for another 5 minutes, then draw it along in strips upon thick cartridge paper to the proper size of the biscuit, and bake them in rather a hot oven; but let them be carefully watched, as they are soon done, and a few seconds over the proper time will scorch and spoil them. These biscuits, or ladies'-fingers, as they are called, are used for making Charlotte russes, and for a variety of fancy sweet dishes.

Time.—5 to 8 minutes, in a quick oven.

Average cost, 1s. 8d. per lb., or ½d. each.

SEED BISCUITS.

1749. INGREDIENTS.—1 lb. of flour, ¼ lb. of sifted sugar, ¼ lb. of butter, ½ oz. of caraway seeds, 3 eggs.

Mode.—Beat the butter to a cream; stir in the flour, sugar, and caraway seeds; and when these ingredients are well mixed, add the eggs, which should be well whisked. Roll out the paste, with a round cutter shape out the biscuits, and bake them in a moderate oven from 10 to 15 minutes. The tops of the biscuits may be brushed over with a little milk or the white of an egg, and then a little sugar strewn over.

Time.—10 to 15 minutes. *Average cost*, 1s.

Sufficient to make 3 dozen biscuits. *Seasonable* at any time.

SIMPLE HARD BISCUITS.

1750. INGREDIENTS.—To every lb. of flour allow 2 oz. of butter, about ½ pint of skimmed milk.

Mode.—Warm the butter in the milk until the former is dissolved, and then mix it with the flour into a very stiff paste; beat it with a rolling-pin until the dough looks perfectly smooth. Roll it out thin; cut it with the top of a glass into round biscuits; prick them well, and bake them from 6 to 10 minutes. The above is the proportion of milk which we think would convert the flour into a stiff paste; but should it be found too much, an extra spoonful or two of flour must be put in. These biscuits are very nice for the cheese course.

Time.—6 to 10 minutes.

Seasonable at any time.

SODA BISCUITS.

1751. INGREDIENTS.—1 lb. of flour, ½ lb. of pounded loaf sugar, ¼ lb. of fresh butter, 2 eggs, 1 small teaspoonful of carbonate of soda.

Mode.—Put the flour (which should be perfectly dry) into a basin; rub in the butter, add the sugar, and mix these ingredients well together. Whisk the eggs, stir them into the mixture, and beat it well, until everything is well incorporated. Quickly stir in the soda, roll the paste out until it is about ½ inch thick, cut it into small round cakes with a tin cutter, and bake them from 12 to 18 minutes in rather a brisk oven. After the soda is added, great expedition is necessary in rolling and cutting out the paste, and in putting the biscuits *immediately* into the oven, or they will be heavy.

Time.—12 to 18 minutes. *Average cost*, 1s.

Sufficient to make about 3 dozen cakes. *Seasonable* at any time.

ALMOND CAKE.

1752. INGREDIENTS.—½ lb. of sweet almonds, 1 oz. of bitter almonds, 6 eggs, 8 tablespoonfuls of sifted sugar, 5 tablespoonfuls of fine flour, the grated rind of 1 lemon, 3 oz. of butter.

Mode.—Blanch and pound the almonds to a paste ; separate the whites from the yolks of the eggs ; beat the latter, and add them to the almonds.   Stir in the sugar, flour, and lemon-rind ; add the butter, which should be beaten to a cream ; and when all these ingredients are well mixed, put in the whites of the eggs, which should be whisked to a stiff froth.   Butter a cake-mould, put in the mixture, and bake in a good oven from 1¼ to 1¾ hour.

Time.—1¼ to 1¾ hour.   *Average cost,* 1s.

Seasonable at any time.

RICH BRIDE OR CHRISTENING CAKE.

1753. INGREDIENTS.—5 lbs. of the finest flour, 3 lbs. of fresh butter, 5 lbs. of currants, 2 lbs. of sifted loaf sugar, 2 nutmegs, ¼ oz. of mace, half ¼ oz. of cloves, 16 eggs, 1 lb. of sweet almonds, ½ lb. of candied citron, ½ lb. each of candied orange and lemon peel, 1 gill of wine, 1 gill of brandy.

Mode.—Let the flour be as fine as possible, and well dried and sifted ; the currants washed, picked, and dried before the fire ; the sugar well pounded and sifted ; the nutmegs grated, the spices pounded ; the eggs thoroughly whisked, whites and yolks separately ; the almonds pounded with a litte orange-flower water, and the candied peel cut in neat slices.   When all these ingredients are prepared, mix them in the following manner.   Begin working the butter with the hand till it becomes of a cream-like consistency; stir in the sugar, and when the whites of the eggs are whisked to a solid froth, mix them with the butter and sugar; next, well beat up the yolks for 10 minutes, and, adding them to the flour, nutmegs, mace, and cloves, continue beating the whole together for ½ hour or longer, till wanted for the oven. Then mix in lightly the currants, almonds, and candied peel with the wine and brandy ; and having lined a hoop with buttered paper, fill it with the mixture, and bake the cake in a tolerably quick oven, taking care, however, not to burn it : to prevent this, the top of it may be covered with a sheet of paper.   To ascertain whether the cake is done, plunge a clean knife into the middle of it, withdraw it directly, and if the blade is not sticky, and looks bright, the cake is sufficiently baked.   These cakes are usually spread with a thick layer of almond icing, and over that another layer of sugar icing, and afterwards ornamented. In baking a large cake like this, great attention must be paid to the heat of the oven; it should not be too fierce, but have a good soaking heat.

Time.—5 to 6 hours. *Average cost,* 2s. per lb.

CHRISTMAS CAKE.

1754. INGREDIENTS.—5 teacupfuls of flour, 1 teacupful of melted butter, 1 teacupful of cream, 1 teacupful of treacle, 1 teacupful of moist sugar, 2 eggs, $\frac{1}{2}$ oz. of powdered ginger, $\frac{1}{2}$ lb. of raisins, 1 teaspoonful of carbonate of soda, 1 tablespoonful of vinegar.

Mode.—Make the butter sufficiently warm to melt it, but do not allow it to oil; put the flour into a basin; add to it the sugar, ginger, and raisins, which should be stoned and cut into small pieces. When these dry ingredients are thoroughly mixed, stir in the butter, cream, treacle, and well-whisked eggs, and beat the mixture for a few minutes. Dissolve the soda in the vinegar, add it to the dough, and be particular that these latter ingredients are well incorporated with the others; put the cake into a buttered mould or tin, place it in a moderate oven immediately, and bake it from $1\frac{3}{4}$ to $2\frac{1}{4}$ hours.

Time.—$1\frac{3}{4}$ to $2\frac{1}{4}$ hours. *Average cost,* 1s. 6d.

COMMON CAKE, suitable for sending to Children at School.

1755. INGREDIENTS.—2 lbs. of flour, 4 oz. of butter or clarified dripping, $\frac{1}{2}$ oz. of caraway seeds, $\frac{1}{4}$ oz. of allspice, $\frac{1}{2}$ lb. of pounded sugar, 1 lb. of currants, 1 pint of milk, 3 tablespoonfuls of fresh yeast.

Mode.—Rub the butter lightly into the flour; add all the dry ingredients, and mix these well together. Make the milk warm, but not hot; stir in the yeast, and with this liquid make the whole into a light dough; knead it well, and line the cake-tins with strips of buttered paper: this paper should be about 6 inches higher than the top of the tin. Put in the dough; stand it in a warm place to rise for more than an hour; then bake the cakes in a well-heated oven. If this quantity be divided in two, they will take from $1\frac{1}{2}$ to 2 hours' baking.

Time.—$1\frac{3}{4}$ to $2\frac{1}{4}$ hours. *Average cost,* 1s. 9d.

Sufficient to make 2 moderate-sized cakes.

ECONOMICAL CAKE.

1756. INGREDIENTS.—1 lb. of flour, $\frac{1}{4}$ lb. of sugar, $\frac{1}{4}$ lb. of butter or lard, $\frac{1}{2}$ lb. of currants, 1 teaspoonful of carbonate of soda, the whites of 4 eggs, $\frac{1}{2}$ pint of milk.

Mode.—In making many sweet dishes, the whites of eggs are not required, and if well beaten and added to the above ingredients, make

an excellent cake, with or without currants. Beat the butter to a cream, well whisk the whites of the eggs, and stir all the ingredients together but the soda, which must not be added until all is well mixed, and the cake is ready to be put into the oven.

CAKE-MOULD.

When the mixture has been well beaten, stir in the soda, put the cake into a buttered mould, and bake it in a moderate oven for 1½ hour.

Time.—1½ hour. *Average cost*, 1s. 3d.

A NICE USEFUL CAKE.

1757. INGREDIENTS.—¼ lb. of butter, 6 oz. of currants, ¼ lb. of sugar, 1 lb. of dried flour, 2 teaspoonfuls of baking-powder, 3 eggs, 1 teacupful of milk, 2 oz. of sweet almonds, 1 oz. of candied peel.

Mode.—Beat the butter to a cream; wash, pick, and dry the currants; whisk the eggs; blanch and chop the almonds, and cut the peel into neat slices. When all these are ready, mix the dry ingredients together; then add the butter, milk, and eggs, and beat the mixture well for a few minutes. Put the cake into a buttered mould or tin, and bake it for rather more than 1½ hour. The currants and candied peel may be omitted, and a little lemon or almond flavouring substituted for them: made in this manner, the cake will be found very good.

Time.—Rather more than 1½ hour. *Average cost*, 1s. 9d.

HONEY CAKE.

1758. INGREDIENTS.—½ breakfast-cupful of sugar, 1 breakfast-cupful of rich sour cream, 2 breakfast-cupfuls of flour, ½ teaspoonful of carbonate of soda, honey to taste.

Mode.—Mix the sugar and cream together; dredge in the flour, with as much honey as will flavour the mixture nicely; stir it well, that all the ingredients may be thoroughly mixed; add the carbonate of soda, and beat the cake well for another 5 minutes; put it into a buttered tin, bake it from ½ to ¾ hour, and let it be eaten warm.

Time.—½ to ¾ hour. *Average cost*, 8d.

Sufficient for 3 or 4 persons. *Seasonable* at any time.

RICH SWEETMEAT GINGERBREAD NUTS.

1759. INGREDIENTS.—1 lb. of treacle, ¼ lb. of clarified butter, 1 lb. of coarse brown sugar, 2 oz. of ground ginger, 1 oz. of candied orange-peel, 1 oz. of candied angelica, $\frac{1}{2}$ oz. of candied lemon-peel, $\frac{1}{2}$ oz. of coriander seeds, $\frac{1}{2}$ oz. of caraway seeds, 1 egg; flour.

Mode.—Put the treacle into a basin, and pour over it the butter, melted so as not to oil, the sugar, and ginger. Stir these ingredients well together, and whilst mixing, add the candied peel, which should be cut into very small pieces, but not bruised, and the caraway and coriander seeds, which should be pounded. Having mixed all thoroughly together, break in an egg, and work the whole up with as much fine flour as may be necessary to form a paste. Make this into nuts of any size, put them on a tin plate, and bake in a slow oven from $\frac{1}{4}$ to $\frac{1}{2}$ hour.

Time.—$\frac{1}{4}$ to $\frac{1}{2}$ hour. *Average cost*, from 1s. to 1s. 4d. per lb.

Seasonable at any time.

THICK GINGERBREAD.

1760. INGREDIENTS.—1 lb. of treacle, $\frac{1}{4}$ lb. of butter, $\frac{1}{4}$ lb. of coarse brown sugar, $1\frac{1}{2}$ lb. of flour, 1 oz. of ginger, $\frac{1}{2}$ oz. of ground allspice, 1 teaspoonful of carbonate of soda, $\frac{1}{4}$ pint of warm milk, 3 eggs.

Mode.—Put the flour into a basin, with the sugar, ginger, and allspice; mix these together; warm the butter, and add it, with the treacle, to the other ingredients. Stir well; make the milk just warm, dissolve the carbonate of soda in it, and mix the whole into a nice smooth dough with the eggs, which should be previously well

GINGERBREAD.

whisked; pour the mixture into a buttered tin, and bake it from $\frac{3}{4}$ to 1 hour, or longer, should the gingerbread be very thick. Just before it is done, brush the top over with the yolk of an egg beaten up with a little milk, and put it back in the oven to finish baking.

Time.—$\frac{3}{4}$ to 1 hour. *Average cost*, 1s. per square.

Seasonable at any time.

SUNDERLAND GINGERBREAD NUTS.

(An Excellent Recipe.)

1761. INGREDIENTS.—$1\frac{3}{4}$ lb. treacle, 1 lb. of moist sugar, 1 lb. of butter, $2\frac{3}{4}$ lbs. of flour, $1\frac{1}{2}$ oz. of ground ginger, $1\frac{1}{2}$ oz. of allspice, $1\frac{1}{2}$ oz. of coriander seeds.

Mode.—Let the allspice, coriander seeds, and ginger be freshly ground; put them into a basin, with the flour and sugar, and mix these ingredients well together; warm the treacle and butter together; then with a spoon work it into the flour, &c., until the whole forms a nice smooth paste. Drop the mixture from the spoon on to a piece of buttered paper, and bake in rather a slow oven from 20 minutes to ½ hour. A little candied lemon-peel mixed with the above is an improvement, and a great authority in culinary matters suggests the addition of a little cayenne pepper in gingerbread. Whether it be advisable to use this latter ingredient or not, we leave our readers to decide.

Time.—20 minutes to ½ hour. *Average cost*, 1*s*. to 1*s*. 4*d*. per lb.

Seasonable at any time.

WHITE GINGERBREAD.

1762. INGREDIENTS.—1 lb. of flour, ½ lb. of butter, ½ lb. of loaf sugar, the rind of 1 lemon, 1 oz. of ground ginger, 1 nutmeg grated, ½ teaspoonful of carbonate of soda, 1 gill of milk.

Mode.—Rub the butter into the flour ; add the sugar, which should be finely pounded and sifted, and the minced lemon-rind, ginger, and nutmeg. Mix these well together ; make the milk just warm, stir in the soda, and work the whole into a nice smooth paste ; roll it out, cut it into cakes, and bake in a moderate oven from 15 to 20 minutes.

Time.—15 to 20 minutes. *Average cost*, 1*s*. 3*d*.

Seasonable at any time.

GOOD HOLIDAY CAKE.

1763. INGREDIENTS.—1½*d*. worth of Borwick's German baking-powder, 2 lbs. of flour, 6 oz. of butter, ¼ lb. of lard, 1 lb. of currants, ½ lb. of stoned and cut raisins, ¼ lb. of mixed candied peel, ½ lb. of moist sugar, 3 eggs, ¾ pint of cold milk.

Mode.—Mix the baking-powder with the flour ; then rub in the butter and lard ; have ready the currants, washed, picked, and dried the raisins stoned and cut into small pieces (not chopped), and the peel cut into neat slices. Add these with the sugar to the flour, &c., and mix all the dry ingredients well together. Whisk the eggs, stir to them the milk, and with this liquid moisten the cake ; beat it up well, that all may be very thoroughly mixed ; line a cake-tin with buttered paper, put in the cake, and bake it from 2¼ to 2¾ hours in a good oven. To ascertain when it is done, plunge a clean knife into the middle of it, and if, on withdrawing it, the knife looks clean, and not sticky, the cake is done. To prevent its burning at the top, a piece of clean paper may be put over whilst the cake is soaking, or being thoroughly cooked in the middle. A steamer, such as is used for steaming potatoes, makes a very good cake-tin, if it be lined at the bottom and sides with buttered paper.

Time.—2¼ to 2¾ hours. *Average cost*, 2*s*. 6*d*.

Seasonable at any time.

LEMON CAKE.

1764. INGREDIENTS.—10 eggs, 3 tablespoonfuls of orange-flower water, ¾ lb. of pounded loaf sugar, 1 lemon, ¾ lb. of flour.

Mode.—Separate the whites from the yolks of the eggs; whisk the former to a stiff froth; add the orange-flower water, the sugar, grated lemon-rind, and mix these ingredients well together. Then beat the yolks of the eggs, and add them, with the lemon-juice, to the whites, &c.; dredge in the flour gradually; keep beating the mixture well; put it into a buttered mould, and bake the cake about an hour, or rather longer. The addition of a little butter, beaten to a cream, we think, would improve this cake.

CAKE-MOULD.

Time.—About 1 hour. *Average cost*, 1s. 4d.

Seasonable at any time.

LUNCHEON CAKE.

1765. INGREDIENTS.—½ lb. of butter, 1 lb. of flour, ½ oz. of caraway seeds, ¼ lb. of currants, 6 oz. of moist sugar, 1 oz. of candied peel, 3 eggs, ½ pint of milk, 1 small teaspoonful of carbonate of soda.

Mode.—Rub the butter into the flour until it is quite fine; add the caraway seeds, currants (which should be nicely washed, picked, and dried), sugar, and candied peel cut into thin slices; mix these well together, and moisten with the eggs, which should be well whisked. Boil the milk, and add to it, whilst boiling, the carbonate of soda, which must be well stirred into it, and, with the milk, mix the other ingredients. Butter a tin, pour the cake into it, and bake it in a moderate oven from ¾ to 1 hour.

Time.—1 to 1½ hour. *Average cost*, 1s. 8d.

Seasonable at any time.

CARBONATE OF SODA.—Soda was called the mineral alkali, because it was originally dug up out of the ground in Africa and other countries: this state of carbonate of soda is called *natron*. But carbonate of soda is likewise procured from the combustion of marine plants, or such as grow on the sea-shore. Pure carbonate of soda is employed for making effervescing draughts, with lemon-juice, citric acid, or tartaric acid. The chief constituent of soda, the alkali, has been used in France from time immemorial in the manufacture of soap and glass, two chemical productions which employ and keep in circulation an immense amount of capital. A small pinch of carbonate of soda will give an extraordinary lightness to puff pastes; and, introduced into the teapot, will extract the full strength of the tea. But its qualities have a powerful effect upon delicate constitutions, and it is not to be used incautiously in any preparation.

A NICE PLAIN CAKE.

1766. INGREDIENTS.—1 lb. of flour, 1 teaspoonful of Borwick's baking-powder, ¼ lb. of good dripping, 1 teacupful of moist sugar,

3 eggs, 1 breakfast-cupful of milk, 1 oz. of caraway seeds, ¼ lb. of currants.

Mode.—Put the flour and baking-powder into a basin; stir these together; then rub in the dripping, add the sugar, caraway seeds, and currants; whisk the eggs with the milk, and beat all together very thoroughly until the ingredients are well mixed. Butter a tin, put in the cake, and bake it from 1½ to 2 hours. Let the dripping be quite clean before using: to insure this, it is a good plan to clarify it. Beef dripping is better than any other for cakes, &c., as mutton dripping frequently has a very unpleasant flavour, which would be imparted to the preparation.

Time.—1½ to 2 hours. *Average cost,* 1s.

Seasonable at any time.

A NICE PLAIN CAKE FOR CHILDREN.

1767. INGREDIENTS.—1 quartern of dough, ¼ lb. of moist sugar, ¼ lb. of butter or good beef dripping, ¼ pint of warm milk, ½ grated nutmeg or ½ oz. of caraway seeds.

Mode.—If you are not in the habit of making bread at home, procure the dough from the baker's, and, as soon as it comes in, put it into a basin near the fire; cover the basin with a thick cloth, and let the dough remain a little while to rise. In the mean time, beat the butter to a cream, and make the milk warm; and when the dough has risen, mix with it thoroughly all the above ingredients, and knead the cake well for a few minutes. Butter some cake-tins, half fill them, and stand them in a warm place, to allow the dough to rise again. When the tins are three parts full, put the cakes into a good oven, and bake them from 1¾ to 2 hours. A few currants might be substituted for the caraway seeds when the flavour of the latter is disliked.

Time.—1¾ to 2 hours. *Average cost,* 1s. 2d.

Seasonable at any time.

COMMON PLUM CAKE.

1768. INGREDIENTS.—3 lbs. of flour, 6 oz. of butter or good dripping, 6 oz. of moist sugar, 6 oz. of currants, ½ oz. of pounded allspice, 2 table-spoonfuls of fresh yeast, 1 pint of new milk.

Mode.—Rub the butter into the flour; add the sugar, currants, and allspice; warm the milk, stir to it the yeast, and mix the whole into a dough; knead it well, and put it into 6 buttered tins; place them near the fire for nearly an hour for the dough to rise, then bake the cakes in a good oven from 1 to 1¼ hour. To ascertain when they are done, plunge a clean knife into the middle, and if on withdrawal it comes out clean, the cakes are done.

Time.—1 to 1¼ hour. *Average cost*, 1s. 8d.

Sufficient to make 6 small cakes.

A NICE PLUM CAKE.

1769. INGREDIENTS.—1 lb. of flour, ¼ lb. of butter, ½ lb. of sugar, ½ lb. of currants, 2 oz. of candied lemon-peel, ½ pint of milk, 1 teaspoonful of ammonia or carbonate of soda.

Mode.—Put the flour into a basin with the sugar, currants, and sliced candied peel; beat the butter to a cream, and mix all these ingredients together with the milk. Stir the ammonia into 2 tablespoonfuls of milk; add it to the dough, and beat the whole well, until everything is thoroughly mixed. Put the dough into a buttered tin, and bake the cake from 1½ to 2 hours.

Time.— 1½ to 2 hours. *Average cost*, 1s. 3d.

Seasonable at any time.

POUND CAKE.

1770. INGREDIENTS.—1 lb. of butter, 1¼ lb. of flour, 1 lb. of pounded loaf sugar, 1 lb. of currants, 9 eggs, 2 oz. of candied peel, ½ oz. of citron, ½ oz. of sweet almonds; when liked, a litttle pounded mace.

Mode.—Work the butter to a cream; dredge in the flour; add the sugar, currants, candied peel, which should be cut into neat slices, and the almonds, which should be blanched and chopped, and mix all these well together; whisk the eggs, and let them be thoroughly blended with the dry ingredients. Beat the cake well for 20 minutes, and put it into a

POUND CAKE.

round tin, lined at the bottom and sides with a strip of white buttered paper. Bake it from 1½ to 2 hours, and let the oven be well heated when the cake is first put in, as, if this is not the case, the currants will all sink to the bottom of it. To make this preparation light, the yolks and whites of the eggs should be beaten separately, and added separately to the other ingredients. A glass of wine is sometimes added to the mixture; but this is scarcely necessary, as the cake will be found quite rich enough without it.

Time.—1½ to 2 hours. *Average cost*, 3s. 6d.

Sufficient.—The above quantity divided in two will make two nice-sized cakes.

Seasonable at any time.

A PAVINI CAKE.

1771. INGREDIENTS.—½ lb. of flour, ½ lb. of ground rice, ½ lb. of raisins stoned and cut into small pieces, ¼ lb. of currants, ¼ lb. of butter, 2 oz. of sweet almonds, ¼ lb. of sifted loaf sugar, ½ nutmeg grated, 1 pint of milk, 1 teaspoonful of carbonate of soda.

Mode.—Stone and cut the raisins into small pieces; wash, pick, and dry the currants; melt the butter to a cream, but without oiling it; blanch and chop the almonds, and grate the nutmeg. When all these ingredients are thus prepared, mix them well together; make the milk warm, stir in the soda, and with this liquid make the whole into a paste. Butter a mould, rather more than half fill it with the dough, and bake the cake in a moderate oven from 1½ to 2 hours, or less time should it be made into 2 cakes.

Time.—1½ to 2 hours. *Average cost*, 1s. 8d.

Seasonable at any time.

RICE CAKE.

1772. INGREDIENTS.—½ lb. of ground rice, ½ lb. of flour, ½ lb. of loaf sugar, 9 eggs, 20 drops of essence of lemon, or the rind of 1 lemon, ¼ lb. of butter.

Mode.—Separate the whites from the yolks of the eggs; whisk them both well, and add to the latter the butter beaten to a cream. Stir in the flour, rice, and lemon (if the rind is used, it must be very finely minced), and beat the mixture well; then add the whites of the eggs, beat the cake again for some time, put it into a buttered mould or tin, and bake it for nearly 1½ hour. It may be flavoured with essence of almonds, when this is preferred.

CAKE-MOULD.

Time.—Nearly 1½ hour. *Average cost*, 1s. 6d.

Seasonable at any time.

QUEEN-CAKES.

1773. INGREDIENTS.—1 lb. of flour, ½ lb. of butter, ½ lb. of pounded loaf sugar, 3 eggs, 1 teacupful of cream, ½ lb. of currants, 1 teaspoonful of carbonate of soda, essence of lemon or almonds to taste.

Mode.—Work the butter to a cream; dredge in the flour, add the sugar and currants, and mix the ingredients well together. Whisk the eggs, mix them with the cream and flavouring, and stir these to the flour; add the carbonate of soda, beat the paste well for 10 minutes, put it into small buttered pans, and bake the cake from ¼ to ½ hour.

Grated lemon-rind may be substituted for the lemon and almond flavouring, which will make the cakes equally nice.

Time. ¼ to ½ hour. *Average cost,* 1s. 9d.

Seasonable at any time.

SAUCER-CAKE FOR TEA.

1774. INGREDIENTS.—¼ lb. of flour, ¼ lb. of *tous-les-mois*, ¼ lb. of pounded white sugar, ¼ lb. of butter, 2 eggs, 1 oz. of candied orange or lemon-peel.

Mode.—Mix the flour and *tous-les-mois* together; add the sugar the candied peel cut into thin slices, the butter beaten to a cream, and the eggs well whisked. Beat the mixture for 10 minutes, put it into a buttered cake-tin or mould, or, if this is not obtainable, a soup-plate answers the purpose, lined with a piece of buttered paper. Bake the cake in a moderate oven from 1 to 1¼ hour, and when cold, put it away in a covered canister. It will remain good some weeks, even if it be cut into slices.

Time.—1 to 1¼ hour. *Average cost,* 1s.

Seasonable at any time.

COMMON SEED-CAKE.

1775. INGREDIENTS.—½ quartern of dough, ¼ lb. of good dripping, 6 oz. of moist sugar, ½ oz. of caraway seeds, 1 egg.

Mode.—If the dough is sent in from the baker's, put it in a basin covered with a cloth, and set it in a warm place to rise. Then with a wooden spoon beat the dripping to a liquid; add it, with the other ingredients, to the dough, and beat it until everything is very thoroughly mixed. Put it into a buttered tin, and bake the cake for rather more than 2 hours.

Time.—Rather more than 2 hours. *Average cost,* 8d.

Seasonable at any time.

A VERY GOOD SEED-CAKE.

1776. INGREDIENTS.—1 lb. of butter, 6 eggs, ¾ lb. of sifted sugar, pounded mace and grated nutmeg to taste, 1 lb. of flour, ¾ oz. of caraway seeds, 1 wineglassful of brandy.

Mode.—Beat the butter to a cream; dredge in the flour; add the sugar, mace, nutmeg, and caraway seeds, and mix these ingredients well together. Whisk the eggs, stir to them the brandy, and beat the cake again for 10 minutes. Put it into a tin lined with buttered paper, and bake it from 1½ to 2 hours. This cake would be equally nice made with currants, and omitting the caraway seeds.

Time.—1½ to 2 hours.   *Average cost, 2s. 6d.*

Seasonable at any time.

BREAD-MAKING IN SPAIN.—The bread in the south of Spain is delicious: it is white as snow, close as cake, and yet very light; the flavour is most admirable, for the wheat is good and pure, and the bread well kneaded. The way they make this bread is as follows:—From large round panniers filled with wheat they take out a handful at a time, sorting it most carefully and expeditiously, and throwing every defective grain into another basket. This done, the wheat is ground between two circular stones, as it was ground in Egypt 2,000 years ago (see No. 117), the requisite rotary motion being given by a blindfolded mule, which paces round and round with untiring patience, a bell being attached to his neck, which, as long as he is in movement, tinkles on; and when it stops, he is urged to his duty by the shout of "*Arre, mula,*" from some one within hearing. When ground, the wheat is sifted through three sieves, the last of these being so fine that only the pure flour can pass through it: this is of a pale apricot-colour. The bread is made in the evening. It is mixed with only sufficient water, with a little salt in it, to make it into dough: a very small quantity of leaven, or fermenting mixture, is added. The Scripture says, "A little leaven leaveneth the whole lump;" but in England, to avoid the trouble of kneading, many put as much leaven or yeast in one batch of household bread as in Spain would last them a week for the six or eight donkey-loads of bread they send every night from their oven. The dough made, it is put into sacks, and carried on the donkeys' backs to the oven in the centre of the village, so as to bake it immediately it is kneaded. On arriving there, the dough is divided into portions weighing 3 lbs. each. Two long narrow wooden tables on trestles are then placed down the room; and now a curious sight may be seen. About twenty men (bakers) come in and range themselves on one side of the tables. A lump of dough is handed to the nearest, which he commences kneading and knocking about with all his might for about 3 or 4 minutes, and then passes it on to his neighbour, who does the same; and so on successively until all have kneaded it, when it becomes as soft as new putty, and ready for the oven. Of course, as soon as the first baker has handed the first lump to his neighbour, another is given to him, and so on till the whole quantity of dough is successively kneaded by them all. The bakers' wives and daughters shape the loaves for the oven, and some of them are very small, and they are baked immediately. The ovens are very large, and not heated by fires *under* them; but a quantity of twigs of the herbs of sweet marjoram and thyme, which cover the hills in great profusion, are put in the oven and ignited. They heat the oven to any extent required; and, as the bread gets baked, the oven gets gradually colder; so the bread is never burned. They knead the bread in Spain with such force, that the palm of the hand and the second joints of the fingers of the bakers are covered with corns; and it so affects the chest, that they cannot work more than two hours at a time.

SNOW-CAKE.

1777. INGREDIENTS.—½ lb. of *tous-les-mois*, ¼ lb. of white pounded sugar, ¼ lb. of fresh or washed salt butter, 1 egg, the juice of 1 lemon.

Mode.—Beat the butter to a cream; then add the egg, previously well beaten, and then the other ingredients; if the mixture is not light, add another egg, and beat for ¼ hour, until it turns white and light. Line a flat tin, with raised edges, with a sheet of buttered paper; pour in the cake, and put it into the oven. It must be rather slow, and the cake not allowed to brown at all. If the oven is properly heated, 1 to 1¼ hour will be found long enough to bake it. Let it cool a few minutes, then with a clean sharp knife cut it into small square pieces, which should be gently removed to a large flat dish to cool before putting away. This will keep for several weeks.

Time.—1 to 1¼ hour.   *Average cost, 1s. 3d.*

Seasonable at any time.

SNOW-CAKE.

(A genuine Scotch Recipe.)

1778. INGREDIENTS.—1 lb. of arrowroot, ½ lb. of pounded white sugar, ½ lb. of butter, the whites of 6 eggs; flavouring to taste, of essence of almonds, or vanilla, or lemon.

Mode.—Beat the butter to a cream; stir in the sugar and arrow-root gradually, at the same time beating the mixture. Whisk the whites of the eggs to a stiff froth, add them to the other ingredients, and beat well for 20 minutes. Put in whichever of the above flavour-ings may be preferred; pour the cake into a buttered mould or tin, and bake it in a moderate oven from 1 to 1½ hour.

Time.—1 to 1½ hour.

Average cost, with the best Bermuda arrowroot, 4s. 6d.; with St. Vincent ditto, 2s. 9d.

Sufficient to make a moderate-sized cake. *Seasonable* at any time.

SCRAP-CAKES.

1779. INGREDIENTS.—2 lbs. of leaf, or the inside fat of a pig; 1½ lb. of flour, ¼ lb. of moist sugar, ⅓ lb. of currants, 1 oz. of candied lemon-peel, ground allspice to taste.

Mode.—Cut the leaf, or flead, as it is sometimes called, into small pieces; put it into a large dish, which place in a quick oven; be careful that it does not burn, and in a short time it will be reduced to oil, with the small pieces of leaf floating on the surface; and it is of these that the cakes should be made. Gather all the scraps together, put them into a basin with the flour, and rub them well together. Add the currants, sugar, candied peel, cut into thin slices, and the ground allspice. When all these ingredients are well mixed, moisten with sufficient cold water to make the whole into a nice paste; roll it out thin, cut it into shapes, and bake the cakes in a quick oven from 15 to 20 minutes. These are very economical and wholesome cakes for children, and the lard, melted at home, produced from the flead, is generally better than that you purchase. To prevent the lard from burning, and to insure its being a good colour, it is better to melt it in a jar placed in a saucepan of boiling water; by doing it in this manner, there will be no chance of its discolouring.

Time.—15 to 20 minutes.

Sufficient to make 3 or 4 dozen cakes.

Seasonable from September to March.

3 K

WHEAT is liable to several diseases, which affect the flour made from it, and render it unfit for good bread. The principal of these are the blight, mildew, and smut, which are occasioned by microscopic fungi, which sow themselves and grow upon the stems and ears, destroying the nutritive principles, and introducing matter of a deleterious kind. The farmer is at the utmost pains to keep away these intruders. Wheat, as well as all kinds of corn, is also very liable to be injured by being stacked before it is quite dry ; in which case it will heat, and become musty in the ricks. In wet harvests it is sometimes impossible to get it sufficiently dried, and a great deal of corn is thus often spoiled. It is generally reckoned that the sweetest bread is made from wheat threshed out before it is stacked ; which shows the importance of studying the best modes of preserving it.

The erudite are not agreed as to the aboriginal country of corn : some say it is Egypt, others Tartary ; and the learned Bailly, as well as the traveller Pallas, affirms that it grows spontaneously in Siberia. Be that as it may, the Phocians brought it to Marseilles before the Romans had penetrated into Gaul. The Gauls ate the corn cooked or bruised in a mortar : they did not know, for a long time, how to make fermented bread.

SCOTCH SHORTBREAD.

1780. INGREDIENTS.—2 lbs. of flour, 1 lb. of butter, ¼ lb. of pounded loaf sugar, ½ oz. of caraway seeds, 1 oz. of sweet almonds, a few strips of candied orange-peel.

Mode.—Beat the butter to a cream, gradually dredge in the flour, and add the sugar, caraway seeds, and sweet almonds, which should

SHORTBREAD.

be blanched and cut into small pieces. Work the paste until it is quite smooth, and divide it into six pieces. Put each cake on a separate piece of paper, roll the paste out square to the thickness of about an inch, and pinch it upon all sides. Prick it well, and ornament with one or two strips of candied orange-peel. Put the cakes into a good oven, and bake them from 25 to 30 minutes.

Time.—25 to 30 minutes. *Average cost*, for this quantity, 2s.

Sufficient to make 6 cakes. *Seasonable* at any time.

Note.—Where the flavour of the caraway seeds is disliked, omit them, and add rather a larger proportion of candied peel.

SODA-CAKE.

1781. INGREDIENTS.—¼ lb. of butter, 1 lb. of flour, ½ lb. of currants, ½ lb. of moist sugar, 1 teacupful of milk, 3 eggs, 1 teaspoonful of carbonate of soda.

Mode.—Rub the butter into the flour, add the currants and sugar, and mix these ingredients well together. Whisk the eggs well, stir them to the flour, &c., with the milk, in which the soda should be previously dissolved, and beat the whole up together with a wooden spoon or beater. Divide the dough into two pieces, put them into buttered moulds or cake-tins, and bake in a moderate oven for nearly an hour. The mixture must be extremely well beaten up, and not allowed to stand after the soda is added to it, but must be placed in the oven immediately. Great care must also be taken that the cakes are quite done through, which may be ascertained by thrusting a knife into the middle of them : if the blade looks bright when withdrawn, they are done. If the tops acquire too much colour before the inside is sufficiently baked, cover them over with a piece of clean white paper, to prevent them from burning.

Time.—1 hour. *Average cost*, 1s. 6d.

Sufficient to make 2 small cakes. *Seasonable* at any time.

SAVOY CAKE.

1782. INGREDIENTS.—The weight of 4 eggs in pounded loaf sugar, the weight of 7 in flour, a little grated lemon-rind, or essence of almonds, or orange-flower water.

Mode.—Break the 7 eggs, putting the yolks into one basin and the whites into another. Whisk the former, and mix with them the sugar, the grated lemon-rind, or any other flavouring to taste; beat them well together, and add the whites of the eggs, whisked to a froth. Put in the flour by degrees, continuing to beat the mixture for $\frac{1}{4}$ hour, butter a mould, pour in the cake, and bake it from $1\frac{1}{4}$ to $1\frac{1}{2}$ hour, This is a very nice cake for dessert, and may be iced for a supper-table, or cut into slices and spread with jam, which converts it into sandwiches.

Time.—$1\frac{1}{4}$ to $1\frac{1}{2}$ hour. *Average cost*, 1s.

Sufficient for 1 cake. *Seasonable* at any time.

SPONGE-CAKE.

I.

1783. INGREDIENTS.—The weight of 8 eggs in pounded loaf sugar, the weight of 5 in flour, the rind of 1 lemon, 1 tablespoonful of brandy.

Mode.—Put the eggs into one side of the scale, and take the weight of 8 in pounded loaf sugar, and the weight of 5 in good *dry* flour. Separate the yolks from the whites of the eggs; beat the former, put them into a saucepan with the sugar, and let them remain over the fire until *milk-warm*, keeping them well stirred. Then put them into a basin, add the grated lemon-rind mixed with the brandy, and stir these well together, dredging in the flour very gradually.

SPONGE-CAKE.

3 K 2

Whisk the whites of the eggs to a very stiff froth, stir them to the flour, &c., and beat the cake well for ¼ hour. Put it into a buttered mould strewn with a little fine sifted sugar, and bake the cake in a quick oven for 1½ hour. Care must be taken that it is put into the oven immediately, or it will not be light. The flavouring of this cake may be varied by adding a few drops of essence of almonds instead of the grated lemon-rind.

Time.—1½ hour. *Average cost,* 1s. 3d.

Sufficient for 1 cake. *Seasonable* at any time.

THE EGYPTIAN, OR MUMMY WHEAT, is not grown to any great extent, owing to its inferior quality; but it is notable for its large produce, and is often cultivated on allotment grounds and on small farms, where quantity rather than quality is desired. At Wix, in Essex, the seed of this wheat has produced, without artificial assistance, four thousandfold; some of the ears have had eleven offshoots, and have contained, altogether, eleven grains in one ear.

EGYPTIAN WHEAT.

II.

1784. INGREDIENTS.—¼ lb. of loaf sugar, not quite ¼ pint of water, 5 eggs, 1 lemon, ½ lb. of flour, ¼ teaspoonful of carbonate of soda.

Mode.—Boil the sugar and water together until they form a thick syrup; let it cool a little, then pour it to the eggs, which should be previously well whisked; and after the eggs and syrup are mixed together, continue beating them for a few minutes. Grate the lemon-rind, mix the carbonate of soda with the flour, and stir these lightly to the other ingredients; then add the lemon-juice, and, when the whole is thoroughly mixed, pour it into a buttered mould, and bake in rather a quick oven for rather more than 1 hour. The remains of sponge or Savoy cakes answer very well for trifles, light puddings, &c.; and a very stale one (if not mouldy) makes an excellent tipsy-cake.

Time.—Rather more than 1 hour. *Average cost,* 10d.

Sufficient to make 1 cake. *Seasonable* at any time.

TO MAKE SMALL SPONGE-CAKES.

1785. INGREDIENTS.—The weight of 5 eggs in flour, the weight of 8 in pounded loaf sugar; flavouring to taste.

Mode.—Let the flour be perfectly dry, and the sugar well pounded and sifted. Separate the whites from the yolks of the eggs, and beat the latter up with the sugar; then whisk the whites until they become rather stiff, and mix them with the yolks, but do not stir them more than is just necessary to mingle the ingredients well together. Dredge in the flour by degrees, add the flavouring; butter the tins well, pour in the batter, sift a little sugar over the cakes, and bake them in rather a quick oven, but do not allow them to take too much colour, as they should be rather pale. Remove them from the tins before they get cold, and turn them on their faces, where let them remain until quite cold, when store them away in a closed tin canister or wide-mouthed glass bottle.

Time.—10 to 15 minutes in a quick oven. *Average cost,* 1*d.* each.
Seasonable at any time.

TEA-CAKES.

1786. INGREDIENTS.—2 lbs. of flour, ½ teaspoonful of salt, ¼ lb. of butter or lard, 1 egg, a piece of German yeast the size of a walnut, warm milk.

Mode.—Put the flour (which should be perfectly dry) into a basin; mix with it the salt, and rub in the butter or lard; then beat the egg well, stir to it the yeast, and add these to the flour with as much warm milk as will make the whole into a smooth paste, and knead it well. Let it rise near the fire, and, when well risen, form it into cakes; place them on tins, let them rise again for a few minutes before putting them into the oven, and bake from ¼ to ½ hour in a moderate oven. These are very nice with a few currants and a little sugar added to the other ingredients: they should be put in after the butter is rubbed in. These cakes should be buttered, and eaten hot as soon as baked; but, when stale, they are very nice split and toasted; or, if dipped in milk, or even water, and covered with a basin in the oven till hot, they will be almost equal to new.

Time.—¼ to ½ hour. *Average cost,* 10*d.*
Sufficient to make 8 tea-cakes. *Seasonable* at any time.

TO TOAST TEA-CAKES.

1787. Cut each tea-cake into three or four slices, according to its thickness; toast them on both sides before a nice clear fire, and as each slice is done, spread it with butter on both sides. When a cake is toasted, pile the slices one on the top of the other, cut them into quarters, put them on a very hot plate, and send the cakes immediately to' table.

TEA-CAKES.

As they are wanted, send them in hot, one or two at a time, as, if allowed to stand, they spoil, unless kept in a muffin-plate over a basin of boiling water.

A NICE YEAST-CAKE.

1788. INGREDIENTS.—1½ lb. of flour, ½ lb. of butter, ½ pint of milk, 1½ tablespoonful of good yeast, 3 eggs, ¾ lb. of currants, ½ lb. of white moist sugar, 2 oz. of candied peel.

Mode.—Put the milk and butter into a saucepan, and shake it round over a fire until the butter is melted, but do not allow the milk to get very hot. Put the flour into a basin, stir to it the milk and butter, the yeast, and eggs, which should be well beaten, and form the whole into a smooth dough. Let it stand in a warm place, covered with a cloth, to rise, and, when sufficiently risen, add the currants, sugar, and candied peel cut into thin slices. When all the ingredients are thoroughly mixed, line 2 moderate-sized cake-tins with buttered paper, which should be about six inches higher than the tin; pour in the mixture, let it stand to rise again for another ½ hour, and then bake the cakes in a brisk oven for about 1½ hour. If the tops of them become too brown, cover them with paper until they are done through. A few drops of essence of lemon, or a little grated nutmeg, may be added when the flavour is liked.

Time.—From 1¼ to 1½ hour. *Average cost*, 2s.

Sufficient to make 2 moderate-sized cakes.

Seasonable at any time.

CHAPTER XXXVI.

GENERAL OBSERVATIONS ON BEVERAGES.

1789. BEVERAGES are innumerable in their variety ; but the ordinary beverages drunk in the British isles, may be divided into three classes :—1. Beverages of the simplest kind not fermented. 2. Beverages, consisting of water, containing a considerable quantity of carbonic acid. 3. Beverages composed partly of fermented liquors. Of the first class may be mentioned,—water, toast-and-water, barley-water, eau sucré, lait sucré, cheese and milk whey, milk-and-water, lemonade, orangeade, sherbet, apple and pear juice, capillaire, vinegar-and-water, raspberry vinegar and water.

1790. Of the common class of beverages, consisting of water impregnated with carbonic acid gas, we may name soda-water, single and double, ordinary effervescing draughts, and ginger-beer.

1791. The beverages composed partly of fermented liquors, are hot spiced wines, bishop, egg-flip, egg-hot, ale posset, sack posset, punch, and spirits-and-water.

1792. We will, however, forthwith treat on the most popular of our beverages, beginning with the one which makes "the cup that cheers but not inebriates."

1793. The beverage called tea has now become almost a necessary of life. Previous to the middle of the 17th century it was not used in England, and it was wholly unknown to the Greeks and Romans. Pepys says, in his Diary,— "September 25th, 1661.—I sent for a cup of tea (a China drink), of which I had never drunk before." Two years later it was so rare a commodity in

England, that the English East-India Company bought 2 lbs. 2 oz. of it, as a present for his majesty. In 1666 it was sold in London for sixty shillings a pound. From that date the consumption has gone on increasing from 5,000 lbs. to 50,000,000 lbs.

1794. Linnæus was induced to think that there were two species of tea-plant, one of which produced the black, and the other the green teas; but later observations do not confirm this. When the leaves of black and green tea are expanded by hot water, and examined by the botanist, though a difference of character is perceived, yet this is not sufficient to authorize considering them as distinct species. The tea-tree flourishes best in temperate regions; in China it is indigenous. The part of China where the best tea is cultivated, is called by us the "tea country." The cultivation of the plant requires great care. It is raised chiefly on the sides of hills; and, in order to increase the quantity and improve the quality of the leaves, the shrub is pruned, so as not to exceed the height of from two to three feet, much in the same manner as the vine is treated in France. They pluck the leaves, one selecting them according to the kinds of tea required; and, notwithstanding the tediousness of the operation, each labourer is able to gather from four to ten or fifteen pounds a day. When the trees attain to six or seven years of age, the produce becomes so inferior that they are removed to make room for a fresh succession, or they are cut down to allow of numerous young shoots. Teas of the finest flavour consist of the youngest leaves; and as these are gathered at four different periods of the year, the younger the leaves the higher flavoured the tea, and the scarcer, and consequently the dearer, the article.

1795. The various names by which teas are sold in the British market are corruptions of Chinese words. There are about a dozen different kinds; but the principal are Bohea, Congou, and Souchong, and signify, respectively, inferior, middling, and superior. Teas are often perfumed and flavoured with the leaves of different kinds of plants grown on purpose. Different tea-farms in China produce teas of various qualities, raised by skilful cultivation on various soils.

1796. Tea, when chemically analyzed, is found to contain woody fibre, mucilage, a considerable quantity of the astringent principle, or tannin, a narcotic principle, which is, perhaps, connected with a peculiar aroma. The tannin is shown by its striking a black colour with sulphate of iron, and is the cause of the dark stain which is always formed when tea is spilt upon buff-coloured cottons dyed with iron. A constituent called *Theine* has also been discovered in tea, supposed to be identical with *Caffeine*, one of the constituents of coffee. Liebig says, "Theine yields, in certain processes of decomposition, a series of most remarkable products, which have much analogy with those derived from uric acid in similar circumstances. . . . The infusion of tea differs from that of coffee, by containing iron and manganese. . . . We have in tea, of many kinds, a beverage which contains the active constituents of the most powerful mineral springs, and, however small the amount of iron may be which we daily take in this form, it cannot be destitute of influence on the vital processes."

1797. Chinese tea has frequently been adulterated in this country, by the admixture of the dried leaves of certain plants. The leaves of the sloe, white·thorn, ash, elder, and some others, have been employed for this purpose ; such as the leaves of the speedwell, wild germander, black currants, syringa, purple-spiked willow-herb, sweet-brier, and cherry-tree. Some of these are harmless, others are to a certain degree poisonous ; as, for example, are the leaves of all the varieties of the plum and cherry tribe, to which the sloe belongs. Adulteration by means of these leaves is by no means a new species of fraud ; and several acts of parliament, from the time of George II., have been passed, specifying severe penalties against those guilty of the offence, which, notwithstanding numerous convictions, continues to the present time.

1798. In the purchase of tea, that should be chosen which possesses an agreeable odour and is as whole as possible, in order that the leaf may be easily examined. The greatest care should be taken that it has not been exposed to the air, which destroys its flavour.

1799. It would be impossible, in the space at our command, to enumerate the various modes adopted in different countries for " making coffee ;" that is, the phrase commonly understood to mean the complete preparation of this delicious beverage for drinking. For performing this operation, such recipes or methods as we have found most practical will be inserted in their proper place ; but the following facts connected with coffee will be found highly interesting.

1800. The introduction of coffee into this country is comparatively of recent date. We are assured by Bruce that the coffee-tree is a native of Abyssinia, and it is said to have been cultivated in that country from time immemorial.

1801. It appears that coffee was first introduced into England by Daniel Edwards, a Turkey merchant, whose servant, Pasqua, a Greek, understood the manner of roasting it. This servant, under the patronage of Edwards, established the first coffee-house in London, in George Yard, Lombard Street. Coffee was then sold at four or five guineas a pound, and a duty was soon afterwards laid upon it of fourpence a gallon, when made into a beverage. In the course of two centuries, however, this berry, unknown originally as an article of food, except to some savage tribes on the confines of Abyssinia, has made its way through the whole of the civilized world. Mahommedans of all ranks drink coffee twice a day ; it is in universal request in France ; and the demand for it throughout the British isles is daily increasing, the more especially since so much attention has been given to mechanical contrivances for roasting and grinding the berry and preparing the beverage.

1802. Of the various kinds of coffee the Arabian is considered the best. It is grown chiefly in the districts of Aden and Mocha ; whence the name of our

Mocha coffee.   Mocha coffee has a smaller and rounder bean than any other, and likewise a more agreeable smell and taste.   The next in reputation and quality is the Java and Ceylon coffee, and then the coffees of Bourbon and Martinique, and that of Berbice, a district of the colony of British Guiana. The Jamaica and St. Domingo coffees are less esteemed.

1803. A considerable change takes place in the arrangement of the constituents of coffee by the application of heat in roasting it.   Independently of one of the objects of roasting, namely, that of destroying its toughness and rendering it easily ground, its tannin and other principles are rendered partly soluble in water ; and it is to the tannin that the brown colour of the decoction of coffee is owing.   An aromatic flavour is likewise developed during torrefaction, which is not perceived in the raw berry, and which is not produced in the greatest perfection until the heat has arrived at a certain degree of temperature ; but, if the heat be increased beyond this, the flavour is again dissipated, and little remains but a bitter and astringent matter with carbon.

1804. The roasting of coffee in the best manner requires great nicety, and much of the qualities of the beverage depends upon the operation.   The roasting of coffee for the dealers in London and Paris has now become a separate branch of business, and some of the roasters perform the operation on a great scale, with considerable skill.   Roasted coffee loses from 20 to 30 per cent. by sufficient roasting, and the powder suffers much by exposure to the air ; but, while raw, it not only does not lose its flavour for a year or two, but improves by keeping.   If a cup of the best coffee be placed upon a table boiling hot, it will fill the room with its fragrance ; but the coffee, when warmed again after being cold, will be found to have lost most of its flavour.

1805. To have coffee in perfection, it should be roasted and ground just before it is used, and more should not be ground at a time than is wanted for immediate use, or, if it be necessary to grind more, it should be kept closed from the air.   Coffee readily imbibes exhalations from other substances, and thus often acquires a bad flavour : brown sugar placed near it will communicate a disagreeable flavour.   It is stated that the coffee in the West Indies has often been injured by being laid in rooms near the sugar-works, or where rum is distilled ; and the same effect has been produced by bringing over coffee in the same ships with rum and sugar.   Dr. Moseley mentions that a few bags of pepper, on board a ship from India, spoiled a whole cargo of coffee.

1806. With respect to the quantity of coffee used in making the decoction, much depends upon the taste of the consumer.   The greatest and most common fault in English coffee is the too small quantity of the ingredient. Count Rumford says that to make good coffee for drinking after dinner, a pound of good Mocha coffee, which, when roasted and ground, weighs only thirteen ounces, serves to make fifty-six full cups, or a little less than a quarter of an ounce to a coffee-cup of moderate size.

RECIPES.

CHAPTER XXXVII.

TO MAKE CHOCOLATE.

1807. INGREDIENTS.—Allow ½ oz. of chocolate to each person; to every oz. allow ½ pint of water, ½ pint of milk.

Mode.—Make the milk-and-water hot; scrape the chocolate into it, and stir the mixture constantly and quickly until the chocolate is dissolved; bring it to the boiling-point, stir it well, and serve directly with white sugar. Chocolate prepared with in a mill, as shown in the engraving, is made by putting in the scraped chocolate, pouring over it the boiling milk-and-water, and milling it over the fire until hot and frothy.

Sufficient.—Allow ½ oz. of cake chocolate to each person.

MILL.

CHOCOLATE AND COCOA.—Both these preparations are made from the seeds or beans of the cacao-tree, which grows in the West Indies and South America. The Spanish, and the proper name, is cacao, not cocoa, as it is generally spelt. From this mistake, the tree from which the beverage is procured has been often confounded with the palm that produces the edible cocoa-nuts, which are the produce of the cocoa-tree (*Cocos nucifera*), whereas the tree from which chocolate is procured is very different (the *Theobroma cacao*). The cocoa-tree was cultivated by the aboriginal inhabitants of South America, particularly in Mexico, where, according to Humboldt, it was reared by Montezuma. It was transplanted thence into other dependencies of the Spanish monarchy in 1520; and it was so highly esteemed by Linnæus as to receive from him the name now conferred upon it, of Theobroma, a term derived from the Greek, and signifying "*food for gods.*" Chocolate has always been a favourite beverage among the Spaniards and Creoles, and was considered here as a great luxury when first introduced, after the discovery of America; but the high duties laid upon it, confined it long almost entirely to the wealthier classes. Before it was subjected to duty, Mr. Bryan Edwards stated that cocoa plantations were numerous in Jamaica, but that the duty caused their almost entire ruin. The removal of this duty has increased their cultivation. (For engraving of cocoa-bean, *see* No. 1816.)

TO MAKE ESSENCE OF COFFEE.

1808. INGREDIENTS.—To every ¼ lb. of ground coffee allow 1 small teaspoonful of powdered chicory, 3 small teacupfuls, or 1 pint, of water.

Mode.—Let the coffee be freshly ground, and, if possible, freshly roasted; put it into a percolater, or filter, with the chicory, and pour *slowly* over it the above proportion of boiling water. When it has all filtered through, warm the coffee sufficiently to bring it to the simmering-point, but do not allow it to boil; then filter it a second time, put it into a clean and dry bottle, cork it well, and it will remain good for several days.   Two tablespoonfuls of this essence are quite sufficient for a breakfast-cupful of hot milk.   This essence will be found particularly useful to those persons who have to rise extremely early ; and having only the milk to make boiling, is very easily and quickly prepared.   When the essence is bottled, pour another 3 tea-cupfuls of *boiling* water slowly on the grounds, which, when filtered through, will be a very weak coffee.   The next time there is essence to be prepared, make this weak coffee boiling, and pour it on the ground coffee instead of plain water : by this means a better coffee will be obtained.   Never throw away the grounds without having made use of them in this manner ; and always cork the bottle well that contains this preparation, until the day that it is wanted for making the fresh essence.

Time.—To be filtered once, then brought to the boiling-point, and filtered again.

Average cost, with coffee at 1*s.* 8*d.* per lb., 6*d.*

Sufficient.—Allow 2 tablespoonfuls for a breakfast-cupful of hot milk.

TO ROAST COFFEE.

(*A French Recipe.*)

1809. It being an acknowledged fact that French coffee is decidedly superior to that made in England, and as the roasting of the berry is of great importance to the flavour of the preparation, it will be useful and interesting to know how they manage these things in France. In Paris, there are two houses justly celebrated for the flavour of their coffee,—*La Maison Corcellet* and *La Maison Royer de Chartres ;* and to obtain this flavour, before roasting they add to every 3 lbs. of coffee a piece of butter the size of a nut, and a dessert-spoonful of powdered sugar : it is then roasted in the usual manner. The addition of the butter and sugar develops the flavour and aroma of the berry ; but it must be borne in mind, that the quality of the butter must be of the very best description.

TO MAKE COFFEE.

1810. INGREDIENTS.—Allow ¼ oz., or 1 tablespoonful, of ground coffee to each person; to every oz. of coffee allow ⅓ pint of water.

Mode.—To make coffee good, *it should never be boiled,* but the boiling water merely poured on it, the same as for tea. The coffee should always be purchased in the berry,—if possible, freshly roasted ; and it should never be ground long before it is wanted for use. There are very many new kinds of coffee-pots, but the method of making the coffee is nearly always the same; namely, pouring the boiling water on the powder, and allowing it to filter through. Our illustration shows one of Loysel's Hydrostatic Urns, which are admirably adapted for making good and clear coffee, which should be made in the following, manner :—Warm the urn with boiling water, remove the lid and movable filter, and place the ground coffee at the bottom of the urn. Put the movable filter over this, and screw the lid, inverted, tightly on the end of the centre pipe. Pour into the inverted lid the above proportion of boiling water, and when all the water so poured has disappeared from the funnel, and made its way down the centre pipe and up again through the ground coffee by *hydrostatic pressure*, un-

LOYSEL'S HYDROSTATIC URN.

screw the lid and cover the urn. Pour back direct into the urn, *not through the funnel*, one, two, or three cups, according to the size of the percolater, in order to make the infusion of uniform strength; the contents will then be ready for use, and should run from the tap strong, hot, and clear. The coffee made in these urns generally turns out very good, and there is but one objection to them,—the coffee runs rather slowly from the tap. This is of no consequence where there is a small party, but tedious where there are many persons to provide for. A remedy for this objection may be suggested; namely, to make the coffee very strong, so that not more than $\frac{1}{3}$ of a cup would be required, as the rest would be filled up with milk. Making coffee in filters or percolaters does away with the necessity of using isinglass, white of egg, and various other preparations to clear it. Coffee should always be served very hot, and, if possible, in the same vessel in which it is made, as pouring it from one pot to another cools, and consequently spoils it. Many persons may think that the proportion of water we have given for each oz. of coffee is rather small; it is so, and the coffee produced from it will be very strong; $\frac{1}{3}$ of a cup will be found quite sufficient, which should be filled with nice hot milk, or milk and cream mixed. This is the *café au lait* for which our neighbours over the Channel are so justly celebrated. Should the ordinary method of making coffee be preferred, use double the quantity of water, and, in pouring it into the cups, put in more coffee and less milk.

Sufficient.—For very good coffee, allow $\frac{1}{2}$ oz., or 1 table-spoonful, to each person.

A VERY SIMPLE METHOD OF MAKING COFFEE.

1811. INGREDIENTS.—Allow ½ oz., or 1 tablespoonful, of coffee to each person; to every oz. allow ⅓ pint of water.

Mode.—Have a small iron ring made to fit the top of the coffee-pot inside, and to this ring sew a small muslin bag (the muslin for the purpose must not be too thin). Fit the bag into the pot, pour some boiling water in it, and, when the pot is well warmed, put the ground coffee into the bag; pour over as much boiling water as is required, close the lid, and, when all the water has filtered through, remove the bag, and send the coffee to table. Making it in this manner prevents the necessity of pouring the coffee from one vessel to another, which cools and spoils it. The water should be poured on the coffee gradually, so that the infusion may be stronger; and the bag must be well made, that none of the grounds may escape through the seams, and so make the coffee thick and muddy.

Sufficient.—Allow 1 tablespoonful, or ½ oz., to each person.

COFFEE.

THE COFFEE PLANT grows to the height of about twelve or fifteen feet, with leaves not unlike those of the common laurel, although more pointed, and not so dry and thick. The blossoms are white, much like those of jasmine, and issue from the angles of the leaf-stalks. When the flowers fade, they are succeeded by the coffee-bean, or seed, which is inclosed in a berry of a red colour, when ripe resembling a cherry. The coffee-beans are prepared by exposing them to the sun for a few days, that the pulp may ferment and throw off a strong acidulous moisture. They are then gradually dried for about three weeks, and put into a mill to separate the husk from the seed.

CAFE AU LAIT.

1812. This is merely very strong coffee added to a large proportion of good hot milk; about 6 tablespoonfuls of strong coffee being quite sufficient for a breakfast-cupful of milk. Of the essence No. 1808, which answers admirably for *café au lait*, so much would not be required. This preparation is infinitely superior to the weak watery coffee so often served at English tables. A little cream mixed with the milk, if the latter cannot be depended on for richness, improves the taste of the coffee, as also the richness of the beverage.

Sufficient.—6 tablespoonfuls of strong coffee, or 2 tablespoonfuls of the essence, to a breakfast-cupful of milk.

TEA AND COFFEE.—It is true, says Liebig, that thousands have lived without a knowledge of tea and coffee; and daily experience teaches us that, under certain circumstances, they may be dispensed with without disadvantage to the merely animal functions; but it is an error, certainly, to conclude from this that they may be altogether dispensed with in reference to their effects; and it is a question whether, if we had no tea and no coffee, the popular instinct would not seek for and discover the means of replacing them. Science, which accuses us of so much in these respects, will have, in the first place, to ascertain whether it depends on sensual and sinful inclinations merely, that every people of the globe have appropriated some such means of acting on the nervous life, from the shore of the Pacific, where the Indian retires from life for days in order to enjoy the bliss of intoxication with koko, to the Arctic regions, where Kamtschat-dales and Koriakes prepare an intoxicating beverage from a poisonous mushroom. We think it, on the contrary, highly probable, not to say certain, that the instinct of man feeling certain blanks, certain wants of the intensified life of our times, which cannot be satisfied or filled up by mere quantity, has discovered, in these products of vegetable life the true means of giving to his food the desired and necessary quality.

CAFE NOIR.

1813. This is usually handed round after dinner, and should be drunk well sweetened, with the addition of a little brandy or liqueurs, which may be added or not at pleasure. The coffee should be made very strong, and served in very small cups, but never mixed with milk or cream. Café noir may be made of the essence of coffee No. 1808, by pouring a tablespoonful into each cup, and filling it up with boiling water. This is a very simple and expeditious manner of preparing coffee for a large party, but the essence for it must be made very good, and kept well corked until required for use.

TO MAKE TEA.

1814. There is very little art in making good tea; if the water is boiling, and there is no sparing of the fragrant leaf, the beverage will almost invariably be good. The old-fashioned plan of allowing a teaspoonful to each person, and one over, is still practised. Warm the teapot with boiling water; let it remain for two or three minutes for the vessel to become thoroughly hot, then pour it away. Put in the tea, pour in from ½ to ¾ pint of *boiling* water, close the lid, and let it stand for the tea to draw from 5 to 10 minutes; then fill up the pot with water. The tea will be quite spoiled unless made with water that is actually *boiling*, as the leaves will not open, and the flavour not be extracted from them; the beverage will consequently be colourless and tasteless,—in fact, nothing but tepid water. Where there is a very large party to make tea for, it is a good plan to have two teapots instead of putting a large quantity of tea into one pot; the tea, besides, will go farther. When the infusion has been once completed, the addition of fresh tea adds very little to the strength; so, when more is required, have the pot emptied of the old leaves, scalded, and fresh tea made in the usual manner. Economists say that a few grains of carbonate of soda, added before the boiling water is poured on the tea, assist to draw out the goodness: if the water is very hard, perhaps it is a good plan, as the soda softens it; but care must be taken to use this ingredient sparingly, as it is liable to give the tea a soapy taste if added in too large a quantity. For mixed tea, the usual proportion is four spoonfuls of black to one of green; more of the latter when the flavour is very much liked; but strong green tea is highly pernicious, and should never be partaken of too freely.

Time.—2 minutes to warm the teapot, 5 to 10 minutes to draw the strength from the tea.

Sufficient.—Allow 1 teaspoonful to each person, and one over.

TEA.—The tea-tree or shrub belongs to the class and order of *Monadelphia polyandria* in the Linnæan system, and to the natural order of *Aurantiaceæ* in the system of Jussieu. Lately it has been made into a new order, the *Theasia*, which includes the Camellia and some other plants. It commonly grows to the height of from three to six feet; but it is said, that, in its wild or native state, it reaches twenty feet or more. In China it is cultivated in numerous small plantations. In its general appearance, and the form of its leaf, it resembles the myrtle. The blossoms are white and fragrant, not unlike those of the wild rose, but smaller; and they are succeeded by soft green capsules, containing each from one to three white seeds. These capsules are crushed for oil, which is in general use in China.

TEA.

AN EXCELLENT SUBSTITUTE FOR MILK OR CREAM IN TEA OR COFFEE.

1815. INGREDIENTS.—Allow 1 new-laid egg to every large breakfast-cupful of tea or coffee.

Mode.—Beat up the whole of the egg in a basin, put it into a cup (or a portion of it, if the cup be small), and pour over it the tea or coffee very hot. These should be added very gradually, and stirred all the time, to prevent the egg from curdling. In point of nourishment, both these beverages are much improved by this addition.

Sufficient.—Allow 1 egg to every large breakfast-cupful of tea or coffee.

TO MAKE COCOA.

1816. INGREDIENTS.—Allow 2 teaspoonfuls of the prepared cocoa to 1 breakfast-cup; boiling milk and boiling water.

Mode.—Put the cocoa into a breakfast-cup, pour over it sufficient cold milk to make it into a smooth paste; then add equal quantities of boiling milk and boiling water, and stir all well together. Care must be taken not to allow the milk to get burnt, as it will entirely spoil the flavour of the preparation. The above directions are usually given for making the prepared cocoa. The rock cocoa, or that bought in a solid piece, should be scraped, and made in the same manner, taking care to rub down all the lumps before the boiling liquid is added.

COCOA-BEAN.

Sufficient—2 teaspoonfuls of prepared cocoa for 1 breakfast-cup, or ¼ oz. of the rock cocoa for the same quantity.

COWSLIP WINE.

1817. INGREDIENTS.—To every gallon of water allow 3 lbs. of lump sugar, the rind of 2 lemons, the juice of 1, the rind and juice of 1 Seville orange, 1 gallon of cowslip pips. To every 4½ gallons of wine allow 1 bottle of brandy.

Mode.—Boil the sugar and water together for ½ hour, carefully removing all the scum as it rises. Pour this boiling liquor on the orange and lemon-rinds, and the juice, which should be strained ; when milk-warm, add the cowslip pips or flowers, picked from the stalks and seeds ; and to 9 gallons of wine 3 tablespoonfuls of good fresh brewers' yeast. Let it ferment 3 or 4 days ; then put all together in a cask with the brandy, and let it remain for 2 months, when bottle it off for use.

Time.—To be boiled ½ hour ; to ferment 3 or 4 days ; to remain in the cask 2 months.

Average cost, exclusive of the cowslips, which may be picked in the fields, 2s. 9d. per gallon.

Seasonable.—Make this in April or May.

ELDER WINE.

1818. INGREDIENTS.—To every 3 gallons of water allow 1 peck of elderberries ; to every gallon of juice allow 3 lbs. of sugar, ½ oz. of ground ginger, 6 cloves, 1 lb. of good Turkey raisins ; ¼ pint of brandy to every gallon of wine. To every 9 gallons of wine 3 or 4 tablespoonfuls of fresh brewer's yeast.

Mode.—Pour the water, quite boiling, on the elderberries, which should be picked from the stalks, and let these stand covered for 24 hours ; then strain the whole through a sieve or bag, breaking the fruit to express all the juice from it. Measure the liquor, and to every gallon allow the above proportion of sugar. Boil the juice and sugar with the ginger, cloves, and raisins for 1 hour, skimming the liquor the whole time ; let it stand until milk-warm, then put it into a clean dry cask, with 3 or 4 tablespoonfuls of good fresh yeast to every 9 gallons of wine. Let it ferment for about a fortnight ; then add the brandy, bung up the cask, and let it stand some months before it is bottled, when it will be found excellent. A bunch of hops suspended to a string from the bung, some persons say, will preserve the wine good for several years. Elder wine is usually mulled, and served with sippets of toasted bread and a little grated nutmeg.

3 L

Time.—To stand covered 24 hours; to be boiled 1 hour.

Average cost, when made at home, 3s. 6d. per gallon.

Seasonable.—Make this in September.

ELDER-BERRY WINE.—The elder-berry is well adapted for the production of wine; its juice contains a considerable portion of the principle necessary for a vigorous fermentation, and its beautiful colour communicates a rich tint to the wine made from it. It is, however, deficient in sweetness, and therefore demands an addition of sugar. It is one of the very best of the genuine old English wines; and a cup of it mulled, just previous to retiring to bed on a winter night, is a thing to be "run for," as Cobbett would say: it is not, however, agreeable to every taste.

ELDER-BERRIES.

GINGER WINE.

1819. INGREDIENTS.—To 9 gallons of water allow 27 lbs. of loaf sugar, 9 lemons, 12 oz. of bruised ginger, 3 tablespoonfuls of yeast, 2 lbs. of raisins stoned and chopped, 1 pint of brandy.

Mode.—Boil together for 1 hour in a copper (let it previously be well scoured and beautifully clean) the water, sugar, *lemon-rinds*, and bruised ginger; remove every particle of scum as it rises, and when the liquor is sufficiently boiled, put it into a large tub or pan, as it must not remain in the copper. When nearly cold, add the yeast, which must be thick and very fresh, and, the next day, put all in a dry cask with the strained lemon-juice and chopped raisins. Stir the wine every day for a fortnight; then add the brandy, stop the cask down by degrees, and in a few weeks it will be fit to bottle.

Average cost, 2s. per gallon. *Sufficient* to make 9 gallons of wine.

Seasonable.—The best time for making this wine is either in March or September.

Note.—Wine made early in March will be fit to bottle in June.

GOOSEBERRY VINEGAR.

(*An Excellent Recipe.*)

1820. INGREDIENTS.—2 pecks of crystal gooseberries, 6 gallons of water, 12 lbs. of foots sugar of the coarsest brown quality.

Mode.—Mash the gooseberries (which should be quite ripe) in a tub with a mallet; put to them the water nearly milk-warm; let this stand 24 hours; then strain it through a sieve, and put the sugar to it; mix it well, and tun it. These proportions are for a 9-gallon cask; and if it be not quite full, more water must be added. Let the mixture be stirred from the bottom of the cask two or three times daily for three or four days, to assist the melting of the sugar; then paste a piece of linen cloth over the bunghole, and set the cask in a warm place, *but not in the sun;* any corner of a warm kitchen is the best situation for it. The following spring it should be drawn off into stone bottles, and the vinegar will be fit for use twelve months after it is made. This will be found a most excellent preparation, greatly superior to much that is sold under the name of the best white wine vinegar. Many years' experience has proved that pickle made with this vinegar will keep, when bought vinegar will not preserve the ingredients. The cost per gallon is merely nominal, especially to those who reside in the country and grow their own gooseberries ; the coarse sugar is then the only ingredient to be purchased.

Time.—To remain in the cask 9 months.

Average cost, when the gooseberries have to be purchased, 1s. per gallon ; when they are grown at home, 6d. per gallon.

Seasonable.—This should be made the end of June or the beginning of July, when gooseberries are ripe and plentiful.

EFFERVESCING GOOSEBERRY WINE.

1821. INGREDIENTS.—To every gallon of water allow 6 lbs. of green gooseberries, 3 lbs. of lump sugar.

Mode.—This wine should be prepared from unripe gooseberries, in order to avoid the flavour which the fruit would give to the wine when in a mature state. Its briskness depends more upon the time of bottling than upon the unripe state of the fruit, for effervescing wine can be made from fruit that is ripe as well as that which is unripe. The fruit should be selected when it has nearly attained its full growth, and consequently before it shows any tendency to ripen. Any bruised or decayed berries, and those that are very small, should be rejected. The blossom and stalk ends should be removed, and the fruit well bruised in a tub or pan, in such quantities as to insure each berry being broken without crushing the seeds. Pour the water (which should be warm) on the fruit, squeeze and stir it with the hand until all the pulp is removed from the skin and seeds, and cover the whole closely for 24 hours ; after which, strain it through a coarse bag, and press it with as much force as can be conveniently applied, to extract the whole of the juice and liquor the fruit may contain. To every 40 or 50 lbs. of fruit one gallon more of hot water may be passed through the *marc*, or husks, in order to obtain any soluble matter that may remain, and be again pressed. The juice should be put into a tub or pan of sufficient size to contain all of it, and the sugar added to it. Let it be well stirred until the sugar is dissolved, and place the pan in a warm situation ; keep it closely covered, and let it ferment for a day or two. It must then be drawn off into clean casks, placed a little on one side for the scum that

arises to be thrown out, and the casks kept filled with the remaining
"must," that should be reserved for that purpose. When the active
fermentation has ceased, the casks should be plugged upright, again
filled, if necessary, the bungs be put in loosely, and, after a few days,
when the fermentation is a little more languid (which may be known
by the hissing noise ceasing), the bungs should be driven in tight, and
a spile-hole made, to give vent if necessary. About November or
December, on a clear fine day, the wine should be racked from its
lees into clean casks, which may be rinsed with brandy. After a
month, it should be examined to see if it is sufficiently clear for
bottling; if not, it must be fined with isinglass, which may be dissolved in some of the wine: 1 oz. will be sufficient for 9 gallons. In
March or April, or when the gooseberry bushes begin to blossom, the
wine must be bottled, in order to insure its being effervescing.

Seasonable.—Make this the end of May or beginning of June, before
the berries ripen.

LEMON SYRUP.

1822. INGREDIENTS.—2 lbs. of loaf sugar, 2 pints of water, 1 oz. of
citric acid, ½ drachm of essence of lemon.

Mode.—Boil the sugar and water together for ¼ hour, and put it
into a basin, where let it remain till cold. Beat the citric acid to a
powder, mix the essence of lemon with it, then add these two ingredients to the syrup; mix well, and bottle for use. Two tablespoonfuls
of the syrup are sufficient for a tumbler of cold water, and will be
found a very refreshing summer drink.

Sufficient—2 tablespoonfuls of syrup to a tumbler-ful of cold water.

LEMON WINE.

1823. INGREDIENTS.—To 4½ gallons of water allow the pulp of
50 lemons, the rind of 25, 16 lbs. of loaf sugar, ½ oz. of isinglass,
1 bottle of brandy.

Mode.—Peel and slice the lemons, but use only the rind of 25 of
them, and put them into the cold water. Let it stand 8 or 9 days,
squeezing the lemons well every day; then strain the water off and
put it into a cask with the sugar. Let it work some time, and when
it has ceased working, put in the isinglass. Stop the cask down; in
about six months put in the brandy and bottle the wine off.

Seasonable.—The best time to make this is in January or February,
when lemons are best and cheapest.

MALT WINE.

1824. INGREDIENTS.—5 gallons of water, 28 lbs. of sugar, 6 quarts of sweet-wort, 6 quarts of tun, 3 lbs. of raisins, ½ lb. of candy, 1 pint of brandy.

Mode.—Boil the sugar and water together for 10 minutes; skim it well, and put the liquor into a convenient-sized pan or tub. Allow it to cool; then mix it with the sweet-wort and tun. Let it stand for 3 days, then put it into a barrel; here it will work or ferment for another three days or more; then bung up the cask, and keep it undisturbed for 2 or 3 months. After this, add the raisins (whole), the candy, and brandy, and, in 6 months' time, bottle the wine off. Those who do not brew, may procure the sweet-wort and tun from any brewer. Sweet-wort is the liquor that leaves the mash of malt before it is boiled with the hops; tun is the new beer after the whole of the brewing operation has been completed.

Time.—To be boiled 10 minutes; to stand 3 days after mixing; to ferment 3 days; to remain in the cask 2 months before the raisins are added; bottle 6 months after.

Seasonable.—Make this in March or October.

HOME-MADE NOYEAU.

1825. INGREDIENTS.—2 oz. of bitter almonds, 1 oz. of sweet ditto, 1 lb. of loaf sugar, the rinds of 3 lemons, 1 quart of Irish whiskey or gin, 1 tablespoonful of clarified honey, ½ pint of new milk.

Mode.—Blanch and pound the almonds, and mix with them the sugar, which should also be pounded. Boil the milk; let it stand till quite cold; then mix all the ingredients together, and let them remain for 10 days, shaking them every day. Filter the mixture through blotting-paper, bottle off for use in small bottles, and seal the corks down. This will be found useful for flavouring many sweet dishes.

Average cost, 2s. 9d.

Sufficient to make about 2½ pints of Noyeau.

Seasonable.—May be made at any time.

ORANGE BRANDY.

(*Excellent.*)

1826. INGREDIENTS.—To every ½ gallon of brandy allow ¾ pint of Seville orange-juice, 1¼ lb. of loaf sugar.

Mode.—To bring out the full flavour of the orange-peel, rub a few lumps of the sugar on 2 or 3 unpared oranges, and put these lumps to the rest. Mix the brandy with the orange-juice, strained, the rinds of 6 of the oranges pared very thin, and the sugar. Let all stand in a closely-covered jar for about 3 days, stirring it 3 or 4 times a day. When clear, it should be bottled and closely corked for a year; it will then be ready for use, but will keep any length of time. This is a most excellent stomachic when taken pure in small quantities; or, as the strength of the brandy is very little deteriorated by the other ingredients, it may be diluted with water.

Time.—To be stirred every day for 3 days.

Average cost, 7s.

Sufficient to make 2 quarts. *Seasonable.*—Make this in March.

A VERY SIMPLE AND EASY METHOD OF MAKING A VERY SUPERIOR ORANGE WINE.

1827. INGREDIENTS.—90 Seville oranges, 32 lbs. of lump sugar, water.

Mode.—Break up the sugar into small pieces, and put it into a dry, sweet 9-gallon cask, placed in a cellar or other storehouse, where it is intended to be kept. Have ready close to the cask two large pans or wooden keelers, into one of which put the peel of the oranges pared quite thin, and into the other the pulp after the juice has been squeezed from it. Strain the juice through a piece of double muslin, and put it into the cask with the sugar. Then pour about 1½ gallon of cold spring water on both the peels and pulp; let it stand for 24 hours, and then strain it into the cask; add more water to the peels and pulp when this is done, and repeat the same process every day for a week: it should take about a week to fill up the cask. Be careful to apportion the quantity as nearly as possible to the seven days, and to stir the contents of the cask each day. On the *third* day after the cask is full,—that is, the *tenth* day after the commencement of making,—the cask may be securely bunged down. This is a very simple and easy method, and the wine made according to it will be pronounced to be most excellent. There is no troublesome boiling, and all fermentation takes place in the cask. When the above directions are attended to, the wine cannot fail to be good. It should be bottled in 8 or 9 months, and will be fit for use in a twelvemonth after the time of making. Ginger wine may be made in precisely the same manner, only, with the 9-gallon cask for ginger wine, 2 lbs. of the best whole ginger, *bruised,* must be put with the sugar. It will be found convenient to tie the ginger loosely in a muslin bag.

Time.—Altogether, 10 days to make it.

Average cost, 2s. 6d. per gallon. *Sufficient* for 9 gallons.

Seasonable. — Make this in March, and bottle it the following January.

RASPBERRY VINEGAR.

1828. INGREDIENTS.—To every 3 pints of the best vinegar allow $4\frac{1}{2}$ pints of freshly-gathered raspberries; to each pint of liquor allow 1 lb. of pounded loaf sugar, 1 wineglassful of brandy.

Mode.—Let the raspberries be freshly gathered; pick them from the stalks, and put $1\frac{1}{2}$ pint of them into a stone jar; pour 3 pints of the best vinegar over them, and let them remain for 24 hours; then strain the liquor over another $1\frac{1}{2}$ pint of fresh raspberries. Let them remain another 24 hours, and the following day repeat the process for the third time; then drain off the liquor without pressing, and pass it through a jelly-bag (previously wetted with plain vinegar), into a stone jar. Add to every pint of the liquor 1 lb. of pounded loaf sugar; stir them together, and, when the sugar is dissolved, cover the jar; set it upon the fire in a saucepan of boiling water, and let it boil for an hour, removing the scum as fast as it rises; add to each pint a glass of brandy, bottle it, and seal the corks. This is an excellent drink in cases of fevers and colds: it should be diluted with cold water, according to the taste or requirement of the patient.

Time.—To be boiled 1 hour. *Average cost*, 1s. per pint.

Sufficient to make 2 quarts.

Seasonable.—Make this in July or August, when raspberries are most plentiful.

RHUBARB WINE.

1829. INGREDIENTS.—To every 5 lbs. of rhubarb pulp allow 1 gallon of cold spring water; to every gallon of liquor allow 3 lbs. of loaf sugar, $\frac{1}{2}$ oz. of isinglass, the rind of 1 lemon.

Mode.—Gather the rhubarb about the middle of May; wipe it with a wet cloth, and, with a mallet, bruise it in a large wooden tub or other convenient means. When reduced to a pulp, weigh it, and to every 5 lbs. add 1 gallon of cold spring water; let these remain for 3 days, stirring 3 or 4 times a day; and, on the fourth day, press the pulp through a hair sieve; put the liquor into a tub, and to every gallon put 3 lbs. of loaf sugar; stir in the sugar until it is quite dissolved, and add the lemon-rind; let the liquor remain, and, in 4, 5, or 6 days, the fermentation will begin to subside, and a crust or head will be formed, which should be skimmed off, or the liquor drawn from it, when the crust begins to crack or separate. Put the wine into a cask, and if, after that, it ferments, rack it off into another cask, and in a fortnight stop it down. If the wine should have lost any of its original sweetness, add a little more loaf sugar, taking care that the cask is full. Bottle it off in February or March, and in the summer it should be fit to drink. It will improve greatly by keeping ; and, should a very brilliant colour be desired, add a little currant-juice.

Seasonable.—Make this about the middle of May.

WELSH NECTAR.

1830. INGREDIENTS.—1 lb. of raisins, 3 lemons, 2 lbs. of loaf sugar, 2 gallons of boiling water.

Mode.—Cut the peel of the lemons very thin, pour upon it the boiling water, and, when cool, add the strained juice of the lemons, the sugar, and the raisins, stoned and chopped very fine. Let it stand 4 or 5 days, stirring it every day ; then strain it through a jelly-bag, and bottle it for present use.

Time.—4 or 5 days. *Average cost,* 1s. 9d.

Sufficient to make 2 gallons.

CLARET-CUP.

1831. INGREDIENTS.—1 bottle of claret, 1 bottle of soda-water, about ½ lb. of pounded ice, 4 tablespoonfuls of powdered sugar, ¼ teaspoon-

ful of grated nutmeg, 1 liqueur-glass of Maraschino, a sprig of green borage.

Mode.—Put all the ingredients into a silver cup, regulating the proportion of ice by the state of the weather : if very warm, a larger quantity would be necessary. Hand the cup round with a clean napkin passed through one of the handles, that the edge of the cup may be wiped after each guest

CLARET-CUP.

has partaken of the contents thereof.

Seasonable in summer.

CLARETS.—All those wines called in England clarets are the produce of the country round Bordeaux, or the Bordelais; but it is remarkable that there is no pure wine in France known by the name of claret, which is a corruption of *clairet*, a term that is applied there to any red or rose-coloured wine. Round Bordeaux are produced a number of wines of the first quality, which pass under the name simply of *vins de Bordeaux*, or have the designation of the particular district where they are made ; as Lafitte, Latour, &c. The clarets brought to the English market are frequently prepared for it by the wine-growers by mixing together several Bordeaux wines, or by adding to them a portion of some other wines ; but in France the pure wines are carefully preserved distinct. The genuine wines of Bordeaux are of great variety, that part being one of the most distinguished in France ; and the principal vineyards are those of Medoc, Palus, Graves, and Blanche, the product of each having characters considerably different.

CHAMPAGNE-CUP.

1832. INGREDIENTS.—1 quart bottle of champagne, 2 bottles of soda-water, 1 liqueur-glass of brandy or Curaçoa, 2 tablespoonfuls of powdered sugar, 1 lb. of pounded ice, a sprig of green borage.

Mode.—Put all the ingredients into a silver cup; stir them together, and serve the same as claret-cup No. 1831. Should the above proportion of sugar not be found sufficient to suit some tastes, increase the quantity. When borage is not easily obtainable, substitute for it a few slices of cucumber-rind.

Seasonable.—Suitable for pic-nics, balls, weddings, and other festive occasions.

CHAMPAGNE.—This, the most celebrated of French wines, is the produce chiefly of the province of that name, and is generally understood in England to be a brisk, effervescing, or sparkling white wine, of a very fine flavour; but this is only one of the varieties of this class. There is both red and white champagne, and each of these may be either still or brisk. There are the sparkling wines (*mousseux*), and the still wines (*non-mousseux*). The brisk are in general the most highly esteemed, or, at least, are the most popular in this country, on account of their delicate flavour and the agreeable pungency which they derive from the carbonic acid they contain, and to which they owe their briskness.

GINGER BEER.

1833. INGREDIENTS.—2½ lbs. of loaf sugar, 1½ oz. of bruised ginger, 1 oz. of cream of tartar, the rind and juice of 2 lemons, 3 gallons of boiling water, 2 large tablespoonfuls of thick and fresh brewer's yeast.

Mode.—Peel the lemons, squeeze the juice, strain it, and put the peel and juice into a large earthen pan, with the bruised ginger, cream of tartar, and loaf sugar. Pour over these ingredients 3 gallons of *boiling* water; let it stand until just warm, when add the yeast, which should be thick and perfectly fresh. Stir the contents of the pan well, and let them remain near the fire all night, covering the pan over with a cloth. The next day skim off the yeast, and pour the liquor carefully into another vessel, leaving the sediment; then bottle immediately, and tie the corks down, and in 3 days the ginger beer will be fit for use. For some tastes, the above proportion of sugar may be found rather too large, when it may be diminished; but the beer will not keep so long good.

Average cost for this quantity, 2s.; or ½d. per bottle.

Sufficient to fill 4 dozen ginger-beer bottles.

Seasonable.—This should be made during the summer months.

LEMONADE.

1834. INGREDIENTS.—The rind of 2 lemons, the juice of 3 large or 4 small ones, ½ lb. of loaf sugar, 1 quart of boiling water.

Mode.—Rub some of the sugar, in lumps, on 2 of the lemons until they have imbibed all the oil from them, and put it with the remainder of the sugar into a jug; add the lemon-juice (but no pips), and pour over the whole a quart of boiling water. When the sugar is dissolved, strain the lemonade through a fine sieve or piece of muslin, and, when cool, it will be ready for use. The lemonade will be much improved by having the white of an egg beaten up in it; a little sherry mixed with it, also, makes this beverage much nicer.

Average cost, 6*d.* per quart.

LEMONADE.—" There is a current opinion among women," says Brillat Savarin, " which every year causes the death of many young women,—that acids, especially vinegar, are preventives of obesity. Beyond all doubt, acids have the effect of destroying obesity; but they also destroy health and freshness. Lemonade is, of all acids, the most harmless; but few stomachs can resist it long. I knew, in 1776, at Dijon, a young lady of great beauty, to whom I was attached by bonds of friendship, great, almost, as those of love. One day, when she had for some time gradually grown pale and thin (previously she had a slight *embonpoint*), she told me in confidence, that, as her young friends had ridiculed her for being fat, she had, to counteract the tendency, been in the habit every day of drinking a large glass of *vinaigre.* She died at eighteen years of age, from the effect of these potions."

TO MAKE NEGUS.

1835. INGREDIENTS.—To every pint of port wine allow 1 quart of boiling water, ¼ lb. of sugar, 1 lemon, grated nutmeg to taste.

Mode.—As this beverage is more usually drunk at children's parties than at any other, the wine need not be very old or expensive for the purpose, a new fruity wine answering very well for it. Put the wine into a jug, rub some lumps of sugar (equal to ¼ lb.) on the lemon-rind until all the yellow part of the skin is absorbed, then squeeze the juice, and strain it. Add the sugar and lemon-juice to the port wine, with the grated nutmeg; pour over it the boiling water, cover the jug, and, when the beverage has cooled a little, it will be fit for use. Negus may also be made of sherry, or any other sweet white wine, but is more usually made of port than of any other beverage.

Sufficient.—Allow 1 pint of wine, with the other ingredients in proportion, for a party of 9 or 10 children.

A PLEASANT DRINK FOR WARM WEATHER.

1836. INGREDIENTS.—To every 1½ pint of good ale allow 1 bottle of ginger beer.

Mode.—For this beverage the ginger beer must be in an effervescing state, and the beer not in the least turned or sour. Mix them together, and drink immediately. The draught is refreshing and wholesome, as the ginger corrects the action of the beer. It does not deteriorate by standing a little, but, of course, is better when taken fresh.

FOR A SUMMER DRAUGHT.

1837. INGREDIENTS.—The juice of 1 lemon, a tumbler-ful of cold water, pounded sugar to taste, ½ small teaspoonful of carbonate of soda.

Mode.—Squeeze the juice from the lemon; strain, and add it to the water, with sufficient pounded sugar to sweeten the whole nicely. When well mixed, put in the soda, stir well, and drink while the mixture is in an effervescing state.

TO MULL WINE.

1838. INGREDIENTS.—To every pint of wine allow 1 large cupful of water, sugar and spice to taste.

Mode.—In making preparations like the above, it is very difficult to give the exact proportions of ingredients like sugar and spice, as what quantity might suit one person would be to another quite distasteful. Boil the spice in the water until the flavour is extracted, then add the wine and sugar, and bring the whole to the boiling-point, when serve with strips of crisp dry toast, or with biscuits. The spices usually used for mulled wine are cloves, grated nutmeg, and cinnamon or mace. Any kind of wine may be mulled, but port and claret are those usually selected for the purpose; and the latter requires a very large proportion of sugar. The vessel that the wine is boiled in must be delicately clean, and should be kept exclusively for the purpose. Small tin warmers may be purchased for a trifle, which are more suitable than saucepans, as, if the latter are not scrupulously clean, they will spoil the wine, by imparting to it a very disagreeable flavour. These warmers should be used for no other purposes.

TO MAKE HOT PUNCH.

1839. INGREDIENTS.—½ pint of rum, ½ pint of brandy, ¼ lb. of sugar, 1 large lemon, ½ teaspoonful of nutmeg, 1 pint of boiling water.

Mode.—Rub the sugar over the lemon until it has absorbed all the yellow part of the skin, then put the sugar into a punchbowl; add the lemon-juice (free from pips), and mix these two ingredients well together. Pour over them the boiling water, stir well together, add the rum, brandy, and nutmeg; mix thoroughly, and the punch will be ready to serve. It is very important in making good punch that all the ingredients are thoroughly

PUNCH-BOWL AND LADLE.

incorporated; and, to insure success, the processes of mixing must be diligently attended to.

Sufficient.—Allow a quart for 4 persons; but this information must be taken *cum grano salis;* for the capacities of persons for this kind of beverage are generally supposed to vary considerably.

PUNCH is a beverage made of various spirituous liquors or wine, hot water, the acid juice of fruits, and sugar. It is considered to be very intoxicating; but this is probably because the spirit, being partly sheathed by the mucilaginous juice and the sugar, its strength does not appear to the taste so great as it really is. Punch, which was almost universally drunk among the middle classes about fifty or sixty years ago, has almost disappeared from our domestic tables, being superseded by wine. There are many different varieties of punch. It is sometimes kept cold in bottles, and makes a most agreeable summer drink. In Scotland, instead of the Madeira or sherry generally used in its manufacture, whiskey is substituted, and then its insidious properties are more than usually felt. Where fresh lemons cannot be had for punch or similar beverages, crystallized citric acid and a few drops of the essence of lemon will be very nearly the same thing. In the composition of "Regent's punch," champagne, brandy, and *veritable Martinique* are required; "Norfolk punch" requires Seville oranges; "Milk punch" may be extemporized by adding a little hot milk to lemonade, and then straining it through a jelly-bag. Then there are "Wine punch," "Tea punch," and "French punch," made with lemons, spirits, and wine, in fantastic proportions. But of all the compounds of these materials, perhaps, for a *summer* drink, the North-American "mint julep" is the most inviting. Captain Marryat gives the following recipe for its preparation :—"Put into a tumbler about a dozen sprigs of the tender shoots of mint; upon them put a spoonful of white sugar, and equal proportions of peach and common brandy, so as to fill up one third, or, perhaps, a little less; then take rasped or pounded ice, and fill up the tumbler. Epicures rub the lips of the tumbler with a piece of fresh pineapple; and the tumbler itself is very often encrusted outside with stalactites of ice. As the ice melts, you drink." The Virginians, says Captain Marryat, claim the merit of having invented this superb compound; but, from a passage in the "Comus" of Milton, he claims it for his own country.

WHISKEY CORDIAL.

1840. INGREDIENTS.—1 lb. of ripe white currants, the rind of 2 lemons, ¼ oz. of grated ginger, 1 quart of whiskey, 1 lb. of lump sugar.

Mode.—Strip the currants from the stalks; put them into a large jug; add the lemon-rind, ginger, and whiskey; cover the jug closely, and let it remain covered for 24 hours. Strain through a hair sieve, add the lump sugar, and let it stand 12 hours longer; then bottle, and cork well.

Time.—To stand 24 hours before being strained; 12 hours after the sugar is added.

Seasonable.—Make this in July.

INVALID COOKERY.

—◆—

CHAPTER XXXVIII.

A FEW RULES TO BE OBSERVED IN COOKING FOR INVALIDS.

1841. LET all the kitchen utensils used in the preparation of invalids' cookery be delicately and *scrupulously clean*, if this is not the case, a disagreeable flavour may be imparted to the preparation, which flavour may disgust, and prevent the patient from partaking of the refreshment when brought to him or her.

1842. For invalids, never make a large quantity *of one thing*, as they seldom require much at a time ; and it is desirable that variety be provided for them.

1843. Always have something in readiness ; a little beef tea, nicely made and nicely skimmed, a few spoonfuls of jelly, &c. &c., that it may be administered as soon almost as the invalid wishes for it. If obliged to wait a long time, the patient loses the desire to eat, and often turns against the food when brought to him or her.

1844. In sending dishes or preparations up to invalids, let everything look as tempting as possible. Have a clean tray-cloth laid smoothly over the tray ; let the spoons, tumblers, cups and saucers, &c., be very clean and bright. Gruel served in a tumbler is more appetizing than when served in a basin or cup and saucer.

1845. As milk is an important article of food for the sick, in warm weather let it be kept on ice, to prevent its turning sour. Many other delicacies may also be preserved good in the same manner for some little time.

1846. If the patient be allowed to eat vegetables, never send them up undercooked, or half raw ; and let a small quantity only be temptingly arranged on a dish. This rule will apply to every preparation, as an invalid is much more likely to enjoy his food if small delicate pieces are served to him.

1847. Never leave food about a sick room ; if the patient cannot eat it when brought to him, take it away, and bring it to him in an hour or two's time. Miss Nightingale says, "To leave the patient's untasted food by his side, from meal to meal, in hopes that he will eat it in the interval, is simply to prevent him from taking any food at all. She says, "I have known patients literally incapacitated from taking one article of food after another by this piece of ignorance. Let the food come at the right time, and be taken away, eaten or uneaten, at the right time, but never let a patient have 'something always standing' by him, if you don't wish to disgust him of everything."

1848. Never serve beef tea or broth with the *smallest particle* of fat or grease on the surface. It is better, after making either of these, to allow them to get perfectly cold, when *all the fat* may be easily removed; then warm up as much as may be required. Two or three pieces of clean whity-brown paper laid on the broth will absorb any greasy particles that may be floating at the top, as the grease will cling to the paper.

1849. Roast mutton, chickens, rabbits, calves' feet or head, game, fish (simply dressed), and simple puddings, are all light food, and easily digested. Of course, these things are only partaken of, supposing the patient is recovering.

1850. A mutton chop, nicely cut, trimmed, and broiled to a turn, is a dish to be recommended for invalids; but it must not be served *with all the fat* at the end, nor must it be too thickly cut. Let it be cooked over a fire free from smoke, and sent up with the gravy in it, between two very hot plates. Nothing is more disagreeable to an invalid than *smoked* food.

1851. In making toast-and-water, never blacken the bread, but toast it only a nice brown. Never leave toast-and-water to make until the moment it is required, as it cannot then be properly prepared,—at least, the patient will be obliged to drink it warm, which is anything but agreeable.

1852. In boiling eggs for invalids, let the white be just set; if boiled hard, they will be likely to disagree with the patient.

1853. In Miss Nightingale's admirable "Notes on Nursing," a book that no mother or nurse should be without, she says,—"You cannot be too careful as to quality in sick diet. A nurse should never put before a patient milk that is sour, meat or soup that is turned, an egg that is bad, or vegetables under-done." Yet often, she says, she has seen these things brought in to the sick, in a state perfectly perceptible to every nose or eye except the nurse's. It is here that the clever nurse appears,—she will not bring in the peccant article; but, not to disappoint the patient, she will whip up something else in a few minutes. Remember, that sick cookery should half do the work of your poor patient's weak digestion.

1854. She goes on to caution nurses, by saying,—"Take care not to spill into your patient's saucer; in other words, take care that the outside bottom rim of his cup shall be quite dry and clean. If, every time he lifts his cup to his lips, he has to carry the saucer with it, or else to drop the liquid upon and to soil his sheet, or bedgown, or pillow, or, if he is sitting up, his dress, you have no idea what a difference this minute want of care on your part makes to his comfort, and even to his willingness for food."

RECIPES.

CHAPTER XXXIX.

TO MAKE ARROWROOT.

1855. INGREDIENTS.—Two teaspoonfuls of arrowroot, 3 tablespoonfuls of cold water, ½ pint of boiling water.

Mode.—Mix the arrowroot smoothly in a basin with the cold water, then pour on it the *boiling* water, *stirring* all the time. The water must be *boiling* at the time it is poured on the mixture, or it will not thicken; if mixed with hot water only, it must be put into a clean saucepan, and boiled until it thickens; but this is more trouble, and quite unnecessary if the water is boiling at first. Put the arrowroot into a tumbler, sweeten it with lump sugar, and flavour it with grated nutmeg or cinnamon, or a piece of lemon-peel, or, when allowed, 3 tablespoonfuls of port or sherry. As arrowroot is in itself flavourless and insipid, it is almost necessary to add the wine to make it palatable. Arrowroot made with milk instead of water is far nicer, but is not so easily digested. It should be mixed in the same manner, with 3 tablespoonfuls of cold water, the boiling milk then poured on it, and well stirred. When made in this manner, no wine should be added, but merely sugar, and a little grated nutmeg or lemon-peel.

Time.—If obliged to be boiled, 2 minutes. *Average cost,* 2d. per pint.

Sufficient to make ½ pint of arrowroot.

MISS NIGHTINGALE says, in her "Notes on Nursing," that arrowroot is a grand dependence of the nurse. As a vehicle for wine, and as a restorative quickly prepared, it is all very well, but it is nothing but starch and water; flour is both more nutritive and less liable to ferment, and is preferable wherever it can be used.

BARLEY GRUEL.

1856. INGREDIENTS.—2 oz. of Scotch or pearl barley, ½ pint of port wine, the rind of 1 lemon, 1 quart and ½ pint of water, sugar to taste.

Mode.—After well washing the barley, boil it in ½ pint of water for ¼ hour; then pour this water away; put to the barley the quart of fresh boiling water, and let it boil until the liquid is reduced to half; then strain it off. Add the wine, sugar, and lemon-peel; simmer for

5 minutes, and put it away in a clean jug. It can be warmed from time to time, as required.

Time.—To be boiled until reduced to half. *Average cost*, 1s. 6d.

Sufficient with the wine to make 1½ pint of gruel.

TO MAKE BARLEY-WATER.

1857. INGREDIENTS.—2 oz. of pearl barley, 2 quarts of boiling water, 1 pint of cold water.

Mode.—Wash the barley in cold water; put it into a saucepan with the above proportion of cold water, and when it has boiled for about ¼ hour, strain off the water, and add the 2 quarts of fresh boiling water. Boil it until the liquid is reduced one half; strain it, and it will be ready for use. It may be flavoured with lemon-peel, after being sweetened, or a small piece may be simmered with the barley. When the invalid may take it, a little lemon-juice gives this pleasant drink in illness a very nice flavour.

Time.—To boil until the liquid is reduced one half.

Sufficient to make 1 quart of barley-water.

TO MAKE BEEF TEA.

1858. INGREDIENTS.—1 lb. of lean gravy-beef, 1 quart of water, 1 saltspoonful of salt.

Mode.—Have the meat cut without fat and bone, and choose a nice fleshy piece. Cut it into small pieces about the size of dice, and put it into a clean saucepan. Add the water *cold* to it; put it on the fire, and bring it to the boiling-point; then skim well. Put in the salt when the water boils, and *simmer* the beef tea *gently* from ½ to ¾ hour, removing any more scum should it appear on the surface. Strain the tea through a hair sieve, and set it by in a cool place. When wanted for use, remove every particle of fat from the top; warm up as much as may be required, adding, if necessary, a little more salt. This preparation is simple beef tea, and is to be administered to those invalids to whom flavourings and seasonings are not allowed. When the patient is very low, use double the quantity of meat to the same proportion of water. Should the invalid be able to take the tea prepared in a more palatable manner, it is easy to make it so by following the directions in the next recipe, which is an admirable one for making savoury beef tea. Beef tea is always better when made the day before it is wanted, and then warmed up. It is a good plan to put the tea into a small cup or basin, and to place this basin in a saucepan of boiling water. When the tea is warm, it is ready to serve.

Time.—½ to ¾ hour. *Average cost*, 6*d*. per pint.

Sufficient.—Allow 1 lb. of meat for a pint of good beef tea.

MISS NIGHTINGALE says, one of the most common errors among nurses, with respect to sick diet, is the belief that beef tea is the most nutritive of all articles. She says, "Just try and boil down a lb. of beef into beef tea; evaporate your beef tea, and see what is left of your beef; you will find that there is barely a teaspoonful of solid nourishment to ½ pint of water in beef tea. Nevertheless, there is a certain reparative quality in it,—we do not know what,—as there is in tea; but it may be safely given in almost any inflammatory disease, and is as little to be depended upon with the healthy or convalescent, where much nourishment is required."

SAVOURY BEEF TEA.

(*Soyer's Recipe.*)

1859. INGREDIENTS.—1 lb. of solid beef, 1 oz. of butter, 1 clove, 2 button onions or ½ a large one, 1 saltspoonful of salt, 1 quart of water.

Mode.—Cut the beef into very small dice; put it into a stewpan with the butter, clove, onion, and salt; stir the meat round over the fire for a few minutes, until it produces a thin gravy; then add the water, and let it simmer gently from ½ to ¾ hour, skimming off every particle of fat. When done, strain it through a sieve, and put it by in a cool place until required. The same, if wanted quite plain, is done by merely omitting the vegetables, salt, and clove; the butter cannot be objectionable, as it is taken out in skimming.

Time.—½ to ¾ hour. *Average cost*, 8*d*. per pint.

Sufficient.—Allow 1 lb. of beef to make 1 pint of good beef tea.

Note.—The meat left from beef tea may be boiled a little longer, and pounded, with spices, &c., for potting. It makes a very nice breakfast dish.

DR. CHRISTISON says that "every one will be struck with the readiness with which certain classes of patients will often take diluted meat juice, or beef tea repeatedly, when they refuse all other kinds of food." This is particularly remarkable in cases of gastric fever, in which, he says, little or nothing else besides beef tea, or diluted meat juice, has been taken for weeks, or even months; and yet a pint of beef tea contains scarcely ¼ oz. of anything but water. The result is so striking, that he asks, "What is its mode of action? Not simple nutriment; ¼ oz. of the most nutritive material cannot nearly replace the daily wear and tear of the tissue in any circumstances." Possibly, he says, it belongs to a new denomination of remedies.

BAKED BEEF TEA.

1860. INGREDIENTS.—1 lb. of fleshy beef, 1½ pint of water, ½ saltspoonful of salt.

Mode.—Cut the beef into small square pieces, after trimming off all the fat, and put it into a baking-jar, with the above proportion of water and salt; cover the jar well, place it in a warm, but not hot oven, and bake for 3 or 4 hours. When the oven is very fierce in the daytime, it is a good plan to put the jar in at night, and let it remain till the next morning, when the tea will be done. It should be strained, and put by in a cool place until wanted. It may also be flavoured with an onion, a clove, and a few sweet herbs, &c., when the stomach is sufficiently strong to take these.

Time.—3 or 4 hours, or to be left in the oven all night.

Average cost, 6d. per pint.

Sufficient.—Allow 1 lb. of meat for 1 pint of good beef tea.

BAKED OR STEWED CALF'S FOOT.

1861. INGREDIENTS.—1 calf's foot, 1 pint of milk, 1 pint of water, 1 blade of mace, the rind of ½ lemon, pepper and salt to taste.

Mode.—Well clean the foot, and either stew or bake it in the milk-and-water with the other ingredients from 3 to 4 hours. To enhance the flavour, an onion and a small quantity of celery may be added, if approved; ½ a teacupful of cream, stirred in just before serving, is also a great improvement to this dish.

Time.—3 to 4 hours. *Average cost,* in full season, 9d. each.

Sufficient for 1 person. *Seasonable* from March to October.

CALF'S-FOOT BROTH.

1862. INGREDIENTS.—1 calf's foot, 3 pints of water, 1 small lump of sugar, nutmeg to taste, the yolk of 1 egg, a piece of butter the size of a nut.

Mode.—Stew the foot in the water, with the lemon-peel, *very gently,* until the liquid is half wasted, removing any scum, should it rise to the surface. Set it by in a basin until quite cold, then take off every particle of fat. Warm up about ½ pint of the broth, adding the butter, sugar, and a very small quantity of grated nutmeg; take it off the fire for a minute or two, then add the beaten yolk of the egg; keep stirring over the fire until the mixture thickens, but do not allow it to boil again after the egg is added, or it will curdle, and the broth will be spoiled.

Time.—To be boiled until the liquid is reduced one half.

Average cost, in full season, 9d. each.

Sufficient to make 1½ pint of broth.

Seasonable from March to October.

CHICKEN BROTH.

1863. INGREDIENTS.—½ fowl, or the inferior joints of a whole one; 1 quart of water, 1 blade of mace, ½ onion, a small bunch of sweet herbs, salt to taste, 10 peppercorns.

Mode.—An old fowl not suitable for eating may be converted into very good broth, or, if a young one be used, the inferior joints may be put in the broth, and the best pieces reserved for dressing in some other manner. Put the fowl into a saucepan, with all the ingredients, and simmer gently for 1½ hour, carefully skimming the broth well. When done, strain, and put by in a cool place until wanted; then take all the fat off the top, warm up as much as may be required, and serve. This broth is, of course, only for those invalids whose stomachs are strong enough to digest it, with a flavouring of herbs, &c. It may be made in the same manner as beef tea, with water and salt only; but the preparation will be but tasteless and insipid. When the invalid cannot digest this chicken broth with the flavouring, we would recommend plain beef tea in preference to plain chicken tea, which it would be without the addition of herbs, onions, &c.

Time.—1½ hour.

Sufficient to make rather more than 1 pint of broth.

NUTRITIOUS COFFEE.

1864. INGREDIENTS.—½ oz. of ground coffee, 1 pint of milk.

Mode.—Let the coffee be freshly ground; put it into a saucepan, with the milk, which should be made nearly boiling before the coffee is put in, and boil both together for 3 minutes; clear it by pouring some of it into a cup, and then back again, and leave it on the hob for a few minutes to settle thoroughly. This coffee may be made still more nutritious by the addition of an egg well beaten, and put into the coffee-cup.

Time.—5 minutes to boil, 5 minutes to settle.

Sufficient to make 1 large breakfast-cupful of coffee.

OUR great nurse Miss Nightingale remarks, that "a great deal too much against tea is said by wise people, and a great deal too much of tea is given to the sick by foolish people. When you see the natural and almost universal craving in English sick for their 'tea,' you cannot but feel that Nature knows what she is about. But a little tea or coffee restores them quite as much as a great deal; and a great deal of tea, and especially of coffee, impairs the little power of digestion they have. Yet a nurse, because she sees how one or two cups of tea or coffee restore her patient, thinks that three or four cups will do twice as much. This is not the case at all; it is, however, certain that there is nothing yet discovered which is a substitute to the English patient for his cup of tea; he can take it when he can take nothing else, and he often can't take anything else, if he has it not. Coffee is a better restorative than tea, but a greater impairer of the digestion. In making coffee, it is absolutely necessary to buy it in the berry, and grind it at home; otherwise, you may reckon upon its containing a certain amount of chicory, *at least*. This is not a question of the taste, or of the wholesomeness of chicory; it is, that chicory has nothing at all of the properties for which you give coffee, and, therefore, you may as well not give it."

THE INVALID'S CUTLET.

1865. INGREDIENTS.—1 nice cutlet from a loin or neck of mutton, 2 teacupfuls of water, 1 very small stick of celery, pepper and salt to taste.

Mode.—Have the cutlet cut from a very nice loin or neck of mutton; take off all the fat; put it into a stewpan, with the other ingredients; stew *very gently* indeed for nearly 2 hours, and skim off every particle of fat that may rise to the surface from time to time. The celery should be cut into thin slices before it is added to the meat, and care must be taken not to put in too much of this ingredient, or the dish will not be good. If the water is allowed to boil fast, the cutlet will be hard.

Time.—2 hours' very gentle stewing. *Average cost*, 6d.

Sufficient for 1 person. *Seasonable* at any time.

EEL BROTH.

1866. INGREDIENTS.—½ lb. of eels, a small bunch of sweet herbs, including parsley; ½ onion, 10 peppercorns, 3 pints of water, 2 cloves, salt and pepper to taste.

Mode.—After having cleaned and skinned the eel, cut it into small pieces, and put it into a stewpan, with the other ingredients; simmer gently until the liquid is reduced nearly half, carefully removing the scum as it rises. Strain it through a hair sieve; put it by in a cool place, and, when wanted, take off all the fat from the top, warm up as much as is required, and serve with sippets of toasted bread. This is a very nutritious broth, and easy of digestion.

Time.—To be simmered until the liquor is reduced to half.

Average cost, 6d.

Sufficient to make 1½ pint of broth.

Seasonable from June to March.

EGG WINE.

1867. INGREDIENTS.—1 egg, 1 tablespoonful and ½ glass of cold water, 1 glass of sherry, sugar and grated nutmeg to taste.

Mode.—Beat the egg, mixing with it a tablespoonful of cold water; make the wine-and-water hot, but not boiling; pour it on the egg, stirring all the time. Add sufficient lump sugar to sweeten the mixture, and a little grated nutmeg; put all into a very clean saucepan, set it on a gentle fire, and stir the contents one way until they thicken, but *do not allow them to boil.* Serve in a glass with sippets of toasted bread or plain crisp biscuits. When the egg is not warmed, the mixture will be found easier of digestion, but it is not so pleasant a drink.

Sufficient for 1 person.

TO MAKE GRUEL.

1868. INGREDIENTS.—1 tablespoonful of Robinson's patent groats, 2 tablespoonfuls of cold water, 1 pint of boiling water.

Mode.—Mix the prepared groats smoothly with the cold water in a basin ; pour over them the boiling water, stirring it all the time. Put it into a very clean saucepan ; boil the gruel for 10 minutes, keeping it well stirred ; sweeten to taste, and serve. It may be flavoured with a small piece of lemon-peel, by boiling it in the gruel, or a little grated nutmeg may be put in ; but in these matters the taste of the patient should be consulted. Pour the gruel in a tumbler and serve. When wine is allowed to the invalid, 2 tablespoonfuls of sherry or port make this preparation very nice. In cases of colds, the same quantity of spirits is sometimes added instead of wine.

Time.—10 minutes.

Sufficient to make a pint of gruel.

INVALID'S JELLY.

1869. INGREDIENTS.—12 shanks of mutton, 3 quarts of water, a bunch of sweet herbs, pepper and salt to taste, 3 blades of mace, 1 onion, 1 lb. of lean beef, a crust of bread toasted brown.

Mode.—Soak the shanks in plenty of water for some hours, and scrub them well ; put them, with the beef and other ingredients, into a saucepan with the water, and let them simmer very gently for 5 hours. Strain the broth, and, when cold, take off all the fat. It may be eaten either warmed up or cold as a jelly.

Time.—5 hours. *Average cost,* 1s.

Sufficient to make from 1½ to 2 pints of jelly.

Seasonable at any time.

LEMONADE FOR INVALIDS.

1870. INGREDIENTS.—½ lemon, lump sugar to taste, 1 pint of boiling water.

Mode.—Pare off the rind of the lemon thinly ; cut the lemon into 2 or 3 thick slices, and remove as much as possible of the white outside pith, and all the pips. Put the slices of lemon, the peel, and lump sugar into a jug ; pour over the boiling water ; cover it closely, and in 2 hours it will be fit to drink. It should either be strained or poured off from the sediment.

Time.—2 hours. *Average cost,* 2d.

Sufficient to make 1 pint of lemonade. *Seasonable* at any time.

NOURISHING LEMONADE.

1871. INGREDIENTS.—1½ pint of boiling water, the juice of 4 lemons, the rinds of 2, ½ pint of sherry, 4 eggs, 6 oz. of loaf sugar.

Mode.—Pare off the lemon-rind thinly, put it into a jug with the sugar, and pour over the boiling water. Let it cool, then strain it; add the wine, lemon-juice, and eggs, previously well beaten, and also strained, and the beverage will be ready for use. If thought desirable, the quantity of sherry and water could be lessened, and milk substituted for them. To obtain the flavour of the lemon-rind properly, a few lumps of the sugar should be rubbed over it, until some of the yellow is absorbed.

Time.—Altogether 1 hour to make it. *Average cost*, 1s. 8d.

Sufficient to make 2½ pints of lemonade. *Seasonable* at any time.

TO MAKE MUTTON BROTH.

1872. INGREDIENTS.—1 lb. of the scrag end of the neck of mutton, 1 onion, a bunch of sweet herbs, ½ turnip, 3 pints of water, pepper and salt to taste.

Mode.—Put the mutton into a stewpan; pour over the water cold, and add the other ingredients. When it boils, skim it very carefully, cover the pan closely, and let it simmer very gently for an hour; strain it, let it cool, take off all the fat from the surface, and warm up as much as may be required, adding, if the patient be allowed to take it, a teaspoonful of minced parsley which has been previously scalded. Pearl barley or rice are very nice additions to mutton broth, and should be boiled as long as the other ingredients. When either of these is added, the broth must not be strained, but merely thoroughly skimmed. Plain mutton broth without seasoning is made by merely boiling the mutton, water, and salt together, straining it, letting the broth cool, skimming all the fat off, and warming up as much as is required. This preparation would be very tasteless and insipid, but likely to agree with very delicate stomachs, whereas the least addition of other ingredients would have the contrary effect.

Time.—1 hour. *Average cost*, 7d.

Sufficient to make from 1⅓ to 2 pints of broth.

Seasonable at any time.

Note.—Veal broth may be made in the same manner; the knuckle of a leg or shoulder is the part usually used for this purpose. It is very good with the addition of the inferior joints of a fowl, or a few shank-bones.

MUTTON BROTH, QUICKLY MADE.

1873. INGREDIENTS.—1 or 2 chops from a neck of mutton, 1 pint of water, a small bunch of sweet herbs, ¼ of an onion, pepper and salt to taste.

Mode.—Cut the meat into small pieces; put it into a saucepan with the bones, but no skin or fat; add the other ingredients; cover the saucepan, and bring the water quickly to boil. Take the lid off, and continue the rapid boiling for 20 minutes, skimming it well during the procees; strain the broth into a basin; if there should be any fat left on the surface, remove it by laying a piece of thin paper on the top: the greasy particles will adhere to the paper, and so free the preparation from them. To an invalid nothing is more disagreeable than broth served with a quantity of fat floating on the top; to avoid this, it is always better to allow it to get thoroughly cool, the fat can then be so easily removed.

Time.—20 minutes after the water boils. *Average cost, 5d.*

Sufficient to make ½ pint of broth. *Seasonable* at any time.

STEWED RABBITS IN MILK.

1874. INGREDIENTS.—2 very young rabbits, not nearly half grown; 1½ pint of milk, 1 blade of mace, 1 dessertspoonful of flour, a little salt and cayenne.

Mode.—Mix the flour very smoothly with 4 tablespoonfuls of the milk, and when this is well mixed, add the remainder. Cut up the rabbits into joints, put them into a stewpan, with the milk and other ingredients, and simmer them *very gently* until quite tender. Stir the contents from time to time, to keep the milk smooth and prevent it from burning. ½ hour will be sufficient for the cooking of this dish.

Time.—½ hour. *Average cost*, from 1s. to 1s. 6d. each.

Sufficient for 3 or 4 meals. *Seasonable* from September to February.

RICE-MILK.

1875. INGREDIENTS.—3 tablespoonfuls of rice, 1 quart of milk, sugar to taste; when liked, a little grated nutmeg.

Mode.—Well wash the rice, put it into a saucepan with the milk, and simmer gently until the rice is tender, stirring it from time to time to prevent the milk from burning; sweeten it, add a little grated nutmeg, and serve. This dish is also very suitable and wholesome for children; it may be flavoured with a little lemon-peel, and a little finely-minced suet may be boiled with it, which renders it more strengthening and more wholesome. Tapioca, semolina, vermicelli, and macaroni, may all be dressed in the same manner.

Time.—From ¾ to 1 hour. *Seasonable* at any time.

TO MAKE TOAST-AND-WATER.

1876. INGREDIENTS.—A slice of bread, 1 quart of boiling water.

Mode.—Cut a slice from a stale loaf (a piece of hard crust is better than anything else for the purpose), toast it of a nice brown on every side, but *do not allow it to burn or blacken.* Put it into a jug, pour the boiling water over it, cover it closely, and let it remain until cold. When strained, it will be ready for use. Toast-and-water should always be made a short time before it is required, to enable it to get cold: if drunk in a tepid or lukewarm state, it is an exceedingly disagreeable beverage. If, as is sometimes the case, this drink is wanted in a hurry, put the toasted bread into a jug, and only just cover it with the boiling water; when this is cool, cold water may be added in the proportion required,—the toast-and-water strained; it will then be ready for use, and is more expeditiously prepared than by the above method.

TOAST SANDWICHES.

1877. INGREDIENTS.—Thin cold toast, thin slices of bread-and-butter, pepper and salt to taste.

Mode.—Place a very thin piece of cold toast between 2 slices of thin bread-and-butter in the form of a sandwich, adding a seasoning of pepper and salt. This sandwich may be varied by adding a little pulled meat, or very fine slices of cold meat, to the toast, and in any of these forms will be found very tempting to the appetite of an invalid.

———

1878. Besides the recipes contained in this chapter, there are, in the previous chapters on cookery, many others suitable for invalids, which it would be useless to repeat here. Recipes, fish simply dressed, light soups, plain roast meat, well-dressed vegetables, poultry, simple puddings, jelly, stewed fruits, &c. &c., all of which dishes may be partaken of by invalids and convalescents, will be found in preceding chapters.

DINNERS AND DINING.

DINNERS AND DINING.

1879. MAN, it has been said, is a dining animal. Creatures of the inferior races eat and drink ; man only dines. It has also been said that he is a cooking animal ; but some races eat food without cooking it. A Croat captain said to M. Brillat Savarin, "When, in campaign, we feel hungry, we knock over the first animal we find, cut off a steak, powder it with salt, put it under the saddle, gallop over it for half a mile, and then eat it." Huntsmen in Dauphiny, when out shooting, have been known to kill a bird, pluck it, salt and pepper it, and cook it by carrying it some time in their caps. It is equally true that some races of men do not dine any more than the tiger or the vulture. It is not a *dinner* at which sits the aboriginal Australian, who gnaws his bone half bare and then flings it behind to his squaw. And the native of Terra-del-Fuego does not dine when he gets his morsel of red clay. Dining is the privilege of civilization. The rank which a people occupy in the grand scale may be measured by their way of taking their meals, as well as by their way of treating their women. The nation which knows how to dine has learnt the leading lesson of progress. It implies both the will and the skill to reduce to order, and surround with idealisms and graces, the more material conditions of human existence ; and wherever that will and that skill exist, life cannot be wholly ignoble.

1880. Dinner, being the grand solid meal of the day, is a matter of considerable importance ; and a well-served table is a striking index of human ingenuity and resource. "Their table," says Lord Byron, in describing a dinner-party given by Lord and Lady Amundeville at Norman Abbey,—

> " Their table was a board to tempt even ghosts
>   To pass the Styx for more substantial feasts.
> I will not dwell upon ragoûts or roasts,
>   Albeit all human history attests
> That happiness for man—the hungry sinner !—
> Since Eve ate apples, much depends on dinner."

And then he goes on to observe upon the curious complexity of the results produced by human cleverness and application catering for the modifications which occur in civilized life, one of the simplest of the primal instincts :—

> " The mind is lost in mighty contemplation
>   Of intellect expended on two courses ;
> And indigestion's grand multiplication
>   Requires arithmetic beyond my forces.
> Who would suppose, from Adam's simple ration,
>   That cookery could have call'd forth such resources,
> As form a science and a nomenclature
> From out the commonest demands of nature ? "

And we may well say, Who, indeed, would suppose it? The gulf between the Croat, with a steak under his saddle, and Alexis Soyer getting up a great dinner at the Reform Club, or even Thackeray's Mrs. Raymond Gray giving "a little dinner" to Mr. Snob (with one of those famous "roly-poly puddings" of hers),—what a gulf it is!

1881. That Adam's "ration," however, was "simple," is a matter on which we have contrary judgments given by the poets. When Raphael paid that memorable visit to Paradise,—which we are expressly told by Milton he did exactly at dinner-time,—Eve seems to have prepared "a little dinner" not wholly destitute of complexity, and to have added ice-creams and perfumes. Nothing can be clearer than the testimony of the poet on these points :—

> " And Eve within, due at her home prepared
> For dinner savoury fruits, of taste to please
> True appetite, and not disrelish thirst
> Of nectarous draughts between. . . . .
> . . . With dispatchful looks in haste
> She turns, on hospitable thoughts intent,
> What choice to choose for delicacy best,
> What order so contrived as not to mix
> Tastes not well join'd, inelegant, but bring
> Taste after taste, upheld with kindliest change—
> *   *   *   *   *
> She *tempers dulcet creams* . . . . .
> . . . . . . *then strews the ground*
> *With rose and odours.*"

It may be observed, in passing, that the poets, though they have more to say about wine than solid food, because the former more directly stimulates the intellect and the feelings, do not flinch from the subject of eating and drinking. There is infinite zest in the above passage from Milton, and even more in the famous description of a dainty supper, given by Keats in his "Eve of Saint Agnes." Could Queen Mab herself desire to sit down to anything nicer, both as to its appointments and serving, and as to its quality, than the collation served by Porphyro in the lady's bedroom while she slept ?—

> " There by the bedside, where the faded moon
> Made a dim silver twilight, soft he set
> A table, and, half-anguish'd, threw thereon
> A cloth of woven crimson, gold, and jet.
> *   *   *   *   *
> While he, from forth the closet, brought a heap
> Of candied apple, quince, and plum, and gourd;
> With jellies smoother than the creamy curd,
> And lucent syrups tinct with cinnamon ;
> Manna and dates, in argosy transferr'd
> From Fez ; and spicèd dainties, every one,
> From silken Samarcand to cedar'd Lebanon."

But Tennyson has ventured beyond dates, and quinces, and syrups, which may be thought easy to be brought in by a poet. In his idyl of "Audley Court" he gives a most appetizing description of a pasty at a pic-nic :—

> " There, on a slope of orchard, Francis laid
> A damask napkin wrought with horse and hound ;
> Brought out a dusky loaf that smelt of home,
> And, half cut down, a pasty costly made,
> Where quail and pigeon, lark and leveret, lay
> Like fossils of the rock, with golden yolks
> Imbedded and injellied."

We gladly quote passages like these, to show how eating and drinking may be surrounded with poetical associations, and how man, using his privilege to turn any and every repast into a "feast of reason," with a warm and plentiful "flow of soul," may really count it as not the least of his legitimate prides, that he is "a dining animal."

1882. It has been said, indeed, that great men, in general, are great diners. This, however, can scarcely be true of any great men but men of action; and, in that case, it would simply imply that persons of vigorous constitution, who work hard, eat heartily; for, of course, a life of action *requires* a vigorous constitution, even though there may be much illness, as in such cases as William III. and our brave General Napier. Of men of thought, it can scarcely be true that they eat so much, in a general way, though even they eat more than they are apt to suppose they do; for, as Mr. Lewes observes, "nerve-tissue is very expensive." Leaving great men of all kinds, however, to get their own dinners, let us, who are not great, look after ours. Dine we must, and we may as well dine elegantly as well as wholesomely.

1883. There are plenty of elegant dinners in modern days, and they were not wanting in ancient times. It is well known that the dinner-party, or symposium, was a not unimportant, and not unpoetical, feature in the life of the sociable, talkative, tasteful Greek. Douglas Jerrold said that such is the British humour for dining and giving of dinners, that if London were to be destroyed by an earthquake, the Londoners would meet at a public dinner to consider the subject. The Greeks, too, were great diners: their social and religious polity gave them many chances of being merry and making others merry on good eating and drinking. Any public or even domestic sacrifice to one of the gods, was sure to be followed by a dinner-party, the remains of the slaughtered "offering" being served up on the occasion as a pious *pièce de résistance;* and as the different gods, goddesses, and demigods, worshipped by the community in general, or by individuals, were very numerous indeed, and some very religious people never let a day pass without offering up something or other, the dinner-parties were countless. A birthday, too, was an excuse for a dinner; a birthday, that is, of any person long dead and buried, as well as of a living person, being a member of the family, or otherwise esteemed. Dinners were, of course, eaten on all occasions of public rejoicing. Then, among the young people, subscription dinners, very much after the manner of modern times, were always being got up; only that they would be eaten not at an hotel, but probably at the house of one of the *heteræ*. A Greek dinner-party was a handsome, well-regulated affair. The guests came in elegantly dressed and crowned with flowers. A slave, approaching each person as he entered, took off his sandals and washed his feet. During the repast, the guests reclined on couches with pillows, among and along which were set small tables. After the solid meal came the "symposium" proper, a scene of music, merriment, and dancing, the two latter being supplied chiefly by young girls. There was a chairman, or symposiarch, appointed by the company to regulate the drinking ; and it was his duty to mix the wine in the "mighty bowl." From this bowl the attendants ladled the liquor into goblets, and, with the goblets, went round and round the tables, filling the cups of the guests.

1884. The elegance with which a dinner is served is a matter which depends, of course, partly upon the means, but still more upon the taste of the master and mistress of the house. It may be observed, in general, that there should always be flowers on the table, and as they form no item of expense, there is no reason why they should not be employed every day.

1885. The variety in the dishes which furnish forth a modern dinner-table, does not necessarily imply anything unwholesome, or anything capricious. Food that is not well relished cannot be well digested ; and the appetite of the over-worked man of business, or statesman, or of any dweller in towns, whose occupations are exciting and exhausting, is jaded, and requires stimulation. Men and women who are in rude health, and who have plenty of air and exercise, eat the simplest food with relish, and consequently digest it well ; but those conditions are out of the reach of many men. They must suit their mode of dining to their mode of living, if they cannot choose the latter. It is in serving up food that is at once appetizing and wholesome that the skill of the modern housewife is severely tasked ; and she has scarcely a more important duty to fulfil. It is, in fact, her particular vocation, in virtue of which she may be said to hold the health of the family, and of the friends of the family, in her hands from day to day. It has been said that "the destiny of nations depends on the manner in which they are fed ;" and a great gastronomist exclaims, "Tell me what kind of food you eat, and I will tell you what kind of man you are." The same writer has some sentences of the same kind, which are rather hyperbolical, but worth quoting :—" The pleasures of the table belong to all ages, to all conditions, to all countries, and to all eras ; they mingle with all other pleasures, and remain, at last, to console us for their departure. The discovery of a new dish confers more happiness upon humanity than the discovery of a new star."

1886. The gastronomist from whom we have already quoted, has some aphorisms and short directions in relation to dinner-parties, which are well deserving of notice :—" Let the number of your guests never exceed twelve, so that the conversation may be general.* Let the temperature of the dining-room be about 68°. Let the dishes be few in number in the first course, but proportionally good. The order of food is from the most substantial to the lightest. The order of drinking wine is from the mildest to the most foamy and most perfumed. To invite a person to your house is to take charge of his happiness so long as he is beneath your roof. The mistress of the house should always be certain that the coffee be excellent ; whilst the master should be answerable for the quality of his wines and liqueurs."

* We have seen this varied by saying that the number should never exceed that of the Muses or fall below that of the Graces.

BILLS OF FARE.

JANUARY.

1887.—DINNER FOR 18 PERSONS.

First Course.

Stewed Eels.

Mock Turtle Soup,
removed by
Cod's Head and Shoulders.

Vase of
Flowers.

Clear Oxtail Soup,
removed by
Fried Filleted Soles.

Red Mullet.

Entrées.

Ragoût of Lobster.

Riz de Veau aux
Tomates.

Vase of
Flowers.

Poulet à la Marengo.

Cotelettes de Pore
à la Robert.

Second Course.

Boiled Turkey and
Celery Sauce.

Roast Turkey.

Pigeon Pie.

Vase of
Flowers.

Tongue, garnished.

Saddle of Mutton.

Boiled Ham.

Third Course.

Charlotte
à la Parisienne.

Cream.

Pheasants,
removed by
Plum-pudding.

Jelly.

Vase of
Flowers.

Jelly.

Snipes,
removed by
Pommes à la Condé.

Mince
Pies.

Cream.

Apricot-Jam
Tartlets.

Maids
of Honour.

We have given above the plan of placing the various dishes of the 1st Course, Entrées, 2nd Course, and 3rd Course. Following this will be found bills of fare for smaller parties; and it will be readily seen, by studying the above arrangement of dishes, how to place a less number for the more limited company. Several *menus* for dinners *à la Russe,* are also included in the present chapter.

1888.—DINNER FOR 12 PERSONS (January).

First Course.

Carrot Soup à la Crécy.   Oxtail Soup.
Turbot and Lobster Sauce.   Fried Smelts, with Dutch Sauce.

Entrees.

Mutton Cutlets, with Soubise Sauce.   Sweetbreads.
Oyster Patties.   Fillets of Rabbits.

Second Course.

Roast Turkey.   Stewed Rump of Beef à la Jardinière.
Boiled Ham, garnished with Brussels Sprouts.
Boiled Chickens and Celery Sauce.

Third Course.

Roast Hare.   Teal.
Eggs à la Neige.   Vol-au-Vent of Preserved Fruit.   1 Jelly.   1 Cream.
Potatoes à la Maître d'Hôtel.   Grilled Mushrooms.

Dessert and Ices.

1889.—DINNER FOR 10 PERSONS (January).

First Course.

Soup à la Reine.
Whitings au Gratin.   Crimped Cod and Oyster Sauce.

Entrees.

Tendrons de Veau.   Curried Fowl and Boiled Rice.

Second Course.

Turkey, stuffed with Chestnuts, and Chestnut Sauce.
Boiled Leg of Mutton, English Fashion, with Capers Sauce and
Mashed Turnips.

Third Course.

Woodcocks or Partridges.   Widgeon.
Charlotte à la Vanille.   Cabinet Pudding.   Orange Jelly.   Blancmange.
Artichoke Bottoms.   Macaroni, with Parmesan Cheese.

Dessert and Ices.

1890.—DINNER FOR 8 PERSONS (January).

First Course.
Mulligatawny Soup.

Brill and Shrimp Sauce.   Fried Whitings.

Entrees.
Fricasseed Chicken.   Pork Cutlets, with Tomato Sauce.

Second Course.
Haunch of Mutton.   Boiled Turkey and Celery Sauce.

Boiled Tongue, garnished with Brussels Sprouts.

Third Course.
Roast Pheasants.

Meringues à la Crême.   Compôte of Apples.   Orange Jelly.

Cheesecakes.   Soufflé of Rice.

Dessert and Ices.

1891.—DINNER FOR 6 PERSONS (January).—I.

First Course.
Julienne Soup.

Soles à la Normandie.

Entrees.
Sweetbreads, with Sauce Piquante.   Mutton Cutlets, with Mashed Potatoes.

Second Course.
Haunch of Venison.

Boiled-Fowls and Bacon, garnished with Brussels Sprouts.

Third Course.
Plum-pudding.   Custards in Glasses.   Apple Tart.

Fondue à la Brillat Savarin.

Dessert.

1892.—DINNER FOR 6 PERSONS (January).—II.

First Course.
Vermicelli Soup.
Fried Slices of Codfish and Anchovy Sauce.   John Dory.

Entrees.
Stewed Rump-steak à la Jardinière.   Rissoles.   Oyster Patties.

Second Course.
Leg of Mutton.   Curried Rabbit and Boiled Rice.

Third Course.
Partridges.
Apple Fritters.   Tartlets of Greengage Jam.   Orange Jelly.   Plum-pudding

Dessert.

1893.—DINNER FOR 6 PERSONS (January).—III.

First Course.
Pea-soup.
Baked Haddock.   Soles à la Crême.

Entrees.
Mutton Cutlets and Tomato Sauce.   Fricasseed Rabbit.

Second Course.
Roast Pork and Apple Sauce.   Breast of Veal, Rolled and Stuffed.
Vegetables.

Third Course.
Jugged Hare.
Whipped Cream.   Blancmange.   Mince Pies.   Cabinet Pudding.

1894.—DINNER FOR 6 PERSONS (January).—IV.

First Course.
Palestine Soup.
Fried Smelts.   Stewed Eels.

Entrees.
Ragoût of Lobster.   Broiled Mushrooms.   Vol-au-Vent of Chicken.

Second Course.
Sirloin of Beef.   Boiled Fowls and Celery Sauce.
Tongue, garnished with Brussels Sprouts.

Third Course.
Wild Ducks.   Charlotte aux Pommes.
Cheesecakes.   Transparent Jelly, inlaid with Brandy Cherries.
Blancmange.   Nesselrode Pudding.

PLAIN FAMILY DINNERS FOR JANUARY.

1895. *Sunday.*—1. Boiled turbot and oyster sauce, potatoes. 2. Roast leg or griskin of pork, apple sauce, brocoli, potatoes. 3. Cabinet pudding, and damson tart made with preserved damsons.

1896. *Monday.*—1. The remains of turbot warmed in oyster sauce, potatoes. 2. Cold pork, stewed steak. 3. Open jam tart, which should have been made with the pieces of paste left from the damson tart; baked arrowroot pudding.

1897. *Tuesday.*—1. Boiled neck of mutton, carrots, mashed turnips, suet dumplings, and caper sauce : the broth should be served first, and a little rice or pearl barley should be boiled with it along with the meat. 2. Rolled jam pudding.

1898. *Wednesday.*—1. Roast rolled ribs of beef, greens, potatoes, and horse-radish sauce. 2. Bread-and-butter pudding, cheesecakes.

1899. *Thursday.*—1. Vegetable soup (the bones from the ribs of beef should be boiled down with this soup), cold beef, mashed potatoes. 2. Pheasants, gravy, bread sauce. 3. Macaroni.

1900. *Friday.*—1. Fried whitings or soles. 2. Boiled rabbit and onion sauce, minced beef, potatoes. 3. Currant dumplings.

1901. *Saturday.*—1. Rump-steak pudding or pie, greens, and potatoes. 2. Baked custard pudding and stewed apples.

1902. *Sunday.*—1. Codfish and oyster sauce, potatoes. 2. Joint of roast mutton, either leg, haunch, or saddle; brocoli and potatoes, red-currant jelly. 3. Apple tart and custards, cheese.

1903. *Monday.*—1. The remains of codfish picked from the bone, and warmed through in the oyster sauce; if there is no sauce left, order a few oysters and make a little fresh; and do not let the fish boil, or it will be watery. 2. Curried rabbit, with boiled rice served separately, cold mutton, mashed potatoes. 3. Somersetshire dumplings with wine sauce.

1904. *Tuesday.*—1. Boiled fowls, parsley-and-butter; bacon garnished with Brussels sprouts, minced or hashed mutton. 2. Baroness pudding.

1905. *Wednesday.*—1. The remains of the fowls cut up into joints and fricas-seed : joint of roast pork and apple sauce, and, if liked, sage-and-onion, served on a dish by itself; turnips and potatoes. 2. Lemon pudding, either baked or boiled.

1906. *Thursday.*—1. Cold pork and jugged hare, red-currant jelly, mashed potatoes. 2. Apple pudding.

1907. *Friday.*—1. Boiled beef, either the aitchbone or the silver side of the round ; carrots, turnips, suet dumplings, and potatoes : if there is a marrow-bone, serve the marrow on toast at the same time. 2. Rice snowballs.

1908. *Saturday.*—1. Pea-soup made from liquor in which beef was boiled ; cold beef, mashed potatoes. 2. Baked batter fruit pudding.

FEBRUARY.

1909.—DINNER FOR 18 PERSONS.

First Course.   *Entrées.*

Fried Eels.

Hare Soup,
removed by
Turbot and Oyster Sauce.

Fried Whitings.

**Vase of
Flowers.**

Oyster Soup,
removed by
Crimped Cod à la Maître
d'Hôtel.

Lobster Patties.

Lark Pudding.

**Vase of
Flowers.**

Fricasseed Chicken.

Filets de Perdrix.

Second Course.   *Third Course.*

Roast Fowls, garnished with Water-cresses.

**Braised Capon.
Boiled Ham, garnished.**

Boiled Fowls and White Sauce.

**Vase of
Flowers.**

**Pâté Chaud.
Haunch of Mutton.**

Meringues.

Orange Jelly.

Victoria Sandwiches.

Ducklings,
removed by
Ice Pudding.

Coffee Cream.

**Vase of
Flowers.**

Blancmange.

Partridges,
removed by
Cabinet Pudding.

Clear Jelly.

Cheese-cakes.

Gâteau de Pommes.

Dessert and Ices.

1910.—DINNER FOR 12 PERSONS (February).

First Course.

Soup à la Reine.   Clear Gravy Soup.

Brill and Lobster Sauce.   Fried Smelts.

Entrees.

Lobster Rissoles.   Beef Palates.   Pork Cutlets à la Soubise.

Grilled Mushrooms.

Second Course.

Braised Turkey.   Haunch of Mutton.   Boiled Capon and Oysters.

Tongue, garnished with tufts of Brocoli.   Vegetables and Salads.

Third Course.

Wild Ducks.   Plovers.

Orange Jelly.   Clear Jelly.   Charlotte Russe.   Nesselrode Pudding.

Gâteau de Riz.   Sea-kale.   Maids of Honour.

Dessert and Ices.

1911.—DINNER FOR 10 PERSONS (February).

First Course.
Palestine Soup.
John Dory, with Dutch Sauce.   Red Mullet, with Sauce Génoise.

Entrees.
Sweetbread Cutlets, with Poivrade Sauce.   Fowl au Béchamel.

Second Course.
Roast Saddle of Mutton.   Boiled Capon and Oysters.
Boiled Tongue, garnished with Brussels Sprouts.

Third Course.
Guinea-Fowls.   Ducklings.
Pain de Rhubarb.   Orange Jelly.   Strawberry Cream.   Cheesecakes.
Almond Pudding.   Fig Pudding.

Dessert and Ices.

1912.—DINNER FOR 8 PERSONS (February).

First Course.
Mock Turtle Soup.
Fillets of Turbot à la Crême.   Fried Filleted Soles and Anchovy Sauce.

Entrees.
Larded Fillets of Rabbits.   Tendrons de Veau with Purée of Tomatoes.

Second Course.
Stewed Rump of Beef à la Jardinière.   Roast Fowls.   Boiled Ham.

Third Course.
Roast Pigeons or Larks.
Rhubarb Tartlets.   Meringues.   Clear Jelly.   Cream.   Ice Pudding.   Soufflé.

Dessert and Ices.

1913.—DINNER FOR 6 PERSONS (February).—I.

First Course.
Rice Soup.
Red Mullet, with Génoise Sauce.   Fried Smelts.

Entrees.
Fowl Pudding.   Sweetbreads.

Second Course.
Roast Turkey and Sausages.   Boiled Leg of Pork.   Pease Pudding.

Third Course.
Lemon Jelly.   Charlotte à la Vanille.   Maids of Honour.
Plum-pudding, removed by Ice Pudding.

Dessert.
3 N 2

1914.—DINNER FOR 6 PERSONS (February).—II.

First Course.
Spring Soup.
Boiled Turbot and Lobster Sauce.

Entrees.
Fricasseed Rabbit.   Oyster Patties.

Second Course.
Boiled Round of Beef and Marrow-bones.
Roast Fowls, garnished with Water-cresses and rolled Bacon.   Vegetables.

Third Course.
Marrow Pudding.   Cheesecakes.   Tartlets of Greengage Jam.
Lemon Cream.   Rhubarb Tart.

Dessert.

1915.—DINNER FOR 6 PERSONS (February).—III.

First Course.
Vermicelli Soup.
Fried Whitings.   Stewed Eels.

Entrees.
Poulet à la Marengo.   Breast of Veal stuffed and rolled.

Second Course.
Roast Leg of Pork and Apple Sauce.   Boiled Capon and Oysters.
Tongue, garnished with tufts of Brocoli.

Third Course.
Wild Ducks.   Lobster Salad.   Charlotte aux Pommes.   Pain de Rhubarb.
Vanilla Cream.   Orange Jelly.

Dessert.

1916.—DINNER FOR 6 PERSONS (February).—IV.

First Course.
Ox-tail Soup.
Cod à la Crême.   Fried Soles.

Entrees.
Lark Pudding.   Fowl Scollops.

Second Course.
Roast Leg of Mutton.   Boiled Turkey and Celery Sauce.   Pigeon Pie.
Small Ham, boiled and garnished.   Vegetables.

Third Course.
Game, when liked.   Tartlets of Raspberry Jam.   Vol-au-Vent of Rhubarb.
Swiss Cream.   Cabinet Pudding.
Brocoli and Sea-kale.

Dessert.

PLAIN FAMILY DINNERS FOR FEBRUARY

1917. *Sunday.*—1. Ox-tail soup. 2 Roast beef, Yorkshire pudding, brocoli, and potatoes. 3. Plum-pudding, apple tart. Cheese.

1918. *Monday.*—1. Fried soles, plain melted butter, and potatoes. 2. Cold roast beef, mashed potatoes. 3. The remains of plum-pudding cut in slices, warmed, and served with sifted sugar sprinkled over it. Cheese.

1919. *Tuesday.*—1. The remains of ox-tail soup from Sunday. 2. Pork cutlets with tomato sauce ; hashed beef. 3. Rolled jam pudding. Cheese.

1920. *Wednesday.*—1. Boiled haddock and plain melted butter. 2. Rump-steak pudding, potatoes, greens. 3. Arrowroot, blancmange, garnished with jam.

1921. *Thursday.*—1. Boiled leg of pork, greens, potatoes, pease pudding. 2. Apple fritters, sweet macaroni.

1922. *Friday.*—1. Pea-soup made with liquor that the pork was boiled in. 2. Cold pork, mashed potatoes. 3. Baked rice pudding.

1923. *Saturday.*—1. Broiled herrings and mustard sauce. 2. Haricot mutton. 3. Macaroni, either served as a sweet pudding or with cheese.

1924. *Sunday.*—1. Carrot soup. 2. Boiled leg of mutton and caper sauce, mashed turnips, roast fowls, and bacon. 3. Damson tart made with bottled fruit, ratafia pudding.

1925. *Monday.*—1. The remainder of fowl curried and served with rice ; rump-steaks and oyster sauce, cold mutton. 2. Rolled jam pudding.

1926. *Tuesday.*—1. Vegetable soup made with liquor that the mutton was boiled in on Sunday. 2. Roast sirloin of beef, Yorkshire pudding, brocoli, and potatoes. 3. Cheese.

1927. *Wednesday.*—1. Fried soles, melted butter. 2. Cold beef and mashed potatoes : if there is any cold boiled mutton left, cut it into neat slices and warm it in a little caper sauce. 3. Apple tart.

1928. *Thursday.*—1. Boiled rabbit and onion sauce, stewed beef and vegetables, made with the remains of cold beef and bones. 2. Macaroni.

1929. *Friday.*—1. Roast leg of pork, sage and onions and apple sauce ; greens and potatoes. 2. Spinach and poached eggs instead of pudding. Cheese and water-cresses.

1930. *Saturday.*—1. Rumpsteak-and-kidney pudding, cold pork and mashed potatoes. 2. Baked rice pudding.

MARCH.

1931.—DINNER FOR 18 PERSONS.

First Course.   *Entrées.*

Red Mullet.	Turtle or Mock Turtle Soup, removed by Salmon and dressed Cucumber. Vase of Flowers. Spring Soup, removed by Boiled Turbot and Lobster Sauce.	Fillets of Whitings.

Vol-au-Vent.	Fricasseed Chicken. Vase of Flowers. Larded Sweetbreads.	Compôte of Pigeons.

Second Course.   *Third Course.*

Boiled Tongue, garnished.	Fore-quarter of Lamb. Braised Capon. Vase of Flowers. Roast Fowls. Rump of Beef à la Jardinière.	Ham.

Apricot Tartlets.	Guinea-Fowls, larded, removed by Cabinet Pudding. Wine Jelly. Vase of Flowers. Italian Cream. Ducklings, removed by Nesselrode Pudding.	Rhubarb Tart.
Custards.		Jelly, in glasses.
Damson Tart.		Cheese-cakes.

Dessert and Ices.

1932.—DINNER FOR 12 PERSONS (March).

First Course.

White Soup.   Clear Gravy Soup.
Boiled Salmon, Shrimp Sauce, and dressed Cucumber.
Baked Mullets in paper cases.

Entrees.

Filet de Bœuf and Spanish Sauce.   Larded Sweetbreads.   Rissoles.
Chicken Patties.

Second Course.

Roast Fillet of Veal and Béchamel Sauce.   Boiled Leg of Lamb.
Roast Fowls, garnished with Water-cresses.
Boiled Ham, garnished with Carrots and mashed Turnips.
Vegetables—Sea-kale, Spinach, or Brocoli.

Third Course.

Two Ducklings.   Guinea-Fowl, larded.
Orange Jelly.   Charlotte Russe.   Coffee Cream.   Ice Pudding.
Macaroni with Parmesan Cheese.   Spinach, garnished with Croûtons.

Dessert and Ices.

1933.—DINNER FOR 10 PERSONS (March).
First Course.
Macaroni Soup.

Boiled Turbot and Lobster Sauce.   Salmon Cutlets.

Entrees.
Compôte of Pigeons.   Mutton Cutlets and Tomato Sauce.

Second Course.
Roast Lamb.   Boiled Half Calf's Head, Tongue, and Brains.

Boiled Bacon-cheek, garnished with spoonfuls of Spinach.   Vegetables.

Third Course.
Ducklings.

Plum-pudding.   Ginger Cream.   Trifle.   Rhubarb Tart.   Cheesecakes.

Fondues, in cases.

Dessert and Ices.

1934.—DINNER FOR 8 PERSONS (March).
First Course.
Calf's-Head Soup.

Brill and Shrimp Sauce.   Broiled Mackerel à la Maître d'Hôtel.

Entrees.
Lobster Cutlets.   Calf's Liver and Bacon, aux fines herbes.

Second Course.
Roast Loin of Veal. Two Boiled Fowls à la Béchamel. Boiled Knuckle of Ham.

Vegetables—Spinach or Brocoli.

Third Course.
Wild Ducks.

Apple Custards.   Blancmange.   Lemon Jelly.   Jam Sandwiches.

Ice Pudding.   Potatoes à la Maître d'Hôtel.

Dessert and Ices.

1935.—DINNER FOR 6 PERSONS (March).—I.
First Course.
Vermicelli Soup.

Soles à la Crême.

Entrees.
Veal Cutlets.   Small Vols-au-Vent.

Second Course.
Small Saddle of Mutton.   Half Calf's Head.

Boiled Bacon-cheek, garnished with Brussels Sprouts.

Third Course.
Cabinet Pudding.   Orange Jelly.   Custards, in glasses.

Rhubarb Tart.   Lobster Salad.

Dessert.

1936.—DINNER FOR 6 PERSONS (March).—II.

First Course.

Julienne Soup.

Baked Mullets.

Entrees.

Chicken Cutlets.   Oyster Patties.

Second Course.

Roast Lamb and Mint Sauce.   Boiled Leg of Pork.

Pease Pudding.   Vegetables.

Third Course.

Ducklings.

Swiss Cream.   Lemon Jelly.   Cheesecakes.   Rhubarb Tart.   Macaroni.

Dessert.

1937.—DINNER FOR 6 PERSONS (March).—III.

First Course.

Oyster Soup.

Boiled Salmon and dressed Cucumber.

Entrees.

Rissoles.   Fricasseed Chicken.

Second Course.

Boiled Leg of Mutton, Caper Sauce.   Roast Fowls, garnished with Water-cresses.

Vegetables.

Third Course.

Charlotte aux Pommes.   Orange Jelly.   Lemon Cream.

Soufflé of Arrowroot.   Sea-kale.

Dessert.

1938.—DINNER FOR 6 PERSONS (March).—IV.

First Course.

Ox-tail Soup.

Boiled Mackerel.

Entrees.

Stewed Mutton Kidneys.   Minced Veal and Oysters.

Second Course.

Stewed Shoulder of Veal.   Roast Ribs of Beef and Horseradish Sauce.

Vegetables.

Third Course.

Ducklings.

Tartlets of Strawberry Jam.   Cheesecakes.   Gâteau de Riz.

Carrot Pudding.   Sea-kale.

Dessert.

PLAIN FAMILY DINNERS FOR MARCH.

1939. *Sunday.*—1. Boiled ½ calf's head, pickled pork, the tongue on a small dish with the brains round it ; mutton cutlets and mashed potatoes. 2. Plum tart made with bottled fruit, baked custard pudding, Baroness pudding.

1940. *Monday.*—1. Roast shoulder of mutton and onion sauce, brocoli, baked potatoes. 2. Slices of Baroness pudding warmed, and served with sugar sprinkled over. Cheesecakes.

1941. *Tuesday.*—1. Mock turtle soup, made with liquor that calf's head was boiled in, and the pieces of head. 2. Hashed mutton, rump-steaks and oyster sauce. 3. Boiled plum-pudding.

1942. *Wednesday.*—1. Fried whitings, melted butter, potatoes. 2. Boiled beef, suet dumplings, carrots, potatoes, marrow-bones. 3. Arrowroot blanc-mange, and stewed rhubarb.

1943. *Thursday.*—1. Pea-soup made from liquor that beef was boiled in. 2. Stewed rump-steak, cold beef, mashed potatoes. 3. Rolled jam pudding.

1944. *Friday.*—1. Fried soles, melted butter, potatoes. 2. Roast loin of mutton, brocoli, potatoes, bubble-and-squeak. 3. Rice pudding.

1945. *Saturday.*—1. Rump-steak pie, haricot mutton made with remains of cold loin. 2. Pancakes, ratafia pudding.

1946. *Sunday.*—1. Roast fillet of veal, boiled ham, spinach and potatoes. 2. Rhubarb tart, custards in glasses, bread-and-butter pudding.

1947. *Monday.*—1. Baked soles, potatoes. 2. Minced veal and rump-steak pie. 3. Somersetshire dumplings with the remains of custards poured round them ; marmalade tartlets.

1948. *Tuesday.*—1. Gravy soup. 2. Boiled leg of mutton, mashed turnips, suet dumplings, caper sauce, potatoes, veal rissoles made with remains of fillet of veal. 3. Cheese.

1949. *Wednesday.*—1. Stewed mullets. 2. Roast fowls, bacon, gravy, and bread sauce, mutton pudding, made with a few slices of the cold meat and the addition of two kidneys. 3. Baked lemon pudding.

1950. *Thursday.*—1. Vegetable soup made with liquor that the mutton was boiled in, and mixed with the remains of gravy soup. 2. Roast ribs of beef, Yorkshire pudding, horseradish sauce, brocoli and potatoes. 3. Apple pudding or macaroni.

1951. *Friday.*—1. Stewed eels, pork cutlets and tomato sauce. 2. Cold beef, mashed potatoes. 3. Plum tart made with bottled fruit.

1952. *Saturday.*—1. Rumpsteak-and-kidney pudding, broiled beef-bones, greens and potatoes. 2. Jam tartlets made with pieces of paste from plum tart, baked custard pudding.

APRIL.

1953.—DINNER FOR 18 PERSONS.

First Course.   *Entrées.*

Fillets of Mackerel.	Spring Soup, removed by Salmon and Lobster Sauce.		Fried Smelts.
	Vase of Flowers.		
	Soles à la Crème.		

Curried Lobster.	Lamb Cutlets and Asparagus Peas.		Oyster Patties.
	Vase of Flowers.		
	Grenadines de Veau.		

Second Course.   *Third Course.*

Stewed Beef à la Jardinière.	Roast Ribs of Lamb.		Boiled Ham.
	Larded Capon.		
	Vase of Flowers.		
	Spring Chickens.		
	Braised Turkey.		

Raspberry-Jam Tartlets.	Clear Jelly.	Ducklings, removed by Cabinet Pudding.	Orange Jelly.	Rhubarb Tart.
		Charlotte à la Parisienne.		
	Victoria Sandwiches.	Vase of Flowers.		Cheese-cakes.
		Raspberry Cream.		
		Nesselrode Pudding.		

Dessert and Ices.

1954.—DINNER FOR 12 PERSONS (April).

First Course.

Soup à la Reine.   Julienne Soup.

Turbot and Lobster Sauce.   Slices of Salmon à la Genévése.

Entrees.

Croquettes of Leveret.   Fricandeau de Veau.

Vol-au-Vent.   Stewed Mushrooms.

Second Course.

Fore-quarter of Lamb.   Saddle of Mutton.   Boiled Chickens and Asparagus Peas.

Boiled Tongue garnished with Tufts of Brocoli.   Vegetables.

Third Course.

Ducklings.   Larded Guinea-Fowls.   Charlotte à la Parisienne.   Orange Jelly.

Meringues.   Ratafia Ice Pudding.   Lobster Salad.   Sea-kale.

Dessert and Ices.

1955.—DINNER FOR 10 PERSONS (April).

First Course.
Gravy Soup.
Salmon and Dressed Cucumber.   Shrimp Sauce.   Fillets of Whitings.

Entrees.
Lobster Cutlets.   Chicken Patties.

Second Course.
Roast Fillet of Veal.   Boiled Leg of Lamb.   Ham, garnished with Brocoli.
Vegetables.

Third Course.
Ducklings.
Compôte of Rhubarb.   Custards.   Vanilla Cream.   Orange Jelly.
Cabinet Pudding.   Ice Pudding.

Dessert.

1956.—DINNER FOR 8 PERSONS (April).

First Course.
Spring Soup.
Slices of Salmon and Caper Sauce.   Fried Filleted Soles.

Entrees.
Chicken Vol-au-Vent.   Mutton Cutlets and Tomato Sauce.

Second Course.
Roast Loin of Veal.   Boiled Fowls à la Béchamel.   Tongue.   Vegetables.

Third Course.
Guinea-Fowl.
Sea-kale.   Artichoke Bottoms.   Cabinet Pudding.   Blancmange.
Apricot Tartlets.   Rice Fritters.   Macaroni and Parmesan Cheese.

Dessert.

1957.—DINNER FOR 6 PERSONS (April).—I.

First Course.
Tapioca Soup.
Boiled Salmon and Lobster Sauce.

Entrees.
Sweetbreads.   Oyster Patties.

Second Course.
Haunch of Mutton.   Boiled Capon and White Sauce.   Tongue.   Vegetables.

Third Course.
Soufflé of Rice.   Lemon Cream.   Charlotte à la Parisienne.   Rhubarb Tart.

Dessert.

1958.—DINNER FOR 6 PERSONS (April).—II.

First Course.
Julienne Soup.

Fried Whitings.   Red Mullet.

Entrees.
Lamb Cutlets and Cucumbers.   Rissoles.

Second Course.
Roast Ribs of Beef.   Neck of Veal à la Béchamel.   Vegetables.

Third Course.
Ducklings.

Lemon Pudding.   Rhubarb Tart.   Custards.   Cheesecakes.

Dessert.

1959.—DINNER FOR 6 PERSONS (April).—III.

First Course.
Vermicelli Soup.

Brill and Shrimp Sauce.

Entrees.
Fricandeau of Veal.   Lobster Cutlets.

Second Course.
Roast Fore-quarter of Lamb.   Boiled Chickens.   Tongue.   Vegetables.

Third Course.
Goslings.

Sea-kale.   Plum-pudding.   Whipped Cream.
Compôte of Rhubarb.   Cheesecakes.

Dessert.

1960.—DINNER FOR 6 PERSONS (April).—IV.

First Course.
Ox-tail Soup.

Crimped Salmon.

Entrees.
Croquettes of Chicken.   Mutton Cutlets and Soubise Sauce.

Second Course.
Roast Fillet of Veal.   Boiled Bacon-cheek garnished with Sprouts.
Boiled Capon.   Vegetables.

Third Course.
Sea-kale.   Lobster Salad.   Cabinet Pudding.   Ginger Cream.
Raspberry Jam Tartlets.   Rhubarb Tart.   Macaroni.

Dessert.

PLAIN FAMILY DINNERS FOR APRIL.

1961. *Sunday.*—1. Clear gravy soup. 2. Roast haunch of mutton, sea-kale, potatoes. 3. Rhubarb tart, custards in glasses.

1962. *Monday.*—1. Crimped skate and caper sauce. 2. Boiled knuckle of veal and rice, cold mutton, mashed potatoes. 3. Baked plum-pudding.

1963. *Tuesday.*—1. Vegetable soup. 2. Toad-in-the-hole, made from remains of cold mutton. 3. Stewed rhubarb and baked custard pudding.

1964. *Wednesday.*—1. Fried soles, anchovy sauce. 2. Boiled beef, carrots, suet dumplings. 3. Lemon pudding.

1965. *Thursday.*—1. Pea-soup made with liquor that beef was boiled in. 2. Cold beef, mashed potatoes, mutton cutlets and tomato sauce. 3. Macaroni.

1966. *Friday.*—1. Bubble-and-squeak, made with remains of cold beef. Roast shoulder of veal stuffed, spinach, potatoes. 2. Boiled batter pudding and sweet sauce.

1967. *Saturday.*—1. Stewed veal with vegetables, made from the remains of the shoulder. Broiled rump-steaks and oyster sauce. 2. Yeast-dumplings.

1968. *Sunday.*—1. Boiled salmon and dressed cucumber, anchovy sauce. 2. Roast fore-quarter of lamb, spinach, potatoes, mint sauce. 2. Rhubarb tart, cheesecakes.

1969. *Monday.*—1. Curried salmon, made with remains of salmon, dish of boiled rice. 2. Cold lamb, rumpsteak-and-kidney pudding, potatoes. 3. Spinach and poached eggs.

1970. *Tuesday.*—1. Scotch mutton broth with pearl barley. 2. Boiled neck of mutton, caper sauce, suet dumplings, carrots. 3. Baked rice-pudding.

1971. *Wednesday.*—1. Boiled mackerel and melted butter or fennel sauce, potatoes. 2. Roast fillet of veal, bacon, and greens. 3. Fig pudding.

1972. *Thursday.*—1. Flemish soup. 2. Roast loin of mutton, brocoli, potatoes; veal rolls made from remains of cold veal. 3. Boiled rhubarb pudding.

1973. *Friday.*—1. Irish stew or haricot, made from cold mutton, minced veal. 2. Half-pay pudding.

1974. *Saturday.*—1. Rump-steak pie, broiled mutton-chops. 2. Baked arrowroot pudding.

MAY.

1975.—DINNER FOR 18 PERSONS.

First Course.   *Entrées.*

Fried Filleted Soles.	Asparagus Soup, removed by Salmon and Lobster Sauce. Vase of Flowers. Ox-tail Soup removed by Brill & Shrimp Sauce.	Fillets of Mackerel, à la Maître d'Hôtel.

Lobster Pudding.	Lamb Cutlets and Cucumbers. Vase of Flowers. Veal Ragoût.	Curried Fowl.

Second Course.   *Third Course.*

Roast Fowls.	Saddle of Lamb. Raised Pie. Vase of Flowers. Braised Ham. Roast Veal.	Boiled Capon and White Sauce.

Almond Cheesecakes.	Plovers' Eggs.	Goslings, removed by College Puddings. Noyeau Jelly. Italian Cream. Vase of Flowers. Inlaid Jelly. Ducklings, removed by Nesselrode Pudding.	Charlotte à la Parisienne.	Lobster Salad. Tartlets.

Dessert and Ices.

1976.—DINNER FOR 12 PERSONS (May).

First Course.
White Soup.   Asparagus Soup.
Salmon Cutlets.   Boiled Turbot and Lobster Sauce.

Entrees.
Chicken Vol-au-Vent.   Lamb Cutlets and Cucumbers.   Fricandeau of Veal.
Stewed Mushrooms.

Second Course.
Roast Lamb.   Haunch of Mutton.   Boiled and Roast Fowls.   Vegetables.

Third Course.
Ducklings.   Goslings.
Charlotte Russe.   Vanilla Cream.   Gooseberry Tart.   Custards.
Cheesecakes.   Cabinet Pudding and Iced Pudding.

Dessert and Ices.

1977.—DINNER FOR 10 PERSONS (May).

First Course.
Spring Soup.
Salmon à la Genévése.   Red Mullet.

Entrees.
Chicken Vol-au-Vent.   Calf's Liver and Bacon aux Fines Herbes.

Second Course.
Saddle of Mutton.   Half Calf's Head, Tongue, and Brains.   Braised Ham.
Asparagus.

Third Course.
Roast Pigeons.   Ducklings.
Sponge-cake Pudding.   Charlotte à la Vanille.   Gooseberry Tart.   Cream.
Cheesecakes.   Apricot-jam Tart.

Dessert and Ices.

1978.—DINNER FOR 8 PERSONS (May).

First Course.
Julienne Soup.
Brill and Lobster Sauce.   Fried Fillets of Mackerel.

Entrees.
Lamb Cutlets and Cucumbers.   Lobster Patties.

Second Course.
Roast Fillet of Veal.   Boiled Leg of Lamb.   Asparagus.

Third Course.
Ducklings.
Gooseberry Tart.   Custards.   Fancy Pastry.   Soufflé.

Dessert and Ices.

1979.—DINNER FOR 6 PERSONS (May).—I.

First Course.
Vermicelli Soup.
Boiled Salmon and Anchovy Sauce.

Entrees.
Fillets of Beef and Tomato Sauce.   Sweetbreads.

Second Course.
Roast Lamb.   Boiled Capon.   Asparagus.

Third Course.
Ducklings.
Cabinet Pudding.   Compôte of Gooseberries.   Custards in Glasses.
Blancmange.   Lemon Tartlets.   Fondue.

Dessert.

1980.—DINNER FOR 6 PERSONS (May).—II.

First Course.
Macaroni Soup.
Boiled Mackerel à la Maître d'Hôtel.   Fried Smelts.

Entrees.
Scollops of Fowl.   Lobster Pudding.

Second Course.
Boiled Leg of Lamb and Spinach.
Roast Sirloin of Beef and Horseradish Sauce.   Vegetables.

Third Course.
Roast Leveret.   Salad.
Soufflé of Rice.   Ramakins.   Strawberry-jam Tartlets.   Orange Jelly.

Dessert.

1981.—DINNER FOR 6 PERSONS (May).—III.

First Course.
Julienne Soup.
Trout with Dutch Sauce.   Salmon Cutlets.

Entrees.
Lamb Cutlets and Mushrooms.   Vol-au-Vent of Chicken.

Second Course.
Roast Lamb.   Calf's Head à la Tortue.   Vegetables.

Third Course.
Spring Chickens.
Iced Pudding.   Vanilla Cream.   Clear Jelly.   Tartlets.   Cheesecakes.

Dessert.

1982.—DINNER FOR 6 PERSONS (May).—IV.

First Course.
Soup à la Reine.
Crimped Trout and Lobster Sauce.   Baked Whitings aux Fines Herbes.

Entrees.
Braised Mutton Cutlets and Cucumbers.   Stewed Pigeons.

Second Course.
Roast Fillet of Veal.   Bacon-cheek and Greens.
Fillet of Beef à la Jardinière.

Third Course.
Ducklings.
Soufflé à la Vanille.   Compôte of Oranges.   Meringues.
Gooseberry Tart.   Fondue.

Dessert.

PLAIN FAMILY DINNERS FOR MAY.

1983. *Sunday.*—1. Vegetable soup. 2. Saddle of mutton, asparagus and potatoes. 3. Gooseberry tart, custards.

1984. *Monday.*—1. Fried whitings, anchovy sauce. 2. Cold mutton, mashed potatoes, stewed veal. 3. Fig pudding.

1985. *Tuesday.*—1. Haricot mutton, made from remains of cold mutton, rump-steak pie. 2. Macaroni.

1986. *Wednesday.*—1. Roast loin of veal and spinach, boiled bacon, mutton cutlets and tomato sauce. 2. Gooseberry pudding and cream.

1987. *Thursday.*—1. Spring soup. 2. Roast leg of lamb, mint sauce, spinach, curried veal and rice. 3. Lemon pudding.

1988. *Friday.*—1. Boiled mackerel and parsley-and-butter. 2. Stewed rump-steak, cold lamb and salad. 3. Baked gooseberry pudding.

1989. *Saturday.*—1. Vermicelli. 2. Rump-steak pudding, lamb cutlets, and cucumbers. 3. Macaroni.

————

1990. *Sunday.*—1. Boiled salmon and lobster or caper sauce. 2. Roast lamb, mint sauce, asparagus, potatoes. 3. Plum-pudding, gooseberry tart.

1991. *Monday.*—1. Salmon warmed in remains of lobster sauce and garnished with croûtons. 2. Stewed knuckle of veal and rice, cold lamb and dressed cucumber. 3. Slices of pudding warmed, and served with sugar sprinkled over. Baked rice pudding.

1992. *Tuesday.*—1. Roast ribs of beef, horseradish sauce, Yorkshire pudding, spinach and potatoes. 2. Boiled lemon pudding.

1993. *Wednesday.*—1. Fried soles, melted butter. 2. Cold beef and dressed cucumber or salad, veal cutlets and bacon. 3. Baked plum-pudding.

1994. *Thursday.*—1. Spring soup. 2. Calf's liver and bacon, broiled beef-bones, spinach and potatoes. 3. Gooseberry tart.

1995. *Friday.*—1. Roast shoulder of mutton, baked potatoes, onion sauce, spinach. 2. Currant dumplings.

1996. *Saturday.*—1. Broiled mackerel, fennel sauce or plain melted butter. 2. Rump-steak pie, hashed mutton, vegetables. 3. Baked arrowroot pudding.

3 o

JUNE.

1997.—DINNER FOR 18 PERSONS.

First Course.

Fillets of Gurnets.

Asparagus Soup,
removed by
Crimped Salmon.

Vase of
Flowers.

Vermicelli Soup,
removed by
Whitebait.

Soles aux fines herbes.

Entrées.

Lobster Patties.

Lamb Cutlets and
Peas.

Vase of
Flowers.

Larded Sweetbreads.

Tendrons de Veau à la Jardinière.

Second Course.

Roast Spring Chickens.

Saddle of Lamb.

Tongue.

Vase of
Flowers.

Ham.

Boiled Calf's Head.

Boiled Capon.

Third Course.

Prawns.

Vol-au-Vent of Strawberries and Cream.

Cheesecakes.

Leveret,
removed by
Ice Pudding.

Wine Jelly.

Vase of
Flowers.

Blancmange.

Goslings,
removed by
Fondues, in cases.

Custards, in glasses.

Plovers' Eggs.

Tartlets.

Dessert and Ices.

1998.—DINNER FOR 12 PERSONS (June).

First Course.

Green-Pea Soup.　　Rice Soup.

Salmon and Lobster Sauce.　　Trout à la Genévése.　　Whitebait.

Entrees.

Lamb Cutlets and Cucumbers.　　Fricasseed Chicken.　　Stewed Veal and Peas.

Lobster Rissoles.

Second Course.

Roast Quarter of Lamb and Spinach.　　Filet de Bœuf à la Jardinière.

Boiled Fowls.　　Braised Shoulder of Lamb.　　Tongue.　　Vegetables.

Third Course.

Goslings.　　Ducklings.

Nesselrode Pudding.　　Charlotte à la Parisienne.　　Gooseberry Tartlets.

Strawberry Cream.　　Raspberry-and-Currant Tart.　　Custards.

Dessert and Ices.

1999.—DINNER FOR 10 PERSONS (June).
First Course.
Julienne Soup.
Salmon Trout and Parsley-and-Butter.   Red Mullet.

Entrees.
Stewed Breast of Veal and Peas.   Mutton Cutlets à la Maintenon.

Second Course.
Roast Fillet of Veal.   Boiled Leg of Lamb, garnished with young Carrots.
Boiled Bacon-cheek.   Vegetables.

Third Course.
Roast Ducks.   Leveret.
Gooseberry Tart.   Strawberry Cream.   Strawberry Tartlets.   Meringues.
Cabinet Pudding.   Iced Pudding.

Dessert and Ices.

2000.—DINNER FOR 8 PERSONS (June).
First Course.
Vermicelli Soup.
Trout à la Genévése.   Salmon Cutlets.

Entrees.
Lamb Cutlets and Peas.   Fricasseed Chicken.

Second Course.
Roast Ribs of Beef.   Half Calf's Head, Tongue, and Brains.   Boiled Ham.
Vegetables.

Third Course.
Roast Ducks.
Compôte of Gooseberries.   Strawberry Jelly.   Pastry.   Iced Pudding.
Cauliflower with Cream Sauce.

Dessert and Ices.

2001.—DINNER FOR 6 PERSONS (June).—I.
First Course.
Spring Soup.
Boiled Salmon and Lobster Sauce.

Entrees.
Veal Cutlets and Endive.   Ragoût of Duck and Green Peas.

Second Course.
Roast Loin of Veal.   Boiled Leg of Lamb and White Sauce.
Tongue, garnished.   Vegetables.

Third Course.
Strawberry Cream.   Gooseberry Tartlets.   Almond Pudding.   Lobster Salad

Dessert.

2002.—DINNER FOR 6 PERSONS (June).—II.

First Course.
Calf's-Head Soup.

Mackerel à la Maître d'Hôtel.　　Whitebait.

Entrees.
Chicken Cutlets.　　Curried Lobster.

Second Course.
Fore-quarter of Lamb and Salad.　　Stewed Beef à la Jardinière.　　Vegetables.

Third Course.
Goslings.

Green-Currant Tart.　　Custards, in glasses.　　Strawberry Blancmange.

Soufflé of Rice.

Dessert.

2003.—DINNER FOR 6 PERSONS (June).—III.

First Course.
Green-Pea Soup.

Baked Soles aux fines herbes.　　Stewed Trout.

Entrees.
Calf's Liver and Bacon.　　Rissoles.

Second Course.
Roast Saddle of Lamb and Salad.　　Calf's Head à la Tortue.　　Vegetables.

Third Course.
Roast Ducks.

Vol-au-Vent of Strawberries and Cream.　　Strawberry Tartlets.

Lemon Blancmange.　　Baked Gooseberry Pudding.

Dessert.

2004.—DINNER FOR 6 PERSONS (June).—IV.

First Course.
Spinach Soup.

Soles à la Crême.　　Red Mullet.

Entrees.
Roast Fillet of Veal.　　Braised Ham and Spinach.

Second Course.
Boiled Fowls and White Sauce.　　Vegetables.

Third Course.
Leveret.

Strawberry Jelly.　　Swiss Cream.　　Cheesecakes.　　Iced Pudding.

Dessert.

PLAIN FAMILY DINNERS FOR JUNE.

2005. *Sunday.*—1. Salmon trout and parsley-and-butter, new potatoes. 2. Roast fillet of veal, boiled bacon-cheek and spinach, vegetables. 3. Gooseberry tart, custards.

2006. *Monday.*—1. Light gravy soup. 2. Small meat pie, minced veal, garnished with rolled bacon, spinach and potatoes. 3. Raspberry-and-currant tart.

2007. *Tuesday.*—1. Baked mackerel, potatoes. 2. Boiled leg of lamb, garnished with young carrots. 3. Lemon pudding.

2008. *Wednesday.*—1. Vegetable soup. 2. Calf's liver and bacon, peas, hashed lamb from remains of cold joint. 3. Baked gooseberry pudding.

2009. *Thursday.*—1. Roast ribs of beef, Yorkshire pudding, peas, potatoes. 2. Stewed rhubarb and boiled rice.

2010. *Friday.*—1. Cold beef and salad, lamb cutlets and peas. 2. Boiled gooseberry pudding and baked custard pudding.

2011. *Saturday.*—1. Rump-steak pudding, broiled beef-bones and cucumber, vegetables. 2. Bread pudding.

2012. *Sunday.*—1. Roast fore-quarter of lamb, mint sauce, peas, and new potatoes. 2. Gooseberry pudding, strawberry tartlets. Fondue.

2013. *Monday.*—1. Cold lamb and salad, stewed neck of veal and peas, young carrots, and new potatoes. 2. Almond pudding.

2014. *Tuesday.*—1. Green-pea soup. 2. Roast ducks stuffed, gravy, peas and new potatoes. 3. Baked ratafia pudding.

2015. *Wednesday.*—1. Roast leg of mutton, summer cabbage, potatoes. 2. Gooseberry and rice pudding.

2016. *Thursday.*—1. Fried soles, melted butter, potatoes. 2. Sweetbreads, hashed mutton, vegetables. 3. Bread-and-butter pudding.

2017. *Friday.*—1. Asparagus soup. 2. Boiled beef, young carrots and new potatoes, suet dumplings. 3. College puddings.

2018. *Saturday.*—1. Cold boiled beef and salad, lamb cutlets and green peas. 2. Boiled gooseberry pudding and plain cream.

JULY.

2019.—DINNER FOR 18 PERSONS.

First Course.   *Entrées.*

First Course box:

Whitebait. | Green-Pea Soup, removed by Salmon and dressed Cucumber. / Vase of Flowers. / Soup à la Reine, removed by Mackerel à la Maître d'Hôtel. | Stewed Trout.

Entrées box:

Lobster Curry en Casserole. | Lamb Cutlets and Peas. / Vase of Flowers. / Chicken Patties. | Scollops of Chickens.

Second Course.   *Third Course.*

Second Course box:

Boiled Capons. | Haunch of Venison. / Pigeon Pie. / Vase of Flowers. / Braised Ham. / Saddle of Lamb. | Spring Chickens.

Third Course box:

Prawns. / Cherry Tart. / Creams. | Roast Ducks, removed by Vanilla Soufflé. / Raspberry Cream. / Vase of Flowers. / Strawberry Cream. / Green Goose, removed by Iced Pudding. | Custards. / Raspberry-and-Currant Tart. / Tartlets.

Dessert and Ices.

2020.—DINNER FOR 12 PERSONS (July).

First Course.

Soup à la Jardinière.   Chicken Soup.

Crimped Salmon and Parsley-and-Butter.   Trout aux fines herbes, in cases.

Entrees.

Tendrons de Veau and Peas.   Lamb Cutlets and Cucumbers.

Second Course.

Loin of Veal à la Béchamel.   Roast Fore-quarter of Lamb.   Salad.

Braised Ham, garnished with Broad Beans.   Vegetables.

Third Course.

Roast Ducks.   Turkey Poult.

Stewed Peas à la Française.   Lobster Salad.   Cherry Tart.

Raspberry-and-Currant Tart.   Custards, in glasses.   Lemon Creams.

Nesselrode Pudding.   Marrow Pudding.

Dessert and Ices.

2021.—DINNER FOR 8 PERSONS (July)

First Course.

Green-Pea Soup.

Salmon and Lobster Sauce.   Crimped Perch and Dutch Sauce.

Entrees.

Stewed Veal and Peas.   Lamb Cutlets and Cucumbers.

Second Course.

Haunch of Venison.   Boiled Fowls à la Béchamel.   Braised Ham.   Vegetables.

Third Course.

Roast Ducks.

Peas à la Française.   Lobster Salad.   Strawberry Cream.   Blancmange.

Cherry Tart.   Cheesecakes.   Iced Pudding.

Dessert and Ices.

2022.—DINNER FOR 6 PERSONS (July).—I.

First Course.

Soup à la Jardinière.

Salmon Trout and Parsley-and-Butter.   Fillets of Mackerel à la Maître d'Hôtel.

Entrees.

Lobster Cutlets.   Beef Palates à la Italienne.

Second Course.

Roast Lamb.   Boiled Capon and White Sauce.

Boiled Tongue, garnished with small Vegetable Marrows.   Bacon and Beans.

Third Course.

Goslings.

Whipped Strawberry Cream.   Raspberry-and-Currant Tart.   Meringues.

Cherry Tartlets.   Iced Pudding.

Dessert and Ices.

2023.—DINNER FOR 6 PERSONS (July).—II.

First Course.

Julienne Soup.

Crimped Salmon and Caper Sauce.   Whitebait.

Entrees.

Croquettes à la Reine.   Curried Lobster.

Second Course.

Roast Lamb.   Rump of Beef à la Jardinière.

Third Course.

Larded Turkey Poult.

Raspberry Cream.   Cherry Tart.   Custards, in glasses.   Gâteaux à la Genévése.

Nesselrode Pudding.

Dessert.

PLAIN FAMILY DINNERS FOR JULY.

2024. *Sunday.*—1. Salmon trout and parsley-and-butter. 2. Roast fillet of veal, boiled bacon-check, peas, potatoes. 3. Raspberry-and-currant tart, baked custard pudding.

2025. *Monday.*—1. Green-pea soup. 2. Roast fowls garnished with water-cresses; gravy, bread sauce; cold veal and salad. 3. Cherry tart.

2026. *Tuesday.*—1. John dory and lobster sauce. 2. Curried fowl with remains of cold fowls, dish of rice, veal rolls with remains of cold fillet. 3. Strawberry cream.

2027. *Wednesday.*—1. Roast leg of mutton, vegetable marrow, and potatoes, melted butter. 2. Black-currant pudding.

2028. *Thursday.*—1. Fried soles, anchovy sauce. 2. Mutton cutlets and tomato sauce, hashed mutton, peas, potatoes. 3. Lemon dumplings.

2029. *Friday.*—1. Boiled brisket of beef, carrots, turnips, suet dumplings, peas, potatoes. 2. Baked semolina pudding.

2030. *Saturday.*—1. Cold beef and salad, lamb cutlets and peas. 2. Rolled jam pudding.

2031. *Sunday.*—1. Julienne soup. 2. Roast lamb, half calf's head, tongue and brains, boiled ham, peas and potatoes. 3. Cherry tart, custards.

2032. *Monday.*—1. Hashed calf's head, cold lamb and salad. 2. Vegetable marrow and white sauce, instead of pudding.

2033. *Tuesday.*—1. Stewed veal, with peas, young carrots, and potatoes. Small meat pie. 2. Raspberry-and-currant pudding.

2034. *Wednesday.*—1. Roast ducks stuffed, gravy, peas, and potatoes; the remains of stewed veal rechauffé. 2. Macaroni served as a sweet pudding.

2035. *Thursday.*—1. Slices of salmon and caper sauce. 2. Boiled knuckle of veal, parsley-and-butter, vegetable marrow and potatoes. 3. Black-currant pudding.

2036. *Friday.*—1. Roast shoulder of mutton, onion sauce, peas and potatoes. 2. Cherry tart, baked custard pudding.

2037. *Saturday.*—1. Minced mutton, rumpsteak-and-kidney pudding. 2. Baked lemon pudding.

AUGUST.

2038.—DINNER FOR 18 PERSONS.

First Course. *Entrées.*

	First Course			Entrées	
Red Mullet.	Mock-Turtle Soup, removed by Broiled Salmon and Caper Sauce. Vase of Flowers. Soup à la Julienne, removed by Brill and Shrimp Sauce.	Perch.	Curried Lobster.	Fricandeau de Veau à la Jardinière. Vase of Flowers. Fillets of Ducks and Peas.	Lamb Cutlets à la Purée de Pommes de Terre.

Second Course. *Third Course.*

	Second Course				Third Course			
Capon à la Financière.	Haunch of Venison. Ham, garnished. Vase of Flowers. Leveret Pie. Saddle of Mutton.	Roast Fowls.	Lobster Salad.	Charlotte à la Vanille. Raspberry Tartlets.	Grouse, removed by Cabinet Pudding. Fruit Jelly. Vase of Flowers. Vol-au-Vent of Pears. Larded Peahen, removed by Iced Pudding.	Custards.	Cheesecakes. Prawns.	

Dessert and Ices.

2039.—DINNER FOR 12 PERSONS (August).

First Course.
Vermicelli Soup.   Soup à la Reine.
Boiled Salmon.   Fried Flounders.   Trout en Matelot.

Entrees.
Stewed Pigeons.   Sweetbreads.   Ragoût of Ducks.
Fillets of Chickens and Mushrooms.

Second Course.
Quarter of Lamb.   Cotelette de Bœuf à la Jardinière.
Roast Fowls and Boiled Tongue.   Bacon and Beans.

Third Course.
Grouse.   Wheatears.
Greengage Tart.   Whipped Cream.   Vol-au-Vent of Plums.   Fruit Jelly.
Iced Pudding.   Cabinet Pudding.

Dessert and Ices.

2040.—DINNER FOR 8 PERSONS (August).

First Course.
Julienne Soup.

Fillets of Turbot and Dutch Sauce.   Red Mullet.

Entrees.
Riz de Veau aux Tomates.   Fillets of Ducks and Peas.

Second Course.
Haunch of Venison.   Boiled Capon and Oysters.   Ham, garnished.   Vegetables.

Third Course.
Leveret.

Fruit Jelly.   Compôte of Greengages.   Plum Tart.   Custards, in glasses.
Omelette soufflée.

Dessert and Ices.

2041.—DINNER FOR 6 PERSONS (August).—I.

First Course.
Macaroni Soup.

Crimped Salmon and Sauce Hollandaise.   Fried Fillets of Trout.

Entrees.
Tendrons de Veau and Stewed Peas.   Salmi of Grouse.

Second Course.
Roast Loin of Veal.   Boiled Bacon, garnished with French Beans.
Stewed Beef à la Jardinière.   Vegetables.

Third Course.
Turkey Poult.

Plum Tart.   Custard Pudding.   Vol-au-Vent of Pears.
Strawberry Cream.   Ratafia Soufflé.

Dessert.

2042.—DINNER FOR 6 PERSONS (August).—II.

First Course.
Vegetable-Marrow Soup.

Stewed Mullet.   Fillets of Salmon and Ravigotte Sauce.

Entrees.
Curried Lobster.   Fricandeau de Veau à la Jardinière.

Second Course.
Roast Saddle of Mutton.   Stewed Shoulder of Veal, garnished with
Forcemeat Balls.   Vegetables.

Third Course.
Roast Grouse and Bread Sauce.

Vol-au-Vent of Greengages.   Fruit Jelly.   Raspberry Cream.
Custards.   Fig Pudding.

Dessert.

PLAIN FAMILY DINNERS FOR AUGUST.

2043. *Sunday.*—1. Vegetable-marrow soup. 2. Roast quarter of lamb, mint sauce, French beans and potatoes. 3. Raspberry-and-currant tart, custard pudding.

2044. *Monday.*—1. Cold lamb and salad, small meat pie, vegetable marrow and white sauce. 2. Lemon dumplings.

2045. *Tuesday.*—1. Boiled mackerel. 2. Stewed loin of veal, French beans and potatoes. 3. Baked raspberry pudding.

2046. *Wednesday.*—1. Vegetable soup. 2. Lamb cutlets and French beans ; the remains of stewed shoulder of veal, mashed vegetable marrow. 3. Black-currant pudding.

2047. *Thursday.*—1. Roast ribs of beef, Yorkshire pudding, French beans and potatoes. 2. Bread-and-butter pudding.

2048. *Friday.*—1. Fried soles and melted butter. 2. Cold beef and salad, lamb cutlets and mashed potatoes. 3. Cauliflowers and white sauce instead of pudding.

2049. *Saturday.*—1. Stewed beef and vegetables, with remains of cold beef ; mutton pudding. 2. Macaroni and cheese.

———

2050. *Sunday.*—1. Salmon pudding. 2. Roast fillet of veal, boiled bacon-cheek garnished with tufts of cauliflowers, French beans and potatoes. 3. Plum tart, boiled custard pudding.

2051. *Monday.*—1. Baked soles. 2. Cold veal and bacon, salad, mutton cutlets and tomato sauce. 3. Boiled currant pudding.

2052. *Tuesday.*—1. Rice soup. 2. Roast fowls and water-cresses, boiled knuckle of ham, minced veal garnished with croûtons ; vegetables. 3. College puddings.

2053. *Wednesday.*—1. Curried fowl with remains of cold fowl ; dish of rice, stewed rump-steak and vegetables. 2. Plum tart.

2054. *Thursday.*—1. Boiled brisket of beef, carrots, turnips, suet dumplings, and potatoes. 2. Baked bread pudding.

2055. *Friday.*—1. Vegetable soup, made from liquor that beef was boiled in. 2. Cold beef and dressed cucumber, veal cutlets and tomata sauce. 3. Fondue.

2056. *Saturday.*—1. Bubble-and-squeak, made from remains of cold beef ; cold veal-and-ham pie, salad. 2. Baked raspberry pudding.

SEPTEMBER.

2057.—DINNER FOR 18 PERSONS.

First Course.   *Entrées.*

First Course box:
Red Mullet & Italian Sauce.

Julienne Soup, removed by Brill and Shrimp Sauce.

Vase of Flowers.

Giblet Soup, removed by Salmon and Lobster Sauce.

Fried Eels.

Entrées box:
Fillets of Chicken and Truffles.

Lamb Cutlets and French Beans.

Vase of Flowers.

Sweetbreads and Tomata Sauce.

Oysters au gratin.

Second Course.   *Third Course.*

Second Course box:
Chickens à la Béchamel.

Saddle of Mutton.

Veal-and-Ham Pie.

Vase of Flowers.

Broiled Ham, garnished with Cauliflowers.

Fillet of Veal.

Braised Goose.

Third Course box:
Custards.   Noyeau Jelly.   Plum Tart.

Partridges, removed by Plum-pudding.

Compôte of Greengages

Vase of Flowers.

Pastry Sandwiches.

Grouse & Bread Sauce, removed by Nesselrode Pudding.

Apple Tart.   Lemon Cream.   Custards.

Dessert and Ices.

2058.—DINNER FOR 12 PERSONS (September).
First Course.
Mock-Turtle Soup.   Soup à la Jardinière.
Salmon and Lobster Sauce.   Fried Whitings.   Stewed Eels.

Entrees.
Veal Cutlets.   Scalloped Oysters.   Curried Fowl.   Grilled Mushrooms.

Second Course.
Haunch of Mutton.   Boiled Calf's Head à la Béchamel.   Braised Ham.
Roast Fowls aux Cressons.

Third Course.
Leveret.   Grouse.
Cabinet Pudding.   Iced Pudding.   Compôte of Plums.   Damson Tart.
Cream.   Fruit Jelly.   Prawns.   Lobster Salad.

Dessert and Ices.

2059.—DINNER FOR 8 PERSONS (September).

First Course.

Flemish Soup.

Turbot, garnished with Fried Smelts.   Red Mullet and Italian Sauce.

Entrees.

Tendrons de Veau and Truffles.   Lamb Cutlets and Sauce Piquante.

Second Course.

Loin of Veal à la Béchamel.   Roast Haunch of Venison.   Braised Ham.

Grouse Pie.   Vegetables.

Third Course.

Roast Hare.

Plum Tart.   Whipped Cream.   Punch Jelly.   Compôte of Damsons.

Marrow Pudding.

Dessert.

2060.—DINNER FOR 6 PERSONS (September).—I.

First Course.

Game Soup.

Crimped Skate.   Slices of Salmon à la Genévése.

Entrees.

Fricasseed Sweetbreads.   Savoury Rissoles.

Second Course.

Sirloin of Beef and Horseradish Sauce.   Boiled Leg of Mutton and Caper Sauce.

Vegetables.

Third Course.

Roast Partridges.

Charlotte Russe.   Apricots and Rice.   Fruit Jelly.   Cabinet Pudding.

Dessert.

2061.—DINNER FOR 6 PERSONS (September).—II.

First Course.

Thick Gravy Soup.

Fillets of Turbot à la Crême.   Stewed Eels.

Entrees.

Vol-au-Vent of Lobster.   Salmi of Grouse.

Second Course.

Haunch of Venison.   Rump of Beef à la Jardinière.

Hare, boned and larded, with Mushrooms.

Third Course.

Roast Grouse.

Apricot Blancmange.   Compôte of Peaches.   Plum Tart.

Custards.   Plum-pudding.

Dessert.

PLAIN FAMILY DINNERS FOR SEPTEMBER.

2062. *Sunday.*—1. Julienne soup.   2. Roast ribs of beef, Yorkshire pudding, horseradish sauce, French beans, and potatoes.   3. Greengage pudding, vanilla cream.

2063. *Monday.*—1. Crimped skate and crab sauce.   2. Cold beef and salad, small veal-and-ham pie.   3. Vegetable marrow and white sauce.

2064. *Tuesday.*—1. Fried soles, melted butter.   2. Boiled fowls, parsley-and-butter; bacon-cheek, garnished with French beans; beef rissoles, made from remains of cold beef.   3. Plum tart and cream.

2065. *Wednesday.*—1. Boiled round of beef, carrots, turnips, and suet dumplings; marrow on toast.   2. Baked damsons and rice.

2066. *Thursday.*—1. Vegetable soup, made from liquor that beef was boiled in.   2. Lamb cutlets and cucumbers, cold beef and salad.   3. Apple pudding.

2067. *Friday.*—1. Baked soles.   2. Bubble-and-squeak, made from cold beef; veal cutlets and rolled bacon.   3. Damson tart.

2068. *Saturday.*—1. Irish stew, rump-steaks and oyster sauce.   2. Somersetshire dumplings.

2069. *Sunday.*—1. Fried filleted soles and anchovy sauce.   2. Roast leg of mutton, brown onion sauce, French beans, and potatoes; half calf's head, tongue, and brains.   3. Plum tart; custards, in glasses.

2070. *Monday.*—1. Vegetable-marrow soup.   2. Calf's head à la maître d'hôtel, from remains of cold head; boiled brisket of beef and vegetables. 3. Stewed fruit and baked rice pudding.

2071. *Tuesday.*—1. Roast fowls and water-cresses; boiled bacon, garnished with tufts of cauliflower; hashed mutton, from remains of mutton of Sunday. 2. Baked plum-pudding.

2072. *Wednesday.*—1. Boiled knuckle of veal and rice, turnips, potatoes; small ham, garnished with French beans.   2. Baked apple pudding.

2073. *Thursday.*—1. Brill and shrimp sauce.   2. Roast hare, gravy, and red-currant jelly; mutton cutlets and mashed potatoes.   3. Scalloped oysters, instead of pudding.

2074. *Friday.*—1. Small roast loin of mutton; the remains of hare, jugged; vegetable marrow and potatoes.   2. Damson pudding.

2075. *Saturday.*—1. Rump-steaks, broiled, and oyster sauce, mashed potatoes; veal-and-ham pie,—the ham may be cut from that boiled on Wednesday, if not all eaten cold for breakfast.   2. Lemon pudding.

OCTOBER.

2076.—DINNER FOR 18 PERSONS.

First Course.   *Entrées.*

Soles à la Normandie.

Mock-Turtle Soup,
removed by
Crimped Cod and Oyster
Sauce.

Vase of
Flowers.

Julienne Soup,
removed by
John Dory and Dutch
Sauce.

Red Mullet.

Oyster Patties.

Sweetbreads and Tomata
Sauce.

Vase of
Flowers.

Fricandeau de Veau and
Celery Sauce.

Stewed Mushrooms.

Second Course.   *Third Course.*

Roast Goose.

Roast Saddle of
Mutton.

Grouse Pie.

Vase of
Flowers.

Ham.

Larded Turkey.

Boiled Fowls and Oyster Sauce.

Custards.   **Gâteau de Pommes.**   **Lobster Salad.**

Pheasants,
removed by
Cabinet Pudding.

Italian Cream.

Vase of
Flowers.

Peach Jelly.

Roast Hare,
removed by
Iced Pudding.

Prawns.   **Compôte of Plums.**   **Apple Tart.**

Dessert and Ices.

2077.—DINNER FOR 12 PERSONS (October).

First Course.
Carrot Soup à la Créci.   Soup à la Reine.
Baked Cod.   Stewed Eels.

Entrees.
Riz de Veau and Tomata Sauce.   Vol-au-Vent of Chicken.
Pork Cutlets and Sauce Robert.   Grilled Mushrooms.

Second Course.
Rump of Beef à la Jardinière.   Roast Goose.   Boiled Fowls and Celery Sauce.
Tongue, garnished.   Vegetables.

Third Course.
Grouse.   Pheasants.
Quince Jelly.   Lemon Cream.   Apple Tart.   Compôte of Peaches.
Nesselrode Pudding.   Cabinet Pudding.   Scalloped Oysters.

Dessert and Ices.

2078.—DINNER FOR 8 PERSONS (October).

First Course.

Calf's-Head Soup.

Crimped Cod and Oyster Sauce.   Stewed Eels.

Entrees.

Stewed Mutton Kidneys.   Curried Sweetbreads.

Second Course.

Boiled Leg of Mutton, garnished with Carrots and Turnips.   Roast Goose.

Third Course.

Partridges.

Fruit Jelly.   Italian Cream.   Vol-au-Vent of Pears.   Apple Tart.

Cabinet Pudding.

Dessert and Ices.

2079.—DINNER FOR 6 PERSONS (October).—I.

First Course.

Hare Soup.

Broiled Cod à la Maître d'Hôtel.   Haddocks and Egg Sauce.

Entrees.

Veal Cutlets, garnished with French Beans.   Haricot Mutton.

Second Course.

Roast Haunch of Mutton.   Boiled Capon and Rice.   Vegetables.

Third Course.

Pheasants.

Punch Jelly.   Blancmange.   Apples à la Portugaise.

Charlotte à la Vanille.   Marrow Pudding.

Dessert.

2080.—DINNER FOR 6 PERSONS (October).—II.

First Course.

Mock-Turtle Soup.

Brill and Lobster Sauce.   Fried Whitings.

Entrees.

Fowl à la Béchamel.   Oyster Patties.

Second Course.

Roast Sucking-Pig.   Stewed Rump of Beef à la Jardinière.   Vegetables.

Third Course.

Grouse.

Charlotte aux Pommes.   Coffee Cream.   Cheesecakes.

Apricot Tart.   Iced Pudding.

Dessert.

PLAIN FAMILY DINNERS FOR OCTOBER.

2081. *Sunday.*—1. Roast sucking-pig, tomata sauce and brain sauce ; small boiled leg of mutton, caper sauce, turnips, and carrots. 2. Damson tart, boiled batter pudding.

2082. *Monday.*—1. Vegetable soup, made from liquor that mutton was boiled in. 2. Sucking-pig en blanquette, small meat pie, French beans, and potatoes. 3. Pudding, pies.

2083. *Tuesday.*—1. Roast partridges, bread sauce, and gravy ; slices of mutton warmed in caper sauce ; vegetables. 2. Baked plum-pudding.

2084. *Wednesday.*—1. Roast ribs of beef, Yorkshire pudding, vegetable marrow, and potatoes. 2. Damson pudding.

2085. *Thursday.*—1. Fried soles, melted butter. 2. Cold beef and salad ; mutton cutlets and tomata sauce. 3. Macaroni.

2086. *Friday.*—1. Carrot soup. 2. Boiled fowls and celery sauce ; bacon-cheek, garnished with greens ; beef rissoles, from remains of cold beef. 3. Baroness pudding.

2087. *Saturday.*—1. Curried fowl, from remains of cold ditto ; dish of rice, rumpsteak-and-kidney pudding, vegetables. 2. Stewed pears and sponge cakes.

2088. *Sunday.*—1. Crimped cod and oyster sauce. 2. Roast haunch of mutton, brown onion sauce, and vegetables. 3. Bullace pudding, baked custards in cups.

2089. *Monday.*—1. The remains of codfish, flaked, and warmed in a maître d'hôtel sauce. 2. Cold mutton and salad, veal cutlets and rolled bacon, French beans and potatoes. 3. Arrowroot blancmange and stewed damsons.

2090. *Tuesday.*—1. Roast hare, gravy, and red-currant jelly ; hashed mutton, vegetables. 2. Currant dumplings.

2091. *Wednesday.*—1. Jugged hare, from remains of roast ditto ; boiled knuckle of veal and rice ; boiled bacon-cheek. 2. Apple pudding.

2092. *Thursday.*—1. Roast leg of pork, apple sauce, greens, and potatoes. 2. Rice snowballs.

2093. *Friday.*—1. Slices of pork, broiled, and tomata sauce, mashed potatoes ; roast pheasants, bread sauce, and gravy. 2. Baked apple pudding.

2094. *Saturday.*—1. Rump-steak pie, sweetbreads. 2. Ginger pudding.

NOVEMBER.

2095.—DINNER FOR 18 PERSONS.

First Course.

Entrées.

Baked Whitings.	Thick Grouse Soup, removed by Crimped Cod and Oyster Sauce.	Fried Smelts.
	Vase of Flowers.	
	Clear Ox-tail Soup, removed by Fillets of Turbot à la Crème.	

Fillets of Leveret.	Poulet à la Marengo.	Ragoût of Lobster.
	Vase of Flowers.	
	Mushrooms sautés.	

Second Course.

Third Course.

Lark Pudding.	Haunch of Mutton.	Roast Fowls.
	Cold Game Pie.	
	Vase of Flowers.	
	Boiled Ham.	
	Boiled Turkey and Celery Sauce.	

Apple Tart.	Pommes à la Condé. Prawns.	Partridges, removed by Plum-pudding.	Vol-au-Vent of Pears.	Apricot Tartlets. Shell-Fish.
		Wine Jelly.		
		Vase of Flowers.		
		Blancmange.		
		Snipes, removed by Charlotte glacée.		

Dessert and Ices.

2096.—DINNER FOR 12 PERSONS (November).

First Course.

Hare Soup.   Julienne Soup.

Baked Cod.   Soles à la Normandie.

Entrees.

Riz de Veau aux Tomates.   Lobster Patties.

Mutton Cutlets and Soubise Sauce.   Croûtades of Marrow aux fines herbes.

Second Course.

Roast Sirloin of Beef.   Braised Goose.   Boiled Fowls and Celery Sauce.

Bacon-cheek, garnished with Sprouts.

Third Course.

Wild Ducks.   Partridges.

Apples à la Portugaise.   Bavarian Cream.   Apricot-jam Sandwiches.

Cheesecakes.   Charlotte à la Vanille.   Plum-pudding.

Dessert and Ices.

2097.—DINNER FOR 8 PERSONS (November).

First Course.

Mulligatawny Soup.

Fried slices of Codfish and Oyster Sauce.   Eels en Matelote.

Entrees.

Broiled Pork Cutlets and Tomata Sauce.   Tendrons de Veau à la Jardinière.

Second Course.

Boiled Leg of Mutton and Vegetables.   Roast Goose.   Cold Game Pie.

Third Course.

Snipes.   Teal.

Apple Soufflé.   Iced Charlotte.   Tartlets.   Champagne Jelly.

Coffee Cream.   Mince Pies.

Dessert and Ices.

2098.—DINNER FOR 6 PERSONS (November).—I.

First Course.

Oyster Soup.

Crimped Cod and Oyster Sauce.   Fried Perch and Dutch Sauce.

Entrees.

Pigs' Feet à la Béchamel.   Curried Rabbit.

Second Course.

Roast Sucking-Pig.   Boiled Fowls and Oyster Sauce.   Vegetables.

Third Course.

Jugged Hare.

Meringues à la Crême.   Apple Custard.   Vol-au-Vent of Pears.

Whipped Cream.   Cabinet Pudding.

Dessert.

2099.—DINNER FOR 6 PERSONS (November).—II.

First Course.

Game Soup.

Slices of Codfish and Dutch Sauce.   Fried Eels.

Entrees.

Kidneys à la Maître d'Hôtel.   Oyster Patties.

Second Course.

Saddle of Mutton.   Boiled Capon and Rice.   Small Ham.   Lark Pudding.

Third Course.

Roast Hare.

Apple Tart.   Pineapple Cream.   Clear Jelly.   Cheesecakes.

Marrow Pudding.   Nesselrode Pudding.

Dessert.

3 P 2

PLAIN FAMILY DINNERS FOR NOVEMBER.

2100. *Sunday.*—1. White soup. 2. Roast haunch of mutton, haricot beans, potatoes. 3. Apple tart, ginger pudding.

2101. *Monday.*—1. Stewed eels. 2. Veal cutlets garnished with rolled bacon; cold mutton and winter salad. 3. Baked rice pudding.

2102. *Tuesday.*—1. Roast fowls, garnished with water-cresses; boiled bacon-cheek; hashed mutton from remains of haunch. 2. Apple pudding.

2103. *Wednesday.*—1. Boiled leg of pork, carrots, parsnips, and pease-pudding; fowl croquettes made with remainder of cold fowl. 2. Baroness pudding.

2104. *Thursday.*—1. Cold pork and mashed potatoes; roast partridges, bread sauce and gravy. 2. The remainder of pudding cut into neat slices, and warmed through, and served with sifted sugar sprinkled over; apple fritters.

2105. *Friday.*—1. Roast hare, gravy, and currant jelly; rump-steak and oyster sauce; vegetables. 2. Macaroni.

2106. *Saturday.*—1. Jugged hare; small mutton pudding. 2. Fig pudding.

2107. *Sunday.*—1. Crimped cod and oyster sauce. 2. Roast fowls, small boiled ham, vegetables; rump-steak pie. 3. Baked apple pudding, open jam tart.

2108. *Monday.*—1. The remainder of cod warmed in maître d'hôtel sauce. 2. Boiled aitchbone of beef, carrots, parsnips, suet dumplings. 3. Baked bread-and-butter pudding.

2109. *Tuesday.*—1. Pea-soup, made from liquor in which beef was boiled. 2. Cold beef, mashed potatoes; mutton cutlets and tomata sauce. 3. Carrot pudding.

2110. *Wednesday.*—1. Fried soles and melted butter. 2. Roast leg of pork, apple sauce, vegetables. 3. Macaroni with Parmesan cheese.

2111. *Thursday.*—1. Bubble-and-squeak from remains of cold beef; curried pork. 2. Baked Semolina pudding.

2112. *Friday.*—1. Roast leg of mutton, stewed Spanish onions, potatoes. 2. Apple tart.

2113. *Saturday.*—1. Hashed mutton; boiled rabbit and onion sauce; vegetables. 2. Damson pudding made with bottled fruit.

DECEMBER.

2114.—DINNER FOR 18 PERSONS.

First Course.   *Entrées.*

Stewed Eels.	Mock-Turtle Soup, removed by Cod's Head and Shoulders and Oyster Sauce. Vase of Flowers. Julienne Soup, removed by Soles aux fines herbes.	Fried Whitings.

Curried Lobster.	Fillets of Grouse and Sauce Piquante. Vase of Flowers. Sweetbreads.	Mutton Cutlets and Soubise Sauce.

Second Course.   *Third Course.*

Roast Goose.	Haunch of Mutton. Ham and Brussels Sprouts. Vase of Flowers. Game Pie. Boiled Turkey and Celery Sauce.	Stewed Beef à la Jardinière.

Apricot Tourte.	Lemon Jelly.	Pheasants, removed by Plum-pudding. Vanilla Cream. Vase of Flowers. Blancmange. Wild Ducks, removed by Iced Pudding.	Tipsy Cake.	Champagne Jelly.	Victoria Sandwiches. Mince Pies.

Dessert and Ices.

2115.—DINNER FOR 12 PERSONS (December).

First Course.

Game Soup.   Clear Vermicelli Soup.

Codfish au gratin.   Fillets of Whitings à la Maître d'Hôtel.

Entrees.

Filet de Bœuf and Sauce Piquante.   Fricasseed Chicken.

Oyster Patties.   Curried Rabbit.

Second Course.

Roast Turkey and Sausages.   Boiled Leg of Pork and Vegetables.

Roast Goose.   Stewed Beef à la Jardinière.

Third Course.

Widgeon.   Partridges.

Charlotte aux Pommes.   Mince Pies.   Orange Jelly.   Lemon Cream.

Apple Tart.   Cabinet Pudding.

Dessert and Ices.

2116.—DINNER FOR 10 PERSONS (December).
First Course.
Mulligatawny Soup.

Fried Slices of Codfish.   Soles à la Crême.

Entrees.
Croquettes of Fowl.   Pork Cutlets and Tomata Sauce.

Second Course.
Roast Ribs of Beef.   Boiled Turkey and Celery Sauce.   Tongue, garnished.

Lark Pudding.   Vegetables.

Third Course.
Roast Hare.   Grouse.

Plum-pudding.   Mince Pies.   Charlotte à la Parisienne.   Cheesecakes.

Apple Tart.   Nesselrode Pudding.

Dessert and Ices.

2117.—DINNER FOR 8 PERSONS (December).
First Course.
Carrot Soup.

Crimped Cod and Oyster Sauce.   Baked Soles.

Entrees.
Mutton Kidneys à la Française.   Oyster Patties.

Second Course.
Boiled Beef and Vegetables.   Marrow-bones.   Roast Fowls and Water-cresses.

Tongue, garnished.   Game Pie.

Third Course.
Partridges.

Blancmange.   Compôte of Apples.   Vol-au-Vent of Pears.

Almond Cheesecakes.   Lemon Pudding.

Dessert and Ices.

2118.—DINNER FOR 6 PERSONS (December).—I.
First Course.
Rabbit Soup.

Brill and Shrimp Sauce.

Entrees.
Curried Fowl.   Oyster Patties.

Second Course.
Roast Turkey and Sausages.   Boiled Leg of Pork.   Vegetables.

Third Course.
Hunters' Pudding.   Lemon Cheesecakes.   Apple Tart.   Custards, in glasses.

Raspberry Cream.

Dessert.

2119.—**DINNER FOR 6 PERSONS (December).—II.**
First Course.
Ox-tail Soup.
Crimped Cod and Oyster Sauce.

Entrees.
Savoury Rissoles.   Fowl Scollops à la Béchamel.

Second Course.
Haunch of Mutton.   Boiled Chickens and Celery Sauce.
Bacon-cheek, garnished with Brussels Sprouts.   Vegetables.

Third Course.
Snipes.
Orange Jelly.   Cheesecakes.   Apples à la Portugaise.
Apricot-jam Tartlets.   Soufflé of Rice.

Dessert.

2120.—**DINNER FOR 6 PERSONS (December).—III.**
First Course.
Vermicelli Soup.
Soles à la Maître d'Hôtel.   Fried Eels.

Entrees.
Pork Cutlets and Tomata Sauce.   Ragoût of Mutton à la Jardinière.

Second Course.
Roast Goose.   Boiled Leg of Mutton and Vegetables.

Third Course.
Pheasants.
Whipped Cream.   Meringues.   Compôte of Normandy Pippins.
Mince Pies.   Plum-pudding.

Dessert.

2121.—**DINNER FOR 6 PERSONS (December).—IV.**
First Course.
Carrot Soup.
Baked Cod.   Fried Smelts.

Entrees.
Stewed Rump-steak à la Jardinière.   Fricasseed Chicken.

Second Course.
Roast Leg of Mutton, boned and stuffed.   Boiled Turkey and Oyster Sauce.
Vegetables.

Third Course.
Wild Ducks.
Fancy Pastry.   Lemon Cream.   Damson Tart, with bottled fruit.
Custards, in glasses.   Cabinet Pudding.

Dessert.

PLAIN FAMILY DINNERS FOR DECEMBER.

2122. *Sunday.*—1. Carrot soup. 2. Roast beef, horseradish sauce, vegetables. 3. Plum-pudding, mince pies.

2123. *Monday.*—1. Fried whitings, melted butter. 2. Rabbit pie, cold beef, mashed potatoes. 3. Plum-pudding cut in slices and warmed; apple tart.

2124. *Tuesday.*—1. Hashed beef and broiled bones, pork cutlets and tomata sauce; vegetables. 2. Baked lemon pudding.

2125. *Wednesday.*—1. Boiled neck of mutton and vegetables; the broth served first with a little pearl barley or rice boiled in it. 2. Bakewell pudding.

2126. *Thursday.*—1. Roast leg of pork, apple sauce, vegetables. 2. Rice snowballs.

2127. *Friday.*—1. Soles à la Crême. 2. Cold pork and mashed potatoes, broiled rump-steaks and oyster sauce. 3. Rolled jam pudding.

2128. *Saturday.*—1. The remains of cold pork curried, dish of rice, mutton cutlets, and mashed potatoes. 2. Baked apple dumplings.

———

2129. *Sunday.*—1. Roast turkey and sausages, boiled leg of pork, pease pudding, vegetables. 2. Baked apple pudding, mince pies.

2130. *Monday.*—1. Hashed turkey, cold pork, mashed potatoes. 2. Mince-meat pudding.

2131. *Tuesday.*—1. Pea-soup made from liquor in which pork was boiled. 2. Boiled fowls and celery sauce, vegetables. 3. Baked rice pudding.

2132. *Wednesday.*—1. Roast leg of mutton, stewed Spanish onions, potatoes. 2. Baked rolled jam pudding.

2133. *Thursday.*—1. Baked cod's head. 2. Cold mutton, roast hare, gravy and red-currant jelly. 3. Macaroni.

2134. *Friday.*—1. Hare soup, made with stock and remains of roast hare. 2. Hashed mutton, pork cutlets, and mashed potatoes. 3. Open tarts, rice blancmange.

2135. *Saturday.*—1. Rumpsteak-and-kidney pudding, vegetables. 2. Mince pies, baked apple dumplings.

2136.—BILL OF FARE FOR A GAME DINNER FOR 30 PERSONS (November).

First Course.

Purée of Grouse.

Hare Soup.

Vase of Flowers.

Soup à la Reine.

Pheasant Soup.

Entrées.

Salmi of Widgeon.

Salmi of Woodcock.

Fillets of Hare en Chevreuil.

Perdrix aux Choux.

Lark Pudding.

Vase of Flowers.

Curried Rabbit.

Fillet of Pheasant and Truffles.

Game Patties.

Salmi of Woodcock.

Salmi of Widgeon.

Second Course.

Cold Pheasant Pie à la Périgord.

Larded Pheasants.

Leveret, larded and stuffed.

Vase of Flowers.

Grouse.

Larded Partridges.

Hot raised Pie of mixed Game.

Third Course.

Snipes.

Golden Plovers.

Wild Duck.

Pintails.

Quails.

Vase of Flowers.

Teal.

Woodcocks.

Snipes. Widgeon. Ortolans.

Entremets and Removes.

Apricot Tart.

Vol-au-Vent of Pears.

Maids of Honour.

Boudin à la Nesselrode.

Dantzic Jelly.

Vase of Flowers.

Charlotte Russe.

Plum-pudding.

Maids of Honour.

Gâteau Génoise glacé.

Compôte of Apples.

Dessert.

Olives.

Preserved Cherries.

Ginger-Ice Cream.

Filberts. Wafers.

Dried Fruit.

Figs.

Strawberry-Ice Cream.

Pineapples.

Grapes.

Pears.

Vase of Flowers.

Apples.

Grapes.

Pears.

Lemon-Water Ice.

Dried Fruit.

Preserved Cherries.

Olives.

Walnuts. Biscuits.

Orange-Water Ice.

Figs.

MENU.

2137.—SERVICE A LA RUSSE (July).

———◇———

Julienne Soup.   Vermicelli Soup.

Boiled Salmon.   Turbot and Lobster Sauce.

Soles-Water Souchy.   Perch-Water Souchy.

Matelote d'Anguilles à la Toulouse.   Filets de Soles à la Normandie.

Red Mullet.   Trout.

Lobster Rissoles.   Whitebait.

Riz de Veau à la Banquière.   Filets de Poulets aux Coucombres.

Canards à la Rouennaise.   Mutton Cutlets à la Jardinière.

Braised Beef à la Flamande.   Spring Chickens.
Roast Quarter of Lamb.   Roast Saddle of Mutton.
Tongue.   Ham and Peas.

Quails, larded.   Roast Ducks.   Turkey Poult, larded.

Mayonnaise of Chicken.   Tomatas.   Green Peas à la Française.

Suédoise of Strawberries.   Charlotte Russe.   Compôte of Cherries.

Neapolitan Cakes.   Pastry.   Madeira Wine Jelly.

Iced Pudding à la Nesselrode.

———

Dessert and Ices.

Note.—Dinners à la Russe differ from ordinary dinners in the mode of serving the various dishes. In a dinner à la Russe, the dishes are cut up on a sideboard, and handed round to the guests, and each dish may be considered a course. The table for a dinner à la Russe should be laid with flowers and plants in fancy flowerpots down the middle, together with some of the dessert dishes. A *menu* or bill of fare should be laid by the side of each guest.

MENU.

2138.—SERVICE A LA RUSSE (November).

Ox-tail Soup.   Soup à la Jardinière.

Turbot and Lobster Sauce.   Crimped Cod and Oyster Sauce.

Stewed Eels.   Soles à la Normandie.

Pike and Cream Sauce.   Fried Filleted Soles.

Filets de Bœuf à la Jardinière.   Croquettes of Game aux Champignons.

Chicken Cutlets.   Mutton Cutlets and Tomata Sauce.

Lobster Rissoles.   Oyster Patties.

Partridges aux fines herbes.   Larded Sweetbreads.

Roast Beef.   Poulets áux Cressons.
Haunch of Mutton.   Roast Turkey.
Boiled Turkey and Celery Sauce.   Ham.

Grouse.   Pheasants.   Hare.

Salad.   Artichokes.   Stewed Celery.

Italian Cream.   Charlotte aux Pommes.   Compôte of Pears.

Croûtes madrées aux Fruits.   Pastry.   Punch Jelly.

Iced Pudding.

Dessert and Ices.

Note.—Dinners à la Russe are scarcely suitable for small establishments; a large number of servants being required to carve, and to help the guests; besides there being a necessity for more plates, dishes, knives, forks, and spoons, than are usually to be found in any other than a very large establishment. Where, however, a service à la Russe is practicable, there is, perhaps, no mode of serving a dinner so enjoyable as this.

SUPPERS.

2139. Much may be done in the arrangement of a supper-table, at a very small expense, provided *taste* and *ingenuity* are exercised. The colours and flavours of the various dishes should contrast nicely; there should be plenty of fruit and flowers on the table, and the room should be well lighted. We have endeavoured to show how the various dishes may be placed; but of course these little matters entirely depend on the length and width of the table used, on individual taste, whether the tables are arranged round the room, whether down the centre, with a cross one at the top, or whether the supper is laid in two separate rooms, &c. &c. The garnishing of the dishes has also much to do with the appearance of a supper-table. Hams and tongues should be ornamented with cut vegetable flowers, raised pies with aspic jelly cut in dice, and all the dishes garnished sufficiently to be in good taste without looking absurd. The eye, in fact, should be as much gratified as the palate. Hot soup is now often served at suppers, but is not placed on the table. The servants fill the plates from a tureen on the buffet, and then hand them to the guests: when these plates are removed, the business of supper commences.

2140. Where small rooms and large parties necessitate having a standing supper, many things enumerated in the following bill of fare may be placed on the buffet. Dishes for these suppers should be selected which may be eaten standing without any trouble. The following list may, perhaps, assist our readers in the arrangement of a buffet for a standing supper.

2141. Beef, ham, and tongue sandwiches, lobster and oyster patties, sausage rolls, meat rolls, lobster salad, dishes of fowls, the latter *all cut up ;* dishes of sliced ham, sliced tongue, sliced beef, and galantine of veal; various jellies, blancmanges, and creams; custards in glasses, compôtes of fruit, tartlets of jam, and several dishes of small fancy pastry; dishes of fresh fruit, bonbons, sweetmeats, two or three sponge cakes, a few plates of biscuits, and the buffet ornamented with vases of fresh or artificial flowers. The above dishes are quite sufficient for a standing supper; where more are desired, a supper must then be laid and arranged in the usual manner.

2142.—BILL OF FARE FOR A BALL SUPPER FOR 60 PERSONS (for Winter).

Lobster Salad.			Lobster Salad.
		BOAR'S HEAD, garnished with Aspic Jelly.	
	Fruited Jelly.	Mayonnaise of Fowl.	Charlotte Russe.
	Small Pastry.	Small Ham, garnished.	Biscuits.
Two Roast Fowls, cut up.		Iced Savoy Cake.	Two Roast Fowls, cut up.
	Vanilla Cream.	Epergne, with Fruit.	Fruited Jelly.
	Prawns.	Two Boiled Fowls, with Béchamel Sauce.	Prawns.
	Biscuits.	Tongue, ornamented.	Small Pastry.
	Custards, in glasses.	Trifle, ornamented.	Custards, in glasses.
		Raised Chicken Pie.	
Lobster Salad.	Fruited Jelly.	Tipsy Cake.	Swiss Cream.
		Roast Pheasant.	
	Meringues.	Epergne, with Fruit.	Meringues.
	Raspberry Cream.	Galantine of Veal.	Fruited Jelly.
	Small Pastry.	Tipsy Cake.	Biscuits.
Two Roast Fowls, cut up.		Raised Game Pie.	Lobster Salad.
	Custards, in glasses.	Trifle, ornamented.	Custards, in glasses.
	Prawns.	Tongue, ornamented.	Prawns.
	Biscuits.	Two Boiled Fowls, with Béchamel Sauce.	Small Pastry.
		EPERGNE, WITH FRUIT.	
	Fruited Jelly.	Iced Savoy Cake.	Blancmange.
Lobster Salad.		Small Ham, garnished.	Two Roast Fowls, cut up.
	Charlotte Russe.	Mayonnaise of Fowl.	Fruited Jelly.
		Larded Capon.	Lobster Salad.

Note.—When soup is served from the buffet, Mock Turtle and Julienne may be selected. Besides the articles enumerated above, Ices, Wafers, Biscuits, Tea, Coffee, Wines, and Liqueurs will be required. Punch à la Romaine may also be added to the list of beverages.

2143.—BILL OF FARE FOR A BALL SUPPER,

Or a Cold Collation for a Summer Entertainment, or Wedding or Christening Breakfast for 70 or 80 Persons (July).

Left margin (vertical): 3 Compôtes of Fruit. — 3 Dishes of Small Pastry. — 3 English Pines.

Left margin (vertical): 4 Blancmanges, to be placed down the table. — 3 Dishes of Small Pastry. — 3 Fruit Tarts. — 20 Small Dishes of various Summer Fruits.

Left margin (vertical): 4 Jellies, to be placed down the table. — 3 Cheesecakes. — 3 Fruit Tarts. — 20 Small Dishes of various Summer Fruits.

Right margin (vertical): 4 Blancmanges, to be placed down the table. — 3 Cheesecakes. — 3 Fruit Tarts. — 20 Small Dishes of various Summer Fruits.

Right margin (vertical): 4 Jellies, to be placed down the table. — 3 Dishes of Small Pastry. — 3 English Pines.

Right margin (vertical): 3 Compôtes of Fruit.

Left dishes	Inner (vertical)	Centre	Inner (vertical)	Right dishes
Dish of Lobster, cut up.		Tongue. Ribs of Lamb. Two Roast Fowls. Mayonnaise of Salmon.		Veal-and-Ham Pie.
Charlotte Russe à la Vanille.	Lobster Salad.	Epergne, with Flowers.	Lobster Salad.	Savoy Cake.
Pigeon Pie.		Mayonnaise of Trout. Tongue, garnished. Boiled Fowls and Béchamel Sauce. Collared Eel. Ham. Raised Pie. Two Roast Fowls. Shoulder of Lamb, stuffed. Mayonnaise of Salmon.		Dish of Lobster, cut up.
Dish of Lobster, cut up.	Larded Capon. / Lobster Salad.	Epergne, with Flowers.	Boar's Head. / Lobster Salad.	Pigeon Pie.
	Lobster Salad.	Mayonnaise of Trout. Tongue. Boiled Fowls and Béchamel Sauce. Raised Pie. Ham, decorated. Shoulder of Lamb, stuffed. Two Roast Fowls. Mayonnaise of Salmon.	Lobster Salad.	
Pigeon Pie.				Dish of Lobster, cut up.
Dish of Lobster, cut up. Savoy Cake.	Lobster Salad.	Epergne, with Flowers.	Lobster Salad.	Charlotte Russe à la Vanille. Veal and Ham Pie.
		Mayonnaise of Trout. Tongue, garnished. Boiled Fowls and Béchamel Sauce. Collared Eel.		Dish of Lobster, cut up.

Note.—The length of the page will not admit of our giving the dishes as they should be placed on the table; they should be arranged with the large and high dishes down the centre, and the spaces filled up with the smaller dishes, fruit, and flowers, taking care that the flavours and colours contrast nicely, and that no two dishes of a sort come together. This bill of fare may be made to answer three or four purposes, placing a wedding cake or christening cake in the centre on a high stand, if required for either of these occasions. A few dishes of fowls, lobster salads, &c. &c., should be kept in reserve to replenish those that are most likely to be eaten first. A joint of cold roast and boiled beef should be placed on the buffet, as being something substantial for the gentlemen of the party to partake of. Besides the articles enumerated in the bill of fare, biscuits and wafers will be required, cream-and-water ices, tea, coffee, wines, liqueurs, soda-water, ginger-beer, and lemonade.

BREAKFASTS.

2144. It will not be necessary to give here a long bill of fare of cold joints, &c., which may be placed on the side-board, and do duty at the breakfast-table. Suffice it to say, that any cold meat the larder may furnish, should be nicely garnished, and be placed on the buffet. Collared and potted meats or fish, cold game or poultry, veal-and-ham pies, game-and-rumpsteak pies, are all suitable dishes for the breakfast-table; as also cold ham, tongue, &c. &c.

2145. The following list of hot dishes may perhaps assist our readers in knowing what to provide for the comfortable meal called breakfast. Broiled fish, such as mackerel, whiting, herrings, dried haddocks, &c.; mutton chops and rump-steaks, broiled sheep's kidneys, kidneys à la mâitre d'hôtel, sausages, plain rashers of bacon, bacon and poached eggs, ham and poached eggs, omelets, plain boiled eggs, œufs-au-plat, poached eggs on toast, muffins, toast, marmalade, butter, &c. &c.

2146. In the summer, and when they are obtainable, always have a vase of freshly-gathered flowers on the breakfast-table, and, when convenient, a nicely-arranged dish of fruit: when strawberries are in season, these are particularly refreshing; as also grapes, or even currants.

LUNCHEONS AND SUPPERS.

2147. The remains of cold joints, nicely garnished, a few sweets, or a little hashed meat, poultry or game, are the usual articles placed on the table for luncheon, with bread and cheese, biscuits, butter, &c. If a substantial meal is desired, rump-steaks or mutton chops may be served, as also veal cutlets, kidneys, or any dish of that kind. In families where there is a nursery, the mistress of the house often partakes of the meal with the children, and makes it her luncheon. In the summer, a few dishes of fresh fruit should be added to the luncheon, or, instead of this, a compôte of fruit or fruit tart, or pudding.

2148. Of suppers we have little to say, as we have already given two bills of fare for a large party, which will answer very well for a smaller number, by reducing the quantity of dishes and by omitting a few. Hot suppers are now very little in request, as people now generally dine at an hour which precludes the possibility of requiring supper; at all events, not one of a substantial kind. Should, however, a bill of fare be required, one of those under the head of DINNERS, with slight alterations, will be found to answer for a hot supper.

BILL OF FARE FOR A PICNIC FOR 40 PERSONS.

2149. A joint of cold roast beef, a joint of cold boiled beef, 2 ribs of lamb, 2 shoulders of lamb, 4 roast fowls, 2 roast ducks, 1 ham, 1 tongue, 2 veal-and-ham pies, 2 pigeon pies, 6 medium-sized lobsters, 1 piece of collared calf's head, 18 lettuces, 6 baskets of salad, 6 cucumbers.

2150. Stewed fruit well sweetened, and put into glass bottles well corked; 3 or 4 dozen plain pastry biscuits to eat with the stewed fruit, 2 dozen fruit turnovers, 4 dozen cheesecakes, 2 cold cabinet puddings in moulds, 2 blanc-manges in moulds, a few jam puffs, 1 large cold plum-pudding (this must be good), a few baskets of fresh fruit, 3 dozen plain biscuits, a piece of cheese, 6 lbs. of butter (this, of course, includes the butter for tea), 4 quartern loaves of household bread, 3 dozen rolls, 6 loaves of tin bread (for tea), 2 plain plum cakes, 2 pound cakes, 2 sponge cakes, a tin of mixed biscuits, ½ lb. of tea. Coffee is not suitable for a picnic, being difficult to make.

Things not to be forgotten at a Picnic.

2151. A stick of horseradish, a bottle of mint-sauce well corked, a bottle of salad dressing, a bottle of vinegar, made mustard, pepper, salt, good oil, and pounded sugar. If it can be managed, take a little ice. It is scarcely necessary to say that plates, tumblers, wine-glasses, knives, forks, and spoons, must not be forgotten; as also teacups and saucers, 3 or 4 teapots, some lump sugar, and milk, if this last-named article cannot be obtained in the neighbourhood. Take 3 corkscrews.

2152. *Beverages.*—3 dozen quart bottles of ale, packed in hampers; ginger-beer, soda-water, and lemonade, of each 2 dozen bottles; 6 bottles of sherry, 6 bottles of claret, champagne à discrétion, and any other light wine that may be preferred, and 2 bottles of brandy. Water can usually be obtained; so it is useless to take it.

attached domestics.

DOMESTIC SERVANTS.

CHAPTER XLI.

2153. IT is the custom of "Society" to abuse its servants,—a *façon de
parler,* such as leads their lords and masters to talk of the weather, and,
when rurally inclined, of the crops,—leads matronly ladies, and ladies just
entering on their probation in that honoured and honourable state, to talk
of servants, and, as we are told, wax eloquent over the greatest plague in
life while taking a quiet cup of tea.   Young men at their clubs, also, we are
told, like to abuse their "fellows," perhaps not without a certain pride and
pleasure at the opportunity of intimating that they enjoy such appendages
to their state.   It is another conviction of "Society" that the race of good
servants has died out, at least in England, although they do order these
things better in France ; that there is neither honesty, conscientiousness,
nor the careful and industrious habits which distinguished the servants of our
grandmothers and great-grandmothers ; that domestics no longer know their
place ; that the introduction of cheap silks and cottons, and, still more
recently, those ambiguous "materials" and tweeds, have removed the land-
marks between the mistress and her maid, between the master and his man.

2154. When the distinction really depends on things so insignificant, this
is very probably the case ; when the lady of fashion chooses her footman
without any other consideration than his height, shape, and *tournure* of his
calf, it is not surprising that she should find a domestic who has no attachment for the family, who considers the figure he cuts behind her carriage,
and the late hours he is compelled to keep, a full compensation for the wages
he exacts, for the food he wastes, and for the perquisites he can lay his
hands on.   Nor should the fast young man, who chooses his groom for his
knowingness in the ways of the turf and in the tricks of low horse-dealers,
be surprised if he is sometimes the victim of these learned ways.   But these
are the exceptional cases, which prove the existence of a better state of
things.   The great masses of society among us are not thus deserted ; there
are few families of respectability, from the shopkeeper in the next street to
the nobleman whose mansion dignifies the next square, which do not contain
among their dependents attached and useful servants ; and where these are
absent altogether, there are good reasons for it.   The sensible master and
the kind mistress know, that if servants depend on them for their means of

living, in their turn they are dependent on their servants for very many of the comforts of life; and that, with a proper amount of care in choosing servants, and treating them like reasonable beings, and making slight excuses for the shortcomings of human nature, they will, save in some exceptional case, be tolerably well served, and, in most instances, surround themselves with attached domestics.

2155. This remark, which is applicable to all domestics, is especially so to men-servants. Families accustomed to such attendants have always about them humble dependents, whose children have no other prospect than domestic service to look forward to; to them it presents no degradation, but the reverse, to be so employed; they are initiated step by step into the mysteries of the household, with the prospect of rising in the service, if it is a house admitting of promotion,—to the respectable position of butler or house-steward. In families of humbler pretensions, where they must look for promotion elsewhere, they know that can only be attained by acquiring the good-will of their employers. Can there be any stronger security for their good conduct,—any doubt that, in the mass of domestic servants, good conduct is the rule, the reverse the exception?

2156. The number of the male domestics in a family varies according to the wealth and position of the master, from the owner of the ducal mansion, with a retinue of attendants, at the head of which is the chamberlain and house-steward, to the occupier of the humbler house, where a single footman, or even the odd man-of-all-work, is the only male retainer. The majority of gentlemen's establishments probably comprise a servant out of livery, or butler, a footman, and coachman, or coachman and groom, where the horses exceed two or three.

DUTIES OF THE BUTLER.

2157. The domestic duties of the butler are to bring in the eatables at breakfast, and wait upon the family at that meal, assisted by the footman, and see to the cleanliness of everything at table. On taking away, he removes the tray with the china and plate, for which he is responsible. At luncheon, he arranges the meal, and waits unassisted, the footman being now engaged in other duties. At dinner, he places the silver and plated articles on the table, sees that everything is in its place, and rectifies what is wrong. He carries in the first dish, and announces in the drawing-room that dinner is on the table, and respectfully stands by the door until the company are seated, when he takes his place behind his master's chair on the left, to remove the covers, handing them to the other attendants to carry out. After the first course of plates is supplied, his place is at the sideboard to serve the wines, but only when called on.

2158. The first course ended, he rings the cook's bell, and hands the dishes from the table to the other servants to carry away, receiving from them the second course, which he places on the table, removing the covers as before, and again taking his place at the sideboard.

2159. At dessert, the slips being removed, the butler receives the dessert from the other servants, and arranges it on the table, with plates and glasses, and then takes his place behind his master's chair to hand the wines and ices, while the footman stands behind his mistress for the same purpose, the other attendants leaving the room. Where the old-fashioned practice of having the dessert on the polished table, without any cloth, is still adhered to, the butler should rub off any marks made by the hot dishes before arranging the dessert.

2160. Before dinner, he has satisfied himself that the lamps, candles, or gas-burners are in perfect order, if not lighted, which will usually be the case. Having served every one with their share of the dessert, put the fires in order (when these are used), and seen the lights are all right, at a signal from his master, he and the footman leave the room.

2161. He now proceeds to the drawing-room, arranges the fireplace, and sees to the lights; he then returns to his pantry, prepared to answer the bell, and attend to the company, while the footman is clearing away and cleaning the plate and glasses.

2162. At tea he again attends. At bedtime he appears with the candles; he locks up the plate, secures doors and windows, and sees that all the fires are safe.

2163. In addition to these duties, the butler, where only one footman is kept, will be required to perform some of the duties of the valet, to pay bills, and superintend the other servants. But the real duties of the butler are in the wine-cellar; there he should be competent to advise his master as to the price and quality of the wine to be laid in; "fine," bottle, cork, and seal it, and place it in the binns. Brewing, racking, and bottling malt liquors, belong to his office, as well as their distribution. These and other drinkables are brought from the cellar every day by his own hands, except where an under-butler is kept; and a careful entry of every bottle used, entered in the cellar-book; so that the book should always show the contents of the cellar.

2164. The office of butler is thus one of very great trust in a household. Here, as elsewhere, honesty is the best policy: the butler should make it his business to understand the proper treatment of the different wines under his charge, which he can easily do from the wine-merchant, and faithfully attend to it; his own reputation will soon compensate for the absence of bribes from unprincipled wine-merchants, if he serves a generous and hospitable master. Nothing spreads more rapidly in society than the reputation of a good wine-cellar, and all that is required is wines well chosen and well cared for; and this a little knowledge, carefully applied, will soon supply.

2165. The butler, we have said, has charge of the contents of the cellars, and it is his duty to keep them in a proper condition, to fine down wine in wood, bottle it off, and store it away in places suited to the sorts. Where wine comes into the cellar ready bottled, it is usual to return the same number of empty bottles; the butler has not, in this case, the same inducements to keep the bottles of the different sorts separated; but where the wine is bottled in the house, he will find his account, not only in keeping them separate, but in rinsing them well, and even washing them with clean water as soon as they are empty.

2166. There are various modes of fining wine : isinglass, gelatine, and gum Arabic are all used for the purpose. Whichever of these articles is used, the process is always the same. Supposing eggs (the cheapest) to be used,—Draw a gallon or so of the wine, and mix one quart of it with the whites of four eggs, by stirring it with a whisk; afterwards, when thoroughly mixed, pour it back into the cask through the bunghole, and stir up the whole cask, in a rotatory direction, with a clean split stick inserted through the bunghole. Having stirred it sufficiently, pour in the remainder of the wine drawn off, until the cask is full; then stir again, skimming off the bubbles that rise to the surface. When thoroughly mixed by stirring, close the bunghole, and leave it to stand for three or four days. This quantity of clarified wine will fine thirteen dozen of port or sherry. The other clearing ingredients are applied in the same manner, the material being cut into small pieces, and dissolved in the quart of wine, and the cask stirred in the same manner.

2167. *To Bottle Wine.*—Having thoroughly washed and dried the bottles, supposing they have been before used for the same kind of wine, provide corks, which will be improved by being slightly boiled, or at least steeped in hot water,—a wooden hammer or mallet, a bottling-boot, and a squeezer for the corks. Bore a hole in the lower part of the cask with a gimlet, receiving the liquid stream which follows in the bottle and filterer, which is placed in a tub or basin. This operation is best performed by two persons, one to draw the wine, the other to cork the bottles. The drawer is to see that the bottles are up to the mark, but not too full, the bottle being placed in a clean tub to prevent waste. The corking-boot is buckled by a strap to the knee, the bottle placed in it, and the cork, after being squeezed in the press, driven in by a flat wooden mallet.

2168. As the wine draws near to the bottom of the cask, a thick piece of muslin is placed in the strainer, to prevent the viscous grounds from passing into the bottle.

2169. Having carefully counted the bottles, they are stored away in their respective binns, a layer of sand or sawdust being placed under the first tier, and another over it; a second tier is laid over this, protected by a lath, the head of the second being laid to the bottom of the first; over this another bed of sawdust is laid, not too thick, another lath; and so on till the binn is filled.

2170. Wine so laid in will be ready for use according to its quality and age. Port wine, old in the wood, will be ready to drink in five or six months; but if it is a fruity wine, it will improve every year. Sherry, if of good quality, will be fit to drink as soon as the "sickness" (as its first condition after bottling is called) ceases, and will also improve; but the cellar must be kept at a perfectly steady temperature, neither too hot nor too cold, but about 55° or 60°, and absolutely free from draughts of cold air.

DUTIES OF THE FOOTMAN.

2171. Where a single footman, or odd man, is the only male servant, then, whatever his ostensible position, he is required to make himself generally useful. He has to clean the knives and shoes, the furniture, the plate; answer the visitors who call, the drawing-room and parlour bells; and do all the errands. His life is no sinecure; and a methodical arrangement of his time will be necessary, in order to perform his many duties with any satisfaction to himself or his master.

2172. The footman only finds himself in stockings, shoes, and washing. Where silk stockings, or other extra articles of linen are worn, they are found by the family, as well as his livery, a working dress, consisting of a pair of overalls, a waistcoat, a fustian jacket, with a white or jean one for times when he is liable to be called to answer the door or wait at breakfast; and, on quitting his service, he is expected to leave behind him any livery had within six months.

2173. The footman is expected to rise early, in order to get through all his dirty work before the family are stirring. Boots and shoes, and knives and forks, should be cleaned, lamps in use trimmed, his master's clothes brushed, the furniture rubbed over; so that he may put aside his working dress, tidy himself, and appear in a clean jean jacket to lay the cloth and prepare breakfast for the family.

2174. We need hardly dwell on the boot-cleaning process: three good brushes and good blacking must be provided; one of the brushes hard, to brush off the mud; the other soft, to lay on the blacking; the third of a medium hardness, for polishing; and each should be kept for its particular use. The blacking should be kept corked up, except when in use, and applied to the brush with a sponge tied to a stick, which, when put away, rests in a notch cut in the cork. When boots come in very muddy, it is a good practice to wash off the mud, and wipe them dry with a sponge; then leave them to dry very gradually on their sides, taking care they are not placed near the fire, or scorched. Much delicacy of treatment is required in cleaning ladies' boots, so as to make the leather look well-polished, and the upper part retain a fresh appearance, with the lining free from hand-marks, which are very offensive to a lady of refined tastes.

2175. Patent leather boots require to be wiped with a wet sponge, and afterwards with a soft dry cloth, and occasionally with a soft cloth and sweet oil, blacking and polishing the edge of the soles in the usual way, but so as not to cover the patent polish with blacking. A little milk may also be used with very good effect for patent leather boots.

2176. Top boots are still occasionally worn by gentlemen. While cleaning the lower part in the usual manner, protect the tops, by inserting a cloth or brown paper under the edges and bringing it over them. In cleaning the tops, let the covering fall down over the boot; wash the tops clean with soap and flannel, and rub out any spots with pumice-stone. If the tops are to be whiter, dissolve an ounce of oxalic acid and half an ounce of pumice-stone in a pint of soft water; if a brown colour is intended, mix an ounce of muriatic acid, half an ounce of alum, half an ounce of gum Arabic, and half an ounce of spirit of lavender, in a pint and a half of skimmed milk "turned." These mixtures apply by means of a sponge, and polish, when dry, with a rubber made of soft flannel.

2177. Knives are now generally cleaned by means of Kent's or Masters's machine, which gives very little trouble, and is very effective; before, however, putting the knives into the machine, it is highly necessary that they be first washed in a little warm (not hot) water, and then thoroughly wiped: if put into the machine with any grease on them, it adheres to the brushes, and consequently renders them unfit to use for the next knives that may be put in. When this precaution is not taken, the machine must come to pieces, so causing an immense amount of trouble, which may all be avoided by having the knives thoroughly free from grease before using the machine. Brushes are also used for cleaning forks, which facilitate the operation. When knives are so cleaned, see that they are carefully polished, wiped, and with a good edge, the ferules and prongs free from dirt, and place them in the basket with the handles all one way.

2178. Lamp-trimming requires a thorough acquaintance with the mechanism; after that, constant attention to cleanliness, and an occasional entire clearing out with hot water: when this is done, all the parts should be carefully dried before filling again with oil. When lacquered, wipe the lacquered parts with a soft brush and cloth, and wash occasionally with weak soapsuds, wiping carefully afterwards. Brass lamps may be cleaned with oil and rottenstone every day when trimmed. With bronze, and other ornamental lamps, more care will be required, and soft flannel and oil only used, to prevent the removal of the bronze or enamel. Brass-work, or any metal-work not lacquered, is cleaned by a little oil and rottenstone made into a paste, or with fine emery-powder and oil mixed in the same manner. A small portion of sal ammoniac, beat into a fine powder and moistened with soft water, rubbed over brass ornaments, and heated over a charcoal fire, and rubbed dry with bran or whitening, will give to brass-work the brilliancy of gold. In trimming moderator lamps, let the wick be cut evenly all round; as, if left higher in one place than it is in another, it will cause it to smoke and burn badly. The lamp should then be filled with oil from a feeder, and afterwards well wiped with a cloth or rag kept for the purpose. If it can be avoided, never wash the chimneys of a lamp, as it causes them to crack when they become hot. Small sticks, covered with wash-leather pads, are the best things to use for cleaning the glasses inside, and a clean duster for polishing the outside. The globe of a moderator lamp should be occasionally washed in warm soap-and-water, then well rinsed in cold water, and either wiped dry or left to drain. Where candle-lamps are used, take out the springs occasionally, and free them well from the grease that adheres to them.

2179. French polish, so universally applied to furniture, is easily kept in condition by dusting and rubbing with a soft cloth, or a rubber of old silk; but dining-tables can only be kept in order by hard rubbing, or rather by quick rubbing, which warms the wood and removes all spots.

2180. Brushing clothes is a very simple but very necessary operation. Fine cloths require to be brushed lightly, and with rather a soft brush, except where mud is to be removed, when a hard one is necessary, being previously beaten lightly to dislodge the dirt. Lay the garment on a table, and brush it in the direction of the nap. Having brushed it properly, turn the sleeves back to the collar, so that the folds may come at the elbow-joints; next turn the lappels or sides back over the folded sleeves; then lay the skirts over level with the collar, so that the crease may fall about the centre, and double one half over the other, so as the fold comes in the centre of the back.

2181. Having got through his dirty work, the single footman has now to clean himself and prepare the breakfast. He lays the cloth on the table; over it the breakfast-cloth, and sets the breakfast things in order, and then proceeds to wait upon his master, if he has any of the duties of a valet to perform.

2182. Where a valet is not kept, a portion of his duties falls to the footman's share,—brushing the clothes among others. When the hat is silk, it requires brushing every day with a soft brush; after rain, it requires wiping the way of the nap before drying, and, when nearly dry, brushing with the soft brush and with the hat-stick in it. If the footman is required to perform any part of a valet's duties, he will have to see that the housemaid lights a fire in the dressing-room in due time; that the room is dusted and cleaned; that the washhand-ewer is filled with soft water; and that the bath, whether hot or cold, is ready when required; that towels are at hand; that hairbrushes and combs are properly cleansed, and in their places; that hot water is ready at the hour ordered; the dressing-gown and slippers in their place, the clean linen aired, and the clothes to be worn for the day in their proper places. After the master has dressed, it will be the footman's duty to restore everything to its place properly cleansed and dry, and the whole restored to order.

2183. At breakfast, when there is no butler, the footman carries up the tea-urn, and, assisted by the housemaid, he waits during breakfast. Breakfast over, he removes the tray and other things off the table, folds up the breakfast-cloth, and sets the room in order, by sweeping up all crumbs, shaking the cloth, and laying it on the table again, making up the fire, and sweeping up the hearth.

2184. At luncheon-time nearly the same routine is observed, except where the footman is either out with the carriage or away on other business, when, in the absence of any butler, the housemaid must assist.

2185. For dinner, the footman lays the cloth, taking care that the table is not too near the fire, if there is one, and that passage-room is left. A table-cloth should be laid without a wrinkle; and this requires two persons: over this the slips are laid, which are usually removed preparatory to placing dessert on the table. He prepares knives, forks, and glasses, with five or six plates for each person. This done, he places chairs enough for the party, distributing them equally on each side of the table, and opposite to each a napkin neatly folded, within it a piece of bread or small roll, and a knife on the right side of each plate, a fork on the left, and a carving-knife and fork at the top and bottom of the table, outside the others, with the rests opposite to them, and a gravy-spoon beside the knife. The fish-slice should be at the top, where the lady of the house, with the assistance of the gentle-man next to her, divides the fish, and the soup-ladle at the bottom: it is some-times usual to add a dessert-knife and fork; at the same time, on the right side also of each plate, put a wine-glass for as many kinds of wine as it is in-tended to hand round, and a finger-glass or glass-cooler about four inches from the edge. The latter are frequently put on the table with the dessert.

2186. About half an hour before dinner, he rings the dinner-bell, where that is the practice, and occupies himself with carrying up everything he is likely to require. At the expiration of the time, having communicated with the cook, he rings the real dinner-bell, and proceeds to take it up with such assist-ance as he can obtain. Having ascertained that all is in order, that his own dress is clean and presentable, and his white cotton gloves are without a stain, he announces in the drawing-room that dinner is served, and stands respect-fully by the door until the company are seated: he places himself on the left, behind his master, who is to distribute the soup; where soup and fish are served together, his place will be at his mistress's left hand; but he must be on the alert to see that whoever is assisting him, whether male or female, are at their posts. If any of the guests has brought his own servant with him, his place is behind his master's chair, rendering such assistance to others as he can, while attending to his master's wants throughout the dinner, so that every guest has what he requires. This necessitates both activity and intelligence, and should be done without bustle, without asking any questions, except where it is the custom of the house to hand round dishes or wine, when it will be necessary to mention, in a quiet and unobtrusive manner, the dish or wine you present.

2187. Salt-cellars should be placed on the table in number sufficient for the guests, so that each may help themselves, or, at least, their immediate neighbours.

DINNERS À LA RUSSE.

2188. In some houses the table is laid out with plate and glass, and ornamented with flowers, the dessert only being placed on the table, the dinner itself being placed on the sideboard, and handed round in succession, in courses of soup, fish, entrées, meat, game, and sweets. This is not only elegant but economical, as fewer dishes are required, the symmetry of the table being made up with the ornaments and dessert. The various dishes are also handed round when hot; but it involves additional and superior attendance, as the wines are also handed round; and unless the servants are very active and intelligent, many blunders are likely to be made. (See p. 954.)

GENERAL OBSERVATIONS.

2189. While attentive to all, the footman should be obtrusive to none; he should give nothing but on a waiter, and always hand it with the left hand and on the left side of the person he serves, and hold it so that the guest may take it with ease. In lifting dishes from the table, he should use both hands, and remove them with care, so that nothing is spilt on the table-cloth or on the dresses of the guests.

2190. Masters as well as servants sometimes make mistakes; but it is not expected that a servant will correct any omissions, even if he should have time to notice them, although with the best intentions : thus it would not be correct, for instance, if he observed that his master took wine with the ladies all round, as some gentlemen still continue to do, but stopped at some one :—to nudge him on the shoulder and say, as was done by the servant of a Scottish gentleman, "What ails you at her in the green gown?" It will be better to leave the lady unnoticed than for the servant thus to turn his master into ridicule.

2191. During dinner each person's knife, fork, plate, and spoon should be changed as soon as he has done with it; the vegetables and sauces belonging to the different dishes presented without remark to the guests; and the footman should tread lightly in moving round, and, if possible, should bear in mind, if there is a wit or humorist of the party, whose good things keep the table in a roar, that they are not expected to reach his ears.

2192. In opening wine, let it be done quietly, and without shaking the bottle; if crusted, let it be inclined to the crusted side, and decanted while in that position. In opening champagne, it is not necessary to discharge it with a pop; properly cooled, the cork is easily extracted without an explosion; when the cork is out, the mouth of the bottle should be wiped with the napkin over the footman's arm.

2193. At the end of the first course, notice is conveyed to the cook, who is waiting to send up the second, which is introduced in the same way as before; the attendants who remove the fragments, carrying the dishes from the kitchen, and handing them to the footman or butler, whose duty it is to arrange them on the table. After dinner, the dessert-glasses and wines are placed on the table by the footman, who places himself behind his master's chair, to supply wine and hand round the ices and other refreshments, all other servants leaving the room.

2194. As soon as the drawing-room bell rings for tea, the footman enters with the tray, which has been previously prepared; hands the tray round to the company, with cream and sugar, the tea and coffee being generally poured out, while another attendant hands cakes, toast, or biscuits. If it is an ordinary family party, where this social meal is prepared by the mistress, he carries the urn or kettle, as the case may be; hands round the toast, or such other eatable as may be required, removing the whole in the same manner when tea is over.

2195. **After each** meal, the footman's place is in his pantry : here perfect order should prevail—a place for everything and everything in its place. A sink, with hot and cold water laid on, is very desirable,—cold absolutely necessary. Wooden bowls or tubs of sufficient capacity are required, one for hot and another for cold water. Have the bowl three parts full of clean hot water; in this wash all plate and plated articles which are greasy, wiping them before cleaning with the brush.

2196. The footman in small families, where only one man is kept, has many of the duties of the upper servants to perform as well as his own, and more constant occupation; he will also have the arrangement of his time more immediately under his own control, and he will do well to reduce it to a methodical division. All his rough work should be done before breakfast is ready, when he must appear clean, and in a presentable state. After breakfast, when everything belonging to his pantry is cleaned and put in its place, the furniture in the dining and drawing rooms requires rubbing. Towards noon, the parlour luncheon is to be prepared; and he must be at his mistress's disposal to go out with the carriage, or follow her if she walks out.

2197. Glass is a beautiful and most fragile article: hence it requires great care in washing. A perfectly clean wooden bowl is best for this operation, one for moderately hot and another for cold water. Wash the glasses well in the first and rinse them in the second, and turn them down on a linen cloth folded two or three times, to drain for a few minutes. When sufficiently drained, wipe them with a cloth and polish with a finer one, doing so tenderly and carefully. Accidents will happen; but nothing discredits a servant in the drawing-room more than continual reports of breakages, which, of course, must reach that region.

2198. Decanters and water-jugs require still more tender treatment in cleaning, inasmuch as they are more costly to replace. Fill them about two-thirds with hot but not boiling water, and put in a few pieces of well-soaped brown paper; leave them thus for two or three hours; then shake the water up and down in the decanters; empty this out, rinse them well with clean cold water, and put them in a rack to drain. When dry, polish them outside and inside, as far as possible, with a fine cloth. To remove the crust of port or other wines, add a little muriatic acid to the water, and let it remain for some time.

2199. When required to go out with the carriage, it is the footman's duty to see that it has come to the door perfectly clean, and that the glasses, and sashes, and linings, are free from dust. In receiving messages at the carriage door, he should turn his ear to the speaker, so as to comprehend what is said, in order that he may give his directions to the coachman clearly. When the house he is to call at is reached, he should knock, and return to the carriage for orders. In closing the door upon the family, he should see that the handle is securely turned, and that no part of the ladies' dress is shut in.

2200. It is the footman's duty to carry messages or letters for his master or mistress to their friends, to the post, or to the tradespeople; and nothing is more important than dispatch and exactness in doing so, although writing even the simplest message is now the ordinary and very proper practice. Dean Swift, among his other quaint directions, all of which are to be read by contraries, recommends a perusal of all such epistles, in order that you may be the more able to fulfil your duty to your master. An old lady of Forfarshire had one of those odd old Caleb Balderston sort of servants, who construed the Dean of St. Patrick more literally. On one occasion, when dispatch was of some importance, knowing his inquiring nature, she called her Scotch Paul Pry to her, opened the note, and read it to him herself, saying, "Now, Andrew, you ken a' aboot it, and needna' stop to open and read it, but just take it at once." Probably most of the notes you are expected to carry might, with equal harmlessness, be communicated to you; but it will be better not to take so lively an interest in your mistress's affairs.

2201. Politeness and civility to visitors is one of the things masters and mistresses have a right to expect, and should exact rigorously. When visitors present themselves, the servant charged with the duty of opening the door will open it promptly, and answer, without hesitation, if the family are "not at home," or "engaged;" which generally means the same thing, and might be oftener used with advantage to morals. On the contrary, if he has no such orders, he will answer affirmatively, open the door wide to admit them, and precede them to open the door of the drawing-room. If the family are not there, he will place chairs for them, open the blinds (if the room is too dark), and intimate civilly that he goes to inform his mistress. If the lady is in her drawing-room, he announces the name of the visitors, having previously acquainted himself with it. In this part of his duty it is necessary to be very careful to repeat the names correctly; mispronouncing names is very apt to give offence, and leads sometimes to other disagreeables. The writer was once initiated into some of the secrets on the "other side" of a legal affair in which he took an interest, before he could correct a mistake made by the servant in announcing him. When the visitor is departing, the servant should be at hand, ready, when rung for, to open the door; he should open it with a respectful manner, and close it gently when the visitors are fairly beyond the threshold. When several visitors arrive together, he should take care not to mix up the different names together, where they belong to the same family, as Mr., Mrs., and Miss; if they are strangers, he should announce each as distinctly as possible.

2202. *Receptions and Evening Parties.*—The drawing-rooms being prepared, the card-tables laid out with cards and counters, and such other arrangements as are necessary made for the reception of the company, the rooms should be lighted up as the hour appointed approaches. Attendants in the drawing-room, even more than in the dining-room, should move about actively but noiselessly; no creaking of shoes, which is an abomination; watching the lights from time to time, so as to keep up their brilliancy. But even if the attendant likes a game of cribbage or whist himself, he must not interfere in his master or mistress's game, nor even seem to take an interest in it. We once knew a lady who had a footman, and both were fond of a game of cribbage,—John in the kitchen, the lady in her drawing-room. The lady was a giver of evening parties, where she frequently enjoyed her favourite amusement. While handing about the tea and toast, John could not always suppress his disgust at her mistakes. "There is more in that hand, ma'am," he has been known to say; or, "Ma'am, you forgot to count his nob;" in fact, he identified himself with his mistress's game, and would have lost twenty places rather than witness a miscount. It is not necessary to adopt his example on this point, although John had many qualities a good servant might copy with advantage.

THE COACHHOUSE AND STABLES.

2203. THE HORSE is the noblest of quadrupeds, whether we view him in his strength, his sagacity, or his beauty. He is also the most useful to man of all the animal creation; but his delicacy is equal to his power and usefulness. No other animal, probably, is so dependent on man in the state of domestication to which he has been reduced, or deteriorates so rapidly under exposure, bad feeding, or bad grooming. It is, therefore, a point of humanity, not to speak of its obvious impolicy, for the owner of horses to overlook any neglect in their feeding or grooming. His interest dictates that so valuable an animal should be well housed, well fed, and well groomed; and he will do well to acquire so much of stable lore as will enable him to judge of these points himself. In a general way, where a horse's coat is habitually rough and untidy, there is a sad want of elbow-grease in the stable. When a horse of tolerable breeding is dull and spiritless, he is getting ill or badly fed; and where he is observed to perspire much in the stables, is overfed, and probably eats his litter in addition to his regular supply of food.

2204. *Stables.*—The architectural form of the stables will be subject to other influences than ours; we confine ourselves, therefore, to their internal arrangements. They should be roomy in proportion to the number of stalls; warm, with good ventilation, and perfectly free from cold draughts; the stalls roomy, without excess, with good and well-trapped drainage, so as to exclude bad smells; a sound ceiling to prevent the entrance of dust from the hayloft, which is usually above them; and there should be plenty of light, coming, however, either from above or behind, so as not to glare in the horse's eye.

2205. *Heat.*—The first of these objects is attained, if the stables are kept within a degree or two of 50° in winter, and 60° in summer; although some grooms insist on a much higher temperature, in the interests of their own labour.

2206. *Ventilation* is usually attained by the insertion of one or more tubes or boxes of wood or iron through the ceiling and the roof, with a sloping covering over the opening, to keep out rain, and valves or ventilators below to regulate the atmosphere, with openings in the walls for the admission of fresh air: this is still a difficulty, however; for the effluvium of the stable is difficult to dispel, and draughts must be avoided. This is sometimes accomplished by means of hollow walls with gratings at the bottom outside, for the exit of bad air, which is carried down through the hollow walls and discharged at the bottom, while, for the admission of fresh air, the reverse takes place: the fresh by this means gets diffused and heated before it is discharged into the stable.

2207. *The Stalls* should be divided by partitions of wood-work eight or nine feet high at the head and six at the heels, and nine feet deep, so as to separate each horse from its neighbour. A hay-rack placed within easy reach of the horse, of wood or iron, occupies either a corner or the whole breadth of the stall, which should be about six feet for an ordinary-sized horse. A manger, formerly of wood, but of late years more generally of iron lined with enamel, occupies a corner of the stall. The pavement of the stall should be nearly level, with a slight incline towards the gutter, to keep the bed dry, paved with hard Dutch brick laid on edge, or asphalte, or smithy clinkers, or rubble-stones, laid in strong cement. In the centre, about five feet from the wall, a grating should be firmly fixed in the pavement, and in communication with a well-trapped drain to carry off the water; the gutter outside the stall should also communicate with the drains by trapped openings. The passage between the stall and the hall should be from five to six feet broad at least; on the wall, opposite to each stall, pegs should be placed for receiving the harness and other things in daily use.

2208. *A Harness-room* is indispensable to every stable. It should be dry and airy, and furnished with a fireplace and boiler, both for the protection of the harness and to prepare mashes for the horses when required. The partition-wall should be boarded where the harness goes, with pegs to hang the various pieces of harness on, with saddle-trees to rest the saddles on, a cupboard for the brushes, sponges, and leathers, and a lock-up corn-bin.

2209. *The furniture* of a stable with coachhouse, consists of coach-mops, jacks for raising the wheels, horse-brushes, spoke-brushes, water-brushes, crest and bit-brushes, dandy-brushes, currycombs, birch and heath brooms, trimming-combs, scissors and pickers, oil-cans and brushes, harness-brushes of three sorts, leathers, sponges for horse and carriage, stable-forks, dung-baskets or wheelbarrow, corn-sieves and measures, horse-cloths and stable pails, horn or glass lanterns. Over the stables there should be accommodation for the coachman or groom to sleep. Accidents sometimes occur, and he should be at hand to interfere.

DUTIES OF THE COACHMAN, GROOM, AND STABLE-BOY.

2210. *The Establishment* we have in view will consist of coachman, groom, and stable-boy, who are capable of keeping in perfect order four horses, and perhaps the pony. Of this establishment the coachman is chief. Besides skill in driving, he should possess a good general knowledge of horses-; he has usually to purchase provender, to see that the horses are regularly fed and properly groomed, watch over their condition, apply simple remedies to trifling ailments in the animals under his charge, and report where he observes symptoms of more serious ones which he does not understand. He has either to clean the carriage himself, or see that the stable-boy does it properly.

2211. *The Groom's* first duties are to keep his horses in condition; but he is sometimes expected to perform the duties of a valet, to ride out with his master, on occasions, to wait at table, and otherwise assist in the house: in these cases, he should have the means of dressing himself, and keeping his clothes entirely away from the stables. In the morning, about six o'clock, or rather before, the stables should be opened and cleaned out, and the horses fed, first by cleaning the rack and throwing in fresh hay, putting it lightly in the rack, that the horses may get it out easily; a short time afterwards their usual morning feed of oats should be put into the manger. While this is going on, the stable-boy has been removing the stable-dung, and sweeping and washing out the stables, both of which should be done every day, and every corner carefully swept, in order to keep the stable sweet and clean. The real duties of the groom follow: where the horses are not taken out for early exercise, the work of grooming immediately commences. "Having tied up the head," to use the excellent description of the process given by old Barrett, "take a currycomb and curry him all over the body, to raise the dust, beginning first at the neck, holding the left cheek of the headstall in the left hand, and curry him from the setting-on of his head all over the body to the buttocks, down to the point of the hock; then change your hands, and curry him before, on his breast, and, laying your right arm over his back, join your right side to his left, and curry him all under the belly near the fore-bowels, and so all over from the knees and back upwards; after that, go to the far side and do that likewise. Then take a dead horse's tail, or, failing that, a cotton dusting-cloth, and strike that away which the currycomb hath raised. Then take a round brush made of bristles, with a leathern handle, and dress him all over, both head, body, and legs, to the very fetlocks, always cleansing the brush from the dust by rubbing it with the currycomb. In the curry-combing process, as well as brushing, it must be applied with mildness, especially with fine-skinned horses; otherwise the tickling irritates them much. The brushing is succeeded by a hair-cloth, with which rub him all over again very hard, both to take away loose hairs and lay his coat; then wash your hands in fair water, and rub him all over while they are wet, as well over the head as the body. Lastly, take a clean cloth, and rub him all over again till he be dry;

then take another hair-cloth, and rub all his legs exceeding well from the knees and hocks downwards to his hoofs, picking and dressing them very carefully about the fetlocks, so as to remove all gravel and dust which will sometimes lie in the bending of the joints." In addition to the practice of this old writer, modern grooms add wisping, which usually follows brushing. The best wisp is made from a hayband, untwisted, and again doubled up after being moistened with water : this is applied to every part of the body, as the brushing had been, by changing the hands, taking care in all these operations to carry the hand in the direction of the coat. Stains on the hair are removed by sponging, or, when the coat is very dirty, by the water-brush ; the whole being finished off by a linen or flannel cloth. The horsecloth should now be put on by taking the cloth in both hands, with the outside next you, and, with your right hand to the off side, throw it over his back, placing it no farther back than will leave it straight and level, which will be about a foot from the tail. Put the roller round, and the pad-piece under it, about six or eight inches from the fore legs. The horse's head is now loosened ; he is turned about in his stall to have his head and ears rubbed and brushed over every part, including throat, with the dusting-cloth, finishing by "pulling his ears," which all horses seem to enjoy very much. This done, the mane and foretop should be combed out, passing a wet sponge over them, sponging the mane on both sides, by throwing it back to the midriff, to make it lie smooth. The horse is now returned to his headstall, his tail combed out, cleaning it of stains with a wet brush or sponge, trimming both tail and mane, and forelock when necessary, smoothing them down with a brush on which a little oil has been dropped.

2212. Watering usually follows dressing ; but some horses refuse their food until they have drunk : the groom should not, therefore, lay down exclusive rules on this subject, but study the temper and habits of his horse.

2213. *Exercise.*—All horses not in work require at least two hours' exercise daily ; and in exercising them a good groom will put them through the paces to which they have been trained. In the case of saddle-horses he will walk, trot, canter, and gallop them, in order to keep them up to their work. With draught horses they ought to be kept up to a smart walk and trot.

2214. *Feeding* must depend on their work, but they require feeding three times a day, with more or less corn each time, according to their work. In the fast coaching days it was a saying among proprietors, that "his belly was the measure of his food ;" but the horse's appetite is not to be taken as a criterion of the quantity of food under any circumstances. Horses have been known to consume 40 lbs. of hay in twenty-four hours, whereas 16 lbs. to 18 lbs. is the utmost which should have been given. Mr. Croall, an extensive coach proprietor in Scotland, limited his horses to 4½ lbs. cut straw, 8 lbs. bruised oats, and 2½ lbs. bruised beans, in the morning and noon, giving them at night 25 lbs. of the following ; viz., 560 lbs. steamed potatoes, 36 lbs. barley-dust, 40 lbs. cut straw, and 6 lbs. salt, mixed up together : under this the horses did their work well. The ordinary measure given to a horse is a peck of oats, about 40 lbs. to the bushel, twice a day, a third feed and a rack-ful of hay, which may be about 15 lbs. or 18 lbs., when he is in full work.

2215. You cannot take up a paper without having the question put, "Do you bruise your oats ?" Well, that depends on circumstances : a fresh young horse can bruise its own oats when it can get them ; but aged horses, after a time, lose the power of masticating and bruising them, and bolt them whole ; thus much impeding the work of digestion. For an old horse, then, bruise the oats ; for a young one it does no harm and little good. Oats should be bright and dry, and not too new. Where they are new, sprinkle them with salt and water ; otherwise, they overload the horse's stomach. Chopped straw mixed with oats, in the proportion of a third of straw or hay, is a good food for horses in full work ; and carrots, of which horses are remarkably fond, have a perceptible effect in a short time on the gloss of the coat.

2216. The water given to a horse merits some attention; it should not be too cold; hard water is not to be recommended; stagnant or muddy water is positively injurious; river water is the best for all purposes; and anything is preferable to spring water, which should be exposed to the sun in summer for an hour or two, and stirred up before using it: a handful of oatmeal thrown into the pail will much improve its quality.

2217. *Shoeing.*—A horse should not be sent on a journey or any other hard work immediately after new shoeing;—the stiffness incidental to new shoes is not unlikely to bring him down. A day's rest, with reasonable exercise, will not be thrown away after this operation. On reaching home very hot, the groom should walk him about for a few minutes; this done, he should take off the moisture with the scraper, and afterwards wisp him over with a handful of straw and a flannel cloth: if the cloth is dipped in some spirit, all the better. He should wash, pick, and wipe dry the legs and feet, take off the bridle and crupper, and fasten it to the rack, then the girths, and put a wisp of straw under the saddle. When sufficiently cool, the horse should have some hay given him, and then a feed of oats: if he refuse the latter, offer him a little wet bran, or a handful of oatmeal in tepid water. When he has been fed, he should be thoroughly cleaned, and his body-clothes put on, and, if very much harassed with fatigue, a little good ale or wine will be well bestowed on a valuable horse, adding plenty of fresh litter under the belly.

2218. *Bridles.*—Every time a horse is unbridled, the bit should be carefully washed and dried, and the leather wiped, to keep them sweet, as well as the girths and saddle, the latter being carefully dried and beaten with a switch before it is again put on. In washing a horse's feet after a day's work, the master should insist upon the legs and feet being washed thoroughly with a sponge until the water flows over them, and then rubbed with a brush till quite dry.

2219. *Harness*, if not carefully preserved, very soon gets a shabby tarnished appearance. Where the coachman has a proper harness-room and sufficient assistance, this is inexcusable and easily prevented. The harness-room should have a wooden lining all round, and be perfectly dry and well ventilated. Around the walls, hooks and pegs should be placed, for the several pieces of harness, at such a height as to prevent their touching the ground; and every part of the harness should have its peg or hook,—one for the halters, another for the reins, and others for snaffles and other bits and metal-work; and either a wooden horse or saddle-trees for the saddles and pads. All these parts should be dry, clean, and shining. This is only to be done by careful cleaning and polishing, and the use of several requisite pastes. The metallic parts, when white, should be cleaned by a soft brush and plate-powder; the copper and brass parts burnished with rottenstone-powder and oil,—steel with emery-powder; both made into a paste with a little oil.

2220. An excellent paste for polishing harness and the leather-work of carriages, is made by melting 8 lbs. of yellow wax, stirring it till completely dissolved. Into this pour 1 lb. of litharge of the shops, which has been pounded up with water, and dried and sifted through a sieve, leaving the two, when mixed, to simmer on the fire, stirring them continually till all is melted. When it is a little cool, mix this with 1½ lb. of good ivory-black; place this again on the fire, and stir till it boils anew, and suffer it to cool. When cooled a little, add distilled turpentine till it has the consistence of a thickish paste, scenting it with any essence at hand, thinning it when necessary from time to time, by adding distilled turpentine.

2221. When the leather is old and greasy, it should be cleaned before applying this polish, with a brush wetted in a weak solution of potass and water, washing afterwards with soft river water, and drying thoroughly. If the leather is not black, one or two coats of black ink may be given before applying the polish. When quite dry, the varnish should be laid on with a soft shoe-brush, using also a soft brush to polish the leather.

2222. When the leather is very old, it may be softened with fish-oil, and, after putting on the ink, a sponge charged with distilled turpentine passed over, to scour the surface of the leather, which should be polished as above.

2223. *For fawn or yellow-coloured leather*, take a quart of skimmed milk, pour into it 1 oz. of sulphuric acid, and, when cold, add to it 4 oz. of hydrochloric acid, shaking the bottle gently until it ceases to emit white vapours; separate the coagulated from the liquid part, by straining through a sieve, and store it away till required. In applying it, clean the leather by a weak solution of oxalic acid, washing it off immediately, and apply the composition when dry with a sponge.

2224. *Wheel-grease* is usually purchased at the shops; but a good paste is made as follows:—Melt 80 parts of grease, and stir into it, mixing it thoroughly and smoothly, 20 parts of fine black-lead in powder, and store away in a tin box for use. This grease is used in the mint at Paris, and is highly approved.

2225. *Carriages* in an endless variety of shapes and names are continually making their appearance; but the hackney cab or clarence seems most in request for light carriages; the family carriage of the day being a modified form of the clarence adapted for family use. The carriage is a valuable piece of furniture, requiring all the care of the most delicate upholstery, with the additional disadvantage of continual exposure to the weather and to the muddy streets.

2226. It requires, therefore, to be carefully cleaned before putting away, and a coach-house perfectly dry and well ventilated, for the wood-work swells with moisture; it shrinks also with heat, unless the timber has undergone a long course of seasoning: it should also have a dry floor, a boarded one being recommended. It must be removed from the ammoniacal influence of the stables, from open drains and cesspools, and other gaseous influences likely to affect the paint and varnish. When the carriage returns home, it should be carefully washed and dried, and that, if possible, before the mud has time to dry on it. This is done by first well slushing it with clean water, so as to wash away all particles of sand, having first closed the sashes to avoid wetting the linings. The body is then gone carefully over with a soft mop, using plenty of clean water, and penetrating into every corner of the carved work, so that not an atom of dirt remains; the body of the carriage is then raised by placing the jack under the axletree and raising it so that the wheel turns freely; this is now thoroughly washed with the mop until the dirt is removed, using a water-brush for corners where the mop does not penetrate. Every particle of mud and sand removed by the mop, and afterwards with a wet sponge, the carriage is wiped dry, and, as soon after as possible, the varnish is carefully polished with soft leather, using a little sweet oil for the leather parts, and even for the panels, so as to check any tendency of the varnish to crack. Stains are removed by rubbing them with the leather and sweet oil; if that fails, a little Tripoli powder mixed with the oil will be more successful.

2227. In preparing the carriage for use, the whole body should be rubbed over with a clean leather and carefully polished, the iron-work and joints oiled, the plated and brass-work occasionally cleaned,—the one with plate-powder, or with well-washed whiting mixed with sweet oil, and leather kept for the purpose,—the other with rottenstone mixed with a little oil, and applied without too much rubbing, until the paste is removed; but, if rubbed every day with the leather, little more will be required to keep it untarnished. The linings require careful brushing every day, the cushions being taken out and beaten, and the glass sashes should always be bright and clean. The wheel-tires and axletree are carefully seen to, and greased when required, the bolts and nuts tightened, and all the parts likely to get out of order overhauled.

2228. These duties, however, are only incidental to the coachman's office, which is to drive; and much of the enjoyment of those in the carriage depends on his proficiency in his art,—much also of the wear of the carriage and horses. He should have sufficient knowledge of the construction of the carriage to know when it is out of order,—to know, also, the pace at which he can go over the road he has under him, without risking the springs, and without shaking those he is driving too much.

2229. Having, with or without the help of the groom or stable-boy, put his horses to the carriage, and satisfied himself, by walking round them, that everything is properly arranged, the coachman proceeds to the off-side of the carriage, takes the reins from the back of the horses, where they were thrown, buckles them together, and, placing his foot on the step, ascends to his box, having his horses now entirely under control. In ordinary circumstances, he is not expected to descend, for where no footman accompanies the carriage, the doors are usually so arranged that even a lady may let herself out, if she wishes it, from the inside. The coachman's duties are to avoid everything approaching an accident, and all his attention is required to guide his horses.

2230. The pace at which he drives will depend upon his orders,—in all probability a moderate pace of seven or eight miles an hour; less speed is injurious to the horses, getting them into lazy and sluggish habits; for it is wonderful how soon these are acquired by some horses. The writer was once employed to purchase a horse for a country friend, and he picked a very handsome gelding out of Collins's stables, which seemed to answer to his friend's wants. It was duly committed to the coachman who was to drive it, after some very successful trials in harness and out of it, and seemed likely to give great satisfaction. After a time, the friend got tired of his carriage, and gave it up; as the easiest mode of getting rid of the horse, it was sent up to the writer's stables,—a present. Only twelve months had elapsed; the horse was as handsome as ever, with plenty of flesh, and a sleek glossy coat, and he was thankfully enough received; but, on trial, it was found that a stupid coachman, who was imbued with one of their old maxims, that "it's the pace that kills," had driven the horse, capable of doing his nine miles an hour with ease, at a jog-trot of four miles, or four and a half; and now, no persuasion of the whip could get more out of him. After many unsuccessful efforts to bring him back to his pace, in one of which a break-down occurred, under the hands of a professional trainer, he was sent to the hammer, and sold for a sum that did not pay for the attempt to break him in. This maxim, therefore, "that it's the pace that kills," is altogether fallacious in the moderate sense in which we are viewing it. In the old coaching days, indeed, when the Shrewsbury "Wonder" drove into the inn yard while the clock was striking, week after week and month after month, with unerring regularity, twenty-seven hours to a hundred and sixty-two miles; when the "Quicksilver" mail was timed to eleven miles an hour between London and Plymouth, with a fine of £5 to the driver if behind time; when the Brighton "Age," "tool'd" and horsed by the late Mr. Stevenson, used to dash round the square as the fifth hour was striking, having stopped at the half-way house while his servant handed a sandwich and a glass of sherry to his passengers,—then the pace was indeed "killing." But the truth is, horses that are driven at a jog-trot pace lose that *élàn* with which a good driver can inspire them, and they are left to do their work by mere weight and muscle; therefore, unless he has contrary orders, a good driver will choose a smart pace, but not enough to make his horses perspire : on level roads this should never be seen.

2231. In choosing his horses, every master will see that they are properly paired,—that their paces are about equal. When their habits-differ, it is the coachman's duty to discover how he can, with least annoyance to the horses, get that pace out of them. Some horses have been accustomed to be driven on the check, and the curb irritates them; others, with harder mouths, cannot be controlled with the slight leverage this affords; he must, therefore, accommodate the horses as he best can. The reins should always be held so that the horses are " in hand ;" but he is a very bad driver who always drives with a tight rein; the pain to the horse is intolerable, and causes him to rear and plunge, and finally break away, if he can. He is also a bad driver when the reins are always slack ; the horse then feels abandoned to himself; he is neither directed nor supported, and if no accident occurs, it is great good luck.

2232. The true coachman's hands are so delicate and gentle, that the mere weight of the reins is felt on the bit, and the directions are indicated by a turn of the wrist rather than by a pull ; the horses are guided and encouraged, and only pulled up when they exceed their intended pace, or in the event of a stumble ; for there is a strong though gentle hand on the reins.

2233. *The Whip*, in the hands of a good driver, and with well-bred cattle, is there, more as a precaution than a "tool" for frequent use ; if he uses it, it is to encourage, by stroking the flanks ; except, indeed, he has to punish some waywardness of temper, and then he does it effectually, taking care, however, that it is done on the flank, where there is no very tender part, never on the crupper. In driving, the coachman should never give way to temper. How often do we see horses stumble from being conducted, or at least "allowed," to go over bad ground by some careless driver, who immediately wreaks that vengeance on the poor horse which might, with much more justice, be applied to his own brutal shoulders. The whip is of course useful, and even necessary, but should be rarely used, except to encourage and excite the horses.

DUTIES OF THE VALET.

2234. *Attendants on the Person.*—"No man is a hero to his valet," saith the proverb; and the corollary may run, "No lady is a heroine to her maid." The infirmities of humanity are, perhaps, too numerous and too equally distributed to stand the severe microscopic tests which attendants on the person have opportunities of applying. The valet and waiting-maid are placed near the persons of the master and mistress, receiving orders only from them, dressing them, accompanying them in all their journeys, the confidants and agents of their most unguarded moments, of their most secret habits, and of course subject to their commands,—even to their caprices ; they themselves being subject to erring judgment, aggravated by an imperfect education. All that can be expected from such servants is polite manners, modest demeanour, and a respectful reserve, which are indispensable. To these, good sense, good temper, some self-denial, and consideration for the feelings of others, whether above or below them in the social scale, will be useful qualifications. Their duty leads them to wait on those who are, from sheer wealth, station, and education, more polished, and consequently more susceptible of annoyance ; and any vulgar familiarity of manner is opposed to all their notions of self-respect. Quiet unobtrusive manners, therefore, and a delicate reserve in speaking of their employers, either in praise or blame, is as essential in their absence, as good manners and respectful conduct in their presence.

2235. Some of the duties of the valet we have just hinted at in treating of the duties of the footman in a small family. His day commences by seeing that his master's dressing-room is in order ; that the housemaid has swept and dusted it properly ; that the fire is lighted and burns cheerfully ; and some time before his master is expected, he will do well to throw up the sash to admit fresh air, closing it, however, in time to recover the temperature which he knows his master prefers. It is now his duty to place the body-linen on the horse before the fire, to be aired properly ; to lay the trousers intended to be worn, carefully brushed and cleaned, on the back of his master's chair ; while the coat and waistcoat, carefully brushed and folded, and the collar cleaned, are laid in their place ready to put on when required. All the articles of the toilet should be in their places, the razors properly set and stropped, and hot water ready for use.

2236. Gentlemen generally prefer performing the operation of shaving themselves, but a valet should be prepared to do it if required; and he should, besides, be a good hairdresser. Shaving over, he has to brush the hair, beard, and moustache, where that appendage is encouraged, arranging the whole simply and gracefully, according to the age and style of countenance. Every fortnight, or three weeks at the utmost, the hair should be cut, and the points of the whiskers trimmed as often as required. A good valet will now present the various articles of the toilet as they are wanted; afterwards, the body-linen, neck-tie, which he will put on, if required, and, afterwards, waistcoat, coat, and boots, in suitable order, and carefully brushed and polished.

2237. Having thus seen his master dressed, if he is about to go out, the valet will hand him his cane, gloves, and hat, the latter well brushed on the outside with a soft brush, and wiped inside with a clean handkerchief, respectfully attend him to the door, and open it for him, and receive his last orders for the day.

2238. He now proceeds to put everything in order in the dressing-room, cleans the combs and brushes, and brushes and folds up any clothes that may be left about the room, and puts them away in the drawers.

2239. Gentlemen are sometimes indifferent as to their clothes and appearance; it is the valet's duty, in this case, where his master permits it, to select from the wardrobe such things as are suitable for the occasion, so that he may appear with scrupulous neatness and cleanliness; that his linen and neck-tie, where that is white or coloured, are unsoiled; and where he is not accustomed to change them every day, that the cravat is turned, and even ironed, to remove the crease of the previous fold. The coat collar,—which where the hair is oily and worn long, is apt to get greasy—should also be examined; a careful valet will correct this by removing the spots day by day as they appear, first by moistening the grease-spots with a little rectified spirits of wine or spirits of hartshorn, which has a renovating effect, and the smell of which soon disappears. The grease is dissolved and removed by gentle scraping. The grease removed, add a little more of the spirit, and rub with a piece of clean cloth; finish by adding a few drops more; rub it with the palm of the hand, in the direction of the grain of the cloth, and it will be clean and glossy as the rest of the garment.

2240. Polish for the boots is an important matter to the valet, and not always to be obtained good by purchase; never so good, perhaps, as he can make for himself after the following recipes:—Take of ivory-black and treacle each 4 oz., sulphuric acid 1 oz., best olive-oil 2 spoonfuls, best white-wine vinegar 3 half-pints: mix the ivory-black and treacle well in an earthen jar; then add the sulphuric acid, continuing to stir the mixture; next pour in the oil; and, lastly, add the vinegar, stirring it in by degrees, until thoroughly incorporated.

2241. Another polish is made by mixing 1 oz. each of pounded galls and logwood-chips, and 3 lbs. of red French wine (ordinaire). Boil together till the liquid is reduced to half the quantity, and pour it off through a strainer. Now take ½ lb. each of pounded gum-arabic and lump-sugar, 1 oz. of green copperas, and 3 lbs. of brandy. Dissolve the gum-arabic in the preceding decoction, and add the sugar and copperas : when all is dissolved and mixed together, stir in the brandy, mixing it smoothly. This mixture will yield 5 or 6 lbs. of a very superior polishing paste for boots and shoes.

2242. It is, perhaps, unnecessary to add, that having discharged all the commissions intrusted to him by his master, such as conveying notes or messages to friends, or the tradesmen, all of which he should punctually and promptly attend to, it is his duty to be in waiting when his master returns home to dress for dinner, or for any other occasion, and to have all things prepared for this second dressing. Previous to this, he brings under his notice the cards of visitors who may have called, delivers the messages he may have received for him, and otherwise acquits himself of the morning's commissions, and receives his orders for the remainder of the day. The routine of his evening duty is to have the dressing-room and study, where there is a separate one, arranged comfortably for his master, the fires lighted, candles prepared, dressing-gown and slippers in their place, and aired, and everything in order that is required for his master's comforts.

FEMALE DOMESTICS.

DUTIES OF THE LADY'S-MAID.

2243. The duties of a lady's-maid are more numerous, and perhaps more onerous, than those of the valet ; for while the latter is aided by the tailor, the hatter, the linen-draper, and the perfumer, the lady's-maid has to originate many parts of the mistress's dress herself: she should, indeed, be a tolerably expert milliner and dressmaker, a good hairdresser, and possess some chemical knowledge of the cosmetics with which the toilet-table is supplied, in order to use them with safety and effect. Her first duty in the morning, after having performed her own toilet, is to examine the clothes put off by her mistress the evening before, either to put them away, or to see that they are all in order to put on again. During the winter, and in wet weather, the dresses should be carefully examined, and the mud removed. Dresses of tweed, and other woollen materials, may be laid out on a table and brushed all over ; but in general, even in woollen fabrics, the lightness of the tissues renders brushing unsuitable to dresses, and it is better to remove the dust from the folds by beating them lightly with a handkerchief or thin cloth. Silk dresses should never be brushed, but rubbed with a piece of merino, or other soft material, of a similar colour, kept for the purpose. Summer dresses of barège, muslin, mohair, and other light materials, simply require shaking ; but if the muslin be tumbled, it must be ironed afterwards. If the dresses require slight repair, it should be done at once : "a stitch in time saves nine."

2244. The bonnet should be dusted with a light feather plume, in order to remove every particle of dust; but this has probably been done, as it ought to have been, the night before. Velvet bonnets, and other velvet articles of dress, should be cleaned with a soft brush. If the flowers with which the bonnet is decorated have been crushed or displaced, or the leaves tumbled, they should be raised and readjusted by means of flower-pliers. If feathers have suffered from damp, they should be held near the fire for a few minutes, and restored to their natural state by the hand or a soft brush.

2245. *The Chausserie*, or foot-gear of a lady, is one of the few things left to mark her station, and requires special care. Satin boots or shoes should be dusted with a soft brush, or wiped with a cloth. Kid or varnished leather should have the mud wiped off with a sponge charged with milk, which preserves its softness and polish. The following is also an excellent polish for applying to ladies' boots, instead of blacking them :— Mix equal proportions of sweet-oil, vinegar, and treacle, with 1 oz. of lamp-black. When all the ingredients are thoroughly incorporated, rub the mixture on the boots with the palm of the hand, and put them in a cool place to dry. Ladies' blacking, which may be purchased in 6*d*. and 1*s*. bottles, is also very much used for patent leather and kid boots, particularly when they are a little worn. This blacking is merely applied with a piece of sponge, and the boots should not be put on until the blacking is dry and hardened.

2246. These various preliminary offices performed, the lady's-maid should prepare for dressing her mistress, arranging her dressing-room, toilet-table, and linen, according to her mistress's wishes and habits. The details of dressing we need not touch upon,—every lady has her own mode of doing so ; but the maid should move about quietly, perform any offices about her mistress's person, as lacing stays, gently, and adjust her linen smoothly.

2247. Having prepared the dressing-room by lighting the fire, sweeping the hearth, and made everything ready for dressing her mistress, placed her linen before the fire to air, and laid out the various articles of dress she is to wear, which will probably have been arranged the previous evening, the lady's-maid is prepared for the morning's duties.

2248. *Hairdressing* is the most important part of the lady's-maid's office. If ringlets are worn, remove the curl-papers, and, after thoroughly brushing the back hair both above and below, dress it according to the prevailing fashion. If bandeaux are worn, the hair is thoroughly brushed and frizzed outside and inside, folding the hair back round the head, brushing it perfectly smooth, giving it a glossy appearance by the use of pomades, or oil, applied by the palm of the hand, smoothing it down with a small brush dipped in bandoline. Double bandeaux are formed by bringing most of the hair forward, and rolling it over frizettes made of hair the same colour as that of the wearer : it is finished behind by plaiting the hair, and arranging it in such a manner as to look well with the head-dress.

2249. Lessons in hairdressing may be obtained, and at not an unreasonable charge. If a lady's-maid can afford it, we would advise her to initiate herself in the mysteries of hairdressing before entering on her duties. If a mistress finds her maid handy, and willing to learn, she will not mind the expense of a few lessons, which are almost necessary, as the fashion and mode of dressing the hair is so continually changing. Brushes and combs should be kept scrupulously clean, by washing them about twice a week : to do this oftener spoils the brushes, as very frequent washing makes them so very soft.

To wash Brushes.

2250. Dissolve a piece of soda in some hot water, allowing a piece the size of a walnut to a quart of water. Put the water into a basin, and, after combing out the hair from the brushes, dip them, bristles downwards, into the water and out again, keeping the backs and handles as free from the water as possible. Repeat this until the bristles look clean ; then rinse the brushes in a little cold water ; shake them well, and wipe the handles and backs with a towel, *but not the bristles,* and set the brushes to dry in the sun, or near the fire ; but take care not to put them too close to it. Wiping the bristles of a brush makes them soft, as does also the use of soap.

To clean Combs.

2251. If it can be avoided, never wash combs, as the water often makes the teeth split, and the tortoiseshell or horn of which they are made, rough. Small brushes, manufactured purposely for cleaning combs, may be purchased at a trifling cost : with this the comb should be well brushed, and afterwards wiped with a cloth or towel.

A good Wash for the Hair.

2252. INGREDIENTS.—1 pennyworth of borax, ½ pint of olive-oil, 1 pint of boiling water.

Mode.—Pour the boiling water over the borax and oil ; let it cool ; then put the mixture into a bottle. Shake it before using, and apply it with a flannel. Camphor and borax, dissolved in boiling water and left to cool, make a very good wash for the hair ; as also does rosemary-water mixed with a little borax. After using any of these washes, when the hair becomes thoroughly dry, a little pomatum or oil should be rubbed in, to make it smooth and glossy.

To make Pomade for the Hair.

2253. INGREDIENTS.—¼ lb. of lard, 2 pennyworth of castor-oil ; scent.

Mode.—Let the lard be unsalted ; beat it up well ; then add the castor-oil, and mix thoroughly together with a knife, adding a few drops of any scent that may be preferred. Put the pomatum into pots, which keep well covered to prevent it turning rancid.

Another Recipe for Pomatum.

2254. INGREDIENTS.—8 oz. of olive-oil, 1 oz. of spermaceti, 3 pennyworth of essential oil of almonds, 3 pennyworth of essence of lemon.

Mode.—Mix these ingredients together, and store away in jars for use.

To make Bandoline.

2255. INGREDIENTS.—1 oz. of gum-tragacanth, ¼ pint of cold water, 3 pennyworth of essence of almonds, 2 teaspoonfuls of old rum.

Mode.—Put the gum-tragacanth into a wide-mouthed bottle with the cold water ; let it stand till dissolved, then stir into it the essence of almonds ; let it remain for an hour or two, when pour the rum on the top. This should make the stock bottle, and when any is required for use, it is merely necessary to dilute it with a little cold water until the desired consistency is obtained, and to keep it in a small bottle, well corked, for use. This bandoline, instead of injuring the hair, as many other kinds often do, improves it, by increasing its growth, and making it always smooth and glossy.

An excellent Pomatum.

2256. INGREDIENTS.—1½ lb. of lard, ½ pint of olive-oil, ½ pint of castor-oil, 4 oz. of spermaceti, bergamot, or any other scent; elder-flower water.

Mode.—Wash the lard well in the elder-flower water; drain, and beat it to a cream. Mix the two oils together, and heat them sufficiently to dissolve the spermaceti, which should be beaten fine in a mortar. Mix all these ingredients together with the brandy and whatever kind of scent may be preferred; and whilst warm pour into glass bottles for use, keeping them well corked. The best way to liquefy the pomatum is to set the bottle in a saucepan of warm water. It will remain good for many months.

To promote the Growth of Hair.

2257. INGREDIENTS.—Equal quantities of olive-oil and spirit of rosemary; a few drops of oil of nutmeg.

Mode.—Mix the ingredients together, rub the roots of the hair every night with a little of this liniment, and the growth of it will very soon sensibly increase.

2258. Our further remarks on dressing must be confined to some general advice. In putting on a band, see that it is laid quite flat, and is drawn tightly round the waist before it is pinned in front; that the pin is a strong one, and that it is secured to the stays, so as not to slip up or down, or crease in the folds. Arrange the folds of the dress over the crinoline petticoats; if the dress fastens behind, put a small pin in the slit to prevent it from opening. See that the sleeves fall well over the arms. If it is finished with a jacket, or other upper dress, see that it fits smoothly under the arms; pull out the flounces, and spread out the petticoat at the bottom with the hands, so that it falls in graceful folds. In arranging the petticoat itself, a careful lady's-maid will see that this is firmly fastened round the waist.

2259. Where sashes are worn, pin the bows securely on the inside with a pin, so as not to be visible; then raise the bow with the fingers. The collar is arranged and carefully adjusted with brooch or bow in the centre.

2260. Having dressed her mistress for breakfast, and breakfasted herself, the further duties of the lady's-maid will depend altogether upon the habits of the family, in which hardly two will probably agree. Where the duties are entirely confined to attendance on her mistress, it is probable that the bed-room and dressing-room will be committed to her care; that, the housemaid will rarely enter, except for the weekly or other periodical cleaning; she will, therefore, have to make her mistress's bed, and keep it in order; and as her duties are light and easy, there can be no allowance made for the slightest approach to uncleanliness or want of order. Every morning, immediately after her mistress has left it, and while breakfast is on, she should throw the bed open, by taking off the clothes; open the windows (except in rainy weather), and leave the room to air for half an hour. After breakfast, except her attendance on her mistress prevents it, if the rooms are carpeted, she should sweep them carefully, having previously strewed the room with moist tea-leaves, dusting every table and chair, taking care to penetrate to every corner, and moving every article of furniture that is portable. This done satisfactorily, and having cleaned the dressing-glass, polished up the furniture and the ornaments, and made the glass jug and basin clean and bright, emptied all slops, emptied the water-jugs and filled them with fresh water, and arranged the rooms, the dressing-room is ready for the mistress when she thinks proper to appear.

2261. The dressing-room thoroughly in order, the same thing is to be done in the bedroom, in which she will probably be assisted by the housemaid to make the bed and empty the slops. In making the bed, she will study her lady's wishes, whether it is to be hard or soft, sloping or straight, and see that it is done accordingly.

2262. Having swept the bedroom with equal care, dusted the tables and chairs, chimney-ornaments, and put away all articles of dress left from yesterday, and cleaned and put away any articles of jewellery, her next care is to see, before her mistress goes out, what requires replacing in her department, and furnish her with a list of them, that she may use her discretion about ordering them. All this done, she may settle herself down to any work on which she is engaged. This will consist chiefly in mending; which is first to be seen to; everything, except stockings, being mended before washing. Plain work will probably be one of the lady's-maid's chief employments.

2263. A waiting-maid, who wishes to make herself useful, will study the fashion-books with attention, so as to be able to aid her mistress's judgment in dressing, according to the prevailing fashion, with such modifications as her style of countenance requires. She will also, if she has her mistress's interest at heart, employ her spare time in repairing and making up dresses which have served one purpose, to serve another also ; or turning many things, unfitted for her mistress to use, for the younger branches of the family. The lady's-maid may thus render herself invaluable to her mistress, and increase her own happiness in so doing. The exigencies of fashion and luxury are such, that all ladies, except those of the very highest rank, will consider themselves fortunate in having about them a thoughtful person, capable of diverting their finery to a useful purpose.

2264. Among other duties, the lady's-maid should understand the various processes for washing, and cleaning, and repairing laces ; edging of collars ; removing stains and grease-spots from dresses, and similar processes, for which the following recipes will be found very useful. In washing—

2265. *Blonde*, fine toilet-soap is used; the blonde is soaped over very slightly, and washed in water in which a little fig-blue is dissolved, rubbing it very gently ; when clean, dry it. Dip it afterwards in very thin gum-water, dry it again in linen, spread it out as flat as it will lie, and iron it. Where the blonde is of better quality, and wider, it may be stretched on a hoop to dry after washing in the blue-water, applying the gum with a sponge ; or it may be washed finally in water in which a lump of sugar has been dissolved, which gives it more the appearance of new blonde.

2266. Lace collars soil very quickly when in contact with the neck ; they are cleaned by beating the edge of the collar between the folds of a fine linen cloth, then washing the edges as directed above, and spreading it out on an ironing-board, pinning it at each corner with fine pins ; then going carefully over it with a sponge charged with water in which some gum-dragon and fig-blue have been dissolved, to give it a proper consistence. To give the collar the same tint throughout, the whole collar should be sponged with the same water, taking care not to touch the flowers.

2267. A multiplicity of accidents occur to soil and spot dresses, which should be removed at once. To remove—

2268. *Grease-spots* from cotton or woollen materials of fast colours, absorbent pastes, purified bullock's-blood, and even common soap, are used, applied to the spot when dry. When the colours are not fast, use fuller's-earth or pulverized potter's-clay, laid in a layer over the spot, and press it with a very hot iron.

2269. For Silks, Moires, and plain or brocaded Satins, begin by pouring over the spot two drops of rectified spirits of wine ; cover it over with a linen cloth, and press it with a hot iron, changing the linen instantly. The spot will look tarnished, for a portion of the grease still remains : this will be removed entirely by a little sulphuric ether dropped on the spot, and a very little rubbing. If neatly done, no perceptible mark or circle will remain ; nor will the lustre of the richest silk be changed, the union of the two liquids operating with no injurious effects from rubbing.

2270. *Fruit-spots* are removed from white and fast-coloured cottons by the use of chloride of soda. Commence by cold-soaping the article, then touch the spot with a hair-pencil or feather dipped in the chloride, dipping it immediately into cold water, to prevent the texture of the article being injured.

2271. *Ink-spots* are removed, when fresh applied to the spot, by a few drops of hot water being poured on immediately afterwards. By the same process, iron-mould in linen or calico may be removed, dipping immediately in cold water to prevent injury to the fabric.

2272. *Wax* dropped on a shawl, table-cover, or cloth dress, is easily discharged by applying spirits of wine.

2273. *Syrups or Preserved Fruits*, by washing in lukewarm water with a dry cloth, and pressing the spot between two folds of clean linen.

2274. *Essence of Lemon* will remove grease, but will make a spot itself in a few days.

To clean Silk or Ribbons.

2275. INGREDIENTS.—$\frac{1}{2}$ pint of gin, $\frac{1}{2}$ lb. of honey, $\frac{1}{2}$ lb. of soft soap, $\frac{1}{2}$ pint of water.

Mode.—Mix the above ingredients together ; then lay each breadth of silk upon a clean kitchen table or dresser, and scrub it well on the soiled side with the mixture. Have ready three vessels of cold water ; take each piece of silk at two corners, and dip it up and down in each vessel, but do not wring it ; and take care that each breadth has one vessel of quite clean water for the last dip. Hang it up dripping for a minute or two, then dab it in a cloth, and iron it quickly with a very hot iron.

To remove Paint-spots from Silk Cloth.

2276. If the fabric will bear it, sharp rubbing will frequently entirely discharge a newly-made paint-stain ; but, if this is not successful, apply spirit of turpentine with a quill till the stains disappear.

To make old Crape look nearly equal to new.

2277. Place a little water in a teakettle, and let it boil until there is plenty of steam from the spout ; then, holding the crape in both hands, pass it to and fro several times through the steam, and it will be clean and look nearly equal to new.

2278. *Linen.*—Before sending linen to wash, the lady's-maid should see that everything under her charge is properly mended; for her own sake she should take care that it is sent out in an orderly manner, each class of garments by themselves, with a proper list, of which she retains a copy. On its return, it is still more necessary to examine every piece separately, so that all missing buttons be supplied, and only the articles properly washed and in perfect repair passed into the wardrobe.

2279. Ladies who keep a waiting-maid for their own persons are in the habit of paying visits to their friends, in which it is not unusual for the maid to accompany them; at all events, it is her duty to pack the trunks; and this requires not only knowledge but some practice, although the improved trunks and portmanteaus now made, in which there is a place for nearly everything, render this more simple than formerly. Before packing, let the trunks be thoroughly well cleaned, and, if necessary, lined with paper, and everything intended for packing laid out on the bed or chairs, so that it may be seen what is to be stowed away; the nicer articles of dress neatly folded in clean calico wrappers. Having satisfied herself that everything wanted is laid out, and that it is in perfect order, the packing is commenced by disposing of the most bulky articles, the dressing-case and work-box, skirts, and other articles requiring room, leaving the smaller articles to fill up; finally, having satisfied herself that all is included, she should lock and cover up the trunk in its canvas case, and then pack her own box, if she is to accompany her mistress.

2280. On reaching the house, the lady's-maid will be shown her lady's apartment; and her duties here are what they were at home; she will arrange her mistress's things, and learn which is her bell, in order to go to her when she rings. Her meals will be taken in the housekeeper's room; and here she must be discreet and guarded in her talk to any one of her mistress or her concerns. Her only occupation here will be attending in her lady's room, keeping her things in order, and making her rooms comfortable for her.

2281. The evening duties of a lady's-maid are pretty nearly a repetition of those of the morning. She is in attendance when her mistress retires; she assists her to undress if required, brushes her hair, and renders such other assistance as is demanded; removes all slops; takes care that the fire, if any, is safe, before she retires to rest herself.

2282. *Ironing* is a part of the duties of a lady's-maid, and she should be able to do it in the most perfect manner when it becomes necessary. Ironing is often badly done from inattention to a few very simple requirements. Cleanliness is the first essential: the ironing-board, the fire, the iron, and the ironing-blanket should all be perfectly clean. It will not be necessary here to enter into details on ironing, as full directions are given in the "Duties of the Laundry-maid." A lady's-maid will have a great deal of ,, ironing-out" to do; such as light evening dresses, muslin dresses, &c., which are not dirty enough to be washed, but merely require smoothing out to remove the creases. In summer, particularly, an iron will be constantly required, as also a skirt-board, which should be covered with a nice clean piece of flannel. To keep muslin dresses in order, they almost require smoothing out every time they are worn, particularly if made with many flounces. The lady's-maid may often have to perform little services for her mistress which require care; such as restoring the colour to scorched linen, &c. &c. The following recipe is, we believe, a very good one.

To restore Whiteness to scorched Linen.

· 2283. INGREDIENTS.—½ pint of vinegar, 2 oz. of fuller's-earth, 1 oz. of dried fowls' dung, ½ oz. of soap, the juice of 2 large onions.

Mode.—Boil all these ingredients together to the consistency of paste; spread the composition thickly over the damaged part, and if the threads be not actually consumed, after it has been allowed to dry on, and the place has subsequently been washed once or twice, every trace of scorching will disappear.

2284. *Furs, Feathers, and Woollens* require the constant care of the waiting-maid. Furs and feathers not in constant use should be wrapped up in linen washed in lye. From May to September they are subject to being made the depositary of the moth-eggs. They should be looked too, and shaken and beaten, from time to time, in case some of the eggs should have been lodged in them, in spite of every precaution; laying them up again, or rather folding them up as before, wrapping them in brown paper, which is itself a preservative. Shawls and cloaks, which would be damaged by such close folds, must be looked to, and aired and beaten, putting them away dry before the evening.

Preservatives against the Ravages of Moths.

2285. Place pieces of camphor, cedar-wood, Russia leather, tobacco-leaves, bog-myrtle, or anything else strongly aromatic, in the drawers or boxes where furs or other things to be preserved from moths are kept, and they will never take harm.

2286. *Jewels* are generally wrapped up in cotton, and kept in their cases; but they are subject to tarnish from exposure to the air, and require cleaning. This is done by preparing clean soap-suds, using fine toilet-soap. Dip any article of gold, silver, gilt, or precious stones into this lye, and dry them by brushing with a brush of soft badgers' hair, or a fine sponge; afterwards with a piece of fine cloth, and, lastly, with a soft leather.

2287. *Epaulettes* of gold or silver, and, in general, all articles of jewellery, may be dressed by dipping them in spirits of wine warmed in a *bain marie*, or shallow kettle, placed over a slow fire or hot-plate.

2288. The valet and lady's-maid, from their supposed influence with their master and mistress, are exposed to some temptations to which other servants are less subjected. They are probably in communication with the trades-people who supply articles for the toilet; such as hatters, tailors, dressmakers, and perfumers. The conduct of waiting-maid and valet to these people should be civil but independent, making reasonable allowance for want of exact punctuality, if any such can be made : they should represent any inconvenience respectfully, and if an excuse seems unreasonable, put the matter fairly to master or mistress, leaving it to them to notice it further, if they think it necessary. No expectations of a personal character should influence them one way or the other. It would be acting unreasonably to any domestic to make them refuse such presents as tradespeople choose to give them ; the utmost that can be expected is that they should not influence their judgment in the articles supplied—that they should represent them truly to master or mistress, without fear and without favour. Civility to all, servility to none, is a good maxim for every one. Deference to a master and mistress, and to their friends and visitors, is one of the implied terms of their engagement ; and this deference must apply even to what may be considered their whims. A servant is not to be seated, or wear a hat in the house, in his master's or mistress's presence ; nor offer any opinion, unless asked for it ; nor even to say "good night," or "good morning," except in reply to that salutation.

To preserve cut Flowers.

2289. A bouquet of freshly-cut flowers may be preserved alive for a long time by placing them in a glass or vase with fresh water, in which a little charcoal has been steeped, or a small piece of camphor dissolved. The vase should be set upon a plate or dish, and covered with a bell-glass, around the edges of which, when it comes in contact with the plate, a little water should be poured to exclude the air.

To revive cut Flowers after packing.

2290. Plunge the stems into boiling water, and by the time the water is cold, the flowers will have revived. Then cut afresh the ends of the stems, and keep them in fresh cold water.

UPPER AND UNDER HOUSEMAIDS.

2291. Housemaids, in large establishments, have usually one or more assistants ; in this case they are upper and under housemaids. Dividing the work between them, the upper housemaid will probably reserve for herself the task of dusting the ornaments and cleaning the furniture of the principal apartments, but it is her duty to see that every department is properly attended to. The number of assistants depends on the number in the family, as well as on the style in which the establishment is kept up. In wealthy families it is not unusual for every grown-up daughter to have her waiting-maid, whose duty it is to keep her mistress's apartments in order, thus abridging the housemaid's duties. In others, perhaps, one waiting-maid attends on two or three, when the housemaid's assistance will be more requisite. In fact, every establishment has some customs peculiar to itself, on which we need not dwell ; the general duties are the *same in all*, perfect cleanliness and order being the object.

DUTIES OF THE HOUSEMAID.

2292. "Cleanliness is next to godliness," saith the proverb, and "order" is in the next degree; the housemaid, then, may be said to be the handmaiden to two of the most prominent virtues. Her duties are very numerous, and many of the comforts of the family depend on their performance; but they are simple and easy to a person naturally clean and orderly, and desirous of giving satisfaction. In all families, whatever the habits of the master and mistress, servants will find it advantageous to rise early; their daily work will thus come easy to them. If they rise late, there is a struggle to overtake it, which throws an air of haste and hurry over the whole establishment. Where the master's time is regulated by early business or professional engagements, this will, of course, regulate the hours of the servants; but even where that is not the case, servants will find great personal convenience in rising early and getting through their work in an orderly and methodical manner. The housemaid who studies her own ease will certainly be at her work by six o'clock in the summer, and, probably, half-past six or seven in the winter months, having spent a reasonable time in her own chamber in dressing. Earlier than this would, probably, be an unnecessary waste of coals and candle in winter.

2293. The first duty of the housemaid in winter is to open the shutters of all the lower rooms in the house, and take up the hearth-rugs of those rooms

CARPET-BROOMS.

which she is going to "do" before breakfast. In some families, where there is only a cook and housemaid kept, and where the drawing-rooms are large, the cook has the care of the dining-room, and the housemaid that of the breakfast-room, library, and drawing-rooms. After the shutters are all opened, she sweeps the breakfast-room, sweeping the dust towards the fire-place, of course previously removing the fender. She should then lay a cloth (generally made of coarse wrappering) over the carpet in front of the stove, and on this should place her housemaid's box, containing black-lead brushes, leathers, emery-paper, cloth, black lead, and all utensils necessary for cleaning a grate, with the cinder-pail on the other side.

2294. She now sweeps up the ashes, and deposits them in her cinder-pail, which is a japanned tin pail, with a wire-sifter inside, and a closely-fitting top. In this pail the cinders are sifted, and reserved for use in the kitchen or under the copper, the ashes only being thrown away. The cinders disposed of, she proceeds to black-lead the grate, producing the black lead, the soft brush for laying it on, her blacking and polishing brushes, from the box which contains her tools. This housemaid's box should be kept well stocked. Having blackened, brushed, and polished every part, and made all clean and bright, she now proceeds to lay the fire. Sometimes it is very difficult to get a proper

STOVE-BRUSHES.   HOUSEMAID'S BOX.

polish to black grates, particularly if they have been neglected, and allowed to rust at all. Brunswick black, which is an excellent varnish for grates, may be prepared in the following manner :—

2295. INGREDIENTS.—1 lb. of common asphaltum, ½ pint of linseed oil, 1 quart of oil of turpentine.

Mode.—Melt the asphaltum, and add gradually to it the other two ingredients. Apply this with a small painter's brush, and leave it to become perfectly dry. The grate will need no other cleaning, but will merely require dusting every day, and occasionally brushing with a dry black-lead brush. This is, of course, when no fires are used. When they are required, the bars, cheeks, and back of the grate will need black-leading in the usual manner.

2296. *Fire-lighting*, however simple, is an operation requiring some skill; a fire is readily made by laying a few cinders at the bottom in open order; over this a few pieces of paper, and over that again eight or ten pieces of dry wood; over the wood, a course of moderate-sized pieces of coal, taking care to leave hollow spaces between for air at the centre; and taking care to lay the whole well back in the grate, so that the smoke may go up the chimney, and not into the room. This done, fire the paper with a match from below, and, if properly laid, it will soon burn up; the stream of flame from the wood and paper soon communicating to the coals and cinders, provided there is plenty of air at the centre.

2297. A new method of lighting a fire is sometimes practised with advantage, the fire lighting from the top and burning down, in place of being lighted and burning up from below. This is arranged by laying the coals at the bottom, mixed with a few good-sized cinders, and the wood at the top, with another layer of coals and some paper over it; the paper is lighted in the usual way, and soon burns down to a good fire, with some economy of fuel, as is said.

2298. Bright grates require unceasing attention to keep them in perfect order. A day should never pass without the housemaid rubbing with a dry leather the polished parts of a grate, as also the fender and fire-irons. A careful and attentive housemaid should have no occasion ever to use emery-paper for any part but the bars, which, of course, become blackened by the fire. (Some mistresses, to save labour, have a double set of bars, one set bright for the summer, and another black set to use when fires are in requisition.) When bright grates are once neglected, small rust-spots begin to show themselves, which a plain leather will not remove ; the following method of cleaning them must then be resorted to :—First, thoroughly clean with emery-paper ; then take a large smooth pebble from the road, sufficiently large to hold comfortably in the hand, with which rub the steel backwards and forwards one way, until the desired polish is obtained. It may appear at first to scratch, but continue rubbing, and the result will be success. The following is also an excellent polish for bright stoves and steel articles :—

2299. INGREDIENTS.—1 tablespoonful of turpentine, 1 ditto of sweet oil, emery powder.

Mode.—Mix the turpentine and sweet oil together, stirring in sufficient emery powder to make the mixture of the thickness of cream. Put it on the article with a piece of soft flannel, rub off quickly with another piece, then polish with a little dry emery powder and clean leather.

2300. The several fires lighted, the housemaid proceeds with her dusting, and polishing the several pieces of furniture in the breakfast-parlour, leaving no corner unvisited., Before sweeping the carpet, it is a good practice to sprinkle it all over with tea-leaves, which not only lay all dust, but give a slightly fragrant smell to the room. It is now in order for the reception of the family ; and where there is neither footman nor parlour-maid, she now proceeds to the dressing-room, and lights her mistress's fire, if she is in the habit of having one to dress by. Her mistress is called, hot water placed in the dressing-room for her use, her clothes—as far as they are under the house-maid's charge—put before the fire to air, hanging a fire-guard on the bars where there is one, while she proceeds to prepare the breakfast.

2301. In summer the housemaid's work is considerably abridged : she throws open the windows of the several rooms not occupied as bedrooms, that they may receive the fresh morning air before they are occupied ; she prepares the breakfast-room by sweeping the carpet, rubbing tables and chairs, dusting mantel-shelf and picture-frames with a light brush, dusting the furniture, and beating and sweeping the rug ; she cleans the grate when necessary, and replaces the white paper or arranges the shavings with which it is filled, leaving everything clean and tidy for breakfast. It is not enough, however, in cleaning furniture, just to pass lightly over the surface ; the rims and legs of tables, and the backs and legs of chairs and sofas, should be rubbed vigorously daily ; if there is a book-case, every corner of every pane and ledge requires to be carefully wiped, so that not a speck of dust can be found in the room.

2302. After the breakfast-room is finished, the housemaid should proceed to sweep down the stairs, commencing at the top, whilst the cook has the charge of the hall, door-step, and passages. After this she should go into the drawing-room, cover up every article of furniture that is likely to spoil, with large dusting-sheets, and put the chairs together, by turning them seat to seat, and, in fact, make as much room as possible, by placing all the loose furniture in the middle of the room, whilst she sweeps the corners and sides. When this is accomplished, the furniture can then be put back in its place, and the middle of the room swept, sweeping the dirt, as before said, towards

BANISTER-BROOM.

STAIRCASE-BROOM.

the fireplace. The same rules should be observed in cleaning the drawing-room grates as we have just stated, putting down the cloth, before commencing, to prevent the carpet from getting soiled. In the country, a room would not require sweeping thoroughly like this more than twice a week; but the house-maid should go over it every morning with a dust-pan and broom, taking up every crumb and piece she may see. After the sweeping she should leave the room, shut the door, and proceed to lay the breakfast. Where there is neither footman nor parlour-maid kept, the duty of laying the breakfast-cloth rests on the housemaid.

2303. Before laying the cloth for breakfast, the heater of the tea-urn is to be placed in the hottest part of the kitchen fire; or, where the kettle is used, boiled on the kitchen fire, and then removed to the parlour, where it is kept hot. Having washed herself free from the dust arising from the morning's work, the housemaid collects the breakfast-things on her tray, takes the breakfast-cloth from the napkin press, and carries them all on the tray into the parlour; arranges them on the table, placing a sufficiency of knives, forks, and salt-cellars for the family, and takes the tray back to the pantry; gets a supply of milk, cream, and bread; fills the butter-dish, taking care that the salt is plentiful, and soft and dry, and that hot plates and egg-cups are ready where warm meat or eggs are served, and that butter-knife and bread-knife are in their places. And now she should give the signal for breakfast, holding herself ready to fill the urn with hot water, or hand the kettle, and take in the rolls, toast, and other eatables, with which the cook supplies her, when the breakfast-room bell rings; bearing in mind that she is never to enter the parlour with dirty hands or with a dirty apron, and that everything is to be handed on a tray; that she is to hand everything she may be required to supply, on the left hand of the person she is serving, and that all is done quietly and without bustle or hurry. In some families, where there is a large number to attend on, the cook waits at breakfast whilst the housemaid is busy upstairs in the bedrooms, or sweeping, dusting, and putting the drawing-room in order.

2304. Breakfast served, the housemaid proceeds to the bed-chambers, throws up the sashes, if not already done, pulls up the blinds, throwing back curtains at the same time, and opens the beds, by removing the clothes, placing them over a horse, or, failing that, over the backs of chairs. She now proceeds to empty the slops. In doing this, everything is emptied into the slop-pail, leaving a little scalding-hot water for a minute in such vessels as require it ; adding a drop of turpentine to the water, when that is not sufficient to cleanse them. The basin is emptied, well rinsed with clean water, and carefully wiped ; the ewers emptied and washed ; finally, the water-jugs themselves emptied out and rinsed, and wiped dry. As soon as this is done, she should remove and empty the pails, taking care that they also are well washed, scalded, and wiped as soon as they are empty.

2305. Next follows bedmaking, at which the cook or kitchen-maid, where one is kept, usually assists ; but, before beginning, velvet chairs, or other things injured by dust, should be removed to another room. In bedmaking, the fancy of its occupant should be consulted ; some like beds sloping from the top towards the feet, swelling slightly in the middle ; others, perfectly flat : a good housemaid will accommodate each bed to the taste of the sleeper, taking care to shake, beat, and turn it well in the process. Some persons prefer sleeping on the mattress ; in which case a feather bed is usually beneath, resting on a second mattress, and a straw paillasse at the bottom. In this case, the mattresses should change places daily ; the feather bed placed on the mattress shaken, beaten, taken up and opened several times, so as thoroughly to separate the feathers : if too large to be thus handled, the maid should shake and beat one end first, and then the other, smoothing it afterwards equally all over into the required shape, and place the mattress gently over it. Any feathers which escape in this process a tidy servant will put back through the seam of the tick ; she will also be careful to sew up any stitch that gives way the moment it is discovered. The bedclothes are laid on, beginning with an under blanket and sheet, which are tucked under the mattress at the bottom. The bolster is then beaten and shaken, and put on, the top of the sheet rolled round it, and the sheet tucked in all round. The pillows and other bedclothes follow, and the counterpane over all, which should fall in grace-ful folds, and at equal distance from the ground all round. The curtains are drawn to the head and folded neatly across the bed, and the whole finished in a smooth and graceful manner. Where spring-mattresses are used, care should be taken that the top one is turned every day. The housemaid should now take up in a dustpan any pieces that may be on the carpet ; she should dust the room, shut the door, and proceed to another room. When all the bedrooms are finished, she should dust the stairs, and polish the handrail of the banisters, and see that all ledges, window-sills, &c., are quite free from dust. It will be necessary for the housemaid to divide her work, so that she may not have too much to do on certain days, and not sufficient to fill up her time on other days. In the country, bedrooms should be swept and thoroughly cleaned once a week ; and to be methodical and regular in her work, the house-maid should have certain days for doing certain rooms thoroughly. For instance, the drawing-room on Monday, two bedrooms on Tuesday, two on Wednesday, and so on, reserving a day for thoroughly cleaning the plate, bedroom candlesticks, &c. &c., which she will have to do where there is no parlour-maid or footman kept. By this means the work will be divided, and there will be no unnecessary bustling and hurrying, as is the case where the work is done any time, without rule or regulation.

2306. Once a week, when a bedroom is to be thoroughly cleaned, the housemaid should commence by brushing the mattresses of the bed before it is made; she should then make it, shake the curtains, lay them smoothly on the bed, and pin or tuck up the bottom valance, so that she may be able to sweep under the bed. She should then unloop the window-curtains, shake them, and pin them high up out of the way. After clearing the dressing-table, and the room altogether of little articles of china, &c. &c., she should shake the toilet-covers, fold them up, and lay them on the bed, over which a large dusting-sheet should be thrown. She should then sweep the room; first of all sprinkling the carpet with well-squeezed tea-leaves, or a little freshly-pulled

SCRUBBING-BRUSH.   grass, when this is obtainable.

After the carpet is swept, and the grate cleaned, she should wash with soap and water, with a little soda in it, the washing-table apparatus, removing all marks or fur round the jugs, caused by the water. The water-bottles and tumblers must also have her attention, as well as the top of the washing-stand, which should be cleaned with soap and flannel if it be marble: if of polished mahogany, no soap must be used. When these

LONG HAIR-BROOM

are all clean and arranged in their places, the housemaid should scrub the floor where it is not covered with carpet, under the beds, and round the wainscot. She should use as little soap and soda as possible, as too free a use of these articles is liable to give the boards a black appearance. In the country, cold soft water, a clean scrubbing-brush, and a willing arm, are all that are required to make bedroom floors look white. In winter it is not advisable to scrub rooms too often, as it is difficult to dry them thoroughly at that season of the year, and nothing is more dangerous than to allow persons to sleep in a damp room. The housemaid should now dust the furniture, blinds, ornaments, &c.; polish the looking-glass; arrange the toilet-cover and muslin; remove the cover from the bed, and straighten and arrange the curtains and counterpane. A bedroom should be cleaned like this every week. There are times, however, when it is necessary to have the carpet up; this should be done once a year in the country, and twice a year in large cities. The best time for these arrangements is spring and autumn, when the bed-furniture requires changing to suit the seasons of the year. After arranging the furniture, it should all be well rubbed and polished; and for this purpose the housemaid should provide herself with an old silk pocket-handkerchief, to finish the polishing.

3 s

2307. As modern furniture is now nearly always French-polished, it should often be rubbed with an old silk rubber, or a fine cloth or duster, to keep it free from smears. Three or four times a year any of the following polishes may be applied with very great success, as any of them make French-polished furniture look very well. One precaution must be taken,—not to put too much of the polish on at one time, and *to rub, not smear* it over the articles.

Furniture Polish.

2308. INGREDIENTS. — ¼ pint of linseed - oil, ¼ pint of vinegar, 1 oz. of spirits of salts, ½ oz. of muriatic antimony.

Mode.—Mix all well together, and shake before using.

Furniture Polish.

2309. INGREDIENTS.—Equal proportions of linseed-oil, turpentine, vinegar, and spirits of wine.

Mode.—When used, shake the mixture well, and rub on the furniture with a piece of linen rag, and polish with a clean duster. Vinegar and oil, rubbed in with flannel, and the furniture rubbed with a clean duster, produce a very good polish.

Furniture Paste.

2310. INGREDIENTS.—3 oz. of common beeswax, 1 oz. of white wax, 1 oz. of curd soap, 1 pint of turpentine, 1 pint of boiled water.

Mode.—Mix the ingredients together, adding the water when cold; shake the mixture frequently in the bottle, and do not use it for 48 hours after it is made. It should be applied with a piece of flannel, the furniture polished with a duster, and then with an old silk rubber.

FURNITURE-BRUSH.

2311. The chambers are finished, the chamber candlesticks brought down and cleaned, the parlour lamps trimmed ;—and here the housemaid's utmost care is required. In cleaning candlesticks, as in every other cleaning, she should have cloths and brushes kept for that purpose alone ; the knife used to scrape them should be applied to no other purpose ; the tallow-grease should be thrown into a box kept for the purpose ; the same with everything connected with the lamp-trimming ; the best mode of doing which she will do well to learn from the tradesman who supplies the oil ; always bearing in mind, however, that without perfect cleanliness, which involves occasional scalding, no lamp can be kept in order.

2312. The drawing and dining-room, inasmuch as everything there is more costly and valuable, require even more care. When the carpets are of the kind known as velvet-pile, they require to be swept firmly by a hard whisk brush, made of cocoanut fibre.

2313. The furniture must be carefully gone over in every corner with a soft cloth, that it may be left perfectly free from dust ; or where that is beyond reach, with a brush made of long feathers, or a goose's wing. The sofas are swept in the same manner, slightly beaten, the cushions shaken and smoothed, the picture-frames swept, and everything arranged in its proper place. This, of course, applies to dining as well as drawing-room and morning-room. And now the housemaid may dress herself for the day, and prepare for the family dinner, at which she must attend.

2314. We need not repeat the long instructions already given for laying the dinner-table. At the family dinner, even where no footman waits, the routine will be the same. In most families the cloth is laid with the slips on each side, with napkins, knives, forks, spoons, and wine and finger glasses on all occasions.

2315. She should ascertain that her plate is in order, glasses free from smears, water-bottles and decanters the same, and everything ready on her tray, that she may be able to lay her cloth properly. Few things add more to the neat and comfortable appearance of a dinner-table than well-polished plate ; indeed, the state of the plate is a certain indication of a well-managed or ill-managed household. Nothing is easier than to keep plate in good order, and yet many servants, from stupidity and ignorance, make it the greatest trouble of all things under their care.

BUTLER'S TRAY AND STAND.

It should be remembered, that it is utterly impossible to make greasy silver take a polish ; and that as spoons and forks in daily use are continually in contact with grease, they must require good washing in soap-and-water to remove it. Silver should be washed with a soapy flannel in one water, rinsed in another, and then wiped dry with a dry cloth. The plate so washed may be polished with the plate-rags, as in the following directions :—Once a week all the plate should receive a thorough cleaning with the hartshorn powder, as directed in the first recipe for cleaning plate ; and where the housemaid can find time, rubbed every day with the plate-rags.

2316. Hartshorn, we may observe, is one of the best possible ingredients for plate-powder in daily use. It leaves on the silver a deep, dark polish, and at the same time does less injury than anything else. It has also the advantage of being very cheap ; almost all the ordinary powders sold in boxes containing more or less of quicksilver, in some form or another; and this in process of time is sure to make the plate brittle. If any one wishes to be convinced of the effect of quicksilver on plate, he has only to rub a little of it on one place for some time,—on the handle of a silver teaspoon for instance, and he will find it break in that spot with very little pressure.

To Clean Plate.
A very excellent method.

2317. Wash the plate well to remove all grease, in a strong lather of common yellow soap and boiling water, and wipe it quite dry ; then mix as much hartshorn powder as will be required, into a thick paste, with cold water or spirits of wine ; smear this lightly over the plate with a piece of soft rag,

PLATE-BRUSH.

and leave it for some little time to dry. When perfectly dry, brush it off quite clean with a soft plate-brush, and polish the plate with a dry leather. If the plate be very dirty, or much tarnished, spirits of wine will be found to answer better than the water for mixing the paste.

Plate-rags for daily use.

2318. Boil soft rags (nothing is better for the purpose than the tops of old cotton stockings) in a mixture of new milk and hartshorn powder, in the proportion of 1 oz. of powder to a pint of milk; boil them for 5 minutes; wring them as soon as they are taken out, for a moment, in cold water, and dry them before the fire. With these rags rub the plate briskly as soon as it has been well washed and dried after daily use. A most beautiful deep polish will be produced, and the plate will require nothing more than merely to be dusted with a leather or a dry soft cloth, before it is again put on the table.

2319. For waiting at table, the housemaid should be neatly and cleanly dressed, and, if possible, her dress made with closed sleeves, the large open ones dipping and falling into everything on the table, and being very much in the way. She should not wear creaking boots, and should move about the room as noiselessly as possible, anticipating people's wants by handing them things without being asked for them, and altogether be as quiet as possible. It will be needless here to repeat what we have already said respecting waiting at table, in the duties of the butler and footman: rules that are good to be observed by them, are equally good for the parlour-maid or housemaid.

2320. The housemaid having announced that dinner is on the table, will hand the soup, fish, meat, or side-dishes to the different members of the family; but in families who do not spend much of the day together, they will probably prefer being alone at dinner and breakfast: the housemaid will be required, after all are helped, if her master does not wish her to stay in the room, to go on with her work of cleaning up in the pantry, and answer the bell when rung. In this case she will place a pile of plates on the table or a dumb-waiter, within reach of her master and mistress, and leave the room.

2321. Dinner over, the housemaid removes the plates and dishes on the tray, places the dirty knives and forks in the basket prepared for them, folds up the napkins in the ring which indicates by which member of the family it has been

CRUMB-BRUSH.

used, brushes off the crumbs on the hand-tray kept for the purpose, folds up the table-cloth in the folds already made, and places it in the linen-press to be smoothed out. After every meal the table should be rubbed, all marks from hot plates removed, and the table-cover thrown over, and the room restored to its usual order. If the family retire to the drawing-room, or any other room, it is a good practice to throw up the sash to admit fresh air and ventilate the room.

2322. The housemaid's evening service consists in washing up the dinner-things, the plate, plated articles, and glasses, restoring everything to its place ; cleaning up her pantry, and putting away everything for use when next required ; lastly, preparing for tea, as the time approaches, by setting the things out on the tray, getting the urn or kettle ready, with cream and other things usually partaken of at that meal.

2323. In summer-time the windows of all the bedrooms, which have been closed during the heat/of the day, should be thrown open for an hour or so after sunset, in order to air them. Before dark they should be closed, the bedclothes turned down, and the night-clothes laid in order for use when required. During winter, where fires are required in the dressing-rooms, they should be lighted an hour before the usual time of retiring, placing a fire-guard before each fire. At the same time, the night-things on the horse should be placed before it to be aired, with a tin can of hot water, if the mistress is in the habit of washing before going to bed. We may add, that there is no greater preservative of beauty than washing the face every night in hot water. The housemaid will probably be required to assist her mistress to undress and put her dress in order for the morrow ; in which case her duties are very much those of the lady's-maid.

2324. And now the fire is made up for the night, the fireguard replaced, and everything in the room in order for the night, the housemaid taking care to leave the night-candle and matches together in a convenient place, should they be required. It is usual in summer to remove all highly fragrant flowers from sleeping-rooms, the impression being that their scent is injurious in a close chamber.

2325. On leisure days, the housemaid should be able to do some needlework for her mistress,—such as turning and mending sheets and darning the house linen, or assist her in anything she may think fit to give her to do. For this reason it is almost essential that a housemaid, in a small family, should be an expert needlewoman ; as, if she be a good manager and an active girl, she will have time on her hands to get through plenty of work.

2326. *Periodical Cleanings.* —Besides the daily routine which we have described, there are portions of every house which can only be thoroughly cleaned occasionally ; at which time the whole house usually undergoes a more thorough cleaning than is permitted in the general way. On these occasions it is usual to begin at the top of the house and clean downwards ; moving everything out of the room ; washing the wainscoting or paint with soft soap and water ; pulling down the beds and thoroughly cleansing all the joints ; "scrubbing" the floor ; beating feather beds, mattress, and paillasse, and thoroughly purifying every article of furniture before it is put back in its place.

2327. This general cleaning usually takes place in the spring or early summer, when the warm curtains of winter are replaced by the light and cheerful muslin curtains. Carpets are at the same time taken up and beaten, except where the mistress of the house has been worried into an experiment by the often-reiterated question, "Why beat your carpets?" In this case she will probably have made up her mind to try the cleaning process, and arranged with the company to send for them on the morning when cleaning commenced. It is hardly necessary to repeat, that on this occasion every article is to be gone over, the French-polished furniture well rubbed and

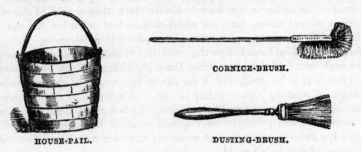

CORNICE-BRUSH.

HOUSE-PAIL.   DUSTING-BRUSH.

polished. The same thorough system of cleaning should be done throughout the house; the walls cleaned where painted, and swept down with a soft broom or feather brush where papered; the window and bed curtains, which have been replaced with muslin ones, carefully brushed, or, if they require it, cleaned; lamps not likely to be required, washed out with hot water, dried, and cleaned. The several grates are now to be furnished with their summer ornaments; and we know none prettier than the following, which the housemaid may provide at a small expense to her mistress:—Purchase two yards and a half of crinoline muslin, and tear it into small strips, the selvage way of the material, about an inch wide; strip this thread by thread on each side, leaving the four centre threads; this gives about six-and-thirty pieces, fringed on each side, which are tied together at one end, and fastened to the trap of the register, while the threads, unravelled, are spread gracefully about the grate, the lower part of which is filled with paper shavings. This makes a very elegant and very cheap ornament, which is much stronger, besides, than those usually purchased.

2328. As winter approaches, this house-cleaning will have to be repeated, and the warm bed and window curtains replaced. The process of scouring and cleaning is again necessary, and must be gone through, beginning at the top, and going through the house, down to the kitchens.

2329. Independently of these daily and periodical cleanings, other occupations will present themselves from time to time, which the housemaid will have to perform. When spots show on polished furniture, they can generally be restored by soap-and-water and a sponge, the polish being brought out by using a little polish, and then well rubbing it. Again, drawers which draw out stiffly may be made to move more easily if the spot where they press is rubbed over with a little soap.

2330. Chips broken off any of the furniture should be collected and replaced, by means of a little glue applied to it. Liquid glue, which is sold prepared in bottles, is very useful to have in the house, as it requires no melting; and anything broken can be so quickly repaired.

2331. Breaking glass and china is about the most disagreeable thing that can happen in a family, and it is, probably, a greater annoyance to a right-minded servant than to the mistress. A neat-handed housemaid may sometimes repair these breakages, where they are not broken in very conspicuous places, by joining the pieces very neatly together with a cement made as follows:—Dissolve an ounce of gum mastic in a quantity of highly-rectified spirits of wine; then soften an ounce of isinglass in warm water, and, finally, dissolve it in rum or brandy, till it forms a thick jelly. Mix the isinglass and gum mastic together, adding a quarter of an ounce of finely-powdered gum ammoniac; put the whole into an earthen pipkin, and in a warm place, till they are thoroughly incorporated together; pour it into a small phial, and cork it down for use.

2332. In using it, dissolve a small piece of the cement in a silver teaspoon over a lighted candle. The broken pieces of glass or china being warmed, and touched with the now liquid cement, join the parts neatly together, and hold in their places till the cement has set; then wipe away the cement adhering to the edge of the joint, and leave it for twelve hours without touching it: the joint will be as strong as the china itself, and if neatly done, it will show no joining. It is essential that neither of the pieces be wetted either with hot or cold water.

USEFUL RECIPES FOR HOUSEMAIDS.

To clean Marble.

2333. Mix with ¼ pint of soap lees, ½ gill of turpentine, sufficient pipe-clay and bullock's gall to make the whole into rather a thick paste. Apply it to the marble with a soft brush, and after a day or two, when quite dry, rub it off with a soft rag. Apply this a second or third time till the marble is quite clean.

Another method.

2334. Take two parts of soda, one of pumice-stone, and one of finely-powdered chalk. Sift these through a fine sieve, and mix them into a paste with water. Rub this well all over the marble, and the stains will be removed; then wash it with soap-and-water, and a beautiful bright polish will be produced.

To clean Floorcloth.

2335. After having washed the floorcloth in the usual manner with a damp flannel, wet it all over with milk and rub it well with a dry cloth, when a most beautiful polish will be brought out. Some persons use for rubbing a well-waxed flannel; but this in general produces an unpleasant slipperiness, which is not the case with the milk.

To clean Decanters.

2336. Roll up in small pieces some soft brown or blotting paper ;. wet them, and soap them well. Put them into the decanters about one quarter full of warm water ; shake them well for a few minutes, then rinse with clear cold water ; wipe the outsides with a nice dry cloth, put the decanters to drain, and when dry they will be almost as bright as new ones.

To brighten Gilt Frames.

2337. Take sufficient flour of sulphur to give a golden tinge to about 1½ pint of water, and in this boil 4 or 5 bruised onions, or garlic, which will answer the same purpose. Strain off the liquid, and with it, when cold, wash, with a soft brush, any gilding which requires restoring, and when dry it will come out as bright as new work.

To preserve bright Grates or Fire-irons from Rust.

2338. Make a strong paste of fresh lime and water, and with a fine brush smear it as thickly as possible over all the polished surface requiring preservation. By this simple means, all the grates and fire-irons in an empty house may be kept for months free from harm, without further care or attention.

German Furniture-Gloss.

2339. INGREDIENTS.—¼ lb. yellow wax, 1 oz. black rosin, 2 oz. of oil of turpentine.

Mode.—Cut the wax into small pieces, and melt it in a pipkin, with the rosin pounded very fine. Stir in gradually, while these two ingredients are quite warm, the oil of turpentine. Keep this composition well covered for use in a tin or earthen pot. A little of this gloss should be spread on a piece of coarse woollen cloth, and the furniture well rubbed with it ; afterwards it should be polished with a fine cloth.

DUTIES OF THE MAID-OF-ALL-WORK.

2340. THE general servant, or maid-of-all-work, is perhaps the only one of her class deserving of commiseration : her life is a solitary one, and in, some places, her work is never done. She is also subject to rougher treatment than either the house or kitchen-maid, especially in her earlier career : she starts in life, probably a girl of thirteen, with some small tradesman's wife as her mistress, just a step above her in the social scale ; and although the class contains among them many excellent, kind-hearted women, it also contains some very rough speci-mens of the feminine gender, and to some of these it occasionally falls to give our maid-of-all-work her first lessons in her multifarious occupations : the mistress's commands are the measure of the maid-of-all-work's duties. By the time she has become a tolerable servant, she is probably engaged in some respectable tradesman's house, where she has to rise with the lark, for she has to do in her own person all the work which in larger establishments is performed by cook, kitchen-maid, and housemaid, and occasionally the part of a footman's duty, which consists in carrying messages.

2341. The general servant's duties commence by opening the shutters (and windows, if the weather permits) of all the lower apartments in the house ; she should then brush up her kitchen-range, light the fire, clear away the ashes, clean the hearth, and polish with a leather the bright parts of the range, doing all as rapidly and as vigorously as possible, that no more time be wasted than is necessary. After putting on the kettle, she should then proceed to the dining-room or parlour to get it in order for breakfast. She should first roll up the rug, take up the fender, shake and fold up the table-cloth, then sweep the room, carrying the dirt towards the fireplace ; a coarse cloth should then be laid down over the carpet, and she should proceed to clean the grate, having all her utensils close to her. When the grate is finished, the ashes cleared away, the hearth cleaned, and the fender put back in its place, she must dust the furniture, not omitting the legs of the tables and chairs ; and if there are any ornaments or things on the sideboard, she must not dust round them, but lift them up on to another place, dust well where they have been standing, and then replace the things. Nothing annoys a particular mistress so much as to find, when she comes down stairs, different articles of furniture looking as if they had never been dusted. If the servant is at all methodical, and gets into a habit of *doing* a room in a certain way, she will scarcely ever leave her duties neglected. After the rug is put down, the table-cloth arranged, and everything in order, she should lay the cloth for breakfast, and then shut the dining-room door.

2342. The hall must now be swept, the mats shaken, the door-step cleaned, and any brass knockers or handles polished up with the leather. If the family breakfast very early, the tidying of the hall must then be deferred till after that meal.   After cleaning the boots that are absolutely required, the servant should now wash her hands and face, put on a clean white apron, and

be ready for her mistress when she comes down stairs.   In families where there is much work to do before breakfast, the master of the house frequently has two pairs of boots in wear, so that they may be properly cleaned when the servant has more time to do them, in the daytime.   This arrangement is, per-

BLACKING-BRUSH BOX.

haps, scarcely necessary in the summer-time, when there are no grates to clean every morning; but in the dark days of winter it is only kind and thoughtful to lighten a servant-of-all-work's duties as much as possible.

2343. She will now carry the urn into the dining-room, where her mistress will make the tea or coffee, and sometimes will boil the eggs, to insure them being done to her liking.   In the mean time the servant cooks, if required, the bacon, kidneys, fish, &c. ;—if cold meat is to be served, she must always send it to table on a clean dish, and nicely garnished with tufts of parsley, if this is obtainable.

2344. After she has had her own breakfast, and whilst the family are finish-ing theirs, she should go upstairs into the bedrooms, open all the windows, strip the clothes off the beds, and leave them to air whilst she is clearing away the breakfast things.   She should then take up the crumbs in a dustpan from under the table, put the chairs in their places, and sweep up the hearth.

2345. The breakfast things washed up, the kitchen should be tidied, so that it may be neat when her mistress comes in to give the orders for the day : after receiving these orders, the servant should go upstairs again, with a jug of boiling water, the slop-pail, and two cloths.   After emptying the slops, and scalding the vessels with the boiling water, and wiping them thoroughly dry, she should wipe the top of the wash-table and arrange it all in order.   She then proceeds to make the beds, in which occupation she is generally assisted by the mistress, or, if she have any daughters, by one of them.   Before commencing to make the bed, the servant should put on a large bed-apron, kept for this purpose only, which should be made very wide, to button round the waist and meet behind, while it should be made as long as the dress.   By adopting this plan, the blacks and dirt on servants' dresses (which at all times it is impossible to help) will not rub off on to the bed-clothes, mattresses, and bed furniture. When the beds are made, the rooms should be dusted, the stairs lightly swept down, hall furniture, closets, &c., dusted.   The lady of the house, where there is but one servant kept, frequently takes charge of the drawing-room herself, that is to say, dusting it ; the servant sweeping, cleaning windows, looking-glasses, grates, and rough work of that sort.   If there are many ornaments and knick-knacks about the room, it is certainly better for the mistress to dust these herself, as a maid-of-all-work's hands are not always in a condition to handle delicate ornaments.

2346. Now she has gone the rounds of the house and seen that all is in order, the servant goes to her kitchen to see about the cooking of the dinner, in which very often her mistress will assist her. She should put on a coarse apron with a bib to do her dirty work in, which may be easily replaced by a white one if required.

2347. Half an hour before dinner is ready, she should lay the cloth, that everything may be in readiness when she is dishing up the dinner, and take all into the dining-room that is likely to be required, in the way of knives, forks, spoons, bread, salt, water, &c. &c. By exercising a little forethought, much confusion and trouble may be saved both to mistress and servant, by getting everything ready for the dinner in good time.

2348. After taking in the dinner, when every one is seated, she removes the covers, hands the plates round, and pours out the beer ; and should be careful to hand everything on the left side of the person she is waiting on.

2349. We need scarcely say that a maid-of-all-work cannot stay in the dining-room during the whole of dinner-time, as she must dish up her pudding, or whatever is served after the first course. When she sees every one helped, she should leave the room to make her preparations for the next course ; and anything that is required, such as bread, &c., people may assist themselves to in the absence of the servant.

2350. When the dinner things are cleared away, the servant should sweep up the crumbs in the dining-room, sweep the hearth, and lightly dust the furniture, then sit down to her own dinner.

2351. After this, she washes up and puts away the dinner things, sweeps the kitchen, dusts and tidies it, and puts on the kettle for tea. She should now, before dressing herself for the afternoon, clean her knives, boots, and shoes, and do any other dirty work in the scullery that may be necessary. Knife-cleaning machines are rapidly taking the place, in most households, of the old knife-board. The saving of labour by the knife-cleaner is very great, and its performance of the work is very satisfactory. Small and large machines are manufactured, some cleaning only four knives, whilst others clean as many as twelve at once. Nothing can be more simple

KNIFE-CLEANING MACHINE.

than the process of machine knife-cleaning ; and although, in a very limited household, the substitution of the machine for the board may not be necessary, yet we should advise all housekeepers, to whom the outlay is not a difficulty, to avail themselves of the services of a machine. We have already spoken of its management in the "Duties of the Footman," No. 2177.

2352. When the servant is dressed, she takes in the tea, and after tea turns down the beds, sees that the water-jugs and bottles are full, closes the windows, and draws down the blinds. If the weather is very warm, these are usually left open until the last thing at night, to cool the rooms.

2353. The routine of a general servant's duties depends upon the kind of situation she occupies; but a systematic maid-of-all-work should so contrive to divide her work, that every day in the week may have its proper share. By this means she is able to keep the house clean with less fatigue to herself than if she left all the cleaning to do at the end of the week. Supposing there are five bedrooms in the house, two sitting-rooms, kitchen, scullery, and the usual domestic offices :—on Monday she should thoroughly clean the drawing-room; on Tuesday, two of the bedrooms; on Wednesday, two more; on Thursday, the other bedroom and stairs; on Friday morning she should sweep the dining-room very thoroughly, clean the hall, and in the afternoon her kitchen tins and bright utensils. By arranging her work in this manner, no undue proportion will fall to Saturday's share, and she will then have this day for cleaning plate, cleaning her kitchen, and arranging everything in nice order. The regular work must, of course, be performed in the usual manner, as we have endeavoured to describe.

2354. Before retiring to bed, she will do well to clean up glasses, plates, &c. which have been used for the evening meal, and prepare for her morning's work by placing her wood near the fire, on the hob, to dry, taking care there is no danger of it igniting, before she leaves the kitchen for the night. Before retiring, she will have to lock and bolt the doors, unless the master undertakes this office himself.

2355. If the washing, or even a portion of it, is done at home, it will be impossible for the maid-of-all-work to do her household duties thoroughly, during the time it is about, unless she have some assistance. Usually, if all the washing is done at home, the mistress hires some one to assist at the wash-tub, and sees to little matters herself, in the way of dusting, clearing away breakfast things, folding, starching, and ironing the fine things. With a little management much can be accomplished, provided the mistress be industrious, energetic, and willing to lend a helping hand. Let washing-week be not the excuse for having everything in a muddle; and although "things" cannot be cleaned so thoroughly, and so much time spent upon them, as ordinarily, yet the house may be kept tidy and clear from litter without a great deal of exertion either on the part of the mistress or servant. We will conclude our remarks with an extract from an admirably-written book, called "Home Truths for Home Peace." The authoress says, with respect to the great wash—"Amongst all the occasions in which it is most difficult and glorious to keep muddle out of a family, 'the great wash' stands pre-eminent ; and as very little money is now saved by having *everything* done at home, many ladies, with the option of taking another servant or putting out the chief part of the washing, have thankfully adopted the latter course." She goes on to say—"When a gentleman who dines at home can't bear washing in the house, but gladly pays for its being done elsewhere, the lady should gratefully submit to his wishes, and put out anything in her whole establishment rather than put out a good and generous husband."

2356. A bustling and active girl will always find time to do a little needle-work for herself, if she lives with consistent and reasonable people. In the summer evenings she should manage to sit down for two or three hours, and for a short time in the afternoon in leisure days. A general servant's duties are so multifarious, that unless she be quick and active, she will not be able to accomplish this. To discharge these various duties properly is a difficult task, and sometimes a thankless office ; but it must be remembered that a good maid-of-all-work will make a good servant in any capacity, and may be safely taken not only without fear of failure, but with every probability of giving satisfaction to her employer.

DUTIES OF THE DAIRY-MAID.

2357. THE duties of the dairy-maid differ considerably in different districts. In Scotland, Wales, and some of the northern counties, women milk the cows. On some of the large dairy farms in other parts of England, she takes her share in the milking, but in private families the milking is generally performed by the cowkeeper, and the dairy-maid only receives the milkpails from him morning and night, and empties and cleans them preparatory to the next milking ; her duty being to supply the family with milk, cream, and butter, and other luxuries depending on the "milky mothers" of the herd.

2358. *The Dairy.*—The object with which gentlemen keep cows is to procure milk un-adulterated, and sweet butter, for themselves and families : in order to obtain this, however, great cleanliness is required, and as visitors, as well as the mistress of the house, sometimes visit the dairy, some efforts are usually made to render it ornamental and picturesque. The locality is usually fixed near to the house ; it should neither be exposed to the fierce heat of the summer's sun nor to the equally unfavourable frosts of winter—it must be both sheltered and shaded. If it is a building apart from the house and other offices, the walls should be tolerably thick, and if hollow, the temperature will be more equable. The walls inside are usually covered with Dutch glazed tiles ; the flooring also of glazed tiles set in asphalte, to resist water ; and the ceiling, lath and plaster, or closely-jointed woodwork, painted. Its architecture will be a matter of fancy : it should have a northern aspect, and a thatched roof is considered most suitable, from the shade and shelter it affords ; and it should contain at least two apartments, besides a cool place for storing away butter. One of the apartments, in which the milk is placed to deposit cream, or to ripen for churning, is usually surrounded by shelves of marble or slate, on which the milk-dishes rest ; but it will be found a better plan to have a large square or round table of stone in the centre, with a water-tight ledge all round it, in which water may remain in hot weather, or, if some attempt at the picturesque is desired, a small fountain might occupy the centre, which would keep the apartment cool and fresh. Round this table the milk-dishes should be ranged; one shelf, or dresser, of slate or marble, being kept for the various occupations of the dairy-maid: it will be found a better plan than putting them on shelves and corners against the wall. There should be a funnel or ventilator in the ceiling, communicating with the open air, made to open and shut as required. Double windows are recommended, but of the lattice kind, so that they may open, and with wire-gauze blinds fitted into the opening, and calico blinds, which may be wetted when additional coolness is required. The other apartment will be used for churning, washing, and scrubbing—in fact, the scullery of the dairy, with a boiler for hot water, and a sink with cold water laid on, which should be plentiful and good. In some dairies a third apartment, or, at least, a cool airy pantry, is required for storing away butter, with shelves of marble or slate, to hold the cream-jars while it is ripening; and where cheeses are made, a fourth becomes necessary. The dairy utensils are not numerous,—*churns, milk-pails* for each cow, *hair-sieves, slices of tin,* milk-pans, marble dishes for cream for family use, scales and weights, a portable rack for drying the utensils, *wooden bowls,* butter-moulds and butter-patters, and *wooden tubs* for washing the utensils, comprising pretty nearly everything.

2359. *Pails* are made of maple-wood or elm, and hooped, or of tin, more or less ornamented. One is required for each cow.

2360. *The Hair-Sieve* is made of closely-twisted horse-hair, with a rim, through which the milk is strained to remove any hairs which may have dropped from the cow in milking.

2361. *Milk-Dishes* are shallow basins of glass, of glazed earthenware, or tin, about 16 inches in diameter at top, and 12 at the bottom, and 5 or 6 inches deep, holding about 8 to 10 quarts each when full.

2362. *Churns* are of all sorts and sizes, from that which churns 70 or 80 gallons by means of a strap from the engine, to the square box in which a pound of butter is made. The churn used for families is a square box, 18 inches by 12 or 13, and 17 deep, bevelled below to the plane of the *dashers,* with a loose lid or cover. The dasher consists of an axis of wood, to which the four beaters or fanners are attached; these fans are simply four pieces of elm strongly dovetailed together, forming an oblong square, with a space left open, two of the openings being left broader than the others; attached to an axle, they form an axis with four projecting blades; the axle fits into supports at the centre of the box; a handle is fitted to it, and the act of churning is done by turning the handle.

2363. Such is the temple in which the dairy-maid presides: it should be removed both from stable and cowhouse, and larder; no animal smells should come near it, and the drainage should be perfect.

2364. The dairy-maid receives the milk from the cowkeeper, each pail being strained through the hair sieve into one of the milk-basins. This is left in the basins from twenty-four to thirty-six hours in the summer, according to the weather; after which it is skimmed off by means of the slicer, and poured into glazed earthenware jars to "turn" for churning. Some persons prefer making up a separate churning for the milk of each cow; in which there is some advantage. In this case the basins of each cow, for two days, would either be kept together or labelled. As soon as emptied, the pails should be scalded and every particle of milk washed out, and placed away in a dry place till next required; and all milk spilt on the floor, or on the table or dresser, cleaned up with a cloth and hot water. Where very great attention is paid to the dairy, the milk-coolers are used larger in winter, when it is desirable to retard the cooling down and increase the creamy deposit, and smaller in summer, to hasten it; the temperature required being from 55° to 50°. In summer it is sometimes expedient, in very sultry weather, to keep the dairy fresh and cool by suspending cloths dipped in chloride of lime across the room.

2365. In some dairies it is usual to churn twice, and in others three times a week : the former produces the best butter, the other the greatest quantity. With three cows, the produce should be 27 to 30 quarts a day. The dairy-maid should churn every day when very hot, if they are in full milk, and every second day in more temperate weather ; besides supplying the milk and cream required for a large establishment. The churning should always be done in the morning : the dairy-maid will find it advantageous in being at work on churning mornings by five o'clock. The operation occupies from 20 minutes to half an hour in summer, and considerably longer in winter. A steady uniform motion is necessary to produce sweet butter ; neither too quick nor too slow. Rapid motion causes the cream to heave and swell, from too much air being forced into it : the result is a tedious churning, and soft, bad-coloured butter.

2366. In spring and summer, when the cow has her natural food, no artificial colour is required ; but in winter, under stall-feeding, the colour is white and tallowy, and some persons prefer a higher colour. This is communicated by mixing a little finely-powdered arnotto with the cream before putting it into the churn ; a still more natural and delicate colour is communicated by scraping a red carrot into a clean piece of linen cloth, dipping it into water, and squeezing it into the cream.

2367. As soon as the butter comes, the milk is poured off, and the butter put into a shallow wooden tub or bowl, full of pure spring water, in which it is washed and kneaded, pouring off the water, and renewing it until it comes away perfectly free from milk. Imperfect washing is the frequent cause of bad butter, and in nothing is the skill of the dairy-maid tested more than in this process ; moreover, it is one in which cleanliness of habits and person are most necessary. In this operation we want the aid of Phyllis's neat, soft, and perfectly clean hand ; for no mechanical operation can so well squeeze out the sour particles of milk or curd.

2368. The operations of churning and butter-making over, the butter-milk is disposed of : usually, in England, it goes to the pigs ; but it is a very wholesome beverage when fresh, and some persons like it ; the disposal, therefore, will rest with the mistress : the dairy-maid's duty is to get rid of it. She must then scald with boiling water and scrub out every utensil she has used ; brush out the churn, clean out the cream-jars, which will probably require the use of a little common soda to purify ; wipe all dry, and place them in a position where the sun can reach them for a short time, to sweeten them.

2369. In Devonshire, celebrated for its dairy system, the milk is always scalded. The milk-pans, which are of tin, and contain from 10 to 12 quarts, after standing 10 or 12 hours, are placed on a hot plate of iron, over a stove, until the cream has formed on the surface, which is indicated by the air-bubbles rising through the milk, and producing blisters on the surface-coating of cream. This indicates its approach to the boiling point : and the vessel is now removed to cool. When sufficiently, that is, quite cool, the cream is skimmed off with the slice: it is now the clouted cream for which Devonshire is so famous. It is now placed in the churn, and churned until the butter comes, which it generally does in a much shorter time than by the other process. The butter so made contains more *caseine* than butter made in the usual way, but does not keep so long.

2370. It is a question frequently discussed, how far it is economical for families to keep cows and make their own butter. It is calculated that a good cow costs from May 1 to October 1, when well but economically kept, £5. 16s. 6d.; and from October 1 to April 30, £10. 2s. 6d. During that time she should produce 227 lbs. of butter, besides the skimmed milk. Of course, if new milk and cream are required, that will diminish the quantity of butter.

2371. Besides churning and keeping her dairy in order, the dairy-maid has charge of the whole produce, handing it over to the cook, butler, or house-maid as required; and she will do well to keep an exact account both of what she receives and how and when she disposes of it.

DUTIES OF THE LAUNDRY-MAID.

2372. THE laundry-maid is charged with the duty of washing and getting-up the family linen,—a situation of great importance where the washing is all done at home; but in large towns, where there is little convenience for bleaching and drying, it is chiefly done by professional laundresses and companies, who apply mechanical and chemical processes to the purpose. These processes, however, are supposed to injure the fabric of the linen; and in many families the fine linen, cottons, and muslins, are washed and got-up at home, even where the bulk of the washing is given out. In country and suburban houses, where greater conveniences exist, washing at home is more common,—in country places universal.

2373. The laundry establishment consists of a washing-house, an ironing and drying-room, and sometimes a drying-closet heated by furnaces. The washing-house will probably be attached to the kitchen; but it is better that it should be completely detached from it, and of one story, with a funnel or shaft to carry off the steam. It will be of a size proportioned to the extent of the washing to be done. A range of tubs, either round or oblong, opposite to, and sloping towards, the light, narrower at the bottom than the top, for convenience in stooping over, and fixed at a height suited to the convenience of the women using them; each tub having a tap for hot and cold water, and another in the bottom, communicating with the drains, for drawing off foul water. A boiler and furnace, proportioned in size to the wants of the family, should also be fixed. The flooring should be York stone, laid on brick piers, with good drainage, or asphalte, sloping gently towards a gutter connected with the drain.

2374. Adjoining the bleaching-house, a second room, about the same size, is required for ironing, drying, and mangling. The contents of this room should comprise an ironing-board, opposite to the light ; a strong white deal table, about twelve or fourteen feet long, and about three and a half feet broad, with drawers for ironing-blankets ; a mangle in one corner, and clothes-horses for drying and airing ; cupboards for holding the various irons, starch, and other articles used in ironing ; a hot-plate built in the chimney, with furnace beneath it for heating the irons ; sometimes arranged with a flue for carrying the hot air round the room for drying. Where this is the case, however, there should be a funnel in the ceiling for ventilation and carrying off steam ; but a better arrangement is to have a hot-air closet adjoining, heated by hot-air pipes, and lined with iron, with proper arrangements for carrying off steam, and clothes-horses on castors running in grooves, to run into it for drying purposes. This leaves the laundry free from unwholesome vapour.

2375. The laundry-maid should commence her labours on Monday morning by a careful examination of the articles committed to her care, and enter them in the washing-book ; separating the white linen and collars, sheets and body-linen, into one heap, fine muslins into another, coloured cotton and linen fabrics into a third, woollens into a fourth, and the coarser kitchen and other greasy cloths into a fifth. Every article should be examined for ink- or grease-spots, or for fruit- or wine-stains. Ink-spots are removed by dipping the part into hot water, and then spreading it smoothly on the hand or on the back of a spoon, pouring a few drops of oxalic acid or salts of sorel over the ink-spot, rubbing and rinsing it in cold water till removed ; grease-spots, by rubbing over with yellow soap, and rinsing in hot water ; fruit- and wine-spots, by dipping in a solution of sal ammonia or spirits of wine, and rinsing.

2376. Every article having been examined and assorted, the sheets and fine linen should be placed in one of the tubs and just covered with lukewarm water, in which a little soda has been dissolved and mixed, and left there to soak till the morning. The greasy cloths and dirtier things should be laid to soak in another tub, in a liquor composed of $\frac{1}{2}$ lb. of unslaked lime to every 6 quarts of water which has been boiled for two hours, then left to settle, and strained off when clear. Each article should be rinsed in this liquor to wet it thoroughly, and left to soak till the morning, just covered by it when the things are pressed together. Coppers and boilers should now be filled, and the fires laid ready to light.

2377. Early on the following morning the fires should be lighted, and as soon as hot water can be procured, washing commenced ; the sheets and body-linen being wanted to whiten in the morning, should be taken first ; each article being removed in succession from the lye in which it has been soaking, rinsed, rubbed, and wrung, and laid aside until the tub is empty, when the foul water is drawn off. The tub should be again filled with lukewarm water, about 80°, in which the articles should again be plunged, and

3 T

each gone over carefully with soap, and rubbed. Novices in the art sometimes rub the linen against the skin; more experienced washerwomen rub one linen surface against the other, which saves their hands, and enables them to continue their labour much longer, besides economizing time, two parts being thus cleaned at once.

2378. After this first washing, the linen should be put into a second water as hot as the hand can bear, and again rubbed over in every part, examining every part for spots not yet moved, which require to be again soaped over and rubbed till thoroughly clean; then rinsed and wrung, the larger and stronger articles by two of the women; the smaller and more delicate articles requiring gentler treatment.

2379. In order to remove every particle of soap, and produce a good colour, they should now be placed, and boiled for about an hour and a half in the copper, in which soda, in the proportion of a teaspoonful to every two gallons of water, has been dissolved. Some very careful laundresses put the linen into a canvas bag to protect it from the scum and the sides of the copper. When taken out, it should again be rinsed, first in clean hot water, and then in abundance of cold water slightly tinged with fig-blue, and again wrung dry. It should now be removed from the washing-house and hung up to dry or spread out to bleach, if there are conveniences for it; and the earlier in the day this is done, the clearer and whiter will be the linen.

2380. Coloured muslins, cottons, and linens, require a milder treatment; any application of soda will discharge the colour, and soaking all night, even in pure water, deteriorates the more delicate tints. When ready for washing, if not too dirty, they should be put into cold water and washed very speedily, using the common yellow soap, which should be rinsed off immediately. One article should be washed at a time, and rinsed out immediately before any others are wetted. When washed thoroughly, they should be rinsed in succession in soft water, in which common salt has been dissolved, in the proportion of a handful to three or four gallons, and afterwards wrung gently, as soon as rinsed, with as little twisting as possible, and then hung out to dry. Delicate-coloured articles should not be exposed to the sun, but dried in the shade, using clean lines and wooden pegs.

2381. Woollen articles are liable to shrink, unless the flannel has been well shrunk before making up. This liability is increased where very hot water is used: cold water would thus be the best to wash woollens in; but, as this would not remove the dirt, lukewarm water, about 85°, and yellow soap, are recommended. When thoroughly washed in this, they require a good deal of rinsing in cold water, to remove the soap.

2382. Greasy cloths, which have soaked all night in the liquid described, should be now washed out with soap-and-water as hot as the hands can bear, first in one water, and rinsed out in a second; and afterwards boiled for two hours in water in which a little soda is dissolved. When taken out, they should be rinsed in cold water, and laid out or hung up to dry.

2383. Silk handkerchiefs require to be washed alone. When they contain snuff, they should be soaked by themselves in lukewarm water two or three hours; they should be rinsed out and put to soak with the others in cold water for an hour or two; then washed in lukewarm water, being soaped as they are washed. If this does not remove all stains, they should be washed a second time in similar water, and, when finished, rinsed in soft water in which a handful of common salt has been dissolved. In washing stuff or woollen dresses, the band at the waist and the lining at the bottom should be removed, and wherever it is gathered into folds; and, in furniture, the hems and gatherings. A black silk dress, if very dirty, must be washed; but, if only soiled, soaking for four-and-twenty hours will do; if old and rusty, a pint of common spirits should be mixed with each gallon of water, which is an improvement under any circumstances. Whether soaked or washed, it should be hung up to drain, and dried without wringing.

2384. Satin and silk ribbons, both white and coloured, may be cleaned in the same manner.

2385. Silks, when washed, should be dried in the shade, on a linen-horse, taking care that they are kept smooth and unwrinkled. If black or blue, they will be improved if laid again on the table, when dry, and sponged with gin, or whiskey, or other white spirit.

2386. The operations should be concluded by rinsing the tubs, cleaning the coppers, scrubbing the floors of the washing-house, and restoring everything to order and cleanliness.

2387. Thursday and Friday, in a laundry in full employ, are usually devoted to mangling, starching, and ironing.

2388. Linen, cotton, and other fabrics, after being washed and dried, are made smooth and glossy by mangling and by ironing. The mangling process, which is simply passing them between rollers subjected to a very considerable pressure, produced by weight, is confined to sheets, towels, table-linen, and similar articles, which are without folds or plaits. Ironing is necessary to smooth body-linen, and made-up articles of delicate texture or gathered into folds. The mangle is too well known to need description.

2389. *Ironing.*—The irons consist of the common flat-iron, which is of different sizes, varying from 4 to 10 inches in length, triangular in form, and from $2\frac{1}{2}$ to $4\frac{1}{2}$ inches in width at the broad end; the oval iron, which is used for more delicate articles; and the box-iron, which is hollow, and heated by a red-hot iron inserted into the box. The Italian iron is a hollow tube, smooth on the outside, and raised on a slender pedestal with a footstalk. Into the hollow cylinder a red-hot iron is pushed, which heats it; and the smooth outside of the latter is used, on which articles such as frills, and plaited articles, are drawn. Crimping- and gauffering-machines are used for a kind of plaiting where much regularity is required, the articles being passed through two iron rollers fluted so as to represent the kind of plait or fold required.

2390. Starching is a process by which stiffness is communicated to certain parts of linen, as the collar and front of shirts, by dipping them in a paste made of starch boiled in water, mixed with a little gum Arabic, where extra stiffness is required.

To make Starch.

2391. INGREDIENTS.—Allow ½ pint of cold water and 1 quart of boiling water to every 2 tablespoonfuls of starch.

Mode.—Put the starch into a tolerably large basin ; pour over it the cold water, and stir the mixture well with a wooden spoon until it is perfectly free from lumps, and quite smooth. Then take the basin to the fire, and whilst the water is *actually boiling* in the kettle or boiler, pour it over the starch, stirring it the whole time. If made properly in this manner, the starch will require no further boiling ; but should the water not be boiling when added to the starch, it will not thicken, and must be put into a clean saucepan, and stirred over the fire until it boils. Take it off the fire, strain it into a clean basin, cover it up to prevent a skin forming on the top, and, when sufficiently cool that the hand may be borne in it, starch the things. Many persons, to give a shiny and smooth appearance to the linen when ironed, stir round two or three times in the starch a piece of wax candle, which also prevents the iron from sticking.

2392. When the "things to be starched" are washed, dried, and taken off the lines, they should be dipped into the hot starch made as directed, squeezed out of it, and then just dipped into cold water, and immediately squeezed dry. If fine things be wrung, or roughly used, they are very liable to tear ; so too much care cannot be exercised in this respect. If the article is lace, clap it between the hands a few times, which will assist to clear it ; then have ready laid out on the table a large clean towel or cloth ; shake out the starched things, lay them on the cloth, and roll it up tightly, and let it remain for three or fours, when the things will be ready to iron.

2393. To be able to iron properly requires much practice and experience. Strict cleanliness with all the ironing utensils must be observed, as, if this is not the case, not the most expert ironer will be able to make her things look clear and free from smears, &c. After wiping down her ironing-table, the laundry-maid should place a coarse cloth on it, and over that the ironing-blanket, with her stand and iron-rubber ; and having ascertained that her irons are quite clean and of the right heat, she proceeds with her work.

2394. It is a good plan to try the heat of the iron on a coarse cloth or apron before ironing anything fine : there is then no danger of scorching. For ironing fine things, such as collars, cuffs, muslins, and laces, there is nothing so clean and nice to use as the box-iron ; the bottom being bright, and never placed near the fire, it is always perfectly clean ; it should, however, be kept in a dry place, for fear of its rusting. Gauffering-tongs or irons must be placed in a clear fire for a minute, then withdrawn, wiped with a coarse rubber, and the heat of them tried on a piece of paper, as, unless great care is taken, these will very soon scorch.

2395. The skirts of muslin dresses should be ironed on a skirt-board covered with flannel, and the fronts of shirts on a smaller board, also covered with flannel ; this board being placed between the back and front.

2396. After things are mangled, they should also be ironed in the folds and gathers ; dinner-napkins smoothed over, as also table-cloths, pillow-cases, and sometimes sheets. The bands of flannel petticoats, and shoulder-straps to flannel waistcoats, must also undergo the same process.

UPPER AND UNDER NURSEMAIDS.

2397. THE nursery is of great importance in every family, and in families of distinction, where there are several young children, it is an establishment kept apart from the rest of the family, under the charge of an upper nurse, assisted by under nursery-maids proportioned to the work to be done. The responsible duties of upper nursemaid commence with the weaning of the child : it must now be separated from the mother or wet-nurse, at least for a time, and the cares of the nursemaid, which have hitherto been only occasionally put in requisition, are now to be entirely devoted to the infant. She washes, dresses, and feeds it ; walks out with it, and regulates all its little wants ; and, even at this early age, many good qualities are required to do so in a satisfactory manner. Patience and good temper are indispensable qualities; truthfulness, purity of manners, minute cleanliness, and docility and obedience, almost equally so. She ought also to be acquainted with the art of ironing and trimming little caps, and be handy with her needle.

2398. There is a considerable art in carrying an infant comfortably for itself and for the nursemaid. If she carry it always seated upright on her arm, and presses it too closely against her chest, the stomach of the child is apt to get compressed, and the back fatigued. For her own comfort, a good nurse will frequently vary this position, by changing from one arm to the other, and sometimes by laying it across both, raising the head a little. When teaching it to walk, and guiding it by the hand, she should change the hand from time to time, so as to avoid raising one shoulder higher than the other. This is the only way in which a child should be taught to walk ; leading-strings and other foolish inventions, which force an infant to make efforts, with its shoulders and head forward, before it knows how to use its limbs, will only render it feeble, and retard its progress.

2399. Most children have some bad habit, of which they must be broken ; but this is never accomplished by harshness without developing worse evils : kindness, perseverance, and patience in the nurse, are here of the utmost importance. When finger-sucking is one of these habits, the fingers are sometimes rubbed with bitter aloes, or some equally disagreeable substance. Others have dirty habits, which are only to be changed by patience, perseverance, and, above all, by regularity in the nurse. She should never be permitted to inflict punishment on these occasions, or, indeed, on any occasion. But, if punishment is to be avoided, it is still more necessary that all kinds of indulgences and flattery be equally forbidden. Yielding to all the whims of a child,—picking up its toys when thrown away in mere wantonness, would be intolerable. A child should never be led to think others inferior to it, to beat a dog, or even the stone against which it falls, as some children are taught to do by silly nurses. Neither should the nurse affect or show alarm at any of the little accidents which must inevitably happen : if it falls, treat it as a trifle; otherwise she encourages a spirit of cowardice and timidity. But she will take care that such accidents are not of frequent occurrence, or the result of neglect.

2400. The nurse should keep the child as clean as possible, and particularly she should train it to habits of cleanliness, so that it should feel uncomfortable when otherwise ; watching especially that it does not soil itself in eating. At the same time, vanity in its personal appearance is not to be encouraged by over-care in this respect, or by too tight lacing or buttoning of dresses, nor a small foot cultivated by the use of tight shoes.

2401. Nursemaids would do well to repeat to the parents faithfully and truly the defects they observe in the dispositions of very young children. If properly checked in time, evil propensities may be eradicated ; but this should not extend to anything but serious defects ; otherwise, the intuitive perceptions which all children possess will construe the act into " spying " and " informing," which should never be resorted to in the case of children, nor, indeed, in any case.

2402. Such are the cares which devolve upon the nursemaid, and it is her duty to fulfil them personally. In large establishments she will have assistants proportioned to the number of children of which she has the care. The under nursemaid lights the fires, sweeps, scours, and dusts the rooms, and makes the beds ; empties slops, and carries up water ; brings up and removes the nursery meals ; washes and dresses all the children, except the infant, and assists in mending. Where there is a nursery girl to assist, she does the rougher part of the cleaning ; and all take their meals in the nursery together, after the children of the family have done.

2403. In smaller families, where there is only one nursemaid kept, she is assisted by the housemaid, or servant-of-all-work, who will do the rougher part of the work, and carry up the nursery meals. In such circumstances she will be more immediately under the eye of her mistress, who will probably relieve her from some of the cares of the infant. In higher families, the upper nurse is usually permitted to sup or dine occasionally at the housekeeper's table by way of relaxation, when the children are all well, and her subordinates trustworthy.

2404. Where the nurse has the entire charge of the nursery, and the mother is too much occupied to do more than pay a daily visit to it, it is desirable that she be a person of observation, and possess some acquaintance with the diseases incident to childhood, as also with such simple remedies as may be useful before a medical attendant can be procured, or where such attendance is not considered necessary. All these little ailments are preceded by symptoms so minute as to be only perceptible to close observation ; such as twitching of the brows, restless sleep, grinding the gums, and, in some inflammatory diseases, even to the child abstaining from crying, from fear of the increased pain produced by the movement. Dentition, or cutting the teeth, is attended with many of these symptoms. Measles, thrush, scarlatina, croup, hooping-cough, and other childish complaints, are all preceded by well-known symptoms, which may be alleviated and rendered less virulent by simple remedies instantaneously applied.

2405. *Dentition* is usually the first serious trouble, bringing many other disorders in its train. The symptoms are most perceptible to the mother: the child sucks feebly, and with gums hot, inflamed, and swollen. In this case, relief is yielded by rubbing them from time to time with a little of Mrs. Johnson's soothing syrup, a valuable and perfectly safe medicine. Selfish and thoughtless nurses, and mothers too, sometimes give cordials and sleeping-draughts, whose effects are too well known.

2406. *Convulsion Fits* sometimes follow the feverish restlessness produced by these causes; in which case a hot bath should be administered without delay, and the lower parts of the body rubbed, the bath being as hot as it can be without scalding the tender skin; at the same time, the doctor should be sent for immediately, for no nurse should administer medicine in this case, unless the fits have been repeated and the doctor has left directions with her how to act.

2407. *Croup* is one of the most alarming diseases of childhood; it is accompanied with a hoarse, croaking, ringing cough, and comes on very suddenly, and most so in strong, robust children. A very hot bath should be instantly administered, followed by an emetic, either in the form of tartar-emetic, croup-powder, or a teaspoonful of ipecacuhana, wrapping the body warmly up in flannel after the bath. The slightest delay in administering the bath, or the emetic, may be fatal; hence, the importance of nurses about very young children being acquainted with the symptoms.

2408. *Hooping-Cough* is generally preceded by the moaning noise during sleep, which even adults threatened with the disorder cannot avoid: it is followed by violent fits of coughing, which little can be done to relieve. A child attacked by this disorder should be kept as much as possible in the fresh, pure air, but out of draughts, and kept warm, and supplied with plenty of nourishing food. Many fatal diseases flow from this scourge of childhood, and a change to purer air, if possible, should follow convalescence.

2409. *Worms* are the torment of some children: the symptoms are, an unnatural craving for food, even after a full meal; costiveness, suddenly followed by the reverse; fetid breath, a livid circle under the eyes, enlarged abdomen, and picking the nose; for which the remedies must be prescribed by the doctor.

2410. *Measles* and *Scarlatina* much resemble each other in their early stages: headache, restlessness, and fretfulness are the symptoms of both.

Shivering fits, succeeded by a hot skin ; pains in the back and limbs, accompanied by sickness, and, in severe cases, sore throat ; pain about the jaws, difficulty in swallowing, running at the eyes, which become red and inflamed, while the face is hot and flushed, often distinguish scarlatina and scarlet fever, of which it is only a mild form.

2411. While the case is doubtful, a dessert-spoonful of spirit of nitre diluted in water, given at bedtime, will throw the child into a gentle perspiration, and will bring out the rash in either case. In measles, this appears first on the face ; in scarlatina, on the chest ; and in both cases a doctor should be called in. In scarlatina, tartar-emetic powder or ipecacuhana may be administered in the mean time.

2412. In all cases, cleanliness, fresh air, clean utensils, and frequent washing of the person, both of nurse and children, are even more necessary in the nursery than in either drawing-room or sick-room, inasmuch as the delicate organs of childhood are more susceptible of injury from smells and vapours than adults.

2413. It may not be out of place if we conclude this brief notice of the duties of a nursemaid, by an extract from Florence Nightingale's admirable "Notes on Nursing." Referring to children, she says :—

2414. "They are much more susceptible than grown people to all noxious influences. They are affected by the same things, but much more quickly and seriously ; by want of fresh air, of proper warmth ; want of cleanliness in house, clothes, bedding, or body ; by improper food, want of punctuality, by dulness, by want of light, by too much or too little covering in bed or when up." And all this in health ; and then she quotes a passage from a lecture on sudden deaths in infancy, to show the importance of careful nursing of children :—"In the great majority of instances, when death suddenly befalls the infant or young child, it is an *accident*; it is not a necessary, inevitable result of any disease. That which is known to injure children most seriously is foul air ; keeping the rooms where they sleep closely shut up is destruction to them ; and, if the child's breathing be disordered by disease, a few hours only of such foul air may endanger its life, even where no inconvenience is felt by grown-up persons in the room."

2415. Persons moving in the best society will see, after perusing Miss Nightingale's book, that this "foul air," "want of light," "too much or too little clothing," and improper food, is not confined to Crown Street or St. Giles's ; that Belgravia and the squares have their north room, where the rays of the sun never reach. "A wooden bedstead, two or three mattresses piled up to above the height of the table, a vallance attached to the frame,—nothing but a miracle could ever thoroughly dry or air such a bed and bedding,"—is the ordinary bed of a private house, than which nothing can be more unwholesome. "Don't treat your children like sick," she sums up ; "don't dose them with tea. Let them eat meat and drink milk, or half a glass of light beer. Give them fresh, light, sunny, and open rooms, cool bedrooms, plenty of outdoor exercise, facing even the cold, and wind, and weather, in sufficiently warm clothes, and with sufficient exercise, plenty of amusements and play ; more liberty, and less schooling, and cramming, and training ; more attention to food and less to physic."

DUTIES OF THE SICK-NURSE.

2416. ALL women are likely, at some period of their lives, to be called on to perform the duties of a sick-nurse, and should prepare themselves as much as possible, by observation and reading, for the occasion when they may be required to perform the office. The main requirements are good temper, compassion for suffering, sympathy with sufferers, which most women worthy of the name possess, neat-handedness, quiet manners, love of order, and cleanliness. With these qualifications there will be very little to be wished for; the desire to relieve suffering will inspire a thousand little attentions, and surmount the disgusts which some of the offices attending the sick-room are apt to create. Where serious illness visits a household, and protracted nursing is likely to become necessary, a professional nurse will probably be engaged, who has been trained to its duties; but in some families, and those not a few let us hope, the ladies of the family would oppose such an arrangement as a failure of duty on their part. There is, besides, even when a professional nurse is ultimately called in, a period of doubt and hesitation, while disease has not yet developed itself, when the patient must be attended to; and, in these cases, some of the female servants of the establishment must give their attendance in the sick-room. There are, also, slight attacks of cold, influenza, and accidents in a thousand forms, to which all are subject, where domestic nursing becomes a necessity; where disease, though unattended with danger, is nevertheless accompanied by the nervous irritation incident to illness, and when all the attention of the domestic nurse becomes necessary.

2417. In the first stage of sickness, while doubt and a little perplexity hang over the household as to the nature of the sickness, there are some things about which no doubt can exist: the patient's room must be kept in a perfectly pure state, and arrangements made for proper attendance; for the first canon of nursing, according to Florence Nightingale, its apostle, is to "keep the air the patient breathes as pure as the external air, without chilling him." This can be done without any preparation which might alarm the patient; with proper windows, open fireplaces, and a supply of fuel, the room may be as fresh as it is outside, and kept at a temperature suitable for the patient's state.

2418. Windows, however, must be opened from above, and not from below, and draughts avoided; cool air admitted beneath the patient's head chills the lower strata and the floor. The careful nurse will keep the door shut when the window is open; she will also take care that the patient is not placed between the door and the open window, nor between the open fireplace and the window. If confined to bed, she will see that the bed is placed in a thoroughly ventilated part of the room, but out of the current of air which is produced by the momentary opening of doors, as well as out of the line of draught between the window and the open chimney, and that the temperature of the room is kept about 64°. Where it is necessary to admit air by the door, the windows should be closed ; but there are few circumstances in which good air can be obtained through the chamber-door ; through it, on the contrary, the gases generated in the lower parts of the house are likely to be drawn into the invalid chamber.

2419. These precautions taken, and plain nourishing diet, such as the patient desires, furnished, probably little more can be done, unless more serious symptoms present themselves ; in which case medical advice will be sought.

2420. Under no circumstances is ventilation of the sick-room so essential as in cases of febrile diseases, usually considered infectious ; such as typhus and puerperal fevers, influenza, hooping-cough, small- and chicken-pox, scarlet fever, measles, and erysipelas : all these are considered communicable through the air ; but there is little danger of infection being thus communicated, provided the room is kept thoroughly ventilated. On the contrary, if this essential be neglected, the power of infection is greatly increased and concentrated in the confined and impure air ; it settles upon the clothes of the attendants and visitors, especially where they are of wool, and is frequently communicated to other families in this manner.

2421. Under all circumstances, therefore, the sick-room should be kept as fresh and sweet as the open air, while the temperature is kept up by artificial heat, taking care that the fire burns clear, and gives out no smoke into the room ; that the room is perfectly clean, wiped over with a damp cloth every day, if boarded ; and swept, after sprinkling with damp tea-leaves, or other aromatic leaves, if carpeted ; that all utensils are emptied and cleaned as soon as used, and not once in four-and-twenty hours, as is sometimes done. "A slop-pail," Miss Nightingale says, "should never enter a sick-room ; everything should be carried direct to the water-closet, emptied there, and brought up clean ; in the best hospitals the slop-pail is unknown." "I do not approve," says Miss Nightingale, "of making housemaids of nurses, —that would be waste of means ; but I have seen surgical sisters, women whose hands were worth to them two or three guineas a week, down on their knees, scouring a room or hut, because they thought it was not fit for their patients : these women had the true nurse spirit."

2422. Bad smells are sometimes met by sprinkling a little liquid chloride of lime on the floor ; fumigation by burning pastiles is also a common expedient for the purification of the sick-room. They are useful, but only in the sense hinted at by the medical lecturer, who commenced his lecture thus :—" Fumigations, gentlemen, are of essential importance ; they make so abominable a smell, that they compel you to open the windows and admit fresh air." In this sense they are useful, but ineffectual unless the cause be removed, and fresh air admitted.

2423. The sick-room should be quiet; no talking, no gossiping, and, above all, no whispering,—this is absolute cruelty to the patient; he thinks his complaint the subject, and strains his ear painfully to catch the sound. No rustling of dresses, nor creaking shoes either; where the carpets are taken up, the nurse should wear list shoes, or some other noiseless material, and her dress should be of soft material that does not rustle. Miss Nightingale denounces crinoline, and quotes Lord Melbourne on the subject of women in the sick-room, who said, "I would rather have men about me, when ill, than women; it requires very strong health to put up with women." Ungrateful man! but absolute quiet is necessary in the sick-room.

2424. Never let the patient be waked out of his first sleep by noise, never roused by anything like a surprise. Always sit in the apartment, so that the patient has you in view, and that it is not necessary for him to turn in speaking to you. Never keep a patient standing; never speak to one while moving. Never lean on the sick-bed. Above all, be calm and decisive with the patient, and prevent all noises over-head.

2425. A careful nurse, when a patient leaves his bed, will open the sheets wide, and throw the clothes back so as thoroughly to air the bed. She will avoid drying or airing anything damp in the sick-room.

2426. "It is another fallacy," says Florence Nightingale, "to suppose that night air is injurious; a great authority told me that, in London, the air is never so good as after ten o'clock, when smoke has diminished; but then it must be air from without, not within, and not air vitiated by gaseous airs." "A great fallacy prevails also," she says, in another section, "about flowers poisoning the air of the sick-room: no one ever saw them over-crowding the sick-room; but, if they did, they actually absorb carbonic acid and give off oxygen." Cut flowers also decompose water, and produce oxygen gas. Lilies, and some other very odorous plants, may perhaps give out smells unsuited to a close room, while the atmosphere of the sick-room should always be fresh and natural.

2427. "Patients," says Miss Nightingale, "are sometimes starved in the midst of plenty, from want of attention to the ways which alone make it possible for them to take food. A spoonful of beef-tea, or arrowroot and wine, or some other light nourishing diet, should be given every hour, for the patient's stomach will reject large supplies. In very weak patients there is often a nervous difficulty in swallowing, which is much increased if food is not ready and presented at the moment when it is wanted: the nurse should be able to discriminate, and know when this moment is approaching."

2428. Diet suitable for patients will depend, in some degree, on their natural likes and dislikes, which the nurse will do well to acquaint herself with. Beef-tea is useful and relishing, but possesses little nourishment; when evaporated, it presents a teaspoonful of solid meat to a pint of water. Eggs are not equivalent to the same weight of meat. Arrowroot is less nourishing than flour. Butter is the lightest and most digestible kind of fat. Cream, in some diseases, cannot be replaced. But, to sum up with some of Miss Nightingale's useful maxims :—Observation is the nurse's best guide, and the patient's appetite the rule. Half a pint of milk is equal to a quarter of a pound of meat. Beef-tea is the least nourishing food administered to the sick ; and tea and coffee, she thinks, are both too much excluded from the sick-room.

THE MONTHLY NURSE.

2429. THE choice of a monthly nurse is of the utmost importance ; and in the case of a young mother with her first child, it would be well for her to seek advice and counsel from her more experienced relatives in this matter. In the first place, the engaging a monthly nurse in good time is of the utmost importance, as, if she be competent and clever, her services will be sought months beforehand ; a good nurse having seldom much of her time disengaged. There are some qualifications which it is evident the nurse should possess : she should be scrupulously clean and tidy in her person ; honest, sober, and noiseless in her movements ; should possess a natural love for children, and have a strong nerve in case of emergencies. Snuff-taking and spirit-drinking must not be included in her habits ; but these are happily much less frequent than they were in former days.

2430. Receiving, as she often will, instructions from the doctor, she should bear these in mind, and carefully carry them out. In those instances where she does not feel herself sufficiently informed, she should ask advice from the medical man, and not take upon herself to administer medicines, &c., without his knowledge.

2431. A monthly nurse should be between 30 and 50 years of age, sufficiently old to have had a little experience, and yet not too old or infirm to be able to perform various duties requiring strength and bodily vigour. She should be able to wake the moment she is called,—at any hour of the night, that the mother or child may have their wants immediately attended to. Good temper, united to a kind and gentle disposition, is indispensable ; and, although the nurse will frequently have much to endure from the whims and caprices of the invalid, she should make allowances for these, and command her temper, at the same time exerting her authority when it is necessary.

2432. What the nurse has to do in the way of cleaning and dusting her lady's room, depends entirely on the establishment that is kept. Where there are plenty of servants, the nurse, of course, has nothing whatever to do but attend on her patient, and ring the bell for anything she may require. Where the number of domestics is limited, she should not mind keeping her room in order ; that is to say, sweeping and dusting it every morning. If fires be necessary, the housemaid should always clean the grate, and do all that is wanted in that way, as this, being rather dirty work, would soil the nurse's dress, and unfit her to approach the bed, or take the infant without soiling its clothes.   In small establishments, too, the nurse should herself fetch things she may require, and not ring every time she wants anything ; and she must, of course, not leave her invalid unless she sees everything is comfortable ; and then only for a few minutes.   When down stairs, and in company with the other servants, the nurse should not repeat what she may have heard in her lady's room, as much mischief may be done by a gossiping nurse.   As in most houses the monthly nurse is usually sent for a few days before her services may be required, she should see that all is in readiness ; that there be no bustle and hurry at the time the confinement takes place. She should keep two pairs of sheets thoroughly aired, as well as night-dresses, flannels, &c. &c.   All the things which will be required to dress the baby the first time should be laid in the basket in readiness, in the order in which they are to be put on ; as well as scissors, thread, a few pieces of soft linen rag, and two or three flannel squares.   If a berceaunette is to be used immediately, the nurse should ascertain that the mattresses, pillow, &c. are all well aired ; and if not already done before she arrives, she should assist in covering and trimming it, ready for the little occupant.   A monthly nurse should be handy at her needle, as, if she is in the house some time before the baby is born, she will require some work of this sort to occupy her time.   She should also understand the making-up of little caps, although we can scarcely say this is one of the nurse's duties.   As most children wear no caps, except out of doors, her powers in this way will not be much taxed.

2433. A nurse should endeavour to make her room as cheerful as possible, and always keep it clean and tidy.   She should empty the chamber utensils as soon as used, and on no account put things under the bed.   Soiled baby's napkins should be rolled up and put into a pan, when they should be washed out every morning, and hung out to dry : they are then in a fit state to send to the laundress ; and should, on no account, be left dirty, but done every morning in this way.   The bedroom should be kept rather dark, particularly for the first week or ten days ; of a regular temperature, and as free as possible from draughts, at the same time well ventilated and free from unpleasant smells.

2434. The infant during the month must not be exposed to strong light, or much air ; and in carrying it about the passages, stairs, &c., the nurse should always have its head-flannel on, to protect the eyes and ears from the currents of air.   For the management of children, we must refer our readers to the following chapters ; and we need only say, in conclusion, that a good nurse should understand the symptoms of various ills incident to this period, as, in all cases, prevention is better than cure.   As young mothers with their first baby are very often much troubled at first with their breasts, the nurse should understand the art of emptying them by suction, or some other contrivance. If the breasts are kept well drawn, there will be but little danger of inflammation; and as the infant at first cannot take all that is necessary, something must be done to keep the inflammation down. This is one of the greatest difficulties a nurse has to contend with, and we can only advise her to be very persevering, to rub the breasts well, and to let the infant suck as soon and as often as possible, until they get in proper order.

THE WET-NURSE.

2435. WE are aware that, according to the opinion of some ladies, there is no domestic theme, during a certain period of their married lives, more fraught with vexation and disquietude than that ever-fruitful source of annoyance, "the Nurse;" but, as we believe, there are thousands of excellent wives and mothers who pass through life without even a temporary embroglio in the kitchen, or suffering a state of moral hectic the whole time of a nurse's empire in the nursery or bedroom. Our own experience goes to prove, that although many unqualified persons palm themselves off on ladies as fully competent for the duties they so rashly and dishonestly undertake to perform, and thus expose themselves to ill-will and merited censure, there are still very many fully equal to the legitimate exercise of what they undertake; and if they do not in every case give entire satisfaction, some of the fault,—and sometimes a great deal of it,—may be honestly placed to the account of the ladies themselves, who, in many instances, are so impressed with the propriety of their own method of performing everything, as to insist upon the adoption of *their* system in preference to that of the nurse, whose plan is probably based on a comprehensive forethought, and rendered perfect in all its details by an ample experience.

2436. In all our remarks on this subject, we should remember with gentleness the order of society from which our nurses are drawn; and that those who make their duty a study, and are termed professional nurses, have much to endure from the caprice and egotism of their employers; while others are driven to the occupation from the laudable motive of feeding their own children, and who, in fulfilling that object, are too often both selfish and sensual, performing, without further interest than is consistent with their own advantage, the routine of customary duties.

2437. Properly speaking, there are two nurses,—the nurse for the mother and the nurse for the child, or, the monthly and the wet nurse. Of the former we have already spoken, and will now proceed to describe the duties of the latter, and add some suggestions as to her age, physical health, and moral conduct, subjects of the utmost importance as far as the charge intrusted to her is concerned, and therefore demanding some special remarks.

2438. When from illness, suppression of the milk, accident, or some natural process, the mother is deprived of the pleasure of rearing her infant, it becomes necessary at once to look around for a fitting substitute, so that the child may not suffer, by any needless delay, a physical loss by the deprivation of its natural food. The first consideration should be as regards age, state of health, and temper.

2439. The age, if possible, should not be less than twenty nor exceed thirty years, with the health sound in every respect, and the body free from all eruptive disease or local blemish. The best evidence of a sound state of health will be found in the woman's clear open countenance, the ruddy tone of the skin, the full, round, and elastic state of the breasts, and especially in the erectile, firm condition of the nipple, which, in all unhealthy states of the body, is pendulous, flabby, and relaxed ; in which case, the milk is sure to be imperfect in its organization, and, consequently, deficient in its nutrient qualities. Appetite is another indication of health in the suckling nurse or mother ; for it is impossible a woman can feed her child without having a corresponding appetite ; and though inordinate craving for food is neither desirable nor necessary, a natural vigour should be experienced at meal-times, and the food taken should be anticipated and enjoyed.

2440. Besides her health, the moral state of the nurse is to be taken into account, or that mental discipline or principle of conduct which would deter the nurse from at any time gratifying her own pleasures and appetites at the cost or suffering of her infant charge.

2441. The conscientiousness and good faith that would prevent a nurse so acting are, unfortunately, very rare ; and many nurses, rather than forego the enjoyment of a favourite dish, though morally certain of the effect it will have on the child, will, on the first opportunity, feed with avidity on fried meats, cabbage, cucumbers, pickles, or other crude and injurious aliments, in defiance of all orders given, or confidence reposed in their word, good sense, and humanity. And when the infant is afterwards racked with pain, and a night of disquiet alarms the mother, the doctor is sent for, and the nurse, covering her dereliction by a falsehood, the consequence of her gluttony is treated as a disease, and the poor infant is dosed for some days with medicines, that can do it but little if any good, and, in all probability, materially retard its physical development. The selfish nurse, in her ignorance, believes, too, that as long as she experiences no admonitory symptoms herself, the child cannot suffer ; and satisfied that, whatever is the cause of its screams and plunges, neither she, nor what she had eaten, had anything to do with it, with this flattering assurance at her heart, she watches her opportunity, and has another luxurious feast off the proscribed dainties, till the increasing disturbance in the child's health, or treachery from the kitchen, opens the eyes of mother and doctor to the nurse's unprincipled conduct. In all such cases the infant should be spared the infliction of medicine, and, as a wholesome corrective to herself, and relief to her charge, a good sound dose administered to the nurse.

2442. Respecting the diet of the wet-nurse, the first point of importance is to fix early and definite hours for every meal; and the mother should see that no cause is ever allowed to interfere with their punctuality. The food itself should be light, easy of digestion, and simple. Boiled or roast meat, with bread and potatoes, with occasionally a piece of sago, rice, or tapioca pudding, should constitute the dinner, the only meal that requires special comment; broths, green vegetables, and all acid or salt foods, must be avoided. Fresh fish, once or twice a week, may be taken; but it is hardly sufficiently nutritious to be often used as a meal. If the dinner is taken early,—at one o'clock, —there will be no occasion for luncheon, which too often, to the injury of the child, is made the cover for a first dinner. Half a pint of stout, with a Reading biscuit, at eleven o'clock, will be abundantly sufficient between breakfast at eight and a good dinner, with a pint of porter at one o'clock. About eight o'clock in the evening, half a pint of stout, with another biscuit, may be taken; and for supper, at ten or half-past, a pint of porter, with a slice of toast or a small amount of bread and cheese, may conclude the feeding for the day.

2443. Animal food once in twenty-four hours is quite sufficient. All spirits, unless in extreme cases, should be avoided; and wine is still more seldom needed. With a due quantity of plain digestible food, and the proportion of stout and porter ordered, with early hours and regularity, the nurse will not only be strong and healthy herself, but fully capable of rearing a child in health and strength. There are two points all mothers, who are obliged to employ wet-nurses, should remember, and be on their guard against. The first is, never to allow a nurse to give medicine to the infant on her own authority: many have such an infatuated idea of the *healing excellence* of castor-oil, that they would administer a dose of this disgusting grease twice a week, and think they had done a meritorious service to the child. The next point is, to watch carefully, lest, to insure a night's sleep for herself, she does not dose the infant with Godfrey's cordial, syrup of poppies, or some narcotic potion, to insure tranquillity to the one and give the opportunity of sleep to the other. The fact that scores of nurses keep secret bottles of these deadly syrups, for the purpose of stilling their charges, is notorious; and that many use them to a fearful extent, is sufficiently patent to all.

2444. It therefore behoves the mother, while obliged to trust to a nurse, to use her best discretion to guard her child from the unprincipled treatment of the person she must, to a certain extent, depend upon and trust; and to remember, in all cases, rather than resort to castor-oil or sedatives, to consult a medical man for her infant in preference to following the counsel of her nurse.

THE

REARING, MANAGEMENT, AND DISEASES OF INFANCY AND CHILDHOOD.

—◆◇◆—

CHAPTER XLII.

Physiology of Life, as illustrated by Respiration, Circulation, and Digestion.

2445. THE infantine management of children, like the mother's love for her offspring, seems to be born with the child, and to be a direct intelligence of Nature. It may thus, at first sight, appear as inconsistent and presumptuous to tell a woman how to rear her infant as to instruct her in the manner of loving it. Yet, though Nature is unquestionably the best nurse, Art makes so admirable a foster-mother, that no sensible woman, in her novitiate of parent, would refuse the admonitions of art, or the teachings of experience, to consummate her duties of nurse. It is true that, in a civilized state of society, few young wives reach the epoch that makes them mothers without some insight, traditional or practical, into the management of infants : consequently, the cases wherein a woman is left to her own unaided intelligence, or what, in such a case, may be called instinct, and obliged to trust to the promptings of nature alone for the well-being of her child, are very rare indeed. Again, every woman is not gifted with the same physical ability for the harassing duties of a mother ; and though Nature, as a general rule, has endowed all female creation with the attributes necessary to that most beautiful and, at the same time, holiest function,—the healthy rearing of their offspring,—the cases are sufficiently numerous to establish the exception, where the mother is either physically or socially incapacitated from undertaking these most pleasing duties herself, and where, consequently, she is compelled to trust to adventitious aid for those natural benefits which are at once the mother's pride and delight to render to her child.

2446. In these cases, when obliged to call in the services of hired assistance, she must trust the dearest obligation of her life to one who, from her social sphere, has probably notions of rearing children diametrically opposed to the preconceived ideas of the mother, and at enmity with all her sentiments of right and prejudices of position.

2447. It has justly been said—we think by Hood—that the children of the poor are not brought up, but *dragged up*. However facetious this remark may seem, there is much truth in it ; and that children, reared in the reeking

3 U

dens of squalor and poverty, live at all, is an apparent anomaly in the course of things, that, at first sight, would seem to set the laws of sanitary provision at defiance, and make it appear a perfect waste of time to insist on pure air and exercise as indispensable necessaries of life, and especially so as regards infantine existence.

2448. We see elaborate care bestowed on a family of children, everything studied that can tend to their personal comfort,—pure air, pure water, regular ablution, a dietary prescribed by art, and every precaution adopted that medical judgment and maternal love can dictate, for the well-being of the parents' hope; and find, in despite of all this care and vigilance, disease and death invading the guarded treasure. We turn to the fœtor and darkness that, in some obscure court, attend the robust brood who, coated in dirt, and with mud and refuse for playthings, live and thrive, and grow into manhood, and, in contrast to the pale face and flabby flesh of the aristocratic child, exhibit strength, vigour, and well-developed frames, and our belief in the potency of the life-giving elements of air, light, and cleanliness receives a shock that, at first sight, would appear fatal to the implied benefits of these, in reality, all-sufficient attributes of health and life.

2449. But as we must enter more largely on this subject hereafter, we shall leave its consideration for the present, and return to what we were about to say respecting trusting to others' aid in the rearing of children. Here it is that the young and probably inexperienced mother may find our remarks not only an assistance but a comfort to her, in as far as, knowing the simplest and best system to adopt, she may be able to instruct another, and see that her directions are fully carried out.

2450. The human body, materially considered, is a beautiful piece of mechanism, consisting of many parts, each one being the centre of a system, and performing its own vital function irrespectively of the others, and yet dependent for its vitality upon the harmony and health of the whole. It is, in fact, to a certain extent, like a watch, which, when once wound up and set in motion, will continue its function of recording true time only so long as every wheel, spring, and lever performs its allotted duty, and at its allotted time; or till the limit that man's ingenuity has placed to its existence as a moving automaton has been reached, or, in other words, till it has run down.

2451. What the key is to the mechanical watch, air is to the physical man. Once admit air into the mouth and nostrils, and the lungs expand, the heart beats, the blood rushes to the remotest part of the body, the mouth secretes saliva, to soften and macerate the food; the liver forms its bile, to separate the nutriment from the digested aliment; the kidneys perform their office; the eye elaborates its tears, to facilitate motion and impart that glistening to the orb on which depends so much of its beauty; and a dewy moisture exudes from the skin, protecting the body from the extremes of heat and cold, and sharpening the perception of touch and feeling. At the same instant, and in every part, the arteries, like innumerable bees, are everywhere laying down layers of muscle, bones, teeth, and, in fact, like the coral zoophyte, building up a continent of life and matter ; while the veins, equally busy, are carrying away the *débris* and refuse collected from where the zoophyte arteries are building,—this refuse, in its turn, being conveyed to the liver, there to be converted into bile.

2452. All these—and they are but a few of the vital actions constantly taking place—are the instant result of one gasp of life-giving air. No subject can be fraught with greater interest than watching the first spark of life, as it courses with electric speed " through all the gates and alleys " of the soft, insensate body of the infant. The effect of air on the new-born child is as remarkable in its results as it is wonderful in its consequence ; but to understand this more intelligibly, it must first be remembered that life consists of the performance of *three* vital functions—RESPIRATION, CIRCULATION, and DIGESTION. The lungs digest the air, taking from it its most nutritious element, the *oxygen*, to give to the impoverished blood that circulates through them. The stomach digests the food, and separates the nutriment—*chyle*—from the aliment, which it gives to the blood for the development of the frame ; and the blood, which is understood by the term circulation, digests in its passage through the lungs the nutriment—*chyle*—to give it quantity and quality, and the *oxygen* from the air to give it vitality. . Hence it will be seen, that, speaking generally, the three vital functions resolve themselves into one,—DIGESTION ; and that the lungs are the primary and the most important of the vital organs ; and respiration, the first in fact, as we all know it is the last in deed, of all the functions performed by the living body.

The Lungs.—Respiration.

2453. The first effect of air on the infant is a slight tremor about the lips and angles of the mouth, increasing to twitchings, and finally to a convulsive contraction of the lips and cheeks, the consequence of sudden cold to the nerves of the face. This spasmodic action produces a gasp, causing the air to rush through the mouth and nostrils, and enter the windpipe and upper portion of the flat and contracted lungs, which, like a sponge partly immersed in water, immediately expand. This is succeeded by a few faint sobs or pants, by which larger volumes of air are drawn into the chest, till, after a few seconds, and when a greater bulk of the lungs has become inflated, the breast-bone and ribs rise, the chest expands, and, with a sudden start, the infant gives utterance to a succession of loud, sharp cries, which have the effect of filling every cell of the entire organ with air and life. To the anxious mother, the first voice of her child is, doubtless, the sweetest music she ever heard ; and the more loudly it peals, the greater should be her joy, as it is an indication of health and strength, and not only shows the perfect expansion of the lungs, but that the process of life has set in with vigour. Having welcomed in its own existence, like the morning bird, with a shrill note of gladness, the infant ceases its cry, and, after a few short sobs, usually subsides into sleep or quietude.

2454. At the same instant that the air rushes into the lungs, the valve, or door between the two sides of the heart—and through which the blood had previously passed—is closed and hermetically sealed, and the blood taking a new course, bounds into the lungs, now expanded with air, and which we have likened to a wetted sponge, to which they bear a not unapt affinity, air being substituted for water. It here receives the *oxygen* from the atmosphere, and the *chyle*, or white blood, from the digested food, and becomes, in an instant, arterial blood, a vital principle, from which every solid and fluid of the body is constructed. Besides the lungs, Nature has provided another respiratory organ, a sort of supplemental lung, that, as well as being a covering to the body, *i*nspires air and *e*xpires moisture ;—this is the cuticle, or skin ; and so intimate is the connection between the skin and lungs, that whatever injures the first, is certain to affect the latter.

2455. *Hence the difficulty of breathing experienced after scalds or burns on the cuticle, the cough that follows the absorption of cold or damp by the skin, the oppressed and laborious breathing experienced by children in all eruptive diseases, while the rash is coming to the surface, and the hot, dry skin that always attends congestion of the lungs, and fever.*

2456. The great practical advantage derivable from this fact is, the knowledge that whatever relieves the one benefits the other. Hence, too, the great utility of hot baths in all affections of the lungs or diseases of the skin ; and the reason why exposure to cold or wet is, in nearly all cases, followed by tightness of the chest, sore throat, difficulty of breathing, and cough. These symptoms are the consequence of a larger quantity of blood than is natural remaining in the lungs, and the cough is a mere effort of Nature to throw off the obstruction caused by the presence of too much blood in the organ of respiration. The hot bath, by causing a larger amount of blood to rush suddenly to the skin, has the effect of relieving the lungs of their excess of blood, and by equalizing the circulation, aud promoting perspiration from the cuticle, affords immediate and direct benefit, both to the lungs and the system at large.

The Stomach.—Digestion.

2457. The organs that either directly or indirectly contribute to the process of digestion are, the mouth, teeth, tongue, and gullet, the stomach, small intestines, the pancreas, the salivary glands, and the liver. Next to respiration, digestion is the chief function in the economy of life, as, without the nutritious fluid digested from the aliment, there would be nothing to supply the immense and constantly recurring waste of the system, caused by the activity with which the arteries at all periods, but especially during infancy and youth, are building up the frame and developing the body. In infancy (the period of which our present subject treats), the series of parts engaged in the process of digestion may be reduced simply to the stomach and liver, or rather its secretion,—the bile. The stomach is a thick muscular bag, connected above with the gullet, and, at its lower extremity, with the commencement of the small intestines. The duty or function of the stomach is to secrete from the arteries spread over its inner surface, a sharp acid liquid called the *gastric juice ;* this, with a due mixture of saliva, softens, dissolves, and gradually digests the food or contents of the stomach, reducing the whole into a soft pulpy mass, which then passes into the first part of the small intestines, where it comes in contact with the bile from the gall-bladder, which immediately separates the digested food into two parts ; one is a white creamy fluid called *chyle,* and the absolute concentration of all nourishment, which is taken up by proper vessels, and, as we have before said, carried directly to the heart, to be made blood of, and vitalized in the lungs, and thus provide for the wear and tear of the system. It must be here observed that the stomach can only digest *solids,* for fluids, being incapable of that process, can only be *absorbed ;* and without the result of digestion, animal, at least human life, could not exist. Now, as Nature has ordained that infantine life shall be supported on liquid aliment, and as, without a digestion the body would perish, some provision was necessary to meet this difficulty, and that provision was found in the nature of the liquid itself, or in other words, THE MILK. The process of making cheese, or fresh curds and whey, is familiar to most persons ; but as it is necessary to the elucidation of our subject, we will briefly repeat it. The internal membrane, or the lining coat of a calf's stomach, having been removed from the organ, is hung up, like a bladder, to dry ; when required, a piece is cut off, put in a jug, a little warm water poured upon it, and after a few hours it is fit for use ; the liquid so made being called *rennet.* A little of this rennet, poured into a basin of warm milk, at once coagulates the greater part, and separates from it a quantity of thin liquor, called *whey.* This is precisely the action that takes place in the infant's stomach after every supply from the breast. The cause is the same in both cases, the acid of the gastric juice in the infant's stomach immediately converting the milk into a soft cheese. It is gastric juice, adhering to the calf's stomach, and drawn out by the water, forming rennet, that makes the curds in the basin. The cheesy substance being a solid, at once undergoes the process of digestion, is separated into *chyle* by the bile, and, in a few hours, finds its way to the infant's heart, to become blood, and commence the architecture of its little frame. This is the simple process of a baby's digestion :—milk converted into cheese, cheese into *chyle,* chyle into blood, and blood into flesh, bone, and tegument—how simple is the cause, but how sublime and wonderful are the effects !

2458. We have described the most important of the three functions that take place in the infant's body—respiration and digestion ; the third, namely, circulation, we hardly think it necessary to enter on, not being called for by the requirements of the nurse and mother ; so we shall omit its notice, and proceed from theoretical to more practical considerations. Children of weakly constitutions are just as likely to be born of robust parents, and those who earn their bread by toil, as the offspring of luxury and affluence; and, indeed, it is against the ordinary providence of Nature to suppose the children of the hardworking and necessitous to be hardier and more vigorous than those of parents blessed with ease and competence.

2459. All children come into the world in the same imploring helplessness, with the same general organization and wants, and demanding either from the newly-awakened mother's love, or from the memory of motherly feeling in the nurse, or the common appeals of humanity in those who undertake the earliest duties of an infant, the same assistance and protection, and the same fostering care.

THE INFANT.

2460. WE have already described the phenomena produced on the new-born child by the contact of air, which, after a succession of muscular twitchings, becomes endowed with voice, and heralds its advent by a loud but brief succession of cries. But though this is the general rule, it sometimes happens (from causes it is unnecessary here to explain) that the infant does not cry, or give utterance to any audible sounds, or if it does, they are so faint as scarcely to be distinguished as human accents, plainly indicating that life, as yet, to the new visitor, is neither a boon nor a blessing; the infant being, in fact, in a state of suspended or imperfect vitality,—a state of *quasi* existence, closely approximating the condition of a *still-birth.*

2461. As soon as this state of things is discovered, the child should be turned on its right side, and the whole length of the spine, from the head downwards, rubbed with all the fingers of the right hand, sharply and quickly, without intermission, till the quick action has not only evoked heat, but electricity in the part, and till the loud and sharp cries of the child have thoroughly expanded the lungs, and satisfactorily established its life. The operation will seldom require above a minute to effect, and less frequently demands a repetition. If there is brandy at hand, the fingers before rubbing may be dipped into that, or any other spirit.

2462. There is another condition of what we may call "mute births," where the child only makes short ineffectual gasps, and those at intervals of a minute or two apart, when the lips, eyelids, and fingers become of a deep purple or slate colour, sometimes half the body remaining white, while the other half, which was at first swarthy, deepens to a livid hue. This condition of the infant is owing to the valve between the two sides of the heart remaining open, and allowing the unvitalized venous blood to enter the arteries and get into the circulation.

2463. The object in this case, as in the previous one, is to dilate the lungs as quickly as possible, so that, by the sudden effect of a vigorous inspiration, the valve may be firmly closed, and the impure blood, losing this means of egress, be sent directly to the lungs. The same treatment is therefore necessary as in the previous case, with the addition, if the friction along the spine has failed, of a warm bath at a temperature of about 80°, in which the child is to be plunged up to the neck, first cleansing the mouth and nostrils of the mucus that might interfere with the free passage of air.

2464. While in the bath, the friction along the spine is to be continued, and if the lungs still remain unexpanded, while one person retains the child in an inclined position in the water, another should insert the pipe of a small pair of bellows into one nostril, and while the mouth is closed and the other nostril compressed on the pipe with the hand of the assistant, the lungs are to be slowly inflated by steady puffs of air from the bellows, the hand being removed from the mouth and nose after each inflation, and placed on the pit of the stomach, and by a steady pressure expelling it out again by the mouth. This process is to be continued, steadily inflating and expelling the air from the lungs, till, with a sort of tremulous leap, Nature takes up the process, and the infant begins to gasp, and finally to cry, at first low and faint, but with every engulp of air increasing in length and strength of volume, when it is to be removed from the water, and instantly wrapped (all but the face and mouth) in a flannel. Sometimes, however, all these means will fail in effecting an utterance from the child, which will lie, with livid lips and a flaccid body, every few minutes opening its mouth with a short gasping pant, and then subsiding into a state of pulseless inaction, lingering probably some hours, till the spasmodic pantings growing further apart, it ceases to exist.

2465. The time that this state of negative vitality will linger in the frame of an infant is remarkable ; and even when all the previous operations, though long-continued, have proved ineffectual, the child will often rally from the simplest of means—the application of dry heat. When removed from the bath, place three or four hot bricks or tiles on the hearth, and lay the child, loosely folded in a flannel, on its back along them, taking care that there is but one fold of flannel between the spine and heated bricks or tiles. When neither of these articles can be procured, put a few clear pieces of red cinder in a warming-pan, and extend the child in the same manner along the closed lid. As the heat gradually diffuses itself over the spinal marrow, the child that was dying, or seemingly dead, will frequently give a sudden and energetic cry, succeeded in another minute by a long and vigorous peal, making up, in volume and force, for the previous delay, and instantly confirming its existence by every effort in its nature.

2466. With these two exceptions,—restored by the means we have pointed out to the functions of life,—we will proceed to the consideration of the child HEALTHILY BORN. Here the first thing that meets us on the threshold of inquiry, and what is often between mother and nurse not only a vexed question, but one of vexatious import, is the *crying* of the child ; the mother, in her natural anxiety, maintaining that her infant *must be ill* to cause it to cry so much or so often, and the nurse insisting that *all* children cry, and that nothing is the matter with it, and that crying does good, and is, indeed, an especial benefit to infancy. The anxious and unfamiliar mother, though not convinced by these abstract sayings of the truth or wisdom of the explanation, takes both for granted ; and, giving the nurse credit for more knowledge and experience on this head than she can have, contentedly resigns herself to the infliction, as a thing necessary to be endured for the good of the baby, but thinking it, at the same time, an extraordinary instance of the imperfectibility of Nature as regards the human infant ; for her mind wanders to what she has observed in her childhood with puppies and kittens, who, except when rudely torn from their nurse, seldom give utterance to any complaining.

2467. We, undoubtedly, believe that crying, to a certain extent, is not only conducive to health, but positively necessary to the full development and physical economy of the infant's being. But though holding this opinion, we are far from believing that a child does not very often cry from pain, thirst, want of food, and attention to its personal comfort ; but there is as much difference in the tone and expression of a child's cry as in the notes of an adult's voice ; and the mother's ear will not be long in discriminating between the sharp peevish whine of irritation and fever, and the louder intermitting cry that characterizes the want of warmth and sleep. All these shades of expression in the child's inarticulate voice every nurse *should* understand, and every mother will soon teach herself to interpret them with an accuracy equal to language.

2468. There is no part of a woman's duty to her child that a young mother should so soon make it her business to study, as the voice of her infant, and the language conveyed in its cry. The study is neither hard nor difficult ; a close attention to its tone, and the expression of the baby's features, are the two most important points demanding attention. The key to both the mother will find in her own heart, and the knowledge of her success in the comfort and smile of her infant. We have two reasons—both strong ones—for urging on mothers the imperative necessity of early making themselves acquainted with the nature and wants of their child : the first, that when left to the entire responsibility of the baby, after the departure of the nurse, she may be able to undertake her new duties with more confidence than if left to her own resources and mother's instinct, without a clue to guide her through the mysteries of those calls that vibrate through every nerve of her nature ; and, secondly, that she may be able to guard her child from the nefarious practices of unprincipled nurses, who, while calming the mother's mind with false statements as to the character of the baby's cries, rather than lose their rest, or devote that time which would remove the cause of suffering, administer, behind the curtains, those deadly narcotics which, while stupefying Nature into sleep, insure for herself a night of many unbroken hours. Such nurses as have not the hardihood to dose their infant charges, are often full of other schemes to still that constant and reproachful cry. The most frequent means employed for this purpose is giving it something to suck,—something easily hid from the mother,—or, when that is impossible, under the plea of keeping it warm, the nurse covers it in her lap with a shawl, and, under this blind, surreptitiously inserts a finger between the parched lips, which possibly moan for drink ; and, under this inhuman cheat and delusion, the infant is pacified, till Nature, balked of its desires, drops into a troubled sleep. These are two of our reasons for impressing upon mothers the *early,* the *immediate* necessity of putting themselves sympathetically in communication with their child, by at once learning its hidden language as a delightful task.

2469. We must strenuously warn all mothers on *no* account to allow the nurse to sleep with the baby, never herself to lay down with it by her side for a night's rest, never to let it sleep in the parents' bed, and on no account keep it, longer than absolutely necessary, confined in an atmosphere loaded with the breath of many adults.

2470. The amount of *oxygen* required by an infant is so large, and the quantity consumed by mid-life and age, and the proportion of carbonic acid thrown off from both, so considerable, that an infant breathing the same air cannot possibly carry on its healthy existence while deriving its vitality from so corrupted a medium. This objection, always in force, is still more objectionable at night-time, when doors and windows are closed, and amounts to a condition of poison, when placed between two adults in sleep, and shut in by bed-curtains ; and when, in addition to the impurities expired from the lungs, we remember, in quiescence and sleep, how large a portion of mephitic gas is given off from the skin.

2471. Mothers, in the fulness of their affection, believe there is no harbour, sleeping or awake, where their infants can be so secure from all possible or probable danger as in their own arms ; yet we should astound our readers if we told them the statistical number of infants who, in despite of their motherly solicitude and love, are annually killed, unwittingly, by such parents themselves, and this from the persistency in the practice we are so strenuously condemning. The mother frequently, on awaking, discovers the baby's face closely impacted between her bosom and her arm, and its body rigid and lifeless ; or else so enveloped in the "head-blanket" and superincumbent bedclothes, as to render breathing a matter of physical impossibility. In such cases the jury in general returns a verdict of "*Accidentally overlaid ;*" but one of "Careless suffocation" would be more in accordance with truth and justice. The only possible excuse that can be urged, either by nurse or mother, for this culpable practice, is the plea of imparting warmth to the infant. But this can always be effected by an extra blanket in the child's crib, or, if the weather is particularly cold, by a bottle of hot water enveloped in flannel and placed at the child's feet; while all the objections already urged—as derivable from animal heat imparted by actual contact—are entirely obviated. There is another evil attending the sleeping together of the mother and infant, which, as far as regards the latter, we consider quite as formidable, though not so immediate as the others, and is always followed by more or less of mischief to the mother. The evil we now allude to is that most injurious practice of letting the child *suck* after the mother has *fallen asleep,* a custom that naturally results from the former, and which, as we have already said, is injurious to both mother and child. It is injurious to the infant by allowing it, without control, to imbibe to distension a fluid sluggishly secreted and deficient in those vital principles which the want of mental energy, and of the sympathetic appeals of the child on the mother, so powerfully produce on the secreted nutriment, while the mother wakes in a state of clammy exhaustion, with giddiness, dimness of sight, nausea, loss of appetite, and a dull aching pain through the back and between the shoulders. In fact, she wakes languid and unrefreshed from her sleep, with febrile symptoms and hectic flushes, caused by her baby vampire, who, while dragging from her her health and strength, has excited in itself a set of symptoms directly opposite, but fraught with the same injurious consequences—"functional derangement."

THE MILK.

2472. As Nature has placed in the bosom of the mother the natural food of her offspring, it must be self-evident to every reflecting woman, that it becomes her duty to study, as far as lies in her power, to keep that reservoir of nourishment in as pure and invigorating a condition as possible; for she must remember that the *quantity* is no proof of the *quality* of this aliment.

2473. The mother, while suckling, as a general rule, should avoid all sedentary occupations, take regular exercise, keep her mind as lively and pleasingly occupied as possible, especially by music and singing. Her diet should be light and nutritious, with a proper sufficiency of animal food, and of that kind which yields the largest amount of nourishment; and, unless the digestion is naturally strong, vegetables and fruit should form a very small proportion of the general dietary, and such preparations as broths, gruels, arrowroot, &c., still less. Tapioca, or ground-rice pudding, made with several eggs, may be taken freely; but all slops and thin potations, such as that delusion called chicken-broth, should be avoided, as yielding a very small amount of nutriment, and a large proportion of flatulence. All purely stimulants should be avoided as much as possible, especially spirits, unless taken for some special object, and that medicinally; but as a part of the dietary they should be carefully shunned. Lactation is always an exhausting process, and as the child increases in size and strength, the drain upon the mother becomes great and depressing. Then something more even than an abundant diet is required to keep the mind and body up to a standard sufficiently healthy to admit of a constant and nutritious secretion being performed without detriment to the physical integrity of the mother, or injury to the child who imbibes it; and as stimulants are inadmissible, if not positively injurious, the substitute required is to be found in *malt liquor*. To the lady accustomed to her Madeira and sherry, this may appear a very vulgar potation for a delicate young mother to take instead of the more subtle and condensed elegance of wine; but as we are writing from experience, and with the avowed object of imparting useful facts and beneficial remedies to our readers, we allow no social distinctions to interfere with our legitimate object.

2474. We have already said that the suckling mother should avoid stimulants, especially spirituous ones; and though something of this sort is absolutely necessary to support her strength during the exhausting process, it should be rather of a *tonic* than of a stimulating character; and as all wines contain a large percentage of brandy, they are on that account less beneficial than the pure juice of the fermented grape might be. But there is another consideration to be taken into account on this subject; the mother has not only to think of herself, but also of her infant. Now wines, especially port wine, very often—indeed, most frequently—affect the baby's bowels, and what might have been grateful to the mother becomes thus a source of pain and irritation to the child afterwards. Sherry is less open to this objection than other wines, yet still *it* very frequently does influence the second participator, or the child whose mother has taken it.

2475. The nine or twelve months a woman usually suckles must be, to some extent, to most mothers, a period of privation and penance, and unless she is deaf to the cries of her baby, and insensible to its kicks and plunges, and will not see in such muscular evidences the griping pains that rack her child, she will avoid every article that can remotely affect the little being who draws its sustenance from her. She will see that the babe is acutely affected by all that in any way influences her, and willingly curtail her own enjoyments, rather than see her infant rendered feverish, irritable, and uncomfortable. As the best tonic, then, and the most efficacious indirect stimulant that a mother can take at such times, there is no potation equal to *porter* and *stout*, or, what is better still, an equal part of porter and stout. Ale, except for a few constitutions, is too subtle and too sweet, generally causing acidity or heartburn, and stout alone is too potent to admit of a full draught, from its proneness to affect the head; and quantity, as well as moderate strength, is required to make the draught effectual; the equal mixture, therefore, of stout and porter yields all the properties desired or desirable as a medicinal agent for this purpose.

2476. Independently of its invigorating influence on the constitution, *porter exerts a marked and specific effect on the secretion of milk, more powerful in exciting an abundant supply of that fluid than any other article within the range of the physician's art;* and, in cases of deficient quantity, is the most certain, speedy, and the healthiest means that can be employed to insure a quick and abundant flow. In cases where malt liquor produces flatulency, a few grains of the "carbonate of soda" may advantageously be added to each glass immediately before drinking, which will have the effect of neutralizing any acidity that may be in the porter at the time, and will also prevent its after-disagreement with the stomach. The quantity to be taken must depend upon the natural strength of the mother, the age and demand made by the infant on the parent, and other causes; but the amount should vary from *one* to *two* pints a day, never taking less than half a pint at a time, which should be repeated three or four times a day.

2477. We have said that the period of suckling is a season of penance to the mother, but this is not invariably the case; and, as so much must depend upon the natural strength of the stomach, and its power of assimilating all kinds of food into healthy *chyle*, it is impossible to define exceptions. Where a woman feels she can eat any kind of food, without inconvenience or detriment, she should live during her suckling as she did before; but, as a general rule, we are bound to advise all mothers to abstain from such articles as pickles, fruits, cucumbers, and all acid and slowly digestible foods, unless they wish for restless nights and crying infants.

2478. As regards exercise and amusement, we would certainly neither prohibit a mother's dancing, going to a theatre, nor even from attending an assembly. The first, however, is the best indoor recreation she can take, and a young mother will do well to often amuse herself in the nursery with this most excellent means of healthful circulation. The only precaution necessary is to avoid letting the child suck the milk that has lain long in the breast, or is heated by excessive action.

2479. Every mother who can, should be provided with a breast-pump, or glass tube, to draw off the superabundance that has been accumulating in her absence from the child, or the first gush excited by undue exertion: the subsequent supply of milk will be secreted under the invigorating influence of a previous healthy stimulus.

2480. As the first milk that is secreted contains a large amount of the saline elements, and is thin and innutritious, it is most admirably adapted for the purpose Nature designed it to fulfil,—that of an aperient; but which, unfortunately, it is seldom permitted, in our artificial mode of living, to perform.

2481. So opposed are we to the objectionable plan of physicking new-born children, that, unless for positive illness, we would much rather advise that medicine should be administered *through* the mother for the first eight or ten weeks of its existence. This practice, which few mothers will object to, is easily effected by the parent, when such a course is necessary for the child, taking either a dose of castor-oil, half an ounce of tasteless salts (the phosphate of soda), one or two teaspoonfuls of magnesia, a dose of lenitive electuary, manna, or any mild and simple aperient, which, almost before it can have taken effect on herself, will exhibit its action on her child.

2482. One of the most common errors that mothers fall into while suckling their children, is that of fancying they are always hungry, and consequently overfeeding them ; and with this, the great mistake of applying the child to the breast on every occasion of its crying, without investigating the cause of its complaint, and, under the belief that it wants food, putting the nipple into its crying mouth, until the infant turns in revulsion and petulance from what it should accept with eagerness and joy. At such times, a few teaspoonfuls of water, slightly chilled, will often instantly pacify a crying and restless child, who has turned in loathing from the offered breast ; or, after imbibing a few drops, and finding it not what nature craved, throws back its head in disgust, and cries more petulantly than before. In such a case as this, the young mother, grieved at her baby's rejection of the tempting present, and distressed at its cries, and in terror of some injury, over and over ransacks its clothes, believing some insecure pin can alone be the cause of such sharp complaining, an accident that, from her own care in dressing, however, is seldom or ever the case.

2483. These abrupt cries of the child, if they do not proceed from thirst, which a little water will relieve, not unfrequently occur from some unequal pressure, a fold or twist in the "roller," or some constriction round the tender body. If this is suspected, the mother must not be content with merely slackening the strings ; the child should be undressed, and the creases and folds of the hot skin, especially those about the thighs and groins, examined, to see that no powder has caked, and, becoming hard, irritated the parts. The violet powder should be dusted freely over all, to cool the skin, and everything put on fresh and smooth. If such precautions have not afforded relief, and, in addition to the crying, the child plunges or draws up its legs, the mother may be assured some cause of irritation exists in the stomach or bowels,—either acidity in the latter or distension from overfeeding in the former ; but, from whichever cause, the child should be "opened" before the fire, and a heated napkin applied all over the abdomen, the infant being occasionally elevated to a sitting position, and while gently jolted on the knee, the back should be lightly patted with the hand.

2484. Should the mother have any reason to apprehend that the *cause* of inconvenience proceeds from the bladder—a not unfrequent source of pain,—the napkin is to be dipped in hot water, squeezed out, and immediately applied over the part, and repeated every eight or ten minutes, for several times in succession, either till the natural relief is afforded, or a cessation of pain allows of its discontinuance. The pain that young infants often suffer, and the crying that results from it, is, as we have already said, frequently caused by the mother inconsiderately overfeeding her child, and is produced by the pain of distension, and the mechanical pressure of a larger quantity of fluid in the stomach than the gastric juice can convert into cheese and digest.

2485. Some children are stronger in the enduring power of the stomach than others, and get rid of the excess by vomiting, concluding every process of suckling by an emission of milk and curd. Such children are called by nurses "thriving children ;" and generally they are so, simply because their digestion is good, and they have the power of expelling with impunity that superabundance of aliment which in others is a source of distension, flatulence, and pain.

2486. The length of time an infant should be suckled must depend much on the health and strength of the child, and the health of the mother, and the quantity and quality of her milk ; though, when all circumstances are favourable, it should never be less than *nine*, nor exceed *fifteen* months ; but perhaps the true time will be found in the medium between both. But of this we may be sure, that Nature never ordained a child to live on suction after having endowed it with teeth to bite and to grind ; and nothing is more out of place and unseemly than to hear a child, with a set of twenty teeth, ask for "the breast."

2487. The practice of protracted wet-nursing is hurtful to the mother, by keeping up an uncalled-for, and, after the proper time, an unhealthy drain on her system, while the child either derives no benefit from what it no longer requires, or it produces a positive injury on its constitution. After the period when Nature has ordained the child shall live by other means, the secretion of milk becomes thin and deteriorated, showing in the flabby flesh and puny features of the child both its loss of nutritious properties and the want of more stimulating aliment.

2488. Though we have said that twelve months is about the medium time a baby should be suckled, we by no means wish to imply that a child should be fed exclusively on milk for its first year ; quite the reverse ; the infant can hardly be too soon made independent of the mother. Thus, should illness assail her, her milk fail, or any domestic cause abruptly cut off the natural supply, the child having been annealed to an artificial diet, its life might be safely carried on without seeking for a wet-nurse, and without the slightest danger to its system.

2489. The advantage to the mother of early accustoming the child to artificial food is as considerable to herself as beneficial to her infant ; the demand on her physical strength in the first instance will be less severe and exhausting, the child will sleep longer on a less rapidly digestible aliment, and yield to both more quiet nights, and the mother will be more at liberty to go out for business or pleasure, another means of sustenance being at hand till her return. Besides these advantages, by a judicious blending of the two systems of feeding, the infant will acquire greater constitutional strength, so that, if attacked by sickness or disease, it will have a much greater chance of resisting its virulence than if dependent alone on the mother, whose milk, affected by fatigue and the natural anxiety of the parent for her offspring, is at such a time neither good in its properties nor likely to be beneficial to the patient.

2490. All that we have further to say on suckling is an advice to mothers, that if they wish to keep a sound and unchapped nipple, and possibly avoid what is called a "broken breast," never to put it up with a wet nipple, but always to have a soft handkerchief in readiness, and the moment that delicate part is drawn from the child's mouth, to dry it carefully of the milk and saliva that moisten it; and, further, to make a practice of suckling from each breast alternately.

Dress and Dressing, Washing, &c.

2491. As respects the dress and dressing of a new-born infant, or of a child in arms, during any stage of its nursing, there are few women who will require us to give them guidance or directions for their instruction; and though a few hints on the subject may not be out of place here, yet most women intuitively "take to a baby," and, with a small amount of experience, are able to perform all the little offices necessary to its comfort and cleanliness with ease and completeness. We shall, therefore, on this delicate subject hold our peace; and only, from afar, *hint* "at what we would," leaving our suggestions to be approved or rejected, according as they chime with the judgment and the apprehension of our motherly readers.

2492. In these days of intelligence, there are few ladies who have not, in all probability, seen the manner in which the Indian squaw, the aborigines of Polynesia, and even the Lapp and Esquimaux, strap down their baby on a board, and by means of a loop suspend it to the bough of a tree, hang it up to the rafters of the hut, or on travel, dangle it on their backs, outside the domestic implements, which, as the slave of her master, man, the wronged but uncomplaining woman carries, in order that her lord may march in unhampered freedom. Cruel and confining as this system of "backboard" dressing may seem to our modern notions of freedom and exercise, it is positively less irksome, less confining, and infinitely less prejudicial to health, than the mummying of children by our grandmothers a hundred, ay, fifty years ago: for what with chin-stays, back-stays, body-stays, forehead-cloths, rollers, bandages, &c., an infant had as many girths and strings, to keep head, limbs, and body in one exact position, as a ship has halyards.

2493. Much of this—indeed we may say all—has been abolished; but still the child is far from being dressed loosely enough ; and we shall never be satisfied till the abominable use of the *pin* is avoided *in toto* in an infant's dressing, and a texture made for all the under garments of a child of a cool and elastic material.

2494. The manner in which an infant is encircled in a bandage called the "roller," as if it had fractured ribs, compressing those organs—that, living on suction, must be, for the health of the child, to a certain degree distended, to obtain sufficient aliment from the fluid imbibed—is perfectly preposterous. Our humanity, as well as our duty, calls upon us at once to abrogate and discountenance by every means in our power.   Instead of the process of washing and dressing being made, as with the adult, a refreshment and comfort, it is, by the dawdling manner in which it is performed, the multiplicity of things used, and the perpetual change of position of the infant to adjust its complicated clothing, rendered an operation of positive irritation and annoyance. We, therefore, entreat all mothers to regard this subject in its true light, and study to the utmost, simplicity in dress, and dispatch in the process.

2495. Children do not so much cry from the washing as from the irritation caused by the frequent change of position in which they are placed, the number of times they are turned on their face, on their back, and on their side, by the manipulations demanded by the multiplicity of articles to be fitted, tacked, and carefully adjusted on their bodies.   What mother ever found her girl of six or seven stand quiet while she was curling her hair ?   How many times nightly has she not to reprove her for not standing still during the process ! It is the same with the unconscious infant, who cannot bear to be moved about, and who has no sooner grown reconciled to one position than it is forced reluctantly into another.   It is true, in one instance the child has intelligence to guide it, and in the other not ; but the *motitory nerves*, in both instances, resent coercion, and a child cannot be too little handled.

2496. On this account alone, and, for the moment, setting health and comfort out of the question, we beg mothers to simplify their baby's dress as much as possible ; and not only to put on as little as is absolutely necessary, but to make that as simple in its contrivance and adjustment as it will admit of ; to avoid belly-bands, rollers, girths, and everything that can impede or confine the natural expansion of the digestive organs, on the due performance of whose functions the child lives, thrives, and develops its physical being.

REARING BY HAND.
Articles necessary, and how to use them.—Preparation of Foods.— Baths.—Advantages of Rearing by Hand.

2497. As we do not for a moment wish to be thought an advocate for an artificial, in preference to the natural course of rearing children, we beg our readers to understand us perfectly on this head ; all we desire to prove is the fact that a child *can* be brought up as well on a spoon dietary as the best example to be found of those reared on the breast ; having more strength, in-deed, from the more nutritious food on which it lives. It will be thus less liable to infectious diseases, and more capable of resisting the virulence of any danger that may attack it ; and without in any way depreciating the nutriment of its natural food, we wish to impress on the mother's mind that there are many cases of infantine debility which might eventuate in rickets, curvature of the spine, or mesenteric disease, where the addition to, or total substitution of, an artificial and more stimulating aliment, would not only give tone and strength to the constitution, but at the same time render the employment of mechanical means totally unnecessary. And, finally, though we would never —where the mother had the strength to suckle her child—supersede the breast, we would insist on making it a rule to accustom the child as early as possible to the use of an artificial diet, not only that it may acquire more vigour to help it over the ills of childhood, but that, in the absence of the mother, it might not miss the maternal sustenance ; and also for the parent's sake, that, should the milk, from any cause, become vitiated, or suddenly cease, the child can be made over to the bottle and the spoon without the slightest appre-hension of hurtful consequences.

2498. To those persons unacquainted with the system, or who may have been erroneously informed on the matter, the rearing of a child by hand may seem surrounded by innumerable difficulties, and a large amount of personal trouble and anxiety to the nurse or mother who undertakes the duty. This, however, is a fallacy in every respect, except as regards the fact of preparing the food ; but even this extra amount of work, by adopting the course we shall lay down, may be reduced to a very small sum of inconvenience ; and as respects anxiety, the only thing calling for care is the display of judgment in the preparation of the food. The articles required for the purpose of feeding an infant are a night-lamp, with its pan and lid, to keep the food warm ; a nursing-bottle, with a prepared teat ; and a small pap saucepan, for use by day. Of the lamp we need hardly speak, most mothers being acquainted with its operation : but to those to whom it is unknown we may observe, that the flame from the floating rushlight heats the water in the reservoir above, in which the covered pan that contains the food floats, keeping it at such a heat that, when thinned by milk, it will be of a temperature suitable for immediate use. Though many kinds of nursing-bottles have been lately invented, and some mounted with India-rubber nipples, the common glass bottle, with the calf's teat, is equal in cleanliness and utility to any ; besides, the nipple put into the child's mouth is so white and natural in appearance, that no child taken from the breast will refuse it. The black artificial ones of caoutchouc or gutta-percha are unnatural. The prepared teats can be obtained at any chemist's, and as they are kept in spirits, they will require a little soaking in warm water, and gentle washing, before being tied securely, by means of fine twine, round the neck of the bottle, just sufficient being left projecting for the child to grasp freely in its lips; for if left the full length, or over long, it will be drawn too far into the mouth, and possibly make the infant heave. When once properly adjusted, the nipple need never be removed till replaced by a new one, which will hardly be necessary oftener than once a fortnight, though with care one will last for several weeks. The nursing-bottle should be thoroughly washed and cleaned every day, and always rinsed out before and after using it, the warm water being squeezed through the nipple, to wash out any particles of food that might lodge in the aperture, and become sour. The teat can always be kept white and soft by turning the end of the bottle, when not in use, into a narrow jug containing water, taking care to dry it first, and then to warm it by drawing the food through before putting it into the child's mouth.

Food, and its Preparation.

2499. The articles generally employed as food for infants consist of arrow-root, bread, flour, baked flour, prepared groats, farinaceous food, biscuit-powder, biscuits, tops-and-bottoms, and semolina, or manna croup, as it is otherwise called, which, like tapioca, is the prepared pith of certain vegetable substances. Of this list the least efficacious, though, perhaps, the most believed in, is arrowroot, which only as a mere agent, for change, and then only for a very short time, should ever be employed as a means of diet to infancy or childhood. It is a thin, flatulent, and innutritious food, and incapable of supporting infantine life with energy. Bread, though the universal *régime* with the labouring poor, where the infant's stomach and digestive powers are a reflex, in miniature, of the father's, should never be given to an infant under three months, and, even then, however finely beaten up and smoothly made, is a very questionable diet. Flour, when well boiled, though infinitely better than arrowroot, is still only a kind of fermentative paste, that counteracts its own good by after-acidity and flatulence.

2500. Baked flour, when cooked into a pale brown mass, and finely powdered, makes a far superior food to the others, and may be considered as a very useful diet, especially for a change. Prepared groats may be classed with arrowroot and raw flour, as being innutritious. The articles that now follow in our list are all good, and such as we could, with conscience and safety, trust to for the health and development of any child whatever.

2501. We may observe in this place, that an occasional change in the character of the food is highly desirable, both as regards the health and benefit of the child; and though the interruption should only last for a day, the change will be advantageous.

2502. The packets sold as farinaceous food are unquestionably the best aliment that can be given from the first to a baby, and may be continued, with the exception of an occasional change, without alteration of the material, till the child is able to take its regular meals of animal and vegetable food. Some infants are so constituted as to require a frequent and total change in their system of living, seeming to thrive for a certain time on any food given to them, but if persevered in too long, declining in bulk and appearance as rapidly as they had previously progressed. In such cases the food should be immediately changed, and when that which appeared to agree best with the child is resumed, it should be altered in its quality, and perhaps in its consistency.

2503. For the farinaceous food there are directions with each packet, containing instructions for the making ; but, whatever the food employed is, enough should be made at once to last the day and night ; at first, about a pint basinful, but, as the child advances, a quart will hardly be too much. In all cases, let the food boil a sufficient time, constantly stirring, and taking every precaution that it does not get burnt, in which case it is on no account to be used.

2504. The food should always be made with water, the whole sweetened at once, and of such a consistency that, when poured out, and it has had time to cool, it will cut with the firmness of a pudding or custard. One or two spoonfuls are to be put into the pap saucepan and stood on the hob till the heat has softened it, when enough milk is to be added, and carefully mixed with the food, till the whole has the consistency of ordinary cream ; it is then to be poured into the nursing-bottle, and the food having been drawn through to warm the nipple, it is to be placed in the child's mouth. For the first month or more, half a bottleful will be quite enough to give the infant at one time ; but, as the child grows, it will be necessary not only to increase the quantity given at each time, but also gradually to make its food more consistent, and, after the third month, to add an egg to every pint basin of food made. At night the mother puts the food into the covered pan of her lamp, instead of the saucepan—that is, enough for one supply, and, having lighted the rush, she will find, on the waking of her child, the food sufficiently hot to bear the cooling addition of the milk. But, whether night or day, the same food should never be heated twice, and what the child leaves should be thrown away.

2505. The biscuit powder is used in the same manner as the farinaceous food, and both prepared much after the fashion of making starch. But when tops-and-bottoms, or the whole biscuit, are employed, they require soaking in cold water for some time previous to boiling. The biscuit or biscuits are then to be slowly boiled in as much water as will, when thoroughly soft, allow of their being beaten by a three-pronged fork into a fine, smooth, and even pulp, and which, when poured into a basin and become cold, will cut out like a custard. If two large biscuits have been so treated, and the child is six or seven months old, beat up two eggs, sufficient sugar to properly sweeten it, and about a pint of skim milk. Pour this on the beaten biscuit in the saucepan, stirring constantly ; boil for about five minutes, pour into a basin, and use, when cold, in the same manner as the other.

3 x 2

2506. This makes an admirable food, at once nutritious and strengthening. When tops-and-bottoms or rusks are used, the quantity of the egg may be reduced, or altogether omitted.

2507. Semolina, or manna croup, being in little hard grains, like a fine millet-seed, must be boiled for some time, and the milk, sugar, and egg added to it on the fire, and boiled for a few minutes longer, and, when cold, used as the other preparations.

2508. Many persons entertain a belief that cow's milk is hurtful to infants, and, consequently, refrain from giving it ; but this is a very great mistake, for both sugar and milk should form a large portion of every meal an infant takes.

TEETHING AND CONVULSIONS.

Fits, &c., the consequence of Dentition, and how to be treated.— The number and order of the Teeth, and manner in which they are cut.—First and Second Set.

2509. About three months after birth, the infant's troubles may be said to begin ; teeth commence forming in the gums, causing pain and irritation in the mouth, and which, but for the saliva it causes to flow so abundantly, would be attended with very serious consequences.   At the same time the mother frequently relaxes in the punctuality of the regimen imposed on her, and, taking some unusual or different food, excites diarrhœa or irritation in her child's stomach, which not unfrequently results in a rash on the skin, or slight febrile symptoms, which, if not subdued in their outset, superinduce some more serious form of infantine disease.   But, as a general rule, the teeth are the primary cause of much of the child's sufferings, in consequence of the state of nervous and functional irritation into which the system is thrown by their formation and progress out of the jaw and through the gums.   We propose beginning this branch of our subject with that most fertile source of an infant's suffering—

Teething.

2510. That this subject may be better understood by the nurse and mother, and the reason of the constitutional disturbance that, to a greater or less degree, is experienced by all infants, may be made intelligible to those who have the care of children, we shall commence by giving a brief account of the formation of the teeth, the age at which they appear in the mouth, and the order in which they pierce the gums.   The organs of mastication in the adult consist of 32 distinct teeth, 16 in either jaw ; being, in fact, a double set.   The teeth are divided into 4 incisors, 2 canine, 4 first and second grinders, and 6 molars ; but in childhood the complement or first set consists of only twenty, and these only make their appearance as the development of the frame indicates the requirement of a different kind of food for the support of the system. At birth some of the first-cut teeth are found in the cavities of the jaw, in a very small and rudimentary form; but this is by no means universal. About the third month, the jaws, which are hollow and divided into separate cells, begin to expand, making room for the slowly developing teeth, which, arranged for beauty and economy of space lengthwise, gradually turn their tops upwards, piercing the gum by their edges, which, being sharp, assist in cutting a passage through the soft parts. There is no particular period at which children cut their teeth, some being remarkably early, and others equally late. The earliest age that we have ever ourselves known as a reliable fact was, *six weeks*. Such peculiarities are generally hereditary, and, as in this case, common to a whole family. The two extremes are probably represented by six and sixteen months. Pain and drivelling are the usual, but by no means the general, indications of teething.

2511. About the sixth month the gums become tense and swollen, presenting a red, shiny appearance, while the salivary glands pour out an unusual quantity of saliva. After a time, a white line or round spot is observed on the top of one part of the gums, and the sharp edge of the tooth may be felt beneath if the finger is gently pressed on the part. Through these white spots the teeth burst their way in the following order :—

2512. Two incisors in the lower jaw are first cut, though, in general, some weeks elapse between the appearance of the first and the advent of the second. The next teeth cut are the four incisors of the upper jaw. The next in order are the remaining two incisors of the bottom, one on each side, then two top and two bottom on each side, but not joining the incisors; and lastly, about the eighteenth or twentieth month, the four eye teeth, filling up the space left between the side teeth and the incisors; thus completing the infant's set of sixteen. Sometimes at the same period, but more frequently some months later, four more double teeth slowly make their appearance, one on each side of each jaw, completing the entire series of the child's first set of twenty teeth. It is asserted that a child, while cutting its teeth, should either dribble excessively, vomit after every meal, or be greatly relaxed. Though one or other, or all of these at once, may attend a case of teething, it by no means follows that any one of them should accompany this process of nature, though there can be no doubt that where the pain consequent on the unyielding state of the gums, and the firmness of the skin that covers the tooth, is severe, a copious discharge of saliva acts beneficially in saving the head, and also in guarding the child from those dangerous attacks of fits to which many children in their teething are liable.

2513. The *Symptoms* that generally indicate the cutting of teeth, in addition to the inflamed and swollen state of the gums, and increased flow of saliva, are the restless and peevish state of the child, the hands being thrust into the mouth, and the evident pleasure imparted by rubbing the finger or nail gently along the gum ; the lips are often excoriated, and the functions of the stomach or bowels are out of order. In severe cases, occurring in unhealthy or scrofulous children, there are, from the first, considerable fever, disturbed sleep, fretfulness, diarrhœa, rolling of the eyes, convulsive startings, laborious breathing, coma, or unnatural sleep, ending, unless the head is quickly relieved, in death.

2514. The *Treatment* in all cases of painful teething is remarkably simple, and consists in keeping the body cool by mild aperient medicines, allaying the irritation in the gums by friction with a rough ivory ring or a stale crust of bread, and when the head, lungs, or any organ is overloaded or unduly excited, to use the hot bath, and by throwing the body into a perspiration, equalize the circulation, and relieve the system from the danger of a fatal termination.

2515. Besides these, there is another means, but that must be employed by a medical man ; namely, scarifying the gums—an operation always safe, and which, when judiciously performed, and at a critical opportunity, will often snatch the child from the grasp of death.

2516. There are few subjects on which mothers have often formed such strong and mistaken opinions as on that of lancing an infant's gums, some rather seeing their child go into fits—and by the unrelieved irritation endangering inflammation of the brain, water on the head, rickets, and other lingering affections—than permit the surgeon to afford instant relief by cutting through the hard skin, which, like a bladder over the stopper of a bottle, effectually confines the tooth to the socket, and prevents it piercing the soft, spongy substance of the gum. This prejudice is a great error, as we shall presently show; for, so far from hurting the child, there is nothing that will so soon convert an infant's tears into smiles as scarifying the gums in painful teething ; that is, if effectually done, and the skin of the tooth be divided.

2517. Though teething is a natural function, and to an infant in perfect health should be unproductive of pain, yet in general it is not only a fertile cause of suffering, but often a source of alarm and danger ; the former, from irritation in the stomach and bowels, deranging the whole economy of the system, and the latter, from coma and fits, that may excite alarm in severe cases ; and the danger, that eventuates in some instances, from organic disease of the head or spinal marrow.

2518. We shall say nothing in this place of "rickets," or "water on the head," which are frequent results of dental irritation, but proceed to finish our remarks on the treatment of teething. Though strongly advocating the lancing of the gums in teething, and when there are any severe head-symptoms, yet it should never be needlessly done, or before being satisfied that the tooth is fully formed, and is out of the socket, and under the gum. When assured on these points, the gum should be cut lengthwise, and from the top of the gum downwards to the tooth, in an horizontal direction, thus ——, and for about half an inch in length. The operation is then to be repeated in a transverse direction, cutting across the gum, in the centre of the first incision, and forming a cross, thus +. The object of this double incision is to insure a retraction of the cut parts, and leave an open way for the tooth to start from—an advantage not to be obtained when only one incision is made ; for unless the tooth immediately follows the lancing, the opening reunites, and the operation has to be repeated. That this operation is very little or not at all painful, is evidenced by the suddenness with which the infant falls asleep after the lancing, and awakes in apparently perfect health, though immediately before the use of the gumlancet, the child may have been shrieking or in convulsions.

Convulsions, or Infantine Fits.

2519. From their birth till after teething, infants are more or less subject or liable to sudden fits, which often, without any assignable cause, will attack the child in a moment, and while in the mother's arms ; and which, according to their frequency, and the age and strength of the infant, are either slight or dangerous.

2520. Whatever may have been the remote cause, the immediate one is some irritation of the nervous system, causing convulsions, or an effusion to the head, inducing coma. In the first instance, the infant cries out with a quick, short scream, rolls up its eyes, arches its body backwards, its arms become bent and fixed, and the fingers parted ; the lips and eyelids assume a dusky leaden colour, while the face remains pale, and the eyes open, glassy, or staring. This condition may or may not be attended with muscular twitchings of the mouth, and convulsive plunges of the arms. The fit generally lasts from one to three minutes, when the child recovers with a sigh, and the relaxation of the body. In the other case, the infant is attacked at once with total insensibility and relaxation of the limbs, coldness of the body and suppressed breathing ; the eyes, when open, being dilated, and presenting a dim glistening appearance ; the infant appearing, for the moment, to be dead.

2521. *Treatment.*—The first step in either case is, to immerse the child in a hot bath up to the chin ; or if sufficient hot water cannot be procured to cover the body, make a hip-bath of what can be obtained ; and, while the left hand supports the child in a sitting or recumbent position, with the right scoop up the water, and run it over the chest of the patient. When sufficient water can be obtained, the spine should be briskly rubbed while in the bath ; when this cannot be done, lay the child on the knees, and with the fingers dipped in brandy, rub the whole length of the spine vigorously for two or three minutes, and when restored to consciousness, give occasionally a teaspoonful of weak brandy and water or wine and water.

2522. An hour after the bath, it may be necessary to give an aperient powder, possibly also to repeat the dose for once or twice every three hours; in which case the following prescription is to be employed. Take ot

Powdered scammony . . .	6 grains.
Grey powder	6 grains.
Antimonial powder	4 grains.
Lump sugar	20 grains.

Mix thoroughly, and divide into three powders, which are to be taken as advised for an infant one year old; for younger or weakly infants, divide into four powders, and give as the other. For thirst and febrile symptoms, give drinks of barley-water, or cold water, and every three hours put ten to fifteen drops of spirits of sweet nitre in a dessert-spoonful of either beverage.

THRUSH, AND ITS TREATMENT.

2523. THIS is a disease to which infants are peculiarly subject, and in whom alone it may be said to be a disease; for when thrush shows itself in adult or advanced life, it is not as a disease proper, but only as a symptom, or accessory, of some other ailment, generally of a chronic character, and should no more be classed as a separate affection than the petechæ, or dark-coloured spots that appear in malignant measles, may be considered a distinct affection.

2524. Thrush is a disease of the follicles of the mucous membrane of the alimentary canal, whereby there are formed small vesicles, or bladders, filled with a thick mucous secretion, which, bursting, discharge their contents, and form minute ulcers in the centre of each vessel. To make this formal but unavoidable description intelligible, we must beg the reader's patience while we briefly explain terms that may appear to many so unmeaning, and make the pathology of thrush fully familiar.

2525. The whole digestive canal, of which the stomach and bowels are only a part, is covered, from the lips, eyes, and ears downwards, with a thin glairy tissue, like the skin that lines the inside of an egg, called the mucous membrane; this membrane is dotted all over, in a state of health, by imperceptible points, called follicles, through which the saliva, or mucus secreted by the membrane, is poured out.

2526. These follicles, or little glands, then, becoming enlarged, and filled with a congealed fluid, constitute thrush in its first stage; and when the child's lips and mouth appear a mass of small pearls, then, as these break and discharge, the second stage, or that of ulceration, sets in.

2527. *Symptoms.*—Thrush is generally preceded by considerable irritation, by the child crying and fretting, showing more than ordinary redness of the lips and nostrils, hot fetid breath, with relaxed bowels, and dark feculent evacuations; the water is scanty and high-coloured; whilst considerable difficulty in swallowing, and much thirst, are the other symptoms, which a careful observation of the little patient makes manifest.

2528. The situation and character of thrush show at once that the cause is some irritation of the mucous membrane, and can proceed only from the nature and quality of the food. Before weaning, this must be looked for in the mother, and the condition of the milk; after that time, in the crude and indigestible nature of the food given. In either case, this exciting cause of the disease must be at once stopped. When it proceeds from the mother, it is always best to begin by physicking the infant through the parent; that is to say, let the parent first take the medicine, which will sufficiently affect the child through the milk: this plan has the double object of benefiting the patient and, at the same time, correcting the state of the mother, and improving the condition of her milk. In the other case, when the child is being fed by hand, then proceed by totally altering the style of aliment given, and substituting farinaceous food, custards, blanc-mange, and ground-rice puddings.

2529. As an aperient medicine for the mother, the best thing she can take is a dessert-spoonful of carbonate of magnesia once or twice a day, in a cup of cold water; and every second day, for two or three times, an aperient pill.

2530. As the thrush extends all over the mouth, throat, stomach, and bowels, the irritation to the child from such an extent of diseased surface is proportionately great, and before attempting to act on such a tender surface by opening medicine, the better plan is to soothe by an emollient mixture; and, for that purpose, let the following be prepared   Take of

Castor oil   .   .   .   .   . 2 drachms.
Sugar   .   .   .   .   .   . 1 drachm.
Mucilage, or powdered gum Arabic   . half a drachm.

Triturate till the oil is incorporated, then add slowly—

Mint-water   .   .   .   .   . One ounce and a half.
Laudanum   .   .   .   .   . Ten drops.

Half a teaspoonful three times a day, to an infant from one to two years old; a teaspoonful from two to three years old; and a dessert-spoonful at any age over that time. After two days' use of the mixture, one of the following powders should be given twice a day, accompanied with one dose daily of the mixture :—

Grey powder .   .   .   .   . 20 grains.
Powdered rhubarb.   .   .   . 15 grains.
Scammony   .   .   .   .   . 10 grains. Mix.

Divide into twelve powders, for one year; eight powders, from one to two;

and six powders, from two to six years old. After that age, double the strength, by giving the quantity of two powders at once.

2531. It is sometimes customary to apply borax and honey to the mouth for thrush ; but it is always better to treat the disease constitutionally rather than locally. The first steps, therefore, to be adopted are, to remove or correct the exciting cause—the mother's milk or food; allay irritation by a warm bath and the castor-oil mixture, followed by and conjoined with the powders.

2532. To those, however, who wish to try the honey process, the best preparation to use is the following :—Rub down one ounce of honey with two drachms of tincture of myrrh, and apply it to the lips and mouth every four or six hours.

2533. It is a popular belief, and one most devoutly cherished by many nurses and elderly persons, that everybody must, at some time of their life, between birth and death, have an attack of thrush, and if not in infancy, or prime of life, it will surely attack them on their death-bed, in a form more malignant than if the patient had been affected with the malady earlier ; the black thrush with which they are then reported to be affected being, in all probability, the petechæ, or purple spots that characterize the worst form, and often the last stage, of typhoid fever.

2534. In general, very little medicine is needed in this disease of the thrush —an alterative powder, or a little magnesia, given once or twice, being all, with the warm bath, that, in the great majority of cases, is needed to restore the mucous membrane to health. As thrush is caused by an excess of heat, or over-action in the lining membrane of the stomach and bowels, whatever will counteract this state, by throwing the heat on the surface, must materially benefit, if not cure, the disease : and that means every mother has at hand, in the form of a *warm bath*. After the application of this, a little magnesia to correct the acidity existing along the surface of the mucous membrane, is often all that is needed to throw the system into such a state as will effect its own cure. This favourable state is indicated by an excessive flow of saliva, or what is called "dribbling," and by a considerable amount of relaxation of the bowels—a condition that must not be mistaken for diarrhœa, and checked as if a disease, but rather, for the day or two it continues, encouraged as a critical evacuant.

2535. Should there be much debility in the convalescence, half a teaspoonful of stee wine, given twice a day in a little barley-water, will be found sufficient for all the purposes of a tonic. This, with the precaution of changing the child's food, or, when it lives on the mother, of correcting the quality of the milk by changing her own diet, and, by means of an antacid or aperient, improving the state of the secretion. Such is all the treatment that this disease in general requires.

2536. The class of diseases we are now approaching are the most important, ooth in their pathological features and in their consequences on the constitution, of any group or individual disease that assails the human body; and though more frequently attacking the undeveloped frame of childhood, are yet by no means confined to that period. These are called Eruptive Fevers, and embrace chicken-pox, cow-pox, small-pox, scarlet fever, measles, milary fever, and erysipelas, or St. Anthony's fire.

2537. The general character of all these is, that they are contagious, and, as a general rule, attack a person only once in his lifetime; that their chain of diseased actions always begins with fever, and that, after an interval of from one to four days, the fever is followed by an eruption of the skin.

CHICKEN-POX, OR GLASS-POX; AND COW-POX, OR VACCINATION.

2538. CHICKEN-POX, or GLASS-POX, may, in strict propriety, be classed as a mild variety of small-pox, presenting all the mitigated symptoms of that formidable disease. Among many physicians it is, indeed, classed as small-pox, and not a separate disease; but as this is not the place to discuss such questions, and as we profess to give only facts, the result of our own practical experience, we shall treat this affection of glass-pox or chicken-pox, as we ourselves have found it, as a distinct and separate disease.

2539. Chicken-pox is marked by all the febrile symptoms presented by small-pox, with this difference, that, in the case of chicken-pox, each symptom is particularly slight. The heat of body is much less acute, and the principal symptoms are difficulty of breathing, headache, coated tongue, and nausea, which sometimes amounts to vomiting. After a term of general irritability, heat, and restlessness, about the fourth day, or between the third and fourth, an eruption makes its appearance over the face, neck, and body, in its first two stages closely resembling small-pox, with this especial difference, that whereas the pustules in small-pox have *flat* and *depressed* centres—an infallible characteristic of small-pox—the pustules in chicken-pox remain *globular*, while the fluid in them changes from a transparent white to a straw-coloured liquid, which begins to exude and disappear about the eighth or ninth day, and, in mild cases, by the twelfth desquamates, or peels off entirely.

2540. There can be no doubt that chicken-pox, like small-pox, is contagious, and under certain states of the atmosphere becomes endemic. Parents should, therefore, avoid exposing young children to the danger of infection by taking them where it is known to exist, as chicken-pox, in weakly constitutions, or in very young children, may superinduce small-pox, the one disease either running concurrently with the other, or discovering itself as the other declines. This, of course, is a condition that renders the case very hazardous, as the child has to struggle against two diseases at once, or before it has recruited strength from the attack of the first.

2541. *Treatment.*—In all ordinary cases of chicken-pox—and it is very seldom it assumes any complexity—the whole treatment resolves itself into the use of the warm bath, and a course of gentle aperients. The bath should be used when the oppression of the lungs renders the breathing difficult, or the heat and dryness of the skin, with the undeveloped rash beneath the surface, shows the necessity for its use.

2542. As the pustules in chicken-pox very rarely run to the state of suppuration, as in the other disease, there is no fear of *pitting* or disfigurement, except in very severe forms, which, however, happen so seldom as not to merit apprehension. When the eruption subsides, however, the face may be washed with elder-flower water, and the routine followed which is prescribed in the convalescent state of small-pox.

2543. Cow-pox, properly speaking, is an artificial disease, established in a healthy body as a prophylactic, or preventive agent, against the more serious attack of small-pox, and is merely that chain of slight febrile symptoms and local irritation, consequent on the specific action of the lymph of the vaccination, in its action on the circulating system of the body. This is not the place to speak of the benefits conferred on mankind by the discovery of vaccination, not only as the preserver of the human features from a most loathsome disfigurement, but as a sanitary agent in the prolongation of life.

2544. Fortunately the State has now made it imperative on all parents to have their children vaccinated before, or by the end of, the twelfth week; thus doing away, as far as possible, with the danger to public health proceeding from the ignorance or prejudice of those parents whose want of information on the subject makes them object to the employment of this specific preventive; for though vaccination has been proved *not* to be *always* an infallible guard against small-pox, the attack is always much lighter, should it occur, and is seldom, if indeed *ever*, fatal after the precaution of vaccination. The best time to vaccinate a child is after the sixth and before the twelfth week, if it is in perfect health, but still earlier if small-pox is prevalent, and any danger exists of the infant taking the disease. It is customary, and always advisable, to give the child a mild aperient powder one or two days before inserting the lymph in the arm; and should measles, scarlet fever, or any other disease arise during the progress of the pustule, the child, when recovered, should be *re-vaccinated*, and the lymph taken from its arm on no account used for vaccinating purposes.

2545. The disease of cow-pox generally takes twenty days to complete its course; in other words, the maturity and declension of the pustule takes that time to fulfil its several changes. The mode of vaccination is either to insert the matter, or lymph, taken from a healthy child, under the cuticle in several places on both arms, or, which is still better, to make three slight scratches, or abrasions, with a lancet on one arm in this manner, „"„ and work into the irritated parts the lymph, allowing the arm to dry thoroughly before putting down the infant's sleeve ; by this means absorption is insured, and the unnecessary pain of several pustules on both arms avoided. No apparent change is observable by the eye for several days; indeed, not till the fourth, in many cases, is there any evidence of a vesicle ; about the fifth day, however, a pink areola, or circle, is observed round one or all of the places, surrounding a small pearly vesicle or bladder. This goes on deepening in hue till the seventh or eighth day, when the vesicle is about an inch in diameter, with a depressed centre ; on the ninth the edges are elevated, and the surrounding part hard and inflamed. The disease is now at its height, and the pustule should be opened, if not for the purpose of vaccinating other children, to allow the escape of the lymph, and subdue the inflammatory action. After the twelfth day the centre is covered by a brown scab, and the colour of the swelling becomes darker, gradually declining in hardness and colour till the twentieth, when the scab falls off, leaving a small pit, or cicatrix, to mark the seat of the disease, and for life prove a certificate of successful vaccination.

2546. In some children the inflammation and swelling of the arm is excessive, and extremely painful, and the fever, about the ninth or tenth day, very high ; the pustule, therefore, at that time, should sometimes be opened, the arm fomented every two hours with a warm bread poultice, and an aperient powder given to the infant.

MEASLES AND SCARLET FEVER, WITH THE TREATMENT OF BOTH.

Measles.

2547. THIS much-dreaded disease, which forms the next subject in our series of infantine diseases, and which entails more evils on the health of childhood than any other description of physical suffering to which that age of life is subject, may be considered more an affection of the venous circulation, tending to general and local congestion, attended with a diseased condition of the blood, than either as a fever or an inflammation ; and though generally classed before or after scarlet fever, is, in its pathology and treatment, irrespective of its after-consequences, as distinct and opposite as one disease can well be from another.

2548. As we have already observed, measles are always characterized by the running at the nose and eyes, and great oppression of breathing ; so, in the mode of treatment, two objects are to be held especially in view ; first, to unload the congested state of the lungs,—the cause of the oppressed breathing ; and, secondly, to act vigorously, both during the disease and afterwards, on the bowels. At the same time it cannot be too strongly borne in mind, that though the patient in measles should on no account be kept unduly hot, more care than in most infantine complaints should be taken to guard the body from *cold,* or any abrupt changes of temperature. With these special observations, we shall proceed to give a description of the disease, as recognized by its usual—

2549. *Symptoms,* which commence with cold chills and flushes, lassitude, heaviness, pain in the head, and drowsiness, cough, hoarseness, and extreme difficulty of breathing, frequent sneezing, defluction or running at the eyes and nose, nausea, sometimes vomiting, thirst, a furred tongue ; the pulse throughout is quick, and sometimes full and soft, at others hard and small, with other indications of an inflammatory nature.

2550. On the third day, small red points make their appearance, first on the face and neck, gradually extending over the upper and lower part of the body. On the fifth day, the vivid red of the eruption changes into a brownish hue ; and, in two or three days more, the rash entirely disappears, leaving a loose powdery desquamation on the skin, which rubs off like dandriff. At this stage of the disease a diarrhœa frequently comes on, which, being what is called " critical," should never be checked, unless seriously severe. Measles sometimes assume a typhoid or malignant character, in which form the symptoms are all greatly exaggerated, and the case from the first becomes both doubtful and dangerous. In this condition the eruption comes out sooner, and only in patches ; and often, after showing for a few hours, suddenly recedes, presenting, instead of the usual florid red, a dark purple or blackish hue ; a dark brown fur forms on the gums and mouth, the breathing becomes laborious, delirium supervenes, and, if unrelieved, is followed by coma ; a fetid diarrhœa takes place, and the patient sinks under the congested state of the lungs and the oppressed functions of the brain.

2551. The unfavourable symptoms in measles are a high degree of fever, the excessive heat and dryness of the skin, hurried and short breathing, and a particularly hard pulse. The sequelæ, or after-consequences, of measles are, croup, bronchitis, mesenteric disease, abscesses behind the ear, ophthalmia, and glandular swellings in other parts of the body.

2552. *Treatment.*—In the first place, the patient should be kept in a cool room, the temperature of which must be regulated to suit the child's feelings of comfort, and the diet adapted to the strictest principles of abstinence. When the inflammatory symptoms are severe, bleeding, in some form, is often necessary, though, when adopted, it must be in the *first stage* of the disease ; and, if the lungs are the apprehended seat of the inflammation, two or more leeches,. according to the age and strength of the patient, must be applied to the upper part of the chest, followed by a small blister ; or the blister may be substituted for the leeches, the attendant bearing in mind, that the benefit effected by the blister can always be considerably augmented by plunging the feet into very hot water about a couple of hours after applying the blister, and kept in the water for about two minutes. And let it further be remembered, that this immersion of the feet in hot water may be adopted at any time or stage of the disease ; and that, whenever the *head* or *lungs* are oppressed, relief will *always* accrue from its sudden and brief employment. When the symptoms commence with much shivering, and the skin early assumes a hot, dry character, the appearance of the rash will be facilitated, and all the other symptoms rendered milder, if the patient is put into a warm bath, and kept in the water for about three minutes. Or, where that is not convenient, the following process, which will answer quite as well, can be substituted :—Stand the child, naked, in a tub, and, having first prepared several jugs of sufficiently warm water, empty them, in quick succession, over the patient's shoulders and body ; immediately wrap in a hot blanket, and put the child to bed till it rouses from the sleep that always follows the effusion or bath. This agent, by lowering the temperature of the skin, and opening the pores, producing a natural perspiration, and unloading the congested state of the lungs, in most cases does away entirely with the necessity both for leeches and a blister. Whether any of these external means have been employed or not, the first internal remedies should commence with a series of aperient powders and a saline mixture, as prescribed in the following formularies ; at the same time, as a beverage to quench the thirst, let a quantity of barley-water be made, slightly acidulated by the juice of an orange, and partially sweetened by some sugar-candy ; and of which, when properly made and cold, let the patient drink as often as thirst, or the dryness of the mouth, renders necessary.

2553. *Aperient Powders.*—Take of scammony and jalap, each 24 grains ; grey powder and powdered antimony, each 18 grains. Mix and divide into 12 powders, if for a child between two and four years of age ; into 8 powders, if for a child between four and eight years of age ; and into 6 powders for between eight and twelve years. One powder to be given, in a little jelly or sugar-and-water, every three or four hours, according to the severity of the symptoms.

2554. *Saline Mixture.*—Take of mint-water, 6 ounces ; powdered nitre, 20 grains ; antimonial wine, 3 drachms ; spirits of nitre, 2 drachms ; syrup of saffron, 2 drachms. Mix. To children under three years, give a teaspoonful every two hours ; from that age to six, a dessertspoonful at the same times ; and a tablespoonful every three or four hours to children between six and twelve.

2555. The object of these aperient powders is to keep up a steady but gentle action on the bowels ; but, whenever it seems necessary to administer a stronger dose, and effect a brisk action on the digestive organs,—a course particularly imperative towards the close of the disease,—two of these powders given at once, according to the age, will be found to produce that effect ; that is, two of the twelve for a child under four years, and two of the eight, and two of the six, according to the age of the patient.

2556. When the difficulty of breathing becomes oppressive, as it generally does towards night, a hot bran poultice, laid on the chest, will be always found highly beneficial. The diet throughout must be light, and consist of farinaceous food, such as rice and sago puddings, beef-tea and toast ; and not till convalescence sets in should hard or animal food be given.

2557. When measles assume the malignant form, the advice just given must be broken through ; food of a nutritious and stimulating character should be at once substituted, and administered in conjunction with wine, and even spirits, and the disease regarded and treated as a case of typhus. But, as this form of measles is not frequent, and, if occurring, hardly likely to be treated without assistance, it is unnecessary to enter on the minutiæ of its practice here. What we have prescribed, in almost all cases, will be found sufficient to meet every emergency, without resorting to a multiplicity of agents.

2558. The great point to remember in measles is, not to give up the treatment with the apparent subsidence of the disease, as the *after-consequences* of measles are too often *more serious*, and to be more dreaded, than the measles themselves. To guard against this danger, and thoroughly purify the system, after the subsidence of all the symptoms of the disease, a corrective course of medicine, and a regimen of exercise, should be adopted for some weeks after the cure of the disease. To effect this, an active aperient powder should be given every three or four days, with a daily dose of the subjoined tonic mixture, with as much exercise, by walking, running after a hoop, or other bodily exertion, as the strength of the child and the state of the atmosphere will admit, the patient being, wherever possible, removed to a purer air as soon as convalescence warrants the change.

2559. *Tonic Mixture.*—Take of infusion of rose-leaves, 6 ounces ; quinine, 8 grains ; diluted sulphuric acid, 15 drops. Mix. Dose, from half a teaspoonful up to a dessertspoonful, once a day, according to the age of the patient.

Scarlatina, or Scarlet Fever.

2560. Though professional accuracy has divided this disease into several forms, we shall keep to the one disease most generally met with, the common or simple scarlet fever, which, in all cases, is characterized by an excessive heat on the skin, sore throat, and a peculiar speckled appearance of the tongue.

2561. *Symptoms.*—Cold chills, shivering, nausea, thirst, hot skin, quick pulse, with difficulty of swallowing ; the tongue is coated, presenting through its fur innumerable specks, the elevated papillæ of the tongue, which gives it the speckled character, that, if not the invariable sign of scarlet fever, is only met with in cases closely analogous to that disease. Between the *second* and *third* day, but most frequently on the *third*, a bright red efflorescence breaks out in patches on the face, neck, and back, from which it extends over the trunk and extremities, always showing thicker and deeper in colour wherever there is any pressure, such as the elbows, back, and hips ; when the eruption is well out, the skin presents the appearance of a boiled lobster-shell. At first, the skin is smooth, but, as the disease advances, perceptible roughness is apparent, from the elevation of the rash, or, more properly, the pores of the skin. On the *fifth* and *sixth* days the eruption begins to decline, and by the *eighth* has generally entirely disappeared. During the whole of this period, there is, more or less, constant sore throat.

2562. The *Treatment* of scarlet fever is, in general, very simple. Where the heat is great, and the eruption comes out with difficulty, or recedes as soon as it appears, the body should be sponged with cold vinegar-and-water, or tepid water, as in measles, poured over the chest and body, the patient being, as in that disease, wrapped in a blanket and put to bed, and the same powders and mixture ordered in measles administered, with the addition of a constant hot bran poultice round the throat, which should be continued from the first symptom till a day or two after the declension of the rash. The same low diet and cooling drink, with the same general instructions, are to be obeyed in this as in the former disease.

2563. When the fever runs high in the first stage, and there is much nausea, before employing the effusions of water, give the patient an emetic, of equal parts of ipecacuanha and antimonial wine, in doses of from a teaspoonful to a tablespoonful, according to age. By these means, nine out of every ten cases of scarlatina may be safely and expeditiously cured, especially if the temperature of the patient's room is kept at an even standard of about sixty degrees.

HOOPING-COUGH, CROUP, AND DIARRHŒA, WITH THEIR MODE OF TREATMENT.

Hooping-Cough.

2564. THIS is purely a spasmodic disease, and is only infectious through the faculty of imitation, a habit that all children are remarkably apt to fall into ; and even where adults have contracted hooping-cough, it has been from the same cause, and is as readily accounted for, on the principle of imitation, as that the gaping of one person will excite or predispose a whole party to follow the same spasmodic example. If any one associates for a few days with a person who stammers badly, he will find, when released from his company, that the sequence of his articulation and the fluency of his speech are, for a time, gone ; and it will be a matter of constant vigilance, and some difficulty, to overcome the evil of so short an association. The manner in which a number of school-girls will, one after another, fall into a fit on beholding one of their number attacked with epilepsy, must be familiar to many. These several facts lead us to a juster notion of how to treat this spasmodic disease. Every effort should, therefore, be directed, mentally and physically, to break the chain of nervous action, on which the continuance of the cough depends.

2565. *Symptoms.*—Hooping-cough comes on with a slight oppression of breathing, thirst, quick pulse, hoarseness, and a hard, dry cough. This state may exist without any change from one to two or three weeks before the peculiar feature of the disease—the *hoop*—sets in. As the characteristics of this cough are known to all, it is unnecessary to enter here, physiologically, on the subject. We shall, therefore, merely remark that the frequent vomiting and bleeding at the mouth or nose are favourable signs, and proceed to the

2566. *Treatment*, which should consist in keeping up a state of nausea and vomiting. For this purpose, give the child doses of ipecacuanha and antimonial wines, in equal parts, and quantities varying from half to one and a half teaspoonful once a day, or, when the expectoration is hard and difficult of expulsion, giving the following cough mixture every four hours. Take of

Syrup of squills	. . . .	½	ounce.
Antimonial wine	. . .	1	ounce.
Laudanum	. . . .	15	drops.
Syrup of Toulou	. . . .	2	drachms.
Water	. . . .	1½	ounce.

Mix. The dose is from half a spoonful to a dessertspoonful. When the cough is urgent, the warm bath is to be used, and either one or two leeches applied over the breastbone, or else a small blister laid on the lower part of the throat.

2567. Such is the medical treatment of hooping-cough ; but there is a moral regimen, based on the nature of the disease, which should never be omitted. And, on the principle that a sudden start or diversion of the mind will arrest a person in the act of sneezing or gaping, so the like means should be adopted with the hooping-cough patient ; and, in the first stage, before the *hooping* has been added, the parent should endeavour to break the paroxysm of the cough by abruptly attracting the patient's attention, and thus, if possible, preventing the cough from reaching that height when the ingulp of air gives the hoop or crow that marks the disease ; but when once that symptom has set in, it becomes still more necessary to endeavour, by even measures of intimidation, to break the spasmodic chain of the cough. Exercise in the open air, when dry, is also requisite, and change of scene and air in all cases is of absolute necessity, and may be adopted at any stage of the disease.

Croup.

2568. THIS is by far the most formidable and fatal of all the diseases to which infancy and childhood are liable, and is purely an inflammatory affection, attacking that portion of the mucous membrane lining the windpipe and bronchial tubes, and from the effect of which a false or loose membrane is formed along the windpipe, resembling in appearance the finger of a glove suspended in the passage, and, consequently, terminating the life of the patient by suffocation ; for, as the lower end grows together and becomes closed, no air can enter the lungs, and the child dies choked. All dull, fat, and heavy children are peculiarly predisposed to this disease, and those with short necks and who make a wheezing noise in their natural breathing. Croup is always sudden in its attack, and rapid in its career, usually proving fatal within three days ; most frequently commences in the night, and generally attacking children between the ages of three and ten years. Mothers should, therefore, be on their guard who have children predisposed to this disease, and immediately resort to the means hereafter advised.

2569. *Symptoms.*—Languor and restlessness, hoarseness, wheezing, and short, dry cough, with occasional rattling in the throat during sleep, the child often plucking at its throat with its fingers ; difficulty of breathing, which quickly becomes hard and laboured, causing great anxiety of the countenance, and the veins of the neck to swell and become knotted ; the voice in speaking acquires a sharp, crowing, or croupy sound, while the inspirations have a harsh, metallic intonation. After a few hours, a quantity of thick, ropy mucus is thrown out, hanging about the mouth, and causing suffocating fits of coughing to expel.

2570. *Treatment.*—Place the child immediately in a hot bath up to the throat ; and, on removal from the water, give an emetic of the antimonial or ipecacuanha wine, and, when the vomiting has subsided, lay a long blister down the front of the throat, and administer one of the following powders every twenty minutes to a child from three to six years of age.

2571. Take of calomel, 12 grains ; tartar emetic, 2 grains ; lump sugar, 30 grains. Mix accurately, and divide into 12 powders. For a child from six to twelve years, divide into 6 powders, and give one every half-hour.

2572. Should the symptoms remain unabated after a few hours, apply one or two leeches to the throat, and put mustard poultices to the feet and thighs, retaining them about eight minutes ; and, in extreme cases, a mustard poultice to the spine between the shoulders, and at the same time rub mercurial ointment into the armpits and the angles of the jaws.

2573. Such is a vigorous and reliable system of treatment in severe cases of croup ; but, in the milder and more general form, the following abridgment will, in all probability, be all that will be required :—First, the hot bath ; second, the emetic ; third, a mustard plaster round the throat for five minutes ; fourth, the powders ; fifth, another emetic in six hours, if needed, and the powders continued without intermission while the urgency of the symptoms continues. When relief has been obtained, these are to be discontinued, and a dose of senna tea given to act on the bowels.

Diarrhœa.

2574. THE diarrhœa with which children are so frequently affected, especially in infancy, should demand the nurse's immediate attention, and when the secretion, from its clayey colour, indicates an absence of bile, a powder composed of 3 grains of grey powder and 1 grain of rhubarb, should be given twice, with an interval of four hours between each dose, to a child from one to two years, and, a day or two afterwards, an aperient powder containing the same ingredients and quantities, with the addition of 2 or 3 grains of scammony. For the relaxation consequent on an overloaded stomach, or acidity in the bowels, a little magnesia dissolved in milk should be employed two or three times a day.

2575. When much griping and pain attend the diarrhœa, half a teaspoonful of Dalby's Carminative (the best of all patent medicines) should be given, either with or without a small quantity of castor oil to carry off the exciting cause.

2576. For any form of diarrhœa that, by excessive action, demands a speedy correction, the most efficacious remedy that can be employed in all ages and conditions of childhood is the tincture of Kino, of which from 10 to 30 drops, mixed with a little sugar and water in a spoon, are to be given every two or three hours till the undue action has been checked. Often the change of diet to rice, milk, eggs, or the substitution of animal for vegetable food, or vice versâ, will correct an unpleasant and almost chronic state of diarrhœa.

2577. A very excellent carminative powder for flatulent infants may be kept in the house, and employed with advantage, whenever the child is in pain or griped, by dropping 5 grains of oil of aniseed and 2 of peppermint on half an ounce of lump sugar, and rubbing it in a mortar, with a drachm of magnesia, into a fine powder. A small quantity of this may be given in a little water at any time, and always with benefit.

THE DOCTOR.

—◦◇◦—

CHAPTER XLIII.

2578. "Time," according to the old proverb, "is money;" and it may also, in many cases, and with equal truthfulness, be said to be life; for a few moments, in great emergencies, often turn the balance between recovery and death. This applies more especially to all kinds of poisoning, fits, submersion in water, or exposure to noxious gases; and many accidents. If people knew how to act during the interval that must necessarily elapse from the moment that a medical man is sent for until he arrives, many lives might be saved, which now, unhappily, are lost. Generally speaking, however, nothing is done—all is confusion and fright; and the surgeon, on his arrival, finds that death has already seized its victim, who, had his friends but known a few rough rules for their guidance, might have been rescued. We shall, therefore, in a series of papers, give such information as to the means to be employed in event of accidents, injuries, &c., as, by the aid of a gentleman of large professional experience, we are warranted in recommending.

List of Drugs, &c., necessary to carry out all Instructions.

2579. We append at once A LIST OF DRUGS, &c., and a few PRESCRIPTIONS necessary to carry out all the instructions given in this series of articles. It will be seen that they are few—they are not expensive; and by laying in a little stock of them, our instructions will be of instant value in all cases of accident, &c.—The drugs are—Antimonial Wine. Antimonial Powder. Blister Compound. Blue Pill. Calomel. Carbonate of Potash. Compound Iron Pills. Compound Extract of Colocynth. Compound Tincture of Camphor. Epsom Salts. Goulard's Extract. Jalap in Powder. Linseed Oil. Myrrh and Aloes Pills. Nitre. Oil of Turpentine. Opium, powdered, and Laudanum. Sal Ammoniac. Senna Leaves. Soap Liniment, Opodeldoc. Sweet Spirits of Nitre. Turner's Cerate.—To which should be added: Common Adhesive Plaster. Isinglass Plaster. Lint. A pair of small Scales with Weights. An ounce and a drachm Measure-glass. A Lancet. A Probe. A pair of Forceps, and some curved Needles.

2580. The following PRESCRIPTIONS may be made up for a few shillings; and, by keeping them properly labelled, and by referring to the remarks on the treatment of any particular case, much suffering, and, perhaps, some lives, may be saved.

2581. *Draught.*—Twenty grains of sulphate of zinc in an ounce and a half of water. This draught is to be repeated in a quarter of an hour if vomiting does not take place.

2582. *Clyster.*—Two tablespoonfuls of oil of turpentine in a pint of warm gruel.

2583. *Liniments.*—1. Equal parts of lime-water and linseed-oil well mixed together. [Lime-water is made thus : Pour 6 pints of boiling water upon ¼ lb. of lime ; mix well together, and when cool, strain the liquid from off the lime which has fallen to the bottom, taking care to get it as clear as possible.] 2. Compound camphor liniment.

2584. *Lotions.*—1. Mix a dessert-spoonful of Goulard's extract and 2 tablespoonfuls of vinegar in a pint of water.—2. Mix ½ oz. of sal-ammoniac, 2 tablespoonfuls of vinegar, and the same quantity of gin or whisky, in half a pint of water.

2585. *Goulard Lotion.*—1 drachm of sugar of lead, 2 pints of rain-water, 2 teaspoonfuls of spirits of wine. For inflammation of the eyes or else-where :—The better way of making Goulard Lotion, if for the eyes, is to add to 6 oz. of distilled water, or water that has been well boiled, 1 drachm of the extract of lead.

2586. *Opodeldoc.* — This lotion being a valuable application for sprains, lumbago, weakness of joints, &c., and it being difficult to procure either pure or freshly made, we give a recipe for its preparation. Dissolve 1 oz. of camphor in a pint of rectified spirits of wine ; then dissolve 4 oz. of hard white Spanish soap, scraped thin, in 4 oz. of oil of rosemary, and mix them together.

2587. *The Common Black Draught.*—Infusion of senna 10 drachms ; Epsom salts 10 drachms ; tincture of senna, compound tincture -of cardamums, compound spirit of lavender, of each 1 drachm. Families who make black draught in quantity, and wish to preserve it for some time without spoiling, should add about 2 drachms of spirits of hartshorn to each pint of the strained mixture, the use of this drug being to prevent its becoming mouldy or decom-posed. A simpler and equally efficacious form of black draught is made by infusing ½ oz. of Alexandrian senna, 3 oz. of Epsom salts, and 2 drachms of bruised ginger and coriander-seeds, for several hours in a pint of boiling water, straining the liquor, and adding either 2 drachms of sal-volatile or spirits of hartshorn to the whole, and giving 3 tablespoonfuls for a dose to an adult.

2588. *Mixtures*—1. *Aperient.*—Dissolve an ounce of Epsom salts in half a pint of senna tea : take a quarter of the mixture as a dose, and repeat it in three or four hours if necessary.

2589. 2. *Fever Mixture.*—Mix a drachm of powdered nitre, 2 drachms of carbonate of potash, 2 teaspoonfuls of antimonial wine, and a tablespoonful of sweet spirits of nitre, in half a pint of water.

2590. 3. *Myrrh and Aloes Pills.*—Ten grains made into two pills are the dose for a full-grown person.

2591. 4. *Compound Iron Pills.*—Dose for a full-grown person: 10 grains made into two pills.

2592. *Pills.*—1. Mix 5 grains of calomel and the same quantity of antimonial powder with a little bread-crumb, and make into two pills. Dose for a full-grown person: two pills.—2. Mix 5 grains of blue pill and the same quantity of compound extract of colocynth together, and make into two pills, the dose for a full-grown person.

2593. *Powders.*—Mix a grain of calomel and 4 grains of powdered jalap together.

2594. In all cases, the dose of medicines given is to be regulated by the age of the patient.

2595. *Abernethy's Plan for making a Bread-and-Water Poultice.*—First scald out a basin; then having put in some boiling water, throw in coarsely-crumbled bread, and cover it with a plate. When the bread has soaked up as much water as it will imbibe, drain off the remaining water, and there will be left a light pulp. Spread it a third of an inch thick on folded linen, and apply it when of the temperature of a warm bath. To preserve it moist, occasionally drop warm water on it.

2596. *Linseed-Meal Poultice.*—"Scald your basin, by pouring a little hot water into it; then put a small quantity of finely-ground linseed-meal into the basin, pour a little hot water on it, and stir it round briskly until you have well incorporated them; add a little more meal and a little more water; then stir it again. Do not let any lumps remain in the basin, but stir the poultice well, and do not be sparing of your trouble. What you do next, is to take as much of it out of the basin as you may require, lay it on a piece of soft linen, and let it be about a quarter of an inch thick."—*Abernethy.*

2597. *Mustard Poultice.*—Mix equal parts of dry mustard and linseed-meal in warm vinegar. When the poultice is wanted weak, warm water may be used for the vinegar; and when it is required very strong, mustard alone, without any linseed-meal, is to be mixed with warm vinegar.

2598. *An ordinary Blister.*—Spread a little blister compound on a piece of common adhesive plaster with the right thumb. It should be put on just thickly enough to conceal the appearance of the plaster beneath. The part from which a blister has been taken should be covered till it heals over with soft linen rags smeared with lard.

Baths and Fomentations.

2599. All fluid applications to the body are exhibited either in a hot or cold form ; and the object for which they are administered is to produce a stimulating effect over the entire, or a part, of the system ; for the effect, though differently obtained, and varying in degree, is the same in principle, whether procured by hot or cold water.

2600. *Heat.*—There are three forms in which heat is universally applied to the body,—that of the tepid, warm, and vapour bath ; but as the first is too inert to be worth notice, and the last dangerous and inapplicable, except in public institutions, we shall confine our remarks to the really efficacious and always attainable one—the

2601. *Warm and Hot Bath.*—These baths are used whenever there is congestion, or accumulation of blood in the internal organs, causing pain, difficulty of breathing, or stupor, and are employed, by their stimulating property, to cause a rush of blood to the surface, and, by unloading the great organs, produce a temporary inflammation in the skin, and so equalize the circulation. The effect of the hot bath is to increase the fulness of the pulse, accelerate respiration, and excite perspiration. In all inflammations of the stomach and bowels, the hot bath is of the utmost consequence ; the temperature of the warm bath varies from 92° to 100°, and may be obtained by those who have no thermometer to test the exact heat, by mixing one measure of boiling with two of cold water.

2602. *Fomentations* are generally used to effect, in a part, the benefit produced on the whole body by the bath ; to which a sedative action is occasionally given by the use of roots, herbs, or other ingredients ; the object being to relieve the internal organ, as the throat, or muscles round a joint, by exciting a greater flow of blood to the skin *over* the affected part. As the real agent of relief is heat, the fomentation should always be as hot as it can comfortably be borne, and, to insure effect, should be repeated every half-hour. Warm fluids are applied in order to render the swelling which accompanies inflammation less painful, by the greater readiness with which the skin yields, than when it is harsh and dry. They are of various kinds ; but the most simple, and oftentimes the most useful, that can be employed, is "Warm Water." Another kind of fomentation is composed of dried poppyheads, 4 oz. Break them to pieces, empty out the seeds, put them into 4 pints of water, boil for a quarter of an hour, then strain through a cloth or sieve, and keep the water for use. Or, chamomile flowers, hemlock, and many other plants, may be boiled, and the part fomented with the hot liquor, by means of flannels wetted with the decoction.

2603. *Cold*, when applied in excess to the body, drives the blood from the surface to the centre, reduces the pulse, makes the breathing hard and difficult, produces coma, and, if long continued, death. But when medicinally used, it excites a reaction on the surface equivalent to a stimulating effect ; as in some cases of fever, when the body has been sponged with cold water, it excites, by reaction, increased circulation on the skin. Cold is sometimes used to keep up a repellent action, as, when local inflammation takes place, a remedy is applied, which, by its benumbing and astringent effect, causes the blood, or the excess of it in the part, to recede, and, by contracting the vessels, prevents the return of any undue quantity, till the affected part recovers its tone. Such remedies are called *Lotions*, and should, when used, be applied with the same persistency as the fomentation ; for, as the latter should be renewed as often as the heat passes off, so the former should be applied as often as the heat from the skin deprives the application of its cold.

2604. *Poultices* are only another form of fomentation, though chiefly used for abscesses. The ingredient best suited for a poultice is that which retains heat the longest ; of these ingredients, the best are linseed - meal, bran, and bread. Bran sewed into a bag, as it can be reheated, will be found the cleanest and most useful ; especially for sore throats.

How to Bleed.

2605. In cases of great emergency, such as the strong kind of apoplexy, and when a surgeon cannot possibly be obtained for some considerable time, the life of the patient depends almost entirely upon the fact of his being bled or not. We therefore give instructions how the operation of bleeding is to be performed, but caution the reader only to attempt it in cases of the greatest emergency. Place a handkerchief or piece of tape rather but not too tightly round the arm, about three or four inches above the elbow. This will cause the veins below to swell and become very evident. If this is not sufficient, the hand should be constantly and quickly opened and shut for the same purpose. There will now be seen, passing up the middle of the fore-arm, a vein which, just below the bend of the elbow, sends a branch inwards and outwards, each branch shortly joining another large vein. It is from the *outer* branch that the person is to be bled. The right arm is the one mostly operated on. The operator should take the lancet in his right hand, between the thumb and first finger, place the thumb of his left hand on the vein below the part where he is going to bleed from, and then gently thrust the tip of the lancet into the vein, and, taking care not to push it too deeply, cut in a gently curved direction, thus ⌣ and bring it out, point upwards, at about half an inch from the part of the vein into which he had thrust it. The vein must be cut lengthways, and not across. When sufficient blood has been taken away, remove the bandage from above the elbow, and place the thumb of the left hand firmly over the cut, until all the bleeding ceases. A small pad of lint is then to be put over the cut, with a larger pad over it, and the two kept in their places by means of a handkerchief or linen roller bound pretty tightly over them and round the arm.

2606. When a person is bled, he should always be in the standing, or at any rate in the sitting, position ; for if, as is often the case, he should happen to faint, he can, in most cases at least, easily be brought to again by the operator placing him flat on his back, and stopping the bleeding. *This is of the greatest importance.* It has been recommended, for what supposed advantages we don't know, to bleed people when they are lying down. Should a person, under these circumstances, faint, what could be done to bring him to again? The great treatment of lowering the body of the patient to the flat position cannot be followed here. It is in that position already, and cannot be placed lower than it at present is—except, as is most likely to be the case, under the ground.

2607. BLEEDING FROM THE NOSE.—Many children, especially those of a sanguineous temperament, are subject to sudden discharges of blood from some part of the body ; and as all such fluxes are in general the result of an effort of nature to relieve the system from some overload or pressure, such discharges, unless in excess, and when likely to produce debility, should not be rashly or too abruptly checked. In general, these discharges are confined to the summer or spring months of the year, and follow pains in the head, a sense of drowsiness, languor, or oppression ; and, as such symptoms are relieved by the loss of blood, the hemorrhage should, to a certain extent, be encouraged. When, however, the bleeding is excessive, or returns too frequently, it becomes necessary to apply means to subdue or mitigate the amount. For this purpose the sudden and unexpected application of cold is itself sufficient, in most cases, to arrest the most active hemorrhage. A wet towel laid suddenly on the back, between the shoulders, and placing the child in a recumbent posture, is often sufficient to effect the object ; where, however, the effusion resists such simple means, napkins wrung out of cold water must be laid across the forehead and nose, the hands dipped in cold water, and a bottle of hot water applied to the feet. If, in spite of these means, the bleeding continues, a little fine wool or a few folds of lint, tied together by a piece of thread, must be pushed up the nostril from which the blood flows, to act as a plug and pressure on the bleeding vessel. When the discharge has entirely ceased, the plug is to be pulled out by means of the thread. To prevent a repetition of the hemorrhage, the body should be sponged every morning with cold water, and the child put under a course of steel wine, have open-air exercise, and, if possible, salt-water bathing. For children, a key suddenly dropped down the back between the skin and clothes, will often immediately arrest a copious bleeding.

2608. SPITTING OF BLOOD, or hemorrhage from the lungs, is generally known from blood from the stomach by its being of a brighter colour, and in less quantities than that, which is always grumous and mixed with the half-digested food. In either case, rest should be immediately enjoined, total abstinence from stimulants, and a low, poor diet, accompanied with the horizontal position, and bottles of boiling water to the feet. At the same time the patient should suck through a quill, every hour, half a wine-glass of water in which 10 or 15 drops of the elixir of vitriol has been mixed, and, till further advice has been procured, keep a towel wrung out of cold water on the chest or stomach, according to the seat of the hemorrhage.

Bites and Stings.

2609. BITES AND STINGS may be divided into three kinds :—1. Those of Insects. 2. Those of Snakes. 3. Those of Dogs and other Animals.

2610. 1. *The Bites or Stings of Insects,* such as gnats, bees, wasps, &c., need cause very little alarm, and are, generally speaking, easily cured. They are very serious, however, when they take place on some delicate part of the body, such as near the eye, or in the throat. *The treatment* is very simple in most cases ; and consists in taking out the sting, if it is left behind, with a needle, and applying to the part a liniment made of finely-scraped chalk and olive-oil, mixed together to about the thickness of cream.

2611. Bathing the part bitten with warm turpentine or warm vinegar is also of great use. If the person feels faint, he should lie quietly on his back, and take a little brandy-and-water, or sal-volatile and water. When the inside of the throat is the part stung, there is great danger of violent inflam- mation taking place. In this case, from eight to twelve leeches should be immediately put to the outside of the throat, and when they drop off, the part to which they had been applied should be well fomented with warm water. The inside of the throat is to be constantly gargled with salt and water. Bits of ice are to be sucked. Rubbing the face and hands well over with plain olive-oil, before going to bed, will often keep gnats and musquitoes from biting during the night. Strong scent, such as eau-de-Cologne, will have the same effect.

2612. 2. *Bites of Snakes.*—These are much more dangerous than the pre- ceding, and require more powerful remedies. The bites of the different kinds of snakes do not all act alike, but affect people in different ways.—*Treatment of the part bitten.* The great thing is to prevent the poison getting into the blood ; and, if possible, to remove the whole of it at once from the body. A pocket-handkerchief, a piece of tape or cord, or, in fact, of anything that is at hand, should be tied tightly round the part of the body bitten ; if it be the leg or arm, immediately *above* the bite, and between it and the heart. The bite should then be sucked several times by any one who is near. There is no danger in this, provided the person who does it has not got the skin taken off any part of his mouth. What has been sucked into the mouth should be immediately spit out again. But if those who are near have suffi- cient nerve for the operation, and a suitable instrument, they should cut out the central part bitten, and then bathe the wound for some time with warm water, to make it bleed freely. The wound should afterwards be rubbed with a stick of lunar caustic, or, what is better, a solution of this—60 grains of lunar caustic dissolved in an ounce of water—should be dropped into it. The band should be kept on the part during the whole of the time that these means are being adopted. The wound should afterwards be covered with lint dipped in cold water. The best plan, however, to be adopted, if it can be managed, is the following :—take a common wine-glass, and, holding it upside down, put a lighted candle or a spirit-lamp into it for a minute or two. This will take out the air. Then clap the glass suddenly over the bitten part, and it will become attached, and hold on to the flesh. The glass being nearly empty, the blood containing the poison will, in consequence, flow into it from the wound of its own accord. This process should be repeated three or four times, and the wound sucked, or washed with warm water, before each application of the glass. As a matter of course, when the glass is removed, all the blood should be washed out of it before it is applied again.—*Constitutional Treatment.* There is mostly at first great depression of strength in these cases, and it is therefore requisite to give some stimulant ; a glass of hot brandy-and-water, or twenty drops of sal-volatile, is the best that can be given. When the strength has returned, and if the patient has not already been sick, a little mustard in hot water should be given, to make him so. If, on the other hand, as is often the case, the vomiting is excessive, a large mustard poultice should be placed over the stomach, and a grain of solid opium swallowed in the form of a pill, for the purpose of stopping it. Only one of these pills should be given by a non-professional person. In all cases of bites from snakes, send for a surgeon as quickly as possible, and act according to the above directions until he arrives. If he is within any reasonable distance, content yourself by putting on the band, sucking the wound, applying the glass, and, if necessary, giving a little brandy-and-water.

2613. 3. *Bites of Dogs.*—For obvious reasons, these kinds of bites are more frequently met with than those of snakes. *The treatment* is the same as that for snake-bites, more especially that of the bitten part. The majority of writers on the subject are in favour of keeping the wound open as long as possible. This may be done by putting a few beans on it, and then by applying a large linseed-meal poultice over them.

Injuries and Accidents to Bones.

2614. *Dislocation of Bones.*—When the end of a bone is pushed out of its natural position, it is said to be dislocated. This may be caused by violence, disease, or natural weakness of the parts about a joint.—*Symptoms.* Deformity about the joint, with unnatural prominence at one part, and depression at another. The limb may be shorter or longer than usual, and is stiff and unable to be moved, differing in these last two respects from a broken limb, which is mostly shorter, never longer, than usual, and which is always more movable.—*Treatment.* So much practical science and tact are requisite in order to bring a dislocated bone into its proper position again, that we strongly advise the reader never to interfere in these cases ; unless, indeed, it is altogether impossible to obtain the services of a surgeon. But because any one of us may very possibly be placed in that emergency, we give a few rough rules for the reader's guidance. In the first place make the joint, from which the bone has been displaced, perfectly steady, either by fixing it to some firm object or else by holding it with the hands; then pull the dislocated bone in a direction towards the place from which it has been thrust, so that, if it moves at all from its unnatural position, it may have the best chance of returning to its proper place. Do not, however, pull or press against the parts too violently, as you may, perhaps, by doing so, rupture blood-vessels, and produce most serious consequences. When you *do* attempt to reduce a dislocated bone, do it as quickly as possible after the accident has taken place, every hour making the operation more difficult. When the patient is very strong, he may be put into a warm bath until he feels faint, or have sixty drops of antimonial wine given him every ten minutes until he feels sickish. These two means are of great use in relaxing the muscles. If the bone has been brought back again to its proper place, keep it there by means of bandages; and if there is much pain about the joint, apply a cold lotion to it, and keep it perfectly at rest. The lotion should be, a dessert-spoonful of Goulard's extract, and two table-spoonfuls of vinegar, mixed in a pint of water. Leeches are sometimes necessary. Unless the local pain, or general feverish symptoms, are great, the patient's diet should be the same as usual. Dislocations may be reduced a week, or even a fortnight, after they have taken place. As, therefore, although the sooner a bone is reduced the better, there is no very great emergency, and as the most serious consequences may follow improper or too violent treatment, it is always better for people in these cases to do too little than too much; inasmuch as the good which has not yet may still be done, whereas the evil that *has* been done cannot so easily be undone.

2615. FRACTURES OF BONES.—*Symptoms.* 1. Deformity of the part. 2. Unnatural looseness. 3. A grating sound when the two ends of the broken bone are rubbed together. 4. Loss of natural motion and power. In some cases there is also shortening of the limb.—Fracture takes place from several causes, as a fall, a blow, a squeeze, and sometimes from the violent action of muscles.—*Treatment.* In cases where a surgeon cannot be procured immediately after the accident, the following general rules are offered for the reader's guidance:—The broken limb should be placed and kept as nearly as possible in its natural position. This is to be done by first pulling the two portions of the bone in opposite directions, until the limb becomes as long as the opposite one, and then by applying a splint, and binding it to the part by means of a roller. When there is no deformity, the pulling is of course unnecessary. If there is much swelling about the broken part, a cold lotion is to be applied. This lotion (*which we will call Lotion No.* 1) may be thus made:—Mix a dessert-spoonful of Goulard's extract and two tablespoonfuls of vinegar in a pint of water. When the leg or arm is broken, always, if possible, get it to the same length and form as the opposite limb. The broken part should be kept perfectly quiet. When a broken limb is deformed, and a particular muscle is on the stretch, place the limb in such a position as will relax it. This will in most cases cure the deformity. Brandy-and-water, or sal-volatile and water, are to be given when the patient is faint. Surgical aid should, of course, be procured as soon as possible.

2616. JOINTS, INJURIES TO.—All kinds of injuries to joints, of whatever description, require particular attention, in consequence of the violent inflammations which are so liable to take place in these parts of the body, and which do so much mischief in a little time. The joint injured should always be kept perfectly at rest ; and when it is very painful, and the skin about it red, swollen, hot, and shining, at the same time that the patient has general feverish symptoms, such as great thirst and headache—leeches, and when they drop off, warm poppy fomentations, are to be applied ; the No. 1 pills abovementioned are to be given (two are a dose for a grown person) with a black draught three hours afterwards. Give also two tablespoonfuls of the fever-mixture every four hours, and keep the patient on low diet. When the injury and swelling are not very great, warm applications, with rest, low diet, and a dose of aperient medicine, will be sufficient. When a joint has received a penetrating wound, it will require the most powerful treatment, and can only be properly attended to by a surgeon. The patient's friends will have to use their own judgment to a great extent in these and in many other cases, as to when leeches, fever-mixture, &c., are necessary. A universal rule, however, without a single exception, *is always to rest a joint well* after it has been injured in any way whatever, to purge the patient, and to keep him on low diet, without beer, unless he has been a very great drinker indeed, in which case he may still be allowed to take a little ; for if the stimulant that a person has been accustomed to in excess be all taken away at once, he is very likely to have an attack of delirium tremens. The quantity given should not, however, be much—say a pint, or, at the most, a pint and a half a day. Rubbing the joint with opodeldoc, or the application of a blister to it, is of great service in taking away the thickenings, which often remain after all heat, pain, and redness have left an injured joint. Great care should be observed in not using a joint too quickly after it has been injured. When the shoulder-joint is the one injured, the arm should be bound tightly to the body by means of a linen or flannel roller, and the elbow raised ; when the elbow, it should be kept raised in the straight position, on a pillow ; when the wrist, it should be raised on the chest, and suspended in a sling ; when the knee, it should be kept in the straight position ; and, lastly, when the ankle, it should be a little raised on a pillow.

2617. BRUISES, LACERATIONS, AND CUTS.—Wherever the bruise may be, or however swollen or discoloured the skin may become, two or three applications of the *extract of lead,* kept to the part by means of lint, will, in an hour or little more, remove all pain, swelling, and tenderness. Simple or clean cuts only require the edges of the wound to be placed in their exact situation, drawn close together, and secured there by one or two slips of adhesive plaster. When the wound, however, is jagged, or the flesh or cuticle lacerated, the parts are to be laid as smooth and regular as possible, and a piece of lint, wetted in the *extract of lead,* laid upon the wound, and a piece of greased lint placed above it to prevent the dressing sticking ; the whole covered over to protect from injury, and the part dressed in the same manner once a day till the cure is effected.

2618. BRUISES AND THEIR TREATMENT.—The best application for a bruise, be it large or small, is moist warmth ; therefore, a warm bread-and-water poultice in hot moist flannels should be put on, as they supple the skin. If the bruise be very severe, and in the neighbourhood of a joint, it will be well to apply ten or a dozen leeches over the whole bruised part, and afterwards a poultice. But leeches should not be put on young children. If the bruised part be the knee or the ankle, walking should not be attempted till it can be performed without pain. Inattention to this point often lays the foundation for serious mischief in these joints, especially in the case of scrofulous persons. In all conditions of bruises occurring in children, whether swellings or abrasions, no remedy is so quick or certain of effecting a cure as the pure extract of lead applied to the part.

Burns and Scalds.

2619. BURNS AND SCALDS being essentially the same in all particulars, and differing only in the manner of their production, may be spoken of together. As a general rule, scalds are less severe than burns, because the heat of water, by which scalds are mostly produced, is not, even when it is boiling, so intense as that of flame ; oil, however, and other liquids, whose boiling-point is high, produce scalds of a very severe nature. Burns and scalds have been divided into three classes. The first class comprises those where the burn is altogether superficial, and merely reddens the skin ; the second, where the injury is greater, and we get little bladders containing a fluid (called serum) dotted over the affected part ; in the third class we get, in the case of burns, a charring, and in that of scalds, a softening or pulpiness, perhaps a complete and immediate separation of the part. This may occur at once, or in the course of a little time. The pain from the second kind of burns is much more severe than that in the other two, although the danger, as a general rule, is less than it is in the third class. These injuries are much more dangerous when they take place on the trunk than when they happen on the arms or legs. The danger arises more from the extent of surface that is burnt than from the depth to which the burn goes. This rule, of course, has certain exceptions ; because a small burn on the chest or belly penetrating deeply is more dangerous than a more extensive but superficial one on the arm or leg. When a person's clothes are in flames, the best way of extinguishing them is to wind a rug, or some thick material, tightly round the whole of the body.

2620. *Treatment of the First Class of Burns and Scalds. — Of the part affected.*—Cover it immediately with a good coating of common flour, or cotton-wool with flour dredged well into it. The great thing is to keep the affected surface of the skin from the contact of the air. The part will shortly get well, and the skin may or may not peel off.—*Constitutional Treatment.* If the burn or scald is not extensive, and there is no prostration of strength, this is very simple, and consists in simply giving a little aperient medicine— pills (No. 2), as follows :—Mix 5 grains of blue pill and the same quantity of compound extract of colocynth, and make into two pills—the dose for a full-grown person. Three hours after the pills give a black draught. If there are general symptoms of fever, such as hot skin, thirst, headache, &c. &c., two tablespoonfuls of fever-mixture are to be given every four hours. The fever-mixture, we remind our readers, is made thus :—Mix a drachm of powdered nitre, 2 drachms of carbonate of potash, 2 teaspoonfuls of antimonial wine, and a tablespoonful of sweet spirits of nitre, in half a pint of water.

2621. *Second Class.   Local Treatment.*—As the symptoms of these kinds of burns are more severe than those of the first class, so the remedies appropriate to them are more powerful. Having, as carefully as possible, removed the clothes from the burnt surface, and taking care not to break the bladders, spread the following liniment (No. 1) on a piece of linen or lint—not the *fluffy* side—and apply it to the part : the liniment should be equal parts of lime-water and linseed-oil, well mixed. If the burn is on the trunk of the body, it is better to use a warm linseed-meal poultice. After a few days dress the wound with Turner's cerate. If the burn is at the bend of the elbow, place the arm in the *straight* position ; for if it is *bent,* the skin, when healed, will be contracted, and the arm, in all probability, always remain in the same unnatural position. This, indeed, applies to all parts of the body ; therefore, always place the part affected in the most *stretched* position possible. — *Constitutional Treatment.* The same kind of treatment is to be used as for the first class, only it must be more powerful. Stimulants are more often necessary, but must be given with great caution. If, as is often the case, there is great irritability and restlessness, a dose of opium (paregoric, in doses of from sixty to a hundred drops, according to age, is best) is of great service. The feverish symptoms will require aperient medicines and the fever-mixture. A drink made of about a tablespoonful of cream of tartar and a little lemon-juice, in a quart of warm water, allowed to cool, is a very nice one in these cases. The diet throughout should not be too low, especially if there is much discharge from the wound. After a few days it is often necessary to give wine, ammonia, and strong beef-tea. These should be had recourse to when the tongue gets dry and dark, and the pulse weak and frequent. If there should be, after the lapse of a week or two, pain over one particular part of the belly, a blister should be put on it, and a powder of mercury and chalk— grey powder, and Dover's powder (two grains of the former and five of the latter) given three times a day. Affections of the head and chest also frequently occur as a consequence of these kinds of burns, but no one who is not a medical man can treat them.

2622. *Third Class.*—These are so severe as to make it impossible for a non-professional person to be of much service in attending to them. When they occur, a surgeon should always be sent for. Until he arrives, however, the following treatment should be adopted:—Place the patient full-length on his back, and keep him warm. Apply fomentations of flannels wrung out of boiling water and sprinkled with spirits of turpentine to the part, and give wine and sal-volatile in such quantities as the prostration of strength requires ; always bearing in mind the great fact that you have to steer between two quicksands—death from present prostration and death from future excitement, which will always be increased in proportion to the amount of stimulants given. Give, therefore, only just as much as is absolutely necessary to keep life in the body.

2623. CONCUSSION OF BRAIN—STUNNING.—This may be caused by a blow or a fall.—*Symptoms.* Cold skin ; weak pulse ; almost total insensibility ; slow, weak breathing ; pupil of eye sometimes bigger, sometimes smaller, than natural ; inability to move ; unwillingness to answer when spoken to. These symptoms come on directly after the accident.—*Treatment.* Place the patient quietly on a warm bed, send for a surgeon, *and do nothing else for the first four or six hours.* After this time the skin will become hot, the pulse full, and the patient feverish altogether. If the surgeon has not arrived by the time these symptoms have set in, shave the patient's head, and apply the following lotion (No. 2) : Mix half an ounce of sal-ammoniac, two tablespoonfuls of vinegar, and the same quantity of gin or whisky, in half a pint of water. Then give this pill (No. 1) : Mix five grains of calomel and the same quantity of antimonial powder with a little bread-crumb, and make into two pills. Give a black draught three hours after the pill, and two tablespoonfuls of the above-mentioned fever-mixture every four hours. Keep on low diet. Leeches are sometimes to be applied to the head. These cases are often followed by violent inflammation of the brain. They can, therefore, only be attended to properly throughout by a surgeon. The great thing for people to do in these cases is—nothing ; contenting themselves with putting the patient to bed, and waiting the arrival of a surgeon.

2624. THE CHOLERA AND AUTUMNAL COMPLAINTS.—To oppose cholera, there seems no surer or better means than cleanliness, sobriety, and judicious ventilation. Where there is dirt, that is the place for cholera ; where windows and doors are kept most jealously shut, there cholera will find easiest entrance ; and people who indulge in intemperate diet during the hot days of autumn are actually courting death. To repeat it, cleanliness, sobriety, and free ventilation almost always defy the pestilence ; but, in case of attack, immediate recourse should be had to a physician. The faculty say that a large number of lives have been lost, in many seasons, solely from delay in seeking medical assistance. They even assert that, taken early, the cholera is by no means a fatal disorder. The copious use of salt is recommended on very excellent authority. Other autumnal complaints there are, of which diarrhœa is the worst example. They come on with pain, flatulence, sickness, with or without vomiting, followed by loss of appetite, general lassitude, and weakness. If attended to at the first appearance, they may soon be conquered ; for which purpose it is necessary to assist nature in throwing off the contents of the bowels, which may be done by means of the following prescription :—Take of calomel 3 grains, rhubarb 8 grains ; mix and take it in a little honey or jelly, and repeat the dose three times, at the intervals of four or five hours. The next purpose to be answered is the defence of the lining membrane of the intestines from their acrid contents, which will be best effected by drinking copiously of linseed tea, or of a drink made by pouring boiling water on quince-seeds, which are of a very mucilaginous nature ; or, what is still better, full draughts of whey. If the complaint continue after these means have been employed, some astringent or binding medicine will be required, as the sub-joined :—Take of prepared chalk 2 drachms, cinnamon-water 7 oz., syrup of poppies 1 oz. ; mix, and take 3 tablespoonfuls every four hours. Should this fail to complete the cure, ½ oz. of tincture of catechu, or of kino, may be added to it, and then it will seldom fail ; or a teaspoonful of the tincture of kino alone, with a little water, every three hours, till the diarrhœa is checked. While any symptoms of derangement are present, particular attention must be paid to the diet, which should be of a soothing, lubricating, and light nature, as instanced in veal or chicken broth, which should contain but little salt. Rice, batter, and bread puddings will be generally relished, and be eaten with advantage ; but the stomach is too much impaired to digest food of a more solid nature. Indeed, we should give that organ, together with the bowels, as little trouble as possible, while they are so incapable of acting in their accustomed manner. Much mischief is frequently produced by the absurd practice of taking tincture of rhubarb, which is almost certain of aggravating that species of disorder of which we have now treated ; for it is a spirit as strong as brandy, and cannot fail of producing harm upon a surface which is rendered tender by the formation and contact of vitiated bile. But our last advice is, upon the first appearance of such symptoms as are above detailed, have *immediate* recourse to a doctor, where possible.

2625. To Cure a Cold.—Put a large teacupful of linseed, with ¼ lb. of sun raisins and 2 oz. of stick liquorice, into 2 quarts of soft water, and let it simmer over a slow fire till reduced to one quart ; add to it ¼ lb. of pounded sugar-candy, a tablespoonful of old rum, and a tablespoonful of the best white-wine vinegar, or lemon-juice. The rum and vinegar should be added as the de-coction is taken ; for, if they are put in at first, the whole soon becomes flat and less efficacious. The dose is half a pint, made warm, on going to bed ; and a little may be taken whenever the cough is troublesome. The worst cold is generally cured by this remedy in two or three days ; and, if taken in time, is considered infallible.

2626. Cold on the Chest.—A flannel dipped in boiling water, and sprinkled with turpentine, laid on the chest as quickly as possible, will relieve the most severe cold or hoarseness.

2627. Substances in the Eye.—To remove fine particles of gravel, lime,

&c., the eye should be syringed with lukewarm water till free from them. Be particular not to worry the eye, under the impression that the substance is still there, which the enlargement of some of the minute vessels makes the patient believe is actually the case.

2628. SORE EYES.—Incorporate thoroughly, in a glass mortar or vessel, one part of strong citron ointment with three parts of spermaceti ointment. Use the mixture night and morning, by placing a piece of the size of a pea in the corner of the eye affected, only to be used in cases of chronic or long-standing inflammation of the organ, or its lids.

2629. LIME IN THE EYE.—Bathe the eye with a little weak vinegar-and-water, and carefully remove any little piece of lime which may be seen, with a feather. If any lime has got entangled in the eyelashes, carefully clear it away with a bit of soft linen soaked in vinegar-and-water. Violent inflammation is sure to follow ; a smart purge must be therefore administered, and in all probability a blister must be applied on the temple, behind the ear, or nape of the neck.

2630. STYE IN THE EYE.—Styes are little abscesses which form between the roots of the eyelashes, and are rarely larger than a small pea. The best way to manage them is to bathe them frequently with warm water, or in warm poppy-water, if very painful. When they have burst, use an ointment composed of one part of citron ointment and four of spermaceti, well rubbed together, and smear along the edge of the eyelid. Give a grain or two of calomel with 5 or 8 grains of rhubarb, according to the age of the child, twice a week. The old-fashioned and apparently absurd practice of rubbing the stye with a ring, is as good and speedy a cure as that by any process of medicinal application ; though the number of times it is rubbed, or the quality of the ring and direction of the strokes, has nothing to do with its success. The pressure and the friction excite the vessels of the part, and cause an absorption of the effused matter under the eyelash. The edge of the nail will answer as well as a ring.

2631. INFLAMMATION OF THE EYELIDS.—The following ointment has been found very beneficial in inflammations of the eyeball and edges of the eyelids:—Take of prepared calomel, 1 scruple ; spermaceti ointment, ½ oz. Mix them well together in a glass mortar ; apply a small quantity to each corner of the eye every night and morning, and also to the edges of the lids, if they are affected. If this should not eventually remove the inflammation, elder-flower water may be applied three or four times a day, by means of an eye-cup. The bowels should be kept in a laxative state, by taking occasionally a quarter of an ounce of the Cheltenham or Epsom salts.

2632. FASTING.—It is said by many able physicians that fasting is a means of removing incipient disease, and of restoring the body to its customary healthy sensations. Howard, the celebrated philanthropist (says a writer), used to fast one day in every week. Napoleon, when he felt his system unstrung, suspended his wonted repast, and took his exercise on horseback.

Fits.

2633. FITS come on so suddenly, often without even the slightest warning, and may prove fatal so quickly, that all people should be acquainted at least with their leading symptoms and treatment, as a few moments, more or less, will often decide the question between life and death. The treatment, in very many cases at least, to be of the slightest use, should be *immediate*, as a person in a fit (of apoplexy for instance) may die while a surgeon is being fetched from only the next street. We shall give, as far as the fact of our editing a work for non-professional readers will permit, the peculiar and distinctive symptoms of all kind of fits, and the immediate treatment to be adopted in each case.

2634. APOPLEXY.—These fits may be divided into two kinds—the *strong* and the *weak*.

2635. 1. *The strong kind.*—These cases mostly occur in stout, strong, short-necked, bloated-faced people, who are in the habit of living well.—*Symptoms.* The patient may or may not have had headache, sparks before his eyes, with confusion of ideas and giddiness, for a day or two before the attack. When it takes place, he falls down insensible; the body becomes paralyzed, generally more so on one side than the other; the face and head are hot, and the blood-vessels about them swollen; the pupils of the eyes are larger than natural, and the eyes themselves are fixed; the mouth is mostly drawn down at one corner; the breathing is like loud snoring; the pulse full and hard.—*Treatment.* Place the patient immediately in bed, with his head well raised; take off everything that he has round his neck, and bleed freely and at once from the arm. If you have not got a lancet, use a pen-knife or anything suitable that may be at hand. Apply warm mustard poultices to the soles of the feet and the insides of the thighs and legs; put two drops of castor oil, mixed up with eight grains of calomel, on the top of the tongue, as far back as possible; a most important part of the treatment being to open the bowels as quickly and freely as possible. The patient cannot swallow; but these medicines, especially the oil, will be absorbed into the stomach altogether independent of any voluntary action. If possible, throw up a warm turpentine clyster (two table-spoonfuls of oil of turpentine in a pint of warm gruel), or, if this cannot be obtained, one composed of about a quart of warm salt-and-water and soap. Cut off the hair, and apply rags dipped in weak vinegar-and-water, or weak gin-and-water, or even simple cold water, to the head. If the blood-vessels about the head and neck are much swollen, put from eight to ten leeches on the temple opposite to the paralyzed side of the body. Always send for a surgeon immediately, and act according to the above rules, doing more or less, according to the means at hand, and the length of time that must necessarily elapse until he arrives. A pint, or even a quart of blood in a very strong person, may be taken away. When the patient is able to swallow, give him the No. 1 pills, and the No. 1 mixture directly. [The No. 1 pills are made as follows :—Mix 5 grains of calomel and the same quantity of antimonial powder with a little bread-crumb : make into two pills, the dose for a full-grown person. For the No. 1 mixture, dissolve an ounce of Epsom salts in half a pint of senna tea: take a quarter of the mixture as a dose.] Repeat these remedies if the bowels are not well opened. Keep the patient's head well raised, and cool as above. Give very low diet indeed : gruel, arrowroot, and the like. When a person is recovering, he should have blisters applied to the nape of the neck, his bowels should be kept well open, light diet given, and fatigue, worry, and excess of all kinds avoided.

2636. 2. *The weak kind.*—*Symptoms.* These attacks are more frequently preceded by warning symptoms than the first kind. The face is pale, the pulse weak, and the body, especially the hands and legs, cold. After a little while, these symptoms sometimes alter to those of the first class in a mild degree.— *Treatment.* At first, if the pulse is *very feeble indeed*, a little brandy-and-water or sal-volatile must be given. Mustard poultices are to be put, as before, to the soles of the feet and the insides of the thighs and legs. Warm bricks, or bottles filled with warm water, are also to be placed under the arm-pits. When the strength has returned, the body become warmer, and the pulse fuller and harder, the head should be shaved, and wet rags applied to it, as before described. Leeches should be put, as before, to the temple opposite the side paralyzed ; and the bowels should be opened as freely and as quickly as possible. Bleeding from the arm is often necessary in these cases, but a non-professional person should never have recourse to it. Blisters may be applied to the nape of the neck at once. The diet in these cases should not be so low as in the former—indeed, it is often necessary, in a day or so after one of these attacks, to give wine, strong beef-tea, &c., according to the condition of the patient's strength.

2637. *Distinctions between Apoplexy and Epilepsy.*—1. Apoplexy mostly happens in people *over thirty*, whereas epilepsy generally occurs under that age ; at any rate for the first time. A person who has epileptic fits over thirty, has generally suffered from them for some years. 2. Again, *in apoplexy*, the body is *paralyzed;* and, therefore, has not the *convulsions which take place in epilepsy.* 3. The peculiar *snoring* will also distinguish apoplexy from epilepsy.

2638. *Distinctions between Apoplexy and Drunkenness.*—1. The known habits of the person. 2. The fact of a person who was perfectly sober and sensible a little time before, being found in a state of insensibility. 3. The absence, in apoplexy, of the *smell of drink* on applying the nose to the mouth. 4. A person in a fit of apoplexy cannot be roused at all ; in drunkenness he mostly can, to a certain extent.

2639. *Distinction between Apoplexy and Hysterics.* — Hysterics mostly happen in young, nervous, unmarried women ; and are attended with convulsions, sobbing, laughter, throwing about of the body, &c. &c.

2640. *Distinction between Apoplexy and Poisoning by Opium.*—It is exceedingly difficult to distinguish between these two cases. In poisoning by opium, however, we find the particular smell of the drug in the patient's breath. We should also, in forming our opinion, take into consideration the person's previous conduct—whether he has been low and desponding for some time before, or has ever talked about committing suicide.

2641. EPILEPSY.—*Falling Sickness.*—These fits mostly happen, at any rate for the first time, to young people, and are more common in boys than girls. They are produced by numerous causes.—*Symptoms.* The fit may be preceded by pains in the head, palpitations, &c. &c. ; but it mostly happens that the person falls down insensible suddenly, and without any warning whatever. The eyes are distorted, so that only their whites can be seen ; there is mostly foaming from the mouth ; the fingers are clinched ; and the body, especially on one side, is much agitated ; the tongue is often thrust out of the mouth. When the fit goes off, the patient feels drowsy and faint, and often sleeps soundly for some time.—*Treatment.* During the fit, keep the patient flat on his back, with his head slightly raised, and prevent him from doing any harm to himself ; dash cold water into his face, and apply smelling-salts to his nose ; loosen his shirt collar, &c. ; hold a piece of wood about as thick as a finger— the handle of a tooth-brush or knife will do as well—between the two rows of teeth, at the back part of the mouth. This will prevent the tongue from being injured. A teaspoonful of common salt thrust into the patient's mouth, during the fit, is of much service. The after-treatment of these fits is various, and depends entirely upon their causes. A good general rule, however, is always to keep the bowels well open, and the patient quiet, and free from fatigue, worry, and excess of all kinds.

2642. *Fainting Fits* are sometimes very dangerous, and at others perfectly harmless ; the question of danger depending altogether upon the causes which have produced them, and which are exceedingly various. For instance, fainting produced by disease of the heart is a very serious symptom indeed ; whereas, that arising from some slight cause, such as the sight of blood, &c., need cause no alarm whatever. The symptoms of simple fainting are so well known that it would be quite superfluous to enumerate them here. The *treatment* consists in laying the patient at full length upon his back, with his head upon a level with the rest of his body, loosening everything about the neck, dashing cold water into the face, and sprinkling vinegar and water about the mouth ; applying smelling-salts to the nose ; and, when the patient is able to swallow, in giving a little warm brandy-and-water, or about 20 drops of sal-volatile in water.

2643. *Hysterics.*—These fits take place, for the most part, in young, nervous, unmarried women. They happen much less often in married women ; and even (in some rare cases indeed) in men. Young women, who are subject to these fits, are apt to think that they are suffering from " all the ills that flesh is heir to ;" and the false symptoms of disease which they show are so like the true ones, that it is often exceedingly difficult to detect the difference. The fits themselves are mostly preceded by great depression of spirits, shedding of tears, sickness, palpitation of the heart, &c. A pain, as if a nail were being driven in, is also often felt at one particular part of the head. In almost all cases, when a fit is coming on, pain is felt on the left side. This pain rises gradually until it reaches the throat, aud then gives the patient a sensation as if she had a pellet there, which prevents her from breathing properly, and, in fact, seems to threaten actual suffocation. The patient now generally becomes insensible, and faints ; the body is thrown about in all directions, froth issues from the mouth, incoherent expressions are uttered, and fits of laughter, crying, or screaming, take place. When the fit is going off, the patient mostly cries bitterly, sometimes knowing all, and at others nothing, of what has taken place, and feeling general soreness all over the body. *Treatment during the fit.* Place the body in the same position as for simple fainting, and treat, in other respects, as directed in the article on Epilepsy. *Always well loosen the patient's stays ;* and, when she is recovering, and able to swallow, give 20 drops of sal volatile in a little water. The *after-treatment* of these cases is very various. If the patient is of a strong constitution, she should live on plain diet, take plenty of exercise, and take occasional doses of castor oil, or an aperient mixture, such as that described as " No. 1," in previous numbers. If, as is mostly the case, the patient is weak and delicate, she will require a different mode of treatment altogether. Good nourishing diet, gentle exercise, cold baths, occasionally a dose of No. 3 myrrh and aloes pills at night, and a dose of compound iron pills twice a day. [As to the myrrh and aloes pills (No. 3), 10 grains made into two pills are a dose for a full-grown person. Of the compound iron pills (No. 4), the dose for a full grown person is also 10 grains, made into two pills.] In every case, amusing the mind, and avoiding all causes of over-excitement, are of great service in bringing about a permanent cure.

2644. LIVER COMPLAINT AND SPASMS.—A very obliging correspondent recommends the following, from personal experience :—Take 4 oz. of dried dandelion root, 1 oz. of the best ginger, ¼ oz. of Columba root ; bruise and boil all together in 3 pints of water till it is reduced to a quart : strain, and take a wine-glassful every four hours. Our correspondent says it is a "safe and simple medicine for both liver complaint and spasms."

2645. LUMBAGO.—A " new and successful mode." of treating lumbago, advocated by Dr. Day, is a form of counter-irritation, said to have been introduced into this country by the late Sir Anthony Carlisle, and which consists in the instantaneous application of a flat iron button, gently heated in a spirit-lamp, to the skin. Dr. Corrigan published, about three years ago, an account of some cases very successfully treated by nearly similar means. Dr. Corrigan's plan was, however, to touch the surface of the part affected, at intervals of half an inch, as lightly and rapidly as possible. Dr. Day has found greater advantages to result from drawing the flat surface of the heated button lightly over the affected part, so as to act on a greater extent of surface. The doctor speaks so enthusiastically of the benefit to be derived from this practice, that it is evidently highly deserving attention.

2646. PALPITATION OF THE HEART.—Where palpitation occurs as symptomatic of indigestion, the treatment must be directed to remedy that disorder ; when it is consequent on a plethoric state, purgatives will be effectual. In this case the patient should abstain from every kind of diet likely to produce a plethoric condition of body. Animal food and fermented liquor must be particularly avoided. Too much indulgence in sleep will also prove injurious. When the attacks arise from nervous irritability, the excitement must be allayed by change of air and a tonic diet. Should the palpitation originate from organic derangement, it must be, of course, beyond domestic management. Luxurious living, indolence, and tight-lacing often produce this affection : such cases are to be conquered with a little resolution.

2647. Poisons

shall be the next subject for remark ; and we anticipate more detailed instructions for the treatment of persons poisoned, by giving a simple LIST OF THE PRINCIPAL POISONS, with their ANTIDOTES OR REMEDIES.

Oil of Vitriol Aquafortis Spirit of Salt	Magnesia, Chalk, Soap-and-Water.
Emetic Tartar	Oily Drinks, Solution of Oak-bark.
Salt of Lemons, or Acid of Sugar	Chalk, Whiting, Lime, or Magnesia and Water. Sometimes an Emetic Draught.
Prussic Acid	Pump on back, Smelling-Salts to nose, Artificial Breathing, Chloride of Lime to nose.
Pearlash Soap-Lees Smelling-Salts Nitre Hartshorn Sal-Volatile	Lemon-Juice and Vinegar-and-Water.
Arsenic Fly-Powder, or White Arsenic. King's Yellow, or Yellow Arsenic	Emetics, Lime-Water, Soap-and-Water, Sugar-and-Water, Oily Drinks.
Mercury Corrosive Sublimate Calomel	Whites of Eggs, Soap-and-Water.
Opium Laudanum	Emetic Draught, Vinegar-and-Water, dashing Cold Water on chest and face, walking up and down for two or three hours.

Lead .... White Lead .... Sugar of Lead .... Goulard's Extract	Epsom Salts, Castor Oil, Emetics.
Copper .... Blue-stone .... Verdigris	Whites of Eggs, Sugar-and-Water, Castor Oil, Gruel.
Zinc	Lime-Water, Chalk-and-Water, Soap-and-Water.
Iron	Magnesia, Warm Water.
Henbane .... Hemlock .... Nightshade .... Foxglove	Emetics and Castor Oil; Brandy-and-Water, ·if necessary.
Poisonous Food	Emetics and Castor Oil.

2648. The symptoms of poisoning may be known for the most part from those of some diseases, which they are very like, from the fact of their coming on *immediately* after eating or drinking something ; whereas those of disease come on, in most cases at least, by degrees, and with warnings. In most cases where poison is known, or suspected, to have been taken, the first thing to be done is to empty the stomach, well and immediately, by means of mustard mixed in warm water, or plain warm salt-and-water, or, better, this draught, which we call No. 1:—Twenty grains of sulphate of zinc in an ounce and a half of water. This draught to be repeated in a quarter of an hour if vomiting does not ensue. The back part of the throat should be well tickled with a feather, or two of the fingers thrust down it, to induce vomiting. The cases where vomiting must not be used are those where the skin has been taken off, and the parts touched irritated and inflamed by the poison taken, and where the action of vomiting would increase the evil. Full instructions are given in the article on each particular poison as to where emetics are or are not to be given. The best and safest way of emptying the stomach is by means of the stomach-pump, as in certain cases the action of vomiting is likely to increase the danger arising from the swollen and congested condition of the blood-vessels of the head, which often takes place. In the hands, however, of any one else than a surgeon, it would be not only useless, but harmful, as a great deal of dexterity, caution, and experience are required to use it properly. After having made these brief introductory remarks, we shall now proceed to particulars.

2649. *Sulphuric Acid,* or *Oil of Vitriol* (a clear, colourless liquid, of an oily appearance).—*Symptoms in those who have swallowed it.* When much is taken, these come on immediately. There is great burning pain, extending from the mouth to the stomach ; vomiting of a liquid of a dark coffee-colour, often mixed with shreds of flesh and streaks of blood ; the skin inside the mouth is taken off, and the exposed surface is at first white, and after a time becomes brownish. There are sometimes spots of a brown colour round the lips and on the neck, caused by drops of the acid falling on these parts. There is great difficulty of breathing, owing to the swelling at the back part of the mouth. After a time there is much depression of strength, with a quick, weak pulse, and cold, clammy skin. The face is pale, and has a very anxious look. When the acid swallowed has been greatly diluted in water, the same kind of symptoms occur, only in a milder degree.—*Treatment.* Give a mixture of magnesia in milk-and-water, or, if this cannot be obtained, of finely powdered chalk, or whiting, or even of the plaster torn down from the walls or ceiling, in milk-and-water. The mixture should be nearly as thick as cream, and plenty of it given. As well as this, simple gruel, milk, or thick flour-and-water, are very useful, and should be given in large quantities. Violent inflammation of the parts touched by the acid is most likely to take place in the course of a little time, and can only be properly attended to by a surgeon; but if one cannot be obtained, leeches, the fever-mixtures (the recipe for which appears repeatedly in previous paragraphs), thick drinks, such as barley-water, gruel, arrowroot, &c., must be had recourse to, according to the symptoms of each particular case and the means at hand. The inflamed condition of the back part of the mouth requires particular attention. When the breathing is very laboured and difficult in consequence, from fifteen to twenty leeches are to be immediately applied to the outside of the throat, and when they drop off, warm poppy fomentations constantly kept to the part. When the pain over the stomach is very great, the same local treatment is necessary; but if it is only slight, a good mustard poultice will be sufficient without the leeches. In all these cases, two tablespoonfuls of the fever-mixture should be given every four hours, and only gruel or arrowroot allowed to be eaten for some days.

2650. *Nitric Acid,* commonly known as *Aqua Fortis,* or *Red Spirit of Nitre* (a straw-coloured fluid, of the consistence of water, and which gives off dense white fumes on exposure to the air).—*Symptoms produced in those who have swallowed it.* Much the same as in the case of sulphuric acid. In this case, however, the surface touched by the acid becomes *yellowish.* The tongue is mostly much swollen.—*Treatment.* The same as for sulphuric acid.

2651. *Muriatic Acid, Spirit of Salt* (a thin yellow fluid, emitting dense white fumes on exposure to the air).—This is not often taken as a poison. The *symptoms* and *treatment* are much the same as those of *nitric acid.*

N.B.—*In no case of poisoning by these three acids should emetics ever be given.*

2652. *Oxalic Acid,* commonly called *Salt of Lemons.*—This poison may be taken by mistake for Epsom salts, which it is a good deal like. It may be distinguished from them by its very acid taste and its shape, which is that of needle-formed crystals, each of which, if put into a drop of ink, will turn it to a *reddish brown,* whereas Epsom salts will not change its colour at all. When a large dose of this poison has been taken, death takes place very quickly indeed.—*Symptoms produced in those who have swallowed it.* A hot, burning, acid taste is felt in the act of swallowing, and vomiting of a *greenish-brown* fluid is produced, sooner or later, according to the quantity and strength of the poison taken. There is great tenderness felt over the stomach, followed by clammy perspirations and convulsions; the legs are often drawn up, and there is generally stupor, from which the patient, however, can easily be roused, and always great prostration of strength. The pulse is small and weak, and the breathing faint.—*Treatment.* Chalk or magnesia, made into a cream with water, should be given in large quantities, and afterwards the emetic draught above prescribed, or some mustard-and-water, if the draught cannot be got. The back part of the throat to be tickled with a feather, to induce vomiting. Arrowroot, gruel, and the like drinks, are to be taken. When the prostration of strength is very great and the body cold, warmth is to be applied to it, and a little brandy-and-water, or sal-volatile and water, given.

2653. *Prussic Acid* (a thin, transparent, and colourless liquid, with a peculiar smell, which greatly resembles that of bitter almonds).—*Symptoms produced in those who have swallowed it.* These come on *immediately* after the poison has been taken, and may be produced by merely *smelling* it. The patient becomes perfectly insensible, and falls down in convulsions—his eyes are fixed and staring, the pupils being bigger than natural, the skin is cold and clammy, the pulse scarcely perceptible, and the breathing slow and gasping. —*Treatment.* Very little can be done in these cases, as death takes place so quickly after the poison has been swallowed, when it takes place at all. The best treatment—which should always be adopted in all cases, even though the patient appears quite dead—is to dash quantities of cold water on the back, from the top of the neck downwards. Placing the patient under a pump, and pumping on him, is the best way of doing this. Smelling-salts are also to be applied to the nose, and the chest well rubbed with a camphor liniment.

2654. ALKALIS: *Potash, Soda,* and *Ammonia,* or common *Smelling-Salts,* with their principal preparations —*Pearlash, Soap Lees, Liquor Potassœ, Nitre, Sal Prunella, Hartshorn,* and *Sal-Volatile.*—Alkalis are seldom taken or given with the view of destroying life. They may, however, be swallowed by mistake. —*Symptoms produced in those who have swallowed them.* There is at first a burning, acrid taste in, and a sensation of tightness round, the throat, like that of strangling; the skin touched is destroyed; retching mostly followed by actual vomiting, then sets in; the vomited matters often containing blood of a dark brown colour, with little shreds of flesh here and there, and always changing vegetable blue colours green. There is now great tenderness over the whole of the belly. After a little while, great weakness, with cold, clammy sweats, a quick weak pulse, and purging of bloody matters, takes place. The brain, too, mostly becomes affected.—*Treatment.* Give two tablespoonfuls of vinegar or lemon-juice in a glassful of water every few minutes until the burning sensation is relieved. Any kind of oil or milk may also be given, and will form soap when mixed with the poison in the stomach. Barley-water, gruel, arrowroot, linseed-tea, &c., are also very useful, and should be taken constantly, and in large quantities. If inflammation should take place, it is to be treated by applying leeches and warm poppy fomentations to the part where the pain is most felt, and giving two tablespoonfuls of the fever mixture every four hours. The diet in all these cases should only consist of arrowroot or gruel for the first few days, and then of weak broth or beef-tea for some time after.

2655. When very strong fumes of smelling-salts have in any way been inhaled, there is great difficulty of breathing, and alarming pain in the mouth and nostrils. In this case let the patient inhale the steam of warm vinegar, and treat the feverish symptoms as before.

2656. *Arsenic.*—Mostly seen under the form of white arsenic, or fly-powder, and yellow arsenic, or king's yellow.—*Symptoms produced in those who have swallowed it.* These vary very much, according to the form and dose in which the poison has been taken. There is faintness, depression, and sickness, with an intense burning pain in the region of the stomach, which gets worse and worse, and is increased by pressure. There is also vomiting of dark brown matter, sometimes mixed with blood; and mostly great thirst, with a feeling of tightness round, and of burning in, the throat. Purging also takes place, the matters brought away being mixed with blood. The pulse is small and irregular, and the skin sometimes cold and clammy, and at others hot. The breathing is painful. Convulsions and spasms often occur.—*Treatment.* Give a couple of teaspoonfuls of mustard in a glass of water, to bring on or assist vomiting, and also use the other means elsewhere recommended for the purpose. A solution, half of lime-water and half of linseed-oil, well mixed, may be given, as well as plenty of arrowroot, gruel, or linseed-tea. Simple milk is also useful. A little castor-oil should be given, to cleanse the intestines of all the poison, and the after-symptoms treated on general principles.

2657. *Corrosive Sublimate.*—Mostly seen in the form of little heavy crystalline masses, which melt in water, and have a metallic taste. It is sometimes seen in powder. This is a most powerful poison.—*Symptoms.* These mostly come on *immediately* after the poison has been taken. There is a coppery taste experienced in the act of swallowing, with a burning heat, extending from the top of the throat down to the stomach; and also a feeling of great tightness round the throat. In a few minutes great pain is felt over the region of the stomach, and frequent vomiting of long, stringy white masses, mixed with blood, takes place. There is also mostly great purging. The countenance is generally pale and anxious; the pulse always small and frequent; the skin cold and clammy, and the breathing difficult. Convulsions and insensibility often occur, and are very bad symptoms indeed. The inside of the mouth is more or less swollen.—*Treatment.* Mix the whites of a dozen eggs in two pints of cold water, and give a glassful of the mixture every three or four minutes, until the stomach can contain no more. If vomiting does not now come on naturally, and supposing the mouth is not very sore or much swollen, an emetic draught, No. 1, may be given, and vomiting induced. (The No. 1 draught, we remind our readers, is thus made:—Twenty grains of sulphate of zinc in an ounce and a half of water; the draught to be repeated if vomiting does not take place in a quarter of an hour.) After the stomach has been well cleaned out, milk, flour-and-water, linseed-tea, or barley-water, should be taken in large quantities. If eggs cannot be obtained, milk, or flour-and-water, should be given as a substitute for them at once. When the depression of strength is very great indeed, a little warm brandy-and-water must be given. In the course of an hour or two the patient should take two tablespoonfuls of castor-oil, and if inflammation comes on, it is to be treated as directed in the article on acids and alkalis. The diet should also be the same. If the patient recovers, great soreness of the gums is almost certain to take place. The simplest, and at the same time one of the best modes of treatment, is to wash them well three or four times a day with brandy-and-water.

2658. *Calomel.*—A heavy white powder, without taste, and insoluble in water. It has been occasionally known to destroy life.—*Symptoms.* Much the same as in the case of corrosive sublimate.—*Treatment.* The same as for corrosive sublimate. If the gums are sore, wash them, as recommended in the case of corrosive sublimate, with brandy-and-water three or four times a day, and keep the patient on *fluids,* such as arrowroot, gruel, broth, or beef-tea, according to the other symptoms. Eating hard substances would make the gums more sore and tender.

2659. *Copper.*—The preparations of this metal which are most likely to be the ones producing poisonous symptoms, are *blue-stone* and *verdigris.* People are often taken ill after eating food that has been cooked in copper saucepans. When anything has been cooked in one of these vessels, *it should never be allowed to cool in it.* — *Symptoms.* Headache, pain in the stomach, and purging; vomiting of green or blue matters, convulsions, and spasms.— *Treatment.* Give whites of eggs, sugar-and-water, castor-oil, and drinks, such as arrowroot and gruel.

2660. *Emetic Tartar.*—Seen in the form of a white powder, or crystals, with a slightly metallic taste. It has not often been known to destroy life.—*Symptoms.* A strong metallic taste in the act of swallowing, followed by a burning pain in the region of the stomach, vomiting, and great purging. The pulse is small and rapid, the skin cold and clammy, the breathing difficult and painful, and the limbs often much cramped. There is also great prostration of strength.—*Treatment.* Promote the vomiting by giving plenty of warm water, or warm arrowroot and water. Strong tea, in large quantities, should be drunk ; or, if it can be obtained, a decoction of oak bark. The after-treatment is the same as that for acids and alkalis ; the principal object in all these cases being to keep down the inflammation of the parts touched by the poison by means of leeches, warm poppy fomentations, fever-mixtures, and very low diet.

2661. *Lead,* and its preparations, *Sugar of Lead, Goulard's Extract, White Lead.*—Lead is by no means an active poison, although it is popularly considered to be so. It mostly affects people by being taken into the system slowly, as in the case of painters and glaziers. A newly-painted house, too, often affects those living in it.—*Symptoms produced when taken in a large dose.* There is at first a burning, pricking sensation in the throat, to which thirst, giddiness, and vomiting follow. The belly is tight, swollen, and painful ; *the pain being relieved by pressure.* The bowels are mostly bound. There is great depression of strength, and a cold skin.—*Treatment.* Give an emetic draught (No. 1, see above) at once, and shortly afterwards a solution of Epsom salts in large quantities. A little brandy-and-water must be taken if the depression of strength is very great indeed. Milk, whites of eggs, and arrowroot are also useful. After two or three hours, cleanse the stomach and intestines well out with two tablespoonfuls of castor-oil, and treat the symptoms which follow according to the rules laid down in other parts of these articles.—*Symptoms when it is taken into the body slowly.* Headache, pain about the navel, loss of appetite and flesh, offensive breath, a *blueness of the edges of the gums ;* the belly is tight, hard, and knotty, and the pulse slow and languid. There is also sometimes a difficulty in swallowing.—*Treatment.* Give five grains of calomel and half a grain of opium directly, in the form of a pill, and half an ounce of Epsom salts in two hours, and repeat this treatment until the bowels are well opened. Put the patient into a warm bath, and throw up a clyster of warmish water when he is in it. Fomentations of warm oil of turpentine, if they can be obtained, should be put over the whole of the belly. The great object is to open the bowels as freely and as quickly as possible. When this has been done, a grain of pure opium may be given. Arrowroot or gruel should be taken in good large quantities. The after-treatment must depend altogether upon the symptoms of each particular case.

2662. *Opium,* and its preparations, *Laudanum, &c.*—Solid opium is mostly seen in the form of rich brown flattish cakes, with little pieces of leaves sticking on them here and there, and a bitter and slightly warm taste. The most common form in which it is taken as a poison, is that of laudanum.— *Symptoms.* These consist at first in giddiness and stupor, followed by insensibility, the patient, however, being roused to consciousness by a great noise, so as to be able to answer a question, but becoming insensible again almost immediately. The pulse is now quick and small, the breathing hurried, and the skin warm and covered with perspiration. After a little time, these symptoms change ; the person becomes *perfectly insensible,* the breathing slow and *snoring,* as in apoplexy, the skin cold, and the pulse slow and full. The pupil of the eye is mostly smaller than natural. On applying his nose to the patient's mouth, a person may smell the poison very distinctly.—*Treatment.* Give an emetic draught (No. 1, see above) directly, with large quantities of warm mustard-and-water, warm salt-and-water, or simple warm water. Tickle the top of the throat with a feather, or put two fingers down it to bring on vomiting, which rarely takes place of itself. Dash cold water on the head, chest, and spine, and flap these parts well with the ends of wet towels. Give strong coffee or tea. Walk the patient up and down in the open air for two or three hours ; the great thing being to keep him from sleeping. Electricity is of much service. When the patient is recovering, mustard poultices should be applied to the soles of the feet and the insides of the thighs and legs. The head should be kept cool and raised.

2663. The following preparations, which are constantly given to children by their nurses and mothers, for the purpose of making them sleep, often prove fatal:—*Syrup of Poppies,* and *Godfrey's Cordial.* The author would most earnestly urge all people caring for their children's lives, never to allow any of these preparations to be given, unless ordered by a surgeon.

2664. The treatment in the case of poisoning by *Henbane, Hemlock, Nightshade,* and *Foxglove,* is much the same as that for opium. Vomiting should be brought on in all of them.

2665. *Poisonous Food.*—It sometimes happens that things which are in daily use, and mostly perfectly harmless, give rise, under certain unknown circumstances, and in certain individuals, to the symptoms of poisoning. The most common articles of food of this description are *Mussels, Salmon,* and certain kinds of *Cheese* and *Bacon.* The general symptoms are thirst, weight about the stomach, difficulty of breathing, vomiting, purging, spasms, prostration of strength, and, in the case of mussels more particularly, an eruption on the body, like that of nettle-rash.—*Treatment.* Empty the stomach well with No. 1 draught and warm water, and give two tablespoonfuls of castor-oil immediately after. Let the patient take plenty of arrowroot, gruel, and the like drinks, and if there is much depression of strength, give a little warm brandy-and-water. Should symptoms of fever or inflammation follow, they must be treated as directed in the articles on other kinds of poisoning.

2666. *Mushrooms,* and similar kinds of vegetables, often produce poisonous effects. The symptoms are various, sometimes giddiness and stupor, and at others pain in and swelling of the belly, with vomiting and purging, being the leading ones. When the symptoms come on quickly after taking the poison, it is generally the head that is affected.—The treatment consists in bringing on vomiting in the usual manner, as quickly and as freely as possible. The other symptoms are to be treated on general principles ; if they are those of depression, by brandy-and-water or sal-volatile ; if those of inflammation, by leeches, fomentations, fever-mixtures, &c. &c.

2667. FOR CURE OF RINGWORM.—Take of subcarbonate of soda 1 drachm, which dissolve in ½ pint of vinegar. Wash the head every morning with soft soap, and apply the lotion night and morning. One teaspoonful of sulphur and treacle should also be given occasionally night and morning. The hair should be cut close, and round the spot it should be shaved off, and the part, night and morning, bathed with a lotion made by dissolving a drachm of white vitriol in 6 oz. of water. A small piece of either of the two subjoined ointments rubbed into the part when the lotion has dried in. No. 1.—Take of citron ointment 1 drachm; sulphur and tar ointment, of each ½ oz.: mix thoroughly, and apply twice a day. No. 2.—Take of simple cerate 1 oz.; creosote 1 drachm; calomel 30 grains: mix and use in the same manner as the first. Concurrent with these external remedies, the child should take an alterative powder every morning, or, if they act too much on the bowels, only every second day. The following will be found to answer all the intentions desired.

2668. *Alterative Powders for Ringworm.*—Take of

Sulphuret of antimony, precipitated .	24 grains.
Grey powder	12 grains.
Calomel	6 grains.
Jalap powder	36 grains.

Mix carefully, and divide into 12 powders for a child from 1 to 2 years old; into 9 powders for a child from 2 to 4 years; and into 6 powders for a child from 4 to 6 years. Where the patient is older, the strength may be increased by enlarging the quantities of the drugs ordered, or by giving one and a half or two powders for one dose. The ointment is to be well washed off every morning with soap-and-water, and the part bathed with the lotion before re-applying the ointment. An imperative fact must be remembered by mother or nurse,—never to use the same comb employed for the child with ringworm, for the healthy children, or let the affected little one sleep with those free from the disease; and, for fear of any contact by hands or otherwise, to keep the child's head enveloped in a nightcap, till the eruption is completely cured.

2669. Scratches.—Trifling as scratches often seem, they ought never to be neglected, but should be covered and protected, and kept clean and dry until they have completely healed. If there is the least appearance of inflammation, no time should be lost in applying a large bread-and-water poultice, or hot flannels repeatedly applied, or even leeches in good numbers may be put on at some distance from each other.

2670. For Shortness of Breath, or Difficult Breathing.—Vitriolated spirits of ether 1 oz., camphor 12 grains: make a solution, of which take a teaspoonful during the paroxysm. This is found to afford instantaneous relief in difficulty of breathing, depending on internal diseases and other causes, where the patient, from a very quick and laborious breathing, is obliged to be in an erect posture.

2671. Sprains.—A sprain is a stretching of the leaders or ligaments of a part through some violence, such as slipping, falling on the hands, pulling a limb, &c. &c. The most common are those of the ankle and wrist. These accidents are more serious than people generally suppose, and often more difficult to cure than a broken leg or arm. The first thing to be done is to place the sprained part in the straight position, and to raise it a little as well. Some recommend the application of cold lotions at first. The editress, however, is quite convinced that *warm* applications are, in most cases, the best for for the first three or four days. These fomentations are to be applied in the following manner :—Dip a good-sized piece of flannel into a pail or basin full of hot water or hot poppy fomentation,—six poppy heads boiled in one quart of water for about a quarter of an hour ; wring it almost dry, and apply it, as hot as the patient can bear, right round the sprained part. Then place another piece of flannel, quite dry, over it, in order that the steam and warmth may not escape. This process should be repeated as often as the patient feels that the flannel next to his skin is getting cold—the oftener the better. The bowels should be opened with a black draught, and the patient kept on low diet. If he has been a great drinker, he may be allowed to take a little beer; but it is better not to do so. A little of the cream of tartar drink, ordered in the case of burns, may be taken occasionally if there is much thirst. When the swelling and tenderness about the joint are very great, from eight to twelve leeches may be applied. When the knee is the joint affected, the greatest pain is felt at the inside, and therefore the greater quantity of the leeches should be applied to that part. When the shoulder is sprained, the arm should be kept close to the body by means of a linen roller, which is to be taken four or five times round the whole of the chest. It should also be brought two or three times underneath the elbow, in order to raise the shoulder. This is the best treatment for these accidents during the first three or four days. After that time, supposing that no unfavourable symptoms have taken place, a cold lotion, composed of a tablespoonful of sal-ammoniac to a quart of water, or vinegar-and-water, should be constantly applied. This lotion will strengthen the part, and also help in taking away any thickening that may have formed about the joint. In the course of two or three weeks, according to circumstances, the joint is to be rubbed twice a day with flannel dipped in opodeldoc, a flannel bandage rolled tightly round the joint, the pressure being greatest at the lowest part, and the patient allowed to walk about with the assistance of a crutch or stick. He should also occasionally, when sitting or lying down, quietly bend the joint backwards and forwards, to cause its natural motion to return, and to prevent stiffness from taking place. When the swelling is very great immediately after the accident has occurred, from the breaking of the blood-vessels, it is best to apply cold applications at first. If it can be procured, oil-silk may be put over the warm-fomentation flannel, instead of the dry piece of flannel. Old flannel is better than new.

2672. CURE FOR STAMMERING.—Where there is no malformation of the organs of articulation, stammering may be remedied by reading aloud with the teeth closed. This should be practised for two hours a day, for three or four months. The advocate of this simple remedy says, "I can speak with certainty of its utility."

4 A

2673. STAMMERING.—At a recent meeting of the Boston Society of Natural History, Dr. Warren stated, "A simple, easy, and effectual cure of stammering." It is, simply, at every syllable pronounced, to tap at the same time with the finger; by so doing, "the most inveterate stammerer will be surprised to find that he can pronounce quite fluently, and, by long and constant practice, he will pronounce perfectly well."

2674. SUFFOCATION, APPARENT.—Suffocation may arise from many different causes. Anything which prevents the air getting into the lungs will produce it. We shall give the principal causes, and the treatment to be followed in each case.

2675. 1. *Carbonic Acid Gas. Choke-Damp of Mines.*—This poisonous gas is met with in rooms where charcoal is burnt, and where there is not sufficient draught to allow it to escape; in coalpits, near limekilns, in breweries, and in rooms and houses where a great many people live huddled together in wretchedness and filth, and where the air in consequence becomes poisoned. This gas gives out no smell, so that we cannot know of its presence. A candle will not burn in a room which contains much of it.—*Effects.* At first there is giddiness, and a great wish to sleep; after a little time, or where there is much of it present, a person feels great weight in the head, and stupid; gets by degrees quite unable to move, and snores as if in a deep sleep. The limbs may or may not be stiff. The heat of the body remains much the same at first.—*Treatment.* Remove the person affected into the open air, and, even though it is cold weather, take off his clothes. Then lay him on his back, with his head slightly raised. Having done this, dash vinegar-and-water over the whole of the body, and rub it hard, especially the face and chest, with towels dipped in the same mixture. The hands and feet also should be rubbed with a hard brush. Apply smelling-salts to the nose, which may be tickled with a feather. Dashing cold water down the middle of the back is of great service. If the person can swallow, give him a little lemon-water, or vinegar-and-water to drink. The principal means, however, to be employed in this, as, in fact, in most cases of apparent suffocation, is what is called *artificial breathing.* This operation should be performed by three persons, and in the following manner:—The first person should put the nozzle of a common pair of bellows into one of the patient's nostrils; the second should push down, and then thrust back, that part of the throat called "Adam's apple;" and the third should first raise and then depress the chest, one hand being placed over each side of the ribs. These three actions should be performed in the following order:—First of all, the throat should be drawn down and thrust back; then the chest should be raised, and the bellows gently blown into the nostril. Directly this is done, the chest should be depressed, so as to imitate common breathing. This process should be repeated about eighteen times a minute. The mouth and the other nostril should be closed while the bellows are being blown. Persevere, if necessary, with this treatment for seven or eight hours—in fact, till absolute signs of death are visible. Many lives are lost by giving it up too quickly. When the patient becomes roused, he is to be put into a warm bed, and a little brandy-and-water, or twenty drops of sal-volatile, given cautiously now and then. This treatment is to be adopted in all cases where people are affected from breathing bad air, smells, &c. &c.

2676. 2. *Drowning.*—This is one of the most frequent causes of death by suffocation.—*Treatment.* Many methods have been adopted, and as some of them are not only useless, but hurtful, we will mention them here, merely in order that they may be avoided. In the first place, then, never hang a person up by his heels, as it is an error to suppose that water gets into the lungs. Hanging a person up by his heels would be quite as bad as hanging him up by his neck. It is also a mistake to suppose that rubbing the body with salt and water is of service.—*Proper Treatment.* Directly a person has been taken out of the water, he should be wiped dry and wrapped in blankets; but if these cannot be obtained, the clothes of the bystanders must be used for the purpose. His head being slightly raised, and any water, weeds, or froth that may happen to be in his mouth, having been removed, he should be carried as quickly as possible to the nearest house. He should now be put into a warm bath, about as hot as the hand can pleasantly bear, and kept there for about ten minutes, artificial breathing being had recourse to while he is in it. Having been taken out of the bath, he should be placed flat on his back, with his head slightly raised, upon a warm bed in a warm room, wiped perfectly dry, and then rubbed constantly all over the body with warm flannels. At the same time, mustard poultices should be put to the soles of the feet, the palms of the hands, and the inner surface of the thighs and legs. Warm bricks, or bottles filled with warm water, should be placed under the armpits. The nose should be tickled with a feather, and smelling-salts applied to it. This treatment should be adopted while the bath is being got ready, as well as when the body has been taken out of it. The bath is not absolutely necessary; constantly rubbing the body with flannels in a warm room having been found sufficient for resuscitation. Sir B. Brodie says that warm air is quite as good as warm water. When symptoms of returning consciousness begin to show themselves, give a little wine, brandy, or twenty drops of sal-volatile and water. In some cases it is necessary, in about twelve or twenty-four hours after the patient has revived, to bleed him, for peculiar head-symptoms which now and then occur. Bleeding, however, even in the hands of professional men themselves, should be very cautiously used—non-professional ones should never think of it. The best thing to do in these cases is to keep the head well raised, and cool with a lotion such as that recommended above for sprains; to administer an aperient draught, and to abstain from giving anything that stimulates, such as wine, brandy, sal-volatile, &c. &c. As a general rule, a person dies in three minutes and a half after he has been under water. It is difficult, however, to tell how long he has actually been *under* it, although we may know well exactly how long he has been *in* it. This being the case, always persevere in your attempts at resuscitation until actual signs of death have shown themselves, even for six, eight, or ten hours.

Dr. Douglas, of Glasgow, resuscitated a person who had been under water for fourteen minutes, by simply rubbing the whole of his body with warm flannels, in a warm room, for eight hours and a half, at the end of which time the person began to show the *first* symptoms of returning animation. Should the accident occur at a great distance from any house, this treatment should be adopted as closely as the circumstances will permit of. Breathing through any tube, such as a piece of card or paper rolled into the form of a pipe, will do as a substitute for the bellows. To recapitulate : Rub the body dry ; take matters out of mouth ; cover with blankets or clothes ; slightly raise the head, and place the body in a warm bath, or on a bed in a warm room ; apply smelling-salts to nose ; employ artificial breathing ; rub well with warm flannels ; put mustard poultices to feet, hands, and insides of thighs and legs, with warm bricks or bottles to armpits. *Don't bleed.* Give wine, brandy, or sal-volatile when recovering, and *persevere till actual signs of death are seen.*

2677. Briefly to conclude what we have to say of suffocation, let us treat of *Lightning.* When a person has been struck by lightning, there is a general paleness of the whole body, with the exception of the part struck, which is often blackened, or even scorched.—*Treatment.* Same as for drowning. It is not, however, of much use ; for when death takes place at all, it is generally instantaneous.

2678. CURE FOR THE TOOTHACHE.—Take a piece of sheet zinc, about the size of a sixpence, and a piece of silver, say a shilling ; place them together, and hold the defective tooth between them or contiguous to them ; in a few minutes the pain will be gone, as if by magic. The zinc and silver, acting as a galvanic battery, will produce on the nerves of the tooth sufficient electricity to establish a current, and consequently to relieve the pain. Or smoke a pipe of tobacco and caraway-seeds. Again—

2679. A small piece of the pellitory root will, by the flow of saliva it causes, afford relief. Creosote, or a few drops of tincture of myrrh, or friar's balsam, on cotton, put on the tooth, will often subdue the pain. A small piece of camphor, however, retained in the mouth, is the most reliable and likely means of conquering the paroxysms of this dreaded enemy.

2680. WARTS.—Eisenberg says, in his "Advice on the Hand," that the hydrochlorate of lime is the most certain means of destroying warts ; the process, however, is very slow, and demands perseverance, for, if discontinued before the proper time, no advantage is gained. The following is a simple cure :—On breaking the stalk of the crowfoot plant in two, a drop of milky juice will be observed to hang on the upper part of the stem ; if this be allowed to drop on a wart, so that it be well saturated with the juice, in about three or four dressings the warts will die, and may be taken off with the fingers. They may be removed by the above means from the teats of cows, where they are sometimes very troublesome, and prevent them standing quiet to be milked. The wart touched lightly every second day with lunar caustic, or rubbed every night with blue-stone, for a few weeks, will destroy the largest wart, wherever situated.

2681. To CURE A WHITLOW.—As soon as the whitlow has risen distinctly, a pretty large piece should be snipped out, so that the watery matter may readily escape, and continue to flow out as fast as produced. A bread-and-water poultice should be put on for a few days, when the wound should be bound up lightly with some mild ointment, when a cure will be speedily completed. Constant poulticing both before and after the opening of the whitlow, is the only practice needed; but as the matter lies deep, when it is necessary to open the abscess, the incision must be made *deep* to reach the suppuration.

2682. WOUNDS.—There are several kinds of wounds, which are called by different names, according to their appearance, or the manner in which they are produced. As, however, it would be useless, and even hurtful, to bother the reader's head with too many nice professional distinctions, we shall content ourselves with dividing wounds into three classes.

2683. 1. *Incised wounds or cuts*—those produced by a knife, or some sharp instrument.

2684. 2. *Lacerated, or torn wounds*—those produced by the claws of an animal, the bite of a dog, running quickly against some projecting blunt object, such as a nail, &c.

2685. 3. *Punctured or penetrating wounds*—those produced by anything running deeply into the flesh; such as a sword, a sharp nail, a spike, the point of a bayonet, &c.

2686. *Class* 1. *Incised wounds or cuts.*—The danger arising from these accidents is owing more to their position than to their extent. Thus, a cut of half an inch long, which goes through an artery, is more serious than a cut of two inches long, which is not near one. Again, a small cut on the head is more often followed by dangerous symptoms than a much larger one on the legs.— *Treatment.* If the cut is not a very large one, and no artery or vein is wounded, this is very simple. If there are any foreign substances left in the wound, they must be taken out, and the bleeding must be quite stopped before the wound is strapped up. If the bleeding is not very great, it may easily be stopped by raising the cut part, and applying rags dipped in cold water to it. All clots of blood must be carefully removed; for, if they are left behind, they prevent the wound from healing. When the bleeding has been stopped, and the wound perfectly cleaned, its two edges are to be brought closely together by thin straps of common adhesive plaster, which should remain on, if there is not great pain or heat about the part, for two or three days, without being removed. The cut part should be kept raised and cool. When the strips of plaster are to be taken off, they should first be well bathed with lukewarm water. This will cause them to come away easily, and without opening the lips of the wound ; which accident is very likely to take place, if they are pulled off without having been first moistened with the warm water. If the wound is not healed when the strips of plaster are taken off, fresh ones must be applied. Great care is required in treating cuts of the head, as they are often followed by erysipelas taking place round them. They should be strapped with isinglass-plaster, which is much less irritating than the ordinary adhesive plaster. Only use as many strips as are actually requisite to keep the two edges of the wound together ; keep the patient quite quiet, on low diet, for a week or so, according to his symptoms. Purge him well with the No. 2 pills (five grains of blue pill mixed with the same quantity of compound extract of colocynth ; make into two pills, the dose for an adult). If the patient is feverish, give him two tablespoonfuls of the fever-mixture three times a day. (The fever-mixture, we remind our readers, is thus made : Mix a drachm of powdered nitre, 2 drachms of carbonate of potash, 2 tea-spoonfuls of antimonial wine, and a tablespoonful of sweet spirits of nitre in half a pint of water.) A person should be very careful of himself for a month or two after having had a bad cut on the head. His bowels should be kept constantly open, and all excitement and excess avoided. When a vein or artery is wounded, the danger is, of course, much greater. These accidents, therefore, should always be attended to by a surgeon, if he can possibly be procured. Before he arrives, however, or in case his assistance cannot be obtained at all, the following treatment should be adopted :—Raise the cut part, and press rags dipped in cold water firmly against it. This will often be sufficient to stop the bleeding, if the divided artery or vein is not dangerous. When an artery is divided, the blood is of a bright red colour, and comes away in jets. In this case, and supposing the leg or arm to be the cut part, a handkerchief is to be tied tightly round the limb *above* the cut ; and, if possible, the two bleeding ends of the artery should each be tied with a piece of silk. If the bleeding is from a vein, the blood is much darker, and does not come away in jets. In this case, the handkerchief is to be tied *below* the cut, and a pad of lint or linen pressed firmly against the divided ends of the vein. Let every bad cut, especially where there is much bleeding, and even although it may to all appearance have been stopped, be attended to by a surgeon, if one can by any means be obtained.

2687. *Class* 2. *Lacerated or torn wounds.*—There is not so much bleeding in these cases as in clean cuts, because the blood-vessels are torn across in a zigzag manner, and not divided straight across. In other respects, however, they are more serious than ordinary cuts, being often followed by inflammation, mortification, fever, and in some cases by locked-jaw. Foreign substances are also more likely to remain in them.—*Treatment.* Stop the bleeding, if there is any, in the manner directed for cuts ; remove all substances that may be in the wound ; keep the patient quite quiet, and on low diet—gruel, arrowroot, and the like ; purge with the No. 1 pills and the No. 1 mixture. (The No. 1 pill : Mix 5 grains of calomel and the same quantity of antimonial powder, with a little bread-crumb, and make into two pills, which is the dose for an adult. The No. 1 mixture : Dissolve an ounce of Epsom salts in half a pint of senna tea. A quarter of the mixture is a dose.) If there are feverish symptoms, give two tablespoonfuls of fever-mixture (see above) every four hours. If possible, bring the two edges of the wound together, *but do not strain the parts, to do this.* If they cannot be brought together, on account of a piece of flesh being taken clean out, or the raggedness of their edges, put lint dipped in cold water over the wound, and cover it with oiled silk. It will then fill up from the bottom. If the wound, after being well washed, should still contain any sand, or grit of any kind, or if it should get red and hot from inflammation, a large warm bread poultice will be the best thing to apply until it becomes quite clean, or the inflammation goes down. When the wound is a very large one, the application of warm poppy fomentations is better than that of the lint dipped in cold water. If the redness and pain about the part, and the general feverish symptoms, are great, from eight to twelve leeches are to be applied round the wound, and a warm poppy fomentation or warm bread poultice applied after they drop off.

2688. *Class* 3. *Punctured or penetrating wounds.*—These, for many reasons, are the most serious of all kinds of wounds.—*Treatment.* The same as that for lacerated wounds. Pus (matter) often forms at the bottom of these wounds, which should, therefore, be kept open at the top, by separating their edges every morning with a bodkin, and applying a warm bread poultice immediately afterwards. They will then, in all probability, heal up from the bottom, and any matter which may form will find its own way out into the poultice. Sometimes, however, in spite of all precautions, collections of matter (abscesses) will form at the bottom or sides of the wound. These are to be opened with a lancet, and the matter thus let out. When matter is forming, the patient has cold shiverings, throbbing pain in the part, and flushes on the face, which come and go. A swelling of the part is also often seen. The matter in the abscesses may be felt to move backwards and forwards, when pressure is made from one side of the swelling to the other with the first and second fingers (the middle and that next the thumb) of each hand.

MEDICAL MEMORANDA.

2689. ADVANTAGES OF CLEANLINESS.—Health and strength cannot be long continued unless the skin—*all* the skin—is washed frequently with a sponge or other means. Every morning is best ; after which the skin should be rubbed very well with a rough cloth. This is the most certain way of preventing cold, and a little substitute for exercise, as it brings blood to the surface, and causes it to circulate well through the fine capillary vessels. Labour produces this circulation naturally. The insensible perspiration cannot escape well if the skin is not clean, as the pores get choked up. It is said that in health about half the aliment we take passes out through the skin.

2690. THE TOMATO MEDICINAL.—To many persons there is something unpleasant, not to say offensive, in the flavour of this excellent fruit. It has, however, long been used for culinary purposes in various countries of Europe. Dr. Bennett, a professor of some celebrity, considers it an invaluable article of diet, and ascribes to it very important medicinal properties. He declares :— 1. That the tomato is one of the most powerful deobstruents of the *materia medica ;* and that, in all those affections of the liver and other organs where calomel is indicated, it is probably the most effective and least harmful remedial agent known in the profession. 2. That a chemical extract can be obtained from it, which will altogether supersede the use of calomel in the cure of diseases. 3. That he has successfully treated diarrhœa with this article alone. 4. That when used as an article of diet, it is almost a sovereign remedy for dyspepsia and indigestion.

2691. WARM WATER.—Warm water is preferable to cold water, as a drink, to persons who are subject to dyspeptic and bilious complaints, and it may be taken more freely than cold water, and consequently answers better as a diluent for carrying off bile, and removing obstructions in the urinary secretion, in cases of stone and gravel. When water of a temperature equal to that of the human body is used for drink, it proves considerably stimulant, and is particularly suited to dyspeptic, bilious, gouty, and chlorotic subjects.

2692. CAUTIONS IN VISITING SICK-ROOMS.—Never venture into a sick-room if you are in a violent perspiration (if circumstances require your continuance there), for the moment your body becomes cold, it is in a state likely to absorb the infection, and give you the disease. Nor visit a sick person (especially if the complaint be of a contagious nature) with *an empty stomach ;* as this disposes the system more readily to receive the contagion. In attending a sick person, place yourself where the air passes from the door or window to the bed of the diseased, not betwixt the diseased person and any fire that is in the room, as the heat of the fire will draw the infectious vapour in that direction, and you would run much danger from breathing it.

2693. NECESSITY OF GOOD VENTILATION IN ROOMS LIGHTED WITH GAS.— In dwelling-houses lighted by gas, the frequent renewal of the air is of great importance. A single gas-burner will consume more oxygen, and produce more carbonic acid to deteriorate the atmosphere of a room, than six or eight candles. If, therefore, when several burners are used, no provision is made for the escape of the corrupted air and for the introduction of pure air from without, the health will necessarily suffer.

LEGAL MEMORANDA.

CHAPTER XLIV.

2694. HUMORISTS tell us there is no act of our lives which can be performed without breaking through some one of the many meshes of the law by which our rights are so carefully guarded; and those learned in the law, when they do give advice without the usual fee, and in the confidence of friendship, generally say, "Pay, pay anything rather than go to law;" while those having experience in the courts of Themis have a wholesome dread of its pitfalls. There are a few exceptions, however, to this fear of the law's uncertanties; and we hear of those to whom a lawsuit is an agreeable relaxation, a gentle excitement. One of this class, when remonstrated with, retorted, that while one friend kept dogs, and another horses, he, as he had a right to do, kept a lawyer; and no one had a right to dispute his taste. We cannot pretend, in these few pages, to lay down even the principles of law, not to speak of its contrary exposition in different courts; but there are a few acts of legal import which all men—and women too—must perform; and to these acts we may be useful in giving a right direction. There is a house to be leased or purchased, servants to be engaged, a will to be made, or property settled, in all families; and much of the welfare of its members depends on these things being done in proper legal form.

2695. PURCHASING A HOUSE.—Few men will venture to purchase a freehold, or even a leasehold property, by private contract, without making themselves acquainted with the locality, and employing a solicitor to examine the titles, ; but many do walk into an auction-room, and bid for a property upon the representations of the auctioneer. The conditions, whatever they are, will bind him; for by one of the legal fictions of which we have still so many, the auctioneer, who is in reality the agent for the vendor, becomes also the agent for the buyer, and by putting down the names of bidders and the biddings, he binds him to whom the lot is knocked down to the sale and the conditions,—the falling of the auctioneer's hammer is the acceptance of the offer, which completes the agreement to purchase. In any such transaction you can only look at the written or printed particulars; any verbal statement of the auctioneer, made at the time of the sale, cannot contradict them, and they are implemented by the agreement, which the auctioneer calls on the purchaser to sign after the sale. You should sign no such contract without having a duplicate of it signed by the auctioneer, and delivered to you. It is, perhaps, unnecessary to add, that no trustee or assignee can purchase property for himself included in the trust, even at auction; nor is it safe to pay the purchase-money to an agent of the vendor, unless he give a written authority to the agent to receive it, besides handing over the requisite deeds and receipts.

2696. The laws of purchase and sale of property are so complicated that Lord St. Leonards devotes five chapters of his book on Property Law to the subject. The only circumstances strong enough to vitiate a purchase, which has been reduced to a written contract, is proof of fraudulent representation as to an encumbrance of which the buyer was ignorant, or a defect in title; but every circumstance which the purchaser might have learned by careful investigation, the law presumes that he did know. Thus, in buying a leasehold estate or house, all the covenants of the original lease are presumed to be known. "It is not unusual," says Lord St. Leonards, "to stipulate, in conditions of sale of leasehold property, that the production of a receipt for the last year's rent shall be accepted as proof that all the lessor's covenants were performed up to that period. Never bid for one clogged with such a condition. There are some acts against which no relief can be obtained; for example, the tenant's right to insure, or his insuring in an office or in names not authorized in the lease. And you should not rely upon the mere fact of the insurance being correct at the time of sale: there may have been a prior breach of covenant, and the landlord may not have waived his right of entry for the forfeiture." And where any doubt of this kind exists, the landlord should be appealed to.

2697. Interest on a purchase is due from the day fixed upon for completing: where it cannot be completed, the loss rests with the party with whom the delay rests; but it appears, when the delay rests with the seller, and the money is lying idle, notice of that is to be given to the seller to make him liable to the loss of interest. In law, the property belongs to the purchaser from the date of the contract; he is entitled to any benefit, and must bear any loss; the seller may suffer the insurance to drop without giving notice; and should a fire take place, the loss falls on the buyer. In agreeing to buy a house, therefore, provide at the same time for its insurance. Common fixtures pass with the house, where nothing is said about them.

2698. There are some well-recognized laws, of what may be called good-neighbourhood, which affect all properties. If you purchase a field or house, the seller retaining another field between yours and the highway, he must of necessity grant you a right of way. Where the owner of more than one house sells one of them, the purchaser is entitled to benefit by all drains leading from his house into other drains, and will be subject to all necessary drains for the adjoining houses, although there is no express reservation as to drains.

Thus, if his nappens to be a leading drain, other necessary drains may be opened into it. In purchasing land for building on, you should expressly reserve a right to make an opening into any sewer or watercourse on the vendor's land for drainage purposes.

2699. CONSTRUCTIONS.—Among the cautions which purchasers of houses, land, or leaseholds, should keep in view, is a not inconsiderable array of *constructive* notices, which are equally binding with actual ones. Notice to your attorney or agent is notice to you ; and when the same attorney is employed by both parties, and he is aware of an encumbrance of which you are ignorant, you are bound by it ; even where the vendor is guilty of a fraud to which your agent is privy, you are responsible, and cannot be released from the consequences.

2700. THE RELATIONS OF LANDLORD AND TENANT are most important to both parties, and each should clearly understand his position. The proprietor of a house, or house and land, agrees to let it either to a tenant-at-will, a yearly tenancy, or under lease. A tenancy-at-will may be created by parol or by agreement ; and as the tenant may be turned out when his landlord pleases, so he may leave when he himself thinks proper ; but this kind of tenancy is extremely inconvenient to both parties. Where an annual rent is attached to the tenancy, in construction of law, a lease or agreement without limitation to any certain period is a lease from year to year, and both landlord and tenant are entitled to notice before the tenancy can be determined by the other. This notice must be given at least six months before the expiration of the current year of the tenancy, and it can only terminate at the end of any whole year from the time at which it began ; so that the tenant entering into possession at Midsummer, the notice must be given to or by him, so as to terminate at the same term. When once he is in possession, he has a right to remain for a whole year ; and if no notice be given at the end of the first half-year of his tenancy, he will have to remain two years, and so on for any number of years.

2701. TENANCY BY SUFFERANCE.—This is a tenancy, not very uncommon, arising out of the unwillingness of either party to take the initiative in a more decided course at the expiry of a lease or agreement. The tenant remains in possession, and continues to pay rent as before, and becomes, from sufferance, a tenant from year to year, which can only be terminated by one party or the other giving the necessary six months' notice to quit at the term corresponding with the commencement of the original tenancy. This tenancy at sufferance applies also to an under-tenant, who remains in possession and pays rent to the reversioner or head landlord. A six months' notice will be insufficient for this tenancy. A notice was given (in Right *v.* Darby, I.T.R. 159) to quit a house held by plaintiff as tenant from year to year, on the 17th June, 1840, requiring him "to quit the premises on the 11th October following, or such other day as his said tenancy might expire." The tenancy had commenced on the 11th October in a former year, but it was held that this was not a good notice for the year ending October 11, 1841. A tenant from year to year gave his landlord notice to quit, ending the tenancy at a time within the half-year; the landlord acquiesced at first, but afterwards refused to accept the notice. The tenant quitted the premises; the landlord entered, and even made some repairs, but it was afterwards held that the tenancy was not determined. A notice to quit must be such as the tenant may safely act on at the time of receiving it; therefore it can only be given by an agent properly authorized at the time, and cannot be made good by the landlord adopting it afterwards. An unqualified notice, given at the proper time, should conclude with "On failure whereof, I shall require you to pay me double the former rent for so long as you retain possession."

2702. LEASES.—A lease is an instrument in writing, by which one person grants to another the occupation and use of lands or tenements for a term of years for a consideration, the lessor granting the lease, and the lessee accepting it with all its conditions. A lessor may grant the lease for any term less than his own interest. A tenant for life in an estate can only grant a lease for his own life. A tenant for life, having power to grant a lease, should grant it only in the terms of the power, otherwise the lease is void, and his estate may be made to pay heavy penalties under the covenant, usually the only one onerous on the lessor, for quiet enjoyment. The proprietor of a freehold— that is, of the possession in perpetuity of lands or tenements—may grant a lease for 999 years, for 99 years, or for 3 years. In the latter case, the lease may be either verbal or in writing, no particular form and no stamps being necessary, except the usual stamp on agreements; so long as the intention of the parties is clearly expressed, and the covenants definite, and well understood by each party, the agreement is complete, and the law satisfied. In the case of settled estates, the court of Chancery is empowered to authorize leases under the 19 & 20 Vict. c. 120, and 21 & 22 Vict. c. 77, as follows:—

> 21 years for agriculture or occupation.
> 40 years for water-power.
> 99 years for building-leases.
> 60 years for repairing-leases.

2703. A lessor may also grant an under-lease for a term less than his own: to grant the whole of his term would be an assignment. Leases are frequently burdened with a covenant not to underlet without the consent of the landlord: this is a covenant sometimes very onerous, and to be avoided, where it is possible, by a prudent lessee.

2704. A lease for any term beyond three years, whether an actual lease or an agreement for one, must be in the form of a deed; that is, it must be "under seal;" and all assignments and surrenders of leases must be in the same form, or they are *void at law*. Thus, an agreement made by letter, or by a memorandum of agreement, which would be binding in most cases, would be valueless when it was for a lease, unless witnessed, and given under hand and seal. The last statute, 8 & 9 Vict. c. 106, under which these precautions became necessary, has led to serious difficulties. "The judges," says Lord St. Leonards, "feel the difficulty of holding a lease in writing, but not by deed, to be altogether void, and consequently decided, that although such a lease is void under the statute, yet it so far regulates the holding, that it creates a tenancy from year to year, terminable by half a year's notice; and if the tenure endure for the term attempted to be created by the void lease, the tenant may be evicted at the end of the term without any notice to quit." An agreement for a lease not by deed has been construed to be a lease for a term of years, and consequently void under the statute; "and yet," says Lord St. Leonards, "a court of equity has held that it may be specifically enforced as an agreement upon the terms stated." The law on this point is one of glorious uncertainty; in making any such agreement, therefore, we should be careful to express that it is an agreement, and not a lease; and that it is witnessed and under seal.

2705. AGREEMENTS.—It is usual, where the lease is a repairing one, to agree for a lease to be granted on completion of repairs according to specification. This agreement should contain the names and designation of the parties, a description of the property, and the term of the intended lease, and all the covenants which are to be inserted, as no verbal agreement can be made to a written agreement. It should also declare that the instrument is an agreement for a lease, and not the lease itself. The points to be settled in such an agreement are, the rent, term, and especially covenants for insuring and rebuilding in the event of a fire; and if it is intended that the lessor's consent is to be obtained before assigning or underleasing, a covenant to that effect is required in the agreement. In building-leases, usually granted for 99 years, the tenant is to insure the property; and even where the agreement is silent. on that point, the law decides it so. It is otherwise with ordinary tenements, when the tenant pays a full, or what the law terms rack-rent; the landlord is then to insure, unless it is otherwise arranged by the agreement.

2706. It is important for lessee, and lessor also, that the latter does not exceed his powers. A lease granted by a tenant for life before he is properly in possession, is void in law; for, although a court of equity, according to Lord St. Leonards, will, "by force of its own jurisdiction, support a *bonâ fide* lease, granted under a power which is merely erroneous in form or ceremonies," and the 12 & 13 Vict. c. 26, and 13 & 14 Vict. c. 19, compel a new lease to be granted with the necessary variations, while the lessor has no power to compel him to accept such a lease, except when the person in remainder is competent and willing to confirm the original lease without variations, yet all these difficulties involve both delay, costs, and anxieties.

2707. In husbandry leases, a covenant to cultivate the land in a husbandlike manner, and according to the custom of the district, is always implied; but it is more usual to prescribe the course of tillage which is to be pursued. In the case of houses for occupation, the tenant would have to keep the house in a tenantable state of repair during the term, and deliver it up in like condition. This is not the case with the tenant at will, or from year to year, where the landlord has to keep the house in tenantable repair, and the tenant is only liable for waste beyond reasonable wear and tear.

2708. INSURANCE.—Every lease, or agreement for a lease, should covenant not only who is to pay insurance, but how the tenement is to be rebuilt in the event of a fire; for if the house were burnt down, and no provision made for insurance, the tenant, supposing there was the ordinary covenant to repair in the lease, would not only have to rebuild, but to pay rent while it was being rebuilt. More than this, supposing, under the same lease, the landlord had taken the precaution of insuring, he is not compelled to lay out the money recovered in rebuilding the premises. Sir John Leach lays it down, that "the tenant's situation could not be changed by a precaution, on the part of the landlord, with which he had nothing to do." This decision Lord Campbell confirmed in a more recent case, in which an action was brought against a lessee who was not bound to repair, and neither he nor the landlord bound to insure; admitting an equitable defence, the court affirmed Sir John Leach's decision, holding that the tenant was bound to pay the rent, and could not require the landlord to lay out the insurance money in rebuilding. This is opposed to the opinion of Lord St. Leonards, who admits, however, that the decision of the court must overrule his *dictum*. Such being the state of the law, it is very important that insurance should be provided for, and that the payment of rent should be made to depend upon rebuilding the house in the event of a fire. Care must be taken, however, that this is made a covenant of the lease, as well as in the agreement, otherwise the tenant must rebuild the house.

2709. The law declares that a tenant is not bound to repair damages by tempest, lightning, or other natural casualty, unless there is a special covenant to that effect in the lease; but if there is a general covenant to repair, the repair will fall upon the tenant. Lord Kenyon lays it down, in the case of a bridge destroyed by a flood, the tenant being under a general covenant to repair, that, "where a party, by his own contract, creates a duty or charge upon himself, he is bound to make it good, because he might have guarded against it in the contract." The same principle of law has been applied to a house destroyed by lightning. It is, therefore, important to have this settled in the insurance clause.

2710. Lord St. Leonards asserts that "his policies against fire are not so framed as to render the company *legally* liable." Generally the property is inaccurately described with reference to the conditions under which you insure. They are framed by companies who, probably, are not unwilling to have a legal defence against any claim, as they intend to pay what they deem a just claim without taking advantage of any technical objection, and intending to make use of their defence only against what they believe to be a fraud, although they may not be able to prove it. " But," says his lordship, " do not rely upon the moral feelings of the directors. Ascertain that your house falls strictly within the conditions. Even having the surveyor of the company to look over your house before the insurance will not save you, unless your policy is correct." This is true ; but probably his lordship's legal jealousy overshoots the mark here. Assurance companies only require an honest statement of the facts, and that no concealment is practised with their surveyor ; and the case of his own, which he quotes, in which a glass door led into a conservatory, rendering it, according to the view of the company, "hazardous," and consequently voiding the policy, when a fire did occur, the company paid, rather than try the question ; but even after the fire they demurred, when called upon, to make the description correct and indorse on the policy the fact that the drawing-room opened through a glass door into conservatories. One of two inferences is obvious here ; either his lordship has overcoloured the statement, or the company could not be the respectable one represented. The practice with all reputable offices is to survey the premises before insurance, and to describe them as they appear ; but no concealment of stoves, or other dangerous accessories or inflammable goods, should be practised. This certainly binds the office so long as no change takes place ; but the addition of any stove, opening, or door through a party wall, the introduction of gunpowder, saltpetre, or other inflammable articles into the premises without notice, very properly "voids the policy." The usual course is to give notice of all alterations, and have them indorsed on the policy, as additions to the description of the property : there is little fear, where this is honestly done, that any company would adopt the sharp practice hinted at in Lord St. Leonards' excellent handy book.

2711. BREAKS IN THE LEASE.—Where a lease is for seven, fourteen, or twenty-one years, the option to determine it at the end of the first term is in the tenant, unless it is distinctly agreed that the option shall be mutual, according to Lord St. Leonards.

2712. NOXIOUS TRADES.—A clause is usually introduced prohibiting the carrying on of any trade in some houses, and of noxious or particular trades in others. This clause should be jealously inspected, otherwise great annoyance may be produced. It has been held that a general clause of this description prohibited a tenant from keeping a school, for which he had taken it, although a lunatic asylum and public-house have been found admissible ; the keeping an asylum not being deemed a trade, which is defined as " conducted by buying and selling." It is better to have the trades, or class of trades objected to, defined in the lease.

2713. FIXTURES.—In houses held under lease, it has been the practice with landlords to lease the bare walls of the tenement only, leaving the lessee to put in the stoves, cupboards, and such other conveniences as he requires, at his own option. These, except under particular circumstances, are the property of the lessee, and may either be sold to an incoming tenant, or removed at the end of his term. The articles which may not be removed are subject to considerable doubt, and are a fruitful source of dispute. Mr. Commissioner Fonblanque has defined as tenants' property all goods and chattels; 2ndly, all articles "slightly connected one with another, and with the freehold, but capable of being separated without materially injuring the freehold;" 3rdly, articles fixed to the freehold by nails and screws, bolts or pegs, are also tenants' goods and chattels; but when sunk in the soil, or built on it, they are integral parts of the freehold, and cannot be removed. Thus, a green-house or conservatory attached to the house by the tenant is not remov-able; but the furnace and hot-water pipes by which it is heated, may be removed or sold to the in-coming tenant. A brick flue does not come under the same category, but remains. Window-blinds, grates, stoves, coffee-mills, and, in a general sense, everything he has placed which can be removed without injury to the freehold, he may remove, if they are separated from the tenement during his term, and the place made good. It is not unusual to leave the fixtures in their place, with an undertaking from the landlord that, when again let, the in-coming tenant shall pay for them, or permit their removal. In a recent case, however, a tenant having held over beyond his term and not removed his fixtures, the landlord let the premises to a new tenant, who entered into possession, and would not allow the fixtures to be removed—it was held by the courts, on trial, that he was justified. A similar case occurred to the writer: he left his fixtures in the house, taking a letter from the landlord, undertaking that the in-coming tenant should pay for them by valuation, or permit their removal. The house was let; the landlord died. His executors, on being applied to, pleaded ignorance, as did the tenant, and on being furnished with a copy of the letter, the executors told applicant that if he was aggrieved, he knew his remedy; namely, an action at law. He thought the first loss the least, and has not altered his opinion.

2714. TAXES.—Land-tax, sewers-rate, and property-tax, are landlord's taxes; but by 30 Geo. II. c. 2, the occupier is required to pay all rates levied, and deduct from the rent such taxes as belong to the landlord. Many landlords now insert a covenant, stipulating that land-tax and sewers-rate are to be paid by the tenants, and not deducted: this does not apply to the property-tax. All other taxes and rates are payable by the occupier.

2715. WATER-RATE, of course, is paid by the tenant. The water-compa-nies, as well as gas-companies, have the power of cutting off the supply; and most of them have also the right of distraining, in the same manner as land-lords have for rent.

2716. NOTICE TO QUIT.—In the case of leasing for a term, no notice is necessary; the tenant quits, as a matter of course, at its termination; or if, by tacit consent, he remains paying rent as heretofore, he becomes a tenant at sufferance, or from year to year. Half a year's notice now becomes necessary, as we have already seen, to terminate the tenancy; except in London, and the rent is under forty shillings, when a quarter's notice is sufficient. Either of these notices may be given verbally, if it can be proved that the notice was definite, and given at the right time. Form of notice is quite immaterial, provided it is definite and clear in its purport.

2717. Tenancy for less than a year may be terminated according to the taking. Thus, when taken for three months, a three months' notice is required; when monthly, a month's notice; and when weekly, a week's notice; but weekly tenancy is changed to a quarterly tenure if the rent is allowed to stand over for three months. When taken for a definite time, as a month, a week, or a quarter, no notice is necessary on either side.

2718. DILAPIDATIONS.—At the termination of a lease, supposing he has not done so before, a landlord can, and usually does, send a surveyor to report upon the condition of the tenement, and it becomes his duty to ferret out every defect. A litigious landlord may drag the outgoing tenant into an expensive lawsuit, which he has no power to prevent. He may even compel him to pay for repairing improvements which he has effected in the tenement itself, if dilapidations exist. When the lessor covenants to do all repairs, and fails to do so, the lessee may repair, and deduct the cost from the rent.

2719. RECOVERY OF RENT.—The remedies placed in the hands of land-lords are very stringent. The day after rent falls due, he may proceed to recover it, by action at law, by distress on the premises, or by action of ejectment, if the rent is half a year in arrear. Distress is the remedy usually applied, the landlord being authorized to enter the premises, seize the goods and chattels of his tenant, and sell them, on the fifth day, to reimburse himself for all arrears of rent and the charges of the distress. There are a few exceptions; but, generally, all goods found on the premises may be seized. The exceptions are—dogs, rabbits, poultry, fish, tools and imple-ments of a man's trade actually in use, the books of a scholar, the axe of a carpenter, wearing apparel on the person, a horse at the plough, or a horse he may be riding, a watch in the pocket, loose money, deeds, writings, the cattle at a smithy forge, corn sent to a mill for grinding, cattle and goods of a guest at an inn; but, curiously enough, carriages and horses standing at livery at the same inn may be taken. Distress can only be levied in the daytime, and if made after the tender of arrears, it is illegal. If tender is made after the distress, but before it is *impounded*, the landlord must abandon the distress and bear the cost himself. Nothing of a perishable nature, which cannot be restored in the same condition—as milk, fruit, and the like, must be taken.

2720. The law does not regard a day as consisting of portions. The popular notion that a notice to quit should be served before noon is an error. Although distraint is one of the remedies, it is seldom advisable in a landlord to resort to distraining for the recovery of rent. If a tenant cannot pay his rent, the sooner he leaves the premises the better. If he be a rogue and won't pay, he will probably know that nine out of ten distresses are illegal, through the carelessness, ignorance, or extortion of the brokers who execute them. Many, if not most, of the respectable brokers will not execute distresses, and the business falls into the hands of persons whom it is by no means desirable to employ.

2721. Powers to relieve landlords of premises, by giving them legal possession, are given by 19 & 20 Vict., cap. 108, to the county courts, in cases where the rent does not exceed £50 per annum, and under the circumstances hereinafter mentioned ; *i.e.* :—

1. Where the term has expired, or been determined by notice to quit.
2. Where there is one half-year's rent in arrear, and *the landlord shall have right by law to enter for the nonpayment thereof.* As proof of this power is required, the importance of including such a power in the agreement for tenancy will be obvious.

In the county courts the amount of rent due may be claimed, as well as the possession of the premises, in one summons.

2722. When a tenant deserts premises, leaving one half-year's rent in arrear, possession may be recovered by means of the police-court. The rent must not exceed £20 per annum, and must be at least three-fourths of the value of the premises. In cases in which the tenant has not deserted the premises, and where notice to quit has been given and has expired, the landlord must give notice to the tenant of his intended application. The annual rent in this case, also, must not exceed £20.

2723. THE I. O. U.—The law is not particular as to orthography; in fact, it distinctly refuses to recognize the existence of that delightful science. You may bring your action against Mr. Jacob Phillips, under the fanciful denomination of Jaycobb Fillipse, if you like, and the law won't care, because the law goes by ear; and, although it insists upon having everything written, things written are only supposed in law to have any meaning when read, which is, after all, a common-sense rule enough. So, instead of " I owe you," persons of a cheerful disposition, so frequently found connected with debt, used to write facetiously I. O. U., and the law approved of their so doing. An I. O. U. is nothing more than a written admission of a debt, and may run thus :—

15th October, 1860.

To Mr. W. BROWN.

I. O. U. ten pounds for coals.

£10.   JOHN JONES.

If to this you add the time of payment, as " payable in one month from this date," your I. O. U. is worthless and illegal; for it thus ceases to be a mere acknowledgment, and becomes a promissory note. Now a promissory note requires a stamp, which an I. O. U. does not. Many persons, nevertheless, stick penny stamps upon them, probably for ornamental effect, or to make them look serious and authoritative. If for the former purpose, the postage-stamp looks better than the receipt stamp upon blue paper. If you are W. Brown, and you didn't see the I. O. U. signed, and can't find anybody who knows Jones's autograph, and Jones won't pay, the I. O. U. will be of no use to you in the county court, except to make the judge laugh. He will, however, allow you to prove the consideration, and as, of course, you won't be prepared to do anything of the sort, he will, if you ask him politely, adjourn the hearing for a week, when you can produce the coalheavers who delivered the article, and thus gain a glorious victory.

2724. APPRENTICES.—By the statute 5 Eliz. cap. 4, it is enacted that, in cases of ill-usage by masters towards apprentices, or of neglect of duty by apprentices, the complaining party may apply to a justice of the peace, who may make such order as equity may require. If, for want of conformity on the part of the master, this cannot be done, then the master may be bound to appear at the next sessions. Authority is given by the act to the justices in sessions to discharge the apprentice from his indentures. They are also empowered, on proof of misbehaviour of the apprentice, to order him to be corrected or imprisoned with hard labour.

2725. HUSBAND AND WIFE.—Contrary to the vulgar opinion, second cousins, as well as first, may legally marry. When married, a husband is liable for his wife's debts contracted before marriage. A creditor desirous of suing for such a claim should proceed against both. It will, however, be sufficient if the husband be served with process, the names of both appearing therein, thus:—John Jones and Ann his wife. A married woman, if sued alone, may plead her marriage, or, as it is called in law, coverture. The husband is liable for debts of his wife contracted for necessaries while living with him. If she voluntarily leaves his protection, this liability ceases. He is also liable for any debts contracted by her with his authority. If the husband have abjured the realm, or been transported by a sentence of law, the wife is liable during his absence, as if she were a single woman, for debts contracted by her.

2726. In civil cases, a wife may now give evidence on behalf of her husband; in criminal cases she can neither be a witness for or against her husband. The case of assault by him upon her forms an exception to this rule.

2727. The law does not at this day admit the ancient principle of allowing moderate correction by a husband upon the person of his wife. Although this is said to have been anciently limited to the use of "a stick not bigger than the thumb," this barbarity is now altogether exploded. He may, notwithstanding, as has been recently shown in the famous Agapemone case, keep her under restraint, to prevent her leaving him, provided this be effected without cruelty.

2728. By the **Divorce and Matrimonial Causes Act, 1857,** a wife deserted by her husband may apply to a magistrate, or to the petty sessions, for an order to protect her lawful earnings or property acquired by her after such desertion, from her husband and his creditors. In this case it is indispensable that such order shall, within ten days, be entered at the county court of the district within which she resides. It will be seen that the basis of an application for such an order is *desertion*. Consequently, where the parties have separated by common consent, such an order cannot be obtained, any previous cruelty or misconduct on the husband's part notwithstanding.

2729. When a husband allows his wife to invest money in her own name in a savings-bank, and he survives her, it is sometimes the rule of such establishments to compel him to take out administration in order to receive such money, although it is questionable whether such rule is legally justifiable. Widows and widowers pay no legacy-duty for property coming to them through their deceased partners.

2730. RECEIPTS for sums above £2 should now be given upon penny stamps. A bill of exchange may nevertheless be discharged by an indorsement stating that it has been paid, and this will not be liable to the stamp. A receipt is not, as commonly supposed, conclusive evidence as to a payment. It is only what the law terms *primâ facie* evidence ; that is, good until contradicted or explained. Thus, if A sends wares or merchandise to B, with a receipt, as a hint that the transaction is intended to be for ready money, and B detain the receipt without paying the cash, A will be at liberty to prove the circumstances and to recover his claim. The evidence to rebut the receipt must, however, be clear and indubitable, as, after all, written evidence is of a stronger nature than oral testimony.

2731. BOOKS OF ACCOUNT.—A tradesman's books of account cannot be received as evidence in his own behalf, unless the entries therein be proved to have been brought under the notice of, and admitted to be correct by the other party, as is commonly the case with the "pass-books" employed backwards and forwards between bakers, butchers, and the like domestic traders, and their customers. The defendant may, however, compel the tradesman to produce his books to show entries adverse to his own claim.

2732. WILLS.—The last proof of affection which we can give to those left behind, is to leave their worldly affairs in such a state as to excite neither jealousy, nor anger, nor heartrendings of any kind, at least for the immediate future. This can only be done by a just, clear, and intelligible disposal of whatever there is to leave. Without being advocates for every man being his own lawyer, it is not to be denied that the most elaborately prepared wills have been the most fruitful sources of litigation, and it has even happened that learned judges left wills behind them which could not be carried out. Except in cases where the property is in land or in leases of complicated tenure, very elaborate details are unnecessary; and we counsel no man to use words in making his will of which he does not perfectly understand the meaning and import.

2733. All men over twenty-one years of age, and of sound mind, and all unmarried women of like age and sanity, may by will bequeath their property to whom they please. Infants, that is, all persons under twenty-one years of age, and married women, except where they have an estate to their " own separate use," are incapacitated, without the concurrence of the husband; the law taking the disposal of any property they die possessed of. A person born deaf and dumb cannot make a will, unless there is evidence that he could read and comprehend its contents. A person convicted of felony cannot make a will, unless subsequently pardoned; neither can persons outlawed; but the wife of a felon transported for life may make a will, and act in all respects as if she were unmarried. A suicide may bequeath real estate, but personal property is forfeited to the crown.

2734. Except in the case of soldiers on actual service, and sailors at sea, every will must be made in writing. It must be signed by the testator, or by some other person in his presence, and at his request, and the signature must be made or acknowledged in the presence of two or more witnesses, who are required to be present at the same time, who declare by signing that the will was signed by the testator, or acknowledged in their presence, and that they signed as witnesses in testator's presence.

2735. By the act of 1852 it was enacted that no will shall be valid unless signed at the foot or end thereof by the testator, or by some person in his presence, and by his direction; but a subsequent act proceeds to say that every will shall, as far only as regards the position of the signature of the testator, or of the person signing for him, be deemed valid if the signature shall be so placed at, or after, or following, or under, or beside, or opposite to the end of the will, that it shall be apparent on the face of it that the testator intended to give it effect by such signature. Under this clause, a will of several sheets, all of which were duly signed, except the last one, has been refused probate; while, on the other hand, a similar document has been admitted to probate where the last sheet only, and none of the other sheets, was signed. In order to be perfectly formal, however, each separate sheet should be-numbered, signed, and witnessed, and attested on the last sheet. This witnessing is an important act: the witnesses must subscribe it in the presence of the testator and of each other; and by their signature they testify to having witnessed the signature of the testator, he being in sound mind at the time. Wills made under any kind of coercion, or even importunity, may become void, being contrary to the wishes of the testator. Fraud or imposition also renders a will void, and where two wills made by the same person happen to exist, neither of them dated, the maker of the wills is declared to have died intestate.

2736. A will may always be revoked and annulled, but only by burning or entirely destroying the writing, or by adding a codicil, or making a subsequent will duly attested ; but as the alteration of a will is only a revocation to the extent of the alteration, if it is intended to revoke the original will entirely, such intention should be declared,—no merely verbal directions can revoke a written will; and the act of running the pen through the signatures, or down the page, is not sufficient to cancel it, without a written declaration to that effect signed and witnessed.

2737. A will made before marriage is revoked thereby.

2738. A codicil is a supplement or addition to a will, either explaining or altering former dispositions; it may be written on the same or separate paper, and is to be witnessed and attested in the same manner as the original document.

2739. WITNESSES.—Any persons are qualified to witness a will who can write their names ; but such witness cannot be benefitted by the will.   If a legacy is granted to the persons witnessing, it is void.   The same rule applies to the husband or wife of a witness ; a bequest made to either of these is void.

2740. FORM OF WILLS.—Form is unimportant, provided the testator's intention is clear. It should commence with his designation ; that is, his name and surname, place or abode, profession, or occupation.   The legatees should also be clearly described.   In leaving a legacy to a married woman, if no trustees are appointed over it, and no specific directions given, " that it is for her sole and separate use, free from the control, debts, and incumbrances of her husband," the husband will be entitled to the legacy.   In the same manner a legacy to an unmarried woman will vest in her husband after marriage, unless a settlement of it is made on her before marriage.

2741. In sudden emergencies a form may be useful, and the following has been considered a good one for a death-bed will, where the assistance or a solicitor could not be obtained ; indeed, few solicitors can prepare a will on the spur of the moment : they require time and legal forms, which are by no means necessary, before they can act.

I, A. B., of No. 10, ——, Street, in the city of —— [gentleman, builder, or grocer, as the case may be,] being of sound mind, thus publish and declare my last will and testament. Revoking and annulling all former dispositions of my property, I give and bequeath as follows :—to my son J. B., of ——, I give and bequeath the sum of ——; to my daughter M., the wife of J., of ——, I give and bequeath the sum of —— [if intended for her own use, add, "to her sole and separate use, free from the control, debts, and incumbrances of her husband"], both in addition to any sum or sums of money or other property they have before had from me. All the remaining property I die possessed of I leave to my dear wife M. B., for her sole and separate use during her natural life, together with my house and furniture, situate at No. 10, —— Street, aforesaid. At her death, I desire that the said house shall be sold, with all the goods and chattels therein [or, I give and bequeath the said house, with all the goods and chattels therein, to ——], and the money realized from the sale, together with that in which my said wife had a life-interest, I give and bequeath in equal moieties to my son and daughter before named. I appoint my dear friend T. S., of ——, and T. B., of ——, together with my wife M. B., as executors to this my last will and testament.

Signed by A. B., this 10th day of October, 1861, in our presence, both being present together, and both having signed as witnesses, in the presence of the testator :—   } A. B.

T. S., Witness.
F. M., Witness.

It is to be observed that the signature of the testator after this attestation has been signed by the witnesses, is not a compliance with the act; he must sign first.

2742. STAMP-DUTIES.—In the case of persons dying intestate, when their effects are administered to by their family, the stamp-duty is half as much more as it would have been under a will. Freehold and copyhold estates are now subject to a special impost on passing, by the Stamp Act of 1857.

2743. The legacy-duty only commences when it amounts to £20 and upwards; and where it is not directed otherwise, the duty is deducted from the legacy.

2744. You cannot compound for past absence of charity by bequeathing land or tenements, or money to purchase such, to any charitable use, by your last will and testament; but you may devise them to the British Museum, to either of the two universities of Oxford and Cambridge, to Eton, Winchester, and Westminster; and you may, if so inclined, leave it for the augmentation of Queen Anne's bounty. You may, however, order your executors to sell land and hand over the money received to any charitable institution.

2745. In making provision for a wife, state whether it is in lieu of, or in addition to, dower.

2746. If you have advanced money to any child, and taken an acknowledgment for it, or entered it in any book of account, you should declare whether any legacy left by will is in addition to such advance, or whether it is to be deducted from the legacy.

2747. A legacy left by will to any one would be cancelled by your leaving another legacy by a codicil to the same person, unless it is stated to be in addition to the former bequest.

2748. Your entire estate is chargeable with your debts, except where the real estate is settled. Let it be distinctly stated out of which property, the real or personal, they are paid, where it consists of both.

2749. Whatever is *devised*, let the intention be clearly expressed, and without any condition, if you intend it to take effect.

2750. Attestation is not necessary to a will, as the act of witnessing is all the law requires, and the will itself declares the testator to be of sound mind in his own estimation ; but, wherever there are erasures or interlineations, one becomes necessary. No particular form is prescribed ; but it should state that the testator either signed it himself, or that another signed it by his request, or that he acknowledged the signature to be his in their presence, both being present together, and signed as witnesses in his presence. When there are erasures, the attestation must declare that—The words interlined in the third line of page 4, and the erasure in the fifth line of page 6, having been first made. These are the acts necessary to make a properly-executed will ; and, being simple in themselves and easily performed, they should be strictly complied with, and always attested.

2751. A witness may, on being requested, sign for testator ; and he may also sign for his fellow-witness, supposing he can only make his mark, declaring that he does so ; but a husband cannot sign for his wife, either as testator or witness, nor can a wife for her husband.